CYCLOPÆDIA

OF

MODERN

WIT AND HUMOR.

CYCLOPÆDIA OF MODERN Wit and Humor.

EDITED BY

W. E. BURTON.

SCOTCH.

Eng.d by W. G. Jackman

James Hogg

N. Y. D. Appleton & C°.

THE

CYCLOPÆDIA

OF

WIT AND HUMOR;

CONTAINING

CHOICE AND CHARACTERISTIC SELECTIONS

FROM THE

WRITINGS OF THE MOST EMINENT HUMORISTS

OF

AMERICA, IRELAND, SCOTLAND,
AND ENGLAND.

Illustrated with Twenty-four Portraits on Steel, and many Hundred Wood Engravings.

EDITED BY

WILLIAM E. BURTON.

VOLUME II.

"I have observed, that in Comedy, the best actor plays the part of the droll, while some scrub rogue is made the hero, or fine gentleman. So, in this Farce of Life, wise men pass their time in mirth, whilst fools only are serious.—BOLINGBROKE.

NEW YORK:
D. APPLETON AND COMPANY,
443 & 445 BROADWAY.
LONDON: 16 LITTLE BRITAIN.
1864.

LIST OF PORTRAITS.—VOL. II.

CYCLOPÆDIA

OF

MODERN WIT AND HUMOR.

SCOTCH.

CYCLOPÆDIA

OF

WIT AND HUMOR.

SCOTCH.

SEEKING THE HOUDY.

BY JAMES HOGG (THE ETTRICK SHEPHERD).

THERE was a shepherd on the lands of Meggat-dale, who once set out riding with might and main, under cloud of night, for that most important and necessary personage in a remote and mountainous country, called by a different name in every country of the world, excepting perhaps Egypt and England; but by the highlanders most expressively termed *bean-glhuine* or *te the toctor*.

The mare that Robin rode was a black one, with a white face like a cow. She had a great big belly, a switch tail, and a back, Robin said, as sharp as a knife; but perhaps this part of the description was rather exaggerated. However, she was laziness itself personified, and the worst thing of all, her foal was closed in at home; for Robin had wiled the mare and foal into the bire with a piece of bread, which he did not give her after all, but put in his pocket in case of farther necessity: he then whipped a hair halter on the mare's head, and the straw sunks on her back, those being the only equipment within his reach; and it having cost Robin a great deal of trouble to get the foal into the bire, he now eyed him with an exulting, and at the same time a malicious, look. "You mischievous rascal," said he, "I think I have you now; stand you there an' chack flees, till I come back to teach you better manners."

Robin then hurried out the mare to the side of the kail-yard dike, and calling out to Jean, his wife, not to be in ower grit a hurry, and to exercise all the patience she was mistress of, he flew on the yaud's back, and off he went at full gallop.

The hair halter that Robin rode with had a wooden snibbelt upon the end of it, as all hair halters had erewhile, when there were no other bridles in Meggat, saving branks and hair halters annexed; consequently with the further end of this halter one could hit an exceeding hard stroke. Indeed, I never saw any thing in my life that hurt so sore as a hair halter and wooden snibbelt at the end of it; and I may here mention, as an instance of its efficacy, that there was once a boy at Hartwood mines, near Selkirk, who killed with a snibbelt two Highland soldiers, who came to press his horses in *the forty-five*.

Well, to this halter and snibbelt Robin had trusted for a rod, there being no wood in Meggat-dale, not so much as a tree: and a more unlucky and dangerous goad he could scarcely have possessed, and that the black mare, with a white face like a cow, felt to her experience. Robin galloped, by the light of the full moon, down by the But-haugh and Glengaber-foot about as fast as a good horse walks; still he was galloping, and could make no more of it, although he was every now and then lending the yaud a yerk on the flank with the snibbelt. But when he came to Henderland, to which place the mare was accustomed to go every week to meet the eggler, then Robin and the mare split in their opinions. Robin thought it the most natural and reasonable thing in the world that the mare should push on to the Sandbed, about eight miles further, to bring home the wise woman to his beloved wife's assistance. The mare thought exactly the reverse, being inwardly convinced that the most natural and reasonable path she could take was the one straight home again to her foal; and without any further ceremony, save giving a few switches with her long ill-shapen tail, she set herself with all her might to dispute the point with Robin.

Then there was such a battle commenced, as never was fought at the foot of Henderland-bank at midnight, either before or since. O, my beloved and respected editor and readers! I wish I could make you understand the humor of this battle as well as I do. The branks were two sticks hung by a head-steel, which, when one drew the halter hard, nipped the beast's nose most terribly; but then they were all made in one way, and could only turn the beast to the near side. Now the black mare did not, or could not, resist this agency of the branks; she turned round as often as Robin liked, but not one step farther would she proceed on the road to Sandbed. So roundabout and roundabout the two went; and the mare, by a very clever expedient, contrived at every circle to work twice her own length nearer home. Saint Sampson! how Robin did lay on with the halter and snibbelt, whenever he got her head round towards the way he wanted her to go! No—round she came again! He cursed her, he flattered her, he reminded her of the precarious state of her mistress, who had so often filled her manger; but all would not do; she thought only of the precarious state of her foal, closed in an old void smearing-house.

Robin, at last, fell upon a new stratagem, which was this, that as the mare wheeled round, whenever her head reached the right point, he hit her a yerk with the wooden snibbelt on the near cheek, to stop that mill-stone motion of hers. This occasioned some furious plunges, but no advancement the right way, till at length he hit her such a pernicious blow somewhere near about the ear, that he brought her smack to the earth in a moment; and so much was he irritated, that he laid on her when down, and nodding like one falling asleep. After two or three prolonged groans, she rose again, and, thus candidly admonished, made no further resistance for the present, but moved on apace to the time of the halter and the snibbelt. On reaching a ravine called the Capper Cleuch, the mare, coming again in some degree to her senses, perceived that she was not where she ought to have been, at least where it was her interest, and the interest of her foal, that she should have been; and raising her white face, she uttered a tremendous neigh. The hills to the left are there steep and rocky, and the night being calm and frosty, first one fine echo neighed out of the hill, then another, and then another. "There are plenty of foals here," thought the old mare; and neighing again even louder than before, she was again answered in the same way; and seeing an old crabbed thorn-tree among the rocks, in the direction whence the echo proceeded, it struck her obtuse head that it was her great lubber of a foal standing on very perilous ground; and off she set at a right angle from the road, or rather a left one, with her utmost speed, braying, as she went, while every scream was returned by her shaggy colt with interest. It was in vain that Robin pulled by the hair halter, and smote her on the cheek with the wooden snibbelt: away she ran through long heath and large stones, with a tremendous and uncultivated rapidity, neighing as she flew. "Wo! ye jaud! Hap-wo! chywooo!" shouted Robin, "Hap-wo! Hap-wo! Devil confound the beast, for I'm gone!"

Nothing would stay her velocity till she stabled herself against a rock over which she could not win, and then Robin lost no time in throwing himself from her back. Many and bitter were the epithets he there bestowed on his old mare, and grievous was the lamentation he made for his wife, as endeavoring to lead back the mare from the rocky hill into the miserable track of a road. No; the plague o' one foot would the mare move in that direction! She held out her long nose, with her white muslin face, straight up to heaven, as if contemplating the moon. She weened that her foal was up among the crags, and put on a resolution not to leave him a second time for any man's pleasure. After all, Robin confessed that he had some excuse for her, for the shadow of the old thorn was so like a colt, that he could scarcely reason himself out of the belief that it was one.

Robin was now hardly set indeed, for the mare would not lead a step; and when he came back to her side to leather her with the snibbelt, she only galloped round him and round him and neighed. "O plague on you for a beast, that ever you were foaled!" exclaimed Robin; "I shall lose a dearly beloved wife, and perhaps a couple of babies at least, and all owing to your stupidity and obstinacy! I could soon run on foot to the Sandbed, but then I cannot carry the widwife home on my back; and could I once get you there, you would not be long in bringing us both home again. Plague on you for a beast, if I winna knock your brains out."

Robin now attacked the mare's white face with the snibbelt, yerk for yerk, so potently, that the mare soon grew madly crazed, and came plunging and floundering from the hill at a great rate. Robin thus found out a secret not before known in this country, on which he acted till the day of his death, namely, "that the best way to make a horse spring forward is to strike it on the face."

Once more on the path, Robin again mounted, sparing neither the mare nor the halter; while the mare, at every five or six paces, entertained him with a bray so loud, with its accompanying nicker, that every one made the hills ring again.

There is scarcely any thing a man likes worse than this constant neighing of the steed he rides upon, especially by night. It makes him start as from a reverie, and puts his whole frame in commotion. Robin did not like it more than other men. It caused him inadvertently to utter some imprecations on the mare, that he confessed he should not have uttered; but it also caused him to say some short prayers for preservation; and to which of these agencies he owed the following singular adventure, he never could divine.

Robin had got only about half a mile farther on his road, when his mare ceased her braying, and all at once stood stone-still, cocking her large ears, and looking exceedingly frightened. "Oho, madam! what's the matter now?" said Robin; "is this another stratagem to mar my journey, for all the haste that you see me in? Get on, my fine yaud, get on! There is nothing uncanny there."

Robin coaxed thus, as well to keep up his own spirits, as to encourage his mare; for the truth is, that his hair began to stand on end with affright. The mare would neither ride, lead, nor drive, one step further; but there she stood, staring, snuffing the wind, and snorting so long, that it was frightsome to hear, as well as to see her. This was the worst dilemma of all. What was our forlorn shepherd to do now? He averred that the mare *would not* go on either by force or art; but I am greatly deceived, if by this time he durst for his life have gone on, even though the mare could have been induced to proceed. He took the next natural expedient, which was that of shouting out as loud as he could bellow, "Hilloa! who's there? Be ye devils, be ye witches, or be ye Christian creatures, rise an' shaw yoursels. I say hilloa! who's there?"

Robin was at this time standing hanging by the mare's hair halter with both his hands, for she was capering and flinging up her white face with such violence, that she sometimes made him bob off the ground; when, behold! at his last call, a being like a woman rose from among some deep heather bushes about twenty yards before him. She was like an elderly female, dressed in a coarse country garb, tall and erect, and there she stood for a space, with her pale face, on which the moon shone full, turned straight towards Robin. He then heard her muttering something to herself; and, with a half-stifled laugh, she stooped down, and lifted something from among the heath, which Robin thought resembled a baby.—"There! the gipsey yaud has been murdering that poor bairn!" thought Robin to himself: "it was nae wonder my auld yaud was frightened!

she kens what's what, for as contrarysome as she is. And murderess though the hizzy be, it is out o' my power to pursue her wi' this positive auld hack, for no another foot nearer her will she move."

Robin never thought but that the mysterious being was to fly from him, or at least go off the road to one side; but in place of that she rolled her baby, or bundle, or whatever it was, deliberately up in a blanket, fastened it up between her shoulders, and came straight to the place where Robin stood hanging by his mare's head. The mare was perfectly mad. She reared, snorted, and whisked her long ill-shaped tail: but Robin held her, for he was a strong young man, and the hair halter must have been proportionably so, else it never could have stood the exercise of that eventful night.

Though I have heard Robin tell the story oftener than once when I was a boy, there was always a confusion here which I never understood. This may be accounted for, in some measure, by supposing that Robin was himself in such perplexity and confusion, that he neither knew well what passed, nor remembered it afterwards. As far as I recollect, the following was the dialogue that passed between the two.

"Wha's this?"

"What need ye speed, goodman? kend fo'k, gin it war daylight."

"I think I'm a wee bit at a loss. I dinna ken ye."

"May be no, for ye never saw me afore. An' yet it is a queer thing for a father no to ken his ain doughter."

"Ay, that wad be a queer thing, indeed. But where are you gaun at this time o' the night?"

"Where am I gaun? where but up to the Craigy-rigg, to get part o' my ain blithemeat. But where are you riding at sic a rate?"

"Why, I'm just riding my whole might for the houdy: an' that's very true, I hae little need to stand claverin here wi' you."

"Ha, ha, ha! daddy Robin! It is four hours sin' ye came frae hame, and ye're no won three miles yet. Why, man, afore ye get to the Sand-bed an' hame again, your doughter will be ready for spaining."

"Doughter! what's a' this about a doughter? Has my dear Jean really a daughter?"

"You may be sure she has, else I could not have been here."

"And has she only ane? for, od! ye maun ken, wifie, that I expectit twa at the fewest. But I dinna understand you. I wish ye may be canny enough, for my white-faced yaud seems to jalouse otherwise."

"Ye dinna ken me, Robin, but ye will ken me. I am Ellen Grieve. I was well brought up, and married to a respectable farmer's son; but he turned out a villain, and, among other qualifications, was a notorious thief; so that I have been reduced to this that you see, to travel the country with a pack, and lend women a helping-hand in their hour o' need. An', Robin, when you and I meet here again, you may be preparing for another world."

"I dinna comprehend ye at a', wifie. No: a' that I can do, I canna comprehend ye. But I understand thus far. It seems ye are a houdy, or a meedwife, as the grit fo'ks will ca' you. Now that's the very thing I want at present, for your helping hand may be needfu' yonder. Come on ahint me, and we'll soon be hame."

I must give the expedition home in Robin's own words.

"Weel, I forces my yaud into the Cleuch-brae, contrary as she was, wi' her white face, for she had learned by this time to take a wee care o' the timmer snibbelt. I was on her back in a jiffey; an' to say truth, the kerlin wi' the pale round face, and the bit lang bundle on her back, wasna slack; for she was on ahint me, bundle and' a', ere ever I kend I was on mysel. But, Gude forgie us! sichan a voyage as we gat! I declare my yaud gae a snore that gart a' the hills ring, an' the verra fire flew frae her snirls. Out o' the Cleuch-brae she sprang as there hadna been a bane or a joint within her hide, but her hale carcass made o' steel springs; an' ower bush, ower brier, ower stock, an' ower stane she flew, I declare, an' so be it, faster than ever an eagle flew through the firmament of the heavens.

"I kend then that I had either a witch or a mermaid on ahint me; but how was I now to get quit o' her. The hair halter had lost a' power, an' I had no other shift left, than to fix by instinct on the mane wi' baith hands, an' cry out to the mare to stop. 'Wo, ye auld viper o' the pit! wo, ye beast o' Bashan!' I cries in outer desperation; but ay the louder I cried, the faster did the glyde flee. She snored, an' she grained, an' she reirdit baith ahint an' afore; an' on she dashed, regardless of a' danger.

"I soon lost sight o' the ground—off gaed my bonnet, an' away i' the wind—off gaed my plaid, an' away i' the wind; an' there was I sitting lootching forret, cleaving the wind like an arrow out of a bow, an' my een rinning, pouring like streams of water from the south. At length we came to the Birk-bush Linn! and alangst the very verge of that awsome precipice, there was my dementit beast, scouring like a fiery dragon. 'Lord preserve me!' cried I, loud out; an' I hadna weel said the word, till my mare gae a tremendous plunge ower something, I never kend what it was, and then down she came on her nose. No rider could stand this concussion, an' I declare, an' so be it, the meedwife lost her haud, and ower the precipice she flew head foremost. I just gat ae glisk o' her as she was gaun ower the top o' the birk-bush like a shot stern, an' I heard her gae a waw like a cat; an' that was the last sight I saw o' her.

"I was then hanging by the mane an' the right hough; an' during the moment that my mare took to gather hersel' up, I recovered my seat, but only on the top o' the shoulder, for I couldna win to the right place. The mare flew on as madly as ever; and frae the shoulder I came on the neck, an' forret, an' forret, piecemeal, till, just as I came to my ain door, I had gotten a grip o' baith the lugs. The foal gae a screed of a nicher; on which the gyde threw up her white face wi' sic a vengeance, that she gart me play at pitch-an'-toss up in the air. The foal nichered, an' the mare nichered, an' out came the kimmers; an' I declare, an' so be it, there was I lying in the gutter senseless, wanting the plaid, an' wanting the bonnet, an' nae meedwife at a'; an' that's the truth, sir, I declare, an' so be it.

"Then they carried me in, an' they washed me, an' they bathed me, an' at last I came to mysel'; an', to be sure, I had gotten a bonny doughter, an' a' things war gaun on *as weel as could be expectit.* 'What hae ye made o' your plaid, Robin?' says ane. Whare's your bonnet, Robin?' says anither. 'But, gudeness guide us! what's come o' the houdy, Robin? Whare's the meedwife, Robin?' cried they a' at aince. I trow this question gart me glower as I had seen a ghaist. 'Och! huh!' cried the wives, an' held up their hands; 'something has happened! something has happened! We see by his looks!—Robin! what has happened? Whare's the meedwife?'

"'Haud your tongue, Janet Reive; an' haud ye your tongue too, Eppie Dickson,' says I, 'an' dinna speer that question at me again; for the houdy is where the Lord will, an' where my white-faced yaud was pleased to pit her, and that's in the howe o' the Birk-bush Linn. Gin she be a human creature, she's a' dashed to pieces: but an' she be nae a human creature, she may gang where she like for me; an' that's true, I declare, an' so be it.'"

Now it must strike every reader, as it did me at first and for many years afterwards, that this mysterious nocturnal wanderer gave a most confused and unintelligible account of herself. She was Robin's daughter; her name was Ellen Grieve; she was married to such and such a man; and had now become a peddler, and acted occasionally as a midwife: and finally, when the two met there again, it would be time for Robin to be preparing for another state of existence. Now, in the first place, Robin never had a daughter till that very hour and instant when the woman rose out of the heather-bush and accosted him. All the rest appeared to him like a confused dream, of which he had no comprehension, save that he could never again be prevailed on to pass that way alone by night; for he had an impression that at some time or other he should meet with her again.

But by far the most curious part of this story is yet to come, and it shall be related in few words. Robin went with some others, as soon as it was day, to the Birk-bush Linn, but there was neither body nor blood to be seen, nor any appearance of a person having been killed or hurt. Robin's daughter was christened by the name of Ellen, after her maternal grandmother, so that her name was actually Ellen Grieve: and from the time that Robin first saw his daughter, there never was a day on which some of her looks did not bring the mysterious midwife to his mind. Thus far the story had proceeded, when I heard it related; for I lived twelve months in the family, and the girl was then only about seven years of age. But, strange to relate, the midwife's short history of herself has turned out the exact history of this once lovely girl's life; and Robin, a few days before his death, met her at the Kirk Cleuch, with a bundle on her back, and recognized his old friend in every lineament and article of attire. He related this to his wife as a secret, but added, that "he did not know whether it was his *real* daughter whom he met or not."

Many are the traditions remaining in the country, relative to the seeking of midwives, or houdies, as they are universally denominated all over the south of Scotland; and strange adventures are related as having happened in these precipitate excursions, which were proverbially certain to happen by night. Indeed it would appear, that there hardly ever was a midwife brought, but some incident occurred indicative of the fate or fortunes of the little forthcoming stranger; but, amongst them all, I have selected this as the most remarkable.

I am exceedingly grieved at the discontinuance of midwifery, that primitive and original calling, in this primitive and original country; for never were there such merry groups in Scotland as the midwives and their kimmers in former days, and never was there such store of capital stories and gossip circulated as on these occasions. But those days are over! and alack, and wo is me! no future old shepherd shall tell another tale of SEEKING THE HOUDY?

LOVE IS LIKE A DIZZINESS.

BY JAMES HOGG.

I LATELY lived in quiet case,
An' ne'er wish'd to marry, O!
But when I saw my Peggy's face,
I felt a sad quandary, O!
Though wild as ony Athol deer,
She has trepann'd me fairly, O!
Her cherry cheeks an' een sae clear
Torment me late an' early, O!
O, love, love, love!
Love is like a dizziness;
It winna let a poor body
Gang about his biziness!

To tell my feats this single week
Wad mak a daft-like diary, O!
I drave my cart outow'r a dike,
My horses in a miry, O!
I wear my stockings white an' blue,
My love's sae fierce an' fiery, O!
I drill the land that I should plough,
An' plough the drills entirely, O!
O, love, love, love! etc.

Ae morning, by the dawn o' day,
I rase to theek the stable, O!
I kuest my coat, and plied away
As fast as I was able, O!

I wrought that morning out an' out,
As I'd been redding fire, O!
When I had done an look'd about,
Gudefaith, it was the byre, O!
O, love, love, love! etc.

Her wily glance I'll ne'er forget,
The dear, the lovely blinkin o't
Has pierced me through an' through the heart,
An' plagues me wi' the prinkling o't.
I tried to sing, I tried to pray,
I tried to drown't wi' drinkin' o't,
I tried wi' sport to drive't away,
But n'er can sleep for thinkin' o't.
O, love, love, love! etc.

Nae man can tell what pains I prove,
Or how severe my pliskie, O!
I swear I'm sairer drunk wi' love
Than ever I was wi' whiskey, O!
For love has raked me fore an' aft,
I scarce can lift a leggie, O!
I first grew dizzy, then gaed daft,
An' soon I'll dee for Peggy, O!
O, love, love, love!
Love is like a dizziness
It winna let a poor body
Gang about his biziness!

MORE THAN A PROVIDENTIAL ESCAPE.—A serving woman, who was sent to bring water for some domestic purposes, returned completely drenched, after what was considered rather an unreasonable length of time. Her mistress demanded what had kept her so long. "Kept me so long!" said the dripping absentee, with a look of surprise, "deed, ye may be glad to see me again; the burn was runnin' frae bank to brae. I missed a fit and fell in, and if it hadna been for Providence and *another woman*, I'd ha'e been drowned."

A WITTY REPLY.—Sir Walter Scott does not seem to have been the fool at school which some have stated. Once, a boy in the same class was asked by the "dominie" what part of speech *with* was. "A noun, sir," said the boy. "You young blockhead," cried the pedagogue, "what example can you give of such a thing?" "I can tell you, sir," interrupted Scott; "you know there's a verse in the Bible which says, 'they bound Samson with *withs*.'"

A HIGHLAND CABINETMAKER.—A young Highlander was apprenticed to a cabinetmaker in Glasgow, and, as a first job, had a chest of veneered drawers to clean and polish. After a sufficient time had elapsed for doing the work assigned him, the foreman inquired whether he was ready with the dressers yet? "Oich no; it's a tough job; I've almost taken the skin off my ain two hand before I'll get it off the drawers." "What!" replied the startled director of plane and chisel, "you are not taking the veneering off, you blockhead?" "What I'll do then? I could not surely put a polish on before I'll teuk the bark aff!"

A DESIDERATUM.—A traveller sitting down to a Scotch breakfast, gratified at the varied display of tempting viands, said to the lassie in attendance, "there is nothing wanting here to prevent me from making a most sumptuous breakfast, but an appetite." "An appetite," said the poor creature, anxious to please, "I dinna ken we ha' sic a thing in a' the house, but I'll rin and ask my mistress."

THE WONDERFU' WEAN.

BY WILLIAM MILLER.

OUR wean's the most wonderfu' wean e'er I saw,
It would tak' me a lang summer day to tell a'
His pranks, frae the mornin' till night shuts his e'e,
When he sleeps like a peerie, 'tween father an' me.
For in his quiet turns, siccan questions he'll speir:
How the moon can stick up in the sky that's sae clear?
What gars the win' blaw? an' whar frae comes the rain?
He's a perfect divert—he's a wonderfu' wean.

Or wha was the first bodie's father? an' wha
Made the very first snaw-show'r that ever did fa'?
An' wha made the first bird that sang on a tree?
An' the water that sooms a' the ships in the sea!—
But after I've tauld as weel as I ken,
Again he begins wi' his wha? an' his when?
An' he looks aye sae watchfu', the while I explain;
He's as auld as the hills—he's an auld-farrant wean.

And folk wha ha'e skill o' the lumps on the head,
Hint there's mae ways than toilin' o' winnin' ane's bread;—
How he'll be a rich man, an' ha'e men to work for him,
Wi' a kyte like a bailie's, shug shugging afore him;
Wi' a face like the moon, sober, sonsy, and douce,
An' a back, for its breadth, like the side o' a house.
'Tweel I'm unco ta'en up wi't, they mak' a' sae plain;
He's just a town's-talk—he's a bye-ord'nar wean.

I ne'er can forget sic a laugh as I gat
To see him put on father's waistcoat and hat?
Then the lang-leggit boots gaed sae far ower his knees,
The tap loops wi' his fingers he grippit wi' ease,
Then he marcht thro' the house, he marcht but, he marcht ben,
Sae like mony mae o' our great-little men,
That I leugh clean outright, for I couldna contain,
He was sic a conceit—sic an ancient-like wean.

But mid a' his daffin sic kindness he shows,
That he's dear to my heart as the dew to the rose;
An' the unclouded hinnie-beam aye in his e'e,
Mak's him every day dearer an' dearer to me.
Though fortune be saucy, an' dorty, an' dour,
An' glooms thro' her fingers, like hills thro' a show'r,
When bodies ha'e got ae bit bairn o' their ain,
He can cheer up their hearts,—he's the wonderfu' wean.

COCKIE-LEERIE-LA.

BY WILLIAM MILLER.

THERE is a country gentleman, who leads a thrifty life,
Ilk morning scrapin' orra things thegither for his wife—
His coat o' glowin' ruddy brown, and wavelet wi' gold—
A crimson crown upon his head, well fitting one so bold.

If ithers pick where he did scrape, he brings them to disgrace,
For, like a man o' mettle, he—siclike meets face to face;
He gi'es the loons a letherin', a crackit croon to claw—
There is nae gaun about the buss wi' Cockie-leerie-la!

His step is firm and evenly, his look both grave and sage—
To bear his rich and stately tail should have a pretty page;
An' tho' he hauds his head fu' hie, he glinteth to the grun,
Nor fyles his silver spurs in dubs wi' glow'rin' at the sun:

And whyles I've thoct had he a haun wharwi' to grip a stickie,
A pair o' specks across his neb, an' roun his neck a dickie,
That weans wad laughin' haud their sides, an' cry—"Preserve us a'!
Ye're some frien' to Doctor Drawblood, douce Cockie-leerie-la!"

So learn frae him to think nae shame to work for what ye need,
For he that gapes till he be fed, may gape till he be dead;
An' if ye live in idleness, ye'll find unto your cost,
That they wha winna work in heat will hunger in the frost.
An' hain wi' care ilk sair-won plack, and honest pride will fill
Your purse wi' gear—e'en far-aff frien's will bring grist to your mill;
An' if, when grown to be a man, your name's without a flaw,
Then rax your neck, and tune your pipes to—Cockie-leerie-la!

THE CHEATERIE PACKMAN.

BY LEITCH RITCHIE.

The beings of the mind are not of clay.—BYRON.

It was yet pretty early in the morning when I arrived at the inn of Skreigh, and never having been in that part of the country before, my heart misgave me at the appearance of the house, and I thought that surely I had mistaken the road, an awful idea to a man who had walked twelve miles before breakfast! It was a huge, gray, dismantled edifice, standing alone in a wild country, and presenting evident traces of a time when the *bawbees* of the traveller might have procured him lodgings within its walls for a longer period than suited his convenience. On entering the parlor, although the "base uses" to which this ancient mansion had returned were clearly indicated by certain gill-stroups scattered about the dirty tables, yet the extraordinary size of the room, the lowness of the walls, and the scantiness of the furniture, kept up in my mind the associations which had been suggested by the exterior; and it was not till the aroma of tea, and the still more "fragrant lunt" of a Finnan haddie had saluted my senses, that the visions of the olden time fled from my eyes.

While busy with my breakfast, another traveller came into the room. He had a pack on his back and an ellwand in his hand, and appeared to be one of those travelling philanthropists—answering to the peddlers of the south—who carry into the holes and corners of the sylvan world the luxuries of the city. Our scene being on the *best side* of the Tweed, I need not say that the body had a sharp eye, an oily face, and a God-fearing look. He sat down over against me, upon one of the tables, to rest his pack, and from his shining shoes and orderly apparel, I judged that he had passed the night in the house, and was waiting to pay his score, and fare forth again upon his journey. There was, notwithstanding, a singular expression of fatigue on his yellow countenance. A common observer would have guessed that he had been brim-*fou* over night, and had risen before he had quite slept off the effects; but to me, who am curious in such matters, there appeared a something in his face which invested with a moral dignity an expression that would otherwise have been ludicrous or pitiable.

Ever and anon he turned a longing eye upon the Finnan haddie, but as often edged himself with a jerk farther away from the temptation; and whenever the landlady came into the room, his remonstrances on her delay, at first delivered in a moaning, heart-broken tone, became at last absolutely cankered. The honest wife, however, appeared determined to extend the hospitality of breakfast to her guest, and made sundry lame excuses for not "bringing ben his score," while she was occupied in displaying upon my table, with the most tempting liberality, the various good things that constitute a Scottish breakfast.

"Are you not for breakfasting, good man," said I, at length, "before you go forth this morning?"

"No, please God," said he, with almost a jump, "no carnal comfort shall pass my lips on this side the mill of Warlock!"

"The mill of Warlock!" repeated I, with surprise, "that should be at least twelve miles from this—and I can tell you, my friend, it is not pleasant travelling so far on an empty stomach. If you have any urgent reason for an abstinence that we of the kirk of Scotland attach no merit to, you should not have loitered in bed till this hour of the morning."

The packman at my reproof, put on a kind of *blate* look, but his features gathering gradually into solemnity—

"Sir," said he, "I *have* urgent reasons for my conduct, and while this weary wife is making out my score, I will, if you desire it, tell you the story." Having eagerly signified my assent, the packman wiped his glistening forehead, and with a heavy sigh began to discourse as follows:—

"Aweel, sir—it was at this time yesterday morning I arrived at the mill of Warlock. The miller was out, and his wife, glad of the opportunity, rampauged over my pack like one demented. She made me turn out every article in my aught, and kept me bargaining about this and that, and flyting by the hour about the price; and after all it came to pass that the jaud (God forgive me!) wanted naething of more value than three ells of riband! You may be sure that I was not that pleased; and what with fatigue, and what with my vexation, while I was measuring the riband, and the wife sklanting round at the looking-glass, I just clipped — by mistake like—a half-ell short. Aweel, ye'll say that was just naething after the fash I had had, and moreover, I stoutly refused the second glass of whiskey she offered me to the douroch; and so, shouldering my pack again, I took the way in an evil hour to the inn of Skreigh.

"It was late at night when I arrived here, and I had been on my legs all day, so that you may think my heart warmed to the auld biggin, and I looked forward to naething waur than a cozy seat by the ingle-side, or chat with the landlady—a douce woman, sir, and not aye so slow as the now, foul fa' her! (God forgive me!) forby, maybe, a half mutchin—or twa: and all these things of a truth I had. Not that I exceeded the second stoup, a practice which I hold to be *contra bonos mores*—but ye'll no understand Latin? ye'll be from the south? Aweel—but there was something mair, ye ken, quite as necessary for a Christian traveller, and a wearied man; and at last, with a great gaunt, I speered at the serving hizzie for my bedroom.

"'Bed-room,' quo' she, 'ye'll no be ganging to sleep here the night?'

"'Atweel,' said the mistress, 'I am unco wae, but every room in the house is fu'. Hout! it's but a step to the town—no abune twal miles and a bittock—and ye ken every inch of the way as weel as the brass nails on your ellwand.' I wish I may be forgi'en for the passion they put me intil! To think of sending me out such a gait my lane, and near the sma' hours!

"'O ye jaud!' cried I, 'if the gudeman was no in the yird the night, ye would craw till a different tune!' and with that such a hullibaloo was raised amang us, that at last the folks began to put in their shouthers at the door in their sarks to speer what was the matter.

"'Aweel, aweel,' said the landlady, in the hinder end, quite forfaughten, a wilfu' man maun hae his way. There is but ae room in the house where there is no a living soul, and it's naething but an auld lumber-room. However, if you can pass the time with another half-mutchin while Jenny and me rig up the bed, it will be as much at your service as a decenter place.' And so, having gotten the battle, I sat myself down again, and Jenny brought in the other stoup—ye'll be saying that was the third; but there's nae rule without an exception, and moreover ye ken, 'three's aye canny.'

"At last and at length, I got into my bed-room, and it was no that ill-looking at all. It was a good sizeable room, with a few sticks of old furniture, forby a large old-fashioned bed. I laid my pack down, as is my custom, by the bedside, and after saying my prayers, put out the candle and tumbled in.

"Aweel, sir, whether it was owing to my being over fatigued, or to the third stoup in defiance of the proverb being no canny, I know not, but for the life of me I could not sleep. The bed was not a bad bed, it was roomy and convenient, and there was not a whish in the house, and not a stime of light in the room. I counted over my bargains for the day, and half wished I had not made the mistake with the miller's wife; I put my hand out at the stock of the bed and felt my pack, amusing myself by thinking what was this lump and that; but still I could not sleep. Then by degrees my other senses, as well as the touch, wearied of being awake and doing nothing—fiend tak them—(God forgive me!) sought employment. I listened as if in spite of myself, to hear whether there was any thing stirring in the house, and looked out of the curtains to see if any light came through the window chinks. Not a whish—not a stime! Then I said my prayers over again, and began to wish grievously that the creature had her half-ell of riband. Then my nose must needs be in the hobble, and I thought I felt a smell. It was not that bad a smell, but it was a smell I did not know, and therefore did not like. The air seemed close—feverish; I threw off the bedclothes, and began to puff and pant. Oh, I did wish then that I had never seen the physiog of the miller's wife!

"I began to be afraid. The entire silence seemed strange, the utter darkness more strange, and the strange smell stranger than all. I at first grasped at the bed-clothes, and pulled them over my head; but I had bottled in the smell with me; and, rendered intolerable by the heat, it seemed like the very essence of typhus. I threw off the clothes again in a fright, and felt persuaded that I was just in the act of taking some awful fever. I would have given the world to have been able to rise and open the window, but the world would have been offered me in vain to do such a thing. I contented myself with flapping the sheet like a fan, and throwing my arms abroad to catch the wind.

"My right hand, which was towards the stock of the bed, constantly lighted upon my pack, but my left could feel naething at all, save that there was a space between the bed and the wall. At last, leaning more over in that direction than heretofore, my hand encountered something a little lower than the surface of the bed, and I snatched it back with a smothered cry. I knew no more than the man in the moon what the something was, but it sent a tingle through my frame, and I felt the sweat begin to break over my brow. I would have turned to the other side, but I felt as heavy to my own muscles as if I had been made of lead; and besides, a fearful curiosity nailed me to the spot. I persuaded myself that it was from this part of the bed that the smell arose. Soon, however, with a sudden desperation, I plunged my hand again into the terrible abyss, and it rested upon a cauld, stiff, clammy face!

"Now, sir, I would have you to ken, that although I cannot wrestle with the hidden sympathies of nature, I am not easily frightened. If the stoutest robber that ever broke breeks—ay, or ran bare, for there be such in the Hielands,—was to lay a finger on my pack, I would haud on like grim death; and it is not to tell, that I can flyte about ae bawbee with the dourest wife in the country-side; but och, and alas! to see me at that moment, on the braid of my back, with my eyes shut, and my teeth set, and one hand on the physiog of a corp! The greatest pain I endured was from the trembling of my body, for the motion forced my hand into closer connection with the horrors of its resting-place; while I had no more power to withdraw it than if it had been in the thumb-screws.

"And there I lay, sir, with my eyes steeked, as if with screw-nails, my brain wandering and confused, and whole rivers of sweat spouting down my body, till at times I thought I had got fou, and was lying sleeping in a ditch. To tell you the history of my thoughts at that time is impossible; but the miller's wife, wo be upon her! she rode me like the night-hag. I think I must have been asleep a part of the time, for I imagined that the wearisome half-ell of riband was tied about my neck like a halter, and that I was on the eve of being choked. I ken not how long I tholed this torment; but at last I heard voices and sounds, as if the sheriffs' officers of hell were about me, and in a sudden agony of great fear, I opened my eyes.

"It was broad morning; the sun was shining into the room; and the landlady and her lasses were riving my hand from the face of the corpse. After casting a bewildered glance around, it was on that fearful object my eyes rested, and I recognized the remains of an old serving lass, who it seems died the day before, and was huddled into that room, to be out of the way of the company."

At this moment the landlady entered the room with his score, and while the packman sat wiping his brow, entered upon her defence.

"Ye ken, sir," said she, "that ye *wad* sleep in the house, and a wilfu' man maun hae his way; but gin ye had lain still, like an honest body wi' a clean conscience, and no gaen rampauging about wi' your hands where ye had no business, the feint a harm it would hae done ye!" The packman only answered with a glance of ire, as he thundered down the bawbees upon the table, and turning one last look upon the Finnan haddie, groaned deeply, and went forth upon his journey.

THE SCOTTISH TEA-PARTY.

BY JOHN DONALD CARRICK.

Now let's sing how Miss M'Wharty,
T'other evening had a party,
  To have a cup of tea;
And how she had collected
All the friends that she respected,
  All as merry as merry could be.
Dames and damsels came in dozens,
With two-three country cousins,
  In their lily-whites so gay;
Just to sit and chitter-chatter,
O'er a cup of scalding water,
  In the fashion of the day.

(*Spoken in different female voices.*) 'Dear me, how hae ye been this lang time, mem?' 'Pretty weel, I thank ye, mem. How hae ye been yoursel?' 'O mem, I've been vera ill wi' the rheumatisms, and though I were your tippet, I couldna be fu'er o' *stitches* than I am; but whan did ye see Mrs. Pinkerton?' 'O mem, I haena seen her this lang time. Did ye no hear that Mrs. Pinkerton and I hae had a difference?' 'No, mem, I didna hear. What was't about, mem?' 'I'll tell you what it was about, mem. I gaed o'er to ca' upon her ae day, and when I gaed in, ye see, she's sitting feeding the parrot, and I says to her, 'Mrs. Pinkerton, how d'ye do, mem?' and she never let on she heard me; and I says again, 'Mrs. Pinkerton, how d'ye do?' I says, and wi' that she turns about, and says she, 'Mrs. M'Saunter, I'm really astonished you should come and ask me how I do, considering the manner you've ridiculed me and my husband in public companies!' 'Mrs. Pinkerton,' quo' I, 'what's that ye mean, mem?' and then she began and gied me a' the ill-mannered abuse you can possibly conceive. And I just says to her, quo' I, 'Mrs. Pinkerton,' quo' I, 'that's no what I cam to hear, and if that's the way ye intend to gae on,' quo' I, 'I wish ye gude morning;' so I comes awa. Now I'll tell ye what a' this was about. Ye see, it was just about the term time, ye ken, they flitted aboon us, and I gaed up on the term morning to see if they wanted a kettle boiled or any thing o' that kind; and when I gaed in, Mr. Pinkerton, he's sitting in the middle o' the floor, and the barber's shaving him, and the barber had laid a' his face round wi' the *white* saip, and Mr. Pinkerton, ye ken, has a very *red* nose, and the red nose sticking through the white saip, just put me in mind o' a *carrot* sticking through a *collyflower;* and I very innocently happened to mention this in a party where I had been dining, and some officious body's gane and tell't Mrs. Pinkerton, and Mrs. Pinkerton's ta'en this *wonderfully* amiss. What d'ye think o' Mrs. Pinks?' 'Deed, mem, she's no worth your while; but did you hear what happened to Mrs. Clapperton the ither day?' 'No, mem. What's happened to her, poor body?' 'I'll tell you that, mem. You see, she was coming down Montrose street, and she had on a red pelisse and a white muff, and there's a bubbly-jock* coming

* Turkey-cock.

out o' the breweree—and whether the red pelisse had ta'en the beast's eye or no, I dinna ken, but the bubbly-jock rins after Mrs. Clapperton, and Mrs. Clapperton ran, poor body, and the bubbly-jock after her, and in crossing the causey, ye see, her fit slippet, and the muff flew frae her, and there's a cart coming past, and the wheel o' the cart gaes o'er the muff, and ae gentleman rins and lifts Mrs. Clapperton, and anither lifts the muff, and when he looks into the muff, what's there, but a wee bit broken bottle, wi' a wee soup brandy in't; and the gentlemen fell a looking and laughing to ane anither, and they're gaun about to their dinner parties and their supper parties, and telling about Mrs. Clapperton wi' the bubbly-jock and the bottle o' brandy. Now it's vera ill done o' the gentlemen to do any thing o' the kind, for Mrs. Clapperton was just like to drap down wi' perfect vexation, for she's a body o' that kind o' laithfu' kind o' disposition, she would just as soon take aquafortis as she would take brandy in ony clandestine kind o' manner!

Each gemman at his post now,
In handing tea or toast now,
  Is striving to outshine;
While keen to find a handle
To tip a little scandal,
  The ladies all combine;
Of this one's dress or carriage,
Or t'other's death or marriage,
  The dear chit-chat's kept up;
While the lady from the table,
Is calling while she's able—
  "Will you have another cup?"

'Dear me, you're no done, mem—you'll take another cup, mem—take out your spoon.' 'Oh no, mem, I never take mair than ae cup upon ony occasion.' 'Toots, sic nonsense.' 'You may toots awa, but it's true sense, mem. And whan did ye see Mrs. Petticraw, mem?' 'Deed, I haena seen her this lang time, and I'm no wanting to see her; she's a body o' that kind, that just gangs frae house to house gathering clashes, and gets her tea here and her tea there, and tells in your house what she hears in mine, and when she begins, she claver clavers on and on, and the claver just comes frae her as if it cam' aff a *clew*, and there's nae end o' her.' 'O you maun excuse her, poor body, ye ken she's lost a' her *teeth*, and her tongue *wearies* in her mouth wantin' *company*.' 'Deed they may excuse her that wants her, for it's no me. Oh! ladies, did ye hear what's happened in Mr. M'Farlane's family? there's an awfu' circumstance happened in that family. Mr. and Mrs. M'Farlane haevna spoken to ane anither for this fortnight, and I'll tell you the reason o't. Mrs. M'Farlane, poor body, had lost ane o' her teeth, and she gaed awa to the dentist to get a tooth put in, and the dentist showed her twa-three kinds o' them, and amang the rest he showed her a Waterloo ane, and she thought she would hae a Waterloo ane, poor body. Weel the dentist puts in ane to her, and the tooth's running in her head a' day, and when she gangs to her bed at nicht, as she tells me—but I'm certain she must have been dreaming—just about ane or twa o'clock o' the morning, mem, just about ane or twa o'clock in the morning, when she looks out o' her bed, there's a *great lang* sodger standing at the bedside, and quo' she, 'Man, what are ye wanting?' she says. Quo' he, 'Mrs. M'Farlane, that's my tooth that ye've got in your mouth.' 'Your tooth!' quo' she, 'the very tooth I bought the day at the dentist's!' 'It does na matter for that,' quo' he, 'I lost it at Waterloo.' 'Ye lost it at Waterloo, sic nonsense!' Weel, wi' that he comes forret to pit his finger into Mrs. M'Farlane's mouth to tak' the teeth out o' her mouth, and she gies a snap, and catch'd him by the finger, and he gied a great scriech and took her a gowf i' the side o' the head, and that waukened her, and when she waukens, what has she gotten but Mr. M'Farlane's finger atween her teeth, and him roaring like to gang out o' his judgment!! Noo, Mr. M'Farlane has been gaun about wi' his thumb in a clout, and looking as surly as a bear, for he thinks Mrs. M'Farlane had done it out o' spite, because he wadna let her buy a sofa at a sale the other day; noo it's vera ill-done o' Mr. M'Farlane to think ony thing o' that kind, as if ony woman would gang and *bite* her ain *flesh* and *blood* if she *kent o't*.'

Miss M'Wharty, with a smile,
Asks the ladies to beguile
  An hour with whist or loo;
While old uncle cries "Don't plague us;
Bring the toddy and the negus—
  We'll have a song or two."
"Oh dear me, uncle Joseph!
Pray do not snap one's nose off;
  You'll have toddy when you're dry,
With a little ham and chicken,
An' some other dainty pickin'
  For the ladies, by-and-by."

'Weel, mem, how's your frien' Mrs. Howdyson coming on in thae times, when there is sae muckle influenza gaun about amang families?' 'Mrs. Howdyson! na, ye maun ask somebody that kens better about her than I do. I ha nae seen Mrs. Howdyson for three months.' 'Dear me! do ye tell me sae? you that used to be like twa sisters! how did sic a wonderfu' change as that come about?' ''Deed, mem, it was a very silly matter did it a'. Some five months since, ye see, mem (but ye maunna be speaking about it), Mrs. Howdyson called on me ae forenoon, and after sitting awhile she drew a paper parcel out o' her muff:—'Ye'll no ken what this is?' said she. 'No,' quo I, 'it's no very likely.' 'Weel, it's my worthy husband's satin breeks, that he had on the day we were married; and I'm gaun awa to Miss Gushat to get her to mak them into a bonnet for mysel, for I hae a great respect for them on account of him that's awa'.' Respect! thinks I to mysel (for about this time she was spoke o' wi' Deacon Purdie), queer kind o' respect!—trying to catch a new guidman wi' a bonnet made out o' the auld ane's breeks!—but I said nothing. Weel, twa or three weeks after this, I was taking a walk wi' anither lady, and wha should we meet but Mrs. Howdyson, wi' a fine, flashy, black satin bonnet on! So, we stopped, and chatted about the weather, and the great mortality that was in the town, and when shaking hands wi' her at parting, I, without meaning ony ill, gae a nod at her bonnet, and happened to say, in my thoughtless kind o' way, 'Is that the breeks?' never mindin' at the time that there was a stranger lady wi' me. Now this was maybe wrang in me, but considering our intimacy, I never dreamed she had ta'en't amiss till twa three Sundays after, I met her gaun to the kirk alang wi' Miss Purdie, and I happened to hae on ane o' thae new fashionable bonnets—really, it was an elegant shaped bonnet! and trimmed in the most tasteful and becoming manner—it was, in short, such a bonnet as ony lady might have been proud to be seen in. Weel, for a' that, mem, we hadna stood lang before she began on my poor bonnet, and called it a' the ugly-looking things she could think o', and advised me to gang hame and change it, for I looked so vulgar and daftlike in't. At length I got nettled at her abuse, for I kent it was a' out o' spite; Mrs. Howdyson, says I, the bonnet may be baith vulgar and daftlike, as you say, but I'm no half sae vulgar or sae daftlike as I wad be, if, like *some folks*, I were gaun to the kirk wi' a *pair o' auld breeks on my head!* So I turns on my heel and left them; but though it was the Sabbath-day, I could not help thinking to mysel—my lady, I trow I've given you a lozenge to sook that'll keep you frae sleeping better than ony confectionary you've ta'en to the kirk wi' ye this while.'

'Weel, ladies, there are some strange kind o' folks to be met with after a'. I've just been listening to your crack, and it puts me in mind of a new married lady I was visiting the ither day. Before she was married, she was one of the dressiest belles we had about the town; and as for changing bonnets, you would seldom meet her twice wi' the same ane on. But now, though she has been little mair than three months married, she has become one of the most idle tawpie drabs that ever was seen, and has so many romantic fancies and stupid conceits about her, that I often canna help pitying the poor husband. Besides, she kens nae mair about house matters than if she had never heard o' sic things. She was an only dochter, you see, and, like the ewe's pet lamb, she got mair *licking* than *learning*. Just to gie ye an instance o' her management,—she told me she was making preparations for a dinner that her husband was going to give in a day or twa, and, amang ither things, she said that he wanted a turkey in ruffles.' 'Turkey in ruffles! quo I, that's a queer kind o' a dish!' 'Queer as it is, I'll manage it.' 'I would like to see it,' quo' I. So wi' that, she rings the bell and orders the servant to bring it ben. Weel, what's this but a turkey; the feathers were aff, to be sure, which showed some sma' glimmering o' sense, but the neck o' the beast was a' done up wi' fine cambric ruffles; these were to be ta'en aff, it seems, till it was roasted, and then it was to get on its finery again, so as to appear in full puff before the company, and this was what she called a turkey in ruffles. 'Dear me, quo' I, this is a way o' *dressing* a turkey I never saw before—I'm thinking the guidman must have meant turkey and truffles.' 'Truffles!' cried she, looking like a bewildered goose, and 'what's truffles, in a' the world?' 'Just look your cookery-book, quo' I, and you'll find that truffles are no made o' cambric muslin.' Now, ladies did you ever hear such ignorance? but, better than that, she went on to tell me how she had sent the servant to the market to buy a hare, to mak soup o': but, says she, 'what do you think the stupid creature did? instead of a hare, she brought me twa rabbits; now, ye ken, mem, rabbits dinna mak guid haresoup.' 'No, quo' I; *hare-soup* made o' *rabbits* may be a rare dish, but it's no to my taste.' 'That's just my opinion; so, as they're gay and white in the flesh, I'm thinking just to make a bit veal-pie o' them;—what do you think o' that for economy?' 'Excellent, quo' I, if you can *manage* it.' 'But,' said she, 'I'm to hae a haggis too, as a novelty to some English gentlemen that are to be of the party; now, I'm thinking of having the bag of the haggis died turkey-red; it's a fancy o' my ain, and I think it would astonish them; besides, it would cut such a dash on the table.' 'Dash on the table! quo' I, nae doubt it would cut a dash on the table;—but wha ever heard o' a turkey-red haggis before?' Now, I think, ladies, if my frien' can either make *hare-soup* or a *veal-pie* out of a pair of *rabbits*, she'll be even a greater genius than Mrs. Howdyson, wi' her new bonnet made out o' a pair of auld breeks!'

So thus to sit and chitter chatter
O'er a cup o' scalding water,
Is the fashion o' the day.

EXTRACTS FROM "THE LAIRD OF LOGAN."

BY JOHN DONALD CARRICK.

The Usual Apology.—Logan happened one evening to be at a convivial party in Irvine, where the toast and the song performed their merry round. A lady present being called on to contribute to the hilarity of the evening, excused herself by saying she had only one song, and it was so threadbare, she was afraid to sing it. "Hoot, madam," cried our wag, "so much the better, for if its threadbare, you'll get the easier through it."

Good Excuse for a Bad Hat.—Logan, like some other eccentrics, seems to have disliked parting with his old habiliments. Visiting London on some occasion, he was met by an acquaintance in one of the fashionable regions of the city, who, observing the Laird to have on a "shocking bad hat," could not refrain from expressing his surprise at his negligence. "Oh," rejoins the wit, "it makes nae difference what I wear here—no ane kens me." This, of course, was a settler. Some short time afterwards, however, the parties met again in Edinburgh, at Logan's old favorite haunt—the old favorite chapeau still maintained its crowning eminence. Now, thinks the assailant, I shall certainly hedge him. "Well, Logan, still sticking to the old hat!" "Hoot, man!" replies the wit, dryly, "what matters what I wear here?—everybody kens me."

Love at Sight.—A servant girl, of no strong intellect, who lived with a lady in the neighborhood of Paisley, one day surprised her mistress by giving up her place. The lady inquired the cause, and found that it was that fertile source of dissension between mistress and maid-servant—a lad. "And who is this lad?" inquired her mistress. "Ou, he's a nice lad—a lad that sits in the kirk just forenant me." "And when does he intend that you and he should be married?" "I dinna ken." "Are you sure he intends to marry you at all?" "I daur say he does, mem." "Have you had much of each other's company?" "No yet." "When did you last converse with him?" "Deed, we hae nae conversed ava yet." "Then how should you suppose that he is going to marry you?" "Ou," replied the simple girl, "he's been lang lookin' at me, and I think he'll soon be speakin'."

AN AUDIBLE WITNESS.

BY ANDREW HENDERSON.

Some years ago, Lord ——— was presiding at a circuit trial in Glasgow, where several females were in succession examined as witnesses. Whether it arose from their unusual exposure in the witness box, (a square structure in the centre of the Court Hall, elevated considerably above the floor,) from fear of their expressions being laughed at, or from whatever cause, certain it is, they spoke so inaudibly and indistinctly, that the jury, again and again, complained, and his lordship as often admonished them to speak out; but, notwithstanding repeated admonitions, they again and again resumed their under tone till of new reminded:—on this account, the patience of the Judge was most severely tried, and by the time the examination was finished, he was visibly suppressing great irritation. At this juncture, there approached through the crowd, towards the witness box, a tall, stout fellow, with a fustian sleeved jacket, capacious corduroy inexpressibles, blue rig-and-fur hose, and strong lumps of shoes, well supplied with tackets—who, with pavier-like thumps, tramped up the wooden steps into the box, laid his bonnet on the seat, and sousing himself down on it, stared about with seeming indifference, as if he had nothing more to do. This uncommon nonchalance his lordship eyed with surprise, and having promptly ordered him to stand up, and administered the oath, he, with a fearful scowl and gruff manner, addressed him: "Witness, let me tell you, that my brother (meaning the other Judge) and I have this day been put to great trouble examining witnesses who would not, or could not, speak above their breath;—now, sir, I see you're a strong young man, and being a carter, as I understand, and accustomed to speak out to your horses, you can have no such apology; and, therefore, let me tell you, once for all, that if you speak not at the top of your voice, you shall be sent down to jail in an instant." Ere this volley was well over, the witness, unconscious of wrong by him to call for such a threat, changed color—stared wildly around—hitched up the headband of his small clothes,—and betrayed such strange symptoms, that his lordship, imputing them to disrespect or indifference, called out, "stand still, sir—mind what I've said to you." This acted like an electric shock on the witness, for he instantly grasped the bar before him, stood stock-still, gaping as petrified. His lordship then resumed his seat, and called out to the witness, "What's your name?" "Bauldy M'Luckie," was instantly roared out in a voice more resembling the discharge of a piece of artillery, than the ordinary action of the vocal organs. The amazement was succeeded by a burst of irrepressible laughter from the audience, and the lengthened bawl of "Si-lence," by the macer, while the effect of it on his lordship was such, that, instinctively dropping the pen, clapping both hands to his ears, and looking daggers at Bauldy, he exclaimed, "What's the meaning of that, sir?" Bauldy, who thought his lordship now meant to quarrel with him for not speaking loud enough, immediately answered in the same tone, "I never spoke louder to the brutes in my life." A perfect explosion of laughter succeeded; which, for some time, defied every effort of the macer and the court to get repressed; even his lordship, whose kindness of heart was well known, smilingly observed, "Surely you don't consider us your brutes, sir,—you should know there's a difference betwixt roaring and speaking. Remember where you're standing, sir." This memento wrought on Bauldy prodigiously—his hands clenched convulsively the bar in front—the perspiration broke in drops on his face—his eyes seemed fixed, and his whole frame fearfully agitated. In vain were questions put to him from both sides of the bar—fruitless were expostulations or threats—his answers were all of the *non mi recordo* class, except two, to which no importance seemed attached by any one, unless Bauldy, namely, "That he staid wi' his mither in the Briggate; and he kent she was aulder than himsel'." Seeing, therefore, that nothing further could be elicited from Bauldy, his lordship imputed it to Bauldy's wish to conceal the truth, in a surly manner ordered him to get away. This operated like a charm; Bauldy and bonnet were instantly in motion. His precipitate tramp down the narrow steps, however, ended rather ungracefully, for having tripped himself, down he came, at length, on the top of a man, whose rueful gestures and looks, under the weight and desperate grasp of Bauldy, found no consolation or apology, other than the convulsive laughter of the audience, and the hasty remark of Bauldy at striding away—"Did ye e'er see sick a cankry buffer as that." On getting outside the court, Bauldy's mother and some cronies were overheard asking him how he had come on;—"Come on," said he, "I thought the auld buffer would hae worried me; he said he would send me down to jail whaur I stood—I lost my sight—and gaed clean doited—I was like to swarf, but I held firm by the bauk, for fear they might knock the boddom frae neath my feet, and send me below in an instant, as he said—yon's nae fun ava. Come awa, lads, my throat's as dry as a whistle, and gi'e me a dram to draik the dust."

CATCHING A TARTAR.

An unpublished Chapter from "the Life of Mansie Wauch, the Tailor."

BY DAVID MACBETH MOIR (DELTA).

From the first moment I clapped eye on the caricature thing of a coat, that Tommy Bodkin had, in my absence, shaped out for Cursecowl the butcher, I foresaw, in my own mind, that a catastrophe was brewing for us; and never did soldier gird himself to fight the French, or sailor prepare for a sea-storm, with greater alacrity, than I did to cope with the bull-dog anger, and buffet back the uproarious vengeance of our heathenish customer.

At first I thought of letting the thing take its natural course, and of threaping down Cursecowl's throat, that he must have been feloniously keeping in his breath, when Tommy took his measure; and, moreover, that as it was the fashion to be straight-laced, Tommy had done his utmost, trying to make him look like his betters; till, my conscience checking me for such a nefarious intention, I endeavored, as became me in the relations of man, merchant, and Christian, to solder the matter peaceably, and show him, if there was a fault committed, that there was no evil intention on my side of the house. To this end, I despatched the bit servant wench, on the Friday afternoon, to deliver the coat, which was neatly tied up in brown paper, and directed—"Mr. Cursecowl, with care," and to buy a sheep's head; bidding her, by way of being civil, give my kind compliments, and enquire how Mr. and Mrs. Cursecowl, and the five little Miss Cursecowls, were keeping their healths, and trusting to his honor in sending me a good article. But have a moment's patience.

Being busy at the time, turning a pair of kuttikins for old Mr. Mooleypouch, the mealmonger, when the lassie came back, I had no mind of asking a sight of the sheep's head, as I aye like the little black-faced, in preference to the white, fat, fozy Cheviot-breed; but, most providentially, I catched a gliskie of the wench passing the shop-window, on the road over to Jacob Coom, the smith's, to get it singed, having been despatched there by her mistress. Running round the counter like lightning, I opened the sneck, and hallooed to her to wheel to the right about, having, somehow or other, a superstitious longing to look at the article. As I was saying, there was a Providence in this, which, at the time, mortal man could never have thought of.

James Batter had popped in with a newspaper in his hand, to read me a curious account of a Mermaid, that was seen singing a Gaelic song, and combing its hair with a tortoiseshell comb, someway terrible far north about Shetland, by a respectable minister of the district, riding home in the gloaming, after a presbytery dinner. So, as he was just taking off his spectacles cannily, and saying to me—"And was not that droll?"—the lassie spread down her towel on the counter, when, lo! and behold! such an abominable spectacle! James Batter observing me run back, and turn white, put on his glasses again, cannily taking them out of his well-worn shagreen case, and, giving a stare down at the towel, almost touched the beast's nose with his own.

"And what in the name of goodness is the matter?" quo' James Batter; "ye seem in a wonderful quandary!"

"The matter!" answered I, in astonishment; looking to see if the man had lost his sight or his senses—"the matter! who ever saw a sheep's head with straight horns, and a visnomy, all colors of the rainbow—red, blue, orange, green, yellow, white, and black?"

"Deed it is," said James, after a nearer inspection; "it must be a lowsy-naturay. I'm sure I have read most of Buffon's books, and I have never heard tell of the like. It's gey and querish."

"Od! James," answered I, "ye take every thing very canny; you're a philosopher, to be sure; but,

I dare say, if the moon was to fall from the lift, and knock down the old kirk, ye would say no more than 'it's gey and queerish.'"

"Queerish, man! do ye not see that?" added I, shoving down his head mostly on the top of it. "Do ye not see that? awful, most awful! extonishing!! Do ye not see that long beard? Who, in the name of goodness, ever was an eye-witness to a sheep's head, in a Christian land, with a beard like an unshaven jew, crying 'owl clowes,' with a green bag over his left shoulder!"

"Dog on it," said James, giving a fidge with his hainches; "Dog on it, as I am a living sinner, that is the head of a Willy goat."

"Willie, or Nannie," answered I, "it's not meat for me; and never shall an ounce of it cross the craig of my family;—that is, as sure as ever James Batter drave a shuttle. Give counsel in need, James; what is to be done?"

"That needs consideration," quo' James, giving a bit hoast. "Unless he makes ample apology, and explains the mistake in a feasible way, it is my humble opinion that he ought to be summoned before his betters. That is the legal way to make him smart for his sins."

At last, a thought struck me, and I saw farther through my difficulties than ever mortal man did through a millstone; but, like a politician, I minted not the matter to James, keeping my tongue cannily within my teeth. I then laid the head, wrapped up in the bit towel, in a corner behind the counter; and, turning my face round again to James, I put my hands into my breeches pockets, as if nothing in the world had happened, and ventured back to the story of the Mermaid. I asked him how she looked—what kind of dress she wore—if she swam with her corsets—what was the color of her hair—where she would buy the tortoiseshell comb—and so on; when, just as he was clearing his pipe to reply, who should burst open the shop-door, like a clap of thunder, with burning cat's een, and a face as red as a soldier's jacket, but Cursecowl himself, with the new killing-coat in his hand,—which, giving a tremendous curse, the words of which are not essentially necessary for me to repeat, being an elder of our kirk, he made play flee at me with such a birr, that it twisted round my neck, and mostly blinding me, made me doze like a tottum. At the same time, to clear his way, and the better to enable him to take a good mark, he gave James Batter a shove, that made him stoiter against the wall, and snacked the good new farthing tobacco-pipe, that James was taking his first whiff out of; crying, at the same blessed moment—"Hold out o' my road, ye long withered wabster. Ye're a pair of havering idiots; but I'll have pennyworths out of both your skins, as I'm a sinner!"

What was to be done? There was no time for speaking, for Cursecowl, foaming like a mad dog with passion, seized hold of the ellwand, which he flourished round his head like a highlander's broad sword; and, stamping about, with his stockings drawn up his thighs, threatened every moment to commit bloody murder.

If James Batter never saw service before, he learned a little of it that day, being in a pickle of bodily terror not to be imagined by living man; but his presence of mind did not forsake him, and he cowered for safety and succor into a far corner, holding out a web of buckram before him,—me crying all the time, "Send for the town-officer! will ye not send for the town-officer?"

You may talk of your General Moores, and your Lord Wellingtons, as ye like; but never, since I was born, did I ever see or hear tell of any thing braver than the way Tommy Bodkin behaved, in saving both our precious lives, at that blessed nick of time, from touch-and-go jeopardy; for, when Cursecowl was rampaging about, cursing and swearing like a Russian bear, hurling out vollies of oaths that would have frighted John Knox, forbye the like of us, Tommy stole in behind him like a wild cat, followed by Joseph Breekey, Jerry Staytape, and Jack Thorl, the three apprentices, on their

stocking holes, and, having strong and dumpy arms, pinned back his elbows like a flash of lightning, giving the other callants time to jump on his back, and hold him like a vice; while, having got time to draw my breath, and screw up my pluck, I ran forward like a lion, and houghed the whole concern—Tommy Bodkin, the three faithful apprentices, Cursecowl, and all, coming to the ground like a battered castle.

It was now James Batter's turn to come up in line; and, though a douce man (being savage for the insulting way that Cursecowl had dared to use him), he dropped down like mad, with his knees on Cursecowl's breast, who was yelling, roaring, and grinding his buck-teeth like a mad bull, kicking right and spurring left with fire and fury; and, taking his Kilmarnock off his head, thrust it, like a battering ram, into Cursecowl's mouth, to hinder him from alarming the neighborhood, and bringing the whole world about our ears. Such a stramash of tumbling, roaring, tearing, swearing, kicking, pushing, cuffing, roughing, and riving about the floor!! I thought they would not have left one another with a shirt on; it seemed a combat even to the death. Cursecowl's breath was chocked up within him like wind in an empty bladder, and when I got a gliskie of his face, from beneath James's cowl, it was growing as black as the crown of my hat. It feared me much that murder would be the upshot, the webs being all heeled over, both of broad cloth, buckram, cassimir, and Welch flannel; and the paper shapings and worsted rounds coiled about their throats and bodies like fiery serpents. At long and last, I thought it became me, being the head of the house, to sound a parley, and bid them give the savage a mouthful of fresh air, to see if he had any thing to say in his defence.

Cursecowl, by this time, had forcible assurance of our ability to overpower him, and finding he had by far the worst of it, was obliged to grow tamer, using the first breath he got to cry out, "A barley, ye thieves, a barley! I tell ye, give me wind. There's not a man in nine of ye!"

Finding our own strength, we saw, by this time, that we were masters of the field; nevertheless we took care to make good terms, when they were in our power; nor would we allow Cursecowl to sit upright, till after he had said, three times over, on his honor as a gentleman, that he would behave as became one.

After giving his breeches-knees a skuff with his loof, to dad off the stoure, he came, right foot foremost, to the counter side, while the laddies were dighting their brows, and stowing away the webs upon their ends round about, saying, "Maister Wauch, how have ye the conscience to send hame such a piece o' wark as that coat to ony decent man? Do ye dare to imagine that I am a Jerusalem spider, that I could be crammed, neck and heels, into such a thing as that? Fye, shame—it would not button on yourself, man, scarecrow-looking mortal though ye be!"

James Batter's blood was now up, and broiling like an old Roman's; so he was determined to show Cursecowl that I had a friend in court, able and willing to keep him at stave's-end. "Keep a calm sough," said James Batter, interfering, "and not miscall the head of the house in his own shop; or, to say nothing of present consequences, by way of showing ye the road to the door, perhaps Maister Sneckdrawer, the penny-writer, 'll give ye a caption paper with a broad margin, to claw your elbow with at your leisure, my good fellow."

"Pugh, pugh," cried Cursecowl, snapping his finger and thumb at James's beak, "I do not value your threatening an ill halfpenny. Come away out your ways to the crown of the causeway, and I'll box any three of ye, over the banny's, for half-a mutchkin. But od'sake, Batter, my man, nobody's speaking to you," added Cursecowl, giving a hack now and then, and a bit spit down on the floor: "go hame, man, and get your cowl washed; I dare say you have pushioned me, so I have no more to say to the like of you. But now, Maister Wauch, just speaking hooly and fairly, do you not think black burning shame of yourself, for putting such an article into any decent Christian man's hand, like mine?"

"Wait a wee—wait a wee, friend, and I'll give ye a lock salt to your broth," answered I, in a calm and cool way; for, being a confidential elder of Maister Wiggie's, I kept myself free from the sin of getting into a passion, or fighting, except in self-defence, which is forbidden neither by law nor gospel; and, stooping down, I took up the towel from the corner, and, spreading it upon the counter, bade him look, and see if he knew an auld acquaintance!

Cursecowl, to be such a dragoon, had some rational points in his character; so, seeing that he lent hear to me with a smirk on his rough red face, I went on: "Take my advice as a friend, and make the best of your way home, killing-coat and all; for the most perfect will sometimes fall into an innocent mistake, and, at any rate, it cannot be helped now. But if ye show any symptom of obstrapulosity, I'll find myself under the necessity of publishing you abroad to the world for what you are, and show about that head in the towel for a wonder to broad Scotland, in a manner that will make customers flee from your booth, as if it was infected with the seven plagues of Egypt."

At sight of the goat's-head, Cursecowl clapped his hand on his thigh two or three times, and could scarcely muster good manners enough to keep him from bursting out a laughing.

"Ye seem to have found a fiddle, friend," said I; "but give me leave to tell you, that ye'll may be find it liker a hanging-match than a musical matter. Are you not aware that I could hand you over to the sheriff, on two special indictments: in the first place, for an action of assault and batterfication, in cuffing me, an elder of our kirk, with a sticked killing-coat, in my own shop; and, in the second place, as a swindler, imposing on his Majesty's loyal subjects, taking the coin of the realm on false pretences, and palming off goat's flesh upon Christians, as if they were perfect pagans."

Heathen though Cursecowl was, this oration alarmed him in a jiffy, soon showing him, in a couple of hurries, that it was necessary for him to be our humble servant: so he said, still keeping the smirk on his face, "Kay, kay, it's not worth making a noise about, after all. Gie me the jacket, Mansie, my man, and it 'll maybe serve my nephew, young Killim, who is as lingit in the waiste as a wasp. Let us take a shake of your paw over the counter, and be friends. Bye-ganes should be bye-ganes."

Never let it be said that Mansie Wauch, though one of the king's volunteers, ever thrust aside the olive branch of peace; so, ill-used though I had been, to say nothing of James Batter, who had got his pipe smashed to crunches, and one of the eyes of his spectacles knocked out, I gave him my fist frankly.

James Batter's birse had been so fiercely put up, and no wonder, that it was not so easily sleeked down; so, for a while, he looked unco glum, till Cursecowl insisted that our meeting should not be a dry one; nor would he hear a single word on me and James Batter not accepting his treat of a mutchkin of Kilbagie.

I did not think James would have been so doure and refractory,—funking and flinging like old Jeroboam; but at last, with the persuasion of the treat, he came to, and, sleeking down his front hair, we all three took a step down to the far end of the close, at the back street, where widow Thompson kept the sign of "The Tankard and the Tappit Hen," Cursecowl, when we got ourselves seated, ordering in the spirits with a loud rap on the table with his knuckles, and a whistle on the landlady through his fore-teeth, that made the roof ring. A bottle of beer was also brought; so, after drinking one another's healths round, with a tasting out of the dram-glass, Cursecowl swashed the rest of the raw creature into the tankard, saying,—"Now take your will o't; there's drink fit for a king; that's real 'pap-in.'"

He was an awful body, Cursecowl, and had a power of queer stories, which, weil-a-wat, did not lose in the telling. James Batter, beginning to brighten up, hodged and leuch like a nine-year-old; and I freely confess, for another, that I was so diverted, that, I dare say, had it not been for his fearsome oaths, which made our very hair stand on end, and were enough to open the stone-wall, we would have both sate from that time to this.

We got the whole story of the Willie-Goat, out and out, it seeming to be, with Cursecowl, a prime matter of diversion, especially that part of it relating to the head, by which he had won a crown-piece from Deacon Paunch, who wagered that the wife and me would eat it, without ever finding out our mistake. But, ah ha, lad!

The long and the short of the matter was this. The Willie-Goat had, for eighteen year, belonged to a dragoon marching regiment, and, in its better days, had seen a power of service abroad; till, being now old and infirm, it had fallen off one of the baggage-carts, and got its leg broken on the road to Piershell, where it was sold to Cursecowl, by a corporal, for half-a-crown and a dram. The four quarters he had managed to sell for mutton, like lightning—this one buying a jigget, that one a back-ribs, and so on. However, he had to weather a gay brisk gale, in making his point good. One woman remarked, that it had an unearthly, rank smell; to which he said, "No, no—ye do not ken your blessings, friend,—that's the smell of venison, for the beast was brought up along with the deers in the Duke's parks." And to another wife, that, after smell—smelling at it, though it was a wee humphed, he replied, "Faith, that's all the thanks folks gets for letting their sheep crop heather among the Cheviot Hills;" and such like lies. But as for the head, that had been the doure business. Six times had it been sold and away, and six times had it been brought back again. One bairn said, that her "mother did na like a sheep's head with horns like these, and wanted it changed for another one." A second one said, that "it had tup's een, and her father liked weather mutton." A third customer found mortal fault with the colors, which, she said, "were not canny, or in the course of nature." What the fourth one said, and the fifth one took leave to observe, I have stupidly forgotten, though, I am sure, I heard both; but I mind one remarked, quite off-hand, as she sought back her money, that, "unless sheep could do without beards, like their neighbors, she would keep the pot boiling with a piece beef, in the mean time." After all this, would any mortal man believe, Deacon Paunch, the greasy Daniel Lambert that he is, had taken the wager, as I before took opportunity to remark, that our family would swallow the bait? But, ah ha, he was off his eggs there.

James and me were so tickled with Cursecowl's wild, outrageous, off-hand, humorsome way of telling his crack, that, though sore with the neighering, none of the two of us ever thought of rising; Cursecowl chapping in first one stoup, and then another, and birling the tankard round the table, as if we had been drinking dub-water. I dare say I would never have got away, had I not slipped out behind Lucky Thompson's back—for she was a broad fat body, with a round-eared mutch, and a full-plaited check apron—when she was drawing the sixth bottle of small beer, with her corkscrew between her knees; Cursecowl lecturing away at the dividual moment, like a Glasgow professor, to James Batter, whose een were gathering straws, on a pliskie he had once, in the course of trade, played on a conceited body of a French sick-nurse, by selling her a lump of fat pork to make beef-tea of to her mistress, who was dwining in the blue Beelzebubs.

Ohone, and woes me, for old Father Adam and the fall of man! Poor, sober, good, honest James Batter was not, by a thousand miles, a match for such company. Every thing, however, has its

moral, and the truth will out. When Nanse and me were sitting at our breakfast next morning, we heard from Benjie, who had been early up fishing for eels at the waterside, that the whole town-talk was concerning the misfortunate James Batter, who had been carried home, totally incapable, far in the night, by Cursecowl and an Irish laborer—that sleeped in Widow Thompson's garret—on a hand-barrow, borrowed from Maister Wiggie's servant-lass, Jenny Jessamine.

THE ASS TURNED GENTLEMAN.

BY ALEXANDER RODGERS.

In the year 17—, before the light of literature and science had made such progress among the peasantry of this country—when our less enlightened forefathers ascribed every phenomenon of nature, which they did not understand, to some supernatural agency, either benevolent or malevolent, as the case might be; and an avowal of disbelief in the existence of witchcraft, necromancy, the black art, hobgoblins, fairies, brownies, etc., would have subjected a person to more annoyance and persecution, than an open avowal of infidelity would do at present—three young men of family set out from Edinburgh, on a pleasure excursion into the country. After visiting Linlithgow, Falkirk, Stirling, and Glasgow, they took up their quarters at the head inn in Midcalder, on their way back to Auld Reekie. Finding a set of youthful revellers there to their mind, they spent several days and nights in drinking and carousing, never dreaming of the heavy bill they were running up with the "kind landlady." The truth flashed upon them at last; and they discovered, when it was too late, that they had not wherewithal to clear their heavy score. A consultation was held by the trio, and many plans for getting rid of their disagreeable situation were proposed and rejected. At last, one of them, more fertile in expedients than the other two, hit upon the following method, which good fortune seemed to favor, of extricating both himself and his brethren:—

"Don't you see yon cadger's ass standing at the door over the way?" said he.

"Yes; but what of that?"

"Come along with me—loose the ass—unburden him of his creels—disengage him from his sunks and branks—put me in his place—equip me with his harness—hang the creels likewise upon me—tie me to the door with his own halter—get another for him—lead him away to the next town—you will get him easily sold—return with the money—pay the bill—and leave me to get out of the halter the best way I can."

The plan was instantly put in practice; the youth was soon accoutred in the ass's furniture, and away went the other two to sell the ass.

In the mean time, out comes the honest cadger from the house, where he had been making a contract with the guidwife for eggs; but the moment he beheld, as he supposed, his ass transformed into a fine gentleman, he held up his hands in the utmost wonder, exclaiming at the same time, "Guid hae a care o' us! what means a' this o't? Speak, in the name o' Gude, an' tell me what ye are—are ye an earthly creature, or the auld thief himsel'?"

"Alas!" responded the youth, putting on a sad countenance, "hae ye forgotten your ain ass? Do ye no ken me now?—me! that has served you sae lang and sae faithfu'; that has trudged and toiled through wat and through dry, mid cauld and hunger; hooted at by blackguard callants—lashed by yoursel'—an' yet ye dinna ken me! Waes me, that ever I becam' your ass! that ever I should, by my ain disobedience, hae cast out wi' my father, an' provoked him to turn me into a stupid creature sic as ye now see me!"

"Sic as I now see ye!—instead o' an ass, I now see a braw young gentleman."

"A braw young gentleman!—O Gude be praised that my father has at last been pleased to restore me to my ain shape, and that I can now see wi' the een, an' speak wi' the tongue o' a man!"

"But wha are ye, my braw lad, and wha is your father?"

"Oh, did you never hear o' Maister James Sandilands, the third son o' the Earl o' Torpichen?"

"Heard o' him! ay, an' kent him too, when he was a bairn, but he was sent awa' abroad when he was young, an' I ne'er heard tell o' him sin' syne."

"Weel, I'm that same Maister James; and ye maun ken that my father learned the black art at the college, an' that I happened to anger him by makin' love to a fine young leddy, against his will, an' that, in short, when he faund out that I was in love wi' her, he turned me into an ass for my disobedience."

"Weel, weel, my man, since that is the case, gae awa' hame, an' gree wi' your father; tak' my blessing wi you, an' I will e'en try to get anither ass, whether your father send me as muckle siller as buy anither ane or no; fare ye weel, an' my blessing gang wi' you."

Away went the youth, released from his bondage, and soon meeting with his comrades, related, to their joint gratification, his strange adventure with the honest cadger. Suffice it to say, that the ass was sold, the bill paid, and the youths got safely back to Edinburgh.

So soon as they got matters arranged, they sent a sum to the worthy cadger, sufficient to purchase three asses. On receiving the money, he lost no time in looking out for another ass, and as next week was "Calder fair," he repaired thither with the full intention of making a purchase. He was not long in the fair, looking about for an animal to suit his purpose, when, behold! he saw with new wonder and astonishment, his own identical old ass! The dumb brute knew him also, and made signs of recognition in the best manner he could. The honest cadger could not contain himself, the tears gushed from his eyes, he looked wistfully in the creature's face, and anxiously cried out, "Gude have a care o' us! hae you and your father cuisten out again?"

THE SCHOOL FOR SCAMPS.

(A "Standard Old Comedy," in Five Acts.) Dedicated to the Legitimists.

BY ANGUS B. REACH.

DRAMATIS PERSONÆ.

LORD BELMONT.	SIR FREDERICK MALISON.
LAWYER VENOM.	OLD GOPUS.
YOUNG GOPUS.	FRANK FRIENDLY.
HODGE COWSLIP.	JERRY COWSLIP (*his son.*)
LADY BELMONT.	MATILDA BELMONT.
MRS. GOPUS.	DORCAS COWSLIP.

ACT I.

SCENE. I.—*A Room in Lord Belmont's House.*

Enter Lord Belmont.

LORD BELMONT. Why did I do it? Why did I forge the deeds which made me the lord of all I see around me? Why did I cause my sister's child to be kidnapped, and sent to sea? Oh, Remorse! Oh, Despair! How the throbbing of a guilty brow shakes the coronet which gilds it. Ha! who's there? My evil genius!

Enter Lawyer Venom.

LAWYER VENOM. How is your Lordship? Plotting mischief? Ha! ha! ha! Nothing like it. I hate all the world; don't you? Here is the instrument for turning the Cowslips out of their cottage—it only wants your signature. [*Gives paper.*

LORD BELMONT. Alas! must I affix it? (*Aside.*) Crime, crime, how thou forcest us on from one villany to another. [*He writes.*

Scene closes.

SCENE II.—*A Street in the Village.*

Enter Old Gopus and Young Gopus.

OLD GOPUS. Stick up, my boy; stick up to Miss Belmont. You are the fellow for her. Gad! when I was your age—

YOUNG GOPUS. Oh! You old heathen! Go along. But do you think she'd have me, dad?

OLD GOPUS. Think. D——, I know it. She'd jump at you like a cat-a-mountain. Phew!

YOUNG GOPUS. I'm in such spirits. (*Sings*) Fal de ral de ral de la.

[*Exeunt both, dancing and singing.*

SCENE III.—*A Room in Lord Belmont's House.*

Enter Lady Belmont and Miss Belmont.

LADY BELMONT. Pr'ythee, child, talk no more. The blood of the Belmonts—

MISS BELMONT. Can never be degraded by an alliance in which love consecrates the heart, and honor seals the hands.

LADY BELMONT. Sir Frederick—

MISS BELMONT. Again that odious name.

Enter Sir Frederick unperceived at back.

SIR FREDERICK (*aside*). Ha! Confusion!

LADY BELMONT. While that Frank Friendly—

MISS BELMONT. Frank Friendly! Heavenly sound!

Enter Frank Friendly, unperceived, at back.

FRANK (*aside*). Ha! Blessings on her!

LADY BELMONT. I tell you you shall be the wife of—

Friendly and Malison coming forward, and both speaking together—

FRIENDLY AND MALISON. Of me.

The two Ladies faint in each other's arms, while the Rivals gaze furiously on each other over them.

DROP FALLS.

ACT II.

SCENE I. *Old Cowslip's Cottage.*

Old Cowslip. Jerry Cowslip. Dorcas.

DORCAS (*weeping*). We be all undone.

JERRY. I zay dom Lawyer Venom. Dang'd an I doant break every boan in his ugly body loike!

OLD COWSLIP. My son. My son. Learn patience from your aged sire.

Enter Lawyer Venom and Bailiffs.

VENOM: Turn 'em out. Turn 'em out. I hate all the world. Ha! ha! ha!

JERRY (*kept back by Dorcas and Old Cowslip*). Leat me get at un, I say.

Enter Friendly.

FRIENDLY. A distressed family! Ha! May the tree of benevolence be ever watered by the tears of gratitude. (*To the Bailiffs*). Sharks, take your prey. [*Flings down purse, and Exit.*

OLD COWSLIP. May an old man's blessing— [*Weeps.*

Scene closes.

SCENE II. *Lord Belmont's House.*

Enter Lord Belmont and Sir Frederick.

LORD BELMONT. Sir Frederick, she shall marry you. I pledge the word of a British nobleman.

Enter Venom.

VENOM. I'll manage it. I shall make Miss Belmont believe that Friendly is in love with Dorcas, and that that was the reason for his late romantic generosity. Ha! ha! ha! I hate all the world.

SIR FREDERICK. Excellent. Come along and concoct the plot. [*Exeunt Sir Frederick and Venom.*

LORD BELMONT (*sinking on a chair*). Villain! villain! villain!

DROP FALLS.

ACT III.

Lord Belmont's Garden.—Enter Friendly and Miss Belmont, talking.

FRIENDLY. It was so. I know not my parents—I never did. My love for you is my only solace—my only comfort.

MISS BELMONT. Be still, bursting heart! Oh, Frank, do you really love me?

FRIENDLY. And can then Miss Belmont doubt the sincerity of my devotion?

MISS BELMONT. Never. For the heart which worships at the shrine is hallowed by the altar. [*Exeunt.*

SCENE II. *The Village.—Enter Jerry Cowslip.*

JERRY. Dang'd if I beant as glad as our red cow in a field of clover, loike.

Enter Venom.

VENOM. Know that Friendly, in the guise of benevolence, seeks to seduce your sister. Ha! ha! ha! [*Exit Venom.*

JERRY. Seduce! Sister Dorcas! It beant possible. But lawyer Venom looked as if he meant it loike. I dunna know what to think. I'm like our donkey Jack between two bundles of hay.

Enter Sir Frederick.

SIR FREDERICK. Friendly wishes to seduce your sister. I am your friend. Take this pistol—(*gives pistol*)—he is in the next field. Adieu. Beware. [*Exit Sir Frederick.*

JERRY. I'm all over woonder loike—seduce sister Dorcas—Noa, noa. There's summut here will prevent it. [*Strikes his waistcoat and exit.*

SCENE III. *A Field.—Enter Friendly and Dorcas.*

FRIENDLY. Nay, nay—open your heart to me as to a friend. You love Sir Frederick.

DORCAS (*sobbing*). Alas! yes!

Enter Jerry at back.

JERRY (*aside*). In tears! blood and 'ounds!

FRIENDLY. Come—come—let me dry those eyes.

JERRY (*rushing forward and presenting pistol.*) Never! The benefactor of the feyther may yet be the seducer of the sister. *Group.*

DROP FALLS.

ACT IV.

SCENE I. *Lord Belmont's House.*

Enter Miss Belmont and Sir Frederick.

MISS BELMONT. My brain is bursting. It cannot be!

SIR FREDERICK. It is. [*Exit Sir Frederick.*

MISS BELMONT. Why did I love him—why do I love him? But no, no—I must tear him from my heart for ever.

Enter Friendly.

FRIENDLY. My dearest Matilda—

MISS BELMONT. Villain—who would beguile one woman of her heart while he robbed another of her honor. [*Exit Miss Belmont.*

FRIENDLY. I'm petrified.

Enter Jerry.

JERRY. And you call yourself a foine gentleman loike? What thof ye have gotten a good coat on your back—ye cannot stroike your heart and say it's all right here. [*Strikes his waistcoat and Exits.*

FRIENDLY. What means this?

Enter Young Gopus.

YOUNG GOPUS (*aside*). Refused! and by a woman I thought I was certain of! (*Sees Friendly*). Ha! there stands my successful rival. (*Aloud*). Sir, if you are not a coward follow me. [*Exit Young Gopus.*

FRIENDLY. I'm goaded to madness—have after you. [*Exit following.*

Enter Old Gopus and Mrs. Gopus.

OLD GOPUS. My son—my boy!

MRS. GOPUS. My boy—my son!

[*The reports of two pistols are heard.*

Mr. and Mrs. Gopus fall into each other's arms, and the Scene closes.

SCENE II. *Lord Belmont's Library.*

Enter Lord Belmont and Venom.

VENOM. My Lord, it must be. Sir Frederick must marry Miss Belmont. I have my reasons for it. If you don't press the marriage, I denounce you to-day, and will see you dragged to gaol to-morrow. Ha! ha! ha! [*Exit Venom.*

LORD BELMONT. Earth open and swallow me!

Enter Miss Belmont.

MISS BELMONT. Papa, papa, release me from the persecution of Sir Frederick.

LORD BELMONT. My child, I cannot. I have pledged my word. To-morrow you will be Lady Malison.

[*Miss Belmont screams and faints. Lord Belmont rings the bell violently. Enter Servants and Lady Belmont, and form a group.*

DROP FALLS.

ACT V.

SCENE I. *A Room in Lord Belmont's House.*

Enter Miss Belmont and Dorcas.

MISS BELMONT. You say so.

DORCAS. Lady, yes, a thousand times yes!

MISS BELMONT. Oh, Friendly, how have I wronged thee! Seek him, Dorcas—bring him hither. (*Exit Dorcas*). Alas! when suspicion rankles in the heart, love, instead of a healing balm, becomes a subtle poison. [*Exit.*

Enter Sir Frederick and Venom.

SIR FREDERICK. An hour after Miss Belmont becomes Lady Malison, the money shall be yours!

VENOM. Agreed! Ha! ha! ha!

Enter Lord Belmont and Lady Belmont.

LORD BELMONT. Is all prepared?

LADY BELMONT. Where is the bride?

MISS BELMONT (*appearing at right*). Here.

VENOM. And the bridegroom. I take it is—

FRIENDLY (*appearing at left*). Here!

ALL. Ha!

LORD BELMONT. What means this intrusion?

SIR FREDERICK. Suffer me to chastise his insolence.

FRIENDLY. Miserable trickster! I know all. Your compact with Venom amongst the rest.

SIR FREDERICK. Ha! betrayed!

VENOM. This is trifling. Lord Belmont, I call upon you to cause this marriage to proceed—else—

LORD BELMONT. I care not. I am weary of life! My daughter shall not marry Sir Frederick.

VENOM. Then your blood be on your own head. I accuse you of having murdered your sister's son.

ALL. Ha!

VENOM. If he be not dead produce him. He will be known by a mole on his left elbow. I have myself had an affidavit taken of its existence.

LORD BELMONT. Alas!

FRIENDLY. Ha! (*strips off his sleeve*) a mole—see—see here!

Enter Old Cowslip, Jerry, and Dorcas.

OLD COWSLIP. I know it—I feel it—I remember him well. Many a time have I dandled him on my knee: it is—it is the true Lord Belmont!

VENOM. Confusion!

LORD BELMONT. Thanks be to heaven. Kneel, kneel my children, and receive my blessing.

[*Friendly and Miss Belmont kneel.*

VENOM. And receive mine. May the Devil take you—I'm off.

[*Is going, when he is stopped by Old Gopus.*

OLD GOPUS. Mr. Venom, your banker has failed.

Enter Young Gopus.

YOUNG GOPUS. Mr. Venom, your house and all your property is burnt.

Enter Mrs. Gopus.

MRS. GOPUS. All—Mr. Venom—except your wife! [*Venom staggers out.*

SIR FREDERICK. I feel I have turned virtuous all of a sudden. Dorcas Cowslip, will you marry me?

[*They embrace.*

JERRY. Dang it—I'm a going clean mad wi' joy loike—who'll marry I?

Enter Abigail.

ABIGAIL. Me! [*They embrace.*

LORD BELMONT. Thus, my children and friends, we see how, on the one hand, virtue is rewarded, and how, on the other, vice is punished—how the watering pot of fertility nourishes the useful tree, and the hatchet of destruction clears away the noxious shrub.

CURTAIN FALLS.

THE LAME PIG.

ANON.

MRS. M'CRIE was simplicity itself, and her heart overflowed with the warmest affections of human nature. Mr. Josiah Flowerdew, of Manchester, had occasion to visit Edinburgh, that free-stone village which Scotsmen call a metropolis, situated a mile or two from Leith, a sea-port town on the river Forth. He had a letter of introduction to the Rev. Dr. and Mrs. M'Crie, and was received by them with all the frank and courteous kindness of their disposition.

One Sunday, after having attended divine service in the Doctor's church, he returned with his hospitable friends to their residence. A nice, hot, tasty, but frugal dinner, was quickly placed upon the table.

"Good folk hunger after the word," observed the old lady, putting a haddock of fourteen inches long, with an ocean of oysters and butter, on Josiah's plate; and tak' a willy waught of that Malaga—it's gusty and priesome; our guidman he was dry in the pulpit, and ye hae as guide right to be dry out of it—hem! Excuse me, Doctor—Lord, sir, ye are filing your hands."

Mr. Josiah was a devoted admirer of the fair sex, and could not, even when an aged and wrinkled face met his gaze, fail to remember, that once the same cheek was dyed with the hue of the rose, and the eyes cast a lustre which would have maddened an anchorite. He therefore, out of devotion to what was past, ate and drank as directed, of what was present. After having in this fashion labored with a vigor and industry which would have done credit to an Irish laborer deepening the Thames, or a student of Stinkomalee ettling at comprehending the last number of the Edinburgh Review, he was constrained, from absolute want of local capacity, to give over—"to cease labor, to dig and to delve," in a horrid brute, of the bird species, which must have been cousin-german to the penguins of the Falkland Island.

"The 'tither leg, Mr. Josiah Powderjew?" said the Doctor. "The 'tither leg, Doctor! May I perish if one joint of the whole carcase has moved the flutter of a gnat's wing," answered Josiah. "Ye are ower genty with the beast, Mr. Flowerdew," observed the old lady. "Doctor, mark ye that, and abuse nae man's gude name. Rive it, sir—Rive it." "It is teugh—it is, of a verity," said the Doctor, as his eye-tooth snapped in a struggle with a tendon which would have held his Majesty's yacht in a hurricane. "And toothsome forbye," observed Mrs. M'Crie; "but it's wrang to sport wi' a human creature's distresses. Na, na, Mr. Josiah, ye needna look sae wae like. Possession, nae doubt, is nine points of the law; but the rightful owner of that yellow stump is lang syne gathered to his forbears. Of a troth, it would be an awfu' moment gin he cam to vindicate his ain."

Mr. Flowerdew shuddered, and for reasons that can very well be understood, agreed most heartily with his hostess. "But as I'm in the land of the living!" continued Mrs. M'Crie, "our taupy lass has a'thegether neglected the syllabub. There it stands, in the pride of its beauty, in the aumry. Surely I've been carried mysell. Doctor, whenever you gae by the hour and five minutes, I'm clean done for ony mair use that day—I can mind naething." "Neither can I, Mrs. M'Crie," observed Mr. Josiah, innocently. "It's a blessing for you, Mr. Josiah," answered the old lady; "if I had minded a' I've heard, I would by this time have been demented." "Right, my dear," replied the Doctor, "the female is the weaker vessel—a cracked pitcher, as a man may say, and in no way fit to be the repository of the wonders of airt and science." "And yet," retorted Mrs. M'Crie, somewhat piqued at the observation, "there are some airts, of the whilk ye are as ignorant as a dead dog—saving the compairishon." "And in what, may I be permitted to ask?" answered the Doctor, with much solemnity; "in what? Ye see, Mr. Lourhew," he added, "I in naewise eschew the inquiry." "Na, then, gudeman," exclaimed the old lady exultingly, "I had you now on the hip—that is—God save us—excuse the expression, Mr. Josiah; we are plain folk." "Madam," answered Mr. Flowerdew, "make no apology. "The recollections of youth are delightful. I have many warm remembrances of the kind. But pray, madam, don't let us lose the advantage of knowing in what matter of lore you transcend the Doctor. Pray be so condescending." "Nay, kind sir," said the old lady, "it's a joke of my own; but, as it is connected lady, "I maun be the expounder of the text mysel. So ye see, Mr. Flowerdew"—

But before the secret is disclosed, we must inform our readers that there is a certain jug or pipkin of earthenware, used in various culinary and detergent purposes in Scotland, called a "pig," and which, from the tenacious kind of earth (laam or loam) of which it is composed, goes by the distinctive name of a "lame pig;" a utensil of which, fifty years ago, to have been ignorant, would have been a confession of stultification as great as if you thought that the Red Sea was rubicund.

"So, sir," continued Mrs. M'Crie, "when I want to make a syllabub—it's grand for a cold, or a kittling in the throat"—

"Madam!"—

"Yes, it's nae doubt of healing virtues," observed the Doctor,—"medicinal in all matters, thoracical, if I may use the expression; and Mr. Towerflew, it has the advantage of being divertive and jocund in the swallow. Sir, I hold in utter execration your sennas and globars; the latter are, of a certy, an abomination before the Lord. I ance had a dose thereof—gin I live to the age of Methusalem, the day will be to me like yestreen: they took a good forty minutes to chow, my inside was curmurring like doos in a dooket. It was most special unsavory, Mr. Sourspew."

"So," continued the old lady, after an impatient pause, "I send to the market, and our Bell brings me a lame pig."

"But why a lame pig?"

"Why a lame pig, sir?—what way no? Sir, naething but a lame pig will answer the purpose."

"I cry your mercy, good lady."

"So our Bell brings me a lame pig. I aye tell

with that very syllabub that our lass has set before you, I shall ask the Doctor again. Ye that ken the three wonnerful things in the warld, yea, the four wonnerful things, and strange, how mak ye the syllabub?" "I tak the lass."—"Whisht, Doctor; gin ye begin that gate," interrupted the old our lass (she has been wi' us these thirteen years come Martinmas; she is the O* of her grandfather, as the Doctor says, when he is facetious,) to pick me out a clean ane."

* O signifies grandchild.

"Very right," said Mr. Josiah. "But I'm afraid you would have but little choice in that respect."

"Ye are wrang, Mr. Cowersew," said the Doctor, "they are aye weel washed outside and in."

"Oh, Doctor, no joking; this is a serious matter."

"Na; there's no joking," observed the old lady. "They are weel scraped wi' a heather ringe."

"A what, madam!"

"A nievefu' o' heather; wi' the whilk you get even to the most extreme corner of the concern."

"No doubt, madam, if you are permitted"—

"Permitted, Mr. Josiah! and gin I buy a pig, may I no do what I chuse wi' it? or wi' ony ither face of clay for which I gave ready cuinzie? Ye have, sir, great character in England for cleanliness, and I am sure that Mrs. Flowerdew never has a pig in her aught for she washes it inside and out, as clean as the driven snaw."

"Nay in that," said Mr. Flowerdew, "I can assure you, you are mistaken. Before the pigs reach us"——

"Weel, weel; ither folk do it, and that is the same thing. So, when Bell comes hame, I says, hand me down the can with the virgin honey, and I drap twa dessert spoonfuls into the pig's mouth"—

"Into its mouth, madam?"

"Ay, to be sure, sir; where would you have it put?—a pig's mouth was nae gien to it for naething—or jelly will do as weel. Na, I've tried your large bergamot preserved pear; but whiles the pig's neck is no that wide to admit of a pear of size, and it's fashious squeezing it in."

"No doubt, madam, and dangerous."

"Yes, gin the neck break; but when ye mell and meddle wi' pigs, ye maun mind ye deal wi' slippery gear."

"Very true, madam."

"Weel, then, our lass carries the pig to the cow, and there she gently milks a pint and a half of warm milk in upon the henny or jelly, or pear, as it may be."

"Into the pig, madam!"

"Ay, into the mouth o't. Surely that's nae kittle matter?"

"Now, madam, as I am an ordinary sinner, that is an operation that would puzzle all Lancashire. Into its mouth!"

"Weel, I'm astonished at you, sir: is there ony mystery or sorcery in Bell hauding a pig wi' the tae hands, and milking a cow with the tither?"

"I really, madam, in my innocence of heart, thought that the pig might have run—"

"Run o'er? Nae doubt? so wud it gin ye filled it o'er fu'. So hame comes the pig"—

"Of itself, madam!"

"Sir! Lord, sir, you speak as if the pig could walk!"

"I beg you a thousand pardons, madam; I truly forgot the milk and jelly. It would be extraordinary if it could."

"Very, sir. So the lass brings me my lame pig."

"Ah, that's another reason. Well, may I be drawn to a thread if I could divine why you preferred a lame pig!"

"Ye needna gang to Rome to learn that; a lame pig is aye fendiest. So I begin to steer and steer the milk and jelly."

"Steer and steer, madam!"

"Ay—mix a' weel up thegether."

"And may I entreat to know with what you stir it?"

"Wi' a spoon, to be sure; ye wadna hae me to do it wi' my fingers?"

"God forbid, madam! I would use, if heaven ever employed me in the manner you mention, a spoon with a most respectably long handle."

"It's better of length, certainly, sir. Naething can escape you, then! Weel, the next thing we do is this, to gently put the pig afore the fire to simmer."

"To simmer!"

"Yes, sir, and there stand or it reeks again. But you must not let it get o'er het: it would burn the milk."

"And the pig too, madam."

"Oh! that's naething. We dinna fash ourselves wi' the pig. What were they made for?"

"Why, truly, madam, I thought, until this day, that I knew something of their history; but I find I have been wofully ignorant."

"We canna reach perfection at ance, as our gudeman says (wha, by-the-bye, is and has been this half hour, as sound as a top). And so, after the pig has simmered and simmered, ye in wi' the spoon again."

"Again, madam!"

"Ay, sir; ye wadna hae it all in a mess at the bottom?"

"Far from it, madam; as far as possible."

"So ye maun gie anither stir or twa, until it sings."

"Sings, madam? And does the pig make no other noise during all this operation?"

"Scarce any other, gin it's a good pig; but all depends on that. I've seen a lame pig, that afore the heat had touched its sides a matter of five minutes, would have gane off in a crack."

"I don't wonder at that in the least, madam."

"You would wonder, if your English pigs had half the value of the Scotch."

"Possibly, madam."

"Of a verity," continued Mrs. M'Crie, "there was a pig played me ance a maist mischancy trick. Ye see, I expected a pairty of our presbytery to denner, and I had sent our Bell out for the maist capacious pig she could grip; and I had poured in the *quantum suff*, as the mediciners say, of het milk on the gooseberries (I was making a posset), and a' went weel; but when I thought it was done to a hair, out lap a het aizle; our Bell (the hizzy!) sprang to the tae side; the pig gaed the tither—a' was ruined."

"And the poor pig—what became of it?"

"Puir, indeed! It wasna worth the minding: its head was dung in, and it gat a sma' fracture on the side; but as it was bonny in its color, and genty in its mak, Bell syned it out in clear water, then rubbed it up wi' a duster, and clapped it on the shelf in the kitchen, where it lies to this blessed day, in peace and quiet, as I may say. In my opinion, sir, the pig hadna been right made."

"Not right made, madam?"

"Not right made, sir. You look surprised. Think you ony body can make a pig?"

"Far from it, madam."

"It would sarely fash you and me, I'm jalousing, Mr. Josiah Flowerdew."

"Admitted, madam; admitted.—But, my dear Mrs. M'Crie, I have just one other thing to ask. You have told me—(here Josiah gave a shudder)—

how the milk and honey gets in. Now, madam, may I be allowed to ask, how you get the syllabub out?"

"How we get it out? Lord, sir, you surprise me! Just the way we put it in. How would you get it out? Sure, there's nae magic in that!"

"Nay, madam, I don't pretend to venture upon any speculations on the point. There are many reasons, no doubt, why the pig would easier let it out than in; and I am quite willing to prefer the mouth. But, after it is out, pray, madam, who eats the syllabub?—or, pray, madam, do you also eat the pig?"

"Ha, ha! Weel, that's guide. Lord, sir, the pig's as hard as a stane!"

"Ged, madam, you are right; I had forgot the frying. But as to the milk and jelly, or the bergamot pear, after the pig's, for whose intestines are they devoted?"

"Sir?"

"Pray, madam, who devours that?" pointing with his finger to the horrid potion before him.

"You, sir, if you will do me that honor."

"Me, madam! Me! Good night, madam. Pray don't waken the doctor. I am particularly engaged. Nay, madam, not a morsel—(I would as soon bolt a barbecued toad, or mouth a curried hedge-hog)—I do entreat you to keep it for the next presbytery. If they resemble our clergy in the south, they are more familiar with pigs than I am.—Well, well?" Mr. Flowerdew was heard to exclaim, as he, in a manner, tumbled down, in his haste, from top to the bottom of the stair, "I have often heard that the Scotch were dirty; but, by all the stripes in a yard of gingham, they were born barbarians!"

"Mr. Dourstew!" exclaimed the Doctor, awakening. "Where are you? Here's my wife with the syllabub. Where are you, Mr. Moorskew?"

"I'm off!" answered Mr. Josiah; and it is said by his friends, that during a long life of some seventy years, no persuasion could induce him ever again to visit Edinburgh. "The lame pig," he would mutter to himself, "the jelly and hot milk! Heaven save me from such a calamity!"

THE MIGRATIONS OF A SOLAN GOOSE.

BY MISS CORBET.

"WELL, Bryce," said Mrs. Maxwell one day to her housekeeper, "what has the gamekeeper sent this week from Maxwell Hall?"—"Why, madam, there are three pair of partridges, a brace of grouse, a woodcock, three hares, a couple of pheasants, and a solan goose."—"A solan goose!" ejaculated the lady; "what could induce him to think I would poison my house with a solan goose?"—"He knows it is a dish that my master is very fond of," replied Mrs. Bryce. "It is more than your mistress is," retorted the lady; "let it be thrown out directly before Mr. Maxwell sees it."

The housekeeper retired, and Mrs. Maxwell resumed her cogitations, the subject of which was how to obtain an introduction to the French noblesse who had recently taken up their abode in Edinburgh. "Good heavens!" said she, as she hastily rung the bell, "how could I be so stupid?—there is nothing in the world that old Lady Crosby is so fond of as a solan goose, and I understand she knows all the French people, and that they are constantly with her.—Bryce," she continued, as the housekeeper obeyed her summons, "is the goose a fine bird?" "Very fine indeed, madam; the beak is broken, and one of the legs is a little ruffled, but I never saw a finer bird." "Well, then, don't throw it away, as I mean to send it to my friend, lady Crosby, as soon as I have written a note." Mrs.

Bryce once more retreated, and Mrs. Maxwell, having selected a beautiful sheet of note paper, quickly penned the following effusion:

"My dear Lady Crosby, permit me to request your acceptance of a solan goose, which has just been sent me from Maxwell Hall. Knowing your fondness for this bird, I am delighted at having it in my power to gratify you. I hope that you continue to enjoy good health. This is to be a very gay winter. By the bye, do you know any one who is acquainted with the French noblesse? I am dying to meet with them. Ever, my dear Lady Crosby, yours truly, M. MAXWELL."

Lady Crosby being out when this billet reached her house, it was opened by one of her daughters. "Bless me, Maria!" she exclaimed to her sister, "how fortunate it was that I opened this note; Mrs. Maxwell has sent mamma a solan goose!" "Dreadful!" exclaimed Eliza; "I am sure if mamma hears of it she will have it roasted immediately, and Captain Jessamy, of the Lancers, is to call to-day, and you know, a roasted solan goose is enough to contaminate a whole parish,—I shall certainly go distracted!" "Don't discompose yourself," replied Maria; "I shall take good care to send it out of the house before mamma comes home; meanwhile, I must write a civil answer to Mrs. Maxwell's note. I dare say she will not think of alluding to it; but, if she should, mamma, luckily, is pretty deaf, and may never be a bit the wiser." "I think," said Eliza, "we had better send the goose to the Napiers, as they were rather affronted at not being asked to our last musical party; I dare say they will make no use of it, but it looks attentive." "An excellent thought," rejoined Maria. No sooner said than done; in five minutes, the travelled bird had once more changed its quarters.

"A solan goose!" ejaculated Mrs. Napier, as her footman gave her the intelligence of Lady Crosby's present. "Pray, return my compliments to her ladyship, and I feel much obliged by her polite attention. Truly," continued she, when the domestic had retired to fulfil this mission, "if Lady Crosby thinks to stop our mouths with a solan goose, she will find herself very much mistaken. I suppose she means this as a peace-offering for not having asked us to her last party. I suppose she was afraid, Clara, my dear, you would cut out her clumsy daughters with Sir Charles." "If I don't, it shall not be my fault," replied her amiable daughter. "I flirted with him in such famous style at the last concert, that I thought Eliza would have fainted on the spot. But what are you going to do with the odious bird?" "Oh, I shall desire John to carry it to poor Mrs. Johnstone." "I wonder, mamma, that you would take the trouble of sending all the way to the Canongate for any such purpose; what good can it do you to oblige people who are so wretchedly poor?" "Why, my dear," replied the lady, "to tell you the truth, your father, in early life, received such valuable assistance from Mr. Johnstone, who was at that time a very rich man, as laid the foundation of his present fortune. Severe losses reduced Mr. Johnstone to poverty; he died, and your father has always been intending, at least promising to do something for the family, but has never found an opportunity. Last year, Mrs. Johnstone most unfortunately heard that he had it in his power to get a young man out to India, and she applied to Mr. Napier on behalf of her son, which, I must say, was a very ill-judged step, as showing that she thought he required to be reminded of his promises, which, to a man of any feeling, must always be a grating circumstance; but I have often observed, that poor people have very little delicacy in such points; however, as your papa fancies sometimes that these people have a sort of claim on him, I am sure he will be glad to pay them any attention that costs him nothing."

Behold, then, our hero exiled from the fashionable regions of the West, and laid on the broad of his back on a table, in a small but clean room, in a humble tenement in the Canongate, where three hungry children eyed with delight his fat legs, his swelling breast and magnificent pinions. "Oh,

mamma, mamma," cried the children, skipping round the table, and clapping their hands, "what a beautiful goose! how nice it will be when it is roasted! You must have a great large slice, mamma, for you had very little dinner yesterday. Why have we never any nice dinners now, mamma?" "Hush, little chatter-box," said her brother Henry, a fine stripling of sixteen, seeing tears gather in his mother's eyes. "My dear boy," said Mrs. Johnstone, "it goes to my heart to think of depriving these poor children of their expected treat, but I think we ought to send this bird to our benefactress, Lady Bethune. But for her, what would have become of us? While the Napiers, who owe all they have to your worthy and unfortunate father, have given us nothing but empty promises, she has been a consoling and ministring angel, and I should wish to take this opportunity of showing my gratitude; trifling as the offering is, I am sure it will be received with kindness." "I am sure of it," replied Henry; "and I will run and buy a few nuts and apples to console the little ones for losing their expected feast."

The children gazed with lengthened faces as the goose was carried from their sight, and conveyed by Henry to the house of Lady Bethune, who, appreciating the motives which had dictated the gift, received it with benevolent kindness. "Tell your mother, my dear," said she to Henry, "that I feel most particularly obliged by her attention, and be sure to say that Sir James has hopes of procuring a situation for you; and if he succeeds, I will come over myself to tell her the good news." Henry bounded away as gay as a lark, while Lady Bethune, after having given orders to her butler to send some bolls of potatoes, meal, and a side of fine mutton, to Mrs. Johnstone, next issued directions for the disposal of the present she had just received.

"La, madam!" exclaimed Mrs. Bryce, as she once more made her appearance before her mistress, "if here be not our identical solan goose come back to us, with Lady Bethune's compliments! I know him by his broken beak and ruffled leg; and as sure as eggs are eggs, that's my master's knock at the door!" "Run, Bryce! fly!" cried Mrs. Maxwell in despair; "put it out of sight! give it to the house-dog!"

Away ran Mrs. Bryce with her prize to Towler; and he, not recollecting that he had any favor to obtain from any one, or that he had any dear friends to oblige, received the present very gratefully, and, as he lay in his kennel,

> Lazily mumbled the bones of the dead;

thus ingloriously terminating the migrations of a solan goose.

A LEGAL PEDANT NONPLUSSED.

ANON.

Isaac M'Gregor was a simple-minded rustic, of a most obliging disposition, with a vein of sarcastic humor, which he could work with very decided effect when occasion required. He rented a small patch of ground that fringed the muir of Kippen, part of the estate of Stirling of Carden. Isaac had never seen much of the great world. With a couple of horses, he contrived to keep the thatch over his shoulders, and the wheels of life in working condition, by carrying whiskey for the far-famed Kepp distillery, the proprietor of which, the late Mr. Cassils, was distantly related to him. Isaac piqued himself on his knowledge of horses, and was generally his own farrier, whether as respected medical treatment, or arming the hoofs of that noble animal against the tear and wear of the road.

Isaac had been witness to the sale of a horse at the fair of Shandon, which, though sold as sound, turned out afterwards to have some defect in the hoof; and an action was raised before the sheriff, and proof allowed, to show that the disease was of long standing, and the fault must have been known to the vender at the time of sale. Isaac was summoned to Dumblane, to give evidence before the sheriff in favor of the defender.

The agent employed by the purchaser was as pompous a "quill driver" as ever scribbled on parchment or small pott. Peter Dudgeon (for that was his name) boasted that he had a more complete knowledge of the English language than any practitioner in sheriff or burgh court, from the Grampians to Cheviot, from his having the whole of Johnson's dictionary at his finger-ends. The words selected by Peter for common use, were remarkable more for the quantity of the alphabet employed in their construction, than from their adaptation to the idea meant to be conveyed.

Peter thought to dash Isaac, and so confuse him at first, that his evidence would want coherence, and therefore be rejected. The officer called out, "Is Isaac M'Gregor in court?" "Yes, sir!" shouted Isaac, in a voice like the report of school-boy artillery. "Come forward, then."

Peter threw himself back into his seat and looked terror, at the same time displaying a frill of cambric of extraordinary depth and longitude. "Your name is Isaac M'Gregor—is it?" "The minister ance ca'd me that, and I haena had ony reason to change 't since, but you needna speir my name, for ye hae kent me ony time this twenty years." "It is only for the information of the court." "Giff that be a', you're abler to tell them than I am—you're glibber in the tongue." "Very well; gentlemen of the court, the deponent's name is Isaac M'Gregor, a most enlightened, ratiocinating, and philosophic carter, from the bloody mires of Lock-Leggin. Notice that, gentlemen! Do you know any thing about the vending, transtulation, or transfer of the quadruped in question?" "I didna bring my dictionary in my pouch this day, or else I micht hae been able to spell your meaning: maybe, my lord judge, ye'll be able to explain what he means, for to me there's just as muckle sense in the blether o' the heather blubber!" "He means to ask, witness, do you know any thing about the sale of the horse, the subject on which you are summoned here?" "Thank you, my lord. Yes, I ken that the horse was selt to Jock Paterson there; and he appeared to me to be weel worth a' the siller he gied for him."

"Well, my sexagenarian friend Isaac," resumed Peter, "how do you know, or how can you satisfy your mind as to the validity of the testimony upon which your powers of perception have chosen to arbitrate so temerariously?" "Och, man! it would tak you a lang time to ken as muckle about horses as I do; ye would need to gang out and eat grass wi' them for seven years, like auld Nebuchadnezzar, afore ye learnt your lesson."

Peter was fairly put out, and got into a violent rage. "My lord, I have asked a plain question, and I must demand a categorical answer, or I shall move that the witness be committed for contempt of court." "I would advise you, Mr. Dudgeon," said the judge, "to put your questions in a more intelligible shape, and I have no doubt but the witness will give you a respectful answer." "That sairs you right, Peter," said the imperturbable Isaac, "and gin I had you in the muir o' Kippen, I would let ye fin' the weight o' that shakle-bane alang the side o' your head—and mak thae hornshottle teeth in your mouth dance the Dusty Miller. Ony mair to spin, ye manifest piece o' impudence?"

"What do you know about the value of a horse?" resumed Peter. "I wonder what I should ken about, if I didna ken about horse—I may say born and brought up amang them—mair than ye can say, Mr. Peter, o' the profession ye hae taen by the hand." "Have you made it your business to become acquainted with the veterinary art, whether as applied to the general anatomy of the horse, or the moral and physical habits of this useful animal; and, to attain the requisite degree of knowledge, have you studied carefully the article on that subject in the Encyclopædia Britannica, and most particularly, as in the minutiæ of detail on the subject, have you bought from your bookseller, a copy of the work, entitled The Horse, published under the sanction and patronage of the society denominating themselves, The Society for Diffusing Useful Knowledge, and made it your study by night and by day?"

"Hech, sirs! nae wonder, Peter, that you're blawing like a bursting haggis, after a' that blabber o' words; you'll hae pitten a' the lair ye e'er got at the cottage in that speech, I'se warrant;—ye mind sin' you and I were at Claymire's school thegether, what a poor fusionless whey-faced shawp o' a creature you war', baith in soul and body, and that you couldna spell your ain name!" "Do you know, then, any thing about the diseases that horses are predisposed to?" "Lang-winded is no ane o' them, at ony rate."

"From your knowledge of the veterinary art, and the profound attention that you have bestowed on the subject, would you presume to say, that a horse's hoof might be the seat of any latent, unmanifested ailment—disease—malady—gangrene or tumor, protected though it be by the crust or wall of the foot, without being visible to the ocular faculty? Now?"

"Did ye hear the thunder down there, lads? Ye may be verra thankfu', Mr. Dudgeon, that ye haena mony teeth left in the front o' your mouth, or thae big words could never hae gotten out." "Really, Mr. Dudgeon," said the Judge, "you are taking up too much time of the court, by useless preliminaries. If you have any of your young men in court, would you allow one of them to take up the examination?" "Very well, my lord."

"William, take up this brief, or case, and farther interrogate that incorrigible carter." "Witness! the next question in my brief or case,—and recollect you are still upon oath, is—Do you suppose it possible for a disease or ailment to exist in the perforating flesh or tendon, without immediately manifesting itself in occasioning lameness by its action in the chamber of the hoof?" "Weel, my lord-judge, after a', are thae twa no a bonny pair? as the craw said o' his claws." The court became perfectly convulsed, so that the sheriff was himself obliged to finish the examinatio*r*

A COOK'S LEGACY.

BY J. D. CARRICK.

Bleak now the winter blaws, thick flee the driftin' snaws,
  A' the warld looks cauld and blae;
Birds wha used to sing, now wi' shiverin' wing,
  Dozen'd sit on the frosted spray;
But though the wintry winds blaw keenly,
  What are the wintry winds to me,
When by the kitchen fire sae cleanly,
  My love is baking a pie for me!

Oh when I think on her cheeks sae greasy,
  Oh when I think on her shoulders fat,
Never a lass have I seen like Leezy,
  She makes my poor heart to go pitty-pat!
All the way hame though never so dreary,
  It charms my heart to think of thee;
How by the kitchen fire sae cheery,
  My love is baking a pie for me.

Some yield their hearts to the charms of beauty,
  Doating with pleasure upon her smile,
But when they've caught their long-wish'd booty,
  'Twill neither make pat nor pan to boil;
And wi' their beauty they aft catch a Tartar—
  Often it happens, as all may see:
Then for beauty, I'll scorn to barter
  The maid that is baking a pie for me.

The Last Debt.—An old man about to die, had his friends around him, when he was desired by his wife to tell what debts were owing to him. "There's —— owes me five shillings for mutton." "Oh," interjected the delighted helpmate, "to see a man at this time o' day, and just gaun to close his last account, hae the use o' his faculties—just say away, James." "Ay, an'— ten shillings for beef." "What a pleasant thing to see a man bein' sensible to the last! ony mair?" "An' a crown for a cow's hide." "Ay," quoth the wife, "sensible yet—weel, James, what was't ye was gaun to say?" "Nae mair," quoth James, "but I am ow'n Jock Tamson twa pounds in balance o' a cow." "Hoot, toot," quoth the wife, "he's a ravin' now—he's just demented—dinna mind ony mair that he says."

THE STUDENT OF JENA.

BY W. E. AYTOUN (BON GAULTIER).

ONCE—'t was when I lived at Jena—
At a Wirthshaus' door I sat;
And in pensive contemplation,
Ate the sausage thick and fat;
Ate the kraut, that never sourer
Tasted to my lips than here;
Smoked my pipe of strong canaster,
Sipped my fifteenth jug of beer;
Gazed upon the glancing river,
Gazed upon the tranquil pool,
Whence the silver-voiced Undine,
When the nights were calm and cool,
As the Baron Fouqué tells us,
Rose from out her shelly grot,
Casting glamour o'er the waters,
Witching that enchanted spot.
From the shadow which the coppice
Flings across the rippling stream,
Did I hear a sound of music—
Was it thought, or was it dream?
There, beside a pile of linen,
Stretched along the daisied sward,
Stood a young and blooming maiden—
'Twas her thrush-like song I heard.
Evermore within the eddy
Did she plunge the white chemise;
And her robes were loosely gathered
Rather far above her knees;

Then my breath at once forsook me,
For too surely did I deem
That I saw the fair Undine
Standing in the glancing stream—
And I felt the charm of knighthood;
And from that remembered day,
Every evening to the Wirthshaus
Took I my enchanted way.
Shortly to relate my story,
Many a week of summer long,
Came I there, when beer-o'ertaken,
With my lute and with my song;
Sung in mellow-toned soprano
All my love and all my woe,
Till the river-maiden answered,
Lilting in the stream below:—
"Fair Undine! sweet Undine!
Dost thou love as I love thee?"
"Love is free as running water,"
Was the answer made to me.

Thus, in interchange seraphic,
Did I woo my phantom fay,
Till the nights grew long and chilly,
Short and shorter grew the day;
Till at last—'t was dark and gloomy,
Dull and starless was the sky,
And my steps were all unsteady,
For a little flushed was I,—
To the well accustomed signal
No response the maiden gave;
But I heard the waters washing,
And the moaning of the wave.

Vanished was my own Undine,
All her linen, too, was gone
And I walked about lamenting,
On the river bank alone.

Idiot that I was, for never
Had I asked the maiden's name.
Was it Lieschen—was it Gretchen?
Had she tin, or whence she came?

So I took my trusty meerschaum,
And I took my lute likewise;
Wandered forth in minstrel fashion,
Underneath the lowering skies;
Sang before each comely Wirthshaus,
Sang beside each purling stream,
That same ditty which I chanted
When Undine was my theme,
Singing, as I sang at Jena,
When the shifts were hung to dry,
"Fair Undine! young Undine!
Dost thou love as well as I?"

But, alas! in field or village,
Or beside the pebbly shore,
Did I see those glancing ankles,
And the white robe, never more;
And no answer came to greet me,
No sweet voice to mine replied;
But I heard the waters rippling,
And the moaning of the tide.

"The moaning of the TIED."

MY WIFE'S COUSIN.

BY W. E. AYTOUN.

Decked with shoes of blackest polish,
And with shirt as white as snow,
After matutinal breakfast
To my daily desk I go;
First a fond salute bestowing
On my Mary's ruby lips,
Which, perchance, may be rewarded
With a pair of playful nips.

All day long across the ledger
Still my patient pen I drive,
Thinking what a feast awaits me
In my happy home at five;
In my small, one-storied Eden,
Where my wife awaits my coming,
And our solitary handmaid
Mutton chops with care is crumbing.

When the clock proclaims my freedom,
Then my hat I seize and vanish;
Every trouble from my bosom,
Every anxious care I banish.
Swiftly brushing o'er the pavement,
At a furious pace I go,
Till I reach my darling dwelling
In the wilds of Pimlico.

"Mary, wife, where art thou, dearest?"
Thus I cry, while yet afar;
Ah! what scent invades my nostrils?—
'Tis the smoke of a cigar!

Instantly into the parlor
Like a maniac I haste,
And I find a young Life-Guardsman,
With his arm round Mary's waist.

And his other hand is playing
Most familiarly with hers;
And I think my Brussels carpet
Somewhat damaged by his spurs.
"Fire and furies! what the blazes!"
Thus in frenzied wrath I call;
When my spouse her arms upraises,
With the most astounding squall.

"Was there ever such a monster,
Ever such a wretched wife?
Ah! how long must I endure it,
How protract this hateful life?
All day long, quite unprotected,
Does he leave his wife at home,
And she cannot see her cousins,
Even when they kindly come!"

Then the young Life-Guardsman, rising,
Scarce vouchsafes a single word,
But with look of deadly menace,
Claps his hand upon his sword;
And in fear I faintly falter—
"This your cousin, then he's mine!
Very glad, indeed, to see you—
Won't you stop with us, and dine?"

Won't a ferret suck a rabbit?—
As a thing of course he stops;
And with most voracious swallow
Walks into my mutton chops.
In the twinkling of a bed-post,
Is each savory platter clear,
And he shows uncommon science
In his estimate of beer.

Half-and-half goes down before him,
Gurgling from the pewter-pot;
And he moves a counter motion
For a glass of something hot.
Neither chops nor beer I grudge him,
Nor a moderate share of goes;
But I know not why he's always
Treading upon Mary's toes.

Evermore, when, home returning,
From the counting-house I come,
Do I find the young Life-Guardsman
Smoking pipes and drinking rum.
Evermore he stays to dinner,
Evermore devours my meal;
For I have a wholesome horror
Both of powder and of steel.

Yet I know he's Mary's cousin,
For my only son and heir
Much resembles that young Guardsman,
With the self-same curly hair;
But I wish he would not always
Spoil my carpet with his spurs;
And I'd rather see his fingers
In the fire, than touching hers.

THE FRIARS OF DIJON.

BY THOMAS CAMPBELL.

When honest men confess'd their sins,
And paid the church genteelly—
In Burgundy two Capuchins
Lived jovially and freely.

They march'd about from place to place,
With shrift and dispensation;
And mended broken consciences,
Soul-tinkers by vocation.

One friar was Father Boniface,
And he ne'er knew disquiet,
Save when condemn'd to saying grace
O'er mortifying diet.

The other was lean Dominick,
Whose slender form, and sallow,
Would scarce have made a candlewick
For Boniface's tallow.

Albeit, he tippled like a fish,
Though not the same potation;
And mortal man ne'er clear'd a dish
With nimbler mastication.

Those saints without the shirts arrived,
One evening late, to pigeon
A country pair for alms, that lived
About a league from Dijon.

Whose supper-pot was set to boil,
On faggots briskly crackling;
The friars enter'd, with a smile
To Jacquez and to Jacqueline.

They bow'd and bless'd the dame, and then
In pious terms besought her,
To give two holy-minded men
A meal of bread and water.

For water and a crust they crave,
Those mouths that even on Lent days
Scarce knew the taste of water, save
When watering for dainties.

Quoth Jacquez, "That were sorry cheer
For men fatigued and dusty;
And if ye supp'd on crusts, I fear,
You'd go to bed but crusty."

So forth he brought a flask of rich
Wine, fit to feast Silenus,
And viands, at the sight of which
They laugh'd like two hyænas.

Alternately, the host and spouse
Regaled each pardon-gauger,
Who told them tales right marvellous,
And lied as for a wager—

'Bout churches like balloons convey'd
With æronautic martyrs;
And wells made warm, where holy maid
Had only dipp'd her garters.

And if their hearers gaped, I guess,
With jaws three inch asunder,
'Twas partly out of weariness,
And partly out of wonder.

Then striking up duets, the freres
Went on to sing in matches,
From psalms to sentimental airs,
From these to glees and catches.

At last, they would have danced outright,
Like a baboon and tame bear,
If Jacquez had not drunk, Good night,
And shown them to their chamber.

The room was high, the host was nigh—
Had wife or he suspicion,
That monks would make a raree-show
Of chinks in the partition?—

Or that two confessors would come,
Their holy ears out-reaching
To conversations as hum-drum
Almost as their own preaching?

Shame on you, Friars of orders gray,
That peeping knelt, and wriggling,
And when ye should have gone to pray,
Betook yourselves to giggling!

But every deed will have its meed:
And hark! what information
Has made the sinners, in a trice,
Look black with consternation.

The farmer on a hone prepares
His knife, a long and keen one;
And talks of killing both the freres,
The fat one, and the lean one.

To-morrow by the break of day,
He orders too, saltpetre,
And pickling-tubs; but, reader, stay,
Our host was no man-eater.

The priests knew not that country-folk
Give pigs the name of friars;
But startled, witless of the joke,
As if they trod on briers.

Meanwhile, as they perspired with dread,
The hair of either craven
Had stood erect upon his head,
But that their heads were shaven.

What, pickle and smoke us limb by limb!
God curse him and his lardners!
St. Peter will bedevil him,
If he saltpetres pardoners.

Yet, Dominick, to die!—the bare
Idea shakes one oddly;—
Yes, Boniface, 'tis time we were
Beginning to be godly.

Would that, for absolution's sake
Of all our sins and cogging,
We had a whip, to give and take
A last kind mutual flogging.

O Dominick, thy nether end
Should bleed for expiation,
And thou shouldst have, my dear fat friend,
A glorious flagellation.

But having ne'er a switch, poor souls,
They bow'd like weeping willows,
And told the Saints long rigmaroles
Of all their peccadillos.

Yet, 'midst this penitential plight
A thought their fancies tickled,
'Twere better brave the window's height,
Than be at morning pickled.

And so they girt themselves to leap,
Both under breath imploring
A regiment of Saints to keep
Their host and hostess snoring.

The lean one lighted like a cat,
Then scampered off like Jehu,
Nor stopp'd to help the man of fat,
Whose cheek was of a clay hue—

Who, being by nature more design'd
For resting than for jumping,
Fell heavy on his parts behind,
That broaden'd with the plumping.

There long beneath the window's sconce,
His bruises he sat pawing,
Squat as the figure of a bronze
Upon a Chinese drawing.

At length he waddled to a sty;
The pigs, you'd thought for game sake,
Came round and nosed him lovingly,
As if they'd known their namesake.

Meanwhile the other flew to town,
And with short respiration
Bray'd like a donkey up and down
Ass-ass-ass-assination!

Men left their beds, and night-capp'd heads
Popp'd out from every casement;
The cats ran frighten'd on the leads;
Dijon was all amazement.

Doors bang'd, dogs bay'd, and boys hurra'd,
Throats gaped aghast in bare rows,
Till soundest sleeping watchmen woke,
And even at last the mayor rose—

Who charging him before police,
Demands of Dominick surly,
What earthquake, fire, or breach of peace
Made all this hurly-burly?

Ass—quoth the priest—ass-assins, Sir,
Are hence a league, or nigher,
About to salt, scrape, massacre,
And barrel up a friar.

Soon at the magistrate's command,
A troop from the gens-d'arm's house,
Of twenty men, rode sword in hand,
To storm the bloody farm's house.

As they were cantering towards the place,
Comes Jacquez to the swineyard,
But started when a great round face
Cried, "Rascal, hold thy whinyard."

'Twas Boniface, as mad's King Lear,
Playing antics in the piggery:—
"And what the devil brought you here,
You mountain of a friar, eh?"

Ah, once how jolly, now how wan,
  And blubber'd with the vapors,
That frantic Capuchin began
  To cut fantastic capers—

Crying, "help, halloo, the bellows blow,
  The pot is on to stew me;
I am a pretty pig, but, no!
  They shall not barbacue me."

Nor was this raving fit a sham;
  In truth, he was hysterical,
Until they brought him out a dram,
  And that wrought like a miracle.

Just as the horsemen halted near,
  Crying, Murderer, stop, ohoy, oh!
Jacquez was comforting the frere
  With a good glass of noyeau—

Who beckon'd to them not to kick up
  A row; but, waxing mellow,
Squeez'd Jacquez' hand, and with a hiccup
  Said, You're a d——d good fellow.

Explaining lost but little breath:—
  Here ended all the matter;
So God save Queen Elizabeth,
  And long live Henry Quatre!

The gens-d'arms at the story broke
  Into horse-fits of laughter,
And, as if they had known the joke,
  Their horses neigh'd thereafter.

Lean Dominick, methinks, his chaps
  Yawn'd weary, worn, and moody;
So may my readers too, perhaps,
  And thus I wish 'em Good day.

CHANGEABLE CHARLIE.

A Tale of the Dominie.

BY ANDREW PICKEN.

It was in the early part of my life, when I was yet in the apprenticeship of my fortune, that I had the teaching of a pleasant boy, whose name was Charlie Cheap. Charlie's father was a weel-speeked witless body, who kept a shop in the largest village near; and having made money by mere want of sense, and selling of the jigs and jags of a country town, was called by the name of John Cheap the Chapman, after the classical story of that personage with which we used to be diverted when we were children; so the old man seeing indications of genius in his son, sent the lad to me to finish his education.

There was not a better-liked boy in the whole school than Charlie Cheap; for though he never would learn any thing effectually, and was the head and ringleader of every trick that was hatched, he had such a laughing, happy disposition, and took his very punishment so good-humoredly, that it went to my heart to think of chastising him; and as for the fool's cap and the broom sceptre, they were no punishment to him, for he never seemed better pleased than when he had them on; and when mounted thus on the top of the black stool, he seemed so delighted, and pulled such faces at the rest of the boys, that no mortal flesh could stand to their gravity near him, and my seat of learning was in danger of becoming a perfect hobbleshow of diversion. How to master this was past my power. But Charlie's versatility ended it by his own will, and before he was half learned in his preliminary humanities, his father and he had taken some scheme into their heads, and he was removed from me and sent to the college.

I know not how it was, but for several years I lost sight of Charlie, until I heard that his father was dead, and that he was now a grown man, and was likely to make a great fortune. This news was no surprise to me, for I now began to make the observation, that the greatest fools that I had the honor of preparing for the world, most generally became the wealthiest men.

It was one day when on a summer tramp, that, entering a decentish town, and looking about at the shop windows, I began to bethink me of the necessity that had fallen upon me, by the tear and wear of the journey, of being at the expense of a new hat, so I entered a magazine of miscellaneous commodities, when who should astonish me in the person of the shopkeeper, but my old pupil Charlie Cheap. "Merciful me! Charlie," said I, "who would have expected to find you at this trade! I thought you had gone to the college to serve your time for a minister of the gospel."

"Indeed," said Charlie, "that was once the intent, but in truth, my head got rather confused with the lair and the logic. I had not the least conjugality to the Greek conjugations, and when I came to the Hebrew, that is read every word backwards, faith, I could neither read it backwards nor forwards, and fairly stuck, and grew a sticked minister. But I had long begun to see that the minister trade was but a poor business, and that a man might wait for the mustard till the meat was all eaten, and so I just took up a chop like my father before me; and faith, Mr. Dominie, I'm making a fortune."

"Well," said I, "I am really happy to hear it, and I hope, besides that, that you like your employment."

"I'm quite delighted with the chop-keeping, Mr. Balgownie; a very different life from chapping verbs in a cauld college. Besides, I am a respected man in the town; nothing but Mr. Cheap here and Mrs. Cheap there, and ladies coming in at all hours of the day, and bowing and becking to me, and throwing the money to me across the counter; I would not wonder if they should make me a baillie yet."

"Well, I am really delighted too," said I, "and from my knowledge of baillies, I would not wonder in the least—so good bye, Mr. Cheap. I think this hat looks very well on me."

"Makes you ten years younger, sir—good bye! wish you your health to wear it."

It might be a twelvemonth after that I was plodding along a country road some ten miles from the fore-mentioned town, when looking over the hedge by my side, I saw a team of horses pulling a plough towards me; and my cogitations were disturbed by the yo-ing and yau-ing of the man who followed it. Something struck me that I knew the voice, and when the last of the men came up, I discovered under the plush waistcoat and farmer's bonnet, my old friend Charlie Cheap.

"Soul and conscience!" cried he, thrusting his clayey hand through the hedge and grasping mine, "if this is not my old master the Dominie!" and truly he gave me the farmer's gripe, as if my hand had been made of cast metal.

"What are you doing here, Charlie?" said I. "Why are you not minding your shop instead of marching there in the furrows at the plough-tail?"

"Chop," said he, "what chop? Na, na, Dominie, I've gotten a better trade by the hand."

"It cannot be possible, Charlie, that ye've turned farmer?"

"Whether it be possible or no, it is true," said Charlie; "but dinna be standing there whistling through the hedge, but come in by the slap at the corner, and ye shall taste my wife's treacle ale."

"Well really," said I, when I had got down into the farm-house, "this is the most marvellous change."

"No change to speak of," said he; "do ye think I was going to be tied up to haberdrabbery all my days? No, no, I knew I had a genius for farming; the chop-keeping grew flat and unprofitable, a chield from England set up next door to me, so a country customer took a fancy for a town life. I sold him my stock in trade, and he sold me the stock on his farm. He stepped in behind the counter, and I got behind the plough, so here I am, happier than ever; besides, harkie! I am making money fast."

"Are you really? But how do you know that?"

"Can I not count my ten fingers? Have I not figured it on black and white over and over again? There's great profits with management such as mine, that I can assure you, sir."

"But how could you possibly learn farming? That, I believe, is not taught at college."

"Pooh! my friend; I can learn any thing. Besides, my wife's mother was a farmer's daughter, and Lizzy herself understands farming already, as if she was reared to it. She makes all the butter, and the children drink all the milk, and we live so happy; birds singing in the morning—cows lowing at night—drinking treacle ale all day; and nothing to do but watch the corn growing. In short, farming is the natural state of man. Adam and Eve were a farmer and his wife, just like me and Lizzie Cheap!"

"But you'll change again shortly, I am afraid, Mr. Cheap."

"That's impossible, for I've got a nineteen years' lease. I'll grow gray as a farmer. Well, good bye, Dominie. Be sure you give us a call the next time ye pass, and get a drink of our treacle ale."

"Well, really this is the most extraordinary thing," said I to myself, as I walked up the lane from the farm house. "I shall be curious to ascertain if he's going to stick to the farming till he's ruined."

I thought no more of Changeable Charlie for above a year, when, coming towards the same neighborhood, I resolved to go a short distance out of my way to pay him a visit. My road lay across a clear country stream, which winded along a pleasant green valley beneath me; and as I drew near the rustic bridge, my ear caught the lively sound of a waterfall, which murmured from a picturesque spot among opening woods, a little way above the bridge. A little mill-race, with its narrow channel of deep, level water, next attracted my notice; and presently after, the regular splash of a water-wheel, and the boom of a corn-mill, became objects of my meditative observation. The mill looked so quaint and rustic by the stream, the banks were so green and the water so clear, that I was tempted to wander towards it, down from the bridge, just to make the whole a subject of closer observation.

A barefooted girl came forth from the house and stared in my face, as a Scottish lassie may be supposed to do at a reasonable man. "Can you tell me," said I, willing to make up an excuse for my intrusion, "if this road will lead me to the farm of Longrigs, which is occupied by one Mr. Cheap?" The lassie looked in my face with a thieveless smile, and, without answering a word, took a bare-legged race into the mill. Presently, a great lumbering miller came out, like a walking bag of flour from beside the hopper, and I immediately saw he was going to address me.

Never did I see such a snowy man. His miller's hat was inch thick with flour; he whitened the green earth as he walked, the knees of his breeches were loose, and the stockings that hung about his heels would have made a hearty meal for a starving garrison.

"What can the impudent rascal be staring at?" I said, and I began to cast my eyes down on my person, to see if I could find any cause in my own appearance, that the miller and his lassie should thus treat me as a world's wonder.

"Ye were asking, I think," he said, "after Charlie Cheap, of the Longrigs?"

"Yes," said I, "but his farm must be some miles from this. Perhaps, as you are the miller of the neighborhood, you can direct me the nearest road to it."

The burley scoundrel first lifted up his eye-winkers, which were clotted with flour, shook out about a pound of it from his bushy whiskers, and then burst into a laugh in my very face as loud as the neighing of a miller's horse.

"Ho, ho, hough!" grinned he, coughing upon me a shower of flour. "Is it possible, Dominie, that ye dinna ken me?" and opening a mouth at least as wide as his own hopper, I began to recognize the exaggerated features of Changeable Charlie.

"Well really," said I, gazing at his grin, and the hills of flour that arose from his cheeks—"really this beats every thing! and so, Charlie, ye're now turned into a miller?"

"As sure's a gun!" said he. "Lord bless your soul, Dominie! do you think I could bear to spread dung and turn up dirt all my life? no! I have a soul above that. Besides, your miller is a man in power. He is an aristocrat over the farmers, and with the power has its privileges too, for he takes a multre out of every man's sack, and levies his revenues like a prime minister. No one gets so soon fat as those that live by the labor of others, as you may see; for the landed interest supports me by day, and my water wheel works for me all night, so if I don't get rich now, the deuce is in it."

"I suppose," said I, following him into the mill, "you are just making a fortune."

"How can I help it?" said he, "making money while I sleep, for I hear the musical click of the hopper in my dreams, and my bairns learn their lessons by the jog of it. I wish every man who has passed a purgatory at college, were just as happy as the miller and his wife. Is not that the case, Lizzy?" he added, addressing his better half, who now came forth hung round by children—"as the song goes,"

Merry may the maid be that marries the miller,
For foul day and fair day, he's aye bringing till her—
His ample hands in ilk man's pock,
His mill grinds muckle siller,
His wife is dress'd in silk and lawn
For he's aye bringing till her.

"But dear me, Mr. Cheap," said I, "what was it that put you out of the farm, where I thought you were so happy, and making a fortune?"

"I was as happy as a man could be, and making money too, and nothing put me out of the farm, although I was quite glad of the change, but just a penny of fair debt, the which, you know, is a good man's case—and a little civil argument about the rent. But every thing turned out for the best, for Willie Happer, the former miller, just ran awa the same week; I got a dead bargain of the mill, and so I came in to reign in his stead. Am I not a fortunate man?"

"Never was a man so lucky," said I; "but do you really mean to be a waiter on the mill-hopper all your days?"

"As long as wood turns round and water runs; but, Lizzy," he added to his wife, "what are you standing glowering there for, and me like to choke? Gang and fetch us a jug of your best treacle ale."

"It surely cannot be," said I to myself when I had left the mill, "that Changeable Charlie will ever adopt a new profession now, but live and die a miller." I was, however, entirely mistaken in my calculation, as I found before I was two years older; and though I have not time, at this present sitting, to tell the whole of Charlie's story—and have a strong suspicion that my veracity might be put in jeopardy, were I to condescend thereto, I am quite ready to take my oath, that after this I found him in not less than five different characters, in all of which he was equally happy and equally certain of making a fortune. Where the mutations of Charlie might have run to, and whither, to speak with a little agreeable stultification, he might not, like another remarkable man, have exhausted worlds and then imagined new, it is impossible to predicate, if Fortune had not, in her usual injustice, put an end to his career of change, by leaving his wife Lizzy a considerable legacy.

The last character then that I found Charlie striving to enact, was that of a gentleman—that is, a man who has plenty of money to live upon, and nothing whatever to do. It did not appear, however, that Charlie's happiness was at all improved by this last change; for, besides that it had taken from him all his private joys, in the *hope* of one day making a fortune, it had raised up a most unexpected enemy, in the shape of old father Time, whom he found it more troublesome and less hopeful to contend with, than all the obstacles that had formerly seemed to stand in his way to the making of an independent fortune.

When the legacy was first showered upon him, however, he seemed as happy under the dispensation as he had been before under any other of his changes. In the hey-dey of his joy, he sent for me to witness his felicity, and to give him my advice as to the spending of his money. This invitation I was thoughtless enough to accept, but it was more that I might pick up a little philosophy out of what I should observe, than from any pleasure that I expected, or any good that I was likely to do. When I got to his house, I was worried to death by all the fine things I was forced to look at, that had been sent to him from Jamaica, and all that from him and his wife I was forced to hear. I tried to impress him concerning the good that he might do with his money, in reference to many who sorely wanted it, but I found that he had too little feeling himself to understand the feelings of others, and that affliction had never yet driven a nail into his own flesh, to open his heart to sympathy. Instead of entering into any rational plans, his wife and he laughed all day at nothing whatever, his children turned the house upside down in their ecstasy at being rich; and, in short, never before had I been so wearied at seeing people happy.

In all this, however, I heard not one single word of thankfulness for this unlooked-for deliverance from constant vicissitude, or one grateful expression to Providence, for being so unreasonably kind to this family, while thousands around them struggled incessantly, in ill-rewarded industry and unavailing anxiety. So I wound up the story of Changeable Charlie in reflective melancholy, for I had seen so many who would, for any little good fortune, have been most thankful and happy, yet never were able to attain thereto; and I inclined to the sombre conclusion, that in this world the wise and virtuous man was often less fortunate, and generally less happy, than the fool.

THE COBBLER.

BY A. WHITELAW.

In the little picturesque village of Duddingstone, which lies sweetly at the foot of Edinburgh's great lion, Arthur-Seat, and which is celebrated for its strawberries and sheep-head broth, flourished, within our own remembrance, a poor and honest mender of boots and shoes, by name Robert Rentoul.

Robin had been a cobbler all his days—to very little purpose. He had made nothing of the business, although he had given it a fair trial of fifty or sixty years. He was born, and cobbled—got married, and cobbled—got children, and cobbled—got old, and cobbled, without advancing a step beyond his last. It "found him poor at first and left him so!" To make the ends meet was the utmost he could do. He therefore bore no great liking to a profession which had done so little for him, and for which he had done so much; but in truth, his want of liking may be considered as much a cause as an effect of his want of success. His mind, in short, did not go with his work; and it was the interest, as well as duty and pleasure, of his good wife, Janet, to hold him to it (particularly when he had given his word of honor to a customer) by all the arts common to her sex,—sometimes by scolding, sometimes by taunting, but oftener—for Janet was a kind-hearted creature—by treating him to a thimbleful of aquavitæ, which he loved dearly, with its proper accompaniments of bread and cheese.

Although, however, Robin did not keep by the shoes with any good heart, he could not be called either a lazy or inefficient man. In every thing but cobbling he took a deep and active interest. In particular, he was a great connoisseur of the weather. Nobody could prophesy snow like Robin, or foretell a black frost. The latter was Robin's delight; for with it came the people of Edinburgh, to hold their saturnalia on Duddingstone Loch, and cobbling, on these great occasions, was entirely out of the question. His rickety table, big-bellied bottle, and tree-legged glass, were then in requisition, for the benefit of curlers and skaters in general, and of himself in particular. But little benefit accrued from these to Robin, although he could always count on one good customer—in himself. On the breaking up of the ice, he regularly found himself poorer than before, and, what was worse, with a smaller disposition than ever to work.

It must have been on some occasion of this kind, that strong necessity suggested to Robin a step for the bettering of his fortunes, which was patronized by the legislature of the day, and which he had heard was resorted to by many with success. Robin resolved to try the lottery. With thirty shillings, which he kept in an old stocking for the landlord, he went to Edinburgh, and purchased a sixteenth. This proceeding he determined to keep a profound secret from every one; but whiskey cannot tolerate secrets; the first half-mutchkin with barber Hugh succeeding in ejecting it; and as the barber had every opportunity, as well as disposition, to spread it, the thing was known to all the village in the lathering of a chin.

Among others, it reached the ears of Mr. Blank, a young gentleman who happened to reside at Duddingstone, and who took an interest in the fortunes of Robin. Mr. B. (unknown to the villagers) was connected with the press of Edinburgh, particularly with a certain newspaper, one copy of which had an extensive circulation in Duddingstone. First of all, the newspaper reached Mr. Blank on the Saturday of its publication; on the Monday it fell into the hands of Robin, who, like the rest of his trade, had most leisure on that day to peruse it; on the Tuesday, the baker had it; on the Wednesday, the tailor; on the Thursday, the blacksmith; on the Friday, the gardener; and on the Saturday the barber, in whose shop it lay till the succeeding Saturday brought another, when it was torn down for suds, leaving not a wreck behind, except occasionally a King's speech, a cure for the rupture, a list of magistrates and town council, or any other interesting passage that took the barber's fancy, which was carefully clipped out, and pasted on the wooden walls of his apartment, to the general satisfaction, instruction, and entertainment of his customers. This newspaper, like Wordsworth's Old Cumberland Beggar, was the means of keeping alive a sympathy and community of feeling among the parties; and in particular, tended to establish a friendly intercourse between Robin Rentoul and Mr. Blank. Robin could count upon his glass every Monday, when he went for "the papers,"—and, except the glass, he liked nothing better than to have what he called "a bother" with Mr. B. himself. Mr. B. soon got from Robin's own mouth all the particulars of the lottery-ticket purchase, even to the very number,—which was 1757, a number chosen by Robin, who had an eye to fatalism, as being the date of the year in which he was born.

A love of mischief or sport suggested to the

young gentleman the wicked thought of making the newspaper a means of hoaxing Robin regarding the lottery ticket. We shall not undertake to defend Mr. Blank's conduct, even on the score of his being, as he was, a very young man. The experiment he made was cruel, although we believe it was done without malignity, and with every resolution that Robin should not be a loser by it. About the time when news of the lottery-drawing was expected, the following paragraph appeared in the newspaper with which Mr. Blank was connected:

"By private accounts from London, we understand that 984 and 1757 are the numbers drawn in the present lottery for the two £20,000 prizes. We know not if any of these lucky numbers have been disposed of in this quarter."

Poor Robin came for his newspaper at the usual time, and in his usual manner. He got his customary glass, but missed his customary "bother" with Mr. Blank, who chose for the present to be out of the way. Home he trudged, carrying the newspaper, the harbinger of his fortune, in the crown of his hat—placed himself on his stool—drew out his spectacles—and began to read, as usual, from the beginning of the first page. It was some time before he reached the paragraph big with his fate. When he saw it, he gave a gasp—took off his spectacles, and began to rub them, as if doubtful that they had deceived him—placed them again deliberately on his nose—read the passage over again, slowly and surely—then quietly laying his hand on a shoe which he had been mending, and which contained a last, made it in a moment spin through the window, carrying casement with it, and passing barely the head of a fishwife who was toiling along with her creel. His wife, Janet, was not at home, so, rushing out of doors, he made way to his old howff, at the sign of the Sheep's Head. The landlady held up her hands at his wild look.

"Send for barber Hughie," he cried, "and Neil the tailor; and I say, Luckie, bring in—let me see—a GALLON o' your best; and some cheese—a HAIL CHEESE—nane o' your halfs and quarters."

"Guide us, Robin! What bee's this in your bonnet? The man's gyte!"

"Look there, woman, at the papers. I've gotten a prize. A twenty thousand pounder. What's the sixteenth o' that, think ye?"

"A prize and nae blank! Eh, wow, Robin, gie's a shake o' your hand. I aye said ye wad come to something. Isy, you slut, rin for the barber,—and Neil—if he's sober—and bring the gudeman too. The mae the merrier."

Robin was soon surrounded by all his cronies of the village, for the news of his good fortune spread with the rapidity of scandal. Innumerable were the shakings of hands, and the pledges of good will and assistance. The Sheep's Head soon became too hot for the company; the village itself was in an uproar, and as halloo followed halloo, Mr. Blank inwardly "shrunk at the sound himself had made." Meanwhile, to have the truth of the statement confirmed, a superannuated lawyer had been despatched on an old blood horse to the lottery office at Edinburgh; and his return, with the intelligence that all was a hoax, spread dismay over the faces of the carousers, and made Robin's heart sink with grief and shame.

A speedy change took place in the conduct of those fair-weather friends who had flocked around the poor cobbler. From being the admired of all beholders, he became on object of scorn and laughtes, till, unable to stand their mocks and jibes, he rushed from their presence, and sought shelter under his own bed-clothes. The only one who stood true was Neil the tailor. He followed Robin to his own house—took him by the hand, and said, "Robin, my man, I promised you a suit o' clothes, o' the best. I ken ye wad hae befriended me had ye got the cash—and—lottery or no lottery—by Jove! I'll keep my word."

Mr. Blank took care to discharge the debt in-

curred at the Sheep's Head, and endeavored, by proffers of money and otherwise, to comfort Robin, and atone in some measure for the injury he had secretly done him. But Robin turned himself in his bed, and would not be comforted. Three days he laid in this plight, when authentic information arrived of the drawing of the lottery. Robin's number was, after all, in reality a lucky one—not, indeed, twenty thousand, but five thousand pounds. The sixteenth of even this was a little fortune to him, and he received it with a sober satisfaction, very different from the boisterous glee which he had formerly displayed, "I'll seek nane o' them this time," he said to his wife, Janet—"except Neil the tailor; *he*, puir body, was the only true-hearted creature amang them a'. I've learnt a lesson by what has taken place. *I ken wha to trust.*"

THE SEARCH AFTER HAPPINESS;

Or, The Quest of Sultaun Solimaun.

BY SIR WALTER SCOTT.

Oh, for a glance of that gay muse's eye,
That lighten'd on Bandello's laughing tale,
And twinkled with a lustre shrewd and sly,
When Giam Battista bade her vision hail!—
Yet fear not, ladies, the *naïve* detail
Given by the natives of that land canorous;
Italian license loves to leap the pale,
We Britons have the fear of shame before us,
And, if not wise in mirth, at least must be decorous.

In the far eastern clime, no great while since,
Lived Sultaun Solimaun, a mighty prince,
Whose eyes, as oft as they perform'd their round,
Beheld all others fixed upon the ground;
Whose ears received the same unvaried phrase,
"Sultaun! thy vassal hears, and he obeys!"
All have their tastes—this may the fancy strike
Of such grave folks as pomp and grandeur like:
For me, I love the honest heart and warm
Of monarch who can amble round his farm,
Or when the toil of state no more annoys,
In chimney corner seek domestic joys—
I love a prince will bid the bottle pass,
Exchanging with his subjects glance and glass;
In fitting time, can, gayest of the gay,
Keep up the jest, and mingle in the lay—
Such Monarchs best our free-born humors suit,
But Despots must be stately, stern, and mute.

This Solimaun, Serendib had in sway—
And where's Serendib? may some critic say—
Good lack, mine honest friend, consult the chart,
Scare not my Pegasus before I start!
If Rennell has it not, you'll find, mayhap,
The isle laid down in Captain Sinbad's map—
Famed mariner! whose merciless narrations
Drove every friend and kinsman out of patience,
Till, fain to find a guest who thought them shorter,
He deign'd to tell them over to a porter—
The last edition see, by Long and Co.,
Rees, Hurst, and Orme, our fathers in the Row.

Serendib found, deem not my tale a fiction—
This Sultaun, whether lacking contradiction—
(A sort of stimulant which hath its uses,
To raise the spirits and reform the juices,
—Sovereign specific for all sorts of cures
In my wife's practice, and perhaps in yours),
The Sultaun lacking this same wholesome bitter,
Of cordial smooth for prince's palate fitter—
Or if some Mollah had hag-rid his dreams
With Degial, Ginnistan, and such wild themes
Belonging to the Mollah's subtle craft,
I wot not—but the Sultaun never laugh'd,
Scarce ate or drank, and took a melancholy
That scorn'd all remedy, profane or holy;
In his long list of melancholies, mad,
Or mazed, or dumb, hath Burton none so bad.

Physicians soon arrived, sage, ware, and tried,
As e'er scrawl'd jargon in a darken'd room;
With heedful glance the Sultaun's tongue they eyed,
Peep'd in his bath, and God knows where beside,
And then in solemn accent spoke their doom,
"His majesty is very far from well."
Then each to work with his specific fell;
The Hakim Ibrahim *instanter* brought
His unguent Mahazzin al Zerdukkaut,
While Roompot, a practitioner more wily,
Relied on his Munaskif all fillfily.
More and yet more in deep array appear,
And some the front assail, and some the rear;
Their remedies to reinforce and vary,
Came surgeon eke, and eke apothecary;

Till the tired Monarch, though of words grown chary,

Yet dropt, to recompense their fruitless labor,
Some hint about a bowstring or a sabre.
There lack'd, I promise you, no longer speeches,
To rid the palace of those learned leeches.

Then was the council call'd—by their advice
(They deem'd the matter ticklish all, and nice,
And sought to shift it off from their own shoulders)
Tartars and couriers in all speed were sent,
To call a sort of Eastern Parliament
Of feudatory chieftains and freeholders—
Such have the Persians at this very day,
My gallant Malcolm calls them *couroultai*;—
I'm not prepared to show in this slight song
That to Serendib the same forms belong—
E'en let the learned go search, and tell me if I'm wrong.

The Omrahs, each with hand on scimetar,
Gave, like Sempronius, still their voice for war—
"The sabre of the Sultaun in its sheath
Too long has slept, nor own'd the work of death;
Let the Tambourgi bid his signal rattle,
Bang the loud gong, and raise the shout of battle.
This dreary cloud that dims our sovereign's day,
Shall from his kindled bosom flit away,
When the bold Lootie wheels his courser round,
And the arm'd elephant shall shake the ground.
Each noble pants to own the glorious summons—
And for the charges—Lo! your faithful Commons!"

The Riots who attended in their places
(Serendib language calls a farmer Riot)
Look'd ruefully in one another's faces,
From this oration arguing much disquiet,
Double assessment, forage, and free quarters;
And fearing these as China-men the Tartars,
Or as the whisker'd vermin fear the mousers,
Each fumbled in the pockets of his trowsers.
And next came forth the reverend Convocation,
Bald heads, white beards, and many a turban green,
Imaum and Mollah there of every station,
Santon, Fakir, and Calendar were seen.
Their votes were various—some advised a Mosque
With fitting revenues should be erected,
With seemly gardens and with gay Kiosque,
To recreate a band of priests selected;
Others opined that through the realm a dole
Be made to holy men, whose prayers might profit
The Sultaun's weal in body and in soul.
But their long-headed chief, the Sheik Ul-Sofit,
More closely touch'd the point;—"Thy studious mood,"
Quoth he, "O Prince! hath thicken'd all thy blood,
And dull'd thy brain with labor beyond measure;
Wherefore relax a space and take thy pleasure,
And toy with beauty, or tell o'er thy treasure;
From all the cares of state, my Liege, enlarge thee,
And leave the burden to thy faithful clergy."

These counsels sage availed not a whit,
And so the patient (as is not uncommon
Where grave physicians lose their time and wit)
Resolved to take advice of an old woman;
His mother she, a dame who once was beauteous,
And still was called so by each subject duteous.
Now whether Fatima was witch in earnest,
Or only made believe, I cannot say—
But she profess'd to cure disease the sternest,
By dint of magic, amulet or lay;
And, when all other skill in vain was shown,
She deem'd it fitting time to use her own.

"*Sympathia magica* hath wonders done;"
(Thus did old Fatima bespeak her son,)
"It works upon the fibres and the pores,
And thus, insensibly, our health restores,
And it must help us here. Thou must endure
The ill, my son, or travel for the cure.
Search land and sea, and get, where'er you can,
The inmost vesture of a happy man:
I mean his SHIRT, my son; which, taken warm
And fresh from off his back, shall chase your harm,
Bid every current of your veins rejoice,
And your dull heart leap light as shepherd-boy's."
Such was the counsel from his mother came;—
I know not if she had some under game,
As doctors have, who bid their patients roam
And live abroad, when sure to die at home;
Or if she thought, that, somehow or another,
Queen-Regent sounded better than Queen-Mother;
But, says the Chronicle (who will go look it?)
That such was her advice—the Sultaun took it.

All are on board—the Sultaun and his train,
In gilded galley prompt to plow the main.
The old Rais was the first who question'd, "Whither?"
They paused—"Arabia," thought the pensive Prince,
"Was call'd The Happy many ages since;—
For Mokha, Rais." And they came safely thither,
But not in Araby, with all her balm,
Not where Judea weeps beneath her palm,
Not in rich Egypt, not in Nubian waste,
Could there the step of Happiness be traced.
One Copt alone profess'd to have seen her smile
When Bruce his goblet fill'd at infant Nile:
She bless'd the dauntless traveller as he quaff'd,
But vanish'd from him with the ended draught.

"Enough of turbans," said the weary King,
"These dolimans of ours are not the thing;
Try we the Giaours, these men of coat and cap, I
Incline to think some of them must be happy;
At least they have as fair a cause as any can,
They drink good wine and keep no Ramazan.
Then northward, ho!"—The vessel cuts the sea,
And fair Italia lies upon her lee.—
But fair Italia, she who once unfurled
Her eagle-banners o'er a conquer'd world,
Long from her throne of domination tumbled,
Lay, by her quondam vassals, sorely humbled,
The Pope himself look'd pensive, pale, and lean,
And was not half the man he once had been.
"While these the priest and those the noble fleeces,
Our poor old boot," they said, "is torn to pieces.
Its tops the vengeful claws of Austria feel,
And the Great Devil is rending toe and heel.
If happiness you seek, to tell you truly,
We think she dwells with one Giovanni Bulli;
A tramontane, a heretic—the buck,
Poffaredio! still has all the luck;
By land or ocean never strikes his flag—
And then—a perfect walking money-bag."
Off set our Prince to seek John Bull's abode,
But first took France—it lay upon the road.

Monsieur Baboon, after much late commotion,
Was agitated like a settling ocean,
Quite out of sorts, and could not tell what ail'd him,
Only the glory of his house had fail'd him;
Besides, some tumors on his noddle biding,
Gave indication of a recent hiding.
Our Prince, though Sultauns of such things are
heedless,
Thought it a thing indelicate and needless,
To ask, if at that moment he was happy.
And Monsieur, seeing that he was *comme il faut*, a
Loud voice muster'd up, for "*Vive le Roi!*"
Then whisper'd, "'Ave you any news of Nappy?"
The Sultaun answered him with a cross question—
"Pray, can you tell me aught of one John Bull,
That dwells somewhere beyond your herring-
pool?"
The query seem'd of difficult digestion.
The party shrugg'd, and grinn'd, and took his snuff,
And found his whole good-breeding scarce enough.

Twitching his visage into as many puckers,
As damsels wont to put into their tuckers
(Ere liberal Fashion damn'd both lace and lawn,
And bade the veil of modesty be drawn),
Replied the Frenchman, after a brief pause,
"Jean Bool!—I vas not know him—yes, I vas;
I vas remember dat, von year or two,
I saw him at von place call'd Vaterloo—
Ma foi! il s'est tres joliment battu,
Dat is for Englishman—m'entendez-vous?
But den he had wit him one damn son-gun,
Rogue I no like—dey call him Vellington."
Monsieur's politeness could not hide his fret,
So Solimaun took leave, and cross'd the strait.

John Bull was in his very worst of moods,
Raving of sterile farms and unsold goods;
His sugar-loaves and bales about he threw,
And on his counter beat the devil's tattoo.
His wars were ended, and the victory won,
But then, 'twas reckoning-day with honest John;
And authors vouch, 'twas still this worthy's way,
"Never to grumble till he came to pay;
And then he always thinks, his temper's such,
The work too little, and the pay too much."
Yet grumbler as he is, so kind and hearty,
That when his mortal foe was on the floor,
And past the power to harm his quiet more,
Poor John had well-nigh wept for Bonaparte!
Such was the wight whom Solimaun salam'd—
"And who are you," John answer'd, "and be
d—d?"

"A stranger, come to see the happiest man—
So, signior, all avouch—in Frangistan."—
"Happy? my tenants breaking on my hand;
Unstock'd my pastures, and untill'd my land;
Sugar and rum a drug, and mice and moths
The sole consumers of my good broadcloths—
Happy?—why, cursed war and racking tax
Have left us scarcely raiment to our backs."—
"In that case, signior, I may take my leave;
I came to ask a favor—but I grieve."—
"Favor?" said John, and eyed the Sultaun hard,
"It's my belief you came to break the yard!—
But, stay, you look like some poor foreign sinner—
Take that to buy yourself a shirt and dinner."—
With that he chuck'd a guinea at his head;
But, with due dignity, the Sultaun said,
"Permit me, sir, your bounty to decline;
A *shirt* indeed I seek, but none of thine.
Signior, I kiss your hands, so fare you well,"—
"Kiss and be d—d," quoth John, "and go to hell!"

Next door to John there dwelt his sister Peg,
Once a wild lass as ever shook a leg
When the blithe bagpipe blew—but, soberer now,
She *doucely* span her flax and milk'd her cow.
And whereas erst she was a needy slattern,
Nor now of wealth or cleanliness a pattern,
Yet once a month her house was partly swept,
And once a week a plenteous board she kept.
And, whereas, eke, the vixen used her claws
And teeth of yore, on slender provocation,
She now was grown amenable to laws,
A quiet soul as any in the nation;
The sole remembrance of her warlike joys
Was in old songs she sang to please her boys.
John Bull, whom, in their years of early strife,
She wont to lead a cat-and-doggish life,
Now found the woman, as he said, a neighbor,
Who look'd to the main chance, declined no labor,
Loved a long grace, and spoke a northern jargon,
And was d—d close in making of a bargain.

The Sultaun enter'd, and he made his leg,
And with decorum courtesy'd sister Peg;
(She loved a book, and knew a thing or two,
And guess'd at once with whom she had to do.)
She bade him "Sit into the fire," and took
Her dram, her cake, her kebbuck from the nook;
Ask'd him "About the news from Eastern parts;
And of her absent bairns, puir Highland hearts!
If peace brought down the price of tea and pepper,
And if the *nitmugs* were grown *ony* cheaper;—
Were there nae *speerings* of our Mungo Park—
Ye'll be the gentleman that wants the sark?
If ye wad buy a web o' auld wife's spinning,
I'll warrant ye it's a weel wearing linen."

Then up got Peg, and round the house 'gan scuttle
In search of goods her customer to nail,
Until the Sultaun strain'd his princely throttle
And halloo'd—"Ma'am, that is not what I ail.
Pray, are you happy, ma'am, in this snug glen?"—
"Happy?" said Peg; "What for d'ye want to ken?
Besides, just think upon this by-gane year,
Grain wadna pay the yoking of the pleugh."—
"What say you to the present?"—"Meal's sae
dear,
To make their *brose* my bairns have scarce
aneugh."—
"The devil take the shirt," said Solimaun,
"I think my quest will end as it began.—
Farewell, ma'am; nay, no ceremony, I beg"—
"Ye'll no be for the linen, then?" said Peg.

Now, for the land of verdant Erin,
The Sultaun's royal bark is steering,
The Emerald Isle, where honest Paddy dwells,
The cousin of John Bull, as story tells.
For a long space had John, with words of thunder,
Hard looks, and harder knocks, kept Paddy under,
Till the poor lad, like boy that's flogged unduly,
Had gotten somewhat restive and unruly.
Hard was his lot and lodging, you'll allow,
A wigwam that would hardly serve a sow;

His landlord, and of middle men two brace,
Had screw'd his rent up to the starving place;
His garment was a top-coat, and an old one,
His meal was a potato, and a cold one;
But still for fun or frolic, and all that,
In the round world was not the match of Pat.
The Sultaun saw him on a holiday,
Which is with Paddy still a jolly day;
When mass is ended, and his load of sins
Confess'd, and Mother Church hath from her binns
Dealt forth a bonus of imputed merit,
Then is Pat's time for fancy, whim, and spirit!
To jest, to sing, to caper fair and free,
And dance as light as leaf upon the tree.

"By Mahomet," said Sultaun Solimaun,
"That ragged fellow is our very man!
Rush in and seize him—do not do him hurt,
But, will he nill he, let me have his *shirt.*"

Shilela their plan was well-nigh after balking
(Much less provocation will set it a-walking),
But the odds that foil'd Hercules foil'd Paddy Whack;
They seized, and they floor'd, and they stripp'd him; Alack!
Up-bubboo! Paddy had not—a shirt to his back!!!
And the King, disappointed, with sorrow and shame,
Went back to Serendib as sad as he came.

Rab's Dream.—Rab was in the habit of occasionally receiving a small gratuity from one of the clergymen of the town. From some cause or other, this had been for some time neglected. One day the clergyman and Rab having met: "Weel, how's a' wi' you the day, Rab?" inquired his reverence. "Deed, sir, I had an awfu' dream last night. I dreamt that I was dead, and that I gaed awa to the guid place; and when I cam' there, I knocked at a big yett, and after I had stood awhile, there was a man, I believe it was the Apostle Peter, looked ower the top o' the yett, and he cries, 'Who's there?' 'It's Rab Hamilton,' says I. 'Where,' says he, 'do ye come from?' Says I, 'Frae the auld town o' Ayr.' 'Hech, mon,' says he, 'I am glad to see you here; for there's neither mon nor woman come here frae that place for the last twa or three years.'"

Obedient Wives.—The people of Greenock are fond of telling stories reflecting on the inland ignorance of the bodies of Paisley.

One of these is to the following effect:—Two cocks, newly sprung into affluence, were prevailed upon by their wives to allow them to pay a visit to Gourock, but only on condition that they were to employ their time well, and take plenty of salt water. Having accompanied their spouses to that village, and seen them properly accommodated, the two gentlemen returned to business, and did not appear again for a week, when observing a surprising apparent decrease in the volume of the ocean, owing to the recess of the tide, one remarked to the other, "Gosh, Jamie, the jauds hae dune weel!"

A Liberal Offer.—A clergyman was presented to a living in the vicinity of Glasgow, who had a protuberance between the shoulders, arising from diseased spine; and a corresponding protrusion of the chest. The parishioners were opposed to a person of such ungainly appearance occupying their pulpit. The presentee heard of the dissatisfaction, and, being a person of some humor and tact, convened a meeting of the malcontents, in order to ascertain their objections. "I have heard," said he, "that my settlement amongst you is not likely to be agreeable; now, as I am not aware of any objection to my opinions or practice—my slender abilities for such a charge I admit—I should just like, as we are all friends and brethren, and have only one object to serve, that you would state your objections." One glanced to another, which was as significantly returned, and silence prevailed for some time, when one stammered out, "Sir, you see—we—you see—sir—sir, I maun speak for my brethren here—dinna like your bodily appearance." "Neither do I," was the reply; "and if ye can get it repaired, I'll be at half the expense myself."

Eng^d by [illegible]

John Wilson

N.Y. D. Appleton & Co.

DR. KITCHINER.

BY JOHN WILSON (CHRISTOPHER NORTH).

FIRST COURSE.

It greatly grieved us to think that Dr. Kitchiner should have died before our numerous avocations had allowed us an opportunity of dining with him, and subjecting to the test-act of our experienced palate his claims to immortality as a Cook and a Christian. The Doctor had, we know, a dread of Us—not altogether unalloyed by delight; and on the dinner to Us, which he had meditated for nearly a quarter of a century, he knew and felt must have hung his reputation with posterity—his posthumous fame. We understand that there is an unfinished sketch of that Dinner among the Doctor's papers, and that the design is magnificent. Yet, perhaps, it is better for his glory that Kitchiner should have died without attempting to imbody in forms the idea of that Dinner. It might have been a failure. How liable to imperfection the *matériel* on which he would have had to work! How defective the instruments! Yes—yes!—happier far was it for the good old man that he should have fallen asleep with the undimmed idea of that unattempted Dinner in his imagination, than, vainly contending with the physical evil inherent in matter, have detected the Bishop's foot in the first course, and died of a broken heart!

"Travelling," it is remarked by our poor dear Doctor in his Traveller's Oracle, "is a recreation to be recommended, especially to those whose employments are sedentary—who are engaged in abstract studies—whose minds have been sunk in a state of morbid melancholy by hypochondriasis, or, by what is worst of all, a lack of domestic felicity. Nature, however, will not suffer any sudden transition; and therefore it is improper for people accustomed to a sedentary life to undertake suddenly a journey, during which they will be exposed to long and violent jolting. The case here is the same as if one accustomed to drink water, should, all at once, begin to drink wine."

Had the Doctor been alive, we should have asked him what he meant by "long and violent jolting." Jolting is now absolutely unknown in England, and it is of England the Doctor speaks. No doubt, some occasional jolting might still be discovered among the lanes and cross-roads; but, though violent, it could not be long: and we defy the most sedentary gentleman living to be more so, when sitting in an easy chair by his parlor fireside, than in a cushioned carriage spinning along the turnpike. But for the trees and hedge-rows all galloping by, he would never know that he was himself in motion. The truth is, that no gentleman can be said, nowadays, to lead a sedentary life, who is not constantly travelling before the insensible touch of M'Adam. Look at the first twenty people that come towering by on the roof of a Highflier or a Defiance. What can be more sedentary? Only look at that elderly gentleman with the wig, evidently a parson, jammed in between a brace of buxom virgins on their way down to Doncaster races. Could he be more sedentary, during the psalm, in his own pulpit?

The Doctor then wisely remarks, that it is "impossible to lay down any rule by which to regulate the number of miles a man may journey in a day, or to prescribe the precise number of ounces he ought to eat; but that nature has given us a very excellent guide in a sense of lassitude, which is as unerring in exercise as the sense of satiety is in eating."

We say the Doctor wisely remarks, yet not altogether wisely; for the rule does not seem to hold always good either in exercise or in eating. What more common than to feel one's self very much fatigued—quite done up as it were, and unwilling to stir hand or foot. Up goes a lark in heaven—tira-lira—or suddenly the breezes blow among the clouds, who forthwith all begin campaigning in the sky—or, quick as lightning, the sunshine in a moment resuscitates a drowned day—or tripping along, all by her happy self, to the sweet accompaniment of her joy-varied songs, the woodman's daughter passes by on her way, with a basket in her hand, to her father in the forest, who has already laid down his axe on the meridian shadow darkening one side of the straight stem of an oak, beneath whose grove might be drawn up five score of plumed chivalry! Where is your "sense of lassitude now, nature's unerring guide in exercise?" You spring up from the mossy wayside bank, and renewed both in mind and body, "rejoicing in nature's joy," you continue to pass over houseless moors, by small, single, solitary, straw-roofed huts, through villages gathered round Stone Cross, Elm Grove, or old Monastic Tower, till, unwearied in lith and limb, you see sunset beautifying all the west, and drop in, perhaps, among the hush of the Cottar's Saturday Night—for it is in sweet Scotland we are walking in our dream—and know not, till we have stretched ourselves on a bed of rushes or of heather, that "kind nature's sweet restorer, balmy sleep," is yet among the number of our bosom friends—alas! daily diminishing beneath fate, fortune, the sweeping scythe-stroke of death, or the whisper of some one poor, puny, idle, and unmeaning word!

Then, as to the "sense of satiety in eating." It is produced in us by three platefuls of hotch-potch—and, to the eyes of an ordinary observer, our dinner would seem to be at an end. But no—strictly speaking, it is just going to begin. About an hour ago did we, standing on the very beautiful bridge of Perth, see that identical salmon, with his back-fin just visible above the translucent tide, arrowing up the Tay, bold as a bridegroom, and nothing doubting that he should spend his honeymoon among the gravel beds of Kinnaird or Moulenearn, or the rocky sofas of the Tummel, or the green marble couches of the Tilt. What has become now of "the sense of satiety in eating!" John—the castors!—mustard—vinegar—cayenne—catchup—peas and potatoes, with a very little butter—the biscuit called "rusk"—and the memory of the hotch-potch is as that of Babylon the Great. That any gigot of mutton, exquisite though much of the five-year-old blackfaced must assuredly be, can, with any rational hopes of success, contend against a haunch of venison, will be asserted by no devout lover of truth. Try the two by alternate platefuls, and you will uniformly find that you leave off after the venison. That "sense of satiety in eating," of which Dr. Kitchiner speaks, was produced by the Tay salmon devoured above—but of all the transitory feelings of us transitory creatures on our transit through this transitory world, in which the Doctor asserts nature will not suffer any sudden transitions, the most transitory ever experienced by us is "the sense of satiety in eating." Therefore, we have now seen it for a moment existing on the disappearance of the hotch-potch—dying on the appearance of the Tay salmon—once more noticeable as the last plate of the noble fish melted away—extinguished suddenly by the vision of the venison—again felt for an instant, and but for an instant—for a brace and a half of as fine grouse as ever expanded their voluptuous bosoms to be devoured by hungry love! Sense of satiety in eating, indeed! If you please, my dear friend, one of the backs—pungent with the most palate-piercing, stomach-stirring, heart-warming, soul-exalting of all tastes—the wild bitter-sweet.

But the Doctor returns to the subject of travelling—and fatigue. "When one begins," he says, "to be low-spirited and dejected, to yawn often and be drowsy, when the appetite is impaired, when the smallest movement occasions a fluttering of the pulse, when the mouth becomes dry, and is sensible of a bitter taste, *seek refreshment and repose*, if you wish to PREVENT ILLNESS, already beginning to take place." Why, our dear Doctor, illness in such a deplorable case as this, is just about to end, and death is beginning to take place. Thank heaven, it is a condition to which we do not remember having very nearly approximated! Who ever saw us yawn? or drowsy? or with our appetite impaired, except on the withdrawal of the table-cloth? or low-spirited, but when the Glenlivet was at ebb? Who dare declare that he ever saw our mouth dry? or sensible of a bitter taste, since we gave over munching rowans? Put your finger on our wrist, at any moment you choose, from June to January, from January to June, and by its pulsation you may rectify Harrison's or Kendal's chronometer.

But the Doctor proceeds—"By raising the temperature of my room to about 65°, a broth diet, and taking a tea-spoonful of Epsom salts in half a pint of warm water, and repeating it every half hour till it moves the bowels twice or thrice, and retiring to rest an hour or two sooner than usual, I have often very speedily got rid of colds," etc.

Why, there may be no great harm in acting as above. A tea-spoonful of Epsom salts in half a pint of warm water, reminds one, somehow or other, of Tims. A small matter works a cockney. It is not so easy—and that the cockneys well know—to move the bowels of old Christopher North. We do not believe that a tea-spoonful of any thing in this world would have any serious effect on old "Ironsides." We should have no hesitation in backing him against so much corrosive sublimate. He would dine out on the day he had bolted that quantity of arsenic;—and would, we verily believe, rise triumphant from a tea-spoonful of Prussic acid.

We could mention a thousand cures for "colds, et cetera," more efficacious than a broth diet, a warm room, a tea-spoonful of Epsom salts, or early roosting. What say you, our dear Dean, to half a dozen tumblers of hot toddy? Your share of a brown jug to the same amount? Or an equal quantity, in its gradual decrease revealing deeper and deeper still the romantic Welsh scenery of the Devil's Punch-Bowl? *Adde tot* small-bearded oysters, all redolent of the salt-sea foam, and worthy, as they stud the Ambrosial brodd, to be licked off all at once by the lambent tongue of Neptune. That antiquated calumny against the character of toasted cheese—that, forsooth, it is indigestible—has been trampled under the march of mind; and therefore you may tuck in a pound of double Gloucester. Other patients, laboring under catarrh, may, very possibly, prefer the roasted how-towdy—or the green goose from his first stubble-field—or why not, by way of a little variety, a roasted mawkin, midway between hare and leveret, tempting as maiden between woman and girl, or, as the Eastern poet says, between a frock and a gown? Go to bed—no need of warming pans—about a quarter before one;—you will not hear that small hour strike—you will sleep sound till sunrise, sound as the Black Stone at Scone, on which the Kings of Scotland were crowned of old. And if you contrive to carry a cold about you next day, you deserve to be sent to Coventry by all sensible people—and may, if you choose, begin taking, with Tims, a tea-spoonful of Epsom salts in a half pint of warm water every half hour, till it moves your bowels twice or thrice; but if you do, be your sex, politics, or religion what they may, never shall ye be suffered to contribute even a bit of Balaam to the Magazine.

SECOND COURSE.

Above all things, continues Dr. Kitchiner, "avoid travelling through the night, which by interrupting sleep, and exposing the body to the night air, is always prejudicial, even in the mildest weather, and to the strongest constitutions." Pray, Doctor, what ails you at the night air? If the night air be, even in the mildest weather, prejudicial to the strongest constitutions, what do you think becomes of the cattle on a thousand hills? Why don't all the bulls in Bashan die of the asthma—or look interesting by moonlight in a galloping consumption? Nay, if the night air be so very fatal, how do you account for the longevity of owls? Have you never read of the Chaldean shepherds watching the courses of the stars? Or, to come nearer our own times, do you not know that every blessed night throughout the year, thousands of young lads and lasses meet, either beneath the milk-white thorn—or on the lea-rig, although the night be ne'er sae wet, and they be ne'er sae weary—or under a rock on the hill—or—no uncommon case—beneath a frozen stack—not of chimneys, but of corn-sheaves—or on a couch of snow—and that they are all as warm as so many pies; while, instead of feeling what you call "the lack of vigor attendant on the loss of sleep, which is as enfeebling and as distressing as the languor that attends the want of food," they are, to use a homely Scotch expression, "neither too haud nor bind," the eyes of the young lads being all as brisk, bold, and bright as the stars in Charles's Wain, while those of the young lasses shine with a soft, faint, obscure, but beautiful lustre, like the dewy Pleiades, over which nature has insensibly been breathing a mist almost waving and wavering into a veil of clouds?

Have you, our dear Doctor, no compassion for those unfortunate blades, who, *nolentes-volentes*, must remain out perennially all night—we mean the blades of grass, and also the flowers? Their constitutions seem often far from strong; and shut your eyes on a frosty night, and you will hear them—we have done so many million times—shivering, ay, absolutely shivering under their coat of hoar-frost! If the night air be indeed what Dr. Kitchiner has declared it to be—Lord have mercy on the vegetable world! What agonies in that field of turnips! Alas, poor Swedes! The imagination recoils from the condition of that club of winter cabbages—and of what materials, pray, must the heart of that man be made, who could think but for a moment on the case of those carrots, without bursting into a flood of tears!

The Doctor avers that the firm, health and fine spirits of persons who live in the country, are not more from breathing a purer air, than from enjoying plenty of sound sleep; and the most distressing misery of "this elysium of bricks and mortar," is the rareness with which we enjoy "the sweets of a slumber unbroke."

Doctor—in the first place, it is somewhat doubtful whether or not persons who live in the country have firmer health and finer spirits than persons who live in towns—even in London. What kind of persons do you mean? You must not be allowed to select some dozen or two of the hairiest among the curates—a few chosen rectors whose faces have been but lately elevated to the purple—a team of prebends issuing sleek from their golden stalls—a picked bishop—a sacred band, the élite of the squirearchy—with a corresponding sprinkling of superior noblemen from lords to dukes—and then to compare them, cheek by jowl, with an equal number of external objects taken from the common run of cockneys. This, Doctor, is manifestly what you are ettling at—but you must clap your hand, Doctor, without discrimination, on the great body of the rural population of England, male and female, and take whatever comes first—be it a poor, wrinkled, toothless, blear-eyed, palsied hag, tottering horizontally on a staff, under the load of a premature old age, (for she is not yet fifty,) brought on by annual rheumatism and perennial poverty;—be it a young, ugly unmarried woman, far advanced in pregnancy, and sullenly trooping to the alehouse, to meet the overseer of the parish poor, who, enraged with the unborn bastard, is about to force the parish bully to marry the parish prostitute;—be it a landlord of a rural inn, with pig eyes peering over his ruby cheeks, the whole machinery of his mouth so deranged by tippling that he simultaneously snorts, stutters, slavers and snores—pot-bellied—shanked like a spindle-strae—and bidding fair to be buried on or before Saturday week;—be it a half-drunk horse-cowper, swinging to and fro in a wraprascal, on a bit of broken-down blood that once won a fifty, every sentence, however short, having but two intelligible words, an oath and a lie—his heart rotten with falsehood, and his bowels burned up with brandy, so that sudden death may pull him from his saddle before he put spurs to his sporting filly that she may bilk the turnpike man, and carry him more speedily home to beat or murder his poor, pale, industrious char-woman of a wife;—be it—not a beggar, for beggars are prohibited from this parish—but a pauper in the sulks, dying on her pittance from the poor-rates, which altogether amount in merry England but to about the paltry sum of, more or less, six millions a year—her son, all the while, being in a thriving way as a general merchant in the capital of the parish, and with clear profits from his business of three hundred pounds per annum, yet suffering the mother that bore him, and suckled him, and washed his childish hands, and combed the bumpkin's hair, and gave him Epsoms in a cup when her dear Jonny-raw had the belly-ache, to go down, step by step, as surely and as obviously as one is seen going down a stair with a feeble hold of the banisters, and stumbling every footfall, down that other flight of steps that consist of flags that are mortal damp and mortal cold, and lead to nothing but a parcel of rotten planks, and overhead a vault dripping

with perpetual moisture, green and slobbery, such as toads delight in crawling heavily through with now and then a bloated leap, and hideous things more worm-like, that go wriggling briskly in and out among the refuse of the coffins, and are heard, by imagination at least, to emit faint angry sounds, because the light of day has hurt their eyes, and the air from the upper world weakened the rank savory smell of corruption, clothing, as with a pall, all the inside walls of the tombs;—be it a man yet in the prime of life as to years, six feet and an inch high, and measuring round the chest forty-eight inches, (which is more, reader, than thou dost by six, we bet a sovereign, member although thou even be'st of the Edinburgh Six Feet Club,) to whom Washington Irving's Jack Tibbets was but a Tims—but then ever so many game-keepers met him all alone in my lord's pheasant preserve, and though two of them died within the month, two within the year, and two are now in the workhouse—one a mere idiot, and the other a madman—both shadows—so terribly were their bodies mauled, and so sorely were their skulls fractured;—yet the poacher was taken, tried, hulked; and there he sits now, sunning himself on a bank by the edge of a wood whose haunts he must thread no more—for the keepers were grim bone-breakers enough in their way—and when they had gotten him on his back, one gouged him like a Yankee, and the other bit off his nose like a Bolton trotter—and one smashed his *os frontis* with the nailed heel of a two pound wooden clog, a Preston Purrer;—so that Master Allonby is now far from being a beauty, with a face of that description attached to a head wagging from side to side under a powerful palsy, while the Mandarin drinks damnation to the Lord of the Manor in a horn of eleemosynary ale, handed to him by the village blacksmith, in days of old not the worst of the gang, and who, but for a stupid jury, a merciful judge, and something like prevarication in the circumstantial evidence, would have been hanged for a murderer—as he was—dissected, and hung in chains;—be it a red-haired woman, with a pug-nose, small fiery eyes, high cheekbones, bulging lips, and teeth like swine-tusks,—bearded—flat-breasted as a man—tall, scambling in her gait, but swift, and full of wild motions in her weather-withered arms, all starting with sinews like whipcord—the Pedestrian Post to and fro the market town twelve miles off—and so powerful a pugilist that she hit Grace Maddox senseless in seven minutes—tried before she was eighteen for child-murder, but not hanged, although the man-child, of which the drab was self-delivered in a ditch, was found with blue finger-marks on its wind-pipe, bloody mouth, and eyes forced out of their sockets, buried in the dunghill behind her father's hut—not hanged, because a surgeon, originally bred a sow-gelder, swore that he believed the mother had unconsciously destroyed her offspring in the throes of travail, if indeed it had ever breathed, for the lungs would not swim, he swore in a basin of water—so the incestuous murderess was let loose; her brother got hanged in due time after the mutiny at the Nore—and her father, the fishmonger—why he went red raving mad as if a dog had bitten him—and died, as the same surgeon and sow-gelder averred, of the hydrophobia, foaming at the mouth, gnashing his teeth, and some said cursing, but that was a calumny, for something seemed to be the matter with his tongue, and he could not speak, only splutter—nobody venturing, except his amiable daughter—and in that particular act of filial affection she was amiable—to hold in the article of death the old man's head;—be it that moping idiot that would sit, where she suffered, on, on, on—night and day for ever, on the selfsame spot, whatever that spot might be on which she happened to squat at morning, mound, wall, or stone—motionless, dumb, and, as a stranger would think, also blind, for the eyelids are still shut—never opened in sun or storm;—yet that figure—that which is now, and has for years been, an utter and hopeless idiot, was once a gay, laughing, dancing, singing girl, whose blue eyes seemed full of light, whether they looked on earth or heaven, the flowers or the stars—her sweet-heart—a rational young man, it would appear—having leapt out upon her suddenly, as she was passing through the churchyard at night, from behind a tomb-stone in a sack which she, having little time for consideration, and being naturally superstitious, supposed to be a shroud, and the wearer thereof, who was an active stripling of sound flesh and blood, to be a ghost or skeleton, all one horrid rattle of bones; so that the trick succeeded far beyond the most sanguine expectation of the Tailor who played the principal part—and sense, feeling, memory, imagination, and reason, were all felled by one blow of fear—as butcher felleth ox—while by one of those mysteries, which neither we, nor you, nor anybody else, can understand, life remained not only unimpaired, but even invigorated; and there she sits, like a clock wound up to go a certain time, the machinery of which being good, has not been altogether deranged by the shock that sorely cracked the case, and will work till the chain is run down, and then it will tick no more;—be it that tall, fair, lovely girl, so thin and attenuated that all wonder she can walk by herself—that she is not blown away even by the gentle summer breeze that woos the hectic of her cheek—dying all see—and none better than her poor old mother—and yet herself thoughtless of the coming doom, and cheerful as a nest-building bird—while her lover, too deep in despair to be betrayed into tears, as he carries her to her couch, each successive day, feels the dear and dreadful burden lighter and lighter in his arms. Small strength will it need to

support her bier! The coffin, as if empty, will be lowered unfelt by the hands that hold those rueful cords!

THIRD COURSE.

Having thus briefly instructed travellers how to get a look at Lions, the Doctor suddenly exclaims —"Imprimis, beware of dogs!" "There have," he says, "been many arguments, *pro* and *con*, on the dreadful disease their bite produces—it is enough to prove that multitudes of men, women and children have died in consequence of having been bitten by dogs. What does it matter whether they were the victims of bodily disease or mental irritation? The life of the most humble human being is of more value than all the dogs in the world—dare the most brutal cynic say otherwise?"

Dr. Kitchiner always travelled, it appears, in chaises; and a chaise of one kind or other, he recommends to all his brethren of mankind. Why, then, this intense fear of the canine species? Who ever saw a mad dog leap into the mail-coach, or even a gig? The creature when so afflicted, hangs his head, and goes snapping right and left at pedestrians. Poor people like us, who must walk, may well fear hydrophobia—though, thank heaven, we have never, during the course of a tolerably long and well-spent life, been so much as once bitten by "the rabid animal!" But what have rich authors, who loll in carriages, to dread from dogs, who always go on foot? We cannot credit the very sweeping assertion, that multitudes of men, women, and children have died in consequence of being bitten by dogs. Even the newspapers do not run up the amount above a dozen per annum, from which you may safely deduct two-thirds. Now, four men, women and children, are not "a multitude." Of those four, we may set down two as problematical —having died, it is true, *in*, but not *of* hydrophobia —states of mind and body wide as the poles asunder. He who drinks two bottles of pure spirits every day he buttons and unbuttons his breeches, generally dies *in* a state of hydrophobia—for he abhorred water, and knew instinctively the jug containing that insipid element. But he never dies at all *of* hydrophobia, there being evidence to prove that for twenty years he had drunk nothing but brandy. Suppose we are driven to confess the other two—why, one of them was an old woman of eighty, who was dying as fast as she could hobble, at the very time she thought herself bitten—and the other a ninety-year old brat, in hooping cough and measles, who, had there not been such a quadruped as a dog created, would have worried itself to death before evening, so lamentably had its education been neglected, and so dangerous an accomplishment is an impish temper. The twelve cases for the year of that most horrible disease, hydrophobia, have, we flatter ourselves, been satisfactorily disposed of—eight of the alleged deceased being at this moment engaged at various handicrafts on low wages indeed, but still such as enable the industrious to live—two having died of drinking—one of extreme old age, and one of a complication of complaints incident to childhood, their violence having, in this particular instance, been aggravated by neglect and a devilish temper. Where, now, the "multitude" of men, women, and children, who have died in consequence of being bitten by mad dogs?

Gentle reader—a mad dog is a bugbear; we have walked many hundred times the diameter and the circumference of this our habitable globe—along all roads, public and private—with stiles or turnpike—metropolitan streets and suburban paths—and at all seasons of the revolving year and day; but never, as we padded the hoof along, met we nor were overtaken by greyhound, mastiff, or cur, in a state of hydrophobia. We have many million times seen them with their tongues lolling out about a yard—their sides panting—flag struck—and the whole dog showing symptoms of severe distress. That such travellers were not mad, we do not assert—they may have been mad—but they certainly were fatigued; and the difference, we hope, is often considerable between weariness and insanity. Dr. Kitchiner, had he seen such dogs as we have seen, would have fainted on the spot. He would have raised the country against the harmless jog-trotter. Pitchforks would have gleamed in the setting sun, and the flower of the agricultural youth of a midland country, forming a levy *en masse*, would have offered battle to a turnspit. The Doctor, sitting in his coach—like Napoleon at Waterloo—would have cried "*Tout est perdu—sauve qui peut?*"—and regalloping to a provincial town, would have found refuge under the gateway of the Hen and Chickens.

"The life of the most humble human being," quoth the Doctor, "is of more value than all the dogs in the world—dare the most brutal cynic say otherwise?"

This question is not put to us; for so far from being the most brutal cynic, we do not belong to the cynic school at all—being an Eclectic, and our philosophy composed chiefly of Stoicism, Epicureanism, and Peripateticism—with a fine, pure, clear, bold dash of Platonicism. The most brutal cynic, if now alive and snarling, must therefore answer for himself—while we tell the Doctor, that so far from holding, with him, that the life of the most humble human being is of more value than all the dogs in the world, we, on the contrary, verily believe that there is many an humble dog whose life far transcends in value the lives of many men, women, and children. Whether or not dogs have souls, is a question in philosophy never yet solved; although we have ourselves no doubt on the subject, and firmly believe that they have souls.

But the question, as put by the Doctor, is not about souls, but about lives; and as the human soul does not die when the human body does, the death of an old woman, middle-aged man, or young child, is no such very great calamity, either to themselves or to the world. Better, perhaps, that all the dogs now alive should be massacred, to prevent hydrophobia, than that a human soul should be lost;—but not a single human soul is going to be lost, although the whole canine species should become insane to-morrow. Now, would the Doctor have laid one hand on his heart and the other on his Bible, and take a solemn oath that rather than one old woman of a century and a quarter should suddenly be cut off by the bite of a mad dog, he would have signed the warrant of execution of all the packs of harriers and fox-hounds, all the pointers, spaniels, setters, and cockers, all the stag-hounds, greyhounds, and lurchers, all the Newfoundlanders, shepherd-dogs, mastiffs, bull-dogs, and terriers, the infinite generation of mongrels and crosses included, in Great Britain and Ireland—to say nothing of the sledge-drawers in Kamschatka, and in the realms slow-moving near the Pole? To clench the argument at once—What are all the old women in Europe, one-half of the men, and one-third of the children, when compared, in value, with any one of Christopher North's Newfoundland dogs—Fro—Bronte—or O'Bronte? Finally, does he include in his sweeping condemnation the whole brute creation, lions, tigers, panthers, ounces, elephants, rhinoceroses, hippopotami, camelopardales, zebras, quaggas, cattle, horses, asses, mules, cats, the ichneumon, cranes, storks, cocks-of-the-wood, geese, and how-towdies?

"Semi-drowning in the sea"—he continues—"and all the pretended specifics, are mere delusions—there is no real remedy but cutting the part out immediately. If the bite be near a bloodvessel, that cannot always be done, nor when done, however well done, will it always prevent the miserable victim from dying the most dreadful of deaths. Well might St. Paul tell us '*beware of dogs.*' First Epistle to Philippians, chap. iii. v. 2."

Semi-drowning in the sea is, we grant, a bad specific, and difficult to be administered. It is not possible to tell *a priori*, how much drowning any particular patient can bear. What is mere semi-drowning to James, is total drowning to John:—Tom is easy of resuscitation—Bob will not stir a muscle for all the Humane Societies in the United Kingdoms. To cut a pound of flesh from the rump of a fat dowager, who turns sixteen stone, is within the practical skill of the veriest bungler in the anatomy of the human frame—to scarify the fleshless spindle-shank of an antiquated spinstress, who lives on a small annuity, might be beyond the scalpel of an Abernethy or a Liston. A large bloodvessel, as the Doctor well remarks, is an awkward neighbor to the wound made by the bite of a mad dog, "when a new excision has to be attempted"—but will any Doctor living inform us how, in a thousand other cases besides hydrophobia, "the miserable victim may always be prevented from dying?" There are, probably, more dogs in Britain than horses; yet a hundred men, women, and children are killed by kicks of sane horses, for one by bites of insane dogs. Is the British army, therefore, to be deprived of its left arm, the cavalry? Is there to be no flying artillery? What is to become of the horse-marines?

FOURTH COURSE.

THE Doctor, of course, is one of those travellers who believe, that unless they use the most ingenious precautions, they will be uniformly robbed and murdered in inns. The villains steal upon you during the midnight hour, when all the world is asleep. They leave their shoes down stairs, and leopard-like, ascend with velvet, or—what is almost as noiseless—worsted steps, the wooden stairs. True, that your breeches are beneath your bolster—but that trick of travellers has long been "as notorious as the sun at noonday;" and although you are aware of your breeches, with all the ready money perhaps that you are worth in this world, eloping from beneath your parental eye, you in vain try to cry out—for a long, broad, iron hand, with ever so many iron fingers, is on your mouth; another, with still more numerous digits, compresses your windpipe, while a low hoarse voice, in a whisper to which Sarah Siddons's was empty air, on pain of instant death enforces silence from a man unable for his life to utter a single word; and after pulling off all the bed-clothes, and then clothing you with curses, the ruffians, whose accent betrays them to be Irishmen, inflict upon you divers wanton wounds with a blunt instrument, probably a crow-bar—swearing by Satan and all his saints, that if you stir an inch of your body before daybreak, they will instantly return, cut your throat, knock out your brains, sack you, and carry you off for sale to a surgeon. Therefore you must use pocket door-bolts, which are applicable to almost all sorts of doors, and on many occasions save the property and life of the traveller. The corkscrew door-fastening the Doctor recommends as the simplest. This is screwed in between the door and the door-post, and unites them so firmly, that great power is required to force a door so fastened. They are as portable as common corkscrews, and their weight does not exceed an ounce and a half. The safety of your bed-room should always be carefully examined; and in case of bolts not being at hand, it will be useful to hinder entrance into the room by putting a table and a chair upon it against the door. Take a peep below the bed, and into the closets, and every place where concealment is possible—of course, although the Doctor forgets to suggest it, into the chimney. A friend of the Doctor's used to place a bureau against the door, and "thereon he set a basin and ewer in such a position as easily to rattle, so that on being shook, they instantly bacame *molto agitato.*" Upon one alarming occasion this device frightened away one of the chambermaids, or some other Paulina Pry, who attempted to steal on the virgin sleep of the travelling Joseph, who all the time was hiding his head beneath the bolster. Joseph, however, believed it was a horrible midnight assassin, with mustaches and a dagger. "The chattering of the crockery gave the alarm, and the attempt, after many attempts, was abandoned."

With all these fearful apprehensions in his mind, Dr. Kitchiner must have been a man of great natural personal courage and intrepidity, to have slept even once in his whole lifetime from home. What danger must we have passed, who used to plump in, without a thought of damp in the bed, or scamp below it—closet and chimney uninspected, door unbolted and unscrewed, exposed to rape, robbery, and murder! It is mortifying to think that we should be alive at this day. Nobody, male or female, thought it worth their while to rob, ravish, or murder us! There we lay, forgotten by the whole world—till the crowing of cocks, or the ringing of bells, or blundering Boots insisting on it that we were a Manchester Bagman, who had taken an inside in the Heavy at five, broke our repose, and Sol, laughing in at the unshuttered and uncurtained window, showed us the floor of our dormitory, not streaming with a gore of blood. We really know not whether to be most proud of having been the favorite child of Fortune, or the neglected brat of Fate. One only precaution did we ever use to take against assassination, and all the other ills that flesh is heir to, sleep where one may, and that was to say inwardly a short fervent prayer, humbly thanking our Maker for all the happiness—let us trust it was innocent—of the day; and humbly imploring his blessing on all the hopes of to-morrow. For, at the time we speak of we were young—and every morning, whatever the atmosphere might be, rose bright and beautiful with hopes that, far as the eyes of the soul could reach, glittered on earth's, and heaven's, and life's horizon!

But suppose that after all this trouble to get himself bolted and screwed into a parad.siacal tabernacle of a dormitory, there had suddenly rung through the house the cry of FIRE—FIRE—FIRE! how was Dr. Kitchiner to get out? Tables, bureaus, benches, chairs, blocked up the only door—all laden with wash-hand basins and other utensils, the whole crockery, shepherdesses of the chimney-piece, double-barrelled pistols with spring bayonets ready to shoot and stab, without distinction of persons, as their proprietor was madly seeking to escape the roaring flames! Both windows are iron-bound, with all their shutters, and over and above tightly fastened with "the corkscrew-fastening, the simplest we have seen." The wind-board is in like manner, and by the same unhappy contrivance, firmly jammed into the jaws of the chimney, so egress to the Doctor up the vent is wholly denied —no fire-engine in the town—but one under repair. There has not been a drop of rain for a month, and the river is not only distant but dry. The element is growling along the galleries like a lion, and the room is filling with something more deadly than back-smoke. A shrill voice is heard crying—"Number five will be burned alive! Number five will be burned alive! Is there no possibility of saving the life of Number five?" The Doctor falls down before the barricade, and is stretched all his hapless length fainting on the floor. At last the door is burst open, and landlord, landlady, chambermaid, and boots—each in a different key—from manly bass to childish treble, demand of Number five if he be a murderer or a madman—for, gentle reader, it has been a—— Dream.

* * * * * * * *

Thus he says that no person should sit down to a hearty meal immediately after any great exertion, either of mind or body—that is, one might say, after a few miles of Plinlimnon or a few pages of the Principia. Let the man, quoth he, "who comes home fatigued by bodily exertion, especially if he feels heated by it, throw his legs upon a chair, and remain quiet, tranquil and composed, that the energy which has been dispersed to the extremities may have time to return to the stomach, when it is required." To all this we say—Fudge! The sooner you get hold of a leg of roasted mutton the better; but meanwhile, off rapidly with a pot of porter—then leisurely on with a clean shirt—wash your face and hands in gelid—none of your tepid water—There is no harm done if you should shave —then keep walking up and down the parlor rather impatiently, for such conduct is natural, and in all things act agreeably to nature—stir up the waiter with some original jest by way of stimulant, and to give the knave's face a well-pleased stare—and never doubting "that the energy which has been dispersed to the extremities" has had ample time to return to the stomach, in God's name fall to! and take care that the second course shall not appear till there is no vestige left of the first—a second course being looked upon by the judicious moralist and pedestrian very much in the light in which the poet has made a celebrated character consider it—

Nor fame I slight—nor for her favors call;
She comes unlook'd for—if she comes at all.

To prove how astonishingly our strength may be diminished by indolence, the Doctor tells us, that meeting a gentleman who had lately returned from India, to his inquiry after his health he replied, "Why, better—better, thank ye—I think I begin to feel some symptoms of the return of a little English energy. Do you know that the day before yesterday I was in such high spirits, and felt so strong, I actually put on one of my stockings myself?"

Here lies interr'd a man of micht,
His name is Malcolm Downie,
He'll lost his life one market nicht,
In fa'ing aff his pounie. Aged 37 years.

EXTRACTS FROM "TOM CRINGLE'S LOG."

BY MICHAEL SCOTT.

One of our crew undertook to be the guide to the agent's house. We arrived before it. It was a large mansion, and we could see lights glimmering in the ground-floor; but it was gaily lit up aloft. The house itself stood back about twenty feet from the street, from which it was separated by an iron railing.

We knocked at the outer gate, but no one answered. At length our black guide found out a bell pull, and presently the clang of a bell resounded throughout the mansion. Still no one answered. I pushed against the door, and found it was open, and Mr. Treenail and myself immediately ascended a flight of six marble steps, and stood in the lower piazza, with the hall, or lower vestibule, before us. We entered. A very well-dressed brown woman, who was sitting at her work at a small table, being with two young girls of the same complexion, instantly rose to receive us.

"Beg pardon," said Mr. Treenail, "pray, is this Mr. ——'s house?"

"Yes, sir, it is."

"Will you have the goodness to say if he be at home?"

"Oh yes, sir, he is dere upon dinner wid company," said the lady.

"Well," continued the lieutenant, "say to him that an officer of his majesty's sloop Torch is below, with dispatches for the admiral."

"Surely, sir,—surely," the dark lady continued; "Follow me, sir; and dat small gentleman,—[Thomas Cringle, Esquire, no less!]—him will better follow me too."

We left the room, and, turning to the right, landed in the lower piazza of the house, fronting the north. A large clumsy stair occupied the easternmost end, with a massive mahogany balustrade, but the whole affair below was very ill lighted. The brown lady preceded us; and, planting herself at the bottom of the staircase, began to shout to some one above—

"Toby! Toby! buccra gentlemen arrive, Toby." But no Toby responded to the call.

"My dear madam," said Treenail, "I have little time for ceremony. Pray usher us up into Mr. ——'s presence."

"Den follow me, gentlemen, please."

Forthwith we all ascended the dark staircase until we

reached the first landing-place, when we heard a noise as of two negroes wrangling on the steps above us.

"You rascal!" sang out one, "take dat; larn you for to teal my wittal!"—then a sharp crack, as if it had smote the culprit across the pate; whereupon, like a shot, a black fellow, in a handsome livery, trundled down, pursued by another servant with a large silver ladle in his hand, with which he was belaboring the fugitive over his flint-hard skull, right against our hostess, with the drumstick of a turkey in his hand, or rather in his mouth.

"Top, you tief!—Top, you tief!—for me piece dat," shouted the pursuer.

"You dam rascal!" quoth the dame. But she had no time to utter another word, before the fugitive pitched, with all his weight, right against her; and at the very moment another servant came trundling down with a large tray-full of all kinds of meats—and I especially remember that two large crystal stands of jellies composed part of his load—so there we were regularly capsized, and caught all of a heap in the dark landing-place, half way up the stairs; and down the other flight tumbled our guide, with Mr. Treenail and myself, and the two blackies, on the top of her, rolling in the descent over, or rather into, another large mahogany tray which had just been carried out, with a tureen of turtle soup in it, and a dish of roast-beef, and platefulls of land-crabs, and the Lord knows what all besides.

The crash reached the ear of the landlord, who was seated at the head of his table in the upper piazza, a long gallery about fifty feet long by fourteen wide, and he immediately rose and ordered his butler to take a light. When he came down to ascertain the cause of the uproar, I shall never forget the scene.

There was, first of all, mine host, a remarkably neat personage, standing on the polished mahogany stair, three steps above his servant, who was a very well-dressed respectable elderly negro, with a candle in each hand; and beneath him, on the landing-place, lay two trays of viands, broken tureens of soup, fragments of dishes, and fractured glasses, and a chaos of eatables and drinkables, and table gear scattered all about, amidst which lay scrambling my lieutenant and myself, the brown housekeeper, and the two negro servants, all more or less covered with gravy and wine dregs.

* * * * * *

Speaking of telegraphing, I will relate an anecdote here, if you will wait until I mend my pen. I had landed at Greenwich wharf on duty—this was the nearest point of communication between Port Royal and the admiral's pen—where, finding the flag-lieutenant, he drove me up in his ketureen to lunch. While we were regaling ourselves, the old signal-man came into the piazza, and with several most remarkable obeisances, gave us to know that there were flags hoisted on the signal mast, at the mountain settlement, of which he could make nothing—the uppermost was neither the interrogative, the affirmative, nor the negative, nor in fact, any thing that with the book he could make sense of.

"Odd enough," said the lieutenant; "hand me the glass," and he peered away for half a minute. "Confound me, if I can make heads or tails of it either; there, Cringle, what do you think? How do you construe it?"

I took the telescope. Uppermost there was hoisted on the signal-mast a large tablecloth, not altogether immaculate, and under it a towel, as I guessed, for it was too opaque for bunting, and too white, although I could not affirm that it was fresh out of the fold either.

"I am puzzled," said I, as I spied away again. Meanwhile, there was no acknowledgment made at our semaphore—"There, down they go," I continued—"Why, it must be a mistake—Stop, here's a new batch going up above the green trees—There goes the tablecloth once more, and the towel, and ——deuce take me, if I can compare the lowermost to any thing but a dishclout—why, it must be a dishclout."

The flags, or substitutes for them, streamed another minute in the breeze, but as there was still no answer made from our end of the string, they were once more hauled down. We waited another minute—"Why, here goes the same signal up again, tablecloth, towel, dishclout, and all—What the *diable* have we got here? A red ball, two pennants under—What can that mean? Ball—it is the *bonnet-rouge*, or I am a Dutchman, with two short streamers"—Another look—"A red nightcap and a pair of stockings, by all that is portentous!" exclaimed I.

"Ah, I see, I see!" said the lieutenant, laughing—"signal-man, acknowledge it."

It was done, and down came the flags in a trice. It appeared, on inquiry, that the washing cart, which ought to have been sent up that morning, had been forgotten; and the admiral and his secretary having ridden out, there was no one who could make the proper signal for it. So, the old housekeeper took this singular method of having the cart dispatched, and it was sent off accordingly.

* * * * * *

At six o'clock we drove to Mr. Pepperpot Wagtail's. The party was a bachelor's one, and, when we walked up the front steps there was our host in person, standing to receive us at the door; while, on each side of him, there were five or six of his visitors, all sitting with their legs cocked up, their feet resting on a sort of surbase, above which the jalousies, or movable blinds of the piazza were fixed.

I was introduced to the whole party *seriatim*—and as each of the cock-legs dropped his *trams*, he started up, caught hold of my hand, and wrung it as if I had been his dearest and oldest friend.

Were I to designate Jamaica as a community, I would call it a hand-shaking people. I have often laughed heartily upon seeing two cronies meeting in the streets of Kingston, after a temporary separation; when about pistol-shot asunder, both would begin to tug and rug at the right hand glove, but it is frequently a mighty serious affair in that hissing hot climate to get the gauntlet off; they approach, —one, a short urbane little man, who would not disgrace St. James's street, being more kiln-dried and less moist in his corporeals than his country friend, has contrived to extract his paw, and holds it out in act to shake:

"Ah! how do you do, Ratoon?" quoth the Kingston man.

"Quite well, Shingles," rejoins the *gloved*, a stout red-faced sudoriferous yam-fed planter, dressed in blue-white jean trousers and waistcoat, with long Hessian boots drawn up to his knee over the former, and a span-new square-skirted blue coatee, with lots of clear brass buttons; a broad-brimmed black silk hat, worn white at the edge of the crown—wearing a very small neckcloth, above which shoots up an enormous shirt collar, the peaks of which might serve for winkers to a starting horse, and

carrying a large whip in his hand—"Quite well, my dear fellow," while he persists in dragging at it —the other *homo* all the while standing in the absurd position of a finger post—at length off comes the glove—piecemeal, perhaps—a finger first, for instance—then a thumb—at length, they tackle to, and shake each other like the very devil—not a sober pump-handle shake, but a regular jiggery jiggery, as if they were trying to dislocate each other's arms—and, confound them, even then they don't let go—they cling like sucker fish, and talk and wallop about, and throw themselves back and laugh, and then another jiggery jiggery.

On horseback, this custom is conspicuously ridiculous—I have nearly gone into fits at beholding two men careering along the road at a handgallop—each on a goodish horse, with his negro boy astern of him on a mule, in clean frock and trousers, and smart glazed hat with broad gold band, with massa's umbrella in a leathern case slung across his shoulders, and his portmanteau behind him on a mail pillion covered with snow-white sheep's fleece—suddenly they would pull up on recognizing each other, when tucking their whips under their arms, or crossing them in their teeth, it may be—they would commence the rugging and riving operation. In this case—Shingle's bit of blood swerves, we may assume—Ratoon rides at him—Shingle fairly turns tail, and starts out at full speed, Ratoon thundering in his rear with stretched-out arm; and it does happen, I am assured, that the hot pursuit oftentimes continues for a mile, before the desired clapperclaw is obtained. But when two lusty planters meet on horseback, then indeed, Greek meets Greek. They begin the interview by shouting to each other, while fifty yards off, pulling away at the gloves all the while—"How are you, Canetop? —glad to see you, Canetop. How do you do, *I hope?*" "How are you, Yamfu, my dear fellow?" their horses fretting and jumping all the time—and if the Jack Spaniards or gadflies be rife, they have, even when denuded for the shake, to spur each other, more like a Knight Templar and a Saracen charging in mortal combat, than two men merely struggling to be civil; and after all they have often to get their black servants alongside to hold their horses, for *shake* they must, were they to break their necks in the attempt. Why they won't shake hands with their gloves on, I am sure *I* can't tell. It would be much cooler and nicer—lots of *Scotchmen* in the community, too.

This hand-shaking, however, was followed by an invitation to dinner from each individual in the company. I looked at Captain Transom, as much as to say, "Can they mean us to take them at their word?" He nodded.

"We are sorry, that being under orders to go to sea on Sunday morning, neither Mr. Cringle nor myself can have the pleasure of accepting such kind invitations."

"Well, when you come back you know—one day you *must* give *me*."

"And I won't be denied," quoth a second.

"Liberty Hall, you know, so to me you must come, no ceremony," said a third—and so on.

At length, no less a man drove up to the door than Judge ——. When he drew up, his servant who was sitting behind on a small projection of the ketureen, came round and took a parcel out of the gig, closely wrapped in a blanket—"Bring that carefully in, Leonidas," said the judge, who now stumped up stairs with a small saw in his hand. He received the parcel, and, laying it down carefully in a corner, he placed the saw on it, and then came up and shook hands with Wagtail, and made his bow very gracefully.

"What—can't you do without your ice and sour claret yet?" said Wagtail.

"Never mind, never mind," said the Judge; and here dinner being announced, we all adjourned to the dining-room, where a very splendid entertainment was set out, to which we sat to, and in the end, as it will appear, we did the utmost justice to it.

The wines were most exquisite. Madeira, for instance, never can be drank in perfection any where out of the tropics.—You may have the wine as good at home, although I doubt it, but then you have not the climate to drink it in—I would say the same of most of the delicate French wines—that is, those that will stand the voyage—Burgundy of course not included; but never mind, let us get along.

All the decanters were covered with cotton bags, kept wet with saltpetre and water, so that the evaporation carried on powerfully by the stream of air that flowed across the room, through the open doors and windows, made the fluids quite as cool as was desirable to worthies sitting luxuriating with the thermometer at 80 or thereby; yet, from the free current, I was in no way made aware of this degree of heat by any oppressive sensation; and I found in the West Indies as well as in the East, although the wind in the latter is more dry and parching, that a current of heated air, if it be moderately dry, even with the thermometer at 95 in the shade, is really not so enervating or oppressive as I have found it in the stagnating atmosphere on the sunny side of Pall Mall, with the mercury barely at 75. A cargo of ice had a little before this arrived at Kingston, and at first all the inhabitants who could afford it, iced every thing, wine, water, cold meats, fruits, and the Lord knows what all; tea, I believe, among other things, (by the way, I have tried this, and it *is* a luxury of its kind;) but the regular old stagers, who knew what was what, and had a regard for their interiors, soon began to eschew the ice in every way, saving and excepting to cool the water they washed their thin faces and hands in; so *we* had no ice, nor did we miss it; but the Judge had a plateful of chips on the table before him, one of which he every now and then popped into his long thin bell-glass of claret, diluting it, I should have thought, in rather a heathenish manner; but *n'importe*, he worked away, sawing off pieces now and then from the large lump in the blanket, (to save the tear and wear attending a fracture,) which was handed him by his servant, so that by eleven o'clock at night, allowing for the water, he must have concealed his three bottles of pure claret, besides garnishing with a lot of white wines. In fine, we all carried on astonishingly, some good singing was given, a practical joke was tried on now and then, by Fyall, and we continued mighty happy. As to the singing part of it,—the landlord, with a bad voice, and worse ear, opened the *rorytory*, by volunteering a very extraordinary squeak; fortunately it was not very long, but it gave him a plea to screw a song out of his right-hand neighbor, who in turn acquired the same right of compelling the person next to him to make a fool of himself; at last, it came to Transom, who, by-the-by, sung exceedingly well, but he had more wine than usual, and essayed to coquet a bit.

"Bring the wet night-cap!" quoth our host.

"Oh, is it that you are at?" said Transom, and he sung as required; but it was all pearls before swine, I fear.

At last, we stuck fast at Fyall. Music! there was not one particle in his whole composition; so the wet nightcap already impended over him, when I sung out, "Let him tell a story, Mr. Wagtail! Let him tell a story!"

"Thank you, Tom," said Fyall; "I owe you a good turn for that, my boy."

"Fyall's story—Mr. Fyall's story!" resounded on all hands. Fyall, glad to escape the song and wet night-cap, instantly began.

"Why, my friends, you all know Isaac Grimm, the Jew snuff merchant and cigar maker, in Harbour street. Well, Isaac had a brother, Ezekiel by name, who carried on business in Curaçoa; you may have heard of him too. Ezekiel was often down here for the purpose of laying in provisions, and purchasing drygoods. You all know that?"

"Certainly!" shouted both Captain Transom and myself in a breath, although we had never heard of him before.

"Hah, I knew it! Well then, Ezekiel was very rich; he came down in August last, in the Pickle schooner, and, as back luck would have it, he fell sick of the fever. 'Isaac,' quoth Ezekiel, 'I am wery sheek; I tink I shall tie!' 'Hope note, dear proder; you hab no vive nor shildir; pity you should tie, Ezekiel. Ave you make your vil, Ezekiel?' 'Yesh; de vill is make. I leavish every ting to you, Isaac, on von condition, dat you send my pody to be pury in Curaçoa. I love dat place; twenty years since I left de Minories; all dat time I cheat dere, and tell lie dere, and lif dere happily. Oh, you most send my pody for its puryment to Curaçoa!' 'I will do dat, mine proder.' 'Den I depart in peace, dear Isaac;' and the Israelite was as good as his word for *once*. He *did die*. Isaac, according to his promise, applied to the captains of several schooners; none of them would take the dead body. 'What shall I do?' thought Isaac, 'de monish mosh not be loss.' So he straightway had Ezekiel (for even a Jew won't keep long in that climate) cut up and packed with pickle into two barrels, marked, 'Prime Mess Pork, Leicester, M'Call and Co., Cork.' He then shipped the same in the Fan-Fan, taking bills of lading in accordance with the brand, deliverable to Mordecai Levi, of Curaçoa, to whom he sent the requisite instructions. The vessel sailed—off St. Domingo she carried away a mast—tried to fetch Carthagena under a jury-spar—fell to leeward, and finally brought up at Honduras.

"Three months after, Isaac encountered the master of the schooner in the streets of Kingston. "Ah, mine goot captain—how is you? you lookish tin—ave you been sheek?' 'No, Moses—I am well enough, thank you—poor a bit, but sound in health, thank God. You have heard of my having carried away the mainmast, and, after kicking about fifteen days on short allowance, having been obliged to bear up for Honduras?' 'I know noting of all dat,' said Isaac; 'sorry for it, captain—very sad, inteed.' 'Sad—you may say that, Moses. But I am honest although poor, and here is your bill of lading for your two barrels of provisions; "Prime mess," *it* says; d——d tough, say I—Howsomdever,' pulling out his purse, 'the present value on Bogle, Jopp and Co.'s wharf, is £5 6s. 8d. the barrel; so there are two doubloons, Moses, and now discharge the account on the back of the bill of lading, will you?' 'Vy should I take payment, captain? if de (pork stuck in his throat like 'amen' in Macbeth's,) 'if de barrel ish lost, it can't be help—de act of God, you know.' 'I am an honest man, Isaac,' continued the captain, 'although a poor one, and I must tell the truth—we carried on with our own as long as it lasted, at length we had to break bulk, and your two barrels being nearest the hatchway, why we ate them first, that's all. Lord, what has come over you?' Isaac grew pale as a corpse. 'Oh, mine Got—mine poor proder, dat you ever was live to tie in Jamaic—Oh tear, oh tear!'"

"Did they eat the head and hands, and ——"

"Hold your tongue, Tom Cringle, don't interrupt me, *you* did not eat them; I tell it as it was told to me. So Isaac Grimm," continued Fyall, "was fairly overcome; the kindly feelings of his nature were at length stirred up, and as he turned away, he wept—blew his nose hard, like a Chaldean trumpet in the new moon; and while the large tears coursed each other down his care-worn cheeks, he exclaimed, wringing the captain's hand, in a voice tremulous and scarcely audible from extreme emotion, 'Oh, Isaac Grimm, Isaac Grimm, tid not your heart mishgive you, ven you vas commit te great blasphemy of invoish Ezekiel, flesh of your flesh, pone of your pone—as *por*—de onclean peast, I mean. If you had put invoish him as *peef*, surely te earthly tabernacle of him, as always sheet in de high places in te sinacogue, would never have peen allow to pass troo te powels of te pershicuting Nazareen. Ah, mine goot captain, mine very tear friend, vat, vat, vat av you done wid de cask, captain?'"

"Oh, most lame and impotent conclusion," sung out the judge, who by this time had become deusedly prosy; and all hands arose, as if by common consent, and agreed that we had got enough.

So off we started in groups. Fyall, Captain Transom, Whiffle, Aaron Bang, and myself, sallied forth in a bunch, pretty well inclined for a lark, you may guess. There are no lamps in the streets in Kingston, and as all the *decent* part of the community are in their *cavies* by half-past nine in the evening, and as it is now "the witching time o' night," there was not a soul in the streets that we saw, except when we passed a solitary townguard, lurking about some dark corner under the piazzas. These same streets, which were wide and comfortable enough in the daytime, had become unaccountably narrow and intricate since six o'clock in the evening, and, although the object of the party was to convoy Captain Transom and myself to our boat at the Ordnance Wharf, it struck me that we were as frequently on a totally different tack.

"I say, Cringle, my boy," stuttered out my superior, *lieutenant* and *captain* being both drowned *in* and equalized *by* the claret—"why, Tom, Tom Cringle, you dog—don't you hear your superior officer speak, sir, eh?"

My superior officer, during this address, was standing with both arms round a pillar of the piazza.

"I am here, sir," said I.

"Ah, I see," said Transom; "let us heave ahead, Tom—now do ye hear?—stand you with your white trousers against the next pillar." The ranges supporting the piazza were at distances of about twenty feet from each other. "Ah, stand there now—I see it." So he weighed from the one he had tackled to, and making a staggering bolt of it, he ran up to the pillar against which I stood, whose position was marked by my white vestments, where he again hooked on for a second or two, until I had taken up a new position.

"There, my boy, that's the way to lay out a warp—right in the wind's eye, Tom—we shall fairly beat those lubbers who are tacking in the stream; nothing like warping in the dead water near the shore—mark that down, Tom—never beat in a tide-way when you can warp up along shore in the dead water. D——n the judge's ice"—(hiccup)—"he has poisoned me with that piece he plopped in my last whitewash of madeira. He a judge! He may be a good crim—criminal judge, but no judge of wine. Why don't you laugh, Tom, eh?—and then his saw—the rasp of a saw I hate—wish it, and a whole nest more, had been in his legal stomach—full of old saws—Shakspere—he, he—why don't you laugh, Tom? Poisoned by the judge, by Jupiter. Now, here we are fairly abreast of them—Hillo! Fyall, what are you after?"

* * * * * *

The next morning had been fixed for duck-shooting, and the overseer and I were creeping along among the mangrove bushes on the shore, to get a shot at some teal, when we saw our friend the pair of compasses crossing the small bay in his boat, towards his little pilot-boat-built schooner, which was moored in a small creek opposite, the bushwood concealing every thing but her masts. My companion, as wild an Irishman as I ever knew, hailed him,—

"Hillo, Obadia—Buckskin—you Yankee rascal, heave-to. Come ashore here—come ashore."

Obed, smoking his pipe, deliberately uncoiled himself—I thought, as he rose, there was to be no end of him—and stood upright in the boat, like an ill-rigged jury-mast.

"I say, Master Tummas, you ben't no friend of mine, I guess, a'ter last night's work; you hears how I coughs?"—and he began to wheezle and crow in a most remarkable fashion.

"Never mind," rejoined the overseer; "if you go round that point, and put up the ducks—by the piper, but I'll fire at you!"

Obed neighed like a horse expecting his oats, which was meant as a laugh of derision. "Do you think your birding-piece can touch me here away, Master Tummas?" And again he *nichered* more loudly than before.

"Don't provoke me to try, you yellow snake, you!"

"Try, and be d——d, and there's a mark for thee," unveiling a certain part of his body, *not* his face.

The overseer, or *busha*, to give him his Jamaica name, looked at me and smiled, then coolly lifted his long Spanish barrel, and fired. Down dropped the smuggler, and ashore came the boat.

"I am mortally wounded, Master Tummas," quoth Obed; and I was confoundly frightened at first, from the unusual proximity of the injured part to his head; but the overseer, as soon as he could get off the ground, where he had thrown himself in an uncontrollable fit of laughter, had the man stripped and laid across a log, where he set his servant to pick out the pellets with a penknife.

A SLIPPERY YOUTH.

"Old Gelid, Longtram, Steady, and myself had been eating *ratoons*, at the former's domicil, and it was about nine in the evening when I got home. We had taken next to no wine, a pint of Madeira a-piece, during dinner, and six bottles of claret between us afterwards, so I went to bed as cool as a cucumber, and slept soundly for several hours, until awakened by my old gander—now do be quiet, Cringle—by my old watchman of a gander, cackling like a hero. I struck my repeater—half past one—so I turned myself, and was once more falling over into the arms of Morpheus, when I thought I saw some dark object flit silently across the open window that looks into the piazza, between me and the deep blue as yet moonless sky. This somewhat startled me, but it might have been one of the servants. Still I got up and looked out, but I could see nothing. It did certainly strike me once or twice, that there was some dark object cowering in the deep gloom caused by the shade of the orange-tree at the end of the piazza, but I persuaded myself it was fancy, and once more slipped into my nest. However, the circumstance had put sleep to flight. Half an hour might have passed, and the deep dark purity of the eastern sky was rapidly quickening into a greenish azure, the forerunner of the rising moon," ("Oh, confound your poetry," said Rubiochico,) "which was fast swamping the sparkling stars, like a bright river flowing over diamonds, when the old gander again set up his gabblement, and trumpeted more loudly than before. 'If you were not so tough, my noisy old cock'—thought I—'next Michaelmas should be your last.' So I now resolutely shut my eyes, and tried to sleep perforce, in which usually fruitless attempt, I was actually beginning to succeed, do you know, when a strong odor of palm oil came through the window, and on opening my eyes, I saw by the increasing light a naked negro standing at it, with his head and shoulders in sharp relief against the pale broad disc of the moon, at that moment just peering over the dark summit of the Long Mountain.

"I rubbed my eyes, and looked again; the dark figure was still there, but as if aware that some one was on the watch, it gradually sank down, until nothing but the round bullet head appeared above the window sill. The stratagem succeeded; the figure, deceived by my feigned snoring and quietude, slowly rose, and once more stood erect. Presently, it slipped one foot into the room, and then another, but so noiselessly that when I saw the black figure standing before me on the floor, I had some misgivings as to its being really a being of this world. However, I had small space for speculation, when it slid past the foot of the bed towards my open bureau—I seized the opportunity—started up—turned the key of the door—and planted myself right between the thief and the open window. 'Now, you scoundrel, surrender, or I will murder you on the spot.' I had scarcely spoken the word, when with the speed of light, the fellow threw himself on me—we closed—I fell—when, clip, he slipped through my fingers like an eel—bolted through the window—cleared the balcony at a bound, and disappeared. The thief had stripped himself as naked as when he was born, and soaped his woolly skull, and smeared his whole corpus with palm oil, so that in the struggle I was charmingly lubricated."

Nicodemus here lay back on his chair, evidently desirous of our considering this the *whole* of the story, but he was not to be let off so easily, for presently Longtram, with a wicked twinkle of his eye, chimed in—

"Ay, and what happened next, old Nic—did nothing follow, eh?"

Nic's countenance assumed an irresolute expression; he saw he was jammed up in the wind, so at a venture he determined to sham deafness—

"Take wine, Lucifer—a glass of Hermitage?"

"With great pleasure," said his satanic majesty. The propitiatory libation, however, did not work, for no sooner had his glass touched the mahogany again, than he returned to the charge.

"Now, Mr. Nicodemus, since you won't, I will tell the company the reason of so nice an old gentleman wearing Baltimore flour in his hair instead of perfumed Mareschal powder, and none of the freshest either, let me tell you; why, I have seen three weevils take flight from your august pate since we sat down to dinner."

Old Nic, seeing he was caught, met the attack with the greatest good humor—

"Why, I will tell the whole truth, Lucifer, if you don't bother."—("The devil thank you," said Longtram.)—"So you must know," continued Nicodemus, "that I immediately roused the servants, searched the premises in every direction without success—nothing could be seen; but at the suggestion of my valet, I lit a small spirit-lamp, and placed it on the table at my bed-side, on which it pleased him to place my brace of Mantons, loaded with slug, and my naked small-sword, so that, thought I, if the thief ventures back, he shall not slip through my fingers again so easily. I do confess that these imposing preparations did appear to me somewhat preposterous, even at the time, as it was not, to say the least of it, very probable that my slippery gentleman would return the same night. However, my servant in his zeal was not to be denied, and I was not so fit to judge as usual, from having missed my customary quantity of wine after dinner the previous day; so, seeing all right, I turned in, thus bristling like a porcupine, and slept soundly until daylight, when I bethought me of getting up. I then rose—slipped on my night-gown—and"—here Nicodemus laughed more loudly than ever,—"as I am a gentleman, my spirit-lamp—naked sword—loaded pistols—my diamond breast-pin, and all my clothes, even unto my unmentionables, had disappeared; but what was the cruelest cut of all, my box of Mareschal powder, my patent puff, and all my pomade divine, had also vanished; and true enough, as Lucifer says, it so happened that from the delay in the arrival of the running ships, there was not an ounce of either powder or pomatum to be had in the whole town, so I have been driven in my extremity—oh, most horrible declension!—to keep my tail on hog's lard and Baltimore flour ever since."

"Well, but"—persisted Lucifer—"who the deuse was the man in the moon? Come, tell us. And what has become of the queue you so tenderly nourished, for you sport a crop, Master Nic, now, I perceive?"

Here Nicodemus was neither to hold nor to bind; he was absolutely suffocating with laughter, as he shrieked out, with long intervals between—

"Why, the robber was my own favorite body-servant, Crabclaw, after all, and be damned to him—the identical man who advised the warlike demonstrations; and as for the pigtail, why, on the very second night of the flour and grease, it was so cruelly damaged by a rat while I slept, that I had to amputate the whole affair, stoop and roop, this very morning." And so saying, the excellent creature fell back in his chair, like to choke from the uproariousness of his mirth, while the tears streamed down his cheeks and washed channels in the floor, as if he had been a tattooed Mandingo.

Thos Hood

CYCLOPÆDIA

OF

MODERN WIT AND HUMOR.

ENGLISH.

Mirth, with thee I mean to live,
Jest and youthful Jollity,
Quips and cranks and wanton wiles,
CYCLOPÆDIA
OF
MODERN
Wit and Humor.
EDITED BY
W. E. BURTON.
ENGLISH.

CYCLOPÆDIA

OF

WIT AND HUMOR.

ENGLISH.

THE PUGSLEY PAPERS.

BY THOMAS HOOD.

A PASTORALE IN A FLAT.

How the following correspondence came into my hands must remain a Waverley mystery. The Pugsley Papers were neither rescued from a garret, like the Evelyn—collected from cartridges like the Culloden,—nor saved, like the Garrick, from being shredded into a snow storm at a Winter Theatre. They were not snatched from a tailor's shears, like the original parchment of Magna Charta. They were neither the Legacy of a Dominie, nor the communications of My Landlord,—a consignment, like the Clinker Letters, from some Rev. Jonathan Dustwich,—nor the waifs and strays of a Twopenny Post Bag. They were not unrolled from ancient papyri. They were none of those that "line trunks, clothe spices," or paper the walls of old attics. They were neither given to me nor sold to me,—nor stolen,—nor borrowed and surreptitiously copied,—nor left in a hackney coach, like Sheridan's play,—nor misdelivered by a carrier pigeon,—nor dreamt of, like Coleridge's Kubla Khan,—nor turned up in the Tower, like Milton's Foundling MS.,—nor dug up—nor trumped up, like the eastern tales of Horam Harum Horam, the son of Asmar,—nor brought over by Rammohun Roy,—nor translated by Doctor Bowring from the Scandinavian, Batavian, Pomeranian, Spanish, or Danish, or Russian, or Prussian, or any other language dead or living. They were not picked from the Dead Letter Office, nor purloined from the British Museum. In short, I cannot, dare not, will not, hint even at the mode of their acquisition; the reader must be content to know, that, in point of authenticity, the Pugsley Papers are the extreme reverse of Lady L.'s celebrated Autographs, which were all written by the proprietor.

No. I.—*From Master* Richard Pugsley *to Master* Robert Rogers, *at Number* 132, *Barbican.*

Dear Bob,—Huzza! Here I am in Lincolnshire! It's good-bye to Wellingtons and Cossacks, Ladies' double channels, Gentlemen's stout calf, and ditto, ditto. They've all been sold off under prime cost, and the old Shoe Mart is disposed of, goodwill and fixtures, for ever and ever. Father has been made a rich Squire of by will, and we've got a house and fields, and trees of our own. Such a garden, Bob! It beats White Conduit.

Now, Bob, I'll tell you what I want. I want you to come down here for the holidays. Don't be afraid. Ask your Sister to ask your Mother to ask your Father to let you come. It's only ninety mile. If you're out of pocket money, you can walk, and beg a lift now and then, or swing by the dickeys. Put on corduroys, and don't care for cut behind. The two prentices, George and Will, are here to be made farmers of, and brother Nick is took home from school to help in agriculture. We like farming very much, it's capital fun. Us four have got a gun, and go out shooting; it's a famous good un, and sure to go off if you don't full cock it. Tiger is to be our shooting dog as soon as he has left off killing the sheep. He's a real savage, and worries cats beautiful. Before Father comes down, we mean to bait our bull with him.

There's plenty of New Rivers about, and we're going a fishing as soon as we have mended our top joint. We've killed one of our sheep on the sly to get gentles. We've a pony, too, to ride upon when we can catch him, but he's loose in the paddock, and has neither mane nor tail to signify to lay hold of. Isn't it prime, Bob? You *must* come.

If your Mother won't give your Father leave to allow you,—run away. Remember, you turn up Gosnell street to go to Lincolnshire, and ask for Middlefen Hall. There's a pond full of frogs, but we won't pelt them till you come, but let it be before Sunday, as there's our own orchard to rob, and the fruit's to be gathered on Monday.

If you like sucking raw eggs, we know where the hens lay, and mother don't; and I'm bound there's lots of birds' nests. Do come, Bob, and I'll show you the wasp's nest, and every thing that can make you comfortable. I dare say you could borrow your father's volunteer musket of him without his knowing of it; but be sure anyhow to bring the ramrod, as we have mislaid ours by firing it off. Don't forget some bird-lime, Bob, and some fish-hooks—and some different sorts of shot—and some gut and some gunpowder—and a gentle-box, and some flints,—some May flies—and a powder horn,—and a landing net and a dog-whistle—and some porcupine quills, and a bullet mould—and a trolling-winch, and a shot-bolt and a tin can. You pay for 'em Bob, and I'll owe it you.

Your old friend and schoolfellow,

RICHARD PUGSLEY.

No. II.—*From the Same to the Same.*

DEAR BOB,—When you come, bring us a 'bacco-pipe to load the gun with. If you don't come, it can come by the waggon. Our Public House is three mile off, and when you've walked there it's out of every thing. Yours, etc.

RICH. PUGSLEY.

No. III.—*From Miss* ANASTASIA PUGSLEY, *to Miss* JEMIMA MOGGRIDGE, *at Gregory House Establishment for Young Ladies, Mile End.*

MY DEAR JEMIMA,—Deeply solicitous to gratify sensibility, by sympathising with our fortuitous elevation, I seize the epistolatory implements to inform you, that, by the testamentary disposition of a remote branch of consanguinity, our tutelary residence is removed from the metropolitan horizon to a pastoral district and its congenial pursuits. In futurity I shall be more pertinaciously superstitious in the astrological revelations of human destiny. You remember the mysterious gipsy at Hornsey Wood? Well, the eventful fortune she obscurely intimated, though couched in vague terms, has come to pass in minutest particulars; for I perceive perspicuously, that it predicted that papa should sell off his boot and shoe business at 133, Barbican, to Clack and Son, of 144, Hatton Garden, and that we should retire, in a station of affluence, to Middlefen Hall, in Lincolnshire, by bequest of our great-great maternal uncle, Pollexfen Goldsworthy Wrigglesworth, Esq., who deceased suddenly of apoplexy at Wisbeach Market, in the ninety-third year of his venerable and lamented age.

At the risk of tedium, I will attempt a cursory delineation of our rural paradise, altho' I feel it would be morally arduous to give any idea of the romantic scenery of the Lincolnshire Fens. Conceive, as far as the visual organ expands, an immense sequestered level, abundantly irrigated with minute rivulets, and studded with tufted oaks, whilst more than a hundred wind-mills diversify the prospect and give a revolving animation to the scene. As for our own gardens and grounds, they are a perfect Vauxhall—excepting of course the rotunda, the orchestra, the company, the variegated lamps, the fireworks, and those very lofty trees. But I trust my dear Jemima will supersede topography by ocular inspection; and in the interim I send for acceptance a graphical view of the locality, shaded in Indian ink, which will suffice to convey an idea of the terrestrial verdure and celestial azure we enjoy, in lieu of the sable exhalations and architectural nigritude of the metropolis.

You who know my pastoral aspirings, and have been the indulgent confidant of my votive tributes to the Muses, will conceive the refined nature of my enjoyment when I mention the intellectual repast of this morning. I never could enjoy Bloomfield in Barbican,—but to-day he read beautifully under our pear tree. I look forward to the felicity of reading Thomson's Summer with you on the green seat, and if engagements at Christmas permit your participation in the bard, there is a bower of evergreens that will be delightful for the perusal of his Winter.

I enclose, by request, an epistolary effusion from sister Dorothy, which I know will provoke your risible powers, by the domesticity of its details. You know she was always in the homely characteristics a perfect Cinderella, though I doubt whether even supernatural agency could adapt her foot to a diminutive vitrified slipper, or her hand for a prince of regal primogeniture. But I am summoned to receive, with family members, the felicitations of Lincolnshire aristocracy; though whatever necessary distinctions may prospectively occur between respective grades in life, they will only superficially affect the sentiments of eternal friendship between my dear Jemima and her affectionate friend,

ANASTASIA PUGSLEY.

No. IV.—*From Miss* DOROTHY PUGSLEY *to the Same.*

MY DEAR MISS JEMIMA.—Providence having been pleased to remove my domestic duties from Barbican to Lincolnshire, I trust I shall have strength of constitution to fulfil them as becomes my new allotted line of life. As we are not sent into this world to be idle, and Anastasia has declined housewifery, I have undertaken the Diary, and the Brewery, and the Baking, and the Poultry, the Pigs, and the Pastry,—and though I feel fatigued at first, use reconciles to labors and trials, more severe than I at present enjoy. Altho' things may not turn out to wish at present, yet all well-directed efforts are sure to meet reward in the end, and altho' I have chumped and churned two days running, and it's nothing yet but curds and whey, I should be wrong to despair of eating butter of my own making before I die. Considering the adulteration committed by every article in London, I was never happier in any prospect, than of drinking my own milk, fattening my own calves, and laying my own eggs. We cackle so much I am sure we new-lay somewhere, tho' I cannot find out our nests; and I am looking every day to have chickens, as one pepper-and-salt colored hen has been sitting these two months. When a poor ignorant bird sets me such an example of patience, how can I repine at the hardest domestic drudgery! Mother and I have worked like horses to be sure ever since we came to the estate; but if we die in it, we know it's for the good of the family, and to agreeably surprise my Father, who is still in town winding up his books. For my own part, if it was right to look at things so selfishly, I should say I never was so happy in my life; though I own I have cried more since coming here than I ever remember before. You will confess my crosses and losses have been unusual trials, when I tell you, out of all my makings, and bakings, and brewings, and preservings, there has been nothing either eatable or drinkable; and what is more painful to an affectionate mind, have half poisoned the whole family with home-made ketchup of toadstools, by mistake for mushrooms. When I reflect that they are preserved, I ought not to grieve about my damsons and bullaces, done by Mrs. Maria Dover's receipt.

Among other things we came into a beautiful closet of old China, which, I am shocked to say, is all destroyed by my preserving. The bullaces and damsons fomented, and blew up a great jar with a violent shock that smashed all the tea and coffee cups, and left nothing but the handles hanging in rows on the tenter-hooks. But to a resigned spirit there's always some comfort in calamities, and if the preserves work and foment so, there's some hope that my beer will, as it has been a month next Monday in the mash tub. As for the loss of the elder wine, candor compels me to say it was my own fault for letting the poor blind animals crawl into the copper; but experience dictates next year not to boil the berries and kittens at the same time.

I mean to attempt cream cheese as soon as we can get cream,—but as yet we can't drive the Cows home to be milked for the Bull—he has twice hunted Grace and me into fits, and kept my poor Mother a whole morning in the pigstye. As I know you like country delicacies, you will receive a pound of my fresh butter when it comes, and I mean to add a cheese as soon as I can get one to stick together. I shall send also some family pork for Governess, of our own killing, as we wring a pig's neck on Saturday. I did hope to give you the unexpected treat of a home-made loaf, but it was forgot in the oven from ten to six, and so too black to offer. However, I hope to surprise you with one by Monday's carrier. Anastasia bids me add she will send a nosegay for respected Mrs. Tombleson, if the plants don't die off before, which I am sorry to say is not improbable.

It's really shocking to see the failure of her cultivated taste, and one in particular, that must be owned a very pretty idea. When we came, there was a vast number of flower roots, but jumbled without any regular order, till Anastasia trowelled them all up, and set them in again, in the quadrille figures. It must have looked sweetly elegant, if it had agreed with them, but they have all dwindled and drooped like deep declines and consumptions. Her dahlias and tulips, too, have turned out nothing but onions and kidney potatoes, and her ten week stocks have not come up in twenty. But as Shakspere says, Adversity is a precious toad—that teaches us Patience is a jewel.

Considering the unsettled state of coming in, I must conclude, but could not resist giving your friendliness a short account of the happy change that has occurred, and our increase of comforts. I would write more, but I know you will excuse my listening to the calls of dumb animals. It's the time I always scald the little pigs' bread and milk, and put saucers of clean water for the ducks and geese. There are the fowls' beds to make with

VERY FOND OF GARDENING.

fresh straw, and a hundred similar things that country people are obliged to think of.

The children, I am happy to say, are all well, baby is a little fractious, we think from Grace setting him down in the nettles, and he was short-coated last week. Grace is poorly with a cold, and Anastasia has got a sore throat, from sitting up fruitlessly in the orchard to hear the nightingale; perhaps there may not be any in the Fens. I seem to have a trifling ague and rheumatism myself, but it may be only a stiffness from so much churning, and the great family wash-up of every thing we had directly we came down, for the sake of grass-bleaching on the lawn. With these exceptions, we are all in perfect health and happiness, and unite in love, with

Dear Miss Jemima's affectionate friend,

DOROTHY PUGSLEY.

No. V.—*From* MRS. PUGSLEY *to* MRS. MUMFORD, *Bucklersbury.*

MY DEAR MARTHA,—In my ultimatum I informed of old Wrigglesworth paying his natural debts, and of the whole Middlefen estate coming from Lincolnshire to Barbican. I charged Mr. P. to send bulletings into you with progressive reports, but between sisters, as I know you are very curious, I am going to make myself more particular. I take the opportunity of the family being all restive in bed, and the house all still, to give an account of our moving. The things all got here safe, with the exception of the Crockery and Glass, which came down with the dresser, about an hour after its arrival. Perhaps if we hadn't overloaded it with the whole of our breakables, it wouldn't have given way,—as it is, we have only one plate left, and that's chipt, and a mug without a spout to keep it in countenance. Our furniture, etc., came by the wagon, and I am sorry to say a poor family at the same time, and the little idle boys with their knives carved and scarified my rosewood legs, and, what is worse, not of the same patterns; but as people say, two Lincolnshire removes are as bad as a fire of London.

The first thing I did on coming down, was to see to the sweeps going up,—but I wish I had been less precipitous, for the sooty wretches stole four good flitches of bacon, as was up the kitchen chimney, quite unbeknown to me. We have filled up the vacancy with more, which smoke us dreadfully, but what is to be cured must be endured. My next thing was to have all holes and corners cleared out, and washed, and scrubbed, being left, like bachelor's places, in a sad state by old single W.; for a rich man, I never saw one that wanted so much cleaning out. There were heaps of dung about, as high as haystacks, and it cost me five shillings a load to have it all carted off the premises; besides heaps of good-for-nothing littering straw, that I gave to the boys for bonfires. We are not all to rights yet, but Rome wasn't built in St. Thomas's day.

It was providential I hampered myself with cold provisions, for except the bacon there were no eatables in the house. What old W. lived upon is a mystery, except salads, for we found a whole field of beet-root, which, all but a few plants for Dorothy to pickle, I had chucked away. As the ground was then clear for sowing up a crop, I directed George to plough it up, but he met with agricultural distress. He says as soon as he whipped his horses, the plough stuck its nose in the earth, and tumbled over head and heels. It seems very odd when ploughing is so easy to look at, but I trust he will do better in time. Experience makes a King Solomon of a Tom noddy.

I expect we shall have bushels upon bushels of corn, tho' sadly pecked by the birds, as I have had all the scarecrows taken down for fear of the children dreaming of them for Bogies. For the same dear little sakes I have had the well filled up, and the nasty sharp iron spikes drawn out of all the rakes and harrows. Nobody shall say to my teeth, I am not a good Mother. With these precautions I trust the young ones will enjoy the country when the gipsies have left, but till then, I confine them to round the house, as it's no use shutting the stable door after you've had a child stole. We have a good many fine fields of hay, which I mean to have reaped directly, wet or shine; for delays are as dangerous as pickles in glazed pans. Perhaps St. Swithen's is in our favor, for if the stacks are put up dampish they won't catch fire so easily, if Swing should come into these parts. The poor boys have made themselves very industrious in shooting off the birds, and hunting away all the vermin, besides cutting down trees. As I knew it was profitable to fell timber, I directed them to begin with a very ugly straggling old hollow tree next the premises, but it fell the wrong way, and knocked down the cow-house. Luckily the poor animals were all in the clover-field at the time. George says it wouldn't have happened but for a violent sow, or rather sow-west,—and it's likely enough, but it's an ill wind that blows nothing to nobody.

THE RAKE'S PROGRESS.

Having writ last post to Mr. P., I have no occasion to make you a country commissioner. Anastasia, indeed, wants to have books about every thing, but for my part and Dorothy's we don't put much faith in authorized receipts and directions, but trust more to nature and common sense. For instance, in fatting a goose, reason points to sage and onions,—why our own don't thrive on it, is very mysterious. We have a beautiful poultry yard, only infested with rats,—but I have made up a poison, that, I know by the poor ducks, will kill them if they eat it.

I expected to send you a quantity of wall-fruit, for preserving, and am sorry you bought the brandy beforehand, as it has all vanished in one night by

WALL FRUIT.

picking and stealing, notwithstanding I had ten dozen of bottles broke on purpose to stick a-top of the wall. But I rather think they came over the pales, as George, who is very thoughtless, had driven in all the new tenter hooks with the points downwards. Our apples and pears would have gone too, but luckily we heard a noise in the dark, and threw brickbats out of the window, that alarmed the thieves by smashing the cowcumber frames. However, I mean on Monday to make sure of the orchard, by gathering the trees,—a pheasant in one's hand is worth two cock sparrows in a bush. One comfort is, the house-dog is very vicious, and wont let any of us stir in or out after dark—indeed, nothing can be more furious, except the bull, and at me in particular. You would think he knew my inward thoughts, and that I intend to have him roasted whole when we give our grand housewarming regalia.

With these particulars, I remain, with love, my dear Dorcas, your affectionate sister,

BELINDA PUGSLEY.

P. S.—I have only one anxiety here, and that is, the likelihood of being taken violently ill, nine miles off from any physical powers, with nobody that can ride in the house, and nothing but an insurmountable hunting horse in the stable. I should like, therefore, to be well doctor-stuff'd from Apothecaries' Hall, by the wagon or any other vehicle. A stitch in the side taken in time saves nine spasms. Dorothy's tincture of the rhubarb stalks in the garden, doesn't answer, and it's a pity now they were not saved for pies.

No. VI.—*From Mrs.* PUGSLEY *to Mrs.* ROGERS.

MADAM,—Although warmth has made a coolness, and our having words has caused a silence—yet as mere writing is not being on speaking terms, and disconsolate parents in the case; I waive venting of animosities till a more agreeable moment. Having perused the afflicted advertisement in the *Times*, with interesting description of person, and ineffectual dragging of New River,—beg leave to say that Master Robert is safe and well,—having arrived here on Saturday night last, with almost not a shoe to his foot, and no coat at all, as was supposed to be with the approbation of parents. It appears, that not supposing the distance between the families extended to him, he walked the whole way

A COOLNESS BETWEEN FRIENDS.

down on the footing of a friend, to visit my son Richard, but hearing the newspapers read, quitted suddenly, the same day with the gipsies, and we haven't an idea what is become of him. Trusting this statement will relieve of all anxiety, remain, madam, your humble servant,

BELINDA PUGSLEY.

No. VII.—*To Mr.* SILAS PUGSLEY, *Parisian Depôt, Shoreditch.*

DEAR BROTHER,—My favor of the present date, is to advise of my safe arrival on Wednesday night, per opposition coach, after ninety miles of discomfort, absolutely unrivalled for cheapness, and a walk of five miles more, through lanes and roads, that for dirt and sludge may confidently defy competition,—not to mention turnings and windings, too numerous to particularize, but morally impossible to pursue on undeviating principles. The night was of so dark a quality as forbade finding the gate, but for the house-dog flying upon me by mistake for the late respectable proprietor, and almost tearing my clothes off my back by his strenuous exertions to obtain the favor of my patronage.

Conscientiously averse to the fallacious statements, so much indulged in by various competitors, truth urges to acknowledge that on arrival, I did not find things on such a footing as to insure universal satisfaction. Mrs. P., indeed, differs in her statement, but you know her success always surpassed the most sanguine expectations. Ever emulous to merit commendation by the strictest regard to principles of economy, I found her laid up with lumbago, through her studious efforts to please, and Doctor Clarke, of Wisbeach, in the house prescribing for it, but I am sorry to add—no abatement. Dorothy is also confined to her bed, by her unremitting assiduity and attention in the housekeeping line; and Anastasia the same, from listening for nightingales, on a fine July evening, but which is an article not always to be warranted to keep its virtue in any climate,—the other children, large and small sizes, ditto, ditto, with Grace too ill to serve in the nursery,—and the rest of the servants totally unable to execute such extensive demands. Such an unprecedented depreciation in health makes me doubt the quality of country air, so much recommended for family use, and whether constitutions have not more eligibility to offer that have been regularly town-made.

Our new residence is a large lonely mansion, with no connection with any other house, but standing in the heart of Lincolnshire fens, over which it looks through an advantageous opening: comprising a great variety of windmills, and drains, and willow-pollards, and an extensive assortment of similar articles, that are not much calculated to invite inspection. In warehouses for corn, etc., it probably presents unusual advantages to the occupier; but candor compels to state that agriculture in this part of Lincolnshire is very flat. To supply language on the most moderate terms, unexampled distress in Spitalfields is nothing to the distress in ours. The corn has been deluged with rain of remarkable durability, without being able to wash the smut out of its ears; and with regard to the expected great rise in hay, our stacks have been burnt down to the ground, instead of going to the consumer. If the hounds hadn't been out, we might have fetch'd the engines, but the hunter threw George on his head, and he only revived to be sensible that the entire stock had been disposed of at an immense sacrifice. The whole amount, I fear, will be out of book,—as the Norwich Union refuses to liquidate the hay, on the ground that the policy was voided by the impolicy of putting it up wet. In other articles I am sorry I must write no alteration. Our bull, after killing the house-dog, and tossing William, has gone wild, and had the madness to run away from his livelihood, and, what is worse, all the cows after him—except those that had burst themselves in the clover-field, and a small dividend, as I may say, of one in the pound. Another item, the pigs, to save bread and milk, have been turned into the woods for acorns, and is an article producing no returns—as not one has yet come back. Poultry ditto. Sedulously cultivating an enlarged connection in the turkey line, such the antipathy to gipsies, the whole breed, geese and ducks inclusive, removed themselves from the premises by night, directly a strolling camp came and set up in the neighborhood. To avoid prolixity, when I came to take stock, there was no stock to take—namely, no eggs, no butter, no cheese, no corn, no hay, no bread, no beer—no water even—nothing but the mere commodious premises, and fixtures, and good-will—and candor compels to add, a very small quantity on hand of the last-named particular.

To add to stagnation, neither of my two sons in the business, nor the two apprentices, have been so diligently punctual in executing country orders with despatch and fidelity, as laudable ambition desires, but have gone about fishing and shooting—and William has suffered a loss of three fingers, by his unvarying system of high charges. He and Richard are likewise both threatened with prosecution for trespassing on the hares in the adjoining landed interest, and Nick is obliged to decline any active share, by dislocating his shoulder in climbing a tall tree for a tom-tit. As for George, tho' for the first time beyond the circumscribed limits of town custom, he indulges vanity in such unqualified pretensions to superiority of knowledge in farming, on the strength of his grandfather having belonged to the agricultural line of trade, as renders a wholesale stock of patience barely adequate to meet its demands. Thus stimulated to injudicious performance, he is as injurious to the best interests of the country, as blight and mildew, and smut and rot, and glanders, and pip, all combined in one texture. Between ourselves, the objects of unceasing endeavors, united with uncompromising integrity, have been assailed with so much deterioration, as makes me humbly desirous of abridging sufferings, by resuming business as a shoe marter at the old-established house. If Clack and Son, therefore, have not already taken possession and respectfully informed the vicinity, will thankfully pay reasonable compensation for loss of time and expense incurred by the bargain being off. In case parties agree, I beg you will authorize Mr. Robins to have the honor to dispose of the whole Lincolnshire concern, tho' the knocking down of Middlefen Hall will be a severe blow on Mrs. P. and family. Deprecating the deceitful stimulus of advertising arts, interest commands to mention,—desirable freehold estate and eligible investment—and sole reason for disposal, the proprietor going to the continent. Example suggests likewise, a good country for hunting for fox-hounds—and a prospect too extensive to put in a newspaper. Circumstances being rendered awkward by the untoward event of the running away of the cattle, etc., it will be best to say—"The stock to be taken as it stands;"—and an additional favor will be politely conferred, and the same thankfully acknowledged, if the auctioneer will be so kind as bring the next market town ten miles nearer, and carry the coach and the wagon once a day past the door. Earnestly requesting early attention to the above, and with sentiments of, etc. R. Pugsley, Sen.

P. S. Richard is just come to hand dripping and half dead out of the Nene, and the two apprentices all but drowned each other in saving him. Hence occurs to add, fishing opportunities among the desirable items.

SALLY SIMPKIN'S LAMENT; OR, JOHN JONES'S KIT-CAT-ASTROPHE.

BY THOMAS HOOD.

"Oh! what is that comes gliding in,
And quite in middling haste?
It is the picture of my Jones,
And painted to the waist.

"It is not painted to the life,
For where's the trowsers blue?
Oh Jones, my dear!—Oh dear! my Jones,
What is become of you?"

"O! Sally dear, it is too true,—
The half that you remark
Is come to say my other half
Is bit off by a shark!

"Oh! Sally, sharks do things by halves,
Yet most completely do!
A bite in one place seems enough,
But I've been bit in two.

"You know I once was all your own
But now a shark must share!
But let that pass—for now to you
I'm neither here nor there.

"Alas! death has a strange divorce
Effected in the sea,
It has divided me from you,
And even me from me!

"Don't fear my ghost will walk o' nights
To haunt, as people say;
My ghost *can't* walk, for, oh! my legs
Are many leagues away!

"Lord! think when I am swimming round,
And looking where the boat is,
A shark just snaps away a *half*,
Without 'a *quarter's* notice.'

"One half is here, the other half
Is near Columbia placed;
Oh! Sally, I have got the whole
Atlantic for my waist.

"But now, adieu—a long adieu!
I've solved death's awful riddle,
And would say more, but I am doomed
To break off in the middle!"

THE LOST HEIR.

BY THOMAS HOOD.

A LOST CHILD ITS OWN CRYER.

One day, as I was going by
That part of Holborn christened High,
I heard a loud and sudden cry
  That chill'd my very blood;
And lo! from out a dirty alley,
Where pigs and Irish wont to rally,
I saw a crazy woman sally,
  Bedaub'd with grease and mud.
She turn'd her East, she turn'd her West,
Staring like Pythoness possest,
With streaming hair and heaving breast,
  As one stark mad with grief.
This way and that she wildly ran,
Jostling with woman and with man—
Her right hand held a frying pan,
  The left a lump of beef.
At last her frenzy seem'd to reach
A point just capable of speech,
And with a tone almost a screech,
  As wild as ocean birds,
Or female Ranter mov'd to preach,
  She gave her "sorrow words."

"O Lord! O dear, my heart will break, I shall go stick stark staring wild!
Has ever a one seen any thing about the streets like a crying lost-looking child?
Lawk help me, I don't know where to look, or to run, if I only knew which way—
A Child as is lost about London streets, and especially Seven Dials, is a needle in a bottle of hay.
I am all in a quiver—get out of my sight, do, you wretch, you little Kitty M'Nab!
You promised to have half an eye to him, you know you did, you dirty deceitful young drab.
The last time as ever I see him, poor thing, was with my own blessed Motherly eyes,
Sitting as good as gold in the gutter, a playing at making little dirt pies.
I wonder he left the court where he was better off than all the other young boys,
With two bricks, an old shoe, nine oyster-shells, and a dead kitten by way of toys.
When his Father comes home, and he always comes home as sure as ever the clock strikes one,
He'll be rampant, he will, at his child being lost; and the beef and the inguns not done!
La bless you, good folks, mind your own consarns, and don't be making a mob in the street;
O serjeant M'Farlane! you have not come across my poor little boy, have you, in your beat?
Do, good people, move on! don't stand staring at me like a parcel of stupid stuck pigs;
Saints forbid! but he's p'r'aps been inviggled away up a court for the sake of his clothes by the prigs;

He'd a very good jacket, for certain, for I bought it myself for a shilling one day in Rag Fair;
And his trousers considering not very much patch'd, and red plush, they was once his Father's best pair.
His shirt, it's very lucky I'd got washing in the tub, or that might have gone with the rest;
But he'd got on a very good pinafore with only two slits and a burn on the breast.
He'd a goodish sort of hat, if the crown was sew'd in, and not quite so much jagg'd at the brim.
With one shoe on, and the other shoe is a boot, and not a fit, and you'll know by that if it's him.
Except being so well dress'd, my mind would misgive, some old beggar woman in want of an orphan,
Had borrow'd the child to go a begging with, but I'd rather see him laid out in his coffin!
Do, good people, move on, such a rabble of boys! I'll break every bone of 'em I come near;
Go home—you're spilling the porter—go home—Tommy Jones, go along home with your beer.
This day is the sorrowfulest day of my life, ever since my name was Betty Morgan.
Them vile Savoyards! they lost him once before all along of following a Monkey and an Organ:
O my Billy—my head will turn right round—if he's got kiddynapp'd with them Italians,
They'll make him a plaster parish image boy, they will, the outlandish tatterdemalions.
Billy—where are you, Billy?—I'm as hoarse as a crow, with screaming for ye, you young sorrow!
And shan't have half a voice, no more I shan't, for crying fresh herrings to-morrow.
O Billy, you're bursting my heart in two, and my life won't be of no more vally,
If I'm to see other folks darlin's, and none of mine, playing like angels in our alley;
And what shall I do but cry out my eyes, when I looks at the old three-legged chair
As Billy used to make coach and horses of, and there a'n't no Billy there!
I would run all the wide world over to find him, if I only know'd where to run.
Little Murphy, now I remember, was once lost for a month through stealing a penny bun,—
The Lord forbid of any child of mine! I think it would kill me raily,
To find my Bill holdin' up his little innocent hand at the Old Bailey.
For though I say it as oughtn't, yet I will say, you may search for miles and mileses
And not find one better brought up, and more pretty behaved, from one end to t'other of St. Giles's.
And if I called him a beauty, it's no lie, but only as a Mother ought to speak;
You never set eyes on a more handsomer face, only it hasn't been washed for a week;
As for hair, tho' its red, it's the most nicest hair when I've time to just show it the comb;
I'll owe 'em five pounds, and a blessing besides, as will only bring him safe and sound home.
He's blue eyes, and not to be call'd a squint, though a little cast he's certainly got;
And his nose is still a good un, tho' the bridge is broke, by his falling on a pewter pint pot;
He's got the most elegant wide mouth in the world, and very large teeth for his age;
And quite as fit as Mrs. Murdockson's child to play Cupid on the Drury Lane Stage.
And then he has got such dear winning ways—but O I never never shall see him no more!
O dear! to think of losing him just after nussing him back from death's door!
Only the very last month when the windfalls, hang 'em, was at twenty a penny!
And the threepence he'd got by grottoing was spent in plums, and sixty for a child is too many.
And the Cholera man came and whitewash'd us all and, drat him, made a seize of our hog.—
It's no use to send the Cryer to cry him about, he's such a blunderin' drunken old dog;
The last time he was fetched to find a lost child, he was guzzling with his bell at the Crown,
And went and cried a boy instead of a girl, for a distracted Mother and Father about Town.
Billy—where are you, Billy, I say? come Billy, come home, to your best of Mothers!
I'm scared when I think of them Cabroleys, they drive so, they run over their own Sisters and Brothers.
Or may be he's stole by some chimbly sweeping wretch, to stick fast in narrow flues and what not,
And be poked up behind with a picked pointed pole, when the soot has ketch'd, and the chimney's red hot.
Oh I'd give the whole wide world, if the world was mine, to clap my two longin' eyes on his face.
For he's my darlin' of darlin's, and if he don't soon come back, you'll see me drop stone dead on the place.
I only wish I'd got him safe in these two Motherly arms, and wouldn't I hug him and kiss him!
Lauk! I never knew what a precious he was—but a child don't not feel like a child till you miss him.
Why, there he is! Punch and Judy hunting, the young wretch; it's that Billy as sartin as sin!
But let me get him home, with a good grip of his hair, and I'm blest if he shall have a whole bone in his skin!"

A FETE AT A COUNTRY SEAT.

FROM "TYLNEY HALL." BY THOMAS HOOD.

For some days previous to the fete, the Hive presented a scene of hurry, scurry, worry, and flurry. As usual, Twigg interfered in every thing; and his voice was heard from all parts of the house, swearing, entreating, threatening, exhorting, directing, or disputing with his wife and daughter on matters of taste. Never in the days of his industry had he labored so unremittingly, so early, and so late; he really slaved bodily like a negro, while Pompey, the true nigger, was set to work on matters far surpassing the dim intelligence of an African brain; the most provoking blunders naturally followed, and the black, as might have been expected from one of his complexion, "played the very devil." Many a tumble he had over the numerous packages from London which encumbered the floors and tables, the stairs and the chairs. It was well the Hive did not happen to be a glass one, such as those which invite the spectator to observe the wonderful order, harmony, regularity, and exact distribution of labor, evinced by its busy inhabitants. Indeed, the House of Industry much more resembled a wasp's nest, where the peevish swarm were all restless and irritated by some recent disturbance. Every body was out of humor. Mrs. Twigg scolded and wept by turns, and threatened to faint, but had not time to spare for fits; and the cook fumed and broiled at her mistress's culinary interference. The coachman sulkily helped in the kitchen, to whip cream instead of horses. The butler quarrelled with the footman; and the housemaids among themselves. The gardener growled and grumbled while he transported his hothouse plants into the open air, cropped all his choicest buds and blossoms to make bouquets and fill baskets, nor did it make him amends for his real flowers, to see artificial ones in wreaths and festoons decorating his favorite "old statues," so that Mercury looked as if he was going to dance in a ballet, and Neptune as if he had just come from Covent Garden. The grooms grew weary of galloping express on coach-horses, as the jealous tradespeople of the village tardily executed, or altogether neglected, the stray orders for forgotten articles which they grumbled "had better have been had down from London like the rest." To crown the confusion, the cub arrived full of boisterous spirits, and began to amuse himself with a whole flock of *larks*, a phrase that indicated those practical jokes, in which persons of limited capacity are so apt to indulge. He locked the butler in his pantry—sent off the footman, when most in request, on frivolous errands—plugged the pipes of keys—fastened chairs together—set tables topsy-turvy—shut the cat in the china-closet—fastened the house-dog to the gate-bell—and then was discovered ranting as Belvidera, with his clumsy person thrust into a new dress that had just been sent home for his sister. 'Tilda screamed and scolded, the mother begged and prayed—but the mischievous spirit of this domestic Caliban was not properly quelled till Twigg senior had ten times turned him out of the business, twenty times cut him off with a shilling, and, at last, given him a sound cuffing with his own fatherly hands.

It seemed impossible that the festive preparation could be completed by the given day; but the time came, and every thing was in order. As the cub had predicted, the governor had rolled a great many entertainments into one. In the centre of the lawn stood a large marquee, containing an ample cold collation, which made a very showy appearance, the principal dishes being kept cold by the new massive silver covers, each surmounted by the family emblem, a bee, big enough for a cockchafer. Above this pavilion waved, or rather should have waved, a broad silken banner, that had often fluttered and flaunted in the procession of the Worshipful Company of Ironmongers, but now, for want of wind, hung down as motion-

less as a piece of hardware. In a line with the marquee was a target for archery, so posted, that whoever missed the butt would have a fair chance of hitting the tent; whilst, for the accommodation of anglers, the margin of the large fish-pond was furnished with sundry elbow-chairs, wherein the sedentary angler might enjoy "the contemplative man's recreation," in the immediate vicinity of a country dance and a pandean band, in those days as fashionable a band as Weippart's or Colinet's at the present time. To accommodate the musicians, the octagon summer-house was fitted up as a temporary orchestra, in front of which stood a column of benches three deep; for Twigg, on personally inviting the pedagogue of Prospect House, and begging a whole holyday for the boys, had embraced that eligible opportunity of borrowing all the school forms. On the opposite side of the garden, the orange trees and exotics from the hothouse formed an avenue up to an arbor, christened, for the occasion, the Temple of Flora, and specially dedicated to the occupation of Miss Twigg, who undertook, in an appropriate fancy dress, to represent the Queen of Flowers. The Hermitage, in a secluded corner of the grounds, had its rustic table furnished with a huge portfolio of colored caricatures; and the paddock was devoted to trapball and cricket, the wicket for the latter game being considerately pitched, so that a barn on one side, and a haystack on the other, would materially assist the fieldsmen in stopping the ball. A whimsical feature remains to be mentioned. In anticipation of syllabub, Daisy, a polled Alderney, was tethered at a corner of the lawn, a stone Cupid seeming ludicrously to keep watch over her, in the capacity of a cowboy.

Such were the festive arrangements over which Twigg glanced with a satisfaction that made him frequently wash his hands without water or soap, while he mentally contrasted the gay scene before him with the humble prospects of his youth. He was dressed in a full court suit of plum color, in which, as Sheriff, he had gone up with an address to the King; his partner, with her *embonpoint* and her pink satin, looked extremely like that hearty and substantial flower, a full-blown cabbage-rose; while 'Tilda, in apple-green silk, festooned with artificial flowers, and her hair wreathed with real ones, appeared actually, as he expressed it, "a cut above human nature."

At the first encounter of husband and wife in their full plumage, she saluted him with a very profound courtesy, which he returned by an elaborate bow, as if in joint rehearsal of the ceremonies to come, and then they mutually congratulated each other on the propitious weather, for the sky was calm and cloudless, though it was rather hot for the season; indeed, as Twigg said, he should have thought it "very hard if a man of his property could not have a fine day for a fete."

One thing puzzled the worthy pair. Few of the neighboring gentry had accepted their invitation, though the Hive was so handy, and they had carriages of their own; whereas the metropolitan families who had been asked, came almost to a fraction, notwithstanding the distance was considerable, and many had to hire vehicles. It was singular, besides, that those who had the farthest to travel arrived first; guests from Bishopsgate, Ludgate, and Cripplegate, came in, and had successively made the tour of the house and grounds before a single soul was announced who belonged to the vicinity. However, the interval was a grateful one, for it allowed the master and mistress of the Hive to feel really "at home" with their former connections, and to indulge in the luxury of civic recollections, unrepressed by the presence of their more aristocratic acquaintance. Mrs. Twigg exhibited to her female friends her drawing-room, bed-rooms, store-room, kitchen, wash-house, brewhouse, and her unprofitable dairy; meanwhile Twigg paraded his old cronies through his dining-room, billiard-room, study, and stables, or trotted them round the grounds, pointing out peeps and prospects, and then rushing back to act as showman to fresh batches, who were successively ushered into the garden by Pompey, his black face opening from ear to ear, like a personification of Coalman's Broad Grins. The coachman, in topboots, assisted the footman; and the gardener, a sort of Jerry Blossom, fancy-dressed in a straw-hat, pea-green coat, skyblue hose, and parsley-and-butter waistcoat, trotted after his master, to give the proper names of the flowers and shrubs, for the proprietor scarcely knew a peony from a pink.

At one o'clock all the company had arrived, excepting the Tyrrels and the Riverses; many of the younger guests coming in fancy dresses, more or less tasteful; there were Swiss, Turkish, and Grecian maids; nuns, Dianas, nymphs, Spanish Dons, troubadours, monks, knights, a shepherd, and no less than three shepherdesses, without a sheep. The air was now become oppressively sultry; but Twigg suffered little from the weather, in comparison with his hot and cold fits of nervousness and anxiety, originating in other causes than the mere novelty of his situation. First, he had to endure a long complimentary oration from Doctor Bellamy, an appropriate answer to which would have cost the hearer more trouble than a speech in common council; then he had to meet the Squire for the first time since smashing his decanters;—the pedagogue from Prospect House was perpetually addressing him with Latin quotations; and he was especially puzzled by the presence of the Rev. Dr. Cobb,—for archery and cricket were sports for laymen, and he could think of no clerical amusement, except inviting the worthy vicar every ten minutes to eat or drink. The occasional absences of his son kept him, besides, in an intermitting fever, for he judged rightly, that the cub, when out of sight, was engaged in mischief; above all, he could not help noticing that a damp hung over the spirits of the whole company, which he vainly tried to dissipate. The town party and the country party refused to amalgamate, and took opposite sides of the garden, like Whigs and Tories; nay, the very sexes seemed to antipathize, and the young ladies planted themselves in clumps on one part of the lawn, while the young gentlemen formed groups elsewhere. Possibly, like the guests at the feast after the manner of the ancients, as recorded in Peregrine Pickle, each individual awaited the example of his neighbor how he was to behave or enjoy himself at so unusual an entertainment; perhaps mirth was depressed by the earnest injunction to be merry of the host and hostess, who did not know that to bid a wit "to be funny," is to desire him to be dull. As Twigg trotted to and fro with the activity and volubility of a flying pieman, he indulged in such patter as the following:—

"My dear Miss Tipper, I declare, as blooming as ever—glad to see you—take an ice—Mrs. Crowder, have you been round the grounds?—Rev. Dr. Cobb, a glass of wine—Pray make free, gentlemen—Liberty Hall, you know—Matilda, Miss Dobbs would like to see Flora's Temple—'Tilda looks well, don't she?—Mr. Deputy, there'll be a collation at four in the tent; but take a snack beforehand—plenty in the dining-room—come, young folks, be merry, be merry—what are you all for?—there's bow and arrows, and cricket and fishing, and dancing on the green, and music—Mrs. Tilby, I know you're fond of vocals—run, Pompey, and desire Mr. Hopkinson for the favor of a song—my dear, do keep an eye on John, he's drunk already, d——n him—Mr. Sparks, a glass of wine—the same with you, Mr. Dowson—here, this way into the green-house—come, hob-a-nob—a pretty scene, isn't it, Sparks, my old boy—and all my own property—Mr. Dowson, I can't help remembering old times; but many's the time Sparks and me has clubbed our shillings together for a treat at Bagnigge Wells. A great change though, say you, from that to this. I little thought when I wrote T. Twigg with a watering-tin, on a dusty pavement, that I should be signing it some day to cheques for thousands. I don't care who knows it, but I wasn't always the warm man I am to-day. Mr. Squire, pray step in—a glass of wine—glad to see you, Mr. Squire—break as much as you please, and I won't say any thing; we shall only be quits—now for a look about again—where the devil is T., junior?—Mr. Danvers, go to my daughter's bower, she'll present you with a bouquet—Dr. Bellamy, a glass of wine—Miss Trimmer, I know you like solitude; and that's the way to the Hermitage. Don't be alarmed at the cow, she's only flapping off the flies—Dr. Cobb, there's lunch in the dining-room—Mr. Cottrel, do go and divide those young ladies—beaux, beaux, what are you about?—come, choose partners, don't let the band play for nothing—Mr. Crump, a glass of wine—"

Such was the style of Twigg's exhortations; who, unlike other lecturers, endeavored to enforce his precepts by practice. He made a dozen ineffectual offers with the trap-bat at the ball, bobbed a fishing line up and down in the fish-pond, seized Mrs. Deputy Dobbs, and cut a brief caper with her on the grass plat, and finally, fitting an arrow to a bow, the shaft escaped from his fingers, and passed through Mrs. Tipper's turban, where it lodged, like a skewer *a la Grecque.* Such a commencement made every one adverse to archery, and particularly as Mrs. Twigg requested that before shooting any more arrows, they would let her put corks on all the points. As to angling, it seemed universally agreed, that on such a day no fish would take a bait; and with regard to dancing, Twigg's tarantula did not bite any more than the fish, whilst the trap-ball and the cricket-ball were as much out of favor as the ball on the lawn. Music itself seemed for once to have lost its charms, and the most popular of Mr. Hopkinson's songs attracted no auditor but Dr. Bellamy, who sat gravely bowing time, and waving his hand in accompaniment of the long, elaborate, rambling cadences then in fashion, and which might aptly be compared to the extraneous flourishes so much in vogue at the same period, when the pen went curveting off from plain pot-hooks and hangers into ornamental swans, ships, dragoons, eagles, and fierce faces in flowing wigs. Indeed, from the evolutions of Old Formality's right hand and fore-finger, their sweeps, and wavings, and circumgyrations, and occasional rapid spinnings, a deaf man would certainly have thought that he was meditating and practising some such caligraphic devices on the empty air.

At last Massa, Baronet Tyrrel was announced by the obsequious Pompey, and the jovial Sir Mark immediately appeared, with his family, including his daughter elect, Grace Rivers, the avocations of the Justice not allowing him to be present so early. The Baronet, delivered from gout, was in excellent health and spirits; Mrs. Hamilton seemed unusually cheerful; Raby and Grace were of course happy in each other's society; and even Ringwood and St. Kitts appeared either to have forgotten their old feud, or to have agreed on an armistice for the day. The host and hostess were loud and eager in their welcome and salutations.

"Oh, Sir Mark Tyrrel, Baronet," exclaimed Mrs. Twigg, in a tone of reproach, "how could you be so behind time? You promised to enjoy a long day."

"To be sure, madam," answered Sir Mark, "to judge by the field, I am rather late at the meet; but no matter—a short burst may be a merry one; and as yet, from all I see, I have lost little sport."

"Sir Mark Tyrrel, Baronet, a glass of wine?" said Mr. Twigg. "A votary of Diana," lisped Miss Twigg, "must be a friend to Flora,—may I offer a bouquet?"

"I shall be proud and happy," returned the gallant Sir Mark, with a bow that belonged to the Hunt Balls; but in stepping hastily forward to receive the nosegay, he unluckily set his right foot with some emphasis on the forepaw of a little Blenheim spaniel that was careering round Flora's green sandals. The poor brute immediately set up a dismal howl, and the Goddess, divesting her hands with little ceremony of the proffered bouquet, caught up the curly favorite, and began to fondle it in her arms.

"D——n the dog!" exclaimed Twigg, with his usual abruptness; "chuck him down again, and give Sir Mark Tyrrel, Baronet, his bow-pot."

"I am really ashamed of her, sir," said the mother, stooping and presenting the flowers herself; "but the little animal's a great darling, a real Marlbro', and a present from Mr. Ringwood."

The Baronet winced at the information, and could have kicked the dog back to Blenheim with all his heart; while Ringwood, Raby, and the Creole exchanged looks of vexation with each other, which gradually altered into smiles, and at last they all laughed in concert. There's a story current on the turf, of a certain jockey who very profitably disposed of three several whips, to as many gentlemen, as the identical whip with which he had won the Derby; and the keeper, or under-keeper of Blenheim had practised a similar imposition on our three collegians, by selling to each of them the only spaniel of that celebrated breed that "was not to be had for love or money." However, each prudently kept the secret. Twigg took the Baronet into the green-house for a glass of wine; Mrs. Twigg invited Mrs. Hamilton to take a peep at the preparations in the marquee, and Matilda led Grace to her temple.

* * * * * *

During this interlude the dulness of the rest of the company had rather increased, and the gaudy flag, that still drooped motionless upon its staff, seemed a proper emblem of their listless and inanimate condition. They stood about the grounds in groups, idle, weary, and dreary, and seemed by common consent to have adopted the line of conduct of the Hon. Mr. Danvers, a sort of exclusive of those days, who, in answer to every proposition of amusement, lisped languidly, "that he preferred to look on."

"It's very odd a man of my property can't have a merry party," thought Twigg, as he looked round on his grand to-do, and saw the festive scene with a visible damp over it, like a wet night at Vauxhall. In the bitterness of his heart he sidled up to Mrs. Twigg, who was standing near the marquee, and said to her, in a low tone, "Our friends, d——n them, are as dull as ditch-water. What the devil can we do with them?"

"Nine, ten, eleven," said Mrs. Twigg, with an abstracted look, and a little nod of her head at each number.

"What the —— is running in your fool's head, madam?" said the master of the Hive.

"Hush;—fourteen, fifteen, sixteen, seventeen," continued Mrs. Twigg, with the action of a Mandarin. "Drat that Pompey; I know there's more heads than plates." And she rushed off to scold the oblivious black. The poor African, indeed, during the last half hour, had fully entitled himself to receive what Twigg, junior, would have called a regular good wigging.

A breath of air displaying for the first time the Ironmongers' banner, it was discovered that the obtuse negro had hoisted it reversed, with all the armorial bearings of that Worshipful Company standing on their heads; and in absurdly attempting to rectify this blunder, by swarming up the staff, down came Pompey, pole, flag, and all, on the dignified head of the Hon. Mr. Danvers, who was indulging his preference for looking on. His next exploit was in bowing and backing to make way for Mr. Justice Rivers, whereby he got a fair roll and tumble over Miss Bower, one of the shepherdesses, who was sitting very pastorally on the grass; and by-and-by, recollecting some neglected previous order, he ran off headlong to execute it, popping down a trayful of ices to thaw and dissolve themselves into a dew, under the broiling sun. A long hundred of such little enormities were committed by the wrong-headed Hottentot; but only imagine the amazement of his mistress, when she saw him gravely conveying a reinforcement of cake and wine to the green-house in a common handbarrow;—and conceive her still greater horror when he came back on the broad grin, with the same vehicle containing the helpless, portly body of the coachman as drunk as the celebrated sow of David. The only possible thing that could be urged in favor of the sot, was, that he was not cross in his cups, for during his progress he persisted in singing a jolly song, quite as broad as it was long, with all the voice that he had left.

"I shall faint away! I shall go wild! I shall die on the spot!" exclaimed the distressed mistress of the Hive. "I wonder where Mr. T. is? That Pompey is enough to—has any body seen Mr. T.? It is really cruel,—what can a woman do with a tipsy man? Do run about, Peter, and look for your master,—Mr. T.! Mr. T.! Mr. T.!"

But no one responded to the invocation, although the whole grounds resounded, gradually, with an universal call for Mr. Twigg. The unhappy lady was in despair—she feared she knew not what. When she last saw him, he had been worked up

by successive mistakes and accidents to an awful pitch of nervous excitement, and she did not feel sure that he had not actually run away in a paroxysm of disgust and horror, leaving her, like Lady Macbeth, to huddle up the banquet as she might. At last a popping sound attracted her to the tent, and there she found the wished-for personage, cursing and swearing in a whisper, and stopping with each thumb a bottle of champagne, which had suffered so from the hot weather, that the fixed air had determined on visiting the fresh.

"Oh, Mr. T., what would you think!"—began the poor hostess, but he cut her short; and the following dialogue ensued:—

"None of your clack, madam; but stop those two bottles"—and he pointed to a couple of long-necked fizzlers; "d——n it, madam, stop 'em tight,—you're making them squirt in my face. There you go agin! Where's Pompey,—where's Peter,—where's John,—what the devil's the use of servants, if they're away when you want 'em—curse the champagne!—Here's a pretty situation for a man of my property!"

"My dear, do only have a little patience—"

"Patience be hanged! I've been standing so, madam, this half hour—till I've got a cramp in both thumbs. I told that rascal, John, never to quit the tent, and you, madam, you,—with your confounded she-gossips—why didn't you come sooner? I'll tell you what—if ever I have a fete again—is any body happy—is any body lively—will any body shoot at the target—or dance on the lawn—or play cricket? No, says you, it's a failure, a regular failure; and as for pleasure, there an't a farthing in the pound!"

The colloquy would doubtless have proceeded much further, but for a succession of female shrieks which arose from all quarters at once, whereat leaving the champagne to take care of itself, the perplexed pair rushed out, with palpitating hearts, to inquire into the nature of this new catastrophe. And truly they beheld a sight to London-bred spectators peculiarly appalling. The human groups that occupied the lawn had disappeared, and in lieu of them, the terrific Alderney was racing about "like mad," with her head up, and her tail bolt upright, and as stiff as a kitchen poker. Driven to wildness by three hours' exposure to a hot sun, and the incessant tormenting stings of insects, poor Daisy had broken her tether, or more probably it had been cut for her by young Twigg, and she immediately began that headlong gallop which cows are apt to take when goaded by the breeze-fly. After running three heats round the lawn, she naturally made for the shades of the shrubbery, but being headed back by the gentlemen, she paused, and looked around for an instant, as if to consider; and then, making up her mind, she suddenly dashed off for the only place of shelter, and rushed headlong into the marquee. An awful crash ensued. Plate clattered, glass jingled, and timber banged! The canvas bulged fearfully on one side, and the moorings giving way, out rushed Daisy, and down fell the tent like a clap-net, decidedly catching the cold fowls, ducks, and pigeons that were under it.

A loud cry of a mixed character arose from the spectators of this lamentable catastrophe. The ladies screamed from terror; the expectant citizens bellowed from hungry disappointment, and some of the younger gentlemen, amateurs of fun, gave a shout that sounded like a huzza!

"She's upset the tables!" shrieked Mrs. Twigg, with her arms working aloft like a telegraph's.

"And there goes every delicacy of the season," exclaimed Mr. Twigg, gazing with the stupefied aspect of an underwriter at a total wreck.

"The new covers ——" groaned the lady.

"All battered and bruised—nothing but dents and bumps," added her husband, in the same tone.

"And the beautiful cut glass—not a bit of it blowed," said the hostess, beginning to whimper.

"Smash'd—shivered to atoms—curse her soul!" cried the host, with the fervor of a believer in the metempsychossi.

"My poor damask table-cloths!" moaned the mistress, with some indications of her old fainting fits.

"Hamstring her!—kill her! knock her on the head!" shouted Twigg, dancing on his tiptoes with excitement, and unconsciously imitating the action of a slaughter-man.

After standing a minute at gaze, the cow had recommenced her career about the lawn, causing a general panic, and nature's first law, the *sauve qui peut* principle, triumphed over all others. Guided by this instinct, Twigg rushed into the green-house, and resolutely shut the door against the cow, as well as against Mrs. Twigg, who had made for the same place of refuge. The corpulent Mr. Deputy Dobbs, by hard running, contrived to place the breadth of the fish-pond between himself and the "infuriated animal,"—the orchestra box, *alias* the octagon summer-house, was crowded with company,—the hermitage, oh, shade of Zimmerman, what a sacrilege! was a perfect squeeze; and Flora had clambered up the lattice-work of her temple, and sat shrieking on the top. All the guests were in safety but one; and every one trembled at the probable fate of Mrs. Tipper, who had been sitting on the end of a form, and was not so alert in jumping up from it as her juniors. The bench, on a mechanical principle well understood, immediately reared up and threw it's rider; and before the unfortunate lady, as she afterwards averred, "could feel her feet, she saw the rampaging cretur come tearing at her, with the black man arter her, making her ten times worser."

The scared Alderney, however, in choosing her course, had no design against Mrs. Tipper, but merely inclined to enjoy a cold bath in the fish-pond, into which she accordingly plunged, accompanied by Pompey, who had just succeeded, after many attempts, in catching hold of the remnant of her tether. In they went—souse!—saluted by a chorus of laughter from the orchestra; and there, floundering up to their necks in water, the black animal and the red one hauled each other about, and splashed and dashed as if an aquatic parody of the combat of Guy of Warwick and Dun Cow had been part of the concerted entertainments.

"Confound the fellow—she'll be drown'd!" cried an angry voice from the greenhouse.

"His livery's dish'd and done for," responded a melancholy voice from the hothouse.

"Oh! my gold-fish will be killed!" cried a shrill tone from the top of the temple; while a vaccine bellow resounded from the pond, intermingled with a volley of African jargon, of which only one sentence could be caught, and it intimated a new disaster.

"O ki! him broke all de fishin'-rods and de lines!"

As Pompey spoke, he exchanged his grasp of the halter, which had become slippery, for a clutch at the tail; an indignity the animal no sooner felt, than with a desperate effort she scrambled out of the pond, and dashed off at full gallop towards the paddock, making a dreadful gap by the way in Flora's display of exotics, whether in tubs or pots. As for Pompey, through not timing his leap with the cow's, he was left sprawling under the rails of the paddock; meanwhile the persecuted Alderney finally took shelter under the shade of the hay-stack.

And now the company, with due caution, came abroad again from roof and shed and leafy recess, like urchins after a shower. Twigg sallied from the green-house, and his helpmate at the same moment issued from the forcing-house, with a face looking perfectly ripe; the octagon summer-house sent forth a congregation like that of a dwarf chapel,—the hermitage was left to the joint tenancy of Raby and Grace, and Flora descended from the roof of her temple, being tenderly assisted in her descent by the enamored Ringwood. By common consent the company all hastened towards the fallen marquee, and clearing away the canvas, they beheld the turf variously strewed,—exactly as if Time,—that Edax Rerum,—had made a miscellaneous meal which had disagreed with him.

In the middle the tables lay on their sides with their legs stretched out like dead horses, and the bruised covers, and knives and forks, were scattered about like battered helmets and masterless weapons after a skirmish of cavalry. The tablecloths were dappled with the purple blood of the grape; and the eatables and drinkables scattered, battered, spattered, shattered, and tattered, all round about, presented a spectacle equally whimsical and piteous. The following are but a few of the objects which the Hon. Mr. Danvers beheld when he looked on.

Item. A huge cold round of beef, surrounded by the froth of a trifle, like an island "begirt with foam," with a pigeon perched on the top instead of a cormorant.

Item. A large lobster, roosting on the branch of an epergne.

Item. A roast duck, seemingly fast asleep, with a cream cheese for a mattress and a cucumber for a bolster.

Item. Brawn, in an ample writing-paper ruff, well sprinkled with claret, reminding the spectator irresistibly of the neck of King Charles the First.

Item. Tipsy-cake, appropriately under the table.

Item. A puddle of cold punch, and a neat's tongue apparently licking it up.

Item. A noble ham, brilliantly powdered with broken glass.

Item. A boiled rabbit smothered in custard.

Item. A lump of *blanc*-mange dyed *purple*.

Item. A shoal of prawns in an ocean of lemonade.

Item. A very fine boiled turkey in a harlequin suit of lobster salad.

Item. A ship of sugar-candy, high and dry on a fillet of veal.

Item. A "hedge-hog" sitting on a "hen's nest." Vide Mrs. Glasse's Cookery for the confectionary devices.

Item. "A floating island," as a new constellation, amongst "the moon and stars in jelly." See Mrs. Glasse again.

Item. A large pound crab, sitting upright against a table, and nursing a chicken between its claws.

Item. A collard eel, uncoiled, and threatening like a boa constrictor to swallow a fowl.

Item. A Madeira pond, in a dish cover, with a duck drowned in it.

Item. A pig's face, with a snout smelling at a bunch of artificial flowers.

Item. A leg of lamb, as yellow as the leg of a boy at Christ's hospital, thanks to the mustard-pot.

Item. A tongue all over "flummery."

Item. An immense Macedoine of all the fruits of the season, jumbled together in jam, jelly, and cream.

Such were some of the objects, interspersed with Serpentines of sherry, Peerless Pools of port, and New Rivers of Madeira, that saluted the eyes of the expectant guests, thus untimely reduced to the feast of reason and the flow of soul. The unfortunate hostess appeared ready to drop on the spot; but, according to Major Oakley's theory, she refrained from fainting among so many broken bottles; whilst Twigg stood with the very aspect and attitude of a baker's journeyman we once saw, just after a stumble which had pitched five rice puddings, two custard ditto, a gooseberry pie, a currant tart, and two dozen cheesecakes into a reservoir of M'Adams's broth from flints. The swamping of his collation on the ait in the Thames was a retail concern to this enormous wreck. His eyebrows worked, his eyes rolled, his lips quivered with inaudible curses, and his fingers twitched, as if eager to be doing something, but waiting for

orders from the will; he was divided, in truth, between a dozen rival impulses, suggesting to him, all at once, to murder the cow, to thrash Pompey, to quarrel with his wife, to disinherit his son, to discharge the cooks, to order everybody's carriage, to send Matilda back to boarding-school, to go to bed suddenly ill, to run away God knew where, to hang himself on the pear-tree, to drown himself in the fish-pond, to burn the marquee, to turn Infidel and deny a Providence, to get dead drunk.

In this strain the indignant Ex-Sheriff was eloquently proceeding, when suddenly, a drop of rain, as big as a bullet, fell splashing on the bald head of the deputy; and then came a flash of lightning so vivid, and a clap of thunder so astounding, that in his confusion the host himself led a retreat into the house, followed by the company en masse. Music was prepared, and the carpet was taken up. Matilda was sulky, and wouldn't sing, and Mr. Hopkinson couldn't, through a cold caught in the octagon summer-house. Mrs. Filby was grumpy about her satin gown, observing, with an angry glance at Miss Sparkes, that if people must jump at claps of thunder, they needn't jump their jellies into other people's laps; and the pedagogue of Prospect House was weary of uttering classical jokes at which nobody laughed. The Honorable Mr. Danvers began to tire of looking on. Deputy Dobbs was disappointed of his accustomed speechifying, for in spite of all his hints, Twigg set his face against toasts, not liking probably to bid gentlemen charge their glasses who had so few to charge. The rest of the Londoners began to calculate the distance of the metropolis. Doctor Cobb had been huffed by Mr. Figgins in a dispute about politics; Squire Ned, for the last half hour, had been making up his mind to steal away; and even the Crumpe family, who had come early on purpose to enjoy a long day, began to agree in their own minds, that it was the longest they had ever known. In short, every body found some good reason for going, and successively they took leave, Doctor Bellamy being the last of the guests that departed, whereby he had the pleasure, and to Old Formality it *was* a pleasure, of bowing them all out.

As the last pair of wheels rattled away, Mrs. Twigg dropped into her chair, and began to relieve her feelings by having what she called a good cry. At the same moment, Twigg threw off his coat, and seizing plate, knife, and fork, began eating like a glutton for a wager, occasionally washing down ham, beef, veal, chicken, jelly, tarts, and fruit, with great gulps of brandy and water. As for Matilda, she threw herself on a sofa, as flat, inanimate, and faded, as the Flora of a Hortus Siccus.

Thus ended a fête especially devoted to enjoyment, but where the spirit of the work did not answer to its dedication. Premeditated pleasures frequently terminate in disappointment; for mirth and glee do not always care to accept a ceremonious invitation; they are friendly familiar creatures that love to drop in. To use a mercantile metaphor, bills at long dates upon happiness are apt to be dishonored when due.

On the morrow, John the coachman found himself out of a situation, whilst Twigg, junior, was provided with a place on the roof of the Highflyer on its road to the metropolis. Pompey was threatened also with dismissal, but as black servants are not as plenty as blackberries, the discharge was not made out; whereas, the gardener, shocked at the havoc among his exotics, and annoyed by the nickname of Jerry Blossom, which his fancy dress had entailed on him, gave warning of his own accord. The cook received a message from her mistress, who was kept in bed by a nervous complaint, that she might suit herself as soon as she pleased; the dairy-maid received a significant hint from the same source, that she must butter the family better if she wished to stay in it; and to Dolly's deep regret, her favorite Daisy, with a bad character for gentleness, was driven off to the nearest market to be sold peremptorily for what she would fetch.

MY AUNT HONOR.

BY AGNES STRICKLAND.

My Aunt Honor was for ten years the reigning beauty of her native village; and even at the end of that period, though the opening charms of early youth had gradually ripened into the more dignified graces of womanhood, and she was a girl no longer, no one could say that the change had caused that diminution in her personal attractions which could afford just reason for the loss of the title. It was but the seasonable expansion of the bud into the flower, and in the eye of every person of taste and sense, my Aunt Honor was a beauty still. How, indeed, could she be otherwise, with her graceful contour of form and face, her noble line of features, brilliant yet reflective; eyes of rich dark hazel; serene brow; coral lips; and clear brunette complexion? But unluckily for poor Aunt Honor, she had two younger sisters in their teens, who, as soon as they were emancipated from boarding-school, began to consider the expediency of making conquests; and finding that very few gentlemen paid much attention to them when their eldest sister was present, they took the trouble of making every one acquainted with the precise date of her baptismal register; after which kind disclosure Aunt Honor lost the title of a beauty, and acquired that of an old maid.

This change of style was, I should apprehend, rather a trial of patience, in the first instance; for Aunt Honor, though she had never exhibited the slightest degree of vanity or presumption, on account of the general admiration she had excited, was nevertheless pleased with the homage paid to her charms—and it was hard to feel herself suddenly deprived of all her flattering privileges at once, and that without the reasonable warning which the faithful mirror gives of the first indications of the sure, yet silent, progress of decay in those who are not so wholly blinded by self-conceit as to be insensible to its ravages. Time had dealt so gently with Aunt Honor, that when the account of his takings and leavings were reckoned, it scarcely appeared that she stood at discount—I am inclined to think the balance was in her favor; but then I had so much reason to love her, that perhaps I was not an impartial judge. How, indeed, could I forget her tender cherishing care of me in my bereaved and sickly childhood, when by the early death of my parents, my brother and myself being left in a comparative state of destitution, were thrown upon the compassion of my mother's family. This was regarded in the light of a serious misfortune by my two young aunts, Caroline and Maria, who might have instructed gray hairs in lessons of worldly wisdom, and both possessed what is vulgarly termed a sharp eye for the main chance. They calculated with a clearness and accuracy truly wonderful at their age—for the elder of the twain had not completed her eighteenth year at the period of which I speak—the expense of our board, clothes, education, and the general diminution of their comforts and chances of forming advantageous matrimonial settlements, which would be occasioned by our residence with my grandfather; and they did not of course forget the great probability of his providing for us in his will, which would naturally take something from their portions of the inheritance. Under the influence of such feelings, they not only used every means in their power to prevent our reception in their father's house, but after we were, through the influence of Aunt Honor, admitted, they treated us with a degree of unkindness that amounted to actual persecution. All our little faults were repeated by them in the most exaggerated terms to my grandmother; and, but for the affectionate protection which Aunt Honor extended towards us, we should have experienced much harshness in consequence of these misrepresentations, but her tenderness made up to us for all deficiencies in other quarters. She was to us in the place of mother, father, and every other tie of kindred: she was by turns our nurse, preceptress, and playfellow. Our love, our duty, our respect, were all lavished on her; she was our kind aunt, our dear aunt, our good aunt; and well do I remember being tied to the leg of the table for a whole morning by my grandmother, as a punishment for exclaiming, in the fulness of my heart, that "she was my pretty aunt, and aunts Maria and Caroline were my two old, ugly, cross aunts." The rage of the injured juniors, by twelve years, may be imagined at this rash proof of my devotion to their eldest sister; nor could Aunt Honor, with any degree of prudence or propriety, interfere to avert the castigation which my young aunts bestowed upon me in the shape of boxes on the ears, too numerous to record, in addition to the penance of being confined to the leg of grandmamma's work-table. Considering me, however, in the light of a martyr in her cause, she made me more than ample amends in private for all I had suffered, and loaded me with the most endearing caresses, while she reproved me for having said such improper things to aunts Caroline and Maria.

My grandmother, who, for the misfortune of her husband, was married long before she knew how to conduct a house with any degree of propriety, was one of those foolish women who occasionally boast of their own early nuptials to their unmarried daughters, with ill-timed remarks on their comparative tardiness in forming suitable matrimonial alliances, which has too often piqued the mortified maidens into contracting most unsuitable matches, that they might avoid the reproach of celibacy: the fruitful source from which so many ill assorted and calamitous marriages have proceeded.

My grandfather, who had formed a very just estimate of his eldest daughter's merits, was wont to observe, in reply to his wife's constant remark, "that Honor would never marry now, poor girl!" "Those women who were most eminently qualified to prove excellent wives, mothers, and mistresses of families, and who were, metaphorically speaking, the twenty thousand pound prizes in the matrimonial lottery, were generally left in the wheel, while the blanks and tickets of trifling value were drawn over and over again; but, for his part, he knew so much of men, that he would recommend all his daughters to remain single." Notwithstanding this declaration of the old gentleman, it was evident enough that he was inwardly chagrined at the unaccountable circumstance of his lovely Honor, his sensible, clever girl, the pride of his eyes, and the darling of his heart, being unmarried at thirty years of age; or as her younger sisters, in the insolence of their only attraction, youth, called her an "old maid."

No! that he would not allow—"thirty"—she was in the prime of her days still, and, in his eyes, as handsome as ever;—certainly wiser and better than when she was in her teens—far more likely to be the choice of a sensible man than either of her younger sisters—and he would bet a hundred guineas that she would be married now before either of them.

"Certainly, papa, if wedlock goes by turn, she ought to be," would Aunt Caroline rejoin, "for you know she is twelve years older than I."

"She might, however, make haste, if she thinks of getting married now," would Aunt Maria add, with a silly giggle, "for she is getting quite venerable; and, for my part, if I do not marry by the time I am one-and-twenty, I am sure I shall consider myself an old maid."

"There will be some wisdom in accustoming yourself to the title betimes, since it may very probably be your portion through life, young lady," retorted my grandfather, on one occasion: "at any rate, no man of taste and sense will be likely to prefer you to such a woman as your sister Honor." But here my grandmother, who always made a sort of party with her younger daughters, interposed, and said, "It really was quite absurd that Honor should put herself so forward in engaging the attention of gentlemen, who might possibly fix their regards on her younger sisters, provided she would but keep a little in the background, and remember that her day was gone by. She had for some unaccountable reason permitted several opportunities of forming a good establishment to slip by, and now she ought to allow her sisters a fair chance in their turn, and submit to her own destiny with a good grace."

And Aunt Honor did submit, not only with a good grace, but with a temper perfectly angelical, not only to a destiny of blighted hopes and wasted feelings, but to all invidious taunts with which it was imbittered by those to whom she had been ever ready to extend her generous kindness, whenever it was required. She never hesitated to sacrifice her own pleasure, if she thought it would be conducive to theirs. Her purse, her ornaments, her talents, and industry, were at their service on all occasions, and though it was far from pleasing to her to be either artfully manœuvred, or rudely thrust out of her place by the juvenile pair, who had formed an alliance offensive and defensive against her, yet she did not attempt to contest with them the usurped rights and privileges of eldership, or to struggle for the ascendency she had hitherto enjoyed in the family; nor did she boast of her youthful charms, or the multiplicity of her former conquests, in reply to the insolence with which she was daily annoyed. She was too dignified to appear to regard these things; yet doubtless she felt them, and felt them keenly; her heart knew its own bitterness, yet suffered it not to overflow in angry, useless retorts. She kept the quiet even tenor of her way, under all provocations, with silent magnanimity; and sought in the active performance of her duties, a resource from vain regrets and fruitless repinings; and if a sigh did occasionally escape her, it was smothered ere fully breathed.

The village in which we resided was one of those dull, stagnating sort of places, in which years pass away without any visible change appearing to be effected. The inhabitants were few, and these, for the most part, beneath us in situation; for my grandfather was a man of family, though his fortune was inadequate to the expenses attendant on entering into that society with which alone he would have permitted his wife and daughters to mix. Latterly, however, my two younger aunts contrived to engage in a general round of expensive visiting with the surrounding gentry, without paying the slightest regard to his disapprobation. Their mother upheld them in this line of conduct, and had recourse to many painful expedients, in order to furnish them with the means of appearing like other young people, as she termed it, and we had all to suffer the pains and penalties of a stinted table in consequence. Aunt Honor was of course excluded from all these gay doings, and her allowance was very irregularly paid, and sometimes wholly diverted from its proper channel, to supply her younger sisters with ball-dresses, or to satisfy the clamorous milliner, who would not depart without the payment of at least a part of the bills my grandmother had imprudently permitted her selfish favorites to contract, when ready money to procure some indispensable piece of finery, to be worn at places of more than ordinary attraction, could not be obtained.

Our house, in former times so quiet and respectable, was now the resort of the thoughtless, the gay, and the extravagant. Our peace was broken by the domiciliary visits of duns, to get rid of whom, a system of falsehood, equivocation, and blandishment, was made use of, which rendered our family despicable in the eyes of servants, and mean even in our own. Aunt Honor reasoned, entreated, and represented the evil and moral injustice of these things in vain. Her mother told her "she was mistress of her own house, and would do as she thought proper," and her two sisters informed her, "that they had no ambition to become old maids like her, which would infallibly be the case if they were confined to the dull solitude which their father preserved, and she appeared inclined to enforce."

Aunt Honor represented, in reply, that they were not pursuing a course very likely to lead to the desired goal of the temple of Hymen; and received, in return, a retort of more than usual aggravation. She was accused of malice, of envy, and an unsisterly desire of depriving the youthful maidens of the pleasure belonging to their time of life; and worse than all, of the opportunity of becoming happy wives and useful members of society. Aunt Honor would have smiled at the folly of the latter inuendoes, had she not felt inclined to weep at their unkindness.

In the midst of one of these scenes, of now almost daily occurrence, the whole party received tickets of invitation to a ball, given by Sir Edward Grosvenor, in honor of having been chosen, after a contested election, as one of the representatives of his native county. Sir Edward Grosvenor, who had passed his youth in India, where he had greatly signalized himself under the banners of the Marquis of Hastings, had only recently returned to England, to take possession of his estates on the death of his elder brother without heir male. Nothing could exceed the exultation of my grandmother and her two youngest daughters, at the prospect of a flattering introduction into the house of so distinguished a character as their wealthy baronet neighbor, of whom fame reported noble things, and who was a very handsome man in the prime of life, not exceeding, as the date of his birth in the baronetage of England stated, his six-and thirtieth year.

Visions of a title, equipage, and wealth, floated over the brains of aunts Caroline and Maria, as their delighted eyes glanced over the tickets. There was but one drawback to these felicitous anticipations—the difficulty of procuring dresses suitable for such an occasion.

They looked in eager inquiry at their mother; she shook her head. "I cannot do any thing to forward your wishes," said she, "for reasons too obvious to you both:"—but after a pause she added, "Your sister Honor can assist you, if she pleases." They both turned to Honor with imploring glances. "In this instance it will not be in my power," observed Honor, gravely.

"You have only just received your quarterly allowance from your father," said her mother.

"I have already appropriated part of the sum to the purchase of a few necessaries for my orphan nephew and niece," replied she, "and the residue, which would be quite inadequate for your purpose, will be barely sufficient to supply me with a simple dress of book-muslin, with shoes and gloves requisite for this occasion."

"For this occasion!" echoed both her sisters in a breath; "surely you do not think of going to the ball?"

"Why not?" demanded Honor, calmly.

"You are so—"

"Old, you would say, Caroline," continued Aunt Honor coolly, finishing the sentence for her; "only, as you happen to want money of me to-day, you are rather more cautious of wounding my feelings than is usual with you."

"Well, but really, Honor, I do not see what good your going to a ball would do."—"None," interposed her mother; "and I thought you had given up these sort of things long ago."

"Is it not your intention to accept the ticket which Sir Edward Grosvenor has sent for you, mamma?" asked Honor.

"Of course it is; your sisters could not, with any degree of propriety, go without me."

"Then I shall do myself the pleasure of accompanying you," said Honor, quietly.

The elder sisters of Cinderella never said more insulting things to that far-famed heroine of fairy lore, to prevent her from trying her chance in fitting the glass slipper, than were uttered by Caroline and Maria to dear Aunt Honor from going to the ball. She listened to them with her usual mildness of temper, yet persevered in her resolution.

I think I never saw her look so beautiful as on that eventful evening, when attired in modest, simple elegance, she was led by my grandfather to the carriage, in spite of all opposition from the adverse parties. I, of course, was not included in the party; but I can readily imagine that the surprise and envy of the mortified sisters of Cinderella, on entering the room where the hitherto despised victim of their persecutions was dancing with her princely partner, did not exceed that of my juvenile aunts, when they beheld the hero of the night—the gallant and admired Sir Edward Grosvenor—greet old Honor, as they disparagingly styled their elder, with the deferential yet tender air of a lover; and passing over, not only themselves, but many others of the young, the fair, the highborn stars of the evening, and entreating to open the ball with her—a distinction which was modestly declined by her, with equal sweetness and propriety, on the plea that there were others of high rank present, who were, according to etiquette, better entitled to that honor.

"Honor!" exclaimed the gallant knight of the

shire, gently possessing himself of her unreluctant hand; "the honor, I trust, is mine; I have long," he added, in a whisper that was meant for no other ear than hers, "sighed to possess this honor, of which the cold considerations of rank and etiquette can never possess sufficient power to deprive me."

Can any one believe that Aunt Honor was fastidious enough to examine too critically the merits of the pun which a faithful lover, under such circumstances, ventured on her name?

There was not, perhaps, one lady in the room that would not have been proud of being the woman to whom Sir Edward Grosvenor addressed that whispered compliment; but there was none to whom it was so well due as to her whom he delighted to honor; for she was the love of his youth, who, for his sake, had faithfully endured years of expectation and delay, with no other assurance of his remembrance and constancy than that hope which keeps alive despair, and survives all the fading flowers of youthful affection—that fond reliance on his regard, which would not suffer her to imagine that he could be false or forgetful. Nor was the object of such devoted love undeserving of feelings like these. He too had had his sufferings: he had endured paternal wrath, expulsion from his home, years of exile, of poverty, and of suspense.

"But it is all over now," he whispered, as he dashed an intrusive tear from his sun-burned cheek. "I suffered for Honor! I fought for Honor! and the residue of my days will, I trust, be passed with Honor!"

It was a proud day for my grandfather, when he bestowed his beloved daughter on Sir Edward Grosvenor at the marriage altar; and he did not fail to take due credit to himself on the verification of his prediction. As for my aunts Caroline and Maria, I think I had better say nothing of their feelings on the occasion; but, for the warning of such of the juvenile readers of these pages who may feel inclined, in the thoughtless presumption of early youth, to brand older—and, perchance, fairer females than themselves—with the contemptuous epithet of old maids, I feel myself compelled to record the mortifying fact, that these two luckless sisters of my honored mother remain at this moment spinsters of forty and forty-two years standing, and have acted as bridesmaids to Lady Grosvenor's youngest daughter, without one opportunity having offered to either of them of changing their forlorn condition.

So far, however, from voluntarily assuming the name of old maids, if unmarried at one-and-twenty, as they engaged to do when, in the fulness of their self-conceit, they imagined such a circumstance out of the bounds of human possibility, neither of them will acknowledge the title at forty; on the contrary, they endeavor to conceal the ravages of time under the affectation and airs of excessive youthfulness.

Libellers.—Literary bravos, supported by illiterate cowards. If the receiver of stolen goods be worse than the thief, so must the purchaser of libels be more culpable than their author. As the peruser of a slanderous journal would write what he reads, had he the talent, so the actual maligner would become a malefactor, had he the opportunity and the courage. "He who stabs you in the dark, with a pen, would do the same with a pen-knife, were he equally safe from detection and the law." A libeller's mouth has been compared to that of a volcano—the lighter portions of what it vomits forth are dissipated by the winds, the heavier ones fall back into the throat whence they were disgorged. The aspersions of libellers may, perhaps, be better compared to fuller's earth, which, though it may seem to dirt you at first, only leaves you more pure and spotless, when it is rubbed off.—*Tin Trumpet.*

PICTORIAL HUMOR.

FROM "NEW READINGS OF OLD AUTHORS." BY — SEYMOUR.

Shakspere.

Poor *Tom's* a-cold.
King Lear. Act 4, Sc. 2.

Lamentings heard i' the air.
Macbeth. Act 2, Sc. 3.

How bravely thou becom'st thy bed, *fresh* lily!
Cymbeline. Act 2, Sc. 2.

You plead in vain. I have *no room* for pity left within me.
Tempest. Act 4, Sc. 2.

THE ENCHANTED NET.

BY FRANK E. SMEDLEY.

Could we only give credit to half we are told,
There were sundry strange monsters existing of old;
As evinced (on the *ex pede* Herculean plan,
Which from merely a footstep presumes the whole man)
By our *Savans* disturbing those very large bones,
Which have turned (for the rhyme's sake, perhaps) into stones,
And have chosen to wait a
Long while hid in *strata*,
While old Time has been dining on empires and thrones.
Old bones and dry bones,
Leg-bones and thigh-bones,
Bones of the vertebræ, bones of the tail,—
Very like, only more so, the bones of a whale;
Bones that were very long, bones that were very short
(They have never as yet found a real fossil merry-thought;
Perchance because mastodons, burly and big,
Considered all funny-bones quite *infra dig.*)
Skulls have they found in strange places imbedded,
Which, at least, prove their owners were very long-headed;
And other queer things,—which 'tis not my intention,
Lest I weary your patience, at present to mention,
As I think I can prove, without further apology,
What I said to be true, sans appeal to geology,
That there lived in the good old days gone by
Things unknown to our modern philosophy,
And a giant was then no more out of the way
Than a dwarf is now in the present day.

Sir Eppo of Epstein was young, brave, and fair;
Dark were the curls of his clustering hair,
Dark the moustache that o'ershadowed his lip,
And his glance was as keen as the sword at his hip;
Though the enemy's charge was like lightning's fierce shock,
His seat was as firm as the wave-beaten rock;
And woe to the foeman, whom pride or mischance
Opposed to the stroke of his conquering lance.
He carved at the board, and he danced in the hall,
And the ladies admired him, each one and all.
In a word, I should say, he appears to have been
As nice a young "ritter" as ever was seen.

He could not read nor write,
He could not spell his name,
Towards being a clerk, Sir Eppo, his (†) mark,
Was as near as he ever came.
He had felt no vexation
From multiplication;
Never puzzled was he
By the rule of three;
The practice he'd had
Did not drive him mad,
Because it all lay
Quite a different way.
The Ass's Bridge, that Bridge of Sighs.
Had (lucky dog!) ne'er met his eyes.
In a very few words he expressed his intention
Once for all to decline every Latin declension,
When persuaded to add, by the good Father Herman,
That most classical tongue to his own native German.
And no doubt he was right in
Point of fact, for a knight in
Those days was supposed to like nothing but fighting;
And one who had learned any language that is hard
Would have stood a good chance of being burned for a wizard.
Education being then never pushed to the verge ye
Now see it, was chiefly confined to the clergy.

'Twas a southerly wind and a cloudy sky,
For aught that I know to the contrary;
If it wasn't, it ought to have been proper*ly*,
As it's certain Sir Eppo, his feather bed scorning,
Thought that *something* proclaimed it a fine hunting morning;
So pronouncing his benison
O'er a cold haunch of venison,
He floored the best half, drank a gallon of beer,
And set out on the Taurus to chase the wild deer.

Sir Eppo he rode through the good greenwood,
And his bolts flew fast and free;
He knocked over a hare, and he passed the lair
(The tenant was out) of a grisly bear;
He started a wolf, and he got a snap shot
At a bounding roe, but he touched it not,
Which caused him to mutter a naughty word
In German, which luckily nobody heard,
For he said it right viciously;
And he struck his steed with his armèd heel,
As though horse-flesh were tougher than iron or steel,
Or any thing else that's unable to feel.

What is the sound that meets his ear?
Is it the plaint of some wounded deer?
Is it the wild-fowl's mournful cry,
Or the scream of yon eagle soaring high?
Or is it only the southern breeze
As it sighs through the boughs of the dark pine trees?
No, Sir Eppo, be sure 'tis not any of these:
And hark, again!
It comes more plain—
'Tis a woman's voice in grief or pain.

Like an arrow from the string,
Like a stone that leaves the sling,
Like a railroad-train with a queen inside,
With directors to poke and directors to guide,
Like the rush upon deck when a vessel is sinking,
Like (I vow I'm hard up for a simile) winking!
In less time than by name you Jack Robinson can call,
Sir Eppo dashed forward o'er hedge, ditch, and hollow,
In a steeple-chase style I'd be sorry to follow,

And found a young lady chained up by the ankle—
Yes, chained up in a cool and business-like way,
As if she'd been only the little dog Tray;
While, the more to secure any knight-errant's pity,
She was really and truly excessively pretty.

Here was a terrible state of things!
Down from his saddle Sir Eppo springs,
As lightly as if he were furnished with wings,
While every plate in his armor rings.
The words that he uttered were short and few,
But pretty much to the purpose too,
As sternly he asked, with lowering brow,
"Who's been and done it, and where is he now?"

'Twere long to tell
Each word that fell
From the coral lips of that demoiselle;
However, as far as I'm able to see,
The pith of the matter appeared to be
That a horrible giant, twelve feet high,
Having gazed on her charms with a covetous eye,
Had stormed their castle, murdered papa,
Behaved very rudely to poor dear mamma,
Walked off with the family jewels and plate,
And the tin and herself at a terrible rate;
Then by way of conclusion
To all this confusion,
Tied her up like a dog
To a nasty great log,
To induce her (the brute) to become Mrs. Gog;
That 'twas not the least use for Sir Eppo to try
To chop off his head, or to poke out his eye,
As he'd early in life done a bit of Achilles
(Which, far better than taking an "Old Parr's life-pill" is),
Had been dipped in the Styx, or some equally old stream,
And might now face unharmed a battalion of Coldstream.

But she'd thought of a scheme
Which did certainly seem
Very likely to pay—no mere vision or dream:—
It appears that the giant each day took a nap
For an hour (the wretch!) with his head in her lap:
Oh, she hated it so! but then what could she do?
Here she paused, and Sir Eppo remarked, "Very true;"
And that during this time one might pinch, punch, or shake him,
Or do just what one pleased, but that nothing could wake him,
While each horse and each man in the emperor's pay
Would not be sufficient to move him away,
Without magical aid, from the spot where he lay.
In an old oak chest, in an up-stairs room
Of poor papa's castle, was kept an heir-loom,
An enchanted net, made of iron links,
Which was brought from Palestine, she thinks,
By her great grandpapa, who had been a Crusader;
If she had but got that, she was sure it would aid her.
Sir Eppo, kind man,
Approves of the plan;
Says he'll do all she wishes as quick as he can;
Begs she won't fret if the time should seem long;
Snatches a kiss, which was "pleasant but wrong;"
Mounts, and taking a fence in good fox-hunting style,
Sets off for her family-seat on the Weil.

The sun went down,
The bright stars burned,
The morning came,
And the knight returned;
The net he spread
O'er the giant's bed,
While Eglantine, and Hare-bell blue,
And some nice green moss on the spot he threw;
Lest perchance the monster alarm should take,
And not choose to sleep from being too *wide awake.*
Hark to that sound!
The rocks around
Tremble—it shakes the very ground;
While Irmengard cries,
And tears stream from her eyes,—
A lady-like weakness we must not despise,
(And here, let me add, I have been much to blame,
As I long ago ought to have mentioned her name):
"Here he comes! now do hide yourself, dear Eppo, pray;
For *my* sake, I entreat you, keep out of his way."
Scarce had the knight
Time to get out of sight
Among some thick bushes, which covered him quite,
Ere the giant appeared. Oh! he was such a fright!
He was very square built, a good twelve feet in height,
And his waistcoat (three yards round the waist) seemed too tight;
While, to add even yet to all this singularity,
He had but one eye, and his whiskers were carroty.

What an anxious moment! Will he lie down?
Ah, how their hearts beat! he seems to frown,—
No, 'tis only an impudent fly that's been teasing
His *snub*lime proboscis, and set him a sneezing.
Attish hu! attish hu!
You brute, how I wish you
Were but as genteel as the Irish lady,
Dear Mrs. O'Grady,
Who, chancing to sneeze in a noble duke's face,
Hoped she hadn't been guilty of splashing his Grace.
Now, look out. Yes, he will! No, he won't! By the powers!
I thought he was taking alarm at the flowers;
But it luckily seems, his gigantic invention
Has at once set them down as a little attention
On Irmengard's part,—done by way of suggestion
That she means to say "Yes," when he next pops the question.

There! he's down! now he yawns, and in one minute more—
I thought so, he's safe—he's beginning to snore;
He is wrapped in that sleep he shall wake from no more.
From his girdle the knight takes a ponderous key;
It fits—and once more is fair Irmengard free.

From heel to head, and from head to heel,
They wrap their prey in that net of steel,
And they *croché* the edges together with care,
As you finish a purse for a fancy-fair,
Till the last knot is tied by the diligent pair.
At length they have ended their business laborious,
And Eppo shouts "Bagged him, by all that is glorious!"

No billing and cooing,
You must up and be doing.
Depend on't, Sir Knight, this is no time for wooing;
You'll discover, unless you progress rather smarter,
That catching a giant's like catching a Tartar:
He still has some thirty-five minutes to sleep,
Close to this spot hangs a precipice steep,
Like Shakspere's tall cliff which they show one at Dover;
Drag him down to the brink, and then let him roll over;
As they scarce make a capital crime of infanticide,
There can't be any harm in a little giganticide.

"Pull him, and haul him! take care of his head!
Oh, how my arms ache—he's as heavy as lead!
That'll do, love—I'm sure I can move him alone,
Though I'm certain the brute weighs a good forty stone.
Yo! heave ho! roll him along
(It's exceedingly lucky the net's pretty strong);
Once more—that's it—there, now, I think
He's done to a turn, he rests on the brink;
At it again, and over he goes
To furnish a feast for the hooded crows;
Each vulture that makes the Taurus his home
May dine upon giant for months to come."

Lives there a man so thick of head
To whom it must in words be said,
How Eppo did the lady wed,
And built upon the giant's bed
A castle, walled and turreted?
We will hope not; or, if there be,
Defend us from his company!

ADVICE TO JOKERS.

A NEW work published in London, entitled, "The Hand-Book of Joking," gives the following advice, which is worthy of remembrance:

"Always let your jokes be well-timed. Any time will do for a good joke, but no time will do for a bad one. Any place will fit, provided the joke itself be fitting, but it never fits if a joke be out of its place. No man can order a joke as he would his coat, at Stultz's, or his boots at Hoby's. Jokes are not only often out of order, but we have known jokers ordered out; in short, any man who attempts to joke out of order, should either be provided with a strait waistcoat, or be kicked out of society. In concocting jokes as in making puddings, each person employs similar materials, but the quality of the dish is entirely dependent on the skill of the artiste. As gold becomes refined by passing through the ordeal of fire, so truth is the purer for being tested by the furnace of fun; for jokes are, to facts, what melting pots are to metal. The utterer of a good joke is a useful member of society, but the maker of a bad one is a more despicable character than the veriest coiner by profession.

"A joke from a gentleman is an act of charity; an uncharitable joke is an ungentlemanly act. The retort courteous is the touchstone of good feeling; the reply churlish the proof of cold-headed stupidity."

A MAN MILLINER.

FROM "TEN THOUSAND A-YEAR." BY SAMUEL WARREN.

About ten o'clock one Sunday morning, in the month of July, 183—, the dazzling sunbeams which had for many hours irradiated a little dismal back attic in one of the closest courts adjoining Oxford street, in London, and stimulated with their intensity the closed eyelids of a young man lying in bed, at length awoke him. He rubbed his eyes for some time, to relieve himself from the irritation he experienced in them; and yawned and stretched his limbs with a heavy sense of weariness, as though his sleep had not refreshed him. He presently cast his eyes on the heap of clothes lying huddled together on the backless chair by the bedside, and where he had hastily flung them about an hour after midnight; at which time he had returned from a great draper's shop in Oxford street, where he served as a shopman, and where he had nearly dropped asleep after a long day's work, while in the act of putting up the shutters. He could hardly keep his eyes open while he undressed, short as was the time it took him to do so; and on dropping exhausted into bed, there he had continued in deep unbroken slumber till the moment he is presented to the reader. He lay for several minutes, stretching, yawning, and sighing, occasionally casting an irresolute eye towards the tiny fireplace, where lay a modicum of wood and coal, with a tinder-box and a match or two placed upon the hob, so that he could easily light his fire for the purposes of shaving and breakfasting. He stepped at length lazily out of bed, and when he felt his feet, again yawned and stretched himself, then he lit his fire, placed his bit of a kettle on the top of it, and returned to bed, where he lay with his eyes fixed on the fire, watching the cracking blaze insinuating itself through the wood and coal. Once, however, it began to fail, so he had to get up and assist it by blowing and bits of paper; and it seemed in so precarious a state that he determined not again to lie down, but sit on the bedside, as he did with his arms folded, ready to resume operations if necessary. In this posture he remained for some time, watching his little fire, and listlessly listening to the discordant jangling of innumerable church-bells, clamorously calling the citizens to their devotions. What passed through his mind was something like the following:—

"Heigho!—Oh, Lord!—Dull as ditch-water!—This is my only holiday, yet I don't seem to enjoy it—the fact is, I feel knocked up with my week's work.—Lord, what a life mine is, to be sure! Here am I, in my eight-and-twentieth year, and for four long years have been one of the shopmen at Dowlas, Tagrag, Bobbin and Company's—slaving from seven o'clock in the morning till ten at night, and all for a salary of £35 a year and my board! And Mr. Tagrag is always telling me how high he's raised my salary. Thirty-five pounds a-year is all I have for lodging, and appearing like a gentleman! Oh, Lord, it can't last, for sometimes I feel getting desperate—such strange thoughts! Seven shillings a-week do I pay for this cursed hole—[he uttered these words with a bitter emphasis, accompanied by a disgustful look round the little room]—that one couldn't swing a cat in without touching the four sides!—Last winter, three of our gents (*i. e.* his fellow-shopmen) came to tea with me one Sunday night; and bitter cold as it was, we made this d—d doghole so hot we were obliged to open the windows! And as for accommodations—I recollect I had to borrow two nasty chairs from the people below, who, on the next Sunday, borrowed my only decanter in return, and, hang them, cracked it!—Curse me, if this life is worth having! It's all the very vanity of vanities, and no mistake! Fag, fag, fag, all one's days, and—what for? Thirty-five pounds a-year, and '*no advance!*' Bah, bells! ring away till you're all cracked!—Now do you think *I'm*

going to be mewed up in church on this the only day out of the seven I've got to sweeten myself in, and sniff fresh air? A precious joke that would be! Whew!—after all, I'd as leave sit here; for what's the use of my going out? Every body I see out is happy, excepting me, and the poor chaps that are like me!—Every body laughs when they see me, and know that I'm only a tallow-faced counter-jumper, for whom it's no use to go out!—Oh, Lord! what's the use of being good-looking, as some chaps say I am?"—Here he instinctively passed his left hand through a profusion of sandy-colored hair, and cast an eye towards the bit of fractured looking-glass that hung against the wall, and which, by faithfully representing to him a by no means plain set of features (despite the dismal hue of his hair) whenever he chose to appeal to it, had afforded him more enjoyment than any other object in the world for years. "Ah, Lord! many and many's the fine gal I've done my best to attract the notice of, while I was serving her in the shop,—that is, when I've seen her get out of a carriage! There has been luck to many a chap like me, in the same line of speculation; look at Tom Tarnish—how did he get Miss Twang, the rich piano-forte maker's daughter?—and now he's cut the shop, and lives at Hackney like a regular gentleman! Ah! that was a stroke! But somehow, it hasn't answered with me yet: the gals don't take! Lord, how I have set my eyes and ogled them—all of them don't seem to dislike the thing—and sometimes they'll smile, in a sort of way that says I'm safe—but 'tis no use, not a bit of it!—My eyes! catch me, by the way, ever nodding again to a lady on the Sunday, that had smiled when I stared at her while serving her in the shop—after what happened to me a month or two ago in the Park! Didn't I feel like damaged goods, just then! But, it's no matter, women are so different at different times!—Very likely I mismanaged the thing.—By the way, what a precious puppy of a chap the fellow was that came up to her at the time she stepped out of her carriage to walk a bit! As for good looks—cut me to ribbons"—another glance at the glass—"no; I ain't afraid there, neither—but, heigh-ho! I suppose he was, as they say, born with a golden spoon in his mouth, and never so many thousand a-year, to make up to him for never so few brains! He was uncommon well dressed though, I must own. What trowsers!—they stuck so natural to him, he might have been born in them. And his waistcoat, and satin stock—what an air! And yet, his figure was nothing *very* out of the way! His gloves, as white as snow! I've no doubt he wears a pair of them a-day—my stars! that's three and sixpence a-day, for don't I know what they cost?—Whew! if I had but the cash to carry on that sort of thing!—And when he had seen her into her carriage—the horse he got on!—and what a tip-top groom—that chap's wages, I'll answer for it, were equal to my salary!" Here was a long pause. "Now, just for the fun of the thing, only suppose luck was to befall me. Say somebody was to leave me lots of cash—many thousands a-year, or something in that line! My stars! wouldn't I go it with the best of them!" Another long pause. "Gad, I really should hardly know how to begin to spend it!—I think, by the way, I'd buy a title to set off with—for what won't money buy? The thing's often done—there was a great biscuit-maker in the city, the other day, made a baronet of, all for his money—and why shouldn't I?" He grew a little heated with the progress of his reflections, clasping his hands with involuntary energy, as he stretched them out to their fullest extent, to give effect to a very hearty yawn, "Lord, only think how it would sound!

"Sir Tittlebat Titmouse, Baronet.

"The very first place I'd go to after I'd got my title, and was rigged out in Stultze's tip-top, should be—our cursed shop, to buy a dozen or two pair of white kid. What a flutter there would be among the poor pale devils as were standing, just as ever, behind the counters, at Dowlas, Tagrag and Co.'s, when my carriage drew up, and I stepped into the shop! Tagrag would come and attend to me himself. No he wouldn't—pride wouldn't let him. I don't know, though; what wouldn't he do to turn a penny, and make two and ninepence into three and a penny. I shouldn't quite come Captain Stiff over him; but I should treat him with a kind of an air, too, as if—hem! how delightful!" A sigh and a pause. "Yes, I should often come to the shop. Gad, it would be half the fun of my fortune! And they would envy me, to be sure! How one should enjoy it! I wouldn't think of marrying till—and yet I won't say either; if I get among some of them out and outers—those first-rate articles—that lady, for instance, the other day in the Park—I should like to see her cut me as she did, with ten thousand a-year in my pocket! Why, she'd be running after *me*, or there's no truth in novels, which I'm sure there's often a great deal in. Oh, of course, I might marry whom I pleased. Who couldn't be got with ten thousand a-year!" Another pause. "I should go abroad to Russia directly; for they tell me there's a man lives there who could dye this hair of mine any color I liked—egad! I'd come home as black as a crow, and hold up my head as high as any of them! While I was about it, I'd have a touch at my eyebrows"—Crash went all his castle-building at the sound of his tea-kettle, hissing, whizzing, sputtering in the agonies of boiling over; as if the intolerable heat of the fire had driven desperate the poor creature placed upon it, who instinctively tried thus to extinguish the cause of its anguish. Having taken it off and placed it upon the hob, and placed on the fire a tiny fragment of fresh coal, he began to make preparations for shaving, by pouring some of the hot water into an old tea-cup, which was presently to serve for the purpose of breakfast. Then he spread out a bit of crumpled whity-brown paper, that had folded up a couple of segars which he had bought over-night for the Sunday's special enjoyment—and which, if he had supposed they had come from any place beyond the four seas, I imagine him to have been slightly mistaken. He placed this bit of paper on the little mantel-piece; drew his solitary, well-worn razor several times across the palm of his left hand; dipped his brush, worn within the third of an inch to the stump, into the hot water; presently passed it over as much of his face as he intended to shave; then rubbed on the damp surface a bit of yellow soap—and in less than five minutes Mr. Titmouse was a shaved man. But mark—don't suppose that he had performed an extensive operation. One would have thought him anxious to get rid of as much as possible of his abominable sandy-colored hair—quite the contrary.

Every hair of his spreading whiskers was sacred from the touch of steel; and a bushy crop of hair stretched underneath his chin, coming curled out on each side of it, above his stock, like two little horns or tusks. An imperial—*i. e.*, a dirt-colored tuft of hair, permitted to grow perpendicularly down the upper lip of puppies—and a pair of promising mustachios, poor Mr. Titmouse had been compelled to sacrifice some time before, to the tyrannical whimsies of his vulgar employers, Messrs. Dowlas and Tagrag, who imagined them not to be exactly suitable appendages for counter-jumpers. So that it will be seen that the space shaved over on this occasion was somewhat circumscribed. This operation over, he took out of his trunk an old dirty-looking pomatum-pot. A little of its contents, extracted on the tips of his two forefingers, he stroked carefully into his eyebrows; then spreading some on the palms of his hands, he rubbed it vigorously into his stubborn hair and whiskers for some quarter of an hour; and then combed and brushed his hair into half a dozen different dispositions—so fastidious in that matter was Mr. Titmouse. Then he dipped the end of a towel into a little water, and twisting it round his right fore-finger, passed it gently over his face, carefully avoiding his eyebrows, and the hair at the top, sides, and bottom of his face, which he then wiped with a dry corner of the towel; and no further did Mr. Tittlebat Titmouse think it necessary to carry his ablutions. Had he been able to "see himself as others saw him," in respect of those neglected regions which lay somewhere behind and beneath his ears, he might not possibly have thought it superfluous to irritate them with a little soap and water; but, after all, he knew best; it might have given him cold; and besides, his hair was very thick and long behind, and might, perhaps, conceal any thing that was unsightly. Then Mr. Titmouse drew from underneath the bed a bottle of Warren's "incomparable blacking," and a couple of brushes, with great labor and skill polishing his boots up to a wonderful point of brilliancy. Having washed his hands, and replaced his blacking implements under the bed, he devoted a few moments to boiling about three teaspoonfuls of coffee (as it was styled on the paper from which he took, and in which he had bought it—whereas it was, in fact, chicory.) Then he drew forth from his trunk a calico shirt, with linen wristbands and collars, which had been worn only twice since its last washing—*i. e.*, on the preceding two Sundays—and put it on, taking great care not to rumple a very showy front, containing three little rows of frills; in the middle one of which he stuck three "studs," connected together with two little gilt chains, looking exceedingly stylish—especially coupled with a span-new satin stock, which he next buckled round his neck. Having put on his bright boots (without, I am sorry to say, any stockings) he carefully insinuated his legs into a pair of white trowsers, for the first time since their last washing; and what with his short straps and high braces, they were so tight that you would have feared their bursting, if he should have sat hastily. I am almost afraid that I shall hardly be believed, but it is a fact, that the next thing that he did was to attach a pair of spurs to his boots;—but, to be sure, it was not *impossible* that he might intend to ride during the day. Then he put on a queer kind of under-waistcoat, which in fact was only a roll-collar of rather faded pea-green silk, and designed to set off a very fine flowered damson-colored silk waistcoat; over which he drew a massive mosaic gold chain (to purchase which he had sold a serviceable silver watch) which had been carefully wrapped up in cotton wool; from which soft depository, also, he drew HIS RING (those must have been sharp eyes that could tell, at a distance, and in a hurry, that it was not diamond), which he placed on the stumpy little finger of his red and thick right hand—and contemplated its sparkle with exquisite satisfaction.

Having proceeded thus far with his toilet, he sat down to his breakfast, spreading the shirt he had taken off upon his lap, to preserve his white trowsers from spot or stain—his thoughts alternating between his late waking vision and his purposes for the day. He had no butter, having used the last on the preceding morning; so he was fain to put up with dry bread—and very dry and teeth-trying it was, poor fellow—but his eye lit on his ring! Having swallowed two cups of his *quasi*-coffee, (eugh! such stuff!) he resumed his toilet, by drawing out of his other trunk his blue surtout, with embossed silk buttons and velvet collar, and an outside pocket in the left breast. Having smoothed down a few creases, he put it on. Then, before him the little vulgar fraction of a glass, he stood twitching about the collar, and sleeves, and front, so as to make them sit well; concluding with a careful elongation of the wristbands of his shirt, so as to show their whiteness gracefully beyond the cuff of his coat-sleeve—and he succeeded in producing a sort of white boundary line between the blue of his coat-sleeve and the red of his hand. At that useful member he could not help looking with a sigh, as he had often done before—for it was not a handsome hand. It was broad and red, and the fingers were thick and stumpy, and very coarse deep wrinkles at every joint. His nails also were flat and shapeless; and he used to be continually gnawing them, till he had succeeded in getting them down to the quick—and they were a sight to set a Christian's teeth on edge. Then he extracted from the first-mentioned trunk a white pocket-handkerchief—an exemplary one, that had gone through four Sundays' show (not *use*, be it understood,) and yet was capable of exhibition again. A pair of sky-colored kid gloves next made their appearance; which, however, showed such barefaced marks of former service as rendered indispensable a ten minutes' rubbing with bread crumbs. His Sunday hat, carefully covered with silver-paper, was next gently removed from its well-worn box—ah, how lightly and delicately did he pass his smoothing hand round its glossy surface! Lastly, he took down a thin black cane, with a gilt head, and full brown tassel, from a peg behind the door—and his toilet was complete. Laying down his cane for a moment, he passed his hands again through his hair, arranging it so as to fall nicely on each side beneath his hat, which he then placed upon his head, with an elegant inclination towards the left side. He was really not bad-looking, in spite of his sandy-colored hair. His forehead, to be sure, was contracted, and his eyes of a very light color, and a trifle too protuberant; but his mouth was rather well-formed, and being seldom closed, exhibited very beautiful teeth; and his nose was of that description which generally passes for a Roman nose. His countenance wore generally a smile, and was expressive of—self-satisfaction; and surely any expression is better than none at all. As for the slightest trace of *intellect* in it, I should be misleading the reader if I were to say any thing of the sort. He was about five feet five inches in height, and rather strongly set, with a little tendency to round shoulders; but his limbs were pliant and his motions nimble.

Here you have, then, Mr. Tittlebat Titmouse to the life—certainly no more than an average sample of his kind. Well—he put his hat on, as I have said; buttoned the lowest two buttons of his surtout, and stuck his white pocket-handkerchief into the outside pocket in front, as already mentioned, disposing it so as to let a little of it appear above the edge of the pocket, with a sort of careful carelessness—a graceful contrast to the blue; drew on his gloves; took his cane in his hand; drained the last sad remnant in his coffee-cup; and, the sun shining in the full splendor of a July noon, and promising a glorious day, forth sallied this poor fellow, an Oxford street Adonis, going forth conquering and to conquer! Petty finery without, a pinched and stinted stomach within; a case of Back *versus* Belly (as the lawyers would say) the plaintiff winning in a canter! Forth sallied, I say, Mr. Titmouse, down the narrow, creaking, close staircase, which he had not quitted before he heard exclaimed from an opposite window, "My eyes, *ain't* that a swell!" He felt how true the observation was, and that at that moment he was somewhat out of his element; so he hurried on, and soon reached the great broad street, apostrophized by the celebrated Opium-Eater, with bitter feeling, as—"Oxford street!—stony-hearted step-mother!—Thou that listenest to the sighs of orphans, and drinkest the tears of children." Here, though his spirits were not just then very buoyant, the poor dandy breathed more freely than when he was passing through the nasty crowded court (Closet Court) which he had just quitted. He passed and met hundreds who, like himself, seemed released for a precious day's interval from intense toil and miserable confinement during the week; but there were not many of them who had any pretensions to vie with him in elegance of appearance—and that was a *luxury!* Who could do justice to the air with which he strutted along? He felt as happy, poor soul, in his little ostentation, as his Corinthian rival in tip-top turnout, after twice as long, and as anxious, and fifty times as expensive preparations for effective public display! Nay, *my* poor swell was greatly the superior of such a one as I have alluded to. Titmouse *did*, to a great degree, bedizen his back at the expense of his belly; whereas, the Corinthian exquisite, too often taking advantage of station and influence, recklessly both satiates his appetite within, and decorates his person without, at the expense of innumerable heart-aching creditors. I do not mean, however, to claim any real merit for Titmouse on this score, because I am not sure how he would act if he were to become

possessed of his magnificent rival's means and opportunities for the perpetration of gentlemanly frauds on a splendid scale. But we shall, perhaps, see by and by. He walked along with leisurely step; for haste and perspiration were vulgar, and he had the day before him.

Observe the careless glance of self-satisfaction with which he occasionally regarded his bright boots, with their martial appendage, giving out a faint tingling sound as he heavily trod the broad flags; his spotless trowsers, his tight surtout, and the tip of white handkerchief peeping accidentally out in front! A pleasant sight it was to behold him in a chance rencontre with some one genteel enough to be recognized—as he stood, resting on his left leg; his left arm stuck upon his hip; his right leg easily bent outwards; his right hand lightly holding his ebon cane, with the gilt head of which he occasionally tapped his teeth; and his eyes, half-closed, scrutinizing the face and figure of each "*pretty gal*" as she passed! This was indeed happiness, as far as his forlorn condition could admit of his enjoying it. He had no particular object in view. A tiff over night with two of his shopmates had broken off a party which they had agreed the Sunday preceding in forming, to go to Greenwich on the ensuing Sunday; and this little circumstance a little soured his temper, depressed as were his spirits before. He resolved to-day to walk straight on, and dine somewhere a little way out of town, by way of passing the time till four o'clock, at which hour he intended to make his appearance in Hyde Park, "to see the fashions," which was his favorite Sunday occupation.

His condition was, indeed, forlorn in the extreme. To say nothing of his *prospects* in life—what was his present condition? A shopman, with £35 a-year, out of which he had to find his clothing, washing, lodging, and all other incidental expenses—his board being found him by his employers. He was five weeks in arrear to his landlady—a corpulent old termagant, whom nothing could have induced him to risk offending, but his overmastering love of finery; for I grieve to say, that this deficiency had been occasioned by his purchase of the ring he then wore with so much pride. How he had contrived to pacify her—lie upon lie as he must have had recourse to—I know not. He was in debt, too, to his poor washerwoman in six or seven shillings for nearly a quarter's washing; and owed five times that amount to a little old tailor, who, with huge spectacles on his nose, turned up to him, out of a little cupboard which he occupied in Closet Court, and which Titmouse had to pass whenever he went to or from his lodgings, a lean, sallow, wrinkled face, imploring him to "settle his small account." All the cash in hand which he had to meet contingencies between that day and quarter-day, which was six weeks off, was about twenty-six shillings, of which he had taken one for the present day's expenses!

Revolving these somewhat disheartening matters in his mind, he passed easily and leisurely along the whole length of Oxford street. No one could have judged from his dressy appearance, the constant smirk on his face, and his confident air, how very miserable that poor dandy was; but three-fourths of his misery were occasioned by the impossibility he felt of his ever being able to indulge in his propensities for finery and display. Nothing better had he to occupy his few thoughts. He had had

only a plain mercantile education, as it is called, *i. e.*, reading, writing, and arithmetic: beyond a very moderate acquaintance with these, he knew nothing whatever; not having read more than a few novels, and plays, and sporting newspapers.

On he walked towards Bayswater; and finding it was yet early, and considering that the farthest he went from town the better prospect there was of his being able, with a little sacrifice of appearances, to get a dinner consistent with the means he carried about with him, viz., one shilling, he pursued his way a mile or two beyond Bayswater, and, sure enough, came at length upon a nice little public-house on the roadside, called the Squaretoes Arms. Very tired, and quite smothered with dust, he first sat down in a small back room to rest himself; and took the opportunity to call for a clothes-brush and shoe-brush, to relieve his clothes and boots from the heavy dust upon them. Having thus attended to his outer man, as far as circumstances would permit, he bethought himself of his inner man, whose cravings he satisfied with a pretty substantial mutton-pie and a pint of porter. This fare, together with a penny to the little girl who waited on him, cost him tenpence; and having somewhat refreshed himself, he began to think of returning to town. Having lit one of his two segars, he sallied forth, puffing along with an air of quiet enjoyment. Dinner, however humble, seldom fails, especially when accompanied by a fair draught of good porter, in some considerable degree to tranquillize the animal spirits; and that soothing effect began soon to be experienced by Mr. Titmouse. The sedative *cause* he erroneously attributed to the segar he was smoking; whereas in fact the only tobacco he had imbibed was from the porter. But, however that might be, he certainly returned towards town in a far calmer and even more cheerful humor than that in which he had quitted it an hour or two before.

THE FIRST-FLOOR LODGER.

ANONYMOUS.

There are two lodged together.—SHAKSPERE.

It so happens that, throughout my life, I have had occasion only for half a house, and, from motives of economy, have been unwilling to pay rent for a whole one; but—there can be on earth, I find, no resting-place for him who is so unhappy as to want only "half a house." In the course of the last eight years, I have occupied one hundred and forty-three different lodgings, running the gauntlet twice through all London and Westminster, and, oftener than I can remember, the "out-parishes" through! As "two removes" are as bad as a fire, it follows that I have gone seventy-one times and a half through the horrors of conflagration! And, in every place where I have lived, it has been my fate to be domiciled with a monster! But my voice shall be heard, as a voice upon the house-top, crying out until I find relief. I have been ten days already in the abode from which I now write, so I cannot, in reason, look to stay more than three or four more. I hear people talk of "the grave" as a lodging (at worst) that a man is "sure of;" but, if there be one resurrection-man alive when I die, as sure as quarter-day, I shall be taken up again.

The first trial I endured when I came to London, was making the tour of all the boarding-houses—being deluded, I believe, *seriatim*, by every prescriptive form of "advertisement."

First, I was lured by the pretence modest—this appeared in *The Times* all the year round. "Desirable circle"—"Airy situation"—"Limited number of guests"—"Every attention"—and "no children."

Next, was the commanding—at the very "head and front" of the *Morning Post*. "Vicinity of the fashionable Squares!"—"Two persons, to increase society"—"Family of condition"—and "Terms at Mr. Sams's, the bookseller's."

Then came the irresistible. "Widow of an officer of rank"—"Unprotected early in life"—"Desirous to extend family circle"—"Flatters herself," etc. Moonshine all together! "Desirable circle"—a bank clerk and five daughters who wanted husbands. Brandy and water after supper, and booby from Devonshire snapt up before my eyes. Little boy, too, in the family, that belonged to a sister who "had died." I hate scandal; but I never could find out where *that* sister had been buried.

"Fashionable Square"—The fire, to the frying-pan! The worst *item*—(on consideration)—in all my experience. Dishes without meat, and beds without blankets. "Terms," "two hundred guineas a-year," and surcharges for night-candle. And, as for dinner! as I am a Yorkshireman, I never knew what it meant while I was in Manchester Square!

I have had two step-mothers, Mr. Editor, and I was six months at a preparatory school, but I never saw a woman since I was born cut meat like Lady Catharine Skinflint! There was a transparency about her slice which (after a good luncheon) one could pause and look at. She would cover you a whole plate with fillet of veal and ham, and not increase the weight of it half an ounce.

And then the Misses Skinflints—for knowledge of anatomy—their cutting up a fowl!—In the puniest half-starved chicken that ever broke the heart of a brood-hen to look at, they would find you side-bone, pinion, drum-stick, liver, gizzard, rump and merry-thought! and, even beyond this critical acquaintance with all admitted—and apocryphal—divisions and distinctions, I have caught the eldest of them actually inventing new joints, that, even in speculation, never before existed!

I understand the meaning now of the Persian salutation—"May your shadow never be less!" I lost mine entirely in about a fortnight that I staid at Lady Skinflint's.

Two more hosts took me "at livery" (besides the "widow" of the "officer of rank")—an apothecary, who made patients of his boarders, and an attorney, who looked for clients among them. I got away from the medical gentleman rather hastily, for I found that the pastry-cook who served the house was his brother; and the lawyer was so pressing about "discounts," and "investments of property," that I never ventured to sign my name, even to a washing-bill, during the few days I was in his house; on quitting the which, I took courage, and, resolving to become my own provider, hired a "First floor," accordingly ("unfurnished") in the neighborhood of Bloomsbury Square.

Mutatio loci, non ingenii.

The *premier coup* of my career amounted to an escape. I ordered a carte blanche outfit from an upholsterer of Piccadilly, determined to have my "apartments" unexceptionable before I entered them; and discovered, after a hundred pounds laid out in painting, decorating, and curtain-fitting, that the "ground landlord" had certain claims which would be liquidated when my property "went in."

This miscarriage made me so cautious, that before I would choose again, I was the sworn horror of every auctioneer and house-agent (so called) in London. I refused twenty offers, at least, because they had the appearance of being "great bargains." Eschewed all houses as though they had the plague, in which I found that "single gentlemen were preferred." Was threatened with three actions for defamation, for questioning the solvency of persons in business. And, at length, was so lucky as to hit upon a really desirable mansion! The "family" perfectly respectable; but had "more room" than was necessary for them. Demanded the "strictest references," and accepted no inmate for "less than a year." Into this most unexceptionable abode I conveyed myself and my property. Sure I should stay for ever, and doubted whether I ought not to secure it at once for ten years instead of one. And before I had been settled in the house three quarters of an hour, I found that the chimneys—every one of them! smoked, from the top to the bottom!

There was guilt, reader, in the landlord's eye, the moment the first puff drove me out of my drawing-room. He made an effort to say something like "damp day;" but the "amen" stuck in his throat. He could not say "amen," when I did cry "God bless us!" The whole building, from the kitchen to the garret, was infected with the malady. I had noticed the dark complexions of the family, and had concluded they were from the West Indies,—they were smoke-dried:—

Blow high, blow low!

I suffered six weeks under excuses, knowing them to be humbug all the while. For a whole month it was "the wind;" but I saw "the wind" veer twice all round the compass, and found, blow which way it would, it still blew down my chimney!

Then we came to "cures." First, there were alterations at the top—new chimney-pots, cowls, hovels—and all making the thing worse. Then we tried at the bottom—grates reset, and flues contracted—still to no purpose. Then we came to burning charcoal; and in four days I was in a de-

cline. Then we kept the doors and windows open; and in one day I got a fit of the rheumatism. And in spite of doors or windows, blowers, registers, or Count Rumford—precaution in putting on coals, or mathematical management of poker—down the enemy would come to our very faces,—poof! poof! —as if in derision! till I prayed heaven that smoke had life and being, that I might commit murder on it at once, and so be hanged; and at length, after throwing every movable I could command at the grate and the chimney by turns, and paying "no cure no pay" doctors by dozens, who did nothing but make dirt and mischief, I sent for a respectable surveyor, paid him for his opinion beforehand, and heard that the fault in the chimneys was "radical," and not to be remedied without pulling the house down!

I paid my twelvemonth's rent, and wished only that my landlord might live through his lease. I heard afterwards, that he had himself been imposed upon; and that the house, from the first fire ever lighted in it, had been a scandal to the neighborhood. But this whole volume would not suffice to enumerate the variety of wretchedness—and smoky chimneys the very least of them!—which drove me a second time to change my plan of life; the numberless lodgings that I lived in, and the inconveniences, greater or lesser, attending each. In one place, my servants quarrelled with the servants of "the people of the house." In another, "the people of the house's" servants quarrelled with mine. Here, my housekeeper refused to stay, because the kitchen was "damp." There, my footman begged I would "provide myself," as there were "rats in his cockloft." Then somebody fell over a pail of water, left upon "my stairs;" and "my maid" declared it was "the other maid" had put it there. Then the cats fought; and I was assured that mine had given the first scratch. On the whole, the disputes were so manifold, always ending to my discomfiture,—for the lady of the mansion would assail me,—I never could get the gentleman to be dissatisfied, (and so conclude the controversy by kicking him down stairs,)—that seeing one clear advantage maintained by the ground possessor, viz., that I, when we squabbled, was obliged to vacate, and he remained where he was, I resolved, once for all, to turn the tables upon mankind at large, and become a "landlord" and a "housekeeper," in my own immediate person.

"*Sir, the gray goose hath laid an egg.—Sir, the old barn doth need repair.—The cook sweareth, the meat doth burn at the fire.—John Thomas is in the stocks; and every thing stays on your arrival.*"

I would not advise any single gentleman hastily to conclude that he is in distress. Bachelors are discontented, and take wives; footmen are ambitious, and take eating-houses. What does either party gain by the change? "We know," the wise man has said, "what we are; but we know not what we may be."

In estimating the happiness of householders, I had imagined all tenants to be like myself,—mild, forbearing, punctual, and contented; but I "kept house" three years, and was never out of hot water the whole time! I did manage, after some trouble, to get fairly into a creditable mansion—just missing one, by a stroke of fortune, which had a brazier's shop at the back of it, and was always shown at hours when the workmen were gone to dinner—and sent a notice to the papers, that a bachelor of sober habits, having "a larger residence than he wanted," would dispose of half of it to a family of respectability. But the whole world seemed to be, and I think is, in a plot to drive me out of my senses. In the first ten days of my new dignity, I was visited by about twenty tax-gatherers, half of them with claims that I had never heard of, and the other half with claims far exceeding my expectations. The householder seemed to be the minister's very milch cow—the positive scape-goat of the whole community! I was called on for house-tax, window-tax, land-tax, and servant's-tax! Poor's-rate, sewers'-rate, pavement-rate, and scavengers'-rate! I had to pay for watering streets on which other people walked; for lighting lamps which other people saw by; for maintaining watchmen who slept all night; and for building churches that I never went into. And—I never knew that the country was taxed till that moment!—these were but a few of the "dues" to be sheared off from me. There was the clergyman of the parish, whom I never saw, sent to me at Easter for "an offering." There was the charity-school of the parish, solicited "the honor" of my "subscription and support." One man came to inform me that I was "drawn for the militia," and offered to "get me off," on payment of a sum of money. Another insisted that I was "chosen constable," and actually brought the *insignia* of office to my door. Then I had petitions to read (in writing) from all the people who chose to be in distress; personal beggars, who penetrated into my parlor, to send to Bridewell, or otherwise get rid of. Windows were broken, and "nobody" had "done it." The key of the street door was lost, and "nobody" had "had it." Then my cook stopped up the kitchen "sink;" and the bricklayers took a month to open it. Then my gutter ran over, and flooded my neighbor's garret; and I was served with notice of an action for dilapidation.

And at Christmas!—Oh! it was no longer dealing with ones and twos!—The whole hundred, on the day after that festival, rose up, by concert, to devour me!

Dustmen, street-keepers, lamplighters, turncocks, postmen, beadles, scavengers, chimney-sweeps—the whole *pecus* of parochial servitorship were at my gate before eleven at noon.

Then the "waits" came—two sets! and fought which should have "my bounty." Rival patrols disputed whether I did or did not lie within their "beat." At one time there was a doubt as to which, of two parishes, I belonged; and I fully expected that (to make sure) I should have been visited by the collectors from both! Meantime the knocker groaned, until very evening, under the dull, stunning, single thumps—each villain would have struck, although it had been upon the head of his own grandfather!—of bakers, butchers, tallow-chandlers, grocers, fishmongers, poulterers, and oilmen! Every ruffian who made his livelihood by swindling me through the whole year, thought himself entitled to a peculiar benefaction (for his robberies) on this day. And

Host! now by my life I scorn the name!

All this was child's play—bagatelle, I protest, and "perfumed," to what I had to go through in the "letting off" of my dwelling! The swarms of crocodiles that assailed me, on every fine day—three-fourths of them, to avoid an impending shower, or to pass away a stupid morning—in the shape of stale dowagers, city coxcombs, "professional gentlemen," and "single ladies!" And all (except a few that were swindlers) finding something wrong about my arrangements! Gil Blas' mule, which was nothing but faults, never had half so many faults as my house. Carlton Palace, if it were to be "let" to-morrow, would be objected to by a tailor. One man found my rooms "too small;" another thought them rather "too large;" a third wished that they had been loftier; a fourth, that there had been more of them. One lady hinted a sort of doubt, "whether the neighborhood was quite respectable;" another asked, "if I had any family;" and, then, "whether I would bind myself not to have any during her stay." Two hundred, after detaining me an hour, had called only "for friends." Ten thousand went through all the particulars, and would "call again to-morrow." At last there came a lady who gave the *coup-de-grace* to my "housekeeping;" she was a clergyman's widow, she said, from Somersetshire; if she had been an "officer's" I had suspected her; but, in an evil hour, I let her in; and—she had come for the express purpose of marrying me! Sometimes she heard a mouse behind the wainscot, and I was called in to scare it. Her canary bird got loose; would I be so good as to catch it? I fell sick, but was soon glad to get well again; for she sent five times a day to ask if I was better; beside pouring in plates of blanc mange, jellies, cordials, raspberry vinegar, fruits fresh from the country, and hasty-puddings made by her own hand. And, at last, after the constant borrowings of books, the eternal interchange of newspapers, and the daily repair of crow-quills, the opinions upon wine, and the corrections of hackney coachmen, I determined to get rid of many troubles at once; I therefore presented Mrs. F—— with my house, and every thing in it, and determined never again, as a man's only protection against female cupidity, to possess even a tooth-brush that I could legally call my own.

This resolution, gentle reader, compelled me to shelter myself in "furnished lodgings," where the most of accommodation, (sublunary!) after all, I believe, is to be found. I had sad work, as you may imagine, to find my way at first. Once I ventured to inhabit (as there was no board in the case) with a surgeon. But, what between the patients and the resurrection-men, the "night bell" was intolerable; and he ordered the watchman, too, I found, to pull it privately six or seven times a-week, in order to impress the neighborhood with an opinion of his practice. From one place I was driven away by a music-master, who gave concerts opposite to me; and at a second, after two days' abiding, I found that a madman was confined on the second floor! Two houses I left because my hostesses made love to me. Three, because parrots were kept in the streets. One, because a cock (who would crow all night) came to live in a yard at the back of me; and another, in which I had staid two months, (and should perhaps have remained till now,) because a boy of eight years old (there is to me no earthly creature so utterly intolerable as a boy of eight years old!) came home from school to "pass the holidays." I had thoughts, I don't care who knows it, of taking him off by poison; and bought two raspberry tarts to give him arsenic in, as I met him on the stairs, where he was, up and down, all day. As it is, I have sent an order to the Seven Dials, to have an "early delivery" of all the "dying speeches" for the next ten years. I did this in order that I may know when he is hanged—a fact I wish particularly to ascertain, because his father and I had an altercation about it.

Experience, however, gives lights; and a "furnished lodging" is the best arrangement among the bad. I had seven transitions last month, but that was owing to accidents; a man who chooses well, may commonly stay a fortnight in a place. Indeed, as I said in the beginning, I have been ten days where I am; and I don't, up to this moment, see clearly what point I shall go away upon. The mistress of the house entertains a pet monkey; and I have got a new footman, who, I understand, plays upon the fiddle. The matter, I suspect, will lie between these two.

I am most nervous myself about the monkey. He broke loose the other day. I saw him escape over the next garden-wall, and drop down by the side of a middle-aged gentleman, who was setting polyanthuses! The respectable man, as was prudent, took refuge in a summer-house; and then he pulled up all the polyanthuses; and then tried to get in at the summer-house window! I think that—

Eh!—Why, what the deuce is all this?—Why, the room is full of smoke!—Thomas!—[*I ring the bell violently.*]—Thomas!—[*I call my new footman.*] Tho-o-mas!—Why, somebody has set the house on fire.

Enter THOMAS.

Indeed no, your honor—indeed—no—it—it's only the chimney.

The chimney! you dog!—get away this moment and put it out.—Stay!—Thomas!—Come back, I say.—What chimney is it?

THOMAS. Only the kitchen chimney, sir.

Only the kitchen chimney! how did you do it?

THOMAS. I was only tuning my fiddle, your honor; and Mary, the housemaid, flung the resin in the fire.

Where's the landlord, sirrah?

THOMAS. He is not at home, sir.

Where's his wife?

THOMAS. She's in fits, sir.

You'll be hanged, to a certainty!—there's a statute for you, caitiff! there is—Come, sir—come—strip, and go up the chimney directly. Strip, or I'll kill you with the toasting-fork, and bury your body in the dust-hole.

[*Enter the cat, with a tail as thick as my arm, galloping round the room.*]

Zounds and death, what's to be done? My life's not insured!—I must get out of the house. [*Rattling of wheels, and cries of "Fire" in the street.*] Here comes the parish engine, and as many thieves with it as might serve six parishes!—Shut the doors below, I say. [*Calling down stairs.*] Don't let 'em in.—Thomas!—The house will be gutted from top to bottom!—Thomas!—Thomas!—Where is that rascally servant of mine?—Thomas! [*Calling in all directions.*] I—I must see, myself.

[*Scene changes to the kitchen. The housemaid in hysterics under the dresser.*]

Pooh! what a smell of sulphur! Thomas!—I remember, it was on a Friday I hired him!—Thomas!—take a wet blanket, you rascal, and get through the garret window. Crawl up the tiles, and muffle the chimney-pot!

THOMAS. [*Down the chimney.*] Sir!

One more peep [*I run up stairs*] from the window. Hark, how they knock without!—Rat-tat-tat-tat! As I live, here are a dozen engines, fifty firemen, and four thousand fools!—I must be off! —Thomas!—[*He enters.*]—I must escape.—Thomas, show me the back door!

THOMAS. There is none, sir.—I've been trying to get out myself.

No back door?

[*Enter the cook, with the monkey on her back. The knocking continued.*]

COOK. Oh law, sir! We shall all be destructed, sir!—Oh dear, where is your honor's double-barrelled gun?

My gun? up stairs. What d'ye want with the gun?

COOK. Oh, sir! if it was to be shot off up the chimney, it would surely put it out.

She's right. Run, Thomas! At the head of the bed. Away with you. Mind—it's loaded—take care what you are about.

There they go!—They have found it.—Now they are down stairs.—Why, the woman has got the gun!—Take it from her!—He don't hear me.—Thomas!—She's going to fire it, as I live!—Yes! she's sitting down in the grate!—Thomas!—With her body half way up the chimney!—Bang! bang! [*Report heard.*] Ah! there she goes backwards!—as black as a soot-bag!—Why, stop her, I say!—Ah! she gets into the street. Thomas!—Margery! —Everybody! The woman will be burned to death! [*Shouts without, and noise of water.*] Ha! [*I run to the window.*] Huzza!—The engines are playing upon her!!! Oh, that footman! he is my fate—and I thought it would be the monkey!

Enter THOMAS.

Come in, you villain. Is the woman burnt?

THOMAS. No, sir, she's only frightened.

Only frightened! you unfeeling creature—but see the monkey—stop him—he's gone off with my gold spectacles.

Reader, if you have compassion, hear a man of five-and-forty's prayer! I can't stay here!—where am I to go to?—If you should think—Thomas!—I must get into a hackney coach!—If you should think—Call me a hackney-coach, sirrah—and ask the man what he charges for it (d'ye hear) by the week.—If you should think that there is any chance of my doing well in Edinburgh or Dublin—I shouldn't like to be above the fifth story (I understand most of your houses run ten), a line to say so would greatly oblige me. As I have no home, at present, except the hackney-coach that I have sent for, I can't say exactly in what place of suffering your let-

It's all up!—Here comes the soot in cart-loads, all over her!—She's killed!—No, egad! she's up and running.—Don't let her come near me.—Margery! What's her name?—She's running towards the street door!—Margery!—Why, she's all on fire, and ter will find me; but, by addressing to the coffee-house, in Rathbone Place, it will somewhere or other come to the hands of

Your very humble servant,

WRINKLETON FIDGET.

POETRY, PUNNING, AND PIETY.—When the Hon. Mrs. Norton was applied to, on Hood's death, for a contribution to the fund then raised for his destitute widow, and headed by Sir Robert Peel with the munificent donation of £50, she promptly sent a liberal subscription with the following lines, (never before published:)

To cheer the widow's heart in her distress,
To make provision for the fatherless,
Is but a Christian's duty, and none should
Resist the heart-appeal of Widow Hood.

Poetry, punning, and piety, all of the genuine sort, are not often thus happily united.

THE VALUE OF A WORD.

FROM "THE LIFE AND TIMES OF FREDERIC REYNOLDS." BY HIMSELF.

WANTING to walk on the pier (at Calais), I asked the *garcon*, who spoke English very tolerably, the French for it. He, thinking as *Milord Anglais* I could mean nothing but *peer*, a lord, replied *paire.* Away I then went, and passing over the market-place, and drawbridge, stumbled on the pier, without having had occasion to inquire my way to it by the *garcon's* novel appellation. There I remained, strutting my half-hour, till dinner-time.

At the *table d'hôte*, the Commandant of the troops of the town sat next me; and among other officers and gentlemen at the table, were the President of the Council at Ratisbon, a Russian count, and several Prussians—in all amounting to about twenty, not one of whom, as it appeared to me, spoke a word of English.

I thought I could never please a Frenchman so much as by praising his town:—'Monsieur,' I said, condescendingly, to the Commandant, 'J'ai vu votre paire,' meaning, 'I have seen your *pier;*' but which he naturally understood, 'I have seen your *père*, father.' This address from a perfect stranger surprised him. 'Il est beau et grand, monsieur,' I continued. The Commandant examined me from head to foot with an astonishment that imparted to me an almost equal share. I saw there was a mistake, and I attempted to explain, by pronouncing very articulately,

'Oui, monsieur, j'ai vu votre *paire*—votre *paire*, sur le havre.'

'Eh bien, monsieur,' replied the Commandant, 'et que vous a-t-il dit?' (What did he say to you?)

I was astounded, and looking round the room for the keeper to the supposed madman, I discovered that the eyes of the whole of the company were upon me.

'Monsieur,' I cried, again attempting to explain, with as much deliberation and precision, and in as good French as I could command—'Monsieur, est-il possible que vous résidez ici, et que vous ne connoissez pas votre *paire*—votre *paire*—si long!'

This speech only increased the incomprehensibility of the whole conversation; and the Commandant beginning, in rather *haut en bas* terms, to demand an explanation, like all cowards, when driven into a corner, I became desperate.

'Monsieur,' I cried, somewhat boisterously, 'il faut que vous connoissez votre *paire!* le *paire* de votre ville, qui est fait de pierre, et a la tête de bois, et a ce moment on travaille a lui racommoder sa fin, a laquelle le vent a fait du mal.'

This was the *coup de grace* to all the decorum; every Frenchman abandoned himself to his laughter, till the room fairly shook with their shouts and even the Commandant himself could not help joining them.

'Allow me, sir,' said a gentleman whom I had not previously observed—

'My dear sir,' interrupted I, 'you are an Englishman, pray, pray explain.'

'Sir,' he replied, 'you have just told this gentleman,' pointing to the Commandant, '*that his father is the father of the whole town, that he is made of stone, but has a wooden head!* and at this moment the workmen are engaged in mending his end, that the wind has damaged.'

I was paralyzed. 'Tell me,' I cried, as if my life depended on an answer, 'what is the French for *pier?*'

'*Jetée*,' he replied, or according to the common people, *pont?*'

I had scarcely sense enough left to assist the Englishman in his good-natured attempts to unravel the error. He succeeded, however, and then commenced in French an explanation to the officers. At this moment the waiter informed me that the St. Omer diligence was about to depart. I rushed from the scene of my disgrace, and stepped into the vehicle, just as the termination of the Englishman's recital exploded an additional *éclat de rire* at my expense.

MIRTH.

FROM "GUESSES AT TRUTH." BY JULIUS AND AUGUSTUS HARE.

*Ridentem dicere verum quid vetat?** In the first place, all the sour faces in the world, stiffening into a yet more rigid asperity at the least glimpse of a smile. I have seen faces, too, which, so long as you let them lie in their sleepy torpor, unshaken and unstirred, have a creamy softness and smoothness, and might beguile you into suspecting their owners of being gentle; but, if they catch the sound of a laugh, it acts on them like thunder, and they also turn sour. Nay, strange as it may seem, there have been such incarnate paradoxes as would rather see their fellow-creatures cry than smile.

But is not this in exact accordance with the spirit which pronounces a blessing on the weeper, and a woe on the laugher?

Not in the persons I have in view. That blessing and woe are pronounced in the knowledge how apt the course of this world is to run counter to the kingdom of God. They who weep are declared to be blessed, not because they weep, but *because they shall laugh;* and the woe threatened to the laughers is in like manner, that *they shall mourn and weep.* Therefore, they who have this spirit in them, will endeavor to forward the blessing and to avert the woe. They will try to comfort the mourner, so as to lead him to rejoice; and they will warn the laugher, that he may be preserved from the mourning and weeping, and may exchange his passing for lasting joy. But there are many who merely in-

* What forbids one to say what is true in a laughing manner?

dulge in the antipathy, without opening their hearts to the sympathy. Such is the spirit found in those who have cast off the bonds of the lower earthly affections, without having risen as yet into the freedom of heavenly love—in those who have stopped short in the state of transition between the two lives, like so many skeletons stripped of their earthly, and not yet clothed with a heavenly body. It is the spirit of Stoicism, for instance, in philosophy, and of vulgar Calvinism, which in so many things answers to Stoicism in religion. They who feel the harm they have received from worldly pleasures, are prone at first to quarrel with pleasure of every kind altogether; and it is one of the strange perversities of our self-will to entertain anger, instead of pity, towards those whom we fancy to judge or act less wisely than ourselves. This, however, is only while the scaffolding is still standing around the edifice of their Christian life, so that they cannot see clearly out of the windows, and their view is broken up into disjointed parts. When the scaffolding is removed, and they look abroad without hindrance, they are readier than any to delight in all the beauty and true pleasure around them. They feel that it is their blessed calling not only to *rejoice always* themselves, but likewise to *rejoice with all who do rejoice* in innocence of heart. They feel that this must be well-pleasing to Him who has filled His universe with ever-bubbling springs of gladness; so that whithersoever we turn our eyes, through earth and sky as well as sea, we behold the ἀνήριθμον γέλασμα* of nature. On the other hand, it is the harshness of an irreligious temper clothing itself in religious zeal, and not seldom exhibiting symptoms of mental disorganization, that looks scowlingly on every indication of happiness and mirth.

Moreover, there is a large class of people who deem the business of life far too weighty and momentous to be made light of; who would leave merriment to children, and laughter to idiots; and who hold that a joke would be as much out of place on their lips as on a grave-stone or in a ledger. Wit and wisdom being sisters, not only are they afraid of being indicted for bigamy were they to wed them both, but they shudder at such a union as incestuous. So, to keep clear of temptation, and to preserve their faith where they have plighted it, they turn the younger out of doors; and if they see or hear of any body taking her in, they are positive he can know nothing of the elder. They would not be witty for the world. Now, to escape being so, is not very difficult for those whom nature has so favored that wit with them is always at zero, or below it. Or, as to their wisdom, since they are careful never to overfeed her, she jogs leisurely along the turnpike-road, with lank and meagre carcass, displaying all her bones, and never getting out of her own dust. She feels no inclination to be frisky, but, if a coach or wagon passes her, is glad, like her rider, to run behind a thing so big. Now, all these people take grievous offence if any one comes near them better mounted, and they are in a tremor lest the neighing and snorting and prancing should be contagious.

Surely, however, ridicule implies contempt; and so the feeling must be condemnable, subversive of gentleness, incompatible with kindness?

Not necessarily so, or universally; far from it. The word *ridicule*, it is true, has a narrow, one-sided meaning. From our proneness to mix up personal feelings with those which are more purely objective and intellectual, we have in great measure restricted the meaning of *ridicule*, which would properly extend over the whole region of the *ridiculous*, the laughable, where we may disport ourselves innocently, without any evil emotion; and we have narrowed it, so that in common usage it mostly corresponds to *derision*, which does indeed involve personal and offensive feelings. As the great business of wisdom in her speculative office is to detect and reveal the hidden harmonies of things, those harmonies which are the sources and the ever-flowing emanations of Law, the dealings of Wit, on the other hand, are with incongruities. And it is the perception of incongruity, flashing upon us, when unaccompanied, as Aristotle observes (*Poet.* c. v.), by pain, or by any predominant moral disgust, that provokes laughter, and excites the feeling of the ridiculous. But it no more follows that the perception of such an incongruity must breed or foster haughtiness or disdain, than that the perception of any thing else that may be erroneous or wrong should do so. You might as well argue that a man must be proud and scornful because he sees that there is such a thing as sin, or such a thing as folly, in the world. Yet, unless we blind our eyes, and gag our ears, and hoodwink our minds, we shall seldom pass through a day without having some form of evil brought in one way or other before us. Besides, the perception of incongruity may exist, and may awaken laughter, without the slightest reprobation of the object laughed at. We laugh at a pun, surely without a shade of contempt either for the words punned upon or for the punster; and if a very bad pun be the next best thing to a very good one, this is not from its flattering any feeling of superiority in us, but because the incongruity is broader and more glaring. Nor, when we laugh at a droll combination of imagery, do we feel any contempt, but often admiration at the ingenuity shown in it, and an almost affectionate thankfulness toward the person by whom we have been amused, such as is rarely excited by any other display of intellectual power, as those who have ever enjoyed the delight of Professor Sedgwick's society will bear witness.

It is true, an exclusive attention to the ridiculous side of things is hurtful to the character, and destructive of earnestness and gravity. But no less mischievous is it to fix our attention exclusively, or even mainly, on the vices and other follies of mankind. Such contemplations, unless counteracted by wholesomer thoughts, harden or rot the heart, deaden the moral principle, and make us hopeless and reckless. The objects toward which we should turn our minds habitually are those which are great, and good, and pure; the throne of virtue, and she who sits upon it; the majesty of truth, the beauty of holiness. This is the spiritual sky through which we should strive to mount, "springing from crystal step to crystal step," and bathing our souls in its living, life-giving ether. These are the thoughts by which we should whet and polish our swords for the warfare against evil, that the vapors of the earth may not rust them. But in a warfare against evil, under one or other of its forms, we are all of us called to engage; and it is a childish dream to fancy that we can walk about among mankind without perpetual necessity of remarking that

* Boundless laughter.

the world is full of many worse incongruities besides those which make us laugh.

Nor do I deny that a laugher may often be a scoffer and a scorner. Some jesters are fools of a worse breed than those who used to wear the cap. Sneering is commonly found along with a bitter splenetic misanthropy; or it may be a man's mockery at his own hollow heart, venting itself in mockery at others. Cruelty will try to season or to palliate its atrocities by derision. The hyena grins in its den; most wild beasts over their prey. But though a certain kind of wit, like other intellectual gifts, may coexist with moral depravity, there has often been a playfulness in the best and greatest men—in Phocion, in Socrates, in Luther, in Sir Thomas More—which, as it were, adds a bloom to the severer graces of their character, shining forth with amaranthine brightness when storms assail them, and springing up in fresh blossoms under the axe of the executioner. How much is our affection for Hector increased by his tossing his boy in his arms, and laughing at his childish fears! Smiles are the language of love; they betoken the complacency and delight of the heart in the object of its contemplation. Why are we to assume that there must needs be bitterness or contempt in them, when they enforce a truth or reprove an error? On the contrary, some of those who have been richest in wit and humor have been among the simplest and kindest-hearted of men. I will only instance Fuller, Bishop Earle, Lafontaine, Matthes Claudius, Charles Lamb. "Le méchant n'est jamais comique," is wisely remarked by De Maistre, when canvassing the pretensions of Voltaire (*Soirées*, i. 273); and the converse is equally true: *Le comique, le vrai comique, n'est jamais méchant.* A laugh, to be joyous, must flow from a joyous heart; but without kindness there can be no true joy. And what a dull, plodding, tramping, clanking would the ordinary intercourse of society be, without wit to enliven and brighten it! When two men meet, they seem to be kept at bay through the estranging effects of absence, until some sportive sally opens their hearts to each other. Nor does any thing spread cheerfulness so rapidly over a whole party, or an assembly of people, however large. Reason expands the soul of the philosopher; imagination glorifies the poet, and breathes a breath of spring through the young and genial; but if we take into account the numberless glances and gleams whereby wit lightens our every-day life, I hardly know what power ministers so bountifully to the innocent pleasures of mankind.

Surely, too, it cannot be requisite, to a man's being in earnest, that he should wear a perpetual frown. Or is there less of sincerity in Nature during her gambols in spring, than during the stiffness and harshness of her wintry gloom? Does not the bird's blithe carolling come from the heart quite as much as the quadruped's monotonous cry? And is it then altogether impossible to take up one's abode with Truth, and to let all sweet homely feelings grow about it and cluster around it, and to smile upon it as on a kind father or mother, and to sport with it, and hold light and merry talk with it, as with a loved brother or sister; and to fondle it, and play with it, as with a child? No otherwise did Socrates and Plato commune with Truth; no otherwise Cervantes and Shakspere. This playfulness of Truth is beautifully represented by Landor, in the conversation between Marcus Cicero and his brother, in an allegory which has the voice and the spirit of Plato. On the other hand, the outcries of those who exclaim against every sound more lively than a bray or a bleat, as derogatory to truth, are often prompted, not so much by their deep feeling of the dignity of the truth in question, as of the dignity of the person by whom that truth is maintained. It is our vanity, our self-conceit, that makes us so sore and irritable. To a grave argument we may reply gravely, and fancy that we have the best of it; but he who is too dull or too angry to smile, cannot answer a smile, except by fretting and fuming. Olivia lets us into the secret of Malvolio's distaste for the Clown.

For the full expansion of the intellect, moreover, to preserve it from that narrowness and partial warp which our proneness to give ourselves up to the sway of the moment is apt to produce, its various faculties, however opposite, should grow and be trained up side by side—should twine their arms together, and strengthen each other by love-wrestles. Thus will it be best fitted for discerning and acting upon the multiplicity of things which the world sets before it. Thus, too, will something like a balance and order be upheld, and our minds preserved from that exaggeration on the one side, and depreciation on the other side, which are the sure results of exclusiveness. A poet, for instance, should have much of the philosopher in him; not, indeed, thrusting itself forward at the surface—this would only make a monster of his work, like the Siamese twins, neither one thing nor two—but latent within; the spindle should be out of sight, but the web should be spun by the Fates. A philosopher, on the other hand, should have much of the poet in him. A historian cannot be great without combining the elements of the two minds. A statesman ought to unite those of all the three. A great religious teacher, such as Socrates, Bernard, Luther, Schleiermacher, needs the statesman's practical power of dealing with men and things, as well as the historian's insight into their growth and purpose. He needs the philosopher's ideas, impregnated and impersonated by the imagination of the poet. In like manner, our graver faculties and thoughts are much chastened and bettered by a blending and interfusion of the lighter, so that "the sable cloud" may "turn her silver lining on the night;" while our lighter thoughts require the graver to substantiate them and keep them from evaporating. Thus Socrates is said, in Plato's *Banquet*, to have maintained that a great tragic poet ought likewise to be a great comic poet—an observation the more remarkable, because the tendency of the Greek mind, as at once manifested in their Polytheism, and fostered by it, was to insulate all their ideas; and, as it were, to split up the intellectual world into a cluster of Cyclades, leading to confusion, is the characteristic of modern times. The combination, however, was realized in himself, and in his great pupil; and may, perhaps, have been so to a certain extent in Æschylus, if we may judge from the fame of his satiric dramas. At all events the assertion, as has been remarked more than once—for instance by Coleridge (*Remains*, ii., 12,)—is a wonderful prophetical intuition, which has received its fulfilment in Shakspere. No heart would have been strong enough to hold the woe of Lear and Othello, except that which had the unquenchable elasticity of Falstaff and the "Midsummer Night's dream." He, too, is an example that the perception of the ridiculous does not necessarily imply bitterness and scorn. Along with his intense humor, and his equally intense piercing insight into the darkest, most fearful depths of human nature, there is still a spirit of universal kindness, as well as universal justice, pervading his works; and Ben Jonson has left us a precious memorial of him, where he calls him "My *gentle* Shakspeare." This one epithet sheds a beautiful light on his character: its truth is attested by his wisdom, which could never have been so perfect unless it had been harmonized by the gentleness of the dove. A similar union of the graver and lighter powers is found in several of Shakspeare's contemporaries, and in many others among the greatest poets of the modern world; in Boccaccio, in Cervantes, in Chaucer, in Göthe, in Tieck; so was it in Walter Scott.

MY HONORABLE FRIEND BOB.

FROM "DAVID DUMPS." BY THOMAS HAYNES BAYLY.

It was at a public school that I first became acquainted with my friend Bob. He was then a little round-faced, curly-pated boy, about ten years of age; and I being two years his senior, and there existing some intimacy between our parents, he was put under my protection.

I soon, fool that I was, became very fond of Bob. We naturally get attached to those who cling to us for support; and every thing was so new to him, poor fellow! that without me he was miserable.

At that very early age, Bob had acquired a taste for extravagance; his money always burnt a hole in his little breeches' pocket; and when it was gone, many a shilling did he borrow of me, and many more did he owe to Mrs. Puffy, the fat vender of pastry, whose residence was "down the street."

At sixteen, I left Doctor Rearpepper's establishment; and many were the tears that poor Bob shed at my departure. He said nothing at all about the nine shillings and fourpence halfpenny that he owed me; but when I said, "Bob, be sure you write to me," I suspect that he almost expected me to add, "and don't forget to enclose the money."

During my residence at Oxford, we never met. At first our interchange of letters was frequent, and the style of our communications most affectionate; but gradually our correspondence flagged, and for a whole year I heard nothing of him. At length, by the coach came a splendidly bound copy of a work which he knew to be my favorite; and in the title-page was written my name, and underneath the words, "From his affectionate and grateful friend Bob."

"Yes," thought I, as I read the inscription, "and still thou art my honorable friend!"

Bob, after so long a period had elapsed, was naturally ashamed to send me the few shillings that he owed me; but he could not be happy till he had spent many pounds on a gift which was intended to repay me. With the parcel, I received a letter announcing his having entered the army, and adding that he was about to join his regiment, which was then on a foreign station. He entreated me not to suppose from his long silence that he had forgotten me; and, in short, there was so much warmth of heart about the whole letter, that Bob was reinstated in my good graces, and I wrote him a most affectionate reply, assuring him that whenever we met he would find me unaltered.

After quitting Oxford, I travelled on the Continent for many months; and on my return to England, I found my friend Bob at a hotel in Bond street, and, in every sense of the words, "a gay man about town."

Ours was more like the reunion of boys after a summer's vacation, than a meeting of men who had seen something of the world. We could talk only of the past, of frolic and of fun; and while arm-in-arm we ranged the streets of the west end, we laughed almost as much, and were really nearly as thoughtless, as in the days when together we ranged the play-ground of old Rearpepper.

Whatever *I* may have been, Bob was indeed unchanged; and not alone in spirits and temper, for I soon found that his old habits had grown with his growth, and strengthened with his strength. He still retained his "sweet tooth," and daily did he lead me into Gunter's or Grange's, (nay, often into both in turn,) and there I saw him indulge as he used of old in the habitation of Mrs. Puffy;—the only difference was, that his dainties were somewhat more refined, and more expensive; for, alas! I soon saw the old injunction, "Put it down to my bill," had by no means fallen into disuse. All other tradespeople were most impartially *dealt with* by Bob in the same way; and I saw him take possession of trinkets, coats, hats, and boots, without considering it requisite to take his purse out of his pocket.

The next morning, Bob ran to my bedside to inform me that he was ordered to India, and must leave London in a day or two. He showed me his letters, and it was evident that he must prepare for his immediate departure.

We breakfasted together; and during the repast, the waiter was continually presenting him with wafered notes; and it appeared that several persons had called, very earnestly wishing to see him. I had my suspicions about these visitations, but said nothing.

Immediately after breakfast, Bob took my arm and requested me to walk with him; and after passing through several streets and squares in unusual silence, and with an appearance of agitation in his manner, he suddenly addressed me.

"There is no alternative," said he; "I must go."

"You must, indeed, Bob," I replied,—"unless you are *detained*."

"Detained!" said Bob, blushing; "how do you mean?"

"Pardon me," I answered, "but really few young men could go on as you have lately done, and be prepared for a departure so sudden. Now, my dear Bob, you know what my finances are; you know I have literally *nothing* to spare; but if, knowing this, you think I can be of temporary use to you, command me."

Bob grasped my arm, and his eyes watered; but he was ashamed to own the extent of his encumbrances, and therefore hastily answered,

"This is like yourself, my dear friend, and at the moment you may indeed serve me by putting your name to a bill."

"Not of large amount, Bob, I trust?"

"No—yes—larger, I fear, than——"

"If it be a large sum, Bob, you know that if your draft is not honored when it becomes due, *I* shall go to prison instead of *you*."

"Never!" said Bob with a fervor and an evidence of deep feeling which I could not distrust.

"Well, then, what is the sum?" said I.

"First, let me tell you some circumstances which press heavily on my heart," said Bob; "not here—come with me this way."

And in solemn silence he led me to Portman Square.

"What can all this mean?" said I, at last.

"Hush!" said Bob; "you see that house?"

And he pointed to a very handsome well-appointed mansion. A footman was standing at the door receiving cards from a lady in a carriage.

"My dear fellow," I exclaimed, "this is news indeed!—you have no occasion of assistance from a poor fellow like *me*."

"Oh!" said Bob, "you have not heard all. She loves me to madness, poor dear girl! But, rich as her father is, were *he* to suppose that I am involved, he would forbid the match."

"A very sensible old man."

"That may be; but there is another obstacle—my rank: Clara will not consent to marry any thing below a captain."

I could not repress a laugh.

"It *is* a foible, perhaps," said Bob, rather piqued; "but it is her only one, and I must humor it. But my promotion depends on my going to India, and—"

"Well, well," said I, "I understand all this; but tell me at once what you wish *me* to do for you."

"To put your name to a draft for one hundred and ninety pounds," faltered Bob.

"Mercy on me! what a sum!" said I. However, it must be done: and when the draft becomes due—"

"See the house?" I replied; "to be sure I do; and what then?"

"That house is owned by one of the wealthiest commoners in England."

"Umph!" said I; "the owner, I suppose, *is* rich."

"He has an only daughter," said Bob.

"Has he?" I answered.

"His sole heiress," added Bob.

"What then?" I replied.

"I am ashamed of having concealed all this so long from so dear a friend," murmured Bob.

"All what?"

"But the secret was not my own."

"What secret?"

"That lovely girl!"

"Upon my word, Bob," I cried, "you put me out of all patience!"

"I have won that girl's affections."

"The heiress?" said I.

"She loves me," whispered Bob.

"I will honorably pay it!"

"If not, to prison I go. And now let us return to our hotel."

"One moment," said Bob: "I love to look at the house."

"At the casket which contains the gem?" said I.

"Yes; and for *your* sake, too, I love to look at it. You see those three windows shaded with sky-blue silk curtains? Oh, *such* a little room *that* is!—and that room I always mean to be your own *exclusively*, when *I* am master of the mansion. Such a room!—the furniture so exquisite!—and such a sweet look out over the square!—But come, we'll talk all that over while we are at dinner."

Before the meal was half finished, Bob seemed quite to have recovered his spirits; and I could not help suspecting, that as the prospect of an immediate separation did not seem to depress him, he loved the lady less than he loved her gold.

"Is she pretty?" said I after a long pause, during which *I* at least had been thinking of her.

"Who?" said Bob, starting.

"I say, is the lady pretty?"

"What lady?" said Bob.

"Why, your love, to be sure."

"Which do you mean?"

"Nonsense, Bob!—I mean the girl you are attached to;—why, man, she who lives in Portman Square."

"O! what *was* I dreaming of!—*very* pretty."

"I can't imagine, Bob," said I, "when you contrived to win your divinity: you and I have been for months almost inseparable, and—"

"Ask no questions," said Bob; "the secret is not my own."

"Not entirely, certainly," I replied. "Is she to inherit the house in Portman Square?"

"To be sure she is: and *such* a house as it is!—and that room which I mean for you! You are fond of a hot bath?"

"Very."

"There is a sky-blue silk sofa in that room; and when you touch a spring, it flies up, (I don't exactly know the principle on which it acts,) and turns into the most delightful bath!"

"Indeed!"

"Yes, a marble bath."

"Marble?"

"White marble without a speck;—she *did* tell me where it came from,—but that's no consequence."

"How very luxurious!" said I.

"Yes; and so very complete!—three cocks!"

"*Three!*" said I: "*two*, you mean."

"No, no,—three," replied Bob: "one for hot water—"

"Yes," said I.

"And one for cold—"

"Well, that makes *two*," said I.

"And one," said Bob, "for *eau-de-Cologne*."

In the evening, I put my name to Bob's draft, and the next morning we parted with mutual expressions of regret.

I missed him sadly; and it so happened, that after he went, many untoward circumstances occurred which, having first materially lowered my resources, next effectually lowered my spirits, and I used to saunter through our old haunts, looking like the ghost of his companion.

When he was gone, I became acquainted with many circumstances connected with his expenditure which perfectly astounded me; and at the end of four months, (exactly two months before it was to become due,) I had every reason to doubt whether the draft for one hundred and ninety pounds would ever be paid.

I was conscious of my own utter inability to pay it; and I therefore existed for a week or two in a state of mental excitement not to be described. One day after breakfast, I sallied forth more dolorous than usual; and after wandering about for some time, I found myself in Portman Square, opposite the identical mansion inhabited by Bob's intended.

"Ah!" thought I, "were Bob now in possession of that house, all would go well with us:—his heart is in the right place, poor fellow! But, alas! before he puts me in possession of that sky-blue apartment, with the hot water and the cold and the *eau-de-Cologne*, I may be in prison, and my name disgraced!"

As I looked towards the balcony of the drawing-room, I saw a female watering some geraniums; and, suddenly turning her head towards me, she seemed to recognize my person, and gave me a familiar nod.

I soon discovered it was my old friend and near connection Mrs. Symmons; and, beckoning me to the window, she exclaimed,

"Oh! I'm delighted to see you!—we only came to town yesterday,—we are on a visit to Mr. Molesworth: pray come in, and I'll introduce you."

I knocked at the hall-door in a state of mind not to be described,—the hall-door of the house in which *I* (*by anticipation*) already possessed a room of my own, with sky-blue curtains, and a new-invented spring sofa bath overflowing with *eau-de-Cologne!* I walked up stairs; and my friend Mrs. Symmons introduced me to Mr. Molesworth, (an old gentleman in a pair of gouty shoes,) his daughter, Miss Molesworth, (a lovely, fair-haired girl of about eighteen,) *her sister Flora*, (still *in* a pinafore, and not *come out*,) *and her two little brothers* (schoolboys in round jackets and duck trousers).

"Dear me!" thought I, "how poor dear Bob was mistaken in supposing her an heiress!"

In this family I spent many happy days; and being, though unknown to her, so well acquainted with the secret of the young lady's heart, I became more intimate with her than I could have been with any one else, without incurring the imputation of "serious intentions." In this instance, however, my knowledge of the fair lady's engagement to another person, (and that person my friend,) made me feel perfectly at my ease; and we became the talk of all our acquaintances, without my being the least aware that we were engaged even in a little flirtation.

To my utter astonishment, Mrs. Symmons came to me one day, (it was the day before that on which Bob's draft was to become due,) and, with a knowing look, asked me why I was so out of spirits? I gave an evasive reply, for I did not choose to own the paltry pecuniary difficulty, which was threatening to overpower me.

"Nonsense!" said Mrs. Symmons; "go boldly, and make your offer: your connections are unexceptionable; and whatever your present income may be, your prospects are excellent. Besides, *she* has enough for both; for, though not an only child, her father can afford to give her a very excellent fortune."

"And pray," I replied, "of what lady are you talking?"

"Miss Molesworth, to be sure;—I *know* she is attached to you."

"You know nothing about the matter," said I; "for I can tell *you* that——"

I hesitated, for I had no right to betray Bob's secret.

"Well," said Mrs. Symmons, "here she comes, and I will leave you together;" and away she went.

"What is the matter?" said Miss Molesworth earnestly, as she entered; "you seem agitated—what has happened?"

"Are we alone?" said I after a pause. "It is better that I should be explicit."

Miss Molesworth started, colored, and cast down her eyes. Had I been a favored lover on the point of making an avowal of attachment, she could not have been more embarrassed.

"Do not be alarmed," said I: "I know all!"

"Sir!" said Miss Molesworth.

"I am Bob's best friend, and I know your secret."

"*My* secret!" she exclaimed.

"Yes, dear lady," I answered: "I am, as I told you before, the most intimate friend of Bob."

"Of Bob!" said she.

"Yes," I replied, taking her hand; "I am Bob's school-fellow."

"And pray, sir," said she, withdrawing her hand, "who *is* Bob?"

"Do not distress yourself," I whispered; "do not think it necessary to conceal any thing from me;—before he left England, Bob told me all."

"All *what?*" cried Miss Molesworth.

"Your mutual attachment,—your engagement," I replied.

Miss Molesworth started up, coloring crimson. At first, she could not articulate, but at last she said,

"I know not, sir, to what I am to attribute this conduct: I have been attached to *no one*, engaged to *no one*,—I know not of whom you speak. I had considered you, sir, in the light of a friend; but now, sir, now——"

She could say no more, but sank on a chair beside me, in a flood of tears.

A mist at that moment fell from my eyes; I saw at once the full extent of Bob's unpardonable falsehood, and the distressing certainty flashed upon my mind that his draft would be dishonored.

Mrs. Symmons entered at the moment, and found us both apparently plunged into the depths of despair. Miss Molesworth was in an instant weeping on her shoulder; and before a quarter of an hour had elapsed, I found myself breathing forth vows of love to the young lady, and exulting in my discovery that her engagement to my friend Bob was a fable.

Miss Molesworth referred me to her father; but I read in her large blue eyes that she did *not* dislike me. I therefore retired to my bed that night full of love and hope, and dreamed of driving my wife in a chariot drawn by six dragons, over the mangled body of Bob.

The next morning, my first thought was of my approaching interview with Mr. Molesworth: but, alas! it was soon followed by my recollection of Bob's draft, and the too great probability that before night I should be in durance vile for the amount. My own resources were at the moment inadequate to meet the demand; and could I ask a rich man to let me marry his daughter, and expect that his first act would be to pay one hundred and ninety pounds to extricate me from a prison!

At length, I made up my mind to walk to Bob's bankers, and at once ascertain the worst. I did so, and on my arrival was astounded at being informed by the clerk that he had provided funds for the payment of the draft!

So far I had wronged my honorable friend; and I was therefore able to appear in Portman Square in excellent spirits.

"The course of" my "true love" did, for a wonder, "run smooth," and, all our preliminaries having been finally arranged, the Molesworths left town for the family seat in Wiltshire, and I remained to arrange some legal and other matters, which would in all probability detain me for a couple of months. I was sitting in my own room rather out of spirits the morning after my true love's departure, when the door opened, and in came—Bob! He was so evidently delighted to see me again, that I could not help receiving him kindly. He spoke of the obligation I had conferred upon him previous to his departure; and after frankly acknowledging the gratification I had felt at his punctuality, I said,

"But how is this? returned after so short an absence!"

"Oh! we are not to go to India, after all; I've been no further than Madeira;—we'll talk that all over another time. I suppose I shall be sent to the West, instead of the East."

"I only regret it on account of your rank; it may retard your marriage."

"*My* marriage!" said Bob, blushing all over.

"Yes; your marriage with the heiress of Portman Square."

"Oh!" cried Bob, starting from his chair and pressing his hand, "never—never, I entreat you, mention that subject again."

"Why so?" said I.

"It is all off," sighed Bob.

"Off!" I exclaimed.

"Yes, the traitress!—But enough,—never name her to me again."

I of course promised to obey him, and for some days we enjoyed ourselves very much in the old way. One morning, he came to me in real distress, and told me that his tailor had threatened to arrest him for the amount of his bill. I offered to go and speak to the man, and endeavor to persuade him to give Bob time.

"If he will only give me a month," said Bob.

"Well," I cried, "I can but try him;" and away I went.

The tailor was inexorable; but he told me that if I would become responsible for the payment of the debt in a month, he would consent to wait; if not, he was determined to arrest Bob that day.

I hesitated for a moment; but, recollecting his prompt payment of the hundred and ninety pounds, I made myself responsible for the amount of the bill, and then returned to congratulate my friend.

When I told him what I had done, he started up and exclaimed, "You do not mean it!—you cannot have made yourself responsible for the amount of that fellow's bill!"

"I have, I assure you," said I.

"Then," said Bob, "*you* will have to pay it; I shall not have the money myself; I never asked you to incur the responsibility,—I never expected it,—and I repeat that you will have to pay it."

"My dear Bob," said I, "it will not be in my power; I am peculiarly situated. At the end of a month, I shall be most particularly engaged—my hands, as it were, will be *tied*, and paying this at that particular period will be out of the question."

Still Bob persisted that he never asked me to become responsible, and it ended in his leaving me in a very ill humor. My engagements with legal persons employed me for days together in the city, and I saw very little of Bob. When we did meet, my manner was cold and restrained; and it was not till within a day or two of the expiration of the month that I had time to think of the very inopportune and annoying responsibility which I had incurred.

That very day, I met Bob, and spoke to him most earnestly and seriously about the payment; but he sighed most deeply, told me how much he lamented my having engaged to make the payment, and pathetically bemoaned the emptiness of his own pockets. The next morning, I called on the tailor, earnestly requesting him to renew the draft for another month, and was then told that my honorable friend had called that very day, and had placed in his hands the sum for which I was responsible!

I went instantly to call upon him, and he received me with laughter, in which I could not resist joining; but I confess I laughed the more from the recollection that my hour of revenge was at hand.

About a fortnight afterwards, (the family of my intended having arrived in town for the wedding, which was to take place the next morning at St. George's Church, Hanover Square,) Bob inquired "*what* it was that seemed to occupy me from morning till night, and *why* it was that we so seldom met?"

"My dear Bob," said I, "it has been a secret!"

"Oh! a secret!"

"Yes; and the secret has not been *entirely* my own."

"Indeed!" said Bob.

"But I will *now* conceal nothing from you: you, I remember, before you went away, confided *your* secret to *me*."

"Oh!—ah!—hem—yes—well?" stammered Bob.

"I am going to be married to-morrow."

"Married!" exclaimed Bob: "tell me all about it; who is she,—do *I* know her?"

"You do *not* know her; but I have heard you *speak of her*."

"Indeed! Where does she live?—is she pretty?—is she rich?"

"There is no time," said I, "to answer your questions at present: I dine with the family at six, and I mean to take you with me. Go and dress, and in half an hour I will call for you in a carriage."

"Where does your intended live?" said Bob as we drove along Oxford Street and turned into Orchard Street.

"Time will show," I replied.

"Where are we now?" said Bob as the carriage made a sudden turn.

"We are in Portman Square," I replied.

"And the lady lives——" faltered Bob.

"In Portman Square," said I.

Bob sat in evident confusion; and when the carriage actually stopped at Mr. Molesworth's house, he said,

"I deserve this—I am quite ashamed of myself. Come, come, turn back and drive home."

"By no means," said I, as the servant gave a thundering knock at the door, and then let down the steps of the carriage.

"Look," said I, pointing upwards, while we waited for the street-door to be opened; "you see those three windows with sky-blue curtains?"

"O! spare me!" cried Bob.

"That room I always mean to reserve *exclusively* for you: there is a wonderful sofa, silken without, and marble within."

"My dear friend!" said Bob imploringly.

"Don't interrupt me," I proceeded;—"an exquisite bath with three cocks; one for hot water, one for cold, and one for *eau-de-Cologne*. But we have no time now to expatiate on its advantages;" and I jumped out of the carriage.

"Why, you *won't* go in!" cried Bob as he breathlessly ran up the steps after me, and vigorously pulled at the tail of my coat.

"Go in!" said I; "to be sure: and you will meet old friends, and show me where you used to meet the lady of your love, and——"

"You are going too far!" whispered Bob: "I see my error; I uttered what was false—forgive me—I am cured. But these servants and the inmates of the house will think us mad!"

"Not at all," I replied. "Speak the truth in future, as I have done to you."

I pressed his hand, and led him up stairs. I saw that he was depressed and humiliated; and when we got to the drawing-room door, he whispered,

"And do *they* know it? I cannot face them."

"They know *nothing*," I replied, "and shall never know from me any thing discreditable to my honorable friend Bob."

"I will never utter a falsehood again," said Bob. And I firmly believe he adhered to his resolution.

READING A TRAGEDY.

FROM "WEEDS OF WITCHERY." BY THOMAS HAYNES BAYLY.

OH, proud am I, exceeding proud, I've mustered the *Elite!*
I'll read them my new Tragedy—no ordinary treat;
It has a deeply-stirring plot—the moment I commence
They'll feel for my sweet Heroine an interest intense;
It never lags, it never flags, it cannot fail to touch;
Indeed, I fear the sensitive may feel it *over* much;
But still a dash of pathos with my terrors I combine,
The bright reward of tragic Bard—the laurel will be mine!

Place chairs for all the company, and, Ma'am, I really think
If you don't send that child to bed, he will not sleep a wink;
I know he'll screech like any thing before I've read a page;
My second act would terrify a creature of that age:
And should the darling, scared by me, become an *Imbecile*,
Though *flatter'd* at the circumstance—how sorry I should feel!
What! *won't* you send the child to bed? well, Madam, we shall see;—
Pray take a chair, and now prepare the laurel crown for me.

Have *all* got pocket-handkerchiefs? your tears will fall in streams:
Place water near to sprinkle over any one who screams;
And pray, good People, recollect, when what I've said controls
Your sympathies, and actually harrows up your souls;
Remember, (it may save you all from suicide, or fits,)
'Tis but a mortal man who opes the flood-gates of his wits!
Retain your intellects to trace my brightest gem, (*my moral*)
And, when I've done, I'm *very* sure you'll wreathe my brow with laurel.

Hem—"*Act the first, and scene the first—a wood—Bumrumpti enters—*
Bumrumpti speaks, 'And have I then escaped from my tormentors?
Revenge! Revenge! oh, were they dead, and *I* a carrion crow,
I'd pick the flesh from off their bones, I'd sever toe from toe!
Shall fair Fryfritta, pledged to me, her plighted vow recall,
And wed with hated Snookums or with *any* man at all!
No—rather perish earth and sea, the sky and—all the rest of it—
For wife to me she swore she'd be, and she *must* make the best of it.'"

Through five long acts—ay, *very* long, the happy Bard proceeds;
Without a pause, without applause, scene after scene he reads!
That *silent* homage glads his heart! it silent well may be;
Not one of all his slumbering friends can either hear or see!
The anxious Chaperon is asleep! the Beau beside the Fair!
The dog is sleeping on the rug! the cat upon the chair!
Old men and babes—the Footman, too! oh, if we crown the Bard,
We'll twine for him the *Poppy* wreath, his only fit reward.

DEADLY NIGHTSHADE.

FROM "WEEDS OF WITCHERY." BY THOMAS HAYNES BAYLY.

I LAY within a strange abode, and on a curtain'd bed,
The lamp upon the tapestry a ghastly glimmer shed;
I could not doze, I could not sleep, I heard the rats and mice;
My head was like a furnace, and my hands and feet like ice.
I thought of all my evil deeds, and wished them all undone,
I longed to hear the merry lark, and see the rising sun;
I heard the hooting of the owl, the ticking of the clock,
And the door did shake, while something seem'd to fidget with the lock!

I wanted much to ring the bell to summon man or maid,
I did not thrust a finger forth, because I was afraid;
I longed to call out lustily, but not a word I said,
I grasped the blankets and the sheets and held them o'er my head.
I heard a most alarming noise, I never heard the like,
Just as the turret-clock struck twelve! a horrid hour to strike!
And down my chimney screeching came a most malignant Fiend—
I sat up trembling in my bed—good gracious, how he grinn'd!

Upon the marble mantelpiece there flared a globe of flame!
And in it danced distorted forms too horrible to name!
And on the hearth the Fiend still sat! I fainted with affright!
But rose next morn to trace the cause the moment there was light.
The Fiend was but a tabby cat! the globe of flame I saw,
A shade of paper for the lamp—such as my sisters draw!
'Twas traced with ghosts and skeletons from charnel-houses damp!
It *isn't* nice to have a Deadly Nightshade for one's lamp!

THE WORLD AS IT IS.

ANONYMOUS.

"What a delightful thing the world is! Lady Lennox's ball, last night—how charming it was!—every one so kind, and Charlotte looking so pretty—the nicest girl I ever saw! But I must dress now. Balfour is to be here at twelve with the horse he wants to sell me. How lucky I am to have such a friend as Balfour!—so entertaining—so good-natured—so devilish clever too—and such an excellent heart! Ah! how unlucky! it rains a little; but never mind, it will clear up; and if it don't—why, there's billiards. What a delightful thing the world is!"

So soliloquized Charles Nugent, a man of twenty-one—a philanthropist—an optimist. Our young gentleman was an orphan, of good family and large fortune; brave, generous, confiding, and open-hearted. His ability was above the ordinary standard, and he had a warm love and a pure taste for letters. He had even bent a knee to Philosophy, but the calm and cold graces with which the goddess receives her servants had soon discontented the young votary with the worship. "Away!" cried he, one morning, flinging aside the volume of La Rochefoucault, which he had fancied he understood; "Away with this selfish and debasing code!—men are not the mean things they are here described—be it mine to think exulting of my species!" My dear Experience, with how many fine sentiments do you intend to play the devil? It is not without reason that Goethe tells us, that though Fate is an excellent, she is also a very expensive schoolmistress.

"Ha! my dear Nugent, how are you?" and Captain Balfour enters the room: a fine, dark, handhome fellow, with something of pretension in his air and a great deal of frankness. "And here is the horse. Come to the window. Does he not step finely? What action! Do you remark his forehand? How he carries his tail! Gad, I don't think you shall have him, after all!" "Nay, my dear fellow, you may well be sorry to part with him. He is superb! Quite sound—eh?" "Have him examined." "Do you think I would not take your word for it? The price?" "Fix it yourself. Prince Paul once offered me a hundred-and-eighty; but to you——" "You shall have it." "No, Nugent—say, a hundred-and-fifty." "I won't be outdone—there's a draft for the 180*l.*" "Upon my soul, I'm ashamed; but you are such a rich fellow. John, take the horse to Mr. Nugent's stables. Where will you dine to-day?—at the Cocoa-tree?" "With all my heart."

The young men rode together. Nugent was delighted with his new purchase. They dined at the Cocoa-tree. Balfour ordered some early peaches. Nugent paid the bill. They went to the Opera. "Do you see that *danseuse*, Florine?" asked Balfour. "Pretty ankle—eh?" "Yes, *comme ça*—but dances awkwardly—not handsome. "What! not handsome? Come and talk to her. She's more admired than any girl on the stage." They went behind the scenes, and Balfour convinced his friend that he ought to be enchanted with Florine. Before the week was out, the *danseuse* kept her carriage, and in return, Nugent supped with her twice a week.

Nugent had written a tale for "The Keepsake;" it was his first literary effort; it was tolerably good, and exceedingly popular. One day, he was lounging over his breakfast, and a tall, thin gentleman, in black, was announced by the name of Mr. Gilpin. Mr. Gilpin made a most respectful bow, and heaved a peculiarly profound sigh. Nugent was instantly seized with a lively interest in the stranger. "Sir, it is with great regret," faltered forth Mr. Gilpin, "that I seek you. I—I—I—" A low, consumptive cough checked his speech. Nugent offered him a cup of tea. The civility was refused, and the story continued. Mr. Gilpin's narration is soon told, when he himself is not the narrator. An unfortunate literary man—once in affluent circumstances—security for a treacherous friend—friend absconded—pressure of unforeseen circumstances—angel wife and four cherub children — a book coming out next season—deep distress at present—horror at being forced to beg—generous sentiments expressed in the tale written by Mr. Nugent forcibly struck him—a ray of hope broke on his mind—and *voila* the causes of Mr. Gilpin's distress and Mr. Gilpin's visit. Never was there a more interesting personification of the afflicted man of letters than Gregory Gilpin. He looked pale, patient, and respectable; he coughed frequently, and he was dressed in deep mourning. Nugent's heart swelled—he placed a bank-note in Mr. Gilpin's hands—he promised more effectual relief, and Mr. Gilpin retired, overpowered with his own gratitude and Mr. Nugent's respectful compassion. "How happy I am to be rich!" said the generous young philanthropist, throwing open his chest.

Nugent went to a conversazione at Lady Lennox's. Her ladyship was a widow, and a charming woman. She was a little of the blue, and a little of the fine lady, and a little of the beauty, and a little

of the coquette, and a great deal of the sentimentalist. She had one daughter, without a shilling; she had taken a warm interest in a young man of the remarkable talents and amiability of Charles Nugent. He sat next her—they talked of the heartlessness of the world—it is a subject on which men of twenty-one and ladies of forty-five are especially eloquent. Lady Lennox complained, Mr. Nugent defended. "One does not talk much of innocence," it is said, or something like it is said, somewhere in Madame d' Epinay's Memoirs, "without being sadly corrupted;" and nothing brings out the goodness of our own hearts more than a charge against the heartlessness of others. "An excellent woman!" thought Nugent; "what warm feelings! — how pretty her daughter is! Oh, a charming family!" Charlotte Lennox played an affecting air; Nugent leaned over the piano; they talked about music, poetry, going on the water, sentiment and Richmond Hill. They made up a party of pleasure. Nugent did not sleep well that night—he was certainly in love. When he rose the next morning, the day was bright and fine; Balfour, the best of friends, was to be with him in an hour; Balfour's horse, the best of horses, was to convey him to Richmond; and at Richmond he was to meet Lady Lennox, the most agreeable of mothers—and Charlotte, the most enchanting of daughters. The *danseuse* had always been a bore—she was now forgotten. "It certainly is a delightful world!" repeated Nugent, as he tied his neckcloth.

It was some time—we will not say how long—after the date of this happy day; Nugent was alone in his apartment, and walking to and fro—his arms folded, and a frown upon his brow. "What a rascal! what a mean wretch!—and the horse was lame when he sold it—not worth ten pounds!—and I so confiding—d—— my folly! *That*, however, I should not mind; but to have saddled me with his cast-off mistress!—to make me the laughing-stock of the world! By heavens, he shall repent it! Borrowed money of me, then made a jest of my good-nature!—introduced me to his club, in order to pillage me!—but, thank God, thank God, I can shoot him yet! Ha! Colonel; this is kind!" Colonel Nelmore, an elderly gentleman, well known in society, with a fine forehead, a shrewd, contemplative eye, and an agreeable address, entered the room. To him Nugent poured forth the long list of his grievances, and concluded by begging him to convey a challenge to the best of friends—Captain Balfour. The Colonel raised his eyebrows. "But,—my dear sir,—this gentleman has certainly behaved ill to you, I allow it—but for what specific offence do you mean to challenge him?" "For his conduct in general." The Colonel laughed. "For saying yesterday, then, that I was grown a d——d bore, and he should cut me in future. He told Selwyn so in the bow-window at White's." The Colonel took snuff. "My good young friend," said he, "I see you don't know the world. Come and dine with me to-day—a punctual seven. We'll talk over these matters. Meanwhile, you cant challenge a man for calling you a bore." "Not challenge him!—what should I do then?" "Laugh—shake your head at him, and say—'Ah! Balfour, you're a sad fellow!'" The Colonel succeeded in preventing the challenge, but Nugent's indignation at the best of friends remained as warm as ever. He declined the Colonel's invitation—he was to dine with the Lennoxes. Meanwhile, he went to the shady part of Kensington Gardens to indulge his reflections. He sat himself down in an arbor, and looked moralizingly over the initials, the dates, and the witticisms, that hands, long since mouldering, have consigned to the admiration of posterity.

A gay party was strolling by this retreat—their laughter and voices preceded them. "Yes," said a sharp, dry voice, which Nugent recognized as belonging to one of the wits of the day—"Yes, I saw you, Lady Lennox, talking sentiment to Nugent—fie! how could you waste your time so unprofitably!" "Ah! poor young man! he is certainly *bien bête*, with his fine phrases and so forth: but 'tis a good creature on the whole, and exceedingly useful!" "Useful!" "Yes; fills up a vacant place at one's table, at a day's warning; lends me his carriage-horses when mine have caught cold; subscribes to my charities for me; and supplies the drawing-room with flowers. In a word, if he were more sensible, he would be less agreeable: his sole charm is his foibles."

Proh Jupiter! what a description, from the most sentimental of mothers, of the most talented, the most interesting of young men. Nugent was thunderstruck; the party swept by; he was undiscovered. He raved, he swore, he was furious. He go to the dinner to-day? No, he would write such a letter to the lady—it should speak daggers! But the daughter: Charlotte was not of the party. Charlotte—oh! Charlotte was quite a different creature from her mother—the most natural, the most simple of human beings, and evidently loved him. He could not be mistaken there. Yes, for her sake he would go to the dinner; he would smother his just resentment.

He went to Lady Lennox's. It was a large party. The young Marquis of Austerly had just returned from his travels. He was sitting next to the most lovely of daughters. Nugent was forgotten. After dinner, however, he found an opportunity to say a few words in a whisper to Charlotte. He hinted a tender reproach, and he begged her to sing "*We met; 'twas in a crowd.*" Charlotte was hoarse—had caught cold. Charlotte could not sing. Nugent left the room. When he got to the end of the street, he discovered that he had left his cane behind. He went back for it, glad (for he was really in love) of an excuse for darting an angry glance at the most simple, the most natural of human beings, that should prevent her sleeping the whole night. He ascended the drawing-room; and Charlotte was delighting the Marquis of Austerly, who leaned over her chair, with *We met; 'twas in a crowd.*" Charlotte Lennox was young, lovely, and artful. Lord Austerly was young, inexperienced, and vain. In less than a month, he proposed, and was accepted.

"Well, well!" said poor Nugent, one morning, breaking from a reverie; "betrayed in my friendship, deceived in my love, the pleasure of doing good is still left to me. Friendship quits us at the first stage of life, Love at the second, Benevolence lasts till death! Poor Gilpin! how grateful he is: I must see if I can get him that place abroad." To amuse his thoughts, he took up a new magazine. He opened the page at a violent attack on himself—on his beautiful tale in the "Keepsake." The satire was not confined to the work; it extended to the author. He was a fop, a coxcomb, a ninny, an intellectual dwarf, a miserable creature, and an abortion. These are pleasant studies for a man out of spirits, especially before he is used to them. Nugent had just flung the magazine to the other end of the room, when his lawyer came to arrange matters about a mortgage, which the generous Nugent had already been forced to raise on his estates. The lawyer was a pleasant, entertaining man of the world, accustomed to the society, for he was accustomed to the wants, of young men. He perceived Nugent was a little out of humor. He attributed the cause, naturally enough, to the mortgage; and to divert his thoughts, he entered first on a general conversation.

"What rogues there are in the world!" said he. Nugent groaned. "This morning, for instance, before I came to you, I was engaged in a curious piece of business enough. A gentleman gave his son-in-law a qualification to stand for a borough; the son-in-law kept the deed, and so cheated the good gentleman out of more than 300*l.* a-year. Yesterday, I was employed against a fraudulent bankrupt—such an instance of long, premeditated, cold-hearted, deliberate rascality! And when I leave you, I must see what is to be done with a literary swindler, who, on the strength of a consumptive cough, and a suit of black, has been respectably living on compassion for the last two years." "Ha!" "He has just committed the most nefarious fraud—a forgery, in short, on his own uncle, who has twice seriously distressed himself to save the rogue of a nephew, and who must now submit to this loss, or proclaim, by a criminal prosecution, the disgrace of his own family. The nephew proceeded, of course, on his knowledge of my client's goodness of heart; and thus a man suffers in proportion to his amiability." "Is his name Gil—Gil—Gilpin?" stammered Nugent. "The same! O-ho! have you been bit too, Mr. Nugent?"

Before our hero could answer, a letter was brought to him. Nugent tore the seal; it was from the editor of the magazine in which he had just read his own condemnation. It ran thus:—

"Sir,—Having been absent from London on unavoidable business for the last month, and the care of the —— Magazine having thereby devolved on another, who has very ill discharged its duties, I had the surprise and mortification of perceiving, on my return this day, that a most unwarrantable and personal attack upon you has been admitted in the number for this month. I cannot sufficiently express my regret, the more especially on finding that the article in question was written by a mere mercenary in letters. To convince you of my concern, and my resolution to guard against such unworthy proceedings in future, I enclose you another, and yet severer attack, which was sent to us for our next number, and for which, I grieve to say, the unprincipled author has already succeeded in obtaining from the proprietors—a remuneration," etc., etc., etc.

Nugent's eyes fell on the enclosed paper; it was in the handwriting of Mr. Gregory Gilpin, the most grateful of distressed literary men.

"You seem melancholy to-day, my dear Nugent," said Colonel Nelmore, as he met his young friend walking with downcast eyes on the old mall of St. James's Park. "I am unhappy, I am discontented; the gloss is faded from life," answered Nugent, sighing. "I love meeting with a pensive man," said the Colonel; "let me join you, and let us dine together, *tête-à-tête*, at my bachelor's house. You refused me some time ago; may I be more fortunate now?" "I shall be but poor company," rejoined Nugent; "but I am very much obliged to you, and I accept your invitation with pleasure."

Colonel Nelmore was a man who had told some fifty years. He had known misfortune in his day, and he had seen a great deal of the harsh realities of life. But he had not suffered nor lived in vain. He was no theorist, and did not affect the philosopher; but he was contented with a small fortune, popular with retired habits, observant for a love of study, and, above all, he did a great deal of general good, exactly because he embraced no particular system.

"Yes," said Nugent, as they sat together after dinner, and the younger man had embosomed to the elder, who had been his father's most intimate friend, all that had seemed to him the most unexampled of misfortunes—after he had repeated the perfidies of Balfour, the faithlessness of Charlotte, and the rascalities of Gilpin—"Yes," said he, "I now see my error; I no longer love my species; I no longer place reliance in the love, friendship, sincerity, or virtue of the world; I will no longer trust myself open-hearted in this vast community of knaves; I will not fly mankind, but I will despise them." The Colonel smiled. "You shall put on your hat, my young friend, and pay a little visit with me:—nay, no excuse; it is only an old lady, who has given me permission to drink tea with her." Nugent demurred, but consented. The two gentlemen walked to a small house in the Regent's Park. They were admitted to a drawing-room, where they found a blind old lady, of a cheerful countenance and prepossessing manners. "And how does your son do!" asked the Colonel, after the first salutations were over, "have you seen him lately?" "Seen him lately! why, you know he rarely lets a day pass without calling on or writing to me. Since the affliction which visited me with blindness, though he has nothing to hope from me, though from my jointure I must necessarily be a burden to one of his limited income, and mixing so much with the world as he does; yet had I been the richest mother in England, and every thing at my own disposal, he could not have been more attentive, more kind to me. He will cheerfully give up the gayest party to come and read to me, if I am the least unwell, or the least out of spirits; and he sold his horses to pay Miss Blandly, since I could not afford from my own income to pay the salary so accomplished a musician asked, to become my companion. Music, you know, is now my chief luxury. Oh, he is a paragon of sons—the world thinks him dissipated and heartless; but if they could see how tender he is to me!" exclaimed the mother, clasping her hands, as the tears gushed from her eyes. Nugent was charmed; the Colonel encouraged the lady to proceed; and Nugent thought he had never passed a more agreeable hour than in listening to her maternal praises of her affectionate son.

"Ah, Colonel!" said he, as they left the house, how much wiser have you been than myself; you have selected your friends with discretion. What would not I give to possess such a friend as that good son must be! But you never told me the lady's name." "Patience," said the Colonel, taking snuff, "I have another visit to pay."

Nelmore turned down a little alley, and knocked at a small cottage. A woman with a child at her breast opened the door; and Nugent stood in one of those scenes of cheerful poverty which it so satisfies the complacency of the rich to behold. "Aha!" said Nelmore, looking round, "you seem comfortable enough now; your benefactor has not done his work by halves." "Blessings on his heart, no! Oh, sir, when I think how distressed he is himself, how often he has been put to it for money, how calumniated he is by the world, I cannot express how grateful I am, how grateful I ought to be. He has robbed himself to feed us, and merely because he knew my husband in youth." The Colonel permitted the woman to run on. Nugent wiped his eyes, and left his purse behind him. "Who is this admirable, this self-denying man?" cried he, when they were once more in the street. "He is in distress himself—would I could relieve him! Ah, you already reconcile me to the world. I acknowledge your motive, in leading me hither; there are good men as well as bad. All are not Balfours and Gilpins! But the name—the name of these poor people's benefactors!"

"Stay," said the Colonel, as they now entered Oxford-street; "this is lucky indeed, I see a good lady whom I wish to accost." "Well, Mrs. Johnson," addressing a stout, comely, middle-aged woman of respectable appearance, who, with a basket on her arm, was coming out of an oil shop; "so have known her since she was that high!" "What, she's good-tempered, I suppose?" said the Colonel sneering. "Good-tempered—I believe it is impossible for her to say a harsh word to any one. There never was so mild, so even-like a temper." "What, and not heartless, eh! this is too good!" "Heartless! she nursed me herself when I broke my leg coming up stairs: and every night before she went to bed, would come into my room with her sweet smile, and see if I wanted any thing." "And you fancy, Mrs. Johnson, that she'll make a good wife: why, she was not much in love when she married." "I don't know as to that, sir, whether she was or not; but I'm sure she is always studying my Lord's wishes, and I heard him myself say this very morning to his brother—'Arthur, if you knew what a treasure I possess.'" "You are very right," said the Colonel, resuming his natural manner; "and I only spoke for the pleasure of seeing how well and how justly you could defend your mistress; she is, truly, an excellent lady—good evening to you."

"I have seen that woman before," said Nugent, "but I can't think where; she has the appearance of being a housekeeper in some family." "She is so." "How pleasant it is to hear of female excellence in the great world," continued Nugent, sighing: "it was evident to see the honest servant was sincere in her praise. Happy husband, whoever he may be!"

They were now at the Colonel's house. "Just let me read this passage," said Nelmore, opening the pages of a French philosopher, and as I do not

you have been laboring in your vocation, I see—making household purchases. And how is your young lady?" "Very well, sir, I'm happy to say," replied the woman, courtseying. "And you are well, too, I hope, sir." "Yes, considering the dissipation of the long season, pretty well, thank you. But I suppose your young mistress is as gay and heartless as ever—a mere fashionable wife, eh!" "Sir," said the woman, bridling up, "there is not a better lady in the world than my young lady; I pronounce French like a native, I will translate as I proceed:

"In order to love mankind—expect but little from them; in order to view their faults, without bitterness, we must accustom ourselves to pardon them, and to perceive that indulgence is a justice which frail humanity has a right to demand from wisdom. Now nothing tends more to dispose us to indulgence, to close our hearts against hatred, to open them to the principles of a humane and soft morality, than a profound knowledge of the human heart—that knowledge which La Rochefoucault possessed. Accordingly, the wisest men have always been the most indulgent," etc.

"And now prepare to be surprised. That good son whom you admired so much—whom you wished you could obtain as a friend, is Captain Balfour—that generous, self-denying man, whom you desired yourself so nobly to relieve, is Mr. Gilpin—that young lady, who, in the flush of health, beauty, dissipation, and conquest, could attend the sick chamber of her servant, and whom her husband discovers to be a treasure, is Charlotte Lennox!"

"Good Heavens!" cried Nugent, "what then am I to believe? has some juggling been practised on my understanding? and are Balfour, Gilpin, and Miss Lennox, after all, patterns of perfection?"

"No, indeed, very far from it: Balfour is a dissipated, reckless man—of loose morality and a low standard of honor; he saw you were destined to purchase experience—he saw you were destined to be plundered by some one—he thought he might as well be a candidate for the profit. He laughed afterwards at your expense—not because he despised you; on the contrary, I believe that he liked you very much in his way; but because, in the world he lives in, every man enjoys a laugh at his acquaintance. Charlotte Lennox saw in you a desirable match; nay, I believe she had a positive regard for you: but she had been taught all her life to think equipage, wealth, and station better than love. She could not resist the temptation of being Marchioness of Austerly—not one girl in twenty could; yet she is not on that account the less good-tempered, good-natured, or less likely to be a good mistress and a tolerable wife. Gilpin is the worst instance of the three. Gilpin is an evident scoundrel; but Gilpin is in evident distress. He was in all probability very sorry to attack you, who had benefited him so largely; but perhaps, as he is a dull dog, the only thing the Magazines would buy of him was abuse. You must not think he maligned you out of malice, out of ingratitude, out of wantonness; he maligned you for ten guineas. Yet Gilpin is a man, who, having swindled his father out of ten guineas, would in the joy of the moment give five to a beggar. In the present case he was actuated by a better feeling; he was serving the friend of his childhood—few men forget those youthful ties, however they trample on others. Your mistake was not the single mistake of supposing the worst people the best—it was the double mistake of supposing commonplace people—now the best—now the worst; in making what might have been a pleasant acquaintance an intimate friend; in believing a man in distress must necessarily be a man of merit; in thinking a good-tempered, pretty girl, was an exalted specimen of Human Nature. You were then about to fall into the opposite extreme—and to be as indiscriminating in suspicion as you were in credulity. Would that I could flatter myself that I had saved you from that—the more dangerous error of the two!"

"You have—my dear Nelmore: and now lend me your philosopher!"

"With pleasure; but one short maxim is as good as all Philosophers can teach you, for Philosophers can only enlarge on it—it is simple—it is this—'TAKE THE WORLD AS IT IS.'"

ON THE INCONVENIENCES RESULTING FROM BEING HANGED.

BY CHARLES LAMB. (ELIA.)

TO THE EDITOR OF THE REFLECTOR.

SIR,—I am one of those unhappy persons whose misfortunes, it seems, do not entitle them to the benefit of pure pity. All that is bestowed upon me of that kind alleviator of human miseries comes dashed with a double portion of contempt. My griefs have nothing in them that is felt as sacred by the bystanders. Yet is my affliction in truth of the deepest grain—the heaviest task that was ever given to mortal patience to sustain. Time, that wears out all other sorrows, can never modify or soften mine. Here they must continue to gnaw as long as that fatal mark——

Why was I ever born? Why was innocence in my person suffered to be branded with a stain which was appointed only for the blackest guilt? What had I done, or my parents, that a disgrace of mine should involve a whole posterity in infamy? I am almost tempted to believe, that, in some preexistent state, crimes to which this sublunary life of mine hath been as much a stranger as the babe that is newly born into it, have drawn down upon me this vengeance, so disproportionate to my actions on this globe.

My brain sickens, and my bosom labors to be delivered of the weight that presses upon it, yet my conscious pen shrinks from the avowal. But out it must——

O, Mr. Reflector! guess at the wretch's misery who now writes this to you, when, with tears and burning blushes, he is obliged to confess that he has been ——HANGED——

Methinks I hear an involuntary exclamation burst from you, as your imagination presents to you fearful images of your correspondent unknown—*hanged!*

Fear not, Mr. Editor. No disembodied spirit has the honor of addressing you. I am flesh and blood, an unfortunate system of bones, muscles, sinews, arteries, like yourself.

Then, I presume, you mean to be pleasant.—That expression of yours, Mr. Correspondent, must be taken somehow in a metaphorical sense——

In the plainest sense, without trope or figure—Yes, Mr. Editor! this neck of mine has felt the fatal noose, these hands have tremblingly held up the corroborative prayer-book,—these lips have sucked the moisture of the last consolatory orange,—this tongue has chanted the doleful cantata which no performer was ever called upon to repeat,—this face has had the veiling night-cap drawn over it——

But for no crime of mine.—Far be it from me to arraign the justice of my country, which, though tardy, did at length recognize my innocence. It is not for me to reflect upon judge or jury, now that eleven years have elapsed since the erroneous sentence was pronounced. Men will always be fallible, and perhaps circumstances did appear at the time a little strong——

Suffice it to say, that after hanging four minutes, (as the spectators were pleased to compute it,—a man that is being strangled, I know from experience, has altogether a different measure of time from his friends who are breathing leisurely about him,—I suppose the minutes lengthen as time approaches eternity, in the same manner as the miles get longer as you travel northward,)—after hanging four minutes, according to the best calculation of the bystanders, a reprieve came, and I was cut DOWN——

Really I am ashamed of deforming your pages with these technical phrases—if I knew how to express my meaning shorter———

But to proceed. My first care after I had been brought to myself by the usual methods, (those methods that are so interesting to the operator and his assistants, who are pretty numerous on such occasions,—but which no patient was ever desirous of undergoing a second time for the benefit of science,) my first care was to provide myself with an enormous stock or cravat to hide the place—you understand me;—my next care was to procure a residence as distant as possible from that part of the country where I had suffered. For that reason I chose the metropolis, as the place where wounded honor (I had been told) could lurk with the least danger of exciting inquiry, and stigmatized innocence had the best chance of hiding her disgrace in a crowd. I sought out a new circle of acquaintance, and my circumstances happily enabling me to pursue my fancy in that respect, I endeavored, by mingling in all the pleasures which the town affords, to efface the memory of what I had undergone.

But, alas! such is the portentous and all-pervading chain of connection which links together the head and members of this great community, my scheme of lying perdu was defeated almost at the outset. A countryman of mine, whom a foolish law-suit had brought to town, by chance met me, and the secret was soon blazoned about.

In a short time, I found myself deserted by most of those who had been my intimate friends. Not that any guilt was supposed to attach to my character. My officious countryman, to do him justice, had been candid enough to explain my perfect innocence. But, somehow or other, there is a want of strong virtue in mankind. We have plenty of the softer instincts, but the heroic character is gone. How else can I account for it, that of all my numerous acquaintance, among whom I had the honor of ranking sundry persons of education, talents, and worth, scarcely here and there one or two could be found who had the courage to associate with a man that had been hanged.

Those few who did not desert me altogether were persons of strong but coarse minds; and from the absence of all delicacy in them, I suffered almost as much as from the superabundance of a false species of it in the others. Those who stuck by me were the jokers, who thought themselves entitled, by the fidelity which they had shown towards me, to use me with what familiarity they pleased. Many and unfeeling are the jests that I have suffered from these rude (because faithful) Achateses. As they passed me in the streets, one would nod significantly to his companion and say, pointing to me, Smoke his cravat, and ask me if I had got a wen, that I was so solicitous to cover my neck. Another would inquire, What news from * * * Assizes? (which you may guess, Mr. Editor, was the scene of my shame,) and whether the sessions was like to prove a maiden one? A third would offer to ensure me from drowning. A fourth would teaze me with inquiries how I felt when I was swinging, whether I had not something like a blue flame dancing before my eyes? A fifth took a fancy never to call me any thing but *Lazarus*. And an eminent bookseller and publisher,—who, in his zeal to present the public with new facts, had he lived in those days, I am confident, would not have scrupled waiting upon the person himself last mentioned, at the most critical period of his existence, to solicit a *few facts relative to resuscitation*,—had the modesty to offer me—guineas per sheet, if I would write, in his Magazine, a physiological account of my feelings upon coming to myself.

But these were evils which a moderate fortitude might have enabled me to struggle with. Alas! Mr. Editor, the women,—whose good graces I had always most assiduously cultivated, from whose softer minds I had hoped a more delicate and generous sympathy than I found in the men,—the women began to shun me. This was the unkindest blow of all.

But is it to be wondered at? How couldst thou imagine, wretchedest of beings, that that tender creature Seraphina would fling her pretty arms about that neck which previous circumstances had rendered infamous? That she would put up with the refuse of the rope, the leavings of the cord? Or that any analogy could subsist between the knot which binds true lovers, and the knot which ties malefactors?

I can forgive that pert baggage Flirtilla, who, when I complimented her one day on the execution which her eyes had done, replied, that, to be sure, Mr. * * was a judge of those things. But from thy more exalted mind, Celestina, I expected a more unprejudiced decision.

The person whose true name I conceal under this appellation, of all the women that I was acquainted with, had the most manly turn of mind, which she had improved by reading and the best conversation. Her understanding was not more masculine than her manners and whole disposition were delicately and truly feminine. She was the daughter of an officer who had fallen in the service of his country, leaving his widow, and Celestina, an only child, with a fortune sufficient to set them above want, but not to enable them to live in splendor. I had the mother's permission to pay my addresses to the young lady, and Celestina seemed to approve of my suit.

Often and often have I poured out my overcharged soul in the presence of Celestina, complaining of the hard and unfeeling prejudices of the world; and the sweet maid has again and again declared, that no irrational prejudice should hinder her from esteeming every man according to his intrinsic worth. Often has she repeated the consolatory assurance, that she could never consider as essentially ignominious an *accident*, which was indeed to be deprecated, but which might have happened to the most innocent of mankind. Then would she set forth some illustrious example, which her reading easily furnished, of a Phocion or a Socrates unjustly condemned; of a Raleigh or a Sir Thomas More, to whom late posterity had done justice; and by soothing my fancy with some such agreeable parallel, she would make me almost to triumph in my disgrace, and convert my shame into glory.

In such entertaining and instructive conversations the time passed on, till I importunely urged the mistress of my affections to name a day for our union. To this she obligingly consented, and I thought myself the happiest of mankind. But how I was surprised one morning on the receipt of the following billet from my charmer:—

Sir,—You must not impute it to levity, or to a worse failing, ingratitude, if, with anguish of heart, I feel myself compelled by irresistible arguments to recall a vow which I fear I made with too little consideration. I never can be yours. The reasons of my decision, which is final, are in my own breast, and you must everlastingly remain a stranger to them. Assure yourself that I can never cease to esteem you as I ought.

Celestina.

At the sight of this paper, I ran in frantic haste to Celestina's lodgings, where I learned, to my infinite mortification, that the mother and daughter were set off on a journey to a distant part of the country, to visit a relation, and were not expected to return in less than four months.

Stunned by this blow, which left me without the courage to solicit an explanation by letter, even if I had known where they were, (for the particular address was industriously concealed from me,) I waited with impatience the termination of the period, in the vain hope that I might be permitted to have a chance of softening the harsh decision by a personal interview with Celestina after her return. But before three months were at an end, I learned from the newspapers that my beloved had—given her hand to another!

Heart-broken as I was, I was totally at a loss to account for the strange step which she had taken; and it was not till some years after that I learned the true reason from a female relation of hers, to whom it seems Celestina had confessed in confidence, that it was no demerit of mine that had caused her to break off the match so abruptly, nor any preference which she might feel for any other person, for she preferred me (she was pleased to say) to all mankind; but when she came to lay the matter closer to her heart, she found that she never should be able to bear the sight—(I give you her very words as they were detailed to me by her relation)—the sight of a man in a nightcap, who had appeared on a public platform—it would lead to such a disagreeable association of ideas! And to this punctilio I was sacrificed.

To pass over an infinite series of minor mortifications, to which this last and heaviest might well render me callous, behold me here, Mr. Editor! in the thirty-seventh year of my existence, (the twelfth, reckoning from my reanimation,) cut off from all respectable connections; rejected by the fairer half of the community,—who in my case alone seem to have laid aside the characteristic pity of their sex; punished because I was once punished unjustly; suffering for no other reason than because I once had the misfortune to suffer without any cause at all. In no other country, I think, but this, could a man have been subject to such a life-long persecution, when once his innocence had been clearly established.

Had I crawled forth a rescued victim from the rack, in the horrible dungeons of the Inquisition,—had I heaved myself up from a half bastinado in China, or been torn from the just-entering, ghastly impaling stake in Barbary,—had I dropt alive from the knout in Russia, or come off with a gashed neck from the half-mortal, scarce-in-time-retracted cimeter of an executioneering slave in Turkey,—I might have borne about the remnant of this frame (the mangled trophy of reprieved innocence) with credit to myself, in any of those barbarous countries. No scorn, at least, would have mingled with the pity (small as it might be) with which what was left of me would have been surveyed.

The singularity of my case has often led me to inquire into the reasons of the general levity with which the subject of hanging is treated as a topic in this country. I say, as a topic: for let the very persons who speak so lightly of the thing at a distance be brought to view the real scene,—let the platform be bona fide exhibited, and the trembling culprit brought forth,—the case is changed; but as a topic of conversation, I appeal to the vulgar jokes which pass current in every street. But why mention them, when the politest authors have agreed in making use of this subject as a source of the ridiculous? Swift, and Pope, and Prior, are fond of recurring to it. Gay has built an entire drama upon this single foundation. The whole interest of the *Beggars' Opera* may be said to hang upon it. To such writers as Fielding and Smollett it is a perfect *bonne-bouche*.—Hear the facetious Tom Brown, in his *Comical View of London and Westminster*, describe the *Order of the Show at one of the Tyburn Executions* in his time:—"Mr. Ordinary visits his

melancholy flock in Newgate by eight. Doleful procession up Holborn-hill about eleven. Men handsome and proper that were never thought so before, which is some comfort, however. Arrive at the fatal place by twelve. Burnt brandy, women, and sabbath-breaking, repented of. Some few penitential drops fall under the gallows. Sheriff's men, parson, pickpockets, criminals, all very busy. The last concluding peremptory psalm struck up. Show over by one."—In this sportive strain does this misguided wit think proper to play with a subject so serious, which yet he would hardly have done if he had not known that there existed a predisposition in the habits of his unaccountable countrymen to consider the subject as a jest. But what shall we say to Shakspere, who, (not to mention the solution which the *Gravedigger* in *Hamlet* gives of his fellow-workman's problem,) in that scene in *Measure for Measure*, where the *Clown* calls upon *Master Barnardine* to get up and be hanged, which he declines on the score of being sleepy, has actually gone out of his way to gratify this amiable propensity in his countrymen; for it is plain, from the use that was to be made of his head, and from *Abhorson's* asking, "Is the axe upon the block, sirrah?" that beheading, not hanging, was the punishment to which *Barnardine* was destined. But Shakspere knew that the axe and block were pregnant with no ludicrous images, and therefore falsified the historic truth of his own drama (if I may so speak), rather than he would leave out such excellent matter for a jest as the suspending of a fellow-creature in mid-air has been ever esteemed to be by Englishmen.

One reason why the ludicrous never fails to intrude itself into our contemplations upon this mode of death, I supppse to be, the absurd posture into which a man is thrown who is condemned to dance, as the vulgar delight to express it, upon nothing. To see him whisking and wavering in the air,

As the wind you know will wave a man;*

to behold the vacant carcass, from which the life is newly dislodged, shifting between earth and heaven, the sport of every gust; like a weathercock, serving to show from which point the wind blows; like a maukin, fit only to scare away birds; like a nest left to swing upon a bough when the bird is flown: these are uses to which we cannot without a mixture of spleen and contempt behold the human carcass reduced. We string up dogs, foxes, bats, moles, weasels. Man surely deserves a steadier death.

Another reason why the ludicrous associates more forcibly with this than with any other mode of punishment, I cannot help thinking to be, the senseless costume with which old prescription has thought fit to clothe the exit of malefactors in this country. Let a man do what he will to abstract from his imagination all idea of the whimsical, something of it will come across him when he contemplates the figure of a fellow-creature in the day-time (in however distressing a situation) in a night-cap. Whether it be that this nocturnal addition has something discordant with daylight, or that it is the dress which we are seen in at those times when we are "seen," as the Angel in Milton expresses it, "least wise,"—this, I am afraid, will always be the case; unless, indeed, as in my instance, some strong personal feeling overpower the ludicrous altogether. To me, when I reflect upon the train of misfortunes which have pursued men through life, owing to that accursed drapery, the cap presents as purely frightful an object as the sleeveless yellow-coat and devil-painted mitre of the San Benitos. An ancestor of mine, who suffered for his loyalty in the time of the civil wars, was so sensible of the truth of what I am here advancing, that on the morning of execution, no entreaties could prevail upon him to submit to the odious dishabille, as he called it, but he insisted upon wearing, and actually suffered in, the identical flowing periwig which he is painted in, in the gallery belonging to my uncle's seat in —— shire.

Suffer me, Mr. Editor, before I quit the subject, to say a word or two respecting the minister of justice in this country; in plain words, I mean the hangman. It has always appeared to me that, in the mode of inflicting capital punishments with us,

* Hieronimo, in the Spanish Tragedy.

there is too much of the ministry of the human hand. The guillotine, as performing its functions more of itself, and sparing human agency, though a cruel and disgusting exhibition, in my mind, has many ways the advantage over *our way*. In beheading, indeed, as it was formerly practised in England, and in whipping to death, as is sometimes practised now, the hand of man is no doubt sufficiently busy; but there is something less repugnant in these downright blows than in the officious barber-like ministerings of *the other*. To have a fellow with his hangman's hands fumbling about your collar, adjusting the thing as your valet would regulate your cravat, valuing himself on his menial dexterity——

I never shall forget meeting my rascal,—I mean the fellow who officiated for me,—in London last winter. I think I see him now,—in a waistcoat that had been mine,—smirking along as he knew me——

In some parts of Germany, that fellow's office is by law declared infamous, and his posterity incapable of being ennobled. They have hereditary hangmen, or had, at least, in the same manner as they had hereditary other great officers of state; and the hangmen's families of two adjoining parishes intermarried with each other, to keep the breed entire. I wish something of the same kind were established in England.

But it is time to quit a subject which teems with disagreeable images——

Permit me to subscribe myself, Mr. Editor,

Your unfortunate friend,

PENSILIS.

A FAREWELL TO TOBACCO.

BY CHARLES LAMB. (ELIA.)

MAY the Babylonish curse
Strait confound my stammering verse,
If I can a passage see
In this word—perplexity,
Or a fit expression find,
Or a language to my mind,
(Still the phrase is wide or scant)
To take leave of thee, GREAT PLANT!
Or in any terms relate
Half my love, or half my hate;
For I hate, yet love, thee so,
That, whichever thing I show,
The plain truth will seem to be
A constrain'd hyperbole,
And the passion to proceed
More from a mistress than a weed.

Sooty retainer to the vine,
Bacchus' black servant, negro fine;
Sorcerer, that mak'st us dote upon
Thy begrimed complexion:
And, for thy pernicious sake,
More and greater oaths to break,
Than reclaimed lovers take
'Gainst women: thou thy siege dost lay
Much too in the female way,
While thou suck'st the lab'ring breath
Faster than kisses or than death.

Thou in such a cloud dost bind us,
That our worst foes cannot find us,
And ill fortune, that would thwart us,
Shoots at rovers shooting at us;
While each man, through thy height'ning steam,
Does like a smoking Etna seem,
And all about us does express
(Fancy and wit in richest dress)
A Sicilian fruitfulness.

Thou through such a mist dost show us,
That our best friends do not know us,
And for those allowed features,
Due to reasonable creatures,
Liken'st us to fell Chimeras,
Monsters that, who see us, fear us;
Worse than Cerberus or Geryon,
Or, who first loved a cloud, Ixion.

Bacchus we know, and we allow
His tipsy rites. But what art thou,
That but by reflex canst show
What his deity can do,
As the false Egyptian spell
Aped the true Hebrew miracle?
Some few vapors thou may'st raise,
The weak brain may serve to amaze,
But to the reins and nobler heart
Canst nor life nor heat impart.

Brother of Bacchus, later born,
The old world was sure forlorn,
Wanting thee, that aidest more
The god's victories than before
All his panthers, and the brawls
Of his piping Bacchanals.
These, as stale, we disallow,
Or judge of *thee* meant: only thou
His true Indian conquest art;
And, for ivy round his dart,
The reformed god now weaves
A finer thyrsus of thy leaves.

Scent to match thy rich perfume
Chemic art did ne'er presume
Through her quaint alembic strain,
None so sov'reign to the brain.
Nature, that did in thee excel,
Framed again no second smell.
Roses, violets, but toys
For the smaller sort of boys,
Or for greener damsels meant;
Thou art the only manly scent.

Stinkingest of the stinking kind,
Filth of the mouth and fog of the mind,

Chs Lamb

Africa, that brags her foyson,
Breeds no such prodigous poison,
Henbane, nightshade, both together,
Hemlock, aconite——

Nay, rather,
Plant divine, of rarest virtue;
Blisters on the tongue would hurt you.
'Twas but in a sort I blamed thee;
None e'er prosper'd who defamed thee;
Irony all, and feign'd abuse,
Such as perplext lovers use,
At a need, when, in despair
To paint forth their fairest fair,
Or in part but to express
That exceeding comeliness
Which their fancies doth so strike,
They borrow language of dislike;
And, instead of Dearest Miss,
Jewel, Honey, Sweetheart, Bliss,
And those forms of old admiring,
Call her Cockatrice and Siren,
Basilisk and all that's evil,
Witch, Hyena, Mermaid, Devil,
Ethiop, Wench, and Blackamoor,
Monkey, Ape, and twenty more;
Friendly Trait'ress, loving Foe,—
Not that she is truly so,
But no other way they know
A contentment to express,
Borders so upon excess,
That they do not rightly wot
Whether it be pain or not.

Or, as men, constrain'd to part
With what's nearest to their heart,
While their sorrow's at the height,
Lose discrimination quite,
And their hasty wrath let fall,
To appease their frantic gall,
On the darling thing whatever,
Whence they feel it death to sever,
Though it be, as they, perforce,
Guiltless of the sad divorce.

For I must (nor let it grieve thee,
Friendliest of plants, that I must) leave thee;
For thy sake, TOBACCO, I
Would do any thing but die,
And but seek to extend my days
Long enough to sing thy praise.
But, as she, who once hath been
A king's consort, is a queen
Ever after, nor will bate
Any title of her state,
Though a widow, or divorced,
So I, from thy converse forced,
The old name and style retain,
A right Katherine of Spain;
And a seat, too, 'mongst the joys
Of the blest Tobacco Boys;
Where, though I, by sour physician,
Am debarr'd the full fruition
Of thy favors, I may catch
Some collateral sweets, and snatch
Sidelong odors, that give life
Like glances from a neighbor's wife;
And still live in the bye-places
And the suburbs of thy graces;
And in thy borders take delight,
An unconquer'd Canaanite.

THE WIT AND HUMOR OF CHARLES LAMB.

COLERIDGE in 1799, went to Germany, and left word to Lamb, that if he wished any information on any subject, he might apply to him, (*i. e.* by letter,) so Lamb sent him the following abstruse propositions, to which, however, Coleridge did not "deign an answer."

Whether God loves a lying angel better than a true man?

Whether the archangel Uriel *could* knowingly affirm an untruth, and whether, if he *could*, he *would?*

Whether the higher order of seraphim illuminati ever *sneeze?*

Whether an immortal and amenable soul may not come *to be damned at last*, and the man never suspect it beforehand?

MOVING.—What a dislocation of comfort is implied in that word moving! Such a heap of little, nasty things, after you think all is got into the cart; old dredging boxes, worn-out trunks, gallipots, vials, things that it is impossible the most necessitous person can ever want, but which women, who preside on these occasions, will not leave behind, if it was to save your soul; they'd keep the cart ten minutes, to stow in dirty pipes and broken matches, to show their economy. They can find nothing you want for many days after you get into your new lodgings. You must comb your hair with your fingers, wash your hands without soap, go about in dirty gaiters.

THE PLEASURES OF LONDON.—Streets, streets, streets, markets, theatres, churches, Covent Gardens; shops sparkling with pretty faces of industrious milliners, neat seamstresses, ladies cheapening, gentlemen behind counters lying, authors in the streets with spectacles (you may know them by their gait), lamps lighted at night, pastry-cook and silversmiths' shops, beautiful Quakers of Pentonville, noise of coaches, dreary cry of mechanic watchmen by night, with bucks reeling home drunk; if you happen to wake at midnight, cries of fire and stop thief; Inns of Court, with their learned air, and stalls and butteries just like Cambridge Colleges; old book stalls, "Jeremy Taylors," "Burtons on Melancholy," and "Religio Medici," on every stall. These are thy pleasures, O London!

NOTHING TO DO.—Positively, the best thing a man can have to do is nothing, and, *next to that*, perhaps, good works.

BRANDY-AND-WATER.—Of this mixture, Charles Lamb said it spoiled two good things.

MISERS.—The passion for wealth has worn out much of its grossness by track of time. Our ancestors certainly conceived of money as able to confer a distinct gratification in itself, not alone considered simply as a symbol of wealth. The oldest poets, when they introduce a miser, constantly make him address his gold as his mistress; as something to be seen, felt, and hugged; as capable of satisfying two of the senses at least. The substitution of a thin, unsatisfying medium for the good old tangible gold, has made avarice quite a Platonic affection in comparison with the seeing, touching, and humbling pleasures of the old Chrysophilities. A bank-note can no more satisfy the touch of a true sensualist in this passion, than Creusa could return her husband's embrace in the shades. A miser is sometimes a grand personification of Fear. He has a fine horror of Poverty; and he is not content to keep Want from the door, or at arm's length—but he places it, by heaping wealth upon wealth, *at a sublime distance.*

PRESENTS.—If presents be not the soul of friendship, doubtless they are the most spiritual part of the body in that intercourse. There is too much narrowness of thinking on this point. The punctilio of acceptance, methinks, is too confined and straitened. I should be content to receive money, or clothes, or a joint of meat from a friend. Why should he not send me a dinner as well as a dessert? I would taste him in the beasts of the field, and through all creation.

CANNIBALS.—Lamb writes to his friend Manning, to dissuade him from going to China, and endeavors to instil the fear of cannibals into his mind: "Some say the Tartars are cannibals, and then conceive a fellow *eating* my friend, and adding the *cool malignity* of mustard and vinegar."

THE BEST KIND OF ACID.—Martin Burney was one day explaining the three kinds of acid, very *lengthily*, to Charles Lamb, when the latter stopped him by saying: "The best of all kind of acid, however, as you know, Martin, is uity—assiduity."

DIRTY HANDS.—Lamb once said to a brother whist player, Martin Burney, whose hands were none of the cleanest, "Martin, if dirt was trumps, what a hand you'd have."

GOOD ACTIONS.—The greatest pleasure I know, is to do a good action by stealth, and to have it found out by accident.

PAYING FOR THINGS.—One cannot bear to pay for articles he used to get for nothing. When Adam laid out his first penny upon nonpareils at some stall in Mesopotamia, I think it went hard with him, reflecting upon his old goodly orchard, where he had so many for nothing.

SIGN FOR A SCHOOL.—A widow friend of Lamb, having opened a preparatory school for children, at Camden Town, said to him, "I live so far from town I must have a sign, I think you call it, to show that I teach children." "Well," he replied, "you can have nothing better than '*The Murder of the Innocents.*'"

A SHARP SET.—The Sexton of Salisbury Cathedral, was telling Lamb, that eight persons had dined together upon the top of the spire; upon which he remarked, that "They must have been sharp set."

PUNNING TRANSLATION.—Coleridge's motto, "*sermoni proprioria,*" was translated by Lamb, as "properer for a sermon."

Hood says that Lamb never affected any spurious gravity. Neither did he ever act the *Grand Senior.* He did not exact that common copy-book respect, which some asinine persons would fain command, on account of the mere length of their years; as if forsooth, what is bad in itself, could be the better for keeping; as if intellects already *mothery,* got any thing but *grand-mothery* by lapse of time!

A COLD.—"Do you know what it is?" asked Lamb of Bernard Barton, describing his own state, "to succumb under an insurmountable *daymare*—'a whoreson lethargy,' Falstaff calls it—an indisposition to do any thing, or to be any thing—a total deadness and distaste—a suspension of vitality—an indifference to locality—a numb soporifical good-for-nothingness—an ossification all over—an oyster-like indifference to passing events—a mind-stupor—a brawny defiance to the needles of a thrusting-in conscience—with a total irresolution to submit to water-gruel processes?"

BOILED MUTTON.—A farmer, Charles Lamb's chance companion in a coach, kept boring him to death with questions as to the state of the crops. At length he put a poser—"And pray, sir, how go turnips?" "Why, that, sir (stammered out Lamb), will depend upon the boiled legs of mutton."

MAKING BOTH ENDS MEET.—While Lamb was clerk at the India House, he used his own pleasure in observing the hours of attendance. The other officials grumbled, and one of the heads of the establishment undertook to lecture the erring Elia. "Mr. Lamb, you come very late every morning." "I do, sir," said Lamb, "but I make up for it by going away very early every afternoon."

"Charles," said Coleridge, one day, to Lamb, "did you ever hear me preach?" "I never heard you do any thing else," said Lamb.

On a cold and drizzling day, a mendicant faced Lamb in the street with an appealing look and outstretched hand. "I have seen better days," said the beggar, in a whining tone. "So have I," said Lamb, shrugging his shoulders, and buttoning up his coat. "This is a very bad day, indeed."

Lamb was reserved amongst strangers. His friend T——, about to introduce him to a circle of new faces, said, "Now will you promise, *Lamb,* not to be as *sheepish* as usual?" Charles replied, with a rustic air, "I *wool.*"

ON PUNS.—"A pun," said Lamb in a letter to Coleridge, in which he eulogized the Odes and addresses of his friends Hood and Reynolds, "is a thing of too much consequence to be thrown in as a make-weight. You shall read one of the addresses twice over and miss the puns, and it shall be quite as good, or better, than when you discover them. A pun is a noble thing *per se.* O never bring it in as an accessary. A pun is a sole digest of reflection; it is entire; it fills the mind; it is as perfect as a sonnet; better. It limps ashamed in the train and retinue of humor—it knows it should have an establishment of its own.

THE BON-VIVANT.

FROM "PERICLES AND ASPASIA." BY WALTER SAVAGE LANDOR.

We had invited Polus to dine with us, and now condoled with him on his loss of appetite. * *

Slaves brought in an ewer of water, with several napkins. They were not lost upon Polus, and he declared that those two boys had more sagacity and intuition than all the people in the theatre. * * *

Supper was served.

"A quail, O best Polus."

"A quail, O wonderful! may hurt me; but being recommended—"

It disappeared.

"The breast of that capon—"

"Capons, being melancholic, breed melancholy within."

"Coriander-seed might correct it, together with a few of those white plump pine-seeds."

"The very desideratum."

It was corrected.

"Tunny under oil, with marjoram and figs, pickled locusts, and pistachios—for your stomach seems delicate."

The field was won; nothing was left upon it.

Another slave came forward, announcing loudly and pompously, "Gosling from Brauron! Sauce, prunes, mustard-seed, capers, fenugreek, sesamum, and squills."

"Squills!" exclaimed Pôlus, "they soothe the chest. It is not every cook that is deep in the secrets of nature. Brauron! an ancient city: I have friends in Brauron; I will taste were it only for remembrance of them."

He made several essays, several pauses.

"But when shall we come to the squills?" said he, turning to the slave; "the qualities of the others are negative."

The whole dish was, presently.

"Our pastry," said I, "O illustrious Polus! is the only thing I can venture to recommend at table; the other dishes are merely on sufferance; but, really our pastry is good; I usually dine entirely upon it."

"Entirely," cried he, in amaze.

"Alas! indeed it is declining. Tunny! tunny! I dare not, O festoon of the Graces! I dare not verily. Chian wine alone can appease its seditions."

They were appeased.

Some livers were offered him, whether of fish or fowl, I know not, for I can hardly bear to look at that dish. He waved them away, but turned suddenly round, and said, "Youth! I think I smell fennel."

"There is fennel, O mighty one!" replied the slave, "and not fennel only, but parsley and honey, pepper and rosemary, garlic from Salamis, and—"

"Say no more, say no more; fennel is enough for moderate men, and brave ones. It reminds me of the field of Marathon."

"With a glass of water," added I, "and some grapes, fresh or dry."

"To accompany you, O divine Aspasia! though in good truth this said pastry is but a sandy sort of road; no great way can be made in it."

The diffident Polus was not a bad engineer however, and he soon had an opportunity of admiring the workmanship at the bottom of the salver.

Two dishes of roast meat were carried to him. I know not what one was, nor could Polus make up his mind upon it: experiment following experiment. Kid, however, was an old acquaintance.

"Those who kill kids," said he, "deserve well of their country, for they grow up mischievous: the Gods, aware of this, make them very eatable. They require some management, some skill, some reflection: mint, shalot, dandelion, vinegar: strong coercion upon 'em. Chian wine, boy!"

"What does Pericles eat?"

"Do not mind Pericles. He has eaten of the quails, and some roast fish, besprinkled with dried bay-leaves for sauce."

"Fish! ay, that makes him so vigilant. Cats—"

Here he stopt, not however without a diversion in his favor from me, observing that he usually dined on vegetables, fish, and some bird: that his earlier meal was his longest, confectionery, honey, and white bread composing it.

"Chian or Lesbian?"

"He enjoys a little wine after dinner, preferring the lighter and subacid."

"Wonderful man!" cried he; "and all from such fare as that!"

Another exquisite letter, again in a different strain:

"Thanks for the verses! I hope Leuconoe was as grateful as I am, and as sensible to their power of soothing.

"Thanks too for the perfumes! Pericles is ashamed of acknowledging he is fond of them; but I am resolved to betray one secret of his: I have caught him several times *trying* them as he called it.

"How many things are there that people pretend to dislike, without any reason, as far as we know, for the dislike or the pretence!

"I love sweet odors. Surely my Cleone herself must have breathed her very soul into these! Let me smell again: let me inhale them into the sanctuary of my breast, lighted up by her love for their reception.

"But, ah, Cleone! what an importunate and exacting creature is Aspasia! Have you no willows fresh-peeled? none lying upon the banks for baskets, white, rounded, and delicate as your fingers! How very fragrant they were formerly! I have seen none lately. Do you remember the cross old Hermesionax? how he ran to beat us for breaking his twigs? and how, after looking in our faces, he seated himself down again, finished his basket, disbursed from a goat-skin a corroded clod of rancid cheese, put it in, pushed it to us, forced it under my arm, and told us to carry it home *with the Gods!* and lifted up both hands and blest us.

"I do not wish *that* one exactly; cheese is the cruellest of deaths to me, and Pericles abhors it."

A CHAPTER ON OLD COATS.

ANONYMOUS.

I LOVE an old coat. By an old coat, I mean not one of last summer's growth, on which the gloss yet lingers, shadowy, and intermittent, like a faint ray of sun-light on the counting-house desk or a clothier's warehouse in Eastcheap, but a real unquestionable antique, which for some five or six years has withstood the combined assaults of sun, dust, and rain, has lost all pretensions to starch, unsocial formality, and gives the shoulders assurance of ease, and the waist of a holiday. Such a coat is my delight. It presents itself to my mind's eye, mixed up with a thousand varying recollections, and not only shadows forth the figures, but recalls the very faces, even to the particular expression of eye, brow, or lip, of friends over whom the waters of oblivion have long since rolled. This, you will say, is strange. Granted; but mark how I deduce my analogy!

In that repository of wit, learning, and sarcasm, the "Tale of a Tub," Swift pertinently remarks, that in forming an estimate of an individual's trade or profession, one should look to his dress. The man himself is nothing: his apparel is the distinguishing characteristic; the outward and visible sign of his inward and spiritual grace. What, adds the satirist, is a lawyer, but a black wig and gown, hung upon an animated peg, like a barber's caxon on a block? What, a judge, but an apt conjunction of scarlet and white ermine, thrown over a similar peg, a little stouter, perhaps, and stuck on a bench? What, a dandy, but a pair of tight persuasives to corns and gentility, exuberant pantaloons, and unimpeachable coat and hat, trimly appended to a moving stick, from a yard and a half, to two yards high, grown in Bond-street, and cut down in the fulness of time in the King's Bench? What, a lord mayor, but a gold chain stuck round the neck of a plump occupier of space? What, a physician, but a black gilt-headed cane, thrust with professional gravity, under the snout of an embodied "Memento Mori?" What, an alderman, but a furred gown and white napkin stuck beneath the triple chin of a polypetalous personification of dyspepsia?—Caxon the barber held opinions similar to these. "Pray, sir," said he to the antiquary, "do not venture near the sands to-night; for when *you* are dead and gone there will be only three *wigs* left in the village!"*

If then we look to the dress—of which the coat, of course, forms the chief feature—as the criterion of a man, it is logically manifest, that the appearance of certain coats will renew the recollection of certain individuals; or suppose we substitute the word "coat" for "man," and it will be equally manifest that a certain coat is *bona fide* a certain man. Now, whenever I see an old coat, brown, rusty, and long-waisted, with the dim metal buttons at the back sewed on so far apart, that if a short-sighted man were to stand upon the one, he could scarcely, according to the ordinary laws of probability, see over to the other; I imagine, on Swift's principle, that I see my fat city friend, Tims, who died of a lord mayor's feast, ten years since come Martinmas. In like manner, whenever I behold a gaunt, attenuated, blue surtout, so perfectly old-fashioned in shape, that I should hardly be justified in making an affidavit before Sir Richard Birnie, that, to the best of my belief, it was younger than the Temple of the Sun at Palmyra; I think that I behold my ancient college-chum, Dickson — the cream of bachelors—the pink of politeness—the most agreeable of tipplers, who expired last year of vexation, the necessary consequence of his having been married a full fortnight to a blue-stocking. Peace to his ashes—he always spoke respectfully of whisky-punch!

Old coats are the indices by which a man's pecu-

* *Vide* Sir Walter Scott's novel of The Antiquary, Vol. I.

liar turn of mind may be pointed out. So tenaciously do I hold this opinion, that, in passing down a crowded thoroughfare, the Strand, for instance, I would wager odds, that in seven out of ten cases, I would tell a stranger's character and calling by the mere cut of his every-day coat. Who can mistake the staid, formal gravity of the orthodox divine, in the corresponding weight, fulness, and healthy condition of his familiar, easy-natured flaps? Who sees not the necessities—the habitual eccentricities of the poet, significantly developed in his two haggard, shapeless old apologies for skirts, original in their genius as "Christabel," uncouth in their build as the New Palace at Pimlico? Who can misapprehend the motion of the spirit, as it slily flutters beneath the quaker's drab? Thus, too, the sable hue of the lawyer's working coat corresponds most convincingly with the color of his conscience; while his thrift, dandyism, and close attention at appearances, tells their own tale in the half-pay officer's smart but somewhat faded exterior.

No lover of independence ventures voluntarily on a new coat. This is an axiom not to be overturned, unlike the safety stage-coaches. The man who piques himself on the newness of such an habiliment, is—till time hath "moulded it into beauty"—its slave. Wherever he goes, he is harassed by an apprehension of damaging it. Hence he loses his sense of independence, and becomes—a Serf! How degrading! To succumb to one's superiors is bad enough; but to be the martyr of a few yards of cloth; to be the Helot of a tight fit; to be shackled by the ninth fraction of a man; to be made submissive to the sun, the dust, the rain, and the snow; to be panic-stricken by the chimney sweep; to be scared by the dust-man; to shudder at the advent of the baker; to give precedence to the scavenger; to concede the wall to a peripatetic conveyancer of eggs; to palpitate at the irregular sallies of a mercurial cart-horse; to look up with awe at the apparition of a giggling servant-girl, with a slop-pail thrust half-way out of a garret-window; to coast a gutter with a horrible anticipation of consequences; to faint at the visitation of a shower of soot down the chimney; to be compelled to be at the mercy of each and all of these vile contingencies! can any thing in human nature be so preposterous, so effeminate, so disgraceful? A truly great mind spurns the bare idea of such slavery; hence, according to the "Subaltern," Wellington liberated Spain in a red coat, extravagantly over-estimated at sixpence, and Napoleon entered Moscow in a green one out at the elbows.

An old coat is the aptest possible symbol of sociality. An old shoe is not to be despised; an old hat, provided it has a crown, is not amiss; none but a cynic would speak irreverently of an old slipper; but were I called upon to put forward the most unique impersonation of comfort, I should give a plumper in favor of an old coat. The very mention of this luxury conjures up a thousand images of enjoyment. It speaks of warm fire-sides,—long flowing curtains—a downy arm-chair—a nicely trimmed lamp—a black cat fast asleep on the hearth-rug—a bottle of old Port (vintage 1812)—a snuff-box—a cigar—a Scotch novel—and, above all, a social independent, unembarrassed attitude. With a new coat, this last blessing is unattainable. Imprisoned in this detestable tunic—oh, how unlike the flowing toga of the ancients!—we are perpetually haunted with a consciousness of the necessities of our condition. A sudden pinch in the waist dispels a philosophic reverie; another in the elbow withdraws us from the contemplation of the poet to the recollection of the tailor; Snip's goose vanquishes Anacreon's dove; while, as regards our position, to lean forward is inconvenient; to lean backward extravagant; to lean sideways impossible. The great secret of happiness is the ability to merge self in the contemplation of nobler objects. This a new coat, as I have just now hinted, forbids. It keeps incessantly intruding itself on our attention. While it flatters our sense of the becoming, it comprises our freedom of thought. While it insinuates that we are the idol of a ball-room, it neutralizes the compliment by a high-pressure power on the short ribs. It bids us be easy, at the expense of respiration; comfortable, with elbows on the rack.

There is yet another light in which old coats may be viewed; I mean as chroniclers of the past, as vouchers to particular events. Agesilaus, King of Sparta, always dated from his last new dress. Following in the wake of so illustrious a precedent, I date from my last (save one) new coat, which was ushered into being during the memorable period of the Queen's trial. Do I remember that epoch from the agitation it called forth? From the loyalty, the radicalism, the wisdom, and the folly it quickened into life?—Assuredly not. I gained nothing by the wisdom. I lost as much by the folly. I was neither the better nor the worse for the agitation. Why, then, do I still remember that period? simply and selfishly from the circumstance of its having occasioned the dismemberment—most calamitous to a poor annuitant!—of the very coat in which I have the honor of addressing this essay to the public. In an olfactory crowd, whom her majesty's wrongs had congregated at Hammersmith, my now invalid habiliment was transformed after the manner of an Ovidian metamorphosis, where the change is usually from the better to the worse, from a coat into a spencer. In a word, some adroit conveyancer eloped with the hinder flaps, and, by so doing, secured a snuff-box which played two waltz tunes.

A THOUSAND YEARS AGO.

BY B. W. PROCTOR (BARRY CORNWALL).

Beauties! there is nothing new
'Neath the changing moon:
Maids are fickle, men are true,
And are vanquished soon!
It was so—(was it not so?)
A thousand thousand years ago!

Gold is still the king of kings;
Life is still too brief;
Love hath still his little wings,
And is still——a thief!
It was so—(was it not so?)
A thousand thousand years ago!

Beauties, help us to a change;
Teach us (simple elves!)
A little art, and how to range,
But——be true, *yourselves*
This may be, though 'twas not so
A thousand thousand years ago.

PICTORIAL HUMOR.

BY JOHN LEECH.

NOT YET.

SHAKSPERE A LITTLE ALTERED.

"He lived not wisely, but too well."

THE BUM-BOAT WOMAN.

BY CAPTAIN GLASCOCK, R. N.

WHAT sounds fall so joyous on the naval ear, always excepting the spirit-stirring cry of "an enemy in sight," as those which announce the nearing of Bum-boat Bet, the pulling-off of Pilchard Poll, or the coming alongside of Coaxing Kate?* Not that we would pay so poor a compliment to the craft, as to place in parallels the friend with the foe of the fleet; but extremes will meet, ay, even in the teeth of the great mathematical saw.

It is true that in Johnson's voluminous work, the word "Bum-boat" is permitted to appear. But, mark! instead of the substantive being made "to stand by itself"—the naval noun to float on its own bottom, to swim freely, fitted and freighted—the lexicographer, in violation of all philological rule, exhibits it a shored-up uncommissioned craft, curtailed of its *fair* proportions, having for supporters two such unsightly and anti-nautical things as a "Bum-bailiff," and "a Bump." † Where was the "bump of order," when the doctor had recourse to such uncongenial juxtaposition?

Among other etymological matters, discussed over a strong Nor-wester in the larboard fore-cock-pit cabin, Pipes, the boatswain, who was a man of letters (for a better A. B. was not borne on the books of any of his Majesty's ships), would have set the lexicographer right as to the due derivation of the title attached to the subject of our present sketch. In his usual familiar and flowing strain, would he thus have enlightened his plodding companion:—"See here, old boy, as regards what *you* calls the derrywation o' the word, but what *I* calls the christ'nin' o' the craft; yer just like all the rest o' the shore-going tribe—and that's preciously out in yer reck'nin'—for you see *that* warn't her *first* name—she went by a name of another natur; and, ye knows, as there's nothin' more nat'ral nor to give a name nearest to the natur of the thing in trade, why, in course, as she never brought nothin' aboard but buns, the craft was never no more nor a reglar-built Bun-boat Woman. But you see, old gemman, as the people afloat soon gets tired of buns, and wanted more substantialer stuff; buns no longer was brought aboard. So when they begins to bring off sogers,* sassingers, soft-tack, beer, butter, soap, eggs, pipes, pigtail, and such like sarviceable stuff, why, in course, 'twas no easy matter to fix upon a name as would suit every article taken on tick: and, as men-o'-war's-men, ye know, never do things hand over hand, in a hurry, but always likes first to *feel* their way, why, they thinks they cou'dn't do better nor go grad'ally to work,—throw the N out of the name, taking the M as next above in lieu. By this, you know, they couldn't make matters worse, whilst, on the tother tack, they was sarvin' *she* as sarved the fleet, by giving the craft a *higher* letter at Lloyd's.† So you see, old boy, they turns it end for end, and converts Bun-boat Woman into *Bum*-boat Woman; and, after all, take it by or large, it's a better name—it sounds more ship-shape—less mincing—less young-ladyish—and sartinly, a rounder and fuller mouthful in a seaman's mouth. There you has it, Doctor, short and sweet—*you* has it as *I* had it." And the Doctor would have had it, as we had it in our youth, years ago. But with derivation a truce. Proceed we with our sketch. We take as a sitter a sister from the Sister Isle.

Reader, permit us to introduce to your favorable

* Celebrated Bum-boat beauties.

† Vide Johnson's Dictionary.

* The name by which men-o'-war's-men designate red herrings.

† At Lloyd's, vessels are estimated by letters affixed to their several names. The letter A stands highest in value.

notice and special protection, "Mother Donovan," of the Cove of Cork,—part owner (for the pig in the parlor pays the rint) of a much-frequented mud edifice located in the East Holy Ground, a patch of Paradise attached to the Great Island, and immediately facing the Spit Sand and Isle of Spike.

Well, we can now take her in all her glory, for at this moment a two-decker—a crack seventy-four gun ship—a stranger returning from a foreign station, possibly short of provisions, or short of water, is suddenly descried under a cloud of canvas, with a brisk breeze, a flood tide, and a flowing sheet, between the towering heads of the harbor's mouth. All Cove is already in a state of excitement. Chaos is come again. Milesian sounds startle the uninitiated ear, but the shriller tones of Mother Donovan outhowl every other hoveller, of either Holy Ground, east or west.

"Oh! murder, murder," she exclaims, "if here isn't a big baste of a man-o'-war, after comin' right into the Cove. Honor! Honor! Be quick!—sack the praties, string the sassingers, and basket the butter. Tim, be stirrin' yer stumps—launch the whaler—where in the dickens is Paddy Molloy? Couldn't he be killin' the ould gander? For the lives o' yees, don't be after lettin Mudder Murphy bate us in gettin' the business aboord."

Some score of bustling competitors are now heard cheering their Paddies, and hurrying their Honors (a name common in the south of Ireland) in the shipment of their marketable goods. Pots, pans, black jacks, red herrings, yellow soap, pails of sky-blue, and barrels of brown stout, are seen descending, or rather bundling, over the high and hanging cliffs, on their way to the boat on the beach.

Mother Donovan, who is a dame of double dimensions—a sort of Lambert in petticoats—with Honor, her "nate niece" (for the mothers afloat, like the fathers of the land, beget *nieces* rather than daughters), seat themselves in the stern-sheets of a white whaler. Both are clad in brown cloaks, called "jocks," with huge hoods covering their unadorned heads—for bonnets are held in utter contempt by the fair of Cove. Honor is a bright brunette, with eyes of hazel hue, flashing fire at every glance; hair black, glossy, and lank, like a skein of sable silk—with a face and figure (saving her feet) perfectly Spanish. And now, in the trying tug to fetch the ship already anchored, may be seen the opposing Paddies, and contending Tims, bending their broad backs to their huge unpliable sweeps (for oars they can hardly be called), sending the salt spray over the bows of their bounding boats, and drenching to the skin the fair sitters abaft. See how the brine stiffens the playful muscles of the mother's mouth, and still straightens the daughter's locks of love! After a tiring tug against wind and tide, the white whaler reaches abreast of the towering liner, in all the busy bustle of furling sails, and of squaring yards.—There she is: the inner boat, lying off on her oars. And now watch the "sheeps-eyes," and imploring glances which Mother Donovan throws at the first-lieutenant, standing stiff as a steeple on the break of the poop, and who tries hard to preserve his official station, and maintain the gravity of his quarter-deck face.

"Honor, darlint! Stand up fornent him. Show him you mane to give him the news. Hould up, child, hould up, and show him the paper."

Honor does as desired; and standing erect in the boat, her dripping locks wafting in the wind, her anxious eyes following every turn and tread of the first-lieutenant. At length, she catches his glance, and extending a bare arm of symmetrical mould, holds in her hand "The Cork Constitution, or Southern Reporter:" and now, in bewitching accents, she exclaims, "Ah, now, that's a dear jintleman—do, do, let us in—ah, now do—isn't it the day's paper I have here for ye? Ah, be marciful! —the saa's mighty salt! mighty tryin to the eyes!"

The eyes of Honor are more trying to the first-lieutenant; still, he assumes no show of favor or affection, and, in a commanding voice, he cries:—"Keep off that boat, master-at-arms; mind, no muslin aboard till the yards are square, and every rope taut as a harp-string."

"There's the raal gintleman—my blessin's wid ye," ejaculates the stout dame, implying by this loudly-delivered benediction—directed to silence the tiring entreaties of her trading opponents—that she is certain of "sarving the ship:"—and so she is —for the word of admission is soon after given by the sentinel pacing his post. "Up wid ye, child—quick!—there's a darlint—and, mind ye" (the caution is loudly delivered), "for the life o' ye, don't part wid de paper till ye place it in his honor's hands.—The Lord love him, and it's himself that *is* the raal gintilman."

A tall topman jumps down the gangway steps, to lend Honor a hand in ascending the side of the lofty ship. Her top-lights dazzle the eyes of the tar, and all her upper works are suited to his taste; but as the giggling girl places her foot on the first step (and the first *step* often mars a match), the conductor breaks out: "There we have it—all alike—fair above, and full below."

"Ah now, mister sailor, lave off your ticklin';" (Jack's only playful—nothing more than freshening her way aloft); "fait, I'll be missin' my futtin', so I will." But no such thing: Honor arrives on the gangway;—and now to *undergo* an overhaul from the master-at-arms.

"Nothing *here*, I hope?" says the searcher, suiting the action to the word.

"Hands off, i' ye plase!" returns the indignant girl, keeping the master-at-arms at arm's length. "It's yer betters that darn't do the likes o' *that!* It's thrúe for me—who d'ye think ye got hould of?"

The man of feeling relents, and the charmer is permitted to pass muster; and next comes, panting and blowing like a lady-whale, the huge and unwieldy owner of the stock-in-trade. After no little of exertion, she finds a footing on deck. She stops to regain her breath,—now throws her eyes aloft,—now directs them on the deck, expressing, by dumb gesticulations, the greatest surprise. Her shoulders are up to her ears, and the elbows of her short arms are pinioned to her side, as she claps, with seeming delight, her small but fleshy hands.

"Oh, murder! murder! what a bu-tee-ful sight it is! Och, thin, isn't she a terrible size intirely!" (she had seen many ships before of a similar size:) "oh, by de book, a big man-o'-war bates every oder sight in nathur."

"Strange sights are sometimes seen in nature," says the official feeler, taking the fair Fatima in hand, and deliberately pursuing his system of search: any thing *here?*"

"Is it game yer makin' of a body? Sure, havn't I got quite enough of my own? Fait, my good man, there's nothin' there but raal, wholesome, solid nathur."

"Can't say; can't always trust to the loom o' natur—tic'larly about the cat-heads:" and so saying, the searcher satisfies himself as to the reality of the trader's natural capacities. As there is nothing contraband traceable about her portly person, she descends the gangway ladder, following her marketable commodities, which are hardly placed between the two allotted guns on the main-deck, ere her baskets of bread, butter, eggs, sausages, apples, together with her pails of milk, are beset by shoals of the younger middies, watering at the mouth to taste the sweets of the sod. An elbowing and scrambling scene ensues; all are pushing for priority of purchase.

"Asy now, asy wid ye," ejaculates the portly purveyor, extending her short arms to preserve her eggs, and prevent, if possible, a crash of her crockery: "asy wid ye; first money, *first* sarved—that's the way we sarves the young gintry afloat."

The young gentry afloat are no sooner "sarved," than a missive from the ward-room summonses the presence of the ladies abaft.

"Who, d'ye say, my good boy, does be wantin' the Bum-boat Woman?"

This interrogation, delivered in accents mild as milk, is put to a young urchin, who pertly replies, "The First Leaftennant."

"Honor! Honor!—the Lord save us! where's the child got to? Honor!" again calls the startled dame, looking around for her lost lamb.

"Here am *I*, mudder—*aunt* I mean;" (for sometimes the outbursting of nature causes Honor to trip on the truth: a *lapsus linguæ* proclaims the parent, and identifies the daughter.)

"Well may the crathur call me mudder. It's myself that's been more than a fader to all her mudder's childer. But sure," she adds, turning to the master-at-arms, "doesn't all the world, ould and young, be now afther callin' me mudder? It's for all the world like puttin' ducks' eggs undher a hin. The young ducklins think, from the care the ould cackler takes of the web-footed crathurs, that the hin must be their raal mudder, whin, at the same time, it's as plain as the nose on yer face, the hin's no more nor their nat'ral aunt:—its thrue for me." —The mother's art corrects the daughter's nature, and now both "aunt" and "niece" are themselves again.

[But, on retiring to her hovel in the Holy Ground —after driving the pig out of the parlor—for secrets are not to be uttered in the presence of the porker —she inflicts on the daughter a moral lecture, upon the impropriety of "*misnaming* her afore the people aboord." "Lucky for me, so it was, the first lift'nint didn't hear the vice (voice) o' ye.—Oh, Honor! Honor! what would he think (an' he had the thought, if I hadn't mended the matter): ye wasn't my nat'ral niece?—Mudder, mudder;—the dickens mudder ye: don't ye know well enough, the navy gintilmen think times is bad wid poor people, when a body is obligated to bring a daughter aboord a man-o'-war? Now, for the futur, larn to call me aunt wid a bould an' asy tongue, an' whinever mudder comes into yer mind, hould yer prate, or muffle yer mouth!"]

"Come, child—throw off the jock—make yerself tidy, an' take the laugh off yer mouth afore ye face the gintlemen. Come, be stirrin'. Follow me—I'll lade the way;" and aft walks the waddling mother, followed by her uncloaked, unbonnetted, and all but unblushing "*niece*." Aware that the ladies are allowed the *entrée*, the sentinel at his post throws open the ward-room door.

"Sarvint, gintlemen. Welcome all to Cove," cries the large "lady," dropping in the door-way her best courtesy. "The blessins on all yer bu-tee-ful, brown, sun-burnt faces; sign for yees, ye've come from furrin parts."

"Good standing color, old girl," returns the first-lieutenant. "Come," he adds familiarly, "bring yourselves both to an anchor."

The chair of the old girl is soon filled, but the younger lass manifests a little of shyness in taking her seat.

"Come, young-un," cries the unsophisticated master, addressing the still standing girl, "come, what are ye ashamed of?—Look at your mother."

"Ah, thin, it *was* her mudder that never *was* ashamed of dacent people."

"Why, are *you* not her mother?" asks the first-lieutenant, throwing at each female alternate glances. "Why, she *must* be yours—she's the very picture of you."

"An' well she might; for it's myself that *was* the very pictur of her mudder;" and here her broad and expansive bosom, like the swell of the sea, heaves and sinks with a heavy sigh—a sigh worthy of a widow in her weeds. But suddenly and adroitly she turns the subject. "Of coorse, gintlemin, ye'll be afther wantin' yer linen washed? It's we that *can* get it up in illegant style. Yer things we'll bleach for yees, whiter than the dhriven snow; an' as for the platin'—may be all the bu-tee-ful ladies at the balls won't be axin' ye, 'Who plates yer bussums, an' who pinches yer frills?'—It's thrue for me."

The plating of the bosoms, and the pinching of the frills, already ensure her the officers' custom; and now, under the influence of a little "ship's" rum (which she "hears is good for the wind"), she not only becomes the more loquacious, but also the more communicative on local matters. She descants on the beauties of the river—no allusion to Honor—but she breaks forth in a figurative strain on the many "big bu-tee-ful sates on both banks of the Lee."

Honor, though less loquacious, is not the less bewitching.—"Lickor never lights on her lip," "The very smell of it always turns her head," and "Tay is her strongest dhrink." But her *naïveté* and playfulness of manner amuses the "nice gintleman" seated by her side, and the silken softness of her jet hair entices his fingers to set right her drooping locks.

"Ah, now, be quiet wid ye;—keep yer fingers to yerself;—fait, I'll be afther lavin' ye, if ye don't lave my hair alone. Ah, m—"

The *lapsus* of mother had nearly escaped; but it is promptly caught, and the substitution of "*aunt*" amends the maternal appeal—to "make the gintleman behave himself."

But the mother's thoughts are otherwise engaged. The liberty taken with her Honor's hair is not the "*liberty* given to broach the beer." Besides she has yet to feel her way touching the prudence of giving the ship's company trust.

"May-be yer honor," she says in an under tone, addressing the officer possessing the power to favor her views,—"may-be yer honor can be tellin' a body when the people's comin' in coorse o' pay?"

"Why, they've three years' whack due," returns the executive chief.

"Poor crathurs! It's the likes o' they that *is* desarvin' o' thrust! May-be it's yer honor," she adds coaxingly, "'ill be now lettin' me broach the beer?" A nod of assent ensues, and the fair traders rise to depart—the mother pouring down blessings on the heads of the several officers assembled, and the daughter declaring, in accents not intended to be lost, "that nicer-mannered and gintaler gintlemen wasn't to be found in the grand fleet!"

And now comes on the tug of "tick." The cooks of the messes, kid in hand, close round the flowing barrel, whilst Honor, as in honor bound, checks the chalking score of the master-at-arms. During each day's detention of the ship in port, the "stout" of the stout dame flows to the same tune; and this "serving" on the score of "trust," serves as an after-claim for a passage to the port at which the ship is ordered to be paid;—and then it is that the mother-wit of the "mother" begins to tell.

On this side of the water, the fair traders afloat are craft altogether of another kind. It is true that some partake of the Dutch build—are bluff in the bows, full abaft, and conveniently formed for stowage: but, still, those who desire to stand well with sea-faring folk, study symmetrical lines, fineness of form, and, particularly, neatness in the rigging, 'low and aloft. But, to drop metaphor, the fair traders (and often the fairest afloat) of Gosport, Portsmouth, and Plymouth, are perfectly aware of the nautical feeling in favor of personal appearance. Hence the *bum*bastic conceit:—

'Tis the business of Beauty to become the beauty of Business.

In their mode of commanding success, the English Bum-boat Women are perfectly opposed to the practice pursued by the sisterhood of the sister isle; and though, to attain their end, the British fair seldom display flashes of wit, they nevertheless have always their wits about them. In short, in the pursuit of business, they adopt the "silent system," trusting more to the power of the eye, than to the power of the tongue.

What an eye had Bumboat Bet! Indeed did it "sound a parley of provocation." Whether in anger or despair, the dropping of her long-lashed lid, was alone sufficient to raise in her favor ten thousand tongues; and, as for Coaxing Kate, she had only to smile—display her bewitching teeth—to command Red at the main,—aye, and obtain immediate admission, were even the fore-topsail loose, and "Blue-Peter" flying at the fore.* And what might not be said of their courage? The weather they encounter, and dangers they brave, in pursuing their work on the waters. But we forget—our sketch is confined to the fair of Erin.

* When it be desired to intimate the ship is about to depart, the fore-topsail is let loose, and the flag, blue-pierced-white, is displayed at the fore.

A BLIND STORY; OR MRS. CLAPPER'S RETURN.

FROM "MANY-COLORED LIFE." ANONYMOUS.

Returning late one evening from Gravesend,
Where she had journeyed with a dear old friend,
Kept till 'twas more than late enough to sup,
Because, like her, the *steam* could not *get up*,
Dame Clapper saw light from her chamber flash
Forth from the sash.
The blind was down but on it fell the shade
Of her loved lord.—Think's she "He's in a fright,
Lest I should not come home to-night;
How glad he'll be to find I have not stayed!"

Thrilling with love, and "all that sort of thing,"
She hastily advanced to knock or ring,
When on the blind another figure fell.
Starting at what she saw,
Fury to seize her soul, rushed out of hell,
She "held her breath for awe."
Then mentally exclaimed, "What's to be done?
Two heads I see, but they approach so nigh,
That in *this case*, two are not in my eye,
Better than one!"

Who can describe her passion's wild alarms,
Fearing her lord was faithless to her charms!
Tears trickling down, she cried with wild affright,
"*Shadows*"—'Tis King Dick's speech from Shakspere's pen—
"Have struck more terror to my soul this night,
Than could the *substance of ten thousand men*."

The knocker now the lady agitated,
And then with somewhat of impatience waited.
No answer was returned by her loved spouse,
And so she knocked again, in such a way,
She nearly *brought down*—so the neighbors say,
If not her *gentleman* at least the *house*.

Still closed against her, did the door remain,
She felt of course at such exclusion shock'd,
And even louder than before she knock'd,
Rang and knock'd,
Rang and knock'd again.

At last the husband ventured to appear;
  Like one just risen from bed in wild surprise,
  Yawning, while almost closed his eyes,
His mouth was nearly stretched from ear to ear.

How lovely, Nature, all thy plan!
  How equitable are thy laws!
If shut the eyes of drowsy man,
  Thy care 'tis to extend his jaws!
This therefore may make up for *that*,
O beauteous scheme of tit for tat!

Of course, at being kept so long, she frown'd,
And he lamented having slept so sound;
But said he joyed to see his bosom's pride—
He lied.

Now to retire he hinted she had best,
Because he was convinced she wanted rest.
Consent she gave, yet paused upon the way,
"With sweet, reluctant, amorous delay,"
She thought a robber's footstep struck her ear,
Which made her for her tender husband fear.

With careless laughter and facetious grin,
  The husband bade her all such notions scout;
"*No thief*," he said, "for robbery could get *in*,
  He dreaded much, "*The murder would come out*."
But all in vain was his advice,
  His tale was found untrue;
His friend detected in a trice,
  And pummelled black and blue.

How long Dame Clapper raved, I have not time
To tell in prose, much less to put in rhyme;
Suffice it then to say her lord's disgrace
Was made complete, and neatly clawed his face.
'Twas then he sighed, "O woe is me!
  Too late the moral comes to mind,
That naughty tricks which *none can see*,
  May be discovered by the *blind*.
"But wives," he added, "who will roam,
  And go and gad about,
Ought to expect when they *come home*,
  To find *their husbands out*."

HAMMERING IT IN.

ANONYMOUS.

Depressed by a severe cold, for which I was indebted to the variable nature of the weather in the last days of November, I. sat, yesterday morning, in a despondent way beside my coffee and dry toast, roasted the soles of my slippers, and read away my digestion over the last murder recounted in the Times. Suddenly, I was startled by the step of a man rushing hurriedly up-stairs; the door of my sitting-room was burst open, and my friend Boulder, flourishing in his hand a heavy hammer, stood before me, and gasped out, "I've done it at last, Smith!. I've done it at last!" Boulder is a most excitable man, with a wife and a large family of boys. I looked aghast for marks of blood upon the hammer—for a trace of human hair in some crack of the handle.

"Which—who—how many?" I shouted.

"My son, Jack," he declared, "is the cause of it

all. He brought it upon me. O Smith, my dear friend, would you have believed I should have ever come to this? Cut me some ham?"

He sat down opposite me in an easy chair, turned up his soles also to the fire, helped himself to a thick slice of bread, and said again,

"Cut me some ham. I must be off to the hills in ten minutes, and it's well to fortify myself, because I may miss dinner to-day."

"Sir! Mr. Boulder!"

"Let me ring for a cup and saucer. There, now, go on with your breakfast, and I'll tell you all about it. I was led to it entirely by that hard-headed fellow, David Page."

"Page?"

"David Page, F. G. S. Hark you! Three weeks ago, Mrs. Boulder came to me and said, 'Peter.' I replied, 'Susannah.' She said, 'Look at Jack's clean shirt.' She showed me a shirt folded neatly, with its front covered with red stains, and holes, and indentations. 'Mercy,' I cried, 'what's the cause of this?' Jack was at school—round the corner, you know—Tickleby's day-school. 'I wish to show you, Mr. B.,' said my old girl, 'Jack's linen drawer.' Followed my wife, looked in the drawer, found it filled up with stones and dirt. In the drawer below that, found clay, sand, and old shells in his Sunday jacket. Caused the dirt to be instantly carried to the dust-hole. Further examined drawers in Jack's room, and, in the corner of one, found a book entitled, 'Advanced Text-Book of Geology, Descriptive and Industrial, by David Page, F. G. S.'"

"'That's what has done it, Peter,' Mrs. B. said. 'That's the book I've seen him reading evening after evening.' 'He shall read no more of it,' said I. 'The book is confiscated.' When Jack came home at dinner-time we had a great disturbance."

Here Boulder gasped over his ham, and I felt painfully nervous. Boulder went on:

"'Jack,' said I, 'you shall never more look on that book.' I put it on my own library table. I peeped into it; I looked into it; I read bits of it; I read more of it; I liked it; I studied it; I threw myself heart and soul into it; I comprehended it; —I bought a hammer."

Here Boulder caught his hammer up and flourished it again. He was evidently stone-mad.

"With this hammer, my boy, I break my way into the treasury of Nature."

Here Boulder brought his hammer down and smashed my tea-cup.

"Ah, good!" he cried, taking a fragment up. "A lucky accident. Look at the crystalline fracture. What's here? Clay. What makes the clay crystalline in its fracture? Fire. Theory of the igneous rocks. Thickness of the ponderable crust of the globe, eight hundred miles. Depth at which most of the rocks ordinarily found at the surface would exist in a molten state, say five and twenty miles. Undercrust of the globe, granite. Here's a bit."

My excitable friend took from the mantel-piece a handsome paper-weight of polished stone.

"Some ass of a man has polished this fine specimen of primitive rock." With one tap of his hammer, Boulder broke it in two. "Observe," he said, "the exquisite fracture."

"Exquisite—confound——"

"Never polish a fine specimen. The geologist, my dear boy, is most particular to show you a clean fracture and nothing else. He breaks a stone, and takes pains not so much as to dim with a finger's touch the brilliance of the broken surface. Now fractures are of various sorts, conchoidal or shell-like, even, uneven, smooth, splintery, hackly. Only look in this beautiful bit of granite, at the silvery gleams of the mica and the suety bits of quartz speckling the solid pudding of the felspar. Quartz is, of simple minerals, one of the hardest. I knock out a little chip of granite, and you will observe that it is impossible to powder the quartz in it by blows of a hammer on the hearth-stone. You perceive the hearth-stone breaks, but the quartz grains remain uncomminuted."

"Mr. Boulder—" I began faintly. I was made somewhat weak and helpless by my cold, or I should have met vigor with vigor.

"Pardon me, Smith; they remain, I say, uncomminuted. Let me advise you to be a geologist. I am going to the hills to-day on an excursion. Come. Ah, you have a cold. Well, I will stop exactly half an hour." Here he pulled out his watch. "I do want you to share my enjoyment. I do want to make you feel the delight caused by the study of geology. I didn't think that I should take it up myself when I turned out Jack's drawers. Page over-persuaded me. He's just the man to bring the science home to you. Ah, Mrs. Boulder doesn't know it, but I've carried up her spare sheets and blankets into one of the attics, and have a most beautiful experiment on the formation of mud-banks from aqueous deposit in her linen chest. I've mixed up in water earth and shells and a shilling's worth of shrimps. In a few days, when I drain the water off, you come over to me, and I'll show you how the top crust of the world is formed, and how the remains of extinct animals get to be mixed with it. Only, if Mrs. B. should by chance go to the chest before the experiment is finished—O those women! those women."

"But now, Smith, as you've a cold, and can't go to the hills, I'll show you how a geologist need go no farther than his own room for a study of incomparably the most glorious of sciences. I'll give you to-day only an elementary lesson. When I come next, we'll go into the thing more completely. Now look here,"—down came the hammer on a corner of my mantelpiece,—"I break off this little bit of metamorphic rock; the character has been destroyed by polishing, but now what beauty have I not revealed."

"Boulder," I cried, "give me your hammer. Let me send your hammer down into the hall."

"Thank you, thank you—I shall be going presently. 'Tis not worth while. Dismiss from your mind what I was just saying about aqueous rocks. Above the igneous you have the metamorphic—you have, to speak familiarly, the mantelpiece upon the paper weight, and not the paper weight upon the mantel-piece."

"I have, have I?"

"To be sure you have. Heat and the pressure of the superincumbent strata have given to these metamorphic rocks their crystalline appearance, though it is believed that they were once deposited by water, and contained fossils of which all trace has been extinguished. Well then, Smith, on the top of the metamorphic rocks on the top of the mantel-piece, we place Sir Roderick Murchison."

"Can it be possible?"

"Yes, Murchison and the Silurian rocks defined

and discovered by him. They used to be called, along with some others, the Greywacke formation."

"O, indeed!"

"Yes. Here we have certain sandstones, shales, limestones, flagstones, and the slates near Bala. By Jove! Smith, you've a slate top to that console table. If it should be Silurian, you happy dog!—if it should be Silurian!"

Up leaped my friend, and up leaped I, but not in time to save the chipping of a rather costly bit of furniture.

"Boulder," I cried, hoarse with rage and rheum together, "break another piece of furniture, and we are enemies for ever!"

"Ah, my boy, you have your enthusiasm yet to come. I'll promise to break nothing of any value. But of what value are these precious polished specimens of yours? Their value's doubled when they show the fracture and the cleavage and that sort of thing. Nay, I'll break nothing more. Well, then, above the Silurian you have the old red sandstone, and then above that—ha! but it's all fair to break coal—above that the coal."

A heavy lump of coal was suddenly whipped out of the coal-scuttle, and being hammered into fragments on the breakfast cloth before I could effectually interfere.

"It is most interesting to search coal for the remains of extinct vegetable life. The markings sometimes are of the most beautiful description. The whole of yesterday I spent in our coal-cellar, and a more delightful day I never——"

A loud knocking at the street-door startled us. Mr. Boulder was picking carefully about the contents of the coal-scuttle, and had spread some choice bits on the rug for further investigation, when a servant appeared to report that Mrs. Boulder wished, if Mr. B. was disengaged, to see him instantly.

"Ah!" said my friend, laying another coal upon the rug. "She has been to the linen press. Smith, go and pacify her."

MR. HIPPY'S VAGARIES.

BY CORNELIUS WEBBE.

Not a sentence—not a syllable of *Trismegistus* shall be lost through my neglect. I am his word-banker—his storekeeper of puns and syllogisms.—CHARLES LAMB.

MR. HIPPY—as he was familiarly called, otherwise Harty Hippisley, Gent.—Mr. Hippy was not a man of wit, though he sometimes approached very nigh to it. A Scotch friend, indeed, once called him "A man of *wet*" (meaning wit). "Yes," said he, turning his eye with a merry twinkle upon his flattering friend, "very *wet*." And he took the hint from his friend's pronunciation to suggest this as the true reading of a couplet by Dryden which has been much disputed—

Great *wet*——

or drinking largely—

Great *wet* to madness nearly is allied,
And thin *potations* do their bounds divide.

He was simply a man of whim, which sometimes had blended up with it much playful pleasantry, and sometimes a spice of true humor to season it; for he was a humorist, or I know not what humor is; an English humorist—the only humorist; and notwithstanding all his real or imagined unhappiness (and he had many good proofs to give as reasons for any momentary iudulgence in complaint), he was, after all, of that happy nature, that though there was at times a savor of salt in his humor, there was no bitterness; nothing that offended the good taste, or hurt the feelings of his friends or associates. He had, in an eminent degree, that rare quality in a man who loved jesting and raillery, and indulged in them, that he could forbear and spare. If he thought a severe thing of any one, he would not give it utterance. He was in that respect, perhaps, a little too tender of others; for he sometimes spared those who did not spare him. I have seen him put down by an impudent dog or conceited booby, and have not a word to say for himself. I heard him once, and never but once, regret that he sometimes felt such an embarrassment and diffidence in society, that "for the life of him he could not say *bo!* to a goose when he met one; and he regretted this the more, because he so often met a goose, and lost so many opportunities for saying *bo!*" But he was eminently a humorist; and felt, I should say, more pleasure in abstaining from severities of tongue than he could have taken in indulging that unruly member in an unbridled and unbitted license. Yet no man, I believe, had a sharper sense of the ridiculous, a keener eye at detecting the faults, and follies, and weaknesses of his fellow-men; and no man was more prompt and prone to pity and be patient with them, let them pass and say nothing, though he thought much upon them. If he could persuade any one out of an error, he spoke; if he saw that that was a hopeless task, he was silent. "Let him that is without sin cast the first stone," was the religious rule that governed and restrained him. He was, I believe, a really benevolent man in the main—if not at all times and in all things; any departure of his from that "even tenor" of a wise man's way nevertheless and notwithstanding. If he ever diverged from that "primrose path," and had to accuse himself with any sins of commission—or sins of omission, which are worse—no man more bitterly regretted them. His humor, his jests and jibes, were therefore innocuous, and hurt not; and this was perhaps their best commendation.

Mr. Hippy could sometimes say severities, but he was best at a quiet reproof. Some one, speaking in contempt of the mind of a mutual associate, said, "You may put all the ideas he has under this goblet." Hippy silently drew from his pocket a Pickering copy of Horace, laid it upon the table, drained his goblet, and turning it over the little volume, the whole works, the wit, the playful humor, and brilliant genius of the beloved friend of Virgil and Mæcenas, and the favored of Augustus, lay under that small crystal dome. The "moral" was obvious.

Among a knot of friends who were amusing themselves with cutting up a foolish acquaintance, he interposed by wishing that they would take a hint from Mrs. Rundell's advice to carvers—that "It is not necessary to cut up the *whole goose*, unless the company is very large." He would often turn aside the shafts of ill-nature and ridicule by some such pleasant reproof.

Being in a drinking party where a dirty wit kept the table in a roar, Hippy sat in silence. His chair neighbor remarked it—"You do not laugh with our facetious friend." "No, sir," sternly replied Hippy, who loved wit much, but decency more;—"I saw a dirty pig this day who had just wallowed in the mire, but I did not feel compelled to hug him; I had too much respect for my white waistcoat." During the same evening, he got into his old "merry cue," and kept his friends amused, and instructed too, without once calling in the aid of the low balderdash which some men mistake for humor. I could soon see that the company were very glad to exchange the cleanly tongue and the wholesome, healthy humor of my merry and wise friend for the cancerous comicalities of the dirty-minded gentleman upon whom he had so lately put an extinguisher. The club-room was full, everybody happy, the ale brisk as a bee—the waiters ditto; the Welsh rare-bits never so large and so good; the "natives," as fresh as a daisy, opened as if they were obliged to the knife that let them loose, and were uncommonly fat and fine. Puggleston was in the chair *pro forma*; Hippy faced him. No singing was allowed, which kept the company select and sensible. Any gentleman who forgot himself so far as to strike up a song, found himself, before verse the first was concluded, in the hands of four stout members of the club, who quietly took him out by the legs and wings, with as much gravity as four undertakers would carry out a departed gentleman, opened the yard door, set little or big warbler down upon the cold stones, and left him there to "*sing* his eyes out;" and when he was thoroughly song-exhausted, and come to a sense of his situation, then, and not till then, was he brought back to his chair with the same grave honors, perfectly sane, and silent, and songless.

Hearing a young friend with good ideas, but an inaptness for uttering them, struggling hard to give expression to a happy thought he had somehow got hold of, he said, "you have hooked a fine fish there, W——; but you do not seem to me to know how to land it. Play with it, boy; give it line; and when you have let it spend its strength, then haul it slowly and steadily, whip your landing-net under it quietly, and lift it on shore."

No man sooner saw through masks and the usual dominoes in which men disguise themselves in the masquerade of life. He penetrated in a moment through the thin disguises of a professing friend of his, who preached benevolence, but stood selfishly still when the time came in which he should stir.—"If," said he, "he was over his dessert, and had split a walnut in halves, and (his dining-room hanging over the river) he saw you drowning under his window, he would not be at the trouble to throw out one-half of the shell if it would save you. But as soon as you were sunk 'full fathoms five,' no man would compete with him in the pathos of his exclamations—no one shed more tears for your lamentable death—and no one return so soon to his cigar and whiskey-toddy, and forget you altogether, as though you had never been."

Sitting composedly after supper, over his concluding glass, he felt a fly travelling slowly down his nose, till it "pulled up," as he expressed it, at the bridge: "Go on," said he, pleasantly, "there is no toll." As I have mentioned his nose, I may as well add, that it was undoubtedly none of the shortest, and he never denied it—he was too conscious and too candid; at any time, as he allowed, it was not a bad sabbath day's journey for any fly in all flydom to travel from the beginning to the end thereof. I remember some one remarking how very low down his spectacles hung upon his nose, and wondering that they did not fall off. "Oh!" said he, "there is no fear of that: my nose is so long, that before my glasses could get to the end of it, I should be sure to overtake them;" and he threw himself back in his chair, and, with Richard, descanted on his own deformity.

He was "a man of an unbounded stomach" for humor; and even in his short fits of spleen and passion there was some unexpected stroke of humor, or some oddity of expression, that diverted you, and made his ill-temper as good as other people's good temper. Seeing him one day with a very long face and lowering brow, and impatient with all about him, I ventured to whisper, "You do not seem to be very happy to day, Hippy?" "Happy!" he shrieked out, glancing a severe eye at me, as though he would look me through, "I only want a pair of tight boots to make me a misanthrope."

Most men, when in pain of body or agony of mind, find a sort of ease in an oath, or in some kind of violence. I have seen my poor friend pale and trembling with pain, and he never seemed so much inclined to laugh; his antic disposition was never so playful, and you were never so sure of something out-of-the-way "to startle and waylay" you. When apparently most melancholy, humor always seemed to be lurking in the corner of his eye, and some preposterous pun lay ready to be perpetrated upon the tip of his tongue.

I was sitting with him one day while a deluging rain was falling, and flooding the street till it looked like a part of the river running at the bottom of it. Suddenly, a great outcry was heard in the regions below, and then a sound of feet hurrying up stairs, and in a moment Mrs. Fondleman burst abruptly into the room, crying out, "Oh, Mr. Hippy, Mr. Hippy!—I'm ruined! I'm drowned! We shall be all swept away! What shall I do?" "What is the matter, madam?" he inquired. "Oh that gully! It's of no more use than a pepper-box or a cullender! I've tried every thing—it's stopped, and nothing never will open it!" It was enough to provoke a saint to see his imperturbable temper: "Nothing will open it, eh?" inquired he. "No—nothing: I've tried every thing," said Mrs. F. "Try Morrison's Pills," said he, "they remove all obstructions!" Mrs. F. looked angry for a moment at his levity, and I know five hundred ladies who would have taught him better manners than to jest at such an unreasonable time; but she knew that her lodger would have his joke if he hanged for it, and so she laughed in lieu of being angry, and he, to reward her good humor, then went down, and with an old fishing-rod puddled about the choked gully till he cleared it. Mrs. F. then thanked him with a hundred curtsies, and was particularly careful of his crumpets at tea-time.

Waiting to get into the pit of Covent Garden theatre, he felt a pick-pocket quietly ease him of his handkerchief. He took no immediate notice of him, but pondered his revenge. The prig did not move away, as is the custom of "the gentle craft" when they have hooked their fish: he was evidently going into the pit too, and only amused himself with taking Hippy's handkerchief to kill time till the doors were opened. But being one of that uneasy order of persons who cannot "let well alone" when all is well, and having a few minutes more to spare, he next turned his attention to Hippy's fob-pocket: then he reckoned it was high time to tell him what he thought of his exclusive attentions; and turning suddenly round and looking him full in the face, he said very coolly, "Have the goodness, sir, to wipe my face." "I wipe your face! Come, I like that uncommon much!" exclaimed the man, "Why should I wipe *your* face, when I've got one of my own to attend to?" asked the born for Botany Bay. "I repeat it," said Hippy, "wipe my face!" Just at this moment, Donaldson, the old theatre-officer, bawled out, "Take care of your pockets, ladies and gentlemen!" Hippy looked in the filch's face significantly, and he took the hint. "If you've lost your wiper," said he, humbly, "it happens very fortinate that I've a wiper to spare: there, I'll lend you one with the utmost mildness;" and so saying he thrust a new silk handkerchief—not Hippy's—into his hand, and sneaked off. "While I was congratulating myself upon making so good an exchange of an old lamp for a new one, and conceitedly chuckling over my success in outwitting a pickpocket, there was a sudden cry of 'Officer! officer!—I'm robbed—I'm robbed!' Another voice cried, 'That's him!' and in a moment more I should have been in custody as a pickpocket, had not old Donaldson, when he approached to seize me, known me, and exclaimed, 'Oh, no, it's not this 'ere old gemman, I'll take my davy! I've known this 'ere gemman these thirty years, off and on—he an't the man!' And he pushed through the crowd to look for the culprit, but the Botany Bay bird had flown; and I have now no doubt, nor had I then, that it was Mr. Allfinger, my furtive friend, who, to give me a Rowland for my Oliver, had pointed me out as the thief, and so got quietly off himself. From which adventure I draw this very important *moral.*—'Never to play with edged tools.'"

I remember his coming into the club-room that night, and telling us this amusing incident in his most amusing manner. He did not often visit the theatres; he had seen the old actors, and did not take very kindly to the new. One of the things which annoyed him most in the modern heroes of the buskin, was their over-ingenuity in finding more in Shakspere's text than Shakspere ever meant. He was so displeased with these perverse fellows, that he said with much bitterness, "Where the good old motto, 'Veluti in speculum,' used to be inscribed, there should now be written 'Commit no new sense.'" This led to a long argument between us, which, as we had not concluded it in the club-room, was continued till we arrived at the doors of our respective domiciles, which were opposite to each other. He claimed the victory in the discussion—I denied it. As he stood knocking at his door, a cock crowed loudly. "Mind," cried Hippy across the street to me, with his usual consideration for the feelings of another, and his usual readiness at a stroke of humor,—"Mind, it was not me that crowed!" I was so much tickled with his pleasantry, that I handsomely acknowledged that he was right in his argument; and he was.

He was always catching you with some hunorous turn of expression, or droll surprise. We were walking together once, when he observed a person

with a striking peculiarity of vision coming on towards us: he was too humane a man, in general, to make deformities playthings for his pleasantry, but he said, "I don't know what that man has done to me that he cannot look me straight in the face: he may have his reasons for it, and perhaps the principal one is—he squints."

Going over a picture-gallery with him one day, there was, of course, that old favorite story of painters, Potiphar and Joseph, among the rest. We passed on, and came to another picture, in which two lovers were seen warmly embracing: it was finely painted, and I stopped before it. "What is the story?" I inquired of Hippy. "Oh, the old one, Potiphar and Joseph!" he replied. "Nay," said I, "Joseph would have nothing to do with her, and tore himself away!"—"Hah! true; but he has thought better of it."

Mr. Hippy was such a thorough humorist that he would even do you "a good turn" in the guise of a joke—tell you of an error, and teach you a lesson, in a pun, and take some pains to work it out and make you see it. His friend Etty, he saw plainly, was killing himself with over-application in his profession, and want of exercise and relaxation. Some men would have preached him into a passion with moral and medical reflections; he took a longer course, but a shorter one in the end. He knew that his friend would at any time go six miles to look at a fine picture, so he committed a pious fraud by telling him that if he would walk with him to the suburbs he would show him a Canaletti. Accordingly, he dragged him out of London into Surrey, and on and on they went, till at last, as they were creeping along the bank of the canal below Camberwell, the fatigued Mr. Etty inquired, "but where is this same Canaletti?" "Oh, ah!" said his waggish companion, who had now perfected the pun, "why, here is the *Canal, Etty!*" and giving him a good-humored push, he almost pushed him into it. Of course, Mr. Etty saw the humor of the lesson, and laughed; and Hippy, to reward his placability, after dragging him over the bridge, and up the pleasant Peckham Rise to sharpen his appetite, gave him a series of "mutton chops to follow," and a bottle of sherry following them again, and a good dish of discourse on the painters who are poets, and the poets who are painters.

In a party where a gentleman was bragging extravagantly, he quietly admonished him, and told him at the same time what he thought of him, by stooping down and patting a parlor pug-dog on the head, and quoting the old saying—"Brag is a good dog;" and then removing his hand to a China dog, on the mantel-piece, and patting that on the head too, adding—"but Hold-his-tongue is a better." My gentleman bragged no more that night—he tried another tack, and plunged into the deep waters of erudition—"He!" said Hippy to me aside,—"a shallow dog, that should not go into a shoe-bath without corks under him!" At length when the smatterer got into the peroration of a dissertation upon "the Digamma," he could no longer bear with the evidently drowning puppy, and sternly said, "Don't go out of your depth, Mr. ——, merely to show us that you cannot swim." He did not often indulge in such a severity, so that he could the better afford it, once in a way. Two or three instances of the like kind occurred to me. I remember we were once talking of a very mawkish man of letters; Hippy very happily described him as always looking like a person of sentiment very sick of a sop in the pan. The fickleness and indecision of an old friend being under discussion—"He?" said he, "why he is as undecided as a feather between four winds."

Hippy, too, would, with other wags, sometimes have his joke out, if he died for it. Having a tolerable appetite, not flinching from his glass, and being naturally disposed to inertness, he fell at last into a state of plethora, and was confined to his second-floor bed-chamber. "You must live lower," said Dr. Fumblepulse, as he fingered his wrist: "You must live lower." Hippy took him literally; and when the Doctor called next day he found him at full feed in the parlor: upon which, the worthy physician remonstrated, and Hippy "explained across the table," and the Doctor laughed at his waggery, and Hippy laughed too, and was of course all the better for it next day.

He hated Dr. Johnson's hatred of puns, and loved them, and the worse they were (as parents love most their worst-favored children) the more he petted them, the more pains he took in "getting them up," and playing and acting them. He once pretended that he had a decided objection to eating oysters, which I thought originated in his antipathy to destroying any creature with life in it; but I was mistaken, it was only one of his whims; for upon being assured by Mr. Plynn, the fishmonger of Fleet-street, that "his natives opened larger than their shells"—"Oh, if that is the case, Mr. Plynn," said he, "it must be quite a happy relief to be released from shells too small for them! Pray, let two dozen of them stretch themselves out on my account." And his conscience being thus humorously satisfied as to the humanity of eating his fellow-natives, as he called them, he sat down to satisfy the cravings of nature.

I caught him once near Spring Gardens, where the cows give up their milk "for a consideration" to the demanding dry mouths of the "babes and sucklings" who make that spot a sort of out-door nursery. He was apparently lost in studious consideration of something serious, about which he now looked infinitely grave, and now chuckled and grinned delightedly. I broke in upon his "brown study," and inquired what it was that so "perplexed" him in the "meanders of his brain." He confessed that he had been filling up the time he had had to wait for his friend Spiffle, "somewhere nigh," by satisfying himself—as logically as he could—that the little stunty Park cowkeeper he had in his eye, and to whom he directed mine, was, though he thought it not, to all intents and purposes a publican; and "thus 'twas done:"—"The dairyman kept his cows in public?" Granted. "They were therefore *public cows?*" Granted again. "The tap-keeper also kept his *public 'owze?*" (*Cocknicè* for public house.) Granted. "If the one was a publican, *cæteris paribus*, the other was a publican?" Not granted; but I laughed, and gave a House of Commons "Oh!" which satisfied him quite as well. Thus would he "trifle time away."

It was Mr. Hippy, who, when his barber was going to sleep while dressing his hair, roused him by vociferously striking up "*Ah comè rapida!*"—("Ah comb me rapider!") When some few years since, a creation of Peers amazed and amused the political world, and among the other lifts, Lord Grosvenor was made Marquis of Westminster, Hippy had no partisan objection to the measure; he only said—"I hope we shall be indulged also with a Marquis of Mile-End and a Viscount-Off-the-Stones!"——Some one censuring a smart, flashy habit he had of wearing his hat cocked on the right side of his head, in a most perilous attitude during blowing weather, he accounted for it satisfactorily, I think:—"You must know, sir, that I am leaving off this hat by degrees; and, as you may observe, I have left it off on the left side already."—Some one attributing the wants of Ireland to rich absenteeism, "No, sir," said he, "it is not absenteeism, but absent-dinnerism which is the misery of the poor Irish."

THE RED FISHERMAN.

BY WINTHROP MACKWORTH PRAED.

Oh flesh, flesh, how art thou fishified!—ROMEO AND JULIET.

THE abbot arose, and closed his book,
  And donned his sandal shoon,
And wandered forth, alone, to look
  Upon the summer moon;
A starlight sky was o'er his head,
  A quiet breeze around;
And the flowers a thrilling fragrance shed,
  And the waves a soothing sound:
It was not an hour, nor a scene, for aught
  But love and calm delight;
Yet the holy man had a cloud of thought
  On his wrinkled brow that night.
He gazed on the river that gurgled by,
  But he thought not of the reeds:
He clasped his gilded rosary,
  But he did not tell the beads;
If he looked to the heaven, 'twas not to invoke
  The Spirit that dwelleth there;
If he opened his lips, the words they spoke
  Had never the tone of prayer.
A pious priest might the abbot seem,
  He had swayed the crosier well;
But what was the theme of the abbot's dream,
  The abbot were loth to tell.

Companionless, for a mile or more,
He traced the windings of the shore.
Oh, beauteous is that river still,
As it winds by many a sloping hill,
And many a dim o'erarching grove,
And many a flat and sunny cove,
And terraced lawns, whose bright arcades
The honeysuckle sweetly shades,
And rocks, whose very crags seemed bowers,
So gay they are with grass and flowers!

But the abbot was thinking of scenery,
  About as much in sooth,
As a lover thinks of constancy,
  Or an advocate of truth.
He did not mark how the skies in wrath
  Grew dark above his head;
He did not mark how the mossy path
  Grew damp beneath his tread;
And nearer he came, and still more near,
  To a pool, in whose recess
The water had slept for many a year,
  Unchanged and motionless;
From the river stream it spread away
  The space of a half a rood;
The surface had the hue of clay
  And the scent of human blood;
The trees and the herbs that round it grew
  Were venomous and foul;
And the birds that through the bushes flew
  Were the vulture and the owl;
The water was as dark and rank
  As ever a Company pumped;
And the perch, that was netted and laid on the bank,
  Grew rotten while it jumped:
And bold was he who thither came
  At midnight, man or boy;
For the place was cursed with an evil name,
  And that name was "The Devil's Decoy!"

The abbot was weary as abbot could be,
And he sat down to rest on the stump of a tree,
When suddenly rose a dismal tone—
Was it a song, or was it a moan?
    "Oh, oh! Oh, oh!
      Above, below!
Lightly and brightly they glide and go;
The hungry and keen on the top are leaping,
The lazy and fat in the depths are sleeping;
Fishing is fine when the pool is muddy,
Broiling is rich when the coals are ruddy!"
In a monstrous fright, by the murky light,
He looked to the left and he looked to the right,
And what was the vision close before him,
That flung such a sudden stupor o'er him?

'Twas a sight to make the hair uprise,
And the life-blood colder run:
The startled priest struck both his thighs,
And the abbey clock struck one!

All alone, by the side of the pool,
A tall man sat on a three-legged stool,

Now an old man's hollow groan
Echoed from the dungeon stone:
Now the weak and wailing cry
Of a stripling's agony!

Cold by this was the midnight air;
But the abbot's blood ran colder,

Kicking his heels on the dewy sod,
And putting in order his reel and rod.
Red were the rags his shoulders wore,
And a high red cap on his head he bore;
His arms and his legs were long and bare;
And two or three locks of long red hair
Were tossing about his scraggy neck,
Like a tattered flag o'er a splitting wreck.
It might be Time, or it might be trouble,
Had bent that stout back nearly double—
Sunk in their deep and hollow sockets
That blazing couple of Congreve rockets,
And shrunk and shrivelled that tawny skin,
Till it hardly covered the bones within.
The line the abbot saw him throw
Had been fashioned and formed long ages ago,
And the hands that worked his foreign vest
Long ages ago had gone to their rest:
You would have sworn, as you looked on them,
He had fished in the flood with Ham and Shem!

There was turning of keys, and creaking of locks,
As he took forth a bait from his iron box.
Minnow or gentle, worm or fly—
It seemed not such to the abbot's eye;
Gaily it glittered with jewel and gem,
And its shape was the shape of a diadem.
It was fastened a gleaming hook about,
By a chain within and a chain without;
The fisherman gave it a kick and a spin,
And the water fizzed as it tumbled in!

From the bowels of the earth,
Strange and varied sounds had birth—
Now the battle's bursting peal,
Neigh of steed, and clang of steel;

When he saw a gasping knight lie there,
With a gash beneath his clotted hair,
And a hump upon his shoulder.
And the loyal churchman strove in vain
To mutter a Pater Noster;
For he who writhed in mortal pain
Was camped that night on Bosworth plain—
The cruel Duke of Glo'ster!

There was turning of keys, and creaking of locks,
As he took forth a bait from his iron box.
It was a haunch of princely size,
Filling with fragrance earth and skies.
The corpulent abbot knew full well
The swelling form, and the steaming smell;
Never a monk that wore a hood
Could better have guessed the very wood
Where the noble hart had stood at bay,
Weary and wounded, at close of day.

Sounded then the noisy glee
Of a revelling company—
Sprightly story, wicked jest,
Rated servant, greeted guest,
Flow of wine, and flight of cork:
Stroke of knife, and thrust of fork:
But, where'er the board was spread,
Grace, I ween, was never said!

Pulling and tugging the fisherman sat;
And the priest was ready to vomit,
When he hauled out a gentleman, fine and fat,
With a belly as big as a brimming vat,
And a nose as red as a comet.

"A capital stew," the fisherman said,
"With cinnamon and sherry!"
And the abbot turned away his head,
For his brother was lying before him dead,
The mayor of St. Edmond's Bury!

There was turning of keys, and creaking of locks,
As he took forth a bait from his iron box:
It was a bundle of beautiful things—
A peacock's tail, and a butterfly's wings,
A scarlet slipper, an auburn curl,
A mantle of silk, and a bracelet of pearl,
And a packet of letters, from whose sweet fold
Such a stream of delicate odors rolled,
That the abbot fell on his face, and fainted,
And deemed his spirit was half-way sainted.

Sounds seemed dropping from the skies,
Stifled whispers, smothered sighs,
And the breath of vernal gales,
And the voice of nightingales;
But the nightingales were mute,
Envious, when an unseen lute
Shaped the music of its chords
Into passion's thrilling words:

"Smile, lady, smile!—I will not set
Upon my brow the coronet,
Till thou wilt gather roses white
To wear around its gems of light.
Smile, lady, smile!—I will not see
Rivers and Hastings bend the knee,
Till those bewitching lips of thine
Will bid me rise in bliss from mine.
Smile, lady, smile!—for who would win
A loveless throne through gilt and sin?
Or who would reign o'er vale and hill,
If woman's heart were rebel still?"

One jerk, and there a lady lay,
A lady wondrous fair;
But the rose of her lip had faded away,
And her cheek was as white and as cold as clay,
And torn was her raven hair.
"Ah, ah!" said the fisher, in merry guise,
"Her gallant was hooked before;"
And the abbot heaved some piteous sighs,
For oft he had blessed those deep blue eyes,
The eyes of Mistress Shore!

There was turning of keys, and creaking of locks,
As he took forth a bait from his iron box.
Many the cunning sportsman tried,
Many he flung with a frown aside;
A minstrel's harp, and a miser's chest,
A hermit's cowl, and a baron's crest,
Jewels of lustre, robes of price,
Tomes of heresy, loaded dice,
And golden cups of the brightest wine
That ever was pressed from the Burgundy vine;
There was a perfume of sulphur and nitre,
As he came at last to a bishop's mitre!
From top to toe the abbot shook,
As the fisherman armed his golden hook;
And awfully were his features wrought
By some dark dream or wakened thought.
Look how the fearful felon gazes
On the scaffold his country's vengeance raises,
When the lips are cracked and the jaws are dry
With the thirst which only in death shall die:
Mark the mariner's frenzied frown
As the swaling wherry settles down,
When peril has numbed the sense and will,
Though the hand and the foot may struggle still.
Wilder far was the abbot's glance,
Deeper far was the abbot's trance:
Fixed as a monument, still as air,
He bent no knee, and he breathed no prayer;
But he signed—he knew not why or how—
The sign of the Cross on his clammy brow.

There was turning of keys, and creaking of locks,
As he stalked away with his iron box.
"Oh, ho! Oh, ho!
The cock doth crow;
It is time for the fisher to rise and go.
Fair luck to the abbot, fair luck to the shrine!
He hath gnawed in twain my choicest line;
Let him swim to the north, let him swim to the south,
The abbot will carry my hook in his mouth!"

The abbot had preached for many years,
With as clear articulation
As ever was heard in the House of Peers
Against emancipation;
His words had made battalions quake,
Had roused the zeal of martyrs;
He kept the court an hour awake,
And the king himself three quarters:
But ever, from that hour, 'tis said,
He stammered and he stuttered,
As if an axe went through his head
With every word he uttered.
He stuttered o'er blessing, he stuttered o'er ban,
He stuttered, drunk or dry;
And none but he and the fisherman
Could tell the reason why!

AN INTERVIEW WITH A PASHA.

FROM "EOTHEN." BY G. W. KINGLAKE.

In the Ottoman dominions there is scarcely any hereditary influence except that which belongs to the family of the Sultan; and wealth, too, is a highly volatile blessing, not easily transmitted to the descendants of the owner. From these causes it results, that the people standing in the place of nobles and gentry, are official personages, and though many (indeed the greater number) of these potentates are humbly born and bred, you will seldom, I think, find them wanting in that polished smoothness of manner, and those well undulating tones which belong to the best Osmanlees. The truth is, that most of the men in authority have risen from their humble stations by the arts of the courtier, and they preserve in their high estate, those gentle powers of fascination to which they owe their success. Yet unless you can contrive to learn a little of the language, you will be rather bored by your visits of ceremony; the intervention of the interpreter, or Dragoman as he is called, is fatal to the spirit of conversation. I think I should mislead you, if I were to attempt to give the substance of any particular conversation with Orientals. A traveller may write and say that, "the Pasha of So-and-So was particularly interested in the vast progress which has been made in the application of steam, and appeared to understand the structure of our machinery—that he remarked upon the gigantic results of our manufacturing industry—showed that he possessed considerable knowledge of our Indian affairs, and of the constitution of the Company, and expressed a lively admiration of the many sterling qualities for which the people of England are distinguished." But the heap of common-places thus quietly attributed to the Pasha, will have been founded, perhaps, on some such talking as this:—

Pasha. The Englishman is welcome; most blessed among hours is this, the hour of his coming.

Dragoman (*to the Traveller*). The Pasha pays you his compliments.

Traveller. Give him my best compliments in return, and say I'm delighted to have the honor of seeing him.

Dragoman (*to the Pasha*). His Lordship, this Englishman, Lord of London, Scorner of Ireland, Suppressor of France, has quitted his governments, and left his enemies to breathe for a moment, and has crossed the broad waters in strict disguise, with a small but eternally faithful retinue of followers, in order that he might look upon the bright countenance of the Pasha among Pashas—the Pasha of the everlasting Pashalik of Karagholookoldour.

Traveller (*to his Dragoman*). What on earth have you been saying about London? The Pasha will be taking me for a mere cockney. Have not I told you *always* to say, that I am from a branch of the family of Mudcombe Park, and that I am to be a magistrate for the county of Bedfordshire, only I've not qualified, and that I should have been a Deputy-lieutenant, if it had not been for the extraordinary conduct of Lord Mountpromise, and that I was a candidate for Goldborough at the last election, and that I should have won easy, if my committee had not been bought. I wish to heaven that if you *do* say anything about me, you'd tell the simple truth.

Dragoman—[*is silent*].

Pasha. What says the friendly Lord of London? is there aught that I can grant him within the Pashalik of Karagholookoldour?

Dragoman (*growing sulky and literal*). This friendly Englishman—this branch of Mudcombe—this head-purveyor of Goldborough—this possible po-

liceman of Bedfordshire is recounting his achievements, and the number of his titles.

PASHA. The end of his honors is more distant than the ends of the earth, and the catalogue of his glorious deeds is brighter than the firmament of Heaven!

DRAGOMAN (*to the Traveller*). The Pasha congratulates your Excellency.

TRAVELLER. About Goldborough? The deuce he does!—but I want to get at his views in relation to the present state of the Ottoman Empire; tell him the Houses of Parliament have met, and that there has been a speech from the throne, pledging England to preserve the integrity of the Sultan's dominions.

DRAGOMAN (*to the Pasha*). This branch of Mudcombe, this possible policeman of Bedfordshire, informs your Highness that in England the talking houses have met, and that the integrity of the Sultan's dominions has been assured for ever and ever, by a speech from the velvet chair.

PASHA. Wonderful chair! Wonderful houses! —whirr! whirr! all by wheels!—whiz! whiz! all by steam!—wonderful chair! wonderful houses! wonderful people!—whirr! whirr! all by wheels! —whiz! whiz! all by steam!

TRAVELLER (*to the Dragoman*). What does the Pasha mean by the whizzing? he does not mean to say, does he, that our Government will ever abandon their pledges to the Sultan?

DRAGOMAN. No, your Excellency; but he says the English talk by wheels and steam.

TRAVELLER. That's an exaggeration; but say that the English really have carried machinery to great perfection; tell the Pasha (he'll be struck with that), that whenever we have any disturbances to put down, even at two or three hundred miles from London, we can send troops by the thousand, to the scene of action, in a few hours.

DRAGOMAN (*recovering his temper and freedom of speech*). His Excellency, this Lord of Mudcombe, observes to your Highness, that whenever the Irish, or the French, or the Indians rebel against the English, whole armies of soldiers, and brigades of artillery, are dropped into a mighty chasm called Euston Square, and in the biting of a cartridge they arise up again in Manchester, or Dublin, or Paris, or Delhi, and utterly exterminate the enemies of England from the face of the earth.

PASHA. I know it—I know all—the particulars have been faithfully related to me, and my mind comprehends locomotives. The armies of the English ride upon the vapors of boiling cauldrons, and their horses are flaming coals!—whirr! whirr! all by wheels!—whiz! whiz! all by steam!

TRAVELLER (*to his Dragoman*). I wish to have the opinion of an unprejudiced Ottoman gentleman, as to the prospects of our English commerce and manufactures; just ask the Pasha to give me his views on the subject.

PASHA (*after having received the communication of the Dragoman*). The ships of the English swarm like flies; their printed calicoes cover the whole earth, and by the side of their swords the blades of Damascus are blades of grass. All India is but an item in the ledger-books of the merchants, whose lumber-rooms are filled with ancient thrones!—whirr! whirr! all by wheels!—whiz! whiz! all by steam!

DRAGOMAN. The Pasha compliments the cutlery of England, and also the East India Company.

TRAVELLER. The Pasha's right about the cutlery (I tried my scimitar with the common officers' swords belonging to our fellows at Malta, and they cut it like the leaf of a novel]. Well [to the Dragoman], tell the Pasha I am exceedingly gratified to find that he entertains such a high opinion of our manufacturing energy, but I should like him to know, though, that we have got something in England besides that. These foreigners are always fancying that we have nothing but ships, and railways, and East Companies; do just tell the Pasha that our rural districts deserve his attention, and that even within the last two hundred years, there has been an evident improvement in the culture of the turnip, and if he does not take any interest about that, at all events you can explain that we have our virtues in the country—that the British yeoman is still, thank God! the British yeoman:—Oh! and by the by, whilst you are about it, you may as well say that we are a truth-telling people, and, like the Osmanlees, are faithful in the performance of our promises.

PASHA [*after hearing the Dragoman*]. It is true, it is true:—through all Feringhistan the English are foremost and best; for the Russians are drilled swine, and the Germans are sleeping babes, and the Italians are the servants of songs, and the French are the sons of newspapers, and the Greeks they are weavers of lies, but the English and the Osmanlees are brothers together in righteousness; for the Osmanlees believe in one only God, and cleave to the Koran, and destroy idols; so do the English worship one God, and abominate graven images, and tell the truth, and believe in a book; and though they drink the juice of the grape, yet to say that they worship their prophet as God, or to say that they are eaters of pork, these are lies,—lies born of Greeks, and nursed by Jews!

DRAGOMAN. The Pasha compliments the English.

TRAVELLER [*rising*]. Well, I've had enough of this. Tell the Pasha, I am greatly obliged to him for his hospitality, and still more for his kindness in furnishing me with horses, and say that now I must be off.

PASHA [*after hearing the Dragoman, and standing up on his Divan*]. Proud are the sires and blessed are the dams of the horses that shall carry his Excellency to the end of his prosperous journey.—May the saddle beneath him glide down to the gates of the happy city, like a boat swimming on the third river of Paradise.—May he sleep the sleep of a child, when his friends are around him, and the while that his enemies are abroad, may his eyes flame red through the darkness—more red than the eyes of ten tigers!—farewell!

DRAGOMAN. The Pasha wishes your Excellency a pleasant journey.

So ends the visit.

"WHICH do you think the merriest place in existence?" "That immediately above the atmosphere that surrounds the earth." "Why so?" "Because I am told that there all bodies *lose their gravity*.

A mother admonishing her son, a lad about seven years of age, told him he should never put off till to-morrow any thing that he could do to-day. The little urchin replied, "Then, mother, let's eat the remainder of the plum pudding to-night."

HINTS TO ARCHERS.

BY CAPTAIN CRAM, H. P. ROYAL HORSE MARINES.—ANON.

With loynes in canvass bow-case tied,
Where arrows stick in mickle pride;
Like ghats of Adam Bell and Clymme
Sol sets—*for fear they'll shoot at him.*—SIR WM. DAVENANT.

I AM an enthusiastic admirer of the long-bow, that "noble weapon of renown." I have made myself acquainted with its history, from the day it was first invented by Apollo to the present time. I have studied minutely the great Ascham's "Five Points of Archery,"—I have practised *standing*, *nooking*, *drawing*, *holding*, and *loosing;* and written practical observations on each movement. I can tell you all about the Target, the Bracer, Quiver, Belt, Pouch, Tassal, and Grease-box; I have attentively read, nay, even learned, by heart, Ascham's "Toxophilus," Strutt's "Sports and Pastimes," Moseley's "Essays on Archery," Roberts' "English Bowman," Barrington's tract in the "Archæologia;" besides every writer of antiquity that has treated, ever so remotely, on the long-bow. The result of my studies will be apparent in the following pages—it will be seen that I am no contemptible shot.

The long-bow is a weapon of the very earliest antiquity; it is supposed to have been introduced into England by the Cretan auxiliaries under Julius Cæsar. The weapon was never much in esteem among the Legions, though after reading the commentaries of the Roman hero, I cannot help suspecting that the "immortal Cæsar" was himself no stranger to its practice.

Although the Romans, as a people, were not celebrated for excellence in the art, yet Suetonius and others give some wonderful accounts of the progress of many of the Emperors. Commodus was an absolute marvel. Herodian says, he would kill a hundred lions in the amphitheatre with a hundred arrows, and never miss, or merely wound, in a single instance. That was not all; he would cause arrows to be made with sharp circular heads, and when the ostrich was urged to full speed, he would remove its head so dexterously, that the unconscious bird would continue running as though nothing had happened! The emperor must have been a devil of a shot, and so was Herodian!

But these were isolated cases.—It was reserved for Britons to carry the palm of archery against the world. In Scotland, the bow was practised as early as in the south, if we may believe one Macpherson—a poet of a very remote age, and the author of Ossian. "Sons of Leith," says Macpherson, "bring the *bows* of our fathers! the sounding *quivers* of Morni!" And in Wales, there were archers of wonderful skill. Giraldus Cambrensis relates, that, during a siege in that country, two soldiers, in haste to regain their tower, were annoyed by the arrows of the Welsh. They succeeded in closing the portals; but were killed notwithstanding; for the arrows went clean through the defence, which was of hardened oak, closely studded, and four inches thick! William de Breusa, himself an archer, likewise relates, that he saw a horse-soldier, clad in complete mail, with buff coat beneath, struck through the hip with an arrow, which not only killed the rider, but, piercing the saddle, killed the horse. "But," says William, "although that might be thought a clever shot, it was nothing to *another* I saw." Another Welshman struck another mailed horseman, in a similar way, and fastened him to the saddle through the hip; but the wounded man turning his horse by the bridle, the same archer dealt another shaft, which, *strange to say*, observes William, passed through the *other* hip, and completely fixed him; and the horse plunged so fearfully, that men marvelled to see so clever a horseman, not knowing the ingenious manner by which he was made to keep his seat! If the gentleman did not affirm that he *saw* these things, I should hardly have believed him. This De Breusa was a member of the "Royal British Bowmen," which society exists to this day, and can produce as good shots as William.

But of all who have conferred lustre on the annals of archery, none are so conspicuous as the bold outlaw of Sherwood, that "most gentle theefe," as Grafton calls him in his Chronicle of Breteyne.—Dr. Hanmer, speaking of the extraordinary things performed by Robin Hood and Little John, says, the latter is reported to have shot an arrow a *mile;* "but I leave these," observes the worthy doctor rather discourteously, "among the *lies of the land.*" I don't know why he should disbelieve it, when many greater things than that have been done, with the help of the long-bow; as any one may see who reads the doctor's "Chronicles of Ireland!"

I would willingly recount the feats of the great archers of former days, but I have no space. I must pass over the great Zosimus, who described *a friend of his* at the battle of Mursa, who had the wonderful gift of discharging three arrows at once, and killing a man with each! Phillippe de Comines and Froissart were great shots, as any one will discover by reading their Chronicles. And Sir John Smith, who tells us of the "valleys which ran with rivers of blood, caused by the slaughter from the Turkish bow." The great Lord Bacon, too, a splendid archer, who writes, "The Turkish bow giveth a very forcible shoot; insomuch that it hath been *known* that the arrow hath pierced clean through a steel target, and a plate of brass *two inches thick!*" I must leave, though unwillingly, the exploits of these great men and good archers, and touch upon the moderns, and with great justice; for, however grand are the recorded feats of former days, I will back the performances of our own times against them, whether for length, strength, or ability.

I believe I have hinted, in my title, that I have the honor to belong to that highly respectable and distinguished corps, the Royal Horse Marines, so called from their always riding at anchor, and from my long service in different countries have had much experience in these matters of which I treat.

I have witnessed the practice of each country, and hardly know to which to award the palm. The Americans take an extraordinary range, and shoot very fearlessly. The French, if not so strong, are peculiarly dexterous; but an Irishman possesses a wonderful facility for shooting round corners, particularly if a tailor is after him. The most extraordinary feat I ever witnessed was of an Irishman, who shot up Holborn Hill, and with such *prodigious force*, that both his eyes went clean through a brick wall! This is a fact; for I saw it. I have known some good shots among the English, particularly the ladies, who draw a very powerful bow; one, particularly, I remember, who shot so far beyond the mark, that her shaft was positively lost in the clouds! She was a member of the "Toxophilite" society, of which the late king was president. Their was another capital English shot, a friend of mine, who belonged to the "Royal Kentish Bowmen;" he used to relate, that once riding from Seven Oaks, he was overtaken by a thunder-storm; he hoped to escape it by giving his horse the reins, and singular enough he just kept a-head of it by about half a yard! In this manner, he galloped at speed five miles, I may say, neck and neck with the thunder-cloud, the rain, or rather torrent, descending exactly upon his horse's crupper all the way; the road behind was literally deluged; as he emphatically observed, it could only be compared to being within half a yard of the falls of Niagara! He was fortunately saved from the cataract by shooting up a gateway. It was a capital shot. If any impertinent doubt was ever expressed at this relation, the archer would say, fiercely, "Sir, if you *want* a lie, *I'll give you one;* but that's a fact, by G—!" and no man was better able; he was one of the best shots I knew.

I mentioned the French as dexterous marksmen. I once knew a gentleman from Gascony—proverbial for its archery; he had been an officer under Napoleon—by the way, I have always remarked the superiority of soldiers and sailors in their management of the weapon. He told me of a duel in which he had been engaged at Paris, where the signal was *un*, *deux*, and to fire at the word *trois*. It must be understood we had been quizzing the Parisians on their affectation in rolling the letter R about their mouths previous to utterance. "My opponent," said the Gascon, "was of the *garde imperial—sacre tonnerre!*—he was a dead shot. I had but one chance, and I watched it narrowly. The second gave the word, *un*, *deux*—but *càde di*, long before he could *finish* the word TROIS, I shot my man dead!" I must observe that my lively friend was equally good with the pistol as with the bow. He was very jealous of the honor of his province, which he never allowed could be exceeded in any thing. Some discourse once took place concerning the height of Monsieur Louis, the French giant, who measured six feet ten inches. "*Tonnerre!*" cried he, "what a shrimp! Why, in my country, I knew a man so tall that he was positively obliged to get up a ladder every morning to shave himself; *he* was a tall man if you like." He admitted that he never knew but one man of that stature, and that he was *a very long way off*. My friend was elected, some years since, a member of the "Royal Edinburgh Society" of Archers, and is an ornament to that distinguished corps. After all, I must in justice say, that the Americans beat us all out of the field. Neither French, English, nor Irish, can compare with them in the use and practice of the long-bow, although I am aware that I risk giving offence to many meritorious and skilful individuals. How does the incredulous cockney stare when he hears of the great sea-serpent! He does not believe it, not he—he little knows it was an archer to whom the glory of the discovery is due. What *can* he know of monsters of the deep, except cod-fish and oysters in sauce! What can he know of the howling wilderness, unless it be wilderness-row! What of roaring cataracts, save that of low water at London Bridge! He can form no idea of the trackless waste by that of Walworth and Newington Butts; or of interminable forests, by that of Epping. His scepticism, therefore, is no scandal; it requires an enlarged mind to comprehend the wonders of America, and to judge of the enterprise of archers by whom it has been explored. A very ingenious friend of mine, and, curious enough, of the same name as myself, a native of Boston, and a splendid shot, has frequently astonished me with the exploits of American archers. He said, that once, when he went into Kentucky to witness a trial of skill, he stayed by the way at a public-house, and observing in the room such an amount of broken ware, and equivocal marks, he was quite convinced, knowing the savage nature of Kentuckian fighting, that a desperate and murderous affray had taken place there. He remarked the servant sweeping the floor, and putting the contents carefully into a basket. Rather surprised, he asked her what she was preserving with such care. "Oh!" said the girl, "nothing very particular, only a few *eyes*." "Eyes?" inquired my friend. "You see," she said, "about fourteen gentlemen went home blind last night, so I was just picking up their eyes, 'cause the gentlemen, when they got sober, may be calling for 'em, I guess!"

My friend Cram I have great respect for, both as an accomplished archer, and an excellent man. He has witnessed some wonderful exertions of the art; indeed, those wherein he has taken an active part, are not to be excelled by any professor of any country whatsoever. I remember, before I went to America, and became intimate with him, I was introduced to his sister, then residing in the county of Down. I forgot to mention he has some Irish blood in his veins, which may, perhaps, account for his superiority in skill and power. His sister, to give me an idea of the wonderful prowess of her beloved brother, gave me a letter to read, which she had received from him on his return to Boston from England. I will give an extract:

"We had a pleasant sort of passage enough, but I missed my sport sadly. We, however, managed to practise with the bow and rifle, and I need not tell you, with some advantage over my less practised companions. Occasionally, when the weather was fine, Captain Mizen, knowing my love of the sport, had the boat lowered, and we mustered up a shooting party. There is capital shooting on the Atlantic, but the game, though plentiful, is by no means varied. During our passage, I met with no other than the "flying fish." One day, I managed, however, to bag fifty brace of these amphibious birds, the sailors rowing us under the very trees in which they build their nests! We sometimes had some good fishing. The dolphin is an extraordinarily rapacious fish; an instance of which I will relate. We caught so many one day that several were thrown into the sea again, and we continued merely for the sake of the sport. One of the fish, by some accident, had his tail cut off, and, being short of bait, I put it upon my hook; in about a minute I hooked a fish, and, much to our surprise, it proved to be the very mutilated dolphin, positively caught by his own tail.

"I must not forget to tell you that we landed at Bermuda, and found the niggers all bald, which I heard was occasioned by the habit of *butting* in

their personal encounters with each other. This fact convinces me that the organ of combativeness is not, as Gall has placed it, behind the ear. The Bermudians are a very singular people. I was informed that those who lived on the other side of the island are quite amphibious, and live for days under water. This is in consequence of their living entirely on fish.—I have no reason to doubt the fact. Fish here is extremely good; but all kinds of meat are inferior to those of England, except pork, which is so excellent that the Bermudians literally eat it till the bristles grow out of their skin!

"The inhabitants have no occasion for lamps or candles of any kind; for the atmosphere, at night, is positively in one blaze of illumination with fire-flies. These beautiful little creatures not only dispel darkness, but when we want to light our cigars we need but catch one of these luciferous insects, and holding it to our tobacco, fire is procured."

I shall forbear quoting more of Mr. Cram's letter; the reader will doubtless be pleased with the spirit of observation displayed throughout. I can myself vouch for the authenticity of his statements; for, not long afterwards, I made the same passage, and witnessed the things he describes. I had the good fortune, likewise, to bring down many coveys of the amphibious birds he mentions—the flying fish, as well as several sea-woodcocks, which, having no dogs, he could not flush. Knowing this, I had taken care to provide myself with a brace of water-dogs, and found them very useful.

I never shall forget the first evening I arrived at Boston. Cram had invited many congenial spirits to meet me, and I never passed a pleasanter time. Of course, our favorite weapon bore a prominent part in the conversation. Cram gave us a very interesting account of a vessel foundering near the coast, which was the means of elucidating a curious fact; he wished to prove a superiority of instinct in the scaly inhabitants of these waters, over those of every other. It was no uncommon thing, he said, after that event, for the fishermen to take a king-fish clothed in a bed-gown of Manchester stripes!—a shark was killed with a Guernsey shirt on; a whole shoal of porpoises were seen with red night-caps; and a guard-fish was hooked that wore a gauze veil! A gentleman, however, from Trinidad, a Mr. Muscovada, denied the intellectual superiority of the American fish over those of the West Indies; "and to prove it," observed Muscovada, "I remember once, after the Thunder frigate was wrecked in the gulf of Paria, one of our whale-boats harpooned a grampus, who, it was found, had the man-of-war's mainsail tied round his neck for a cravat? What do you think of that?" said he. Cram was floored.

But the most curious sporting anecdote I remember was told me by Cram, one evening, over our brandy-and-water; as he was the party concerned, it may be relied on. We were speaking of England, and I was relating to him the different societies of Bowmen.

Among other persons, the name of his sister was introduced, and he mentioned several interesting anecdotes of her skill, when she was a member of the "Hainault Foresters." I happened to mention having been much pleased with the letter he had written to his sister, which I had the good fortune to read, and, at his wish, related the points of it. "Ah! my dear Captain," said he, "that letter was written under very singular circumstances; I never knew till this moment what I wrote, although, from your repetition, I have only related the facts as they occurred." I expressed some surprise, and he continued: "The fact was, I had been to a party that day, and had so astonished the natives with my skill upon our weapon, that I believe I over-exerted myself. When I returned, I commenced writing to my sister, as the packet was about to sail, and I remember well writing the words 'My dear sister;' and when I tell you, that I wrote the whole of that communication to which you allude fast asleep, I tell you nothing more than the fact; and what is more, actually folded, directed, and sealed it, and should not have waked, had I not—*burnt my fingers with the wax!*"

THE MOUNTEBANK DOCTOR.

BY LUKE RODEN.

I RESUME my task with the description of a character now entirely extinct, but which sixty years ago was one of no trifling importance—the Mountebank Doctor. As yet quack medicines were not! A few established formulæ had been handed down to us by our ancestors; but the mystery which excited curiosity was not an ignorance of their ingredients, but rather admiration of the wonderful precautions to be observed in their preparation. Plants were to be gathered in the wane of the moon, and especially three days before the new moon, and with the midnight dew upon them. Then the extraordinary multiplicity of ingredients—even the College of Physicians retained preparations originally consisting of two hundred and fifty or three hundred articles, which, in mercy to the apothecaries of those days (for, as yet, "chemists" also were not) they cut down to seventy or eighty. Next, the wonderful accuracy of the instructions, which, instead of the vague directions of ounces and drachms, were worded thus:—Hikery pikery, two pen'orth; cinnamon, one pen'orth; rhubarb, three pen'orth; marjoram, a handful; penny-royal, half a handful; white pepper, a pinch—and so on. Ladies of fortune passed their time in collecting large volumes of these valuable prescriptions, and every visitor was solicited for an addition to the treasure, as in the present day for a contribution to an album. I have seen many of these Thesauri; but as caligraphy was not cultivated in those days, and the orthography was ad libitum, they were often as obscure as the books of the Sybils.

The comprehensive character of some of these prescriptions was admirable. I remember one indeed in a book called "The Englishman's Treasure," published by the serjeant-surgeon to King Henry the Eighth, to Edward the Sixth, Queen Mary, and Queen Elizabeth, which is thus headed, "A Remedy for an Inward Ail." No one ever trumped this till the advent of Dr. Morrison with his pills—"an infallible cure for all diseases, medical or surgical."

There were occasions, however, in which even the medical album failed to afford relief to the tenant farmers and their laborers, though its treasures were bestowed and superintended by the Lady Bountiful of the district. In such cases, there was no resource but to wait for *the Doctor*, who made his regular rounds at stated seasons, and especially at fairs and wakes; and his arrival was anticipated with a degree of anxiety and confidence which those only can appreciate who enjoy the double blessing of credulity and ignorance. Often have I superintended the erection of the stage on which the miracle-worker was to display his nostrums. I had a female friend, whose house was exactly facing it. She had been housekeeper to a nobleman, and retired on an independence. I had the honor to be an especial favorite of the old lady, and have often had the happiness to be made ill by the quantity of custard, sugared bread and butter, toffy, barley sugar, and above all, furmity, which she prepared with unsurpassable skill. The last delicacy perhaps is unknown in the present day;—it deserves preservation in the records of gastronomy. It was composed of wheat boiled quite tender—deprived of its skin, and flavored with cream, yolk of egg, cinnamon, sugar, chopped raisins, candied lemon peel, and various other dainties. I went from time to time to the window to watch the preparations for the doctor, as children in the present day wait the drawing up of the curtain for a pantomime, then back to my furmity and custard; then again to the window, in blissful alternation. At last, the great man appeared, and furmity and custard were abandoned—not, however, till I had eaten enough to make me ill next day.

"A think a see him noo," as Mathews' old Scotchwoman says. He was a tall, spare man, punctiliously dressed in black, with, of course, *diamond* shoe and knee buckles, a brilliant handled sword by his side, long lace ruffles to his wrists, his fingers covered with rings, a profusion of frill forming a cataract of lace and cambric from his neck to his waist; while his satin waistcoat was only fastened with one button, that it might be displayed to advantage: his hair frizzed out on both sides of his head to the greatest possible extent, and surmounted by a small three-cornered hat; an immense silk bag, supposed to contain his long hair, but really, as in the present court dress, only fastened to the collar of his coat. Add to all these attractions, a face well rouged, and an immense gold-headed cane, and you have a perfect picture of the doctor of the last century.

The polished gentleman was accompanied by his servant—his Jack Pudding—exactly in dress, manners, and language, the clown at a circus. His business was to lay plans for jokes, which, of course, had been arranged beforehand with his master, and which were not always the most decent, but which never failed to raise a loud laugh among the clowns who composed the audience. The *Doctor* exhibited a few of the common conjurer tricks with the pulse glass, the air-pump, etc., and then proceeded to business. For all the ailments that man or woman ever felt or fancied, he had infallible remedies,—consumption, king's evil, gout, rheumatism, lumbago, jaundice, bile, (or as he pleased to call it, the boils,) and a thousand others were easily conquered; and I remember often hearing him lament that there was nobody *ill enough* to afford scope for the full power of his art. "Thirty-five did I cure of the most inveterate jaundice in the town of Birmigham, where I stayed only two days."

"A lie," said the clown, (or Merry Andrew, as he was called, putting his hand to the side of his mouth, and affecting to speak to the mob in a stage whisper,) "A lie," said he, "there were only twenty-nine."

"Seven did I cure in the little village of Brently, where I only stopped to bait my horses half an hour—"

"Another lie," said the Merry Andrew, "there were only eight, and one of them was beginning to get better."

Thus did he go on, through all the ills that flesh is heir to, sometimes condescending to give details of the most terrific cases, when, having worked up his audience to breathless horror at the sufferings he described, he would exclaim, "Now who would be such a fool as to run the risk of all this, when by spending three and sixpence for this little bottle of 'Preservative Elixir of Life,' he can be sure of escaping it for ever,"—and he held up one of the bottles with which his table was covered.

After some story of unusual pathos, I recollect seeing people tumble up the steps by half dozens to possess themselves of the treasure, and put down their money with the greatest alacrity and satisfaction,—and as in Homœopathy and Morrison's universal medicines, many of the better classes, who, in their sober moments, ridiculed the folly of others who put faith in a mountebank, carried away by the enthusiasm of the orator, pushed forward to partake of the blessings, or sent others for a large supply to distribute among the deserving poor. If the quack had been more than usually successful, he would generously give a supper to a select number of the farmers and principal tradesmen of the town, and when (as a matter of course) they were all thoroughly drunk, he generally contrived to make them disburse such a sum for "stuff" as abundantly covered the expenses of the entertainment.

The bandying of jokes between the Merry Andrew and the crowd, formed a large part of the fun. Sometimes the doctor would affect ignorance of an obvious deception, and let the clumsy clowns enjoy a temporary triumph, when he would make the man a present of a bottle of his Preservative Elixir, saying that it would be a pity such a clever fellow should ever be ill; but he generally contrived to have his revenge before the termination of the day's proceedings.

On one occasion, a great gawky lumbering clodhopper thought he had devised a mode of turning the laugh against the Doctor. He mounted the stage, and on being questioned as to his disorder, said, very gravely, "Why, I'm a liar."—"Sad disorder, sir, but perfectly curable," said the doctor. "Well, but (said the man) I've a worser nor that, I've lost my memory."—"Quite curable also," added the Doctor, "but I must make my preparations. Come again after dinner, and I will be ready for you; but pay down five shillings." The man, who had intended to have his fun gratis, resisted, but the Doctor declared he never let any one down from the stage till he had paid something. "Besides (said the Doctor) how can I trust you; you say you are a liar, and have no memory; so you will either break your promise or forget all about it." A loud laugh from the crowd expressed their acquiescence in the justice of the claim, and the poor devil, *nolens volens*, was compelled to lay down the cash. No one supposed he would come again, but the fool still hoped that he might turn the tables, and presented himself at the appointed hour.

The Doctor received him with great gravity, and addressing the audience, said, "Gentlemen may think it a joke, but I assure them on the honor of a gentleman, that it is a very serious affair; and I hereby engage to return the money, if the bystanders do not acknowledge the cure, and that I am fairly entitled to the reward." The man sat down —was furnished with a glass of water—the Doctor produced a box of flattened black pills; and to show that they were perfectly innocent, affected to swallow three or four himself. He then gave one to the man, who, after many wry faces *bit into it*—started up, spitting and sputtering, and exclaimed, "Why, hang me, if it isn't cobbler's wax!" Yes, it is true that the Doctor had procured his pills at a neighboring cobbler's stall!

"There," said the Doctor, lifting up both hands, "Did anybody ever witness so sudden, so miraculous a recovery? He's evidently cured of lying, for he has told the truth instantly; and as to memory! my good fellow, (said he, patting him on the back,) if you ever forget this, call on me, and I'll return you the money."

THE DEFEATED DUELLIST.

An unlooked-for termination to an intended tragedy, occurred a few years ago, at Portsmouth. Captain Adamson was constantly complaining that his subaltern did not treat him with sufficient respect, but the more he pointed out the necessity for his being accosted with the defence due to his age and superior rank, the more waggishly familiar would Ridley's language and manner become.

Adamson, for a considerable portion of his life, had held some post at an isolated corner of one of the West India islands, and being the "head buckra" while there, acquired an idea of his own importance, with which on his revisiting Britain he was reluctant to part. He was in the main, however, a kindly disposed person, but very illiterate, and not overblest with natural sagacity, yet, despite the constant freedoms of Ridley, the captain was never so happy as when in his sub's company.

One day, nevertheless, the superior opined that his lieutenant had carried the joke too far. The head and front of his offending was that of having called Adamson "Jimmy," in the presence of some ladies, at whose house the captain flattered himself he was a welcome guest, not only for his amusing conversation, but from his rank in the army.

"If ever you presume to call me so again, I shall take serious notice of it," he spluttered; "James would be quite bad enough, young sir, but Jimmy ——it is not to be borne—and I'll show you that I could, if I liked, bring you to a court-martial for using language to your superior unbecoming the character of an officer and a gentleman."

"Court-martial, indeed!" replied Ridley; "try it, my jolly old boy; why, you are known *only* by the name of Jimmy, and hang me but I think you were christened Jimmy."

"I shall not bear this insolence; you shall hear from me."

A friend of the captain's waited on Ridley, informing him that his presence was expected on South-Sea Common, at the hour of eight on the following morning.

Before the clock struck, Adamson, his second, and a surgeon, to show that the bold challenger was determined to bring matters to a sanguinary issue, were seen on the ground. The morning was raw and cold, a heavy sea-mist came rolling over the flat, much to the discomfort of one who had resided so long in the tropics. The trio remained at the post for an hour, yet Ridley came not; then Adamson, apologizing for having given his companions so much unnecessary trouble, took leave of them, and made his way to the barracks, breathing vows of vengeance against the man whose conduct had forced him to seek the only means left of insuring future respect, yet who had shrunk from giving him any satisfaction; instead of which, the air and exercise had given him a ferocious appetite, and his inward man betokened, by certain grumblings, that he required his morning meal with as little delay as possible.

On entering his room, he found to his disagreeable surprise that no preparations had been made for his breakfast, his grate was empty, all looked cheerless and uncomfortable.

"What is the reason of this shameful neglect, sir?" he demanded from his servant.

"Why, please, sir, Mr. Ridley's man came and said as how I wasn't to get breakfast ready, but when you come in from your walk I was to give you this."

Adamson glanced at the note presented; it was in Ridley's hand. Some new insult, doubtless; he dared not open it while even the eye of the servant was on him. Desiring the man to quit the room, he broke the seal and read as follows:—

"My Dear Jimmy—How could you think that I should be such a fool as to leave my warm bed to go out in the damp air for the purpose of shooting at you? Lord love your dear stupid head! Did I establish my character in Spain for nothing? Ask any man in the service who knows me, whether I can't afford to refuse fighting with my James. I hope the sea-breezes have cooled your fever and made you hungry. I have a capital breakfast ready for you—tea, coffee, hot-rolls, broiled ham, eggs, and what I know you dote on—a red-herring stuffed with bird's-eye peppers. Come along at once, for by the god of war, I shan't wait for you half as long as you were fool enough to cool your heels expecting me—likely. What! fire at my own captain? my friend Jimmy? Impossible.

Yours as ever, Fred. Ridley.

"P. S.—If you don't make haste, your West India favorite will be over-done."

Perfectly astonished at this epistle, half dying with emptiness, and really feeling a strong regard for the offender, Adamson did not think it necessary to deliberate, but went directly to his subaltern's room, the savory steam of the viands urging his steps; he tapped at the door. "Mr. Ridley," attempted Adamson; "this is very extraordinary——"

"Warm yourself, Jimmy."

"I really ought to be offended, but——"

"Eat, Jimmy."

"You are so fond of a joke that——"

"Drink, Jimmy."

He interrupted the captain's every speech by plying him with good things; and when he saw that the cravings of nature were satisfied, said to him in a tone of mock gravity.

"Now, my dear Jimmy, take my advice; keep this little piece of folly of yours entirely to yourself, or you will be laughed at more than ever."

The butt did *not* take counsel. It was to his unwisely detailing, that the garrison owed the diversion occasioned by the story of this defeated duel.

HOW I WENT UP THE JUNG-FRAU, AND CAME DOWN AGAIN.

(BY PETER TWITTERS, PHILOSOPHER, CAMDEN TOWN.)

[From his own private Diary, which he kept for publication in the *Times*, only they didn't put it in.]

ANONYMOUS.

July 25th.—Determined to ascend the Jung-Frau mountain, which is totally inaccessible and impossible to climb. Difficulties only add fuel to the fire of a Briton's determination. Was asked what I should do when I got to the top. Replied, come down again. That's what every body does who goes up high hills. Engaged guides, porters, etc. Provided ourselves with necessaries, such as ladders, umbrellas, skates for the glaciers, ropes, brandy, camp stools, etc., and started. Quite a sensation in the village. Landlord of hotel with tears in his eyes asked me to pay my bill before I went. Didn't. Began the ascent; ground became steepish, as may be seen by the illustration. Hard work. Suppose such a gradient would puzzle Mr. Stephenson. Talking of Stephenson, the whole party puffing and blowing like so many locomotives. Pulled out our camp-stools and tried to sit down on them. Ground so steep that we all lost our balance, and tumbled down to the bottom of the slope. Never mind. Gathered ourselves up, and at it again. Recovered our former position, and getting higher, found the slope still more excessive. In fact, it was a wonder to me how we managed it at all. Approached the glacier region, and found it rather softish. Unpleasant consequence of which is that the whole of our party sink up to the neck in half-melted sludge. Scrambling out again with much ado, we feel chilly, and refresh with brandy. Being apprehensive of the avalanches, we keep a sharp look-out and dodge them. At one time six huge masses of moving snow fell together, but we watch our chance and slip between them with the greatest dexterity.

Next danger a really dreadful one. Arrive at a fearful precipice, the edge very much overhanging the base, so that it formed a species of cave. Called a council of war. Council of war were for going home again. Rebuked them, and pointing to rough edges of the rock, proposed to try to crawl to summit. Set to work accordingly. Dangerous business, but succeeded. On the top of this tremendous cliff, discovered a vast chasm or crevice, which appeared to bar all further progress. Guides in despair. Much too wide to jump. Looked down. Crevice did not appear to have any bottom in particular. Called another council of war, and at the same moment, a violent squall of wind and snow sweeping by, put up my umbrella, when, horrible to relate, the storm caught it, and lifted me into the air; the principal guide, who caught my leg being carried up also, and in a moment we were hurried, in the very thick of the squall, and deafened by its howling, across the abyss, and landed on the further bank. The guides on the other side now flung across the rope, which we caught, and fastened to a rock, and one of their number, unfortunately the heaviest, proceeded to come across. The remaining two, however, not having strength to support his weight, he fairly pulled them into the crevice, so that we were obliged to drag up the whole three. Found that we were now not far from the summit. Saw it before us rising in a sharp peak against the blue

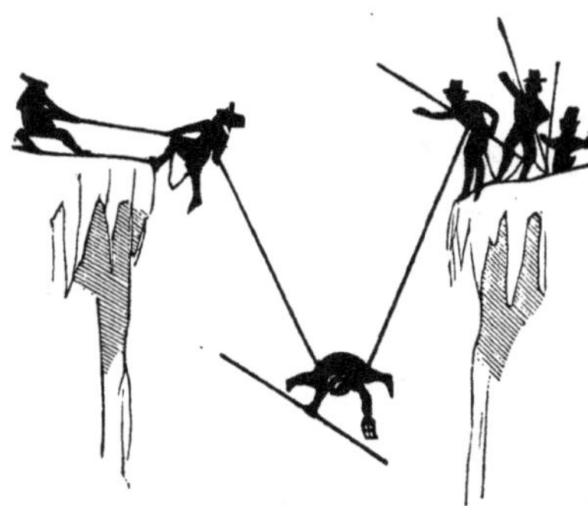

sky. More of the steep slope work. Guides at last become so dreadfully exhausted that I have to drag up the whole four. Terribly hard work. Nothing but my splendid muscular development would have enabled me to go through with it. Ice decidedly too rough for skating over, as may be seen by the following diagram.

Close to the summit, when another dreadful crevice with a high rock on the opposite side threatens to stop our progress. Surmounted the difficulty by a daring gymnastic feat, performed as follows:—Standing on each other's shoulders, the lowest man let his body incline over the cliff, so that I, as highest, reached the edge of the opposite rock, and made fast the rope to a projection, as in this cut.

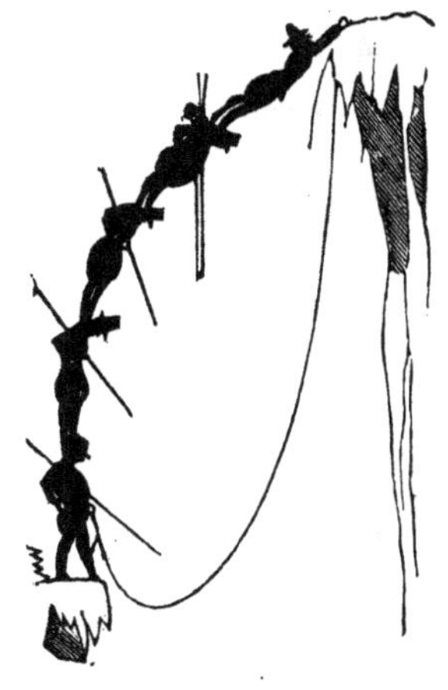

Thus we happily got over, and in half an hour reached the extreme peak of the Jung-Frau, where we clustered together and gave three British cheers, while half a dozen eagles flew round and round us.

Had no time to make scientific experiments; but ascertained that the strength of alcohol is not diminished in any sensible degree by the extreme rarification of the air at great heights.

Having got up, prepared to go down again, an operation which was performed in a much quicker style than the other. Started down a slippery slope, and missing our footing, and not being able to stop ourselves, proceeded in this manner, down at least 2000 feet, before we were brought up by a ridge of rocks, composed of uncommonly hard granite, against which we rebounded like footballs. Up, however, and at it again. Came to another difficulty; found ourselves in a dreadful gully or ravine, with no sort of exit but a narrow cleft, down which poured a tremendous cataract, into an awful black and foaming pool 500 feet below. There was nothing for it but to fling ourselves into the torrent, allow ourselves to go over the waterfall, and take our chance in the cauldron—which we did, in the manner shown below. The exploit was quite dreadful, from the roar of the water, and the speed with which we were hurled through the air, and soused at least 100 fathoms (for I counted them) into the pool below, where, after we had reached the surface, we were whirled about for at least an hour and a quarter before we managed to emerge. Found the experience I had picked up in the Holborn swimming baths of little avail in descending this cataract, but was only too happy to escape at any price. The rest of the journey was comparatively easy, owing to a very happy thought of mine. Happening to see a roundish-shaped avalanche roll past, remembered the globe tricks in the circus, where Signor Sadustini kept his balance on a big wooden ball going down an in-

clined plane. Communicated the notion to guides, waited for the next avalanche, jumped on it as it passed, and went down like winkin, always keeping our places upon the top of the ball, which gradually increased to such a size, that it carried off several chalets beneath us. But that, of course, we had nothing to do with; keeping our places as well as Sadustini himself, until the huge snow-ball came to a full stop in the midst of a pine forest, where we clambered out of the snow, and after several hours' hard walking, reached the village, where we were greeted by a deputation of the authorities, headed by the hotel-keeper holding my bill in his hand, who delivered an address of congratulation, and inquired when it would be convenient for me to settle. Postponing, however. considerations of business to those of festivity, a romantic rural *fête* was got up in honor of our return, The happy peasantry poured in from all sides, singing, "Come arouse us, arouse us, we merry Swiss boys." The notary had a table in the corner, which is always usual. The *Seigneur du Village* and his lady sat on a rustic throne. All the peasants had jerkins and breeches, and bright stockings, with lots of ribands, and all the peasantesses had short muslin petticoats and pink satin shoes. Choosing then, as a partner, the loveliest and the most virtuous—I was particular about the last—I opened the ball.

THE LAMPLIGHTER'S STORY.

BY CHARLES DICKENS.

"If you talk of Murphy and Francis Moore, gentlemen," said the lamplighter who was in the chair, "I mean to say that neither of 'em ever had any more to do with the stars than Tom Grig had."

"And what had *he* to do with 'em?" asked the lamplighter who officiated as vice.

"Nothing at all," replied the other; "just exactly nothing at all."

"Do you mean to say you don't believe in Murphy, then?" demanded the lamplighter who had opened the discussion.

"I mean to say that I believe in Tom Grig," replied the chairman. "Whether I believe in Murphy or not, is a matter between me and my conscience; and whether Murphy believes in himself or not, is a matter between him and *his* conscience. Gentlemen, I drink your healths."

The lamplighter who did the company this honor, was seated in the chimney corner of a certain tavern, which has been, time out of mind, the Lamplighter's House of Call. He sat in the midst of a circle of lamplighters, and was the cacique or chief of the tribe.

If any of our readers have had the good fortune to behold a lamplighter's funeral, they will not be surprised to learn that lamplighters are a strange and primitive people; that they rigidly adhere to old ceremonies and customs which have been handed down among them from father to son since the first public lamp was lighted out of doors; that they intermarry, and betroth their children in infancy; that they enter into no plots or conspiracies (for who ever heard of a traitorous lamplighter?); that they commit no crimes against the

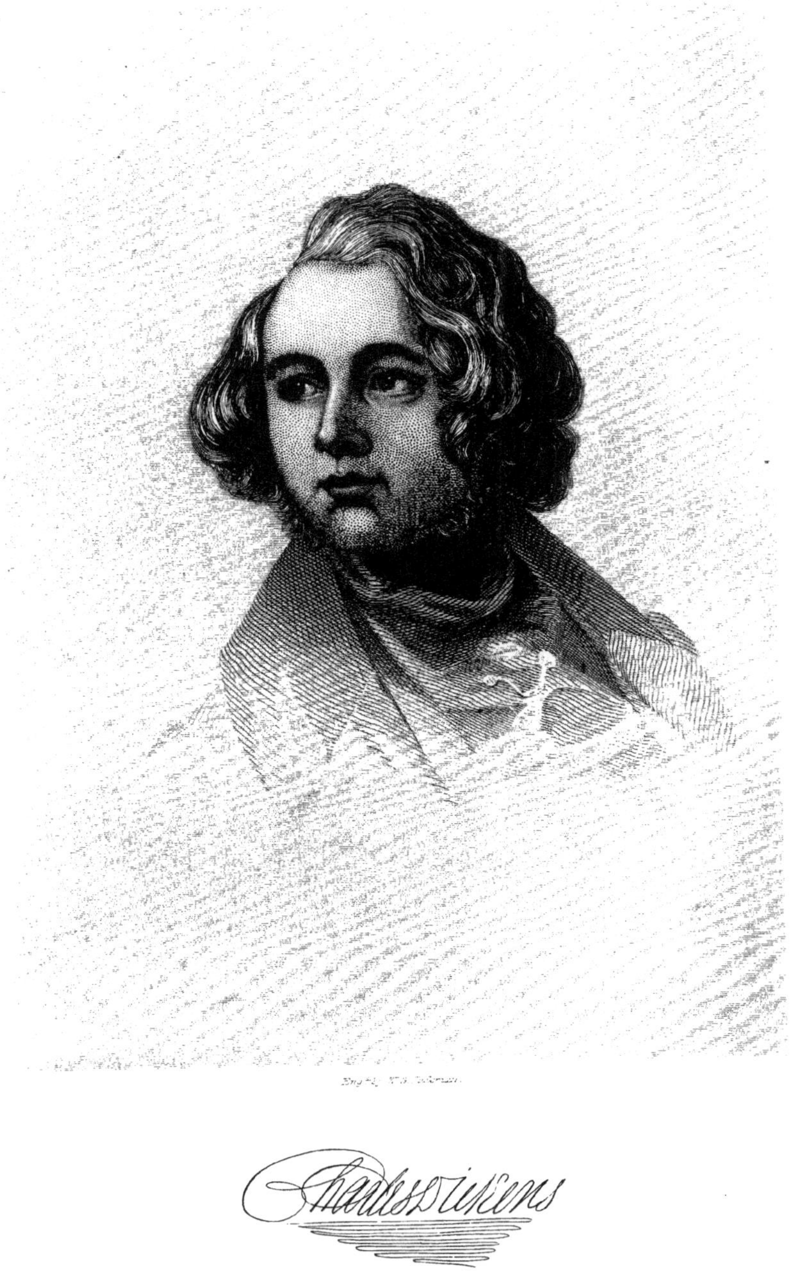
Charles Dickens

laws of their country (there being no instance of a murderous or burglarious lamplighter); that they are, in short, notwithstanding their apparently volatile and restless character, a highly moral and reflective people: having among themselves as many traditional observances as the Jews, and being, as a body, if not as old as the hills, at least as old as the streets. It is an article of their creed that the first faint glimmering of true civilization shone in the first street light maintained at the public expense. They trace their existence and high position in the public esteem, in a direct line to the heathen mythology; and hold that the history of Prometheus himself is but a pleasant fable, whereof the true hero is a lamplighter,

"Gentlemen," said the lamplighter in the chair, "I drink your healths."

"And perhaps, sir," said the vice, holding up his glass, and rising a little way off his seat and sitting down again, in token that he recognized and returned the compliment, "perhaps you will add to that condescension by telling us who Tom Grig was, and how he came to be connected in your mind with Francis Moore, Physician."

"Hear, hear, hear!" cried the lamplighters generally.

"Tom Grig, gentlemen," said the chairman, "was one of us; and it happened to him as it don't often happen to a public character in our line, that he had his what-you-may-call-it cast."

"His head?" said the vice.

"No," replied the chairman, "not his head."

"His face, perhaps?" said the vice. "No, not his face." "His legs?" "No, not his legs." Nor yet his arms, nor his hands, nor his feet, nor his chest, all of which were severally suggested.

"His nativity, perhaps?"

"That's it," said the chairman, awakening from his thoughtful attitude at the suggestion. "His nativity. That's what Tom had cast, gentlemen."

"In plaster?" asked the vice.

"I don't rightly know how it's done," returned the chairman, "but I suppose it was."

And there he stopped, as if that were all he had to say; whereupon there arose a murmur among the company, which at length resolved itself into a request, conveyed through the vice, that he would go on. This being exactly what the chairman wanted, he mused for a little time, performed that agreeable ceremony which is popularly termed wetting one's whistle, and went on thus:

"Tom Grig, gentlemen, was, as I have said, one of us; and I may go further, and say he was an ornament to us, and such a one as only the good old times of oil and cotton could have produced. Tom's family, gentlemen, were all lamplighters."

"Not the ladies, I hope?" asked the vice.

"They had talent enough for it, sir," rejoined the chairman, "and would have been, but for the prejudices of society. Let women have their rights, sir, and the females of Tom's family would have been every one of 'em in office. But that emancipation hasn't come yet, and hadn't then, and consequently they confined themselves to the bosoms of their families, cooked the dinners, mended the clothes, minded the children, comforted their husbands, and attended to the housekeeping generally. It's a hard thing upon the women, gentlemen, that they are limited to such a sphere of action as this; very hard.

"I happen to know all about Tom, gentlemen, from the circumstance of his uncle by the mother's side, having been my particular friend. His (that's Tom's uncle's) fate was a melancholy one. Gas was the death of him. When it was first talked of, he laughed. He wasn't angry; he laughed at the credulity of human nature. 'They might as well talk', he says, 'of laying on an everlasting succession of glow-worms;' and then he laughed again, partly at his joke, and partly at poor humanity.

"In course of time, however, the thing got ground, the experiment was made, and they lighted up Pall Mall. Tom's uncle went to see it. I've heard that he fell off his ladder fourteen times that night from weakness, and that he would certainly have gone on falling till he killed himself, if his last tumble hadn't been into a wheel-barrow which was going his way, and humanely took him home. 'I foresee in this,' says Tom's uncle faintly, and taking to his bed as he spoke—'I foresee in this,' he says, 'the breaking up of our profession. There's no more going the rounds to trim by daylight, no more dribbling down of the oil on the hats and bonnets of ladies and gentlemen when one feels in spirits. Any low fellow can light a gaslamp. And it's all up.' In this state of mind, he petitioned the government for—I want a word again, gentlemen—what do you call that which they give to people when it's found out, at last, that they've never been of any use, and have been paid too much for doing nothing?"

"Compensation?" suggested the vice.

"That's it," said the chairman. "Compensation. They didn't give it him though, and then he got very fond of his country all at once, and went about saying that gas was a death-blow to his native land, and that it was a plot of the radicals to ruin the country and destroy the oil and cotton trade for ever, and that the whales would go and kill themselves privately, out of sheer spite and vexation at not being caught. At last, he got right down cracked; called his tobacco-pipe a gas-pipe; thought his tears were lamp-oil; and went on with all manner of nonsense of that sort, till one night he hung himself on a lamp-iron in Saint Martin's Lane, and there was an end of *him*.

"Tom loved him, gentlemen, but he survived it. He shed a tear over his grave, got very drunk, spoke a funeral oration that night in the watch-house, and was fined five shillings for it, in the morning. Some men are none the worse for this sort of thing. Tom was one of 'em. He went that very afternoon on a new beat: as clear in his head, and as free from fever as Father Mathew himself.

"Tom's new beat, gentlemen, was—I can't exactly say where, for that he'd never tell; but I know it was in a quiet part of town, where there was some queer old houses. I have always had it in my head that it must have been somewhere near Canonbury Tower in Islington, but that's a matter of opinion. Whereever it was, he went upon it, with a bran new ladder, a white hat, a brown holland jacket and trowsers, a blue neck-kerchief, and a sprig of full-blown double wall-flower in his button-hole. Tom was always genteel in his appearance, and I have heard from the best judges, that if he had left his ladder at home that afternoon, you might have took him for a lord.

"He was always merry, was Tom, and such a singer, that if there was any encouragement for native talent, he'd have been at the opera. He was on his ladder, lighting his first lamp, and singing to himself in a manner more easily to be conceived than described, when he hears the clock strike five, and suddenly sees an old gentleman with a telescope in his hand, throw up a window and look at him very hard.

"Tom didn't know what could be passing in this old gentleman's mind. He thought it likely enough that he might be saying within himself, 'Here's a new lamplighter—a good-looking young fellow—shall I stand something to drink?' Thinking this possible, he keeps quite still, pretending to be very particular about the wick, and looks at the old gentleman sideways, seeming to take no notice of him.

"Gentlemen, he was one of the strangest and most mysterious-looking files that ever Tom clapped his eyes on. He was dressed all slovenly and untidy, in a great gown of a kind of bed-furniture pattern, with a cap of the same on his head; and a long old flapped waistcoat; with no braces, no strings, very few buttons—in short, with hardly any of those artificial contrivances that hold society together. Tom knew by these signs, and by his not being shaved, and by his not being over-clean, and by a sort of wisdom not quite awake, in his face, that he was a scientific old gentleman. He often told me that if he could have conceived the possibility of the whole Royal Society being boiled down into one man, he should have said the old gentleman's body was that Body.

"The old gentleman claps the telescope to his eye, looks all round, sees nobody else in sight, stares at Tom again, and cries out very loud:

"'Hal-loa!'

"'Holloa, sir,' says Tom from the ladder; 'and holloa again, if you come to that.'

"'Here's an extraordinary fulfilment,' says the old gentleman, 'of a prediction of the planets.'

"'Is there?' says Tom, 'I'm very glad to hear it.'

"'Young man,' says the old gentleman, 'you don't know me.'

"'Sir,' says Tom, 'I have not that honor; but I shall be happy to drink your health, notwithstanding.'

"'I read,' cries the old gentleman, without taking any notice of this politeness on Tom's part—'I read what's going to happen, in the stars.'

"Tom thanked him for the information, and begged to know if any thing particular was going to happen in the stars, in the course of a week or so; but the old gentleman, correcting him, explained that he read in the stars what was going to happen on dry land, and that he was acquainted with all the celestial bodies.

"'I hope they're all well, sir,' says Tom,—'every body.'

"'Hush!' cries the old gentleman. 'I have consulted the book of Fate with rare and wonderful success. I am versed in the great sciences of astrology and astronomy. In my house here, I have every description of apparatus for observing the course and motion of the planets. Six months ago, I derived from this source, the knowledge that precisely as the clock struck five this afternoon, a stranger would present himself—the destined husband of my young and lovely niece—in reality of illustrious and high descent, but whose birth would be enveloped in uncertainty and mystery. Don't tell me yours isn't,' says the old gentleman, who was in such a hurry to speak that he couldn't get the words out fast enough, 'for I know better.'

"Gentlemen, Tom was so astonished when he heard him say this, that he could hardly keep his footing on the ladder, and found it necessary to hold on by the lamp-post. There *was* a mystery about his birth. His mother had always admitted it. Tom had never known who was his father, and some people had gone so far as to say that even *she* was in doubt.

"While he was in this state of amazement, the old gentleman leaves the window, bursts out of the house-door, shakes the ladder, and Tom, like a ripe pumpkin, comes sliding down into his arms.

"'Let me embrace you,' he says, folding his arms about him, and nearly lighting up his old bed-furniture gown at Tom's link. 'You're a man of noble aspect. Every thing combines to prove the accuracy of my observations. You have had mysterious promptings within you,' he says; 'I know you have had whisperings of greatness, eh?' he says.

"'I think I have,' says Tom—Tom was one of those who can persuade themselves to any thing they like—'I have often thought I wasn't the small beer I was taken for.'

"'You were right,' cries the old gentleman, hugging him again. 'Come in. My niece awaits us.'

"'Is the young lady tolerable good-looking, sir?' says Tom, hanging fire rather, as he thought of her playing the piano, and knowing French, and being up to all manner of accomplishments.

"'She's beautiful!' cries the old gentleman, who was in such a terrible bustle that he was all in a perspiration. 'She has a graceful carriage, an exquisite shape, a sweet voice, a countenance beaming with animation and expression; and the eye,' he says, rubbing his hands, 'of a startled fawn.'

"Tom supposed this might mean, what was called among his circle of acquaintance, 'a game eye;' and, with a view to this defect, inquired whether the young lady had any cash.

"'She has five thousand pounds,' cries the old gentleman. 'But what of that? what of that? A word in your ear. I'm in search of the philosopher's stone. I have very nearly found it—not quite. It turns every thing to gold; that's its property.'

"Tom naturally thought it must have a deal of property; and said that when the old gentleman did get it, he hoped he'd be careful to keep it in the family.

"'Certainly,' he says, 'of course. Five thousand pounds! What's five thousand pounds to us? What's five millions?' he says. 'What's five thousand millions? Money will be nothing to us. We shall never be able to spend it fast enough.'

"'We'll try what we can do, sir,' says Tom.

"'We will,' says the old gentleman. 'Your name?'

"'Grig,' says Tom.

"The old gentleman embraced him again, very tight; and without speaking another word, dragged him into the house in such an excited manner, that it was as much as Tom could do to take his link and ladder with him, and put them down in the passage.

"Gentlemen, if Tom hadn't been always remarkable for his love of truth, I think you would still have believed him when he said that all this was like a dream. There is no better way for a man to find out whether he really is asleep or awake, than calling for something to eat. If he's in a dream, gentlemen, he'll find something wanting in the flavor, depend upon it.

"Tom explained his doubts to the old gentleman, and said if there was any cold meat in the house, it would ease his mind very much to test himself at once. The old gentleman ordered up a venison pie, a small ham, and a bottle of very old Madeira. At the first mouthful of pie, and the first glass of wine, Tom smacks his lips and cries out, 'I'm awake—wide awake;' and to prove that he was so, gentlemen, he made an end of 'em both.

"When Tom had finished his meal (which he never spoke of afterwards without tears in his eyes), the old gentleman hugs him again, and says, 'Noble stranger! let us visit my young and lovely niece.' Tom, who was a little elevated with the wine, replies, 'The noble stranger is agreeable!' At which words the old gentleman took him by the hand, and led him to the parlor; crying as he opened the door, 'Here is Mr. Grig, the favorite of the planets!'

"I will not attempt a description of female beauty, gentlemen, for every one of us has a model of his own that suits his own taste best. In this parlor that I'm speaking of, there were two young ladies; and if every gentleman present will imagine two models of his own in their places, and will be kind enough to polish 'em up to the very highest pitch of perfection, he will then have a faint conception of their uncommon radiance.

"Besides these two young ladies, there was their waiting-woman, that under any other circumstances Tom would have looked upon as a Venus; and besides her, there was a tall, thin, dismal-faced young gentleman, half man and half boy, dressed in a childish suit of clothes very much too short in the legs and arms; and looking, according to Tom's comparison, like one of the wax juveniles from a tailor's door, grown up and run to seed. Now, this youngster stamped his foot upon the ground, and looked very fierce at Tom, and Tom looked fierce at him—for to tell the truth, gentlemen, Tom more than half suspected that when they entered the room he was kissing one of the young ladies; and for any thing Tom knew, you observe, it might be *his* young lady—which was not pleasant.

"'Sir,' says Tom, 'before we proceed any further, will you have the goodness to inform me who this young Salamander'—Tom called him that for aggravation, you perceive, gentlemen—'who this young Salamander may be?'

"'That, Mr. Grig,' says the old gentleman, 'is my little boy. He was christened Galileo Isaac Newton Flamstead. Don't mind him. He is a mere child.'

"'A very fine child, too,' says Tom—still aggravating, you'll observe—'of his age, and as good as fine, I have no doubt. How do you do, my man?' with which kind and patronizing expressions, Tom reached up to pat him on the head, and quoted two lines about little boys, from Doctor Watts' Hymns, which he had learned at a Sunday School.

"It was very easy to see, gentlemen, by this youngster's frowning, and by the waiting-maid's tossing her head and turning up her nose, and by the young ladies turning their backs and talking together at the other end of the room, that nobody but the old gentleman took very kindly to the noble stranger. Indeed, Tom plainly heard the waiting-woman say of her master, that so far from being able to read the stars as he pretended, she didn't believe he knew his letters in 'em, or at best that he had got further than words in one syllable; but Tom, not minding this (for he was in spirits after the Madeira), looks with an agreeable air towards the young ladies, and kissing his hand to both, says to the old gentleman, 'Which is which?'

"'This,' says the old gentleman, leading out the handsomest, if one of 'em could possibly be said to be handsomer than the other—'this is my niece, Miss Fanny Barker.'

"'If you'll permit me, Miss,' says Tom, 'being a noble stranger and a favorite of the planets, I will conduct myself as such.' With these words, he kisses the young lady in a very affable way, turns to the old gentleman, slaps him on the back, and says, 'When's it to come off, my buck?"

"The young lady colored so deep, and her lip trembled so much, gentlemen, that Tom really thought she was going to cry. But she kept her feelings down, and turning to the old gentleman, says, 'Dear uncle, though you have the absolute disposal of my hand and fortune, and though you mean well in disposing of 'em thus, I ask you whether you don't think this is a mistake? Don't you think, dear uncle,' she says, 'that the stars must be in error? Is it not possible that the comet may have put 'em out?'

"'The stars,' says the old gentleman, 'couldn't make a mistake if they tried. Emma,' he says to the other young lady.

"'Yes, papa,' says she.

"'The same day that makes your cousin Mrs. Grig, will unite you to the gifted Mooney. No remonstrance—no tears. Now, Mr. Grig, let me conduct you to that hallowed ground, that philosophical retreat, where my friend and partner, the gifted Mooney of whom I have just now spoken, is even now pursuing those discoveries which shall enrich us with the precious metal, and make us masters of the world. Come, Mr. Grig,' he says.

"'With all my heart, sir,' replies Tom; 'and luck to the gifted Mooney, say I—not so much on his account as for our worthy selves!' With this sentiment, Tom kissed his hand to the ladies again, and followed him out; having the gratification to perceive, as he looked back, that they were all hanging on by the arms and legs of Galileo Isaac Newton Flamstead, to prevent him from following the noble stranger, and tearing him to pieces.

"'Gentlemen, Tom's father-in-law that was to be, took him by the hand, and having lighted a little lamp, led him across a paved court-yard at the back of the house, into a very large, dark, gloomy room: filled with all manner of bottles, globes, books, telescopes, crocodiles, alligators, and other scientific instruments of every kind. In the centre of this room was a stove or furnace, with what Tom called a pot, but which in my opinion was a crucible, in full boil. In one corner was a sort of ladder leading through the roof; and up this ladder the old gentleman pointed, as he said in a whisper:

"'The observatory. Mr. Mooney is even now watching for the precise time at which we are to come into all the riches of the earth. It will be necessary for he and I, alone in that silent place, to cast your nativity before the hour arrives. Put the day and minute of your birth on this piece of paper, and leave the rest to me.'

"'You don't mean to say,' says Tom, doing as he was told and giving him back the paper, 'that I'm to wait here long, do you? It's a precious dismal place.'

"'Hush!' says the old gentleman, 'it's hallowed ground. Farewell!'

"'Stop a minute,' says Tom, 'what a hurry you're in. What's in that large bottle yonder?'

"'It's a child with three heads,' says the old gentleman; 'and every thing else in proportion.

"'Why don't you throw him away?' says Tom. 'What do you keep such unpleasant things here for?'

"'Throw him away!' cries the old gentleman. 'We use him constantly in astrology. He's a charm.'

"'I shouldn't have thought it,' says Tom, 'from his appearance. *Must* you go, I say?'

"The old gentleman makes him no answer, but climbs up the ladder in a greater bustle than ever. Tom looked after his legs till there was nothing of him left, and then sat down to wait; feeling (so he used to say) as comfortable as if he was going to be made a freemason, and they were heating the pokers.

"Tom waited so long, gentlemen, that he began to think it must be getting on for midnight at least, snd felt more dismal and lonely than ever he had done in all his life. He tried every means of whiling away the time, but it never had seemed to move so slow. First he took a nearer view of the child with three heads, and thought what a comfort it must have been to its parents. Then he looked up a long telescope which was pointed out of the window, but saw nothing particular, in consequence of the stopper being on at the other end. Then he came to a skeleton in a glass case, labelled, 'Skeleton of a gentleman—Prepared by Mr. Mooney,'—which made him hope that Mr. Mooney might not be in the habit of preparing gentlemen that way without their own consent. A hundred times, at least, he looked into the pot where they were boiling the philosopher's stone down to the proper consistency, and wondered whether it was nearly done. 'When it is,' thinks Tom, 'I'll send out for sixpenn'orth of sprats, and turn 'em into gold fish for a first experiment.' Besides which, he made up his mind, gentlemen, to have a country-house and a park; and to plant a bit of it with a double row of gas-lamps a mile long, and go out every night with a French-polished mahogany ladder, and two servants in livery behind him, to light 'em for his own pleasure.

"At length and at last, the old gentleman's legs appeared upon the steps leading through the roof, and he came slowly down: bringing along with him the gifted Mooney. This Mooney, gentlemen, was even more scientific in appearance than his friend; and had, as Tom often declared upon his word and honor, the dirtiest face we can possibly know of, in this imperfect state of existence.

"Gentlemen, you are all aware that if a scientific man isn't absent in his mind, he's of no good at all. Mr. Mooney was so absent, that when the old gentleman said to him, 'shake hands with Mr. Grig,' he put out his leg. 'Here's a mind, Mr. Grig!' cries the old gentleman in a rapture. 'Here's philosophy! Here's rumination! Don't disturb him,' he says, 'for this is amazing!'

"Tom had no wish to disturb him, having nothing particular to say; but he was so uncommonly amazing, that the old gentleman got impatient, and determined to give him an electric shock to bring him to—'for you must know, Mr. Grig,' he says, 'that we always keep a strongly charged battery, ready for that purpose.' These means being resorted to, gentlemen, the gifted Mooney revived with a loud roar, and he no sooner came to himself, than both he and the old gentleman looked at Tom with compassion, and shed tears abundantly.

"'My dear friend,' says the old gentleman to the Gifted, 'prepare him.'

"'I say,' cries Tom, falling back, 'none of that, you know. No preparing by Mr. Mooney, if you please.'

"'Alas!' replies the old gentleman, 'you don't understand us. My friend, inform him of his fate. —I can't.'

"The Gifted mustered up his voice, after many efforts, and informed Tom that his nativity had been carefully cast, and he would expire at exactly thirty-five minutes, twenty-seven seconds, and five-sixths of a second, past nine o'clock, A. M., on that day two months.

"Gentlemen, I leave you to judge what were Tom's feelings at this announcement, on the eve of matrimony and endless riches. 'I think,' he says in a trembling way, 'there must be a mistake in the working of that sum. Will you do me the favor to cast it up again?'—'There is no mistake,' replies the old gentleman, 'it is confirmed by Francis Moore, Physician. Here is the prediction for to-morrow two months.' And he showed him the page, where sure enough were these words—'The decease of a great person may be looked for, about this time.'

"'Which,' says the old gentleman, 'is clearly you, Mr. Grig.'

"'Too clearly,' cries Tom, sinking into a chair, and giving one hand to the old gentleman, and one to the Gifted. 'The orb of day has set on Thomas Grig for ever!'

"At this affecting remark, the Gifted shed tears again, and the other two mingled their tears with his, in a kind—if I may use the expression—of Mooney and Co.'s entire. But the old gentleman recovering first, observed that this was only a reason for hastening the marriage, in order that Tom's distinguished race might be transmitted to posterity; and requesting the Gifted to console Mr. Grig during his temporary absence, he withdrew to settle the preliminaries with his niece immediately.

"And now, gentlemen, a very extraordinary and remarkable occurrence took place; for as Tom sat in a melancholy way in one chair, and the Gifted sat in a melancholy way in another, a couple of doors were thrown violently open, the two young ladies rushed in, and one knelt down in a loving attitude at Tom's feet, and the other at the Gifted's. So far, perhaps, as Tom was concerned—as he used to say—you will say there was nothing strange in this; but you will be of a different opinion when you understand that Tom's young lady was kneeling to the Gifted, and the Gifted's young lady was kneeling to Tom.

"'Halloa! stop a minute!' cries Tom; 'here's a mistake. I need condoling with by sympathizing woman, under my afflicting circumstances; but we're out in the figure. Change partners, Mooney.'

"'Monster!' cries Tom's young lady, clinging to the Gifted.

"'Miss!' says Tom. 'Is *that* your manners?'

"'I abjure thee!' cries Tom's young lady. 'I renounce thee. I never will be thine. Thou,' she says to the Gifted, 'art the object of my first and all-engrossing passion. Wrapt in thy sublime visions, thou hast not perceived my love; but, driven to despair, I now shake off the woman, and avow it. Oh, cruel, cruel man!' With which reproach, she laid her head upon the Gifted's breast, and put her arms about him in the tenderest manner possible, gentlemen.

"'And I,' says the other young lady, in a sort of ecstasy that made Tom start,—'I hereby abjure my chosen husband too. Hear me, Goblin!'—this was to the Gifted—'Hear me! I hold thee in the deepest detestation. The maddening interview of this one night has filled my soul with love—but not for thee. It is for thee, for thee, young man,' she cries to Tom. 'As Monk Lewis finely observes, Thomas, Thomas, I am thine; Thomas, Thomas, thou art mine: thine for ever, mine for ever!' With which words, she became very tender likewise.

"Tom and the Gifted, gentlemen, as you may believe, looked at each other in a very awkward manner, and with thoughts not at all complimentary to the two young ladies. As to the Gifted, I have heard Tom say often, that he was certain he was in a fit, and had it inwardly.

"'Speak to me! oh, speak to me!' cries Tom's young lady to the Gifted.

"'I don't want to speak to anybody,' he says, finding his voice at last, and trying to push her away. 'I think I had better go. I'm—I'm frightened,' he says, looking about as if he had lost something.

"'Not one look of love!' she cries. 'Hear me, while I declare—'

"'I don't know how to look a look of love,' he says, all in a maze. 'Don't declare any thing. I don't want to hear anybody.'

"'That's right!' cries the old gentleman (who it seems had been listening). 'That's right! Don't hear her. Emma shall marry you to-morrow, my friend, whether she likes it or not, and *she* shall marry Mr. Grig.'

"Gentlemen, these words were no sooner out of his mouth, than Galileo Isaac Newton Flamstead (who it seems had been listening too) darts in, and spinning round and round, like a young giant's top, cries, 'Let her. Let her. I'm fierce; I'm furious. I give her leave. I'll never marry anybody after this—never. It isn't safe. She is the falsest of the false,' he cries, tearing his hair and gnashing his teeth; 'and I'll live and die a bachelor.'

"'The little boy,' observed the Gifted gravely, 'albeit of tender years, has spoken wisdom. I have been led to the contemplation of woman-kind, and will not adventure on the troubled waters of matrimony.'

"'What!' says the old gentleman, 'not marry my daughter! Won't you, Mooney? Not if I make her? Won't you? Won't you?'

"'No,' says Mooney, 'I won't. And if anybody asks me any more, I'll run away, and never come back again.'

"'Mr. Grig,' says the old gentleman, 'the stars must be obeyed. You have not changed your mind because of a little girlish folly—eh, Mr. Grig?'

"Tom, gentlemen, had had his eyes about him, and was pretty sure that all this was a device and trick of the waiting-maid, to put him off his inclination. He had seen her hiding and skipping about the two doors, and had observed that a very little whispering from her pacified the Salamander directly. 'So,' thinks Tom, 'this is a plot—but it won't fit.'

"'Eh, Mr. Grig?' says the old gentleman.

"'Why, sir,' says Tom, pointing to the crucible, 'if the soup's nearly ready—'

"'Another hour beholds the consummation of our labors,' returned the old gentleman.

"'Very good,' says Tom, with a mournful air. 'It's only for two months, but I may as well be the richest man in the world even for that time. I'm not particular. I'll take her, sir. I'll take her.'

"The old gentleman was in a rapture to find Tom still in the same mind, and drawing the young lady towards him by little and little, was joining their hands by main force, when all of a sudden, gentlemen, the crucible blows up with a great crash; everybody screams; the room is filled with smoke; and Tom, not knowing what may happen next, throws himself into a fancy attitude, and says, 'Come on, if you are a man!' without addressing himself to anybody in particular.

"'The labors of fifteen years!' says the old genman, clasping his hands and looking down upon the Gifted, who was saving the pieces, 'are destroyed in an instant!'—And I am told, gentlemen, by-the-bye, that this same philosopher's stone would have been discovered a hundred times at least, to speak within bounds, if it wasn't for the one unfortunate circumstance that the apparatus always blows up, when it's on the very point of succeeding.

"Tom turns pale when he hears the old gentleman expressing himself to this unpleasant effect, and stammers out that if it's quite agreeable to all parties, he would like to know exactly what has happened, and what change has really taken place in the prospects of that company.

"'We have failed for the present, Mr. Grig,' says

the old gentleman, wiping his forehead, 'and I regret it the more, because I have in fact invested my niece's five thousand pounds in this glorious speculation. But don't be cast down,' he says, anxiously—'in another fifteen years, Mr. Grig—'

"Oh!' cries Tom, letting the young lady's hand fall. 'Were the stars very positive about this union, sir?'

"'They were,' says the old gentleman.

"'I am sorry to hear it,' Tom makes answer, 'for it's no go, sir.

"'No what?' cries the old gentleman.

"'Go, sir,' says Tom fiercely. 'I forbid the banns.' And with these words—which are the very words he used—he sat himself down in a chair, and, laying his head upon the table, thought with a secret grief of what was to come to pass on that day two months.

"Tom always said, gentlemen, that that waiting-maid was the artfullest minx he had ever seen; and he left it in writing in this country when he went to colonize abroad, that he was certain in his own mind she and the Salamander had blown up the philosopher's stone on purpose, and to cut him out of his property. I believe Tom was in the right, gentlemen; but whether or no, she comes forward at this point, and says, 'May I speak, sir?' and the old gentleman answering 'Yes, you may,' she goes on to say that 'the stars are no doubt quite right in every respect, but Tom is not the man.' And she says, 'Don't you remember, sir, that when the clock struck five this afternoon, you gave Master Galileo a rap on the head with your telescope, and told him to get out of the way?' 'Yes I do,' says the old gentleman. 'Then,' says the waiting maid, 'I say he's the man, and the prophecy is fulfilled.' The old gentleman staggers at this, as if somebody had hit him a blow on the chest, and cries, 'He! why, he's a boy!' Upon that, gentlemen, the Salamander cries out that he'll be twenty-one next Lady-day; and complains that his father has always been so busy with the sun round which the earth revolves, that he has never taken any notice of the son that revolves round him; and that he hasn't had a new suit of clothes since he was fourteen; and that he wasn't even taken out of nankeen frocks and trowsers till he was unpleasant in 'em; and touches on a good many more family matters to the same purpose. To make short of a long story, gentlemen, they all talk together, and cry together, and remind the old gentleman that as to the noble family, his own grandfather would have been a lord mayor if he hadn't died at a dinner the year before; and they show him by all kinds of arguments that if the cousins are married, the prediction comes true every way. At last, the old gentleman, being quite convinced, gives in; and joins their hands; and leaves his daughter to marry anybody she likes; and they are all well pleased; and the Gifted as well as any of them.

"In the middle of this little family party, gentlemen, sits Tom all the while, as miserable as you like. But, when every thing else is arranged, the old gentleman's daughter says, that their strange conduct was a little device of the waiting-maid's to disgust the lovers he had chosen for 'em, and will he forgive her? and if he will, perhaps he might even find her a husband—and when she says that, she looks uncommon hard at Tom. Then the waiting maid says that, oh dear! she couldn't abear Mr. Grig should think she wanted him to marry her; and that she had even gone so far as to refuse the last lamplighter, who was now a literary character (having set up as a bill-sticker;) and that she hoped Mr. Grig would not suppose she was on her last legs by any means, for the baker was very strong in his attentions at that moment, and as to the butcher, he was frantic. And I don't know how much more she might have said, gentlemen (for, as you know, this kind of young women are rare ones to talk), if the old gentleman hadn't cut in suddenly, and asked Tom if he'd have her, with ten pounds to recompense him for his loss of time and disappointment, and as a kind of bribe to keep the story secret.

"'It don't much matter, sir,' says Tom, 'I ain't long for this world. Eight weeks of marriage, especially with this young woman, might reconcile me to my fate. I think,' he says, 'I could go off easy, after that.' With which, he embraces her with a very dismal face, and groans in a way that might move a heart of stone—even of philosopher's stone.

"Egad,' says the old gentleman, 'that reminds me—this bustle put it out of my head—there was a figure wrong. He'll live to a green old age—eighty-seven at least!'

"'How much, sir?' cries Tom.

"'Eighty-seven!' says the old gentleman.

"Without another word, Tom flings himself on the old gentleman's neck; throws up his hat; cuts a caper; defies the waiting-maid; and refers her to the butcher.

"'You won't marry her!' says the old gentleman, angrily.

"'And live after it!' says Tom. 'I'd sooner marry a mermaid, with a small-tooth comb and looking-glass.'

"'Then take the consequences,' says the other.

"With those words—I beg your kind attention here, gentlemen, for it's worth your notice—the old gentleman wetted the forefinger of his right hand in some of the liquor from the crucible that was spilt on the floor, and drew a small triangle on Tom's forehead. The room swam before his eyes, and he found himself in the watch-house."

"Found himself *where?*" cried the vice, on behalf of the company generally.

"In the watch-house," said the chairman. "It was late at night, and he found himself in the very watch-house from which he had been let out that morning."

"Did he go home?" asked the vice.

"The watch-house people rather objected to that," said the chairman; "so he stopped there that night, and went before the magistrate in the morning. 'Why, you're here again, are you?' says the magistrate, adding insult to injury; 'we'll trouble you for five shillings more, if you can conveniently spare the money.' Tom told him he had been enchanted, but it was of no use. He told the contractors the same, but they wouldn't believe him. It was very hard upon him, gentlemen, as he often said, for was it likely he'd go and invent such a tale? They shook their heads and told him he'd say anything but his prayers—as indeed he would; there's no doubt about that. It was the only imputation on his moral character that ever *I* heard of."

THE CAB-DRIVER AND THE MAN ABOUT TOWN.

FROM "THE PICKWICK CLUB." BY CHARLES DICKENS (BOZ).

"CAB!" said Mr. Pickwick.

"Here you are, sir," shouted a strange specimen of the human race, in a sackcloth coat, and apron of the same, who with a brass label and number round his neck, looked as if he were catalogued in some collection of rarities. This was the waterman. "Here you are, sir. Now, then, fust cab!" And the fust cab having being fetched from the public house, where he had been smoking his first pipe, Mr. Pickwick and his portmanteau were thrown into the vehicle.

"Golden Cross," said Mr. Pickwick.

"Only a bob's vorth, Tommy,"—cried the driver, sulkily, for the information of his friend the waterman, as the cab drove off.

"How old is that horse, my friend?" inquired Mr. Pickwick, rubbing his nose with the shilling he had reserved for the fare.

"Forty-two," replied the driver, eyeing him askant.

"What!" ejaculated Mr. Pickwick, laying his hand upon his note-book. The driver reiterated his former statement. Mr. Pickwick looked very hard at the man's face, but his features were immovable, so he noted down the fact forthwith.

"And how long do you keep him out at a time?" inquired Mr. Pickwick, searching for further information.

"Two or three veeks," replied the man.

"Weeks!" said Mr. Pickwick in astonishment—and out came the note-book again.

"He lives at Pentonwil when he's at home," observed the driver coolly, "but we seldom takes him home on account of his veakness."

"On acccount of his weakness;" reiterated the perplexed Mr. Pickwick.

"He always falls down, when he's took out o' the cab," contined the driver, "but when he's in it, we bears him up werry tight, and takes him in werry short, so as he can't werry well fall down, and we've got a pair o' precious large wheels on; so ven he *does* move, they run after him, and he must go on—he can't help it."

Mr. Pickwick entered every word of this statement in his note-book, with the view of communicating it to the club, as a singular instance of the tenacity of life in horses, under trying circumstances. The entry was scarcely completed when they reached the Golden Cross. Down jumped the driver, and out got Mr. Pickwick. Mr. Tupman, Mr. Snodgrass, and Mr. Winkle, who had been anxiously waiting the arrival of their illustrious leader, crowded to welcome him.

"Here's your fare," said Mr. Pickwick, holding out the shilling to the driver.

What was the learned man's astonishment, when that unaccountable person flung the money on the pavement, and requested in figurative terms to be allowed the pleasure of fighting him (Mr. Pickwick) for the amount!

"You are mad," said Mr. Snodgrass.

"Or drunk," said Mr. Winkle.

"Or both," said Mr. Tupman.

"Come on," said the cab-driver, sparring away like clock-work. "Come on—all four on you."

"Here's a lark!" shouted half a dozen hackney coachmen. "Go to vork, Sam,"—and they crowded with great glee round the party.

"What's the row, Sam?" inquired one gentleman in black calico sleeves.

"Row!" replied the cabman, "What did he want my number for?"

"I didn't want your number," said the astonished Mr. Pickwick.

"What did you take it for, then?" inquired the cabman.

"I didn't take it," said Mr. Pickwick, indignantly.

"Would any body believe," continued the cab-driver, appealing to the crowd,—"Would any body believe as an informer 'ud go about in a man's cab, not only takin' down his number, but ev'ry word he says into the bargain," (a light flashed upon Mr. Pickwick—it was the note-book.)

"Did he, though?" inquired another cabman.

"Yes, did he," replied the first, "and then, arter aggerawatin' me to assault him, gets three witnesses here to prove it. But I'll give it him, if I've six months for it. Come on,"—and the cabman dashed his hat upon the ground, with a reckless disregard of his own private property, and knocked Mr. Pickwick's spectacles off, and followed up the attack with a blow on Mr. Pickwick's nose, and another on Mr. Pickwick's chest, and a third in Mr. Snodgrass's eye, and a fourth, by way of variety, in Mr. Tupman's waistcoat, and then danced into the road, and then back again to the pavement, and finally dashed the whole temporary supply of breath out of Mr. Winkle's body; and all in half a dozen seconds.

"Where's an officer?" said Mr. Snodgrass.

"Put 'em under the pump," suggested a hot pieman.

"You shall smart for this," gasped Mr. Pickwick.

"Informers," shouted the crowd.

"Come on," cried the cabman, who had been sparring without cessation the whole time.

The mob had hitherto been passive spectators of the scene, but as the intelligence of the Pickwickians being informers was spread among them, they began to canvass with considerable vivacity the propriety of enforcing the heated pastry-vender's proposition: and there is no saying what acts of personal aggression they might have committed, had not the affray been unexpectedly terminated by the interposition of a new comer.

"What's the fun?" said a rather tall, thin young man, in a green coat, emerging suddenly from the coach yard.

"Informers!" shouted the crowd.

"We are not," roared Mr. Pickwick, in a tone, which, to any dispassionate listener, carried conviction with it.

"Ain't you, though—ain't you?" said the young man, appealing to Mr. Pickwick, and making his way through the crowd, by the infallible process of elbowing the countenances of its component members.

That learned man, in a few hurried words, explained the real state of the case.

"Come along, then," said he of the green coat, lugging Mr. Pickwick after him by main force, and talking the whole way. "Here No. 924, take your fare, nad take yourself off—respectable gentleman, —know him well—none of your nonsense—this way, sir—where's your friends?—all a mistake, I see—never mind—accidents will happen—best regulated families —never say die — down upon your luck—pull him up—put that in his pipe—like the flavor— d——d rascals." And with a lengthened string of similar broken sentences, delivered with extraordinary volubility, the stranger led the way to the travellers' waiting room, whither he was closely followed by Mr. Pickwick and his disciples.

"Here, waiter," shouted the stranger, ringing the bell with tremendous violence, "glasses round—brandy and water, hot and strong, and sweet, and plenty —eye damaged, sir? Waiter; raw beef-steak for the gentleman's eye—nothing like raw beef-steak for a bruise, sir; cold lamp-post very good, but lamp-post inconvenient—d——d cold standing in the open street half an hour, with your eye against a lamp-post—eh,—very good—ha! ha!" And the stranger, without stopping to take breath, swallowed at a draught full half a pint of the reeking brandy and water, and flung himself into a chair with as much ease, as if nothing uncommon had occurred.

While his three companions were busily engaged in proffering their thanks to their new acquaintance, Mr. Pickwick had leisure to examine his costume and appearance.

He was about the middle height, but the thinness of his body, and the length of his legs, gave him the appearance of being much taller. The green coat had been a smart dress garment in the days of swallow-tails, but had evidently in those times adorned a much shorter man than the stranger, for the soiled and faded sleeves scarcely reached to his wrists. It was buttoned closely up to his chin, at the imminent hazard of splitting the back; and an old stock, without a vestige of shirt collar, ornamented his neck. His scanty black trousers displayed here and there those shiny patches which bespeak long service, and were strapped very tightly over a pair of patched and mended shoes, as if to conceal the dirty white stockings, which were nevertheless distinctly visible. His long black hair escaped in negligent waves from beneath each side of his old pinched-up hat; and glimpses of his bare wrist might be observed, between the tops of his gloves and the cuffs of his coat sleeves. His face was thin and haggard; but an indescribable air of jaunty impudence and perfect self-possession pervaded the whole man.

Such was the individual, on whom Mr. Pickwick gazed through his spectacles (which he had fortunately recovered), and to whom he proceeded, when his friends had exhausted themselves, to return, in chosen terms, his warmest thanks for his recent assistance.

"Never mind," said the stranger, cutting the address very short, "said enough,—no more; smart chap that cabman—handled his fives well; but if I'd been your friend in the green jemmy—damn me—punch his head,—'cod I would,—pig's whisper—pieman too,—no gammon."

This coherent speech was interrupted by the entrance of the Rochester coachman, to announce that "The Commodore" was on the point of starting.

"Commodore!" said the stranger, starting up, "my coach,—place booked,—one outside—leave you to pay for the brandy and water,—want change for a five,—bad silver—Brummagem buttons—won't do—no go—eh?" and he shook his head most knowingly

Now it so happened that Mr. Pickwick and his three companions had resolved to make Rochester their first halting place too; and having intimated to their new-found acquaintance that they were journeying to the same city, they agreed to occupy the seat at the back of the coach, where they could all sit together.

"Up with you," said the stranger, assisting Mr. Pickwick on to the roof with so much precipitation, as to impair the gravity of that gentleman's deportment very materially.

"Any luggage, sir?" inquired the coachman.

"Who—I? Brown paper parcel here, that's all—other luggage gone by water,—packing-cases, nailed up—big as houses—heavy, heavy, d——d heavy," replied the stranger, as he forced into his pocket as much as he could of the brown paper parcel, which presented most suspicious indications of containing one shirt and a handkerchief.

"Heads, heads, take care of your heads," cried the loquacious stranger, as they came out under the low archway, which in those days formed the entrance to the coach yard. "Terrible place—dangerous work—other day—five children—mother—tall lady, eating sandwiches—forgot the arch—crash—knock—children look round—mother's head off—sandwich in her hand—no mouth to put it in—head of a family off—shocking, shocking. Looking at Whitehall, sir,—fine place—little window—somebody else's head off there, eh, sir?—he didn't keep a sharp look-out enough either—eh, sir, eh?"

"I was ruminating," said Mr. Pickwick, "on the strange mutability of human affairs."

"Ah! I see—in at the palace door one day, out at the window the next. Philosopher, sir?"

"An observer of human nature, sir," said Mr. Pickwick.

"Ah, so am I. Most people are when they've little to do and less to get. Poet, sir?"

"My friend, Mr. Snodgrass has a strong poetic turn," said Mr. Pickwick.

"So have I," said the stranger. "Epic poem,—ten thousand lines—revolution of July—composed it on the spot—Mars by day—Apollo by night,—bang the field-piece, twang the lyre."

"You were present at that glorious scene, sir?" said Mr. Snodgrass.

"Present! think I was; fired a musket, fired with an idea,—rushed into a wine shop—wrote it down—back again—whiz, bang—another idea—wine shop again—pen and ink—back again—cut and slash—noble time, sir. Sportsman, sir?" abruptly turning to Mr. Winkle.

"A little, sir," replied that gentleman.

"Fine pursuit, sir,—fine pursuit.—Dogs, sir?"

"Not just now," said Mr. Winkle.

"Ah! you should keep dogs—fine animals—sagacious creatures—dog of my own once—Pointer—surprising instinct—out shooting one day—entering inclosure—whistled—dog stopped—whistled again—Ponto—no go: stock still—called him—Ponto, Ponto—wouldn't move—dog transfixed—

staring at a board—looked up, saw an inscription—'Gamekeeper has orders to shoot all dogs found in this inclosure'—wouldn't pass it—wonderful dog—valuable dog that—very."

"Singular circumstance, that," said Mr. Pickwick. "Will you allow me to make a note of it* ?"

"Certainly, sir, certainly—hundred more anecdotes of the same animal.—Fine girl, sir" (to Mr. Tracy Tupman, who had been bestowing sundry anti-Pickwickian glances on a young lady by the road side).

"Very!" said Mr. Tupman.

"English girls not so fine as Spanish—noble creatures—jet hair—black eyes—lovely forms—sweet creatures—beautiful."

"You have been in Spain, sir?" said Mr. Tracy Tupman.

"Lived there—ages."

"Many conquests, sir?" inquired Mr. Tupman.

"Conquests! Thousands. Don Bolaro Fizzgig—Grandee—only daughter—Donna Christina—splendid creature—loved me to distraction—jealous father—high-souled daughter—handsome Englishman—Donna Christina in despair—prussic acid—stomach pump in my portmanteau—operation performed—old Bolaro in ecstasies—consent to our union—join hands and floods of tears—romantic story—very."

"Is the lady in England now, sir?" inquired Mr. Tupman, on whom the description of her charms had produced a powerful impression.

"Dead, sir—dead," said the stranger, applying to his right eye the brief remnant of a very old cambric handkerchief. "Never recovered the stomach pump—undermined constitution—fell a victim."

"And her father?" inquired the poetic Snodgrass.

"Remorse and misery," replied the stranger. "Sudden disappearance—talk of the whole city—search made everywhere—without success—public fountain in the great square suddenly ceased playing—weeks elapsed—still a stoppage—workmen employed to clean it—water drawn off—father-in-law discovered sticking head first in the main pipe, with a full confession in his right boot—took him out, and the fountain played away again as well as ever."

"Will you allow me to note that little romance down, sir?" said Mr. Snodgrass, deeply affected.

"Certainly, sir, certainly,—fifty more, if you like to hear 'em—strange life mine—rather curious history—not extraordinary, but singular."

* Although we find this circumstance recorded as a "singular" one, in Mr. Pickwick's note-book, we cannot refrain from humbly expressing our dissent from that learned authority. The stranger's anecdote is not one quarter so wonderful as some of Mr. Jesse's "Gleanings." Ponto sinks into utter insignificance before the dogs whose actions he records.

In this strain, with an occasional glass of ale, by way of parenthesis, when the coach changed horses, did the stranger proceed, until they reached Rochester bridge, by which time the note-books, both of Mr. Pickwick and Mr. Snodgrass, were completely filled with selections from his adventures.

"Magnificent ruin!" said Mr. Augustus Snodgrass, with all the poetic fervor that distinguished him, when they came in sight of the fine old castle.

"What a study for an antiquarian," were the very words which fell from Mr. Pickwick's mouth, as he applied his telescope to his eye.

"Ah! fine place," said the stranger, "glorious pile—frowning walls—tottering arches—dark nooks—crumbling staircases—old cathedral too—earthly smell—pilgrims' feet worn away the old steps—little Saxon doors—confessionals like money-takers' boxes at theatres—queer customers, those monks—Popes, and Lord Treasurers' and all sorts of old fellows, with great red faces, and broken noses, turning up every day—buff jerkins too—matchlocks—sarcophagus—fine place—old legends too—strange stories: capital;" and the stranger continued to soliloquize until they reached the Bull Inn, in the High Street, where the coached stopped.

"Do you remain here, sir?" inquired Mr. Nathaniel Winkle.

"Here—not I—but you'd better—good house—nice beds—Wright's next house, dear—very dear—half a-crown in the bill, if you look at the waiter—charge you more if you dine at a friend's than they would if you dined in the coffee room—rum fellows—very."

Mr. Winkle turned to Mr. Pickwick, and murmured a few words; a whisper passed from Mr. Pickwick to Mr. Snodgrass, from Mr. Snodgrass to Mr. Tupman, and nods of assent were exchanged. Mr. Pickwick addressed the stranger.

"You rendered us a very important service, this morning, sir," said he; "will you allow us to offer a slight mark of our gratitude by begging the favor of your company at dinner?"

"Great pleasure—not presume to dictate, but broiled fowl and mushrooms—capital thing! What time?"

"Let me see," replied Mr. Pickwick, referring to his watch, "it is now nearly three. Shall we say five?"

"Suit me excellently," said the stranger, "five precisely—till then—care of yourselves;" and lifting the pinched-up hat a few inches from his head, and carelessly replacing it very much on one side, the stranger, with half the brown paper parcel sticking out of his pocket, walked briskly up the yard, and turned into the high street.

SAM WELLER'S VALENTINE.

FROM "THE PICKWICK CLUB." BY CHARLES DICKENS (BOZ).

Sam had solaced himself with a most agreeable little dinner, and was waiting at the bar for the glass of warm mixture, in which Mr. Pickwick had requested him to drown the fatigues of his morning's walks, when a young boy of about three feet high, or thereabouts, in a hairy cap and fustian overalls, whose garb bespoke a laudable ambition to attain in time the elevation of an hostler, entered the passage of the George and Vulture, and looked first up the stairs, and then along the passage, and then into the bar, as if in search of somebody to whom he bore a commission; whereupon the barmaid, conceiving it not improbable that the said commission might be directed to the tea or table spoons of the establishment, accosted the boy with

"Now, young man, what do *you* want?"

"Is there anybody here, named Sam?" inquired the youth, in a loud voice of treble quality.

"What's the tother name?" said Sam Weller, looking round.

"How should I know?" briskly replied the young gentleman below the hairy cap.

"You're a sharp boy, you are," said Mr. Weller; "only I wouldn't show that wery fine edge too much, if I was you, in case any body took it off. What do you mean by comin' to a hot-el, and asking after Sam, vith so much politeness as a vild Indian?"

"Cos an old gen'lm'n told me to," replied the boy.

"What old gen'lm'n?" inquired Sam, with deep disdain.

"Him as drives a Ipswich coach, and uses our parlor," rejoined the boy. He told me yesterday mornin' to come to the George in Wultur this arternoon, and ask for Sam."

"It's my father, my dear," said Mr. Weller, turning with an explanatory air to the young lady in the bar; blessed if I think he hardly knows wot my other name is. Vell, young brockily sprout, wot then?"

"Why then," said the boy, "you was to come to him at six o'clock to our 'ouse, 'cos he wants to see you—Blue Boar, Leaden'all Markit. Shall I say you're comin'?"

"You *may* wenture on that 'ere statement, sir," replied Sam. And thus empowered, the young gentleman walked away, awakening all the echoes in George Yard as he did so, with several chaste and extremely correct imitations of a drover's whistle, delivered in a tone of peculiar richness and volume.

Mr. Weller, having obtained leave of absence from Mr. Pickwick, who, in his then state of excitement and worry, was by no means displeased at being left alone, set forth long before the appointed hour; and having plenty of time at his disposal, sauntered down as far as the Mansion House, where he paused and contemplated, with a face of great calmness and philosophy, the numerous cads and drivers of short stages who assemble near that famous place of resort to the great terror and confusion of the old-lady population of these realms. Having loitered here, for half an hour or so, Mr. Weller turned, and began wending his way towards Leadenhall Market, through a variety of bye streets and courts. As he was sauntering away his spare time, and stopped to look at almost every object that met his gaze, it is by no means surprising that Mr. Weller should have paused before a small stationer's and print-seller's window; but without further explanation it does appear surprising that his eyes should have no sooner rested on certain pictures which were exposed for sale therein, than he gave a sudden start, smote his right leg with great vehemence, and exclaimed with energy, "If it hadn't been for this, I should ha' forgot all about it, till it was too late!"

The particular picture on which Sam Weller's eyes were fixed, as he said this, was a highly colored representation of a couple of human hearts skewered together with an arrow, cooking before a cheerful fire, while a male and female cannibal in modern attire, the gentleman being clad in a blue coat and white trowsers, and the lady in a deep red pelisse with a parasol of the same, were approaching the meal with hungry eyes, up a serpentine gravel path leading thereunto. A decidedly indelicate young gentleman, in a pair of wings and nothing else, was depicted as superintending the cooking; a representation of the spire of the church in Langham Place, appeared in the distance; and the whole formed a "valentine," of which, as a written inscription in the window testified, there was a large assortment within, which the shopkeeper pledged himself to dispose of to his countrymen generally, at the reduced rate of one and sixpence each.

"I should ha' forgot it; I should certainly ha' forgot it!" said Sam; and so saying, he at once stepped into the stationer's shop, and requested to be served with a sheet of the best gilt-edged letter-paper, and a hard-nibbed pen which could be warranted not to splutter. These articles having been promptly supplied, he walked on direct towards Leadenhall Market at a good round pace, very different from his recent lingering one. Looking round him, he there beheld a sign-board on which the painter's art had delineated something remotely resembling a cerulean elephant with an aquiline nose in lieu of trunk. Rightly conjecturing that this was the Blue Boar himself, he stepped into the house, and inquired concerning his parent.

"He won't be here this three-quarters of an hour or more," said the young lady who superintended the domestic arrangements of the Blue Boar.

"Very good, my dear," replied Sam. "Let me have nine pen'orth o' brandy and water luke, and the inkstand, will you, miss?"

The brandy and water luke and the inkstand having been carried into the little parlor, and the young lady having carefully flattened down the coals to prevent their blazing, and carried away the poker to preclude the possibility of the fire being stirred, without the full privity and concurrence of the Blue Boar being first had and obtained, Sam Weller sat himself down in a box near the stove, and pulled out the sheet of gilt-edged letter-paper, and the hard-nibbed pen. Then, looking carefully at the pen to see that there were no hairs in it, and dusting down the table, so that there might be no crumbs of bread under the paper, Sam tucked up the cuffs of his coat, squared his elbows, and composed himself to write.

To ladies and gentlemen who are not in the habit of devoting themselves practically to the science of penmanship, writing a letter is no very easy task, it being always considered necessary in such cases for the writer to recline his head on his left arm so as to place his eyes as nearly as possible on a level with the paper, and while glancing sideways at the letters he is constructing, to form with his tongue imaginary characters to correspond. These motions, although unquestionably of the greatest assistance to original composition, retard in some degree the progress of the writer, and Sam had unconsciously been a full hour and a half writing words in small text, smearing out wrong letters with his little finger, and putting in new ones which required going over very often to render them visible through the old blots, when he was roused by the opening of the door and the entrance of his parent.

"Vell, Sammy," said the father.

"Vell, my Prooshan Blue," responded the son, laying down his pen. "What's the last bulletin about mother-in-law?"

"Mrs. Veller passed a wery good night, but is uncommon perwerse and unpleasant this mornin'—

signed upon oath—S. Veller, Esquire, Senior. That's the last vun as was issued, Sammy," replied Mr. Weller, untying his shawl.

"No better yet?" inquired Sam.

"All the symptoms aggerawated," replied Mr. Weller, shaking his head. "But wot's that you're a doin' of—pursuit of knowledge under difficulties —eh, Sammy?'

'I've done now," said Sam with slight embarrassment; "I've been a writin'."

"So I see," replied Mr. Weller. "Not to any young 'ooman, I hope, Sammy."

"Why it's no use a sayin' it ain't," replied Sam. "It's a walentine."

"A what!" exclaimed Mr. Weller, apparently horror-stricken by the word.

"A walentine," replied Sam.

"Samivel, Samivel!" said Mr. Weller, in reproachful accents, "I didn't think you'd ha' done it. Arter the warnin' you've had o' your father's wicious perpensities, arter all I've said to you upon this here wery subject; arter actiwally seein' and bein' in the company o' your own mother-in-law, vich I should ha' thought was a moral lesson as no man could ever ha' forgotten to his dyin' day! I didn't think you'd ha' done it, Sammy, I didn't think you'd ha' done it." These reflections were too much for the good old man. He raised Sam's tumbler to his lips, and drank off its contents.

"Wot's the matter now!" said Sam.

"Never mind, Sammy," replied Mr. Weller, "it'll be a wery agonizin' trial to me at my time of life, but I'm pretty tough, that's vun consolation, as the wery old turkey remarked ven the farmer said he wos afeerd he should be obliged to kill him, for the London market."

"Wot'll be a trial?" inquired Sam.

"To see you married, Sammy—to see you a deluded wictim, and thinkin' in your innocence that it's all wery capital," replied Mr. Weller. "It's a dreadful trial to a father's feelin's, that 'ere, Sammy."

"Nonsense," said Sam. "I ain't a goin' to get married, don't you fret yourself about that; I know you're a judge o' these things. Order in your pipe, and I'll read you the letter—there."

We cannot distinctly say whether it was the prospect of the pipe, or the consolatory reflection that a fatal disposition to get married ran in the family and couldn't be helped, which calmed Mr. Weller's feelings, and caused his grief to subside. We should be rather disposed to say that the result was attained by combining the two sources of consolation, for he repeated the second in a low tone, very frequently; ringing the bell meantime, to order in the first. He then divested himself of his upper coat; and lighting the pipe and placing himself in front of the fire with his back towards it, so that he could feel its full heat, and recline against the mantel-piece at the same time, turned towards Sam, and, with a countenance greatly mollified by the softening influence of tobacco, requested him to "fire away."

Sam dipped his pen into the ink to be ready for any corrections, and began with a very theatrical air——

"'Lovely——.'"

"Stop," said Mr. Weller, ringing the bell. "A double glass o' the inwariable, my dear."

"Very well, sir," replied the girl; who with great quickness appeared, vanished, returned, and disappeared.

"They seem to know your ways here," observed Sam.

"Yes," replied the father, "I've been here before, in my time. Go on, Sammy."

"'Lovely creetur,'" repeated Sam.

"'Tain't in poetry, is it?" interposed the father.

"No, no," replied Sam.

"Wery glad to hear it," said Mr. Weller. "Poetry's unnat'ral; no man ever talked in poetry 'cept a beadle on boxin' day, or Warren's blackin', or Rowland's oil, or some o' them low fellows; never you let yourself down to talk poetry, my boy. Begin again, Sammy."

Mr. Weller resumed his pipe with critical solemnity, and Sam once more commenced, and read as follows.

"'Lovely creetur i feel myself a damned'—.'

"That ain't proper," said Mr. Weller, taking his pipe from his mouth.

"No; it ain't damned," observed Sam, holding the letter up to the light, "it's 'shamed,' there's a blot there—'I feel myself ashamed.'"

"Wery good," said Mr. Weller. "Go on."

"'Feel myself ashamed, and completely cir—' I forget wot this here word is," said Sam, scratching his head with the pen, in vain attempts to remember.

"Why don't you look at it, then?" inquired Mr. Weller.

"So I *am* a lookin' at it," replied Sam, "but there's another blot; here's a 'c,' and a 'i,' and a 'd.'"

"Circumwented, p'raps," suggested Mr. Weller.

"No, it ain't that," said Sam, "circumscribed, that's it."

"That ain't as good a word as circumwented, Sammy," said Mr. Weller, gravely.

"Think not?" said Sam.

"Nothin' like it," replied his father.

"But don't you think it means more?" inquired Sam.

"Vell, p'raps it is a more tenderer word," said Mr. Weller, after a few moments' reflection. "Go on, Sammy."

"'Feel myself ashamed and completely circumscribed in a dressin' of you, for you *are* a nice gal, and nothin' but it.'"

"That's a wery pretty sentiment," said the elder Mr. Weller, removing his pipe to make way for the remark.

"Yes, I think it is rayther good," observed Sam, highly flattered.

"Wot I like in that 'ere style of writin'," said the elder Mr. Weller, "is, that there ain't no callin' names in it,—no Wenuses, nor nothin' o' that kind; wot's the good o' callin' a young 'ooman a Wenus or a angel, Sammy?"

"Ah! what, indeed?" replied Sam.

"You might jist as vell call her a griffin, or a unicorn, or a king's arms at once, which is wery vell known to be a col-lection o' fabulous animals," added Mr. Weller.

"Just as well," replied Sam.

"Drive on, Sammy," said Mr. Weller.

Sam complied with the request, and proceeded as follows; his father continuing to smoke, with a mixed expression of wisdom and complacency, which was particularly edifying.

"'Afore I see you I thought all women was alike.'"

"So they are," observed the elder Mr. Weller, parenthetically.

"'But now,' continued Sam, 'now I find what a reg'lar soft-headed, ink-red'lous turnip I must ha' been, for there ain't nobody like you though I like you better than nothin' at all.' I thought it best to make that rayther strong," said Sam, looking up.

Mr. Weller nodded approvingly, and Sam resumed:

"'So I take the privilidge of the day, Mary, my dear—as the gen'lem'n in difficulties did, ven he valked out of a Sunday,—to tell you that the first and only time I see you your likeness was took on my hart in much quicker time and brighter colors than ever a likeness was took by the profeel macheen (wich p'raps you may have heerd on Mary my dear) altho it *does* finish a portrait and put the frame and glass on complete with a hook at the end to hang it up by and all in two minutes and a quarter.'"

"I am afeerd that werges on the poetical, Sammy," said Mr. Weller, dubiously.

"No it don't," replied Sam, reading on very quickly, to avoid contesting the point.

"'Except of me, Mary my dear, as your walentine, and think over what I've said.—My dear Mary I will now conclude.' That's all," said Sam.

"That's rayther a sudden pull up, ain't it, Sammy?" inquired Mr. Weller.

"Not a bit on it," said Sam; "she'll vish there wos more, and that's the great art o' letter writin'."

"Well," said Mr. Weller, "there's somethin' in that; and I wish your mother-in-law 'ud only conduct her conwersation on the same gen-teel principle. Ain't you a goin' to sign it?"

"That's the difficulty," said Sam; "I don't know what *to* sign it."

"Sign it—Veller," said the oldest surviving proprietor of that name.

"Won't do," said Sam. "Never sign a walentine with your own name."

"Sign it 'Pickvick,' then," said Mr. Weller; "it's a wery good name, and an easy one to spell."

"The wery thing," said Sam. "I *could* end with a werse; what do you think?"

"I don't like it, Sam," rejoined Mr. Weller. "I never know'd a respectable coachman as wrote poetry, 'cept one, as made an affectin' copy o' werses the night afore he wos hung for a highway robbery; and *he* wos only a Cambervell man, so even that's no rule."

But Sam was not to be dissuaded from the poetical idea that had occurred to him, so he signed the letter—

"Your love-sick
Pickwick."

And having folded it, in a very intricate manner, squeezed a down-hill direction in one corner: "To Mary, Housemaid, at Mr. Nupkins's Mayor's, Ipswich, Suffolk;" and put into his pocket, wafered, and ready for the General Post.

ONE PEEP WAS ENOUGH; OR, THE POST-OFFICE.

BY LETITIA ELIZABETH LANDON (L. E. L.)

All places have their peculiarities: now that of Dalton was discourse—that species of discourse, which Johnson's Dictionary entitles "conversation on whatever does not concern ourselves." Everybody knew what everybody did, and a little more. Eatings, drinkings, wakings, sleepings, walkings, talkings, sayings, doings—all were for the good of the public; there was not such a thing as a secret in the town.

There was a story of Mrs. Mary Smith, an ancient dame who lived on an annuity, and boasted the gentility of a back and front parlor, that she once asked a few friends to dinner. The usual heavy antecedent half-hour really passed quite pleasantly; for Mrs. Mary's windows overlooked the market-place, and not a scrag of mutton could leave it unobserved; so that the extravagance or the meanness of the various buyers furnished a copious theme for dialogue. Still, in spite of Mr. A.'s pair of fowls, and Mrs. B.'s round of beef, the time seemed long, and the guests found hunger growing more potent than curiosity. They waited and waited; at length the fatal discovery took place—that in the hurry of observing her neighbor's dinners, Mrs. Smith had forgotten to order her own.

It was in the month of March that an event happened which put the whole town in a commotion—the arrival of a stranger, who took up his abode at the White Hart; not that there was any thing remarkable about the stranger; he was a plain, middle-aged, respectable-looking man, and the nicest scrutiny (and heaven knows how narrowly he was watched) failed to discover any thing odd about him. It was ascertained that he rose at eight, breakfasted at nine, ate two eggs and a piece of broiled bacon, sat in his room at the window, read a little, wrote a little, and looked out upon the road a good deal; he then strolled out, returned home, dined at five, smoked two cigars, read the morning Herald (for the post came in of an evening), and went to bed at ten. Nothing could be more regular or unexceptionable than his habits; still it was most extraordinary what could have brought him to Dalton. There were no chalybeate springs, warranted to cure every disease under the sun; no ruins in the neighborhood, left expressly for antiquarians and pic-nic parties; no fine prospects, which, like music, people make it matter of conscience to admire; no celebrated person had ever been born or buried in its environs; there were no races, no assizes—in short, there was "no nothing." It was not even summer; so country air and fine weather were not the inducements. The stranger's name was Mr. Williams, but that was the extent of their knowledge; and, shy and silent, there seemed no probability of learning any thing more from himself. Conjecture, like Shakspere, "exhausted worlds, and then imagined new." Some supposed he was hiding from his creditors, others that he had committed forgery; one suggested that he had escaped from a mad-house, a second that he had killed some one in a duel; but all agreed that he came there for no good.

It was the twenty-third of March, when a triad of gossips were assembled at their temple, the post-office. The affairs of Dalton and the nation were settled together; newspapers were slipped from their covers, and not an epistle but yielded a portion of its contents. But on this night all attention was concentrated upon one, directed to "John Williams, Esq., at the White Hart, Dalton." Eagerly was it compressed in the long fingers of Mrs. Mary Smith of dinnerless memory; the fat landlady of the White Hart was on tip-toe to peep, while the post-mistress, whose curiosity took a semblance of official dignity, raised a warning hand against any overt act of violence. The paper was closely folded, and closely written in a cramped and illegible

hand; suddenly Mrs. Mary Smith's look grew more intent—she had succeeded in deciphering a sentence; the letter dropped from her hand. "Oh, the monster!" shrieked the horrified peeper. Landlady and post-mistress both snatched at the terrible scroll, and they equally succeeded in reading the following words—"We will settle the matter to-morrow at dinner, but I am sorry you persist in poisoning your wife, the horror is too great." Not a syllable more could they make out; but what they had read was enough. "He told me," gasped the landlady, "that he expected a lady and gentleman to dinner—oh the villain! to think of poisoning any lady at the White Hart; and his wife, too —I should like to see my husband poisoning me!" Our hostess became quite personal in her indignation.

"I always thought there was something suspicious about him; people don't come and live where nobody, knows them, for nothing," observed Mrs. Mary Smith.

"I dare say," returned the post-mistress, "Williams is not his real name."

"I don't know that," interrupted the landlady; "Williams is a good hanging name: there was Williams who murdered the Marr's family, and Williams who burked all those poor dear children; I dare say he is some relation of theirs; but to think of his coming to the White Hart—it's no place for his doings, I can tell him; he shan't poison his wife in my house; out he goes this very night—I'll take the letter to him myself."

"Lord! Lord! I shall be ruined, if it comes to be known that we take a look into the letters;" and the post-mistress thought in her heart that she had better let Mr. Williams poison his wife at his leisure. Mrs. Mary Smith, too, reprobated any violent measures; the truth is, she did not wish to be mixed up in the matter; a gentlewoman with an annuity and a front and back parlor was rather ashamed of being detected in such close intimacy with the post-mistress and the landlady. It seemed likely that poor Mrs. Williams would be left to her miserable fate.

"Murder will out," said the landlord, the following morning, as he mounted the piebald pony, which, like Tom Tough, had seen a deal of service; and hurried off in search of Mr. Crampton, the nearest magistrate.

Their perceptions assisted by brandy and water, he and his wife had sat up long past "the witching hour at night," deliberating on what line of conduct would be most efficacious in preserving the life of the unfortunate Mrs. Williams; and the result of the deliberation was to fetch the justice, and have the delinquent taken into custody at the very dinner-table which was intended to be the scene of his crime. "He has ordered soup to-day for the first time; he thinks he could so easily slip poison into the liquid. There he goes; he looks like a man that has got something on his conscience," pointing to Mr. Williams, who was walking up and down at his usual slow pace. Two o'clock arrived, and with it a hack chaise; out of it stept, sure enough, a lady and gentleman. The landlady's pity redoubled—such a pretty young creature, not above nineteen!—"I see how it is," thought she, "the old wretch is jealous." All efforts to catch her eye were in vain, the dinner was ready, and down they sat. The hostess of the White Hart, looked alternately out of the window, like sister Ann, to see if any one was coming, and to the table to see that nothing was doing. To her dismay, she observed the young lady lifting a spoonful of broth to her mouth! She could restrain herself no longer; but catching her hand, exclaimed, "Poor dear innocent, the soup is poisoned!"—All started from the table in confusion, which was yet to be increased:—a bustle was heard in the passage, in rushed a whole party, two of whom, each catching an arm of Mr. Williams, pinioned them down to his seat. "I am happy, madam," said the little bustling magistrate, "to have been under heaven the instrument of preserving your life from the nefarious designs of that disgrace to humanity." Mr. Crampton paused in consequence of three wants—want of words, breath, and ideas.

"My life!" ejaculated the astonished lady.

"Yes, madam, the ways of Providence are inscrutable—the vain curiosity of three idle women has been turned to good account." And the eloquent magistrate proceeded to detail the process of inspection to which the fatal letter had been subjected; but when he came to the terrible words—"We will settle the matter to-morrow at dinner; but I am sorry you persist in poisoning your wife" —he was interrupted by bursts of laughter from the gentleman, from the injured wife, and even from the prisoner himself. One fit of merriment was followed by another, till it became contagious, and the very constables began to laugh too.

"I can explain all," at last interrupted the visitor. "Mr. Williams came here for that quiet so necessary for the labors of genius; he is writing a melodrama called 'My Wife'—he submitted the last act to me, and I rather objected to the poisoning of the heroine. This young lady is my daughter, and we are on our way to the sea-coast. Mr. Williams is only wedded to the Muses."

The disconcerted magistrate shook his head, and muttered something about theatres being very immoral.

"Quite mistaken, sir," said Mr. Williams. "Our soup is cold; but our worthy landlady roasts fowls to a turn—we will have them and the veal cutlets up, you will stay and dine with us—and, afterwards, I—shall be proud to read 'My Wife' aloud, in the hope of your approval, at least, of your indulgence"—and with the same hope, I bid farewell to my readers.

Cool.—A farmer, suspecting that his wood-pile was robbed, sat up to watch. In the night, he heard a noise, and, looking out, saw a lazy neighbor endeavoring to carry off a large log. "You're a pretty fellow," said the owner, "to come here, and steal my wood while I sleep." "And you're a pretty fellow," said the thief, "to stay up there, and see me breaking my back with lifting, and never offer to help me."

Logic.—A man once made a bet, that he could prove that *this side* of the river was *the other side*. Pointing to the opposite shore, he asked, "Is not that *one* side of the river?" "Yes." Well, a river has but two sides—if that is one side, of course this is *the other side*." His antagonist, dumbfounded by such logic, paid the money, and began to think with Macbeth, that "nothing is but what is not."

CURIOUS OPINIONS OF A TURK.

FROM "NINEVEH AND BABYLON." BY A. H. LAYARD.

THE time was drawing near for my departure. Once more I was about to leave the ruins amidst which I had spent so many happy hours, and to which I was bound by so many pleasant and solemn ties; and probably to return no more.

I only waited the arrival of Abde, the late Pasha of Bagdad, who was now on his way to his new government of Diarbekir. He was travelling with a large company of attendants, as without a strong escort, it was scarcely prudent to venture on a journey. It was doubly necessary for me to have proper protection, as I took with me the valuable collection of bronzes and other small objects discovered in the ruins. I gladly, therefore, availed myself of this opportunity of joining so numerous and powerful a caravan.

At length, after the usual eastern delays, the Pasha arrived at Mosul. He remained encamped outside the town for two or three days, and during that time visited the excavations, his curiosity having been excited by the description he had received of the wondrous idols dug out of the ruins. He marvelled at what he saw, as a Turk marvels at strange things which he can neither understand nor explain. It would be in vain to speak to him of the true objects of such researches, the knowledge they impart, the lessons they teach or the thoughts they beget.

In these pages I have occasionally indulged in reflections suggested by the scenes I have had to describe, and have ventured to point out the moral of the strange tale I have had to relate. I cannot better conclude than by showing the spirit in which eastern philosophy and Mussulman resignation contemplate the evidences of ancient greatness and civilization, suddenly rising up over the midst of modern ignorance and decay. A letter in my possession contained so true and characteristic a picture of the feelings that such an event excites in the mind of a good Mohammedan, that I here give a literal translation of its contents. It was written to a friend of mine by a Turkish Cadi, in reply to some inquiries as to the commerce, population, and remains of antiquity of an ancient city, in which dwelt the head of the land. These are its words:—

"*My illustrious Friend and Joy of my Liver!*

"The thing you ask of me is both difficult and useless. Although I have passed all my days in this place, I have neither counted the houses nor have I inquired into the number of the inhabitants; and as to what one person loads on his mules, and the other stows away in the bottom of his ship, that is no business of mine. But, above all, as to the previous history of this city, God knows the amount of dirt and confusion the infidels may have eaten before the coming of the sword of Islam. It were unprofitable for us to inquire into it. 'Oh, my soul! oh, my lamb! seek not after the things which concern thee not. Thou camest to us and we welcomed thee: go in peace.

"Of a truth, thou hast spoken many words; and there is no harm done, for the speaker is one, and the listener is another. After the fashion of thy people, thou hast wandered from one place to another, until thou art happy and content in none. We (praise be to God) were born here, and never desire to quit it. Is it possible then that the idea of a general intercourse between mankind should make any impression on our understandings? God forbid!

"Listen, oh my son! There is no wisdom equal unto the belief in God! He created the world, and shall we liken ourselves unto him in seeking to penetrate into the mysteries of his creation? Shall we say, behold this star spinneth round that star, and this other star with a tail goeth and cometh in so many years! Let it go! He from whose hand it came will guide and direct it.

"But thou wilt say unto me, Stand aside, oh man, for I am more learned than thou art, and have seen more things. If thou thinkest that thou art in this respect better than I am, thou art welcome. I praise God that I seek not that which I require not. Thou art learned in the things I care not for; and as for that which thou hast seen, I defile it. Will much knowledge create thee a double belly, or wilt thou seek Paradise with thine eyes?

"Oh, my friend! If thou wilt he happy, say, There is no god but God! Do no evil, and thus wilt thou fear neither man nor death; for surely thine hour will come!

"The meek in spirit (El Fakin)

"IMAUN ALIZADE."

On the 28th of April, I bid a last farewell to my faithful Arab friends, and with a heavy heart turned from the ruins of ancient Nineveh.

THE LOTTERY TICKET.

ANONYMOUS.

THAT once fruitful source of pleasing although delusive hopes, the Lottery, is now no more. A despotic act of parliament has given the death-blow to thousands of happy pictures of the imagination, that were hitherto wont to amuse, for a time at least, those earnest suitors of Fortune, who, if they did not actually enjoy her smiles, flattered themselves that they were on the high road to her favors. A stern moralist, indeed, may expatiate on the baneful influence of Lotteries, not only as a species of gambling, but as tending to cherish expectations, which, in a fearful majority of cases, must terminate in disappointment. Yet the very same persons scruple not to hold out as incentives to good conduct examples of success, that must create hopes equally deceptive. The apprentice is taught to cherish the idea, that however humble his fortune, he may one day become Lord Mayor; the midshipman is excited to emulation by the example of Nelson, and told that he ought not to despair of rising to the highest honors in his profession; and whatever be the career in which the youthful adventurer starts for fortune or for fame, it is considered not merely pardonable, but meritorious in him, to propose to himself the attainment of the greatest prize it has to bestow. There is a Russian proverb which says, 'He is a bad soldier that does not expect to become a general;' yet were a whole army to consist of individuals combining the talents of an Alexander, a Cæsar, and a Napoleon, it would be as impossible that all should be commanders, as that in a Lottery every speculator should gain the grand prize.

But, the "Lucky Corner" is gone; or, rather, though the identical house stands there yet, it no longer conjures up in the passers-by, dreams of sudden affluence, and of hoards of gold. There, at the forked triple way, Fortune seemed with open arms to invite all who approached the spot, pointing with one hand to the Bank, and with the other to the wealthy Lombard land. The Lottery, too, whatever be alleged against it in other respects, must be admitted to have frequently furnished an expedient to the novelist and dramatist, and enabled them to extricate a hero from poverty and raise him at once to affluence, without killing a distant relative, or bringing an old uncle from India. A lottery ticket has, also, without doubt, given rise to many a strange incident, and it is hoped that the one I am now about to relate will not be found wholly unamusing.

Mr. Richard Fogrum, or, as his old acquaintance would more familiarly than respectfully designate him, Dick Fogrum, or, as he was sometimes styled on the superscription of a letter from a tradesman or poor relation, Richard Fogrum, Esq., had for some years retired from business, although he had not yet passed what is called the middle age; and, turning his back on his shop, where he had made, if not a considerable fortune, at least a handsome competency, rented a small house at Hackney, or, as he was pleased to term it, in the country. His establishment united a due attention to comfort, with economy and prudence. Beside a kitchen-maid and an occasional charwoman or errand boy, Mr. Fogrum possessed, in the person of the trusty Sally Sadlins, an excellent superintendent of his little *menage*. Sally was not exactly *gouvernante*, or housekeeper, at least she assumed none of the dignity attached to such a post; she seemed indeed hardly to have a will or opinion of her own, but had so insensibly accommodated herself to her employer's ways and humors, that by degrees the apparent distance between master and servant diminished, and as Sally, though far from talkative herself, was a good listener, Mr. Fogrum began to find a pleasure in relating to her all the little news and anecdotes he usually picked up in his daily walk.

Let it not, however, be supposed that there was any thing equivocal in the kind of unconscious courtesy which existed between these two personages; a single glance at Sally would have convinced the most ingenious fabricator of scandal, and dealer in innuendoes, that here there was no foundation on which to build even the slightest surmise of the kind, for both Sally's person and face were to her a shield that would have rebutted any notion of the sort. Alas! that nature, so extolled by every poet for her impartiality, should be at times so capricious in her favors, and bestow her gifts so grudgingly, even on those whose very sex entitles them to be considered fair! "Kind goddess," as Will of Avon styles thee, surely thou didst in this instance behave most unfairly, bestowing on Sally Sadlins an elevation of figure that, had she been of the other sex, might have raised her to the rank of a corporal of grenadiers. Yet, if thou gavest her an aspiring stature, thou gavest her no aspiring thoughts; and if thou didst deny to her softness of person, fortunately for her peace, thou didst not gift her with the least susceptibility of heart. If Sally was not *loveable*, there was no woman on earth who could possibly have regretted it less. Indeed, I may safely aver, the idea of love never for an instant entered her head, much less had a single twinge of it ever touched her heart. She had heard people talk of love; and she supposed—if indeed she ever bestowed a thought on the subject—that there must be something in the world so called, otherwise people would not have invented a name for it: but she could no more pretend to say what it was, than to describe the ingredients of the air she breathed:—In short, Sally was the most guileless, simple, and disinterested of mortals that ever entered beneath the roof of a single gentleman, to be the first servant where there was no mistress.

Well, therefore, might Mrs. Thoms, who was aware that elderly gentlemen in her "dear" uncle's situation, are not always gifted with that discretion that beseems their years, but sometimes commit themselves to wedlock, in an unwary moment, to the no small prejudice of their affectionate relatives;—well, I say, might the prudent Mrs. Thoms congratulate herself on having found such a treasure, so invaluable a jewel, as Sally Sadlins. She was certain that from this quarter, at least, there was nothing to be apprehended—nothing to intercept her "dear" uncle's three per cents from what she considered the legitimate object of their destination. Some alarm, indeed, had been excited in her mind, by hearing that Mr. Fogrum had been seen rather frequently of late knocking at the door of Mrs. Simpson; but then again she thought that he could not possibly be led thither by any other motive than that of chatting away an hour with the widow of an old friend; beside, this lady was not likely either to lead, or to be led, into matrimony. In her younger days Mrs. Simpson might have been pretty, but none of her acquaintance could recollect *when*. She still patched; yet the patch was applied not where coquetry would have placed it, but where necessity dictated, namely, over the left eye. Mrs. Thoms therefore consoled herself with the reflection, that it was better her uncle should knock at Mrs. Simpson's door than at that of a more attractive fair one.—No! her uncle, she was perfectly satisfied, would never marry.

"What have you got there, Sally?" said Mr. Fogrum to his housekeeper, one day, as she drew something from her pocket, while standing before the side-board opposite to him. "An't please you, sir," replied Sally, in a meek, but not very gentle voice, "it's a bit o' summat I was going to show you. You know, sir, my uncle Tim took leave of me yesterday, before he goes to sea again, and so he gave me this paper, which he says may chance turn up trumps, and make me comfortable for life."

"Well, let me see what it is, Sally—is it the old fellow's will?—Hum!—why, Sally, this is a Lottery ticket!—a whole Lottery ticket; yet I will venture to say not worth more than the rag of paper 'tis printed on. I have myself tried the Lottery, times and often, ere now, and never got any thing but—disappointment.—'A blank, sir, a blank'—that was the only answer I ever obtained from them. What could possibly induce your uncle to lay out his cash in so foolish a manner? 'Tis never worth either keeping or thinking about. No. 123, confound it! I know it well, I once purchased a share of it myself—the very first I ever bought, when I was quite a lad; and well do I recollect that I chose it out of a whole heap, and thought myself very fortunate in obtaining one with such a sequence of figures—one, two, three."

Most composedly did Sally take the ticket again, not at all disconcerted at this denunciation of ill-luck, but on the contrary, with a calmness worthy of a stoic. 'Tis true, she did not, like Patience on a monument, absolutely smile at grief; but then, Sally never smiled; nor would a smile perhaps, if the rigidity of her face would have permitted such a relaxation of its muscles, have tended greatly to heighten the attraction of her countenance.

Her master in the meanwhile continued eating and wondering, and wondering and eating, until he could neither eat nor wonder more; but dismissing Sally with the dinner things, turned himself quietly to the fire, and took his pipe.

Mrs. Thoms was sitting one morning cogitating on some mischief that she again began to apprehend from the Widow Simpson, in consequence of certain intelligence she had the day before received, respecting that lady's designs upon the person of her uncle, when she was suddenly startled from her reverie by a loud rapping at the door, and instantly afterwards who should enter the parlor, but the very subject of her meditations—Mrs. Simpson herself.

The appearance of so unusual a visitor would alone have sufficed to surprise her; but there was something in the good lady's manner and countenance, that denoted she came upon a very important errand.

"Why, Mrs. Thoms," exclaimed she, almost breathless, as soon as she entered, "have you heard?—your uncle"—

"Good heavens!" cried Mrs. Thoms, "what do you mean?—what has happened?—my poor dear uncle—ill—dying!"

"Compose yourself, Mrs. Thoms—not dying—but I thought you might have heard"——

"Heard what?—some accident, I suppose?—poor dear man!"

"No: no accident," returned the widow, who by this time had somewhat recovered her breath; "but something very strange—most unaccountable. What you may think of it, I know not; but for my part I think that Mr. Fogrum has acted—I shall not say how."

"And pray, ma'am," said Mrs. Thoms, who now began to think that it was some quarrel between them, of which the widow came to inform her, "what has Mr. Fogrum done, that you should come in this strange manner, and make so great a fuss about it? It is some nonsense, after all, I dare say."

"Nonsense, forsooth!—well, I declare!—however, it certainly is no business of mine, ma'am," returned Mrs. Simpson, quite nettled at her reception; "and as I suppose you know what has taken place, and approve of it, I have nothing further to say."

Mrs. Thoms now became unaffectedly alarmed,

and apprehending she knew not what, requested to be informed what had happened, without further delay.

"Why, ma'am, then, Mr. Fogrum is——married, that's all."

To describe the effect those words had upon Mrs. Thoms, would be impossible, and to paint the expression of her countenance, equally unavailing.

"Married!" screamed she out, at length, as soon as she could draw her breath, "Married!—impossible—to whom?"

"To whom?—to Sally Sadlins, ma'am."

"To Sally Sadlins!—impossible—you must be joking."

"Not I, I assure you. I'm not a person, Mrs. Thoms, to make such jokes. I myself saw them, less than an hour ago, pass by my window in a post-chaise together, and then learnt the whole story from those who saw them step into it, at the church door."

"Oh! Mrs. Simpson, how have I been deceived in that insinuating hussy, Sally Sadlins! She who seemed so staid, so discreet—so very unlikely a person.—What an old fool *he* must be, to marry so vulgar a frump!"

"Nay, do not agitate yourself, my dear ma'am," said Mrs. Simpson, who, now having disburthened herself of her secret, and her own mortification being perhaps carried off by that of Mrs. Thoms's, which acted as a conductor to it, had quite regained her composure—"for my part, I hope he may not repent of his match."

"Oh! Thoms," exclaimed the other lady, as her husband entered the room, "here is news for us!—my silly old uncle has actually, this very morning, married his maid-servant!"

"That is most confoundedly unlucky," cried Thoms, "though I much doubted whether all your management in manœuvring, for which you gave yourself so much credit, would be to any purpose."

"But who could dream of such a thing!—I have no patience with him for having married as he has done."

"Well, my dear, there is no helping it; and perhaps after all, since he is married, it is quite as well for us that he has chosen as he has."

While Mrs. Thoms was ejaculating and bewailling—now abusing poor Sally as an artful seducing woman, who, under the mask of the greatest simplicity, had contrived to work upon her uncle's weakness—and anon venting her reproaches against the latter, for suffering himself to be thus duped,—a post-chaise was seen rolling along on the road to ——, with the identical pair seated in it, who were the subject of this invective and clamor. The intelligence, of which Mrs. Simpson had been the unwelcome messenger, was, in fact, correct in every particular; for Richard Fogrum, single man, and Sally Sadlins, spinster, had that very morning been lawfully united in wedlock, although, but a few days before, had any one prognosticated such an event, they would no more have believed it possible than Mrs. Thoms herself.

"Now, my dear Sally," said the somewhat stale Benedick, laying his hand, rather gently than amorously, on that of the bride, for which, by the bye, it was really no match in size—"I doubt not but my niece will be in a towering passion when she hears of this: however, no matter; let her, and the rest of the world say what they please. I do not see why a man may not just as well follow his own fancies as those of other persons. Besides, Sally, though folks may think that I might have made a more advantageous match, in point of fortune at least, they may perhaps be in error. I have a piece of intelligence to communicate, of which, perhaps, you little dream. You recollect that Lottery ticket?—well! passing the 'Lucky Corner,' by the Mansion-House, two days ago, I beheld, pasted up at the window, 'No. 123, 20,000*l.*!!' Ha! ha! Sally; well did I recollect those figures again—one, two, three! they follow each other as naturally as A, B, C. So home I came, but determined to say nothing of the matter till now."

The reader has already been informed that Sally was the most phlegmatic of her sex; still it may be supposed that such an interesting disclosure would have elicited some ejaculation of exultation, even from the lips of a stoic. Yet Sally, with wonderful composure, merely replied, "La! now that is curious."

"Curious! yes, but I assure you it is quite true; I am not joking."

"Well; what an odd turn things do sometimes take!"

"Odd, indeed! for who would have thought that my identical unlucky number, 123, should bring you—I may say us, Sally,—twenty thousand pounds!"

"But, sir, Mr. Fogrum, you are mistaken, I mean to say"——

"No mistake at all, my dear—quite certain of it—took down the number in my pocket-book—see

here—123, 20,000*l.*! Is not that the number of your ticket?"

"Yes, but"——

"But, what?"

"Why, you won't hear me, Mr. Fogrum," said Sally, mildly. "I was only going to say, that two months ago—I sold the ticket."

"How!—what!—sold!" groaned out poor Fogrum, and sunk gasping against the side of the chaise.

"Now pray don't distress yourself, Mr. Fogrum," said Sally, without the least visible emotion, or any change in her tone; "did you not, yourself, tell me it was not worth keeping; so I thought—'well, master must know better about these matters than I, therefore I may as well make something of it while I can;' so I changed it away for this nice white shawl, which the man said was quite a bargain—only do feel how fine it is."

"Sally!—woman!—a bargain?—twenty thousand pounds!"

Here let me drop the curtain, for none but a master-hand could do justice to the bridegroom's feelings, and I will not impair the effect by attempting to heighten it. I have only to add, that Mr. Fogrum eventually regained his usual composure, and was once known even to relate the story himself over a glass of his best whisky, as a droll anecdote in his life.

Matrimony made no visible alteration in his *menage*, nor in his bride, for the only difference it caused with respect to the latter, was that she sat at table instead of standing by the side-board,—that she was now called Mrs. Fogrum, instead of Sally Sadlins.

Oxford Jokes.—A gentleman entered the room of Dr. Barton, Warden of Merton College, and told him that Dr. Vowel was dead. "What!" said he, "Dr. Vowel dead! thank heaven it was neither U nor I."

Wetheral, the Master of University College, went to Dr. Lee, then sick in bed, and said—"So, Dr. Everleigh has been egged on to matrimony." "Has he?" said he; "why, then, I hope the yoke will sit easy."

A HUSBAND'S VENGEANCE.

A Melting Tale.

BY SHIRLEY BROOKS.

Mrs. Mornington Swale had contrived to get together a very amusing set, but how she had managed it was one of those questions which, if put, indicate the possession of an inquiring rather than a practical mind. For, in the first place, nobody knew, and in the second, nobody cared.

Indeed, the lady herself was a kind of mystery; and if she had not given such very pleasant parties, it is probable that the carelessness we have alluded to might have been superseded by a spirit of interrogation. Her name was in the Court Guide corrected up to April, and that was all. She never talked about her father, or her mother, or any other of the young people mentioned in the long list at the end of the prayer-book, as folks one must not marry; nor did she ever vaunt acquainttance with the Peerage, friendship with the Baronetage, or intimacy with the Landed Commoners, as usual with genteel people of a certain order. When she had a box at the Opera, which happened about three times in the season, she never pretended to know who all the subscribers around her were; and when we add that she insisted on listening to the music instead of chattering during its performance, we shall convince every reader of elegance that she was "not the sort of person to know." Nevertheless, a good many people held an opposite opinion, and proved that they did so, by coming to her parties.

Mrs. Mornington Swale's beauty,—for though not a very young woman, she *was* beautiful—was of the commanding order. Her height, queenly aspect, and glossy black braids, struck terror into the minds of youngish men, and made them very needlessly stammer out greater nonsense than they had intended. Her arrangements were a little despotic, and it was not easy, even if you wished, to escape the partner or the companion to the supper-table whom she had selected for you. Everybody was a little afraid of her, and that is the truth.

Her parties were, as aforesaid, very pleasant. She did not fill her rooms with negative eligibles—men who could only dress, and women who could only simper. She always infused a large quantity of character into her reunions;—not that the individuals were much in themselves, but in the aggregate they gave a tone to the party. We used to meet a popular actor or two—generally dull creatures enough, who spent the evening in alternately droning and snarling upon dramatic matters. We had authors—small authors, but still men who occasionally rushed into print, and wished to be thought eccentric, and usually got tipsy at supper. We had very small poets, who utterly disbelieved in Byron and Moore, but believed a little in one another, and violently in themselves, and wrote stumbling odes about skipping-ropes and public executions. We had second-rate concert singers, chiefly with stubby fingers, who contributed greatly to the harmony of the evening, and sneered in corners at each other's performance. We had a few young barristers, who, by way of advertising their profession, mangled over every thing with much elaborateness of manner, and blocked up the doorways, and talked about "moot points," to the discomfiture of the listeners. And there was a fat German Count, who always came, aud who had moustaches and a very pensive expression, and was greatly addicted to declaring that he wanted something to love him. Now, when the usual litter of a ball-room is diversified with shreds and patches such as we have mentioned, there is sure to be some fun; and our opinion is, that fun is better than formality, any day in the week.

But *apropos* of days in the week, it was a curious fact that there was certain days on which Mrs. Mornington Swale was never at home; never was seen out, and never gave a party. And this was brought to our minds by the extraordinary incident which we are about to relate.

Mrs. Mornington had assembled one of the very best of her parties. There was an excellent show of pretty faces, and an acre or so of white waistcoats, and much polking. The actors were there, grumbling, and the authors were putting themselves in mild attitudes, and the poets were gazing sternly at nothing, and the singers were looking spiteful, and the barristers were squabbling outside the door, and the fat German Count was telling a young lady, with a Norma wreath, that he wanted somebody to love him. The evening was going off remarkably well, and a large double quadrille had just been formed. Mrs. Mornington Swale was standing up, at the top, with a very indifferent young poet, who would have made a very invaluable scarecrow.

We were just going to begin *La Poule*, when a very loud voice was heard in the hall, announcing that somebody, whose lungs were clearly in excellent order, was determined to come up stairs. And presently a group of the barristers was scattered forward into the room, and rushing after them, and into the very centre of the quadrille, came a very short, very stout, and very sturdy man, in the dirtiest dress ever seen, his brawny arms bared to the elbows, and his whole apparel saturated with grease. He glared round upon us all—the effect was dramatic. Nobody remembered to faint, an oversight for which several young ladies never forgave themselves. Mrs. Mornington Swale stood petrified.

"Now, *Sue*," said the stranger, confronting her. "Now, Sue." And this to *her!* Some of us half expected that he would be annihilated. But she continued aghast.

"Mark my words, Sue," continued the unknown, suddenly seating himself on the carpet, with a bang which made the lustres rattle, "I told you that if ever you dared to stay away from me on a melting-day, I'd come for you myself. Now you come along. I've got a cab."

He scrambled from the floor, and seized her by the wrist. Since the abduction of Don Juan by the statue, there never was so appalling a situation. But, apparently stupified, Mrs. Mornington Swale silently yielded. They disappeared together, without further explanation.

But we agreed that though we had lost our hostess, there would be no sense in losing our time.

So the German Count and the young lady with the Norma wreath stood up in the place of the departed. The quadrille was danced, and so were other quadrilles, and supper was eaten, and all went merrily—so merrily, that the German Count was discovered at six in the morning, endeavoring to make a lamp-post in Bedford Square admit that he wanted somebody to love him. But Mrs. Mornington Swale is as much a mystery as ever, and what is worse, she has given no more parties.

ST. MICHAEL'S EVE.

BY EDMOND H. YATES.

I WILL tell to you a story, for in winter time we bore ye
With many an ancient legend and tale of bygone time;
And methinks that there is in it enough to pass a minute,
So, to add to my vain glory, I have put it into rhyme.

As I heard it you shall hear it,—by one whom I revere, it
Was told me, as in childhood upon his knee I sat.
It treats of days long vanished,—of the times of James the Banished,
Of periwig and rapier, and quaint three-cornered hat.

Sir Walter Ralph de Guyon, of a noble house the scion,
Though his monarch was defeated, still held bravely to his cause,
And foremost in the slaughter by the Boyne's ill-fated water
Was seen his knightly cognizance,—a bear with bloody paws.

But when the fight was over, escaping under cover
Of the darkness and confusion, to England he returned,
As well might be expected, dispirited, dejected,
But his rage within him smouldered, nor ever brightly burned.

Save when his daughter Alice would say in playful malice,
That she loved the gallant Orange much better than the Green;
And that as a maid she'd tarry, till she found a chance to marry
With one true to William, her bold king, and Mary, her good queen.

Then Sir Walter's brow would darken, and he'd mutter, "Alice, hearken,
By *my* child no such treason shall be spoken e'en in jest;
And bethink you, oh, my daughter! there is one across the water
Who shall one day have his own again, though now he's sore distressed."

Little knew he that each even, 'twixt the hours of six and seven,
Just below his daughter's casement a whistle low was blown;

And that soon as e'er it sounded through the wicket-gate she bounded,
And was clasped in the embrace of one of bold "King William's Own."

Ay! De Ruyter was a gentleman, and high-bred were his people;
No chapel-going folks were they, but loved a church and steeple!
His blood, of every good Dutch race contained a little sprinkle—
A Knickerbocker was his sire, his aunt a Rip Van Winkle;
And so well he danced and sang, and kissed and talked so wondrous clever,
He gave this maiden's heart a twist, and conquer'd it for ever!
And being thus a captain gay, "condemned to country quarters,"
A favorite of his royal lord, adorned with stars and garters,
He saw this young maid,
As one day on parade
He was gaily attired, all jackboots and braid.
He stared, she but glanced,
Her charms it enhanced;
She passed him quickly, he rested entranced!
No orders he utters,
But vacantly mutters
(Though clamoring round him his underlings gabble hard),
"She's to me Eloisa; to her I'll be Abelard!"

And ever since that hour, whene'er he had the power,
Across to bold Sir Walter's the captain bent his path;
At the garden-gate he met her—upon his knee he set her—
And, vanquished by the daughter's love, forgot the father's wrath:

Till when on the day in question, with a view to aid digestion,
Some retainers of Sir Walter, who with their lord had dined,
Bethought of promenading, what by Gamp is called the "garding,"
And, during their researches, what think ye they should find?

But a gallant captain kneeling, and apparently appealing,
To a dame who, to all seeming, was encouraging his suit;
All dishevelled were her tresses by the warmth of his caresses,
And her eye with love was *liquid*, although her voice was *mute!*

"A prize! a prize!" quoth these Papist spies,—
"A prize for our gallant lord!"
And before poor De Ruyter awoke from surprise
They had pinioned his arms, they had bandaged his eyes;
And when he recovered, his first surmise
Was "At length, I am thoroughly floored!"
For assistance he calls, but they gag him,
And off to Sir Walter they drag him;
While Abraham Cooper,
A stalwart old trooper,
Expresses a hope that they'll "scrag" him.
He conceives it "a pretty idea, as
To think that these Dutch furrineerers
Should come here a-courtin',
On our manors sportin';
A set of young winkers and leerers!"

Sir Walter's brow grew black as night,
He doubted if he heard aright;
"What, to *my* daughter kneeling *here!*
Methinks thou'rt daring, cavalier,
To venture 'neath the gripe of one
Whose ancient race, from sire to son,
Has ever, e'en in face of death,
Upheld that pure and holy faith
By thee and thine denied!
Or think'st thou that, to bow the knee
And whisper words of gallantry
To one of English blood and birth,
Were pastime meet for hour of mirth?
God's life! before to-morrow's sun
Gilds yonder wood, thy race is run;
Nought care I for thy foreign king,
From yon tall oak thy corpse shall swing,
Let good or ill betide!"

Away he is hurried,
All worried and flurried,
And locked in a chamber, dark, dirty, and small.
Huge barriers of iron
The windows environ,
And the door leads but into the banqueting-hall.
The banqueting-hall is soon gaily lit up,
For Sir Walter loved dearly a well-filled cup,
And sent to invite
Each guest that night,
With "Where you have dined, boys, why there you shall sup."

In the banqueting-hall,
Both great and small,
The cavalier knights, the retainers tall,
Together are gathered—one and all.

The red wine has flowed and taken effect
On all, save poor Alice, who, *distraite*, deject,
Has refused to take part in this riotous revel,
And wished those who did with the—Father of Evil.

The mirth was at its loudest, the humblest and the proudest
Were hobnobbing together, as though the dearest friends;
While some for wine were bawling, there were others loudly calling
For a song,—that ancient fiction which e'er to misery tends;

When Sir Walter grasped the table—rose, as well as he was able—
And entreated for a moment that his guests would give him heed:
"'Tis St. Michael's Eve,—a time accursed by a crime
Committed by my ancestor—a ruthless, bloody deed!

"For during times of danger, a sable-armored stranger
One night had roused the castle, and shelter had implored;
Much gold, he said, he carried, and now too late had tarried,
To risk the chance of robbers, or to cross the neighboring ford.

"He was shown into a bedroom, since that period called the Red Room,
(You can see it," said Sir Walter, "for yonder is the door;
And there, in our safe keeping, the Dutchman now is sleeping);
And from that room the stranger never, never issued more.

"But throughout this ancient castle, each terror-stricken vassal
Heard shriek on shriek resounding in the middle of the night;
And with the dawn of morning would each have 'given warning,'
But for one little obstacle yclept the 'feudal right.'

"So no murm'ring e'er was uttered, and old Sir Brandreth muttered
That his visitor had left him as soon as break of day;
But one thing worth attention Sir Brandreth *didn't* mention,—
He didn't take his armor; there in the room it lay.

"And there it lies at present; but each credulous old peasant
Will tell you that upon this night the spectre walks abroad;
'Tis just about his hour, if he really have the power,
We now shall see him. Heavens! he enters, by the Lord!"

Bang! clash!
With a terrible crash,
Flies open the bedroom door;
And out stalks a figure,
To their eyes much bigger
Than great Gog or Magog, more black than a nigger,
In armor accoutred from head to heel,—
Black rusty old armor, not polished steel.
His vizor is down, but he takes a sight,
Though he moves not his eyes to the left or right;
He says not a word, but he walks straight on,
The hall doors ope at his step! he's gone!
He clanks 'cross the court-yard, and enters the stable;
His footsteps are heard by the guests 'neath the table,
For there they have hidden them every one.

There, shivering and shaking, they waited till the breaking
Of the daylight showed the power of all ghosts was at an end;
Then one by one uprising, declared it was surprising
That, overcome by liquor, each had dropped down by his friend;

Till the heart of each was lightened by finding that as frightened
As he himself were all by the spiritual sight;
But their courage and their strength coming back to them at length,
They hasten to the prisoner's room, and find it vacant quite!

Yes! De Ruyter had departed! for while lying all downhearted,
And thinking of poor Alice, he remembered just in time
The spectre-walking legend—he had heard it from a "peagant"
(Excuse the Gampism, reader, but I use it for the rhyme);

And on the instant bright'ning, he proceeded, quick as lightning,
To dress him in the armor which the sable knight had left;
And he listened to the host, till, at mention of the ghost,
He burst upon the drinkers, of their senses nigh bereft.

He called Alice to the stable; then, as fast as he was able,
Galloped off towards his quarters; thence to London hastened on;
There was married to his charmer, thence sent back the sable armor,
And asked Sir Walter's sanction to the good deed he had done.

My tale is nearly ended. Sir Walter, much offended
At the hoax played off upon him, would not listen for awhile;
But regretting much his daughter, came at length to town and sought her,
For he missed her childish prattle and her fond endearing smile.

And then, on this occasion, a grand reconciliation
He had with young De Ruyter—ever after they were friends.
So having now related the tale to me as stated,
I take my humble leave of you, and here my story ends.

"WHO MILKED MY COW?" OR, THE MARINE GHOST.

BY EDWARD HOWARD, R. N.

Captain the honorable Augustus Fitzroy Fitzalban, of that beautiful ship his Majesty's frigate Nænia, loved many things. The first lieutenant, the doctor, the marine officer, the officer and the midshipman of the morning watch, had all assembled to breakfast in the cabin. They had not forgotten their appetites, particularly the gentlemen of the morning watch. They were barbarous and irate in their hunger, as their eyes wandered over cold fowl and ham, hot rolls, grilled kidneys, and devilled legs of turkey.

"By all the stars in heaven," said the honorable commander, "no milk again this morning! Give me, you rascally steward," continued the captain, "a plain, straightforward, categorical answer. Why does this infernal cow, for which I gave such a heap of dollars, give me no milk?"—"Well, sir," said the trembling servitor; "if, sir, you must have a plain answer, I really—believe—it is—because—I don't know."

"A dry answer," said the doctor, who was in most senses a dry fellow.

"You son of a shotten herring!" said the captain, "can you milk her?"—"Yes, sir."

"Then why, in the name of all that is good, don't you?"—"I do, sir, but it won't come."

"Then let us go," said the captain, quite resignedly, "let us go, gentlemen, and see what ails this infernal cow; I can't eat my breakfast without milk, and breakfast is the meal that I generally enjoy most."

So he, leading the way, was followed by his company, who cast many a longing, lingering look behind.

Forward they went to where the cow was *stalled* by capstan-bars, as comfortably as a prebendary, between two of the guns on the maindeck. She seemed in excellent condition; ate her nutritious food with much appetite; and, from her appearance, the captain might have very reasonably expected, not only an ample supply of milk and cream for breakfast and tea, but also a sufficient quantity to afford him custards for dinner.

Well, there stood the seven officers of his Majesty's naval service round the arid cow, looking very like seven wise men just put to sea in a bowl.

"Try again," said the captain to his servant. If the attempt had been only fruitless, there had been no matter for wonder; it was milkless.

"The fool can't milk," said the captain; then turning round to his officers despondingly, he exclaimed, "gentlemen, can any of you?"

Having all protested that they had left off, some thirty, some forty, and some fifty years, according to their respective ages, and the marine officer saying that he never had had any practice at all, having been brought up by hand, the gallant and disappointed hero was obliged to order the boatswain's mates to pass the word fore and aft, to send every one to him who knew how to milk a cow.

Seventeen Welshmen, sixty-five Irishmen, (all on board,) and four lads from Somersetshire made their appearance, moistened their fingers, and set to work, one after the other; yet there was no milk.

"What do you think of this, doctor?" said the captain to him, taking him aside.

"That the animal has been milked a few hours before."

"Hah! If I was sure of that. And the cow could have been milked only by some one who *could* milk?"

"The inference seems indisputable."

The captain turned upon the numerous aspirants for lacteal honors with no friendly eye, exclaiming sorrowfully, "Too many to flog, too many to flog. Let us return to our breakfast; though I shall not be able to eat a morsel or drink a drop. Here, boatswain's mate, pass the word round the ship that I'll give five guineas reward to any one who will tell me who milked the captain's cow."

The gentlemen then all retired to the cabin, and, with the exception of the captain, incontinently fell upon the good things. Now, the midshipman of that morning's watch was a Mr. Littlejohn, usually abbreviated into Jack Small. When Jack Small had disposed of three hot rolls, half a fowl, and a

pound of ham, and was handing in his plate for a well devilled turkey's thigh, his eye fell compassionately upon his fasting captain, and his heart opening to the softer emotions as his stomach filled with his host's delicacies, the latter's want of the milk of the cow stirred up within him his own milk of human kindness.

"I am very sorry that you have no appetite," said Jack Small, with his mouth very full, and quite protectingly, to his skipper; "very sorry, indeed, sir; and, as you cannot make your breakfast without any milk, I think, sir, that the midshipmen's berth could lend you a bottle."

"The devil they can, younker. Oh, oh! It's good and fresh, hey?"

"Very good and fresh, sir," said the midshipman, ramming down the words with a large wadding of hot roll.

"We must borrow some of it, by all means," said the captain; "but let the midshipmen's servant bring it here himself."

The necessary orders having been issued, the bottle of milk and the boy appeared.

"Did you know," said Captain Fitzalban, turning to his first lieutenant, "that the midshipmen's berth was provided with milk, and that too after being at sea a month?"—"Indeed I did not; they are better provided than we are, at least in this respect, in the ward-room."

"Do you think,—do you think," said the captain, trembling with rage, "that any of the young blackguards dare milk my cow?"—"It is not easy to say what they dare not do."

However, the cork was drawn, and the milk found not only to be very fresh indeed, but most suspiciously new. In the latitude of the Caribbean Islands, liquids in general are sufficiently warm, so the captain could not lay much stress upon that.

"As fine milk as ever I tasted," said the captain.

"Very good indeed, sir," said the midshipman, overflowing his cup and saucer with the delicious liquid.

"Where do the young gentlemen procure it?" resumed the captain, pouring very carefully what remained after the exactions of John Small into the cream-jug, and moving it close to his own plate.—"It stands us rather dear, sir," said Mr. Littlejohn, —"a dollar a bottle. We buy it of Joe Grummet, the captain of the waisters."

The captain and first lieutenant looked at each other unutterable things.

Joe Grummet was in the cabin in an instant, and the captain bending upon him his sharp and angry glances. Joseph was a sly old file, a seaman to the backbone; and let the breeze blow from what quarter of the compass it would, he had always an eye to windward. Fifty years had a little grizzled his strong black hair, and, though innovation had deprived him of the massive tail that whilom hung behind, there were still some fancy curls that corkscrewed themselves down his weather-stained temples; and, when he stood before the captain, in one of these he hitched the first bend of the immense forefinger of his right hand. He hobbled a little in his gait, owing to an unextracted musket-ball that had lodged in his thigh; consequently he never went aloft, and had been, for his merits and long services, appointed captain of the waist.

The Honorable Augustus Fitzroy Fitzalban said to the veteran mariner quickly, and pointing at the same time to the empty bottle, "Grummet, you have milked my cow!"—"Unpossible, sir!" said Grummet, bobbing at a bow; "downright unpossible, your honor."

"Then, pray, whence comes the fresh milk you sell every morning to the young gentlemen?"—"Please your honor, I took two or three dozen of bottles to sea with me on a kind o' speculation."

"Grummet, my man, I am afraid this will turn out a bad one for you. Go and show your hands to the doctor, and he'll ask you a few questions."

So Joseph Grummet went and expanded his flippers before the eyes of the surgeon. They were nearly as large and as shapely as the fins of a porpoise, and quite of the color. They had been tanned and tarred till their skin had become more durable than boot-leather, and they were quite rough enough to have rasped close-grained wood.

"I don't think our friend could have milked your cow, Captain Fitzalban," said the doctor; "at least, not with his hands: they are rather calculated to draw blood than milk.'

Joseph rolled his eyes about and looked his innocence most pathetically. He was not yet quite out of danger.

Now there was every reason in the world why this cow should give the captain at least a gallon of milk per diem—but one, and that he was most anxious to discover. The cow was in the best condition; since she had been embarked, the weather had been fine enough to have pleased Europa herself; she had plenty of provender, both dry and fresh. There were fragrant clover closely packed in bags, delicious oat-cakes—meal and water, and fine junks of juicy plantain.—The cow throve, but gave no milk!

"So you brought a few dozen bottles of milk to sea with you as a venture?" continued the man of medicine in his examination.—"I did, sir."

"And where did you procure them?"—"At English Harbor, sir."

"May I ask of whom?"—"Madame Juliana, the fat free Negro woman."

"Now, my man," said the doctor, looking a volume and a half of Galen, and holding up a cautionary fore-finger—"now, my man, do not hope to deceive *me*. How did you prevent the acetous fermentation from taking place in these bottles of milk?"

The question certainly was a puzzler. Joe routed with his fingers among his hair for an answer. At length he fancied he perceived a glimmering of the doctor's meaning; so he hummed and ha-ed, until, the doctor's patience being exhausted, he repeated more peremptorily, "How did you prevent acetous fermentation taking place in these bottles of milk?"

"By paying ready money for them, sir," said the badgered seaman, boldly.

"An excellent preventative against fermentation certainly," said the captain, half smiling. "But you answer the doctor like a fool."

"I was never accused of such a thing, please your honor, before, sir," said tarrybrecks, with all his sheets and tacks aboard.

"Very likely, my man, very likely," answered the captain, with a look that would have been invaluable in a vinegar manufactory. "How did you prevent this milk from turning sour?"

"Ah, sir!" said Grummet, now wide awake to his danger: "if you please, sir, I humbly axes your pardon, but that's my secret."

"Then by all that's glorious I'll flog it out of you."

"I humbly hopes not, sir. I am sure your honor wôn't flog an old seaman who has fought with Howe and Nelson, and who was wounded in the sarvice before your honor was born; you won't flog him, sir, only because he can't break his oath."

"So you have sworn not to divulge it, hey?"

"Ah, sir; if I might be so bold as to say so, your honor's a witch!"

"Take care of yourself, Joseph Grummet; I do advise you to take care of yourself. Folly is a great betrayer of secrets, Joseph. Cunning may milk cows without discovery: however, I will never punish without proof. How many bottles of this excellent milk have you yet left?"—"Eight or ten, sir, more or less, according to sarcumstances."

"Well! I will give you a dollar a-piece for all you have."

At this proposition Joseph Grummet shuffled about, not at all at his ease, now looking very sagacious, now very foolish, till, at last, he brought down his features to express the most deprecating humility of which their iron texture was capable, and he then whined forth, "I would not insult you, sir, by treating you all as one as a midshipman. No, your honor: I knows the respect that's due to you, —I couldn't think of letting you, sir, have a bottle under three dollars—it wouldn't be at all respectful like."

"Grummet," said Captain Fitzalban, "you are not only a thorough seaman, but a thorough knave. Now, have you the conscience to make me pay three dollars a bottle for my own milk?"—"Ah, sir, you don't know how much the secret has cost me."

"Nor do you know how dearly it may cost you yet."

Joseph Grummet then brought into the cabin his remaining stock in trade, which, instead of eight or ten, was found to consist only of two bottles. The captain, though with evident chagrin, paid for them honorably; and whilst the milkman *pro temp.* was knotting up the six dollars in the tie of the handkerchief about his neck, the skipper said to him, "Now, my man, since we part such good friends, tell me your candid opinion concerning this cow of mine?"—"Why, sir, I thinks as how it's the good people as milks her."

"The good people, who the devil are they?"—"The fairies, your honor."

"And what do they do with it?"—"Very few can tell, your honor; but those who gets it are always desarving folks."

"Such as old wounded seamen, and captains of the waist especially. Well, go along to your duty. Look out! *cats* love milk."

So Joseph Grummet went forth from the cabin shrugging up his shoulders, with an ominous presentiment of scratches upon them. The captain, the Honorable Augustus Fitzroy Fitzalban, gave the marine officer orders to place a sentry night and day over his cow, and then dismissed his guests.

The honorable commander was, for the rest of the day, in a most unconscionable ill-humor. The ship's sails were beautifully trimmed, the breeze was just what it ought to have been. The heavens above, and the waters below, were striving to outsmile each other. What then made the gallant captain so miserable? He was thinking only of the temerity of the man who had dared to *milk his cow*.

The first lieutenant touched his hat most respectfully to the Honorable Captain Augustus Fitzroy Fitzalban, and acquainted him that the sun indicated it to be twelve o'clock.

"Milk my cow!" said the captain abstractedly.

"Had not that better be postponed till to-morrow morning, Captain Fitzalban?" said the lieutenant, with a very little smile; "and in the mean time may we strike the bell, and pipe to dinner?"

The captain gazed upon the gallant officer sorrowfully, and, as he shook his head, his looks said as plainly as looks could speak, and with the deepest pathos, "They never milked *his* cow."

"Do what is necessary," at last he uttered; then pulling his hat more over his eyes, he continued to pace the quarter-deck.

Now, though the Honorable Captain Augustus Fitzroy Fitzalban was the younger son of a nobleman, and enjoyed a very handsome patrimony, and his temper had been thoroughly spoiled by that process that is too often called education, yet his heart was sound, English, and noble. He revolted from doing an unjust action; yet he smarted dreadfully under the impression that he was cheated and laughed at to his very face. He did not think that Joseph Grummet had milked his cow, but he felt assured that the same milk-dealing Joseph knew who did; yet was he too humane to introduce the Inquisition on board his ship by extracting the truth by torture.

The Honorable Captain Fitzroy Fitzalban slept late on the succeeding morning. He had been called at daylight, *pro forma*, but had merely turned from his left side to his right, muttering something about a cow. It must be supposed that the slumbers of the morning indemnified him for the horrors of the night, for breakfast was on the table, and the usual guests assembled, when the captain emerged from the after-cabin.

There was no occasion to ask the pale and trembling steward if the cow had given any milk that morning.

The breakfast remained untouched by the captain, and passed off in active silence by his guests. Not wishing to excite more of the derision of Jack than was absolutely necessary, the captain, when he found that the various officers whom he had invited to breakfast had sufficiently "improved the occasion," as the methodists say, turned to the first lieutenant, who was again his guest, and asked him if nothing had transpired on the over-night to warrant a suspicion as to the lacteal felony.

The first luff looked very mysterious, and not wholly disposed to be communicative upon the subject. He had been piously brought up, and was not at all inclined to be sarcastic upon the score of visions or the visitation of ghosts; yet, at the same time, he did not wish to subject himself to the ridicule of his captain, who had rationally enough postponed his belief in apparitions until he had seen one. Under these difficulties, he replied hesitatingly, that a ghost had been reported as having "come on board before daylight in the morning, without leave."

"A ghost, Mr. Mitchell, come on board, and I not called!" said the indignant captain: "By heaven, sir, I would have turned out a guard of honor to have received him! I would have sooner had a visit from his spirituality than from his Excellency the Spanish Ambassador.—The service, sir, has come to a pretty pass, when a ghost can come on board, and leave the ship too, I presume, without even so much as the boatswain to pipe the side. So the ghost came, I suppose, and milked my cow?"

The first lieutenant, in answer, spoke with all manner of humility. He represented that he had been educated as a seaman and as an officer, and not for a doctor of divinity; therefore he could not pretend to account for these preternatural visitations. He could only state the fact, and that not so well as the first lieutenant of marines. "He begged, therefore, to refer to him."

That officer was immediately sent for, and he made his appearance accompanied by one of the sergeants, and then it was asserted that, when the guard went round to relieve the sentries, they found the man who had been stationed over the cow, lying on the deck senseless in a fit, and his bayonet could nowhere be found. When by the means of one of the assistant-surgeons, who had been immediately summoned, he had been sufficiently recovered to articulate, all the explanation they could get from him was, that he had seen a ghost; and the very mention of the fact, so great was his terror, had almost caused a relapse.

"Send the poltroon here immediately: I'll ghost him!" cried the enraged captain. In answer to this he was informed, that the man lay seriously ill in his hammock in the sick-bay, and that the doctor was at that very moment with the patient.

"I'll see him myself," said the captain.

As the honorable captain, with his *cortege* of officers, passed along the decks on his way to the sick-bay, he thought—or his sense of hearing most grievously deceived him—that more than once he heard sneering and gibing voices exclaim, "Who milked my cow?" but the moment he turned his head in the direction from whence the sounds proceeded, he saw nothing but visages the most sanctimonious: indeed they, instead of the unfortunate sentry, appeared to have seen the ghost. The captain's amiability that morning might have been expressed by the algebraical term—minus a cipher.

When the skipper hauled alongside the sick man, he found that the doctor, having bled him, was preparing to blister his head, the ship's barber at the time being occupied in very sedulously shaving it. The patient was fast putting himself upon an equality to contend with his supernatural visitant, by making a ghost of himself. He was in a high fever and delirious,—unpleasant things in the West Indies! All the captain could get from him was, "The devil—flashes of fire—milk cow—horrible teeth—devil's cow—ship haunted—nine yards of blue flame—throw cow overboard—go to heaven—kicked the pail down—horns tipped with red-hot iron," and other rhapsodies to the same effect.

From the man the captain went to the cow; but she was looking excessively sleek, and mild, and amiable, and eating her breakfast with the relish of an outside mail-coach passenger. The captain shook his head, and thought himself the most persecuted of beings.

When this self-estimated injured character gained the quarter-deck, he commenced ruminating on the propriety of flogging Joseph Grummet; for, with the loss of his cow's milk, he had lost all due sense of human kindness. But, as the Lords of the Admiralty had lately insisted upon a report being forwarded to them of every punishment that took place, the number of lashes, and the crime for which they were inflicted, the Honorable the Captain Augustus Fitzroy Fitzalban thought that a report would look rather queer running thus: "Joseph Grummet, captain of the waist, six dozen, because my cow gave no milk," or, "because private marine Snickchops saw a ghost," or, "for selling the midshipmen sundry bottles of milk;" and this last imagination reminded him that there was one of this highly-gifted class walking to leeward of him. "Mr. Littlejohn!" said the captain with a voice that crawled over the nerves like the screeching of an ill-filed saw.

Small Jack touched his hat with more than usual respect to the exasperated officer, and then, stepping to windward, humbly confronted him.

The captain was too angry for many words; so, looking fearfully into the happy countenance of the reefer, and pointing his fore-finger down perpendicularly, he laconically uttered, "Milk this morning?" —"Yes, sir."

"Good?"

The well-breakfasted midshipman licked his lips, and smiled.

"Grummet?"—"Yes, sir."

"Tell the boatswain's mate to send him aft."—"Ay, ay, sir."

All that forenoon, the captain kept officers and men exercising the great guns, running them in and out, pointing them here and there;—sail-trimmers aloft—boarders on the starboard bow—firemen down in the fore-hold: the men had not a moment's respite, nor the officers either. How potently in their hearts they d——d the cow, even from the tips of her horns unto the tuft at the end

of her tail. Five secret resolves were made to poison her that hard-worked morning. Mr. Small Jack, who was stationed at the foremast main-deck guns near her, gave her a kick every time the order came from the quarter-deck to ram home wad and shot.

And there stood the captain of the waist, with his hat in his hand, opposite to the captain of the ship. There was some difference between those two captains:—one verging upon old age, the other upon manhood. The old man with but two articles of dress upon his person, a canvas shirt and a canvass pair of trousers,—for in those latitudes shoes and stockings are dispensed with by the foremast men, excepting on Sundays and when mustering at divisions; the other gay, and and almost gorgeous, in white jeans, broadcloth, and gold. There they stood, the one the personification of meekness, the other of haughty anger. However firm might have been the captain's intentions to convict the man before him by an intricate cross-examination, his warmth of temper defeated them at once, for the old seaman looked more than usually innocent and sheepish. This almost stolid equanimity was sadly provoking

"You insolent scoundrel!—who milked my cow last night?"—"The Lord in heaven knows, your honor. Who could it be, sir, without it was the ghost who has laid that poor lad in his sick hammock?"

"And I suppose that the ghost ordered you to hand the milk to the young gentlemen when he had done?"—"Me, sir! Heaven save me! I never se'ed a ghost in my life."

"Hypocrite! the bottle you sold the midshipmen!"—"One your honor, I brought from Antigua, and which I overlooked yesterday."

"I shall not overlook it when I get you to the gangway. Go, Mr. Littlejohn, give orders to beat to quarters the moment the men have had their time."

Well, this sweltering work, under a tropical sun, proceeded till noon, the captain alternately swearing at the officers for want of energy, and exclaiming to himself indignantly, "How dare they milk my cow! There must be several concerned. Send the carpenter aft. Mr. Wedge, rig both the chain-pumps,—turn the water on in the well. Waisters! man the pumps. Where's that Grummet? Boatswain's mates, out with your colts and lay them over the shoulders of any man that shirks his duty: keep a sharp eye on the captain of the waist."

And thus the poor fellows had, for a finish to their morning's labor, a half-hour of the most overpowering exertion to which you can set mortal man,—that of working at the chain-pumps. When Mr. Littlejohn saw elderly Joseph Grummet stripped to the waist, the perspiration streaming down him in bucketfuls, and panting as it were for his very life, he, the said Small Jack, very rightly opined that no milk would be forthcoming next morning.

At noon the men were as usual piped to dinner, with an excellent appetite for their pork and pease, and a thirsty relish for their grog; for which blessings they had the cow alone to thank. They were very ungrateful.

No sooner was the hour of dinner over than the captain all of a sudden discovered that his ship's company were not smart enough in reefing top-sails. So at it they went, racing up and down the rigging, tricing up and laying out, lowering away and hoisting, until six bells, three o'clock, when the angry and hungry captain went to his dinner. He had made himself more unpopular in that day than any other commander in the fleet.

The dinner was unsocial enough. When a man is not satisfied with himself, it is rarely that he is satisfied with any body else. Now the whole ship's company, officers as well as men, were divided into parties, and only two, respecting this affair of the cow; one believed in a supernatural, the other in a roguish agency; in numbers they were about equal, so that the captain stood in the pleasant predicament of being looked upon in a sinful light by one half of his crew, and in a ludicrous one by the other.

However, as the night advanced, and the marine who had seen the cow-spirit grew worse, the believers in the supernatural increased rapidly; and, as one sentinel was found unwilling to go alone, the cow had the distinguished compliment of a guard of honor of two all night. The captain, with a scornful defiance of the spiritual, would allow of no lights to be shown, or of no extraordinary precautions to be taken. He only signified his intentions of having himself an interview with the ghost, and for that purpose he walked the deck till midnight; but the messenger from the land of spirits did not choose to show himself so early.

Let me hear no more any querulous talk of the labor of getting butter to one's bread—no person could have toiled more than the Honorable Captain Augustus Fitzroy Fitzalban to get milk for his breakfast.

The two sentries were relieved at twelve o'clock, and, for a quarter of an hour after, every thing remaining dark and quiet about the haunted cow, the captain went below and turned in, joyfully anticipative of milk and cream in the morning. He left, of course, the most positive orders that the moment the ghost appeared, he should be called.

Mr. Mitchell, the pious first lieutenant, remained on deck, determined to see the sequel; told the master he was much troubled in spirit, and he thought, with all due deference to the articles of war, and respect for the captain, that he was little better than an infidel, and an over bold tempter of God's providence. The master remarked in reply, that it was an affair entirely out of soundings; but very sagely concluded that they should see what they should see, even if they saw nothing.

It was a beautiful night—darkly, yet, at the same time, brightly beautiful. There was no moon. The pure fires above were like scintillations from the crown of God's glory. Though the heavens were thus starred with splendors, it was deeply, though clearly, dark on the ocean. There was a gentle breeze that was only sufficient to make the sails draw, and the noble frigate walked stately, yet majestically onwards.

Forward on the main-deck the darkness was Cimmerian. When lights had been last there, at the relieving of the sentinels, the cow had laid herself quietly down upon her litter, and seemed to be in a profound sleep; the first hour after midnight was passed, and all was hushed as death, save those noises that indicate what else would be absolute silence more strongly. There was the whispering ripple of the sea, the dull creaking of the tiller-ropes, and the stealthy step of the sentinels: these sounds, and these only, were painfully distinct. One bell struck, and its solemn echoes seemed to creep through the decks as if on some errand of death, and the monotonous cry of the look-outs fell drearily on the ear.

The first lieutenant and the officers of the watch had just begun to shake off their dreamy and fearful impressions, to breathe more freely, and to walk the deck with a firmer tread, when, from what was supposed to be the haunted spot, a low shriek was heard, then a bustle, followed by half-stifled cries of "The guard! the guard!"

The officers of the watch jumped down on to the main-deck, the midshipmen rushed into the cabin to call the captain, and men with and without lights rushed forward to the rescue.

Deep in the darkness of the manger, there glared an apparition that might more than justify the alarm. The spot where the phantom was seen, (we pledge ourselves that we are relating facts,) was that part of a frigate which seamen call "the eyes of her," directly under the foremost part of the forecastle, where the cables run through the hawse-holes, and through which the bowsprit trends upwards. The whole place is called the manger. It is very often appropriated to the use of pigs, until they take their turn for the butcher's knife. This was the strange locality that the ghost chose to honor with its dreadful presence.

From the united evidences of the many who saw this ghastly avatar, it appeared only to have thrust its huge head and a few feet of the forepart of its body through the hawse-hole, the remainder of its vast and voluminous tail hanging out of the ship over its bows. The frightful head and the glaring sockets of its eyes were distinctly marked in lineaments of fire. Its jaws were stupendous, and its triple row of sharp and long-fanged teeth seemed to be gnashing for something mortal to devour. It cast a pale blue halo of light around it, just sufficient to show the outlines of the den it had selected in which to make its unwelcome appearance. Noise it made none, though several of the spectators fancied that they heard a gibbering of unearthly sounds; and Mr. Littlejohn swore the next day upon his John Hamilton Moore, that it mooed dolefully like a young bullock crossed in love.

To describe the confusion on the main-deck, whilst officers, seamen, and marines were gazing on this spectre, so like the fiery spirit of the Yankee sea-serpent, is a task from which I shrink, knowing that language cannot do it adequately. The first lieutenant stood in the middle of the group, not merely transfixed, but paralysed with fear; men were tumbling over each other, shouting, praying, swearing. Up from the dark holds, like shrouded ghosts, the watch below, in their shirts, sprang from their hammocks; and for many, one look was enough, and the head would vanish immediately in the dark profound. The shouting for lights, and loaded muskets and pistols was terrible; and the orders to advance were so eagerly reiterated, that none had leisure to obey them.

But the cow herself did not present the least imposing feature in this picture of horror. She formed, as it were, the barrier between mortality and spirituality—all beyond her was horrible and spectral; by her fright she seemed to acknowledge the presence of a preternatural being. Her legs were stiff and extended, her tail standing out like that of an angered lion, and she kept a continued strain upon the halter with which she was tethered to a ring-bolt in the ship's side.

By this time, several of the ward-room officers, and most of the midshipmen, had reached the scene of action. Pistols were no longer wanting, and loaded ones too. Three shots were fired into the manger, with what aim it is impossible to specify, at the spectre. They did not seem to annoy his ghostship in the least; without an indication of his beginning to grow hungry might be deemed so. As the shot whistled past him, he worked his huge and fiery jaws most ravenously.

"Well," said the second lieutenant, "let us give the gentleman another shot, and then come to close quarters. Mr. Mitchell you have a pistol in your hand: fire!"

"In the name of the Holy Trinity!" said the superstitious first; "there!" Bang! and the shot took effect deep in the loins of the unfortunate cow.

At this precise moment, Captain the Honorable Augustus Fitzroy Fitzalban rushed from his cabin forward, attired in a rich flowered silk morning-gown, in which scarlet predominated. He held a pistol cocked in each hand; and, as he broke through the crowd, he bellowed forth lustily, "Where's the ghost? let me see the ghost!" He was soon in the van of the astonished gazers; but, disappointed Fitzalban! he saw no ghost, because, as the man says in the Critic, "'twas not in sight."

Immediately the honorable captain had gained his station, the much wronged and persecuted cow, galled by her wound, with a mortal effort snapped the rope with which she was fastened, and then, lowering her horned head nearly level with the deck, and flourishing her tail after the manner that an Irishman flourishes his shillelah before he commences occipital operations, she rushed upon the crowded phalanx before her. At this instant, as if its supernatural mission had been completed, the spirit vanished.

The ideal having decamped, those concerned had to save themselves from the well followed up assaults of the real. The captain flew before the pursuing horns, d—ning the cow in all the varieties of condemnation. But she was generous, and she attached herself to him with an unwonted, or rather an unwanted, fidelity. Lanterns were crushed and men overthrown, and laughter now arose amidst the shouts of dismay. The seamen tried to impede the progress of the furious animal by throwing down before her lashed-up hammocks, and by seizing her behind by the tail: but, woe is me! the Honorable the Captain Augustus Fitzroy Fitzalban could not run so fast in his variegated and scarlet flowered silk dressing-gown as a cow in the agonies of death; for he had just reached that asylum of safety, his cabin door, when the cow took him up very carefully with her horns, and first giving him a monitory shake, then with an inclination to port, she tossed him right over the ward-room sky-light, and deposited him very gingerly in the turtle-tub that stood lashed on the larboard side of the half-deck. This exertion was her last; for immediately after falling upon her knees, and then gently rolling over, to use an Homeric expression, her soul issued from her wound, and sought the shades below appropriated to the souls of cows.

In the mean time, the captain was sprawling about, and contending with his turtle for room, and he stood a very good chance of being drowned even in a tub; but assistance speedily arriving, he was drawn out, and thus the world was spared a second tale of a tub. But there was something in the spirit of the aristocratic Fitzalban that neither cows, ghosts, nor turtle-haunted water could subdue. Wet as he was, and suffering also from the contusions of the cow's horns, he immediately ordered more light, and proceeded to search for the ghost,—prolific parent of all his mishaps.

Well escorted, he visited the manger, but the most scrutinizing search could discover nothing extraordinary. The place seemed to have been undisturbed, nor once to have departed from its usual solitariness and dirt. There was not even so much as a smell of sulphur on the spot where the spectre had appeared, nor were there any signs of wet, which, supposing the thing seen had been a real animal, would have been the case, had it come from the sea through one of the hawse-holes. The whole affair was involved in the most profound mystery. The honorable captain, therefore, came to the conclusion that nothing whatever had appeared, and that the whole was the creation of cowardice.

Hot with rage, and aguish with cold, he retired to his cabin, vowing all manner of impossible vengeance, muttering about court-martials, and solemnly protesting that Mr. Mitchell, the first lieutenant, should pay him for the cow that he had so wantonly shot.

Blank were the countenances of many the next morning. The first lieutenant was not, as usual, asked to breakfast. There was distrust and division in his Majesty's ship Nænia, and the Honorable the Captain Augustus Fitzroy Fitzalban had several severe contusions on his noble person, a bad cold, and no milk for breakfast; an accumulation of evils that one of the aristocracy ought not to be obliged to bear. Though Mr. Mitchell did not breakfast with the captain, Jack Small, alias Small Jack, alias Mr. Littlejohn, did. The only attempt of the captain that morning at conversation was as follows. With a voice that croaked like a raven's at the point of death, evidence *externe* of an abominable sore-throat, the captain merely said to the reefer, pointing his forefinger downwards, as he did the day before, "*Milk?*"

Mr. Littlejohn shook his head dolefully, and replied, "No, sir."

"My cow died last night," said the afflicted commander, with a pathos that would have wrung the heart of a stone statue—if it could have heard it.

"If you please, sir," said the steward, "Mr. Mitchell sends his compliments, and would be very glad to know what you would have done with the dead cow."—"My compliments to Mr. Mitchell, and *he* may do whatever he likes with it. He shot it, and must pay me for it: let him eat it if he will."

The first lieutenant and the captain were, after this, not on speaking terms for three months. Several duels had very nearly been fought about the ghost; those who had not seen it, branding those who had with an imputation only a little short of cowardice; those who had seen it, becoming for a few weeks very religious, and firmly resolving henceforward to get drunk only in pious company. The carcase of the cow was properly dressed and cut up, but few were found who would eat of it; the majority of the seamen thinking that the animal had been bewitched: the captain, of course, would take none of it, unless Mr. Mitchell would permit him to pay him for it at so much per pound, as he pertinaciously pretended to consider it to be the property of the first lieutenant. Consequently, the animal was nearly shared between the midshipmen's berth and the mess of which Joseph Grummet, the captain of the waist, was an unworthy member.

The day following the death of the cow, Joseph Grummet was found loitering about the door of the young gentlemen's berth.

"Any milk to-morrow, Joseph?" said the caterer.—"No, sir," with a most sensible shake of the head.

"Oh!—the cow has given up the ghost!"—"*And somebody else too!*" This simple expression seemed to have much relieved Joe's overcharged bosom: he turned his quid in his mouth with evident satisfaction, grinned, and was shortly after lost in the darkness forward.

There never yet was a ghost story that did not prove a very simple affair when the key to it was found. The captain of the Nænia never would believe that any thing uncommon was ever seen at all. He was, however, as much in the wrong as those who believed that they had seen a ghost. The occurrence could not be forgotten, though it ceased to be talked of.

Two years after, the ship came to England, and was paid off. Joseph Grummet bagged his notes and his sovereigns with much satisfaction; but he did not jump like a fool into the first boat, and rush ashore to scatter his hard-earned wages among Jews, and people still worse: he stayed till the last man, and anxiously watched for the moment when the pennant should be hauled down. When he saw this fairly done, he asked leave to speak to the captain. He was ushered into the cabin, and he there saw many of the officers who were taking leave of their old commander.

"Well, Grummet," said the skipper, "what now?"

"Please your honor, you offered five guineas to anybody who would tell you who milked the cow."

"And so I will gladly," said the captain, pleasantly, "if the same person will unravel the mystery of the ghost." And he turned a triumphant look upon the believers in spirits who stood around him.

"I milked your cow, sir."

"Ah! Joseph, Joseph! it was unkindly done. But with your hands?"—"We widened a pair of Mr. Littlejohn's kid-gloves, sir."

"I knew that little rascal was at the bottom of it! but there is honor in the midshipmen's berth still. What is the reason that they thus sought to deprive me of my property?"—"You wouldn't allow them to take any live stock on board that cruise, sir."

"So—so—wild justice, hey? But come to the ghost."—"Why, sir, I wanted to have the cow unwatched for a quarter of an hour every middle watch; so I took the shark's head we had caught a day or two before, scraped off most of the flesh, and whipped it in a bread-bag,—it shone brighter in the dark than stinking mackerel:—so I whips him out when I wants him, and wabbles his jaws about. I was safely stowed under the bowsprit from your shot; and when your honor walked in on one side of the manger, I walked, with my head under my arm, out of the other."

"Well, Joseph, there are your five guineas: and, gentlemen," said the Honorable the Captain Augustus Fitzroy Fitzalban, bowing to his officers, "I wish you joy of your ghost!"

BOXIANA.

ANON.

I HATE the very name of *box;*
It fills me full of fears;
It minds me of the woes I've felt,
Since I was young in years.

They sent me to a Yorkshire school,
Where I had many knocks;
For there my schoolmates *box'd* my ears,
Because I couldn't box.

I pack'd my *box;* I pick'd the locks,
And ran away to sea;
And very soon I learnt to *box*
The compass merrily.

I came ashore—I call'd a coach,
And mounted on the *box;*
The coach upset against a post,
And gave me dreadful knocks.

I soon got well; in love I fell,
And married Martha Cox;
To please her will at fam'd *Box* Hill,
I took a country *box.*

I had a pretty garden there,
All border'd round with *box;*
But, ah, alas! there liv'd next door,
A certain Captain Knox.

He took my wife to see the play;—
They had a private *box:*
I jealous grew, and from that day,
I hated Captain Knox.

I sold my house,—I left my wife;
And went to Lawyer Fox,
Who tempted me to seek redress
All from a jury *box.*

I went to law, whose greedy maw
Soon emptied my strong *box;*
I lost my suit, and cash to boot,
All thro' that crafty Fox.

The name of *box* I therefore dread,
I've had so many shocks;
They'll never end,—for when I'm dead,
They'll nail me in a *box.*

THE LAST STAGE COACHMAN.

BY W. WILKIE COLLINS.

HE Last Stage Coachman! It falls upon the ear of every one but a shareholder in railways, with a boding, melancholy sound. In spite of our natural reverence for the wonders of science, our hearts grow heavy at the thought of never again beholding the sweet-smelling nosegay, the unimpeachable top-boots, and fair white breeches; once so prominent as the uniform of the fraternity. With all our respect for expeditious and business-like travelling, we experience a feeling nearly akin to disgust, at being marshalled to our places by a bell and a fellow with a badge on his shoulder; instead of hearing the cheery summons "Now then, gentlemen," and being regaled by a short and instructive conversation with a ruddy-faced personage in a dustless olive-green coat and prismatic belcher handkerchief. What did we want with smoke? Had we not the coachman's cigar, if we were desirous of observing its shapes and appearances? Who would be so unreasonable as to languish for steam, when he could inhale it on a cool, autumnal morning, naturally concocted from the backs of four blood horses? Who!—Alas! we may propose questions and find out answers to the end of the chapter, and yet fail in reforming the perverted taste of the present generation; we know that the attempt is useless, and we give up in sorrowful and philosophic resignation, and proceed undaunted by the probable sneers of railway directors, to the recital of—

A VISION.

Methought I walked forth one autumn evening, to observe the arrival of a stage coach. I wandered on, yet nothing of the kind met my eye. I tried many an old public road—they were now grass-grown and miry, or desecrated by the abominable presence of a "station." I wended my way towards a famous roadside inn: it was desolate and silent, or in other words, "To Let." I looked for "the commercial room:" not a pot of beer adorned the mouldering tables, and not a pipe lay scattered over the wild and beautiful seclusions of its once numerous "boxes." It was deserted and useless; the voice of the traveller rung no longer round its walls, and the merry horn of the guard startled no more the sleepy few, who once congregated round its hospitable door. The chill fire-place and broad, antiquated mantel-piece, presented but one bill—the starting time of an adjacent railroad; surmounted by a representation of those engines of destruction, in dull, frowsy lithograph.

I turned to the yard. Where was the ostler with his unbraced breeches and his upturned shirt sleeves? Where was the stable boy with his wisp of straw and his sieve of oats? Where were the coquettish mares and the tall blood horses? Where was the manger and the stable door?—All gone—all disappeared; the buildings dilapidated and tottering—of what use is a stable to a stoker? The ostler and the stable boy had passed

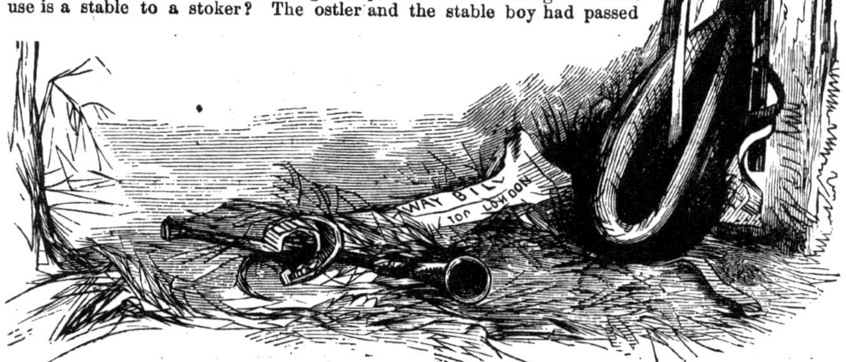

away—what fellowship have either with a boiler? *The inn yard was no more!* The very dunghill in its farthest corner was choked by dust and old bricks; and the cock, the pride of the country round, clamored no longer on the ruined and unsightly wall. I thought it was possible that he had satisfied long since the cravings of a railway committee; and I sat down on a ruined water-tub to give way to the melancholy reflections called up by the sight before me.

I know not how long I meditated. There was no officious waiter to ask me, "What I would please to order?" No chambermaid to simper out, "This way, Sir,"—not even a stray cat to claim acquaintance with the calves of my legs, or a horse's hoof to tread upon my toe. There was nothing to disturb my miserable reverie, and I anathematized railways without distinction or exception.

The distant sound of slow and stealthy footsteps at last attracted my attention. I looked to the far end of the yard. Heavens above! a stage coachman was pacing its worn and weedy pavement.

There was no mistaking him—he wore the low-crowned, broad-brimmed, whitey-brown, well-brushed hat; the voluminous checked neckcloth; the ample-skirted coat; the striped waistcoat; the white cords; and last, not least, the immortal boots. But alas! the calf that had once filled them out, had disappeared; they clanked heavily on the pavement, instead of creaking tightly and noisily whereever he went. His waistcoat, evidently once filled almost to bursting, hung in loose, uncomfortable folds about his emaciated waist; large wrinkles marred the former beauty of the fit of his coat; and his face was all lines and furrows, instead of smiles and jollity. The spirit of the fraternity had passed away from him—he was the stage coachman only in dress.

He walked backwards and forwards for some time without turning his head one way or the other, except now and then to peer into the deserted stable, or to glance mournfully at the whip he held in his hand; at last, the sound of the arrival of a train struck upon his ear!

He drew himself up to his full height, slowly and solemnly shook his clenched fist in the direction of the sound, and looked—Oh that look! it spoke annihilation to the mightiest engine upon the rail, it scoffed at steam, and flashed furious derision at the largest terminus that ever was erected; it was an awfully comprehensive look—the concentrated essence of the fierce and deadly enmity of all the stage coachmen in England to steam conveyance.

To my utter astonishment, not, it must be owned, unmixed with fear, he suddenly turned his eyes towards my place of shelter, and walked up to me.

"That's the rail," said he, between his set teeth.

"It is," said I, considerably embarrassed.

"D——n it!" returned the excited stage coachman.

There was something inexpressibly awful about this execration; and I confess I felt a strong internal conviction that the next day's paper would teem with horrible railway accidents in every column.

"I did my utmost to hoppose 'em," said the stage coachman, in softened accents. "I wos the *last* that guv' in; I kep' a losing day after day, and yet I worked on; I was determined to do my dooty, and I drove a coach the last day with an old hooman and a carpet bag inside, and three little boys and seven whopping empty portmanteaus outside. I wos determined my last kick to have *some* passengers to show to the rail, so I took my wife and children 'cos nobody else wouldn't go, and then we guv' in. Hows'ever, the last time as *I* wos on the road, I didn't go and show 'em an empty coach—we wasn't full, but we wasn't empty; we wos game to the last!"

A grim smile of triumph lit up the features of the deposed coachman, as he gave vent to this assertion. He took hold of me by the button-hole, and led the way into the house.

"This landlord wos an austerious sort of a man," said he; "he used to hobserve, that he only wished a Railway Committee would dine at his house, he'd pison 'em all, and emigrate; and he'd ha' done it, too!"

I did not venture to doubt this, so the stage coachman continued:

"I've smoked my pipe by the hour together in that fire-place; I've read 'The Times' advertisements and Perlice Reports in that box till I fell asleep; I've walked up and down this here room a saying all sorts of things about the rail, and a busting for happiness. Outside this wery door I've bin a drownded in thankys from ladies for never lettin' nobody step through their band-boxes. The chambermaids used to smile, and the dogs used to bark, wherever I came.—But it's all over now—the poor feller as kep' this place takes tickets at a Station, and the chambermaids makes scalding hot tea behind a mahogany counter for the people as has no time to drink it in!"

As the stage coachman uttered these words, a contemptuous sneer puckered his sallow cheek. He led me back into the yard; the ruined appearance of which looked doubly mournful, under the faint rays of moonlight that every here and there stole through the dilapidated walls of the stable. An owl had taken up his abode, where the chief ostler's bedroom had once rejoiced in the grotesque majesty of huge portraits of every winner of every "Derby," since the first days of Epsom. The bird of night flew heavily off at our approach, and my companion pointed gloomily up to the fragments of mouldy, worm-eaten wood, the last relics of the stable loft.

"He wos a great friend of mine, was that h'ostler," said the coachman, "but he's left this railway-bothered world—he was finished by the train."

At my earnest entreaty to hear further, he continued,

"When this h'old place wos guv' up and ruinated, the h'ostler, as 'ud never look at the rail before, went down to have a sight of it, and as he wos a leaning his elbows on the wall, and a wishing as how he had the stabling of all the steam h'ingines (he'd ha' done 'em justice!) wot should he see, but one of his osses as wos thrown out of employ by the rail, a walking along jist where the train was coming. Bill jumped down, and as he wos a leading of him h'off, up comes the train, and went over his leg and cut the 'os in two—'Tom,' says he to me when we picked him up; 'I'm a going eleven mile an hour, to the last stage as is left for me to do. I've always done my dooty with the osses; I've bin and done it now—bury that ere poor os and me out of the noise of the rail.' We got the surgeons to him, but he never spoke no more, Poor Bill! Poor Bill!"

This last recollection seemed too much for the stage coachman, he wrung my hand, and walked abruptly to the farthest corner of the yard.

I took care not to interrupt him, and watched him carefully from a distance.

At first, the one expression of his countenance was melancholy; but by degrees, other thoughts came crowding from his mind, and mantled on his woe-begone visage. Poor fellow, I could see that he was again in imagination the beloved of the ladies and the adored of the chambermaids: a faint reflection of the affable, yet majestic demeanor, required by his calling, flitted occasionally over his pinched, attenuated features; and brightened the cold, melancholy expression of his countenance.

As I still looked, it grew darker and darker, yet the face of the stage coachman was never for an instant hidden from me. The same artificial expression of pleasure characterized its lineaments as before. Suddenly I heard a strange, unnatural noise in the air—now it seemed like the distant trampling of horses; and now again, like the rumbling of a heavily laden coach along the public road. A faint, sickly light, spread itself over that part of the heavens whence the sounds proceeded; and after an interval, a fully equipped stage coach appeared in the clouds, with a railway director strapped fast to each wheel, and a stoker between the teeth of each of the four horses.

In place of luggage, fragments of broken steam carriages, and red carpet bags filled with other mementoes of railway accidents, occupied the roof. Chance passengers appeared to be the only tenants of the outside places. In front sat Julius Cæsar and Mrs. Hannah Moore; and behind, Sir Joseph Banks and Mrs. Brownrigge. Of all the "insides," I could, I grieve to say, see nothing.

On the box, was a little man with fuzzy hair and large iron-gray whiskers; clothed in a coat of engineers' skin, with gloves of the hide of railway police. He pulled up opposite my friend, and bowing profoundly, motioned him to the box seat.

A gleam of unutterable joy irradiated the stage coachman's countenance, as he stepped lightly into his place, seized the reins, and with one hearty "good night," addressed to an imaginary inn-full of people, started the horses.

Off they drove! my friend in the plenitude of his satisfaction cracking the whip every instant, as he drove the phantom coach into the air. And amidst the shrieks of the railway directors at the wheel, the groans of *James Watt*, the bugle of the guard, and the tremendous cursing of the invisible "insides," fast and furiously disappeared from my eyes.

NEIGHBOR NELLY.

ANONYMOUS.

I'M in love with Neighbor Nelly,
 Though I know she's only ten;
While I am eight-and-forty,
 And the *marriedest* of men.
I've a wife that weighs me double,
 I've three daughters all with beaux;
I've a son with noble whiskers,
 Who at me turns up his nose.

Though a Squaretoes and a Buffer,
 Yet I've sunshine in my heart;
Still, I'm fond of cakes and marbles—
 Can appreciate a tart,
I can love my Neighbor Nelly
 Just as though I were a boy,
And would hand her cakes and apples
 From my depths of corduroy.

She is tall, and growing taller;
 She is vigorous of limb;
(You should see her play at cricket
 With her little brother Jim!)
She has eyes as blue as damsons;
 She has pounds of auburn curls:
She regrets the game of leap-frog
 Is prohibited to girls!

I adore my Neighbor Nelly;
 I invite her into tea,
And I let her nurse the baby,
 Her delightful ways to see.
Such a darling bud of woman!
 Yet remote from any teens—
I have learnt from Neighbor Nelly
 What the girl's doll instinct means.

O, to see her with the baby,
 (He adores her more than I,)
How she choruses his crowing,
 How she hushes every cry!
How she loves to pit his dimples,
 With her light forefinger deep;
How she boasts, as one in triumph,
 When she gets him off to sleep!

We must part, my Neighbor Nelly,
 For the summers quickly flee,
And the middle-aged admirer,
 Must, too soon, supplanted be.
Yet, as jealous as a mother,
 A suspicious, canker'd churl—
I look vainly for the setting
 To be worthy such a pearl!

THE NEW TALE OF A TUB.

BY F. W. N. BAYLEY.

THE Orient day was fresh and fair,
A breeze sang soft in the ambient air,
Men almost wondered to find it there
Blowing so near Bengal,
Where waters bubble as boiled in a pot,
And the gold of the sun spreads melting hot,
And there's hardly a breath of wind to be got
At any price at all!
Unless, indeed, when the great Simoom
Gets up from its bed with the voice of doom;
And deserts no rains e'er drench
Rise up and roar with a dreadful gust,
Pillars of sand and clouds of dust
Rushing on drifted, and rapid to burst,
And filling all India's throat with thirst
That its Ganges couldn't quench!

No great Simoom rose up to-day,
But only a gentle breeze,
And that of such silent and voiceless play
That a lady's bustle
Had made more rustle
Than *it* did among the trees!
'Twas not like the breath of a British vale,
Where each Green acre is blessed with a Gale
Whenever the natives please;
But it was of that soft inviting sort,
That it tempted to revel in pic-nic sport
A couple of Bengalese!

Two Bengalese,
Resolved to seize
The balmy chance of that cool-wing'd weather,
To revel in Bengal ease together.
One was tall, the other was stout,
They were natives both of the glorious East,
And both so fond of a rural feast,
That off they roam'd to a country plain
Where the breeze roved free about,
That during its visits brief, at least,
If it never were able to blow again,
It might blow upon their blow-out!

The country plain gave a view as small
As ever man clapped his eyes on,
Where the sense of sight did easily pall,
For it kept on seeing nothing at all,
As far as the far horizon!
Nothing at all!—Oh! what do I say,
Something certainly stood in the way,
(Though it had neither cloth nor tray,
With its "tiffin" I wouldn't quarrel,)
It was a sort of hermaphrodite thing,
(—It might have been filled with sugar or ling
But is very unfit for a Muse to sing,—)
Betwixt a tub and a barrel!

It stood in the midst of that Indian plain,
Burning with sunshine—pining for rain,
—A parenthesis balanced 'twixt pleasure and pain,—
And as stiff as if it were starching:
When up to it, over the brown and green
Of that Indian soil, were suddenly seen
Two gentlemen anxiously marching!
Those two gentlemen were, if you please,
The aforesaid couple of Bengalese!
And the Tub or Barrel that stood beyond—
For short we will call it Tub!—
Contained with pride,
In its jolly inside,
The prize of which they were dotingly fond,
The aforesaid gentlemen's grub!

"Leave us alone—come man or come beast,"
Said the eldest, "We'll soon have a shy at the feast!"

They are now at their pic-nic with might and with main.
But what do we see in the front of the plain?
A jungle, a thicket of bush, weed, and grass,
And in it reposing—eh—no! not an ass—
Not an ass, not an ass, that could not come to pass;
No donkey, no donkey, no donkey at all,
But superb in his slumber, a Royal Bengal!
Tho' Royal, he wasn't a king!
No such thing!
He didn't rule lands from the Thames to the Niger,
But he did hold a reign
O'er that jungle and plain,
And, besides, was a very magnificent Tiger!

There he lay, in his skin so gay,
His passions at rest, and his appetites curbed;
A Minister Prime,
In his proudest time,
Asleep, was never less undisturbed;
For who would come to shake him?
Oh! it's certain sure, in his dream demure,
That none would dare to wake him.
Only the Royal snore may creep
Over the dreams of a Tiger's sleep!

The Bengalese, in cool apparel,
Meanwhile have reached their pic-nic barrel;
In other words, they have tossed the grub
Out of their great provision Tub,
And standing it up for shelter,
Sit guzzling underneath its shade,
With a glorious dinner ready-made,
Which they're eating helter-skelter!
Ham and chicken, and bread and cheese,
They make a pass to spread on the grass.
They sit at ease, with their plates on their knees,
And now their hungry jaws they appease,
And now they turn to the glass;
For Hodgson's ale
Is genuine pale,

And the bright champagne
Flows not in vain,
The most convivial souls to please
Of these very thirsty Bengalese!

Ha! one of the two has relinquished his fork,
And wakes up the Tiger by drawing a cork!

Blurting and spirting!
List! O list!
Perhaps the Tiger thinks he is hiss'd!
Effervescing and whizzed and phizzed!
Perhaps his Majesty thinks he is quizzed!
Or haply deems,
As he's roused from his dreams,
That his visions have come to a thirsty stop,
And resolves to moisten his throat with a drop!

At all events, with body and soul,
He gives in his jungle a stretch and a roll,
Then regally rises to go for a stroll,
With a temperate mind,
For a beast of his kind,
And a tail uncommonly long behind!
He knows of no water,
By field or by flood;
He does not seek slaughter,
He does not scent blood;
No! the utmost scope
Of his limited hope,
Is, that these
Bengalese,
When they find he arrives,
May not rise from their pic-nic and run for their lives,
But simply bow on that beautiful plain,
And offer Sir Tiger a glass of champagne!
"From my jungle it true is
They 'woke me, I think,
So the least they can do is
To give me some drink."

Gently Tiger crouches along,
Humming a kind of animal song,
A sweet subdued familiar lay
As ever was warbled by beast of prey;
And all so softly, tunefully done,
That it made no more sound
Than his shade on the ground:
So the Bengalese heard it, never a one!

Gently Tiger steals along,
"Mild as a moon-beam," meek as a lamb;
What so suddenly changes his song
From a tune to a growl?
"'Och, by my sowl,'
Nothing on earth but the smell of the ham!"
He quickens his pace,
The "illigant baste,
And he's running a race
With himself for a taste.
And he's taken to roaring and given up humming,
Just to let the two Bengalese know he is coming!

What terrors seize
The Bengalese!
As the roar of the tiger reaches the ear,
Their hair is standing on end with fear;
"Short-and-stout," with *his* hair all gray,
Has a rattling note, in his jolly old throat:
If choking his laugh with a truss of hay,
He couldn't more surely have stifled the gay.
While "Tall-and-thin," with *his* hair all carroty,
Looks thrice as red, with fright, as his head
And his face bounds plump, at a single jump,
Into horror, and out of hilarity!
All they can hear, in their terrible fear,
Behind and before, is the Tiger's roar;
Again and again—over the plain.
Clearer and clearer—nearer and nearer!
Into the tub, now, its way it has found,
Where its echoes keep rolling round and round,
Till out of the bung-hole they bursting come,
Like a regiment of thunders escaped from a drum!

If an earthquake had shattered a thousand kegs,
The terrified Bengalese couldn't —i' fegs—
Have leapt more rapidly on to their legs.
He's at 'em, he's on 'em, the jungle guest:
When a man's life by peril is prest,
His wits will sometimes be at their best;
So the presence of Tiger, I find,
Inspires our heroes with presence of mind!
There's no time to be lost,
Down the glasses are tost;
The Bengalese have abandon'd their grub,
And they're dodging their gentleman round the Tub!
Active and earnest, they nowhere lodge,
And he can't get at them because of their dodge;
"Short-and-stout" and "Tall-and-thin"
Never before such a scrape were in;
Nor ever yet used—can you well have a doubt of it?—
So uncommonly artful a dodge to get out of it!

Tiger keeps prowling,
Howling and growling;
He feels himself that their dodge is clever;
But the quick fresh blood of the Bengalese,
Nicer and nicer he snuffs on the breeze!
The more they practise their dodge recitals,
The more he longs to dine on their vitals!
His passion is up! his hunger is keen!
His jaws are ready! his teeth are clean!
And sharpen'd their limbs to sever!
The fire is flashing in light from his eyes!
In his own peculiar manner he cries—
The while they shine—
"If I mean to dine,
I had better begin,"
And then, with a grin,
And a voice the loudest that ever was heard,
He roars, "Never trust to a Tiger's word,
If this dodge shall last much longer!
No, no, no, no,—it shall be no go!
There's a way of disturbing this Tub's repose;
So down on your knees,
You Bengalese,
And prepare to be eaten up, if you please—

Here goes!
Here goes! here goes!" and he gave a spring;
The gentlemen, looking for no such thing,
Might have fallen a prey to the Tiger's fling.
But a certain inter*ference*,
Which bursts from their most intelligent Tub,
May enable them yet to return to their grub,
On the self-same plain a *year* hence!
The Tub, tho' empty of roll and ration,
Is full of a certain preservation—
Of which,—though it does not follow
In every case of argumentation,—
It *is* full because it is hollow!
For, not having a top, and no inside things,
It turns top-heavy when Tiger springs!
And, making a kind of a balancing pause,
Keeps holding the animal up by his claws,
In a manner that seems to fret it;
While "Short-and-stout," in a state of doubt,
Keeps on his belly a sharp look-out;
And "Tall-and-thin," with an impudent grin,
Exults in his way,
As much as to say,
"I only wish you may get it!
But much as I *may* respect your agility,
I don't see at present the great probability!"

The Tiger has leapt up, heart and soul.
It's clear he means to go the whole
Hog, in his hungry efforts to seize
The two defianceful Bengalese!
But the Tub! the Tub!
Ay, there's the rub!
At present he's balanced atop of the Tub,
His fore legs inside,
And the rest of his hide,
Not weighing so much as his head and his legs,
And having no hand in
A pure understandin'
Of the just equilibrium of casks and of kegs,
Not bred up in attics,
Nor taught mathematics,
To work out the problems of Euclid with pegs!
He has plunged with the impetus wild of a lover,
And the tub has loomed large, balanced, paused, and turned over!

The Tiger at first had a hobby-horse-ride,
But now he is decently quartered inside;
And the question is next, long as fortune may frown on him,
How the two Bengalese are to keep the tub down on him!
'Bout this there's no blunder,
The Tiger is under
The Tub!
My verse need not run
To the length of a sonnet,
To tell how the Bengalese
Both jumped upon it,
While the beautiful barrel
Keeps acting as bonnet
To the Tiger inside,
Who no more in his pride
Can roam over jungle and plain,
But sheltered alike from the sun and the rain,
Around its interior his sides deigns to rub
With a fearful hub-hub,
And longs for his freedom again!

The two Bengalese,
Not at all at their ease,
Hear him roar,
And deplore
Their prospects as sore,
Forgetting both pic-nic and flask:
Each wondering, dumb,
What of both will become,
Helps the other to press on the cask;
Resign'd to their fate,
But increasing their weight,
By action of muscle and sinew,
In order that forcibly you, Mr. Tub,
Whom their niggers this morning
Roll'd here with their grub,
May still keep the Tiger with*in* you!

On the top of the Tub,
In the warmest of shirts,
The thin man stands!
While the fat by his skirts
Holds—anxiously puffing and blowing;
And the thin peers over the top of the cask,
"Is there any hope for us?"
As much as to ask,
With a countenance cunning and knowing;
And just as he mournfully 'gins to bewail,
In a grief-song that ought to be *sung* whole,
He twigs the long end of the old Tiger's tail
As it twists itself out of the bung-hole!
Then sharp on the watch,
He gives it a catch,
With the Tiger's tail clenched fast in his fist,
And his own coat-tail grasped fast to assist,
Stands "Tall-and-thin," with "Short-and-stout,"
Both on the top of the Tub to scout,
Tiger within, and they without,
And both in a pretty pickle!
The Tiger begins by giving a bound;
The Tub's half-turn'd, but the men are found
To have very carefully jump'd to the ground—
At trifles they must not stickle!
It's no use quaking and turning pale,
Pluck and patience must now prevail,
They must keep a hold on the Tiger's tail,
And neither one be fickle!

And shouts to the Tiger,
"You've now got your match;
You may rush and may riot, may wriggle and roar,
But I'm blest if I'll let your tail go any more!"
It's as safe as a young roasted pig in a larder,
And no two Bengalese could hold on by it harder!"
There they must pull if they pull for weeks,
Straining their stomachs and bursting their cheeks,
While Tiger alternately roars and squeaks,
Trying to break away from 'em;
They must keep the Tub turned over his back
And never let his long tail get slack,
For fear he should win the day from 'em.

Yes! yes! they must hold him tight,
From night till morning! from morn till night!
Mustn't stop to eat! mustn't stop to weep!
Mustn't stop to drink! mustn't stop to sleep!
No cry! no laugh! no rest! no grub!
Till they starve the Tiger under the Tub!
Till the animal dies,
To his own surprise,
With two Bengalese, in a deadly quarrel,
And his tail thrust through the hole of a barrel!

Oh, dear! oh, dear! it's very clear
They can't live so—but *they daren't let go!*
Fate for a pitying world to wail,
Starving behind a Tiger's tail!
If Invention be Necessity's Son,
Now let him tell them what's to be done.
What's to be done! ha! I see a grin
Of joy on the face of "Tall-and-thin."
Some new device he has hit in a trice,
The which he is telling all about
To the gratified gentleman "Short-and-stout."

What's to be done! what precious fun,
Haven't they found out what's to be done!
See! see! what glorious glee!
Note! mark! what a capital lark,
Tiger and Tub, and bunghole and all
Baffled by what is about to befall;
Excellent! marvellous! beautiful! O!
Isn't it now an original go!
What, stop! I'm ready to drop!
Hold! stay! I'm fainting away!
Laughter I'm certain 'll kill me to-day;
And "Short-and-stout" is bursting his skin,
And almost in fits is "Tall-and-thin,"
And Tiger is free, yet they do not quail,
Tho' temper has all gone wrong with him;
No! they've TIED A KNOT IN THE TIGER'S TAIL,
AND HE CARRIES THE TUB ALONG WITH HIM;
He's a freehold for life, with a tail out of joint,
And has made his last CLIMAX
A TRUE KNOTTY POINT.

A DAY OF DISTRESS.

BY MARY RUSSELL MITFORD.

It was a glorious June morning; and I got up gay and bright, as the Americans say, to breakfast in the pretty summer-room overlooking the garden, which, built partly for my accommodation and partly for that of my geraniums, who make it their winter residence, is as regularly called the green-house as if I and my several properties—sofas, chairs, tables, chiffonières, and ottomans—did not inhabit it during the whole of the fine season; or as if it were not in its own person a well-proportioned and spacious apartment, no otherways to be distinguished from common drawing-rooms than by being nearly fronted with glass, about which out-of-door myrtles, passion-flowers, clematis, and the Persian honeysuckle, form a most graceful and varied framework, not unlike the festoons of flowers and foliage which one sees round some of the scarce and high-prized tradesmen's cards, and ridotto tickets of Hogarth and Bartolozzi. Large glass folding-doors open into the little garden, almost surrounded by old buildings of the most picturesque form — the buildings themselves partly hidden by clustering vines, and my superb bay-tree, its shining leaves glittering in the sun on one side, whilst a tall pear-tree, garlanded to the very top with an English honeysuckle in full flower, breaks the horizontal line of the low cottage-roof on the other; the very pear-tree being, in its own turn, half concealed by a splendid pyramid of geraniums erected under its shade. Such geraniums! It does not become us poor mortals to be vain—but really, my geraniums! There is certainly nothing but the garden into which Aladdin found his way, and where the fruit was composed of gems, that can compare with them. This pyramid is undoubtedly the great object from the green-house; but the common flowerbeds which surround it, filled with roses of all sorts, and lilies of all colors, and pinks of all patterns, and campanulas of all shapes, to say nothing of the innumerable tribes of annuals, of all the outlandish names that ever were invented, are not to be despised even beside the gorgeous exotics, which, arrranged with the nicest attention to color and form, so as to combine the mingled charms of harmony and contrast, seem to look down proudly on their humble compeers.

No pleasanter place for a summer-breakfast—always a pretty thing, with its cherries, and strawberries, and its affluence of nosegays and posies—no pleasanter place for a summer breakfast-table than my green-house! And no pleasanter companion, with whom to enjoy it, than the fair friend, as bright as a rose-bud, and as gay as a lark—the saucy, merry, charming Kate, who was waiting to partake our country fare. The birds were singing in the branches; bees, and butterflies, and myriads of gay, happy insects were flitting about in the flower-beds; the haymakers were crowding to their light and lively labor in a neighboring meadow; whilst the pleasant smell of the newly-mown grass blended with that of a bean-field in full blossom still nearer, and with the thousand odors of the garden—so that sight, and sound, and smell, were a rare compound of all that is delightful to the sense and the feeling.

Nor were higher pleasures wanting. My pretty friend, with all her vivacity, had a keen relish of what is finest in literature and in poetry. An old folio edition of that volume of Dryden called his "Fables," which contains the glorious rifacimenti of parts of Chaucer, and the best of his original poems, happened to be on the table; the fine description of Spring in the opening of the Flower and the Leaf, led to the picture of Eden in the Paradise Lost, and that again to Comus, and Comus to Fletcher's Faithful Shepherdess, and Fletcher's Faithful Shepherdess to Shakspere, and As You Like It. The bees and the butterflies, culling for pleasure or for thrift the sweets of my geraniums, were but types of Kate Leslie and myself roving amidst the poets. This does not sound much like a day of distress; but the evil is to come.

A gentle sorrow did arrive, all too soon, in the shape of Kate Leslie's pony-phaeton, which whisked off that charming person as fast as her two long-tailed Arabians could put their feet to the ground. This evil had, however, substantial consolation in the promise of another visit very soon; and I resumed, in peace and quietness, the usual round of idle occupation which forms the morning employment of a country gentlewoman of small fortune: ordered dinner—minced-veal, cold ham, a currant-pudding, and a salad—if any body happens to be curious on the score of my housekeeping; renewed my bean-pots; watered such of my plants as wanted most; mended my gloves; patted Dash; looked at the Times; and was just sitting down to work, or to pretend to work, when I was most pleasantly interrupted by the arrival of some morning visitors—friends from a distance—for whom, after a hearty welcome and some cordial chat, I ordered luncheon, with which order my miseries began.

"The keys, if you please, ma'am, for the wine and the Kennet ale," said Anne, my female factotum, who rules, as regent, not only the cook and the under-maid and the boy, but the whole family, myself included, and is an actual housekeeper in every respect, except that of keeping the keys. "The keys, ma'am, if you please," said Anne; and then I found that my keys were not in my right-hand pocket, where they ought to have been, nor in my left-hand pocket, where they might have been, nor in either of my apron-pockets, nor in my work-basket, nor in my reticule—in short, that my keys were lost!

Now these keys were only two in number, and small enough in dimensions; but then the one opened that important part of me, my writing-desk; and the other contained within itself the specific power over every lock in the house, being no other than the key of the key-drawer; and no chance of picking them—for alas! alas! the locks were Bramah's! So, after a few exclamations, such as, What can have become of my keys? Has any one seen my keys? Somebody must have run away with my keys!—I recollected that however consolatory to myself such lamentations might be, they would, by no means, tend to quench the thirst of my guests. I applied myself vigorously to remedy the evil all I could by sending to my nearest neighbors (for time were pressing, and our horse and his master out for the day) to supply, as well as might be, my deficiency. Accordingly I sent to the public-house for their best beer, which, not being Kennet ale, would not go down; and to the good-humored wives of the shoemaker and the baker for their best wine. Fancy to yourselves a decanter of damson-wine arriving from one quarter, and a jug of parsnip-wine, fresh from the wood, tapped on purpose, from the other! And this for drinkers of Burgundy and Champagne! Luckily the water was good, and my visitors were good-natured, and comforted me in my affliction, and made a jest of the matter. Really they are a nice family, the St. Johns, especially the two young men, to whom I have, they say, taught the taste of spring-water.

This trouble passed over lightly enough. But scarcely were they gone before the tax-gatherer came for money—locked up in my desk! What will the collector say?—And the justice's clerk for warrants, left under my care by the chairman of the bench, and also safely lodged in the same safe repository. What will their worships say to this delinquency? It will be fortunate if they do not issue a warrant against me in my own person! My very purse was left by accident in that unlucky writing-desk; and when our kind neighbors, the Wrights, sent a melon, and I was forced to borrow a shilling to give the messenger, I could bear my loss no longer, and determined to institute a strict search on the instant.

But before the search could begin, in came the pretty little roly-poly Sydneys and Murrays, brats from seven downwards, with their whole train of nurses, and nursery-maids, and nursery-governesses, by invitation, to eat strawberries; and the strawberries were locked up in a cupboard, the key of which was in the unopenable drawer! And good farmer Brookes, he too called, sent by his honor for a bottle of Hollands—the right Schiedam; and the Schiedam was in the cellar; and the key of the cellar was in the Bramah-locked drawer! And the worthy farmer, who behaved charmingly for a man deprived of his gin, was fain to be content with excuses, like a voter after an election; and the poor children were compelled to put up with promises, like a voter before one; to be sure, they had a few pinks and roses to sweeten their disappointment; but the strawberries were as uncomeatable as the Schiedam.

At last, they were gone; and then began the search in good earnest. Every drawer, not locked, every room that could be entered, every box that could be opened, was ransacked over and over again for these intolerable keys.

All my goods and chattels were flung together in heaps, and then picked over (a process which would make even new things seem disjointed and shabby), and the quantities of trumpery thereby disclosed, especially in the shape of thimbles, needle-cases, pincushions, and scissors, from the different work-baskets, work-boxes, and work-bags (your idle person always abounds in working materials), was astounding. I think there were seventeen pincushions of different patterns—beginning with an old boot and ending with a new guitar. But what was there not? It seemed to me that there were pocketable commodities enough to furnish a second-hand bazaar! Every thing was there, except my keys.

For four hours did I and my luckless maidens perambulate the house, whilst John, the boy, examined the garden; until we were all so tired that we were forced to sit down from mere weariness. Saving always the first night of one of my own tragedies, when, though I pique myself on being composed, I can never manage to sit still; except on such an occasion, I do not think I ever walked so much at one time in my life. At last, I flung myself on a sofa in the green-house, and began to revolve the possibility of their being still in the place where I had first missed them.

A jingle in my apron-pocket afforded some hope, but it turned out to be only the clinking of a pair of garden-scissors against his old companion, a silver pencil-case—and that prospect faded away. A slight opening of Dryden's heavily-bound volume gave another glimmer of sunshine, but it proved to be occasioned by a sprig of myrtle in Palamon and Arcite—Kate Leslie's elegant mark.

This circumstance recalled the recollection of my pretty friend. Could she have been the culprit? And I began to ponder over all the instances of unconscious key-stealing that I had heard of amongst my acquaintance. How my old friend, Aunt Martha, had been so well known for that propensity as to be regularly sought after whenever keys were missing; and my young friend, Edward Harley, from the habit of twisting something round his fingers during his eloquent talk (people used to provide another eloquent talker, Madame de Staël, with a willow-twig for the purpose), had once caught up and carried away a key, also a Bramah, belonging to a lawyer's bureau, thereby, as the lawyer affirmed, causing the loss of divers lawsuits to himself and his clients. Neither Aunt Martha nor Edward had been near the place; but Kate Leslie might be equally subject to absent fits, and might, in a paroxysm, have abstracted my keys; at all events it was worth trying. So I wrote her a note to go by post in the evening (for Kate, I grieve to say, lives above twenty miles off), and determined to await her reply, and think no more of my calamity.

A wise resolution! but, like many other wise resolves, easier made than kept. Even if I could have forgotten my loss, my own household would not have let me.

The cook, with professional callousness, came to demand sugar for the currant-pudding—and the sugar was in the store-room—and the store-room was locked; and scarcely had I recovered from this shock, before Anne came to inform me that

there was no oil in the cruet, and that the flask was in the cellar, snugly reposing, I suppose, by the side of the Schiedam, so that if for weariness I could have eaten, there was no dinner to eat—for without the salad who would take the meat? However, I being alone, this signified little; much less than a circumstance of which I was reminded by my note to Kate Leslie, namely, that in my desk were two important letters, one triple, and franked for that very night; as well as a corrected proof-sheet, for which the press was waiting; and that all these despatches were to be sent off by post that evening.

Roused by this extremity, I carried my troubles and my writing-desk to my good friend the blacksmith—a civil, intelligent man, who sympathized with my distress, sighed, shook his head, and uttered the word Bramah!—and I thought my perplexity was nearly at its height, when, as I was wending slowly homeward, my sorrows were brought to a climax by my being overtaken by one of the friends whom I admire and honor most in the world—a person whom all the world admires—who told me, in her prettiest way, that she was glad to see me so near my own gate, for that she was coming to drink tea with me.

Here was a calamity! The Lady Mary H., a professed tea-drinker—a green-tea-drinker, one (it was a point of sympathy between us) who took nothing but tea and water, and, therefore, required that gentle and lady-like stimulant in full perfection. Lady Mary come to drink tea with me; and I with nothing better to offer her than tea from the shop—the village-shop—bohea, or souchong, or whatever they might call the vile mixture. Tea from the shop for Lady Mary! Ill luck could go no further: it was the very extremity of small distress.

Her ladyship is, however, as kind as she is charming, and bore our mutual misfortune with great fortitude; admired my garden, praised my geraniums, and tried to make me forget my calamity. Her kindness was thrown away. I could not even laugh at myself, or find beauty in my flowers, or be pleased with her for flattering them. I tried, however, to do the honors by my plants; and, in placing a large night-scented stock, which was just beginning to emit its odor, upon the table, I struck against the edge, and found something hard under my belt.

"My keys! my keys!" cried I, untying the ribbon, as I heard a most pleasant jingle on the floor; and the lost keys, sure enough, they were; deposited there, of course, by my own hand; unfelt, unseen, and unsuspected, during our long and weary search. Since the adventure of my dear friend, Mrs. S., who hunted a whole morning for her spectacles whilst they were comfortably perched upon her nose, I have met with nothing so silly and so perplexing.

But my troubles were over—my affliction was at an end.

The strawberries were sent to the dear little girls; and the Schiedam to the good farmer; and the warrants to the clerk. The tax-gatherer called for his money; letters and proofs went to the post, and never in my life did I enjoy a cup of Twining's green tea so much as the one which Lady Mary and I took together after my day of distress.

THE PERSIANS IN LONDON.

FROM "THE ADVENTURES OF HAJJI BABA." BY JAMES MORIER.

We had been so much taken up by our various visitings, that we scarcely had had time to reflect that we were Mussulmans, and that we were living among infidels. Such had been the dissipation in which we passed our days, that the duties of praying and washing at our appointed times were daily becoming lax, to the horror of Mohamed Beg, who being a strict observer of our faith, did not cease upbraiding us for our neglect, and strongly upheld the necessity of keeping ourselves pure from the contagious example of those around us, who, in fact, appeared to live in the world without any religion at all. He had been anxious to settle the true direction of the *kebleh*,* which he had never yet done in England to his satisfaction. His *kebleh nemah*, or compass, had unfortunately been broken; and he was doubtful whether any compass we might procure from the deriders of our faith would set us in the right way; and even whether it might not purposely mislead us, by pointing to some impure spot instead of the sacred shrine of our holy Prophet. Then, to his utter dismay, he had not seen the sun once since our arrival; and he was seriously apprehensive that the accounts which, in Persia, were currently believed concerning Frangistan were about being realized, and that England, in fact, had no sun. He therefore began to give up all hope of settling his kebleh, until one morning, with joy painted in his countenance, he rushed into the presence of the ambassador, followed by many of the servants, exclaiming, "*Mujdeh!* good news! the sun is come! the sun is here!" and, in fact, upon looking up, amidst a yellow atmosphere, composed of smoke and vapor, there we saw it sure enough. But many of us were inclined to doubt whether this could be the glorious luminary that we had in Persia, for there nobody had an eye strong enough to brave its brilliancy; whereas, here we gazed upon it at our ease, quite as well as if it were a moon. However, having satisfied ourselves that it was, in fact, the sun, we were all very happy; and seeing that this auspicious sight took place upon a white day,* the fifteenth of the month, we exclaimed, "*Mobarek!* good fortune!" to the ambassador; while Mohamed Beg became convinced that he had acquired the true direction of the land of our faith.

But this joy of ours at seeing the sun was the cause of confirming many of the English in their ignorance concerning our religion. We were taken for worshippers of fire, and they concluded that we

* The point to which Mahomedans turn in prayer—Mecca.

* Superstitious people in Persia make a distinction between lucky and unlucky days, which they call black and white days; the eighteenth, eleventh, and fifteenth of every month are white days.

adored the sun. One of their khans, a lord of great consequence, who sat in the king's assembly, and gave his opinion upon things fitting and things unfitting, never approached the ambassador without saying, "Well, sir! no sun yet!" One day, when it was freezing, he found the ambassador seated near the fire, warming himself. "Oh, sir," said he, "I see you are worshipping the fire!" Upon this, Mirza Firouz, in wrath, exclaimed to me, who was standing before him, "What words are these? He does not know, that if we were worshippers of fire, it would not be the offensive smoky fires of his country.* Even the Guebres, who are scarcely good enough to manure our fields, are scrupulous as to the purity of their fire; what then must we be, who look upon them as the uncleanest of infidels?" Then turning to the mehmandar, he said, "For the love of Allah! tell the khan that we never worship fire in our country except when it is cold;" to which Mohamed Beg, who was also in the room, added, "And tell him that our holy prophet, blessed be his name! hath ordained, in the forty-first surai of *the* Book, "worship not the sun, neither the moon; but worship God who hath created them." This did not seem to satisfy the khan, but he entered into a long explanation, through the mehmandar, about an ancient infidel who seemed to know a great deal more about our country than any of our own historians; and who, in spite of all we could say to the contrary, had made him and all England believe that we worshipped fire; and, moreover, that we cut our horses' throats in honor of the sun.

"Ha, ha!" exclaimed the ambassador, who was always ready for a joke; "seeing that you have no sun in your country, to whose honor, may I ask, do you cut your horses' tails?"

The khan then went his way, rubbing his hands, saying that fire was a very good thing.

Deploring the ignorance of the nation we were doomed to live with, we determined no longer to lose sight of what was due to our religion, but to adhere to the practice of those ordinances decreed by our blessed Prophet, and to stand forth as champions of the true faith; accordingly we determined to kill our own mutton. The English servants, when they saw Hassan, the cook, about to cut the throat of a sheep in one of the apartments of the house, exclaimed against the filth that such a custom would create; but when they heard Mohamed Beg roaring out the *Bismillah*, and otherwise explaining our law, which forbids man to eat that out of which the blood hath not flowed, they opened the eyes of astonishment, and dropped the head of acquiescence. The ambassador also ordained that every fowl, for the future, was to have its throat cut, and to be thrown on the ground to bleed to death, after the Persian manner; so that, by the blessing of Allah, we might eat our food without endangering our consciences.

Having established these customs, we began to pray and eat more at our ease than we had done since we left our country; although we were convinced that, living in an impure country, our prayers could not be of the same avail, no, not by one-half, as those made upon our own soil. Mohamed Beg threatened us with a double allowance of praying, which would not fail to be decreed to us by the mollahs the moment we reached Persia, saying there was no *behesht*, no paradise, for those whose entreaties to the throne of Allah came from a land "overrun with swine, and overflown with wine," for they would be arrested before they came to the gates of the highest heaven. This operated agreeably upon our spirits, and made most of us cease praying; "for," said we, "if we are to pray double upon returning to Persia, what use is there in praying at all while we are in England?" Right happy were we at this scheme, notwithstanding the solemn looks of Mohamed Beg, who wagged his head to and fro, and exhorted us never to lose sight of the dignity of Mahomedans, and of the duties which our faith enjoined.

We now ventured to walk through the streets, although our dress and appearance attracted much observation; but as we proceeded through the great labyrinth of the city, we began to fear that we should never find our way back. We had nothing by which to direct our steps, for every house appeared the same in our eyes. All the doors were alike, and the windows of the same shapes. There was neither bath, nor caravanserai, nor barber's shop, nor even a dunghill, that we could discover, from whence we could take a fresh departure; but when we got into a great street it was interminable, and one might walk more in a straight line than in the *Chahar Bagh* of Ispahan. We lost ourselves so frequently, even at short distances from our own home, that I determined to adopt a plan which I had practised with success in the forests of Mazanderan, when I was prisoner among the Turcomans. There I cut notches in the trees as I went, and by this means recovered myself if I lost my way. Here I provided myself with a piece of chalk, and marking every corner, I at length succeeded to walk great distances, and to find my way back without the help of any one. But these excursions were hazardous, for we were among a strange people, and scarcely a day passed without an adventure. Once I had strolled to some distance with Mohamed Beg; and as good luck would have it, our walk took us into green fields. There were many people walking to and fro; it was probably a Christian festival; the day happened to be fine, and the sun shone almost as bright as in our country. We came to a beautiful spot, with grass smooth as a carpet, and Mohamed Beg exclaimed, "Allah! Allah! what a charming place for saying one's prayers." At this moment a clock of one of the mosques struck the English noon, and he could no longer resist. "There is the *zohor*, noon," said he, "and although we have no muezzin to make the profession of faith, and to call us to prayer, still let us not disregard the notice. Here is water at hand; we will wash, and then make our devotions." To say the truth, I never had been a great sayer of prayers. Since the days when I was a prisoner in the sanctuary at Kom, where I had prayed enough for the remainder of my life, and where I had had a surfeit of genuflexion, I had always played at "hide and seek" with my religious duties, never going upon my knees unless there was danger in not doing so. The absence of all such necessity in this unholy country was to me one of its greatest attractions, and therefore I cared not to leave it. But at the same time I did not wish to offend my companion; and although I re-

* The Guebres keep up their sacred fire with fuel that produces neither smoke nor smell. They do not allow bones, ordure, or filth of any sort, to be mixed with it; and will not even permit it to be lighted by blowing with the mouth, for fear of any impure odor.

fused his invitation, yet I assured him that I would wait until he had finished his devotions.

He first washed his hands, arms, feet, and back of his ears, in an adjoining stream, and having ascertained the direction of Mecca, he sat down and combed his beard. He then took from his person his seals, rings, looking-glass, and every thing of value which he had about him, and taking the piece of holy earth,* together with his beads, from his breast, he placed them before him, and put himself in the first attitude of prayer. By this time the infidels began to gather round us. What they took us for, it is difficult to say; most likely for jugglers, for they all looked with intense interest at the different trinkets which Mohamed Beg had displayed on the grass. As he stood up with his feet joined together, emphatically pronouncing the *fatheh*,† upon raising his hands before him, I verily believe that they expected to see him vault into the air, or make a somerset, as I have seen some of their own mountebanks do in the street; but when he merely went through his prostrations, touching the piece of holy earth, inscribed with the names of our blessed Prophet and the twelve Imans, with his forehead, they seemed quite disappointed; and one of them had the insolence to take it up and hand it about to his fellows to look at. Upon this my Persian pride was aroused. Reprobate as I was, I could not see ourselves so insulted, and a bit of our holy Mecca so abused. I darted forward to snatch the relic from the hand of one of the infidels; my effort was received with loud hootings. Mohamed Beg, now in wrath, got upon his legs, and, heedless of any thing but the insults offered his religion, drew his knife, and would have buried it in the bowels of one of the infidels, when he received a blow which must have been inflicted by some unseen agent, some *dive*, or some English *gin*, which was thrown so exactly into the very centre of his stomach, that his wrath was soon turned into vomiting; his beard became distended, his face turned white, and his eyes streamed. Never had prayer been so little propitious. Instead of pouring forth blessings, his mouth consoled itself with curses; and whenever he could take breath, it was refreshing to hear him devote the whole English nation to perdition, and announce to them that their fathers were now roasting in the fires of *Jehanum*.

Our situation was not very enviable, particularly when we saw an inclination on the part of the surrounding mob to proceed to something more violent than beating Mohamed Beg's stomach. There was one man more violent than the rest, who performed many feats, the object of which we could in no wise understand; he clenched his fist, put it close to my nose, and then took off his coat. This I conceived implied hostility, although I knew that taking off a hat implied the contrary. To my astonishment, I saw another man in the crowd step forward, and also divest himself of his coat; strange compliments, thought I, but I was soon undeceived. In one of the parties I recognized one of the English servants employed by the ambassador; and had scarcely had time to make myself known to him, when, to our extreme horror and amazement, Mohamed Beg and I saw a fight between these two men, the equal of which we had never before seen, not even by the shah's best *pehlivans*. They fought with great vigor and resolution; but our servant in a very short time was the victor. His blows fell thicker upon his antagonist's face than upon the feet of a sufferer under the bastinado in Persia, until every feature was lost, and he begged for mercy. After he was well beaten, they both shook hands, and walked off apparently good friends. We, however, could not recover our astonishment, nor could we at all comprehend the object of our servant's interference, although he assured us that he only fought out of compliment to us. We had frequently before heard of the hospitality of the Arabs to a stranger; of his killing his last sheep for his entertainment; of his depriving himself of

* The Persians at prayers place before them a piece of clay, said to be part of the soil of Mecca, and which is stamped with holy invocations.

† The first prayer in the Koran.

every thing rather than his guest should suffer; but that he should stand up and fight, and run the chance of losing his eyes, or getting his nose knocked off, or his head broken for the stranger, that we had never yet heard. And yet we had seen this very act performed by an infidel, whom in our minds we condemned to eternal punishments. Mohamed Beg puzzled his head for a long while how to find some satisfactory reason for this phenomenon; but all he could discover was, that the beating which had most likely been intended for him, had, by the interposition of fate, fallen on another. We returned home making many exclamations, and astonished the ambassador by a recital of all we had witnessed.

* * * * * * * *

It appears that the king goes willingly every year in state, surrounded by all the majesty and magnificence of a crowned head, to open the deliberations of the council, and even to invite them to settle how much he ought to spend; how many ministers, what number of generals, how many troops, what quantities of ships, what ambassadors to maintain, in short, how many expenses of every description he ought to incur. They even have the audacity, we were assured, to settle in what manner he ought to support his own wife. If one half of this were true, we concluded that we might as well believe the other half; and, in order to be convinced with his own eyes, the ambassador willingly accepted an invitation to be present at the ceremony of opening the council, which, from what we could learn, resembled in some measure the great *selam-i-aum*, the great prostration of the people before the shah in Persia, on the festival of the *No Rouz*.

The mehmandar informed the Mirza Firouz that the number of persons admitted to the shah's presence on this occasion was restricted to a certain few; and therefore it was proposed that neither I nor any of his Persian suite should be of the party. Accordingly we saw him depart, accompanied only by the mehmandar; but we determined to make our way to the scene of action, in order to observe the passage of the royal procession. The whole city was in motion. Never before had we seen such an assemblage of infidels. We, a handful of true believers, looked indeed rather insignificant in the great mass; but we were proud of being such, and would not have given one hair of our beards for the millions of black hats that waved to and fro before us. We posted ourselves under a tree in a garden leading to the house of assembly. Several avenues bordered the road through which the king was to pass; and, in order to keep it clear, on each side were posted cavalry, mounted upon superb horses. For the time being, we attracted more attention than any thing else, and were beginning to feel the insolence of the crowd, when luckily their attention was soon after diverted from us by the approach of the king, and we opened all our eyes to see his majesty pass. Before the procession had reached us about a *maidan*, we heard strange and unaccountable sounds, which we took for the English mode of paying homage to their monarch; sounds which in some measure assimilated to the greetings made by the Arabian women upon the approach of a great personage. They were a mixture of cries, groans, and hisses. As the great coach in which the king sat drew near, the rush of the crowd was immense, and immediately there issued from the thousands that stood near us such a shower of hisses, that we felt sure that no king could be more beloved by his people than this. So much loyalty was instantaneous in its effect; it was as catching as fear; and, almost involuntarily, we added our most unaffected hisses to those of the surrounding crowd, the hue of our faces almost becoming black with the exertion. All the collected serpents of the plains of *Mogan* in a rage could not exceed the noise we made. We became the point of observation to all beholders. But what was our astonishment, I may add consternation, when, instead of meeting with the encouragement and commendation we expected, we found ourselves surrounded by a host of men, with short painted sticks in their hands, backed by some individuals of the

cavalry, who most unceremoniously invited us to dislodge from our tree, and to walk away with them to places unknown!

"What do these men want?" exclaimed Mohamed Beg; "what dirt do they eat?"

"Shall I give them a taste of the knife?" asked Aga Beg, the master of the horse.

"Use no violence, by your child's soul!" exclaimed I, "or they will strike our stomachs, as they did Mohamed Beg's."

The scene becoming much confused, we were about being very awkwardly situated, when a well-dressed Frank stepped up, and, seeing who we were, immediately interfered, and explained to the men with painted sticks, that whatever we might have done it must have been through ignorance. He released us from their superintendence; and having kindly accompanied us to our home, we there explained all that had happened; and then to our confusion we found, that, instead of paying honor and respect to the shah of England, we had in fact been treating him worse than a dog. "*La illaha, illallah!* There is but one God!" exclaimed Mohamed Beg. "What a country is this! Who ever thought of abusing one's king to his face too! Let us leave this people; they are too bad. One never sees them pray; their wives are without shame; and they heap abomination upon their own king's head!"

"By my soul," exclaimed Aga Beg, "I thought that hissing was the Frank mode of doing honor. We have all made a feast of abomination!"

"But pray, sir," said I to the gentleman who had escorted us home, "tell me by what chance is it that the English people receive their king after this manner!"

"The popularity of our king," said he, "depends upon circumstances, which no human power can control. The people are ignorant, and are led by designing demagogues. Bread is dear, they hiss the king; trade is dull, they hiss the king; they hate peace, they hiss the king; the queen behaves ill, they hiss the king. The following year, perhaps, bread is cheap and trade brisk, they cheer the king; his ships or his armies gain a victory, they smother him with kindness; his ministers make good speeches, and talk of reducing taxes, they will lay down their lives for him. Who can account," said he, "for popular favor, or popular disfavor? It is as uncertain as the wind that blows."

"I tell you what sir," said I, taking hold of the tip of my beard, and holding it out to him, "do you see this?"

"Yes," answered he, "I see it."

"Well then, by this I swear, and I can swear by nothing more sacred, that if the people of Teheran, upon the presence of their shah, were even to spit in his presence, or to do any thing by look or speech that indicated disrespect, he would order a *katl-i-aum*, a general massacre, to take place, and would not leave one rogue of them to look at the sun the next morning. By all the Imams, it is as true as I stand here."

The gentleman at this speech opened his eyes with astonishment, and seeing perhaps how cheap we held other people's heads, he made us a low bow, and took his leave.

By this time the ambassador had returned, and when we had related to him and to the mehmandar the adventures of the morning, they consoled us by laughing at our beards, and said, that if we expected to find in the English mob the same servility which existed in the Persian, we were much mistaken. "They are as different," said they, "as the dirty puddle in which a camel drinks is to the sea, which at one hour is agitated by a hurricane, at another lulled into a dead calm."

Mohamed Beg answered, for his part, that he would rather belong to the puddle, if what he had seen to-day and the day before, when he had been so mauled, were acts illustrative of the people of England.

The ambassador then described his adventures. Never had man seen so much in so short a space of time. A king on a throne; dresses of all descriptions; gold, silver, velvet; sticks, swords, and gold maces; men with most extraordinary wigs sprinkled with dust; a multitude of *omrahs*, with scarlet and ermine cloaks; a rush of men, with a *kedkhoda*, covered with false hair, at their head; and to crown all, women! "Oh such women!" said he, "I was in love with them all; they were all unveiled; I saw much flesh whiter than snow; eyes that killed; and teeth which smiled delight!"

We had never before seen our ambassador in such a state. But there was one fair creature above the rest, of whose charms he raved; he had never conceived that any thing human could be so beautiful; his heart was on fire. It was plain that this circumstance alone had reconciled him to a residence among the infidels; and now we learned to appreciate the truth of that saying of our immortal Sheikah, "Be you seated in the most lonely shade of the valley of the angel of death, and let love be your companion, the desert will appear a paradise, and your wretchedness will seem beatitude." He called her his *jalibelleloob*;* swore that the leaf of her eye † was more tender than that of the rose; that she was more brilliant than a moon fourteen days old; ‡ and that she was in the very eyeball § of her age; in short, he made one believe that she was a very phœnix, "The one of ones."

* * * * * *

There seemed now to pervade one new and universal impulse throughout the city to congregate in a thousand different manners, for objects which to us were totally novel. The men sought the women, and the women received the men. In the morning they met at occasional visits to talk upon matters of little importance; then they congregated in troops on horseback, or in carriages; they then dispersed, and separated into different companies to eat; and although by the time they had done this, it was our time for going to bed, yet again they met in larger and more numerous assemblies, to dance, or to sit, or to be pressed together in masses in a manner difficult to explain. In this we were told they followed their own pleasure; nor were these great meetings at all for the honor of their king, as our principal ones generally are, but purely for their own gratification. When we meet in large bodies it is usual to attend our shah; and although we do congregate and eat together occasionally, yet whoever thought of doing so in the unbounded manner of England?

The mehmandar came into the ambassador's room the day after his appearance at the house of parliament, and said, "Here are five invitations to dinner to-day." "Allah, Allah!" exclaimed the

* Ravisher of hearts. † The eyelid.
‡ An Eastern image for mistress. § Pinnacle.

ambassador, "five invitations! who can eat five dinners in one day?"

"It is not necessary to eat them all," answered the mehmandar; "it is enough that you accept one. You eat one dinner, but you may go to as many evening assemblies afterward as you please. Here is a whole handful of invitations."

We remained perfectly astonished. "Who can go through such labor," said we, "and then live? We are Persians; we go to sleep when the last prayers have been chanted, and we wake with the dawn. How is this?"

"You will soon get accustomed to our manners," said the mehmander. "We make little distinction between day and night at this season."

Without more difficulty, the ambassador, accompanied by the mehmandar and myself, went to the dinner in question, which was given by one of the viziers. He dressed himself in his best, putting on the cap of ceremony with the shawl round it, and girding himself with his diamond-hilted dagger. He had found it more convenient to adopt the shoes of the Franks (excepting on very great occasions, when he preserved our own high-heeled slippers), because it was impossible for him to be always accompanied by his shoe-bearer. He intimated that I was to accompany him, and accordingly I also made my person as fit to be seen as possible.

No one came to inform us that the entertainment was ready; no one said the *Bismillah!* but we went straight to the vizier's house; and we were announced by very loud knocks on a closed door, inflicted by strong servants. Other servants having appeared from within, we were invited to walk in. The ambassador's name was then called out at stated intervals, until we were ushered into the hall of meeting. Here, at the threshold, we were received by the vizier, who himself was walking about as well as most of his guests, for there appeared to be perfect liberty on that score. We then went to the vizier's wife, who seemed to be quite as much at home as her husband, and did her best by sweet smiles to make us welcome. There were several other khanums, very civil and handsome. If any portion of a veil had been thrown over them, to hide certain parts of their very white persons, I should have been in a fever of love at once; but as it was, I scarcely thought of them as women. The conversation began by every person present appearing anxious to know whether we had seen the sun on that day; for it was ascertained that it had been seen, but whether for one hour, or only half an hour, there appeared to be some serious doubts. The ambassador, evidently tired at this constant allusion to our supposed worship of the sun, turned off the observation by a compliment to the vizier's wife. "You do not want a sun in your country," said he, "when you have such suns as the khanum's eyes to give light and joy to the world!"

When this was interpreted, it produced a universal cry of approbation, and was immediately taken up, with the greatest good humor, by the vizier himself, who said, "If his excellency is to be an apostate, and if he is to worship these suns (pointing to the lady's eyes) instead of his own, we must look about us. We must begin building harems, and manufacturing veils."

Upon this, a great deal of agreeable joking took place, which animated the whole party, and indeed gave us an insight into the English character we had never before acquired. We, Persians, who are so fond of a good saying, were delighted to find that so much merriment could exist among persons who usually live in a fog; and the ambassador, who thought that there might be some etiquette among them as to who should launch the first joke, seeing that they were in general so taciturn, willingly ventured to break the spell, and never lost an opportunity for the future of putting in his word whenever he could do so with propriety.

The entrance of a person with white dust on his head to invite us to the feast, put an end for a time to the good humor that had broken out; and when the company stood up, we discovered that there existed among the English to the full as much etiquette about precedence as in our country. But Allah! Allah! who, let me say, were the objects of it? Mohamed Beg, when I related the fact, would not believe it. Women!—they, the women took precedence. They walked out of the room first, while the men seemed to struggle for the privilege of leading them forwards. Every honor was intended towards our ambassador; he was invited to make his way with the vizier's wife, his right hand placed in her left; and considering that this was the first time he had performed such a ceremony, he really did it amazingly well. Without even thinking of washing our hands before we began to eat, both men and women proceeded to the scene of action. What we Mussulmans were to do with our left hands was always a subject of deep consideration; but in a country of infidels we took liberties that no other emergency could ever sanction.

We entered a large room, in the centre of which was spread a table more curiously ornamented than any we had yet seen. Around this we placed ourselves, but not without of the difficulty of etiquette. I avow, that saving our own beards, which looked out of character among the smooth chins that wagged round the board, I was delighted at the sight. 'Tis true that much more noise was heard than during one of our entertainments; for the unceasing activity of the servants with creaking shoes, the clash of plates, the ringing of glasses, the slashing and cutting with sharp instruments, and, above all, the universal talking of the assembly, created a din to which we were little accustomed, and which in Persia would be esteemed as highly indecorous.* But it was an enlivening sight; and excepting the absence of a Hafiz to chant the luxuries of our wine, of the excellence of which even our blessed Prophet could have had no idea, the entertainment would have been perfect. Of what the numerous dishes were composed, I did not give myself the trouble to consider; and without pausing to inquire whether the mutton had properly bled, or whether the poultry had died the true death, I eat whatever came in my way. I certainly made one or two scrutinizing pauses at a new sort of flesh, and which I fancied might be that of the unclean beast; but "in the name of Allah!" said I, "what is the use of sticking about pollution, when we have now been steeped in it ever since we have lived among the infidels?" and so I ate of every thing that was offered to me. If Mohamed Beg had been with us,

* Persian servants in attendance at an entertainment are scarcely heard. They do their work without shoes; and as there is no handing of plates, and no changing of knives and forks, the quiet is great compared to the din of our tables.

he would have been blowing over his shoulders during the whole of the entertainment. The ambassador seemed to be as much at his ease as any one of the most experienced eaters of a dinner among the English themselves. He managed the spoons, knives, claws, and pincers, with surprising dexterity. I must own that I was not so fortunate, for I made one or two mistakes merely from the force of previous habit, which evidently had an unfavorable effect upon those around me. I shared my neighbor's bread, which is here looked upon as offensive as it is otherwise in Persia. I drank out of his glass; and once I presented a bit with my fingers from a dish before me, at which he made a start as if I had offered poison. Although we did not sit with our knees double, but were quite at our ease upon chairs, with legs pendant, yet the great length of the entertainment almost killed me. At length there was a general move, but to my astonishment, the women only took their departure. This was the nearest approach to our own customs which I had yet seen, and I asked my neighbor why this distinction was made? why the women alone went? He seemed puzzled for an explanation. "Is it thus ordained in your scriptures," said I, "or is it ordered by your king?" Still he was at a loss for an answer; and I concluded that this might be a custom borrowed from Islam. My neighbor hinted that the absence of the women left the men at greater liberty to talk and drink wine. "Ah, then," said I, "you must have adopted that maxim of the East, which saith, "first dinner, then conversation;" but if drinking be your object, this is not the way to set about it. Do as we do in Persia; get up betimes in the morning; go into a garden; seat yourself near a running stream; put flowers on your head; have songsters and nightingales; drink till your senses are gone; wait till they return; then drink again, and take no thought of time; let day and night be the same, until at length you have so completely soaked yourself with wine, that it is time to cry out, 'Enough! enough!'"

Whether my neighbor understood my attempt to explain myself in English, I know not, but he eyed me with astonishment.

At length, the dinner was over, and with unwashed hands we proceeded to the room of assembly, where we found the vizier's wife and her khanums ready again to receive us.

RESPECTABILITY.

ANONYMOUS.

"Pray, what do you mean by 'Respectability?'
Is it wisdom or worth, sir? or rank or gentility?
Is it rough sound sense? or a manner refined?
Is it kindness of heart? or expansion of mind?
Is it learning or talent, or honor, or fame,
That you mean by that phrase (so expressive) to name?"—
"No, no—these are not, sir, the things now in vogue:
A 'respectable man,' sir, may be a great rogue,—
A 'respectable person' may be a great fool,—
Have lost even the little he picked up at school,—
Be a glutton, adulterer, deep drowned in debt,—
May forfeit his honor, his best friend forget,—
May be a base sycophant, tyrant, or knave—
But a livery-servant, at least, he must have:
In vice he may vie with the vilest of sinners—
But he *must* keep a cook, and give capital dinners.

THE ENTHUSIAST IN ANATOMY.

BY JOHN OXENFORD (BALZAC D'ANOIS).

The youth, whom we shall call "Tom,"—and nothing *but* "Tom,"—was one of those individuals who labor with a fierce, burning anxiety, to burst through the trammels imposed upon them by a limited education,—one of those votaries of science, whose energy seems to grow all the more, because it has nothing to feed upon. He was very slightly formed, and had eyes so bright and shining, that when one gazed on him, one was inclined to overlook all his other thin, sharply-defined features. Never was there a more complete appearance of a clear intelligence in a corporeal form.

The few half-pence which Tom was enabled to save from his scanty earnings at a laborious trade, he regularly expended at the book-stall, and on one occasion was highly delighted at picking up a small book on Anatomy. The work was one of those that had long been superseded by more modern and better treatises, and the little plates were as ill and coarsely done as possible. Nevertheless, with him it had not the disadvantage of comparison. He thought it a mine of science yet unexplored, and he suffered his whole soul to be absorbed by it.

In a few weeks, he had transferred the entire contents of the work into his own brain; and though he invariably carried the book in his pocket, it was more out of respect to it, as an old friend, than from any further benefit to be derived from it. The names of every bone, cartilage, ligament, and muscle, of which he had read, were deeply imprinted in his mind; and he could have passed with glory through the sharpest examination, provided it had been based on the contents of the little book.

But Tom, in spite of his knowledge, was too intelligent not to perceive the defective state of his acquirements. He soon felt that his anatomy was, after all, a science of names rather than of things; that though he could have described accurately all the intricate bones of the skull, and all the muscles of the extremities, his descriptions would have been little more than a repetition of words committed to memory. He had not seen a single real object connected with his science. If he could but have set eyes upon a skeleton, what an advantage it would have been.

We once read of a celebrated anatomist, who, far from admiring human beauty, regarded the skin as an impertinent obstacle to the acquisition of science, concealing, as it does, the play of the muscles. Whether such a clear notion as this ever entered the mind of our hero, we cannot say; but certainly if some tall lean beggar passed him on the road, he would clutch convulsively at his knife, and follow the man with a sad wistful look.

One autumnal evening, he sat in the ale-house parlor, watching the smoke of his pipe, and indulging in his own reflections; for though the conversation in the room was noisy and animated, it had no interest for him. Devoted to his own pursuits, births, deaths, and marriages were to him things of nought, and he paid no heed to the constant discussions which were held in the village on the extraordinary case of old Ebenezer Grindstone, who had been thought extremely rich, but in whose house not a farthing had been found after his decease, to the great disappointment of his creditors.

Soon, however, there was such a violent dash of rain against the window, that even Tom was compelled to start, when he saw the door open, and a stranger enter, completely muffled in a cloak. The new-comer stood before the fire, as if to dry himself, and seemed to be of the same taciturn disposition as Tom, for he made no answer to the different questions that were addressed to him, nor did he even condescend to look at the speakers. The shower having ceased, and the moon shining brightly through the window, the stranger walked out again, without the sign of leave-taking.

"That be a queer chap," said the ostler, "I'll run and see where he's going,"—and he followed the stranger, who had awakened a curiosity in every one except Tom. Scarcely five minutes had elapsed, when the ostler rushed into the room, pale as death.

"Udds huddikins!" said he; and it was not before a glass of spirits had been poured down his throat, that he could state the cause of his alarm. "Old chap just gone out—got no proper face like—only a death's head—he just looked round on me in the moon-light."

"Do you mean to say," exclaimed Tom, "that he is nothing but a skeleton?"

"Aye—sure I do," said the ostler.

"And which way did he go?"

"Why, towards the church-yard, sure," said the ostler. Tom waited for no more, but dashing down his pipe, he rushed out of the room, and tore along the road to the church-yard. When he had got there, he saw the stranger standing by the tomb of old Ebenezer Grindstone. The moon was shining full upon him, and as Tom approached, the cloak fell down, leaving nothing but a bare skeleton before him.

"Thank my stars!" exclaimed Tom, "I have seen a skeleton at last!"

"Young man," said the skeleton, in a hollow voice, while it hideously moved its jaws, "attend!"

"How beautifully," cried Tom, enraptured, "can I see the play of the lower maxillary!"

"Attend!" repeated the skeleton; "but, rash man, what are you about?" it added, turning suddenly round. The fact is, Tom was running his finger down the vertebræ, and counting to see if their number corresponded with that given in his book. "Seven cervical, twelve dorsal," he cried with immense glee.

The skeleton lost all patience, and, raising its arm, shook its fist angrily at Tom, who, with his eyes fixed on the elbow, merely shouted his joy, at perceiving the "ginglymoid" movement.

The skeleton, who had been accustomed to terrify other people, was completely amazed at the scientific position taken by the young anatomist. In fact, the most extraordinary scene that can be conceived presently occurred; for the apparition, feeling panic-struck at Tom's coolness and scientific spirit, darted away from him, and endeavored to escape by dodging among the tombstones. Tom was too anxious to pursue his studies to allow him-

self to be baffled in this way; and putting forth all his strength, soon overtook the skeleton, and held him tight. A conversation ensued, in the course of which the skeleton explained that he was Old Grindstone himself, who had buried a quantity of money under ground, and could not rest in peace till it was dug up and distributed among the creditors. This office he requested Tom to perform.

"It will be some trouble," said Tom, "and the affair is none of mine—but look ye—I'm willing to comply with your request, if, as a reward, you will allow me to come and study you every night for the next month. You may then retire to rest for as long a time as you please."

"Agreed," said the skeleton; and, quite recovered from his alarm, he shook hands with Tom in ratification of the bargain.

Tom found the money, distributed it among the creditors, and passed every night for the next month in the old church-yard, observing his beloved skeleton, which, as it moved into any position he desired, gave him an opportunity of studying the motion of the bones, in a way that had not been enjoyed by any other anatomist.

The young enthusiast, sitting at midnight with the strange assistant to his pursuits, would have been a delightful sight, had any one possessed the courage to stop and look at the party. When the month had expired, Tom and his good friend shook hands and parted with great regret; but Tom had completely retained in his mind all he had seen, and laid the foundation of that profound anatomical science by which he was afterwards so much distinguished.

It is needless to state that the above is the early history of the celebrated Dr. ——, and that all other accounts are baseless fabrications.

THE SHORT COURTSHIP.

WITH AN ILLUSTRATION BY GEORGE CRUIKSHANK.

As a gentleman was passing along one of the more retired streets of London, he stumbled over the body of an old man, whom, on examination, he found in a state of excessive inebriation, and who had, in consequence, tumbled down and rolled into the kennel. He had not gone many yards further when he found an old woman very nearly in the same circumstances. It immediately struck Mr. L. that this was some poor old couple, who, overcome with the fatigues of the day, had indulged too freely in some restorative beverage, whether Hodges' or Deady's the historian does not say. Full of this idea, and animated by his own charitable disposition, Mr. L. soon made arrangements for the reception of the poor couple into a neighboring public house, where the landlord promised that the senseless pair should be undressed and placed in a warm and comfortable bed. To bed they were put. Mr. L. left them lying side by side, snoring in concert, and likely to pass together a more harmonious night than perhaps would have been the case, had they possessed the full enjoyment of their senses. L. journeyed homewards, filled with the satisfaction arising from the performance of a kind deed, and never reflected that there was a possibility of his having joined a pair whom the laws of God had not made one. The fact was, that the old man and the old woman were perfect strangers to each other, and their being found in a similar situation was purely accidental. In London, however extraor-

Eng^d by W. G. Jackman

George Cruikshank

dinary it may appear, many poor folks get drunk at night, especially Saturday night, and what is not less wonderful, they are in this state often unable to preserve their balance—the laws of gravity exert their influence, and the patient rolls into the kennel. Soundly—soundly did this late united pair sleep and snore till morning—when the light broke in upon them, and disclosed the secret. Imagine the consternation of the old lady when the fumes of intoxication were dissipated, and she opened her eyes upon her snoring partner:—where she was, or how she had been put there, she knew not. It was clear she was in bed with a man, and that was an event which had never happened to her before,—so she set up a scream, and roused the old gentleman, whose astonishment was not a jot less than the lady's. She sat np on end in bed, staring at him; he moved himself into a similar situation, and riveted his eyes upon her, and so they remained for a few instants, both full of perfect wonderment. At last it struck the poor lady that this was some monster of a man, who had succeeded in some horrible design upon her honor; the idea in a moment gave her the look and manner of a fury; she flung out of bed, and roared aloud to the admiration of all the inmates of the house, who, attracted by her first screams, were already peeping in at the door of the room. "Make me an honest woman, thou wretch," she cried,—"Villain that thou are,—make an honest woman of me, or I'll be the death of thee;"—down she sat upon the bed stocks, and as she attempted to dress herself, she interlarded her occupation with calling for vengeance upon her horrible seducer, who sat trembling at the other side of the bed, vainly attempting in his fright to insinuate his legs into his old tattered breeches. The landlord at last interfered with the authority of his station; and, on inquiry, found that no breach had been made which could not be easily repaired. The old gentleman was asked if he had any objection to take his fair bedfellow for a helpmate during the remainder of his life; he stammered out his acquiescence as well as he could, and the enraged virgin consented to smooth down her anger on satisfaction being made to her injured honor. The bargain was soon struck; the happy pair were bundled off to church, amidst the laughing shouts of the mob, where a parson waited to make good the match too precipitately formed by our charitable friend.

FRIGHTS.

ILLUSTRATED BY GEORGE CRUIKSHANK.

We propose to give illustrations of frights familiar to every family, and susceptible of description. Let us take a night scene, conjured up by a sudden alarm of

THIEVES!

'Tis moonlight, and "the very houses seem asleep," out-houses and all. The "quiet family" has attained its utmost pitch of quietness. All sleep soundly, where no sound is heard. A breathless hush pervades the domicile. On a sudden, there is a smart crash, a rattling sound, below. This sleeper starts up in bed; that, darts further under the clothes. "What's that?" is the inward question of everybody. The thought of thieves occurs to each in turn; one is certain that the area-door has been forced open; another is sure that the back-parlor sash has been raised. They lie still, with panting hearts, and listen. Again there is a noise; it is like creaking footsteps on the stairs, or the opening of drawers; then all is silent again, and the noise is renewed.

At last, one little quaking Miss ventures, half-stifled, to whisper, "Sarah, are you awake?" And Sarah faintly answers, "Yes, did you hear that?" and both busy themselves in the bed, and dare not breathe. And then they hear a door open softly, and they utter a loud cry of terror; and then in another minute the door of their own room opens, and with a loud scream they start up—only to see their dear good mama with a candle in her hand; but she is pale and frightened, and desires to know if *they* had made the noise—but they had not;

only they distinctly heard somebody getting in at the back-door, or the parlor-window. Then papa commands the whole assembled family "not to be frightened," and shakes dreadfully—with cold—as he looks at his blunderbuss, and avows his determination to proceed down-stairs. And then there is a "hush!" and a general listening. Yes, there *is* a noise still, and to the stairs he advances; while his better-half lights his way, and holds his garments tight to check his desperate enthusiasm; and the eldest daughter hardly ventures beyond the chamber-door, but with astonishing boldness and exemplary daring springs a rattle; and the others hold on each by each, taking fresh fright from one another's fears. What an amount of suffering, dread, terror—is in the bosom of the little quiet family, as down to the scene of danger they creep with tortoise-pace! And what is all this anxiety, this trepidation, this sickness of the heart, for? What has occasioned so terrific a commotion! Perhaps the tongs have fallen down, and the clatter has filled their ears with all sorts of imaginary noises! Perhaps the cat is clawing at a string tied to the latch of the pantry-door; or, perhaps, the stupid little kitten, having got her tail into the catch of the last new patent mouse-trap, has dragged that excellent invention off the dresser, and is whisking round at intervals in a wearying and vain endeavor to extricate her unprehensile appendage! "Dear me! well, I declare, how I have been frightening myself!" cries every member of the shivering family; and the very next night, should the same noises be heard, the whole frightened family would start, turn pale, quake, wonder, pant, scream, and spring rattles, exactly as before. When Fear has once taken possession, Experience does not always make folks wise. Let us take for another example of the daily domestic romance—

THE STRANGE CAT.

How vividly, among the events of our boyish days, do we remember the "strange cat" that got into the lumber-room at the top of the house! Our elder brother and "the boy" had endeavored to dislodge the animal, which figured in their description as a thing of intense blackness and monstrous dimensions, with great frightful staring green eyes, horrid long claws, and such a tail! Not "frightened of cats" were we, for we had a favorite one of our own; but *this*—it trebled in magnitude and horror the wildest and most savage inhabitants of the then Exeter 'Change. Their own fears had magnified the "strange cat" into a monster; and then they wilfully enlarged the picture to terrify *us*—a feat, in which they succeeded, as we dared not go to the upper rooms alone. For two or three days this "reign of terror" lasted, when, a favorable opportunity being watched for, the "young master" and the "young man" marched up, broom and brush in hand, to hunt out this strange secreted intruder—this black tiger of the upper wilderness. As for our tiny self, we had ventured part of the way up-stairs to witness the result, imagining that the enemy would make its exit by an attic window.

Oh, horror! A loud knocking was heard above; a tremendous shouting next arose, succeeded instantly by an appalling cry of "Here it comes!" This was, shall we say *enough?* it was too much; we turned and *flew* down stairs—the last "flight" of stairs being, with the aid of the handrail, but one leap. The street door! No, we could not open it. Against it, then, we set our back, in an agony of fear, and uttered a cry that would have terrified a whole legion of cats. The hunters were in full cry. Down came the wild animal, followed by brooms and brushes, bounding and rattling over the stairs —a clatter that rent the roof. What saw we then? Not a poor, half-starved, *frightened* animal leaping over the banisters to get out of *our* way, and to escape through the garden door; no, of this piteous, this actual spectacle, we saw nothing; but, in its place—*This*

This little "tail piece" expanded to the dimensions of a full-sized Newfoundland dog, surrounded by a blaze of fire, will convey some idea of what, in the extremity of misapprehension, we actually did see.

A FULL-DRESS PARTY.

DESIGNED BY GEORGE CRUIKSHANK.

WILL YOU BE OUR VIS-A-VIS?"

A TOAD IN A HOLE.

FROM "THREE COURSES AND A DESSERT." BY — CLARKE.

THE Friars of Fairoak were assembled in a chamber adjoining the great hall of their house: the Abbot was seated in his chair of eminence, and all eyes were turned on Father Nicodemus. Not a word was uttered, until he who seemed to be the object of so much interest, at length ventured to speak. "It behooveth not one of my years, perchance," said he, "to disturb the silence of my elders and superiors; but, truly, I know not what meaneth this meeting; and surely my desire to be edified is lawful. Hath it been decided that we should follow the example of our next-door neighbors, the Arroasian Friars, and, henceforth, be tongue-tied? If not, do we come here to eat, or pray, or hold council? Ye seem somewhat too grave for those bidden to a feast, and there lurk too many smiles about the faces of many of ye, for this your silence to be a prelude to prayers. I cannot think we are about to consult on aught; because, with reverence be it spoken, those who pass for the wisest among us, look more silly than is their wont. But if we be here to eat, let us eat; if to pray, let us pray; and if to hold council, what is to be the knotty subject of our debate?"

"Thyself," replied the Abbot.

"On what score?" inquired Nicodemus.

"On divers scores," quoth the Abbot; "thy misdeeds have grown rank; we must even root them out of thee, or root thee out of our fraternity, on which thou art bringing contumely. I tell thee, Brother Nicodemus, thy offences are numberless as the weeds which grow by the way-side. Here be many who have much to say of thee; speak, Brother Ulick!"

"Brother Nicodemus," said Father Ulick, "hath, truly, ever been a gross feeder."

"And a lover of deep and most frequent potations," quoth Father Edmund.

"And a roamer beyond due bounds," added Father Hugo.

"Yea, and given to the utterance of many fictions," muttered his brother.

"Very voluble also, and not altogether of so staid an aspect as becometh one of his order and mellow years," drawled Father James.

"To speak plainly—a glutton," said the first speaker.

"Ay, and a drunkard," said the second.

"Moreover, a night-walker," said the third.

"Also a liar," said the fourth.

"Finally, a babbler and a buffoon," said the fifth.

"Ye rate me roundly, brethren," cried Nicodemus; "and, truly, were ye my judges, I should speedily be convicted of these offences whereof I am accused; but not a man among you is fitted to sit in judgment on the special misfeasance with which he chargeth me. And I will reason with you, and tell you why. Now, first, to deal with Brother Ulick—who upbraideth me with gross feeding:—until he can prove that his stomach and mine are of the same quality, clamor, and power digestive, I will not, without protest, permit him to accuse me of devouring swinishly. He is of so poor and weak a frame, that he cannot eat aught but soppets, without suffering the pangs of indigestion, and the nocturnal visits of incubi, and more sprites than tempted Saint Anthony. It is no virtue in him to be abstemious; he is enforced to avoid eating the tithe of what would be needful to a man of moderate stomach; and, behold, how lean he looks! Next, Brother Edmund hath twitted me with being a deep drinker. Now, it is well known that Brother Edmund must not take a second cup after his repast; being so puny of brain, that if he do, his head is racked with myriads of pains and aches on the morrow, and it lieth like a log on his shoulder,—if perchance he be enabled to rise from his pallet. Shall he, then, pronounce dogmatically on the quantity of potation lawful to a man in good health? I say, nay. Brother Hugo, who chargeth me with roaming, is lame; and his brother, who saith that I am an utterer of fictions, hath a brain which is truly incompetent to conceive an idea, or to comprehend a fact. Brother James, who arraigneth me of volubility, passeth for a sage pillar of the church; because, having naught to say, he looks grave and holds his peace. I will be tried, if you will, by Brother James, for gross feeding; he having a good digestion and an appetite equal to mine own: or by Brother Hugo, for drinking abundantly; inasmuch as he is wont to solace himself, under his infirmity, with a full flask: or by Brother Ulick, for the utterance of fictions; because he hath written a history of some of The Fathers, and admireth the blossoms of the brain: or by Brother Edmund, for not being sufficiently sedate; as he is, truly, a comfortable talker himself, and, although forced to eschew wine, of a most cheerful countenance. By Hugo's brother I will be tried on no charge, seeing that he is, was, and ever will be—in charity I speak it—an egregious fool. Have ye aught else to set up against me, brethren?"

"Much more, Brother Nicodemus," said the Abbot, "much more, to our sorrow. The cry of our vassals hath come up against thee; and it is now grown so loud and frequent, that we are unwillingly enforced to assume our authority, as their lord and thy superior, to redress their grievances and correct thy errors."

"Correct *me!*" exclaimed Father Nicodemus; "why, what say the rogues? Dare they throw blur, blain, or blemish on my good name? Would that I might hear one of them!"

"Thou shalt be gratified; call in John of the Hough."

In a few moments, John of the Hough appeared, with his head bound up, and looking alarmed as a recently-punished hound when brought again into the presence of him by whom he has been chastised.

"Fear not," said the Abbot; "fear not, John o' the Hough, but speak boldly; and our benison or malison be on thee, as thou speakest true or false."

"Father Nicodemus," said John o' the Hough, in a voice rendered almost inaudible by fear, "broke my head with a cudgel he weareth under his cloak."

"When did he do this?" inquired the Abbot.

"On the feast of St. James and Jude; oft before, and since, too, without provocation; and, lastly, on Monday se'nnight."

"Why, thou strangely perverse varlet, dost thou say it was I who beat thee?" demanded the accused friar.

"Ay, truly, most respected Father Nicodemus."

"Dost thou dare to repeat it? I am amazed at thy boldness—or, rather, thy stupidity—or, perhaps, at thy loss of memory. Know, thou naughty hind, it was thyself who cudgelled thee! Didst thou not know that if thou wert to vex a dog ho would snap at thee?—or hew and hack a tree, and not fly, it would fall on thee?—or grieve and wound the feelings of thy ghostly friend Father Nicodemus, he would cudgel thee? Did I rouse myself into a rage? Did I call myself a thief? Answer me, my son; did I?"

"No, truly, Father Nicodemus."

"Did I threaten, if I were not a son of Holy Mother Church, to kick myself out of thy house? Answer me, my son; did I?"

"No, truly, Father Nicodemus.

"Am I less than a dog, or a tree? Answer me, my son; am I?"

"No, truly, Father Nicodemus; but, truly, also—"

"None of thy buts, my son; respond to me with plain aye or no. Didst thou not do all these things antecedent to my breaking thy sconce?"

"Aye, truly, Father Nicodemus."

"Then how canst thou say *I* beat thee? Should I have carried my staff to thy house, did I not know thee to be a churl, and an enemy to the good brotherhood of this house? Was I to go into the lion's den without my defence? Should I have demeaned myself to phlebotomize thee with my cudgel (and doubtless the operation was salubrious) hadst thou not aspersed me? Was it for me to stand by, tamely, with three feet of blackthorn at my belt, and hear a brother of this religious order, betwitted as I was by thee, with petty larceny? Was it not thine own breath, then, that brought the cudgel upon thy caput? Answer me, my son."

"Lead forth John of the Hough, and call in the miller of Hornford," said the Abbot, before John of the Hough could reply. "Now, miller," continued he, as soon as the miller entered, "what hast thou to allege against this our good brother, Nicodemus?"

"I allege," replied the miller, "that he is naught."

"Oh! thou especial rogue!" exclaimed Father Nicodemus; "dost *thou* come here to bear witness against me? I will impeach thy testimony by one assertion, which thou canst not gainsay; for the evidence of it is written on thy brow, thou brawny villain! Thou bearest malice against me, because I, some six years ago, inflicted a cracked crown on thee, for robbing this holy house of its lawful meal. I deemed the punishment adequate to the offence, and spoke not of it to the Abbot, in consideration of thy promising to mend thy ways. Hadst thou not well merited that mark of my attention to the interests of my brethren, the whole lordship would have heard of it. And didst thou ever say I made the wound? Never; thy tale was that some of thy mill-gear had done it. But I will be judged by any here, if the scar be not of my blackthorn's making. I will summon three score, at least, who shall prove it to be my mark. Let it be viewed with that on the head of thy foster-brother, John of the Hough—I will abide by the comparison. Thou hast hoarded malice in thy heart from that day; and now thou comest here to vomit it forth, as thou deemest, to my undoing. But, be sure, caitiff, that

I shall testify upon thy sconce hereafter; for I know thou art rogue enough to rob if thou canst, and fool enough to rob with so little discretion as to be easily detected; and even if my present staff be worn out, there be others in the woods:—ergo—"

"Peace, Brother Nicodemus!" exclaimed the Abbot; "approach not a single pace nearer to the miller; neither do thou threaten nor browbeat him, I enjoin thee."

"Were it not for the reverence I owe to those who are round me, and my unwillingness to commit even so trifling a sin," said Nicodemus, "I would take this slanderous and ungrateful knave betwixt my finger and thumb, and drop him among the hungry eels of his own mill-stream. I chafe apace: lay hands on me, brethren!—for I wax wroth, and am sure, in these moods,—so weak is man—to do mischief ere my humor subside."

"Speak on, miller," said the Abbot; "and thou, Brother Nicodemus, give way to thine inward enemy, at thy peril."

"I will tell him—an' you will hold him back, and seize his staff," said the miller,—"how he and the roystering boatman of Frampton Ferry—"

"My time is coming!" exclaimed Nicodemus, interrupting the miller; "bid him withdraw, or he will have a sore head at his supper."

"They caroused and carolled," said the miller, "with two travellers, like skeldring Jacks o' the flagon, until—"

"Lay hands on Nicodemus, all!" cried the Abbot, as the enraged friar strode towards the miller; "lay hands on the madman at once!"

"It is too late," said Nicodemus, drawing forth a cudgel from beneath his cloak; "do not hinder me now, for my blackthorn reverences not the heads of the holy fraternity of Fairoak. Hold off, I say!" exclaimed he, as several of his brethren roughly attempted to seize him; "hold off, and mar me not in this mood; or to-day will, hereafter, be called the Feast of Blows. Nay, then, if you will not, I strike—may you be marked, but not maimed!" The friar began to level a few of the most resolute of those about him as he spoke. "I will deal lightly as my cudgel will let me," pursued he. "I strike indiscriminately, and without malice, I protest. May blessings follow these blows! Brother Ulick, I grieve that you have thrust yourself within my reach. Look to the Abbot, some of ye, for,—miserable me!—I have laid him low. Man is weak, and this must be atoned for by fasting. Where is the author of this mischief? Miller, where art thou?"

Father Nicodemus continued to lay about him very lustily for several minutes; but, before he could deal with the miller as he wished, Friar Hugo's brother, who was on the floor, caught him by the legs, and suddenly threw him prostrate. He was immediately overwhelmed by numbers, bound hand and foot, and carried to his own cell; where he was closely confined, and most vigilantly watched, until the superiors of his order could be assembled. He was tried in the chamber which had been the scene of his exploits: the charge of having rudely raised his hand against the Abbot, and belabored the holy brotherhood, was fully proved; and, ere twenty-four hours had elapsed, Father Nicodemus found himself enclosed, with a pitcher of water and a loaf, in a niche of a stone wall, in the lowest vault of Fairoak Abbey.

He soon began to feel round him, in order to ascertain if there were any chance of escaping from the tomb to which he had been consigned: the walls were old, but tolerably sound; he considered, however, that it was his duty to break out if he could; and he immediately determined on making an attempt. Putting his back to the wall, which had been built up to enclose him for ever from the world, and his feet against the opposite side of the niche, he strained every nerve to push one of them down. The old wall at length began to move; he reversed his position, and with his feet firmly planted against the new work, he made such a tremendous effort, that the ancient stones and mortar gave way behind him. The next moment he found himself lying on his back, with a quantity of rubbish about him, on the cold pavement of a vault, into which sufficient light glimmered, through a grating, to enable him to ascertain that he was no longer in any part of Fairoak Abbey.

The tongue-tied neighbors to whom Nicodemus

had alluded, when he broke silence at that meeting of his brethren which terminated so unfortunately, were monks of the same order as those of Fairoak Abbey; among whom, about a century and a half before the time of Nicodemus, such dissensions took place, that the heads of the order were compelled to interfere; and under their sanction and advice, two-and-twenty monks, who were desirous of following the fine example of the Arroasians of St. Augustin,—who neither wore linen nor ate flesh, and observed a perpetual silence,—seceded from the community, and elected an Abbot of their own. The left wing of Fairoak Abbey was assigned to them for a residence, and the rents of a certain portion of its lands were set apart for their support. Their first care was to separate themselves, by stout walls, from all communication with their late brethren; and up to the days of Nicodemus, no friendly communion had taken place between the Arroasian and its mother Abbey.

Nicodemus had no doubt but that he was in one of the vaults of the silent monks: in order that he might not be recognized as a brother of Fairoak, he took off his black cloak and hood, and even his cassock and rochet, and concealed them beneath a few stones, in a corner of the recess from which he had just liberated himself. With some difficulty, he reached the inhabited part of the building; after terrifying several of the Arroasians, by abruptly breaking upon their meditations, he at length found an old white cloak and hood, arrayed in which he took a seat at the table of the refectory, and, to the amazement of the monks, tacitly helped himself to a portion of their frugal repast. The Superior of the community, by signs, requested him to state who and what he was; but Nicodemus, pointing to the old Arroasian habit which he now wore, wisely held his peace. The good friars knew not how to act:—Nicodemus was suffered to enter into quiet possession of a vacant cell; he joined in their silent devotions, and acted in every respect as though he had been an Arroasian all his life.

By degrees the good monks became reconciled to his presence, and looked upon him as a brother. He behaved most discreetly for several months; but at length having grown weary of bread, water, and silence, he, one evening, stole over the garden-wall, resolving to have an eel-pie and some malmsey, spiced with a little jovial chat, in the company of his trusty friend, the boatman of Frampton Ferry. His first care, on finding himself at large, was to go to the coppice of Fairoak, and cut a yard of good blackthorn, which he slung by a hazel gad to his girdle, but beneath his cassock. Resuming his path towards the Ferry, he strode on at a brisk rate for a few minutes; when, to his great dismay, he heard the sound of the bell which summoned the Arroasians to meet in the chapel of their Abbey.

"A murrain on thy noisy tongue!" exclaimed Nicodemus, "on what emergency is thy tail tugged, to make thee yell at this unwonted hour? There is a grievous penalty attached to the offence of quitting the walls, either by day or by night; and as I am now deemed a true Arroasian, by Botolph, I stand here in jeopardy; for they will assuredly discover my absence. I will return at once, slink into my cell, and be found there afflicted with a lethargy, when they come to search for me; or, if occasion serve, join my brethren boldly in the chapel."

The bell had scarcely ceased to toll, whon Nicodemus reached the garden-wall again; he clambered over it, alighted safely on a heap of manure, and was immediately seized by half a score of the stoutest among the Arroasians. Unluckily for Nicodemus, the Superior himself had seen a figure, in the costume of the Abbey, scaling the garden-wall, and had immediately ordered the bell to be rung, and a watch to be set, in order to take the offender in the fact, on his return. The mode of administering justice among the Arroasians, was much more summary than in the Abbey of Fairoak. Nicodemus was brought into the Superior's cell, and divested of his cloak; his cassock was then turned down from his belt, and a bull's-hide thong severely applied to his back, before he could recover himself from the surprise into which his sudden capture had thrown him. His wrath rose, not gradually as it did of old,—but in a moment, under the pain and indignity of the thong, it mounted to its highest pitch. Breaking from those who were holding him, he plucked the blackthorn he had cut, from beneath his cassock, and without either benediction or excuse, silently but severely belabored all present, the Superior himself not excepted. When his rage and strength were somewhat exhausted, the prostrate brethren rallied a little, and with the aid of the remainder of the community, who came to their assistance, they contrived to despoil Nicodemus of his staff, and to secure him from doing further mischief.

The next morning, Nicodemus was stripped of his Arroasian habit; and, attired in nothing but the linen in which he had first appeared among the brethren, he was conducted, with very little ceremony, to the vaults beneath the Abbey. Every member of the community advanced to give him a parting embrace, and the Superior pointed with his finger to a recess in the wall. Nicodemus was immediately ushered into it, the wall was built up behind him, and once more he found himself entombed alive.

"But that I am not so strong as I was of yore, after the lenten fare of my late brethren," said Nicodemus, "I should not be content to die thus, in a coffin of stones and mortar. What luck hast thou here, Nicodemus?" continued the friar, as, poking about the floor of his narrow cell, he felt something like a garment, with his foot. "By rood and by rochet, mine own attire!—the cloak and cassock, or I am much mistaken, which I left behind me when I was last here; for surely these are my old quarters! I did not think to be twice tenant of this hole; but man is weak, and I was born to be the bane of blackthorn. The lazy rogues found this niche ready-made to their hands, and, truth to say, they have walled me up like workmen. Ah, me! there is no soft place for me to bulge my back through now. Hope have I none: but I will betake me to my anthems; and perchance, in due season, I may light upon some means of making egress."

Nicodemus had, by this time, contrived to put on his cassock and cloak, which somewhat comforted his shivering body, and he forthwith began to chant his favorite anthem in such a lusty tone, that it was faintly heard by the Fairoak Abbey cellarman, and one of the friars who was in the vaults with him, selecting the ripest wines. On the alarm being given, a score of the brethren betook themselves to the vaults; and, with torches in their hands, searched every corner for the anthem-singer, but without success. At length the cellarman ventured to observe, that, in his opinion, the sounds came from the wall; and the color left the cheeks of all as the recollection of Nicodemus flashed upon them. They gathered round the place where they had enclosed him, and soon felt satisfied that the awful anthem was there more distinctly heard than in any other part of the vault. The whole fraternity soon assembled, and endeavored to come to some resolution as to how they ought to act. With fear and trembling, Father Hugo's brother moved that they should at once open the wall: this proposal was at first rejected with contempt, on account of the known stupidity of the person with whom it originated; but as no one ventured to suggest any thing, either better or worse, it was at last unanimously agreed to. With much solemnity, they proceeded to make a large opening in the wall. In a few minutes, Father Nicodemus appeared before them, arrayed in his cloak and cassock, and not much leaner or less rosy than when they bade him, as they thought, an eternal adieu, nearly a year before. The friars shouted, "A miracle! a miracle!" and Nicodemus did not deem it by any means necessary to contradict them. "Ho, ho!" brethren," exclaimed he, "you are coming to do me justice at last, are you? By faith and troth, but you are tardy! Your consciences, methinks, might have urged you to enact this piece of good-fellowship some week or two ago. To dwell ten months and more in so dark and solitary a den, like a toad in a hole, is no child's-play. Let the man who doubts, assume my place, and judge for himself. I ask no one to believe me on my bare word. You have wronged me, brethren, much; but I forgive you freely."

"A miracle! a miracle!" again shouted the amazed monks. They most respectfully declined the proffered familiarities of Nicodemus, and still gazed on him with profound awe, even after the most incredulous among them were convinced, by the celerity with which a venison pasty, flanked by a platter of brawn, and a capacious jack of Cyprus wine vanished before him, in the refectory, that he was truly their Brother Nicodemus, and still in the flesh. Ere long, the jolly friar became Abbot of Fairoak: he was dubbed a saint after his decease; but as no miracles were ever wrought at his shrine, his name has since been struck out of the calendar.

THE DEAF POSTILION.

FROM "THREE COURSES AND A DESSERT." BY — CLARKE.

In the month of January, 1804, Joey Duddle, a well-known postilion on the North Road, caught a cold, through sleeping without his night-cap; deafness was, eventually, the consequence; and, as it will presently appear, a young fortune-hunter lost twenty-thousand pounds, and a handsome wife, through Joey Duddle's indiscretion, in omitting, on one fatal occasion, to wear his sixpenny woollen night-cap.

Joey did not discontinue driving, after his misfortune; his eyes and his spurs were, generally speaking, of more utility in his monotonous avocation, than his ears. His stage was, invariably, nine miles up the road, or, "a short fifteen" down towards Gretna; and he had repeated his two rides so often, that he could have gone over the ground blindfold. People in chaises are rarely given to talking with their postilions; Joey knew, by experience, what were the two or three important questions in posting, and the usual times and places when and where they were asked; and he was always prepared with the proper answers. At those parts of the road, where objects of interest to strangers occurred, Joey faced about on his saddle, and if he perceived the eyes of his passengers fixed upon him, their lips in motion, and their fingers pointing towards a gentleman's seat, a fertile valley, a beautiful stream, or a fine wood, he naturally enough presumed that they were in the act of inquiring what the seat, the valley, the stream, or the wood was called; and he replied according to the fact. The noise of the wheels was a very good excuse for such trifling blunders as Joey occasionally made; and whenever he found himself progressing towards a dilemma, he very dexterously contrived, by means of a sly poke with his spur, to make his hand-horse evidently require the whole of his attention. At the journey's end, when the gentleman he had driven produced a purse, Joey, without looking at his lips, knew that he was asking a question, to which it was his duty to reply "Thirteen and sixpence," or "Two-and-twenty shillings," according as the job had been, "the short up," or "the long down." If any more questions were asked, Joey suddenly recollected something that demanded his immediate attention; begged pardon, promised to be back in a moment, and disappeared, never to return. The natural expression of his features indicated a remarkably taciturn disposition; almost every one with whom he came in contact, was deterred, by his physiognomy, from asking him any but necessary questions; and as he was experienced enough to answer, or cunning enough to evade these, when he thought fit, but few travellers ever discovered that Joey Duddle was deaf. So blind is man in some cases, even to his bodily defects, that Joey, judging from his general success in giving correct replies to the queries propounded to him, almost doubted his own infirmity; and never would admit that he was above one point beyond a little hard of hearing."

On the first of June, in the year 1806, about nine

o'clock in the morning, a chaise and four was perceived approaching towards the inn kept by Joey's master, at a first-rate Gretna-Green gallop. As it dashed up to the door, the post-boys vociferated the usual call for two pair of horses in a hurry; but, unfortunately, the innkeeper had only Joey and his tits at home; and as the four horses which brought the chaise from the last posting-house, had already done a double job that day, the lads would not ride them on, through so heavy a stage as "the long down."

"How excessively provoking!" exclaimed one of the passengers; "I am certain that our pursuers are not far behind us. The idea of having the cup of bliss dashed from my very lips,—of such beauty and affluence being snatched from me, for want of a second pair of paltry posters, drives me frantic!"

"A Gretna-Green affair, I presume, sir," observed the inquisitive landlord.

The gentleman made no scruple of admitting that he had run away with a fair young creature who accompanied him, and that she was entitled to a fortune of twenty thousand pounds;—"one half of which," continued the gentleman, "I would freely give,—if I had it,—to be, at this instant, behind four horses, scampering away, due north, at full speed."

"I can assure you, sir," said the landlord, "that a fresh pair of such animals as I offer you, will carry you over the ground as quick as if you had ten dozen of the regular road-hacks. No man keeps better cattle than I do, and this pair beats all the others in my stables by two miles an hour. But in ten minutes, perhaps, and certainly within half an hour—"

"Half an hour! half a minute's delay might ruin me," replied the gentleman; I hope I shall find the character you have given your cattle a correct one; dash on, postilion."

Before this short conversation between the gentleman and the innkeeper was concluded, Joey Duddle had put-to his horses,—which were, of course, kept harnessed,—and taken his seat, prepared to start at a moment's notice. He kept his eye upon the innkeeper, who gave the usual signal of a rapid wave of the hand, as soon as the gentleman ceased speaking; and Joey Duddle's cattle, in obedience to the whip and spur, hobbled off at that awkward and evidently painful pace, which is, perforce, adopted by the most praiseworthy post-horses for the first ten minutes or so of their journey. But the pair, over which Joey, presided, were, as the innkeeper had asserted, very speedy; and the gentleman soon felt satisfied, that it would take an extraordinary quadruple team to overtake them. His hopes rose at the sight of each succeeding milestone; he ceased to put his head out of the window every five minutes, and gazed anxiously up the road; he already anticipated a triumph,—when a crack, a crush, a shriek from the lady, a jolt, an instant change of position, and a positive pause occurred, in the order in which they are stated, with such suddenness and relative rapidity, that the gentleman was, for a moment or two, utterly deprived of his presence of mind by alarm and astonishment. The bolt which connects the fore-wheels, splinter-bar, springs, fore-bed, axle-tree, et cetera, with the perch, that passes under the body of the chaise, to the hind wheel-springs and carriage, had snapped asunder; the whole of the fore parts were instantly dragged onwards by the horses; the braces, by which the body was attached to the fore-springs, gave way; the chaise fell forward, and of course, remained stationary with its contents, in the middle of the road; while the Deaf Postilion rode on, with his eyes intently fixed on vacuity before him, as though nothing whatever had happened.

Alarmed, and indignant in the highest degree, at the postilion's conduct, the gentleman shouted with all his might such exclamations as any man would naturally use on such an occasion; but Joey, although still but at a little distance, took no notice of what had occurred behind his back, and very complacently trotted his horses on at the rate of eleven or twelve miles an hour. He thought the cattle went better than ever; his mind was occupied with the prospect of a speedy termination to his journey; he felt elated at the idea of outstripping the pursuers,—for Joey had discrimination enough to perceive, at a glance, that his passengers were runaway lovers,—and he went on very much to his own satisfaction. As he approached the inn, which terminated "the long down," Joey, as usual, put his horses upon their mettle, and they, having nothing but a fore-carriage and a young lady's trunk behind them, rattled up to the door at a rate unexampled in the annals of posting, with all the little boys and girls of the neighborhood hallooing in their rear.

It was not until he drew up to the inn door, and alighted from his saddle, that Joey discovered his disaster; and nothing could equal the utter astonishment which his features then displayed. He gazed at the place where the body of his chaise, his passengers, and hind-wheels ought to have been, for above a minute; and then suddenly started down the road on foot, under an idea that he must very recently have dropped them. On reaching a little elevation, which commanded above two miles of the ground over which he had come, he found, to his utter dismay, that no traces of the main body of his chaise were perceptible; nor could he discover his passengers, who had, as it appeared in the sequel, been overtaken by the young lady's friends. Poor Joey immediately ran into a neighboring hay-loft, where he hid himself, in despair, for three days; and when discovered, he was, with great difficulty, persuaded by his master, who highly esteemed him, to resume his whip and return to his saddle.

THE FORCE OF CIRCUMSTANCES.

BY MARK LEMON.

MY name is John Jones. I dare say you have seen it in the newspapers under the head of "POLICE," "*A gentleman in trouble*," "*More knocker stealing*," "*Fashionable amusement*," etc. Somebody has said that all men are mad upon some subject or the other. Quite right, depend upon it. My monomania is door-knockers, with an occasional furor for bell-handles. I've a museum, which I shall be glad to show any gentleman who will leave his card with the publisher. There he will see specimens arranged according to dates and localities. I shall bequeath my collection to the Ironmongers' Company, with permission to melt down any quantity it may be thought desirable to devote to a bust of the founder of this *unique* exhibition. You now know who I am.

Last winter I had a few fellows at my rooms. The sleet beating at the window had induced every one to make his grog as hot and strong as possible. The odorous tobacco-smoke wreathed itself about the room, and made the argand lamp on the table look like the sun in a London fog. Frank Fitch was on the sofa, singing "The Light of other Days," whilst Harry Fletcher was roaring out "*Il Tomba*," accompanying himself on the shovel and tongs. In fact, the evening was growing delightful, when Bob (my man) brought in a ticket from an elderly gentleman from the country. I looked at it, and saw "Mr. Thomas Thompson, Birkenhead!" My uncle! He to whom I was indebted for my quarterly allowance, and from whom I expected 3,000*l*. a year. I don't care what your opinions may be upon things in general, but you *must* acknowledge that this was awkward.

I scorn a deceit: so, emptying my glass, I went as straight as I could to my uncle. There he stood, on the little mat in the passage, dressed in the same prim blue coat, and pepper-and-salt trousers, that I remembered to have seen him in when a lump of sugar was the Havana of existence. We shook hands heartily with each other, and I was not a little surprised at his request to join the party above. I was in no humor to deny him any thing, and accordingly Mr. Thomas Thompson was formally introduced to Mr. Frank Fitch and party.

My uncle seemed bent upon making himself agreeable, and in order to do so, he begged to offer a few observations on organic remains, diluvial gravel, and some few other geological phenomena. In spite of the horror depicted in every countenance at this announcement, he proceeded to recapitulate the absurdities of many of the exploded cosmogonies of Calcot and others, discussed Hutton's theory, the elements of matter *à parte ante*, the destruction of mountains by atmospheric corrosion, and, I have no doubt, would have favored us with a few chapters of Buckland had not his auditors, one by one, shirked away, shrouded in their own smoke.

When we were left together, my uncle paused, and producing a large pocket-book, took therefrom sundry slips cut from newspapers daily and weekly. Having spread them on the table before him, he politely requested my attention to the information which they contained. I obeyed him, and found that all had relation to myself; they were all headed "police," and ended with—"Mr. John Jones was fined five shillings and discharged."

"John," said my uncle, "I am very angry with you—so angry, that if you continue in your present course, I must make some alteration in the disposition of my property. These occurrences are disgraceful."

"Oh! my dear sir," I exclaimed, "it is not my fault; it is the confounded police. They will be so officious."

"It is their duty to be so," answered my uncle. "Our police force is an examplar to every other nation. Active and intelligent, they have produced,

I may say, a moral revolution, and I honor every member of it. Now, John, I will give you an hour's advice. When a young man—"

But perhaps you will allow me to omit Mr. Thomas Thompson's maxims and opinions for young men studying for the bar—excellent as they are,—and be content with an observation which he made as he paused on the step of my door—his arm within my arm—preparatory to our departure for his inn, where he had asserted I should pass the night.

"Jack, my dear boy, avoid brawls; they degrade a gentleman to the level of a blackguard. During a somewhat riotous youth"—(dear old soul! he was never out of a bed after ten, in his life)—"I never was in the custody of the watch, nor did I ever contribute a single crown to the reigning sovereign of my country as a fine for vinous excitement. I would not encounter such evils to be made president of the British Association for Scientific Purposes!"

As my own opinions were so diametrically opposed to my uncle's, I thought it becoming on my part to bow and remain silent.

We had walked about five minutes, when our attention was directed to a man and woman disputing in language highly objectionable to the excellent old gentleman who was my companion.

"Dear me, Jack, that's very wrong," said my uncle. "What does it mean?"

"It means that if the lady don't go to her residence in five minutes, the gentleman proposes to try the effect of physical force," replied I.

"Good gracious! and he's doing it," exclaimed my uncle. The woman roared out most lustily; and the brutal fellow was about to repeat his violence, when my uncle laid his hand gently on the ruffian's shoulder, and remarked very mildly—

"My good sir, you must not do that!"

"Why mustn't he? he's my lawful husband, you old wagabone," cried the woman, "and he's a right to hit me if I desarve it, and I do desarve it. Give him in charge, Bill—Here! Police! Police! Murder!" screamed the virago.

Experience suggested to me the policy of absquatilating. "Run, sir," said I to Mr. Thompson.

"Run, sir!" replied my uncle, with a look of disdain that would have insured an antique Roman a statue!

It was too late to argue, for two area gates opened at the moment, and a policeman rushed upon us from each side of the street.

"Now then?" said Bull's-eye 22.

"What is it?" asked Bull's-eye 23.

"That old un's been 'salting my missis, and I gives him in charge," said the tender husband.

"And the t'other helped him, I suppose," inquired 22.

"Yes," answered the affectionate wife.

I was silent. *Experientia docet.*

"Allow me to explain," said Mr. Thompson, placing his fore-finger on the cuff of the policeman's coat.

"You see this, Figgs?" said 23, "striking me in the execution of my duty;" and producing his staff, he shook it awfully in the face of my uncle.

Mr. Thompson possessed a full bushel of virtues—standard measure; nevertheless he had one failing; he was very peppery, and the indignity now offered him shook the cayenne from him very considerably.

"What do you mean, you scoundrel?" shouted my uncle, as the policeman jerked him along. "This is a land of freedom—secured to the meanest subject—in the realm—by Magna Charta—wrung from the ty—rant—John—at Run—ny—mede—June the twelfth—twelve hundred—and—fifteen—when the barons—"

My uncle had nearly completed his abridgment of the history of England when we reached the station-house. The inspector was an old acquaintance of mine." "Ah, Mr. John Jones," he exclaimed, "havn't seen you for a month—what's the charge—the usual, I suppose? Drunk and disorderly?"—and then the two bull's-eyes proceeded to give a most lively and minute account of a series of violent assaults upon themselves and the lady before alluded to.

"Perjurers! rascals!" roared Mr. Thompson, "I am a peaceable man—"

"Very," said the inspector, continuing to write in the charge-book: "assaulting Mary Somers and the police."

"A lie, sir—a base lie, sir!"

"Thomas Thompson, drunk and disorderly," muttered the inspector.

"Drunk, sir? I never was drunk in my life!"

"Ah, we know all about that; nobody never is drunk—eh, Mr. Jones?" said the inspector, winking at me.

Mr. Thompson had now become furious, and was occupying the entire attention of four of the police.

"Search him," said the inspector.

"I'll not be searched; no man shall search me!" screamed Mr. Thompson, whilst his arms were stretched out like the letter Y; and two more of the police emptied his pockets in a twinkling. I had hitherto been amused at my uncle's position—I now felt seriously anxious for him. His face was the color of a peony, and his legs were in full play, as though he were indulging in a fit of convulsions. I remonstrated with the inspector, but my character was too well known to obtain any indulgence (beyond procuring a messenger for bail), and we were consequently marched off to the cell, and turned in among some six or eight "disorderlies," to whom Mr. Thompson rendered himself particularly disagreeable by the detail of his wrongs and his vociferations through the grating in the door of the cell. The bail at length arrived; and having been frequently employed in the same capacity, was accepted without delay. The cell-door was opened, and our janitor called out, "John Jones's bail."

I instantly stepped out, expecting my uncle's name would be the next; but the officer pausing, I said, "Well, there's Mr. Thompson!"

"Incapable of taking care of himself—can't let him out till the morning," answered the man, turning the key in the lock.

My uncle's fury is indescribable. He kicked the door—abused the police—vowed all manner of actions—recited the whole of Magna Charta, until he fell back exhausted upon a huge coal-heaver, who had laid himself down to sleep on the floor of the cell. I remained during the night in the station-house. In the morning, Mr. Thompson and myself were placed at the bar. I saw that the magistrate recognized me, and judged that the fact was not very likely to prejudice him in our favor. The charge was read over, and the evidence given; my uncle continually denying the assertions made, and being as continually compelled to be silent by the surly usher of the court.

"I shall fine them," said the magistrate, in the mildest tone imaginable, "twenty shillings each for the assault on the woman, three pounds each for the assault on the police, and five shillings for being intoxicated. And," continued his worship, "it pains me exceedingly to see a gentleman of your age and apparent respectability placed in such a disgraceful position."

Mr. Thompson was in a frenzy—talked about dying in jail—appealing to the House of Lords, and all those other expedients which are the boast of a wronged Briton. The result of his remarks was, that the magistrate remanded Mr. Thompson for a few hours, until he was sufficiently recovered from his debauch to be discharged. Mr. Thompson was then dragged from the bar, for walk he would not.

My uncle was released in the course of the day, and started in the evening for Birkenhead. Within a year, the excellent old gentleman was no more! Before he died, he had altered his will, but it was to make me his sole heir, as he stated "that I look upon my excellent nephew, John Jones, as a martyr, and the victim of that organized tyranny—the London Police!"

Poor dear uncle! whilst I write this, a tear falls upon the paper, and——

I beg your pardon, but Fitch has just run in to say that the surgeon at the corner of the street has mounted a brass knocker of extraordinary dimensions.—Brass-knockers are very scarce, and some lucky dog may get the start of me. Bob, my hat!

A FRIGHTFUL NARRATIVE.

(BY AN OLD BACHELOR) BY MARK LEMON.

Felix Williers was my first and dearest friend. He was little as a boy, and little as a man; the only great thing about him was his heart, and that was large enough for an elephant. He had but one fault, and that was a desperate one—he was always in love. Jilting did him no good; if one woman played him false, he instantly made a declaration to another. Fair or dark, short or tall, fat or slim, were all the same to Williers; his heart was like a carpet-bag—you could cram any amount of love into it. I used to tell him it would be his ruin—so it was—that is, it will be. When he married, I cut him. Self-preservation is the first law of nature, and I didn't know but matrimony was catching. I called him a fool, and he said I was a brute. I never saw Felix for twenty years afterwards.

Last Sunday, I had the blues; I do have them sometimes, particularly when my shirts have no buttons; and I found two in that state on the day to which I allude.

Whenever I'm in the blues, I always call upon a friend; if I don't get rid of the megrims myself, I give them to somebody else; and really *there is* some pleasure in being sympathized with. Well! I thought I'd hunt up Williers. I thought that twenty years were quite enough to owe a man a grudge, even for marrying.

Williers lives at Highgate, so I made the best of my way there. I used to like Highgate once. I was then nineteen, and Mary Spiller was——no matter, I don't regret it now. Well, I found out Williers's house, and just as I was about to ring the bell, I saw Felix and his family turn the corner. I'd been told that he had "his quiver full" of children—that one of his sons was "as big as a giant," and all that sort of thing, but I never thought that poor Williers was so be-offspringed as I found him.

I shall not describe our meeting; he seemed to forget that any thing had ever occurred, and I'm sure I never made a heartier dinner than I did at his table.

There's Felix and his family—and yet he declares that he's happy.

After a glass or two of port, we walked into the garden, and then back into the house. As I passed the door of a small room, I paused, paralysed—positively paralysed—by the objects which met my eye. Williers perceived my embarrassment, and then, with the air of a man who feels that he hath "done the state some service," boldly threw open the door, and requested me to follow him. Deliberately—smilingly—did poor Williers place in a row the objects which had excited my horror. As he did so, he said emphatically—

"Those shoes are—

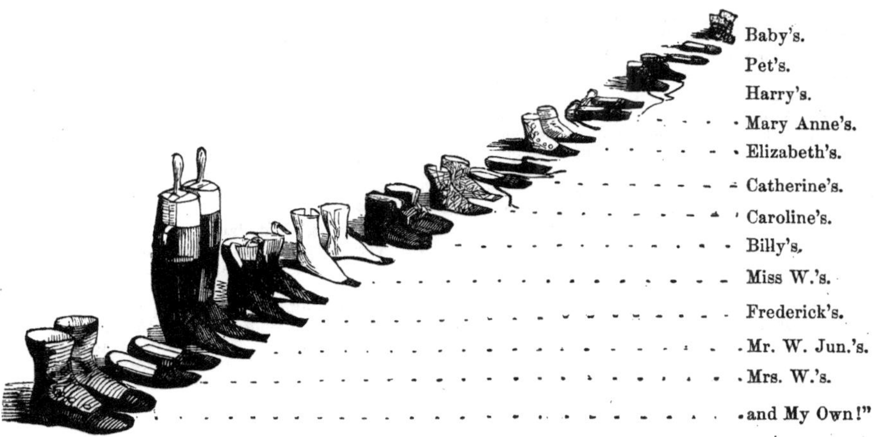

Baby's.
Pet's.
Harry's.
Mary Anne's.
Elizabeth's.
Catherine's.
Caroline's.
Billy's.
Miss W.'s.
Frederick's.
Mr. W. Jun.'s.
Mrs. W.'s.
and My Own!"

The recollection of *that* scene has overpowered me. Should my tea and muffins restore me, I will let you know all that occurred until I got into the omnibus. * * * * *

HORRIBLE DELUSIONS.

BY MARK LEMON.

Every one who has visited Brighton must know Trumper Terrace. It is one of the most quiet localities of the town, and is easily recognized by the green verandahs over the dining-room windows, and by the brilliant brass knobs which ornament the centre of the modest green doors. The small gardens in front are astronomically laid out in full-moons, half-moons, and stars, with neat gravelly ways between them. During the season the houses are let out to emigrants from the metropolis, at proportionably moderate rents, considering that each proprietor keeps a full-buttoned page for the use of the lodgers, who are always persons of the highest respectability, and without "incumbrances" as children are appropriately designated.

If you have half an hour to spare, let me introduce you to Mrs. Abbott, of 48, Trumper Terrace. This is Mrs. Abbott, and a lady of the Gamp school of oratory, full-blown as a peony, and nearly as red. Fifty-two, are you not, Mrs. Abbott? No—only forty-seven, but parish registers are invariably wrong. I believe you are a widow, and have kept a lodging-house two-and-twenty years? You have done pretty well at the business? Pretty well. I thought so. You would rather not say how you realized your profits? Very well, we have no particular object in inquiring. You have a daughter? Married? Recently, I believe? Would you oblige us with a history of her courtship, or at least so much as relates to Mr. Bosberry, your son-in-law's horrible delusions? I knew you would. We *do* wish it, upon my honor. I don't mind sitting in a draught, and would rather not take a glass of ginger-wine before dinner. Hem! Mrs. Abbott speaks.

"It's two years ago come Tuesday, that I was sitting where you may be now, turning a brown holland sofa cover, for which they charge sixteen pence to wash, whereas only one side was dirty, and I thought I would have the benefit of the one which was not, when Bloomfield, our page as was then, but who is now grown into Lord Lobsky's family, and wears a sky-blue livery, and his hair in powder, perhaps you know 'em? Hem! I thought you might. Well, as I was saying, Bloomfield announces a gentleman to look at the apartments. I rolled up the sofa cover, and telling him to show the gentleman into the next room, put it into the *chiffonière*, the very one at your back, sir, and went to the person so announced, and found a very mild, gentlemanly young man, attired in deep mourning, about three-and-twenty, with a small riding-whip in his hand, and light auburn hair rather inclined to be carroty."

"'Mrs. Abbott,' says he.

"'Yes, sir,' says I.

"'You've apartments to let?'

"'Yes, sir,' says I. 'Two pun' ten a-week, washing extra, including boot-cleaning and attendance, without firing, and the use of the piano.'

"'My name is Mr. Bosberry,' says he, 'and I engage your apartments on those terms, having just lost a distant relation, and shall take possession to-morrow, having received a legacy of considerable amount; and when my man brings my luggage, be kind enough to let a fire be lighted in both rooms.'

"'Sir, it shall be done,' says I, 'but without a reference or a deposit, I shouldn't like, as it is usual—'

"'I beg pardon,' said he, 'for forgetting it. There's a five-pound note, with my name and address on that card, which though it's a country note, is as good as the Bank of England, and any body knows me in Coleman-street, London.'"

And Mr. Bosberry took your apartments, I believe, Mrs. Abbott, and continued to occupy them for many months, during which time he formed an attachment for your daughter Julia, proposed for her, was accepted, and had arranged every thing for the joyful occasion, when the circumstances occurred which you will now relate to us. You were about to say that Mr. Bosberry was of rather a jealous temperament, and that on the twelfth day preceding the wedding, he called you into the room and said—Pray go on, Mrs. Abbott.

"'Mrs. Abbott,' says he, 'I shall be married in London.'

"'In London!' I shrieks; and down I set on that ottoman where Mary has left the dust-pan and a bundle of fire-wood, which you will excuse.

"'Yes, ma'am,' says Mr. Bosberry, 'for Miss Abbott seems lately, ma'am, to be holding a daily levee and drawing-room of all the male population of Brighton.'

"'Sir,' says I, of course feeling naturally all my maternal dignity rising in my throat, and choking my utterance, so that I could not speak without coughing, 'Julia is above suspicion, and has received from her cradle, as well as five years' board and tuition under Mrs. Roscommon's finishing academy, an education above the ordinary, and which would render her incapable of such conduct as you attribute to that unoffending girl,' who that instant entered the room, and took a seat accordingly. But I fear I'm boring you and your friend, and as the washerwoman has just drove up to the door in her cart, and I've not made out the book, perhaps you'll tell him the rest and allow me to wish you good morning."

Good morning, Mrs. Abbott.

So if you'll stroll with me to the pier, I will continue this disjointed narrative.

Bosberry was resolute; he vowed they should leave Brighton on the morrow, or he would do something desperate. The ladies were fain to succumb, and Mrs. Abbott, with an eye to business, stuck up in the window a bill of "Apartments to let," within an hour of the foregoing conversation.

"Bloomfield," exclaimed Bosberry, "say Miss Abbott is out; say I am out to every body that calls to-day."

Rat-tat-tat, went the knocker instantly, as though to test the page's fidelity.

"Out, sir, all on 'em out, sir," said Bloomfield, in a very loud voice.

"Indeed! Tell Mr. Bosberry that Mr. Jackson called," said the visitor, and bang went the door.

"Jackson! I lent him ten pounds yesterday, and he's called to pay me. Here! Hi! Jackson, old boy," cried Bosberry, from the Verandah. "At home to you, of course. Here, come in at the window; give me your hand; up you are!" and Mr. Jackson was handed in accordingly.

He had called to discharge his obligation; there was the note. Bosberry went into an inner room to place the money in his desk, and judge of his horror when, reflected in the mirror, he saw Jackson whispering to Julia, Julia smiling on Jackson, and both affectionately pressing the hands of each other. In a state of mind "more easily imagined than described," he returned into the front room, and, with a smile as ghastly as a gorgon's, requested Jackson to take some wine.

"No wine, thank you," said Jackson, "but if my dear young friend would favor me with a cup of coffee, I should be greatly obliged."

"Viper!" thought Bosberry; "but I won't be done; he shall not stop here.—Jackson," said he, *sotto voce*, "I have a most particular appointment with Captain Hamstringer, and Julia detests him so much, that I know not how to get away. It is already five minutes past the hour. Can you take me out?"

"I'll do it," said Jackson, winking violently at Bosberry, and then continuing, in a loud voice, "By the bye, I have just parted from old Bonus, our director; he told me he wished to see you immediately; I quite forgot to name it before. You'll find him at The Ship. Now, make no stranger of me," continued Jackson, in answer to Bosberry's negative gesticulations; "go, I insist upon it," and half by force, half by persuasion, the unhappy man was compelled to leave the house in possession of the enemy.

Jackson remained in earnest conversation with Julia for something more than an hour, when, again pressing her hand to his lips, he took his departure. How happy that conversation had made Julia!

Jackson had just left the house, when a *sort* of a gentleman applied to see the apartments. The applicant was very showily dressed, and might have served as the embodiment of one of those poetical advertisements (the tailor very properly invoking the nine) of Schneider art which daily tempt the unwary. A naval cap, anchored and laced, was placed jauntily on one side of his head, and contrasted somewhat oddly with the brass spurs which adorned the heels of his boots. Bloomfield, who always acted as groom of the chamber (until the appearance of a nibble, when his mistress was ordered to be summoned), was delighted with him. He thought him a "perfect gent," and as such looked forward to much fun and many stray sixpences. The stranger seemed particularly pleased with all the arrangements, especially admiring the weight of the forks and spoons, which Bloomfield assured him "was real silver, and none of your 'lectrifying, which took all the steam out of a boy to make 'em look decent." Mr. Bosberry's gold watch on the mantel-piece was also honored with the stranger's warmest commendations; and Bloomfield had the interest of the establishment too much at heart to inform the gentleman that the watch did not go with the lodgings.

"Let me see your missis," said the stranger; "if we can hagree about terms, I think the hapartments will do."

Bloomfield rushed from the room, delighted.

The stranger was evidently a genius, for the moment the boy had gone, he performed three rapid acts of eccentricity. He twisted the bolt from the French window; he drained Mr. Bosberry's decanter, which stood upon the table, and appropriated that gentleman's best hat, which by chance was on the sideboard! He also looked wistfully at the watch, the spoons, and the forks, and shrugging his shoulders muttered, "No, not now—them lodging-house keepers have heyes like 'awks."

Mrs. Abbott requested the stranger's presence in the parlor, where all matters of business must have been speedily arranged, as very shortly after the eccentric gentleman was seen walking on the Pier, and observed to borrow the contents of an old gentleman's pocket—the said old gentleman being at the time up to his eyes in the parliamentary debate on the Corn Laws.

But where was Bosberry? Flitting round and about Trumper Terrace like a perturbed spirit. He had watched Jackson leave the house; he had noted every minute of his stay; he had seen the eccentric gentleman enter the once happy No. 48; had seen him in the parlor, and of course had placed him to the account of the faithless Julia. But he had not seen pretty little Julia Johnson (Miss Abbott's cousin and namesake) at the door, and heard her give the faintest rat-a-tat imaginable.

"Oh, Julia!" exclaimed Julia Johnson, as she rushed into the arms of Julia Abbott, "Jackson has told you all; I have just received his note—here it is; and he assures me his father has consented to our being married in a month, and that John would meet me here at nine o'clock—and there he is—I'm sure that's his knock."

It was Jackson, sure enough. Bosberry saw him! One hour, ten minutes, and thirty-nine seconds did Bosberry watch for his departure, but in vain. At the fortieth second he—but we must not anticipate events.

"We can never thank you enough, dear Julia," said Jackson, again pressing Miss Abbott's hands to his lips; "but for you how few would have been our meetings; but now all will be well; in a month she will be mine, never to be separated from me but by death! Oh, Julia!—etc., etc., etc."

"There, see him to the door, do," said Miss Abbott; "of course you have something to say to each other; but, dearest, wrap my shawl over your head, there's a dreadful draught in our passage—Mr. Bosberry nearly caught his death there before we were quite engaged." And the considerate girl bounded up to the second floor like a—like a—bird.

Miss Abbott was right; Jackson and his Julia had much to say on their way to the street-door: and it was during their "happy converse" that Bosberry's patience exhausted itself.

"By jingo! I will know the worst!" he exclaimed; "she's a flirt—a coquette: I will listen at the keyhole—any thing to bring detection home to her. Ah! the balcony!" And stealthily as a cat he clambered into the dining-room.

All was still; the last streak of sunlight was fading in the horizon. Bosberry could not discern the objects in the room: he lighted a taper. The first thing which struck him was the exhausted decanter. The next object which caught his attention was the eccentric gentleman's abandoned cap. Bosberry shook with rage and agony.

"Another admirer! Oh, Jul—" and the word stuck as fast in his throat as a fish-bone; for at that moment he heard voices at the street-door. What was that?—a kiss! He crept to the window, and there he saw the perfidious Jackson again attempt to embrace a figure enveloped in a shawl! Ah! he knew that shawl too well—the gaslight showed him the pattern; a pale blue pine-apple on a white ground! He gave it to Julia on her last birth-day. He staggered almost insensible from the window, and buried his face in the sofa pillow.

Miss Abbott called "Bloomfield!"

"Hark! that's her voice!"

"Take this letter to the Bedford Hotel, and if the gentleman is within, wait for an answer."

"What gentleman *ought* she to know at the Bedford?" mentally ejaculated the distracted Bosberry. "What's this? My writing case! Yes, and here, on the blotting-paper, is" (and he held the tell-tale sheet before the candle) "T-h-o-s. B-l-a-c-k, E-s-q., B-e-d-f—," and he read no more.

"Some one must be sacrificed," he exclaimed, hastily producing a brace of pistols, and proceeding to load them; "there must be a wretch in the house now—if he's—not too big, I will immolate him on the altar of—. Zounds! I've rammed a nut into the pistol instead of a bullet—no matter—and now there's the taper gone out—but revenge is sweet. Why did I love her—why?" and throwing himself on the sofa, he continued, for upwards of an hour, to upbraid himself vainly and incoherently, until he was aroused by a noise at the window.

"What's that? A man in the balcony?"

Yes, it was the eccentric gentleman returned no doubt (as he assured Bosberry) with a bull's-eye lantern to look for the cap he had so strangely left behind him.

Bosberry's calmness was getting awful.

"Sir," said he, "this subterfuge shall not save you—this sort of thing is getting unbearable—I must take some decisive steps—your card, sir."

The eccentric gentleman seemed puzzled by this request; but, after a moment's hesitation, produced a card-case, and handed the required pasteboard to Bosberry, who read aloud firmly and distinctly the name of "THOMAS BLACK."

"Enough," said Bosberry, "I understand the purport of your visit—take your choice, sir (and he pointed to the pistols on the table), for I am desperate."

"What do you mean? I haint going to fight," exclaimed the stranger. "Call the perlice if you like, but no fire-harms—I don't resist."

"Coward," said Bosberry, with more dignity than he had before exhibited, "I demand SATISFACTION!"

"Satisfaction! the man's a hass," replied the stranger, seizing a pistol. "Come, let me go, mister—I hain't a going to be shot at neither."

"Never! I shall—" cried Bosberry, but recollecting that one of the pistols only was loaded with ball, he altered the proposed form of the sentence into—"shall it be said that I took a mean advantage of an enemy. You may go, sir! to-morrow you shall hear from me! but I'll trouble you for that pistol, as I do not wish to spoil the pair."

"Don't you," said the eccentric stranger, making a retrograde movement to the windows, "but ye're not a-going to pop at me when my back's turned, so here's off."

Bosberry instantly rushed upon him, and a fearful struggle ensued, during which the pistol, either by accident or design, was discharged, and the pier-glass (48-in. by 56-in.) was shivered into a thousand pieces.

The noise brought all the family into the room! There lay Bosberry, in the centre of the room, covered with the fragments of the dessert, and rendered helpless by the weight of the inverted table, placed thus by the eccentric gentleman, who had retreated as he had entered, by the window.

* * * *

"And now, having told you all I think and feel," said Bosberry, after the necessary screaming and fainting had subsided, "I beg to remark that this is the work of your friend, ma'am—of *your* friend, ma'am," and he looked at Julia.

"Of m-y-y-y friend," sobbed out Miss Abbott.

"Yes—your friend—Mr. Thomas Bl——"

"Mr. Thomas Black," announced Bloomfield.

"Why, he's never dared to come back," cried Bosberry, as a very respectable elderly gentleman was ushered into the room. It was the same that the eccentric gentleman had "eased" of pocket-handkerchief and card-case in the morning.

"Uncle!" cried Julia.

"Brother!" cried Mrs. Abbott. "Welcome home from India!"

Yes! quite true; Mr. Thomas Black, after a long sojourn in the East, had come down to Brighton to seek out his relatives, the Abbotts. His name announced in the "Arrivals," had informed Mrs. Abbott of his whereabouts, and Julia had written accordingly. Bosberry was bothered.

"But Jackson—the shawl—"

"Was worn by me," said Miss Johnson. "Mr. Jackson is my—"

"Affianced husband," exclaimed Mrs. Abbott; "and if it hadn't been for some people such an event had *never* been, now foully suspected and sought to be injured in name and fame."

Bosberry was more bothered—more so, when a police officer (introduced by Bloomfield) requested his attendance in the morning to give what evidence he could against the eccentric gentleman, who was then at the station-house, laboring under something more than a suspicion of theft.

Bosberry fell on his knees * * *

If you refer to the Supplement of the *Times*, September 31, 1847, and look for "Marriages," you will read as follows:—

"On the 29th, at St. Buckleton's, Brighton, Augustus Brown Bosberry, Esq., to Julia, only daughter of Mrs. Rackstraw Abbott, of Trumper Terrace."

"On the same day, at the same place, John Jackson, Esq., to Julia, ninth daughter of Peter Johnson, Esq., of the Dyke, Brighton."

THE BARBER OF STOCKSBAWLER.

A Tale of the Supernatural.

BY MARK LEMON.

At the little town of Stocksbawler, on the Lower Rhine, in the year of grace 1830, resided one Hans Scrapschins, an industrious and close-shaving barber. His industry met with due encouragement from the bearded portion of the community; and the softer sex, whose greatest fault is fickleness, generally selected Hans for the honor of new-fronting them, when they had grown tired of the ringlets nature had bestowed, and which time had frosted.

Hans continued to shave and thrive, and all the careful old burghers foretold of his future well-doing; when he met with a misfortune, which promised for a time to shut up his shop and leave him a beggar. He fell in love.

Neighbors warned Hans of the consequences of his folly; but all remonstrance was vain. Customers became scarce, wearing out their patience and their wigs together; the shop became dirty, and winter saw the flies of summer scattered on his show-board.

Agnes Flirtitz was the prettiest girl in Stocksbawler. Her eyes were as blue as a summer's sky, her cheeks as rosy as an autumn sunset, and her teeth as white as winter's snow. Her hair was a beautiful flaxen—not a *drab*—but that peculiar sevenpenny-moist-sugar tint which the poets of old were wont to call golden. Her voice was melodious; her notes *in alt.* were equal to Grisi's: in short, she would have been a very desirable, lovable young lady, if she had not been a coquette.

Hans met her at a festival given in commemoration of the demise of the burgomaster's second wife —I beg pardon, I mean in celebration of his union with his third bride. From that day, Hans was a lost barber. Sleeping, waking, shaving, curling, weaving, or powdering, he thought of nothing but Agnes. His love-dreams placed him in all kinds of awkward predicaments.

And Agnes—what thought she of the unhappy barber? Nothing, except that he was a presumptuous puppy, and wore very unfashionable garments. Hans received an intimation of this latter opinion; and, after sundry quailings and misgivings, he resolved to dispose of his remaining stock in trade, and, for once, dress like a gentleman. The measure had been taken by the tailor, the garments had been basted and tried on, and Hans was standing at his door in a state of feverish excitement, awaiting their arrival in a completed condition (as there was to be a *fête* on the morrow, at which Agnes was to be present), when a stranger requested to be shaved. Hans wished him at the——next barber's; but there was something so unpleasantly positive in the visitor's appearance, that he had not the power to object, so politely bowed him into the shop. The stranger removed his cap, and discovered two very ugly protuberances, one on each side of his head, and of most unphrenological appearance. Hans commenced operations—the lather dried as fast as he laid it on, and the razor emitted small sparks as it encountered the bristles on the stranger's chin. Hans felt particularly uncomfortable, and not a word had hitherto passed on either side, when the stranger broke the ice by asking rather abruptly, "Have you any schnapps in the house?" Hans jumped like a parched pea. Without waiting for a reply, the stranger rose, and opened the cupboard. "I never take any thing stronger than water," said Hans, in reply to the "Pshaw!" which broke from the stranger's lips as he smelt at the contents of a little brown pitcher. "More fool you," replied his customer. "Here, taste that—some of the richest grape-blood of

Rheinga;" and he handed Hans a small flask, which the sober barber respectfully declined. "Ha! ha! and yet you hope to thrive with the women," said the stranger. "No wonder that Agnes treats you as she does. But drink, man! drink!"

The stranger took a pipe, and coolly seated himself again in his chair, hung one leg over the back of another, and striking his finger briskly down his nose, elicited a flame that ignited his tobacco, and then he puffed, and puffed, till every moth in the shop coughed aloud. The uneasiness of Hans increased, and he looked towards the door with the most cowardly intention; and, lo! two laughing, dimpled faces were peeping in at them. "Ha! how are you?" said the stranger; "come in! come in!" and to Hans's horror, two very equivocal damsels entered the shop. Hans felt scandalized, and was about to make a most powerful remonstrance, when he encountered the eye of his impertinent customer; and, from its sinister expression, he thought it wise to be silent. One of the damsels seated herself upon the stranger's knee, whilst the other looked most coaxingly to the barber; who, however, remained proof to all her winks and blinks, and "wreathed smiles."

"'Sblitzen!" exclaimed the lady, "the man's an icicle!"

"Hans, you're a fool!" said the stranger; and his inamorata concurred in the opinion. The flask was again proffered—the eye-artillery again brought into action, but Hans remained constant to pump-water and Agnes Flirtitz.

The stranger rubbed the palm of his hand on one of his head ornaments, as though he were somewhat perplexed at the contumacious conduct of the barber; then rising, he gracefully led the ladies out. As he stood, with one foot on the step of the door, he turned his head scornfully over his shoulder and said, "Hans, you are nothing but—a barber; but before I eat, you shall repent of your present determination."

"What security have I that you will keep your word?" replied Hans, who felt emboldened by the outside situation of his customer, and the shop poker, of which he had obtained possession.

"The best in the world," said the stranger. "Here, take these!" and placing both rows of his teeth in the hands of the astonished Hans, he quietly walked up the street with the ladies.

The astonishment of Hans had somewhat subsided, when Stitz, the tailor, entered with the so-much and the so-long-expected garments. The stranger was forgotten; the door was bolted, the clothes tried on, and they fitted to a miracle. A small three-cornered piece of looking-glass was held in every direction by the delighted tailor, who declared this performance his *chef-d'œuvre;* and Hans felt, for the first time in his life, that he looked like a gentleman. Without a moment's hesitation, or the slightest hint at discount for ready money, he gave the tailor his last thaler, and his old suit of clothes, as per contract; shook Stitz's hand at parting, till every bone of the tailor's fingers ached for an hour afterwards, bolted the door, and went to bed the poorest but happiest barber in Stocksbawler.

After a restless night, Hans rose the next morning with the oddest sensation in the world. He fancied that the bed was shorter, the chairs lower, and the room smaller, than on the preceding day; but attributing this feeling to the feverish sleep he had had, he proceeded to put on his pantaloons. With great care he thrust his left leg into its proper division, when, to his horror and amazement, he found that he had grown *two feet at least during the*

night; and that the pantaloons which had fitted so admirably before, were now only knee-breeches. He rushed to the window with the intention of breaking his neck by a leap into the street, when his eye fell upon the strange customer of the preceding day, who was leaning against the gable-end of the house opposite, quietly smoking his meerschaum. Hans paused; then thought, and then concluded that having found an appetite, he had repented of his boast at parting, and had called for his teeth. Being a good-natured lad, Hans shuffled down stairs, and opening the door, called him to come over. The stranger obeyed the summons, but honorably refused to accept of his teeth, except on the conditions of the wager. To Hans' great surprise he seemed perfectly acquainted with the phenomenon of the past night, and good-naturedly offered to go to Stitz, and inform him of the barber's dilemma. The stranger departed, and in a few moments the tailor arrived, and having ascertained by his inch-measure the truth of Hans' conjectures, bade him be of good cheer, as he had a suit of clothes which would exactly fit him. They had been made for a travelling giant, who had either forgotten to call for them, or suspected that Stitz would require the *gelt* before he gave up the broadcloth.

The tailor was right—they did fit—and in an hour afterwards Hans was on his way to the *fête.* When he arrived there, many of his old friends stood agape for a few moments; but, as stranger things had occurred in Germany than a man growing two feet in one night, they soon ceased to notice the alteration in Hans' appearance. Agnes was evidently struck with the improvement of the barber's figure, and for two whole hours did he enjoy the extreme felicity of making half-a-dozen other young gentlemen miserable, by monopolizing the arm and conversation of the beauty of Stocksbawler. But pleasure, like fine weather, lasts not for ever; and, as Hans and Agnes turned the corner of a path, his eye again encountered the stranger. Whether it was from fear or dislike, he knew not, but his heart seemed to sink, and so did his body; for, to his utter dismay, he found that he had shrunk to his original proportions, and that the garment of the giant hung about him in any thing but graceful festoons. He felt that he was a human telescope, that some infernal power could elongate or shut up at pleasure.

The whole band of jealous rivals set up the "Laughing Chorus," and Agnes, in the extremity of her disgust, turned up her nose till she nearly fractured its bridge, whilst Hans rushed from the scene of his disgrace, and never stopped running until he opened the door of his little shop, threw himself into a chair, and laid his head down upon an old "family Bible" which chanced to be upon the table. In this position he continued for some time, when, on raising his head, he found his tormentor and the two ladies, grouped like the Graces, in the centre of the apartment.

"Well, Scrapschins," said the gentleman, "I have called for my teeth. You see I have kept my promise." Hans sighed deeply, and the ladies giggled.

"Nay, man, never look so glum! Here, take the flask—forget Agnes, and console yourself with the love of—"

The conclusion of this harangue must for ever remain a mystery; for Hans, at this moment, took up the family volume which had served him for a pillow, and dashed it at the heads of the trio. A scream, so loud that it broke the tympanum of his left ear, seemed to issue from them simultaneously—a thick vapor filled the room, which gradually cleared off, and left no traces of Hans' visitors but three small sticks of stone brimstone. The truth flashed upon the barber—his visitor was the far-famed Mephistopheles. Hans packed up his remaining wardrobe, razor, strop, soap-dish, scissors, and combs, and turned his back upon Stocksbawler for ever. Four years passed away, and Hans was again a thriving man, and Agnes Flirtitz the wife of the doctor of Stocksbawler. Another year passed on, and Hans was both a husband and a father; but the coquette who had nearly been his ruin had eloped with the *chasseur* of a travelling nobleman.

LAUGH AND GET FAT!

BY —— FITZGERALD.

Lack we motives to laugh? Are not all things, any thing, every thing, to be laughed at? And if nothing were to be seen, felt, heard, or understood, we would laugh at it too.—MERRY BEGGARS.

THERE'S nothing here on earth deserves
  Half of the thought we waste about it;
And thinking but destroys the nerves,
  When we could do so well without it:
If folks would let the world go round,
  And pay their tithes, and eat their dinners,
Such doleful looks would not be found,
  To frighten us poor laughing sinners:
Never sigh when you can sing,
But laugh, like me, at every thing!

One plagues himself about the sun,
  And puzzles on, through every weather,
What time he'll rise,—how long he'll run,—
  And when he'll leave us altogether:
Now matters it a pebble-stone,
  Whether he shines at six or seven?
If they don't leave the sun alone,
  At last they'll plague him out of heaven!
Never sigh when you can sing,
But laugh, like me, at every thing!

Another spins from out his brains
  Fine cobwebs, to amuse his neighbors,
And gets, for all his toils and pains,
  Reviewed and laughed at for his labors:
Fame is *his* star! and fame is sweet;
  And praise is pleasanter than honey,—
I write at just so much a sheet,
  And Messrs. Longman pay the money!
Never sigh when you can sing,
But laugh, like me, at every thing!

My brother gave his heart away
  To Mercandotti, when he met her;
She married Mr. Ball one day—
  He's gone to Sweden to forget her!
I had a charmer, too—and sighed
  And raved all day and night about her;
She caught a cold, poor thing! and died,
  And I—am just as fat without her!
Never sigh when you can sing,
But laugh, like me, at every thing!

For tears are vastly pretty things,
  But make one very thin and taper;
And sighs are music's sweetest strings,
  But sound most beautiful—on paper!
"Thought" is the Sage's brightest star,
  Her gems alone are worth his finding;
But as I'm not particular,
  Please God, I'll keep on "never-minding."
Never sigh when you can sing,
But laugh, like me, at every thing!

Oh! in this troubled world of ours,
  A laughter mine's a glorious treasure;
And separating thorns from flowers,
  Is half a pain and half a pleasure:
And why be grave instead of gay?
  Why feel a-thirst while folks are quaffing?
Oh! trust me, whatsoe'er they say,
  There's nothing half so good as laughing!
Never sigh when you can sing,
But laugh, like me, at every thing!

THE DEMON GOOSEBERRY.

A COUNTRY TALE. BY CHARLES HOOTON.

BEING in my own person a great patron of all institutions calculated to promote learning and science of any kind, I some years ago became a subscriber to the Great Hammaway Horticultural Society,—a ociety, which, as appears by its title, has for its object the improvement of the various breeds of apples, quinces, and pot-herbs.

In this situation, it has been my good fortune to encounter, face to face, many of those ingenious fellows, who, through the medium of societies like ours, render themselves notorious, and obtain a great name in the world, by growing prodigious Titan-like cabbages and gooseberries.

Now I consider it a certain sign of great personal merit to be able to produce such large vegetables and berries, according to the well-known saying, that every man is known by his fruit. The grower of the finest specimens of any kind is therefore the most superlative genius, and that is the reason we always reward such by medals and copper tea-kettles; it being expedient that the genius of science and arts should patronize her votaries by rewards. At the same time, entertaining a strong belief in phrenology, I have always held a strong private opinion that the growers of particular vegetables and fruits were some way or other endowed with an organ corresponding with the peculiar kind of culture in which they excelled. This opinion has been confirmed by the observation and experience of many years. Thus, I have found that those members of our society who, on the average, (and it is only through general and comprehensive observations such truths can be arrived at,) took the greatest number of prizes for the biggest cabbages, possessed, one with another, a large cabbage-organ in the skull, which, by its great preponderance over the ordinary thinking faculties, rendered them in a manner unfit for much rational conversation. The pith of their brains appeared to represent the crumpled heart of a cabbage; insomuch, that a man in conversation found no difficulty in imagining he was being addressed by an animated winter-green, or a civil gentlemanly savoy. While such as became most famed for the largest and best potatoes —Long Kidneys or Yorkshire Reds—had invariably, (I speak advisedly,) heads like a bag of those roots; or, in other words, as rugged and lumpy as a village pebble-paved causeway.

Upon the whole, I have ever found all classes of the great growers, strange mortals,—"Rum'uns to look at,"—and in company much inclined to the contemplation of red and black earths, bone, horse, and pig manures, grubs, larvæ, and slugs. Yet have I also generally found their acquaintance well worth cultivating; and having been tolerably successful in that pursuit, can now boast of as extensive a friendship with the great growers, as any horticulturist in the three kingdoms. It has even crossed my mind that some day I would sit down and write their biographies;—classing them under the respective heads of Turnip, Leek, Carrot, Gooseberry, and the like; just in the same manner as other great men are classed, as Painters, Poets, Astronomers, etc. Whether this seed of the mind will ever shoot beyond the present paper, time alone can tell. But that the reader may be the better enabled to judge of the interest attached to such a work, let me particularly draw his attention to the following sketch of Titus,—one of the most talented and enterprising members of the Hammaway Horticultural Society.

Now, Hammaway, the place of my residence, though according to law a market-town, is yet in magnitude and trade scarcely superior to many a village in the same county. That is, it may be properly resembled to a great booby, who is making his transit from lad to manship. About two thousand of its souls weave stockings for the London market;—thus, just enabling themselves to maintain each a coat out at elbows,—a face like a peggy-lantern's, which serves no turn but that of frightening the respectable inhabitants,—a wife who is always mopping her floor,—and a matter of about, on the average, fifteen children apiece.

Hammaway is, as it were, fenced about by small

garden-plots, or rather whole fields divided into squares like a chess-board, separated by stunted hedges, and let to the poor souls above named, to whom they become like little Edens,—snippings of the garden of Paradise itself. Having but one day in a week which they can devote to cultivation, and that the day which the curate demands, but demands in vain,—you may see from ten to fifteen hundred of them on a summer's Sunday morning, all anxious to make the best of time, with their coats off,—perhaps laid on the hedges or suspended by the nape on an upright stick like a scare-crow, —delving, raking, hoeing, planting, uprooting, and watering, at a rate which might mislead a stranger to believe they were working in the last stage of desperation for their lives. This, however, their generous enthusiasm leads them to esteem in no other light than as admirable exercise and relaxation after the week's toil; and knowing their time is short, and that the day of rest (even though it happen to be the longest in the year) must soon be over, they in general scarcely allow themselves time to return to their homes for dinner. Such, however, as do trespass on their amusement so far, usually swallow their meals as nearly all of a lump as the orifice of the throat will allow,—(and that, by the bye, with your hardworking man is not small,)—and without waiting to digest them, hurry back to their garden plots at a rate most nearly resembling a foot race between a couple of hundreds or so of competitors at one and the same time. Whilst those who remain behind and pass the whole blissful time amongst their broccolis and potatoes, may be observed, at about one o'clock, to snatch a few minutes of time, rest on their spades, pull a dry crust out of their pockets, stuff it into their mouths like a bung, take a swig at the watering-pan, and then at it again.

Such is about the manner in which the generality of our population dispose of their Sundays. Though we are not without some of those ale, pipe, and political poor men who carry their profanation of those days so far as to retire to their places called summer-houses,—that is to say, small stud and mud erections, about the size of the now departed watchman's boxes, composed of three sides, a door, and a tile lid on the top,—and spend all the hours between morning and night in drinking, shouting, and maintaining a continual tainted smell in the otherwise pure summer atmosphere, of rank and pestiferous sham-tobacco smoke.

But amongst this multitude of amateur tillers of the earth, whom to look at when engaged in their interesting operations, the spectator might imagine not worth, to purchase, five shillings per hundred, are to be found some of the brightest ornaments, the most shining stars of the Hammaway Horticultural Society,—men who reflect lustre on their native town, and are looked upon by strangers, whenever such happen to see them.

I have said that our raisers of Herculean fruit are for the most part a knot of strange-looking scrubs. One Mr. Jeffrey Todds, for instance, nearly the oldest member of the society, is as remarkable a vessel to look at as soul ever set eyes on. You would think him all stem and ramifications, like a huge leaf animated; and when engaged in his garden, hunting snails out of his banks, the cunningest eyesight might be defied to distinguish him from the barks of the old willows about him; an effect to which, beyond a doubt, his pepper-and-salt long coat contributes, although there is still something of that impalpable green and yellowness in his phiz so characteristic of aged barks, and which I suppose he has unconsciously acquired by his continual intercommunication and cheek-by-jowlship with them. His head, from being as bald as the ivory top of a walking-stick, has the appearance of an immense yellow pumpkin; or, lest this simile should be not sufficiently comprehended by the reader, is in other words about the size of a grocer's tea canister. On the other hand, the dark oily countenance of Mr. James Swinburn, another of our most highly respected members, reminds one of nothing so much as a spring evening's moist slug.

But not a soul of them all, no, not one of the delving race within our society, is for an instant to be compared to the late great, and also personally tall Titus. For the ardor of his genius in the pursuit, the splendor of his various growths, the amount of prizes awarded to him, and his disastrous and most extraordinary death,—he must be considered as much superior to all others, as is the poplar of the meadow in height above all other trees. He was the life and soul of our society, or, more correctly speaking, the very apple of its eye. But alas! he is gone, and we are left blind on the best side of the society's face.

At our general meetings, he was always distinguishable above others, as conspicuously as was his fruit above theirs. Nature having taken more than usual mother's care to manure and water him so well during his growth, that when arrived at his standard height, he measured six feet four from the ground to the topmost part of his trunk. Unfortunately he threw out no branches,—in other words, he left no family behind him,—or we might now have had a cutting of that excellent tree engrafted upon the society. I knew him during a period of fourteen or fifteen summers, and from lengthened observation can confidently assert that a greater enthusiast in any pursuit never crossed my widest path. Weather had not the least visible effect upon him. He went to his garden amid thunder-storms, with the same punctuality as in sunshine,—during floods and frosts equally as in dry weather and hot. I have known him when his garden, like the borders of the Nile, has been covered with water all over nearly knee deep, take off his shoes and stockings, hang them round his neck, roll up his trousers like two thick rings or ferrules round his lower extremities, in the greatest unconcern, and with equal pleasure as at other times. It was not for the purpose of *doing* any thing, but only to see the state of the case, and report the depth of water in the gardens to the nightly visitors (members of course) at the sign of "The Frog and Tadpole," near Scum Ditch, on an outskirt of Hammaway, close upon the gardens. The society on such occasions entertained great fears lest he should jeopardize his valuable existence by cold, resulting in consumption; and indeed, on two occasions of remarkably heavy floods, accompanied by piercing blasts, formally passed a resolution forbidding him to wade about his plot until land again appeared. He seemed to bow to the society's wishes, but was afterwards detected privately splashing about as usual. A vote of censure was passed on the commission of the second offence, merely to maintain the outward dignity of the society; though even those individuals who voted in its favor, did so under feelings of no ordinary nature. Once, he happily discovered a thief getting up trees out of the softened and muddy ground, and under the pretence of arresting him, gave him a sound thrashing first, and then lugged him off to the constable. For this exploit a special reward was agreed upon for Titus, and after a comfortable supper, the chairman concluded a flowery speech by presenting him in the name of the society with a new three-legged iron pot.

The constancy of his attendance at his garden, daylight permitting, was astonishing. Exactly at five minutes after six in the evening, he was regularly to be seen crossing the short moor between Hammaway and his garden; and at dusk, be that whatever hour it might, he was as regularly to be observed returning home with a sprig of green or a flower stuck in the corner of his mouth, and a second in some favored button-hole. So constant indeed was he to his minute of going there, that many of those inhabitants of the lower end of the town, who dwelt too far off the church to hear the clock strike, were long in the habit of setting their Dutch clocks and watches by him; as well perceiving that while he had a spring left to keep him going, he was as truly to be depended on as the sun himself.

Some few weeks previous to our last summer-show of fruit, Titus went to his garden as usual. A drizzly soaking evening it was; and throughout the whole range of garden plots, scarcely a soul was to be seen, save himself. In the dusk and mistiness of coming night, his long scrambling limbs, his height, and awkward postures, seemed to resemble him to some strange bogle dabbling and fishing for frogs amidst a swamp; for such the low dewy gardens then appeared when viewed from the surrounding eminences. To the astonishment of all Hammaway, he did not return to his home until full an hour later than his regular time; that is, until it had become almost dark.

At that time, he was met by a belated market-woman, coming at an unusual pace along the road across the common, which, to her terrified gaze, his gaunt legs seemed to swallow up as he strode. Beside him was a creature like a man, but so diminutive, that the coat-laps of Titus occasionally flapped in his face. Yet that tall worthy could not outstrip him. Such a man had never before been seen in our parts, except in a penny show at the annual fair; and as the woman passed them she overheard —unless her senses deceived her—she overheard Titus exclaim energetically to the little biped by his side,—"Done!—I'll take it!"

At that moment, the feet of the dwarf thing struck fire on the pebble stones over which they walked, and the market-woman smelt brimstone as plainly as the nose was on her face. This latter circumstance was however afterwards declared to be no miracle; since it was confidently asserted, though the housewives of Hammaway would never hear of it, that she carried from market that night no less than three-pennyworths of the old-fashioned matches in her basket.

This encounter soon became known and enlarged in all its suspicious circumstances and horrors. Some wisely declared they had their thoughts as well as other folks. Some again spoke outright, and avowed their belief that Titus had done neither more nor less than consort with the devil, for the sake of forcing his gooseberries by and through the aid of that old gentleman's underground hotbed, —it being notorious that up to the point of time of which I am speaking, Titus had been most low in spirits, in consequence of the unusual backwardness of his fruit; while afterwards he mounted up to the highest pinnacle of hope, being frequently heard to declare his solemn conviction that, late as it was, he should take every individual prize for the berries, rough and smooth.

Many had the curiosity afterwards to lie in wait when Titus went to his garden of an evening, in anticipation of seeing him once more enjoying the society of his strange companion, and, if possible, of tracing out where he came from and whither he vanished to; but in every instance were they disappointed,—he never came again.

Instead, perhaps, the little man transacted his business at a distance; for true it was that on the following morning a small and curious box was discovered on the table of the house, by his wife, who rose before daylight to wash her own and her husband's linen. It was a box of no fashion at all, as far as this earth is concerned, having four sides, every one of which was triangular. After much fearful consideration, she was about to exhibit her temerity by opening it, when her hand was arrested by the sound of something coming down her narrow staircase. She looked in that direction, and beheld the smallest black cat—at least it walked on all fours—with the largest development of eyes she had ever seen during the course of her mortal pilgrimage. How was this? *they* kept no cat, either white or black; and, of course, Titus's lady had no recollection whatever at such a critical moment, that stray cats are as desperately determined to put their heads in anywhere, as was her own gigantic lord to stride away to his garden. Instead of washing, she flew off to bed again in terror, without waiting to split open the box; though not without inly promising to do so as soon as broad daylight came. She fell asleep; and on awakening again found that Titus was missing. He had risen by the earliest peep of morning, and carried the box away to his garden, where none but his gooseberry-bushes and cabbage-stumps could be privy to the contents. When he returned home to breakfast, he threw the box *empty* on the floor, telling his wife she might appropriate it, if any use for such a queer-shaped article could be found; but she resolutely avowed it should never be adopted in her house, not even for a match-box, unless Titus would first declare what it had contained.

"Nothing to do *you* any harm," was his reply; and beyond which neither coaxing, threatening, nor reasoning could extort a word. This made the wife still more suspicious: she resolved, by the aid of Providence, to convince herself at least of the nature of the place beyond this world, from whence she believed the three-cornered thing had come; and therefore seizing an opportunity after that morning meal, when Titus had gone to work, she called in one or two of her neighbors as witnesses, informed them of all that had passed, upon which she hung her own interpretations and suspicions, and then, whilst fearfully they all stood round, she seized the box with her tongs, and cast it into the fire. The general expectation was, that it would either explode and vanish in smoke, or else shoot suddenly off in furiously hissing blue flames.

Neither of these events, to the mortal disappointment of the assembly, took place. Instead, the stubborn stuff would scarcely burn at all. After considering awhile about this very unwoodlike phenomenon, they discovered this strange fact to be the most natural and probable; for if it really did come from —— (they here looked infernally horrible at one another,) nothing under the sun could be clearer than that it must necessarily be fire-proof.

In a fright of conviction, Mistress Titus took the box off the coals, and flung it far beyond a neighboring ditch, lest, if cast amongst other refuse, it should charm and bedevil the Christian heap of that commodity, which lay before her cottage door.

From being himself an object of universal suspicion, Titus now found that a thousand curious eyes were turned upon his gooseberries. All expected to see wonders; whilst the extraordinary reports that were spread about respecting them, and which doubtless originated with some prying souls who had crept clandestinely into his garden, and taken a stolen view, tended nothing towards diminishing the general anxiety. It was confidently declared that they were of a fiery red, as though the skins enclosed a hot coal; that they were as hard as hoofs, and the prickles on some of them like hedgehogs' quills.

At length, as the time of exhibition drew nigh, Titus triumphantly invited several connoisseurs of berries to inspect his trees. To their amazement they found the previously incredible reports in all respects true, save with reference to the size of the fruit. Therein, indeed, had the current tales either fallen short, or the berries themselves had since far outgrown their description. They were really ponderous; and adjudged in some instances to weigh as much as thirty-three or four pennyweights. Our inspectors almost doubted their own senses, and began to fancy it possible that some magical delusion was being practised upon their otherwise experienced optics. The matter appeared the more astonishing, when we reflect how dwindled and diminutive appeared the same berries in the early part of the season. What stimulating, miraculous manure must that box have contained in its bowels! Or, was it manure? Was it not rather an elixir drawn from demon-distilled earths, of which a few drops invigorated more than many barrowsful of limes, bones, or salts? But if these thoughts entered their minds spontaneously at the first glance, what did they not think when Titus informed them that he had changed the names of all his bushes? When he led them round his borders, and pointed out "The Dark Fiery," "The Brimstone King," "The Devil's Black;" and even, when he came to christen the biggest of all, "The Great Infernal Rough?" then in truth did they stand aghast, each with his eyes on Titus, as though doubting whether he beheld man or demon.

The day of trial was nigh. Titus had in all opinions of course thrown the idea of competition completely aside, for who could hope to approach even within distance of his Infernal Rough? Nay, his inferior Dark Fiery and Brimstone King were plainly more than a match for the best of all their Imperial Greens and Reds.

It was evident that as many copper kettles would fall to his lot as might set him up with stock for a small brazier's shop. Hence envy, that terrible sprite, crept into the soul of the society, and at one time seriously threatened its very existence. A secret conspiracy against him was laid and hatched by two rival growers, which broke out on the identical night preceding the eventful morn of exhibition.

That night, dreamily unconscious of the gooseberry desolation to which he should awaken on the morrow, poor Titus lay quietly on his woollen mattrass, beholding happy visions of angelic horticulturists, berries as big as beer-barrels, and cart-loads of prizes shooting down their golden loads before his own house door. He awoke by peep of dawn. His mind was full of gooseberries, and he could shut his eyes no more that morning. So, getting up in haste to contemplate those resplendent productions, he strode down to his garden some hours before breakfast time. The gate was open, the trees broken, fruit stripped off and trampled under foot along the pathways! Titus saw, and fell prone to the earth.

Later in the day, his wife went down to see after him, and discovered him as described above, extended on his *bed*, with the watering-pot, that faithful attendant, by his side. Having obtained assistance, she had him conveyed home. Doctor Quassia, of Hammaway, was called in, who administered stimulants of all sorts to effect his recovery; and amongst the rest,—as knowing the proper restoratives for fainting country people—tickled his nose with a cockrel's feather, and his ears with a bunch of nettles. By these additional means he was brought back again to his senses.

Everybody in Hammaway, however anxious before, were now more anxious than ever to pump out the secret of raising such astounding berries. Titus was deeply questioned, but he remained as mute as his own bed-post—a circumstance which gave additional force to the preconceived general opinion, that he had sold himself to ——

No matter who—for what right, ye "purity of election" people, has a man to sell himself to anybody?

They also considered in addition, that the ——, i. e., the same gentleman just alluded to, had cheated him before his time; for who, asked they, ever dealt with—(the reader may here insert the name of any gentleman he pleases,) without eventually finding himself on the wrong side of the post?

All this was very excellent, but the grand secret remained still as unfathomable a secret as before.

Meantime, Titus took his gooseberries so much to heart that he weighed himself down beneath the burden of them; and that sensitive organ, that single wheel upon which life rolls along—I mean his heart—gave evident symptoms that its oil was out, its axle broken, and that it would shortly cease to move at all. Tokens like these alarmed everybody; and lest Titus should slip off unexpectedly, and carry his mystery along with him, to bury it in that deeper mystery, the grave, he was besought, exhorted, conjured, and prayed, to clear his dying body of the charge which, according to common repute, lay at his door; the more especially as at the same time he might be making known one of the greatest discoveries in horticulture ever yet discovered by the greatest discoverers. Titus rolled round his eyes, but said nothing.

The people of Hammaway were perplexed beyond measure. Men, women, and children alike in their degree; though the gardeners especially were at their wit's end.

At length, when it became evident how surely Death had informed Titus that very shortly he should make a call upon him, Mr. Canticle, the curate, was called in, as the man most likely of all men within the Wapentake, to over-match the ——

"Well, what happened?"

"You shall hear."

The curate lodged himself upon the edge of the bedstead on which the fallen Corinthian capital of our society lay, and after several minutes spent in silent rumination—in chewing as it were the cud of his mind—he thus spoke:

"My friend," said he, "it is now high time to inform thee that thy feet are hastening to tread the ground of another world. It may be, the ground of a far more blissful garden than this, upon which thy fleshly heart has been fixed; or, it may be the ground of that dreadful place which is said to be bottomless."

Titus groaned from the bottom of his spirit.

"Speak!" cried the curate, "for this very moment may be thy last. Hadst thou any pact with the devil?"

"No, upon my soul!" groaned Titus again in the hollow voice of an expiring winter's blast. "No, no!—it was only ——"

He *died* before the secret could be delivered.

All the philosophers of Hammaway laid their heads together immediately afterwards, in order to debate, consult, and divine, what words they could be which poor Titus left unrevealed. But as no tolerable evidence could be obtained touching the character, residence, or occupation, of the diminutive biped, who, it was presumed, had furnished the deceased with the queer-shaped box, they finally arrived at the sagacious decision, that "it was totally impossible to decide at all."

Such a conclusion was worth nothing. The reader is at perfect liberty to speculate upon the subject for himself.

EXTRACTS FROM "DOCTOR SYNTAX IN SEARCH OF THE PICTURESQUE."

BY WILLIAM COMBE.

The school was done, the bus'ness o'er,
When tir'd of Greek and Latin lore,
Good Syntax sought his easy chair,
And sat in calm composure there.
His wife was to a neighbor gone,
To hear the chit-chat of the town;
And left him the unfrequent power
Of brooding through a quiet hour.
Thus, while he sat, a busy train
Of images besieged his brain.
Of church-preferment he had none;
Nay, all his hope of that was gone:
He felt that he content must be
With drudging in a curacy.
Indeed, on ev'ry Sabbath-day,
Through eight long miles he took his way,
To preach, to grumble, and to pray;
To cheer the good, to warn the sinner,
And, if he got it,—eat a dinner:
To bury these, to christen those,
And marry such fond folks as chose
To change the tenor of their life,
And risk the matrimonial strife.
Thus were his weekly journeys made,
'Neath summer suns and wintry shade;
And all his gains, it did appear,
Were only thirty pounds a-year.
Besides, th' augmenting taxes press,
To aid expense and add distress;
Mutton and beef, and bread and beer,
And ev'ry thing was grown so dear;
The boys, too, always prone to eat,
Delighted less in books than meat;
So that, when holy Christmas came,
His earnings ceas'd to be the same,
And now, alas! could do no more,
Than keep the wolf without the door.
E'en birch, the pedant master's boast,
Was so increas'd in worth and cost,
That oft, prudentially beguil'd,
To save the rod, he spar'd the child.
Thus, if the times refus'd to mend,
He to his school must put an end.
How hard his lot! how blind his fate!
What shall he do to mend his state?
Thus did poor Syntax ruminate;
When, as the vivid meteors fly,
And instant light the gloomy sky,
A sudden thought across him came,
And told the way to wealth and fame;
And, as th' expanding vision grew
Wider and wider to his view,
The painted fancy did beguile
His woe-worn phiz into a smile:
But, while he pac'd the room around,
Or stood immers'd in thought profound,
The Doctor, 'midst his rumination,
Was waken'd by a visitation
Which troubles many a poor man's life—
The visitation of his wife.
Good Mrs. Syntax was a lady,
Ten years, perhaps, beyond her hey-day;
But though the blooming charms had flown
That grac'd her youth, it still was known
The love of power she never lost,
As Syntax found it to his cost;
For as her words were used to flow,
He but replied or YES or NO.
Whene'er enrag'd by some disaster,
She'd shake the boys and cuff the master;
Nay, to avenge the slightest wrong,
She could employ both arms and tongue;
And, if we list to country tales,
She sometimes would enforce her nails.
Her face was red, her form was fat,
A round-about, and rather squat;
And when in angry humor stalking,
Was like a dumpling set a-walking.
'Twas not the custom of this spouse
To suffer long a quiet house:
She was among those busy wives,
Who hurry-scurry through their lives;
And make amends for fading beauty,
By telling husbands of their duty.

'Twas at this moment, when, inspir'd,
And by his new ambition fir'd,
The pious man his hands uprear'd,
That Mrs, Syntax re-appear'd:
Amaz'd she look'd, and loud she shriek'd,
Or, rather like a pig she squeak'd,

To see her humble husband dare
Thus quit his sober ev'ning chair,
And pace, with varying steps, about,
Now in the room, and now without.
At first, she did not find her tongue,
(A thing which seldom happen'd long,)
But soon that organ grew unquiet,
To ask the cause of all this riot.
The Doctor smil'd, and thus address'd
The secrets of his lab'ring breast——

"Sit down, my love, my dearest dear,
Nay, prithee do, and patient hear;
Let me, for once, throughout my life,
Receive this kindness from my wife;
It will oblige me so:—in troth,
It will, my dear, oblige us both;
For such a plan has come athwart me,
Which some kind sprite from Heav'n has brought me,
That if you will your counsels join,
To aid this golden scheme of mine,
New days will come—new times appear,
And teeming plenty crown the year:
We then on dainty bits shall dine,
And change our home-brew'd ale for wine;
On summer days to take the air,
We'll put our Grizzle to a chair;
While you, in silks and muslins fine,
The grocer's wife shall far outshine,
And neighb'ring folks be forc'd to own,
In this fair town you give the ton."
"Oh! tell me," cried the smiling dame,
"Tell me this golden road to fame:
You charm my heart, you quite delight it."—
"*I'll make a* TOUR—*and then I'll* WRITE IT.
You well know what my pen can do,
And I'll employ my pencil too:—
I'll ride and *write*, and *sketch*, and *print*,
And thus create a real mint;
I'll *prose* it here, I'll *verse* it there,
And *picturesque* it ev'ry where:
I'll do what all have done before;
I think I shall—and somewhat more;
At Doctor *Pompous* give a look;
He made his fortune by a book,
And if my volume does not beat it,
When I return I'll fry and eat it.

Next week the boys will all go home,
And I shall have a month to come.
My clothes, my cash, my all prepare;
While *Ralph* looks to the grizzle mare.
Tho' wond'ring folks may laugh and scoff,
By this day fortnight I'll be off;
And when old Time a month has run,
Our bus'ness, *Lovey*, will be done.
I will in search of fortune roam,
While you enjoy yourself at home."

The story told, the Doctor eas'd
Of his grand plan, and Madam pleas'd,
No pains were spar'd by night or day
To set him forward on his way:
She trimm'd his coat—she mended all
His various clothing, great and small;
And better still, a purse was found
With twenty notes, of each a pound.
Thus furnish'd, and in full condition
To prosper in his expedition;
At length the ling'ring moment came,
That gave the dawn of wealth and fame.
Incurious *Ralph*, exact at four,
Led Grizzle, saddled, to the door;
And soon, with more than common state,
The Doctor stood before the gate.
Behind him was his faithful wife;—
"One more embrace my dearest life!"
Then his gray palfrey he bestrode,
And gave a nod, and off he rode.
"Good luck! good luck!" she loudly cried;
"*Vale! O Vale!*" he replied.
* * * * * *

A heap of stones the Doctor found,
Which loosely lay upon the ground,
To form a seat, where he might trace
The antique beauty of the place;
But, while his eye observ'd the line
That was to limit the design,
The stones gave way, and—sad to tell!—
Down from the bank he headlong fell.
The slush, collected for an age,
Receiv'd the venerable Sage;
For, at the time, the ebbing flood
Was just retreating from the mud:
But, after floundering about,
Syntax contriv'd to waddle out,
Half-stunn'd, amaz'd, and cover'd o'er
As seldom wight had been before.
O'erwhelm'd with filth, and stink, and grief,
He saw no house to give relief;
And thus, amid the village din,
He ran the gauntlet to the inn.
An angler threw his hook so pat,
He caught at once the Doctor's hat;
A bathing boy who naked stood,
Dash'd boldly in the eddying flood,
And, swimming onward like a grig,
Soon overtook the Doctor's wig.
Grizzle had trac'd the barren spot,
Where not a blade of grass was got;
And, finding nought to tempt her stay,
She to the Dragon took her way.
The ostler cried, "Here's some disaster,—
The mare's return'd without her master!"
But soon he came, amid the noise
Of men and women, girls and boys:
Glad in the inn to find retreat
From the rude insults of the street.
* * * * * *

To that warm inn they quickly hied,
Where Syntax, by the fire-side,
Sat in the landlord's garments clad,
But neither sorrowful nor sad,
Nor did he waste his hours away,
But gave his pencil all its play,
And trac'd the landscapes of the day.

Crown'd with success the following day
The Doctor homeward took his way;
And on the morrow he again
Was borne by Grizzle o'er the plain;
But Grizzle, having liv'd in clover,
Symptoms of spirit did discover,
That more than once had nearly thrown
Her deep-reflecting master down;
Nor, till they'd travell'd half the day,
Did he perceive he'd lost his way:
Nor, to that moment, did he find
That Grizzle, by some chance unkind,
Had left her ears and tail behind.
"Ne'er mind, good beast," he kindly said;
"What though no ears bedeck your head:
What though the honors of your rump
Are dwindled to a naked stump,
Now, rais'd in purse as well as spirit,
Your master will reward your merit."
Another day they journey'd on;
The next, and lo! the work was done.

Some days before, (I had forgot
To say,) a letter had been wrote,
To tell how soon he should appear,
And re-embrace his dearest dear;
But not one solitary word
Of his good fortune he preferr'd.

"Yes, home is home, where'er it be,
Or, shaded by the village-tree,
Or where the lofty domes arise,
To catch the passing stranger's eyes."
'Twas thus he thought, when, at the gate,
He saw his Doll impatient wait;
Nor, as he pass'd the street along,
Was he unnotic'd by the throng;
For not a head within a shop
But did through door or window pop.
He kiss'd his dame, and gravely spoke,
As now he brooded o'er a joke;
While she to know, impatient burn'd,
With how much money he return'd.
"Give me my pipe," he said, "and ale,
And in due time you'll hear the tale."

He sat him down his pipe to smoke,
Look'd sad, and not a word he spoke;
But madam soon her speech began,
And in discordant tones it ran:—

"I think, by that confounded look,
You have not writ your boasted book;
Yes, all your money you have spent,
And come back poorer than you went;
Yes, you have wander'd far from home,
And here a beggar you are come;
But bills from all sides are in waiting,
To give your Reverence a baiting:
I do not mean to scold and rail;
But I'll not live with you in jail.
So long a time you've staid away,
That the Town-Curate you must pay;
For, while from home you play'd the fool,
He kindly came to teach the school;
And a few welcome pounds to earn,
By flogging boys to make them learn:
But I must say, you silly elf!
You merit to be flogg'd yourself;
And I've a mind this whip shall crack
Upon your raw-bon'd lazy back.

Yes, puff away—but 'tis no joke
For all my schemes to end in smoke.
What, tongue-tied booby! will you say
To Mrs. Dress'em?—Who will pay
Her bill for these nice clothes?—Why, zounds!
It borders upon twenty pounds."

Thus, as she vehemently prated,
And the delighted Doctor rated,
From a small pocket in his coat
He unobserv'd drew forth a note,
And throwing it upon the table,
He said, "My dear, you'll now be able
To keep your mantua-maker quiet;
So cease, I beg, this idle riot:
And, if you'll not make such a pother,
I'll treat you with its very brother:
Be kind—and I'll not think it much
To show you half-a-dozen such."

She started up in joy's alarms,
And clasp'd the Doctor in her arms;
Then ran to bid the boys huzza,
And give them all a holiday.

"Such is the matrimonial life,"
Said Syntax;—"but I love my wife
Just now with horsewhip I was bother'd,
And now with hugging I am smother'd;
But wheresoe'er I'm doom'd to roam,
I still shall say—that *home is home!*

Again her dear the Dame caress'd,
And clasp'd him fondly to her breast:
At length, amidst her am'rous play,
The Doctor found a time to say—
"The fatted calf I trust you've slain,
To welcome Syntax home again."
"No," she replied, "no fatted calf;
We have a better thing by half;
For with expectation big
Of your return, we kill'd a pig;
And a rich haslet at the fire,
Will give you all you can desire;
The sav'ry meat myself will baste,
And suit it to my deary's taste."
"That dish," he cried, "I'd rather see,
Than *fricandeau* or *fricassee.*
Oh," he continued, "what a blessing:
To have a wife so fond of dressing;
Who with such taste and skill can work,
To dress herself, and dress the pork."
She now return'd to household care,
The dainty supper to prepare.

"Yes, puff away—but 'tis no joke,
"For all my schemes to end in smoke."

VILLAGE CHORISTERS.

FROM "PROVINCIAL SKETCHES."

ANONYMOUS.

A PIG in a string is a troublesome article to manage; two pigs in a string are more troublesome still, to a degree, perhaps, in proportion to the squares of their distances—a ram in a halter is also proverbial for obstinacy,—mules are celebrated for their pertinacity, and donkeys for their stupidity; but all the pigs, rams, mules, and asses in the world, put together, would be more easily managed than a company of singers in a village church. About four miles from Loppington there is a village called Snatcham. The living is but small, and the rector resides and performs his duty without the aid of a curate. You cannot imagine a milder and more gentle creature than this excellent clergyman. He is quite a picture, either for pen or pencil. He is not more than five feet four inches in height, somewhat stout, but not very robust; he is nearly seventy years of age—perhaps quite, by this time; his hair, what little is left of it, is as white as silver; his face is free from all wrinkles either of care or age; his voice is slender, but musical with meekness. The practical principle of his demeanor has always been—any thing for a quiet life. He would not speak a harsh word, or think an unkind thought to or of any human being; but he is now and then tempted to think that when the Apostle Paul recommended the Christians to live peaceably with all men, he put in the saving clause "if possible," with particular reference to village choristers. Snatcham choir is said to be the best in the county; such at least is the opinion of the choristers themselves; and he must be a bold man who should say to the contrary. They are no doubt very sincere when they say that they never heard any better than themselves; for, to judge from their singing, you would not imagine that they had ever heard any one else. Snatcham church does not boast an organ, and it is well it does not, for if it did, the whole choir would insist upon playing on it all at once; but instead of an organ, it has a band of music, which has been gradually increasing for some years past. It commenced about thirty-five years ago, with a pitch-pipe, which was presently superseded by a flute. It was soon found, however, that the dulcet notes of a single flute were quite lost amid the chaos of sounds produced by the vocal efforts of the choir; so a second flute was added by way of reinforcement; but all the flutes in the world would be no match for the double bass voice of Martin Grubb, the Snatcham butcher, under whose burly weight and hurly-burly notes the whole music-gallery trembled and shook. To give pungency to the instrumental department, therefore, a hautboy was added; but the vocalists felt it a point of honor to outscream the instruments, and the miscellaneous voice of James Gripe, the miller's son, who sang tenor, treble, or counter-tenor, just as it happened, was put into requisition for extra duty to match the hautboy. James Gripe could sing very loud; but the louder he sang, the more you heard that kind of noise that is produced by singing through a comb. It used to be said of him that he sang as if he had studied music in a mill during a high wind. To the two flutes and the hautboy were added two clarionets, because two of Gripe's younger brothers were growing up, and had a fancy for music. Young Grubb, the son of the butcher, began soon to exhibit musical talents, and accompanied his father at home on the violoncello, which instrument, with the leave of the rector, was added to the church band in a very short time,—a time too short, I believe, for the perfection of the performance.

The rector, dear good man, never refused his leave to any thing, especially to what the singers asked; they might have had leave to introduce a wagon and eight horses, if they had asked—but still the rector did not like it; and every time he was called upon to christen a child for one of his parishioners, he trembled lest the young one should have a turn for music, and introduce into the gallery some new musical abomination. It was next discovered that only one bass to so many treble instruments was not fair play, so to the violoncello was added a bassoon, and to the bassoon a serpent. What next?—nothing more at present; but if the movement party retain its ascendency, triangles and kettle-drums may be expected. The present state of Snatcham choir is as follows. In the first place, there is Martin Grubb, the butcher, a stout robust man of about fifty years of age, having a round head and a red face, with strong, straight, thick brownish-gray hair, combed over his forehead, and reaching to his very eyebrows. He is the oldest, the wealthiest, and the most influential man in the choir. He sings bass, and is said to be the life and soul of the party, though there are no great symptoms of life and soul in his face, which is about as full of expression as a bullock's liver. Then there is young Martin Grubb, who is a bit of a dandy, with black curling hair, and whiskers of the same pattern, pale face, thin lips, long chin, and short nose; his instrument is the violoncello. James Gripe is leader of the treble voices, with occasional digressions, as above noticed. And, in addition to the two younger Gripes, Absalom and Peter, who play the two clarionets, there are Onesiphorus Bang, the shoemaker, who plays the first flute; Issachar Crack, a rival shoemaker, who plays the second flute; Cornelius Pike, the tobacco-pipe maker, who plays the bassoon; Alexander Rodolpho Crabbe, the baker, who plays the hautboy; Gregory Plush, the tailor, who plays the serpent, together with divers others, men, boys, and girls, who make up the whole band.

This renowned choir has for a long time considered itself the *ne plus ultra* of the musical profession, and consequently equal to the performance of any music that was ever composed. The old-fashioned psalm tunes are therefore all banished from Snatcham church, to the great grief of the worthy rector, whose own voice is almost put out of tune by hearing Sternhold and Hopkins sung to the tunes of "Lovely nymph, assuage my anguish," and such like Vauxhall and Sadler's Wells music. The members of the choir, too, like other political bodies, have not much peace within, unless they have war without. If any attack be made upon their privileges, they stick together like a swarm of bees; but at other times, they are almost always at loggerheads one with another. Old Martin Grubb wields a precarious sceptre, for James Gripe is mightily tenacious of his rights, and resists, tooth and nail, the introduction or too frequent use of those tunes which superabound with bass solos. Grubb and Gripe, by way of an attempt at compromising the matter, have latterly been in the habit of taking it by turns to choose the tunes; and their alternate choice puts one very much in mind of the fable of the fox and the stork, who invited one another to dinner, the fox preparing a flat dish, of which the stork could not avail himself, and the stork in return serving up dinner in a long-necked bottle, too narrow to admit the fox's head. When James Gripe chooses the tune, he flourishes away in tenor and treble solos, leaving the butcher as mute as a fish; but when the choice devolves on Martin Grubb, he pays off old scores by a selection of those compositions which most abound in bass solos. And in such cases it not unfrequently happens that Martin, in the delighted consciousness of a triumph over his tenor, treble, and counter-tenor rival, growls and roars with such thundering exultation, that the gallery quivers beneath him, while his son saws away at his violoncello as though he would cut it in half, from very ecstasy. Cornelius Pike and Gregory Plush also spend as much breath as they can spare, and perhaps a little more than they can spare conveniently, in filling the vast cavities of their respective serpent and bassoon.

All this disturbs and distresses the feelings of the worthy pastor, who thinks it possible, and feels it desirable, that public devotion should be conducted with a little less noise. It appears, indeed, and no doubt the choristers, one and all, think so, that Snatcham church and Sternhold and Hopkins's psalms were all made to show forth the marvellous talents of the Snatcham choristers. They think that all the people who attend there come merely for the music, and that the prayers and the sermon have no other use or object than just to afford the singers and other musicians time to take breath, and to give them an opportunity of looking over and arranging their books for the next outbreak of musical noise. So little attention do the Snatcham choristers pay to any other part of the service than that in which themselves are concerned, that during the whole course of the prayers, and in all the sermon time, they are whispering to one another, and conning over their music books, sometimes almost audibly buzzing out some musical passage, which seems to require elucidation peradventure to some novice; and Master Grubb the younger is so delighted with his violoncello, that he keeps hugging the musical monster with as much fondness and grace as a bear hugs its cubs, and every now and then, in pleasing anticipation of some coming beauties, or in rapturous recollection of some by-gone graces, he tickles the sonorous strings with his clumsy fingers, bringing forth whispers of musical cadences loud enough to wake the drowsy, and to disturb the attentive part of the congregation. And then the good rector casts up to the music-gallery a look, not of reproof, but of expostulation, and thereupon Master Grubb slips his hands down by his sides, and turns his eyes up to the ceiling, as if wondering where the sound could possibly come from.

The supplicatory looks of the music-baited clergyman are on these occasions quite touching, and most mutely eloquent: they seem to say, "Pray spare me a little;—suffer me to address my flock. I do not interrupt your music with my preaching, why should you interrupt my preaching with your music? My sermons are not very long, why will not you hear them out? I encroach not on your province, why will you encroach upon mine? Let me, I pray you, finish my days on earth as pastor of this flock, and do not altogether fiddle me out of the church." But the hearts of the "village musicianers" are as hard as the nether millstone; they have no more bowels than a bassoon, no more brains than a kettle-drum.

Another grievance is, that these Snatcham choristers have a most intense and villainous provincialism of utterance: it is bad enough in speaking, but in singing they make it ten times worse; for they dilate, expand, and exaggerate their cacophony, till it becomes almost ludicrous to those who are not accustomed to it. The more excited they are, whether it be by joy or anger, the more loudly they sing, the more broadly they blare out their provincial intonations; and it is very seldom indeed that they ascend their gallery without some stimulus or other of this nature. If they all be united together in the bonds of amity and good-will; if Martin Grubb have suspended his jealousy of Gripe, and if Gripe no longer look with envy and hatred upon Grubb; if some new tune be in preparation wherewith to astonish and enrapture the parishioners; if there be in the arrangement tenors and trebles enough to satisfy the ambition of Gripe, and bass enough to develop the marvellous powers of Grubb;—there is a glorious outpouring of sound and vociferation, which none but the well-disciplined ears of the Snatcham parishioners can possibly bear. The walls of Snatcham church must be much stronger than those of Jericho, or they would have been roared to rubbish long ere this. But if the agreement of the choir be the parent of noise, their disagreement is productive of much more. More than once the Gripe and the Grubb factions have carried their animosity so far as to start two different tunes at the same time. And what can be done in such a case? Who is in the wrong? If the Grubb faction were to yield, they would betray a consciousness that they had not acted rightly in their selection of a tune; and if the Gripe faction were to withdraw from the contest, or to chime in with the Grubbs, they would seem to show the white feather: so they battle it out with all their might and main, and each party must sing and play as loud as possible, in order to drown the noise of the other. After church time, the Grubbs throw all the blame upon the Gripes, and the Gripes retort the charge upon the Grubbs, and a man had need have the wisdom of a dozen Solomons to judge between them. So excited with passion, and puffing, and singing, and playing, have the parties sometimes been after a *flare-up* of this kind, that they have looked as tired as two teams of horses just unharnessed from two opposition stage-coaches;—nay, the very instruments themselves have appeared exhausted, and an active imagination might easily believe that the old big burly bassoon, standing in a lounging attitude in one corner of the gallery, was panting for want of breath. Such explosions as these, however, do not frequently occur, and it is well they do not; when they do, a reconciliation generally takes place soon after, and an apology is made to the good pastor, more, perhaps, from compassion to his infirmities, than out of respect to his office or his years; and his mild reply is generally to the following effect:—"Ah, well, my good friends, I think another time you will find it more easy to sing all one tune: I marvel much that ye don't put one another out by this diversity of singing."

There is also another mode in which the parties manifest their discrepancy of opinion, or discordancy of feeling, and that is by the silence of half the choir. Now one would think that such an event would be a joy and a relief to the good man, who loves quiet; and so it is physically, but not morally: for though his ears are relieved from one half of the ordinary musical infliction, yet he is mentally conscious that evil thoughts are cherished in the breasts of the silent ones, that they who sing are not praising God in their songs, and that they who sing not, are not praising him by their silence.

But the climax of the abominations of the Snatcham choristers I have yet to record, and I hope that by their follies other choirs, if there be any so absurd, will take warning. It has been already said, that this celebrated Snatcham choir made it a great point to obtain leave from their rector for all the abominations and absurdities which they were accustomed to inflict upon the parish, under the guise of music; but the arrogant importunity of their solicitation was such, that they seemed to bid defiance to refusal, so that their asking leave was after the fashion of the beggar in Gil Blas, who held his musket in the direction of the donor's head. At a large town in the county in which Snatcham is situated, there had been a musical festival, the directors of which, in order to give *éclat* to their advertisements, had used all manner of means to swell the number of performers. For this purpose they had sought every hedge and ditch, and highway and byway in the county, to pick up every individual who had the slightest pretension whatever to musical talent. In such a search, of course the Snatcham choir could not by any possibility be overlooked. They were accordingly retained for the choruses, in consequence of which they underwent much musical drilling; nor were they a little pleased at the honor thus thrust upon them. They of course distinguished themselves, though I must say that the wisest thing chorus singers can do is not to distinguish themselves; but the Snatcham choir, it is said, actually did distinguish themselves, especially in the Hallelujah Chorus, and so fascinated were they with that chorus, and their own distinguished manner of singing it, that they resolved unanimously to perform it at Snatcham church. This was bad enough; but this was not the worst, for nothing would serve them but they would have it, of all days in the year, on Good Friday!

On the evening of the day before, the whole body of the choristers, vocal and instrumental, went up to the rectory, and demanded an audience of their worthy pastor. The good man trembled at their approach, and his heart sank within him at the announcement that they had something very particular to say to him. He thought of harp, flute, psaltery, dulcimer, sackbut, and all kinds of music, and his ears tingled with apprehension of some new enormity about to be added to the choir, in shape of some heathenish instrument. It was a ludicrous sight, and enough to make the pastor laugh, had he been at all disposed to merriment, to see the whole choir seated in his parlor, and occupying, after a fashion, every chair in the room; for if they were never harmonious in any thing else, they were perfectly harmonious as to their mode of sitting: they were all precisely in the same attitude, and that attitude was—sitting on the very outward edge of the chair, with their hats carefully held between their knees, their mouths wide open, and their eyes fixed upon vacancy. At the entrance of the clergyman they all rose, bowed with simultaneous politeness, and looked towards Martin Grubb as their mouthpiece. Martin Grubb, with his broad heavy hand, smoothed his locks over his forehead, and said—"Hem!"

"Well, Mr. Grubb," replied the rector, "you and your friends, I understand, have something particular to say to me."

"Why yes, sir," said Mr. Grubb, "we are called upon you by way of deputation like, just to say a word about singing; and for the matter of that, we have been practising a prettyish bit of music out of Handel, what they sung at the musical festival, called the Hallelujah Chorus; and as our choir sung it so well at the festival as to draw all eyes upon us, we have been thinking, sir, with your leave, if you please, and if you have no objection, that we should just like to sing it at church."

"At church?"

"Yes, sir, if you please, at church, to-morrow. The Hallelujah Chorus you know, sir, being part of the Messiah, we thought it would be particular appropriate; and we are all perfect in our parts, and there's two or three chaps out of the next parish that are coming over to Snatcham to see their friends, and they'll help us you know, sir, and every thing is quite ready, and rehearsed, and all that; and we hope, sir, you won't have no objection, because we can never do it so proper as with them additional voices what's coming to-morrow, and there will be such lots of people come to church on purpose to hear us, that they will all be so disappointed if we don't sing it."

Here James Gripe, somewhat jealous of his rival's eloquence, and taking advantage of Martin's pausing for a moment to recover breath, stepped forward, saying—"No, sir, we hope you won't refuse us your leave, because all the people so calculate upon hearing it, that they will go away in dudgeon if so be they are disappointed, and mayhap they will never come to church again, but go among the methodishes, or some of them outlandish sexes; and it would be a pity to overthrow the established church just for the matter of a stave or two of music."

The rector sighed deeply, but not audibly, and replied, saying, in a tone of mild expostulation—"But to-morrow, my friends, is Good Friday, a day of extraordinary solemnity, and scarcely admitting even the most solemn music in its service."

"Exactly so," interrupted Martin Grubb, "that's the very thing I say, sir, and therefore the Hallelujah Chorus is the most peculiar appropriate; it's one of the most sollumest things I ever heard,—it's quite awful and grand—enough to make the hair of one's head stand upright with sublimity."

"'Tis indeed, sir," added James Gripe, "you may take my word for it, sir."

"Perhaps," returned Martin Grubb, "your reverence never heard it; now, if so be as you never heard it, mayhap you don't know nothing about it, in which case we can, if you please, with your permission, sing you a little bit of it, just to give you an idea of the thing."

The poor persecuted pastor looked round upon his tormentors in blank amazement, and saw them with their ruthless mouths wide open, and ready to inflict upon him the utmost penalty of their awful voices. In tremulous tones the worthy man exclaimed—"No, no, no; pray don't—pray don't—don't trouble yourselves—I beg you will not. I know the piece of music to which you refer, and I think if you could perform it on any other day than Good Friday——"

Singers are a peculiarly irritable class of persons, and the slightest opposition or contradiction irritates and disturbs them, so that at the very moment that the rector uttered a sentence at all interfering with their will, they all surrounded him with clamorous and sulky importunity, and set to work with all diligence to demolish his objections.

"Please, sir," said Martin Grubb, shaking his big head with a look of dogged wilfulness, "I don't see how it's to be done. The Hallelujah Chorus requires a lot of extra voices what isn't to be got every day; and if we tells them chaps as is coming over to-morrow to help us, that we don't want their help, they may take tiff, and never come over to Snatcham again."

"But perhaps," the pastor meekly replied, "they may assist you in the grave and sober singing of some serious and well-known psalms, in which all the congregation may unite."

On hearing this, the broad-faced butcher expanded his features into a contemptuous sort of a grin, and said—"Come, now, that is a good one, as if reg'lar scientific singers would come all the way to Snatcham just to sing old psalm tunes!"

Mr. Gripe also said—"He! he! he!"

"He! he! he!" is a very conclusive kind of argument; and so the rector of Snatcham felt it to be, for he could not answer it, nor refute it, nor evade it. He looked this way and that way, up to the ceiling and down to the floor, towards Mr. Gripe and towards Mr. Grubb; but neither ceiling nor floor, nor Gripe nor Grubb, afforded him any relief from his painful embarrassment. The exulting singers saw that he was posed, and that now was the time to push home their victory, and overwhelm the rector by their united importunities. So they all crowded round him at once, and almost all at once began to assail him with such a torrent of reasons and argumentation, that he had not a word to say for himself.

"Please, sir," said Onesiphorus Bang, "I ha'n't got nothing else ready to play."

"Nor I neither," said Issachar Crack.

"Please, sir," said Alexander Rodolpho Crabbe, "we never like to do nothing without your leave, and we hope you won't compel us to do so now. My wife says she'll never come to church again, if the Hallelujah Chorus is not performed to-morrow."

"And I declare," said Gregory Plush, "that for my part, I never wish to touch the serpent again, if we mayn't do that piece of music."

Absalom and Peter Gripe also said the same as touching the clarionets; and James Gripe then looked at the rector with a quaintly interrogative aspect, which, without uttering a word, seemed to say—"There, sir, what will you do without Absalom and Peter's clarionets?" Now, for his own part, the worthy pastor would have been glad to get rid of the whole clamor of their music, for these choristers were always at loggerheads either with one another, or with all the rest of the parish.

The rector, thus overwhelmed with argument and eloquence, with pathos and importunity, found himself compelled to yield, which he did with the worst grace imaginable. Away went the choristers, rejoicing in the triumph of music, and full of glee at the thought of the wonderful figure they should cut on the morrow, when, assisted by the "chaps from the next village," they astonished the natives with the Hallelujah Chorus.

That night neither the singers nor the rector slept: the former were kept awake by the anticipation of musical glory, and the latter was made restless by the dread of musical absurdity. Good Friday came:—the whole village looked more like a scene of festivity than of fasting. The "chaps from the next village," as Martin Grubb called them, were as gay as so many larks: there was such a display of blue coats and yellow buttons as never was seen before. The singing gallery was full to suffocation, and the church itself was crowded. The squire of the parish was present, and his family also were present with him, and the singers were so happy that they could hardly contain themselves. They did not mind the prayers: they had heard them before, and did not think them half so well worth hearing as the Hallelujah Chorus. There was such a rustling of leaves, of music books, and such a buzz of whispering voices, that the worthy rector could hardly be heard. The choristers had arranged that the Hallelujah Chorus should be sung immediately before the sermon, and they thought that the prayers would never be over: they were as impatient as a young horse in harness.

At length the prayers were finished, and the merciless choristers let loose upon the congregation to inflict whatever musical torture they pleased. Away they burst with relentless and resistless fury. There was such scraping, and blowing, and roaring, and growling, and screaming, as never was heard; the powers of every voice, and of every instrument, were exerted to the utmost of their capability;—there was such an infinite variety of articulation of hallelowya, holleluyear, allyluyer, and ahmen, and awmen, and ameen, that none but the initiated could form a guess what the singers were about. The patient and afflicted rector sat still in the pulpit, waiting till the storm should be over: he knew that it could not last for ever, and that they must soon sing themselves hoarse or out of breath. There is an Irish proverb which says, "Single misfortunes never come alone:" this was verified in the present case; for a misunderstanding occurred, which produced a double infliction of the music. Messrs. Grubb, Gripe, Crabbe, Bang, Crack, and their friends, when performing at the cathedral, had observed that one or two parts of the performance had been encored by a signal from his grace the Duke of ——, who was present as patron, and this signal consisted of the silent waving or lifting up of a white pocket-handkerchief. Now, unfortunately, just as the band was bringing its mighty performance to a close, the squire of the parish most innocently drew his handkerchief out of his pocket; but happening to draw it forth with a peculiar grace, or with what Mr. Grubb and his friends thought a peculiar grace, they were most graciously pleased to take it for granted that it must be a signal for a repetition of the chorus; and therefore, just at the moment when the good rector was pleasing himself with the thought that the absurd display was over, they all burst forth again with renewed vigor. He thought that they were absolutely mad; he looked; he sighed; he shook his head; but he was only answered by halleluyear, allyluyer; and when they had finished the second time, he was half afraid that they would begin again, and sing it the third time. When the service was over, the good man took the liberty to hint to his musical parishioners that he thought they had performed a work of supererogation in performing the chorus twice. They themselves felt that they had somewhat encroached, but they laid the blame upon the squire, whose slightest wish, they thought, should be obeyed. The squire was very sorry when he found what mischief he had inadvertently done, and promised that he would take care, in future, not to pull out his handkerchief again in singing time.

ERRORS OF THE PRESS.

BY A REPORTER.

I once had occasion to report that a certain "noble lord was confined to his house with a *violent cold*." Next morning I found his lordship represented to be "confined with a *violent scold!*"

In the same way, on the occasion of a recent entertainment, I had said, "that the first point of attraction and admiration, were *her ladyship's looks*." This compliment was transferred by the printer to *her ladyship's cooks*.

My praises of the "*Infant Lyra*" (a juvenile musician), were converted to a panegyric on the "*infant lyar*."

In an account of General Sandanha's conduct at Oporto, I observed that he "*behaved like a hero*," while the printer made it appear that he "*behaved like a hare!*"

"We," says the John Bull, "often suffer in this way. About two years since, we represented Mr. Peel as having joined a party of *fiends* in Hampshire, for the purpose of shooting *peasants;* and only last week, in a Scotch paper, we saw it gravely stated that a *surgeon* was taken alive in the river, and sold to the inhabitants at tenpence a pound."

THE BATTLE OF THE YATCHES; OR THE VICTORY OF THE YANKEE YACHT, AMERICA.

A Pathetic Copy of Verses made by a British Tar, at Spithead.

OH, weep ye British sailors true,
  Above or under hatches,
Here's Yankee Doodle's been and come,
  And beat our crackest yatches!
They started all to run a race,
  And wor well timed with watches;
But oh! they never had no chance
  Had any of our yatches.

The Yankee she delayed at first,
  Says they, "She'll never catch us,"
And flung up their tarpaulin hats—
  The owners of the yatches!
But presently she walked along;
  "O dear," says they, "she'll match us!"
And stuck on their tarpaulin hats,
  The owners of the yatches.

Then deep we ploughs along the sea,
  The Yankee scarcely scratches;
And cracks on every stitch of sail
  Upon our staggering yatches.
But one by one, she passes us,
  While bitterly we watches,
And utters imprecations on
  The builder of our yatches.

And now she's quite hull down a-head,
  Her sails like little patches,
For sand barges and colliers we
  May sell our boasted yatches.
We faintly hear the Club-house gun—
  The silver cup she snatches—
And all the English Clubs are done,
  The English Clubs of yatches!

They say she didn't go by wind,
  But wheels, and springs, and satches;
And that's the way she weathered on
  Our quickest going yatches.
But them's all lies, I'm bound to say,—
  Although they're told by batches—
'Twas bulk of hull, and cut of sail,
  That did for all our yatches.

But novelty, I hear them say,
  Fresh novelty still hatches!
The Yankee yatch the keels will lay
  Of many new Club yatches.
And then we'll challenge Yankee land,
  From Boston Bay to Natchez,
To run their crackest craft agin
  Our spick and span new yatches.

THE LONG CANE.—A traveller, among other narrations of wonders of foreign parts, declared he knew a cane a mile long. The company looked incredulous, and it was evident they were not prepared to swallow it, even if it should have been a sugar cane. "Pray what kind of a cane was it?" asked a gentleman, sneeringly. "It was a hurricane," replied the traveller.

A FAIR RETORT.—Some English officers asked the chaplain for a toast. "The King of France!" "What, our foe?" said the Colonel. "You live by him," said the chaplain. The colonel took the first opportunity of giving, "The Devil!" "Do you mean to affront me?" said the chaplain. "You live by him," said the colonel, very coolly.

THE TREASURY OF RAMPSINITUS.

BY JOHN SOUTH PHILLIPS, M. A.

CHAPTER I.

Of all the quaint tales that to reading invite us,
The quaintest I know is about Rampsinitus:
As told by Herodotus, in his mood chirpy,
(One hundred and twenty-first chapter, Euterpe.)
First of all, then, we read, after Proteus was dead,
That Prince Rampsinitus was king in his 'stead;
So vast were his treasures of silver, no wonder
His Majesty wished to secure them from plunder;
And determined at once, with this object alone,
He would have a grand chamber constructed of stone.
The architect's name I regret I can't tell,
But he thought he might *build his own fortune* as well;
And being, it seems, at all dodges a dab,
He contrived in the chamber a movable slab;
Thus the building was quickly completed, we're told,
And the king stored within it his silver and gold.
Well, time rolled along, till one very fine day
This architect found he must Nature's debt pay;
So he summoned at once his two sons to his bed,
And, after some puffing and wheezing, he said—
"My boys! with your welfare alone in my view,
I have done what but very few fathers would do."
In short, the old fellow explained them his trick;
Gave the size and the place of the movable brick,
And told them that, bearing this well in their mind,
They could draw the king's money whenever inclined;
So, calling his progeny to his bedside,
The governor blessed them, and afterwards—died.
The funeral over, a period brief
Sufficed the bereaved ones for mourning and grief;
They felt they had each a proud mission to fill,
And began to act up to their late father's will;
To the chamber they came, under cover of night,
Found the slab, as their parent had told them, all right;
Slipped it out from the wall—then slipped quietly in,
And succeeded in pocketing plenty of tin.

CHAPTER II.

ELL, matters went smooth, and all seemed to be right,
Till the King found the great privy purse growing light;
So he called the Lord Keeper to fetch him the key,
And proceeded at once to his stone treasury;
On opening the door, just conceive his surprise!
His Majesty scarce could believe his own eyes,
When he saw the wholesale disappearance of tin,
Yet the chamber safe sealed, both without and within,
Indeed, it was clearly no case of house-breaking,
For the house was not broke—he was quite in a taking.
But when, on a second and third visitation,
He constantly found there was fresh depredation,
He issued his mandate for man-traps and gins
To be made, and set craftily all round the bins.

* * * * * *

By and by came the thieves: one went in as before,
And proceeded to plunder the Royal store,
But when just in the act—O, my goodness! bang—snap!
The unfortunate fellow was caught in the trap;
So, seeing at once he was doomed for eternity,
With the greatest sang froid he called his *fraternity:*
"You see my sad fix, my dear brother," he said,
"Come in, if you love me, and cut off my head;
For, should *I* be discovered, sure my recognition
Would bring *you* as well as myself to perdition,"

To this, with much feeling, the other replied:
"You speak like a book, sir, it can't be denied;
'Tis, of course, most unpleasant one's brother to kill,
But since you're so pressing, I'll do as you will."
So, refitting the slab, after doing the job,
He departed for home with his poor brother's nob.

CHAPTER III.

At the first break of dawn rose the King from his bed,
And hastily off to his Treasury sped,
Dumbfounded he stood, in the direst amaze,
At the dread apparition that there met his gaze;
The thief's headless body still baffled detection,
A trunk "left till called for," without a direction.

And when, searching the building, all proved safe and sound,
And nowhere could inlet or outlet be found,
Posed, puzzled, perplexed, at a loss what to do,
He, at last, to the following expedient flew.
Embarrassed at first with this absence of crest,
He did what he could with his *arms* and the rest.
So, nailing the trunk to the wall, as a *hatchment*,
He stationed police, (letter A. 1. detachment),
With orders—that any one given to grief,
Or showing compassion at all for the thief,
They should take into custody, handcuff, and bring
At once to my Lord Rampsinitus the King.
The body had scarce been suspended a day,
When the Mother "took on" in a terrible way,
Attacked the Survivor—said, somehow or other,
He *must* and *should* bring home the corpse of his Brother;
With a threat: that, on failing to do her good pleasure,
She'd go straight to the King, and tell who had his treasure.

CHAPTER IV.

When his mother continued this fiery tirade,
And all he could say to her failed to persuade,
He saw *thus* together they never could lodge,
And finally hit on the following dodge:
By hook or by crook, or from some of his cronies,
He collected a lot of *Jerusalem ponies*,
Filled some goat-skins with wine, slung 'em over their backs,
And started his posse of asinine hacks;
Well—nothing had happened his march to retard,
Till he found himself near to the *dead-body-guard*,
When he slyly unfastened a goat-skin or two,
And out gushed the wine (as, of course, it would do);
He then boxed his own ears—out a bellowing burst—
Seemed quite at a loss to which ass to go first—
Like "*a John*" *out of place* he was fairly *non plus*,
When the dead-body-guard made a general rush;
Each man with his pewter—and reasoning thus:
"What is sorrow to *him*, is a godsend to *us*."
Well—our hero feigned fury to perfect his *ruse*,
And loaded them all with the choicest abuse,
Till they took to consoling him under his sorrow,
And said: "Never mind, you'll be better to-morrow."
So, pretending at length to regain his composure,
He picketed his troop in a joining enclosure:
After some conversation, and mutual chaff,
They actually managed to get him to laugh:
Till they worked on his noble and generous mind,
To give them a bottle of *sherry white wine*,
Whereupon they all voted a snug bivouac,
And cheerily gave one another the *sack;*
Till, in merriment, one took his host by the throttle,
And swore he should help them to finish the bottle:
Pretending to yield to this *urgent* request,
After some hums and haws, he sat down with the rest;
So high was their glee, and so hearty their greeting,
He felt himself bound to continue his treating;
In short, the whole guard got excessively drunk,
And down in the arms of Morpheus sunk.

The night was far spent—to the *right about face*
He shaved the policemen—a badge of disgrace;
And leaving them thus *demi-whiskered* and drunk,
He detached from the building his late brother's trunk,
Slung it over his asses, and thus undetected
Got home, having done as his mother directed.

CHAPTER V.

When the news that the body was stolen away
Came to Royalty's ear, 'twas the devil to pay—
The King in his fury said,Cost what it might,
He'd die or discover this mischievous wight;—
It was this that at last he determined to do:
(Though, between you and me, I believe it untrue)
To the *drawing-room* levees he made an exception,
And bade the Princess hold a *bed-room reception*,
Bade her entertain all, and not be particular,
But first to demand a *confession auricular;*
To compel them to tell her—each one mother's son—
The sharpest and wickedest act he had done;
The man that should own the affair of the thief,
She should grapple him tightly, and bring him to grief.
The fair Princess Royal no cavilling made,
But her father's injunctions most strictly obeyed.—

Well, matters remained *statu quo* for a season,
Till the thief heard the fun, and at once knew the reason:
In his sleeve the *arch-dodger* complacently laughed,
And determined to outdo the king in his craft:
With the arm of a man very recently dead
Hidden under his cloak, on his errand he sped;
Came before the Princess, and, when asked like the rest,
He freely at once to her Highness confessed:
"The *wickedest* act of my lifetime," he said,
"Was when I cut off my poor trapped brother's head;
The *sharpest* was when, having made the guard drunk,
I took down from the building, and *packed up his trunk*."

This said—she remembered her father's command,
And laid hold, as she thought, of the gentleman's hand;
But, in fact, nothing else than the arm of the dead,
Which he left her, and out through the palace-gate fled.

CHAPTER VI.

WHEN this wonderful news to the King was conveyed,
He was stunned at the wisdom and daring displayed;
And heralds were sent, in his Majesty's name,
Through the length and the breadth of his realm to proclaim—
Personal safety, and I don't know what,
If only the man to the King could be got:
Well, the thief, with firm trust in his Majesty's honor,
Presented himself;—says the King, "You're a stunner:
I give you my own royal daughter to wife,

As the knowingest chap I have seen in my life;
For Egyptians are classed above all other men,
But I'm hanged if you ain't a cut above them."

OLD FRIENDS WITH NEW FACES.

NOT BY MARTIN F. TUPPER.

COINED metal impels the feminine horse.

It is painful to be in attendance for the pumps of departed individuals.

Loveliness lies not beneath the superficies of the exterior cuticle.

Let every man pursue the bent of his own genius, as the elderly matron observed, while saluting her vaccine favorite.

An equestrian mendicant will journey towards the realms of his Satanic Majesty.

Too great a number of culinary assistants may impair the flavor of the *consommé.*

A pebble, in a state of circumvolution, acquires not the lichens of mural vegetation.

Royalty may be contemplated with impunity, even by a feline quadruped.

No vendor of the finny tribe announces that her piscatory spoil is so decomposed as to offend the olfactory nerves.

Why should the smaller domestic utensils accuse the larger of nigrotude?

Feathered bipeds of similar plumage will live gregariously.

Those, the illumining apertures of whose messuages are vitrified, should never project fragments of granite.

The capital of the Papal States was not constructed in a diurnal revolution of the globe.

THE STREET-CONJUROR.

BY HAL. WILLIS.

SINCE the decline of fairs, which, for the last ten or twelve years, have gradually lost their charms in the eyes of a "discerning public," the Street-Conjuror, obtaining a precarious livelihood upon the voluntary contributions of an admiring crowd, has evidently gained considerable patronage. In all quarters of the town, he may now be seen enacting his wonders, for the entertainment of a gaping mob, composed of all grades.

There stands the grinning errand-boy, the foremost of the motley circle, losing his employer's time and letting his commission go "clean out" or his head, rubbing against a chimney-sweep, regardless of the sooty contamination; and divers dirty boys bent upon no errand in the world but idleness and mischief. Servants-of-all-work, transfixed to the spot by curiosity, with mugs for the dinner beer, or a dish for the chops or steaks, in one hand, and twirling a latch-key upon the thumb of the other. All excited by the wonders, and expressing their pleasurable surprise in broken exclamations or "Well, then, I never!" and "That beats every think as I ever seed!" while the outermost circle of the congregation, like a rich fringe to a shabby cape, is made up of the more respectable class of middling people.

Probably, stationed at the gas-lamp, at a sufficient distance to prevent any vulgar contact, and still at the same time near enough to witness the dexterity of the performer, appears a young clerk, with a penny Cuba 'twixt his lips, and "preserved" in a fashionable Macintosh, who half patronizes the exhibition by casting a copper ostentatiously in the air, with, for him, the expressive encomium of "Dem the fallow!"

It may be a weakness, but we must confess that we always mix ourselves up in these audiences; for the efforts and exertions of these itinerant vagabonds create an indescribable excitement—a sort of melancholy pleasure—that leaves, we trust, no unprofitable impression on the mind. The faded finery of the tawdry little jacket or vest—the soiled white "tights" and the muddy high-low boots—and the sallow complexion of the loud-voiced performer—are all sad, very sad! He looks like a "soiled remnant" of the scattered company of the once-splendid Richardson, the emperor of showmen; and when we recall to mind the annual display which feasted our devouring eyes at the Fair of St. Bartholomew, we sigh to think of the sorrowful changes relentless Time hath wrought. The familiar tricks—the repetition of the oft-repeated jokes (as threadbare as the speaker)—bring fresh to our pondering mind those happy days when "trifles light as air" were wont to tickle us to laughter.

How has he fallen from his "high estate!" The brilliant prince, all glittering with spangles, whose splendid habiliments excited our wonder, now trudges in the filthy mud!

The romance of our infant mind has evaporated like a dream! The cold and vulgar reality serves only to create our commiseration. Paint seldom conceals the ravages of dissipation in the hard-featured and haggard countenance. We—not uncharitably, but reasonably—conclude, from his appearance, that half his time is perhaps passed in the public streets, and the other half wasted in the public-house. He has no huge caravan now to transport him from place to place; the whole implements of his vocation are carried about with him. An old rusty sword, some balls, a dish or plate, a pack of dirty cards, and some broad-bladed knives, comprise nearly all his available "properties;" and, certainly, when the stock is considered, the interest he derives from it is greater far than the proceeds of any joint-stock bank in the three kingdoms.

His rude oratory, and the cunning manner in which he excites the curiosity of his audience, and contrives to extract the reluctant pence from their pockets, are admirable specimens of seductive eloquence, and worthy a better cause.

The most earnest and successful appeal, to the largest audience, seldom or never brings more than a shilling or eighteen-pence to his exchequer.

These contributions, however, as he repeats his performances so frequently, would produce an ample sum; but, unfortunately, our climate is so unfavorable to *al fresco* entertainments, that he is very often "*rained* in" (like a runaway horse) for days together. In the winter season, indeed, he is rarely visible: he appears to "go out" with the butterflies. Whether, like them, he is transformed to a "*little grub*," we know not; but the probability is that he lives upon *short commons*.

In this profession, as in many others, there are different grades; some exercising their feats unaided, while others have the able and attractive assistance of music and a confederate, who usually enacts a *rôle* similar to the clown in the circle.

We shall endeavor, as far as the power of our pen will permit, to describe one of the latter class:—One September afternoon, we were attracted by a motley mob of boys and girls and "children of a larger growth," who were following closely upon the heels of two men. They were both dressed in shabby great-coats. The head of one was adorned with a cloth cap; the other sported a very "deteriorated" white hat, that, in the palmy days of Hunt, might have surmounted the caput of a respectable radical. A countenance smeared with white and red appeared ludicrously enough in such a guise. He bore a huge drum at his back, and a canvas bag in his hand, while his companion carried a ladder about eight feet high on his shoulders, and led a juvenile Arabian pony (*vulgò*, a donkey) in a string. We, of course, joined the idlers.

Arriving at one of the broadest of the many streets which run into the City-road, the leader of the mob halted.

A moment's consultation, and an evident excitement in the crowd ensued. At last, the drum was placed upon the ground—the young donkey was tied to one of the rowels of the prostrate ladder, and in the meanwhile the "company" began to encircle them—the urchins "punching" their way to the best and foremost places. Cards, cups and balls, and other mystic machinery, were brought to light from the capacious bag, and displayed in order, with rather a tiresome precision, to the expectant beholders.

At length, all was ready. The white hat was thrown aside, and then the envious coat that concealed a very dirty cotton garb of white and red. The boys shouted, for it *was* a real clown, after all—albeit the muddy lace-up boots, with hob-nailed soles and heels, rather "derogated" from the dignity of the character.

"Now, sirrah, beat the drum," said the conjuror, doffing his cap and coat, and exhibiting a short muscular, ill-made figure, arrayed in a loose pair of white tights, garnished with strips of red and green tape, and a very confined dark velvet vest, through the arm-holes of which his shirt-sleeves flowed full and free;—"Now, sirrah, beat the drum."

"Beat the donkey, sir?" inquired the fool (a very old fool, by the bye, averaging about fifty), and hereupon there was *such* a shout!

"No, sirrah; the drum, the drum!"

"What for, sir? He ain't done nothing, I'm sure."

"That's the very reason, sirrah, he ought to be beaten, and for which I shall beat you, if you don't instantly obey; so, set to work."

"To work!—you don't mean it."

"I do."

"It's a big fib, for you mean me to play, I know."

"Well, play away, then."

"Please, sir, I've lost my drum-sticks," replied the fool; "perhaps you'll lend me a pair?" pointing to his master's legs.

"No, sirrah, I want 'em to support me."

"Then I only wonder how you manage to live upon such a slight support. Why, it's as bad as the *Di-e-tittery* of the workhouses."

A burst of "popular feeling" followed this allusion.

"Come, sirrah, no talking; take the pipes and drum, and summon our friends to witness our astonishing feats of legerdemain and balancing, which we confidently hope will be thought worthy of their patronage and support."

"Hear, hear!" exclaimed the fool. And forthwith he thrust the Pandean pipes in the breast of his waistcoat, and began blowing away to the very noisy accompaniment of the drum.

The master, meanwhile, begging his audience to enlarge the circle, commenced throwing up the balls, first two, then three, and lastly four, with a facility and precision which would not have disgraced the manual dexterity of the celebrated Indian jugglers.

And now, drawing four broad-bladed knives from the apparently inexhaustible bag, he played with them in the same manner, the fool still keeping up the time.

The crowd gradually became more dense, and a few pence were from time to time cast into the circle.

Having finished his second performance, he bade the clown produce the money-bag, who, putting down his drum, drew out a small one, about the size of a shilling, with a long bobbin to it.

"What's this for, sirrah?" said his master.

"For the sovereigns," replied the fool.

"Nonsense. Where's the one for the small change?" inquired his master.

The clown then brought forth a large leathern bag from the capacious pocket of his nether garment.

"It's all very well," said he, "but I'm such a loyal man that when I get one good *sovereign* I'm never desirous of seeing any *change*;" and proceeding to collect the pence, he continued, "This is what mother used to call 'picking up a livelihood.'" A laugh followed this sally, and, better than all, some liberal hand threw three pennyworth of coppers, which fell upon the shoulders of the clown. Turning quickly towards the donor, he exclaimed, "Sir, the shower of your benefits has not fallen upon a barren soil. I have not words to express my gratitude. I can truly say," rubbing his shoulders, "that I am struck by your liberality. Now, master, go on, and while you raise the wind, I'll not cease to blow, depend on't." And delivering the bag into the conjuror's hand, he recommenced his music. Now shuffling, and cutting, and flapping the cards, "as the manner is," the conjuror paraded round the circle, requesting one of his audience to draw a card, "anywhere, no matter which," as he said. A boy took a card. "Look at it," said he, "you'll remember it? Now place it in the pack, take it in your own hands, and shuffle it. There, don't be afraid; mix 'em well together. Now, you're sure it's there?" "Yes, quite," replied the boy. "Presto! begone," exclaimed the conjuror, casting up his eyes with a mysterious air, and "snapping" the cards with his right hand. He then bade him name the card aloud.

"The Jack—the Jack o' Clubs," said the boy.

"The Jack of Clubs, eh! Now look;" and then displaying the cards one by one upon the ground, the identical card was found—wanting. "Are you quite sure, young gentleman, that you put it into the pack again?"

"That I am," replied the lad confidently, at the same time coloring up to the eyes, as if he were really under the suspicion of having purloined it.

"Well the card isn't worth much, but the pack will be spoiled without it. Come, I'll give anybody a penny who will produce it."

And taking up the leathern bag for the reward, he suddenly drew out, instead of the penny, the missing card! This delusion was so well executed that there was a general murmur of applause.

He next threw a rusty sword into the air, and catching it as it descended, balanced it on his chin and forehead, walking about the ring; then placing a pewter platter on the hilt, and beating it swiftly round with his hand, he raised it aloft, whirling with the rapidity of a smoke-jack, and striking the point of the weapon in the bowl of a table-spoon, took the handle between his teeth, and moving his head backwards and forwards (with that action so peculiar to the goose!) he walked with arms a-kimbo across the primitive *parterre* of his chosen theatre, to the admiration of the spectators. This being concluded, "Now, sirrah," said he, "while I prepare the infant prodigy, get your dinner."

"That's the ticket," exclaimed the fool, putting down his drum and pipes with alacrity, and tenderly addressing the former, he warned it to be quiet:—"Unless anybody hits you, don't make a noise, now, but be *dumb, dumb!* And there's the pipes—which although rather the worse for wear, I hope nobody won't smoke 'em!"

"Now, sirrah, be quick, and don't keep the *donkey* waiting," said his master.

"I'll not keep *you* a minute," replied the clown, and hereat all the boys laughed immoderately, and the bigger folks tittered. Proceeding to the bag, he drew out a wooden bowl, filled with strips of white paper.

"Here's lining for a man's trunk!" said he, "but I suppose I must chew it, whether I *choose* or no; so here goes;" and he forthwith began filling his mouth with the shreds.

"It's sweet and clean, at any rate," said his master.

"I think it's a little *foul*, for if here ain't a bone!" cried he, arresting his masticatory operations; and putting the forefinger and thumb of his right hand to his jaws, he drew out what is technically termed a "barber's pole," which he gradually extended, projecting it from his lips four or five feet! Taking it in his hand, and spitting out the paper, which he had crammed into his capacious mouth, he held it up to the laughing crowd; "If that ain't enough to choke an alderman!—mind me if I don't discharge the cook, that's all, for attempting to *dish* me, instead of the dinner. No more made dishes for me; my *standing* dish in future, depend on't, shall not be *stationary*."

Having replaced the bowl and its contents, he proffered his services to his master, who having securely tied the donkey's legs to the ladder, with the fool's assistance, raised him on his chin, and held him *in equilibrio* in the air.

"Ain't my master clever?" said the fool, "and yet all the world must see that he's *below* an ass! You laugh—you're tickled—but there's a moral in this that none of you see. I'll expound: That man and that ass are a type of the world as it wags. For how many asses are daily supported by the ability of clever men! The Temperance Society will tell you that asses alone get 'elevated.' Don't believe 'em! Drunkenness may make a beast of a man, but let me tell you every thing is good in moderation. They tell you to drink water, and promise you length of years, which is as much as to say that if you drink water, your *ears* will increase to the length of a donkey's!—pah! when the spirit is fled the man is dead, and all arguments are weak that are wanting in—spirit! But I must assist my master; the greatest fool can give a man a *lift* upon occasion." Having released the conjuror and the donkey, which appeared very stupid and inert, the master stood in the midst of the circle, to take a little breath after his feat."

"Now, calf, leave the donkey," said he.

"Calf indeed!" replied the indignant fool, "I'll show you I can make a little *wheel* before I'm dead, at any rate;" and casting a hoop adroitly over his master's head, he exclaimed, "There, now; there's a little wheel in a jiffy."

"How do you mean, sirrah?"

"Why, that 'ere hoop's the tire, and you're the *knave*," to be sure, replied he.

"But where's the spokes, man?"

"Why, you're the *spokes*-man, everybody must allow," quickly answered the fool; and his master, picking up the hoop and throwing it at him, he caught it, and began trundling it round the area formed by the spectators.

"What *are* you about, sirrah?"

"Playing at hoop," replied the fool; "will you hide?"

"I'll *hide* you," said his master. "Come, strike up;" and the buffoon immediately resumed his musical instruments, and began blowing his pipes, and throwing and swinging about his drumsticks, after the most approved mode of the Moorish drummer.

The conjuror then took a large blue and white dish, and began whirling it to and fro, up and down, to the nervous amazement of the throng, who expected every moment to see it fall, and dashed to pieces on the ground. At last, placing it between his legs, he looked up, and pretended to cast it in the air. Up went his hand, and the dish was gone! All eyes were upturned towards the sky, expecting to see the dish skimming the air; and so adroitly was the deception executed, that they all laughed heartily at their disappointment; for the conjuror had merely passed it from one hand to the other, and now quietly laid it down.

Placing a sort of leathern cup, with a strap, upon his forehead, which projected like the horn of a rhinoceros, he grasped a wooden ball, about the size of an orange, and began tossing it in the air, about as high as the copings of the adjoining houses; and at last in its descent, caught it in the cup! He repeated the apparently dangerous experiment; for, in its fall, should he miss it, the ball certainly threatened to "put him out of countenance." Having caught it for the third time, he appealed to the generosity of a "British public" for more contributions. A few more pence were scattered.

"That's your sort!" exclaimed the fool, seizing the large bag, and beginning to collect the tribute; "down with your dust! If any lady or gentleman wishes to contribute a piece of silver, I've a hand 'open *as* day to melting charity.' Only consider my master's family. Here's a big drum; and here's the pipes, which cost, I don't know how much and a great deal more; and then there's the ass, myself and himself, and a large family of small children at home, who are admiring the beautiful eyes of an old potato, and smelling a red herring! Pray tip; for master owes me the last fortnight's wages, and there's my washerwoman all 'in the suds;' and when she asks me, 'Dick, how are you off for soap?' poor creature, she'll look blue-bags at me if I don't shell out the browns. Washerwomen, of all women in the world, can do the least without '*coppers*,' you know. Thank'e, sir, thank'e."

Having made a tolerably good collection, he looked round the circle before tying up the contribution:—

"I do not wish to disappoint the generosity of any individual: before I draw the string, is there any one who wishes to bestow a mite?"

"No, no; go on!" shouted a boy from the crowd, who had contributed nothing, and was impatient of the delay.

"We shall go on directly," replied the fool. "Ladies and gentlemen, the fireworks are all over!"

Hereupon there was a general movement in the crowd, and they gradually separated; while the Street-Conjuror and his merry colleague resumed their walking attire, and took up their paraphernalia preparatory to a repetition of their gambols in some favorable spot in the vicinity.

THE STRANGER I MET AT MY CLUB.

A Tale of the Isle of Wight.

ANONYMOUS.

At the club of which I am a member, "The Whitechapel Athenæum," we are allowed to bring strangers with us to dinner—a very great convenience, every one must allow, to our friends. I live in that neighborhood; I am not ashamed to confess it. In fact, I have been so long in business, and have seen such a variety of things in my life, that I am too old to be ashamed of any thing. At any rate, I am above the paltry affectation of many of my neighbors, who consider it something mighty ungenteel to remain in town at this season of the year, and give out to all their friends that they are gone to Margate or Gravesend, when I know for a certainty that they have never budged from their own homes. One of them—I don't choose to mention names—a drysalter by trade, a leading member of our club—in fact, the only one who endeavored to exclude me when I was a candidate for admission—put a ticket in his window with "Gone to Brighton for the season," written on it; when, I declare, I have seen him almost every day slinking through by-lanes and alleys into his back-shop. All this, I say, I am above. I stay in town the whole year round, and dine at my club every day. The club, however, it must be confessed, has a very desolate appearance all August and September; piles of uncut newspapers blocking up every table, windows badly cleaned, floors scarcely sanded above once a week, and if by any chance a member does come in, he looks for all the world as if he were detected in a forgery. The steward of the club has gone on leave of absence; the butler is never to be found; dear me! the very waiters seem asleep; and you have to wait at least half an hour for your pint of wine. However, in spite of all these inconveniences, it is better to dine there than at a chop-house; and, accordingly, every day, summer and winter, punctually at five o'clock, I take my seat at the little square table, up at the middle window looking directly opposite into the London Hospital.

One day last week I had dined—mutton chop, I remember, and pot of porter—and was picking my teeth very leisurely to give William time to get me my pint of sherry, when my attention was called to the other end of the room by a gentleman making a speech. He was a stranger; a stout man, about my own age—fifty or thereabouts—and he had been brought in by a friend, a member of the club with whom I am not acquainted. They had dined together very quietly—cold beef and pickles, William said, exactly at three—and, in fact, so little noise had they made, that I was not aware of their presence in the room. All of a sudden, I heard a speech proceeding with the most amazing volubility. I was so far off I could not catch a word of it, but I perceived from the gestures he made use of, and the risings and fallings of his voice, that he was an accomplished orator. His whole audience was his friend—a mercer from Cornhill—a very quiet, respectable man, who certainly looked amazed at the performance. It lasted, I should think, twenty minutes; at the end of which time, the gentleman sat down and knocked very loudly with both hands on the table, and kicked with all his might upon the floor. Shortly after that, he volunteered a song; 'twas "Will Watch, the bold Smuggler," and very well he sang it, bestowing at the end the same hearty marks of approbation on it that he had formerly done on the speech.

My wine was now put before me, and I placed my tooth-pick in my pocket. Before I had finished one-half of the decanter—I drank very slowly—the mercer from Cornhill slipped off, and I thought I perceived by the doggedly determined manner with which he fixed his hat on his head, that he had no intention of returning. The stranger waited very patiently for some time, but at last, looking all round, and seeing nobody but me, he carried his decanter—I declare to heaven it was entirely empty—up to the table I was sitting at, and making me a very polite bow, proposed, as we were both enjoying our wine, that we should do so in company.

"Company, my dear sir," he continued, drawing in his chair, and filling up his glass out of *my* decanter; "company, sir, is indispensable to me. 'Tis even recommended for my health."

"Indeed, sir," I said, keeping a firm hold of my wine, for he had finished his glass in a moment, and looked very dangerously at the decanter again.

"Yes, sir; I am liable to low spirits. I have such a lot of sensibility; 'tis quite distressing to see me sometimes. Nice club this is."

"Very——"

"I think of belonging to it myself. 'Twill be a charming resource against the agonies of recollection, the woes of memory, and the grief of a too sensitive, too sympathizing heart. You don't help yourself to the wine."

"I have had enough, sir," I said, as repulsively as I could.

"Nonsense! Enough? why, you've had nothing. Let me help you." So saying, he fairly got possession of my pint decanter, and divided the contents of it equally between us.

"This is the fine free and easy way I like to see things carried on in clubs. What are clubs? Confraternities of congenial souls. If I belonged to a club, there is not a member in all whose woes I would not have a share."

"And in his bottle, too," I said, with a sneer.

"Good! good! Well, that *does* deserve something. Waiter, a bottle of port. Ah, sir! how charming it is to meet with a good-humored, pleasant, agreeable, witty companion, such as you! 'twas a capital hit about the bottle—I took it at once."

"So I saw, sir. You took every drop of it."

"Good again! Waiter, why the devil don't you bring that bottle of port? Alas! sir, you must excuse me. I am dreadfully subject to low spirits. But, thank heaven, here comes William with the wine."

He poured out a glass, and after looking at it for some time, swallowed it off in a twinkling.

"Medicine, sir—purely as medicine I drink it. It enables me to bear up. I should die without it—ennui—blue devils—hypochondriasis——"

"And thirst, sir?" I said; but somehow the extraordinary familiarity of the man's manner disarmed my dislike, and I filled up my glass, and accompanied my observation with a smile.

"Capital again! You have said three very witty things. I declare to heaven, sir, I *am* ashamed of myself, but I can't laugh. No, sir; the effort would choke me. I have one fatal remembrance, one sorrow, but you know the lines——"

"Indeed, sir?" I asked, inquiringly.

"True. I have thought of suicide; but 'tis so common, 'tis become vulgar; my shoemaker cut his throat last week. I will tell you my story, sir; after that judge if I have no cause for regret."

"Happy to hear it, sir."

The stranger drew his chair more confidentially close to the table, filled up our glasses, and then said—

"Do you know the Isle of Wight, sir?"

"No."

"Did you ever hear of old Sniggs, of Waterlane?"

"No."

"Did you ever hear of Captain Hoskins, of Harridon Lodge?"

"No."

"Good heavens! what a man you must be! The Isle of Wight is the loveliest place in the world, sir. All the Undercliff is a slice out of Eden; hundreds of people go there every year, pretending to be in bad health—'tis only to enjoy the scenery and eat prawns. Dr. Clarke calls it the British Madeira; 'tis the only homebrewed I ever heard of, which is better than the original. Ah! 'tis indeed a charming spot, and five-and-twenty years ago, 'twas still more beautiful than now. I was young then; thin, elegant, genteel; grief had not swelled me; nor tears reddened the point of my nose. And, then, old Sniggs—you never heard of old Sniggs?"

"No, sir; never."

"Curious;—a d—d old hunks as ever was, but such a sweet creature his daughter! Ah, Julia! How playful she used to be at church! We always flirted immensely all the time of the psalms. And Hoskins—never heard of Hoskins?"

"Never."

"Odd again;—a dog, sir. A handsome, laughing, jolly, swearing, whiskered, infernal fellow, sir. He was six feet two—without a shilling—he had spent two fortunes—and, as bad luck would have it, went down to the Isle of Wight."

"To eat prawns, sir?"

"No—to catch gudgeons, sir. He caught *me*—the rascal! That's my story, sir."

"What is, sir? I have heard no story yet."

"No! How slow you must be. Don't you see it all? But I'll tell it you, sir, word for word. Pray, sir, do you ever lend money to a friend?"

This was too much, and I determined to stop the man's impertinence at once. The idea of asking me for a loan after ten minutes' acquaintance! I could not help thinking he was a swindler.

"No, sir," I said: "I would not lend a shilling to the dearest friend I have in the world; no, not to keep him from starving. And, as to trusting a stranger with a sixpence, sir, I should consider he was insulting me if he hinted at such a thing."

"Give me your hand," exclaimed the stranger, "give me your hand. I am proud to have met you—you will be a happy man all your days—you are a gentleman—a wise man. Would to heaven I had always thought as you do! Ah! sir, you shall hear. Old Sniggs was worth a hundred and fifty thousand pounds—Julia his only child. I, sir, lived next door to them in Finsbury Square, and flirted with the daughter every Sunday at church. Could any thing be more agreeable? Yet, somehow or other, we never could scrape up an acquaintance. A she dragon, in the shape of an old housekeeper, always guarded that fairest of Hesperian apples—plums, I should say, for you perceive she was heiress to a plum and a half—and nothing I could do could get the better of her vigilance. I worried, and teazed, and fretted myself to such a degree that I nearly tormented myself into a consumption. Change of scene—mild air—were recommended to me by the faculty, and I set off by the Portsmouth coach for the village of Steephill, at the back of the Isle of Wight. I got a charming bed-room and parlor at a farmer's cottage—oh, 'twas Paradise!—and the hostess made the most delicious hams in the world. Every morning at breakfast I had magnificent slices—sometimes hot, sometimes cold—exquisite prawns, with an occasional lobster. My health grew gradually better, but I still mused a good deal about Julia. Even then, sir, solitude was my aversion, and you may guess my gratification when one day I was visited by a tall handsome young man, dressed in a style that had once been fashionable—trowsers slightly patched about the knees—coat not quite entire about the elbows, for the benefit of the fresh air; and yet his *tout ensemble* showing he was a gentleman—a perfect gentleman. He was romantic, and had stationed himself at the 'Crab and Lobster,' a delicious retreat from the cares of life, just under St. Boniface Down. He begged the honor of my acquaintance. I went of course and dined with him that very day—cold lamb and salad—and vowed eternal friendship, and I was assisted on my homeward way at half-past eight. He was certainly a delightful fellow; no ceremony—no reserve—full of jokes. He came into my bedroom one morning before I was up, and clapped on my new coat—an olive green, I remember, with bright brass buttons—and, all I could say, I never could get it back again. Oh! he was full of fun! He did the same with my trowsers: 'pon my soul, 'twould have killed you with laughing to have heard how comically he spoke about the trick. I love him yet—the rascal! —though he has been the cause of all my misery. 'Twas Hoskins;—I need scarcely tell you his name; you guessed who it was, didn't you?"

"No, sir; I had no idea."

"Well; he and I for about a week were happier than any two men since the fall. We rambled about the sweet vales of Bonchurch—dived into the coves of Ventnor;—we were seldom separate for an hour in the day. Would to Jupiter we had never been separate a moment! Of course we had no secrets with each other. I was come to the island to recover the tone of my mind and stomach, after a disappointment in love; he had come to those deep solitudes and awful dells to avoid the impertinence of his duns. We nearly succeeded in both. I became ruddy as a peony rose, and was hungry five times a day, and he lost the very recollection of wine merchants and tailors. How he rallied me about Julia! how he laughed at the name of Sniggs! But he always particularly impressed on me the necessity of never despairing. We formed together a plan of the campaign by which I was to obtain my wishes. He was to come up and live with me in London—to drive about in my phaeton—cabs are a new invention—and, if possible, obtain an introduction to her himself; and trust to him for pleading the cause of his friend! Nothing could be nicer; I was only anxious to proceed to work, and to return to London immediately. As a preparatory step, I wrote to several of his creditors, and became responsible for his debts. Couldn't do less, you know, for a gentleman who was to get me a wife with a hundred and fifty thousand pounds. It seemed very odd to me all this time that Hoskins—gay, lively, handsome fellow—had never been in love. It seemed to give me too much the advantage over him, but he didn't seem to mind it much. He was as proud of himself as if he had been in love with a dozen. At last, one day—'twas the sixth of our acquaintance—he came to me and said, 'Teddy,' said he, 'will you make my fortune?'

"'Certainly, Hosky, my boy,' said I; 'but how?'

"'Lend me twenty pounds. The oddest thing in the world has just happened to me.'

"I happened only to have twenty-five pounds left; gave him four fives without a word; and kept the other.

"'What is it?' I said.

"'Why, as I was just rambling along below Grove's Inn, there passed me a carriage containing two or three ladies. They were evidently strangers; 'twas a Newport fly; and after they had passed me about twenty yards, the driver stopped, and one of the ladies—rather demure-looking, and somewhat dowdily dressed—came up and spoke to me.

"'Did you know her?' I asked.

"'Never saw her in my life before; but she said to me, "I take the liberty of addressing you, sir, perceiving you to be a gentleman—"'

"'By Jupiter, Hosky! my coat and trowsers——'

"'To inform you,' continued the old woman, 'of our dilemma. We are living at present in Southampton: we have come over here for a two days' tour, and, unluckily, we have just this moment discovered that we have brought no money with us.'

"'And what did you say, Hosky, my boy?' asked I.

"'Say? why, that I was delighted to have the opportunity of being useful—that I would walk direct to my hotel and bring them whatever sum they required. They have gone on to Shanklin, and as they return this way, I shall present them with the twenty pounds you have given me.'

"'Hadn't you better let me do it myself?' I asked; for I thought, sir, as the money was mine, I might as well have all the merit of helping those damsels in distress. But Hoskins was resolved; and insisted on giving me a note of hand for the amount, in order, as he said, that he might hand it to the ladies with a safe conscience. Noble fellow Hoskins was—wasn't he? Well, sir, when I asked him what more he intended to do, what do you think he told me sir? Why, that he intended to marry the old woman!

"'The *old* woman, Hosky!' says I. 'Why do you fix on her?'

"'Because she is dowdily dressed, and asked me for money, she *must* be rich.'

"'Why?' said I, in surprise. 'Because she is ill-dressed and hasn't a farthing in her pocket?'

"'Exactly,' nodded my friend Hoskins—oh, he was a knowing dog. 'If she were really poor, she would be finely dressed, and have rather sunk through the earth than have confessed her poverty to a stranger. She must be rolling in money—at least, I'll marry her on the chance.'

"So I laughed at him, and he rubbed his hands. You never saw two fellows so jolly in your life. Hoskins with the pockets of *my* trowsers stuffed with *my* bank-notes, and buttoning up the bosom of *my* olive-green coat. Short-sighted mortal! Confound me if I ever laugh again! Let me fill your glass again, sir.

"You had better, sir," said I; "for you've emptied it this moment—by mistake, of course."

"Good again! But now my miseries begin. Sir, there is a landslip just below a place called Undermount Cottage, leading down to a beautiful beach. Never was so sweet a spot. High hills frowning above, rugged rocks, shelving glens, quite made for lovers to play hide-and-seek in. Well, sir, that smooth expanse of sand, that richly-wooded shore, that quiet, 'blest retirement, friend to life's decline'—that is, friend to all who are laboring in a consumption, sir—that scene, I say, was the witness of my distraction. Hoskins was a famous sailor, and had hired a boat, which I paid for at the rate of a guinea a week. By way of passing off the time till the old lady's return we resolved to row out and lift up the prawn-pots. No amusement can be so delightful, sir, as catching prawns in the midst of the finest scenery in the world; for

Oh, if there be an Elysium on earth,
It is this, it is this, it is this!

When we were returning, the tide was running out at the rate of sixty miles an hour—sad work pulling against such a racer. But when we had got within a few yards of the shore, who should Hoskins see, just peeping over the cliff, but the identical old lady that had spoken to him in the morning. She waved her hand; he kissed his in return; when —excuse me, sir, till I've swallowed this bumper— just at her elbow, smiling and smirking exactly as we use to do at church, appeared Julia—*my* Julia— 'twas, indeed, Miss Sniggs. My heart jumped into my mouth in a moment, and filled it so completely that there was no room for the tongue to move. Indeed, I believe there was no room for it in the mouth at all, and that it hung out like a dog's in the hot days of July. How I panted to be sure! for you will observe that Hoskins was a capital steersman; and always when we rowed out I held the oars and he the helm; but whether my panting proceeded most from the exertion of rowing against tide, or from seeing Julia so unexpectedly, I cannot at this distance of time exactly remember. The silence lasted for some time, and nothing was to be heard but the prodigiously loud kisses that Hoskins kept constantly impressing on the palm of his hand. At last I pulled my tongue within my lips.

"'Heavens!" I cried, 'that's my Julia!'

"'*Your Julia!*' says Hosky—'which? the old lady in the cotton shawl, straw bonnet, and dingy-colored gown?'

"'No, no; the angel looking over her shoulder in the pink silk scarf—the old one's the housekeeper.'

"'That's she, is it?' said Hosky. 'And a devilish nice angel she is too. Then, my dear Teddy, that alters the whole business; but here we are ashore, my boy. Give me the oars; you stay in the boat and I'll jump to land and keep her steady.'

"Saying this, Hosky—fine active fellow—tossed the two oars ashore, and leaped himself to land; but, instead of keeping the boat steady by the rope in the bow, what do you think he did?—I must really have some brandy-and-water. Why, he gave the boat an infernal kick with his prodigiously long leg, and hollowed after me as the tide caught hold of the Naiad—that was its name, sir—and ran off with it like a run-away hunter—

"'Pleasant voyage to you, Teddy! I hope to tell you some news of the fair Julia when you come back.'

"What could I do, sir? Nothing. I swore a little; but it did me no good. Every minute the tide seemed to go faster and faster; and the boat, being left entirely to itself—for, you remember, Hosky threw the oars ashore—tossed and tumbled so horribly among the little short waves, sometimes turning its side, sometimes its stern, that I began rapidly to, become sick. In the mean time Hosky joined a party on the cliff: I saw him lift off his hat as if he had been a prince; I saw my bright brass buttons glancing in the sun: I saw him put his hand in my breeches pocket, and pull out my fives! Gracious Heavens! fancy my feelings! And just as I had to turn aside to conceal the emotion that the unusual jerking of the boat had produced in my interior, I caught a glimpse of the party winding slowly up the landslip—Hosky being between the two ladies, and Julia leaning on his arm!"

"It was very awkward, sir," I said, as the stranger endeavored to bury his recollections in another bumper; "but, of course, you explained every thing on your return?"

"Return, sir! I never returned: at least it was fourteen years before I came back again. The tide, sir, I tell you, was running like Eclipse, and I was as sick as a dog. I lay down, sir, at the bottom of the boat, I raged—I raved—I swore; and, at last, when evening came on, I was in the middle of the sea, half mad with sickness and vexation; and, at last, I fell asleep. I awakened, sir, perishing with hunger and thirst—my tongue gets parched when I think of it—fill up, sir—and I feel as if I had no dinner—do you allow a Welsh rabbit at this club, sir?—but what what was I to do? I was still weltering in the pathless deep, and expected every moment to be run down by a ship or swallowed up by a whale. Nothing would do, sir. I shut my eyes and tried to sleep again. At last, I was fairly awakened by a thwack across the shoulders with the flat end of an oar—'twas daylight, sir: I saw several little boats all round me, and a place before me which I imagined was St. Helen's. 'Hallo! my boy,' I cried to the huge fellow, dressed in a hairy cap, who had the oar uplifted in act to fall again, 'don't strike so hard, but lend me a couple of oars and I'll give you half a guinea when we get to the Salutation.' By heavens, sir, I never was so surprised in my life. I had fallen among a fleet of French fishermen, and the little town I had fancied was St. Helen's was Dieppe. Nice fellow Hoskins was, to play me such a trick! Napoleon and all the marshals, I suppose, were deucedly alarmed at such an invasion, for they clapped me into prison directly; and there I was, sir—only imagine my condition—till the year eighteen hundred and fifteen. This happened, sir, in eighteen hundred and one. There was, I, sir, kept in close confinement: little to eat; nothing to drink; not a soul to speak to —for I never could pick up the language; and all because I went to the Isle of Wight to recover my good spirits, and lent money to a friend."

"And what did you do when you came back, sir?"

"Ate beefsteaks and drank porter, the first half year, without a moment's intermission, night and day. At the end of that time, I went into St. Dunstan's, and shed a few tears over my mother's grave. She had died of a fit of apoplexy and a broken heart, about a year after my disappearance; and the sight of the old pulpit and the pew where I had had such fun, laughing to Julia, in my younger days, brought the whole scene back into my memory; but no, it had never left it: I thought of her incessantly, and wondered what had become of her. If she is still Miss Sniggs, thought I, all may be well yet; but how was I to hear of her? Her old father had died, or the trade in Water-lane had been sold; for he was nowhere to be found in the Directory. I then tried to find out Hoskins: I went carefully to the Fleet and the King's Bench as the most likely places to discover him; but he was not there. I looked back to all the cases before the magistrates, and all the convictions at the Old Bailey: he was nowhere to be found. Years and years passed on, and the search was still useless; when, at last—your glass is empty, sir—the appalling truth burst upon me: I was a ruined man, sir—happiness destroyed for life, and the Pleasures of Hope a *liber expurgatus*—Miss Sniggs was married! The way I discovered it was this: it had struck me very forcibly that a pilgrimage to the scene of my misery would be a pleasing occupation for a man of my musing and melancholy turn of mind. I mounted once more, sir, the Portsmouth coach; crossed over to Ryde; jumped into one of the open flies that are always kept ready at the pier; traversed the island, and arrived at the old place—the dear little cottage where I had smoked so many pipes with Hosky—the Crab and Lobster. The whole journey took but nine hours—think of that, sir. Fleet-street at nine in the morning, Bonchurch at six at night; but there I was, sir, after an absence of more than five-and-twenty years. Wyld, the landlord, sir, had no idea I was an old friend with a new face, or rather with a face newly done up—for I had neither red nose nor wrinkles when I had seen him last. Ah! 'twas indeed a melancholy retrospection; but the prawns were charming as ever, and the scenery—no, not improved, that's impossible—but just the same as when I left it. How I rambled all that evening, till it was time for supper! What news I heard from my host!—a town built at Ventnor; a castle built at Steephill; a fairy palace built at East End; villas rising like poetical dreams every week upon Bonchurch. Ah! thought I, as I tumbled into bed, why the deuce shouldn't I build a villa? Next morning I revisited the Landslip—fatal spot—and determined to rear my modest mansion on some gentle promontory commanding the whole scene. When once I resolve on a thing, sir, 'tis always more than half done already. A gentleman of the name of Page, a builder at Ventnor, showed me all the grounds. We agreed about terms. Such a heavenly place I chose! just under the jutting cliff, two hundred and fifty feet high, buried amidst a profusion of 'plants of all scent and flowers of every hue;' and that very day I had fifteen men employed in clearing out the foundation. When I was standing superintending their operations, I was delighted—petrified, I own, at the same time—to see a gentleman and lady approaching me from behind a clump of magnificent magnolias, at that moment in full bloom. The gentleman seemed about three or four-and-twenty years old; the lady—fair as the first that fell of womankind—about eighteen. What a nice pleasant fellow was the gentleman! what a charming creature was the wife! Who do you think they were, sir?—Let me propose their healths in a bumper—the bottle's done.—Why they were the Marquis and Marchioness of Marylebone. They were living in the upper cottage—a fascinating couple! In a few minutes, we were as intimate as possible—real marquises are always so good-humored—they invited me to dine with them that day. I went. Pretty little dinner—soup, fish, lamb, and a pudding—quite rural, you perceive; and, after a few turns of the wine, I began to tell the marquis and his lady—she staid with us all the time—the story of my misfortune. Gracious Powers! in the most pathetic part of all, her ladyship went into a fit—a positive, veritable, *bonâ fide* fit! Thank heaven! 'twas only of laughter. The marquis nearly burst, sir—he had to unbutton his waistcoat. I paused; I looked at the beaming face of the marchioness—what splendid white teeth she has! The reddened face and swelled eyes of the marquis! I could not understand it. Her ladyship was the first to speak.

"'How delighted,' she cried, 'mamma will be to see you! Oh, we have heard the story a hundred times from papa!'

"'Mamma—papa!' I exclaimed. 'Your ladyship is very good—may I ask——'

"'My good sir,' said the marquis, 'are you not aware that that lady was Miss Hoskins, the daughter of your old friend?'

"'And her mother, my Lord Marquis?'

"'Miss Sniggs.'

"Do you hear that, sir? The marquis actually looked at me with a smile upon his face when he told me that most diabolical fact.

"'So Hoskins married my Julia!' I exclaimed, in my despair; 'got all the old gentleman's money; has a marquis for his son-in-law—and all these things *ought* to have happened to me—*would* have happened to me, no doubt, if I had never gone to the island, or lent twenty pounds to a friend! 'Madam,' said I to the marchioness, 'I am enraged more than ever against your father when I perceive he has robbed me of so fair and exquisite a daughter.' She laughed, 'But,' I continued, 'nothing is left for me but to bury myself in this desert, and mourn over the unluckiness of my destiny.'

"'You shall do no such thing,' said the marquis; 'we shall all come down and see you when your new house is finished. Captain Hoskins and my fair mother-in-law will accompany us; he is adding a new wing to Harridon Lodge, and will be delighted to leave his work-people."

"'Well, then, my Lord,' I said, ''twill be ready by October. I have ordered the cellar to be finished first, and wrote off this morning to old Giberne, in Broad street, to stock me with good wine; and if you do come, I will do all I can to make you happy.'

"'Will you take us out in a boat?' inquired the marchioness, with a malicious smile.

"'No, I'm —— but I never swear; or, if I do, I will have an extra couple of oars chained to the thwarts.'

"If you can come down and join us, sir, about the tenth of October, I shall be delighted. I am but a silent hypochondriac; but I will do every thing to make it pleasant for you. Are you fond of shell-fish, sir? Bathing? Sailing? Shooting? Riding? Driving? We have them all, sir; but my grief is getting the better of me again, sir—I must ring for another bottle."

While the stranger was giving his orders to William, and ordering in a couple of lobsters for supper, I took the opportunity of following the example that had been given me by his friend, the mercer from Cornhill, and getting, very quietly, possession of my hat and stick, I wended my way home. If he persists in wishing to be a member of the Whitechapel Athenæum, I will black-ball him to a certainty. Strangers are not allowed to pay for any thing they eat or drink; and I found, next day, a bill scored up against me—the mercer having cautioned them that he would not be responsible—for two bottles of port, three glasses of brandy-and-water, fourteen cigars, two lobsters, and six dozen pandores—in all thirty-two shillings and sixpence. I am going to propose, at the next general meeting, that no member be permitted to bring a friend, or, if he does bring him, that he shall be answerable for his expenses.

PICTORIAL HUMOR.

BY — SEYMOUR.

Shakspere.

That man received his charge from me.
Richard III.

Who is it in the press that calls?
Julius Cæsar.

This is the strangest tale that ever I saw.
I. Henry IV.

Put this in any liquid thing you will.
Romeo and Juliet.

THE TWO TOMKINSES.

An Equivoque.

BY RICHARD BRINSLEY PEAKE.

How many a droll error has occurred by the incident of two different persons, bearing the same name, happening to reside in the same street! And yet, in many streets of London, there may be three or four Smiths, or a half-a-dozen Joneses, or Browns. Letters and parcels are constantly delivered at the wrong houses, and great confusion created; sometimes important and disagreeable secrets are divulged. The gist of our story will rest on the fact, that in a Crescent not a hundred miles from the Commercial Road, there lived two persons of the name of Tomkins; we shall call the crescent "Commercial Crescent:" at No. 20, dwelt Mr. Jonas Tomkins; and at No. 30, resided Mr. Josiah Tomkins. They were both professionally occupied in the mercantile way; but in their manners and habits were very distinct persons. Jonas Tomkins was a quiet, primitive man, who, absorbed in his business, had mixed very little in the world, though he was not without an inclination to partake of the good things of it. Mrs. Jonas Tomkins, his *cara sposa*, had of latter years been tinged with the methodistical persuasion that the sins of mankind are so enormous, that it is quite impossible that any one can be saved; therefore, it is indispensable that all human beings should remain depressed, miserable, without hope, and without enjoyment. These principles were strongly inculcated by the pastor of a neighboring Ebenezer

Chapel, who contrived to make a very good living out of the weakness of the nerves of his flock, which consisted principally of females. This minister's name was Ghoule.

Now, as for Mr. Josiah Tomkins, he was a portly, sleek fellow, with a profusion of whisker, quite a contrast to Jonas Tomkins; very much attached to cigars and port wine, rowing on the Thames, shilling promenade concerts, tripe suppers, and whiskey punch.

Mr. and Mrs. Jonas Tomkins were seated at breakfast, one morning; the lady busied with the teapot, the gentleman with the *Times*, from which he was culling the "ship news."

He read, "ARRIVED, the Illustrious, from Batavia," and began to wonder if there was any consignment for him, for he had endeavored to extend his connections to all parts of the habitable globe.

"Ah, my dear," said Mrs. Tomkins, "I wish you could avoid an annoyance, where we really have no connection. Here we live, at No. 20, Commercial Crescent, and, unluckily for us, there is another Tomkins resides at No. 30, and the mistakes that continually occur between the two houses are perfectly unbearable. You, my love, are generally a well-behaved person, but as for the other, he is little better than a bear."

Jonas Tomkins acknowledged that there had been some odd coincidences occasioned by the same names in the same crescent.

Mrs. Tomkins sighed, and said, "I know that our Christmas Norfolk turkey, and the sausages, went by the 'Parcels Delivery Company' to the Tomkins at 30, in the crescent, for we never saw any of them."

To which Jonas replied, with a smile, "But you know, my dear, we were even with him, for we took in an immense cod-fish, and a barrel of oysters, here, from somebody unknown: it was directed '*J. Tomkins, Esq., Commercial Crescent*,' and uncommonly good it was."

Mrs. Tomkins sighed more deeply than before; she pondered whether, or not, unpremeditated or accidental sin would be eventually visited by condign punishment.

The postman knocked at the door, always an interesting occurrence to a merchant.

The first letter opened by Mr. Jonas Tomkins was one that had undergone fumigation; and Mrs. Tomkins regarded it with some alarm, for, she remarked that it looked as if it had the yellow fever. But Jonas pacified her by stating that it came from his Batavian correspondents, Messrs. Murgatroyd, Crombie, and Crossline, and that it was perfectly safe from infection.

The letter was addressed to "Mr. Tomkins."

"SIR,—Per Illustrious, we beg to introduce to your notice the Rev. T. Faraway, who has been for some time a zealous missionary at this and the neighboring settlements; he is a man of unexceptionable merit, and has been at incredible pains in educating the natives. He is accompanied to England by a young prince of Bantam, who, from the best of motives, a desire to increase his knowledge, has voluntarily taken the long voyage. The prince is of a most amiable disposition, agreeable in his manners, and mild in his deportment; any attentions that you can bestow on him will be thankfully acknowledged by,

"Your most obedient servants,"
Etc., etc., etc.

Now Mr. Jonas Tomkins had every reason to show civility to the firm of Murgatroyd, Crombie, and Crossline, and Mrs. Tomkins was rather pleased with the notion of an introduction to the learned missionary.

Benjamin, Mr. Tomkins's footboy, brought in a note, which he stated had been left at the door by one of the Dock porters.

Tomkins glanced his spectacled eye over it; it was worded as follows:—

"Mr. Faraway, Asiatic missionary, begs to inform Mr. J. Tomkins, that he is at the Dock Hotel with his protégé, the Prince of Bantam."

Mr. Tomkins could not conveniently leave the house himself, expecting persons to call on important business, so he determined to send one of his clerks, a young conceited puppy, named Bright; so he told Benjamin to go into the counting-house and tell Mr. Bright he was wanted.

This Mr. Bright was a character, a downright cockney, but who imagined that he overflowed with talent, though in reality there never was a greater oaf.

Mrs. Tomkins said, "If I were you, dear, I would not send Mr. Bright."

"Why not, my love?" replied Tomkins, "Bright is a clever fellow."

"Too clever," continued the lady; "so accomplished, he is always making some absurd mistake."

"My dear," said Tomkins, "Mr. Bright marches with the march of intellect; and notwithstanding that he clips his English a little, he can deliver a lecture on any subject, from mesmerism to meteorology."

"I grant," replied Mrs. Tomkins, "that Mr. Bright knows quite as much about one as the other; he has lately been reading the articles under letter M, in the 'Penny Cyclopædia.'"

Benjamin now came in with a slip of paper; Mr. Bright had just stepped out, but had left this notice on his desk:—

"Gone down to the *singeing*-class; back in ten minutes."

In ten minutes, Bright returned, when Jonas Tomkins gave him a slight reprimand for selecting a time of day for his singing-lesson, when his presence was necessary in the counting-house.

"Here, Sir, read these two letters," said Tomkins, handing them to Bright; "you must run down to the Dock Hotel, and meet the persons mentioned in this letter, a Mr. Faraway, a missionary, and a young Prince of Bantam, who have just landed from a vessel in the river. Behave with all possible respect to them; don't stare in that way, nor get into one of your theories, as you call them; don't make any mistake, and be back as soon as you can."

Bright set off, smiling with contempt at the bare idea that *he* could possibly make a mistake; he, who was a sort of minister for foreign affairs for the whole house—who went and tasted cheese for Mr. Tomkins; bought balls of cotton, peppermint lozenges, and all the new tracts for Mrs. Tomkins. He had been latterly employing his thoughts on the varieties of the human race, and it much gratified him to find that he had to make the acquaintance of a real Bantam.

Bright had a great notion of becoming a scientific lecturer, but in what branch, he had not precisely made up his mind.

The same day that the missionary and his pupil arrived, an American ship came into the port of London, the George Washington; she had some passengers on board, amongst whom was a Mr. Charles Langford, rather a dandy Englishman, who had journeyed over the United States, and a Yankee wine and spirit merchant, by name, Ichabod P. Buggins, who was accompanied, in the shape of "help," or servant, by a free negro, who was known at Boston by the elegant cognomen of Apollo Hyacinth. These three persons took up their quarters, on landing, at the Dock Hotel; to which house of entertainment we will now change our scene.

Mr. Faraway, the missionary, had sent to an emporium for ready-made clothes, that the young prince under his charge might not suffer from the change of climate, in the slight vestments he had brought from his own country. As the prince had a very slender, flexible figure, like most Asiatics, there was a great difficulty in fitting him, and ready-made clothes rarely fit well at first; one of those small-waisted surtouts that are strained tightly over a sort of block at the tailor's door to attract the admiration of exquisites, however, was tried on, and succeeded; but the waistcoat and trousers, poor things, had to be deceived into the notion that they would fit, and they were very much "*taken in*."

When the missionary had got his prince disguised as a gentleman, he rang the bell for the waiter, who, on making his appearance, was asked if he had sent a porter with the letter to Mr. Tomkins; the waiter replied in the affirmative. Mr. Faraway then inquired if the waiter knew Mr. Tomkins. The waiter said smartly, "Yes, sir; lives at No. 30, Commercial Crescent; often comes here, sir, to sup and smoke his cigar." "Will you show us the way to Commercial Crescent?"—"Yes, sir; certainly, sir; not far to walk, sir. Go now, sir, please." And the waiter preceded the missionary and the prince towards the premises of Josiah Tomkins.

Josiah had also finished his breakfast, red herrings and toast, eggs and hung beef, water-cresses, and a small glass of brandy, and had lighted a cheroot to digest every thing. He then opened his letters, one from a New York correspondent was thus indited:

"Dear Tomkins,—I beg to introduce to you Mr. Ichabod P. Buggins, an eminent wine and spirit merchant of Boston, who is proceeding to the port of London; you will find him a fellow after your own heart, and of a very jovial turn.

"If you can induce him to tell you some of his crack stories, he will make you split yonr sides with laughter; ask him to relate to you the comical history of the Mulatto girl. Mr. Buggins is accompanied to England by a free black, who is a great character in his way, but he is so confounded sly, that it is not easy to set his tongue in motion."

"Ay, ay," said Josiah; "I suppose they will call, and I must give Mr. I. P. Buggins a bit of dinner, and a bottle of port."

We will now return to the Dock Hotel, where Mr. Charles Langford was inquiring of the waiter where his companion was who had come on shore with him from the George Washington. The waiter replied that Mr. I. P. Buggins had gone to the Carolina Coffee House, but had left word that he would soon be back, and that his black servant was warming himself in No. 5.

Mr. Charles Langford now proceeded to state, that if it had not been for the intrepidity of that black man, he should have been drowned that very morning; for as the ship was being towed by a steam-tug past Blackwall, Mr. Langford perceived some beautiful ladies, and such a time had elapsed since he had seen an English lady (the most comely in the world), he was anxious to peep at them; but, overbalancing himself with the weight of his telescope, he slipped over the side of the vessel into the Thames, where he decidedly would have become food for white-bait, if blacky had not jumped after him like a large Newfoundland dog, and positively saved Mr. Langford from a watery grave.

"The brave fellow," continued Langford, "as well as myself, was completely sopped through; I had my change of clothes at hand on board; but as I was apprehensive that Apollo might take cold after so devoted an action, I immediately made him strip, and dress himself in my silk dressing-gown, cap, trousers, and slippers, in which he came ashore. Ask him to walk in here."

The waiter went to call Apollo, and when he entered, an extraordinary looking being he was. He had a shining black face, like a new iron stewpan; a beautiful set of grinders, perfect masters of their business; and an expression of rich humor was spread over the ebony countenance. He was attired in a showy silk dressing-gown, tied round the waist by a bandana handkerchief; he wore over his black woolly head an embroidered Greek smoking-cap; had white worsted stockings, and yellow morocco slippers. These habiliments were all the property of Mr. Langford, whose taste, as we have before hinted, was somewhat of the splendid order. When Apollo Hyacinth came in, Langford exclaimed with emotion, "My brave benefactor! how can I ever repay my debt of gratitude to you?" To which the negro replied, "Telly how, Massa Langfud, if we shipmate agen; spose I fall overboard; well! den you jump and dive for me."—"I will, I will, my generous fellow," said Langford; "that is, if they ever catch me at sea again." Apollo grinned, and showing all the white ivory keys of his piano-forte, replied, "Hi, hi, Massa Langfud, de salt water no agree wid you; you not brought up to de sea; though you brought up ebery ting else;—werry bad derangement, dat."

Here Mr. Bright had walked into the Dock Hotel, to make his own observations.

Charles Langford continued his expressions of gratitude; "You, for your glorious and gallant conduct, deserve to be a prince."

Bright instantly thought to himself, "That is the Prince of Bantam—what a picturesque costume!"

Langford said: "But for your arms, I should decidedly have perished."

Bright's ideas quickened, "Saved him from the savages, I suppose."

"But I do not think I shall ever venture on the ocean again," remarked Langford.

To which Apollo replied, "Anoder time, come oberland—dat my 'wice."

"Long overland journey from Bantam," thought Mr. Bright.

"After your praiseworthy exertions," said Langford, "you would probably like some refreshment?"

The eyes of Apollo glistened, and he answered, "No dejection to 'ittle rum, sar."

Bright, who was a Temperance Society person, reflected on the barbarous acquired taste of royalty.

Langford rang the bell for some rum, and carelessly inquired of Apollo, where was the companion of their voyage.

"O! he is far away," replied Apollo.

Bright glanced at his letters, and muttered, "Faraway, the missionary's name;" and now he was convinced that it was all correct.

The waiter re-entered with the rum in a decanter, and glass; Langford, pouring out, said, "Now, my noble heart, will you have it mixed with some water?"

"Tank you, no," rejoined Apollo; "me took de water dis mornin'. Try de rum, now, all by 'umsef."

"It is not that I would grudge it you," said Langford, "but rum is a powerfully acting spirit; so, in regard to your precious health, do not take too much."

"Neber fear," answered Apollo, "my 'pinion is, too much rum is *just enuff!*"

"Mercy on us!" ejaculated Bright, "his friend the missionary has not inculcated the principles of temperance in his pupil;" and he was not a little astonished at beholding the prince swallow down, with apparent zest, several more glasses.

Here a plain-looking man, in a dark suit of clothes, and with a very shrewd eye, and a broad-brimmed hat, entered the room. He had the appearance of foreign travel about him.

"Oh! you are both here, I guess," said Mr. Ichabod P. Buggins (for it was the worthy spirit merchant).

"That's the missionary," conjectured Bright; and he determined to have his ears open, as to the mode in which he would address the prince, his pupil.

"What an eternal confounded smell of New England rum," remarked the venerable missionary.

Apollo was uneasy. The Prince of Bantam whispered to the waiter, "Take 'um dam bottle away."

"What, you've been at it, have you?" said Ichabod, in a peremptory tone.

Mr. Bright saw that his reverence was about to rebuke his highness.

Ichabod continued. "I calculate that rum will set you chattering; now, what's the use of all my preaching to you?"

At the word "preaching," Bright was positively assured that he was correct in his suppositions.

Mr. Buggins fixed his eye on his highness, and said sharply, "Do you happen to know the reason why monkeys are no good? Because they chatter all day long. How many years, you dingy rascal, have you been under my paternal care? How many larrupings have I been compelled to give you, to keep you under proper control?"

Bright could not avoid thinking that the missionary was very severe on the young prince, and he recollected the treatment of the poor South American Indians by the Spanish Jesuits. When Mr. Langford, seeing Apollo rather cast down, exclaimed loudly, "Remember, sir, the noble daring of the person you are abusing, who possesses, I know, noble qualities of heart."

On hearing this eulogium, Bright imagined it to be just the precise time to introduce himself; so, with some very queer bows, he said, smiling, "Gentlemen, my name is Bright—Mr. Bright—I am principal clerk to Mr. Tomkins, merchant, of Commercial Crescent, and I am sent by that highly respectable individual to conduct you to his residence."

"I had a letter of recommendation to Mr. Tomkins, Commercial Crescent, though I never saw him," replied I. P. Buggins, "and I have sent my letter to him."

"We are quite aware of the letters, much revered sir," remarked Bright. Buggins stared; but was more astonished when Bright added, pointing to Apollo, "his royal highness will of course accompany you."

Buggins whistled, thinking to himself, "This dandy clerk believes himself a wag."

Bright turned now to Apollo, who, from the effects of the rum, was holding himself steady by the back of a chair, and said, "I am quite ready, your highness."

Apollo Hyacinth was half affronted. "De man of culler, sar, know him place in society, and behave himself 'cordingly;" (and here he hiccuped in the clerk's countenance;) "rum gone de wrong way; so when I address a gentleplum, I always (another loud hiccup) say—waiter, bring de udder glass of rum."

"Well," thought Bright, "if these are the manners of the royal family of Bantam, what brutes the lower orders of the natives must be."

Mr. I. P. Buggins now shook his fellow traveller, Langford, heartily by the hand, and told Mr. Bright that he was prepared to accompany him to Mr. Tomkins's, in Commercial Crescent. He then addressed the negro, "You keep a little distance behind, d'ye hear? for I don't fancy to be seen in the streets of a foreign and enlightened country, tramposing about with such a scarecrow."

Here Bright offered his arm to his highness, who, when they got into the street, staggered as if he had business on both sides of the way. It is but justice to say that Mr. Bright did all he could to ingratiate himself with royalty, by pointing out the steeples of Poplar and Limehouse churches, the rotunda of the Thames Tunnel, and that wonderful route through chimney-pots and beggarly bedchambers, the Blackwall Railway.

The waiter of the Dock Hotel had left Mr. Faraway and the native of Bantam at the door of Josiah Tomkins, No. 30, Commercial Crescent, where they were admitted by a smart-looking housemaid, and introduced into the presence of the fat and florid Josiah.

"I received the letter of recommendation this morning, and am happy to see you; are you going to make a long stay in London?"

Mr. Faraway replied that his stay entirely depended on the Colonial Missionary Society.

"Oh, do business with them, eh? Well, it is all right, they must eat and drink too, like other people. Perhaps you would like your young black fellow to go down in the kitchen?"

Mr. Faraway appeared surprised, but stated merely that the young man was his constant companion.

Josiah now rung for the luncheon-tray, being of opinion that eating and drinking go a great way to fill up gaps not only in the stomach, but in conversation, for Mr. Ichabod P. Buggins did not appear to be very communicative, and his free negro never opened his mouth, and was particularly ill at ease in his new clothes.

The tray appeared with cold fowl, wine, etc., etc., and Josiah insisted that his visitors should partake of the fare, and he poured out some port for them. But he was rather astonished that Mr. Ichabod Buggins, the jovial companion, should arise, as did his negro, while he recited the longest "grace before meat" that he had ever heard; in fact, Josiah thought that it never would have ended. So, winking at his supposed humorous guest, he said, "Come, that was a tolerably long-winded one!" Faraway looked as if he found himself in very ungodly company, but tasted the wine.

"Will you allow me to ask you a professional question, sir?" said Josiah Tomkins, smacking his lips, after sipping his glass.

"I am all attention, sir," meekly replied Faraway.

"Well, now, give me your candid opinion; what do you think of our port?"

The missionary answered, "The port of London is considered the finest in the world."

"They put such a quantity of brandy in it, for the London market. Fill your glass, sir; but you never drink that wine at New York?"

"I cannot say I ever did, sir," said Mr. Faraway.

"Ay, you are more in the spirit way," remarked Josiah.

The missionary owned that it was the calling he had followed for some years past.

"Then," said Josiah with a knowing wink, "you must be up to a thing or two in whiskeys?"

"I do not rightly comprehend you, Mr. Tomkins."

"Why," continued Josiah, "you get through all your business so easily—you have no duties to care about."

"Pardon me, sir," said Farwaay, somewhat discomposed, "that avowal would be a grievous stain upon my professional character; my duties have ever been attended to scrupulously."

"What! you always adhere to the customs?"

"No," answered the missionary, "it is my vocation, gradually, if I find it possible, to alter or do away with the customs of the remote countries to which I am despatched."

"You are a fellow after my own heart," said Josiah, filling Mr. Faraway's glass. "D—n all customs and custom-house officers. Come, we will change the subject, as I see it is unpleasant to you."

"The oath you uttered was objectionable, sir," remarked Mr. Faraway.

"Oh! ha! ha! you are a capital fellow—you object to a stray d—n that slipped out accidentally, but you don't mind doing the revenue. Change the subject. My correspondent informed me, in the letter you sent this morning, that both you and your free negro yonder (who don't take to his wine, perhaps he would like some grog better) were devilish funny chaps, if you could be drawn out; but you are both corked up very close indeed. Shall we have a bowl of punch? Ay—and"—(here Josiah winked wickedly)—"ha! ha! ha! I must insist on it."

"Insist on what, sir?" asked Mr. Faraway gravely.

Josiah Tomkins poked the missionary in the ribs, and chuckled out, "Tip us the story of the Mulatto wench."

Faraway was aghast.

"Capital face for it," continued Josiah, "you

know you can be a comical old cock when you like it. Why, my dear fellow, your introductory letter says so."

The missionary was much excited, and said, "I beg to state, sir, that I have ever endeavored to set a straight example. This young person, who has accompanied me to Europe, and whose moral character will bear the strictest investigation, looks up to me for precept. In former days, the calling I follow was at first undertaken in a barbarous spirit."

"Peach brandy?" inquired Josiah.

"Hear me, sir," continued Faraway. "But now, owing to the cordial co-operation of a large class of my countrymen, numerous formidable impediments have been removed; an entrance and location among strange nations have been effected; we everywhere find brethren to welcome us. We have given the heathen nearly all the useful literature we possess; we have been the introducers of the art of printing amongst them. In some places, the entire fabric of idolatry is shaken, and the blessings of Christian morality have been widely diffused."

Josiah stared, but said, "I beg your pardon, Mr. Buggins, but I have been very much deceived in you."

"BUGGINS, sir?" repeated the missionary.

"Yes, Buggins; Ichabod P. Buggins. Look at this letter."

And here stopped the *equivoque;* a mistake had evidently occurred, but Mr. Faraway was at a loss to account for it, until Josiah said that, "Perhaps it was the other Tomkins in Commercial Crescent, at No. 20, that you were to visit. Are you not from New York, sir?"

"No, sir; I arrived to-day, in the Illustrious, from Batavia."

"Then," said Josiah, "where the deuce are *my* guests; perhaps at Jonas Tomkins's? What a bit of fun! I had better go and knock at No. 20, and take these gentlemen with me."

We will now return to the dwelling of Mr. Jonas Tomkins, where Mrs. Tomkins was waiting with some curiosity the return of Mr. Bright. In the hope of exciting the good opinion of the expected missionary, she had spread her tracts, with the most alluring titles, on the table and sofa. At length, Bright tapped at the door, and said that the Prince of Bantam and the Rev. Mr. Faraway were in the parlor. Mr. Jonas Tomkins was sent for from the counting-house.

"Well, Bright, what sort of people are they?—the prince?"

Bright replied, "Rummy!"

"Rummy?"

"Werry," said Bright.

"And Mr. Faraway, the missionary?" said Mrs. Tomkins.

"Ah!" cried Bright, "that proves what a edicated mind is over uncultiwated ignorance. Although the prince is a prince, his reverence, the missionary orders him about like bricks."

"Indeed!"

"And I don't wonder at it, for his royal highness drinks rum like a fish."

"How disappointed I am," said Tomkins. "But you had better introduce them at once."

So Mr. Bright went down, and begged the parties to walk up stairs into the drawing-room. When they entered, Bright attempted a very ceremonious introduction; "Mrs. Tomkins, I have the honor. Gentlemen, that is Mrs. Tomkins, and that is Mr. Tomkins."

Jonas, advancing to Ichabod, said, "I am proud, reverend sir, to take you by the hand, and your young friend."

I. P. Buggins interfered, and remarked that Mr. Tomkins need not exactly shake hands with the black, as it was not the custom in their part of the globe. "Besides," added Ichabod, with an odd twist of his face, "they perspire marking-ink."

So Jonas and Mrs. Tomkins saluted his highness with several bows and curtsies, but were utterly astonished when the missionary said rather petulantly,—

"Now, there's no needcessity to be bowing to that nigger."

Mrs. Tomkins could not help thinking that this was strange conduct to a prince.

"He knows how to conduct himself in his station. The critter is as cunning as Sam Slick's bear, and he always comes down a tree stern foremost; he's aware how many pounds his hams weigh, and he calculates if he carried 'em up in the air, they might be too heavy with him."

"Berry true, berry true. Hi! hi! hi!" grinned Apollo.

"Hold your black tongue," said his reverence.

Mr. and Mrs. Jonas Tomkins stared at each other in evident distress. Mrs. Tomkins, in an endeavor to turn the conversation, inquired if they had experienced an agreeable passage.

"By no manner of means," replied the missionary; "three parts across, the wind was enough to blow the devil's horns off."

Mrs. Tomkins started with horror, and she ejaculated, "I declare I thought that missionaries were always of a mild character?" To which Ichabod answered, "I've generally *heerd* that they are; but I see no reason why I should be so."

Jonas reflected how an absence from the society of one's native land may pervert even a missionary; the trio continued conversing; Mr. and Mrs. Tomkins quite embarrassed by the replies of Ichabod, who wondered what it all meant.

Mr. Bright finding himself, as he expressed it, "Nothing and nobody," and entirely disapproving of the missionary's doctrine, determined to exchange a few words with his royal pupil, who was seated near the door, pressing his black puddings of fingers against his forehead.

Bright approached him, bowing: "Pray, your highness, may I ask you a question?"

Apollo gazed at him with a stupidly drunken eye.

Bright continued: "It is a question on which I am anxious to be correctly informed. Do all our little Bantam cocks come from Bantam?"

"How de debble should I know," was the elegant reply of his highness.

Mr. Bright pitied the ignorance of a prince of the blood, who was not acquainted with his own commercial exports.

"What hour 'um hab dinner?" inquired the prince languidly.

"Five o'clock," said Bright.

Apollo touched his stomach, and then replaced his ball of worsted in his palm.

Mrs. Tomkins, now taking Jonas aside, whispered, "What could your Batavian correspondents mean by writing about his agreeable manners and mild deportment?"

"I suppose the torrid climate has heated all their brains," replied Jonas.

Mrs. Tomkins then whispered again, emphatically, "I shall speak to the missionary myself."

"Do, dear."

Mrs. Tomkins then approached Ichabod, and asked him if he was acquainted with the Rev. Wolfe Ghoule. She received a reply in the negative; when she stated that he was author of several of the excellent works on the table—"Tight Stays for Short-breathed Sinners," "The Luxury of Penitent Tears," "Stony Hearts Split," "The Preacher of All-work."

Mr. Buggins replied that he never read any thing of the sort. At this candid reply Mrs. Tomkins was surprised, fancying that the lucubrations of the Rev. Wolfe Ghoule had, by their merits, made their way to every foreign clime.

"Will you allow me to have a little serious conversation with you, sir?"

"Quite ready, Marm," said Ichabod. "It's no use to have the chalks without you can keep the tallies."

Mrs. Tomkins thought this was a strange phrase for a divine, but continued: "My husband is rather of a convivial nature."

"Ay, ay," said Buggins, "then let him deal with me."

"That is just what I want him to do," replied the lady. "In truth, I am sorry to say it, but Mr. Tomkins never thinks of his end."

"That's a bad beginning," said Ichabod.

"I am aware," remarked Mrs. Tomkins, "that gentlemen of your calling are models of temperance."

Buggins nodded his head, but imagined that was not the case with wine and spirit merchants in general; in fact, he knew several who swallowed all their profits.

Mrs. Tomkins then said, "If you would be induced to quit the dinner-table, as you do not care about wine" (Ichabod grimaced), "and indulge me with some of your serious discourse over a cup of tea" (Ichabod made another wry face), "it might, sir, satisfy my doubts."

"As to that, Marm," replied Buggins, "people doubts so now, I don't doubt but, some day or other, they will doubt whether every thing ain't a doubt."

(Buggins had read this elegant aphorism in Sam Slick.)

Mrs. Tomkins said, "I confess myself quite unsettled in my mind, and I should wish to benefit by your matured opinion. Might I ask—would you favor me with a sight of your articles?"

"My articles, Marm," replied Ichabod, "by all means, with the greatest pleasure;" and he fumbled about for a well-worn pocket-book, from which he pulled out a printed paper; this he handed to Mrs. Tomkins, who was in a state of excitement of pious curiosity, but imagine her astonishment when the following list met her eye:—

"WINE AND SPIRIT STORE,

"61, Common Street, Boston, 61.

"Ichabod P. Buggins warrants all articles delivered from his store genuine as imported, at the following low prices (English currency):—

"Champagnes, from 60 to 66.
"Clarets (*first growth*) 48 to 54.
"Prime East India Madeira, 56 to 64.
"Guinnes's Dublin Stout } Quarts, 8.
"Hodson's Pale Ale } Pints, 4.
"Brandies, Rums, Whiskeys, Gins (No. 1, Letter A).

"Nota Bene.—Bottles, jars, and hampers to be returned."

Mrs. Tomkins dropped the articles, and she might have been knocked down with a straw.

A loud rapping at the street door, and Mr. Josiah Tomkins sent up his card; he was accompanied by Mr. Faraway and the Prince of Bantam. A long explanation of the absurd mistake took place, and, as dinner was ready, Jonas Tomkins begged that the whole party would favor him with their company, which invitation was accepted, Apollo Hyacinth being consigned to the care of Benjamin at the kitchen fire.

The result was a merry afternoon; the only really long face in company being that of poor Bright.

THE THEATRICAL MANAGER.

BY RICHARD BRINSLEY PEAKE.

How little do various grades of the public dream (whether seated aristocratically and in perfect comfort in private boxes, respectably and equally comfortable in the public boxes, conveniently in the pit, or most commodiously in the gallery, where gentlemen may sit with their coats off, if they like it) of the toil, care, misery, and vicissitude, of the caterer for their pleasure. Like other masters of stages, it may be said "it is all in the day's work;" but the Theatrical Stage Director has to work by night as well as by day; when other professions are seated quietly in their homes for the evening, then commences the most anxious and active business of the Manager. His domestic comforts are sadly invaded; and when once engaged in the avocations of a theatre, the enjoyment of an hour's ease must not confidently be relied on. We will first enumerate the imperative qualities which the Manager of a Theatre ought to possess; and we detail them without exaggeration.

His temper must be as equally mixed as a bowl of punch; but that is only a simple comparison. We must go to actual contradistinctions, to enable him to have a chance to pursue his course.

He must be firm, yet supple; bold, yet cautious; liberal, yet sparing; he must possess penetration, yet see no further than is necessary. Whether he is asleep or not, he must always be wide awake. He should be a man of education, and be able to calculate tenpenny nails; he should know Shakspere and the "Trader's Price Book" by heart. He should be accomplished as a painter, a musician, and an author; and yet he must have achieved that point of knowledge of being able to tell how many tallow candles go to the pound, and how far that pound will go. His tact must be divided between judgment in the decision of dramas to be accepted, and Birmingham ornaments; the merits of actors, and cotton velvets; the favorable notice of the press, and the foil-merchant's account. He must have a pretty notion of tailoring, ladies' dress-making, and the armory; in short he must be a factotum.

We will endeavor rapidly to sketch his duties; in fact, as if the manager himself had kept a journal:—

"Arrived at the theatre at ten o'clock; not late, considering I was here until half-past one this morning. Look at rehearsal-call, stuck up in the passage: 'New ballet at ten: every body concerned —properties, scenes, firework-maker, Mr. Pringle, répétiteur.'

"Very wet day. All the ladies of the corps de ballet, including the coryphées, assembled with their hair in papers, looking like ghosts with bad colds, being kept up so late every night in the frost scene in the pantomime. Sneezing and low grumbling in all directions; each person attending literally to the words of the call; every body looking 'concerned.'

"Groupings commence to a single violin, and the loud thumping of the ballet-master's stick to keep time. Most of the sylphs and fairies rehearsing in their street-clogs, some with umbrellas. Go to my room adjoining the stage, the chimney of which smokes; but obliged to keep the door closed, because I hate to be overlooked. The table covered with letters, and the daily papers. Peep at superscriptions of the letters, to guess whether or not they may be disagreeable; endeavor to open that likely to be least offensive first. D—n the fiddling and the stamping—but they are unavoidable; and read Note, No. 1:—

MY DEAR SIR—On my return home yesterday, I cannot conceal my surprise and mortification on finding that the part of *Lady Anne* has been sent to me. There must surely be some mistake, as it was expressly stipulated in my engagement that the *Queen* is my property. If any other lady in the theatre had been cast for the *Queen* but the one that has been so favored, I might not have felt the insult so deeply; but, believe me, I never will play second to Miss ——, who has throughout her theatrical career, endeavored assiduously to blight my prospects, and mar my success with the public; to the favor of which public I ever look forward with anxious pride, knowing that on their kind support I am to rest my professional welfare. You are at liberty to make this letter public, if you please. I have, therefore, sent the part of *Lady Anne* back, and shall in justice expect to perform the *Queen*.

I am, my dear sir, yours most sincerely,
* * * *

P. S.—The man omitted to leave the play-bills at my lodgings this morning: but it is the way I am generally used in this world.

"'Oh, ah! she objects to play *Lady Anne*. Very well, I will make her go on for the *Duchess of York*, and that will bring the lady to her senses.' Read Note, No. 2:—

DEAR ——. At your request I have read Mr. Drudge's farce. It has some capital situations, and is throughout full of fun; it is also very original. But I think that the author has committed an error, in imagining for one moment that I would play the part you have named that he intended for me. You are perfectly well aware that, as *I* stand with the public, *I* must be *the* feature. Now, there are several other prominent and good parts in the farce, which would materially deteriorate from my "peculiar effects." If Mr. Drudge will, however, take the farce back again, and cut these other characters down to ribbons, I have no objection to look at it once more, and see what can be done. It is in my engagement to decline any thing which I think will not contribute to my advantage; and you know I am inflexible on that point.

Is it true, that we all played to less than forty pounds, first and second price, last night? If so, heaven help you.

Yours always, faithfully,
* * * *

"Open Note, No. 3 (anonymous, enclosing a ticket):—

SIR—If you will take the trouble to go, or send somebody on whose judgment you can depend, on Thursday next, to Mr. Pym's private theatre, in Wilson street, Gray's Inn Lane, I think you would be much gratified with the performance of a young gentleman who will act *Barbarossa* on that night. His friends impartially think his talents superior to any one at present on the stage, Macready or Kean excepted; he is cleverer than Warde or Phelps, and has got a much louder voice than the late Mr. Pope. There is only one drawback (and that might not be particular) to his becoming a first-rate actor, and this drawback is candidly pointed out to you, *as you may not see it*—he has a club-foot. Begins at half-past seven.

"'You are quite right, my friend; I certainly shall not see it.'

"(*A knock at the door:*) 'Come in. What is it?' 'Can you see Mr. Fatton?' 'What Mr. Fatton?' 'The master of the supernumeraries.' 'Send him in. Now Fatton, what is the matter? Make haste, for I am busy.' 'Sir, there's *a strike* with the children in the theatre.' 'So there ought to be, Mr. Fatton, if you did your duty properly, and kept a birch rod.' 'Yes, sir; but all their fathers and mothers come on me, and threaten to punch my head; now you know it is not my fault.' 'Well, what is this strike, as you call it?' 'The girls who are to fly in the new ballet won't have the wires affixed to them, unless they are raised to eighteenpence a night: their mothers won't let them endanger their lives under that sum! Now, sir, we should be in a great scrape at night, if this were to happen; worse than they were in at the other house, with the boys in the storm.' 'What was that, Fatton?' 'Didn't you hear that, sir? Oh; there were sixty boys, who stood on the stage under a very large canvas, painted to represent the sea. Now these boys were placed alternately, and were to rise and fall, first gradually and then violently, to represent the motion of the waves in a storm; and in the first three nights of the piece it had a powerful effect; but, after that, the manager reduced the water-rate, that is to say, he lowered the salary of each wave to sixpence per night. The boys took their places under the canvas sea; and when the prompter gave the signal for the storm, the water was stagnant—instead of the ship striking, it was the waves that *struck.* The sub-manager, in a fury, inquired the cause; when the principal billow said, "We won't move a peg unless you pay us a shilling a night, for it wears out our corduroys so."' 'Gad, I think that must have been the *deep,* deep sea! Well, promise the girls the eighteenpence; but I will be even with them, I will keep them dangling in the sky-borders in a thorough draught all the night. Tell them so.'—(*Exit Fatton.*)

"Take up newspaper; look to article under the head of 'The Drama.' 'Something agreeable, I dare say.'—(*Reads.*)

—— Theatre.—If we condescend to call the attention of the public to the management, or rather mismanagement of this theatre, it is only to express our utter contempt of the system at this period in operation. Does Mr. —— imagine that such miserable trash as that which was presented within these classic walls last night, can possibly attract an audience possessed of common sense? No; 'reform it altogether.' The plot of the new piece brought forward was so confused and inextricable, that we will not attempt to detail it to our readers: the whole affair was insufferably dull, and was deservedly condemned.

"'Bravo!' (*Rings bell.*) 'Send the free-list clerk to me. I rather think that the critic who wrote this precious paragraph was absent from the performance. Pray, did the * * * * card come in last night?' 'No sir.' 'Was Mr. * * * * here? You can tell by the signature on your book.' 'No, sir.' 'He is too good a judge to *pay.*' 'There was no one from that paper last night, sir.' 'I thought so; that will do.'

"'This is a *bitter* notice: here is a *better* in the * * * *. Ay, ay, this will balance the last; and then the immense difference of the circulation of the journal—double—two to one.'—(*Reads paragraph.*)

—— Theatre.—Another triumphant instance of deserved success was last night achieved by the management of this theatre; in fact, we do not remember at any period being more gratified, we may almost say electrified, with admiration of the gorgeous effects, which have never been surpassed even in this notoriously splendid establishment. The appointments were of the most picturesque order, and reflect the highest credit on the tact, industry, and stage knowledge of Mr. ——, who, it must be confessed, on these occasions is never at fault. The scenery, from the magic pencil of ——, was marvellously illusive: the performers exerted themselves energetically and successfully, and there was a long continued call for the author at the fall of the curtain, who, however, had the good taste not to appear. This drama will undoubtedly, have a good run, and must attract large half-prices.

"'What is this? A three-cornered, perfumed billet.' 'Yes, sir; and a Frenchman is waiting for an answer to it.'

Hotel, Sablonière, Lestere-squar

Madlle. Augustine Entrechat present she complement at Mr. ——, and has the honneur to inform that elle arrive in Londres las night, to fulfil son engagement. She could feel much gratifie if Mr. —— will send her 2,500 francs by de messinger, as she has to envoyer to the Douane for the pack cases containin her superb costume and garderobes. Madlle. Augustine Entrechat give notice to Mr. —— that she cannot consent to appeer at the spectacle until she receive 2,500 francs.

Monsieur, je vous salué

Augustine Entrechat.

"'Plague take the extortion of the foreigners. Never mind, the blessed English *will* wait; must pay her, or she will not dance, and she is announced. Where's the cheque-book? That's the way the money goes—takes French leave!'

Enter Stage Manager.

"'What is the matter now? you look quite alarmed; what mare's nest have you turned up. Sit down; whatever it is, take it coolly, man.' 'Mrs. —— cannot sing to-night!'—'The devil she cannot, what ails her?' 'I don't know! there's an official note from her husband, and we shall have to change the performances.'

Dear Sir—When Mrs. —— came home last night, she was attacked with spasms, and has been excessively unwell. She tells me, it will be impossible for her to perform this evening; so I give you timely notice that you may substitute something else. If you should require a medical certificate, our professional attendant shall forward you one.

Yours ever, and very sorry for it,

To —— Esq., Stage Manager, * * * *
—— Theatre.

"'But I see through it all; she does not like her part in the new piece; and this is the second night of it too; and I have laid out 1,000*l.* in getting it up; and because the tenor has the best part, she has put her monkey up. But I will not be so treated. She cocked up her nose at the music from the first rehearsal. "My compliments to Mr.——, and I do require a medical certificate." What is to be done? don't all speak at once.'

'Can Miss —— be ready in the part by night?' —'No, nor by this night three weeks.' 'Perhaps Miss —— might try it?'—'Bless your heart, no; she is over head and ears in love, and cannot get a word perfect. Never knows a line of any thing; she hardly remembers to come to the treasury for her salary, on Saturday morning.' 'It is rare to find such remissness.'—' What do you think of Mrs. —— getting through it, without the music?'—'I should as soon think of a water-butt getting through it.' 'Something must be done.'—'I am glad you have come to that conclusion.' 'Oh! here is the medical certificate, all ready cut and dried, I see; the old story [*reads*]:—

I hereby certify that Mrs. —— is laboring under severe hoarseness and oppression of the chest—

"She thinks nothing of my chest! I don't wonder at her oppression of the chest. —— supped with the family after last night's performance, and he told me, she ate half a duck, a salad, some stewed oysters, and a slice of cake, and drank bottled porter, besides the punch!" [*reads*]

She is under extreme excitement; and I do not think it safe to advise that she should leave her house, to attend her professional duties, this evening.

(signed) J. W. Twaddle.

I cannot alter the performances; the box-book is better taken than usual. Be so kind, my dear ——, as just to step up to their house, and see if she is really ill, or only shamming. Tell her she must come out to night: coax her, flatter her, any thing; tell her she looks too pretty to be an invalid! Say I am in a state bordering on mental derangement, and that the whole fate of the season depends on the run of the new piece! Stay, tell her the Queen is coming expressly to hear her sing, and a royal command must be obeyed. Run all the way.

* * * * * * *

"'But here is —— come back. Now, have you succeeded in persuading her to appear?' 'I had not—and yet I have.' 'How did you manage it, my good fellow?' 'Quite by accident. I went up to her bedside and used every entreaty. She certainly did look rather unwell.' 'So would any body, after swallowing such a supper.' 'She told me in a low voice, that if she was an angel from heaven, she could not sing to-night; that it was barbarous and unjust to require it; that it would endanger her very life; that her medical attendant had just quitted the room, and told her so; in short, and she spoke much louder, that she would not come out to save you and the whole theatre from destruction!' 'Then how did you persuade her?' 'You shall hear; just where the doctor had been sitting, I saw a small note on the floor, so I quietly picked it up, and to my infinite satisfaction found that it had been written by Mrs. ——'s husband, to the doctor; and he had I presume dropped it by accident; so I took the liberty to glance my eye over it. And here it is.'

Dear Twaddle—Write me a certificate that Mrs. —— is too unwell to act to-night. The Manager has forced her into one of the *muff parts* again, which will really injure her with the public. I assure you she is quite *feverish* enough for you safely to write the certificate; for what with something that has disagreed with her, and the confounded passion she has been in, she will do you no discredit. Do you want our orders for any night this week? if so, say. Regards to Mrs. T.

Yours ever,

To Mr. Twaddle, Apothecary. * * * *

P. S.—Hoarseness and sore throat is the go.

"'Bravo, bravo! excellent.' 'So I thought I would just show the lady that I had this interesting letter of her husband, which I also told her I should carry to you. She jumped up, like a parched pea, and made me pledge my honor that I would not lead her into such a dilemma, and that she would endeavor to get out, even at the risk of her precious life, and crawl into a coach, supported by pillows, and come down and perform; but that there must be a line in the play-bill of the night, announcing to the public her severe indisposition; and that she must leave out all the music, and not to have to change her dress. In short, I promised every thing—and she will be here.' 'We must give her the line in the bills, for our own sake. Send to the printer.'

"Where is the bed of roses on which I imagined I should recline?"

"But my dear fellow, are you not going home to your dinner?"—'Isn't this enough to take away all appetite for a dinner! besides, to-morrow is Saturday; and I must inspect and sign every one of these for payment.' 'What is that mass of papers?'—'Merely the weekly outlay, to be settled at the treasury to-morrow; only the salaries of the company—the band, the chorus, dancers, painters, property-makers, wardrobes, dressers, housekeeper, cleaners, watchmen, firemen, carpenters, copyists, soldiers, supernumeraries, children, bill deliverers, lampmen, gas-lighters, printer, advertisements, candles, oil, hair-dressers, military band, licenses, ironmongery, turnery, basket-work, colors, music paper, stationery, tinman, florist, drapery, hosiery, timber, laceman, ropes, canvas, brushes, authors, and law expenses, box-keepers, money-takers, cheque-takers, candle-stickers, police, call-boy, and coal-porter, besides a portion of nondescripts which cannot possibly be imagined any where else than behind the curtain of a theatre!'"

THE UNLUCKY PUPPY.

FROM "DOGS' TALES." BY RICHARD BRINSLEY PEAKE.

My mother was a pointer bitch, coal-black and comely; I never knew my male parent, but I have some notion that he followed the profession of a shepherd's cur; and his humble but enamored addresses were accepted by the pointress, seeing that she could not well avoid them, as she wore a handsome chain round her accurately proportioned neck, with the other end of which she was attached to her domicile, a neat cottage-formed residence, called a kennel.

I had four brothers and sisters of various different sizes, but I was the only one of my family that in the least resembled my mother; and I soon missed all my little round woolly misshapen companions, and never to any certainty ascertained their fate; only being a shrewd dog, I conjectured that the master of these puppies, having a decided detestation of hydrophobia, determined on accustoming these animals, early in life, to taking water, and in doing so, drowned them.

My mother being well fed, I was soon in a thriving condition, and grew apace: I have little further recollection of this happy period of my life, than that I was always hungry, that my mouth watered everlastingly, and that I had acquired a habit of gnawing every thing that came in my way, even to my mother's tail, who used by an angry growl to resent this unwarrantable liberty from a child to its parent.

My first disgrace was occasioned by my master's man of all work, Joe Banger, having left a pair of leather inexpressibles, which he had most charmingly clean-balled, until they were of a perfect batter-pudding color, on the steps in the stable; he had been employed on them for four hours at least, and master was going out next day with Mr. Conyers's hounds. These leathers looked so inviting, that I could not resist ascending the steps and dragging them down; when I lugged them into a dark corner of the stable, under a manger, and enjoyed myself by shaking them well, and biting a number of holes all over them.

I never had such fun in my life; but I do not think that either Joe Banger or master enjoyed the joke at all, for when the breeches were missed, there was a great outcry as to where they could have possibly vanished; so I looked up at Joe with a knowing and glistening eye, and barked as loud as I could, and wagged my tail, until I at last had the good fortune to attract his attention to the spot where I had so ingeniously nibbled the leather; whereupon Joe seized me by the ear, and with a whip gave me such a lashing and larupping, that to this very day I have not forgotten it. I winced: I shrieked: I howled: even the horses turned their heads from their racks to see what was the matter. The noise I made brought our master into the yard, who, upon hearing the calamity that had befallen him, ordered Joe Banger to recommence the flogging. Oh! well did he deserve the name of Banger.

My mother crept into her kennel, shaking with fear, but occasionally peeping out with some anxiety, whether for the terrible correction of her dear little doggy, or having some remote notion that she was going to be soundly chastised herself.

Then I was tied up by the throat, and not properly understanding the nature of the fastening, I nearly choked myself forty times in an hour.

This event gave me the character of an unlucky young dog: and the next affair that happened proved that I was one; for, one morning early, when the poultry were wandering and picking about the yard, my tender mother made a sudden snatch at a fine old cock, and pulled his tail right out; the cock escaped with the loss of his semi-circular plumes, some of which most unluckily were blown across the yard to the corner where I was tied up; when, as usual, in my simplicity, I began to play with and nibble them, considering a feather a mere trifle; when Joe, coming down from the loft in which he slept, saw the cock looking like a monstrous fool without his tail, and he also beheld unlucky me in the act of gnawing a portion of it. Out came the fatal whip again, and Mr. Banker operated on me more lustily than he did before.

This was barely forgot, when my master, who was going to take a walk of some nine miles for the purpose of angling for chub, determined that I should accompany him, that he might see what I was made of. Never shall I forget my delight in having that horrible halter removed from my throat, and being aware that I was about to have a run across the fields.

Notwithstanding the rebuffs and beatings I had endured, I followed my master with sincere pleasure; but being unused to go out with any one, it happened that he was always stumbling over me, treading on my paws, or kicking me out of the way. When we got into a field, I saw for the first time in my life a cow, with her calf. I own I was rather frightened at so large an animal as the cow appeared to me; but thinking that the calf was a mild looking little buffer, I went up to have some fun with it; when somehow or other, the cow got her horns under my ribs, and I soon felt myself flying in the air like a bird, only I came down at some distance, heavily on my back. I got up and shook myself. Turning round to have another look at the calf, I saw the cow coming at a canter again after me, flourishing her tail in all directions; so I prudently wriggled myself under a fence, out of her reach.

I perceived that my master admired my ingenuity, for he smiled. After a couple of hours' run, during which I caught a butterfly, and fell into a muddy ditch, we arrived at the stream where the angling was to be commenced, and my master with great patience unpacked his tackle; but nothing could induce me to keep at a sufficient distance from the water, but another flogging with the rod.

My master then baited his line with some ox-brains he had brought in a tinpot with him, and started off on his pastime, ever and anon favoring me with a menacing look, if I gave the slightest indication of following him.

A turn in the river took him out of sight, behind a plantation of osiers, when observing that he had left the pot of brains on the bank, and that the flies were beginning to buzz and hover over it, I went to drive them away, and unluckily smelt the bait; in two seconds, the whole of it was licked up and swallowed.

Presently, I saw my master returning: he had walked nine miles, there was no possibility of procuring more bait, he had no brains, and he had nine miles to go home again: his time and his sport lost; and all through me, accursed, unlucky puppy! He resolved to shoot me.

Sulkily, he put up his angling apparatus, and returned towards his domicile by a different route, for the purpose of procuring some bread and cheese and ale.

He accordingly entered a small inn, and called for what he wanted, and was served in a very dilatory manner by a red-haired, blowsy female, who seemed distressed by having too much to do.

I scented something in the house of exquisite savor, which proved to proceed from a dinner of the parish officers of Great Framingham, who had met to arrange their accounts and affairs, and to fix the day for the next feast, as well as to settle a very considerable diminution of the allowance of food and clothing to the paupers, in conjunction with a rise of the poor's rate, to meet the tavern bills. These worthy functionaries had dispatched a substantial repast, at which a turbot from Billingsgate had assisted; and were now taking their wine and punch, while deeply deploring the severity of the times.

I saw my master munching his bread and cheese moodily; he was too savage at my conduct to deign to throw me a crumb: so, finding that he was not communicative, I took the earliest opportunity of wandering out of the room.

In the passage, on a wooden bench, stood a pile of about three dozen dirty plates, placed on each other, that certainly had been very incautiously deposited there; for on the bottom plate but two, was the picked drum-stick of a fowl, which put the whole quantity of crockery rather out of proper equilibrium.

I had not partaken of any thing since the brains. The leg of the fowl was extended from the plates most temptingly, and I made a snap at it, pulling it away—it was mine, but what was the consequence? down came the three dozen plates off the bench

smash on the tiled floor. I never heard such a clatter in my born days, so I involuntarily dropped my tail between my legs, and scampered off with the bone.

"Whose cursed dog is that?" bawled the red-haired waitress; "Drat the dog, whose is it?" no reply: "There's at least five and thirty shillings' worth of plates broken all to pieces."

At last, it occurred to the landlord to ask the gentleman who had the bread and cheese in the parlor, "if the dog was his'n?" My master, who had overheard the whole affair, thought it politic to disown me.

Oh! how I enjoyed that fowl's bone—how sweet was the marrow; but alas! how soon it all vanished; I wished that fowls had as many legs as spiders. But now I perceived my master trudging homewards, so I ran after him; as I passed the public house, the blowsy maid set up an outcry against me; a shower of stones quickly followed me, and a brute of a blacksmith threw his hammer at my carcase so dextrously, that the heavy blow knocked me over and over. I however contrived to hobble home after my master, on three legs.

My master was, I think, deciding upon my fate, whether I was to be hanged, shot, or to take a little Prussic acid; when a letter arrived from a friend who had taken a cottage in one of the numberless colonies on the western outskirts of London, and who asked the assistance of my master to procure him a yard dog.

Thus was I reprieved; the size of my bony paws, and the width of my jaws, denoted, for I had not done growing, that I should be a large dog.

So the next morning I was to be tied under the wagon of the Hatfield Broadoak carrier, and thus to be conducted on my way to my new place. The journey to town *under* a wagon is extremely irksome; I wanted to run after the birds, but I only knocked my nose against the revolving wheel; the road was very dusty, and I had the advantage of the scrapings of the heavy hoofs of four horses sent constantly into my eyes; if I paused for a moment to avoid it, I endured a pull at the neck, which I verily thought would take my head out by the roots. A flock of sheep met the wagon, which was then stopped by the driver, and I had to bear with the affrighted hustle of some hundred and fifty of these woolly creatures, when presently the drover's dog, who had the charge of them, sprung upon me, turned me over on my back, and bit me through the ancle.

At length, after a wearisome journey, I was untied from the cart at an inn in Bishopsgate street, and was not a little surprised at the appearance of the vast metropolis: here I found that I was to be received by my new master, who was a sharp looking little man, suffering from some nervous affection, for he winked his eyes, and gave a sniff with his nose, several times in a minute. He paid the driver for my carriage, such as it was, and humanely gave me a drink of water from a stable pail: he then led me out of the yard with the same chain and strap with which I had been decorated for my travels, and we proceeded together for a short time with mutual regard. Presently, I discovered that I was the stronger animal of the two. He looked at me, as much as to say, "You have the advantage of me," which I returned with a glance, "I intend to keep it;" and I shortly put this principle in action; for, passing a butcher's shop, I raised myself on my hinder legs, attracted by an agreeable scent; I snapped at a veal sweet-bread, and swallowed it almost whole. The butcher came out, and demanded the value of the article; and it was not until my master was threatened with the introduction to a "P No. 158," that he could be induced to pay eighteen pence for my slight repast.

After a fidgety walk, we at length arrived at the villa residence of the family, where I was introduced to the yard; and was almost immediately, through the kindness of the lady of the house, accommodated with some mutton-chop bones, and a lump of outside rind of bacon, full of black bristles.

"This is a place after my own heart," thought I; "it will be my own fault if I am not comfortable."

The name of my new, nervous master, was Pennyfeather: both he and his amiable spouse imagined by my appearance, and what I was likely to become, that they had been fortunate in popping on an eligible yard-dog; but *nous verrons*, as I once heard a French puppy say.

After I had been domiciled for a week, I was voted, not only by every member of the family, but by the neighboring inhabitants, as a thorough nuisance; for whether I fancied I was learning to sing, or whether it proceeded from habit, I howled long and dismally, daily, at daybreak. A gentleman next door, who had invalids in his house, called and remonstrated, that for seven mornings his family had been deprived of sleep, and suggested that it would probably prevent my vocal efforts if I was let loose. Mr. Pennyfeather, who had been equally annoyed, was ready to adopt any plan to keep me quiet; he accordingly released me from my strap and chain, for which I was so grateful that I scratched his velvet waistcoat all to pieces, and tore his eye glass from his neck. He let me out at the gate into the road, where I amused myself for some time walking behind a policeman, who wondered what I wanted. I then saw three boys in paper caps, and clothes spotted with colors in distemper; they looked like merry fellows, so I thought I would go and have some fun with them, particularly as each of them carried a large slice of bread and butter for breakfast. I soon discovered that they were young artists belonging to a paper hanging manufactory; they invited me into their *atélier*, and while one of the boys tickled my palate with small pieces of bread, the other ingenious artists applied their stencil plates on each of my sides, and down my back, and produced, with their sized colors, a most elegant drawing-room pattern all over me; white ground, with roses, keeping me near the fire on which their distemper colors were warming. I soon dried into a picturesque appearance; then, painting my four legs a very light green, and covering my ears and tail with a coating of Dutch metal, they turned me out of the manufactory. I must say that I felt my skin sticky and rather tightly drawn, and the Dutch metal on my ears dazzled my eyes, but I resolved to make my way home. On my way, I discovered that I attracted considerable notice. A milkwoman with her pails, on seeing me, set off running as fast as she could; I thought it was to entice me to follow her, so I scampered after her. She was a little, superstitious, Welsh woman, and subsequently owned that she took me for one of the devil's imps; she loosened her yoke and pails as I approached her, and dropped them. As I always had a predilection for milk, I certainly did not neglect the opportunity of drinking to my heart's content, and overturning both tin cans. I then went quietly back to Mr. Pennyfeather's, and sat on the steps at the door until the family should arise.

One of Mr. Peter Pennyfeather's nervous peculiarities was an utter dislike to have anybody staring about his premises. I, thinking that it was growing late, reminded Mr. Pennyfeather of the time of day by uttering a prolonged yell; this brought the heads of the neighbors and their domestics out of windows and doors, and they all seemed wonderfully surprised at my appearance.

A crowd of work-people, going to their employment, and a number of gaping idlers, male and female, now stood round Mr. Pennyfeather's door, evidently delighted with the gay fancy pattern with which I was decorated; and, indeed, I looked as if I was attired in a rich Turkey carpet, but the gold ears and tail were the objects of general remark. Pennyfeather, hearing the buzzing conversation outside, to his horror, perceived that some novelty had collected a large number of spectat[illegible] in front of his house. I became impatient, and standing on my hinder legs, with my fore paws on the door, I by accident touched the knocker with my snout, which gave rise to a double rap. This feat caused a prodigious roar of laughter from the mob.

The affair was soon buzzed about, and the dairyman who employed the Welsh milkmaid, called on Mr. Pennyfeather for the sum of seven shillings and eight pence, for the milk I had overturned and destroyed.

Peter Pennyfeather called a cabinet council with his better half and family, and it was unanimously agreed that I was to be got rid of—then was debated the how, or when. It was thus decided.

The butcher's boy knew another boy, who was accquainted with a man who was looking out for a yard-dog at Richmond. This was enough; at seven o'clock at night the butcher took a half crown in his pocket and me in a strap. I was delivered to the man, a costermonger, who immediately put-to a valuable five-and-twenty shilling horse to his cart, to the seat of which I was tied, and I had rather a jolting ride to Richmond.

Arriving at the gentleman's house, who was looking out for a yard-dog, there was some demur about taking me in, as it was imagined from my appearance, that I had the distemper—and I had it sure enough, although I was hearty and healthy.

Well, a bargain having been struck up, I was left by the costermonger, and fastened to a staple in the yard.

Now, I am a dog of steady principles, as all the foregoing facts must abundantly prove; and I did not cease to recollect the kindness of the Pennyfeather family, so I determined to make my way back again. I set to work diligently to gnaw the strap through, bolted over a dwarf wall, into the garden, jumped on a spring gun, which exploded without putting a shot in my locker, though it shattered about forty panes of glass in a newly-erected green-house; I scratched my way safely through a holly hedge, which took off a considerable portion of my paint and gilding, and I was soon again on the high road. As I passed the market gardeners' laborers going very early to their work, I observed that they invariably got out of my way, and seized the first large stone they could find.

I no sooner made my way back to Mr. Pennyfeather's door, than I thought it would be proper to announce my return by a long melodious howl.

The butcher's boy was immediately sent for, and catechised. He swore that he put the dog in safe custody on the preceding night, and promised in the evening to come and take me away again. The lad was indignant at having his honor suspected, but secretly made up his mind to sell me to somebody else.

At eight o'clock the butcher arrived, and putting on a stronger noose, he led me through the lanes to Kensington, at the moment quite undecided how he should dispose of me, when chance put in his way an advantageous offer. In the High street, he overheard a woman, an itinerant purveyor of dogs' and cats' meat, bewailing that somebody had enticed away the dog that had drawn her cart for three years, and that the loss was irreparable to her. She had, however, the harness and a muzzle with her, and the butcher taking the lady aside, he exhibited me, when, after much haggling, she agreed to purchase me for eighteen pence. In a trice, I was harnessed and muzzled. I felt a piece of cold rusty iron stretched across my tongue, and strongly fastened to my head-gear; this was attached to a strap bridle, and the lady wishing the butcher "good night," lugged me off in triumph.

I passed about three months in this miserable state of bondage, beaten and starved; for, upon the principle of the adage, "That the shoemaker's wife is the worst shod," so the cats'-meat dealer's dog was the worst fed. I never had a morsel given to me that could possibly be sold.

There was not the slightest increase of respect or affection between my mistress and myself. At length, I was relieved from her tyranny. In the course of her rambles, she had formed an acquaintance with a fat hoary old cripple, who at some early period of life had the misfortune to lose both his legs. For many years after that, he obtained a good income by playing on a cracked clarionet, seated in a go-cart drawn by a single dog. This dog could go no longer, seeing that he died; and the cart would not go without the dog. In brief, I was promoted to the cart, *vice* Cæsar deceased. Here, however, began new troubles. For, oh, such a clarionet!

It has been asserted that dogs do not like music, that at certain notes many will howl. As regards myself, I now had the opportunity of proving the fact.

My present master,—oh, what an inexorable slave driver!—I had to drag his heavy trunk, surmounted by a capacious chest, all over the streets and suburbs of London; all day, drag, drag, drag, by the sides of the gutters. The old rascal had two instruments; his cracked clarionet, and a hard thonged whip. With the one, his intention was to amuse the public; with the other, to torture me. Whenever he ran down several notes in "Maggy Lauder," I invariably howled, I could not help myself: then out came the other instrument; and the tone and flourishes of that about my ears were distinctly heard, and the music was of such a nature, that it was as distinctly felt.

My master was a musical hypocrite of uncommon tact; he knew the houses well where he was encouraged, and where he was sure to be paid to go away. He was perfectly aware at what residence the hundred and fourth Psalm would be acceptable, or where "Nix my dolly pals, fake away," would be preferred. Oh! how I have execrated the old impostor, when he has turned from a low public house, seethed in gin, where he has been clarioneting, "The black joke," and going round the corner, where he knew dwelt what is called a serious family, he would plaintively commence the "Evening Hymn." Dog as I was, I scorned him.

My tale is coming towards an end. I had dragged my old bagpipe of a master out of the Hyde Park end of London; and toiled on, he getting all the pence, I all the annoyance, until I came to the corner of a well known lane, that recalled my early reminiscences. He was in the middle of blowing "The blue bonnets over the border," when I was seized with an irresistible desire once more to behold the inmates of a house wherein I had passed some felicitous hours.

Without, therefore, caring for my driver, (who by the way was drunk,) I set off at full speed down the lane, dragging the cart and musician behind me, and followed by a number of boys, who had surrounded us, out of curiosity.

Some of the little Pennyfeathers seeing this strange sight, ran in to tell their parents: and the old lady and gentleman ventured out to the door, he winking and sniffing as usual. I stopped suddenly before the house, so suddenly that the intoxicated clarionet player fell over, and upset the cart, tearing away a portion of the harness, from which I rapidly disengaged myself, and instantly set up my well known and much dreaded howl. I was so altered in my person, that it was with difficulty that I was recognized; the favorite howl, which I repeated, effected that.

Here was a *tableau!* My master's trunk and clarionet prostrate in the gutter; all the Pennyfeathers in mute astonishment, in various attitudes; I, mad for joy at my release, jumping up to lick Mr. Pennyfeather's face; his utter horror thereat; the arrival of the butcher's boy, attracted by the crowd, with a cleaver in his hand; the advent of two policemen to convey the remains of the drunken beggar to the station house; my determination to be again received as an inmate; Mr. Pennyfeather's decided objection to that measure, expressed by showing the butcher's boy another half-crown; the butcher's boy's attempt to seize me; my boundless

anger excited; the butcher's cruel grasp revenged by my biting him through the hand; the butcher's upraised cleaver! Oh! oh!—it fell, and though intended for my head, cut off two-thirds of my tail!

Maddened with pain, I ran, I know not whither, but out of reach of my pursuers—looked on the world with disgust—and became a vagrant as you now see me.

Here the UNLUCKY DOG turned round, and remarked,

"THIS IS THE END OF MY TAIL."

THE YOUNG PHILANTHROPIST AND THE OLD BRUTE.

A Story for the Time to Come.

BY J. B. BUCKSTONE.

IT was a bitter night in January; few and shivering were the pedestrians of the streets of London; icebergs floated on the river, a sharp north-easterly wind cut every half-clad and homeless creature to the bone; the chimes of Westminster Abbey tolled the hour of eleven; their very sounds seemed to tremble and die in the freezing air, as they were listened to by a figure leaning against the low wall that faced a gloomy and moated building on that side of the Thames called Millbank. The form was that of a woman: her face had been buried in her hand till the chiming of the hour roused her from her position: she looked earnestly towards the miserable building, walked or rather tottered a few paces, then turned and gazed again.

"Three weeks only gone," she exclaimed, "of the long, long year that must pass before I may ever see him again—I shall not live till the end of it—I cannot—I feel that I cannot;"—and she drew a thin and tattered cloak closely around her, as the ruthless wind swept by upon that desolate bank: the cry of a child was heard beneath her wretched garment: she strove in vain to hush it, till the cold-stricken infant's screams struck terror into the heart of its miserable mother.

"What can I do to help you, dear?" was her sobbing question. "You are cold, you must be, for I am shivering from head to foot—I have not tasted food to-day, and nothing have I for *you*, poor dear! where Nature teaches you to turn for nourishment: it were better that we both lie down to die—if we can but fall asleep on such a night as this, neither of us will ever wake again." And she sank by the road-side, exhausted.

The cries of the child were silenced for a time, and she appeared to strive to invite slumber; but in vain; for, suddenly starting up, she said, "He *will* be again at liberty; the bitter lesson he has known will make him more cautious, he will not again be the dupe of wretches; and if some good Christian would but listen to my sad story, and relieve me for a time, all may yet be well. No, no, I must strive against this affliction: though I could not help crawling, even on this wretched night, to look upon the dark walls that surround my husband, and the father of my child. God help me! for I am afraid none upon earth will."

She moved forwards with great rapidity, till she reached one of those lonely streets near the Abbey. An old man walked hurriedly by her, well wrapped up and defended against the weather—his mouth carefully covered to avoid a thick fog which had suddenly followed the subsiding of the wind. In spite of his precautions, the foul air penetrated to his lungs, and a violent cough compelled him to pause. The woman whom he had passed, approached him, and exclaimed—"Pray, Sir, look with pity on the poor and houseless on such a wretched night!"

To this appeal no reply was given; the old man hastened on, the woman seemed to gain courage, and kept pace with him; he waved her back with his hand:—she stopped, uttered a piteous groan, and looked after the cruel one who had so repulsed her. He arrived at the door of a dirty old-fashioned house, knocked and rang. Before the door could be opened, the woman was again at his side—"For heaven's sake, Sir," she said earnestly, "be charitable—I have no home, and this poor child"—He did not allow her to conclude the appeal, but in a harsh voice bade her "go away;" she sank on her knees to him; he laughed, muttered the word "impostor!" and again rang the bell. A severe-looking female appeared at the door, bearing a light. "Martha," said the old man, as he entered the house, "give that woman in charge to the police." The request, however, was not complied with, the door was instantly closed; the noise of bolts and chains was heard—and, as the morning dawned, a young female, and an infant clasped in her arms, were discovered on the step of that door *frozen to death!*

Who can she be? anxiously inquired the crowd that gathered round the old man's house.

They were bearing away the bodies, when a person knocked to inquire if the inmate of the dwelling knew any thing of the sad catastrophe. The old man appeared at the door; his hair and beard, the latter of a week's growth, were gray; his eyes were deeply set in his head, and overshadowed by white and bushy brows; and, as he thrust forth his withered countenance in order to reply to the question put to him, it assumed an expression of such ferocity, that the bystanders shrank in more fear from the face of that living man, than from the placid countenances of the dead before them. "Do you know any thing about them?" was the question. "No," croaked the old man, "I do not, except that the woman was a beggar, and followed me last night as I came home late from the city: had my servant done as I desired her, this might not have happened. Now begone, and don't create a disturbance before my house."

He disappeared, the door was sharply closed, and the crowd bearing the dead passed on. "An old brute!" remarked one; "*he* gave her nothing, I'll be bound, and they say that he is worth thousands."

* * * * * *

It was a lovely morning in spring; the fruit-trees were clothed in blossom, the graceful laburnum drooped in golden beauty, the birds sang gaily in the green hedges; the French windows of a small but elegant villa on the river side were open, and a young man walked forth upon the lawn, to enjoy that genial and delightful day; he was attended by his valet; and, basking in the rays of the sun, sipping his chocolate, took a letter from the pocket of his elegantly-figured morning gown, and, giving it to the man, desired him to deliver it in the course of the day as directed. "It contains," said he "a trifle for the widow of the poor fisherman who was drowned last week;" and, added he, "see that my half-yearly subscription for the relief of the houseless poor be paid to-morrow;" and with a smile he gave his empty cup to the valet, and passed with an air of contentment into his garden, where his gardener was working; the young man approached him—"Are you happy now, Thomas?" was the question put to the laborer.

"Quite, Sir, and I shall ever bless the day that I met you. If you had not taken me without a character, my little family must have gone to the work house," was the reply.

"Well," added the young man, "whether the charge against you were false or not—"

"Quite false, Sir," interrupted the man.

"Whether it was false or not, I hope that my kindness in receiving you into my service will make you grateful, and that your gratitude will teach you honesty while you are with me: I believe the charge of theft made against you in your last place to be unfounded, and trust that your good conduct here will prove it so."

"It shall, Sir, and Heaven bless you!" was the reply of the wrinkled gardener. And the young man passed on, with a light step and a cheek flushed with the consciousness of a heart possessing every charitable feeling for human nature. He walked to the front of his villa, and hung over the gate opening to the high-road: while looking with satisfaction on all around, a beautiful girl approached the gate, carrying a letter; she blushed as she presented it to him. It was from her father, an industrious tradesman in the neighborhood, who, in losing his wife, had, in his sorrow, suffered his business to be neglected. He became the inmate of a prison, leaving his eldest daughter, the bearer of the letter, and two younger children, unprotected: his misfortunes reached the ears of the young philanthropist now hanging over the gate. The tradesman's debts were paid, and his family reinstated in their old house and business. This letter was one of thanks: he perused it with pleasure, asked the young girl into his house, directed the servants to offer her refreshments, and put a bank-note into her hand as she departed. The girl trembled, curtsied, and went home.

The young man reclined in his easy chair, and, surveying himself in a *Psyche* before him, was, for the moment, the happiest man in existence; the blessings and praises of all who had experienced his kindness rang in his ears. "Every body respects me," said he; "respects me! they love me!"—and, in the joy of his heart, he sprang into a light wherry that was moored at the extremity of his lawn, and pulled gaily with the tide down the river. "How delightful it is," thought he, "to have wealth and apply it as I do! How every one must talk of me! I should like to hear what they say; but that is impossible;" and, with a sigh, he landed at Chelsea, trusted his wherry to the care of a waterman, to whom he flung a guinea, and to "Poor Jack" a crown. Both stared after him in astonishment. "I wonder what *they* will say of me?" thought he to himself.

His cab had followed him on the river-side; he leaped into it, his smart tiger hung on, behind, and his fine horses nobly stepped out towards town. He dined at one of his clubs, and reading over the advertisements in the newspaper after dinner, his constant custom, with a view to discover some new case of distress which he could delight himself by relieving, found one object of compassion perishing for want in the neighborhood of Walworth. Not a moment was to be lost: he would fly to her relief; and ten minutes more found him crossing Waterloo Bridge in his way to the abode of wretchedness. The evening was as clear, and as calm, as the morning had been beautiful. He thought again, with heartfelt satisfaction, on all the good that he had done, and on that which he was going to do, and, as he complacently looked upwards to the brightly shining stars, "Oh lovely worlds," he exclaimed; "if you are the abodes of the blessed, surely I may hope to inhabit one of you, when it may be my lot to quit this less favored planet!" His reveries were interrupted by observing a man ascend the parapet of the bridge within a few yards of him, who flung his arms wildly in the air, and seemed preparing to plunge into the rolling tide beneath; the young philanthropist rushed towards him, seized him by the coat—a shrill and unearthly scream burst from the frustrated suicide, as he firmly held him back. Three or four passengers crossed over to the spot from the most frequented side of the bridge; the man was dragged from the parapet, and flung upon the ground.

"He is drunk!" was the observation of the passengers, as they passed on, leaving the young man alone with the desperate stranger.

"Why are you so rash? what is your trouble? Tell me, and I will relieve you if I can."

The man staggered exhausted against the balustrades; he panted for breath. The question was repeated.

"You can do me no service," said the unknown. "I wish to die."

"Why?"

"Sir," said the stranger, "I am the manager of a theatre; to-morrow is Saturday, and I cannot pay my salaries;" and the would-be suicide glanced at the philanthropist with a strange leer.

"What sum do you require?"

"A hundred pounds."

"Is that all?"

"All!" added the manager with a look of despondency. "How can I face my people without that all? How many families will go dinnerless on Sunday, now that I am without that all!"

"Ha!" thought the philanthropist, "how many families then will bless my name if I supply him with the means of paying them!" "You shall have the sum that you require," said the young man: "lead me to a place where I can obtain pen and ink, and I will instantly write you a check."

"You will!" replied the manager, rubbing his hands with glee. "You have not only saved my life, but have sustained my character for punctuality in my payments, without which a manager, from having it in his power to be the pettiest of all petty tyrants, suddenly becomes the most insignificant creature on the face of the earth. Follow me, my kind, my best friend; it is a non-play night—the anniversary of Charles the Martyr; the actors only suffer for that event nowadays—poor devils!" and the manager again rubbed his hands, and seemed to chuckle at something that tickled his fancy mightily. He led the way; they arrived at the theatre, entered it by a small door in a back street, and were soon seated in a dark and dingy room, the walls of which were hung with files of play-bills. An office table with a desk upon it occupied the centre of the apartment; some faded damask chairs, with dirty white and gold arms and legs, completed the rest of the furniture. On the table were several soiled manuscripts and paper parcels tied up and directed.

"These are rejected dramas," said the manager, as he perceived his friend eyeing them. "Every man to whom I return one of those parcels is henceforth my enemy for life." He then threw himself into a chair, and assumed a look of vast importance. "There are pen, ink and paper," said he.

"And there," added the young man, "is the check."

"Attend in the treasury to-morrow," said the manager, "and behold the gratified faces of my company; for," said he, in his ear, "they do not expect a halfpenny. You will hear what they say."

"Shall I?" exclaimed the philanthropist, and his face flushed with delight.

The manager now fixed his eyes on his friend, and seemed to read his very soul.

"I have no doubt," said he, "that you have done many kind actions like this?"

"Yes," replied the young man.

"And you find every body grateful?"

"I think I do."

"And in your own circle of course you are beloved?"

"I believe I am."

"And the objects of your charity reverence you?"

"I believe they do."

"But you wish," said the manager, his eyes twinkling with an arch expression; "you wish, I dare say, to hear what is really said of you?"

"To confess the truth, it would greatly gratify me."

"Well, sir," added the manager, "you have this night done me a great kindness; perhaps it is in my power to return the favor by giving you your wish."

"What!" exclaimed the young man; "give me to hear what is really said of me—is it possible?"

"Possible!" said the manager, and he burst into a laugh, so long and so loud, that the philanthropist doubted the sanity of the Thespian ruler; but as he laughed so merrily, his countenance underwent a complete change, the clothes in which he was attired seemed to become uninhabited, like the dresses in the opening of a Christmas pantomime before the changes to the motley group take place —his head sank into his coat—his coat into his nether garments—they, in their turn, fell into his stockings, and, sitting on the ground before the bewildered young man, appeared an odd little figure, about three feet in height—his legs most grotesquely bowed, and supporting a very corpulent body. His head was large, his nose long and hooked, and a mouth, that alternately expanded from ear to ear, and instantaneously drew up into a small oval of the size of an egg; he held a brown tin ear-trumpet in his hand, his dress was a tightly-fitting suit of yellow, spotted with black, and, at the first glance, he looked like a huge frog; his face, however, was red and jolly, and his little black eyes seemed on fire with delight.

"Don't be alarmed," said he; "a theatre is the legitimate place for transformation, and where could I undergo mine in a more befitting locality? I am the embodied organ of inquisitiveness; many, many years ago I was an insignificant lump on the cranium of the last wife of the great Blue-beard. At her death, I was released from obscurity, and took my place amongst the myriads of liberated organs of every human passion that throngs the invisible air. These little eyes of mine, when I wish to pry into any matter that interests me, I can expand to the size of the crown of your hat." And he immediately gave an evidence of the truth of his boast, by fixing on the alarmed philanthropist a pair of immense black orbs, which he as suddenly reduced to their former twinkling dimensions. Again he laughed long and loud at the astonishment of the young man.

"Behold," said he, pointing to his tin tube, "when I apply this instrument to my ear, I can plainly distinguish all that is said of me amongst my companions behind my back." He placed it to his ear:—"That's right," said he, with a grin. "Go on—defame!—detract!—backbite!—I can hear you—those infernal organs of destructiveness and philoprogenitiveness are giving me a fine character. I know that I am far from a paragon of excellence, but really not such a wretch as my friends wish to make me out. Ah! now I see you have an inkling to try my trumpet; take it, my friend:—don't be alarmed, it won't bite you."

He handed his tube to the young man, who instinctively applied it to the proper organ—he immediately turned pale.

"What do they say?" inquired the embodied organ.

"Is it possible?" ejaculated the philanthropist.

"My friend," said the little gentleman, in the suit of spotted yellow, "What is the matter?"

"I hear a dozen voices reviling me."

"Indeed! what do they say?"

"I relieved a fisherman's young widow this morning, and her friends are persuading her that I have a base motive for my charity."

"And she believes them, no doubt," said the ex-manager.

"She does: her reply is 'who'd have thought it?' and I plainly hear her simper of satisfaction.

Another peal of laughter from the bow-legged gentleman shook the apartment.

"Try again," said he; "better luck next time."

The young man's face once more paled with rage.

"What now?" inquired the owner of the tube.

"My gardener, that I took into my service without a character, is talking to his wife. The man was accused of theft, was starving, and I took pity on him."

"Well, what does *he* say of you?"

"His opinion is, that as I seem so rich, and have taken him without a character, if I don't work a private still, he is almost sure that I am one of the swell mob, and he shall begin to look about him—a wretch!"

The little gentleman rolled about the floor in ecstasies: again the tube was at the eager ear of the young man, whose countenance reflected his vexation.

"What now?" inquired the man with the mouth, in a burlesque tone of commiseration.

"A party of friends, to whom I gave a splendid

dinner last week, are discussing my charitable disposition."

"And what do they say?"

"They attribute all that I have done to ostentation. Even my subscription to the Society for the Relief of the Houseless Poor cannot escape their sneers. 'Poor young man!' says one, 'he feels gratified at reading his name among the list of subscribers.'"

"Ah!" responded the owner of the tube, with a profound sigh:—"How bitter it is, sometimes, to listen to the truth;" and then he grinned again from ear to ear, his mouth immediately afterwards assuming its oval form, as he cast a sidelong glance at the mortified philanthropist. "Can you hear any thing further?" said he.

"Yes."

"What?"

"The tradesman whom I released from prison is talking to his daughter—a beautiful girl, who brought me a letter of thanks from her father this morning."

"Indeed! You are the subject of their discourse, no doubt. What may they say?"

"The father is asking his girl how I behaved to her; she replies, 'most kindly, and that she thinks I pressed her hand at parting, when I presented her with money.'"

"And the father, what says he?"

"Pooh!—psha!—no such thing."

"The father says so?"

"No, no, 'tis my reply to his ridiculous assertion."

"And what is that?"

"He tells his daughter, that if she minds how she plays her cards, she may be my wife; and ascribes all my kindness to him, my releasing him from prison, my paying his debts, and re-establishing him in business, to——to"

"What?"

"Being smitten with the girl's charms. He desires her to be constant in her attendance at church—to take her little sister only with her, and he has no doubt that some afternoon I may offer my arm, which she must timidly take."

"Oh, dear—oh, dear!" sighed the owner of the tube, "what a world it is!"

The young man's face now turned red with fury.

"Any thing more?" asked the embodied organ. "Who is speaking of you now?"

"The man by the river-side, to whom I gave the care of my wherry, and Jack-in-the-water; they are gossiping over a cool tankard at the Adam and Eve—they are speaking of me."

"What do they say?"

"The devil," exclaimed the philanthropist, and he dashed the tube on the ground; it seemed to fly into a thousand pieces—a loud clap of thunder shook the building. The young man received a violent blow, and fell stunned upon the floor. On recovering, the white lines with which the shutters of the room were ruled told him that it was break of day. He groped about in fear and astonishment, and, when recollection of the incidents of the past night returned to him, he anxiously sought the door of the apartment, and explored his way thence through the dark wings of the play-house:—the night-porter had opened the stage-door, and was surveying the state of the weather on the pavement. The philanthropist darted unobserved into the street, called a hackney-coach, and in two hours was stretched upon his bed, with an aching head, and a heart bursting with vexation.

* * * * * *

Forty years and more glided away. The Young Philanthropist of the elegant villa on the banks of the Thames, and the Old Brute of the lonely street near the Abbey, were one and the same person, changed only by years and a matured knowledge of the world.

A BOLD TRANSLATOR.

In certain clubs in London, it has been found useful to check the inclination to classical quotation, by introducing a *translator*, to which position some well-known humorist is generally appointed. When any gentleman indulges in Horatian or Virgilian rhapsodies, or introduces a pedantic or out-of-the way phrase of foreign origin, a cry of "Translator!" brings that functionary to the rescue—his duty being to paraphrase the meaning, if possible, but at the same time invest it with some ridiculous association.

Mr. Paul Bedford, a well known comedian, was at one time the Translator of a certain society near Drury Lane. A gentleman conversed learnedly on the classical meaning of the word *Omnibus*. "Translator," said the President, very gravely, "what is the English for omnibus?" "Shillibeer!" replied Bedford instantly.

A certain musician having been seen flirting with a fair one at the box-door of Drury Lane Theatre, was charged, on entering the club, with inconstancy towards the fair proprietor of his heart and hand. "*Non*," he exclaimed, "*Je suis fidèle!*" The translator was instantly called for, who rendered it thus,—"*I am a fiddler.*" The person in question was celebrated for his artistic excellence on "the merry bit of wood."

The translator, when called on to explain the hackneyed phrase, "*De mortuis nil nisi bonum*," answered, "It is the watchword of the resurrection men—'when dead, how nicely we'll bone 'em!'" (*i. e.* steal them.)

The conversation turning on a speaker, who, at a public meeting, had notes handed up to him, "from which hints he spoke," a gentleman adverting to it used the phrase, "*Gladiator in arenâ.*" "Translator!" sounded loudly, on all sides; when the ingenious gentleman explained that it arose from the destruction of a woman by a Roman, who *devoured* her, and, in the joy of a successful revenge, declared, he was "*glad he ate her* in the arena."

Talking of antediluvian and pre-adamite relics, the Megatherium was named. Some skeptical persons present denied that such an animal ever existed. "Translator," cried the president, "what animals existed before Adam's time?" "Nothing but one *chay-hoss* (chaos)," said the erudite officer. Nor was this the only use made of this word; for, in a learned dispute as to Bryant's denial of Troy and its siege, the Translator was called on to name the earliest conflict on record. "It was in the reign of chaos," he replied, "when nihil *fit.*"

A "PAGE" OF PHRENOLOGY.

BY P. LEIGH (PAUL PRENDERGAST).

How delightful is the pursuit of natural science! To study the habits and manners of ants,—to contemplate the industrious spider—little weaver that never starves for want of employ,—to observe the "busy bee," instinct with that appetite for sweets which it shares with the equally happy, but alas! the less industrious truant, collecting the saccharine principle "from every opening flower,"—to form a continually increasing circle of acquaintance with the verdant inhabitants of the vegetable kingdom, and the interesting inmates of the Zoological Gardens; these, indeed, are the occupations which render life one summer's day; which enhance the beatitude, and sweeten the tea-cup of domestic bliss. To the reflective and observant mind, the blow-fly, blue marauder, regaling itself on the sirloin destined to grace to-morrow the family board; the mouse, tiny thief, luxuriating in fancied secret on the new Stilton in the larder; nay, even the unbidden cockroach helping himself to the Christmas pie,—become objects of instructive survey.

Actuated by an appetite for useful knowledge, which has prompted the foregoing reflections, I connected myself some years ago with a literary and scientific society, which had been formed at Islington, where I reside, among a small but respectable circle of friends. Our members are inclusive of several ladies—among them, of Mrs. Brown, the amiable partner of my lot, with whom I have lived in an uninterruped state of felicity for a longer time than, perhaps, she will allow me to state. The predilections of Mrs. B. are precisely similar to my own; and having no family, we are enabled to devote the greater part of our time to indulgence in our favorite pursuits.

Our society meets at the house of each member in rotation, at half-past six precisely. After an exhilarating cup of tea, we proceed to business, and a lecture is delivered by the host of the evening, on the composition of water, the nature and properties of steam, the construction of the barometer and thermometer, or some other improving and entertaining subject. Sometimes our recreations are diversified and enlivened by a discourse from one of our number, who is a young medical man, on the conformation of the skeleton, the circulation of the blood, and the like arcana of the healing art. At our last meeting, we were gratified with a paper on hydraulics, as exemplified by the common pump.

One evening, our young professional friend, whose name I may mention is Mr. John Hunter Dummer, obliged us with a lecture on the sciences of mesmerism and phrenology. Never having had the means, previously, of acquiring any information on these subjects, I had formed no opinion respecting them; I therefore hailed the opportunity thus afforded me of enlarging my stock of ideas. Mr. Dummer very much disposed me to believe that there was something in the doctrines which he advocated, particularly as he appealed in confirmation of them to facts, which, as he with great truth remarked, were stubborn things. Resolved, as he recommended, to make observation of Nature the test of truth, I took home with me a phrenological bust, accompanied by a card, descriptive of the different organs, which he was so kind as to lend me.

On arriving at our little domicile, I immediately commenced my researches by examining the head of Mrs. B. The first point in her organization which struck me, was the great fulness of the occiput or back of the head. On comparing notes with the bust, I found that this was the region of the organ termed "Philoprogenitiveness." I looked out "Philoprogenitiveness" upon the card, where I found the results of its predominance described as follows:—

"*Very Large.*—Extreme fondness for children and young creatures in general. Apt to lead to indulging and spoiling youth, also to petting and caressing small animals. Often occasions extreme desire for offspring, and regret at the non-enjoyment of that supposed blessing."

This was very singular. Mrs. B. had at that very moment Tiny, a little King Charles's spaniel, whom she washes and combs every morning with her own hands, and has fed so bountifully that he has become quite corpulent in her lap; and Tib, her favorite tortoise-shell, was purring behind her chair. The next evening the little Edwardses over the way, whom she is continually regaling with sugar-plums and raspberry jam, were coming to tea, to meet our little nephews and nieces; and I could not but be interestingly reminded of the circumstance, that the sole affliction of my good lady is that no olive branches have graced our otherwise unique mahogany.

I next remarked her considerable prominence at "Tune," and recollected with a fond sigh of retrospection, that the circumstance which, in youth's gay morn, fixed my destiny for life, was hearing her sing in a summer-house at Brixton, "O 'tis the melody we heard in former years!"

I found, also, "Alimentiveness," or the organ of appetite for food, very highly developed, and remembered that she had that very morning inquired, with a languishing gaze upon vacancy, when ducks and green peas would be reasonable enough for our circumstances. Her predilection for bubble and squeak occurred, in addition, to my mind; as did moreover, ("Constructiveness" was large, too,) her proficiency in the preparation of jellies, pickles, preserves, and in the other mysteries of the culinary art.

"Causality," the organ of perceiving the relation of cause and effect, was moderate in size. Accordingly, Mrs. B. has always experienced a difficulty in understanding the dependence of the boiling point of water on elevation above the level of the sea, and the connection between lobster-salad and indigestion. She is moreover prone, when asked to assign a reason for such and such a fact, to answer, "Because it is." I had inquired of her a few days before, why corned beef was sometimes variegated on its exterior, and she gave me that reply.

These striking coincidences at once rendered me a zealous convert to phrenology. I then tried to mesmerize my partner, and she very soon became a sleeping one; but as in about half an hour she suddenly awoke with a start, and wanted to know if it was not almost supper time, I am not quite sure that the sleep was not simply natural.

The next day, I examined the heads of our domestics,—not without some opposition on the part of the cook, who, I imagine, at first misapprehended my object. She had a very large "Destructiveness," and, certainly, her temper is none of the most equable. The housemaid was deficient in "Order;" a defect which her stockings, exhibiting the chasm vulgarly called a potato—her shoes, which were down at heel—and the general hue of her visage, which once induced a wag, who visited at my house, to say, that she must have been cleaning her face with the blacking-brush—abundantly exemplified; and which the dusty condition of the mantelpiece, the litter usually observable in the passage, and the inadequately rinsed breakfast cups, had too often borne out before.

Our knife, errand, and foot-boy, or page, was endowed with an extraordinary "Locality," which, among other things, occasions a desire for change of place. I had never observed any indications of the faculty in the boy; but he came a few days afterwards to give warning, wishing to change his place, as he said, to better himself—but, as I am convinced, acting under the influence of his "Locality."

When he was gone, I made up my mind to choose his successor on phrenological principles; one of the chief uses of phrenology having been stated by Mr. Dummer to be, its applicability to the selection of servants. Accordingly, I rejected numerous applicants for his situation, who came with the best recommendations, not finding their organizations in conformity with their alleged character; and, finally, made choice of one, whose head, in my judgment, was to be depended on. He seemed to have a fine moral development, with particularly large "Wit," "Form," "Imitation," "Constructiveness," "Adhesiveness," "Marvellousness," and, as I thought, "Ideality."

When I inquired what his name was, he answered, "Bill Summers." I considered his substitution of "Bill" for "William" as a proof of the facetious tendency of his mind—which, admiring innocent mirth rather than otherwise, I considered by no means a disqualification on his part for my service.

I soon found that the disposition to humorous manifestations was really very strong in this young gentleman, and was manifested in a variety of ways. If his fellow-servants asked him for any thing, he would often playfully demand whether they did not wish they might get it? At the same time, he generally put his thumb up to his nose, and twiddled his extended fingers. He would inquire of young passers-by at the area railings, of whom he had no previous acquaintance, the state of the health of their maternal parents? whether those relatives were aware of their being from home? if they had disposed of their mangles? and many similar questions, which, though they had rather the semblance of impertinence, were no doubt dictated by a pure love of drollery.

This "Wit" or "Mirthfulness," acting along with "Imitation," and perhaps "Tune," oftentimes occasioned him to indulge in the utterance of various noises, which I supposed were intended to resemble the cries of different animals. Of these, a favorite one was a note something like the call of the lapwing, another was similar to that of the turkey. The duck he imitated to perfection

"Constructiveness," the organ of manual adroitness, he evinced by a singular dexterity in flinging stones, which sometimes excited my admiration, in spite of my perception of the dangerous tendency of the amusement. He was very fond also of piling little grottos with oyster-shells, which he collected while going on errands. His "Marvellousness," or "Wonder," was very apt to make him loiter in order to stare at sights. This habit sometimes occasioned us a little inconvenience; but then how interesting it was to observe the exemplification of truth! He was always especially attracted by the performance of *Punch*, which gratified the dramatic turn arising from his "Imitation," and was also a rich treat to his "Mirthfulness."

The faculty last mentioned in him was eminently practical, and the cook and housemaid had often to complain of its results, which were, sticking needles point uppermost in their chairs, putting chopped horse-hair in their beds, insects on the sly down their backs, and other like pleasantries. A neighbor, an antiquated spinster, one day sent in to complain that he had singed her cat's whiskers, and shaved its tail; but upon a careful admeasurement, finding "Benevolence" to be decidedly large, I acquitted him of so cruel a joke.

Of his well developed "Form," whereon the talent for drawing depends, I observed a manifestation very shortly after his arrival. I was looking out of a back window which commanded a view of the yard, and the knife-shed therein situated, where he had some work to do. This he had temporarily abandoned, and was engaged in making a sketch in white chalk upon the wall. First he drew a perpendicular line about two feet long, then a transverse one three-fourths shorter, at right angles with the top of it. The former he connected with the latter by a diagonal stroke, commencing at the termination of the one, and joining the other some four inches down its length. From the point of the scalene triangle thus formed, he dropped a fourth line about half a foot in length, and this he joined at its termination to the lateral part of a small irregular circle, beneath and united to which he described a larger oval, with a short horizontal line trifurcate at the end extended from either side, and two similar lines, but longer, a little inclined outwardly, depending from below it—thus:

Having completed this design, which, as will be seen, was a pictorial commentary on the law of capital punishment, he put his hands into his pockets under his apron, and fell to capering and whistling in high glee at the success of his performance; but, upon turning round, and catching sight of me at the window, he hastily resumed his employment. I had called Mrs. Brown, to show the amusement which I derived from witnessing his proceedings, and we both agreed that the subject which he had chosen for illustration—the tendency and reward of crime—was in complete harmony with his large "Conscientiousness," and strongly indicative of his moral sense.

His "Adhesiveness" was shown in the delight which he evidently derived from the interchange of ideas with the butcher and baker boys at the area, wherein he would sometimes spend more time than I quite approved of.

In one respect, however, I was at a loss to reconcile his character with his development. He seemed, as I said, to have large "Ideality," the protuberance indicative of the poet. Nevertheless, he never made any verses that I knew of, and though he knew a few songs, they were principally of the description termed "Negro Melodies," which can hardly be said to be of a poetical or sentimental character. Indeed, they were, for the most part, scarcely intelligible—there was one, in particular, in which one "Josey" was invited to "jim along." I could make no head or tail of it.

To make sure that my phrenological estimate had been correct, I induced him, by the present of five shillings, to allow his head to be shaved, and to let me trace out the different organs thereon in ink. I chose some of Mrs. Brown's marking ink for the purpose, which being principally composed of nitrate of silver or lunar caustic, was ineffaceable by ablution. I mapped out the bare scalp in exact conformity with the bust, and was confirmed in the conviction that I had made no mistake.

Shortly afterwards, several spoons were missing. The cook and housemaid, on being taxed with the theft, indignantly denied it; and the idea that so well organized a boy as William was capable of such a delinquency, was preposterous. Mrs. B. had a tame magpie, and having read in various books of natural history of the propensity of this creature to pilfer and secrete such articles, we determined, not without great reluctance on my wife's part, that the bird's neck should be wrung—an operation which was performed by William, and which he appeared to undertake with greater readiness than could have been predicted from his large "Benevolence."

We had occasionally before observed the marks of smutty fingers on the exterior of mince and apple pies, and had fancied that an undue diminution had taken place in their contents during their reservation in the larder. At length, too, the beer, which it was William's province to fetch, began to assume a much more aqueous character than is consistent with Barclayian integrity. This circumstance, in spite of our preconceived opinion of the lad's honesty, gradually induced us to question his pretensions to that virtue; at last, Mrs. Brown, having lost a brooch, and a diligent search having been vainly instituted in the other servants' boxes, the bed-room of Master William was examined, under the auspices of F 34, when, to our astonishment and confusion, the brooch and two or three of the spoons, with a pawnbroker's duplicate for the rest, were discovered behind a loose brick in the chimney.

The youth was with little loss of time conveyed, in the charge of F to the Clerkenwell Police-office, and thence in a van to Newgate. Before he left, we called in Mr. Dummer to look at his head, and explain its discordance with what he had turned out to be. And now comes the climax of my narration, which I record for the benefit of inexperienced phrenologists. What I had marked out as "Ideality" was declared by Mr. D. to be in reality "Acquisitiveness," which, in this instance was so large as to come three inches in advance of its legitimate boundary, and to occupy the place of the former organ. Here, therefore, as that gentleman remarked, was one of those beautiful exceptions which prove a rule.

William is now in Australia. I have determined, in future, not to trust to my own skill as a manipulator in determining on a servant's character; but, instead, shall have some recourse for that purpose to the assistance of a practised professor of phrenology. The guinea thus laid out will be well spent in the purchase of a guarantee against deception and loss.

The cook and housemaid, who, indignant at having been suspected, had given us warning, both declared that the boy was not only a thief, but an incorrigible storyteller. This feature of his character was beautifully accordant with his great "Marvellousness." On the whole, I consider my phrenological experiment to have been highly satisfactory.

SOME RECOLLECTIONS OF GRIMALDI.

ANONYMOUS.

An attempt to describe Mr. Grimaldi's Clown has always proved a failure: his humor could not be tied down to pen, ink, and paper; it was an essence too subtle to yield to mere phraseology. His eyes, large, globular, and sparkling, rolled in a riot of joy; his mouth, capacious, yet with a never-ending power of extension, could convey all sorts of physical enjoyment and distaste; his nose was not the mere bowsprit appendage we find that respectable feature to be in general: it was a vivacious excrescence capable of exhibiting disdain, fear, anger, even joy. We think we see him now screwing it on one side; his eyes, nearly closed, but twinkling forth his rapture; and his tongue a little extended in the fulness of his enjoyment; his chin he had a power of lowering, we will not say to what button of his waistcoat, but certainly the drop was an alarming one.

It always appeared to us that Grimaldi *moved his ears;* and this, anatomically speaking, is not an impossibility. Be it as it may, the way in which he drew down his lower jaw on any sudden surprise gave this effect to the auricular organs. Speech would have been thrown away in his performance of Clown; every limb of him had a language. What eloquent legs were his! Look at him approaching that cottage of gentility; the man is changed: see how he stands looking at the window, at which hangs a bonnet: his back is toward you; but it tells the tale, the lady within is to be won. Look how he bends toward the balcony—Romeo in red and white: see how mincingly he puts forth his foot, and passes his hand over his garments; he must woo in another shape; he turns round in utter bewilderment; anon, a boy passes—he plays at marbles with him, first for money, then for his jacket; he wins it: a dandy passes—he abstracts his coat tails: a miller—he steals a sack: he has stolen yonder chimney-pot, and made a hat; taken that dandizette's shawl, and converted it into a waistcoat: the sack becomes white ducks; the tails render the jacket a coat; a cellar-door iron ring forms an eye-glass; and he moves, an admirable caricature of the prevailing fashion of the day.

Then, was there ever such a coach-builder? Go to school, Mr. Houlditch; for, with a coal-scuttle and a few cheeses, Grimaldi would construct you a vehicle at a moment's notice. Is his vegetable man unforgotten? He was no paltry humorist who conceived the notion of making a melon into a head, and turnips and radishes do the duty of hands and fingers. His love-making—what infinite variety in his approaches? His boisterous freedom with the London fish-dealer; his sailor-like jollity at Portsmouth; his exquisite nonchalant air when attired as a dandy; and his undeniable all-overishness when as Clown, he meant to impress, being suddenly smitten by the beauty of his fair enslaver. It was all what we had an hundred times seen, without the innate ridiculousness of the things being made apparent to us. Grimaldi had looked on the follies of humanity, and fairly turned the seamy side without.

Then, his treatment of that old man villanous, "yclept Pantaloon," whom, old and infirm as he is, no one pities at all, though he is treated by all the persons of the medley drama in a way that no elderly gentleman should be expected to endure. We applauded and rejoiced in those vices in Grimaldi that we hated in the Pantaloon; here is a bone for your metaphysicians to pick: we were quite blind to the moral delinquency of Mons. Clown's habits; he was a thief—we loved him, nevertheless; a coward, a most detestable coward—still we loved him: he was cruel, treacherous, unmanly, ungenerous, greedy, and the truth was not in him—yet, for all this, multiplied up to murder, if you would, we loved him, and rejoiced in his successes. Clown, (Grimaldi's Clown we mean,) Punch, and Falstaff (Shakspere can afford to be put in any company), are all darlings of our souls, though, if we reason about the matter, we find them to be all most incomprehensible vagabonds. Grimaldi had certainly studied the gamut of merriment, and knew every note of its compass, and could discourse most excellent music. He was the finest practical satirist we ever had, —Hogarth in action;* during his day there were an hundred clever men, but no single Clown. Follet was a jumper only; Laurent was ingenious, not humorous; Bradbury was a man of great strength, but his was very dreary merriment; Kirby was too confined; Bristow, Hartland, and that school, were mere imitators of the great original; Paulo and Southby, both clever, never stood the slightest chance in competition with him; and young Joe was only the shadow of the shade of that Grimaldi that our boyhood recalls; he only approached to an imitation of the style of his father in his latter and weaker day.

Pantomimes are now virtually extinct; Stanfield and Roberts have made picture galleries of them. Be it so. Grimaldi will in a few years be but a name; and our children's children must be content to take the tale of his merits on the credit of their ancestors. We believe in Garrick, whom we never saw, and those to come may believe in Grimaldi; for, though in a low department of art, he was the most wonderful creature of his day, and far more unapproachable in his excellence than Kean or Kemble in theirs. He sleeps well, and had happily quitted the stage ere pantomimes had been driven from it: he was a harmless, and a kind man, had many friends, and few enemies.—*Sit tibi terra levis!*

* Remember his scene when he opens three oysters, and finds an apt excuse for eating them all; his dagger scene; his duel; his skeleton scene, *cum multis aliis.*

THEODORE HOOK.

FROM THE MEMOIR OF THE REV. RICHARD HARRIS BARHAM.

About this time Mr. Barham found opportunities of renewing his acquaintance with one who, in many respects, was to be ranked among the most extraordinary men of his age, the late Mr. Theodore Hook. To say nothing of this gentleman's unequalled happiness in impromptu versification, conveying, as he not unfrequently did, a perfect epigram in every stanza—a talent, by the way, which sundry rivals have affected to consider mere knack, and one of whom still bears in his side the *lethalis arundo* of James Smith, for his bungling effort at imitation; to pass by that particular province of practical humor* with which his name is so commonly associated, and in which he was *facilè princeps*, Mr. Hook yet possessed depth and originality of mind, little dreamed of, probably, by those who were content to bask in the sunshine of his wit, and to gaze with wonder at the superficial talents which he exhibited at table, but sufficient, nevertheless, to place him far beyond the station of a mere sayer of good things, or "diner-out of the first water." To those indeed who have never been fortunate enough to witness those extraordinary displays, no description can convey even a faint idea of the brilliancy of his conversational powers, of the inexhaustible prodigality with which he showered around puns, bon mots, apt quotations, and every variety of anecdote; throwing life and humor into all by the exquisite adaptation of eye, tone, and gesture to his subject. His writings fail to impress one in any way commensurate with his society.

Of the few sketches of him that have been given in novels, not one can claim the merit of being more than a most shadowy resemblance. It needs a graphic skill, surpassing his own, to draw his portrait with any approach to correctness: indeed, it were well nigh as easy to depict on canvas the diamond's blaze, as to portray that intensity of genius, that dazzling vivacity of spirit, which distinguished him even among the peers of intellect. Nowhere, perhaps, is failure more conspicuous than in the miserable and meagre attempt in "Coningsby." Not the faintest glow of humor, not one flash of wit, not an ebullition of merriment breaks forth from first to last; the author, in utter incapacity for the task, contents himself with simply observing, "Here Mr. Lucian Gay (the name under which Hook is introduced) was vastly amusing—there he made the table roar," etc., much in the manner of the provident artist, who, to obviate mistake, affixed the notice to his painting: "This is the lion—this is the dog." Of the moral portraiture, we will venture to say that it is as unjust as the material is weak. For a more accurate estimate of his character and position, and for an account of the main incidents of his life,

* Much as Mr. Barham, with all reasonable and right-thinking people, condemned this practice of playing practical jokes, there was something so original and irresistibly ludicrous in the positions brought about by Theodore Hook's humor, as to draw a smile from the most unbending. The only thing of the kind in which Mr. B. was ever personally engaged was as a boy at Canterbury, when, with a school-fellow, now a gallant major, "famed for deeds of arms," he entered a Quakers' meeting-house: looking round at the grave assembly, the latter held up a penny tart, and said solemnly, "Whoever speaks first shall have this pie."—"Go thy way," commenced a drab-colored gentleman, rising,—"go thy way, and"—— "The pie's yours, sir," exclaimed D——, placing it before the astounded speaker, and hastily effecting his escape.

we may refer the reader to an able, though not over indulgent, article in "The Quarterly Review."

Of what occurred, at that which appears to have been Mr. Barham's first interview with his old companion after their separation at college, we have a somewhat detailed account:—

"November 6th.—Passed one of the pleasantest evenings I ever spent at Lord ——'s. The company, beside the host and hostess, consisted of Mr. Cannon, Mr. C. Walpole, Mr. Hill, generally known as 'Tom Hill,' Theodore Hook, and myself. It was Hook's first visit there, and none of the party but myself, Cannon, and Hill, who were old friends of his, had ever seen him before. While at dinner he began to be excessively amusing. The subject of conversation was an absurdly bombastic prologue, which had been given to C——, of D. L. T., to get by heart, as a hoax, beginning—

> When first the drama's muse by freedom reared,
> In Grecian splendor unadorned appeared, etc.

"Gattie, whose vanity is proverbial, was included in the joke. The stage-manager, who had the arranging of it, offered him also some equally ridiculous lines, which he said the author of the new comedy had written for himself, but that he had not sufficient nerve to deliver them.

"'No man on the stage has such nerve as I,' interrupted Gattie.

"'Then it must be spoken in five characters; the dresses to be thrown off one after the other.'

"'No performer can change his dress so quickly as I can,' quoth Gattie.

"'Then I am afraid of the French dialect and the Irish brogue.'

"'I'm the only Frenchman and Irishman on the stage,' roared Gattie.

"The hoax was complete, and poor Gattie sat up the whole night to learn the epilogue; went through three rehearsals with five dresses on, one over the other, as a Lady, a Dutchman, a Highlander, a Teague, and lastly, as 'Monsieur Tonson come again.' All sorts of impediments were thrown in his way, such as sticking his breeches to his kilt, etc. The time at length arrived, when the stage-manager informed him with a long face, that Colman, the licenser, instigated, no doubt, by Mathews, who trembled for his reputation, had refused to license the epilogue: and poor Gattie, after waiting during the whole of the interlude, in hopes that the license might yet come down, was obliged to retire most reluctantly and disrobe.

"Hook took occasion from this story to repeat part of a prologue which he once spoke as an amateur, before a country audience, without one word being intelligible from the beginning to the end. He afterwards preached part of a sermon in the style of the Rev. ——, of Norwich, of whom he gave a very humorous account; not one sentence of the harangue could be understood, and yet you could not help, all through, straining your attention to catch the meaning. He then gave us many absurd particulars of the Berners street hoax, which he admitted was contrived by himself and Henry H——, who was formerly contemporary with me at Brazenose, and whom I knew there, now a popular preacher. He also mentioned another of a similar character, but previous in point of time, of which he had been the sole originator. The object of it was a Quaker who lived in Henrietta street, Covent Garden. Among other things brought to his house were the dresses of a Punch and nine blue devils, and the body of a man from Lambeth-bone house, who had the day before been found drowned in the Thames.

"In the evening, after Lady —— had sung, 'I've been roaming,' Hook placed himself at the pianoforte, and gave a most extraordinary display of his powers, both as a musician and an improvisatore. His assumed object was to give a specimen of the burlettas formerly produced at Sadlers' Wells, and he went through the whole of one which he composed upon the spot. He commenced with the tuning of the instruments, the prompter's bell, the rapping of the fiddlestick by the leader of the band, and the overture, till, the curtain being supposed to rise, he proceeded to describe:—

"The first scene.—A country village—cottage (O. P.)—church (P. S.) Large tree near wing. Bridge over a river occupying the centre of the background. Music.—Little men in red coats seen riding over bridge. Enter—Gaffer from cottage, to the symphony usually played on introducing old folks on such occasions. Gaffer, in recitative, intimates that he is aware that the purpose of the Squire in thus early

> A crossing over the water,
> Is to hunt not the stag, but my lovely daughter.

Sings a song and retires, to observe Squire's motions, expressing a determination to balk his intentions;

> For a peasant's a man, and a squire's no more,
> And a father has feelings, though never so poor.

'Enter Squire with his train.—Grand chorus of huntsmen—'Merry toned horn, Blythe is the morn,' 'Hark forward, away, Glorious day,' 'Bright Phœbus,' 'Aurora,' etc., etc.

"The Squire dismisses all save Confidant, to whom, in recitative, he avows his design of carrying off the old man's daughter, then sings under her window. The casement up one pair of stairs opens. Susan appears at it, and sings—asking whether the voice which has been serenading her is that of her 'true blue William, who on the seas,—is blown about by every breeze.' The Squire hiding behind the tree she descends to satisfy herself; is accosted by him, and refuses his offer: he attempts force. The old man interferes, lectures the Squire, locks up his daughter, and exit (P. S.) Squire sings a song expressive of rage and his determination to obtain the girl, and exit (P. S.)

"Whistle—Scene changes with a slap.—Public-house door; sailors carousing with long pig-tails, checked shirts, glazed hats, and blue trousers. Chorus—'Jolly tars, Plough the main,—Kiss the girls, Sea again.' William, in recitative, states that he has been 'With brave Rodney,' and has got 'Gold galore;' tells his messmates he has heard a land-lubber means to run away with his sweetheart, and asks their assistance. They promise it.

> Tip us your fin! We'll stick t'ye, my hearty,
> And beat him! Haven't we beat Boneyparty?

Solo, by William, 'Girl of my heart, Never part. Chorus of sailors—'Shiver my timbers,' 'Smoke, and fire, d—n the Squire,' etc., etc. (Whistle—scene closes—slap.)

"Scene—the village as before. Enter Squire; reconnoitres in recitative; beckons on gipsies, headed by confidant in red. Chorus of gipsies entering —'Hark! hark! Butchers' dogs bark! Bow, wow, wow. Not now, not now.' 'Silence, hush!

Behind the bush. Hush, hush, hush.' 'Bow, wow, wow.' 'Hush, hush.' 'Bow, wow.' 'Hush! hush! hush!!' Enter Susan from cottage. Recitative,

What can keep father so long at market?
The sun has set, although it's not quite dark yet.
— Butter and eggs,
— Weary legs.

"Gipsies rush on and seize her; she screams; Squire comes forward. Recitative affettuoso—'She scornful, imploring, furious, frightened!' Squire offers to seize her; True Blue rushes down and interposes; Music agitato; Sailors in pig-tails beat off gipsies; Confidant runs up the tree; True Blue collars Squire. Enter Gaffer:—

Hey-day! what's all this clatter;
William ashore?—why what's the matter?

"William releases Squire, turns to Sue; she screams and runs to him; enbrace; 'Lovely Sue; Own True Blue;' faints; Gaffer goes for gin; she recovers, and refuses it; Gaffer winks, and drinks it himself; Squire, Recitative—'Never knew, about True Blue; constant Sue;' 'Devilish glad, here, my lad; what says dad?' William, recitative—'Thank ye, Squire; heart's desire; roam no more; moored ashore.' Squire joins lovers—'Take her hand; house, and bit of land; my own ground;

And for a portion here's two hundred pound!

Grand chorus huntsmen, gipsies, and sailors with pig-tails; Solo, Susan—'Constant Sue; own True Blue.' Chorus; Solo, William—'Dearest wife, laid up for life.' Chorus; Solo, Squire—'Happy lovers, truth discovers.' Chorus; Solo, Gaffer—'Curtain draws, your applause.' Grand Chorus; huntsmen, gipsies, sailors in pig-tails; William and Susan in centre; Gaffer (O. P.), Squire (P. S), retires singing,

Blithe and gay—Hark away!
Merry, merry May.
Bill and Susan's wedding day."

Such is a brief sketch, or skeleton, thrown together from memory, of one of those extemporaneous melo-dramas with which Hook, when in the vein, would keep his audience in convulsions for the best part of an hour. Perhaps had his *improvisatising* powers been restricted to that particular class of composition, the impromptu might have been questioned; but he more generally took for subjects of his drollery the company present, never succeeding better than when he had been kept in ignorance of the names of those he was about to meet; but, at all times, the facility with which he wrought in what had occurred at table, and the points he made bearing upon circumstances impossible to have been foreseen, afforded sufficient proof that the whole was unpremeditated. Neither in this, nor in any other of his conversational triumphs, was there any thing of trickery or effort. No abruptness was apparent in the introduction of an anecdote; no eager looking for an opportunity to fire off a pun, and no anxiety touching the fate of what he had said. In fact, he had none of the artifice of the professional wit about him, and none of that assumption and caprice which minor 'Lions' exhibit so liberally to their admirers. It may be fairly said, as he knew no rival, so he has left no successor:

Natura lo fece, e poi ruppe la stámpa.

"March 13, 1828.—Lord ——, Sir A. B——, Theodore Hook, Stephen Price and Cannon dined here. Cannon told a story of a manager at a country theatre, who, having given out the play of 'Douglas,' found the whole entertainment nearly put to a stop by the arrest of 'Young Norval' as he was entering the theatre. In this dilemma, no other performer of the company being able to take the part, he dressed up a tall, gawky lad who snuffed the candles, in a plaid and philabeg, and pushing him on the stage, advanced himself to the footlights with the book in his hand, and addressed the audience with, 'Ladies and Gentlemen—

This young gentleman's name is Norval. On the Grampian hills
His father feeds his flock, a frugal swain,
Whose constant care was to increase his store,
And keep his only son (this young gentleman) at home.
For this young gentleman had heard,' etc.

And so on through the whole of the play, much to the delectation of the audience.

"In the evening, Hook went to the piano, and played and sang a long extempore song, principally levelled against Cannon, who had gone up earlier than the rest, and fallen asleep on the sofa in the drawing-room. Sir A. B——, who now met the former for the first time, expressed a wish to witness more of his talent as an improvisatore, and gave him Sir Christopher Wren* as a subject, on which he immediately commenced and sang, without a moment's hesitation, twenty or thirty stanzas to a different air, all replete with humor.

"March 23.—Dined at Sir A. B——'s, who was summoned away to attend the king. * * * * Hook made but one pun: on Walpole's remarking that, of two paintings mentioned, one was 'a shade above the other in point of merit,' he replied, 'I presume you mean to say it was a *shade over* (*chêf d'œuvre*).'

"He told us an amusing story of his going down to Worcester, to see his brother, the dean, with Henry H—— (his companion in many of his frolics). They arrived separately at the coach, and taking their places inside, opposite to each other, pretended to be strangers. After some time, they began to hoax their fellow travellers—the one affecting to see a great many things not to be seen, the other confirming it and admiring them.

"'What a beautiful house that on the hill!' cried H——, when no house was near the spot; 'it must command a most magnificent prospect from the elevation on which it stands.'

"'Why, yes,' returned Hook, 'the view must be extensive enough, but I cannot think those windows in good taste; to run out bay windows in a Gothic front, in my opinion, ruins the effect of the whole building.'

"'Ah! that is the new proprietor's doings,' was the reply, 'they were not there when the Marquis had possession.' Here one of their companions interfered; he had been stretching his neck for some time, in the vain hope of getting a glimpse of the mansion in question, and now asked,

"'Pray, Sir, what house do you mean? I don't see any.'

"'That, Sir, with the turrets and large bay windows on the hill,' said Hook, with profound gravity, pointing to a thick wood.

"'Dear me,' returned the old gentleman, bobbing about to catch the desired object, 'I can't see it for those confounded trees.'

"The old gentleman, luckily for them, proved an indefatigable asker of questions, and the answers

* Mr. Barham's house was situated in St. Paul's Churchyard.

he received, of course, added much to his stock of genuine information.

"'Pray, Sir, do you happen to know to whom that house belongs?' inquired he, pointing to a magnificent mansion and handsome park in the distance.

"'That, Sir,' replied Hook, 'is Womberly Hall, the seat of Sir Abraham Hume, which he won at billiards from the Bishop of Bath and Wells.'

"'You don't say so!' cried the old gentleman in pious horror, and taking out his pocket-book, begged his informant to repeat the name of the seat, which he readily did, and it was entered accordingly—the old gentleman shaking his head gravely the while, and bewailing the profligacy of an age in which dignitaries of the church encouraged gambling to so alarming an extent.

"The frequency of the remarks, however, made by the associates on objects which the eyesight of no one else was good enough to take in, began at length to excite some suspicion, and Hook's bursting suddenly into a rapturous exclamation at 'the magnificent burst of the ocean' in the midst of an inland country—a Wiltshire farmer who had been for some time staring alternately at them and the window, thrust out his head, and after reconnoitring for a couple of minutes, drew it in again, and looking full in the face of the sea-gazer, exclaimed with considerable emphasis,

"'Well, now, then, I'm d—d if I think you can see the ocean, as you call it, for all you pretends,'—and continued very sulky all the rest of the way."

One more instance of Mr. Theodore Hook's innate love of hoaxing.

"December 8.—Hook called, and in the course of conversation gave me an account of his going to Lord Melville's trial with a friend. They went early, and were engaged in conversation when the peers began to enter. At this moment, a country-looking lady, whom he afterwards found to be a resident at Rye, in Sussex, touched his arm and said,—

"'I beg your pardon, sir, but pray who are those gentlemen in red now coming in?'

"'Those, Ma'am,' returned Theodore, 'are the Barons of England; in these cases the junior Peers always come first.'

"'Thank you, Sir, much obliged to you. Louisa, my dear! (turning to a girl about fourteen) tell Jane (about ten), those are the Barons of England, and the Juniors, (that's the youngest, you know) always goes first. Tell her to be sure and remember that, when we get home.'

"'Dear me, Ma!' said Louisa, 'can that gentleman be one of the *youngest?* I am sure he looks very old.'

"'Human nature,' added Hook, 'could not stand this; any one, though with no more mischief in him than a dove, must have been excited to a hoax.'

"'And pray, Sir,' continued the lady, 'what gentlemen are these?' pointing to the Bishops who came next in order, in the dress which they wear on state occasions, viz., the rochet and lawn sleeves over their doctors' robes.

"'Gentlemen, Madam!' said Hook, 'these are not gentlemen; these are ladies, elderly ladies—the Dowager Peeresses in their own right.'

"The fair inquirer fixed a penetrating glance upon his countenance, saying, as plainly as an eye can say, 'Are you quizzing me or no?' Not a muscle moved; till at last, tolerably well satisfied with her scrutiny, she turned round and whispered,—

"'Louisa, dear, the gentleman *says* that these are elderly ladies and Dowager Peeresses in their own right. Tell Jane not to forget that.'

"All went on smoothly, till the Speaker of the House of Commons attracted her attention by the rich embroidery of his robes.

"'Pray, Sir,' said she, 'and who is that fine-looking person opposite?'

"'That, Madam,' was the answer, 'is Cardinal Wolsey!'

"'No, Sir!' cried the lady, drawing herself up, and casting at her informant a look of angry disdain, 'we knows a little better than that; Cardinal Wolsey has been dead many a good year!'

"'No such thing, my dear Madam, I assure you,' replied Hook, with a gravity that must have been almost preternatural, 'it has been, I know, so reported in the country, but without the least foundation in fact; those rascally newspapers will say any thing.'

"The good old gentlewoman appeared thunderstruck, opened her eyes to their full extent, and gasped like a dying carp; *vox faucibus hæsit;* seizing a daughter with each hand, she hurried without a word from the spot."

HIRING A COOK.

FROM "THE MAN OF MANY FRIENDS." BY THEODORE HOOK.

In the morning, the old gentleman received the visits of sundry tradesmen, to whom he had given orders for different articles of dress; and Wilson, who was fully installed in his high office, presented for his approbation, Monsieur Rissolle, "without exception, the best cook in the United Kingdom."

The particular profession of this person, the Colonel, who understood very little French, was for some time puzzled to find out; he heard a vocabulary of dishes enumerated with grace and fluency, he saw a remarkably gentlemanly-looking man, his well-tied neckcloth, his well-trimmed whiskers, his white kid gloves, his glossy hat, his massive chain encircling his neck, and protecting a repeating Breguet, all pronouncing the man of ton; and when he came really to comprehend that the sweet-scented, ring-fingered gentleman before him, was willing to dress a dinner on trial, for the purpose of displaying his skill, he was thunderstruck.

"Do I mistake?" said the Colonel: "I really beg pardon—it is fifty-eight years since I learned French—am I speaking to—a—(and he hardly dared to pronounce the word)—cook?"

"Oui, Monsieur," said M. Rissolle; "I believe I have de first reputation in the profession; I live four years wiz de Marqui de Chester, and je me flatte dat, if I had not turn him off last months, I should have superintend his cuisine at dis moment."

"Oh, you have discharged the Marquis, sir?" said the Colonel.

"Yes, mon Colonel, I discharge him; because he cast affront upon me, insupportable to an artist of sentiment."

"Artist!" *mentally ejaculated* the Colonel.

"Mon Colonel, de Marqui had de mauvais goût one day, when he had large partie to dine, to put salt into his soup, before all his compagnie."

"Indeed," said Arden; "and, may I ask, is that considered a crime, sir, in your code?"

"I don't know Code," said the man, "Morue?—dat is salt enough without."

"I don't mean *that*, sir," said the Colonel; "I ask, is it a crime for a gentleman to put salt into his soup?"

"Not a crime, mon Colonel," said Rissolle, "but it would be de ruin of me, as cook, should it be known to the world,—so I told his Lordship I must leave him; that de butler had said, dat he saw his Lordship put de salt into de soup, which was to proclaim to the universe dat I did not know de propre quantite of salt required to season my soup."

"And you left his Lordship for *that?*" inquired the astonished country gentleman.

"Oui, sir, his Lordship gave me excellent character; I go afterward to live wid my Lord Trefoil, very good, respectable man, my Lord, of good family, and very honest man, I believe—but de king, one day, made him his governeur in Ireland, and I found I could not live in dat devil Dublin."

"No!"

"No, mon Colonel—it is fine city?" said Rissolle—"good place—but dere is no Italian Opera."

"How shocking!" said Arden, "and you left his Excellency on *that* occount?"

"Oui, mon Colonel."

"Why, his Excellency managed to live there without an Italian Opera," said Arden.

"Yes, mon Colonel, c'est vrai—but I presume he did not know dere was none when he took the place—I have de character from my lord, to state why I leave him."

Saying which, he produced a written character from Lord Trefoil, who, being a joker, as well as a minister, had actually stated the fact related by the unconscious turnspit, as the reason for their separation.

"And pray, sir," said the Colonel, "what wages do you expect?"

"Wajes! Je n'entend pas, mon Colonel," an-answered Rissolle; "do you mean de stipend—de salarie?"

"As you please," said Arden.

"My Lor Trefoil," said Rissolle, "give to me seven hundred pounds a-year, my wine, and horse and tilbury, with small tigre for him."

"Small what, sir?" exclaimed the astonished Colonel.

"Tigre," said Rissolle, "little man-boy, to hold de horse."

"Ah!" said Arden, "seven hundred pounds a-year, and a tiger!"

"Exclusive of de pâtisserrie, mon Colonel, I never touch dat departement, but I have de honor to recommend Jenkin, my sister's husband, for the *pâtisserrie*, at five hundred pound, and his wine. Oh Jenkin is dog ship at dat, mon Colonel."

"Oh! exclusive of pastry," said the Colonel, emphatically.

"Oui, mon Colonel," said Rissolle.

"Which is to be contrived for five hundred pounds per annum, additional. Why, sir, the rector of my parish, a clergyman, and a gentleman, with an amiable wife and seven children, has but half the sum to live upon."

"Dat is hard," said Rissolle, shrugging up his shoulders.

"Hard—it *is* hard, sir," said Arden; "and yet you will hear the men who pay their cooks seven hundred a-year for dressing dinners, get up in their places in Parliament, declaim against the exorbitant wealth of the Church of England, and tell the people that our clergy are over-paid."

"Poor clergie! mon Colonel," said the man, "I pity your clergie; but den, you don't remember de science and experience dat it require to make an omelette soufflé."

"The devil take your omelette, sir," said Arden; "do you mean seriously and gravely to ask me seven hundred pounds a-year for your services?"

"Oui, vraiment, mon Colonel," said Rissolle, at the same moment gracefully taking snuff from a superb gold box.

"Why then, d——n it, sir, I can't stand this any longer," cried the irritated novice in the fashionable world; "seven hundred pounds! make it guineas, sir, and I'll be *your* cook for the rest of my life."

The noise of this annunciation, the sudden leap taken by Monsieur Rissolle, to avoid something more serious than words, which he anticipated from the irate Colonel, brought Wilson into the room, who, equally terrified with his Gallic friend at the symptoms of violent anger which his master's countenance displayed, stood wondering at the animation of the scene; when Arden, whose rage at the *nonchalance* of Rissolle, at first impeded his speech, uttered with an emphasis not to be misunderstood—

"Good morning—sir—seven hundred——"

What the rest of this address might have been it is impossible to say, for before it was concluded Rissolle had left the apartment, and Wilson closed the door.

A CHAPTER ON PUNS.

BY THEODORE HOOK.

There is one class of people who, with a depravity of appetite not excelled by that of the celebrated Anna Maria Schurman, who rejoiced in eating spiders, thirst after puns. If you fall in with these, you have no resource but to indulge them to their hearts' content; but, in order to rescue yourself from the imputation of believing punning to be wit, quote the definition of Swift, and be like him, as inveterate a punster as you possibly can, immediately after resting every thing, and hazarding all, upon the principle, that the worse the pun the better.

In order to be prepared for this sort of *punic* war, (for the disorder is provocative and epidemic,) the moment any one gentleman or lady has, as they say in Scotland, "let a pun," every body else in the room who can, or cannot do the same, sets to work to endeavor to emulate the example. From that period, all rational conversation is at an end, and a jargon of nonsense succeeds, which lasts till the announcement of coffee, or supper, or the carriages, puts a happy termination to the riot.

Addison says, "one may say of a pun, as the countryman described his nightingale, that it is *vox et præterea nihil*, a sound, and nothing but a sound;" and, in another place he tells us that "the greatest authors in their most serious works make frequent use of puns; the sermons of Bishop Andrews, and the tragedies of Shakspere are full of them; if a sinner was punned into repentance as in the latter, nothing is more usual than to see a hero weeping and grumbling for a dozen lines together;" but he also says, "it is indeed impossible to kill a weed which the soil has a natural disposition to produce. The seeds of punning are in the minds of all men, and though they may be subdued by reason, reflection, and good sense, they will be very apt to shoot up in the greatest genius that is not broken and cultivated by the rules of art."

Here is something like a justification of the enormity; and, as the pupil is to mix in all societies, he may as well be prepared.

Puns may be divided into different classes; they may be made in different ways, introduced by passing circumstances, or by references to by-gone events; they may be thrown in *anecdotically*, or conundrumwise. It is to be observed that feeling, or pity, or commiseration, or grief, are not to stand in the way of a pun—that personal defects are to be made available, and that sense, so as the sound answers, has nothing to do with the business.

If a man is pathetically describing the funeral of his mother or sister, or wife, it is quite allowable to call it a "black-*burying* party," or to talk of a "fit of *coffin*;" a weeping relative struggling to conceal his grief may be likened to a commander of "*private tears*;" throw in a joke about the phrase of "funerals *performed*," and a re-*hearsal;* and wind up with the anagram *real-fun*, funeral.

I give this instance first, in order to explain that nothing, however solemn the subject, is to stand in the way of a pun.

It is allowable, when you have run a subject dry in English, to hitch in a bit of any other language which may sound to your liking. For instance, on a fishing party. You say fishing is out of your *line;* yet, if you did not keep *a float*, you would deserve a *rod;* and if anybody affects to find fault with your joke, exclaim "Oh, vous *bête!*" There you have *line*, *rod*, *float*, and *bait* ready to your hand. Call two noodles from the city in a punt, endeavoring to catch small fry, "*East Angles;*" or, if you please, observe that "the *punters* are losing the fish," "catching nothing but a cold," or that "the fish are too deep for them." Call the Thames a "*tidy*" river; but say you prefer the *Isis* in hot weather.

Personal deformities or constitutional calamities are always to be laid hold of. If any body tells you that a dear friend has lost his sight, observe that it will make him more hospitable than ever, since now he would be glad *to see any body.* If a clergyman breaks his leg, remark that he is no longer a clergyman, but a *lame man.* If a poet is seized with apoplexy, affect to disbelieve it, although you know it to be true, in order to say—

Poeta nascitur non *fit;*

and then, to carry the joke one step further, add, "that it is not a *fit* subject for a jest." A man falling into a tan-pit you may call "sinking in the *sublime;*" a climbing boy suffocated in a chimney meets with a *sootable* death; and a pretty girl having caught the small-pox is to be much *pitted.* On the subject of the ear and its defects, talk first of something in which *a cow sticks*, and end by telling the story of the man who, having taken great pains to explain something to his companion, at last got into a rage at his apparent stupidity, and exclaimed, "Why, my dear Sir, don't you comprehend? the thing is as plain as A, B, C." "I dare say it is," said the other; "but I am D, E, F."

It may be as well to give the beginner something of a notion of the use he may make of the most ordinary words, for the purposes of quibbleism. For instance, in the way of observation:—The loss of a hat is always *felt*;—if you don't like sugar, you may *lump* it;—a glazier is a *panes*-taking man; —candles are burnt because *wick-ed* things always come to *light*;—a lady who takes you home from a party is kind in her *carriage*, and you say "nunc est *ridendum*" when you step into it; if it happen to be a chariot, she is a *charitable* person:—birds'-nests and King-killing are synonymous, because they are *high trees on*; a Bill for building a bridge should be sanctioned by the Court of *Arches* as well as the House of *Piers*;—when a man is dull, he goes to the sea-side to *Brighton*;—a Cockney lover, when sentimental, should live in *Heigh Ho-burn*;—the greatest fibber is the man most to *re-lie* upon;—a dean expecting a bishopric looks *for lawn*; a *sui*cide kills pigs, and not himself;—a butcher is a gross man, but a fig-seller is a *grocer*;—Joshua never had a father or mother, because he was the sun of *Nun*;—your grandmother and great-grandmother were your *aunt's sisters*;—a leg of mutton is better than Heaven, because nothing is better than Heaven, and a leg of mutton is better than nothing.

Races are matters of *course*. An ass never can be a horse, although he may be a *mayor*;—the Venerable Bede was the mother of Pearl;—a baker makes bread when he *kneads* it; a doctor cannot be a doctor all at once, because he comes to it by *degrees*;—a man hanged at Newgate has taken a *drop* too much;—the *bridle* day is that on which a man leads a woman to the *halter*; never mind the aspirate; punning's all fair, as the archbishop said in the dream.

Puns interrogatory are at times serviceable. You meet a man carrying a hare: ask him if it is his own *hare*, or a wig?—there you stump him. Why is Parliament street like a compendium? Because it goes to *a bridge*. Why is a man murdering his mother in a garret a worthy person? Because he is above committing a crime. Instances of this kind are innumerable; and if you want to render your question particularly pointed, you are, after asking it once or twice, to say "D'ye give it up?"—then favor your friends with the solution.

Puns scientific are effective whenever a scientific man or men are in company, because, in the first place, they invariably hate puns, especially those which are capable of being twisted into jokes which have no possible relation to the science of which the words to be joked upon are terms; and because, in the next place, dear, laughing girls, who are wise enough not to be sages, will love you for disturbing the self-satisfaction of the philosophers, and raising a laugh or titter at their expense.

Where there are three or four geologists of the party, if they talk of their scientific tours made to collect specimens, call the old ones "ninny-hammers," and the young ones "chips of the old block;" and then inform them that claret is the best specimen of *quartz* in the world. If you fall in with a botanist who is holding forth, talk of the quarrels of flowers as a sequel to the loves of the plants, and say they decide their differences with *pistols*. In short, sacrifice every thing to the pursuit of punning, and, in the course of time, you will acquire such a reputation for waggery, that the whole company will burst into an immoderate fit of laughing if you only ask the servants for bread, or say "No" to the offer of a cutlet.

AN HONEST PRACTICAL JOKE.

FROM "ODD PEOPLE." BY THEODORE HOOK.

SHORTLY after the Peace of 1748, and shortly before his own death, the Duke of Montague had noticed a man, whose air and dress were military—for in those days, most wisely, did men wear the costume of the profession to which they belonged—the latter having evidently suffered either during the late campaign, or the still later period of tranquillity; walking in the Mall of St. James's Park, apparently caring for nobody; in fact, seeing nobody; every body, however, seeing *him*, and as he appeared remarkably depressed in spirits, generously resolved rather to laugh at him than otherwise.

Well—as the Duke of Montague was full of fun—and as nobody, at least of his day, ever equalled him in practical trickeries; he resolved, having seen this meagre-faced, melancholy animal crawling about, to make him a subject for one of his jokes. As the big boy said of the little one at the boarding-school, "hit him again, Bill, he han't got no friends!"—so the Duke said to himself, "now all my wig-singeing, and nose-blacking exploits, will be completely outdone by the *rig* (that was the favorite word in the year 1739) I shall run upon this unhappy devil with the tarnished lace."

When a joker wants to joke practically, it adds very much to the point of the jest to select as a victim somebody upon whom the joke will have the most powerful possible effect, and, therefore, the Duke, who was resolved upon his jest, took care to set his emissaries at work, in order to ascertain how he could hit him hardest, and cure him of the Don Quixote-like march, which he thought proper to make up and down the park.

His grace's jackal—and where is there a human lion without one—wriggled and twisted himself about, grinned, showed his teeth, made himself amiable, and at last, got an opportunity of boring himself out a sort of talking acquaintance with the gaunt hero of the Mall. It turned out that the unhappy man had appropriated the small fortune he had secured with his wife to the purchase of a commission in the army, and had behaved, as they say, "uncommon well" upon several occasions. But what was *he* among so many? And after all his unnoticed—and probably unnoticeable—exertions in destroying his fellow-creatures for the good of society, there came a peace—and the unfortunate gentleman with the grizzly wig, tarnished lace, and somewhat thin-kneed inexpressibles, was considerably the worse for the same; inasmuch as besides the infliction of half-pay, he had, out of his pittance, to support, or endeavor to support, a wife and two fine children, all living and thriving as well as they could at Chesterfield, in Derbyshire—the spire of the church of which town, by some malconformation of the lead wherewith it is covered, would make any man, tee-totaller, or not, who looked at it, think that he was not quite right in his vision.

All these imbranglements conduced very much to the pleasure which the Duke anticipated in playing his trick upon his new victim—a trick which, be it observed, for the exceedingly high military offices he held, the Duke was, perhaps, the man best calculated in the world to execute. The Duke had taken his measures to ascertain all the facts connected with the object of his joke, whose cognomen in the Mall was "Grizzlewig," and, being too good a soldier to think of springing a mine before the train was securely laid, it was not for some days after he had made up his mind to the frolic, that he sent a confidential member of his household to invite old Grizzlewig to dinner; but the mere sending the invitation was nothing—the mad-brained Duke could not obtain all the pleasure he desired from the surprise, which Grizzlewig must inevitably exhibit at the message, unless he himself witnessed the effect; and therefore, this Master-general of the Ordnance, this Knight of the Garter, and Grand Master of the Order of the Bath, who moreover was Master of the Great Wardrobe, and *a Member of the College of Physicians*, took the trouble to watch his envoy, in order to behold the result of his mission.

Poor Grizzlewig was seated, as was his wont after his walk, on one of the now exploded and comfortless seats in the Mall, thinking more of being *in* the King's Bench than *upon* it, when the messenger of the Duke approached him. He addressed him, but was not noticed—he was prepared for insult, and the word Grizzlewig was all he expected to hear; but, upon a gentle repetition of an appeal from his confidential man, the Duke, who was at a convenient distance, saw Grizzlewig start as from a slumber, the moment he understood the nature of the invitation.

The poor gentleman looked astonished—stared about—shook his head as if to rouse himself from a nap, in which he had been favored with too sweet a dream. But, when awakened to a consciousness of the real state of affairs, his spirits sunk as much as on the first blush of the thing they had risen. "The Duke of Montague," thought he, "is a joker—I am selected to be his victim." Still, for a park-fed gentleman on half-pay, the opportunity of dining with a nobleman, so highly connected and with such power in the army, was not to be lost. "Laughed at or not laughed at," said poor Grizzlewig, "I must go;" and although the Duke had, *à la distance*, seen the effect the invitation produced, all that he heard from his messenger was, 'that the gentleman would be too proud and too happy to dine with his grace the next day, as invited.

Then came a difficulty with our poor friend as to his dress: in these times, that point is by no means distressing. The servants who wait upon a company, nowadays, are generally better dressed than the company themselves; and if rank and talent are to give the tone, the higher one looks the worse it is: we see our greatest men in rank wearing clothes, which their, "own men" would not condescend to, and talent in the most exalted degree, wrapped in rags, which till now have been appropriated to the scarecrows, whose "danglings" out of doors at night, have been more serviceable to agriculture, than those of their present wearers appear to have been to *husbandry*, within.

In those days, however, Monmouth-street, now lost to society and history, afforded the temporary means of shining in temporary splendor on the shortest notice. Whether the invited of the Duke availed himself of the opportunity of thus burnishing up for the occasion, we know not; or whether he made a glorious effort at the renovation of his well-known wig,

> Which smart when fate was kind,
> Toupeed before and bagg'd behind,
> Now, spoil'd of all its jaunty pride,
> Hangs loose and lank on every side,

history does not record; but what we do know is, that at about three o'clock—late hours for those days—our hero arrived at the Duke of Montague's, and was ushered into his grace's presence, till which moment, I believe, he never was fully satisfied of the reality of the invitation.

Nothing could equal the warmth and amenity of the Duke's reception; in short, it went beyond the ordinary courtesy and graciousness of a great man to a small one; but in a very few minutes, to poor Grizzlewig's astonishment, the Duke, leaving a much more aristocratic visitor, took him aside, and with an *empressement* which was extremely staggering, said,

"You will, I am sure, excuse me; but—I know it is rather an impertinent question—are you—forgive me—are you conscious of having created a sensation in the heart of any lady who has seen you occasionally, and—"

"Sir?" said the visitor.

"Come, come, come," said the Duke, "don't deny it. No man is blind enough, or dull enough, not to know when and where he has planted his blow; you *must* remember."

"Upon my word, sir," replied the guest, who began to think that his suspicions as to having been invited only to be laughed at were correct, "I know of no such thing!"

"Well," said the Duke, "then *I* must let you into the secret. There *is* a lady—a married woman—I like to be frank—and with a family; but she *has*—you'll say, as I might perhaps, there is no accounting for tastes—she has set her heart upon meeting you. And I will at once tell you what may, perhaps, diminish your surprise at having received an invitation from a stranger—your accepting which, gives me the greatest pleasure—that it was to gratify *her* wish, I sent to beg of you to come to me to-day."

"Sir," said the overwhelmed half-pay officer, "I am confident that your grace would do nothing either to wound my feelings, or degrade me in my own estimation. I, sir, have a wife and family, dependent on me, to whom I am devotedly attached; the thoughts which your grace's observations would naturally inspire, never enter my mind; I have but one hope, one wish, in the world, and that is centred in my family. I have—"

"Ay, ay," interrupted the Duke, "I admire your feelings. I respect your affection for your family; but this introduction, this acquaintance, need not at all interfere with those, now we are in London."

"Yes, sir," said the half-pay captain, "I am—in hopes of getting employed—else—"

"Ah," said the Duke, "I never talk of business here; as for *that*, we must take some other time to discuss it. I merely speak of this *affaire de cœur*, and you must let me have *my* way; if the lady is exceedingly disagreeable, turn her off and break her heart; but I do assure you, upon my honor, that her attachment to you is something so romantic, that I could not resist the opportunity of bringing you together."

"Sir," said the officer, "I—really—but—"

"I tell you nothing but truth," said the Duke, "wait and see how much it will be for your advantage."

Dinner was announced: no lady appeared, but when the *battants* were thrown open, and the Duke, and our poor friend Grizzlewig, of the park, entered the dining-room, judge the half-pay officer's surprise, when he beheld his own wife and his two darling children.

in its effect, by his placing the children one on either side of him, and treating them with every kindness and attention.

"Come," said his grace, "let us drink wine together; let us be happy; take no thought of yesterday, my good sir, nor of to-morrow; suffice it to say, that here we are met, and may meet again."

All these attempts to compose and assure his grace's visitors were unavailing, except as far as the younger ones were concerned, who appeared exceedingly well satisfied to take "the goods the gods provide;" and, without comprehending the extent

"There," said his grace, "that is the lady who has the extraordinary prepossession in your favor, and two younger ones, not much behind her in affection."

It is impossible to describe the feelings of the little party.

"Come," said the Duke, "sit down, sit down, and let us dine; you shall talk afterwards, and explain all this to each other, and whatever may be wanting in the narrative, I hope to be able to furnish."

The officer's wife, although prepared for what was to happen, and therefore not so completely taken aback as her husband, could scarcely support herself, while the two children, unfettered and unrestrained by the laws of etiquette, ran to their astonished father, and clung round him, in all the warmth of youthful affection.

The course of the Duke's proceeding had been, as soon as he had ascertained the merits and claims of his guest, to trace out the residence of his lady and the children, and to send a trusty person down to her, for the purpose of bringing them up to town; at the same time preventing the possibility of her communicating the history to her husband.

To describe the astonishment, the anxiety, the agitation, of poor dear Grizzlewig, when he found himself all at once thus domesticated, as it were, in the house of one of the magnates of the land, would be impossible. The Duke had invited but two friends to witness the scene. which was heightened

of the kindness with which they found themselves treated, naturally followed the advice which the noble lord had offered to their parents.

While dinner was in progress, the Duke got on with his guests tolerably well; but he anticipated the awkwardness which must ensue after the servants had left the room, and the party was left as it were to itself, although the presence of the two guests, gentlemen who were in the habit of partaking of his grace's hospitality, was purposely secured, in order to prevent the expression of surprise and gratitude of the strangers, which, however much excited and created by what had already passed, were destined to receive a new stimulus by a sequel to the frolic extant, as far as it had already gone.

Dinner was scarcely ended, and nothing like the possibility of inquiry or explanation had been permitted to occur, when the Duke's attorney—his *homme d'affaires*, the defender of his rights, and the champion of his wrongs—was announced: a nice, good, smug-looking "gent," who was welcomed by the Duke, and placed next to the elder daughter of poor dear Grizzlewig, who was, to all appearance, still in a state, not exactly of somnambulism, for he seemed riveted to his seat by astonishment, but of somnolency; feeling and thinking, even up to the last moment, that all the passing events were the mere fancies of a vision; being himself constantly hindered from saying any thing upon the subject, by the admirable tact of the Duke, who kept his retainers always ready to start some new topic of conversation, so as to baffle any effort of the astonished half-pay officer to lead to the point by which his whole mind was occupied.

The joke, however, as we have just hinted, was not at its height; for after some preliminary observations from the noble host, his grace, addressing himself to the attorney, inquired whether he had "brought it with him;" an inquiry which was very respectfully answered in the affirmative.

"Then," said the Duke, "we had better send for pen and ink, and proceed to business without delay."

Whereupon, the half-pay officer gave his wife a family look, as much as to say, that he thought they ought to retire; but the diffidence of the lady prevented her taking any decisive step, and she preferred risking the passive impropriety of staying where she was, to the active measure of quitting the room, ignorant as she was of the ways of the house, not only in the moral, but in the literal and mechanical sense of the words, and wholly at a loss whither she was to go if she ventured to move from where she was.

The Duke was too much a man of the world not to see how extremely uncomfortable his guests were becoming, and how well his frolic was "progressing"—it pleased him mightily, and his pleasure was considerably heightened, when the attorney, going close to his chair, began in a low voice, reciting some part of the bond or deed, or whatever it was, which his noble client was about to execute; during which ceremony, his grace kept his eyes so constantly fixed upon his embarrassed visitors, as to make them exactly as he hoped and wished, perfectly miserable.

"You had better read it out," said the Duke; "it is by no means a mark of good-breeding to whisper before one's visitors—people always take things to themselves; and as they *are* here—"

"My Lord Duke," said the officer, in a perfect agony of confusion, "pray permit us to quit the room—I am quite conscious of the intrusion, but really—I—my love—let us retire," added he to his wife.

"Stay where you are, my good sir," said the Duke; "you have often heard of my frolics—I like a joke, and I mean to enjoy one to-day, and at your expense."

The unfortunate gentleman began to think that the Duke was a most barbarous and unprincipled person, who could take such pains as he evidently had done, to put him and his family in a most unpleasant position. His wife, however, seemed better contented with the course affairs were taking, and made no effort to obey her lord and master's mandate for retreat.

"Read, sir, read," said the Duke to the attorney, who accordingly began in an audible voice, and with good emphasis, to recite the contents and conditions of the deed which he held in his hand, and which, in its recital, caused the most extraordinary emotions on the part of the half-pay officer and his wife that can be imagined, until, by the time it was concluded, they were both drowned in tears. The husband, supporting his wife's head upon his palpitating breast, and the two children clinging round them, crying with all their hearts and souls without knowing why, except that their fond parents had set them the example.

By the deed, which they had just heard with such surprise and emotion, the Duke settled upon the worthy distressed persons before him, an annuity which afforded them a competency; and so secured, as regarded survivorship, that the two children who were yet unconscious of their change of fortune, must eventually reap the benefit thus munificently bestowed on their father and mother.

The scene which followed is one which cannot be described, and which was so embarrassing to the noble donor, that he broke it up by announcing, himself, that coffee was ready; and in return for the acknowledgments and fervent expressions of gratitude on the part of the recipients, merely entreated them to say nothing about it; declaring upon his honor, that if he could have found a more agreeable or satisfactory way of employing either his time or his money, he should not have played them such a trick.

We presume there scarcely exists a human being so squeamish or fastidious as to find fault with a practical joke, qualified and characterized as this was. Every man has a right to do good after his own fancy; and if he can so contrive as to make his benevolence to others produce amusement to himself, nobody surely ought to object to the *modus operandi.*

ADVENTURE WITH THEODORE HOOK.

BY LORD WILLIAM LENOX.

Alas poor Yorick! I knew him, Horatio; a fellow of infinite jest, of most excellent fancy.—Hamlet.

The recurrence to my mind of the tender musings of the melancholy prince, followed by the more solemn reflection that my three agreeable companions in the well-remembered adventure I am about to relate are all now past that bourne which Hamlet speaks of, is almost sufficient to set me moralizing at the very opening of my story. That, however, must not be: for gravity and dulness would convey but a poor tribute to the memory of the jovial trio whose company I enjoyed on the occasion referred to.

As no cloud was on our spirits, so no cloud was on the morning; it was a lovely one in the spring of 183–. We met, by appointment, to proceed to Epsom for the week; the remainder of the "we" consisting of poor Theodore Hook, the late Stephen Price, and another choice spirit, also departed,—one whose talents and kindness of heart, evinced both in public and private life, entitle him to more than the brief, but honoring tribute, which I must here content myself with paying to his character.

The worthy American, wrapped in a huge fur coat, was comfortably ensconced in the corner of a small britschka, grumbling, however, not a little at the English climate,—"One day, *sir*, hot enough to roast an ox; following morning at freezing point, *sir*."

"Come along," said the friend last alluded to; "come along, King Stephen, or we shall be late—hate to be late!" Suiting the action to the word, he took the remaining place in the ex-manager's britschka.

"Hook and I, then, will go together," I observed, as my buggy drove up to the door.

"Of course; *Hook* and *eye* always go together," was the response of my companion, as he got into into the vehicle.

Thus commenced the sport; and off we went. To repeat all that was said during our drive would form a large edition of facetiæ; the celebrated abridgment of the statutes, in fifty volumes folio, would be nothing to it; it was a regular running fire. Pun, anecdote, song, improviso; jests, a century old, disinterred, as good as new; venerable Joe Millers, revived and decked out in modern fashionable attire; jokes, manufactured on the spot, of every conceivable variety and pattern, some bad enough to take rank with the very best. So far from recounting them, I despair of conveying an idea of their profusion. The plainest of pedestrians, or the commonest name over a shop door, was sufficient to start him off.

"Ah!" said my companion, "'Hawes, Surgeon;' that reminds me of two lines I made on a sawbone of that name during the severe winter of 1814:—

> Perpetual freezings and perpetual thaws,
> Though bad enough for *hips*, are good for *Hawes*.

As we reached Vauxhall bridge, "I wonder if this bridge pays?" I remarked. "Go over it, and you'll be *tolled*," replied the ever-ready punster.

"So," said he, addressing the gatekeeper, who was hoarse, "You haven't recovered your voice yet?" "No, sir," was the answer, "I've caught a fresh cold." "But why did you catch a *fresh* one?" asked Hook; "why didn't you have it *cured?*"

On we went, from subject to subject, and pun to pun. To show that the unmisgiving perpetrator of pleasantries innumerable never flinched or threw a chance away, the sign of the "Three Ravens," at Sutton, as we passed it, suggested the reflection—"That fellow must be *raven* mad!"

Immediately after, we discerned a party of laborers employed in sinking a well. "What are you about?" inquired Hook. "Boring for water," replied a gaping clod. "Water's a bore at any time," rejoined Hook; "besides, you're quite wrong—remember the proverb, 'Let *well* alone.'"

These must serve to convey a passing notion of the spirit of my companion's commentary on every object we encountered; and this spirit carried us gaily into the town of Epsom, which we found crowded to excess. Streams of many-colored life were everywhere mingling and separating. High life and low life; the thorough-bred team, the barouche and four, the light dennet, the heavy bus, the gaudy van, the hack cab, and the tilted cart. But to describe this scene would be to go over old ground, as it has been pictured a thousand times; and the reader, perhaps, will prefer returning with our party to the house we had engaged for the week.

On arriving at the gate, we found seated on a rustic bench a certain individual, having a cigar in his mouth, and by his side a glass of water, with (for this should not be altogether omitted) just a sufficient quantity of Glenlivet in it to destroy, as he said, the animalculæ it might contain. His countenance brightened at our approach.

"Ha! Dean!" said Theodore.

"Ha! Hookems!" responded the other; "have you brought the ginnums, and the mackerelums?"

"I have, most reverend. But where were you last Sunday? I missed you at your accustomed haunt-lunch after chapel."

"Lame, lame—could not get there."

"As usual," said Hook. "Why's the Dean like England? D'ye give it up?—eh!—Because *he* expects every man to do *his* duty."

Dinner was shortly after announced. The cloth was removed, amidst a rapid shower of smart, caustic, and witty sayings, droll stories, retort, and repartee; the wine circulated freely, the tide of good humor "knew no retiring ebb." Plays and politics, wine and women, debts and duels, were discussed with an absence of all restraint; and then commenced a call for a song. This was pretty soon responded to by the accomplished Theodore, whose talent in this respect is no secret to the world, although the world unfortunately possesses so little evidence of it beyond the assertions of the more fortunate few who enjoyed his intimacy, and witnessed the astonishing ease with which he composed while he sung. In this instance, he took for the subject of his song, the worthy manager of New York and Drury Lane celebrity; and after preparing us by ringing the changes on his name, he broke into a measure, and gave us the following, which, however, I cannot pretend to say is strictly *verbatim et literatim*:—

THEODORE HOOK'S SONG.

Come, fill your glasses up, while I sing a song of *prices*,
And show men's market-value at the date of last advices;
For since 'tis pretty clear, you know, that ev'ry man has *his* price,
'Tis well to make inquiries before the terms are *riz*, Price.

Some shabby rogues there are, that are knock'd down at a low price,
Some blockheads so superlative, they can't be sold at no price;
Some, free of soul in youth, sell in middle life at half price,
And some go when they're old—why the devil don't you laugh, Price?

The world is but an Auction;—if to day we fetch a shy price,
To-morrow turns the lot about, and shows us worth a high price;
You want to know what Learning's worth—you ask me what is Wit's price?
I answer, "Push the claret here, whatever may be *its* price!"

The shortest actors now contrive to get a rather long price,
And singers too, although sometimes they're hardly worth a song, Price;
With fiddlers, dancers, fresh from France, well liking a John Bull price,
Though some, when they get nothing, may be said to fetch their full price.

Where'er you sell, whate'er you sell, when selling seek a higher price;
But times are changed, I need not say, when you become the buyer, Price;
For then this truth should in your mind be uppermost and clear, Price,
There are some things and persons that at nothing would be dear, Price.

Don't buy a politician, don't have him at a loan, Price;
Nor lawyers, when they tell you, you may take them at your own price;
Nor doctors, who, if fashionable, always fetch an even price;
And clear of these, the "de'il himsel" shall never fetch a Stephen Price.

Your sneaking, sour, insidious knaves—I hope you wont find many, Price,—
Your Cantwells on the stage of life, don't buy 'em in at any price;
Go, sell your brains, if brains you have, and sell 'em at a fair price,
But *give* your hearts away, my boys—*don't sell 'em* at whate'er price.

And be men's prices what they may, I now shall just make bold, Price,
To sing it in your presence,—there is nothing like the Old Price;
As each man has his own, since the days of Madame Eve, Price,
Why we have *ours*—and here he is!—Your health, my jolly STEPH. PRICE!

"Bravo, *sir!*" exclaimed the delighted hero of the song, at its conclusion. *Sir*, will you take forty pounds a-night, *sir*, to appear at Drury Lane in your own very particular and devilishly admired piece of 'Killing no Murder?'"

"Forty pounds a-night!" cried Hook;—"no, I wouldn't take *half* the money to commit such a barbarity; nay, *ten* pounds a-night shouldn't tempt me. Killing may *be* no murder, when the regular actors combine to destroy an author's production; but for the dramatist to appear himself in his own farce, to assist at the assassination of his own child—to slaughter his tender offspring in public with malice aforethought—this is the worst of killing—

Murder most foul, as in the best it is,
But this most foul, strange and unnatural.

"What d'ye say, *sir?*"

"Nothing; but I make up for it by singing." And here, with barely the pause of a minute, followed another song on the then forthcoming Derby, ending with a line which not even the best sporting prophet of our day could have improved upon either in neatness of point or truth of prediction; for, in allusion to the winner in the approaching race, (Mr. Forth being the owner of the horse,) the singer felicitously prophesied,

The *Forth* shall be first!

About ten o'clock at night, a ramble through the town was proposed, and Hook, Price, and myself strolled towards the "Spread Eagle," to hear the state of the odds on the approaching Derby. Just as we reached the door of that most excellent hostellerie, I was accosted by a man dressed in a gaudy livery, light green coat, belcher handkerchief, a huge gold hatband, white corduroy "shorts," and glazed top-boots, who, placing in my hands a card, hoped that he should have the honor of conducting me to his master's house. By the aid of a large red lamp at a surgeon's door, looking like a bull's eye bloodshot, I read the card; it ran as per margin.

CORINTHIAN CLUB.
FOSTER'S COTTAGE,
Woodcot Green.
FRENCH HAZARD.
BANK 5000!!!

"Let's have some fun!" exclaimed Hook, on reading this; "Price and I will be *drunk* on the premises. Come along, Stephen!" And in a regular gin-broken voice, he hiccupped out the words of Iago's song:—

King *Stephen* was a worthy peer,
His breeches cost him but a crown;
He held them sixpence all too dear,
With that he called the tailor—loun.

The "touter" of the real Pandemonium now approached, and again importuned us; seeing the reeling state of my companions, he suggested a glass of iced soda, which he declared was always ready with the supper at the cottage.

"Hurrah for the cottage!" said Hook; "but what shall I do with my hundred-pound note?—I must deposit that at home."

"Never mind that, *sir*," responded the manager; "I'll insure you against losing *that* hundred." And well he might, seeing that the hundred pound note was a "forgery of the brain"—a draft on the bank of fiction, merely circulated to raise us in the estimation of the members of the Corinthian Club.

Reeling, shouting, singing, we approached Woodcot Green, and passing a small public house, our guide pointed out the hall of Eblis. "Excuse me, gentleman, one moment," he said; and rushing into the bar of the "Running Horse," returned almost instantaneously with a quart bottle peeping out of his coat pocket. "Brandy, *sir*," said Price (*aside*); "I smell it, sir." "All righ' !" whispered Hook.

The room we entered was dirty and ill-lighted; the dingy walls and barred windows formed a *locale* not ill-associated with the crime and wretchedness it harbored. The party assembled consisted of four individuals, two croupiers and two "bonnets," which, for the benefit of the uninitiated, I beg to mention are confederates dressed as players, to assist in pigeoning the public. In the centre of the room hung a gaudy lamp, which threw its oily rays on a large oblong table covered with green baize, on which was painted various figures and directions for those who "stood the hazard of the die;" small bowls of maple wood, two wooden rakes, and sundry counters, formed its furniture. On a side table, graced by a cloth whose particular hue it might be difficult to define, the supper was spread: it consisted of a huge, coarse-looking ham, a few slices of raw, gristly beef, and a bowl of gritty-looking salad. Then there were two bottles of home-made gooseberry called champagne, a few ditto of soda in a stable pail, and the identical brandy that we had seen purchased at the "Running Horse."

"Now, gentlemen, make your game!" exclaimed the croupier, taking his station on a high-backed chair at the side of the table: "we bet the odds against nicks and doublets—the dice, Mr. Dunlop."

Upon which, Mr. Dunlop, who was vice-croupier, opened a packet of dice, containing three pair, and shook them together in one of the bowls. Hook took the box, and, putting a few half-crowns upon the table, cried, "Seven's the main!" "Seven's a nick," said the croupier, at the same time paying the stake. "Eight's the main!" "Eight the caster has to five, eight with the quatres; no gentleman on the doublets." Again the stake was paid.

During this proceeding, I rather fancied Mr. Dunlop, who had raked the dice towards him, fingered them in a peculiar manner. In my zeal to prevent Price putting down his money, I trod so heavily upon his gouty foot, as to wring from him an exclamation; but he took the hint, and putting his money "contre," waited the result of the throw. "Seven's the main!" cried the caster. "Deuce ace!" shouted the croupier, raking up the winnings; "the caster's out."

"Give me the dice," drawled out one of the "bonnets,"—"five's the main!" "Seven the caster has to five—die down, Mr. Dunlop!" for, in the throwing, one of the dice (as I thought, purposely,) went off the table.

"I've got it," he continued, as he went on throwing—"six to four in favor of the caster—we take it in halves.' "I'll bet it!" exclaimed Hook. Up came a deuce ace, two's, three ace aces. I tried in vain to see a four, five, or a six, and determined at the end of the throw to inspect the dice, but the "bonnet" was too wary; for as he threw tray deuce, he, in a pretended passion, anathematized the dice, and threw them into the corner of the room, where they were immediately pounced upon by Mr. Tomkins, the livery servant.

"Will any gentleman take any refreshment?" asked the croupier; "we've a beautiful ham.—Tomkins, offer the gentlemen some soda and brandy."

After this oblation, the other "bonnet," who was called Captain Denscol, took the box, and appeared, as far as I could judge, to hold one between his third finger and the box, making a prodigious rattling with the other.—"Seven's the main!"

The two *bona fide* players, Hook and Price, went against him, despite my looks and nudges, though the result would have been equally the same, as the caster could evidently land the dice as he pleased. —"Seven's a nick!"

"A cup of weak tea!" said the croupier;—"A glass of sherry and water!" exclaimed Mr. Dunlop; —"Tomkins, open the champagne!" In a minute, a pop and a whiz were heard, and as the ballad says—

The juice of ripe (gooseberries) flow'd in our glasses.

The senses of my companions being rather more under control than they had intended them to appear, the little we "imbibed" did not disorder our wits to the anticipated extent. We were more than a match for our antagonists, kept our eyes quite open, watched all their movements, and avoided defeat. After some perseverance, it was pretty clear to the knaves that we were further off than ever from being victims to their devices, however knowingly laid, or dexterously executed. Nay, Price had even realized a small capital and was proposing our departure, when the rural Crocky, addressing himself to me, said, in a tone of impertinence, "Do you or do you not, *gentlemen*, intend giving us our revenge?"

"Certainly not," I replied, "at a public gaming-table; such a thing is unheard of."

"Nor you?" addressing himself to the American.

"I'll see you——

I shall not say exactly what he said,
Because it might astonish ears polite.

"Nor you?" turning to the illustrious and fearless Theodore, who at once burst forth—

Revenge! he cries, and the traitor dies!

shouted Hook, stamping his foot, and giving an imitation of an evergreen English singer, in a celebrated passage from an opera then greatly in vogue.

"Good night, gentlemen," said King Stephen.

"Waiter, what's to pay for the brandy?"

"D—— the brandy, sir!" said the man with the diamond broach, adjusting his substitute for a three-and-fourpenny gossamer fiercely upon his head; "we neither want your money nor your company." And up he rose, rake in hand from his seat. His companions also rose, muttering to each other, and evidently working themselves into an intensity of passion.

"I told you what it would come to," said the landlady; "you had better leave the house without making any disturbance—a set of horse-jockeys coming here, to disturb quiet honest people!"

At another time, I should have thought of the old Latin adage—

Dat veniam corvis, vexat censura columbas—

but I had no time for classical quotation; for a fray was obviously about to ensue, concerning which, feeling indignant at the insolence and rascality with which we were treated, I was totally indifferent, except, indeed, on poor Price's account, whose thews and sinews were ill-qualified for such an adventure. I started up, however, on seeing the others rise, and silently turned my cuffs down—an indication that I was ready if necessary. "You sha'nt leave the house," said the croupier, advancing towards me. "That remains to be proved," I replied, suiting the action to the word, i. e., putting myself in a posture of defence.

Stephen Price, meanwhile, as he saw the tallest "leg" confront him, behaved with the stoutest mettle, or as Hook would have said, "metal:" for, to my infinite amusement, he seized the *poker*, and brandishing it in the air, exclaimed after the manner, and (as was once observed on a similar imitation) "*very much after*" the manner of the celebrated Mackay, the only representative of Scotch characters I ever saw—"Ma conscience! what would the deacon, my father, say?"

Upon this, Hook, seizing the top of a small saucepan, which he employed as a target, and the tongs, which he flourished sword-fashion in the most grotesque way, assumed the form of the Dougal creature, rushed forward, and, throwing himself on one knee, raised his eyes to the ceiling; then, putting himself into a regular Coburg Theatre cut-and-thrust attitude, spluttered forth some mock Gaelic, ending with "Her nainsell has eaten the town praed at the Cross o' Glasgow, and py her troth she'll fight for Baillie Sharvie at the Clachan of Aberfoil—tat will she e'en!" This said, seconding his words with deeds, he made his weapon clatter awfully about the ears of the tall "leg."

The fray now became general. Greek met Greek, and the tug of war was terrible; the tables were overthrown, the dice-boxes rattled against the win-

dows, counters flew, and above all tongs clattered. Hook's voice was heard, shouting passages from half-a-dozen plays at a time :—

Lay on Macduff!
Approach thou like the rugged ruffian Bill,
The armed Mendoza, or the late Dutch Sam!
Oh, this is sweet,
When in one line two crafts together meet!
Come, Signor Roderigo, I'm for you!
Nay, I'll so maul you and your toasting irons,
That you shall think the devil has come from (or rather to) hell.

"Hands off! murder! *po*lice!" exclaimed the landlady, rushing in, followed by a slip-shod kitchen wench. With the presence of the fury, strange to say, came peace, spreading her wings over the scene of strife and desolation. It was not, of course, our wish to protract the fray, and our adversaries seemed equally disposed to capitulate. We stood still; a truce was by common consent established. One of them, acting on the principle of a commissioner in a late national affray, proposed the suspension of hostilities, provided we would refund the numerous dollars we had won; thus, as in China, making it a most "dolorous" affair. This mercantile proposition, however, we declined, and commenced a retreat which, like that of the great warrior of the age, was in our estimation so well conducted, as to "eclipse the very glory of our advance."

So signal a victory was not, of course, to be gained without incurring a few casualties in the Anglo-American force. Our return of wounded was—Field Marshal Hook, slightly; Manager Price, severely in his gouty foot; myself, not at all dangerously. The loss sustained by the enemy cannot be so accurately reported; but it is certain that the heads of several "legs" were broken, and various glasses were numbered with the incurable. We had succeeded in capturing sundry rakes, dice-boxes, maple bowls, and other implements of the war against society; but these prizes were subsequently abandoned, and left scattered over the battle-field.

* * * Of those who laughed with me that day, none remain. They have illustrated, in their own fate, the brevity of that life which they helped to make cheerful:—the eccentric divine, the whim-loving American, the kind-hearted friend,—some there are who yet miss them; but for poor Hook, whose facetiousness enlivened the dullest, who with the convivial was most jovial of all,—*he* is missed, not by a circle, by a party, merely—

Society droops for the loss of his jest.

MEMS. FOR DINERS OUT.

BY LORD WM. LENOX.

Never arrive late at a dinner-party, your host and hostess are apt to get "fussy" at the probability of the dinner being spoilt, and will vent their spleen upon their absent guests. As a matter of course, extol your Amphytrion's house and furniture, not forgetting a considerable portion of "soft solder" to the hostess in praise of her "lovely progeny." Ascertain, if possible, the names and occupations of all the guests, so that you may be prepared to throw in an appropriate word to any one you may chance to get next to. If an antiquated damsel, doomed to single-blessedness (query, wretchedness), talk of the folly of youthful marriages, dwell upon the absurdity of being taken from the school-room to the altar, and run the changes upon "childish attachments," "too young to know their own minds," and "marry in haste, and repent at leisure." If a poet, poetess, author or authoress, is placed next to you, quote a line, or sentence, if possible, of their last work, and talk of it as one of the most talented productions of the season. Censure the severity of critics, which will draw forth a reply from the author of "the kindness shown to their unpretending volume." If the work is dull, tell the writer the right-minded public will, in time, appreciate, despite of what the snarling critics may say. If the author has been guilty of "plagiarism," give him or her a catalogue raisonnée of noble and talented plagiarists, throwing in the reply of Charles the Second, who, when urged not to patronize one of Dryden's plays, as having been stolen from other works, replied, "Steal me such another, and I'll patronize it as much as I do honest John's." If you find yourself next to a youthful poetess, you may say of her work what Sir James Mackintosh said of Corinne, "I swallow it slowly, that I may taste every drop." If chance places a military man next to you, lead him on to talk of drills and pipe-clay—*the* duke and the peninsula, of course pronouncing the corps to which your neighbor belongs to be one of the finest in her majesty's service. If a naval hero is your neighbor, talk of Nelson, Howe, and Collingwood, and listen to his yarns of the sea, and dangers of the deep. If a traveller is placed next to you, journey with him over his beaten track, and urge him to publish his journals. With a lawyer, be *brief;* they are more accustomed to talk than to listen. With a turf-hunter, drop in accidentally that you thought you saw him the day before in the park, which will give him a cue, to commence his narrations of high-bred dames and nobles with whom he is on the most intimate terms. In short, suit your conversation to your company. Respecting anecdotes, have a certain number stored up in your memory, ready to do their duty when called upon: but be particularly careful never to lug in one of them out of place, but be equally prompt, whenever an opportunity occurs, to avail yourself of it. Thus, the conversation turns upon Wellington, you immediately begin—"I heard a most characteristic anecdote of the great man lately: Commander Hall of her majesty's yacht, who had 'done the state some service' in China, was anxious to be presented to the hero of a hundred fights, upon an occasion in which the duke went on board the Victoria and Albert. The name of the commander was mentioned to the duke, who said he should be delighted to be introduced to the gallant officer. The *vainqueur des vainqueurs* went through the yacht, and was about to leave it, when he turned round to the captain, and said, introduce me to your commander. The ceremony took place. 'Happy to know you, Commander Hall. You are a brave fellow; fought like a hero in the Nemesis, in China. Gallant, gallant. God bless you,' holding out his hand at the same time. The son of Neptune warmly grasped the veteran warrior's hand, exclaiming, 'I would rather have that blessing than that of the Archbishop of Canterbury, and all the bishops put together.'"

After telling your story, wait (as the professed actors do) for the applause, and do not be carried away by it, or be led to tell another story, until an equally favorable opportunity occurs. If the subject turns upon politics, quote Sheridan and the pure elector of that immaculate borough of Stafford. "So, Mr. Sheridan, you are about to give us reform; that's right, only think, in some towns there are poor fellows, I hear say, that get nothing at all for their votes; that an't right, and wants reforming altogether. Talking of reform," you may continue, "I must tell you a most extraordinary circumstance that occurred during the last reign. Lord —— paid a visit to Bedlam; among the inmates was a poor woman, who happened to ask his lordship his name, 'Oh,' replied the latter, 'I'm Mr. Smith,' giving a travelling name. Nothing more occurred until a few months afterwards, when the same noble lord paid another visit to the same place. The woman already alluded to approached his lordship, and in a voice that savored little of insanity, said, 'You gave me a false name when last you were here; but let that pass.' The kind-hearted nobleman assured the poor sufferer that he had meant no harm. She proceeded, 'No, you are too warm-hearted to mean to act unkindly; but will you do me a favor? I am mad—I feel it—I know it, although often I am perfectly collected, yet I should not be safe at large; but will you tell the king, mad, insane as I often am, I never was half so mad as he was when he put his name to the Reform bill.'" An electioneering anecdote or two may follow this; but be sure they are short and pithy—always bear in mind the Prince of Denmark's instructions to the players, *vide* Hamlet.

In some societies jocose stories tell well. The best way of introducing them is to mention poor James Smith, and the never-to-be-forgotten Theodore. Then you may rattle off a volley of their best sayings—"Walking one day with Hook, in winter, we passed a shop with the name of Hawes: 'Oh,' said Theodore, 'fine weather for the surgeons—a *nice* practice, I've no doubt, during the frost—

> Perpetual freezings and perpetual thaws,
> Though bad for *Hips*, are good for *Haws.*

Before I had finished laughing, the name of Thurtell, the murderer of Weare, was named. 'Ay,' asked Hook, 'of course you know why he used an air-gun?' 'No,' I replied. 'Because he wished to kill Weare without *Noyse;* or,' he continued, 'like an old coat?—because he was the worse for *wear*' (Weare). Our conversation then turned upon the burning of the Exeter Theatre. 'Ay,' said Hook, 'That's quite theatrical—*enter* a fire; *exit* a theatre,'" (Exeter Theatre.)

Be careful of risking a pun as your own; you can introduce it in the following manner—"A friend of mine said a tolerable good thing last week," then give your pun; if it flashes in the pan, you of course add, "Well, I myself did not see the wit of it, though all the party laughed." If it goes off brilliantly, when asked, who's your friend? you may say, "One's often worst friend, myself."

Reader, study the above axioms, and I have no doubt you will shortly become a truly popular diner-out.

A Fool's Answer.—"How shameful it is that you should fall asleep," said a dull preacher to a drowsy audience, "whilst that poor idiot is awake and attentive." "I would have been asleep, too, said the fool, "if I had not been an idiot."

Useful Hint.—The art of conversation consists in the exercise of two fine qualities. You must originate, and you must sympathise; you must possess, at the same time, the habits of communicating and listening. The union is rare, but irresistible.

DELICATE ATTENTIONS.

BY JOHN POOLE.

"Why, Gingerly!" exclaimed Tom Damper, as he entered the public drawing-room at Mrs. Bustle's Boarding House, at Brighton; "Why Gingerly! this is one of the finest days of the season, all the world is out enjoying it, yet here are you, at three o'clock, sitting alone, on the self-same chair, in the self-same attitude, and looking through the self-same pane of glass, as at eleven this morning when I left you. What ails you?"

Gingerly made no reply; but breathed on one of the panes of glass, drew the letter B on it with his forefinger, and heaved a sigh.

"You are the oddest fellow in the universe," continued Damper. "We have been here nearly a month, yet, since about the third day after our arrival, you have hardly stirred out of the house."

"It is a very nice house," said Gingerly; and he heaved a heavier sigh than before.

"It was at my recommendation you came to it," said Damper; "but though I am not insensible to the merits of the inside of it, its outside also has many charms for me. Again I ask, what ails you?"

"Damper!" said Gingerly.

"Well."

"Damper!" repeated Gingerly, with a sigh.

"You said that before."

"Damper—were you ever in love?"

"I was never out of it till I had turned five-and-forty; but being, at this present talking, within two months of fifty, and a bachelor moreover, I should think myself a fool were I in such a scrape now. You, who are by five years my senior, of course are not."

Gingerly made no reply; but, sighing profoundly, took his handkerchief from his pocket and smeared out the large, flourishing B which he had just before drawn. There was a pause of a minute.

"Damper—may I trust you with a secret?"

"Yes—so it be not a love confidence."

"In that case, my dear friend, I shall have nothing to thank you for."

"Seriously now, my dear Gingerly, do you mean to say you are in love?"

Gingerly expended another sigh, again turned towards his favorite pane, and re-instated his big bouncing B.

"O, Damper!" at length he exclaimed, "if you had a heart you would feel for me."

"I should if I saw you hanging, or drowning, or suffering under any reasonable trouble; but to feel for an old bachelor of fifty-five in love, and for the first time in his life, too!—Ridiculous! But, come; I suppose I must listen to you, so tell me all about it."

"And who so proper as you for the confidence, when you are to blame for the accident!"

"I!" exclaimed Damper, with unfeigned surprise.

"Yes, you," answered Gingerly; "because, but for your recommendation, I never should have set foot in Mrs. Bustle's boarding-house."

"So, then, it is some one in this house, who has smitten your susceptible old heart?" said Damper, with a laugh. And he continued: "I think I can name the tender fair one."

"To be sure you can," replied Gingerly.

"It is old Widow Swillswallow, who eats and drinks from morning till night, and is heard by all in the house, snoring from night till morning."

"Faugh!" exclaimed Gingerly, with a shudder of disgust.

"Or old Miss Fubsworth, who was born on the day of the coronation of George the Third?"

"Absurd!" exclaimed Gingerly.

"Then it must be old Widow Waddilove; for she is the only other lady-lodger here."

"Preposterous!" cried Gingerly, somewhat angrily. "Old *this*, and old *that!* Is there nobody else you can think of?"

"There is but one other," replied Damper; "in which case I am sorry for you. You have not the slightest chance in that quarter; for Mrs. Bustle is engaged to be married to Captain O'Popper."

"*Mistress* Bustle! Pooh! Can't you think of *one* more."

"There is not one more, except, indeed, her daughter, Betsy."

"Well?" said Gingerly.

"Well?" echoed Damper. "You can't be thinking of her."

"And why not? She is very pretty."

"True," replied Damper; "but you forget that she is also very young."

"No," said Gingerly; "that's the very thing I am thinking about. She is eighteen: a delicious age! Surely, now, you don't pretend that a girl of eighteen is too young for me?"

"Not a day," replied Damper, somewhat drily; "but I, who am your junior, should think myself too old for a girl of eighteen."

"I don't care for that, my good friend. I am my own master, have an unencumbered nine hundred a-year, am not troubled with a relation in the world—and—and—in short, I'm resolved to marry Betsy Bustle." Saying which, he flourished half-a-dozen B's with an air of unconquerable determination.

Damper gave him a twirl round, and stared him full in the face.

"Gingerly," said he; "if your head were not as bald of hair as an apple, I should advise you to go this moment and get it shaved, for you are mad—stark, staring mad. Fifty-five and eighteen! If you *do* marry Miss Bustle, my fine fellow, look out for squalls."

"Of course," replied Gingerly, with a look of extreme simplicity; "I must expect that our children will squall just the same as other people's."

"You misunderstand me; I say if you do marry Betsy Bustle, remember that there is already a lover in the case."

"Damper, don't say so," cried Gingerly.

"There is," continued the consoling friend; "there is, or I am much mistaken. A favored lover too: favored by the daughter, by the mother, and, which is of no little importance, by Captain O'Popper also—the Captain, as you know, being as much master here as if he and Mrs. Bustle were already united."

Gingerly turned pale, and big drops rolled from his brow. For some time he was unable to speak. At length, with faltering voice, he inquired of Damper what grounds he had for his belief.

"Chiefly this," replied the latter: "I have frequently heard her speak to her mother about a certain George; and from the tone in which she always utters the name ——"

"Then I am the happiest man alive!" joyfully exclaimed Gingerly. "My name is George."

"But," said the imperturbable friend, "she sometimes speaks of him as '*young* George."

"And what then? I never told her my age; and she is not obliged to know that I am fifty, or so. I tell you what, Damper; that I am the object of her tender thoughts I am now certain—that is to say, *almost* certain. Now I would have proof of it, and *that* you must obtain for me."

"I have already told you I will have nothing to do with a love confidence," coolly replied Damper.

"But you must, my dear Damper; for this once you must—unless you wish to see your poor friend throw himself from the head of the chain-pier souse into the sea."

As Gingerly uttered these words with something like earnestness, his friend, unwilling to be accessory to such a catastrophe, consented, after some further entreaty, to undertake the task:—not without thinking to himself that should Gingerly actually marry the girl, he would be the greatest fool in the universe—excepting only the girl herself for marrying him.

"Now," said Gingerly, "I must first of all confess to you that I am the most timid man alive—I mean in love matters—and that is why I have never popped the question to mortal woman. Indeed, as to popping the question at all, it is a thing I could not do, were I to live a thousand years. Pop! To a delicate-minded man the very word itself is a horrid word. I could as soon pop a pistol at a woman's head, as the question at her heart. No: if I succeed, as I am sure I shall, in ensnaring the heart of my charming Betsy, it will be, not by any daring manœuvre, but by sly approaches, by little gallantries, by delicate attentions, such as the female heart only can appreciate, such as no female heart can resist."

"And when do you mean to begin?" said Damper.

"I shall astonish you, my dear fellow, I know I shall: I *have* begun. I have already made one step in advance, and I flatter myself you will give me some credit for the ingenuity of it. You know the new novel that every body is talking about—'The Timid Lover.' Well; the hero, Mortimer Saint-Aubyn de Mowbray Fitz-Eustaceville, is a character exactly resembling me—timid as I am—something younger, to be sure; but that does not signify—and the heroine is very much like Miss Bustle. Yesterday I bought the book—paid a guinea and-a-half for it, as I hope to be saved: and sent it anonymously to Betsy—*anonymously*—do you mark the delicate attention?"

"I do," replied Damper; "but, for the life of me, I can't discover the ingenuity of the proceeding."

"It consists in this—and that is the point you must assist me in. Nearly at the end of the first volume there is a situation of great interest, where the timid lover first hints at his passion for the heroine. I put a piece of paper into the book to mark the place, and Miss Bustle *must* have noticed it. Now I want you to draw from her whether, in reading that passage—for I saw her reading it last night—she thought of me. If she did, she is mine. That I call both delicate and ingenious."

At this moment Miss Betsy entered the room, and, greatly to the satisfaction of Gingerly, with a volume of "The Timid Lover" in her hand. Gingerly whispered to his friend that now was the time for the experiment; he cast a look of ludicrous tenderness at the young lady, stammered a few words which were utterly unintelligible, and went out for a walk; but with the intention of soon returning to learn the result of Damper's inquiries.

"What a funny gentleman!" exclaimed Miss Bustle, as Gingerly made his retiring bow.

"Funny!" thought Damper; "that is not a very promising epithet for the timid lover."

"His manners are much altered since he first came here," continued Miss Bustle. "*Then* he was very talkative; *now* he scarcely ever utters a word. And he gives one such comical looks, too! Captain O'Popper said yesterday that one would think he is casting sheep's eyes at somebody or other—though I don't know what that means. But he is a nice old man, after all. I wonder, though, he does not wear a wig; his old bald head shines so one can almost see one's face in it. I don't think such a *very* bald head is pretty."

It will not be expected that Damper was much encouraged by these observations to proceed on his friend's behalf; but, having undertaken his cause, he resolved against abandoning it.

"Miss Bustle," said he, "you are mistaken concerning Mr. Gingerly on one point: he is not old—not remarkably old."

"Dear me!" exclaimed Miss Bustle; "how one may be deceived by appearances! He looks a great deal older than my poor, dear, dead-and-gone grandpapa, who was sixty-three when he died."

"He is nothing like so old as that," said Damper; "and then, Miss Bustle—and then, he is rich." This last word did Damper emphasize in a way to produce an effect—and so it did.

"Rich!" responded Miss Bustle; "is he indeed? Lord! how I should like to have *him*—for a grandpapa. I dare say he is very kind to *his* grandchildren."

The learned advocate perceiving that he had taken nothing by his motion, fell back upon the point on which he had been chiefly instructed; and merely explaining by the way, that as his friend was unmarried, it was impossible he should have children, and that, therefore, grandchildren were out of the question, he went at once to the subject of the book.

"Is that a new work you are reading, Miss Bustle?"

"Yes, Sir; it is the 'Timid Lover,' and is only just out."

"You are fortunate in getting it so early from a circulating-library," observed Damper, pretending ignorance of the fact.

"Anxious as I was to read it, I might have waited six weeks for it had I depended on the library, and after all, perhaps, have been obliged to read the third volume first. No, Sir, it is a present; and, although it came anonymously, I know very well who sent it. What delicate attention! Oh!" And here the young lady placed her hand upon her heart, and sighed.

Bravo! thought Damper; this will do. "And pray Miss," said he, "is there not in it one situation of peculiar interest? I mean that where the timid lover first hints at his passion for the heroine?"

"It is charming," replied Miss Betsy; "It absolutely drew tears from me!"

"And did you think of no one—*no one*—whilst you were reading it?" inquired Damper.

"Indeed I did; and I'll tell you in confidence, who it was. I thought all the way through of Mr. Gingerly."

"Well, thought Damper; there is no accounting for the freaks of the heart! And that my old friend should make a conquest of one of the prettiest girls in Brighton!"

"The two characters are so alike! except," continued Miss Bustle, "that Mr. Gingerly is *rather* the elder of the two."

"Yes, yes; I admit that my friend is a little older than the hero, Mortimer Saint-Aubyn de Mowbray Fitz-Eustaceville is represented to be."

"What!" exclaimed Miss Betsy, bursting into an immoderate fit of laughter; "think of him as the divine Fitz-Eustaceville! Shocking! No; what made me think of him was the nasty old rival, Lord Grumblethorpe, who comes in at the critical moment, and prevents the declaration of love. But Fitz-Eustaceville is so like a certain person! But wasn't it a delicate attention, Mr. Damper, on the part of the *friend* who sent me the books? And, then, to put a slip of paper into that very place! Oh! it speaks volumes!!"

At this moment, Mr. Gingerly returned; and Miss Bustle being summoned by a servant to go to her mamma, he and Mr. Damper were left together.

"Well," eagerly cried the timid lover; "well, have you sounded her?"

"I have," was the reply.

"She has read the passage in question?"

"Every syllable of it."

"Did it produce any effect upon her?"

"Tremendous!"

"Did she cry? That's the great point. Did she cry?"

"A bucket-full!"

"You delight me, my dear Damper. Did she notice the bit of paper? Did she speak of me? Did she remark upon the delicate attention?"

"Yes, yes, yes, yes," impatiently replied Damper. "And, now, pray don't tease me any more about it."

"But my dear, dear Damper; did she speak much about me? and what was it she said?"

"Why—not much; but what she did say was quite conclusive."

"I told you so: I knew that by a little ingenious contrivance, by a few delicate attentions, I should make my way to her heart."

"Now, my good friend," said Damper gravely, "prepare yourself for a——" Damper's speech, the tendency of which would doubtless have been to undeceive his self-deluded friend, was cut short by the dinner bell; and, as they descended to the dining-room, Gingerly declared his intention to spare neither pains nor expense to win (in his own delicate way) the affections of Miss Betsy Bustle. Damper sighed for the infatuation of poor Gingerly, and resolved, in his own mind, to save him from any aggravated disappointment, by repeating to him, at the earliest opportunity, and word for word, all that had passed in his conversation with the young lady.

When the friends entered the dining-room, they found the places, all except two, occupied. These were near the head of the table, at which was seated Mrs. Bustle. Captain O'Popper did the honors at the bottom. At his left was the lovely Betsy, and next to her was a young man of about three-and-twenty. This gentleman wore a blue frock-coat of military cut, a buff waistcoat, and a military stock. He was dark; not ill-looking; had a profusion of black hair; huge whiskers; and mustachios of the fiercest:—such, indeed, as might well have excited the envy of one of Napoleon's Old Guard. He smelt strong of cigar, and was clerk to an attorney at Shoreham. This personage was no other than George—*the* George—Mr. George Hobnill.

Gingerly cast a longing look towards the end of the table where was seated his beloved, but there was not a vacant place within eight of her. Mr. Hobnill, who occupied the seat for which the former would have given one of his ears, and whom he now saw for the first time, he inwardly wished —a long way further off than Shoreham.

"Mr. Gingerly," cried Mrs. Bustle, "as I know you are a lady's man, I have reserved *that* seat for you. You are fortunate to-day in having a lady on each side of you." This she uttered in a tone of patronage: at the same time pointing to a vacant chair between Gingerly's prime horrors—Old Widow Swillswallow and Miss Fubsworth. Damper was placed next to Widow Waddilove.

"Come, Mr. G.," mumbled Miss Fubsworth, "come between us ladies. We old folks are always best together."

The earth did not open and swallow Mr. Gingerly at a gulp, as he wished it might, for at the moment of the utterance of these words, his eyes met those of Miss Bustle.

The dinner was provided with the usual boarding-house munificence. First, was served a huge white earthenware tureen, full to the brim of a thin nankeen-colored liquid, on the surface of which floated a few chips of toasted bread. Mrs. Bustle, as she distributed this in copious portions amongst the company, commended her cook for her culinary ability in general, but chiefly praised her for the excellence of her "gravy soup!"

"The only good gravy-soup in all Brighton," exclaimed Captain O'Popper; "and I'm just waiting to hear who'll say the con*trar*y." This proposition, uttered with an unquestionable brogue, was universally granted: at least, nobody *said* the contrary.

Then came three soles to be divided amongst fifteen bodies. This seemed to be a difficult operation; but Mrs. Bustle performed it with a degree of ingenuity which would have done honor to the mistress of any boarding-house in England. Two or three times, in the course of her occupation, she took occasion to say that this was "the poorest fish-day she had ever known in Brighton."

"The only three soles in the market—barring the other three we let go to the Pavilion," said the Captain.

Next appeared, at one end of the table, a roast leg of mutton; and, at the other, a dish containing some five or six mutton-chops—very broad and very thick, with long tails of fat and gristle depending from the narrow ends of them. These were interspersed with thick slices of raw onion, and were described by Mrs. Bustle as "Cutlets *ally* sauce *peekong*"—a dish for which her cook was "particularly famous!"

"*Peekong!*" responded the Captain. "You may well say *peekong*, Madam! and I don't think there's anybody here will contradict *that*."

The dinner was completed by an enormous [looking] gooseberry pie, which derived its name from the half-pint of gooseberries discovered at the bottom of the dish when, after some difficulty, a breach had been effected through the thick, hard crust over the top of it; together with twelve stringy radishes, one lettuce divided into quarters, and a small glass bowl-full of lumps of yellow-looking cheese, of mouse-trap size and Mac-adam substance.

"Shy fare again, to-day!" muttered a quiet little gentleman at table.

"Shy what, Sir!" exclaimed the Captain. "What's shy, Sir? And, by the powers! is it 'shy' you are saying?"

"I—I only spoke, Captain," mildly replied the gentleman.

"I'm satisfied, Sir," said Captain O'Popper.

"I declare, Mr. Gingerly," said Mrs. Bustle, "you have eaten no dinner: I really believe you are in love."

Gingerly was preparing a languishing look for the especial service of Miss Betsy, when the effort was paralyzed by the Captain's——

"Mr. Gingerly in love! Ha, ha, ha! At his time of life! Ha, ha, ha! Well! better late than never, eh! my old Trojan? Ah! those sheep's eyes of your own, Daddy Gingerly! I say, Miss Fubsworth!—Mrs. Swillswallow!—take care of your hearts, ladies! Or, come, Daddy; is it Mrs. Waddilove you may happen to be after?"

"Sir, I—a—I beg, Sir—a—I must desire—" said Gingerly, (assuming as dignified an air as his mingled confusion and vexation would allow)—"these liberties Sir,—a—I——"

The Captain, a good-natured man at heart, perceiving that he had given pain, apologised—though with far better intention than tact.

"Mr. Gingerly, Sir; I'm sorry you have taken seriously what I meant only in joke." [Mr. Gingerly bowed, and the Captain continued.] "I was wrong though, and I'm prepared to confess it." Here Mr. Gingerly bowed again.] "I had no right to take a freedom with a perfect gentleman like you, Sir,"—[Mr. Gingerly bowed almost down to the table,]—"who are old enough to be my grandfather;"—[Mr. Gingerly did *not* bow.]—"and I ask your pardon."

Two maid-servants coming into the room with the dessert—one bringing a plate of apples, and the other a plate of biscuits?—diverted the attention of the company from the affair; and Mr. Gingerly availed himself of that opportunity to be seized with a fit of coughing, and to cover his face with his handkerchief. When he had recovered from this attack, he had the gratification of hearing the following portion of a conversation between Mr. Hobnill and Miss Bustle. As it was carried on in an under-tone he heard no more of it than is here reported.

"Now don't deny it, George."

"*Paw* my life, not the slightest ide*or*."

"I'm certain * * because * * Fitz-Eustaceville * * slip of paper * * if any one else *dared*, the consequences would * * Captain O' Popper * * style of the thing * * so like you, you creature!"

"If you won't believe me, I can't help * * *Paw* my honor * * piece of im*pawt*inence * * horsewhip * * really not the least ide*or*."

"Now it's of no use, George * * sweetly pretty * * I knew you'd deny it * * if you were to swear it, I wouldn't * * folly to deny * * you have a right, dear George, and of course * * been any one else * * insolent monster! * * delicate attention."

"* * * will think so, why aw, * * "

"Now that's quite sufficient to * * O, George! * * elegant expedient * * fully appreciated * * even had I ever given you cause to doubt; but, *now* * * susceptible heart * * so *very* delicate an attention * *yes, dear George, for ever!"

Could there have been the smallest doubt upon any disinterested mind as to the *filling-up* of this short conversation, or to the terms upon which it implied the whisperers to stand in relation to each other, it must have been removed by the unequivocal twist with which Mr. Hobnill indulged his mustachios at its conclusion. But Gingerly was not in a condition to think rationally. How could he? He was in love. He complained of the oppressiveness of the heat; expressed his conviction that the thermometer must suddenly have risen from seventy-five to a hundred; drew his handkerchief from his pocket, and wiped the perspiration from his glossy, bald head. The next minute, he wondered what could make him feel so cold. Damper recommended him to leave the room. It was not the room, however, that produced these extraordinary sensations in him; it was part of the company. But lovers, like drowning men, will catch at the slightest chance of salvation. "I will have proof more relative than this," mentally ejaculated he. He bethought him of the torn paper in Zadig, one-half of which, when read by itself, was a cutting satire, but, when joined to the other, the whole turned out to be nothing more than an innocent love poem. So may it be in this case, thought he: there was something which, certainly, was not quite agreeable in what I did hear; but had I heard all that passed it would have been a different affair. And, hereupon, he rubbed his hands and proposed to Damper that they should have a bottle of port together. The wine was brought; and, according to the amiable fashion of boarding-houses, it played pendulum across the table, vibrating between him and his partner. And did he not invite the ladies on either side of him to take wine? No. And out of this marked neglect of them, he drew occasion for a delicate hint as to the real direction which his affections had taken. He filled a glass, gave it to a servant, and, in a hesitating, indistinct way, said something to her; at the same time pointing in the direction where Miss Bustle was placed. The girl crossed the room, and stood, with the salver in her hand, between the young lady (who was intently occupied in paring an apple) and Mr. Hobnill. To Gingerly this was an awful moment. He felt that he was committing a declaration. His tongue clove to the roof of his mouth: not a syllable could he utter. He screwed his lips up to the circumference of a pin-hole, looked hearts and darts, but dared not, for some time, raise his eyes from the table; and when, at length, he did, they met those of Mr. Hobnill!

"Yow are vastly *paw*lite. With great plea*shaw*," said Mr. Hobnill, as he took the glass. "Your good health, Mr. Ginjawberry."

Ere Mr. Ginjawberry, (as he was miscalled by his rival) had recovered from the shock occasioned by the failure of this delicate little attention, (to say nothing of seeing his wine swallowed by the man of all others for whom he could heartily have wished it had been poison,) Miss Betsy had finished her operation on the apple.

"There, George," said she, as she presented it to Hobnill, "haven't I done it nicely for you?"

"Whatever *you* do, *must* be nicely done," replied the favored youth.

"Now, George, that is so like you: you do say the most elegant things!"

Gingerly swallowed the glass of wine which stood before him; filled again and swallowed that; filled again and would have done the same thing, had not Damper, who had observed him, proposed that they should walk.

Betsy, who had caught the word, intimated to her mamma that, as she had not been out all day, she also should like a walk. Gingerly, emboldened by what he could not help considering as a delicate hint on the part of the young lady, and, perhaps, rendered somewhat less diffident by the wine he had taken, asked permission to offer the young lady his arm.

"Surely," said Mrs. Bustle.

Gingerly was on his legs in an instant; and cast a look at his friend Damper, which, literally interpreted, meant, "What is your opinion of affairs *now?*"

"O dear! mamma," exclaimed Miss Betsy, "impossible! only think!—The idea, you know!"

"Nonsense! my love," replied Mrs. Bustle; "there can be no sort of impropriety in your walking with Mr. Gingerly."

"Confound her impudence," muttered Gingerly.

"None in the least, Betsy," said the Captain; "it is not as if——"

"Captain O'Popper," said Gingerly, eagerly interrupting him, as if apprehensive of a disagreeable conclusion to the speech; "Captain O'Popper, I—a —Miss Bustle and I—a—" Then turning to Hobnill, he said in a taking-it-for-granted tone and with somewhat of an air of triumph,—"You are going back to Shoreham, Sir."

"*Paw* my life," replied Hobnill (half addressing himself to Betsy)—"*Paw* my life, I hardly—I am not *paw*sitively obliged, but—"

"No, no, George," said Betsy; "there is no occasion for your returning to-night. Come and take *one* turn with this gentleman and me on the Chain-pier; and when we have brought him home again, I shall want you to walk with me to my Aunt Heathfield's at Preston."

"I am afraid, my love," said the considerate mamma, "you will be too tired to go to Preston this evening, if you walk much now."

"So I should, mamma," eagerly replied Miss Bustle; "so I think I had better walk by-and-by instead. Hadn't *we*, George?"

"Tired!" exclaimed the Captain. "It's mighty ridiculous for *young* people to talk about being tired. What is it you are made of? Why, look at Mr. Gingerly there! He does not appear to be very strong on the pins; yet I dare say he, even at his age, could contrive to walk that much."

Again was Gingerly seized with a fit of coughing, which compelled him to conceal his face with his handkerchief.

"I hope, my dear Gingerly," said Damper to him, as they were taking a stroll along the Marine Parade, "I hope that, by what you have observed this afternoon, you are cured of your folly. I speak to you as a friend, and with a friend's freedom. I observed all that passed, though, for want of opportunity, I made no remark to you upon it. 'Tis clear the girl likes that vulgar puppy, that impudent attorney-ling, and looks on him as an Apollo upon earth. Rely on it you have not a chance. You have *his* black bushy head, huge whiskers, and fierce mustachios, together with your own superabundant thirty-odd years against you. So give it up, my dear fellow; like a sensible man, give it up at once."

"No," replied Gingerly; "I am more determined upon the point than before. The affair is taking precisely the turn I could have wished. I did not expect her to surrender at the first shot—I should have been disgusted if she had done so. But her reserve! her modesty! Did you not observe her timid acquiescence in my invitation to walk?"

"'Timid acquiescence,' you call it! Unequivocal repugnance."

"Maiden coyness, I tell you. And then, that natural little piece of girlish hypocrisy, resorted to for the purpose of concealing her *real* feelings! Did you mark that? I mean her *pretending* to prefer a walk with that insignificant, impertinent, ill-bred, vulgar——! D—n the ugly rascal!—Damper, if Mrs. Bustle allows fellows of that sort to sit down at her table, no gentleman will remain in her house. We'll go home at once and tell her so. No, no: George Gingerly is not the man to give in to a rival of *that* stamp."

"Go on, if you will," said Damper; "but the further you proceed, the more uncomfortable you will find yourself."

"By dint of delicate attentions," said Gingerly, "I'll carry her against the world!"

"And well have your 'delicate attentions' already served you!" exclaimed the consoling Damper. "The first—the book—has turned to the advantage of the amiable Mr. George Hobnill, who, spite of his own resolute abnegation, is enjoying the entire credit of it."

"Not he!" replied Gingerly; "a coarse-minded fellow, like that, would never be suspected of any thing half so elegant. Though—ahem! it is possible I might have cut that a little too fine. But the second—the wine—what say you to that? Fifty guineas to a shilling, if that Hobnill, or hobnail, or whatever his vulgar name may be, had not swallowed it at the very moment when——But I'll punish the fellow, if I meet him again. I'll overwhelm him with ridicule, and break his heart that way: I'll *call* him Hobnail!"

It was half-past nine. they returned to their quarters at Mrs. Bustle's. In the drawing-room they found the Captain and Mrs. Bustle, in one corner, playing cribbage; and, in another, was the quiet little gentleman, fast asleep, with a newspaper on his knee. Reclining on a sofa was a youngish man, evidently dressed *at* some leader of fashion who unquestionably knew what he himself was about; whilst the costume of the imitator, approaching, though but very little, towards caricature, proved that he (the imitator) did not. This exquisite was engaged in picking his teeth; and (as a subsidiary employment) skimming a new novel which he had just procured from a circulating library. For the benefit of future readers, as well as to exhibit his own fine taste and profound judgment, he occasionally made a pencil-note in the margin. These notes were brief but pithy: as "What stuff!" "Not so bad." "You don't say so?" "I shouldn't wonder!" "*Tolarible* good!" "*Abommanubble* bad!" The commentator (as he afterwards turned out to be) was one of the "Sweetly-pootty-petturn-Mem" gentlemen from the Emporium of Fashion in Regent Street. But the principal group in the room consisted of four elderly ladies in petticoats, and three other old women in trowsers, who were squabbling at a game of pennyloo, and, in the best-bred way imaginable, accusing each other of cheating!

Gingerly looked around him in the hope of finding Miss Betsy, but she was not present. "Then," thought he, "she is fatigued by her walk and has retired for the night."

As the clock struck ten, the Captain said to Mrs. Bustle, "This is rather too late for Betsy to be out."

"Not at all," replied Mrs. Bustle; "George, you know, is with her."

A certain Irish officer in the Life-Guards, whose nerves were not easily disordered, said, when endeavoring to illustrate the effect produced upon him by some sudden and terrible shock, "It threw me into such a state, (and truth compels me to confess it,) that, by Jasus! you might have knocked me down with a poker!"

An instrument of much less power would have served to prostrate Mr. Gingerly, upon hearing the words uttered by Mrs. Bustle.

Five minutes passed away—ten—fifteen—twenty! but no Betsy appeared. Gingerly now computed the time by seconds, and each second appeared to him an hour. He went to the window and peeped: he went to the door and listened. His bald head was steaming—he consulted the thermometer, and was astonished to find that it indicated no more than 74°. At length, at eleven o'clock, Miss Betsy, accompanied by *her* George, returned.

"And how did you find your Aunt Heathfield?" inquired Mrs. Bustle.

"Quite well, Mamma. And I have promised to go to her on Saturday and remain till Monday. And George is to come and take me there; and then he is to come over and pass the Sunday with us; and then George is to come on Monday and bring me home again. And, O Mamma! Cousin Harriet is come home from school, for good; and she is so delighted with George!—now don't deny it, George dear; you know it's true—indeed, I told her that if I were not *certain*, I should be jealous."

"Come Gingerly," whispered Damper to him, "go to bed." But Gingerly was riveted to the spot.

"And, O Mamma," continued the young lady; "we went into M'Seedling's Nursery, and saw such beautiful flowers: George insisted upon buying some for me. I chose four myrtles, four jessamines, four red-roses, and four such beautiful white rose-trees! But they would not sell them for less than a guinea-and-a-half; and, although they are such *loves*, I would not allow him to give so much for them. A guinea-and-a-half again, indeed! That would be too much."

"Too much," exclaimed the Captain; "by the Powers! and I think so too. He had better save his money for the *occasion*." Again Damper whispered his friend "to bed."

"Well," said Betsy, "I have such a passion for flowers, that scatter the road with them and I'm sure it would lead to my heart."

Gingerly's countenance brightened. "Come," said he to Damper, (at the same time rubbing his hands,) "I *will* go to bed."

He wished "good night" generally. "Good night to *you*, Mister—Hob-*nail*," said he to his rival; and brought up with a significant "Ahem!" But no effect was produced by the perpetration of this heart-breaking ridicule.

"Good night, Mr. Ginjawbread," replied Hobnill, and there was a general laugh.

Utterly confused, bowing very low, placing his hand upon his heart, and attempting to look—a look!—he stammered forth, "May light slum—Miss Bet—I mean Miss Eliz—Miss—May your downy pil—Oh! Miss Bets—goo—good afternoon." He left the room; and as he closed the door he fancied he heard a titter, and something about "sheep's eyes." When he had reached his room, he rang for a servant, to whom he gave particular orders to call him at five o'clock!

Seven o'clock of the following morning found Gingerly at M'Seedling's nursery. The plants which had been selected by the charming Miss Betsy Bustle stood in a place apart, exactly as she left them. As he beheld them, Gingerly's heart palpitated.

"What is your price for these plants?" inquired Gingerly.

"Maybe you're wanting them, Sir," said M'Seedling; "if so, ye'll no find their like within ten mile round."

"What is the price of them?" repeated Gingerly.

"I refused thirty-five shillings for them yester-e'en, which was offered me by a young *mee*litary gentleman and his wife, as I guess."

"D—n the military gentleman!" impatiently exclaimed Gingerly; who, although he knew how much it was that M'Seedling had actually demanded for his plants, yet he did not choose, by correcting the man's memory, to expose his own knowledge of what had occurred on the previous evening. "D—n the military gentleman. What do you ask for that lot of plants?"

"Weel, Sir," replied the nurseryman; "I'm just thinkin' I canna in conscience tak' less than twa *pund*——"

Gingerly's hand was instantly in his pocket.

"Ten," added the wily professor of the most innocent and most ancient calling on earth.

Gingerly paid the man the sum he demanded, though not without a passing reflection in his own mind on the unsettled meaning of the term 'conscience.'

"Now," said Gingerly, "I have paid you handsomely for these things, and I shall expect in return that my instructions will be strictly attended to concerning the delivery of them. They must be left at Mrs. Bustle's boarding-house, at Brighton, at half-past nine precisely. Should the carrier be asked who sent them, he must say he doesn't know. He must simply leave the plants, and, along with them, this card." Saying which, he took a card from his pocket; and, having scratched through his own name so carefully as to allow of its being read, he wrote on the other side: "These, the fairest of the vegetable creation, to the fairest of the human creation."

There! thought Gingerly, as he retraced his steps to Brighton; I think, my *military* gentleman, I have now done *your* business for you. The hint about strewing the road to her heart with flowers was pretty plain: and I have strewed it to the tune of two-pound-ten. The card is ingeniously contrived, though sending it is a bold step, certainly; but it will prevent mistake. At any rate, Master Hobnail, you shall not smuggle my trophies this time, "These, the fairest of the vegetable creation, to the fairest of the human creation!" That's a touch above an attorney's clerk, I flatter myself. A delicate attention, and elegantly contrived!

For reasons best known to himself, Gingerly, on this particular occasion, took his breakfast at the York. His walk had given him an appetite, which he inflicted, in all its vigor, upon the cold chicken, and ham, and eggs, and rolls, which were placed before him. This ended, he returned to Mrs. Bustle's; and appeared in the dining-room just as the general breakfast was served. The party consisted of the same persons as were assembled at dinner on the day before, and Hobnill was seated next to Miss Betsy as upon that occasion. Gingerly was so fortunate as to find a chair immediately opposite to his idol, and next to him was his friend Damper.

"Don't you take any thing, Mr. Gingerly?" said Mrs. Bustle to him, after he had sat some time unoccupied at table.

"I——I'll take half a cup of weak tea, thank you, Madam," replied he, in a tender tone, and with a sigh.

"But don't you eat any thing, Sir?"

"I——I have no appetite," was the reply, with the same accompaniments.

"Then, decidedly, you *are* in love," continued the lady.

By the most fortunate concurrence of circumstances—(fortunate for Gingerly's cause)—even whilst Mrs. Bustle was uttering these words, Jenny, one of the maids, entered the room.

"Please, mum," said Jenny, "hasn't nobody ordered no flowers to be sent here?"

Gingerly turned pale, and his heart beat against his side as if it would have jumped through his waistcoat.

"Not that I am aware of," replied Mrs. Bustle. And, having looked inquiringly round the table without receiving any reply, she continued: "No, Jenny; it is a mistake: they are not for here."

Jenny went out, but presently returned. "Please mum, the man says he is sure on it as how they are for here; he says Mrs. Bustle's boarding-house, quite distinct: and he had a card to leave along with them, only he had the misfort'n' to lose it by the way, which, howsomever, isn't of no consequence, as he has found the house without it."

Gingerly's heart sank in his bosom.

"Do go, Betsy, my love, and see what all this is about," said Mrs. Bustle.

Betsy obeyed. Scarcely had she left the room, when, with eyes sparkling with joy, she bounded in again.

"O, George!" she exclaimed, "How *very* foolish of you! It is a delicate attention, truly delicate, indeed! but you shouldn't have done it."

"Done it! done what?" inquired George.

"Now, how silly it is of you to pretend astonishment, George, dear—Go, Jenny, and see those flowers taken *very* carefully up into my room.—O, Mamma! they are such loves!—It is very foolish of you, George: but, certainly, never any thing in my life gave me half so much pleasure!"

"*Paw* my life, Betsy, I'm *paw*fectly ignorant of what you mean;" said Hobnill.

"You ridiculous creature! where is the use of your denying it, when they are the very plants, every one of them, which I selected last night, and you tried to bargain for."

"I *saw*lemly decl*aor*——."

"What's the meaning of all this?" exclaimed Captain O'Popper. "If you didn't send Betsy those plants, Mr. George, why, somebody else did; and as nobody else has the smallest right in the universal world to take such a liberty, that other somebody, whoever he may be, is an impertinent fellow. There's a bit of logic for you. But I'll beat about till I discover who this somebody is; and then we shall see whether Mr. Somebody or Captain O'Popper is the best man at ten paces."

"Lord, Sir!" said Betsy, "it *is* George.—Now—now, hold your tongue, George, and don't deny it, unless you'd make me very angry. I knew them every one again the instant I saw them. Besides," added she, (at the same time bestowing upon him a tender look, and gently placing the tips of her delicate fingers on his arm,)—"besides, dear George, it is so completely your style of thing!"

George, finding denial to be in vain, relinquished the contest. He looked at his watch, rose from table, and announced the necessity of his return to Shoreham.

That's something, and be hanged to him, thought Gingerly.

"And *must* you go back this morning, George?" inquired Betsy. "Well, if you must——But just stop a moment." She ran out of the room, and, after the lapse of a few minutes, returned with a handful of flowers. "Here, George," she said (as she placed one of them in his button-hole, and put the others, carefully made up in a sheet of writing paper, into his hand) "take these. I plucked some of the most beautiful of them for you, for no one has a better right to them than *you*. Good bye, George!—And, George; be sure you come back to dinner to-day, for I shall want you to walk with me to Aunt Heathfields again this evening."

The feelings of poor Gingerly, during this scene, may be (to use a phrase, the originality of which is not insisted upon) may be more easily conceived than described. The rival having fairly taken his departure, Gingerly rose from his seat, walked to the window, back again to the table, resumed his seat, rose, walked towards the fire-place, once more to the window, then to the door, and—out he rushed.

"Is your friend ill?" said Mrs. Bustle to Damper.

"I fear so," replied Damper; "I'll follow him." But Damper knew very well the cause of his friend's disorder.

Damper sought Gingerly all over the house, but he was nowhere to be found. He then went out—paced the Marine Parade—traversed the Steyne—East Cliff—West Cliff—up one street—down another—looked into all the libraries—but to no purpose. He neither saw, nor could he hear, any thing of Gingerly. He became alarmed. He went to the Chain Pier, and walked, hurriedly, to the end of it. But there was no Gingerly. "Can he have been so rash!" exclaimed Damper. One of the men belonging to the Pier was sitting smoking a pipe on the signal-gun. Damper approached him. With some hesitation, Damper said, "Pray—pray, my good friend—have you seen an elderly gentleman throw himself into the sea within these two hours?"

The man deliberately took his pipe from his mouth, did what smokers are in the habit of doing upon such an occasion, and, after leisurely scratching his head, said—

"An elderly gentleman, Sir?—Let me see!—an *elderly* gentleman. Why—a—no, Sir, I can't say as I have. But if I should see e'er a one in the course of the a'ternoon, where shall I have the pleasure of letting you know?"

Damper retraced his steps, and soon, to his great

joy, met Gingerly. The latter allowed him no time to speak, but thus, at once, accosted him:—

"It is awful! truly awful! Would you believe it? That rascally attorney's clerk who walked off with those flowers—with the credit of the little act of gallantry, too—they were my flowers—it was I who sent them."

"I would have sworn it," replied Damper. "To repeat Miss Betsy's words, it was 'so completely your style of thing.' But let me congratulate you on finding you alive: I began to fear you had committed some desperate act."

"Why, no, I have not yet done so. An ingenious expedient has occurred to me;—I'll try it—I don't think it can fail, for the dear girl has a great deal of feeling."

"True," replied Damper, "but not one particle for you. Be wise, book a place in the four o'clock coach, and return to town. All your ingenious expedients, all your delicate attentions, have turned to the advantage of the interesting Hobnill; and take my word for it that——"

"I won't listen to any thing you can say," cried Gingerly, interrupting him. "This *cannot* fail—at least if you will second me in it."

For some time Damper refused to have any thing more to do with the affair; but, upon Gingerly's promise that, should his next delicate attention be no more successful than the others, he would abandon the pursuit of the fair Betsy, and return to his quiet chambers in Lyon's Inn, Damper undertook to assist him. Thus pledged, he listened patiently to Gingerly's instructions; the result of which is now to be shown.

"You seem agitated, Mr. Damper," said Betsy, who was sitting alone in the drawing room when he entered.

"Why, the fact is, Miss Bustle—I—I am afraid to acquaint you with it, but sooner or later you must know it;" replied Damper, who was almost ashamed of the ridiculous commission he had undertaken.

"Good heavens! what has happened?" exclaimed she.

"Why—this morning, a gentleman, a *certain* gentleman, went into Tuppen's Library. Scarcely had he entered, when he heard another gentleman mention your name in a way not altogether respectful. This, the gentleman,—that is to say, the *certain* gentleman,—could not endure. He struck the other; a challenge ensued; within an hour afterwards they met on the downs; exchanged shots; and the gentleman, your champion, was wounded."

"Wounded! who was it?" inquired Miss Bustle.

Now comes the trial, thought Damper.—"It is one," said he, "who takes the deepest interest in every thing that concerns you. In short—for the circumstances of the case compel me to speak out—he entertains for you the most unbounded affection; and, as you already possess his heart, he has authorized me to——"

Betsy Bustle fainted; Damper rang the bell violently. In a moment there was Mrs. Bustle, *sal volatile*, Captain O'Popper, hartshorn, George Hobnill, burnt brown paper, and all the lodgers. In the midst of the confusion Gingerly (with a lackadaisical air, and his left arm in a sling) entered the room, and stood, unperceived, behind the crowd which was pressing about the fair fainter. Not a little delighted was he at the effect produced by this, his last, and most ingenious expedient.

"Betsy, my child, what *is* the matter?" cried Mrs. Bustle.

"Betsy, my de*or*, what *is* the matter?" echoed George.

Either these sounds, or the burnt brown paper, or the hartshorn, or the *sal volatile*, or perhaps, the suffocating pressure of the persons about her—a circumstance inevitable on occasions of this nature—revived her. She opened her eyes; and the first object she beheld was George, kneeling at her side, and officiating as administerer of the burnt brown paper aforesaid. She burst into a flood of tears. As soon as she was sufficiently recovered to speak, she threw herself into his arms, and exclaimed:

"Oh! George! how *could* you be so foolish as to expose your dear, your precious life, on my account? Had any thing fatal happened to you, I should have gone distracted! But whereabouts are you wounded?"

"Wounded!" exclaimed George, in utter amazement; "wounded! What an ide*or*! *Paw* my honor I——"

"Now don't deceive me, George; let me know the worst. But your endeavoring to conceal it from me is so like you! It is so *very* delicate. Oh! Mamma! after this, can you refuse to——?"

"I understand you, my dear child: you have my consent; and, with the consent of George's parents, the banns shall be published on Sunday."

"George," said the Captain, "I didn't think you had so much in you. But you are a brave fellow; so, as to the consent, by the powers! I say *ditto* to that. And Mrs. Bustle," said he in a whisper to the lady; "as we are both in a consenting mood, let us consent to marry one another at the same time."

"Oh! Captain!" was the lady's laconic, but expressive, reply.

Gingerly, pale, and trembling from head to foot with rage and disappointment, was about to rush forward and explain; but he was restrained by an admonitory gesture from his friend.

"My dear Gingerly," said Damper, taking him aside; "remember your promise: the four o'clock coach and Lyon's Inn. Keep your own counsel: so shall you appear ridiculous in the eyes of none but of an old and trusty friend. Your ingenious contrivances, from first to last, have all turned to the advantage of your rival; nor have you the credit of being even suspected of the smallest of them. If you are resolved to marry, say '*Will you?*' to the first woman you may happen to meet; for, rely on it, at your time of life, you are not likely to entrap a female heart by DELICATE ATTENTIONS.'

BITS.—"Are you looking for any one in particular?" as the mite said to the microscope.

"You can't make a noise here," as the wooden pavement said to the omnibus.

Why should a quill pen never be used in inditing secret matters? Because it is apt to *split*.

"Young men taken in and done for," as the shark said to the ship's crew.

"I'm particularly uneasy on this point," as the fly said when the young gentleman stuck him on the end of a needle.

THE WOOING OF MASTER FOX.

BY SIR EDWARD LYTTON BULWER.

[The tale of the Fox's Wooing has been composed to give the English reader an idea of the species of novel not naturalized amongst us, though frequent among the legends of our Irish neighbors; in which the brutes are the only characters drawn—drawn, too, with shades of distinction as nice and subtle as if they were the creatures of the civilized world.]

In the time of which I am about to speak, there was no particular enmity between the various species of brutes; the dog and the hare chatted very agreeably together, and all the world knows that the wolf, unacquainted with mutton, had a particular affection for the lamb. In these happy days, two most respectable cats, of very old family, had an only daughter; never was kitten more amiable or more seducing; as she grew up she manifested so many charms, that in a little while she became noted as the greatest beauty in the neighborhood: her skin was of the most delicate tortoise shell, her paws were smoother than velvet, her whiskers were twelve inches long at the least, and her eyes had a gentleness altogether astonishing in a cat. But if the young beauty had suitors in plenty during the lives of monsieur and madame, the number was not diminished, when, at the age of two years and a half, she was left an orphan, and sole heiress to all the hereditary property. In fine, she was the richest marriage in the whole country. Without troubling you with the adventures of the rest of her lovers, with their suit, and their rejection, I come at once to the two rivals most sanguine of success—the dog and the fox.

Now, the dog was a handsome, honest, straightforward, affectionate fellow. "For my part," said he, "I don't wonder at my cousin's refusing Bruin the bear, and Gauntgrim the wolf: to be sure they give themselves great airs, and call themselves '*noble*,' but what then? Bruin is always in the sulks, and Gauntgrim always in a passion; a cat of any sensibility would lead a miserable life with them: as for me, I am very good-tempered when I'm not put out; and I have no fault except that of being angry if disturbed at my meals. I am young and good looking, fond of play and amusement, and altogether as agreeable a husband as a cat could find in a summer's day. If she marries me, well and good; she may have her property settled on herself: if not, I shall bear her no malice; and I hope I sha'n't be too much in love to forget that there are other cats in the world.'

With that, the dog threw his tail over his back, and set off to his mistress, with a gay face on the matter.

Now the fox heard the dog talking thus to himself—for the fox was always peeping about, in holes and corners, and he burst out a-laughing when the dog was out of sight.

"Ho, ho, my fine fellow!" said he; "not so fast, if you please: you've got the fox for a rival, let me tell you."

The fox, as you very well know, is a beast that can never do any thing without a manœuvre; and as, from his cunning, he was generally very lucky in any thing he undertook, he did not doubt for a moment that he should put the dog's nose out of joint. Reynard was aware that in love one should always, if possible, be the first in the field, and he, therefore, resolved to get the start of the dog and arrive before him at the cat's residence. But this was no easy matter; for though Reynard could run faster than the dog for a little way, he was no match for him in a journey of some distance. "However," said Reynard, "those good-natured creatures are never very wise; and I think I know already what will make him bait on his way."

With that, the fox trotted pretty fast by a short cut in the woods, and getting before the dog, laid himself down by a hole in the earth, and began to howl most piteously.

The dog, hearing the noise, was very much alarmed; "See now," said he, "if the poor fox has not got himself into some scrape! Those cunning creatures are always in mischief; thank heaven, it never comes into my head to be cunning!" And the good-natured animal ran off as hard as he could to see what was the matter with the fox.

"Oh, dear!" cried Reynard; "what shall I do, what shall I do! my poor little sister has fallen into this hole, and I can't get her out—she'll certainly be smothered." And the fox burst out a-howling more piteously than before.

"But, my dear Reynard," quoth the dog very simply, "why don't you go in after your sister?"

"Ah, you may well ask that," said the fox; "but, in trying to get in, don't you perceive that I have sprained my back, and can't stir? Oh, dear! what shall I do if my poor little sister is smothered!"

"Pray don't vex yourself," said the dog; "I'll get her out in an instant:" and with that he forced himself with great difficulty into the hole.

Now, no sooner did the fox see that the dog was fairly in, than he rolled a great stone to the mouth of the hole, and fitted it so tight, that the dog, not being able to turn round and scratch against it with his fore-paws, was made a close prisoner.

"Ha, ha!" cried Reynard, laughing outside; "amuse yourself with my poor little sister, while I go and make your compliments to Mademoiselle the Cat."

With that Reynard set off at an easy pace, never troubling his head what became of the poor dog. When he arrived in the neighborhood of the beautiful cat's mansion, he resolved to pay a visit to a friend of his, an old magpie that lived in a tree, and was well acquainted with all the news of the place. "For," thought Reynard, "I may as well know the blind side of my mistress that is to be, and get round it at once."

The magpie received the fox with great cordiality, and inquired what brought him so great a distance from home.

"Upon my word," said the fox, "nothing so much as the pleasure of seeing your ladyship, and hearing those agreeable anecdotes you tell with so charming a grace: but, to let you into a secret—be sure it don't go farther—"

"On the word of a magpie," interrupted the bird.

"Pardon me for doubting you," continued the fox; "I should have recollected that a pie was a proverb for discretion. But, as I was saying, you know her majesty the lioness?"

"Surely," said the magpie, bridling.

"Well; she was pleased to fall in—that is to say —to—to—take a caprice to your humble servant, and the lion grew so jealous that I thought it prudent to decamp. A jealous lion is no joke, let me assure your ladyship. But mum's the word."

So great a piece of news delighted the magpie. She could not but repay it in kind, by all the news in her budget. She told the fox all the scandal about Bruin and Gauntgrim, and she then fell to work on the poor young cat. She did not spare her foibles, you may be quite sure. The fox listened with great attention, and he learned enough to convince him, that however much the magpie might exaggerate, the cat was very susceptible to flattery, and had a great deal of imagination.

When the magpie had finished, she said, "But it must be very unfortunate for you to be banished from so magnificent a court as that of the lion?"

"As to that," answered the fox, "I consoled myself for my exile with a present his majesty made me on parting, as a reward for my anxiety for his honor and domestic tranquillity; namely, three hairs from the fifth leg of the amoronthologosphorus. Only think of that, ma'am!"

"The what?" cried the pie, cocking down her left ear.

"The amoronthologosphorus."

"La!" said the magpie; "and what is that very long word, my dear Reynard?"

"The amoronthologosphorus is a beast that lives on the other side of the river Cylinx; it has five legs, and on the fifth leg there are three hairs, and whoever has those three hairs can be young and beautiful for ever."

"Bless me! I wish you would let me see them," said the pie, holding out her claw.

"Would that I could oblige you, ma'am; but it's as much as my life's worth to show them to any but the lady I marry. In fact, they only have an effect on the fair sex, as you may see by myself, whose poor person they utterly fail to improve: they are, therefore, intended for a marriage present, and his majesty the lion thus generously atoned to me for relinquishing the tenderness of his queen. One must confess that there was a great deal of delicacy in the gift. But you'll be sure not to mention it."

"A magpie gossip, indeed!" quoth the old blab.

The fox then wished the magpie good night, and retired to a hole to sleep off the fatigues of the day, before he presented himself to the beautiful young cat.

The next morning, heaven knows how! it was all over the place that Reynard the fox had been banished from court for the favor shown him by her majesty, and that the lion had bribed his departure with three hairs that would make any lady whom the fox married young and beautiful for ever.

The cat was the first to learn the news, and she became all curiosity to see so interesting a stranger, possessed of "qualifications" which, in the language of the day, "would render any animal happy!" She was not long without obtaining her wish. As she was taking a walk in the wood, the fox contrived to encounter her. You may be sure that he made her his best bow; and he flattered the poor cat with so courtly an air that she saw nothing surprising in the love of the lioness.

Meanwhile let us see what became of his rival, the dog.

"When the dog found that he was thus entrapped, he gave himself up for lost. In vain he kicked with his hind-legs against the stone—he only succeeded in bruising his paws; and at length he was forced to lie down, with his tongue out of his mouth, and quite exhausted. "However," said he, after he had taken breath, "it won't do to be starved here, without doing my best to escape; and if I can't get out one way, let me see if there is not a hole at the other end." Thus saying, his courage, which stood him in lieu of cunning, returned, and he proceeded on in the same straightforward way in which he always conducted himself. At first the path was exceedingly narrow, and he hurt his sides very much against the rough stones that projected from the earth. But by degrees the way became broader, and he now went on with considerable ease to himself, till he arrived in a large cavern, where he saw an immense griffin sitting on his tail, and smoking a huge pipe.

The dog was by no means pleased at meeting so suddenly a creature that had only to open his mouth to swallow him up at a morsel; however he put a bold face on the danger, and walking respectfully up to the griffin, said, "Sir, I should be very much obliged to you if you would inform me the way out of these holes into the upper world."

The griffin took the pipe out of his mouth, and looked at the dog very sternly.

"Ho, wretch!" said he, "how comest thou hither? I suppose thou wantest to steal my treasure: but I know how to treat such vagabonds as you, and I shall certainly eat you up."

"You can do that if you choose," said the dog; "but it would be very unhandsome conduct in an animal so much bigger than myself. For my own part, I never attack any dog that is not of equal size: I should be ashamed of myself if I did. And as to your treasure, the character I bear for honesty is too well known to merit such a suspicion."

"Upon my word," said the griffin, who could not

help smiling for the life of him, "you have a singularly free mode of expressing yourself;—and how, I say, came you hither?"

Then the dog, who did not know what a lie was, told the griffin his whole history,—how he had set off to pay his court to the cat, and how Reynard the fox had entrapped him into the hole.

When he had finished, the griffin said to him, "I see, my friend, that you know how to speak the truth; I am in want of just such a servant as you will make me, therefore stay with me and keep watch over my treasure when I sleep."

"Two words to that," said the dog. "You have hurt my feelings very much by suspecting my honesty, and I would much sooner go back into the wood and be avenged on that scoundrel the fox, than serve a master who has so ill an opinion of me. I pray you, therefore, to dismiss me, and to put me in the right way to my cousin the cat."

"I am not a griffin of many words," answered the master of the cavern, "and I give you your choice—be my servant, or be my breakfast; it is just the same to me. I give you time to decide till I have smoked out my pipe."

The poor dog did not take so long to consider. "It is true," thought he, "that it is a great misfortune to live in a cave with a griffin of so unpleasant a countenance: but, probably, if I serve him well and faithfully, he'll take pity on me some day, and let me go back to earth, and prove to my cousin what a rogue the fox is; and as to the rest, though I would sell my life as dear as I could, it is impossible to fight a griffin with a mouth of so monstrous a size."—In short, he decided to stay with the griffin.

"Shake a paw on it," quoth the grim smoker; and the dog shook paws.

"And now," said the griffin, "I will tell you what you are to do—look here;" and, moving his tail, he showed the dog a great heap of gold and silver, in a hole in the ground, that he had covered with the folds of his tail; and also, what the dog thought more valuable, a great heap of bones of very tempting appearance.

"Now," said the griffin, "during the day, I can take very good care of these myself; but at night it is very necessary that I should go to sleep: so when I sleep, you must watch over them instead of me."

"Very well," said the dog. "As to the gold and silver, I have no objection; but I would much rather you would lock up the bones, for I'm often hungry of a night, and—"

"Hold your tongue," said the griffin.

"But, Sir," said the dog, after a short silence, "surely nobody ever comes into so retired a situation! Who are the thieves, if I may make boid to ask?"

"Know," answered the griffin, "that there are a great many serpents in this neighborhood, they are always trying to steal my treasure; and if they catch me napping, they, not contented with theft, would do their best to sting me to death. So that I am almost worn out for want of sleep."

"Ah!" quoth the dog, who was fond of a good night's rest, "I don't envy you your treasure, Sir."

At night, the griffin, who had a great deal of penetration, and saw that he might depend on the dog, laid down to sleep in another corner of the cave; and the dog, shaking himself well, so as to be quite awake, took watch over the treasure. His mouth watered exceedingly at the bones, and he could not help smelling them now and then; but he said to himself,—"A bargain's a bargain, and since I have promised to serve the griffin, I must serve him as an honest dog ought to serve."

In the middle of the night, he saw a great snake creeping in by the side of the cave, but the dog set up so loud a bark that the griffin awoke, and the snake crept away as fast as he could. Then the griffin was very much pleased, and he gave the dog one of the bones to amuse himself with; and every night the dog watched the treasure, and acquitted himself so well, that not a snake, at last, dared to make its appearance;—so the griffin enjoyed an excellent night's rest.

The dog now found himself much more comfortable than he expected. The griffin regularly gave him one of the bones for supper; and, pleased with his fidelity, made himself as agreeable a master as a griffin could do. Still, however, the dog was secretly very anxious to return to earth; for, having nothing to do during the day but to doze on the ground, he dreamed perpetually of his cousin the cat's charms; and, in fancy, he gave the rascal Reynard as hearty a worry as a fox may well have the honor of receiving from a dog's paws. He awoke panting—alas! he could not realize his dreams.

One night, as he was watching as usual over the treasure, he was greatly surprised to see a beautiful little black and white dog enter the cave; and it came fawning to our honest friend, wagging its tail with pleasure.

"Ah! little one," said our dog, whom, to distinguish, I will call the watch-dog, "you had better make the best of your way back again. See, there is a great griffin asleep in the other corner of the cave, and if he wakes, he will either eat you up or make you his servant, as he has made me."

"I know what you would tell me," says the little dog; "and I have come down here to deliver you. The stone is now gone from the mouth of the cave, and you have nothing to do but to go back with me. Come, brother, come."

The dog was very much excited by this address. "Don't ask me, my dear little friend," said he; "you must be aware that I should be too happy to escape out of this cold cave, and roll on the soft turf once more: but if I leave my master, the griffin, those cursed serpents, who are always on the watch, will come in and steal his treasure—nay, perhaps, sting him to death." Then the little dog came up to the watch-dog, and remonstrated with him greatly, and licked him caressingly on both sides of his face; and, taking him by the ear, endeavored to draw him from the treasure: but the dog would not stir a step, though his heart sorely pressed him. At length the little dog, finding it all in vain, said, "Well then, if I must leave, good by; but I have become so hungry in coming down all this way after you, that I wish you would give me one of those bones; they smell very pleasantly, and one out of so many could never be missed."

"Alas!" said the watch-dog, with tears in his eyes, "how unlucky I am to have eat up the bone my master gave me, otherwise you should have had it and welcome. But I can't give you one of these, because my master has made me promise to watch over them all, and I have given him my paw on it. I am sure a dog of your respectable appearance will say nothing farther on the subject."

Then the little dog answered pettishly, "Pooh, what nonsense you talk! surely a great griffin can't miss a little bone, fit for me;" and nestling his nose under the watch-dog, he tried forthwith to bring up one of the bones.

On this, the watch-dog grew angry, and, though with much reluctance, he seized the little dog by the nape of the neck and threw him off, but without hurting him. Suddenly, the little dog changed into a monstrous serpent, bigger even than the griffin himself, and the watch-dog barked with all his might. The griffin rose in a great hurry, and the serpent sprang upon him ere he was well awake. I wish you could have seen the battle between the griffin and the serpent, how they coiled and twisted, and bit and darted their fiery tongues at each other. At length, the serpent got uppermost, and was about to plunge his tongue into that part of the griffin which is unprotected by his scales, when the dog, seizing him by the tail, bit him so sharply, that he could not help turning round to kill his new assailant, and the griffin, taking advantage of the opportunity, caught the serpent by the throat with both claws, and fairly strangled him. As soon as the griffin had recovered from the nervousness of the conflict, he heaped all manner of caresses on the dog for saving his life. The dog told him the whole story, and the griffin then explained, that the dead snake was the king of the serpents, who had the power to change himself into any shape he pleased. "If he had tempted you," said he, "to leave the treasure but for one moment, or to have given him any part of it, ay, but a single bone, he would have crushed you in an instant, and stung me to death ere I could have waked; but none, no, not the most venomous thing in creation, has power to hurt the honest!"

"That has always been my belief," answered the dog; "and now, sir, you had better go to sleep again, and leave the rest to me."

"Nay," answered the griffin, "I have no longer need of a servant; for now that the king of the serpents is dead, the rest will never molest me. It was only to satisfy his avarice that his subjects dared to brave the den of the griffin."

Upon hearing this, the dog was exceedingly delighted; and raising himself on his hind-paws, he begged the griffin most movingly to let him return to earth, to visit his mistress the cat, and worry his rival the fox.

"You do not serve an ungrateful master," answered the griffin. "You shall return, and I will teach you all the craft of our race, which is much craftier than the race of that pettifogger the fox, so that you may be able to cope with your rival."

"Ah, excuse me," said the dog, hastily, "I am equally obliged to you: but I fancy honesty is a match for cunning any day; and I think myself a great deal safer in being a dog of honor than if I knew all the tricks in the world."

"Well," said the griffin, a little piqued at the dog's bluntness, "do as you please; I wish you all possible success."

Then the griffin opened a secret door in the side of the cavern, and the dog saw a broad path that led at once into the wood. He thanked the griffin with all his heart, and ran wagging his tail into the open moonlight. "Ah, ah! master fox," said he, "there's no trap for an honest dog that has not two doors to it, cunning as you think yourself."

With that, he curled his tail gallantly over his left leg, and set off on a long trot to the cat's house. When he was within sight of it, he stopped to refresh himself by a pool of water, and who should be there but our friend the magpie!

"And what do *you* want, friend?" said she, rather disdainfully, for the dog looked somewhat out of case after his journey.

"I am going to see my cousin the cat," answered he.

"*Your* cousin! marry come up," said the magpie; "don't you know she is going to be married to Reynard the fox? This is not a time for her to receive the visits of a brute like you."

These words put the dog in such a passion, that he very nearly bit the magpie for her uncivil mode of communicating such bad news. However, he curbed his temper, and, without answering her, went at once to the cat's residence.

The cat was sitting at the window, and no sooner did the dog see her than he fairly lost his heart; never had he seen so charming a cat before: he advanced, wagging his tail, and with his most insinuating air; when the cat, getting up, clapped the window in his face—and lo! Reynard the fox appeared in her stead.

"Come out, thou rascal!" said the dog, showing his teeth: "come out, I challenge thee to single combat; I have not forgiven thy malice, and thou seest that I am no longer shut up in the cave, and unable to punish thee for thy wickedness."

"Go home, silly one!" answered the fox, sneering; "thou hast no business here, and as for fighting thee—bah!" Then the fox left the window and disappeared. But the dog, thoroughly enraged, scratched lustily at the door, and made such a noise, that presently the cat herself came to the window.

"How now!" said she, angrily; "what means all this rudeness? Who are you, and what do you want at my house?"

"O, my dear cousin," said the dog, "do not speak so severely. Know that I have come here on purpose to pay you a visit; and, whatever you do, let me beseech you not to listen to that villain Reynard—you have no conception what a rogue he is!"

"What!" said the cat, blushing; "do you dare to abuse your betters in this fashion? I see you have a design on me. Go, this instant, or—"

"Enough, madam," said the dog, proudly; "you need not speak twice to me—farewell."

And he turned away very slowly, and went under a tree, where he took up his lodgings for the night. But the next morning there was an amazing commotion in the neighborhood; a stranger, of a very different style of travelling from that of the dog, had arrived at the dead of the night, and fixed his abode in a large cavern, hollowed out of a steep rock. The noise he had made in flying through the air was so great, that it had awakened every bird and beast in the parish; and Reynard, whose bad conscience never suffered him to sleep very soundly, putting his head out of the window, perceived, to his great alarm, that the stranger was nothing less than a monstrous griffin.

Now the griffins are the richest beasts in the world; and that's the reason they keep so close under ground. Whenever it does happen that they pay a visit above, it is not a thing to be easily forgotten.

The magpie was all agitation,—what could the griffin possibly want there? She resolved to take a peep at the cavern, and accordingly she hopped timorously up the rock, and pretended to be picking up sticks for her nest.

"Holla, ma'am!" cried a very rough voice, and she saw the griffin putting his head out of the cavern. "Holla! you are the very lady I want to see; you know all the people about here—eh!"

"All the best company, your lordship, I certainly do," answered the magpie, dropping a courtesy.

Upon this, the griffin walked out; and smoking his pipe leisurely in the open air, in order to set the pie at her ease, continued—

"Are there any respectable beasts of good families settled in this neighborhood?"

"O most elegant society, I assure your lordship," cried the pie. "I have lived here myself these ten years, and the great heiress, the cat yonder, attracts a vast number of strangers."

"Humph—heiress, indeed! much you know about heiresses!" said the griffin. "There is only one heiress in the world, and that's my daughter."

"Bless me! has your lordship a family? I beg you a thousand pardons. But I only saw your lordship's own equipage last night, and did not know you brought any one with you."

"My daughter went first, and was safely lodged before I arrived. She did not disturb you, I dare say, as I did; for she sails along like a swan: but I have the gout in my left claw, and that's the reason I puff and groan so in taking a journey."

"Shall I drop in upon Miss Griffin, and see how she is after her journey?" said the pie, advancing.

"I thank you, no. I don't intend her to be seen while I stay here—it unsettles her; and I'm afraid of the young beasts running away with her, if they once heard how handsome she was: she's the living picture of me, but she's monstrous giddy! Not that I should care much if she did go off with a beast of degree, were I not obliged to pay her portion, which is prodigious; and I don't like parting with money, ma'am, when I've once got it. Ho, ho, ho!"

"You are too witty, my lord. But if you refused your consent?" said the pie, anxious to know the whole family history of so grand a seigneur.

"I should have to pay the dowry all the same. It was left her by her uncle the dragon. But don't let this go any farther."

"Your lordship may depend on my secrecy. I wish your lordship a very good morning."

Away flew the pie, and she did not stop till she got to the cat's house. The cat and the fox were at breakfast, and the fox had his paw on his heart. "Beautiful scene!" cried the pie; the cat colored, and bade the pie take a seat.

Then off went the pie's tongue, glib, glib, glib, chatter, chatter, chatter. She related to them the whole story of the griffin and his daughter, and a great deal more besides, that the griffin had never told her.

The cat listened attentively. Another young heiress in the neighborhood might be a formidable rival. "But is the griffiness handsome?" said she.

"Handsome!" cried the pie; "oh! if you could have seen the father!—such a mouth, such eyes, such a complexion; and he declares she's the living picture of himself! But what do you say, Mr. Reynard? you, who have been so much in the world, have, perhaps, seen the young lady!"

"Why, I can't say I have," answered the fox, waking from a revery; "but she must be wonderfully rich. I dare say that fool, the dog, will be making up to her."

"Ah! by the way," said the pie, "what a fuss he made at your door yesterday; why would you not admit him, my dear?"

"Oh!" said the cat, demurely, "Mr. Reynard says that he is a dog of very bad character, quite a fortune-hunter; and hiding the most dangerous disposition to bite under an appearance of good nature. I hope he won't be quarrelsome with you, dear Reynard!"

"With me? O the poor wretch, no!—he might bluster a little; but he knows that if I'm once angry, I'm a devil at biting;—but one should not boast of one's self."

In the evening, Reynard felt a strange desire to go and see the griffin smoking his pipe; but what could he do? There was the dog under the opposite tree, evidently watching for him, and Reynard had no wish to prove himself that devil at biting which he declared he was. At last, he resolved to have recourse to stratagem, to get rid of the dog.

A young buck of a rabbit, a sort of provincial fop, had looked in upon his cousin the cat, to pay her his respects, and Reynard, taking him aside, said, "You see that shabby-looking dog under the tree? He has behaved very ill to your cousin the cat, and you certainly ought to challenge him—forgive my boldness—nothing but respect for your character induces me to take so great a liberty; you know I would chastise the rascal myself, but what a scandal it would make! If I were already married to your cousin, it would be a different thing. But you know what a story that cursed magpie would hatch out of it!"

The rabbit looked very foolish: he assured the fox that he was no match for the dog; that he was very fond of his cousin, to be sure; but he saw no necessity to interfere with her domestic affairs;—and, in short, he tried all he possibly could to get out of the scrape: but the fox so artfully played on his vanity—so earnestly assured him that the dog was the biggest coward in the world, and would make a humble apology, and so eloquently represented to him the glory he would obtain for manifesting so much spirit, that at length the rabbit was persuaded to go out and deliver the challenge.

"I'll be your second," said the fox; "and the great field on the other side the wood, two miles hence, shall be the place of battle: there we shall be out of observation. You go first, I'll follow in half an hour—and I say—hark!—in case he does accept the challenge, and you feel the least afraid, I'll be in the field, and take it off your paws with the utmost pleasure; rely on *me*, my dear sir!"

Away went the rabbit. The dog was a little astonished at the temerity of the poor creature; but on hearing that the fox was to be present, willingly consented to repair to the place of conflict. This readiness the rabbit did not at all relish; he went very slowly to the field, and seeing no fox there, his heart misgave him, and while the dog was putting his nose to the ground to try if he could track the coming of the fox, the rabbit slipped into a burrow, and left the dog to walk back again.

Meanwhile the fox was already at the rock; he walked very soft-footedly, and looked about with extreme caution, for he had a vague notion that a griffin-papa would not be very civil to foxes.

Now there were two holes in the rock—one below, one above, an upper story and an under; and while the fox was peering about, he saw a great claw from the upper rock beckoning to him.

"Ah, ah!" said the fox, "that's the wanton young griffiness, I'll swear."

He approached, and a voice said—

"Charming Mr. Reynard! Do you not think you could deliver an unfortunate griffiness from a barbarous confinement in this rock?"

"Oh heavens!" cried the fox, tenderly, "what a beautiful voice! and, ah, my poor heart, what a lovely claw! Is it possible that I hear the daughter of my lord, the great griffin?"

"Hush, flatterer! not so loud, if you please. My father is taking an evening stroll, and is very quick of hearing. He has tied me up by my poor wings in the cavern, for he is mightily afraid of some beast running away with me. You know I have all my fortune settled on myself."

"Talk not of fortune," said the fox; "but how can I deliver you? Shall I enter and gnaw the cord?"

"Alas!" answered the griffiness, "it is an immense chain I am bound with. However, you may come in and talk more at your ease."

The fox peeped cautiously all round, and seeing no sign of the griffin, he entered the lower cave and stole up stairs to the upper story; but as he went on, he saw immense piles of jewels and gold, and all sorts of treasure, so that the old griffin might well have laughed at the poor cat being called an heiress. The fox was greatly pleased at such indisputable signs of wealth, and he entered the upper cave, resolved to be transported with the charms of the griffiness.

There was, however, a great chasm between the landing-place and the spot where the young lady was chained, and he found it impossible to pass; the cavern was very dark, but he saw enough of the figure of the griffiness to perceive, in spite of her petticoat, that she was the image of her father, and the most hideous heiress that the earth ever saw!

However, he swallowed his disgust, and poured forth such a heap of compliments that the griffiness appeared entirely won. He implored her to fly with him the first moment she was unchained.

"That is impossible," said she; "for my father never unchains me except in his presence, and then I cannot stir out of his sight."

"The wretch!" cried Reynard, "what is to be done?"

"Why, there is only one thing I know of," answered the griffiness, "which is this—I always make his soup for him, and if I could mix something in it that would put him fast to sleep before he had time to chain me up again, I might slip down, and carry off all the treasure below on my back."

"Charming!" exclaimed Reynard; "what invention! what wit! I will go and get some poppies directly."

"Alas!" said the griffiness, "poppies have no effect upon griffins. The only thing that can ever put my father fast to sleep is a nice young cat boiled up in his soup; it is astonishing what a charm that has upon him! But where to get a cat?—it must be a maiden cat too!"

Reynard was a little startled at so singular an opiate. "But," thought he, "griffins are not like the rest of the world, and so rich an heiress is not to be won by ordinary means."

"I do know a cat—a maiden cat," said he, after a short pause; "but I feel a little repugnance at the thought of having her boiled in the griffin's soup. Would not a dog do as well?"

"Ah, base thing!" said the griffiness, appearing to weep, "you are in love with the cat, I see it; go and marry her, poor dwarf that she is, and leave me to die of grief."

In vain the fox protested that he did not care a straw for the cat; nothing could now appease the griffiness, but his positive assurance that, come what would, poor puss should be brought to the cave, and boiled for the griffin's soup.

"But how will you get her here?" said the griffiness.

"Ah, leave that to me," said Reynard. "Only put a basket out of the window, and draw it up by a cord; the moment it arrives at the window, be sure to clap your claw on the cat at once, for she is terribly active."

"Tush!" answered the heiress; "a pretty griffiness I should be if I did not know how to catch a cat!"

"But this must be when your father is out," said Reynard.

"Certainly: he takes a stroll every evening at sunset."

"Let it be to-morrow, then," said Reynard, impatient for the treasure.

This being arranged, Reynard thought it time to decamp. He stole down the stairs again, and tried to filch some of the treasure by the way: but it was too heavy for him to carry, and he was forced to acknowledge to himself that it was impossible to get the treasure without taking the griffiness (whose back seemed prodigiously strong) into the bargain.

He returned home to the cat, and when he entered her house, and saw how ordinary every thing looked after the jewels in the griffin's cave, he quite wondered how he had ever thought the cat had the least pretensions to good looks.

However, he concealed his wicked design, and his mistress thought he had never appeared so amiable.

"Only guess," said he, "where I have been?—to our new neighbor the griffin; a most charming person, thoroughly affable, and quite the air of the court. As for that silly magpie, the griffin saw her character at once; and it was all a hoax about his daughter: he has no daughter at all. You know, my dear, hoaxing is a fashionable amusement among the great. He says he has heard of nothing but your beauty, and on my telling him we were going to be married, he has insisted upon giving a great ball and supper in honor of the event. In fact, he is a gallant old fellow, and dying to see you. Of course I was obliged to accept the invitation."

"You could not do otherwise," said the unsuspecting young creature, who, as I before said, was very susceptible to flattery.

"And only think how delicate his attentions are," said the fox. "As he is very badly lodged for a beast of his rank, and his treasure takes up the whole of the ground floor, he is forced to give the fête in the upper story, so he hangs out a basket for his guests, and draws them up with his own claw. How condescending! But the great *are* so amiable!"

The cat, brought up in seclusion, was all delight at the idea of seeing such high life, and the lovers talked of nothing else all the next day;—when Reynard, towards evening, putting his head out of the window, saw his old friend the dog lying as usual and watching him very grimly. "Ah, that cursed creature! I had quite forgotten him; what is to be done now? he would make no bones of me if he once saw me set foot out of doors."

With that, the fox began to cast in his head how he should get rid of his rival, and at length he resolved on a very notable project: he desired the cat to set out first, and wait for him at a turn in the road a little way off. "For," said he, "if we go together, we shall certainly be insulted by the dog; and he will know that, in the presence of a lady, the custom of a beast of my fashion will not suffer me to avenge the affront. But when I am alone, the creature is such a coward that he would not dare say his soul's his own: leave the door open, and I'll follow immediately."

The cat's mind was so completely poisoned against her cousin that she implicitly believed this account of his character, and accordingly, with many recommendations to her lover not to sully his dignity by getting into any sort of quarrel with the dog, she set off first.

The dog went up to her very humbly, and begged her to allow him to say a few words to her; but she received him so haughtily, that his spirit was up; and he walked back to the tree more than ever enraged against his rival. But what was his joy when he saw that the cat had left the door open! "Now, wretch," thought he, "you cannot escape me!" So he walked briskly in at the back door. He was greatly surprised to find Reynard lying down in the straw, panting as if his heart would break, and rolling his eyes in the pangs of death.

"Ah, friend," said the fox, with a faltering voice, "you are avenged, my hour is come; I am just going to give up the ghost: put your paw upon mine, and say you forgive me."

Despite his anger, the generous dog could not set tooth on a dying foe.

"You have served me a shabby trick," said he: "you have left me to starve in a hole, and you have evidently maligned me with my cousin: certainly, I meant to be avenged on you; but if you are really dying, that alters the affair."

"Oh, oh!" groaned the fox very bitterly; "I am past help; the poor cat is gone for Doctor Ape, but he'll never come in time. What a thing it is to have a bad conscience on one's death-bed! But, wait till the cat returns, and I'll do you full justice with her before I die."

The good-natured dog was much moved at seeing his mortal enemy in such a state, and endeavored as well as he could to console him.

"Oh, oh!" said the fox; "I am so parched in the throat—I am burning;" and he hung his tongue out of his mouth, and rolled his eyes more fearfully than ever.

"Is there no water here?" said the dog, looking round.

"Alas, no!—yet stay—yes, now I think of it, there is some in that little hole in the wall; but how to get at it!—It is so high that I can't, in my poor weak state, climb up to it; and I dare not ask such a favor of one I have injured so much."

"Don't talk of it," said the dog: "but the hole's very small. I could not put my nose through it."

"No; but if you just climb up on that stone, and thrust your paw into the hole, you can dip it into the water, and so cool my poor parched mouth. Oh, what a thing it is to have a bad conscience!"

The dog sprang upon the stone, and, getting on his hind-legs, thrust his front paw into the hole; when suddenly Reynard pulled a string that he had concealed under the straw, and the dog found his paw caught tight to the wall in a running noose.

"Ah, rascal!" said he turning round; but the fox leaped up gaily from the straw, and fastening the string with his teeth to a nail in the other end of the wall, walked out, crying, "Good-by, my dear friend; have a care how you believe hereafter in sudden conversions!"—So he left the dog on his hind-legs to take care of the house.

Reynard found the cat waiting for him where he had appointed, and they walked lovingly together till they came to the cave. It was now dark, and they saw the basket waiting below; the fox assisted the poor cat into it. "There is only room for one," said he, "you must go first!" Up rose the basket; the fox heard a piteous mew, and no more.

"So much for the griffin's soup!" thought he.

He waited patiently for some time, when the griffiness, waving her claw from the window, said cheerfully, "All's right, my dear Reynard; my papa has finished his soup, and sleeps as sound as a rock! All the noise in the world would not wake him now, till he has slept off the boiled cat—which won't be these twelve hours. Come and assist me in packing up the treasure; I should be sorry to leave a single diamond behind."

"So should I," quoth the fox. "Stay, I'll come round by the lower hole: why, the door's shut! pray, beautiful griffiness, open it to thy impatient adorer."

"Alas, my father has hid the key! I never know where he places it: you must come up by the basket; see, I will lower it for you."

The fox was a little loth to trust himself in the same conveyance that had taken his mistress to be boiled; but the most cautious grow rash when money's to be gained, and avarice can trap even a fox. So he put himself as comfortably as he could into the basket, and up he went in an instant. It rested, however, just before it reached the window, and the fox felt, with a slight shudder, the claw of the griffiness stroking his back.

"Oh, what a beautiful coat!" quoth she, caressingly.

"You are too kind," said the fox; "but you can feel it more at your leisure when I am once up. Make haste, I beseech you."

"Oh, what a beautiful bushy tail! Never did I feel such a tail!"

"It is entirely at your service, sweet griffiness," said the fox; "but pray let me in. Why lose an instant?"

"No, never did I feel such a tail! No wonder you are so successful with the ladies."

"Ah, beloved griffiness, my tail is yours to eternity, but you pinch it a little too hard."

Scarcely had he said this, when down dropped the basket, but not with the fox in it; he found himself caught by the tail, and dangling half way down the rock, by the help of the very same sort of pulley wherewith he had snared the dog. I leave you to guess his consternation; he yelped out as loud as he could,—for it hurts a fox exceedingly to be hanged by his tail with his head downwards,—when the door of the rock opened, and out stalked the griffin himself, smoking his pipe, with a vast crowd of all the fashionable beasts in the neighborhood.

"Oho, brother," said the bear, laughing fit to kill himself; "who ever saw a fox hanged by the tail before?"

"You'll have need of a physician," quoth Doctor Ape.

"A pretty match, indeed; a griffiness for such a creature as you!" said the goat, strutting by him.

The fox grinned with pain, and said nothing. But that which hurt him most was the compassion of a dull fool of a donkey, who assured him with great gravity that he saw nothing at all to laugh at in his situation!

"At all events," said the fox at last, "cheated, gulled, betrayed as I am, I have played the same trick to the dog. Go and laugh at him, gentlemen; he deserves it as much as I can, I assure you."

"Pardon me," said the griffin, taking the pipe out of his mouth; "one never laughs at the honest."

"And see," said the bear, "here he is."

And indeed the dog had, after much effort, gnawed the string in two, and extricated his paw: the scent of the fox had enabled him to track his footsteps, and here he arrived, burning for vengeance, and finding himself already avenged.

But his first thought was for his dear cousin.

"Ah, where is she?" he cried, movingly; "without doubt that villain Reynard has served her some scurvy trick."

"I fear so, indeed, my old friend," answered the griffin, "but don't grieve: after all, she was nothing in particular. You shall marry my daughter the griffiness, and succeed to all the treasure; ay, and all the bones that you once guarded so faithfully."

"Talk not to me," said the faithful dog. "I want none of your treasure; and, though I don't mean to be rude, your griffiness may go to the devil. I will run over the world but I will find my dear cousin."

"See her then," said the griffin; and the beautiful cat, more beautiful than ever, rushed out of the cavern, and threw herself into the dog's paws.

A pleasant scene this for the fox!—he had skill enough in the female heart to know that it may excuse many little infidelities,—but to be boiled alive for a griffin's soup!—no, the offence was inexpiable.

"You understand me, Mr. Reynard," said the griffin, "I have no daughter, and it was me you made love to. Knowing what sort of a creature a magpie is, I amused myself with hoaxing her,—the fashionable amusement at court, you know."

The fox made a mighty struggle, and leaped on the ground, leaving his tail behind him. It did not grow again in a hurry.

"See," said the griffin, as the beasts all laughed at the figure Reynard made running into the wood, "the dog beats the fox, with the ladies, after all; and cunning as he is in every thing else, the fox is the last creature that should ever think of making love."

The dog and the cat lived very happily ever afterwards. Indeed the nuptial felicity of a dog and cat is proverbial!

TOO HANDSOME FOR ANY THING.

BY SIR E. L. BULWER.

Mr. Ferdinand Fitzroy was one of those models of perfection of which a human father and mother can produce but a single example,—Mr. Ferdinand Fitzroy was therefore an only son. He was such an amazing favorite with both his parents that they resolved to ruin him; accordingly, he was exceedingly spoiled, never annoyed by the sight of a book, and had as much plum-cake as he could eat. Happy would it have been for Mr. Ferdinand Fitzroy could he always have eaten plum-cake, and remained a child. "Never," says the Greek Tragedian, "reckon a mortal happy till you have witnessed his end." A most beautiful creature was Mr. Ferdinand Fitzroy! Such eyes—such hair—such teeth—such a figure—such manners, too,—and such an irresistible way of tying his neckcloth! When he was about sixteen, a crabbed old uncle represented to his parents the propriety of teaching Mr. Ferdinand Fitzroy to read and write. Though not without some difficulty, he convinced them,—for he was exceedingly rich, and riches in an uncle are wonderful arguments respecting the nurture of a nephew whose parents have nothing to leave him. So our hero was sent to school. He was naturally (I am not joking now) a very sharp, clever boy; and he came on surprisingly in his learning. The schoolmaster's wife liked handsome children.—"What a genius will Master Ferdinand Fitzroy be, if you take pains with him!" said she to her husband.

"Pooh, my dear, it is of no use to take pains with *him*."

"And why, love?"

"Because he is a great deal too handsome ever to be a scholar."

"And that's true enough, my dear!" said the schoolmaster's wife.

So, because he was too handsome to be a scholar, Mr. Ferdinand Fitzroy remained the lag of the fourth form!

They took our hero from school.—"What profession shall he follow?" said his mother.

"My first cousin is the Lord Chancellor," said his father, "let him go to the bar."

The Lord Chancellor dined there that day; Mr. Ferdinand Fitzroy was introduced to him; his Lordship was a little, rough-faced, beetle-browed, hard-featured man, who thought beauty and idleness the same thing—and a parchment skin the legitimate complexion for a lawyer.

"Send him to the bar!" said he, "no, no, that will never do!—Send him into the army; he is much too handsome to become a lawyer."

"And that's true enough, my Lord!" said the mother. So they bought Mr. Ferdinand Fitzroy a cornetcy in the —— Regiment of Dragoons.

Things are not learned by inspiration. Mr. Ferdinand Fitzroy had never ridden at school, except when he was hoisted; he was, therefore, a very indifferent horseman; they sent him to the riding-school, and every body laughed at him.

"He is a d——d ass!" said Cornet Horsephiz, who was very ugly; "a horrid puppy!" said Lieutenant St. Squintem, who was still uglier; "if he does not ride better, he will disgrace the regiment!" said Captain Rivalhate, who was very good-looking; "if he does not ride better, we will cut him!" said Colonel Everdrill, who was a wonderful martinet; "I say, Mr. Bumpemwell (to the riding-master), make that youngster ride less like a miller's sack."

"Pooh, sir, *he* will never ride better."

"And why the d——l will he not?"

"Bless you, Colonel, he is a great deal too handsome for a cavalry officer!"

"True!" said Cornet Horsephiz.

"Very true!" said Lieutenant St. Squintem.

"We must cut him!" said the Colonel.

And Mr. Ferdinand Fitzroy was accordingly cut.

Our hero was a youth of susceptibility—he quitted the —— Regiment, and challenged the Colonel. The Colonel was killed!

"What a terrible blackguard is Mr. Ferdinand Fitzroy!" said the Colonel's relations.

"Very true!" said the world.

The parents were in despair!—They were not rich; but our hero was an only son, and they sponged hard upon the crabbed old uncle!

"He is very clever," said they both, "and may do yet."

So they borrowed some thousands from the uncle, and bought his beautiful nephew a seat in Parliament.

Mr. Ferdinand Fitzroy was ambitious, and desirous of retrieving his character. He fagged like a dragon—conned pamphlets and reviews—got Ricardo by heart—and made notes on the English Constitution.

He rose to speak.

"What a handsome fellow!" whispered one member.

"Ah, a coxcomb!" said another.

"Never do for a speaker!" said a third, very audibly.

And the gentlemen on the opposite benches sneered and *heared!*—Impudence is only indigenous in Milesia, and an orator is not made in a day. Discouraged by his reception, Mr. Ferdinand Fitzroy grew a little embarrassed.

"Told you so!" said one of his neighbors.

"Fairly broke down!" said another.

"Too fond of his hair to have any thing in his head," said a a third, who was considered a wit.

"Hear, hear!" cried the gentleman on the opposite benches.

Mr. Ferdinand Fitzroy sat down—he had not shone; but, in justice, he had not failed. Many a first-rate speaker had began worse; and many a county member had been declared a phœnix of promise upon half his merit.

Not so, thought the heroes of corn laws.

"Your Adonises never make orators!" said a crack speaker with a wry nose.

"Nor men of business either," added the chairman of a committee, with a face like a kangaroo's.

"Poor devil!" said the civilest of the set. "He's a deuced deal too handsome for a speaker! By Jove, he is going to speak again—this will never do; we must cough him down!"

And Mr. Ferdinand Fitzroy was accordingly coughed down.

Our hero was now seven or eight and twenty, handsomer than ever, and the adoration of all the young ladies at Almack's.

"We have nothing to leave you," said the parents, who had long spent their fortune, and now lived on the credit of having once enjoyed it.—"You are the handsomest man in London; you must marry an heiress."

"I will," said Mr. Ferdinand Fitzroy.

Miss Helen Convolvulus was a charming young lady, with a hare-lip and six thousand a-year. To Miss Helen Convolvulus then our hero paid his addresses.

Heavens! what an uproar her relations made about the matter. "Easy to see his intentions," said one: "a handsome fortune-hunter, who wants to make the best of his person!"—"handsome is that handsome does," says another; "he was turned out of the army, and murdered his Colonel;"—"never marry a beauty," said a third; "he can admire none but himself;" "will have so many mistresses," said a fourth;"—"make you perpetually jealous," said a fifth;—"spend your fortune," said a sixth; "and break your heart," said a seventh.

Miss Helen Convolvulus was prudent and wary. She saw a great deal of justice in what was said; and was sufficiently contented with liberty and six thousand a-year, not to be highly impatient for a husband; but our heroine had no aversion to a lover; especially to so handsome a lover as Mr. Ferdinand Fitzroy. Accordingly, she neither accepted nor discarded him; but kept him on hope, and suffered him to get into debt with his tailor, and his coachmaker, on the strength of becoming Mr. Fitzroy Convolvulus. Time went on, and excuses and delays were easily found; however, our hero was sanguine, and so were his parents. A breakfast at Chiswick, and a putrid fever carried off the latter, within one week of each other; but not till they had blessed Mr. Ferdinand Fitzroy, and rejoiced that they had left him so well provided for.

Now, then, our hero depended solely upon the crabbed old uncle and Miss Helen Convolvulus;—the former, though a baronet and a satirist, was a banker and a man of business:—he looked very distastefully at the Hyperian curls and white teeth of Mr. Ferdinand Fitzroy.

"If I make you my heir," said he—"I expect you will continue the bank."

"Certainly, sir!" said the nephew.

"Humph!" grunted the uncle, "a pretty fellow for a banker!"

Debtors grew pressing to Mr. Ferdinand Fitzroy, and Mr. Ferdinand Fitzroy grew pressing to Miss Helen Convolvulus. "It is a dangerous thing," said she, timidly, "to marry a man so admired,—will you always be faithful?"

"By heaven!" cried the lover—

"Heigho!" sighed Miss Helen Convolvulus, and Lord Rufus Pumilion entering, the conversation changed.

But the day of the marriage was fixed; and Mr. Ferdinand Fitzroy bought a new curricle. By Apollo, how handsome he looked in it! A month before the wedding-day, the uncle died. Miss Helen Convolvulus was quite tender in her condolences—"Cheer up, my Ferdinand," said she, "for your sake, I have discarded Lord Rufus Pumilion!" "Adorable condescension!" cried our hero; "but Lord Rufus Pumilion is only four feet two, and has hair like a peony."

"All men are not so handsome as Mr. Ferdinand Fitzroy!" was the reply.

Away goes our hero, to be present at the opening of his uncle's will.

"I leave," said the testator (who, I have before said, was a bit of a satirist), "my share of the bank, and the whole of my fortune, legacies excepted, to"—(here Mr. Ferdinand Fitzroy wiped his beautiful eyes with a cambric handkerchief, exquisitely *brodé*) "my natural son, John Spriggs, an industrious, pains-taking youth, who will do credit to the bank. I did once intend to have made my nephew Ferdinand my heir; but so curling a head can have no talent for accounts. I want my successor to be a man of business, not beauty; and Mr. Ferdinand Fitzroy is a great deal too handsome for a banker; his good looks will, no doubt, win him any heiress in town. Meanwhile, I leave him, to buy a dressing case, a thousand pounds."

"A thousand devils!" said Mr. Ferdinand Fitzroy, banging out of the room. He flew to his mistress. She was not at home. "Lies," says the Italian proverb, "have short legs;" but truths, if they are unpleasant, have terrible long ones! The next day Mr. Ferdinand Fitzroy received a most obliging note of dismissal.

"I wish you every happiness," said Miss Helen Convolvulus, in conclusion—"but my friends are right; you are much too handsome for a husband!"

And the week after, Miss Helen Convolvulus became Lady Rufus Pumilion.

"Alas! sir," said the bailiff, as a day or two after the dissolution of Parliament, he was jogging along

with Mr. Ferdinand Fitzroy, in a hackney coach bound to the King's Bench,—"Alas! sir, what a pity it is to take so handsome a gentleman to prison!"

THE BOX TUNNEL.

A Fact.

BY CHARLES READE.

The 10.15 train glided from Paddington, May 7, 1847. In the left compartment of a certain first-class carriage were four passengers; of these, two were worth description. The lady had a smooth, white, delicate brow, strongly-marked eyebrows, long lashes, eyes that seemed to change color, and a good-sized delicious mouth with teeth as white as milk. A man could not see her nose for her eyes and mouth, her own sex could and would have told us some nonsense about it. She wore an unpretending grayish dress, buttoned to the throat, with lozenge-shaped buttons, and a Scotch shawl that agreeably evaded the responsibility of color. She was like a duck, so tight her plain feathers fitted her; and there she sat, smooth, snug, and delicious, with a book in her hand, and a *soupçon* of her snowy wrist just visible as she held it. Her opposite neighbor was what I call a good style of man—the more to his credit, since he belonged to a corporation, that frequently turns out the worst imaginable style of young man. He was a cavalry officer aged twenty-five. He had a moustache, but not a very repulsive one; not one of those sub-nasal pig-tails, on which soup is suspended like dew on a shrub; it was short, thick, and black as a coal. His teeth had not yet been turned by tobacco smoke to the color of tobacco juice, his clothes did not stick to nor hang on him, they sat on him; he had an engaging smile, and, what I liked the dog for, his vanity, which was inordinate, was in its proper place, his heart, not in his face, jostling mine and other people's, who have none:—in a word, he was what one oftener hears of than meets—a *young gentleman.* He was conversing in an animated whisper with a companion, a fellow-officer—they were talking about, what it is far better not to do, women. Our friend clearly did not wish to be overheard, for he cast, ever and anon, a furtive glance at his fair *vis-à-vis*, and lowered his voice. She seemed completely absorbed in her book, and that reassured him. At last, the two soldiers came down to a whisper, and in that whisper (the truth must be told) the one who got down at Slough, and was lost to posterity, bet ten pounds to three, that he who was going down with us to Bath and immortality, would not kiss either of the ladies opposite upon the road.—"Done!" "Done!" Now, I am sorry a man I have hitherto praised, should have lent himself, even in a whisper, to such a speculation: but "nobody is wise at all hours," not even when the clock is striking five-and-twenty; and you are to consider his profession, his good looks, and, the temptation—ten to three.

After Slough, the party was reduced to three; at Twyford, one lady dropped her handkerchief; Captain Dolignan fell on it like a tiger, and returned it like a lamb; two or three words were interchanged on that occasion. At Reading, the Marlborough of our tale made one of the safe investments of that day, he bought a "Times" and a "Punch"; the latter was full of steel-pen thrusts and wood-*cuts*. Valor and beauty deigned to laugh at some inflated humbug or other punctured by Punch. Now laughing together thaws our human ice; long before Swindon, it was a talking match—at Swindon, who so devoted as Captain Dolignan—he handed them out—he souped them—he tough-chickened them—he brandied and cochinealed* one, and he brandied and burnt-sugared the other; on their return to the carriage, one lady passed into the inner compartment to inspect a certain gentleman's seat on that side the line.

Reader, had it been you or I, the beauty would have been the deserter, the average one would have stayed with us, till all was blue, ourselves included: not more surely does our slice of bread and butter, when it escapes from our hand, revolve it ever so often, alight face downwards on the carpet. But this was a bit of a fop, Adonis, dragoon —so Venus remained in *tête-à-tête* with him. You have seen a dog meet an unknown female of his species; how handsome, how *empressé*, how expressive he becomes:—such was Dolignan after Swindon, and to do the dog justice, he got handsomer and handsomer; and you have seen a cat conscious of approaching cream,—such was Miss Haythorn: she became demurer and demurer: presently, our Captain looked out of the window and laughed: this elicited an inquiring look from Miss Haythorn. "We are only a mile from the Box Tunnel."—"Do you always laugh a mile from the Box Tunnel?" said the lady.

"Invariably."

"What for?"

"Why! hem! it is a gentleman's joke."

"Oh! I don't mind it's being silly, if it makes me laugh." Captain Dolignan thus encouraged, recounted to Miss Haythorn the following: "A lady and her husband sat together going through the Box Tunnel—there was one gentleman opposite: it was pitch dark; after the tunnel, the lady said, 'George, how absurd of you to salute me going through the tunnel.' 'I did no such thing!'—'You didn't?'—'No! why?'—'Why, because somehow I thought you did!'" Here Captain Dolignan laughed, and endeavored to lead his companion to laugh, but it was not to be done. The train entered the tunnel.

Miss Haythorn. "Ah!"

Dolignan. "What is the matter?"

Miss Haythorn. "I am frightened."

Dolignan (moving to her side), "Pray do not be alarmed, I am near you."

Miss Haythorn. "You *are* near me, very near me indeed, Captain Dolignan."

Dolignan. "You know my name!"

Miss Haythorn. "I heard your friend mention it. I wish we were out of this dark place."

Dolignan. "I could be content to spend hours here, reassuring you, sweet lady."

Miss Haythorn. "Nonsense!"

Dolignan. Pweep! (Grave reader, do not put your lips to the cheek of the next pretty creature you meet, or you will understand what this means.)

Miss Haythorn. "Ee! Ee! Ee!"

Friend. "What is the matter?"

Miss Haythorn. "Open the door! open the door!"

There was a sound of hurried whispers, the door was shut and the blind pulled down, with hostile sharpness.

If any critic falls on me for putting inarticulate sounds in a dialogue as above, I answer with all the insolence I can command at present, "Hit boys as big as yourself," bigger perhaps, such as Sophocles, Euripides, and Aristophanes; they began it, and I learned it of them, *sore* against my will.

Miss Haythorn's scream lost a part of its effect, because the engine whistled forty thousand murders at the same moment; and fictitious grief makes itself heard when real cannot.

Between the tunnel and Bath, our young friend had time to ask himself whether his conduct had been marked by that delicate reserve which is supposed to distinguish the perfect gentleman.

With a long face, real or feigned, he held open the door,—his late friends attempted to escape on the other side,—impossible! they must pass him. She whom he had insulted (Latin for kissed) deposited somewhere at his foot a look of gentle blushing reproach; the other, whom he had not insulted, darted red-hot daggers at him from her eyes, and so they parted.

It was, perhaps, fortunate for Dolignan that he had the grace to be friends with Major Hoskyns of his regiment, a veteran laughed at by the youngsters, for the Major was too apt to look coldly upon billiard balls and cigars; he had seen cannon balls and linstocks. He had also, to tell the truth, swallowed a good bit of the mess-room poker, but with it some sort of moral poker, which made it as impossible for Major Hoskyns to descend to an ungentleman-like word or action, as to brush his own trowsers below the knee.

Captain Dolignan told this gentleman his story in gleeful accents; but Major Hoskyns heard him coldly, and as coldly answered that he had known a man to lose his life for the same thing; "*That* is nothing," continued the Major, "but unfortunately he deserved to lose it."

At this, the blood mounted to the younger man's temples, and his senior added, "I mean to say he was thirty-five: you, I presume, are twenty-one!"

"Twenty-five."

"That is much the same thing; will you be advised by me?"

"If you will advise me."

"Speak to no one of this, and send White the £3 that he may think you have lost the bet."

"That is hard when I won it!"

"Do it for all that, sir."

Let the disbelievers in human perfectibility know that this dragoon, capable of a blush, did this virtuous action, albeit with violent reluctance: and this was his first damper. A week after these events he was at a ball. He was in that state of factitious discontent which belongs to us amiable English. He was looking, in vain, for a lady, equal in personal attractions to the idea he had formed of George Dolignan as a man, when suddenly there glided past him a most delightful vision! a lady whose beauty and symmetry took him by the eyes—another look: "It can't be!"—"Yes, it is!" Miss Haythorn! (not that he knew her name!) but what an apotheosis!

The duck had become a pea-hen—radiant, daz-

* This is supposed to allude to two decoctions called port-and sherry, and imagined by one earthly nation to partake of a vinous nature.

zling, she looked twice as beautiful, and almost twice as large as before. He lost sight of her. He found her again. She was so lovely she made him ill—and he, alone, must not dance with her, speak to her. If he had been content to begin her acquaintance the usual way, it might have ended in kissing; but having begun with kissing, it must end in nothing. As she danced, sparks of beauty fell from her on all around, but him—she did not see him; it was clear she never would see him—one gentleman was particularly assiduous; she smiled on his assiduity; he was ugly, but she smiled on him. Dolignan was surprised at his success, his ill taste, his ugliness, his impertinence. Dolignan at last found himself injured: "Who was this man?" "and what right had he to go on so?" "He had never kissed her, I suppose," said Dolly. Dolignan could not prove it, but he felt that somehow the rights of property were invaded. He went home and dreamed of Miss Haythorn, and hated all the ugly successful.* He spent a fortnight, trying to find out who this beauty was,—he never could encounter her again. At last, he heard of her in this way; a lawyer's clerk paid him a little visit, and commenced a little action against him, in the name of Miss Haythorn, for insulting her in a railway train.

The young gentleman was shocked; endeavored to soften the lawyer's clerk; that machine did not thoroughly comprehend the meaning of the term. The lady's name, however, was at least revealed by this untoward incident; from her name to her address was but a short step; and the same day, our crest-fallen hero lay in wait at her door—and many a succeeding day, without effect. But one fine afternoon, she issued forth quite naturally, as if she did it every day, and walked briskly on the nearest Parade. Dolignan did the same, he met and passed her many times on the Parade, and searched for pity in her eyes, but found neither look, nor recognition, nor any other sentiment; for all this she walked and walked, till all the other promenaders were tired and gone,—then her culprit summoned resolution, and taking off his hat, with a voice tremulous for the first time, besought permission to address her. She stopped, blushed, and neither acknowledged nor disowned his acquaintance. He blushed, stammered out how ashamed he was, how he deserved to be punished, how he *was* punished, how little she knew how unhappy he was; and concluded by begging her not to let all the world know the disgrace of a man, who was already mortified enough by the loss of her acquaintance. She asked an explanation; he told her of the action that had been commenced in her name; she gently shrugged her shoulders, and said, "How stupid they are." Emboldened by this, he begged to know whether or not a life of distant unpretending devotion would, after a lapse of years, erase the memory of his madness—his crime!

"She did not know!"

"She must now bid him adieu, as she had some preparations to make for a ball in the crescent, where *every body was to be.* They parted, and Dolignan determined to be at the ball, where every body was to be. He was there, and after some time he obtained an introduction to Miss Haythorn, and he danced with her. Her manner was gracious. With the wonderful tact of her sex, she seemed to have commenced the acquaintance that evening. That night, for the first time, Dolignan was in love. I will spare the reader all a lover's arts, by which he succeeded in dining where she dined, in dancing where she danced, in overtaking her by accident, when she rode. His devotion followed her even to church, where our dragoon was rewarded by learning there is a world where they neither polk nor smoke,—the two capital abominations of this one.

He made acquaintance with her uncle, who liked him, and he saw at last with joy, that her eye loved to dwell upon him, when she thought he did not observe her.

It was three months after the Box Tunnel, that Captain Dolignan called one day upon Captain Haythorn, R. N., whom he had met twice in his life, and slightly propitiated by violently listening to a cutting-out expedition; he called, and in the usual way asked permission to pay his addresses to his daughter. The worthy Captain straightway began doing Quarter-Deck, when suddenly he was summoned from the apartment by a mysterious message. On his return, he announced, with a total change of voice, that "It was all right, and his visitor might run alongside as soon as he chose." My reader has divined the truth; this nautical commander, terrible to the foe, was in complete and happy subjugation to his daughter, our heroine.

As he was taking leave, Dolignan saw his divinity glide into the drawing-room. He followed her, observed a sweet consciousness which encouraged him; that consciousness deepened into confusion—she tried to laugh, she cried instead, and then she smiled again; and when he kissed her hand at the door it was "George" and "Marian," instead of Captain this and Miss the other. A reasonable time after this (for my tale is merciful and skips formalities and torturing delays)—these two were very happy—they were once more upon the railroad, going to enjoy their honeymoon all by themselves. Marian Dolignan was dressed just as before—duck-like, and delicious; all bright, except her clothes: but George sat beside her this time instead of opposite; and she drank him in gently from under her long eye-lashes. "Marian," said George, "married people should tell each other all. Will you ever forgive me if I own to you—no—"

"Yes! yes!"

"Well then! you remember the Box Tunnel," (this was the first allusion he had ventured to it)—"I am ashamed to say—I had bet 3*l.* to 10*l.* with White, I would kiss one of you two ladies," and George, pathetic externally, chuckled within.

"I know that, George; I overheard you;" was the demure reply.

"Oh! you overheard me? impossible."

"And did you not hear me whisper to my companion? I made a bet with her."

"You made a bet, how singular! What was it?"

"Only a pair of gloves, George."

"Yes, I know, but what about it?"

"That if you did, you should be my husband, dearest."

"Oh!—but stay—then you could not have been

* When our successful rival is ugly, the blow is doubly severe, crushing—we fall by bludgeon: we who thought the keenest rapier might perchance thrust at us in vain.

so very angry with me, love;—why, dearest, then who brought that action against me?"

Mrs. Dolignan looked down.

"I was afraid you were forgetting me! George, you will never forgive me!"

"Sweet angel—why here is the Box Tunnel!"

Now reader—fie!—no! no such thing! You can't expect to be indulged in this way, every time we come to a dark place—besides, it is not the thing. Consider, two sensible married people—no such phenomenon, I assure you, took place. No scream issued in hopeless rivalry of the engine—this time!

THE NEW CAPTAIN.

FROM "THE ARETHUSA." BY CAPTAIN CHAMIER, R. N.

In 1806, the Arethusa was in Portsmouth harbor, undergoing repairs. She had been, like most of his Majesty's ships in those stirring times, actively employed in annoying the enemy; the shot and shell of the French batteries had passed over and through her; the singly contested action had been fought, and there was no frigate more honored in song than the "saucy Arethusa."

It was when she removed to Spithead, previous to her starting on another cruise, that her captain, in endeavoring to reach the shore during a heavy gale of wind, was upset in his gig and drowned; and as the body drifted on shore, the coroner and the undertaker did all that was requisite, "save the lapidary's scrawl." It was a sad accident; but sad accidents in active minds are shortly forgotten—they never remain to corrode the heart, which in seamen, during war, beats too highly and too quickly to allow of the rust of life arising from misfortunes to impede its machinery.

The Arethusa was all a-taunto, top-gallant yards across, her red ensign shining in the breeze; and now the pendant was masthead high, for the late captain had been buried, and the first lieutenant almost imagined himself the actual commander; but as he had received some gentle hints that a man half his age was about to take charge of the ship, he thought it best to forget his disappointment,—the decks received a higher polish from the holystone, the ropes were all taut, the yards well squared, and the Arethusa attracted the attention of all parties for her neatness aloft, and her clean, man-of-war-like appearance.

It was about noon, when the people were at dinner, that a smart young man, in plain clothes, came alongside.

"Keep off in that shore-boat!" said the marine on the gangway.

"Have the kindness," said the gentleman in the boat, "to give this note to the first lieutenant."

"What's all this?" said the midshipman of the watch. (The officer of the watch was playing the flute below.)

"A shore-boat, sir," said the marine; "got something for the first lieutenant."

This brought the midshipman to the gangway, who, seeing a remarkably dandified young man telling the boatman to go alongside without his leave, he resolved to cool this intruder on marine discipline.

"Sentry!" said Mr. Weazel, (whose face was not a little altered since we last left him; he being now about five-and-twenty years old, and having one or two distinguishing marks in the shape of grog-blossoms on his nose; whilst his left hand was not quite so ready for mischief as formerly, he having lost two fingers in Trafalgar, and obtained, not his promotion, but the sobriquet of 'Three-fingered Jack,')—"keep that long-togged gentleman off!"

"Keep off in that boat!" roared the marine, "or I'm blessed if I don't fire into you!"

"That's all right enough," said Weazel; "you see the gentleman is ready dressed for *a ball.*"

"Very likely," said the gentleman; "but I am not much inclined to *dance attendance* here."

"Dance ten dances!" said the old quarter-master, "why, his legs ar'n't thick enough for scrub-broom handles! although I'm blessed if he does not stand as stiff in the boat as a midshipman on half-pay."

"None of your impudence, M'Donald, if you please," replied Weazel; "the only thing stiff such old toddles as you like is your grog."

"I'm thinking," said M'Donald, "that there are two of us in that boat, Mr. Weazel."

"Will you have the kindness to take this card to the first lieutenant?" asked the gentleman.

"Will you have the kindness, sir," said Weazel, mimicking the gentleman's manner, "to tell me if you take me for your footman? and be d——d to you!"

"I dare say before long," replied the gentleman, apparently a little irritated, "you will obey my orders, or I shall discharge you."

"That may be," said Weazel, "so by way of being to windward, I'll just *discharge* you now; so *go off*, or this shower of rain may wet the powder in the pan, and hinder the marine's musket from being discharged, by way of *turning you off.*"

"Come, sir," said the gentleman, "I cannot stand this nonsense any more; you will tell the first lieutenant that I desire to see him."

"Well," said Weazel, "that does beat cock-fighting!—But, stop a moment. I say, you, sir, with the top-chain over the shoulders of your mast, are you the new captain's steward?"

"No, sir," answered the gentleman.

"Are you his footman then?"

"No, sir, I am not."

"Are you the old captain's undertaker?—because if you are, you may heave and *Paul* where you are."

"No, sir, I am neither one nor the other; but I am—"

"Oh! never mind who you are, my fine fellow," interrupted Weazel; "if you are not the live captain's steward or the dead captain's undertaker, you must be a Whitechapel bird-catcher; so hop your twig, my boy, or you'll find we have plenty of cats to catch such birds as you are. I wonder what you would take for your watch without the wheels of it?"

"By the Lord! my fine fellow!" said the stranger, "you shall remember that word, and watch and watch shall you have time to think of it."

"It's a *repeater*," said Weazel, "and I dare say you got it on tick; it looks like a second-hand German warming-pan, and the case is large enough for the boatswain's 'baccy-box! Now, Moses, or Aaron, or who the devil you may be of the lost tribes and lost beards, if you take us for any of the *Men-asses*, you are mistaken! I dare say, now, you are some of John Doe's men, without your top-boots, come to nab the first lieutenant; but we know how to weather the Nab-light, however deep it may appear to be surrounded. Here's the first lieutenant coming up the hatchway; so, Catchpoll, look out!"

"Who are you talking to over the gangway, Mr. Weazel? I thought I told you before that I would have nothing of this kind. Have the men had their time to dinner?"

"Not quite, sir," replied Weazel, in a very different tone of voice from that in which he had been amusing himself.

The first lieutenant came to the gangway, and seeing a gentleman—for a gentleman is always known—bobbing about in a shore-boat in a drizzling rain, and hearing from the sentry, who had been giggling away on his post, that the stranger wished to see him, he ordered the boat alongside, and a smart-looking, well-made man of about one-and-twenty, stood on the Arethusa's quarter-deck. That he was a sailor was obvious; no landsman steps up the side, touches his hat, and gives that footing of consequence which a man does from long habit during a professional life.

The first lieutenant, Mr. Jones, returned the salute; and looking at the card, took off his hat and made a low bow. Weazel saw something was wrong, and sheered over to the other side.

"I am appointed to the command of this frigate," said the stranger, "and I was anxious to see her without being known. I shall come on board and read my commission to-morrow; in the mean time, let me look round; and let me beg of you, Mr. Jones, not to mention who I am. I have a great desire, if possible, to repay that young gentleman for some of his civility in his own coin, and I would rather see the people I am to command without their knowing their future captain. If I stop in the midshipman's berth, leave me there."

"Shall I send the shore-boat away?"

"Certainly. I must pay him first, though.—What's your fare, my lad?"

"Three shillings, sir; and I hope your honor will give me something to drink for waiting."

"Three shillings for coming out to Spithead! There's half-a crown, and shove off directly."

"Well," said the boatman as he looked at the money, "you're a pretty chap to call yourself a gentleman!—why, you would skin a flea for its hide and tallow! Take care of him," said he to Weazel; "he's all outside show, like a marine's mess. I dare say he would let a poor fellow pull him to St. Helen's, and then ask for change out of a sixpence." And here the voice grew weaker in the distance; although every now and then such words as "nip-cheese," "herring-bones," "hung-in-chains," and such like fag-ends of the long volleys, reached the ship, until the boatman thought he could no longer be heard, and resting upon his oars he relieved his throat.

Murray at last stood in the position he had so long pictured to himself; he was the captain of the Arethusa. He looked aloft from the quarter-deck, saw the neat-rigged masts, the yards square, the ropes taut—such as a man-of-war should be, in appearance and efficiency; and he remembered the launch, and the little fairy who christened her;—for he had been present when the Arethusa many years before had been launched;—and Amelia, then a mere child, had gone through that ceremony; but that fairy had grown a woman, and seemed, from his father's affection for her, to be likely to cheat him of his birthright. The sister of the man who had struck him!—he bit his lip as the thought occurred to him; and he fancied his revenge but half complete, since Hammerton had never been heard of from the day he had sailed. He considered himself wronged, and he felt he was unrevenged, since the object of his hate might have died uninsulted.

But Murray was himself now a captain; the Arethusa was under his command; the war raged fiercely; the battle of Trafalgar, for he was in it, had led to his promotion; the naval glory of Great Britain was raised upon the highest pinnacle; the ships of England swept the seas; and although in arrogance we did not equal the Dutch, who on a former occasion, carried brooms at their mastheads —a signal now that the vessel is for sale,—yet the long pendants of our ships were to be seen in every sea, in every clime. By Murray's side was his first lieutenant; and although the captain was out of uniform, he felt his own situation, and knew how to profit by it. "Mr. Jones," he began, "this Weazel played me the first frolic ever practised upon me. When I first entered on board the Tribune, he was then a midshipman of four years' standing; and after nine years' separation I find him in the same situation, with as little chance of advancement. What, Mr. Jones, is his general character?"

"He is, sir," replied the first lieutenant, "the life and soul of the ship—foremost in danger, ready for mischief, always excessively innocent, and every day getting into scrapes,—he nearly got into one for talking to you over the gangway, for that is expressly against my orders."

"He took care to have the whole of the conversation to himself," remarked Murray, "and after calling me Moses and Aaron, a bum-bailiff come to arrest you, and so forth, he finished by calling my watch a German warming-pan, or a boatswain's tobacco-box."

"He is not very partial to the Israelites; for it was but yesterday he shaved off the beard of one in the midshipman's berth, and stuck it on the collar of the Jew's coat, remarking that bear-skin collars were coming into fashion; he then lashed him up in a hammock, took him into the cable-tier, stowed him away in the heart of it, and then told him he ought to be very happy, as he resembled his namesake whilst living and whilst dead; in the one instance, because he was always in pursuit of the promised land; and in the other, 'because no man knew of his burying-place even unto this day.' On the Jew being released, he threatened to bring an action against him, upon which Weazel immediately knocked him down, 'by way of commencing the action,' as he said. Finding the poor fellow hurt, he poured some raw rum down his throat, telling him to make the best of 'the spirit of the law.'"

"I should like to see him at some of his tricks again," replied Murray; "and if he asks me to dinner with him after his abuse of me, I certainly will avail myself of the honor. Let us see the between-decks, Mr. Jones; and be kind enough not to give me the honor of an introduction."

Captain Murray expressed himself much pleased with the good order of the frigate; there was no useless lumber about the decks, every thing was in its place, and the ship might have gone into action five minutes after she was clear of St. Helen's. The main-deck was the main-deck of a ship for service as well as for show, and the lower deck exhibited that pride of seamen, the neatness of their messes; the men appeared stout, young, and clean seamen; and to use a common expression, though rarely true, you might have eaten your dinner off her decks, and never felt the grate of a sand-grain.

"This, sir," said Mr. Jones, "is the midshipman's berth," as he put his head inside the door.

The young *gentlemen* had just made preparations for dinner. In those days, the tablecloth did its duty for three or four days, without being relieved; and before Monday evening the whiteness had been pretty well superseded by the lines of dirt which the expectant heroes of the navy had rubbed from between the prongs of their forks; some, indeed, preferred the easier and less laborious mode of plunging the fork through the tablecloth, leaving two large holes,—for three or four prongs were in those days considered useless, and green peas never in fashion in the midshipman's berth. A japanned tin jug, familiarly called a "black-jack," was in the centre of the table, and contained swipes,—a liquor by no means the most intoxicating, it having been proved that a man might drown himself in such miserable beverage before he could get drunk upon it. The bread barge contained its weight of hard flinty biscuits; and the mess, which was a republican one without a caterer, exhibited all the signs of bad government and starving populations which agitation produces. The strongest seemed to profit by this general disorganization, and the weaker suffered in proportion. Each one daily prepared to help himself to the large half-baked piece of beef upon the "after you" principle, which may be thus explained:—When the poor wretch of a boy made his appearance with the dinner, the dish was instantly seized by one of the quickest and the strongest; another immediately called out, "After you!" whilst another, distancing a stuttering companion, had "After you!" out before the poor fellow laboring under the impediment could get out the word "After." So it proceeded; the last one getting but a very slender allowance to feed a voracious appetite, and each receiving the dish to help himself as his turn stood, on the "after you" principle. It was, however, considered a point of honor never to give the dish out of its turn; although Weazel, if he failed in capturing the beef on its passage, generally went upon the cutting-out system; he would draw the attention of his victim to some object, whilst he helped himself from the plate nearest to him. Hence civil discords soon grew high, and not unfrequently blows were repeated instead of grace.

"Will you sit down, sir," said Weazel, addressing the captain, "and make yourself quite at home."

No one had seen the first lieutenant's approach, and all hands were beating the devil's tattoo with their knives and forks on the plates, keeping an inharmonious accompaniment by singing the "Roast Beef of Old England." Mr. Jones on hearing the invitation retired, and Captain Murray entered the berth.

"I am very glad, sir," replied Murray, "to find that you do not consider me as either the live captain's steward or footman, or the dead captain's undertaker; and I shall have much pleasure in accepting your invitation."

"No grabbing now," said Weazel,—"a strange gentleman's here; and manners, you know," in a whispering tone to his messmates. And then addressing Murray, he said, "The dinner will be here in a minute. Here, boy, put the beef before me, and the potatoes within hail. Hold the gentleman's plate, boy. Where the devil have you been educated?—don't you know common behavior?—Do you like the outside piece, sir?"

"Thank you," said Murray, "any piece will do for me."

"Hold the plate nearer, and be d——d to you,

you stinking hound!" said Weazel to the boy; "you have no more manners than a kangaroo! There—don't capsize the gravy down that gentleman's collar!—A potato, sir? I am sorry we have nothing better to offer you; but unfortunately the boy, who is the clumsiest cub in creation, fell down on the main-deck, upset the soup, and left the fish for the cat to eat.—Now, gentlemen," he continued, addressing his messmates as he put about a pound in his own plate, "help yourselves, and remember *manners*."

"After you, Tom!" "After you, Harris!" "After you, Walcot!" "After you, Smith!" was instantly vociferated; and Captain Murray soon saw that, at any rate, if his ship was in good order, his midshipman's berth was in rather a revolutionary state, and required some alterations to protect the youngster from the overbearing power of the oldster. In a minute, the bone was picked as clean as if half a dozen dogs had been at it; the potatoes vanished, the black-jack was empty, and the bread barge capsized. Murray now intimated that he would take a little piece more; and Weazel, who was always ready, said, "Boy, run up to the galley and bring down the turkey." A smile played upon the lips of all his messmates; but Weazel, with consummate coolness, continued as he saw the boy gaping at him, "What the devil is the matter!—has the poulterer forgot to send it?—or has that rascally cook let it fall in the ashes? Tell him I'll report him to the first lieutenant, and the new captain may exercise his powers of eloquence in his maiden speech to the ship's company. I am very sorry, sir," he continued, addressing the stranger, "but we will endeavor to make amends in another way. Boy, bring the dessert, and take care not to injure the branches of the cherry-tree. Tell the captain

of the fore-top to stand by as a scarecrow to frighten the blackbirds. You must see our garden aloft, sir; it's a wonderful invention—much on the plan, as the clergyman of the flag-ship said, of the hanging gardens of Babylon;—it's quite extraordinary how our fruit trees ripen, and how we avoid blights and late frosts. Perhaps, after dinner, you would walk round, and I'll desire the gardeners to be in waiting."

Captain Murray kept his countenance well, although he remembered that Weazel had played him this very trick years ago, and he was perfectly aware that he now destined him to be the scarecrow, and the gardener the captain of the top.

"I shall have much pleasure," replied Murray; "but I cannot conceive how I could have passed unnoticed the garden, for Mr. Jones—"

"Oh, Mr. Jones," interrupted Weazel, "is much too knowing to show the garden; he has such a variety of South American plants which he wishes to bring to perfection before he allows them to be seen."

Here the boy entered, and having taken his cue from Weazel, said, "Gardener says, sir, that one of the fore-top men is in the report for having picked all the cherries, and that a flight of sparrows and blackbirds have eaten up all but a few gooseberries, which Mr. Jones has ordered him to keep for the new captain."

"Curse the new captain!" said Weazel. "By the Lord! the service is come to a pretty pass when the gooseberries are to be kept for the new captain! But, sir," said he to Murray, "so it always is; the active and industrious starve, in order that the slothful and indolent may fatten. As sure as ever I'm first lord of the admiralty, I'll do away with all gardens on board a ship, and make the captain sow mustard and cress on the sills of the ports for the good of the ship's company."

"Clear away, boy," said a rubicund-nosed oldster, "and clap the grog on the table. The only dessert we shall get to-day is some of Bounty Bligh's bread-fruit, or midshipman's nuts, which grow better in an oven than in the fore-top."

The cloth was removed and the greasy oak table brought to view. It had divers proofs of long service; each oldster mixed a pretty strong portion of grog, taking it out of an old lime-juice bottle, most of them preferring a cup, for there were only two glasses or tumblers belonging to the mess. Weazel of course apologized; he was the very cream of civility whenever he intended mischief. It was the last roll of the ship before she rounded the Isle of Wight that smashed all their glasses; and owing to the confusion in refitting the ship, it was judged better not to receive the new glass on board until they should be ready for sea.

"You seem," said Murray, ready to lead Weazel on, "to spend a very jovial life, and to make amends for wanting the amusements of the landsman by some constant occupation. How do you generally pass your evenings?"

"Pretty well and comfortably," replied Weazel. "When we have no theatre open, or no tight-rope dancing, we play at Able Whackets."

"Able Whackets!" replied Murray, "what can that be?"

"The most delightful game ever invented," said Weazel; "it keeps the attention alive, and warms the hands of the players more than any other; and I'll teach it to you, if you like; but take a glass of grog first. When you are on board a ship, you must do as sailors do; and 'grog' you know, or at least I know,—'grog is the liquor of life.' Perhaps you would like a glass better than that cup; but Balderson and myself think that there is no use in showing how much we take—or rather how little, for fear our messmates would force us to take more.

Now, then, Harris, hand out the 'good books,' and let's get round the board of green cloth."

A slight explanation of this game may not be amiss, in order to show how very easy it is for a man to pay off a debt of revenge without incurring suspicion. A handkerchief is twisted up as hard as a rope, and this is called the "good money" by which you are to pay off all debts; the cards are called "good books," (they are called elsewhere the "devil's books," and as far back as memory can trace, the four of clubs has been called "the devil's bed-post;") they are dealt out exactly, and the hands count the same as at Commerce. The great art of the game is never to miscall any thing. For instance, if a person were to designate the hand, as the hand, another would call out "Watch;" and the person having made the blunder would have to hold out his hand and receive one blow upon it from every player, just as hard as he thought proper to inflict it, the culprit being told the reason of the punishment by the man who called out "Watch," saying before he struck him, "This is for calling the good thing *flipper* out of its proper name;" a hand being a flipper; thus, the table is the "board of green cloth," etc., every thing having a professional name. It is obvious that the young beginner is likely to catch the most blows; and Weazel, completely blinded by Murray's manners, sought to pay him off for the "rowing" he got from Mr. Jones for talking to him over the gangway.

Murray, who knew the game well, readily agreed to the proposition; and Weazel having explained to him the game, warning him that when he had a good hand he ought to "stand Able," which gave him the privilege of inflicting three hard cuts upon the person who held the worst hand, they dealt the cards round once or twice to explain the game, and they then "served them out" properly, every one of the midshipmen being determined to pay off "the long-togged gentleman with the chain round his neck."

Perfectly aware of Weazel's character, Murray acted accordingly, and kept a guarded silence, inflicting the punishments gently, in order to show a lenient disposition, and then made a mistake purposely; upon which Weazel called out "Watch," and gave a wink to his messmates. "Hold out your flipper," said Weazel; "I demand the good money—this is for calling the 'good books' out of their names;" and smack came the hard-twisted handkerchief upon Murray's hand with all the force Weazel could bestow upon it; and it required some courage to keep it steady to meet the blows of the others, for they all served him out according to their utmost power, the last man keeping the "good money warm," as the term is. Lord Byron has since said,

> And if we do but wait the hour,
> There never yet was human power
> Which could evade, if unforgiven,
> The patient search and vigil long
> Of him who treasures up a wrong.

Murray was like the bard's watchful man; and Weazel, equally alert, was never off his guard. At last Weazel "stood Able" upon a sequence—"king, queen, and knave;" and Murray "stood Able" upon aces. When the hands were exposed, Weazel had the worst; for each, by some good luck, had got better cards, and the victim was called to receive punishment. Murray having demanded the "good money," desired him to hold out his flipper, and he began,—"This is for the loss of the good game called Able Whackets, this is for the same, and this is for *my* standing Able and *your* losing the game;" and at each time fell a stroke which nearly cut his hand off. At the expiration of this, Weazel withdrew his hand to offer it to the next. "Avast there!" said Murray; "hold out your flipper again!" and he received three more most powerful cuts for Weazel's having stood Able and having lost the game. The tears started in his eyes when he found that Murray used the good money with the swing of a proficient, and amply repaid him for his former unkindness; whilst Weazel, irritated by the laugh of his messmates, who perceived the stranger to be an adept, gave way to his wrath, and got watched "three times more." Some jeered him when he offered his maimed flipper, and refused it as being so much mutilated as not to offer a fair mark; and as the blows so hardly and so constantly inflicted led to abuse, and abuse to a promise of satisfaction, Murray contrived to give the conversation a turn by inquiring when the ship was to sail, as he should be happy to meet the gentlemen again.

"Oh, sail!" said Weazel, whose tongue was not idle, for his wrath had subsided at the idea of satisfaction and the prospect of working an eyelet-hole in the coat of his enemy,—"Sail! why, when we get our new captain on board."

"Who is to command this fine frigate?" said Murray.

"Some booby of a lord's son, dry-nursed by a fat lieutenant, and put under the guidance of Jones to keep out of mischief."

"Why does it follow," said Murray, "that the captain must be the booby you would make him?"

"Because," said Weazel, "merit is never rewarded. Here am I, old enough to command any frigate in the service, having lost two fingers at Trafalgar, been wrecked, badgered, buffeted, swamped in a boat cutting out; cut out of my own promotion by having been knocked overboard and believed drowned, four years past; been mate of the deck, had charge of a watch, and being, though I say it myself, the best hand at dry holystoning a lower-deck in the navy. Now I'll bet a dish of ham and eggs for four, with grog to wash it down, that the skipper who is sent on 'board to be acting captain under Jones is not older than you are to-day, and knows no more of a ship than you do!"

"That may be, and yet he may be a very proper man to command a frigate. Why, you would not like a man as old as a Spanish mule, and perhaps just as obstinate, to command you! I know you all like young slim fellows like myself."

"Do you?" said Weazel; "then you are much mistaken! Every thing is fancy; I fancy being commanded by a man older than myself—one who has been longer at sea, seen more service—one I can respect from his seniority, and in whom I can have confidence from his services. Now you are younger than me; and although I fancy, from the way you handled that handkerchief and gave me such striking proofs of your power, that you have been at sea, yet I should just as soon sail under the orders of the bumboat woman as under yours. So now, no offence, you know; as the hands are turned up, I shall turn out of this."

"Mr. Weazel," said a quartermaster, popping his head in the berth.

"Well?" replied Weazel.

"Mr. Jones says you are to go on shore with the dockyard party in the launch."

"Curse Mr. Jones, and the launch, and the dockyard party too!"

"At any rate," said Murray, rising to depart, "you are variable enough. Poor Mr. Jones, who is to dry-nurse the captain, is old enough to suit you —is entitled to your respect from his long service, and yet you don't seem to have much confidence in his orders. However, I will not be the cause of your delay; so, good evening young gentlemen. I dare say I shall have the pleasure of seeing you again."

"D——n me if ever I want to see you again!" said Weazel.

"Nor I," said Walcot.

"Nor I," said Harris; "he plays too good a knife and fork; and notwithstanding his gold chain, I don't think he has had a blow-out for the last fortnight; he's as thin as a herring, and twists about like an eel, but by the Lord Harry, he hits hard!"

Murray overheard these unfavorable remarks; but he well knew that midshipmen's remarks were harmless enough. Mr. Jones was on deck carrying on the duty; and Murray saw by the way one or two of the officers returned the salute as he got on the quarter-deck, that Jones had given a hint that the new captain was for show. The gig was manned, and Weazel saw the shore-going gentleman take hold of the yoke-lines and steer the boat as well as any man in the navy."

"That gentleman," said Mr. Jones to Weazel, "has known you before. I suppose you shook hands with him after dinner?"

"Not exactly, sir; but he made my hands shake. We played at Able Whackets, and I fancy I got off second-best."

"Had you a midshipman on board the Tribune of the name of Murray?"

"Yes, sir," replied Weazel; "and a gallant fellow he was, but a precious snob to be sure; he was the son of some old lord mayor, and was placed under the protection of a Mr. Hammerton, who gave me a considerable hiding because I stowed his blankets away the first night."

"How did he get on down below with you?" continued Jones.

"Ate very well, I thank you, sir—a mighty stretching appetite. I was in hopes of showing him the garden in the foretop, or the cow in the main-top; but the dockyard party—"

"—Will save you a little repentance. Mr. Weazel, that gentleman is Captain Murray, of the Arethusa."

"Whew!" went Weazel, as he slipped down the side; "a pretty kettle of fish I've made of it!"

THE SPOILED CHILD.

BY R. H. HORNE.

By the side of a deep-bosomed, smouldering Christmas fire, in the oak-panelled drawing-room of an old manor-house in Herefordshire, sat two mild-featured grandmammas, awaiting, with placid dignity, the advent of the dinner-hour. Their figures rose with equal state from their massy brocaded gowns, though their style and effect were different. One grandmamma was exceeding thin; the other grandmamma excelled in fat. Kind hearts looked out from both their faces; nor would this have been quite possible to any hearts *less* kind, for each face was surrounded and surmounted with an embattled cap, thick set with richly notched, though faded, ribbons, and five rows deep in starched point lace; so that each respected head bore a close resemblance to a *bouquet* of thistles exulting in a strong white frost.

They were beguiling the time with grave, yet pleasing conversation, till "papa" and "mamma" were dressed, and the rest of the family, with sundry guests, arrived; and the subject they discussed was the never-enough-to-be-repeated one, of how many perfections were displayed in the pretty person of their dear grandchild, and how many more were to be expected, from the constant care, attention, devotion, and universal admiration and flattery, bestowed upon the beauty and "bringing up" of little Darling Petkin.

A loud scream from the excellent lungs (lungs not to be equalled, of their size, in power of announcement) of the dear child upstairs, was quickly followed by the descent of the same in the arms of his maid, to be carried to the front door to meet a carriagefull of aunts, another full of friends of the family, and sundry uncles on horseback, whose approach he had seen from the nursery window. In less than a couple of minutes, the whole concourse came dancing and crowing into the drawing-room, with Darling Petkin in the centre, mounted upon the left shoulder of Uncle Benjamin, where he sat with a drum slung round his neck, which he furiously beat with both sticks, screaming in vainglorious delight, and never caring to perceive that each blow of the drumstick in his right hand "took" his uncle's left ear in its way upwards. At length the general tumult ceased, and, in the pause occasioned by all the party "taking their breath," the shrill voice of Darling Petkin enunciated, with all the air of a little pagod just come to light, "Yah! on'y nook a' ME!

"Only look at me!" How often do we hear this from children; how seldom do we find the claim upon general attention and admiration made in vain! We begin to fear, that where we are fond of a child (and the same principle applies to a pet dog, horse, or favorite of any kind), there is always a natural tendency towards spoiling it a *little;* that is, towards rendering it vain, exacting, wilful, useless, or disagreeable, by the excess of our manifestations of admiration, and the concessions we make to all its sayings and doings, however capricious and hurtful. Our present business, however, is not so much with the good children, the pretty good, or the not-so-very-good-neither children, but the tip-top specimen of a——"On'y nook" at the portrait!

The tumult having subsided, the uncles and aunts were enabled to offer a few words of recognition and merry-Christmas-wishing to the two grandmammas, and, at the same time, to perceive that

Mr. and Mrs. Meredith (we beg Darling Petkin's pardon! we mean papa and mamma) had entered the room. The family now commenced a kind and solicitous conversation together, on the various gains, losses, changes, and prospects, which had occurred to each other since they met last Christmas; and this interesting conversation and affectionate intercourse was allowed to continue uninterrupted almost to the extent of fifteen minutes, during the whole of which time Darling Petkin was busily and silently occupied alone, in a distant corner, eating greedy handfuls of many-colored "hundreds and thousands," varied by sundry dips into paper packets brought him by Uncle Ben, containing bullseyes, kisses, hardbake, almond sugar-plums, alicumpane, barley sugar, gingerbread, white sugar-candy, pipe peppermint, lollipop squibs, a quire-and-a-half of parliament, and everlastings. These little tokens of remembrance and affection, without which the giver would have met with a very different reception, were deposited in Darling Petkin's hands by mamma, to go and put away in his own pretty cupboard and drawers, and to take out only a little from each packet every day after dinner.

When the various greetings of the family had been exchanged, Aunt Nancy, looking at her watch, and observing that it wanted half-an-hour of dinner, drew a roll of paper from her pocket, and making a great deal of rustling in unfolding it, besides manifesting a more than usually grave look, she thus produced a silence fraught with expectation, during which she cast an interrogative glance around.

"Oh! *do*, Aunt Nancy!" exclaimed several voices apparently proceeding from minds previously instructed, or else very rapidly sympathetic; "oh! *do* read it."

"Pray do!—yes, pray do!" murmured papa and mamma, and several friends of the family. Aunt Nancy bowed her head with an air of self-complacency, which she intended for general respect, and commenced reading:—

"'The production of a rational essay on infant education, is at once an undertaking and an event of the most——'"

Rub-dub-a-dub!—such were the sounds evidently intended to accompany Aunt Nancy's learned recitative; for Darling Petkin, having eaten hardbake and lollipops till he was nearly sick, suddenly came to the perception that he was no longer an object of interest to the company present, who, instead of being solely occupied with him, were actually going on very well among themselves without him! He, therefore, jumped up, seized his drum, and began to strut knee-foremost round the room, and through the seated party, beating it with all his might, sometimes on the head, sometimes with a "tack-tacking" noise on the tin sides or wooden rim, and bloating out his cheeks and stomach as he ejaculated a "row-de-dow" as semi-chorus to the "rub-a-dub" of his belabored instrument. Aunt Nancy's theoretic essay was, therefore, compelled to proceed with an *obligato* accompaniment on the drum, by the celebrated Darling Petkin.

"'The production of a rational'"—rack, tack-a-tack, dub, dub!—"'a rational system of'"—rub!—"'infant'"—dub!—"'education:' my dearest child! pray stop for only a *few* minutes!"—rub-a-dub-a-dub!—"'The production,' I repeat, 'of a national system of'"—row-de-dow!—"'of infant education'—my darling, pray wait a minute!—'is at once an undertaking and an event of'"—ti-ti-rub!—"'the most'"—ri-tum-dub!—"'vital importance,'"—Rub-a-dub! a-dub!, dub-dub-doo!—"'It is of most vital importance, not only to one's own country, but to the'"—row-de-dow!—"'world at large. Instead of the erroneous'"—tack-a-rack, a-rack!—"'methods hitherto practised,'"—row-dow-de-dow!—"'the profound system I have adopted of always permitting a child to'"—rub-a-dub, a-dub!—"'to have its own way in every thing'"—ri-tum-ti!—"'is one, easy of accomplishment; and the results are equally'"—rum-ti-tum, ti-tum—"'easy to be foreseen.'"—Row-de-dow, de-dow, doodle-doo!

"'But, as they grow up, there is the'"—rub!—"'there is the'"—rub!—"'there is'—my dear, sweet child! do, pray be quiet—only *one* moment!—'there,' I say, 'is the'"—rub!—"'in fact, the very greatest'"—dub-a-dub!—"'necessity that the adult should, of its own good'"—row, de-dow, de-dow!—"'of its own good sense, should see the propriety, as well as prudence, of'"—ti-tiddley-ti!—"'of acting on a totally different plan.'"—Tack-a-rack, dub, dub!—"My dearest little boy!"—row-de-dow, de-dow, toodle-loo!—"poor grandmamma!"—ti-rub!—"her head aches, Darling Pet!"—yah! row-de-dow, de-dow, rub-a-doo!—"Oh fie! Uncle Ben!—see! he's got the other drum, to help Darling beat his tatoo!"—Tra! tra-a-a-a, ti-rum! tra, tra-a-a-ti-dum!—rub, *dub*-a-rub-a-rub, rub-de-doo! tra-a-a-a-a-a-a-rub, *dub*-a-rub-a-rub, rub-de-doo! hurra-a-a!

It is not very necessary to inform the reader that Aunt Nancy's learned essay on infant education was quite overwhelmed; and the discomfited spinster replaced it in her pocket, with a look expressive of very mixed and confusing thoughts and emotions. "Bless his dear, sweet face!" murmured mamma, "what a color he *has* got!—he's so fond of his drum, Aunt Nancy?" Whereupon, every body in the room, except one personage, uttered some ejaculation of admiration; and Uncle Benjamin, and two of the aunts, ran and covered him with kisses, and then carried him round the room on their crossed arms.

The one personage who did not contribute his voice to the applause of Darling Petkin's performance, was a corpulent, elderly gentleman, who had arrived in his own carriage at the same time as the batch of uncles and aunts, but of whom we have no more been able to take any notice up to the present moment, than were the company assembled. Mr. Scrope Bellyfield had, therefore, sat in pompous silence, with an expression of much disgust and irritation. He was evidently very vain of his great, fat person; and wore a high-crested, rich-curling, dark brown wig, not unlike the head-dress of George IV. Mr. Scrope Bellyfield was, moreover, a great exacter of all sorts of admiration and attention: first, because, to do him justice, he was really a man of superior understanding, education, and great general information; and, secondly, because he possessed immense wealth and influence, and "commanded" the votes of half the "independent freeholders" in his county. For this county, Mr. Meredith was most anxious to be returned to parliament; and, as the day of election was approaching, he had recently sought the friendship and advice of Mr. Scrope Bellyfield, who seemed disposed to exert himself exclusively in his favor. Mr. Meredith, and the whole family, were, consequently, anxious to show him every attention on the present occasion, although they had not yet been able to find any opportunity, except in helping him to alight from his carriage.

Mr. Meredith had stood rubbing his hands, with an obsequious preparatory air, beside the arm-chair of Mr. Scrope Bellyfield, during the lecture which had just been drummed into the ears of the party, as though he would fain have entered into some very interesting and deferential conversation; but the corpulent visitor was too irritated, and sat with an expression of assumed abstraction, pretending not to see him.

The dinner bell now resounded from the hall, and the whole party made a show of escorting Mr. Bellyfield, as they adjourned to the dining-room; but somehow or other, it happened that Darling Petkin got in the very centre of the group, and fairly carried off "the attention." They all took their seats at the table, Mr. Bellyfield being placed at the right hand of "mamma," who had Darling Petkin upon her knee. Grandmamma Meredith it was observed, had not taken her place; whereupon, Mr. Meredith informed the family that she had retired, with a bad headache, to lie down for an hour or two. "Ah!" murmured mamma, "she has been complaining a good deal of late; the weather, you see,—the cold is too much for her; she will be better when she has been bled: John has gone off for Dr. Mayton. *Shall* I help you to a little soup, Mr. Bellyfield?"

"Thank you, madam," replied the great gentleman in a formal voice, bowing his red face almost down into his plate.

"Me, too, mamma!—me, too!"

"Yes, my dear!—there love!—I'll just give him a spoonful to begin with: I know Mr. Bellyfield will excuse it."

"Me, mamma! me!"

"Yes, my darling!—bless the child! the sweetmeats have made him *so* thirsty. Now, Mr. Bellyfield."

"Oh, no sort of hurry, madam!" ejaculated the gentleman: and down went his face again towards his plate, with preposterous courtesy.

It would be too arduous a task to ourselves, and too provocative to our readers, were we to attempt to give a progressive description of the scene which continued through this most trying dinner. During the whole time did the victorious Darling Petkin sit, and persist in sitting, on mamma's knee; interrupting every attempt she made to address any body but himself; fretfully engrossing all her attention; and, in his unceasing attempts to engross the attention of every body else, as he had always been permitted to do, thoroughly confusing and defeating all general conversation. The effect upon the spirits of every body present, mamma and Uncle Ben perhaps excepted, was that of unmitigated and unconquerable exhaustion and disgust. But no one had the "cruelty" to say so; and few of the family admitted the fact to themselves. What all the visitors thought, was easy to perceive; what Mr. Bellyfield, in particular, thought and felt, we dare not venture to conjecture. He enjoyed the reputation throughout the country of being an excellent companion in all societies: a man who possessed "a fund of anecdote" and urbanity. Certainly, on the present occasion, he manifested no signs whatever of any thing of the kind. He made no movement, except to eat, and to bow his head when papa and the uncles asked him to do them the honor of taking wine; and he never opened his mouth, except to reply in monosyllables. His face, charged with color, presented the peculiarly ominous black-redness of long-suppressed breath; his manner was characterized by terrible composure; his silence was like the preliminary pause before the explosion of some capacious mine.

We pass over the dinner: the recollection of it has a choking effect. The dessert was placed upon the table; the guests now bethought them of merry Christmas, and were anxious to talk of old times. But there was no doing any thing with Darling Petkin in the room, except to listen and admire, or endure and be silent. There he sat, on mamma's knee, who was ready to faint from exhaustion, yet did not possess enough fortitude to send him to bed; there he sat, with his sweetmeats before him, his cheeks, mouth, and chin, begrimed with colored sugars, tart, cake, and orange, all of which he insisted continually upon having kissed; there he sat, with messed hands, and "sticky" fingers, catching at the contents of every dish in his reach, or that he caused to be brought within his reach; then, flinging the conglomeration about the table, or into the plates of those who were nearest; and, finally, wiping his grimy little paws on mamma's satin dress, or on her cheek, and throat, under pretence of playful fondness.

The crawling clock-hands eventually worked their way into the middle of the fatigued night, and Darling Petkin's eyes became heavy, as he made the preparatory movement to go to sleep in mamma's arms. It was now thought a little effort might cautiously be made to try and get him up stairs without her, so that she might have half an hour's respite to devote to her guests and family. The little effort was made in the following manner:—

"My sweetest!" murmured mamma, pressing the child closer to her bosom; "will my sweetest go to his bed?"

"No, I sarnt—sarnt go-a-bed."

"Aunt Nancy," pursued mamma, "has got a little finger that knows it's time Darling went to his own pretty bed. Little finger, what's o'clock?"

Here the accomplished theorist on infant education held up her gifted digit.

"There! Aunt Nancy's little finger says it's very late; and Darling will be so glad to go to his bed—won't he?"

"No, no, no!" squealed the peevish Petkin.

"My precious lamb! how feverish his dear face and hands are! *do* go to his bed."

"Ay, do goey, love;" echoed Aunt Nancy, in the tenderest voice; "Oh! don't beat mamma; you've hit her on the chin--see! you've made poor mamma ky!—poor mamma!"

Here poor mamma made a show of crying, during which the sweet lamb settled himself in her lap, and fell fast asleep. He was thus carried up to bed. Now, in good sooth, did all present, shifting themselves in their seats, take a fresh breath, and reverting to merry Christmas, prepare to have a pleasant hour, and toast old times. Even Mr. Scrope Bellyfield, showed signs of emerging from his pompous austerity and smouldering silence, and gazed at "poor mamma," with an expression in which some commiseration for her pale, worn face, was mingled with contempt and irritation at her moral weakness. Mr. Meredith now began to get alive, and pulling down his waistcoat and wristbands, and stretching his arms, called for fresh decanters of wine and clean glasses. The table was also cleared, and covered afresh with plates of oranges, olives, cakes, dried fruits, etc. "And now," quoth Mr. Meredith, rising with a bumper in his hand, and looking towards Mr. Scrope Bellyfield, "And now, I have to propose a toast!"

A loud yell from the nursery arrested Mr. Meredith's progress. Darling Pet, having had his sleepy face washed before being placed in his bed, had so completely recovered himself as to insist upon coming down stairs again. He was now heard on his way, beating his drum, and singing and shouting, as he descended. Papa, however, began his speech again, in hopes of finishing before the accompaniment overwhelmed him.

"I have to propose"—rub-a-dub-dub!—"a toast to you all,"—ti, rub-a-dub, rub!—"which, I'm sure you must drink with delight."—Row-de-dow, rack-a-tack too! "It is the health of a guest, who has honored us here with his"—rub-a-dub-dub, doodle-doo!—"a gentleman, whose well-known urbanity, and fund of anecdote, is the universal——"

The tumultuous entrance of Darling Petkin, here rendered the speaker quite inaudible, and "poor papa," casting a deplorable look at deplorable mamma, fairly gave it up, and sat down.

The Spoiled Child was in his night-gown and night-cap; his drum was slung round his neck; he had a sword at his side, and a drumstick in one hand, while he used a wooden gun as a drumstick in the other. In the very middle of the table did he insist upon being placed, with his drum before him, and then he commenced an uproar and havoc on every thing within his range, such as we shall refrain from attempting to describe. At length, by a whirl of his gun, the sweet lamb smote a tall candle, which, falling sideways, touched the head-dress of Grandmamma Thompson, and set it all in a blaze. With a loud screaming, "Take me, mamma!" (while Uncle Ben extinguished the fiery old crown) the sweet lamb flew along the table to mamma's expanded arms, and, in doing so, overturned a heavy cut-glass decanter, which rolled off the table, and fell with one edge upon the toe of Mr. Scrope Bellyfield!

"Base urchin!" ejaculated the long-smouldering and now agonized and infuriate gentleman, jumping up with a rapidity never to be anticipated from one so corpulent, and extending his right arm, the clenched fist whereof trembled above the table with passion; "Base urchin! is it to see and hear your yells and antics that I am invited to this place today! Was I inveigled here to enjoy your pretty play and prattle close to my elbow all dinner-time! —to feel continual gouts of gravy, and bits of fat and sweetmeat dropped upon my knees!—to have filbert maggots tossed into my waistcoat, and orange juice and pips shot and squirted into my very face!—Mr. Meredith!—Sir!—this is not to be endured. Talk of system—theory—infant education, indeed! your advisers are lamentably in the dark. There is not one idea entertained upon the subject by that child's grandmammas, uncles, aunts, nor, give me leave to say, Sir, by his papa or mamma, which is not directly the opposite of right. I wish distinctly to say, that the whole system of behavior and treatment adopted towards that creature, is as wrong and injurious to him now, and will be for his future life, as possible. A more ruinous system could scarcely be invented by the most elaborate intention of mischief. You think I say all this only because he has flung a decanter upon my toe; but I don't. It is the pain, Sir, which has shot the truth out of me all of a lump. I say again, a more complete specimen of an atrocious 'Spoiled Child' I never read or heard of—with all my 'fund of anecdote;'—so base an urchin I never saw in the most tormenting dream!"

With these words, Mr. Scrope Bellyfield floundered out of the room, and left the house, never again to set foot in it. Mr. Meredith never had the satisfaction of writing M. P. after his name: he saw it was of no use to stand an election.

AN OVERCHARGE.—A RESUSCITATED JOE, VERSIFIED.

Some twenty years ago—it may be more—
  When Bonaparte was in lofty station,
He vow'd he'd fly his eagles on the shore,
  And freedom give to all the British nation.

Now, John Bull relished not this kind intention;
  He knew *that eagles were much given to peck;*
So thanked the Emperor for his attention,
  Yet firm resolved his progress he would check.

From John o' Groat to Cornwall's austral end,
  A race of volunteers immediate springs,
And valiant hearts their country to defend,
  Who swore they'd clip th' Imperial eagle's wings.

Sam Miles, a lad with heart of British Oak,
  (His head was somewhat of a softer mould,)
Among the awkward squad his station took,
  And in a moment grew a soldier bold.

The drill was over—well he'd play'd his part;
  Now homeward to his loving spouse he hies;
Explain'd the mysteries of the martial art,
  And held the musket to her gazing eyes.

"Come here, my love; I'll quickly fire the piece,
  And you shall hear the wondrous noise it makes."
He loaded—twirled the rod about with grace,
  And, soldier-like, his footing firmly takes.

He touched the trigger, but the piece was dumb,
  For why? our hero had forgot to prime!
He scratched his head, and after many a hum,
  "There's not enough," so charged another time.

Yet all was hush; his efforts were in vain—
  A third he tried—nor yet the fourth was right—
He charged and rammed, and rammed and charged again,
  Till down the tenth he forced with all his might.

But now a ray of reason glanced his soul,
  "I see—I see my error—never fear!
All's right, my love; I quite forgot the hole—
  I ought t' have put a little priming here."

He fired—bang! with a tremendous sound;
  The piece was burst and straight to atoms flew,
Laid one brave warrior sprawling on the ground,
  And by his side, unhurt, his wife so true.

After a while, the wife began to rise;
  Sam seized her fast—roared out with voice of wo,
"Janet, Janet, keep still, and shut your eyes,
  'Tis only once! *she's nine times more to go!*"

SEAMEN ON SHORE.

BY LEIGH HUNT.

The sole business of a seaman on shore, who has to go to sea again, is to take as much pleasure as he can. The moment he sets his foot on dry ground, he turns his back on all salt beef and other salt-water restrictions. His long absence, and the impossibility of getting land pleasures at sea, put him upon a sort of desperate appetite. He lands, like a conqueror taking possession. He has been debarred so long, that he is resolved to have that matter out with the inhabitants. They must render an account to him of their treasures, their women, their victualling stores, their entertainments, their every thing; and in return, he will behave like a gentleman, and scatter his gold.

His first sensation at landing, is the strange firmness of the earth, which he goes treading in a sort of heavy light way, half wagoner and half dancing-master, his shoulders rolling, and his feet touching and going; the same way, in short, in which he keeps himself prepared for all the chances of the vessel, when on deck. There is always this appearance of lightness of foot and heavy strength of upper works, in a sailor. And he feels it himself. He lets his jacket fly open, and his shoulder slouch, and his hair grow long, to be gathered into a heavy pig-tail; but when full-dressed, he prides himself on a certain gentility of toe, on a white stocking and a natty shoe, issuing lightly out of the flowing blue trowser. His arms are neutral, hanging and swinging in a curve aloof; his hands half open, as if they had just been handling ropes, and had no object in life but to handle them again. He is proud of appearing in a new hat and slops, with a Belcher handkerchief flowing loosely round his neck, and the corner of another out of his pocket. Thus equipped, with pinchbeck buckles in his shoes (which he bought for gold), he puts some tobacco in his mouth, not as if he were going to use it directly, but as if he stuffed it in a pouch on one side, as a pelican does fish, to employ it hereafter; and so, with Bet Monson at his side, and perhaps a cane or whanghee twisted under his other arm, sallies forth to take possession of the Lubberland. He buys every thing that he comes athwart—nuts, gingerbread, apples, shoe-strings, beer, brandy, gin, buckles, knives, a watch (two, if he has money enough), gowns and handkerchiefs for Bet and his mother and sisters, dozens of "Superfine Best Men's Cotton Stockings," dozens of "superfine Best Women's Cotton Ditto," best good Check for Shirts (though he has too much already), infinite needles and thread (to sew his trowsers with some day), a footman's laced hat, Bear's Grease, to make his hair grow (by way of joke), several sticks, all sorts of Jew articles, a flute (which he can't play, and never intends), a leg of mutton, which he carries somewhere to roast, and for a piece of which the landlord of the Ship makes him pay twice what he gave for the whole; in short, all that money can be spent upon, which is every thing but medicine gratis, and this he would insist on paying for. He would buy all the painted parrots on an Italian's head, on purpose to break them, rather than not spend his money. He has fiddles and a dance at the Ship, with oceans of flip and grog; and gives the blind fiddler tobacco for sweetmeats, and half-a-crown for treading on his toe. He asks the landlady, with a sigh, after her daughter Nance, who first fired his heart with her silk stockings; and finding that she is married and in trouble, leaves five crowns for her, which the old lady appropriates as part payment for a shilling in advance. He goes to the Port playhouse with Bet Monson, and a great red handkerchief full of apples, gingerbread nuts, and fresh beef; calls out for the fiddlers and Rule Britannia; pelts Tom Sikes in the pit; and compares Othello to the black ship's cook in his white nightcap. When he comes to London, he and some messmates take a hackney-coach, full of Bet Monsons and tobacco-pipes, and go through the streets smoking and lolling out of window. He has

ever been cautious of venturing on horseback, and among his other sights in foreign parts, relates with unfeigned astonishment how he has seen the Turks ride: "Only," says he, guarding against the hearer's incredulity, "they have saddle-boxes to hold 'em in, fore and aft, and shovels like for stirrups." He will tell you how the Chinese drink, and the Negurs dance, and the monkeys pelt you with cocoa-nuts; and how King Domy would have built him a mud hut and made him a peer of the realm, if he would have stopped with him, and taught him to make trowsers. He has a sister at a "School for Young Ladies," who blushes with a mixture of pleasure and shame at his appearance; and whose confusion he completed by slipping fourpence into her hand, and saying loud that he has "no more copper" about him. His mother and elder sisters at home doat on all he says and does; telling him, however, that he is a great sea-fellow, and was always wild ever since he was a hop-o'-my-thumb, no higher than the window locker. He tells his mother that she would be a duchess in Paramaboo; at which the good old portly dame laughs and looks proud. When his sisters complain of his romping, he says that they are only sorry it is not the baker. He frightens them with a mask made after the New Zealand fashion, and is forgiven for his learning. Their mantel-piece is filled by him with shells and sharks' teeth; and when he goes to sea again, there is no end of tears, and "God bless you's!" and home-made-gingerbread.

His officer on shore does much of all this, only, generally speaking, in a higher taste. The moment he lands, he buys quantities of jewelry and other valuables, for all the females of his acquaintance; and is taken in for every article. He sends in a cart-load of fresh meat to the ship, though he is going to town next day; and calling in at a chandler's for some candles, is persuaded to buy a dozen of green wax, with which he lights up the ship at evening; regretting that the fine moonlight hinders the effect of the color. A man, with a bundle beneath his arm, accosts him in an under tone; and, with a look in which respect for his knowledge is mixed with an avowed zeal for his own interest, asks if his Honor will just step under the gangway here, and inspect some real India shawls. The gallant lieutenant says to himself, "This fellow knows what's what, by his face;" and so he proves it, by being taken in on the spot. When he brings the shawls home, he says to his sister with an air of triumph, "There, Poll, there's something for you; only cost me twelve, and is worth twenty if it's worth a dollar." She turns pale—"Twenty what, my dear George? Why, you haven't given twelve dollars for it, I hope?" "Not I, by the Lord." "That's lucky; because you see, my dear George, that all together is not worth more than fourteen or fifteen shillings." "Fourteen or fifteen what! Why it's real **India**, en't it? Why the fellow told me so; or I'm sure I'd as soon"—(here he tries to hide his blushes with a bluster)—I'd as soon have given him twelve douses on the chaps as twelve guineas." "Twelve guineas!" exclaims the sister; and then drawling forth, "Why—my—dear—George," is proceeding to show him what the articles would have cost at Condell's, when he interrupts her by requesting her to go and choose for herself a tea-table service. He then makes his escape to some messmates at a coffee-house, and drowns his recollection of the shawls in the best wine, and a discussion on the comparative merits of the English and West-Indian beauties and tables. At the theatre afterwards, where he has never been before, he takes a lady at the back of one of the boxes for a woman of quality; and when, after returning his long respectful gaze with a smile, she turns aside and puts her handkerchief to her mouth, he thinks it is in derision, till his friend undeceives him. He is introduced to the lady; and ever afterwards, at the first sight of a woman of quality (without any disparagement either to those charming personages), expects her to give him a smile. He thinks the other ladies much better creatures than they are taken for; and for their parts, they tell him, that if all men were like himself, they would trust the sex again:—which, for aught we know, is the truth. He has, indeed, what he thinks a very liberal opinion of ladies in general; judging them all, in a manner, with the eye of a seaman's experience. Yet he will believe nevertheless in the "true-love" of any given damsel whom he seeks in the way of marriage, let him roam as much, or remain as long at a distance, as he may. It is not that he wants feeling; but that he has read of it, time out of mind, in songs; and he looks upon constancy as a sort of exploit, answering to those which he performs at sea. He is nice in his watches and linen. He makes you presents of cornelians, antique seals, cocoa-nuts set in silver, and other valuables. When he shakes hands with you, it is like being caught in a windlass. He would not swagger about the streets in his uniform, for the world. He is generally modest in company, though liable to be irritated by what he thinks ungentlemanly behavior. He is also liable to be rendered irritable by sickness; partly because he has been used to command others, and to be served with all possible deference and alacrity; and partly, because the idea of suffering pain, without any honor or profit to get by it, is unprofessional, and he is not accustomed to it. He treats talents unlike his own with great respect. He often perceives his own so little felt, that it teaches him this feeling for that of others. Besides, he admires the quantity of information which people can get, without travelling like himself; especially when he sees how interesting his own becomes, to them as well as to every body else. When he tells a story, particularly if full of wonders, he takes care to maintain his character for truth and simplicity, by qualifying it with all possible reservations, concessions, and anticipations of objection; such as "in case, at such times as, so to speak, as it were, at least, at any rate." He seldom uses sea-terms but when jocosely provoked by something contrary to his habits of life; as for instance, if he is always meeting you on horseback, he asks if you never mean to walk the deck again; or if he finds you studying day after day, he says you are always overhauling your log-book. He makes more new acquaintances, and forgets his old ones less, than any other man in the busy world; for he is so compelled to make his home everywhere, remembers his native one as such a place of enjoyment, has all his friendly recollections so fixed upon his mind at sea, and has so much to tell and to hear when he returns, that change and separation lose with him the most heartless part of their nature. He also sees such a variety of customs and manners, that he becomes charitable in his opinions altogether; and charity, while it diffuses the affections, cannot let the old ones go. Half the secret of human intercourse is to make allowance for each other.

When the Officer is superannuated or retires, he becomes, if intelligent and inquiring, one of the most agreeable old men in the world, equally welcome to the silent for his card-playing, and to the conversational for his recollections. He is fond of astronomy and books of voyages, and is immortal with all who know him for having been round the world, or seen the transit of Venus, or had one of his fingers carried off by a New Zealand hatchet, or a present of feathers from an Otaheitan beauty.

Not elevated by his acquirements above some of his humbler tastes, he delights in a corner-cupboard holding his cocoa-nuts and punch-bowl; has his summer-house castellated and planted with wooden cannon; and sets up the figure of his old ship, the Britannia, or the Lovely Nancy, for a statue in the garden; where it stares eternally with red cheeks and round black eyes, as if in astonishment at its situation.

Chaucer, who wrote his Canterbury Tales about four hundred and thirty years ago, has among his other characters in that work a SHIPMAN, who is exactly of the same cast as the modern sailor,—the same robustness, courage, and rough-drawn virtue, doing its duty, without being very nice in helping itself to its recreations. There is the very dirk, the complexion, the jollity, the experience, and the bad horsemanship. The plain unaffected ending of the description has the air of a sailor's own speech; while the line about the beard is exceedingly picturesque, poetical, and comprehensive. In copying it out, we shall merely alter the old spelling, where the words are still modern.

A shipman was there, wonned far by west;
For aught I wot, he was of Dartmouth.
He rode upon a rouncie, as he couth,*
All in a gown of falding to the knee.
A dagger hanging by a lace had he,
About his neck, under his arm adown:
The hot summer had made his hew all brown:
And certainly he was a good felaw.
Full many a draught of wine he hadde draw
From Bordeaux ward, while that the chapman slep
Of nice conscience took he no keep.
If that he fought and had the higher hand,
By water he sent 'em home to every land.
But of his craft, to reckon well his tides,
His streames and his strandes him besides.

* He rode upon a hack-horse, as well as he could.

His harborough, his moon, and his lode manage,
There was not such from Hull unto Carthage.
Hardy he was, and wise, I undertake;
With many a tempest had his beard been shake.
He knew well all the heavens, as they were,
From Gothland to the Cape de Finisterre,
And every creek in Briton and in Spain.
His barge ycleped was the Magdelain.

When about to tell his Tale, he tells his fellow-travellers that he shall clink them so merry a bell,

That it shall waken all this company:
But it shall not be of philosophy,
Nor of physick, nor of terms quaint of law;
There is but little Latin in my maw.

The story he tells is a well-known one in the Italian novels, of a monk who made love to a merchant's wife, and borrowed a hundred francs of the husband to give her. She accordingly admits his addresses, during the absence of her good man on a journey. When the latter returns, he applies to the cunning monk for repayment, and is referred to the lady; who thus finds her mercenary behavior outwitted.

ST. VALENTINE'S DAY.

BY LEIGH HUNT.

THE day's at hand, the young, the gay,
The lover's and the postman's day,
The day when, for that only day,
February turns to May,
And pens delight in secret play,
And few may hear what many say.
Be it dull, or be it fine,
Come with those bright eyes of thine;
Come, and make the season shine
For the day, sweet Valentine!

Now are formed sweet annual fates:
Now the birds elect their mates;
Now from dawn love goeth blind,
Till its own true love it find:
He'll not ope his eyes, nor she,
Till themselves encounter'd be,
Fearing bond compulsory;
Fearing Jones and fearing Jenkins,
And so they go with constant blinkings.
"And how should they their true love know?"
Oh, by answers, soft and low;
Or by some such touch of hand,
As only love can understand;
Or a kiss (if safe from spies)
Bolder for the blindest eyes.
Gentle love, made bold with mirth,
Is the sweetest thing on earth.
Come, with those kind eyes of thine,
And make it bold, sweet Valentine!

Now, the servant maiden stops,
Doating on the stationers' shops,
Where she sees the hearts and darts,
Bleeding sweet as cherry tarts:
She'll to-day have one herself,
Or close on Dick the pantry shelf.
Come, with those kind eyes of thine;
Come, and bring him, Valentine!

Now the postman may not choose
But wear out his winter shoes,
Knocking here, and knocking there,
Till a pulse fills all the air,
And the breathless blushes rise
Under letter-reading eyes.
Anne has one, and Jane another,
Flying from their snatching brother.
Oh, may loving freedom meet
As much pardon and heart-heat,
As impertinence meets ire,
And a thrust into the fire.
Come, and see that hearts combine
The P's and Q's, O Valentine!

And thou *dost* come. Lo! I hear
Pinions; and thy birds appear
Two and two. (Some larks from Dunstable
Clear the way, and act as constable.)
Cupids mingle with the birds,
Luring on, with winged words,
Youths and maidens, also pair'd,
Simple-cheek'd, and gentle hair'd,
But squeezing (simple though they be)
Each other's hands excessively.
You can't conceive how hard they do it,
Though their faces may not show it.
Hymen, then, hung all with rings,
Danceth to their jingellings,
In a robe of saffron hue,
Like the crocus, now that's new.
Golden robes, and rings, and hair—
Angel-like, he burns the air.
And then thou comest, O thou priest,
Whose sweet creed hath never ceased,
Christian truly and benign,
Orthodoxest Valentine!

THE MONTHLY NURSE.

BY LEIGH HUNT.

THE MONTHLY NURSE—taking the class in the lump, without such exceptions as will be noticed before we conclude—is a middle-aged, motherly sort of a gossipping, hushing, flattering, dictatorial, knowing, ignorant, not very delicate, comfortable, uneasy, slip-slop kind of a blinking individual, between asleep and awake, whose business it is—under Providence and the doctor—to see that a child be not ushered with too little officiousness into the world, nor brought up with too much good sense during the first month of its existence. All grown people, with her (excepting her own family), consist of wives who are brought to bed, and husbands who are bound to be extremely sensible of the supremacy of that event; and all the rising generation are infants in laced caps, not five weeks old, with incessant thirst, screaming faces, thumpable backs, and red little minnikin hands tipped with hints of nails. She is the only maker of caudle in the world. She takes snuff ostentatiously, drams advisedly, tea incessantly, advice indignantly, a nap when she can get it, cold whenever there is a crick in the door, and the remainder of whatsoever her mistress leaves to eat or drink, provided it is what somebody else would like to have. But she drinks rather than eats. She has not the relish for a "bit o' dinner" that the servant-maid has; though nobody but the washer-woman beats her at a "dish o' tea," or that which "keeps cold out of the stomach," and puts weakness into it. If she is thin, she is generally straight as a stick, being of a condition of body that not even drams will tumefy. If she is fat, she is one of the fubsiest of the cosy; though rheumatic withal, and requiring a complexional good-nature to settle the irritabilities of her position, and turn the balance in favor of comfort or hope. She is the victim of watching; the arbitress of her superiors; the servant, yet rival, of doctors; the opposer of innovations; the regretter of all old household religions as to pap-boats, cradles, and swatches; the inhabitant of a hundred bed-rooms; the Juno Lucina of the ancients, or goddess of child-birth, in the likeness of a cook-maid. Her greatest consolation under a death (next to the corner-cupboard, and the not having had her advice taken about a piece of flannel) is the handsomeness of the corpse; and her greatest pleasure in life, is when lady and baby are both gone to sleep, the fire bright, the kettle boiling, and her corns quiescent. She then first takes a pinch of snuff, by way of pungent anticipation of bliss, or as a sort of concentrated essence of satisfaction; then a glass of spirits—then puts the water in the tea-pot—then takes another glass of spirits (the last having been a small one, and the coming tea affording a "counteraction")—then smooths down her apron, adjusts herself in her arm-chair, pours out the first cup of tea, and sits for a minute or two staring at the fire, with the solid complacency of an owl,—perhaps not without something of his snore, between wheeze and snuff-box.

Good and ill-nature, as in the case of every one else, make the great difference between the endurability, or otherwise, of this personage in your house; and the same qualities, in the master and mistress, together with the amount of their good sense, or the want of it, have a like reaction. The good or ill, therefore, that is here said of the class in general, becomes applicable to the individual accordingly. But as all people will get what power they can, the pleasant by pleasant means, and the unpleasant by the reverse, so the office of the Monthly Nurse, be her temper and nature what it will, is one that emphatically exposes her to temptation that way; and her first endeavor, when she comes into a house, is to see how far she can establish an undisputed authority on all points. In proportion to her success or otherwise in this object, she looks upon the lady as a charming, reasonable, fine, weak, cheatable creature, whose husband (as she tells him) "can never be too grateful for her bearing such troubles on his account;" or as a Frenchified conceited madam, who will turn out a deplorable match for the poor gentleman, and assuredly be the death of the baby with her tantrums about "natural living," and her blasphemies against rum, pieces of fat, and Daffy's Elixir. The gentleman in like manner—or "master," as the humbler ones call him—is, according as he behaves himself, and receives her revelations for gospel, a "sweet good man,"—"quite a gentleman,"—"just the very model of a husband for mistress," etc., etc.; or, on the other hand, he is a "very strange gentleman,"—"quite an oddity,"—one that is "not to be taught his own good,"—that will "neither be led nor *druv*,"—that will "be the death of mistress with his constant *fidge-fidge* in and out of the room,"—and his making her "laugh in that dreadful manner," and so forth;—and, as to his "pretending to hold the baby, it is like a cow with a candlestick." "Holding the baby," indeed, is a science, which she reckons to belong exclusively to herself; she makes it the greatest favor to visitor or servant to let them venture upon a trial of it; and affable intimations are given to the oldest mothers of families, who come to see her mistress, how they will do well to receive a little instruction on that head, and not venture to substitute their fine-spun theories for her solid practice; for your Monthly Nurse (next to a positive grandson) is the greatest teacher of your grandmother how to suck eggs, in the world; and you may have been forty years in the habit of sticking a pin, and find your competency come to nothing before the explanatory pity of her information.

Respecting the "doctor," her thoughts cannot be so bold or even so patronizing. She is confessedly second to him, while he is present; and when he has left the room, a spell remains upon her from his superior knowledge. Yet she has her hearty likes or dislikes of him too, and on the same grounds of self-reference. If she likes him, there "never *was* such a beautiful doctor," except perhaps Sir William, or Doctor Buttermouth (both dead), and always excepting the one that recommended herself. He is a "fine man"—so patient—so without pride—and yet "so firm like;"—nobody comes near him for a difficult case—for a fever case—for the management of a "violent lady." If she dislikes him, he is "queer"—"odd"—"stubborn"—has the "new ways,"—very proper, she has no doubt, but not what she has been used to, or seen practised by the doctors about court. And whether she likes him or not, she has always a saving grace for herself, of superiority to all other nurses, in point of experience and good luck. She has always seen a case of more difficulty than the one in hand, and knows what was done for it; and Doctor Gripps, who is "always" called in to such cases, and who is a very pleasant though rough sort of gentleman, calls her his "other right hand," and "the *jewel* that rhymes to *gruel*."

Armed with these potential notions in general, and the strongest possible sense of her viceroyalty over master and mistress for the time being, she takes possession of the new room and the new faces; and the motto of her reign—the *Dieu et Mon Droit* of her escutcheon—is "During the month." This phrase she has always at hand, like a sceptre, wherewith to assert her privileges, and put down objection. "During the month," the lady is not to read a book. "During the month," nobody is to lay a finger on the bed for the purpose of making it, till her decree goes forth. "During the month," the muffle of the knocker is at her disposal. And "During the month," the husband is to be nobody, except as far as she thinks fit, not even (for the first week or so) to his putting his head in at the door. You would take him to be the last man who had had any thing to do with the business. However, for her own sake, she generally contrives to condescend to become friends with him, and he is then received into high favor—is invited to tea with his wife, at some "unusually early" period; and Nurse makes a bit of buttered toast for "master" with her own hand, and not only repeats that "baby is as like him as two peas" (which it always is, the moment it is born, if the lady's inclination is supposed to set that way), but tells him that she fears he is "a sad charming gentleman," for that "mistress talks of him in her sleep." The phrases commonest in her mouth are mostly of an endearing or flattering sort, with an implication, in the tone, of her right to bestow them; and she is very aristocratic in her ideas. She tells the lady in her hour of trial, as the highest encouragement to fortitude she can think of, that "the Queen must suffer the same;" and the babies are always kings and queens, loves, darlings, jewels, and poppets. Beauties also, be sure:—and as all babies are beautiful, and the last always more beautiful than the one before it, and "the child is father to the man," mankind, according to Nurse, ought to be nothing but a multitude of Venuses and Adonises; aldermen should be mere Cupids full grown; and the passengers in Fleet Street, male and female, slay one another, as they go, with the unbearableness of their respective charms. But she has also modes of speech, simply pathetic or judicious. If the lady, when her health is inquired after, is in low spirits, she is described as "taking *on so*;" if doing well, it must not be too well, for the honor of the importance of the case, and the general dignity of ailment; and hence the famous answer, "as well as can be expected." By the time the baby arrives at the robustness of a fortnight old, and appears to begin to smack its lips, it is manifestly the most ill-used of infant elegancies, if a series of random hits are not made at its mouth and cheeks with a piece of the fat of pig; and, when it is sleepy and yet will "not go to sleep" (which is a phenomenon usually developed about the time that Nurse wants her tea), or when it is "fractious" for not having had *enough* pig, or from something else which has been counteracted, or any thing but the sly sup of gin lately given it, or the pin which is now running into its back, it is equally clear, that if Daffy, or Godfrey, or rocking the chair will not do, a perpetual thumping of the back, and jolting of its very soul out will; and, accordingly, there lies the future lord or lady of the creation, prostrate across the nurse's knees, a lump in a laced cap and interminable clothes, getting redder and redder in the face, ejaculating such agonies between grunt and shout as each simultaneous thump will permit, and secretly saluted by its holder with "brats," and "drat it," and "was there ever such an 'obstropulous' little devil!" while her lips are loud in deprecation of the "naughty milk," or the "naughty cat" (which is to be beaten for its ill-behavior); and "Dordie" (Georgy) is told to "go" to a mysterious place, called "Bye-Bye;" or the whole catechism of nursery interrogation is gone through, from the past tenses of the amenities of "Was it a poppet then?" and "Did it break its pretty heart?" up to the future glories of "Shall it be a King then?" "Shall it be a King Pepin?" "Shall it be a Princy-wincy?" a "Countess?" a "Duchess?" "Shall it break the fine gentlemen's hearts with those beautiful blue eyes?" In the midst of tragi-comic burlesque of this sort, have risen upon the world its future Marses and Apollos, its Napoleons, its Platos, and its Shaksperes.

Alas! that it should be made a question (ridiculed indeed by the shallow, the nurse among them, but very seriously mooted by philosophers) whether in that first and tenderest month of existence, the little bundle of already made organs, sensations, and passions, does not receive impressions from this frivolous elderly "nobody," which may affect the temper and disposition of the future man or woman! whether the "beautiful fury,"—though we confess we never saw such a phenomenon—whether the crash in the china closet, or the sacrifice of a daughter's happiness to a father's will and obstinacy, had not its first seeds sown in the lap of this poppet-dandling simpleton. Not its "first," we apprehend. Those, we take it, are of far earlier origin, the little creature being much older than is generally supposed, when it comes under the influence of this its third, and most transitory, and not always most foolish modifier. But we have no doubt that she contributes her portion of effect. This is, however, what she herself can by no means comprehend. "As if any treatment" (she thinks) "except in the article of rum and sugar, and the mode of holding, can be of consequence to one so young!" She is nevertheless very diligent in looking for "marks" about his body, and tracing them to influences on the mother's mind; and yet she cannot see that the *then* impressible little creature is still impressible. Heaven and earth are to come together if the piece of fat is not supplied, or the clothes are not of the proper fashion; but the sudden affrightment, the secret blow, the deadening jolt to sleep, or the giving way to nothing but the last rage, these are to be of no importance. She has no doubt, nevertheless, that its brothers and sisters are all impressible, whatever the infant may be; and accordingly, with her usual instinct of the love of power, she generally contrives do as much inconsiderate harm to them as possible, and lays the seeds of jealousy in their minds—if none be there already—by telling them that they must now cease to look upon themselves as the only important persons in the family, for that "a little stranger has come to put their noses out of joint." Pleasing and picturesque introduction to the fraternal affections!

Do not despise her; no, not even when portrayed as in our artist's picture, under her worst aspect, for a warning. Engage not such a nurse as that if you can help it; yet pity while you refuse her, for perhaps she would not have had that aspect, but for the unnatural sleeplessness to which her duties forced her, nor have been given to that poison by her side, but for some aggravation of care occasioned by domestic troubles of her own. Even she—even that wretched incontinent face and burly person—has once been an infant, as we all have,—perhaps flattered for her beauty, (who would now think it?) the darling and the spoil of some weak mother like herself. Thus are errors propagated, till we discover that personal reproach and satire are of little use, and that it is systems which are to be better taught, before individuals can improve. Poor old nurse! Strange indeed would it be to begin with reprobating her! Let us see that she does as little harm as may be, crown (or *half* crown) her with fees for her caudle, and dismiss her as fast as possible, with a deprecation of her sciatica.

A CHAPTER ON HATS.

BY LEIGH HUNT.

We know not what will be thought of our taste in so important a matter, but we must confess we are not fond of a new hat. There is a certain insolence about it: it seems to value itself upon its finished appearance, and to presume upon our liking before we are acquainted with it. In the first place, it comes home more like a marmot or some other living creature, than a manufacture. It is boxed up, and wrapt in silver paper, and brought delicately. It is as sleek as a lap-dog. Then we are to take it out as nicely, and people are to wonder how we shall look in it. Maria twitches one this way, and Sophia that, and Caroline that, and Catharine t'other. We have the difficult task, all the while, of looking easy, till the approving votes are pronounced; our only resource (which is also difficult) being to say good things to all four; or to clap the hat upon each of their heads, and see what pretty milk-women they make. At last, the approving votes are pronounced; and (provided it is fine) we may go forth. But how uneasy the sensation about the head! How unlike the old hat, to which we had become used, and which must now make way for this fop of a stranger! We might do what we liked with the former. Dust, rain, a gale of wind, a fall, a squeeze,—nothing affected it. It was a true friend, a friend for all weathers. Its appearance only was against it: in every thing else it was the better for wear. But if the roads or the streets are too dry, the new hat is afraid of getting dusty: if there is wind, and it is not tight, it may be blown off into the dirt; we may have to scramble after it through dust or mud; just reaching it with our fingers, only to see it blown away again. And if rain comes on! Oh ye gallant apprentices, who have issued forth on a Sunday morning, with Jane or Susan, careless either of storms at night-fall, or toils and scoldings next day! Ye, who have received new hats and boots but an hour before ye set out; and then issue forth triumphantly, the charmer by your side! She, with arm in yours, and handkerchief in hand, blushing, or eating gingerbread, trips on: ye, admiring, trudge; we ask ye, whether love itself has prevented ye from feeling a certain fearful consciousness of that crowning glory, the new and glossy hat, when the first drops of rain announce the coming of a shower! Ah, hasten, while yet it is of use to haste; ere yet the spotty horror fixes on the nap! Out with the protecting handkerchief, which, tied round the hat, and flowing off in a corner behind, shall gleam through the thickening night like a superb comet! Trust not the tempting yawn of stable-yard or gate-way, or the impossible notion of a coach! The rain will continue; and, alas! ye are not so rich as in the morning. Hasten! or think of a new hat becoming a rain-spout! Think of its well-built crown, its graceful and well-measured fit, the curved-up elegance of its rim, its shadowing gentility when seen in front, its arching grace over the ear when beheld sideways! Think of it also the next day! How altered, how dejected!

How changed from him,
That life of measure and that soul of rim!

Think of the paper-like change of its consistence; of its limp sadness—its confused and flattened nap, and of that polished and perfect circle, which neither brush nor hot iron shall restore!

We have here spoken of the beauties of a new hat; but abstractedly considered, they are very problematical. Fashion makes beauty for a time. Our ancestors found a grace in the cocked hats now confined to beadles, Chelsea pensioners, and coachmen. They would have laughed at our chimney-tops with a border: though upon the whole we do think them the more graceful of the two. The best modern covering for the head was the imitation of the broad Spanish hat in use about thirty years back, when Mr. Stothard made his designs for the *Novelist's Magazine*. But in proportion as society has been put into a bustle, our hats seem to have narrowed their dimensions: their flaps were clipped off more and more till they became a rim; and now the rim has contracted to a mere nothing; so that what with our close heads and our tight succinct mode of dress, we look as if we were intended for nothing but to dart backwards and forwards on matters of business, with as little hinderance to each other as possible.

This may give us a greater distaste to the hat than it deserves; but, good-looking or not, we know of no situation in which a new one can be said to be useful. We have seen how the case is during bad weather: but if the weather is in the finest condition possible, with neither rain nor dust, there may be a hot sunshine; and then the hat is too narrow to shade us: no great evil, it is true; but we must have our pique out against the knave, and turn him to the only account in our power:—we must write upon him. For every other purpose, we hold him as naught. The only place a new hat can be carried into with safety, is a church; for there is plenty of room there. There also takes place its only union of the ornamental with the useful, if so it is to be called: we allude to the preparatory ejaculation whispered into it by the genteel worshipper, before he turns round and makes a bow to Mr. and Mrs. Jones and the Miss Thompsons. There is a formula for this occasion; and doubtless it is often used, to say nothing of extempore effusions: but there are wicked imaginations, who suspect that instead of devouter whisperings, the communer with his lining sometimes ejaculates no more than Swallow, St. James's-street; or, Augarde and Spain, Hatters, No. 51 Oxford-street, London:—after which he draws up his head with infinite gravity and preparation, and makes the gentle recognitions aforesaid.

But wherever there is a crowd, the new hat is worse than useless. It is a pity that the general retrenchment of people's finances did away with the flat opera hat, which was a very sensible thing. The round one is only in the way. The matting over the floor of the opera does not hinder it from getting dusty; not to mention its chance of a kick from the inconsiderate. But from the pit of the other theatres, you may bring it away covered with sawdust, or rubbed up all the wrong way of the nap, or monstrously squeezed into a shapeless lump. The least thing to be expected in a pressure, is a great poke in its side like a sunken cheek.

Boating is a mortal enemy to new hats. A shower has you fast in a common boat; or a sail-line, or an inexperienced oar, may knock the hat off: and then fancy it tilting over the water with the tide; soaked all the while beyond redemption, and escaping from the tips of your outstretched fingers, while you ought all to be pulling the contrary way home.

But of all wrong boxes for a new hat, avoid a mail-coach. If you keep it on, you will begin nodding perhaps at midnight, and then it goes jamming against the side of the coach, to the equal misery of its nap and your own. If you take it off, where is its refuge? Will the clergyman take the least heed of it, who is snoring comfortably in one corner in his night-cap? Or will the farmer, jolting about inexorably? Or the regular traveller, who, in his fur-cap and infinite knowledge of highway conveniences, has already beheld it with contempt? Or the old market-woman, whom it is in vain to request to be tender? Or the young damsel, who wonders how you can think of sleeping in such a thing? In the morning, you suddenly miss your hat, and ask after it with trepidation. The traveller smiles. They all move their legs, but know nothing of it; till the market-woman exclaims, "Deary me! Well—lord, only think! A hat is it, sir? Why I do believe,—but I'm sure I never thought o' such a thing more than the child unborn,—that it must be a hat then which I took for a pan I've been a buying; and so I've had my warm foot in it, Lord help us, ever since five o'clock this blessed morning!"

It is but fair to add, that we happen to have an educated antipathy to the hat. At our school, no hats were worn, and the cap is too small to be a substitute. Its only use is to astonish the old ladies in the street, who wonder how so small a thing can be kept on; and to this end we used to rub it into the back or side of the head, where it hung like a worsted wonder. It is after the fashion of Katharine's cap in the play: it seems as if

> Moulded on a porringer:
> Why, 'tis a cockle, or a walnut-shell,
> A knack, a toy, a trick, a baby's cap;
> A custard coffin, a bauble.

But we may not add

> I love thee well, in that thou likest it not;

Ill befall us, if we ever dislike any thing about thee, old nurse of our childhood! How independent of the weather used we to feel in our old friar's dress, —our thick shoes, yellow worsted stockings, and coarse long coat or gown! Our cap was oftener in our hand than on our head, let the weather be what it would. We felt a pride as well as pleasure, when everybody else was hurrying through the streets, in receiving the full summer showers with uncovered poll, sleeking our glad hair like the feathers of a bird.

It must be said for hats in general, that they are a very ancient part of dress, perhaps the most ancient; for a negro, who has nothing else upon him, sometimes finds it necessary to guard off the sun with a hat of leaves or straw. The Chinese, who carry their records farther back than any other people, are a hatted race, both narrow-brimmed and broad. We are apt to think of the Greeks as a bare-headed people; and they liked to be so; but they had hats for journeying in, such as may be seen on the statues of Mercury, who was the god of travellers. They were large and flapped, and were sometimes fastened round under the chin like a lady's bonnet. The Eastern nations generally wore turbans, and do still, with the exception of the Persians, who have exchanged them for large conical caps of felt. The Romans copied the Greeks in their dress, as in every thing else; but the poorer orders wore a cap like their boasted Phrygian ancestors, resembling the one which the reader may see about the streets upon the bust of Canova's Paris. The others would put their robes about their heads, upon occasion,—after the fashion of the hoods of the middle ages, and of the cloth head-dresses which we see in the portraits of Dante and Petrarch. Of a similar mode are the draperies on the heads of our old Plantagenet kings and of Chaucer. The velvet cap which succeeded, appears to have come from Italy, as seen in the portraits of Raphael and Titian; and it would probably have continued till the French times of Charles the Second, for our ancestors, up to that period, were great admirers of Italy, had not Philip the Second of Spain come over to marry our Queen Mary. The extreme heats of Spain had forced the natives upon taking to that ingenious compound of the hat and umbrella, still known by the name of the Spanish hat. We know not whether Philip himself wore it. His father, Charles the Fifth, who was at the top of the world, is represented as delighting in a little humble-looking cap. But we conceive it was either from Philip, or some gentleman in his train, that the hat and feather succeeded among us to the cap and jewels of Henry the Eighth. The ascendency of Spain in those times carried it into other parts of Europe. The French, not requiring so much shade from the sun, and always playing with and altering their dress, as a child does his toy, first covered the brim with feathers, then gave them a pinch in front; then came pinches up at the side; and at last appeared the fierce and triple-daring cocked hat. This disappeared in our childhood, or only survived among the military, the old, and the reverend, who could not willingly part with their habitual dignity. An old beau or so would also retain it, in memory of its victories when young. We remember its going away from the heads of the foot-guards. The heavy dragoons retained it till lately. It is now almost sunk into the mock-heroic, and confined, as we before observed, to beadles and coachmen, etc. The modern clerical beaver, agreeably to the deliberation with which our establishments depart from all custom, is a cocked hat with the front flap let down, and only a slight pinch remaining behind. This is worn also by the judges, the lawyers being of clerical extraction. Still, however, the true cocked-hat lingers here and there with a solitary old gentleman; and wherever it appears in such company, begets a certain retrospective reverence. There was a something in its connection with the high-bred drawing-room times of the seventeenth century; in the gallant though quaint ardor of its look; and in its being lifted up in salutations with that deliberate loftiness, the arm arching up in front and the hand slowly raising it by the front angle with finger and thumb—that could not easily die. We remember, when our steward at school, remarkable for his inflexible air of precision and dignity, left off his cocked hat for a round one; there was, undoubtedly, though we dared only half confess it to our minds, a sort of diminished majesty about him. His infinite self-possession began to look remotely finite. His Crown Imperial was a little blighted. It was like divesting a column of its capital. But the native stateliness was there, informing the new hat. He

> had not yet lost
> *All* his original beaver: nor appeared
> Less than arch-steward ruined, and the excess
> Of glory obscured.

The late Emperor Paul had conceived such a sense of the dignity of the cocked hat, aggravated by its having been deposed by the round one of the French republicans, that he ordered all persons in his dominions never to dare be seen in public with round hats, upon pain of being knouted and sent to Siberia.

Hats being the easiest part of the European dress to be taken off, are doffed among us out of reverence. The Orientals, on the same account, put off their slippers instead of turbans, which is the reason why the Jews still keep their heads covered during worship. The Spanish grandees have the privilege of wearing their hats in the royal presence, probably in commemoration of the free spirit in which the Cortes used to crown the sovereign; telling him (we suppose in their corporate capacity) that they were better men than he, but chose him of their own free will for their master. The grandees only claim to be as good men, unless their families are older. There is a well-known story of a picture, in which the Virgin Mary is represented with a label coming out of her mouth, saying to a Spanish gentleman who has politely taken off his hat, "Cousin, be covered." But the most interesting anecdote connected with a hat belongs to the family of the De Courceys, Lords Kinsale. One of their ancestors, at an old period of our history, having overthrown a huge and insolent champion, who had challenged the whole court, was desired by the king to ask him some favor. He requested that his descendants should have the privilege of keeping their heads covered in the royal presence, and they do so to this day. The new lord, we believe, always comes to court on purpose to vindicate his right. We have heard, that on the last occasion, probably after a long interval, some of the courtiers thought it might as well have been dispensed with: which was a foolish as well as a jealous thing, for these exceptions only prove the royal rule. The Spanish grandees originally took their privilege instead of receiving it; but, when the spirit of it had gone, their covered heads were only so many intense recognitions of the king's dignity, which it was thought such a mighty thing to resemble. A Quaker's hat is a more formidable thing than a grandee's.

THE FISH, THE MAN, AND THE SPIRIT.

BY LEIGH HUNT.

TO FISH.

You strange, astonish'd-looking, angled-faced,
Dreary-mouth'd, gaping wretches of the sea,
Gulping salt water everlastingly,
Cold-blooded, though with red your blood be graced,
And mute, though dwellers in the roaring waste;
And you, all shapes beside, that fishy be,
Some round, some flat, some long, all devilry,
Legless, unloving, infamously chaste;
O scaly, slippery, wet, swift, staring wights,
What is't ye do? What life lead? eh, dull goggles?
How do ye vary your vile days and nights?
How pass your Sundays? Are ye still but joggles
In ceaseless wash? Still nought but gapes, and bites,
And drinks, and stares, diversified with boggles?

A FISH ANSWERS.

Amazing monster! that, for aught I know,
With the first sight of thee didst make our race
For ever stare! O flat and shocking face,
Grimly divided from the breast below!
Thou, that on dry land horribly dost go
With a split body and most ridiculous pace
Prong after prong, disgracer of all grace,
Long-useless-finn'd, haired, upright, unwet, slow!

O breather of unbreathable, sword-sharp air,
How canst exist? How bear thyself, thou dry
And dreary sloth? What particle canst share
Of the only blessed life, the watery?
I sometimes see of ye an actual *pair*
Go by!! link'd fin by fin!!! most odiously.

THE FISH TURNS INTO A MAN, AND THEN INTO A SPIRIT, AND AGAIN SPEAKS.

Indulge thy smiling scorn, if smiling still,
O man! and loathe, but with a sort of love;
For difference must itself by difference prove,
And, with sweet clang, the spheres with music fill.
One of the spirits am I, that at their will
Live in whate'er has life—fish, eagle, dove—
No hate, no pride, beneath nought, nor above,
A visitor of the rounds of God's sweet skill.

Man's life is warm, glad, sad, 'twixt loves and graves,
Boundless in hope, honor'd with pangs austere,
Heav'n-gazing; and his angel-wings he craves:—
The fish is swift, small-needing, vague yet clear,
A cold sweet silver life, wrapp'd in round waves,
Quicken'd with touches of transporting fear.

[As the transition from the ludicrous to the grave, in these verses, might otherwise appear too violent, the reader will permit me to explain how they arose. The first sonnet was suggested by a friend's laughing at a description I was giving him of the general aspect of fish (in which, by the way, if any body is curious, let him get acquainted with them in Mr. Yarrell's excellent work on "British Fishes," now in course of publication); the secon sonnet, being a lover of fair play, I thought but a just retort to be allowed to those fellow-creatures of ours, who so differ with us in eyeballs and opinions; and the third, not liking to leave a quarrel unsettled, and having a tendency to push a speculation as far as it will go, especially into those calm and heavenward regions from which we always return the better, if we calmly enter them, naturally became as serious as the peace of mind is, with which all speculations conclude that have harmony and lovingness for their real object. The fish, in his retort, speaks too knowingly of his human banterer, for a fish; but it will be seen, that a Spirit animates him for the purpose.]

JOHN KEMBLE'S RUFFLE.

Once, in a barn, the strolling wardrobe's list
Had but one ruffle left for Hamlet's wrist.
Necessity, which has no law, they say,
Could, with one ruffle, but one arm display.
"What's to be done?" the hero said and sighed.
"Shift hands each scene," a brother buskin cried;
"Now in the pocket keep the left from sight,
While o'er your breast you keep your ruffled right;
Now in your robe your naked right repose,
While down your left the dingy cambric flows;
Thus, tho' half skilled, as well as half-array'd,
You'll make one change that Garrick never made."

THE MODEL FAST MAN.

BY HORACE MAYHEW.

You know him at once by his being the noisiest, the most conspicuous person wherever he is. His dress, too, never fails to attract public notice. He is unhappy if not seen—he is miserable if not heard.

In the street he flourishes a little stick, which, for want of something better to do, he rattles against the railings. He stares ladies in the face, and takes his hat off to carriages, and delights in kissing his hand to some old dowager who is looking out of a drawing-room window. A sedan-chair is his great amusement. He stops the porters, and asks them what they will take him to Buckingham Palace and back again for? He directs a hackney-coach to drive as fast as possible to the British Museum, and to ask Sir Henry Ellis to be kind enough to put it under a glass-case among the Fossils. He takes a card that is offered to him by a street conjuror, and gives him in return one of his own, with an intimation that he "shall be happy to see him at any time between two and four." He walks behind fat old ladies, and is very loud in his praises "of the jolly mad bull there is in the next street." He rings area-bells and inquires "if they could oblige him with the loan of a cucumber-slicer for five minutes." He removes any pewter-pot he finds, and knocks at the door to ask "if it belongs to them: it was hanging outside the railings, and might be stolen by some unprincipled person." News-venders are his especial favorites. He calls them from the other side of the way to ask "if they have got the *Independent Doorknocker* of 1856; if not, he should like to see the third edition of the *Times* to-morrow." He makes cruel faces to little babies as they hang over their nurses' shoulders, and is flattered if he makes them cry. If he meets with twins, he is happy indeed. He shouts into sausage shops as he passes by—"D'ye want any cats, dogs, or kittens, to-day?" He hails an omnibus, and while it is stopping, turns down the next street; and he looks at a cabman till he drives up to him, when he wonders what the "cabbie" wants: he was only admiring his handsome whiskers. If he finds a looking-glass, he adjusts his toilet in it, and takes off his hat, and bows to himself, exclaiming, "On my word, you are looking remarkably well; I never saw you look better." He looks at the milliners through the shop-windows, and darts at them his most piercing smiles. He stares at the watch-makers at their work, with intense curiosity, and talks to them with his fingers, till they get up and leave their stools with great indignation. If he meets the Lord Mayor's carriage with three footmen on the footboard, he is sure to call out "Whip behind!" and he laughs his loudest if the coachman should unconsciously lay his whip across their calves. He is very rich in noises. His "Va-ri-e-ty" is unequalled at two o'clock in the morning; and his collection of "Ri-too-loorals," and "Rum-ti-oddities," and select choruses, is not to be surpassed by the oldest *habitué* of the Coal-hole. He whistles, too, through his fingers; and can bark, crow, and bray quite naturally, especially inside Exeter Hall, or any place where he shouldn't do it. One of his proudest achievements is to enter an omnibus crowded with females, and to display on his knees a large jar, marked "Leeches." He delights, too, in sprinkling cayenne-pepper and snuff on the floor of a dancing-party after supper, or in going behind the cornet-à-piston, and making him laugh during a long solo, when the struggling laughter, oozing out in short gasps through the valves, nearly sends him into fits. He glories in sending in six "brandies warm" to the chairman and different gentlemen on the platform of a Temperance Meeting. He makes a practice of ringing the bells of all doctors, as he walks home at night.

In the theatre, he slams the box-door, and shouts "Box-keeper!" with the most stentorian lungs. He is vociferous in his applause, and sparkles up at the prospect of a row. He likes to sneeze during the pathetic parts, and shouts "Brayvo, Wright!" when the old father is blessing his long-lost child. He revels in a burlesque with plenty of Amazons in it. He cries out "*Encore!*" at every thing, but Hicks especially.

In respectable society he is awkward, and generally very quiet. He does not dance, not knowing what to say to his partner. He hangs about the door and staircase, and consoles himself with the cakes and wine; he leaves early, for "he is dying for a pipe and a drop of beer."

In his appearance he selects the gayest fast colors, and the more the merrier. His shirt is curiously illuminated with pink ballet-girls. He has the winner of the Derby in his pocket-handkerchief. His boots are very delicate, only keeping body and sole together with the aid of large mother-of-pearl buttons. He revels in a white hat. His trowsers are of the chess-board pattern. His shirt-pin is an enormous gooseberry, that would make the fortune of a penny-a-liner. His coat has a Newmarket expression, of the very deepest green. He is above gloves, but encourages a glass, suspended by some magic process in his left eye.

His accomplishments are various. He carries in his waistcoat pocket the stump of a clay pipe, the bowl of which is quite black. He can walk along the parapet of Waterloo Bridge. He can sleep in the station-house upon an emergency. He can slide, skate, and box a little, and play the French horn. He can win a game of billiards, and give you twenty. He is "up to a dodge or two" at cards. He can imitate all the actors, and a brick falling down the chimney. He can fry a pancake in his hat, and light a cigar at a lamp-post. He can manage a pair of sculls, and tool a tandem through Smithfield Market. He can talk slang with a novelist, and "chaff an 'University Man' off his legs." He can also "do a bill," and many other things, as well as persons, that ought not to be done. He is proficient in all the gentish graces of life, and knows "a small wrinkle or two" of every thing. High life, low life, gambling life, sporting life, fashionable life, every kind of life he is intimately acquainted with, particularly fast life. This consists in his beginning the day six hours after everybody else, and finishing it six hours later. It implies the knowledge, on his part, of the Polka, with certain embellishments, and a constant attendance at Casinos, and other places where that knowledge can be displayed. It involves, also, a course of theatres, sporting-houses, masquerades, singing-taverns, cigar-shops, cider-cellars, and early coffee-houses. To all of these the Model Fast Man is an accomplished guide. He condemns every thing as *slow* that does not keep pace with the rapidity with which he runs, or rather gallops, through life; and he annihilates everybody as slow who presumes to live like a rational creature. All books are slow—Shakspere is slow—all domestic, all quiet enjoyments are slow. The country is very slow, and so are sisters. He even calls the railways slow. His great impulse is, "Fast bind, fast find," and he sighs that society is not bound by the same fast law. He is without shame, as he is without gentlemanly feeling. He is familiar with servants, is very facetious with conductors, calls policemen by their letters, jokes with waiters, and does not care how he insults an inferior. Impudence, to him, is fun—brutality, the excess of refinement—giving pain, his most exquisite enjoyment. His highest notion of humor is saying to every thing, "I believe you, my bo-o-o-y." In the morning—that is, the afternoon—he is feverish; in the evening—that is to say, four o'clock in the morning—he is what he calls "fresh." His first call is for soda-water, his last for brandy. Such is the great beginning, and such the grand end, of the existence of the Model Fast Man.

A MODEL IRISH SPEAKER.

BY HORACE MAYHEW.

How have we been treated for the last ten thousand years by the cold-blooded Saxon? My hair stands on end to tell you. (*Cheers.*) Hasn't England so managed matters in her own favor that she receives the light of the sun two-and-twenty minutes before she permits a single ray to come to us? (*A Voice; "It's true!"*) England may boast of her own enlightenment; but is this justice to Ireland? (*Tremendous Cries of "No! No!"*) I have next to accuse England of keeping aloof from us fully sixty miles at the nearest point. Talk of our Union after that! (*Vociferous cheering, which lasted several hours.*) No, my countrymen, it is only a parchment Union, a lying thing, made of the skin of the innocent sheep; but, before we go to bed this night, we'll see that bit of parchment torn into countless strips, so that every tailor in Ireland shall have, to-morrow morning, a remnant of it in his hands, to measure twelve millions of happy Irishmen with. (*At this point the proceedings were interrupted by six persons being carried out of the room who had fainted. They are supposed to be tailors.*) Well, sir, I denounce from this place the atrocious cupidity of England, by which she monopolizes the tin mines entirely, almost all the iron and coal, and thus cramps, sir, our native industry and commerce. Why has not Ireland her own iron and coal? (*Cries of "Why not?"*) I ask again, why have we no tin? (*"Shame! shame!"*) and no brass? no zinc? no salmon? no elephants? no periwinkles? no king? (*Immense cheering, during which the honorable speaker sat down and slept for a quarter of an hour, and then continued.*) Oh! my beloved countrymen, I have had a most beautiful vision. I thought I saw every field of Ireland covered with dancing corn, and embroidered with the most beautiful sheep, whose wool was more exquisite than all the Berlin wool that was ever made in England (*Cheers*); and I thought, my countrymen, its rivers were filled with more salmon and more periwinkles than ever carolled on the muddy Saxon shore (*Cheers*); and I thought, my countrymen, that on the brow of every other hill the mighty elephant was reposing under the peaceful shade of the shamrock (*more cheers*); and again, I thought the corner of each field was filled with more iron, and tin, and brass, than would suffice to build a railway from here to the bottom of England's perdition (*Laughter and Cheers*); and I thought—may the beautiful vision be never effaced from the iris of my weeping eyes!—that there were no dark clouds such as now lower o'er our bright country; but that the whole scene, so intensely Irish, was illumined, as if with a resplendent sun, with our own gas. (*Enthusiastic shouts, the echoes of which have not yet subsided in the neighborhood of the Castle.*) Oh! oh! when will this vision be realized? When shall we see the poor Irishman—the finest peasant of the world—boiling his potato? Ah! the plundering Saxon cannot wring *that* from us; though no thanks to the monster for the blight—(*Shame*)—boiling his potato, I say, with his own coal, in a pot made of his own iron, and eat it on a plate made of his own pewter, with a knife bought with his own tin. Never! never! until the Repeal is carried. (*Three cheers for Repale.*) Do you think you'll ever have it? ("*We will; we will.*") Believe me, in all sincerity, you never will, until you pull up the lamp-posts and make bayonets of them, and have wrenched off every knocker and bell-pull, and melted them into bullets and cannon-balls. (*Cheers.*) I know I am talking sedition; but I dare them to come and tear the shoestrings out of my boots, before I unsay a single word of what I have said. (*Frantic applause.*) They dare not prosecute me. It would be the proudest moment for Ireland, if they would; for then, College Green would be crowded with Irish kings. (*Cheers.*) The British oak would be supplanted with the four-leaved shamrock of Ireland. (*Cheers.*) The Queen of England would be an Irishwoman—(*Cheers*)—and I should die happy in the thought that the majestic tree of Repeal had been watered with my blood, and blossomed, and borne such golden fruit, that unborn nations, far from beyond the poles, were coming on their knees to taste them. (*It is impossible to describe the enthusiasm which broke out when the Hon. Gentleman resumed his seat on the ledge of the window. As many as had hats, threw them into the air; those who had coats, took them off, and dragged them along the ground; whilst a few of the hardiest natives were observed to bury their faces in their coat-tails and weep audibly. The cheering was kept up till a very late hour, and the meeting broke up a little before daylight, after giving ninety-nine cheers, and a little one in, "for the blessed cause of Repale."*)

OUR DOMESTIC PARLIAMENT.

The Debate on the Supplies.

BY HORACE MAYHEW.

All the members of the family being assembled at breakfast, the Housekeeping Book was laid upon the table, and the House (No. 289, Berkeley Square,) resolved itself into a committee to take into consideration the weekly supplies. Mr. Flint was in the arm-chair.

The Butcher's, the Baker's, and Greengrocer's Bills were read for the first, second, and third times, and passed.

The Brougham, Gig, and Family Carriage Estimates were advanced a stage; after which

Mrs. Flummery rose. She said that she had been requested by her daughter, (Mrs. Flint,) who, poor creature! could not come down to breakfast, owing to a nervous headache, to lay before Mr. Flint the estimate of the household expenses of the past week. They amounted to 4*l.* 17*s.* 6¾*d.* She need not say, they had been framed with the strictest regard to economy. There were thirteen mouths to fill, besides a canary and three cats, and she defied any one to say that the housekeeping expenses could be done for less. There was a slight deficiency, she regretted to say, in the week as compared with the one preceding, but on the whole the accounts were flattering. The decrease was to be attributed mainly to the fact of Mr. Flint having brought home clients twice (*A cry of "Only once."*) She would not be interrupted—yes, twice, if not three times, to dinner. However, there was a good stock of cold meat in the larder; and she hoped, by dint of hashes and stews, and the friendly aid of pickles, that the returns of the succeeding week would show a proportionate decrease on the victualling department. There was a slight saving in the item of puddings and pies, for it was found absolutely necessary to reduce this part of the expenditure, so as to bring the disbursements as nearly as possible within the receipts. It must be recollected that meat never was dearer, and that potatoes were very scarce, and that milk had risen a halfpenny in each pint the last week. The boys, too, were growing; all the children had been home for the holidays; and yet, notwithstanding these drawbacks, there had been a hot joint every day of the week. (*Sensation.*) There was a small balance in hand of 3*s.* 9¼*d.*; but against this there was a bill that had to be met, for cigars and brandy, and a lemon, the Chair (Mr. Flint) had had with a few friends the night he was to have taken her daughter and self to the Opera. But she would not allude to that painful circumstance. Brandy and cigars were always chargeable, thank goodness, on the privy purse. (*A cry of "No, no."*) She said, most emphatically, yes, yes, yes. She had nothing more to say. Only she could not help complimenting the House upon having in its employ the talented lady at the head of the home department. The duties of the Exchequer had never, to her knowledge, been discharged with such satisfaction. There was scarcely a bill remaining over. She was acquainted with many houses, but she must say she had never known one in which the business was conducted with half the respectability, or the same amount of servants kept up on the same revenue, as that of the honorable lady whose chair she now filled.—(*Vehement coughing.*)—The hon. gentleman in the chair might cough as he pleased, but she would tell him to his face that he ought to be proud of such a treasure. (*Mrs. Flummery sat down amid a loud clatter of tea-spoons, and the* *youngest members of the House crowded round her, to congratulate her upon her effective speech.*)

MR. FLINT, after a pause, came to the table, and said, that in glancing his eye over the disbursements, he noticed an item of 1*l.* 17*s.* 6*d.* under the head of Sundries. He had found it to occur lately, every week. What were Sundries? He insisted upon knowing. He objected *in toto* to the vagueness of such a definition, and certainly should not allow it to pass.

MRS. FLUMMERY begged to explain. Sundries comprised an endless variety of small sums that it would be impossible to specify separately. It included birdseed for the canary, cat's meat for the Home department, halfpence to the crossing-sweepers, soap, charity sermons, beggars, gruel, nutmegs for the hon. gentleman's toddy,—in fact, Sundries took in no end of miscellaneous articles, that it would be impossible to enumerate individually. Besides, what was one pound odd for Sundries? Why, in many houses she could mention the Sundries came to 5*l.* regularly every week.

MR. FLINT. That has nothing to do with it. I allow a certain sum every week for the housekeeping, and I expect it to be done for that money. But I tell you, Mrs. Flummery, ever since you have been in the house, the expenses have been gradually increasing. No wonder, with such extravagance to answer for, that the lady (Mrs. Flint) whom you represent, was too unwell this morning to undertake her duties at the head of the breakfast-table. (*One or two members get up and leave the room.*)

MRS. FLUMMERY. Very well; pray go on, Mr. Flint. These are all the thanks a poor soul gets for working both day and night to save a halfpenny. On my word, you have your nasty brandy and cigars—

MR. FLINT. Nonsense, madam. You know well enough they don't form part of the expenses. I tell you what it is, Mrs. Flummery; such extravagance as yours will drive me into the workhouse.

MRS. FLUMMERY. Very well. You'll break my poor daughter's heart; that's all, Mr. Flint. The fool that she was, ever to marry such a man! I'm sure she slaves her very soul out to please you. You deny her even the money for your meat and drink, and yet you can afford to give 100*l.* to the stupid Anti-Corn-Law League. Didn't you begrudge her a box at the opera? and yet you can have your filthy brandy—

MR. FLINT. I tell you the brandy has nothing to do with it.

MRS. FLUMMERY. Very well, sir, keep the housekeeping yourself. There is always this scene every time the supplies are debated, and before the children, too! Psha! I'm ashamed of you, that I am. Eliza, poor dear soul, is tired of this work. I'm sure I am, most heartily. We both of us resign—we throw up our situations, and you may get whom you can to fill them.

MR. FLINT. Why, here's 15*s.* 6*d.* for fruit. Didn't I say I'd have no more dessert?

MRS. FLUMMERY. Just as you like, sir.

MR. FLINT. I see 3*s.* 6*d.* too, for cabs; I don't allow that. What do I give Mrs. Flint 10*l.* a year for, if I'm to pay for all her cabs?

MRS. FLUMMERY. I have nothing more to say, sir. The cabs were for the dear children, when they returned from the dentist's. The fruit, sir, includes the lemon you had for your disgraceful toddy. I have nothing more to say—only, if you expect thirteen mouths to be filled for nothing, you had better contract with the Poor Law Union to do it.

MR. FLINT. Zounds, woman! is a man to be ruined and not say a word about it? I have borne this too long. Your wilful waste—your cabs—your sundries, and cats and canaries, are enough to—

MRS. FLUMMERY. (*Beginning to cry.*) This is too much, Mr. Flint. I'm sure my poor dear daughter and myself save every farthing we can, and to be treated in this way! It's brutal (*cries*). I do not care much about it myself—but I do feel for Eliza. (*Emotion in the house.*) No one knows how she toils, and slaves, and deprives herself of every comfort but myself. She won't even take sugar in her tea—she hasn't a bonnet fit to be seen in—she goes nowhere—(*Incipient hysterics.*)

MR. FLINT. Come, come, my dear Mrs. Flummery, don't say another word about it. I've been harsh; but here's the cheque, and if the doctor calls to-day and says Eliza is well enough to go to the opera—

MRS. FLUMMERY (*still in tears.*) I'm sure the doctor was only saying yesterday, "You need restoratives, Mrs. Flummery; you should have your two glasses of port to your luncheon, and a something nice and warm for your supper;" but, I said, "No, Eliza, I can do without it, and Flint, dear, would only complain of the expense." (*The children gather round Mrs. Flummery and begin kissing her.*)

MR. FLINT. No, indeed, he wouldn't do any such thing. Have any thing you like, my good Mrs. Flummery. Come, dry up your tears and put on your bonnet. We'll go down to the Opera House and choose the box.

MRS. FLUMMERY. But I cannot walk!

MR. FLINT. Well, then, we'll have a cab.

MRS. FLUMMERY. But I want to call at Madame Lucretia's to choose a new bonnet for Eliza, and see Jullien to see what night he is disengaged.

MR. FLINT. What for?

MRS. FLUMMERY. Why, for the evening party you promised the dear girls.

MR. FLINT. Oh, dear! you'll drive me into the workhouse. Now, don't cry. I'll do any thing—only don't cry. (*Mr. Flint leaves the arm-chair, and the House adjourns at eleven,* A. M., *for a week.*)

THE MISERIES OF A COMIC WRITER.

BY HORACE MAYHEW.

REPEATEDLY being called upon, in the midst of a strange party, "to say something funny."

Having half-a-dozen scrap-books put into your hand, for "an *impromptu.*"

Being expected, wherever you go, to sing a comic song.

Never being allowed to be in the least unwell; or to look serious, without a dozen people asking, "Why, what's the matter with you?"

Being the 'especial confidant of everybody's bad jokes, and being made the favorite victim for the "capital thing," some one is sure to have "heard yesterday."

Asking for "some potatoes," or some common-place thing, and finding the whole room roar at it incessantly for ten minutes.

Making desperate love to a pretty girl, who only laughs, and says, "La! Mr. Smith, you're always joking."

Being saluted as you go into a room with "Bravo! Here's Smith. Now we shall have something good."

Being introduced as "the young gentleman who does all the funny things in the *Penny Magazine*."

Being suspected of turning every thing you see into ridicule, and putting everybody you meet into print.

A pause of five minutes, in the hopes of hearing you speak, and being asked, at last, whilst everybody is getting ready to grin, "what you think of the weather?"

Being condemned to hear, every day of your life, that the man who would "make a pun would pick a pocket!"

Being invited to meet a "very clever young gentleman who has written a farce."

Laboring under the conventional notion that it is not customary for a comic writer ever to pay anybody, that he generally goes to bed tipsy, and that he cannot write unless he has a bottle of gin at his side.

Hearing mothers continually say to their daughters, "My dear, you must not believe a word he says."

Being invited out, and finding it is to give a "candid opinion"—father, mother, brothers, and sisters being all present—"upon a number of droll things little William has been doing upon *Paradise Lost*." You are obliged to say they are "very clever for a boy," and you are then asked if you cannot get them inserted in *Punch?*"

Being confidently asked, "if it is true you drink much?"

Being asked most seriously by a young lady, "if the incident you described of being locked up in a sponging-house, and escaping up the chimney over the roof of the next house, really occurred to you?"

In short, being suspected of doing all the blackguard, out-of-the way, outrageous, improbable, impossible stupid things you describe.

THE CHEMIST'S CAT.

BY HORACE MAYHEW.

Mr. Celsus Phipps was a chemist, not one of your ordinary men, who put their trust in huge colored glass bottles, and drive a large trade in lozenges. No, Phipps was an experimental chemist, and he acquainted the public with the fact by means of an inscription to that effect over his door, while he confirmed the neighbors in the belief by occasional explosions, more or less violent. On one occasion, he went so far as to blow the roof off his house, but that, he said, "was an accident." Moreover, Phipps was a licentiate of Apothecaries' Hall, and jobbed the paupers at 1½*d.* a head, including pills and plasters. Mr. Phipps's establishment was evidently the home for natural philosophy. Experiments abandoned by every one else were eagerly sought after by Phipps; and he had a valuable auxiliary in his cat.

When science slumbered, the cat might be seen comfortably dozing on the door-step; but when any thing new in medicine or chemistry turned up, the cat had an active life of it. The poor thing had taken poison enough to kill hundreds of rich husbands, and antidotes sufficient to restore double the number. It had a stomach-pump kept for its especial use. You might generally guess when anything extraordinary had happened, by missing the cat from its usual place, and seeing Dick, Mr. Phipps's boy, who had the job of holding it during the experiments, with slips of diachilon plaster all over his face and hands. It had become familiar with prussic acid and arsenic in all their insinuating forms, and had some slight knowledge of the smaller operations of surgery: still it went purring about, and was always at hand on an emergency, ready to have any drug tested on its person. Phipps was proud of it. "My cat, Tom, sir," he would say, "has done more for its fellow animal, man, than all the philanthropists that ever taught people to be discontented."

All went on smoothly till the introduction of ether, when Phipps determined to see if he could extract a tooth from a person under its influence. The cat, of course, was to be the especial patient. Dick was summoned, Tom caught, the ether administered, and Phipps selected one of the largest tusks. But the ether could not have taken proper effect; for, with a frightful yell, Tom freed himself from Dick's grasp, favoring him at the same time with severe marks of his esteem, which made him roar, and disappeared, *à la Harlequin*, through the plate glass window, doing immense damage to the chemicals and Galenicals displayed therein.

But Tom soon came back, for no one would have him. Science, who labels some men F. R. S.'s, or tags half the alphabet to the end of their names, had not forgotten to mark her humble follower, the cat. He had lost one ear in some acoustic experiment,—one eye was closed for ever, from having the operation for squinting practically illustrated some dozen times,—and he was lame in one of his hind legs, the tendon having been cut to exemplify the method of operating for club-foot,—while his coat, once remarkably glossy, had such a second-hand, seedy appearance, that it would not have tempted a Jew.

At last, he died, a martyr to science. Phipps had invented some wonderful pulmonic lozenge, containing a great deal of morphia, which was to cure coughs at first sight. Tom had been rather asthmatic for some time, owing to inhaling noxious gases; so Phipps gave him a good dose to begin with. Next morning, he was found very fast asleep, and extremely rigid in his limbs. Dick suggested that he was dead, but his master indignantly repudiated the idea; so Tom was kept, in the full expectation that he would one day start up quite lively, till at length the moth got into his coat, and Phipps was compelled to consign his furry friend to a grave in the garden. Phipps never had his usual spirits again. His experiments were at an end;

for though he would sometimes furtively introduce some drug or other into Dick's tea or beer, that young gentleman soon found it out, and took his meals ever afterwards with his mother, who was the proprietress of a veal and ham pie dépôt in an adjacent court. Phipps wanders about the College of Surgeons a melancholy man, and amuses himself dreaming over experiments he would perform if he could only get such another cat! He is not best pleased, however, when he meets any young friend of Dick's, who violates private confidence, by running after him and inquiring at the very top of his voice, "Who killed the cat?"

THE DAWN WHEN UNADORNED ADORNED THE MOST.

BY HORACE MAYHEW.

"NINETY-TWO IN THE SHADE."

Bright blew the wind, and plaintive rose the air,
Dark was the morning, but the night was fair;
A misty shade hung over great and small,
Afraid to rise, yet unprepared to fall.
Birds clustered shivering amid the trees;
Thermometers stood still at twelve degrees;
The wolf was dormant in his mountain lair;
The tiger strutted forth to take the air;
The elephant upon his mossy bed
Reposed instinctively his monstrous head;
Even the windmill paused, as if it found
Not yet the time for turning itself round.
The thunder through the air with caution crept;
The very chamois looked before it leapt;
The nightingale went forth long ere 'twas dark;
The early morn was ready for the lark.
The cuckoo nestled in the budding rose;
The pink was dying in cornelian throes.
The dahlia, with the thickening gloom upon her,
Looked nightlier than the nightshade (Bella Donna);
And all was silent in the distant glen,
Save that tremendous hum—the hum of men!

THE UNIVERSAL PHILANTHROPIST.

Philanthropy, how pleasant is thy name!
How often have I set up half the night
Some panegyric on thee to indite,
Until I've warmed myself into a flame
Enough to melt my heart within my frame.
Yes, on the subject I delight to dwell,
Penning those sentiments that always tell—
Calling on wealth to wear the blush of shame,
Because 'tis sometimes slow to "give, give, give"
The means whereby the famished poor may live.
Philanthropy! thy dictates I obey,
To pay thee homage I shall never cease;
(*To "Poor Man"*)
"Give you a penny! Nonsense! get away;
If you're not off I'll call for the police!"

MISS THIMBLEBEE'S BOARDING SCHOOL.

FROM "WHOM TO MARRY AND HOW TO GET MARRIED." BY THE BROTHERS' MAYHEW.

When Papa found that it was no use talking to me, he determined upon sending me to school, where, as he said, the occupation of my studies would soon drive all silly, sentimental ideas from my head; and I declare if in less than a week my mother hadn't found out a "highly genteel" finishing establishment for young ladies, at Turnham-Green, whither, as soon as all my things had been got ready, I was transported; and where poor, dear Mamma, with tears in her eyes, handed *me* over to the Misses Thimblebee till the next holidays, and *my* six towels, and a silver fork and spoon, to them—for ever!

I hadn't been long at Turnham Green, before I found out that the Misses Thimblebee's was no ordinary establishment. It was the boast of both ladies that no vulgar tradesman's daughter had ever polluted the exquisitely refined atmosphere of "Chesterfield House"—even though they had had several advantageous offers upon the "mutual advantage" system. Indeed, they referred with great pride to their heroic refusal to allow the eldest girl of a highly fashionable butcher at the west end to mingle in their select circle, notwithstanding her fond parent had generously consented to estimate the blessings and graces of French and Italian, Music and Dancing, and Berlin-wool work, at several hundred pounds—of beef and mutton—per quarter. No! the Misses Thimblebee were in no way anxious to devote their energies to the rearing of young plebeian "mushrooms," though nothing on earth would have given them greater pleasure than to have bestowed their talents upon the training of budding ducal "Strawberry-leaves." At Chesterfield House, young ladies rehearsed the parts they were intended to *act* at Almack's. There the rough block of the child of nature received its finishing touches, and was converted into the highly polished statue of fashionable society—fit for an ornament to any drawing-room. There the grave of departed nature was adorned with all kinds of artificial flowers; and there, Woman—tutored in all the fascinations of the ball-room—was taught to shine at night like the glow-worm; in order to attract her mate by the display of a brilliance that had no warmth in it.

The Misses Thimblebee, though in their prospectuses they passed as two maiden sisters (the only daughters of a deceased clergyman at the west end of the metropolis), were, to tell the truth, not both in a state of "single blessedness,"—as the rougher sex delight to call it. Miss Grace Thimblebee still dawdled on in all the slow purity of spinsterhood; but Miss Prudence—her younger sister—had, in the flighty moments of her thirty-fifth year, been imprudent enough to rush blindly into matrimony with a certain gay commercial traveller, of the name of Dawes—though if ever she allowed herself to allude to the occupation of that "bad, bad man," she always dropped the "commercial," and spoke of him as a "great traveller," who had unfortunately been led astray, and ruined his "fine intellect and noble figure" by an over fondness for the bottle. On condition that he should not come near the school, Miss Prudence allowed her husband a very respectable annuity; but still the poor thing lived in constant dread of seeing the hopeless prodigal some fine morning force an entrance into the highly moral precincts of Chesterfield House, and demand to be instantly furnished with all the ready cash she had on the premises, and which she knew he would be certain to declare was *his* by law. The very first half I was there, after he had sent—every day for a whole fortnight—a fresh letter, unpaid, with "immediate," written in large characters, and with three notes of admiration after it, on the envelope, he one afternoon, whilst we were at lessons, doing velvet painting, marched into the school-room, smelling disgustingly of spirits and tobacco, with his eyes all heavy and red, and seating himself down on one of the forms among the young ladies, said, he had "just dropped in about *that* small matter," and vowed with a horrible oath, that he wouldn't "leave the place until he had got what was justly his own." Then, I declare, if the monster didn't begin whistling and winking at some of the girls in the first class, and pinching the arm of the "*Native de Paris*," and telling her never to mind him, for he was "only honest Jack Dawes." As far as I could judge—considering the fright I was in—the monster must have been upwards of six feet high, in his "stout men's," and at least a good ell-wide across the shoulders, with very large, bushy, sandy whiskers, and little or no color in his face, except at the end of his nose, which was almost as deep as beet.root. Nor was there any getting rid of the red-nosed giant, until poor Miss Prudence had gone up stairs, and brought down some bank-notes, which the brute took, saying, he'd make shift with them for the present; and adding, that he was glad to see his "old girl was not neglecting her duties," and that he "was sorry he couldn't stop and dine with the ladies that day;" he staggered out of the room, singing, "Nine cheers for the girls that we love." After this, Miss Grace gave us a long lecture upon "the wreck that once remarkably fine man had made of himself by the use of ardent spirits," and hoped that "the disgusting scene we had just witnessed would act as a warning to us all, and make us 'look before we leapt' into matrimony."

The first day I was at Chesterfield House, upon my word, if my whole time wasn't completely taken up in telling the stupid girls "what my Pa was," and "what kind of a carriage we kept," and how many servants we had," and "whether I had any brothers or not;" and when I informed them, that I had "only one,"—then it was, "Is he good looking?" and "had the dear got black or blue eyes," and "what was the color of the pet's hair?" and "did it curl naturally or not?" and was the "angel in long-tailed coats yet, and out of turn-down collars or not?" and "did Ma intend the beauty for the army or the church; or did I think she'd make a duck of an impudent-young-monkey of a midshipman of him, in a gold lace cap, and tiddy-ickle ringlets, like that charming rogue of a brother of Miss Ghearding that left last half, and whom Miss Thimblebee had ordered to quit the house, at least a dozen times, for his tricks.

I declare, too, if I had to unpack my box once, I had to do it twenty times; for they would one after another make me show them my things, while they kept exclaiming, "Oh! goodness! what a duck of a clear muslin!" and "Mi! what a dear, dear poppet of a riband—whatever did it come to a yard, love?"—then, "What a divine lutestring! Did I get it at that paradise of a Howell and James's?"—afterwards, "Well! there *is* a superb chemisette—only look! They never saw such exquisite open work, and such a little pet of an edging. Lor! if it wasn't the very best Valenciennes! Oh! what delightful extravagance, dear!"—next it was, "What a heavenly crinoline! oh! it was fit for an angel—it was *so* beautiful and full. Did I have it sent over to me from Paris?"—then, again, "Gracious! if I hadn't got some sweeties, and a whole tin case full of acidulated drops, too, as they lived!—Oh! how nicey! Do let me taste only just *one*—there's a dear—I'll give you some of mine the next time they send me any;"—after that, "Do open this fixture for me—there's a love—just to let me see if it's the same as I use, and whether the directions say it's to be put on with an old tooth-brush like mine, dear;" and lastly, "Wouldn't I just draw the cork of that lovely nosegay of a mille-fleurs, only to let them have one smell?" and then, "As it was open, and some of the finest they'd ever smelt in all their days, would I mind pouring just half a drop down their bosoms, like a good-natured pet as I was?"

When they'd all seen my box, some of the big girls took me down into the play-ground, and there we walked up and down, with our arms round each other's waists, while they told me they were "so glad I'd come that day I didn't know;" for I was to sleep in the long room, and they were going to have "such a bit of fun" there that night, I couldn't tell. What did I think? They were going to get up, and have a grand feast, after they had gone to bed, and they'd heard Miss Thimblebee let down the night-bolt in her room; and if I chose to be my share towards it, and let them have—like a dear—that pot of tamarinds I'd got in my trunk, they didn't mind letting me go partners—only I was to be sure and not say a word about it to the girls in the other rooms, for they were enemies, and the nasty spiteful things would be sure to go and tell—especially that red-haired Miss Coburn, who had such a long tongue, and was such a tell-tit, there was no trusting her with any thing, although she had been pinched till she was black and blue for it. So they wouldn't have it come to her ears for ever so much, for they had made up their minds that it should be the grandest feast they had had "that half." Only to fancy, too! they had got Susan, for an old pair of Miss M'Taggart's satin shoes, to go out and fetch them half-a-dozen large fourpenny mutton pies from the pastry-cook's, and a shilling box of ginger-beer powders, which they had all subscribed for. Wouldn't it be nice? and they'd got cook, who was a dear old thing, to give them a whole nightcap full of flour on the sly; and Emma Strong'i'th'arm, who had won the prize for morals last half, had made yesterday—which was a half holiday—ever so many sweet cakes in the wash-hand basin. And the best of it was, they'd agreed to try and do some fritters at night with some of the peaches Miss Clanricard had had sent her from home. Didn't I think it would be a good game? Of course, I said yes, and they could have a bit of my plum-cake as well, if they liked; but they told me Miss Thimblebee always made it a rule to have all the cakes the young ladies brought with them cut up for tea, which they all agreed was a great shame—saying, it was all very well for the greedy pigs of little girls, but they did think *they* were old enough to know when they'd had enough, and they ought to be allowed to keep their own good things to themselves, and share them among the girls who slept in their room just as they pleased.

Accordingly, that night, after we had heard the Miss Thimblebees go up to their room, and Susan had taken up the plate-basket, and the glasses of hot elder wine and rusks, which they were accustomed to sup upon in bed, we remained quiet until we fancied they were fast asleep, and then slipping on our wrappers, we lighted the candle-ends we had bought of cook. While some of us went to work on tip-toe, laying the sheet which we used for a tablecloth, and setting the tooth-glasses for tumblers, and the scissors for knives, and cleaning the tops of our pomatum pots for plates, Miss Strong'i'th'arm, who was the best cook in the room, began beating up with the end of a tooth-brush the batter for the fritters in the bottom of the soap-dish, which she washed out expressly for the occasion; and when it was all ready, the clever creature fried them quite nicely on a slate over the brisk fire of six ends of candles.

"Do come and eat them whilst they're hot, there's dears," whispered Miss Strong'i'th'arm, as soon as they were done; and after we had burnt some brown paper, to take away the smell of the frying, down we sat on the floor, as hungry as poets, and devoured as much as one and a half a-piece—giving two to the cook. After this came the second course, of delicious mutton pies; and this was followed by a remove, of beautiful sweet cakes and tamarinds; in the middle of which, *that* Miss Waterford—who is a rare merry one—said, bowing across the sheet to me, "Will you allow me the honor of taking a glass of ginger-beer with you, Miss De Roos;" and then, I declare, if Miss Rawlinson—who is so fond of a bit of fun—didn't get up and say in a whisper, "Will you be so good as to fill your tooth glasses, I have a toast to propose;" and when we had stood up in our wrappers, and put the tartaric acid into the ginger-beer powder, she asked us in, a low voice, "Are you all mixed? Then, here's 'THE LADIES! God bless 'em!'" Whereupon we all emptied our glasses, and cried out, "Hip, hip, hurra! hurra! hurra-a-a-a-a!" as faintly as we possibly could. This done, we put all the things by in the foot-pan, and jumped into bed, and began telling stories to each other; when Miss Howard told us all about how she had once dressed in her brother Henry's clothes, and turned up all her hair, and made herself a pair of moustachios with burnt cork—and how then she had gone out at dusk, and walked ever such a way down Portland-place, all by herself—'pon her word and honor she had!—and nobody knew her from a real man; and how, when she came back, even their maid didn't recognize her, and threatened to scream if she dared to kiss her; and, at last, how, when her hat fell off, and the girl found out who it was, she said she ought to be ashamed of herself, to impose upon a poor servant girl in that way—though she couldn't help allowing that Miss Howard made one of the most good-lookingest and wickedest young gentlemen she had ever set eyes upon. Oh! it was such a good bit of fun, we didn't know; and she wished she'd been born a boy—that was all! After this, Miss Cabell remembered how, once, when Uncle Ben came to stop a week at her Pa's in Hampshire, she and her sister Kate, who was married, used to stitch up the tops of his stockings together, and sew up the bottoms of the lining of his trousers, and flour the inside of his nightcap, and either make him an apple-pie bed, or else put the hair broom down at the bottom inside of it, and play him a whole number of such funny tricks, no one could tell. Oh, it was the best game she had ever had in all her life, and she did like romping *so!* And thus we went on, talking away, till we heard the market-gardeners' carts and the mail-coaches going past the door on their way to town, and could see the daylight looking quite gray through the cracks in the shutters.

Next morning, we were all of us so tired that when the bell rang for us to get up, as we were allowed an hour to dress, we remained in bed, and didn't move till it only wanted ten minutes to the time for us to be in the school-room for prayers, so that when we made our appearance down stairs we all looked such slovens there was a fine to-do. First of all, Miss Grace Thimblebee called up Miss Strong-'i'th'arm, and asked her how she could have the audacity to think of appearing before her without having bandolined her hair, and what she expected would ever become of her if she went on in that way? and then having ordered her to translate the whole of the description of the plates in the last week's "PETIT COURIER DES DAMES," she told her to take herself up stairs immediately after prayers, and make her hair look something like a Christian's. Then she turned round to Miss Cabell, and said, "Come here, child, and let me see your hands, that you're rubbing in that furious way, for they look disgustingly red; and well indeed they might," she added, "for I can plainly see that you never slept in your gloves with the pate d'Amande inside of them. Where on earth do you expect to go with hands like those, you bad, bad child? You'll please to stand in a corner, and hold your arms up over your head for a whole hour, immediately after prayers." And when she had done with her, she turned round again, and said, "Miss Rawlinson, your forehead looks extremely low this morning, and your eyebrows much closer than they were a week ago; I'm half afraid you haven't used your tweezers for these many days past. It's a wonder to me that the ground doesn't open and swallow you up, you wicked, wicked girl! There, go along with you, and just to teach you in future to remove all superfluous hair from between your parting and eyebrows, you will please to get by heart the first six pages of the second chapter of 'THE HANDBOOK OF THE TOILET.'" "Miss Howard," then she went on, "just step this way, if you please. Your dress seems to hang down behind you, as if you had no more bend in your back than an old oak chair. Why, you uncivilized little heathen — you! You've got no crinoline on, as I hope to be saved! Were there ever such girls! But I must put a stop to these evil ways; so you'll remember, Miss Howard, to be able to repeat to me the first five-and-twenty rules of your 'ETIQUETTE FOR THE LADIES,' before you taste a mouthful of luncheon. And, Miss Waterford," she continued, "Why are you hiding behind Miss M'Taggart in that way? Oh, I see! you are afraid I should discover how thin your hair is, I suppose? How often, now, am I to tell you that if your mamma desires you to wear ringlets, you must throw as much of your back hair into your front curls as you can, or you never will appear to have a luxuriant head of it? If you go on in this way, I'm sure I won't take upon myself to say what your latter end will be. All I can tell you is, I shan't be able to rest easy in my bed until I see a very great alteration in your looks. So you will please to stop in the school during play hours, and devote your leisure to the translation of the first of TIMOTHY, into elegant Italian."

At half past two, the bell rang for our *goûté à la fourchette*, when we were expected to make a hearty meal, so that we might appear to be remarkably delicate, small eaters at dinner time, (which never took place till six o'clock,) and Miss Strong'i'-th'arm told me, that though we were allowed beer at luncheon, still it was to be considered a profound secret, and that Miss Grace Thimblebee had once put Miss Howard in the stocks, and kept her on bread and water for three whole days, for asking at dinner for a glass of the disgusting beverage, which she said no lady of the least pretensions to breeding was supposed to know even the taste of. During lunch, I unfortunately said, I would take a little cabbage, as I saw a vegetable dish of very nice white-heart summer ones upon the table. No sooner had the words fallen from my lips, than Miss Prudence (she objected to our calling her Mrs. Dawes) dropped her knife and fork, and looking at me with all her eyes, inquired, "*What* did you say you'd take, Miss De Roos?" "A little cabbage, if you please, ma'am," I replied, quite innocently. "Cabbage! cabbage!" she echoed, "I don't know such a word in the English language, and yet I am not generally considered to be *utterly* ignorant of my mother tongue. Pray, what may you mean by the term?"

"I only wanted some of the vegetables opposite to Mademoiselle de Nemours," I answered.

"Then you will not have any," she returned; "and that, perhaps, will make you remember for the future, that those vegetables are only known here, as well as in all other fashionable circles, by the name of Greens. Cabbage! cabbage!—I suppose I shall soon be doomed to hear you ask for a piece of horrid, horrid cheese. What *do* you expect will become of you, if you go on in this way?"

After lunch we all laid down on our backs for an hour on the boards, so as to improve our figure, and prevent any roundness in our shoulders; then we had lessons in personal deportment. and after this came a slight lecture on the art of stepping into a carriage like a lady; on the conclusion of which, we adjourned to the bottom of the play-ground, where the body of an old landau was fixed up under a shed, so that we might put into practice the valuable precepts that had just been expounded to us. This done, we were dismissed to dress ourselves for the evening, for which we were allowed an hour; and at ten minutes to six, we all entered the drawing-room, whence, as soon as dinner was announced to be on the table, we handed down each other, descending the stairs in couples to the dining-room.

Here I got myself, if possible, into worse disgrace than ever; for, unfortunately for me, there was some very nice *soupe Julienne*, and it was so much to my taste, that when Miss Grace Thimblebee said, "Miss de Roos, now do allow me to send you a little more soup," I replied, "Thank you: since you're *so* pressing I *will* take a little more, if you please, ma'am;" and immediately I had said so, I never saw such mental agony expressed in a human countenance before. "Do I live to hear one of my pupils say that she will take twice of soup," she groaned. "Oh, that it should come to this! that *I*, who have devoted the whole of my energies to the refinement of my sex—that *I* should be doomed to have my heart-strings snapt asunder by any such unheard-of barbarisms! Surely, Miss de Roos, you must have been brought up in the backwoods of America! But you will be pleased to go through the whole of the tenth edition of my little book of "HOW TO LIVE UPON TWO HUNDRED A-YEAR, *so as to make it appear a thousand;*" and until you can repeat all its valuable precepts by heart, you will not dine at this table again. It is a moral duty that I owe to the other young ladies."

"But, ma'am," I replied, "you yourself pressed me to take some more!"

"Of course I did; good breeding required as much from *me*," she answered; "but I never expected that *you* would be ill-bred enough to think for one moment that I meant you to take me at my word. I suppose next, that if I *pressed* you to wear your best gloves at evening service, you would be stupid and prodigal enough to do as I requested."

I declare though, she had no sooner done lecturing me, than observing little red-haired Miss Coburn convey some peas to her mouth by means of her knife, she fell into a state of greater horror than ever.

"Miss Coburn! Miss Coburn!" she screamed; "*do* you want to drive your faithful preceptress to a premature grave! I'm sure if I have made you once go over the sixty-eighth maxim of 'ETIQUETTE FOR THE LADIES,' I must have made you do it at least a hundred times; and yet it only seems as if the golden rules and inestimable truths of that little treasure of a book were entirely thrown away upon you. Now, what does that very sixty-eighth maxim tell you the lady of fashion used to say were her feelings on seeing a person raise her knife to her mouth?"

Miss Coburn remained silent in evident forgetfulness of what the lady of fashion really did say.

"Oh, you don't know, don't you," Miss Thimblebee continued; "then I shall fine you sixpence out of your pocket-money, though I regret to state, you have been fined so often that you have no more to receive this quarter. However, perhaps Miss Smythe Smythe will oblige us all by instructing you on this interesting point."

And immediately Miss Smythe Smythe started off with—"Please ma'am—the—lady—of—fashion—used—to—say—that—she—never—saw—a—person—guilty—of—this—ugly—habit—without—a shudder,—as—every—minute—she—expected—to see—the—head—of—the—unfortunate—severed—from—the—body."

"Very pretty indeed! thank you! Miss Smythe Smythe," said Miss Grace. "We are all of us very much obliged to you, I'm sure; and after dinner you may come to me for a card of merit."

We had only just been helped for the first time to the second course, and had scarcely finished what was on our plates, when Miss Grace Thimblebee said to her sister at the end of the table, "Prudence, my love, can I send you a little more?" and no sooner had Miss Prudence, of course, replied, "No more, I thank you, dearest," than Miss Grace ran her eyes round the table, nodding her head to each of us as quickly as she could, saying, "Nor you?—nor you?—nor you?—n'you?—n'you? n'you?—n'you? Then you may take away, Susan. I'm glad to see my pets are such small eaters."

After dinner, we had to sit down to knit anti-macassars and window-curtains; and when the evenings were long, Miss Thimblebee *would* make us amuse ourselves either with Berlin-wool work or velvet painting, or embroidery, or japanning, or wax flowers, and other odd nick-nackeries; and though the materials for them were regularly charged for in the half-year's bill, still the articles themselves when finished were considered to be the property of the Misses Thimblebee. "Idleness, my dear children," Miss Grace would say, "is the root of all evil, and consequently I am never so well pleased as when I see my sweet girls like a united family, innocently—ay, and I may add profitably—engaged in some lady-like pas-time (not *parse*-time, you will observe, Miss de Roos)."

And well the thin, old, turbaned thing *might* be pleased with seeing us engaged so innocently—ay, and profitably,—as well indeed, too, she MIGHT add; for to tell the truth, "her sweet girls" had managed to supply her with gratuitous window curtains, and chair and sofa cushions and covers for most of the apartments in Chesterfield House; while the grand reception room for all the parents and guardians had been entirely stocked with furniture and ornaments—from the large worked ottoman which stood in the middle of the room, down to the two superb bouquets of wax flowers which graced each end of the mantel-piece—and free of all expense, by "the lady-like exertions of her united family."

Whilst we sat there at that stupid knitting, dropping one and missing two, and letting go three, and throwing off four, and then taking up five, and casting off six, or something just as intellectual and amusing, it was the established rule that we should talk nothing but French; and in order to enforce the practice, the "*Native de Paris*," as she was called, always remained in the room with us. However, to tell the truth, the "*Native de Paris*" wasn't of much use amongst us, for we were not long in finding out that she had entered this world *via* the Surrey side of the Thames, and was rather "*une native de Peckham Rye;*" and though she now chose to give herself a fine French name, still in common gratitude to her godfathers and godmothers, or even in common honesty to the parents of her pupils, she should have added to her grand "ANGELIQUE DE NEMOURS," "*née* SALLY COCKLE;" and, perhaps, it wouldn't have been so much amiss if, while she was about it, she had affixed to the title, "*and cousin to the Misses Thimblebee by their mother's side*," into the bargain. But we liked her the best of the whole of the teachers, for though we were all taught to look up to her as our French mistress, still poor Angelique couldn't help looking down upon herself as a mere French pupil. And well, indeed, she might; for, to be candid, her pure Parisian accent had such a strong Bow-bell twang, that I doubt very much if she could have made herself understood at even a Boulogne *table d'hôte*. So, finding that she was incapable of expressing herself in good sound French, she always made a point of speaking her mind in bad broken English, in which she was materially assisted by a strong lisp, and that Babel-like confusion of the v's and the w's which appertains to the true London dialect.

Thus matters went on for upwards of three

months; and although every half hour through the day some fresh study was introduced, and I learned an infinity of accomplishments, still I cannot at this present time call to mind that I was taught any knowledge. Miss Thimblebee was constantly reminding me that I was receiving the finished education of a perfect lady, though, when I *was* finished, and had left her school, I was totally ignorant of all that was really useful, or truly admirable. Thus matters went on, then, until one day, just as we had finished our morning lessons, and Miss Thimblebee had quitted the school-room, Miss Prudence, who had remained behind, requested silence, and then told us she had a few words to say to us before we retired to the play-ground, on the subject of a joyful event, in which she was sure we all felt equally interested with herself.

To be brief, she was happy to inform us that that day month was the birthday of her dear, dear sister, and our faithful preceptress, Miss Grace Thimblebee. She could read in our eyes how the pleasurable intelligence had gratified us, and how we were all planning in our hearts, like sweet good girls as we were, some little fond surprise, which should be a tangible proof of our love, and worthy the acceptance of that exemplary woman, whom to know, she would add, was to adore. Well, she would not stand between us and our generous feelings, but would forthwith place in Miss Strong'i'th'-arm's hand a money-box, for the reception of subscriptions—however trifling they might be—for it was the sentiment that gave each offering its value and not the amount—though at the same time it might be as well to mention that nothing under five shillings would be received."

After she had gone, I asked Miss Strong'i'th'arm "What we had better buy for Miss Thimblebee with the money?" But she told me, "I needn't trouble my head about that, as Miss Prudence would be sure to lay the money out herself; adding it was only last half that Miss Grace Thimblebee had made very nearly the same speech to them on behalf of her sister Prudence, and indeed it was a rule with the two ladies once a year to do a similar turn one for the other, for by such means they had amassed a very handsome service of plate out of their joint birthdays.

About three days before the joyful event, Miss Prudence came into the school-room, and having unlocked the money box and put the contents into a reticule, which she had brought with her for the purpose, told us, after she had reckoned the amount, that she had hoped she should have been able to have presented her sister with a very neat silver liqueur stand, (which Miss Grace had much admired,) but as she regretted to find the subscription was not so liberal as it had been on former occasions, she must content herself with a small set of silver shells for scolloped oysters, (which she knew her sister was excessively fond of for supper.) Further, she had prepared a short congratulatory and complimentary address, begging Miss Thimblebee's acceptance of the trifling token of our affection and esteem. This she purposed should be spoken by the two youngest ladies in their establishment, on the joyful occasion, when there would be a little *réunion*, just a "*dannce*," a glass of negus and a cake or so, for she intended to treat us all as friends, and make no stupid fuss with us. Then giving the copy of the address to Miss Strongi'th'arm, she said, "Perhaps she would be kind enough to see that Miss Coburn and Miss Smythe Smythe got it off by heart as soon as possible, taking care that they were quite perfect in the hard words, and that they paid particular attention to their stops."

On the evening of the joyful event, the drawing-room was lighted up, and the carpet removed; while the forms which had been brought up from the schoolroom were, by means of a covering of green baize, converted into rout seats. The music mistress had been invited to join in the festivities of the evening; and immediately she made her appearance, she was asked if she would be good enough to oblige them with just one of her beautiful quadrilles, and then handed to the piano, which she never left the whole evening through. The dancing master had been likewise asked to make one of the happy party; and as soon as *he* set foot in the room, he was requested to act as master of the ceremonies. The company consisted of the whole of the teachers, and only one mother and an aunt out of all the parents and relations, though every one of them had been invited; "but unfortunately," as Miss Thimblebee said, at least ten times in the course of the evening, "they had all previous engagements, which they regretted would deprive them of the pleasure of being present on the joyful occasion." However, there were several young gentlemen from a neighboring establishment, who, though of rather too tender an age to please us, still looked particularly clean and uneasy, and had all been elaborately curled and pumped for the joyful event. Their entrance was immediately followed by quadrilles and a strong smell of rose hair oil. After one or two dances, in which the young gentlemen went through the different steps with their eyes intently watching each movement of their feet, Miss Thimblebee asked Miss Rawlinson—whose mamma was *the* one present—if she would be so kind as to oblige the company with her "Gavotte?" When, by dint of saying one-two-three-four to herself, that young lady had accomplished this feat, Miss Howard was requested to let her aunt see how charmingly she was getting on with her music, and to be good enough to play the "Battle of Prague" for them. As soon as she had finished, and been highly complimented for the beauty of her "cries of the wounded," Miss Strong-i'th'arm and Miss Waterford kindly consented to favor the visitors with one of their charming Italian duets; and after a long consultation with the music mistress, at last decided upon singing their beautiful "*La ci darem la mano*," which went off delightfully. Then came a fearful pause; for Miss Prudence had retired with little Miss Coburn and little Miss Smythe Smythe, followed by Miss Strongi'th'-arm, while Miss Thimblebee, who appeared to be greatly astonished at their all leaving the room together in such a mysterious way, wondered what it could mean, and drew the attention of the visitors to a table strewn with our crayon drawings, where Miss Cabell's head of Andromache was much admired by all, excepting Miss Rawlinson's mamma, who said that she thought the pencilling was neither so firm nor so free as that in the sheet of noses by her daughter; indeed, to be candid—and with the young, she was sure Miss Thimblebee would agree with her, it was much better to be so,—she thought the shading down the sides of the cheeks, and under the chin, looked too much like hair to please her; and surely *the* tear she was shedding was a *leetle* out of proportion; while, to tell the truth,

Thos Ingoldsby.

she never did think much of the original; nor did she ever like the subject; nor was she at all pleased with the way in which it was treated. So Miss Thimblebee, to take *the* parent's attention from the drawings, dexterously asked Miss Clanricard who Andromache was? and just as that young lady was informing the guests that "Please, ma'am, Andromache-was-the-wife-of-Hector-of-Troy-and-she-was-so-fond-of-her-husband-that-she—" when, unfortunately, Miss Strongi'th'arm entered the room, followed by little Miss Coburn and Miss Smythe Smythe, bearing the silver scollop-shells on one of the ottoman cushions out of the reception room.

"Why, bless me! what *is* the meaning of this, my dears?" cried Miss Thimblebee, retiring and seating herself in the embroidered easy chair which one of the girls had wheeled into the middle of the room for her.

Then Miss Coburn and Miss Smythe Smythe each made a profound 'curtsy to the enthroned lady, and nearly dropped the silver shells in so doing. After this they both began, in a sing-song tone,—

"We humbly approach you, Miss Grace Thimblebee, our much-respected and beloved mistress, on this, the anniversary of your natal day, to offer you (will you mind your stops, Miss Coburn, whispered Miss Prudence,) to offer you our heartfelt con—congratulations ('One,' said Miss Coburn in an undertone to herself, minding her stops, and so marking a comma,) and to breathe a hope (one,) and prayer (one,) that your valuable existence may be spared for many revolutions of this globe to come (one, two;) and—a—a—a—('That you will condescend to accept,' "Oh you bad child! where *is* your head?" whispered Miss Prudence to Miss Smythe Smythe,) and that you will condescend to accept," continued the young lady, in a half-crying tone, "this paltry token of our profound gratitude (one,) and esteem (one, two;) which (one,) however insignificant its real worth may be (one,) we feel convinced you will attach no trifling value to (one,) as the testimony of the admiration and respect of the young and innocent for the virtues (one,) beauty (one,) accomplishments (one,) and learning of one who is so bright an ornament to her sex (one,) and so kind to her pupils (one, two, three, four.) And please, ma'am, that's all."

"Very nicely spoken, indeed. Thank you, young ladies," exclaimed Miss Prudence; and then taking Miss Smythe Smythe aside, she added in an undertone, "I'll make you suffer for this to-morrow, Miss! —that I will!" then turning round to the company with a 'bland smile, she said, putting her hand up, "Sh-sh-sh-sh-sh!"

Immediately, Miss Thimblebee rose from her chair, and taking a small slip of paper from her pocket, she occasionally spoke and occasionally read as follows:—

"Beloved pupils and respected parents"—but suddenly remembering that there was only one present, she corrected herself—"parent, I should have said; I can assure you the presentation of this little token of your profound gratitude and esteem, has taken me so much by surprise—that—that," [looking at the paper] "I cannot find words to express the feelings that this simple silver liqueur stand —no, scollop shells I should say, has—dear me, no —*have* of course, I mean—but," she added, crumpling up the paper, which had caused her to make so many mistakes, "my feelings quite overpower me—you see—so I can only say—a—a—that I am extremely obliged—you know—for this—a—a— whatever is the word—I've got it on the tip of my tongue—this—a—a—a—what-d'ye-call-it: on this my—a—a—a—no matter what—birthday, so I return you all my very best thanks." And then down she sat quite in a puff.

THE SPECTRE OF TAPPINGTON.

FROM THE "INGOLDSBY LEGENDS." BY RICHARD HARRIS BARHAM.

"It is very odd, though; what can have become of them?" said Charles Seaforth, as he peeped under the valance of an old-fashioned bedstead, in an old-fashioned apartment of a still more old-fashioned manor-house; "'t is confoundedly odd, and I can't make it out at all. Why, Barney, where are they?—and where the d—l are you?"

No answer was returned to this appeal; and the lieutenant, who was, in the main, a reasonable person,—at least as reasonable a person as any young gentleman of twenty-two in "the service" can fairly be expected to be,—cooled when he reflected that his servant could scarcely reply extempore to a summons which it was impossible he should hear.

An application to the bell was the considerate result; and the footsteps of as tight a lad as ever put pipe-clay to belt, sounded along the gallery.

"Come in!" said his master.—An ineffectual attempt upon the door reminded Mr. Seaforth that he had locked himself in.—By Heaven! this is the oddest thing of all," said he, as he turned the key and admitted Mr. Maguire into his dormitory.

"Barney, where are my pantaloons?"

"Is it the breeches?" asked the valet, casting an inquiring eye round the apartment;—"is it the breeches, sir?"

"Yes; what have you done with them?"

"Sure then your honor had them on when you went to bed, and it's hereabout they'll be, I'll be bail;" and Barney lifted a fashionable tunic from a cane-backed arm-chair, proceeding in his examination. But the search was vain; there was the tunic aforesaid,—there was a smart-looking kerseymere waistcoat; but the most important article of all in a gentleman's wardrobe was still wanting.

"Where *can* they be?" asked the master, with a strong accent on the auxiliary verb.

"Sorrow a know I knows," said the man.

"It *must* have been the Devil, then, after all, who has been here and carried them off!" cried Seaforth, staring full into Barney's face.

Mr. Maguire was not devoid of the superstition of his countrymen, still he looked as if he did not quite subscribe to the *sequitur*.

His master read incredulity in his countenance. "Why, I tell you, Barney, I put them there, on that arm-chair, when I got into bed; and, by

Heaven! I distinctly saw the ghost of the old fellow they told me of, come in at midnight, put on my pantaloons, and walk away with them."

"May be so," was the cautious reply.

"I thought, of course, it was a dream; but then, —where the d—l are the breeches?"

The question was more easily asked than answered. Barney renewed his search, while the lieutenant folded his arms, and, leaning against the toilet, sunk into a reverie.

"After all, it must be some trick of my laughter-loving cousins," said Seaforth.

"Ah! then, the ladies!" chimed in Mr. Maguire, though the observation was not addressed to him; "and will it be Miss Caroline, or Miss Fanny, that's stole your honor's things?"

"I hardly know what to think of it," pursued the bereaved lieutenant, still speaking in soliloquy, with his eye resting dubiously on the chamber-door. "I locked myself in, that's certain; and—but there must be some other entrance to the room —pooh! I remember—the private staircase; how could I be such a fool?" and he crossed the chamber to where a low oaken doorcase was dimly visible in a distant corner. He paused before it. Nothing now interfered to screen it from observation; but it bore tokens of having been at some earlier period concealed by tapestry, remains of which yet clothed the walls on either side of the portal.

"This way they must have come," said Seaforth; "I wish with all my heart I had caught them!"

"Och! the kittens!" sighed Mr. Barney Maguire.

But the mystery was yet as far from being solved as before. True, there *was* the "other door;" but then that, too, on examination, was even more firmly secured than the one which opened on the gallery,—two heavy bolts on the inside effectually prevented any *coup de main* on the lieutenant's *bivouac* from that quarter. He was more puzzled than ever; nor did the minutest inspection of the walls and floor throw any light upon the subject: one thing only was clear,—the breeches were gone! "It is *very* singular," said the lieutenant.

* * * *

Tappington (generally called Tapton) Everard is an antiquated but commodious manor-house in the eastern division of the county of Kent. A former proprietor had been High-sheriff in the days of Elizabeth, and many a dark and dismal tradition was yet extant of the licentiousness of his life, and the enormity of his offences. The Glen, which the keeper's daughter was seen to enter, but never known to quit, still frowns darkly as of yore; while an ineradicable bloodstain on the oaken stair yet bids defiance to the united energies of soap and sand. But it is with one particular apartment that a deed of more especial atrocity is said to be connected. A stranger guest—so runs the legend—arrived unexpectedly at the mansion of the "Bad Sir Giles." They met in apparent friendship; but the ill-concealed scowl of their master's brow told the domestics that the visit was not a welcome one. The banquet, however, was not spared; the wine-cup circulated freely,—too freely, perhaps,—for sounds of discord at length reached the ears of even the excluded serving-men, as they were doing their best to imitate their betters in the lower hall. Alarmed, some of them ventured to approach the parlor; one, an old and favored retainer of the house, went so far as to break in upon his master's privacy. Sir Giles, already high in oath, fiercely enjoined his absence, and he retired; not, however, before he had distinctly heard from the stranger's lips a menace that "There was that within his pocket which could disprove the knight's right to issue that or any other command within the walls of Tapton."

The intrusion, though momentary, seemed to have produced a beneficial effect; the voices of the disputants fell, and the conversation was carried on thenceforth in a more subdued tone, till, as evening closed in, the domestics, when summoned to attend with lights, found not only cordiality restored, but that a still deeper carouse was meditated. Fresh stoups, and from the choicest bins, were produced; nor was it till at a late, or rather early hour, that the revellers sought their chambers.

The one allotted to the stranger occupied the first floor of the eastern angle of the building, and had once been the favorite apartment of Sir Giles himself. Scandal ascribed this preference to the facility which a private staircase, communicating with the grounds, had afforded him, in the old knight's time, of following his wicked courses unchecked by parental observation; a consideration which ceased to be of weight when the death of his father left him uncontrolled master of his estate and actions. From that period, Sir Giles had established himself in what were called the "state apartments;" and the "oaken chamber" was rarely tenanted, save on occasions of extraordinary festivity, or when the yule log drew an unusually large accession of guests around the Christmas hearth.

On this eventful night, it was prepared for the unknown visitor, who sought his couch heated and inflamed from his midnight orgies, and in the morning was found in his bed a swollen and blackened corpse. No marks of violence appeared upon the body; but the livid hue of the lips, and certain dark-colored spots visible on the skin, aroused suspicions which those who entertained them were too timid to express. Apoplexy, induced by the excesses of the preceding night, Sir Giles's confidential leech pronounced to be the cause of his sudden dissolution: the body was buried in peace; and though some shook their heads as they witnessed the haste with which the funeral rites were hurried on, none ventured to murmur. Other events arose to distract the attention of the retainers; men's minds became occupied by the stirring politics of the day, while the near approach of that formidable armada, so vainly arrogating to itself a title which the very elements joined with human valor to disprove, soon interfered to weaken, if not obliterate, all remembrance of the nameless stranger who had died within the walls of Tapton Everard.

Years rolled on: the "Bad Sir Giles" had himself long since gone to his account, the last as it was believed of his immediate line; though a few of the older tenants were sometimes heard to speak of an elder brother, who had disappeared in early life, and never inherited the estate. Rumors, too, of his having left a son in foreign lands were at one time rife; but they died away, nothing occurring to support them; the property passed unchallenged to a collateral branch of the family, and the secret, if secret there were, was buried in Denton churchyard, in the lonely grave of the mysterious stranger. One circumstance alone occurred, after a long-intervening period, to revive the memory of these transactions. Some workmen employed in grubbing an old plantation, for the purpose of raising on its site a modern shrubbery, dug up, in the execution of their task, the mildewed remnants of what seemed to have been once a garment. On more minute inspection, enough remained of silken slashes and a coarse embroidery, to identify the relics as having once formed part of a pair of trunk hose; while a few papers which fell from them, altogether illegible from damp and age, were by the unlearned rustics conveyed to the then owner of the estate.

Whether the squire was more successful in deciphering them was never known; he certainly never alluded to their contents; and little would have been thought of the matter but for the inconvenient memory of one old woman, who declared she heard her grandfather say that when the "stranger guest" was poisoned, though all the rest of his clothes were there, his breeches, the supposed repository of the supposed documents, could never be found. The master of Tapton Everard smiled when he heard Dame Jones's hint of deeds which might impeach the validity of his own title in favor of some unknown descendant of some unknown heir; and the story was rarely alluded to, save by one or two miracle-mongers, who had heard that others had seen the ghost of old Sir Giles, in his night-cap, issue from the postern, enter the adjoining copse, and wring his shadowy hands in agony, as he seemed to search vainly for something hidden among the evergreens. The stranger's death-room had, of course, been occasionally haunted from the time of his decease; but the periods of visitation had latterly become very rare,—even Mrs. Botherby, the housekeeper, being forced to admit that, during her long sojourn at the manor, she had never "met with any thing worse than herself;" though as the old lady afterwards added upon more mature reflection, "I must say I think I saw the devil *once.*"

Such was the legend attached to Tapton Everard, and such the story which the lively Caroline Ingoldsby detailed to her equally mercurial cousin, Charles Seaforth, lieutenant in the Hon. East India Company's second regiment of Bombay Fencibles, as arm-in-arm they promenaded a gallery decked with some dozen grim-looking ancestral portraits, and, among others, with that of the redoubted Sir Giles himself. The gallant commander had that very morning paid his first visit to the house of his maternal uncle, after an absence of several years passed with his regiment on the arid plains of Hindostan, whence he was now returned on a three years' furlough. He had gone out a boy,—he returned a man; but the impression made upon his youthful fancy by his favorite cousin remained unimpaired, and to Tapton he directed his steps, even before he sought the home of his widowed mother, —comforting himself in this breach of filial decorum by the reflection that, as the manor was so little out of his way, it would be unkind to pass, as it were, the door of his relatives, without just looking in for a few hours.

But he found his uncle as hospitable and his cousin more charming than ever; and the looks of one, and the requests of the other, soon precluded the possibility of refusing to lengthen the "few hours" into a few days, though the house was at the moment full of visitors.

The Peterses were there from Ramsgate; and Mr., Mrs., and the two Miss Simpkinsons, from Bath, had come to pass a month with the family; and Tom Ingoldsby had brought down his college friend, the Honorable Augustus Sucklethumbkin, with his groom and pointers, to take a fortnight's shooting. And then there was Mrs. Ogleton, the rich young widow, with her large black eyes, who, people did say, was setting her cap at the young squire, though Mrs. Botherby did not believe it; and, above all, there was Mademoiselle Pauline, her *femme de chambre*, who "*mon-Dieu*'d" every thing and every body, and cried "*Quel horreur!*" at Mrs. Botherby's cap. In short, to use the last-named and much respected lady's own expression, the house was "choke-full" to the very attics,—all, save the "oaken chamber," which, as the lieutenant expressed a most magnificent disregard of ghosts, was forthwith appropriated to his particular accommodation. Mr. Maguire, meanwhile, was fain to share the apartment of Oliver Dobbs, the squire's own man; a jocular proposal of joint occupancy having been at first indignantly rejected by "Mademoiselle," though preferred with the "laste taste in life" of Mr. Barney's most insinuating brogue.

* * * *

"Come, Charles, the urn is absolutely getting cold; your breakfast will be quite spoiled: what can have made you so idle?" Such was the morning salutation of Miss Ingoldsby to the *militaire* as he entered the breakfast-room, half an hour after the latest of the party.

"A pretty gentleman, truly, to make an appointment with," chimed in Miss Frances. "What is become of our ramble to the rocks before breakfast?"

"Oh! the young men never think of keeping a promise now," said Mrs. Peters, a little ferret-faced woman with underdone eyes.

"When I was a young man," said Mr. Peters, "I remember I always made a point of——"

"Pray, how long ago was that?" asked Mr. Simpkinson from Bath.

"Why, sir, when I married Mrs. Peters, I was—let me see—I was——"

"Do pray hold your togue, P., and eat your breakfast!" interrupted his better half, who had a mortal horror of chronological references; "it's very rude to tease people with your family affairs."

The lieutenant had by this time taken his seat in silence,—a good-humored nod, and a glance, half-smiling, half-inquisitive, being the extent of his salutation. Smitten as he was, and in the immediate presence of her who had made so large a hole in his heart, his manner was evidently *distrait*, which the fair Caroline in her secret soul attributed to his being solely occupied by her *agrémens*,—how would she have bridled had she known that they only shared his meditations with a pair of breeches!

Charles drank his coffee and spiked some half-dozen eggs, darting occasionally a penetrating glance at the ladies, in hope of detecting the supposed waggery by the evidence of some furtive smile or conscious look. But in vain; not a dimple moved indicative of roguery, nor did the slightest elevation of eyebrow rise confirmative of his suspicions. Hints and insinuations passed unheeded,—more particular inquiries were out of the question:—the subject was unapproachable.

In the mean time, "patent cords" were just the thing for a morning's ride; and, breakfast ended, away cantered the party over the downs, till, every faculty absorbed by the beauties, animate and inanimate, which surrounded him, Lieutenant Seaforth of the Bombay Fencibles, bestowed no more thought upon his breeches than if he had been born on the top of Ben Lomond.

* * * *

Another night had passed away; the sun rose brilliantly, forming with his level beams a splendid rainbow in the far-off west, whither the heavy cloud, which for the last two hours had been pouring its waters on the earth, was now flying before him.

"Ah! then, and it's little good it'll be the claning of ye," apostrophized Mr. Barney Maguire, as he deposited in front of his master's toilet, a pair of "bran-new" jockey boots, one of Hoby's primest fits, which the lieutenant had purchased in his way through town. On that very morning had they come for the first time under the valet's depurating hand, so little soiled, indeed, from the turfy ride of the preceding day, that a less scrupulous domestic might, perhaps, have considered the application of "Warren's Matchless," or oxalic acid, altogether superfluous. Not so, Barney: with the nicest care had he removed the slightest impurity from each polished surface, and there they stood rejoicing in their sable radiance. No wonder a pang shot across Mr. Maguire's breast, as he thought on the work now cut out for them, so different from the light labors of the day before; no wonder he murmured with a sigh, as the scarce-dried window-panes disclosed a road now-inch-deep in mud, "Ah! then, it's little good the claning of ye!"—for well had he learned in the hall below that eight miles of a stiff clay soil lay between the manor and Bolsover Abbey, whose picturesque ruins,

Like ancient Rome, majestic in decay,

the party had determined to explore. The master had already commenced dressing, and the man was fitting straps upon a light pair of crane-necked spurs, when his hand was arrested by the old question,—"Barney, where are the breeches?"

They were nowhere to be found!

* * * *

Mr. Seaforth descended that morning, whip in hand, and equipped in a handsome green riding-frock, but no "breeches and boots to match" were there: loose jean trowsers, surmounting a pair of diminutive Wellingtons, embraced, somewhat incongruously, his nether man, *vice* the "patent cords," returned, like yesterday's pantaloons, absent without leave. The "top-boots" had a holiday.

"A fine morning after the rain," said Mr. Simpkinson from Bath.

"Just the thing for the 'ops," said Mr. Peters. "I remember when I was a boy—"

"Do hold your tongue, P.," said Mrs. Peters,—advice which that exemplary matron was in the constant habit of administering to "her P.," as she called him, whenever he prepared to vent his reminiscences. Her precise reason for this, it would be difficult to determine, unless, indeed, the story be true which a little bird had whispered into Mrs. Botherby's ear,—Mr. Peters, though now a wealthy man, had received a liberal education at a charity school, and was apt to recur to the days of his muffin-cap and leathers. As usual, he took his wife's hint in good part, and "paused in his reply."

"A glorious day for the ruins!" said young Ingoldsby. "But, Charles, what the deuce are you about?—you don't mean to ride through our lanes in such toggery as that?"

"Lassy me!" said Miss Julia Simpkinson, "won't you be very wet?"

"You had better take Tom's cab," quoth the squire.

But this proposition was at once overruled; Mrs. Ogleton had already nailed the cab, a vehicle of all others the best adapted for a snug flirtation.

"Or drive Miss Julia in the phaeton?" No; that was the post of Mr. Peters, who, indifferent as an equestrian, had acquired some fame as a whip while travelling through the midland counties for the firm of Bagshaw, Snivelby, and Ghrimes.

"Thank you, I shall ride with my cousins," said Charles with as much *nonchalance* as he could assume,—and he did so; Mr. Ingoldsby, Mrs. Peters, Mr. Simpkinson from Bath, and his eldest daughter with her *album*, following in the family coach. The gentleman-commoner "voted the affair d—d slow," and declined the party altogether in favor of the game-keeper and a cigar. "There was no fun in looking at old houses!" Mrs. Simpkinson preferred a short *séjour* in the still-room with Mrs. Botherby, who had promised to initiate her in that grand *arcanum*, the transmutation of gooseberry jam in Guava jelly.

* * * *

"Did you ever see an old abbey before, Mr. Peters?"

"Yes, miss, a French one; we have got one at Ramsgate; he teaches the Miss Joneses to parley-voo, and is turned of sixty."

Miss Simpkinson closed her album with an air of ineffable disdain.

* * * *

"Caroline," said Charles, "I have had some very odd dreams since I have been at Tappington."

"Dreams, have you?" smiled the young lady,

arching her taper neck like a swan in pluming. "Dreams, have you?"

"Ay, dreams,—or dream, perhaps, I should say; for, though repeated, it was still the same. And what do you imagine was the subject?"

"It is impossible for me to divine," said the tongue;—"I have not the least difficulty in guessing," said the eye as plainly as ever eye spoke.

"I dreamt—of your great grandfather!"

There was a change in the glance—"My great grandfather?"

"Yes, the old Sir Giles, or Sir John, you told me about the other day: he walked into my bedroom in his short cloak of murrey-colored velvet, his long rapier, and his Raleigh-looking hat and feather, just as the picture represents him; but with one exception."

"And what was that?"

"Why his lower extremities, which were visible, were—those of a skeleton."

"Well."

"Well, after taking a turn or two about the room, and looking round him with a wistful air, he came to the bed's foot, stared at me in a manner impossible to describe,—and then he—he laid hold of my pantaloons; whipped his long bony legs into them in a twinkling; and, strutting up to the glass,

seemed to view himself in it with great complacency. I tried to speak, but in vain. The effort, however, seemed to excite his attention; for, wheeling about, he showed me the grimmest-looking death's head you can well imagine, and with an indescribable grin strutted out of the room."

"Absurd! Charles. How can you talk such nonsense?"

"But, Caroline,—the breeches are really gone."

* * * *

On the following morning, contrary to his usual custom, Seaforth was the first person in the breakfast parlor. As no one else was present, he did precisely what nine young men out of ten so situated would have done; he walked up to the mantel-piece, established himself upon the rug, and subducting his coat-tails one under each arm, turned towards the fire that portion of the human frame which it is considered equally indecorous to present to a friend or an enemy. A serious, not to say anxious, expression was visible upon his good-humored countenance, and his mouth was fast buttoning itself up for an incipient whistle, when little Flo, a tiny spaniel of the Blenheim breed,—the pet object of Miss Julia Simpkinson's affections,—bounced out from beneath a sofa, and began to bark at—his pantaloons.

They were cleverly "built," of a light gray mixture, a broad stripe of the most vivid scarlet traversing each seam in a perpendicular direction from hip to ankle,—in short, the regimental costume of the Royal Bombay Fencibles. The animal, educated in the country, had never seen such a pair of breeches in her life—*Omne ignotum pro magnifico!* The scarlet streak, inflamed as it was by the reflection of the fire, seemed to act on Flora's nerves as the same color does on those of bulls and turkeys; she advanced at the *pas de charge*, and her vociferation, like her amazement, was unbounded. A sound kick from the disgusted officer changed its character, and induced a retreat at the very moment when the mistress of the pugnacious quadruped entered to the rescue.

* * * *

The conference between the young gentlemen was neither brief in its duration nor unimportant in its result. The subject was what the lawyers call tripartite, embracing the information that Charles Seaforth was over head and ears in love with Tom Ingoldsby's sister; secondly, that the lady had referred him to "papa" for his sanction; thirdly, and lastly, his nightly visitations, and consequent bereavement. At the two first items Tom smiled auspiciously;—at the last, he burst out into an absolute "guffaw."

"Steal your breeches!—Miss Bailey over again, by Jove," shouted Ingoldsby. "But a gentleman, you say,—and Sir Giles too.—I am not sure, Charles, whether I ought not to call you out for aspersing the honor of the family!"

"Laugh as you will, Tom,—be as incredulous as you please. One fact is incontestable,—the breeches are gone! Look here—I am reduced to my regimentals; and if these go, to-morrow I must borrow of you!"

Rochefoucault says, there is something in the misfortunes of our very best friends that does not displease us;—assuredly we can, most of us, laugh at their petty inconveniences, till called upon to supply them. Tom composed his features on the instant, and replied with more gravity, as well as with an expletive, which, if my Lord Mayor had been within hearing, might have cost him five shillings.

"There is something very queer in this, after all. The clothes, you say, have positively disappeared. Somebody is playing you a trick; and ten to one your servant has a hand in it. By the way, I heard something yesterday of his kicking up a bobbery in the kitchen, and seeing a ghost, or something of that kind, himself. Depend upon it, Barney is in the plot!"

It now struck the lieutenant at once, that the usually buoyant spirits of his attendant had of late been materially sobered down, his loquacity obviously circumscribed, and that he, the said lieutenant, had actually rung his bell three several times that very morning before he could procure his attendance. Mr. Maguire was forthwith summoned, and underwent a close examination. The "bobbery" was easily explained. Mr. Oliver Dobbs had hinted his disapprobation of a flirtation carrying on between the gentleman from Munster and the lady from the Rue St. Honoré. Mademoiselle had boxed Mr. Maguire's ears, and Mr. Maguire had pulled Mademoiselle upon his knee, and the lady had *not* cried *Mon Dieu!* And Mr. Oliver Dobbs said it was very wrong; and Mrs. Botherby said it was "scandalous," and what ought not to be done in any moral kitchen;—and Mr. Maguire had got hold of the Honorable Augustus Sucklethumbkin's powder-flask, and had put large pinches of the best double Dartford into Mr. Dobbs's tobacco-box; —and Mr. Dobbs's pipe had exploded, and set fire to Mrs. Botherby's Sunday cap—and Mr. Maguire had put it out with the slop-basin, "barring the wig;"—and then they were all so "cantankerous," that Barney had gone to take a walk in the garden; and then—then Mr. Barney had seen a ghost!!

"A what? you blockhead?" asked Tom Ingoldsby.

"Sure then, and it's meself will tell your honor the rights of it," said the ghost-seer. "Meself and Miss Pauline, sir,—or Miss Pauline and meself, for the ladies come first anyhow,—we got tired of the hobstropylous skrimmaging among the ould servants, that didn't know a joke when they seen one: and we went out to look at the comet, that's the rory-bory-alehouse, they calls him in this country, —and we walked upon the lawn,—and divil of any alehouse there was there at all; and Miss Pauline said it was because of the shrubbery maybe, and why wouldn't we see it better beyonst the trees? —and so we went to the trees, but sorrow a comet did meself see there, barring a big ghost instead of it."

"A ghost? And what sort of a ghost, Barney?"

"Och, then, divil a lie I'll tell your honor. A tall ould gentleman he was, all in white, with a shovel on the shoulder of him, and a big torch in his fist,—though what he wanted with that it's meself can't tell, for his eyes were like gig-lamps, let alone the moon and the comet, which wasn't there at all;—and 'Barney,' says he to me,—'cause why he knew me,—'Barney,' says he, 'what is it your'e doing with the *colleen* there, Barney?'—Divil a word did I say. Miss Pauline screeched, and cried murther in French, and ran off with herself; and of course meself was in a mighty hurry after the lady, and had no time to stop palavering with him any way; so I dispersed at once, and the ghost vanished in a flame of fire!"

Mr. Maguire's account was received with avowed incredulity by both gentlemen; but Barney stuck to his text with unflinching pertinacity. A reference to Mademoiselle was suggested, but abandoned, as neither party had a taste for delicate investigations.

"I'll tell you what, Seaforth," said Ingoldsby, after Barney had received his dismissal, "that there is a trick here is evident; and Barney's vision may possibly be a part of it. Whether he is most knave or fool, you best know. At all events, I will sit up with you to-night, and see if I can convert my ancestor into a visiting acquaintance. Meanwhile, your finger on your lip!"

* * * *

'Twas now the very witching time of night,
When churchyards yawn, and graves give up their dead.

Gladly would I grace my tale with a decent horror, and therefore I do beseech the "gentle reader" to believe, that if all the *succedanea* to this mysterious narrative are not in strict keeping, he will ascribe it only to the disgraceful innovations of modern degeneracy upon the sober and dignified habits of our ancestors. I can introduce him, it is true, into an old and high-roofed chamber, its walls covered on three sides with black oak wainscoting, adorned with carvings of fruit and flowers long anterior to those of Grinling Gibbons; the fourth side is clothed with a curious remnant of dingy tapestry, once elucidatory of some Scriptural history, but of *which* not even Mrs. Botherby could determine. Mr. Simpkinson, who had examined it carefully, inclined to believe the principal figure to be either Bathsheba, or Daniel in the lions' den; while Tom Ingoldsby decided in favor of the King of Bashan. All, however, was conjecture, tradition being silent on the subject.—A lofty arched portal led into, and a little arched portal led out of, this apartment; they were opposite each other, and each possessed the security of massy bolts on its interior. The bedstead, too, was not one of yesterday, but manifestly coeval with days ere Seddons was, and when a good four-post "article" was deemed worthy of being a royal bequest. The bed itself, with all the appurtenances of palliasse, mattresses, etc., was of far later date, and looked most incongruously comfortable; the casements, too, with their little diamond-shaped panes and iron binding, had given way to the modern heterodoxy of the sash-window. Nor was this all that conspired to ruin the costume, and render the room a meet haunt for such "mixed spirits" only as could condescend to don at the same time an Elizabethan doublet and Bond street inexpressibles.

With their green morocco slippers on a modern fender, in front of a disgracefully modern grate, sat two young gentlemen, clad in "shawl-pattern" dressing gowns and black silk stocks, much at variance with the high, cane-backed chairs which supported them. A bunch of abomination called a cigar, reeked in the left-hand corner of the mouth of one, and in the right-hand corner of the mouth of the other;—an arrangement happily adapted for the escape of the noxious fumes up the chimney, without that unmerciful "funking" each other, which a less scientific disposition of the weed would have induced. A small pembroke table filled up the intervening space between them, sustaining, at each extremity, an elbow and a glass of toddy;— thus in "lonely pensive contemplation" were the two worthies occupied, when the "iron tongue of midnight had tolled twelve."

"Ghost-time's come?" said Ingoldsby, taking from his waistcoat pocket a watch like a gold half-crown, and consulting it as though he suspected the turret-clock over the stables of mendacity.

"Hush!" said Charles; "did I not hear a footstep?"

There was a pause: there *was* a footstep—it sounded distinctly—it reached the door—it hesitated, stopped, and—passed on.

Tom darted across the room, threw open the door, and became aware of Mrs. Botherby toddling to her chamber at the other end of the gallery, after dosing one of the housemaids with an approved julep from the Countess of Kent's "Choice Manual."

"Good night, sir!" said Mrs. Botherby.

"Go to the d—l!" said the disappointed ghost-hunter.

An hour—two—rolled on, and still no spectral visitation; nor did aught intervene to make night hideous; and when the turret-clock sounded at length the hour of three, Ingoldsby, whose patience and grog were alike exhausted, sprang from his chair, saying—

"This is all infernal nonsense, my good fellow. Deuce of any ghost shall we see to-night; it's long past the canonical hour. I'm off to bed; and as to your breeches, I'll insure them for the next twenty-four hours at least, at the price of the buckram."

"Certainly.—Oh! thank'ee;—to be sure!" stammered Charles, rousing himself from a reverie, which had degenerated into an absolute snooze.

"Good night, my boy! Bolt the door behind me; and defy the Pope, the Devil, and the Pretender!—"

Seaforth followed his friend's advice, and the next morning came down to breakfast dressed in the habiliments of the preceding day. The charm was broken, the demon defeated; the light grays with the red stripe down the seams were yet *in rerum naturâ*, and adorned the person of their lawful proprietor.

Tom felicitated himself and his partner of the watch on the result of their vigilance; but there is a rustic adage, which warns us against self-gratulation before we are quite "out of the wood."—Seaforth was yet within its verge.

* * * *

A rap at Tom Ingoldsby's door the following morning startled him as he was shaving:—he cut his chin.

"Come in, and be d—d to you!" said the martyr, pressing his thumb on the scarified epidermis. —The door opened, and exhibited Mr. Barney Maguire.

"Well, Barney, what is it?" quoth the sufferer, adopting the vernacular of his visitant.

"The master, sir——"

"Well, what does he want?"

"The loanst of a breeches, plase your honor."

"Why, you don't mean to tell me—By heaven, this is too good!" shouted Tom, bursting into a fit of uncontrollable laughter. "Why, Barney, you don't mean to say the ghost has got them again?"

Mr. Maguire did not respond to the young squire's risibility; the cast of his countenance was decidedly serious.

"Faith, then, it's gone they are, sure enough! Hasn't meself been looking over the bed, and under the bed, and *in* the bed, for the matter of that, and divil a ha'p'orth of breeches is there to the fore at all:—I'm bothered entirely!"

"Hark'ee! Mr. Barney," said Tom, incautiously removing his thumb, and letting a crimson stream "incarnadine the multitudinous" lather that plastered his throat,—"this may be all very well with your master, but you don't humbug *me*, sir:—tell me instantly what have you done with the clothes?"

This abrupt transition from "lively to severe" certainly took Maguire by surprise, and he seemed for an instant as much disconcerted as it is possible to disconcert an Irish gentleman's gentleman.

"Me? is it meself, then, that's the ghost, to your honor's thinking?" said he, after a moment's pause, and with a slight shade of indignation in his tones: "is it I would stale the master's things,—and what would I do with them?"

"That you best know:—what your purpose is I can't guess, for I don't think you mean to 'stale' them, as you call it; but that you are concerned in their disappearance, I am satisfied. Confound this blood!—give me a towel, Barney."

Maguire acquitted himself of the commission. "As I've a sowl, your honor," said he, solemnly, "little it is meself knows of the matter; and after what I seen——"

"What you've seen? Why, what *have* you seen? —Barney, I don't want to inquire into your flirtations; but don't suppose you can palm off your saucer eyes and gig-lamps upon me!"

"Then, as sure as your honor 's standing there I saw him: and why wouldn't I, when Miss *Pauline* was to the fore as well as meself, and——"

"Get along with your nonsense,—leave the room, sir!"

"But the master!" said Barney, imploringly; "and without a breeches!—sure he'll be catching cowld!—"

"Take that, rascal!" replied Ingoldsby, throwing a pair of pantaloons at, rather than to, him; "but don't suppose, sir, you shall carry on your tricks here with impunity; recollect there is such a thing as a treadmill, and that my father is a county magistrate."

Barney's eye flashed fire,—he stood erect, and was about to speak; but, mastering himself, not without an effort, he took up the garment, and left the room as perpendicular as a quaker.

* * * *

"Ingoldsby," said Charles Seaforth, after breakfast, "this is now past a joke; to-day is the last of my stay; for, notwithstanding the ties which detain me, common decency obliges me to visit home after so long an absence. I shall come to an immediate explanation with your father on the subject nearest my heart, and depart while I have a change of dress left. On his answer will my return depend! in the mean time tell me candidly,—I ask it in all seriousness, and as a friend,—am I not a dupe to your well-known propensity to hoaxing? have you not a hand in ——"

"No, by Heaven! Seaforth; I see what you mean: on my honor, I am as much mystified as yourself; and if your servant ——"

"Not he:—if there be a trick, he at least is not privy to it."

"If there *be* a trick? Why, Charles, do you think ——"

"I know not *what* to think, Tom. As surely as you are a living man, so surely did that spectral anatomy visit my room again last night, grin in my face, and walk away with my trousers; nor was I able to spring from my bed, or break the chain which seemed to bind me to my pillow."

"Seaforth!" said Ingoldsby, after a short pause, "I will—but hush! here are the girls and my father. —I will carry off the females, and leave you a clear field with the governor: carry your point with him, and we will talk about your breeches afterwards."

Tom's diversion was successful; he carried off the ladies *en masse* to look at a remarkable specimen of the class *Dodecandria Monogynia*,—which they could not find;—while Seaforth marched boldly up to the encounter, and carried "the governor's" outworks by a *coup de main*. I shall not stop to describe the progress of the attack; suffice it that it was as successful as could have been wished, and that Seaforth was referred back again to the lady. The happy lover was off at a tangent; the botanical party was soon overtaken; and the arm of Caroline, whom a vain endeavor to spell out the Linnæan name of a daffy-down-dilly had detained a little in the rear of the others, was soon firmly locked in his own.

What was the world to them,
Its noise, its nonsense, and its 'breeches' all?

Seaforth was in the seventh heaven; he retired to his room that night as happy as if no such thing as a goblin had ever been heard of, and personal chattels were as well fenced in by law as real property. Not so Tom Ingoldsby: the mystery—for mystery there evidently was,—had not only piqued his curiosity, but ruffled his temper. The watch of the previous night had been unsuccessful, probably because it was undisguised. To-night he would "ensconce himself,"—not indeed "behind the arras,"—for the little that remained was, as we have seen, nailed to the wall,—but in a small closet which opened from one corner of the room, and, by leaving the door ajar, would give to its occupant a view of all that might pass in the apartment. Here did the young ghost-hunter take up a position, with a good stout sapling under his arm, a full half-hour before Seaforth retired for the night. Not even his friend did he let into his confidence, fully determined that if his plan did not succeed, the failure should be attributed to himself alone.

At the usual hour of separation for the night, Tom saw, from his concealment, the lieutenant enter his room, and, after taking a few turns in it, with an expression so joyous as to betoken that his thoughts were mainly occupied by his approaching happiness, proceed slowly to disrobe himself. The coat, the waistcoat, the black silk stock, were gradually discarded; the green morocco slippers were kicked off, and then—ay, and then—his countenance grew grave; it seemed to occur to him all at once that this was his last stake,—nay, that the very breeches he had on were not his own,—that to-morrow morning was his last, and that if he lost *them* ——. A glance showed that his mind was made up; he replaced the single button he had just abducted, and threw himself upon the bed in a state of transition,—half chrysalis, half grub.

Wearily did Tom Ingoldsby watch the sleeper by the flickering light of the night-lamp, till the clock, striking one, induced him to increase the narrow opening which he had left for the purpose of observation. The motion, slight as it was, seemed to attract Charles's attention; for he raised himself suddenly to a sitting posture, listened for a moment, and then stood upright upon the floor. Ingoldsby was on the point of discovering himself, when, the light flashing full upon his friend's countenance, he perceived that, though his eyes were open, "their sense was shut,"—that he was yet under the influence of sleep. Seaforth advanced slowly to the toilet, lit his candle at the lamp that stood on it, then, going back to the bed's foot, appeared to search eagerly for something which he could not find. For a few moments he seemed restless and uneasy, walking round the apartment and examining the chairs, till, coming fully in front of a large swing-glass that flanked the dressing-table, he paused, as if contemplating his figure in it. He now returned towards the bed; put on his slippers, and, with cautious and stealthy steps, proceeded towards the little arched doorway that opened on the private staircase.

As he drew the bolt, Tom Ingoldsby emerged from his hiding-place; but the sleep-walker heard him not; he proceeded softly down stairs, followed at a due distance by his friend; opened the door which led out upon the gardens; and stood at once among the thickest of the shrubs, which there clustered round the base of a corner turret, and screened the postern from common observation. At this moment, Ingoldsby had nearly spoiled all by making a false step: the sound attracted Seaforth's attention,—he paused and turned; and, as the full moon shed her light directly upon his pale and troubled features, Tom marked, almost with dismay, the fixed and rayless appearance of his eyes:—

There was no speculation in those orbs
That he did glare withal.

The perfect stillness preserved by his follower seemed to reassure him; he turned aside; and from the midst of a thickset laurustinus, drew forth a gardener's spade, shouldering which he proceeded with greater rapidity into the midst of the shrubbery. Arrived at a certain point where the earth seemed to have been recently disturbed, he set himself heartily to the task of digging, till, having thrown up several shovelfuls of mould, he stopped, flung down his tool, and very composedly began to disencumber himself of his pantaloons.

Up to this moment, Tom had watched him with a wary eye; he now advanced cautiously, and, as his friend was busily engaged in disentangling himself from his garment, made himself master of the spade. Seaforth, meanwhile, had accomplished his purpose: he stood for a moment with

His streamers waving in the wind,

occupied in carefully rolling up the small-clothes into as compact a form as possible, and all heedless of the breath of heaven, which might certainly be supposed, at such a moment, and in such a plight, to "visit his frame too roughly."

—He was in the act of stooping low to deposit the pantaloons in the grave which he had been digging for them, when Tom Ingoldsby came close behind him, and with the flat side of the spade—

* * * *

The shock was effectual;—never again was Lieutenant Seaforth known to act the part of a somnambulist. One by one, his breeches,—his trousers,—his pantaloons,—his silk-net tights,—his patent cords,—his showy grays with the broad red stripe of the Bombay Fencibles, were brought to light,—rescued from the grave in which they had been buried like the strata of a Christmas pie; and, after having been well aired by Mrs. Botherby, became once again effective.

The family, the ladies especially, laughed;—the Peterses laughed;—the Simpkinsons laughed;—Barney Maguire cried "Botheration!" and *Ma'm-selle Pauline*, "*Mon Dieu!*"

Charles Seaforth, unable to face the quizzing which awaited him on all sides, started off two hours earlier than he had proposed:—he soon returned, however, and having, at his father-in-law's request, given up the occupation of rajah-hunting and shooting nabobs, led his blushing bride to the altar.

Mr. Simpkinson from Bath did not attend the

ceremony, being engaged at the Grand Junction Meeting of *Sçavans*, then congregating from all parts of the known world in the city of Dublin. His essay, demonstrating that the globe is a great custard, whipped into coagulation by whirlwinds, and cooked by electricity,—a little too much baked in the Isle of Portland, and a thought underdone about the Bog of Allan,—was highly spoken of, and narrowly escaped obtaining a Bridgewater prize.

Miss Simpkinson and her sister acted as bridesmaids on the occasion; the former wrote an *epithalamium*, and the latter cried "Lassy me!" at the clergyman's wig. Some years have since rolled on; the union has been crowned with two or three tidy little offshoots from the family tree, of whom Master Neddy is "grand-papa's darling," and Mary-Anne mamma's particular "Sock." I shall only add, that Mr. and Mrs. Seaforth are living together quite as happily as two good-hearted, good-tempered bodies, very fond of each other, can possibly do: and that, since the day of his marriage, Charles has shown no disposition to jump out of bed, or ramble out of doors o'nights,—though, from his entire devotion to every wish and whim of his young wife, Tom insinuates that the fair Caroline does still occasionally take advantage of it so far as to "slip on the Breeches."

A HOPEFUL YOUTH.

FROM "MY COUSIN NICHOLAS." BY RICHARD HARRIS BARHAM.

I CANNOT say that the manners of my new friend made a very favorable impression upon me; nay, I must own that with respect to my cousin Nicholas, my temper was even more fastidious. In vain did that facetious young gentleman exhibit some of the choicest specimens of his wit for my entertainment; in vain were the most jocose feats of practical ingenuity, feats which convulsed all the grooms and footmen in the house with laughter, brought forward to amuse me; in vain did he tie the wheel of a post-chaise, which had drawn up at a door in the village, to one of the legs of an adjacent fruit-stall, and occasion in consequence a most ludicrous subversion of the fragile fabric on the sudden movement of the vehicle, to the utter consternation of a profane old apple-woman, who loaded the unknown malefactor with her bitterest execrations; in vain did he even exercise his humor on my own person, putting drugs of a cathartic quality into my soup, or removing the linchpins from a pony-chaise, which I was fond of driving about the grounds, and thereby occasioning me an unexpected descent from my triumphal car, accomplished with far more of precipitation than grace—still, I was so weak as to remain insensible to his merit, and even to look upon these sprightly sallies with some degree of anger and indignation. I have little doubt but that I must have appeared to him a very dull dog, and should in all probability have soon incurred his supreme contempt, but for an event which, I have since had reason to imagine, changed in some degree the nature of his feelings toward me.

The last accounts from Spain had stated the approximation of the two contending armies, and the public journals did not hesitate to speculate on the probability of an approaching engagement. These conjectures derived much additional strength from the contents of private dispatches; and, among others, of letters received by my mother from her husband, who, from his situation in Lord ——'s staff, had good grounds for supposing such a circumstance to be very likely to take place. My mother's anxiety was, of course, extreme; nor could I fail to partake of the same feelings, when, one morning, the rest of the family being already assembled at breakfast, my cousin Nicholas, who was usually later than any other of the party, entered the room.

His countenance, unlike its usual expression, was serious, and even solemn; his step slow and hesitating, while a degree of disorder was visible in his whole demeanor. He took his seat at the breakfast-table in silence, and began to occupy himself with his teacup, bending down his head, as if with the intention of shading his countenance from the observation of the company. My uncle at this moment inquired for the newspaper, the invariable concomitant of his morning meal, and was answered by the butler that he had placed it on the table as usual, before any of the family had come down, except Mr. Bullwinkle, whom he thought he had seen engaged in its perusal.

"And pray, Mr. Nick, what have you done with it?" cried Sir Oliver. "I did not know you had been up so early."

"Done with it, sir?" stammered my cousin. "Nothing, sir—that is, nothing in particular. I have left it in my own room, I dare say; I can fetch it, if you wish me, sir—that is—but perhaps you will like to read it after breakfast?"—and his eye glanced significantly toward my mother.

Its expression was not to be mistaken. She caught the alarm instantly, and rising from her chair, while her trembling limbs scarce sufficed to bear her weight, and her face turned ashy pale, exclaimed, "There is news from Spain! I am sure of it—and Stafford is killed!"

Her words were electrical, and a simultaneous conviction of their truth blanched every cheek.

"Killed!" returned my cousin Nicholas. "No, my dear aunt—that is—I hope not; but—there has been an action—a severe one, and it is as well to be prepared—"

Mrs. Stafford's worst fears were confirmed: she fainted, and was carried from the room. In the confusion of the moment, no one thought of inquiring into the sad particulars of the disaster that had overwhelmed us. Sir Oliver first asked the question, and demanded to see the fatal paper. My cousin immediately complied with the requisition, and produced it from his pocket; saying, coolly, as he put it into his father's hand, that "he was sorry to see his aunt so discomposed, as his uncle Stafford might not, after all, be killed, or even wounded, as his name certainly was not in the list of either the one or the other."

"Not in the list!" roared Sir Oliver. "Then what the d—l did you mean, you young rascal, by alarming us all in this manner?" and stood with an expression of countenance in which joy, surprise, and anger, were most ludicrously commingled; while I, as the conviction that my ingenious cousin had merely been once more indulging his taste for pleasantry flashed upon my mind, sprung forward in the heat of my indignation, and, with a tolerably well-directed blow of my arm, levelled that jocose young gentleman with the floor.

A yell, shrill and piercing as that of the fabled mandrake, when torn by the hand of violence from its parent earth, accompanied his prostration, and the ill-concealed triumph which had begun to sparkle in his eye at the success of his stratagem, gave way to a strong aprearance of disgust at this forcible appeal to his feelings. But Sir Oliver, with all his partiality for his heir, was at this moment too angry to take up his cause: he ordered him instantly out of the room, while I hurried off to console my mother with the intelligence that the fears she had been so cruelly subjected to were altogether groundless, and that the affair, to use a frequent and favorite phrase of my cousin Nicholas, was "nothing but a jolly good hoax from beginning to end."

I found my mother still suffering severely under the impression that the blood of her beloved husband had mingled with that of many of his brave countrymen in crimsoning the plains of Talavera. Painful as it was to witness her distress, I almost dreaded to inform her that she had been imposed upon, lest the sudden transition from despair to extreme joy, on finding her apprehensions for his safety entirely groundless, should prove too much for her agitated mind, and plunge her perhaps into a situation still more to be dreaded than that state of insensibility from which she was now beginning slowly to emerge.

Fortunately, while I was yet meditating on the best method of conveying the happy news to her with the caution it required, Dr. Drench was ushered into the apartment. The worthy old butler, on seeing the condition in which his mistress had been borne from the breakfast parlor, had hurried, unbidden, in search of that gentleman's assistance, and had luckily found him at his own house, which was situate scarcely a hundred yards distant from the avenue leading to the Hall. When he arrived, the good doctor was in the very act of mounting his galloway, a tight little Suffolk punch of more "bone" than "mettle," in order to pay a visit to a patient. Of course, no persuasion was necessary, under the circumstances, to induce him to alter his route for the present; and, having stored his pockets with a profusion of the usual restoratives, a very few minutes brought him to Mrs. Stafford's bedside. Taking him aside to the window, I, in as few words as possible, recounted to him the cause of my mother's sudden indisposition, together with the real state of the case, the assurance of which would, I was persuaded, prove the most effectual remedy for her disorder; then, leaving it to his discretion to announce the glad tidings in the manner most befitting the occasion, I retired from the room. The worthy doctor, not being blessed with a very keen relish for the ridiculous, was at first a good deal shocked at my narration, and, in the simplicity of his heart, cursed my cousin Nicholas for "a mischievous young cub;" but then it may be observed in palliation, that Drench was but a plain man, with very little taste for humor. By his care and skill, however, together with the judicious way in which he communicated to his patient, after a free use of the lancet, the information which had indeed nearly again overwhelmed her, such beneficial effects were produced as to warrant him, on joining us in the parlor below, in holding out the strongest hopes that no ulterior consequences of a more serious or unpleasant nature would attend the execution of my cousin's frolic.

Sir Oliver pressed the doctor strongly to stay and partake of our family dinner; this invitation, however, frankly as it was proffered, he thought fit most positively to decline. Indeed, ever since the surreptitious abduction of his queue, which had taken place on the memorable occasion of the party formerly mentioned, he had been rather shy of committing his person within the four walls of Underdown Hall, except under circumstances of professional emergency. He had by this time, after infinite care and pains, succeeded in rearing another pigtail to a size and longitude nearly coequal with those of its lamented predecessor. It was once again *totus teres atque rotundus*, and its proprietor was, therefore, not without reason, especially apprehensive lest the scissors of my cousin Nicholas, scarcely less fatal than those of the Parcæ, might once more subject this cherished appendage to the unpleasant ceremony of a divorce. Despite, therefore, the Circæan allurements of a fine haunch of forest mutton, his favorite joint, Dr. Drench shook me cordially by the hand, bowed to Sir Oliver and the captain, and quitted the house.

My uncle, whose love and regard for his sister, always sincere, were, perhaps, greater at this than at any former period of his life, was truly rejoiced to find that no seriously unpleasant effects were likely to ensue from what, now his apprehensions were allayed, he began to consider as a pardonable, though somewhat too lively, ebullition of youthful vivacity; he had even begun to explain to the captain, for the five hundredth time, what a *desideratum* it was that a boy should have a little mischief—a "little spice of the d—l," as he phrased it, "in him;" the captain, in no wise relaxing from his accustomed taciturnity, was very composedly occupying himself in arranging the men upon the backgammon board, and neither assented nor demurred to a proposition which he had so often heard laid down by his host before; while I, in that restless, fidgety state of mind which one feels when subsiding agitation has not yet quite sunk into composure, was endeavoring to divert the unpleasant current of my thoughts by turning over the leaves of the last new novel, brought by Miss Kitty Pyefinch from the circulating library at Underdown, when a strange medley of voices and confusion of sounds, portending some new calamity, and proceeding from the outward hall, arrested my attention, caused even the imperturbable captain to raise his eyes from his game, and drew from Sir Oliver Bullwinkle the abrupt exclamation, "What the devil's that?"

The sounds evidently and rapidly approached; in a few seconds, the parlor door flew open, and a figure, which, by its general outline only, could be recognized as that of Drench, occupied the vacant space, while the background of the picture was filled up by an assemblage of sundry domestics, bearing clothes-brushes and rubbers of various descriptions, and exhibiting a set of countenances in every one of which respect, and a strong inclination to risibility, manifestly contended for the mastery.

The unexpected appearance of such a phenomenon excited scarcely less surprise and astonishment in my own mimd than in that of Sir Oliver, who stood gazing on the apparition with symptoms of the most undisguised amazement, till a voice, broken by passion, and impeded by the mud, which filled the mouth of the speaker, stammered out:

"Look here, Sir Oliver! I beg you will look here —this is another of the tricks of your precious son Nicholas. His behavior is unbearable—he is a pest to the whole neighborhood, Sir Oliver."

"Why, what on earth is all this about? What is the matter, my good friend?"

"Matter!—the devil's the matter—almost dislocating my neck's the matter. I'm a plain man, Sir Oliver"—no one who looked in poor Drench's face could gainsay the assertion—"I am a plain man, and I now tell you plainly, that if you do not curb that young man's propensity to mischief, some time or other he will come to be hanged! Only see what a pickle I am in!"

The last sentence was uttered in a lachrymose whine, so different from the highly-raised tone in which the former part of the invective had been pronounced, that my uncle, who had begun to bristle at hearing the lineal heir of Sir Roger de Bullwinkle consigned thus unceremoniously to the superintendence of Mr. Ketch, was immediately mollified, and his attention being thus pointedly attracted to the rueful appearance exhibited by the doctor, his anger was forthwith subdued. Dr. Drench was a little punchy figure of a man, standing about five feet nothing, plump and round as a pill; he was placed opposite to Sir Oliver, dilating his height to the very utmost, and if he did not on this occasion add a cubit to his stature, it was manifestly from sheer inability, and not from any want of inclination; his snuff-colored coat, black-silk waistcoat, kerseymeres, and "continuations," no longer boasted that unsullied purity, in all the pride of which they had quitted Underdown Hall not half an hour before; a thick incrustation of dark blue mud, agreeably relieved by spots of the most vivid crimson, now covered them with plastic tenacity, rendering their original tints scarcely discernible by the most microscopic eye. Nor had the visage of the unfortunate gentleman escaped much better, since, but for the sanguine current which flowed down the lower part of his face in a double stream, he might not unaptly have been compared to the "Man with the Iron Mask," so completely had the aforesaid incrustation adapted itself to the contour of his features.

If Pope's assertion be correct, when, following Ariosto, he pronounces that all things lost on earth are treasured in the moon, the doctor's well-brushed beaver was, in all probability, by this time safely laid up in that poetical repository of missing chattels, for below it was unquestionably nowhere to be found: its place, however, was supplied by a cap of the same adhesive material as that which decorated his face and habiliments, affording strong presumptive evidence that whatever portion of his person had first emerged from the ditch he had so lately evacuated, his head had at all events taken precedence on his entry into it. His pigtail, too—that darling object of his fondest affection, to guard whose sacred hairs from the remotest chance of violation, he had so reluctantly declined the Baronet's proffered cheer—stood forth no longer a splendid specimen of the skill of Humphrey Williams, sole *friseur* to the village of Underdown, but now exhibited indeed but a melancholy resemblance to the real appendage of that unclean animal from which it had metaphorically derived its designation.

Rueful, indeed, was the appearance of the worthy disciple of Galen, as he underwent the scrutinizing gaze of Sir Oliver, who found it very convenient at the same time to have recourse to a family snuff-box which he usually carried about his person. In this mode of proceeding he was imitated by the captain, who now for the first time broke silence to request the favor of a pinch from the well-known *tabatiere*, after which a more specific inquiry was instituted into the predisposing and proximate causes of Dr. Drench's disaster.

Those causes were, alas! but too soon made manifest.

My cousin Nicholas, it seems, had encountered the doctor at the Hall door, on his return, and had stopped him to make inquiries respecting the health of his patient, whose indisposition he vehemently deplored, uttering a thousand regrets that a silly joke of his own should have produced it. For this, he declared he should never be able to forgive himself; although, as he protested, it had never entered his imagination that the trick could have been attended with consequences so alarming. Touched by his remorse, the good doctor comforted him with the information that, if nothing occurred to produce a relapse, his aunt would not, he trusted, be so serious a sufferer as he had at first feared; he then seized the opportunity to read his young penitent a short but energetic lecture on the folly and wickedness (so he expressed himself) of thus terrifying, or even inconveniencing others, merely to gratify a silly and mischievous propensity.

My cousin Nicholas listened to these well-intended and well-delivered observations, with the profoundest attention; he heaved a sigh at their conclusion, and with a becoming gravity assented to their justice, at the same time volunteering a promise that this offence should be his last. Pleased with the effect of his own oratory, and nothing doubting that the contrition of the youthful offender was, for the moment at least, sincere, Dr. Drench put one foot into the stirrup attached to his galloway, which a groom had now led out, and throwing his leg over the saddle, failed to remark that his proselyte had taken the opportunity afforded by his back being turned for the nonce, to introduce a large thistle beneath the tail of the quadruped on whose back he had now attained so perilous an elevation.

The effect was obvious and immediate: utterly unaccustomed to any application of a similar description, and highly resenting the indignity thus offered to his person, Punch, as sober a gelding as any in the three kingdoms, instantly evinced his sense of the degradation to which he had been subjected, by violent and repeated calcitrations, of no common altitude, and distributed in every possible direction. Becoming every moment more eager to relieve himself from so disgraceful and inconvenient an adjunct as that which now encumbered and annoyed his rear, he at length took the resolution of starting off at score, and soon deviated so much from his usually rectilinear mode of progression as to convey his hapless rider to the edge of a large sewer, into which all the filth and drainings of the Hall stables, together with other not less noisome concomitants, eventually flowed. Here, on the very brink of this abyss, an unlucky curvet, describing an angle of forty-five degrees, dismounted the hapless equestrian, and precipitated him head-foremost into the centre of the "vast profound."

But for the groom, who had brought the doctor his horse, and who had witnessed the whole of the foregoing scene, poor Dr. Drench would probably have encountered a fate compared with which, the not altogether dissimilar end of the "Young princes murther'd in the Tower" might have been esteemed a merciful dispensation; since, whether we subscribe to Walpole's "Doubts" or not, there is no reason to imagine that the means employed for the suffocation of the royal innocents was attended by that "rank compound of villainous smells" which served, in the present case, to heighten the catastrophe. By his assistance the sufferer was, with some difficulty, extricated from the imminent peril into which he had been plunged, and was reconducted to the Hall, whither he once more repaired for the double purpose of complaint and depuriation.

These particulars were, not without some little trouble, at length collected from the soiled lips of the indignant doctor, and confirmed by the supplementary attestation of the servant who had observed the transaction, and whose levity in giving his evidence—the fellow absolutely grinned—drew down upon him a well-merited rebuke from the court. A summons was instantly dispatched, commanding the immediate attendance of the accused; but my cousin Nicholas was at this precise moment nowhere to be found.

That considerate young gentleman, on witnessing the "Descent of Drench," being well aware that liberty unexpectedly recovered is, in nine instances out of ten, abused, and most apt to degenerate into licentiousness, hastily followed the enfranchised steed, with a view to prevent any mischief which might accrue to himself or others from this his sudden manumission. The end of the avenue, which opened on the high-road near to the entrance of the village of Underdown, presented a formidable barrier to the further progress of the liberated nag, in the shape of a lofty gate, flanked on each side by a thick plantation of evergreens. To leap it was out of the question, as poor Punch held fox-hunting in utter abomination, and had never cleared any thing more formidable than a gutter in his life; to escape on either side was impossible—the shrubs were absolutely impervious; so, having discovered during a moment of hesitation, what the headlong precipitation of his flight had hitherto prevented him from perceiving, namely, that he had long since got rid of his old tormentor, the thistle—all these considerations, joined with the recollection that he had neither galloped so long nor so fast at any one time during the last fourteen years, induced the philosophic Punch to await quietly my cousin's approach, and once more to surrender his newly-acquired freedom without making a single struggle to retain it.

Having thus possessed himself of a horse, my cousin Nicholas thought he would take a ride.

Many reasons concurred to render his availing himself of the opportunity particularly advisable; in the first place, horse-exercise is strongly recommended by the faculty, and has a tendency toward bracing the nerves; then, it happened to be a remarkably fine day; inclination prompted, opportunity courted him, and he was, moreover, morally certain, from the situation in which he had last beheld him, that the owner of his Pegasus stood in no sort of need of him at present; in addition to all which, an undefined suspicion had by this time entered my cousin's head, that certain disputatious bickerings might, by possibility, arise at the Hall out of the circumstances which had so lately taken place, and that a controversy might ensue, in which he might find himself personally involved to an extent somewhat greater than would be altogether pleasant to his feelings. Now, my cousin Nicholas hated argument and squabbling about trifles, nor was he ever known to enjoy a joke at his own expense.

Any of these motives, if taken separately, would have been sufficient: there was no resisting them all in combination; so my cousin cantered away, and, having a pretty taste enough for the picturesque, was highly delighted by several charming prospects of the surrounding country which he encountered in the course of his ride. So much, indeed, did they engross his attention, that time slipped away unheeded, and he did not reach Underdown Hall, on his return, till long after the hour which had dismissed the doctor to his own "Sweet Home," as well scoured, scrubbed, and scraped, as if he had gone through a regular course of brick-dust, sand, and emery paper.

THE DEVIL AND DR. BUCKLAND.

ANONYMOUS.

As Buckland was boring for quartz and feldspar,
And lignite in Pevensey level,
The downward geologist ventured too far,
And struck the red tiles of the Devil.

"How now?" quoth the demon, aroused by the shock,
You've broken my vitrified casement;
My pavement *Mosaic* was primitive rock,
Till you came to batter its basement.

"Hie elsewhere, and dig for your stratified stuff,
Your laminate, yellow, and blue;
Your miocene, pliocene, gypsum, and stuff,
Or I'll soon make a fossil of you.

"Don't stand with your hammer there, tapping about;
Learn, mortal, to quake at my power!
Know then, that I'm Beelzebub, roaming about,
Intent upon whom to devour!"

"Come, come," quoth the other, "this vaporing smother,
Your pepper is rather too strong;
Your horns and your hoofs are infallible proofs
Of the genus to which you belong.

"I feel not a jot of alarm for myself,
I go from your appetite free;
For, ruminant, mild, graminivorous elf,
I know that you can't devour *me*."

ECCENTRICITIES OF THE EARL OF BRIDGEWATER.

THE following account of the late eccentric nobleman who bore this title, was published in a Paris paper in October, 1826.—No one has higher claims to a distinguished place in the history of eccentricity than M. Egerton, who has for several years borne the name of Lord Bridgewater. Those who have once seen this meagre personage drag himself along, supported by two huge lacqueys, with his sugar-loaf hat slouched down over his eyes, cannot fail to recognize him. An immense fortune enables him to gratify the most extravagant caprices that ever passed through the head of a rich Englishman. If he be lent a book, he carries his politeness so far as to send it back, or rather have it conducted home in a carriage. He gives orders that two of his most stately steeds be harnessed to one of his chariots, and the volume, reclining at ease in milord's seat arrives, attended by four footmen in costly livery, at the door of its astonished owner. His carriage is frequently to be seen filled with his dogs. He bestows great care on the feet of these dogs, and orders them boots, for which he pays as dearly as for his own. Lord Bridgewater's costume is an excellent one for the bootmaker; for besides the four feet of his dogs, the supply of his own two feet must give constant employment to several operatives. He puts on a new pair of boots every day, carefully preserving those he has once worn, and ranging them in order; he commands that none shall touch them, but himself takes great pleasure in observing how much of the year he has each day passed, by observing the state of his boots. Lord Egerton is a man of few acquaintance, and very few of his countrymen have got as far as his dining-hall. His table, however, is constantly set out with a dozen covers, and served by a suitable attendance. Who then are his privileged guests? No less than a dozen of favorite dogs, who daily partake of milord's dinner, seated very gravely in chairs, each with a napkin round his neck. These honorable quadrupeds, as if grateful for such delicate attentions, comport themselves during the time of the repast with a decency and decorum which would do more than honor to a party of gentlemen; but if, by chance, one of them should, without due consideration, obey the natural instinct of his appetite, and transgress any one of the rules of good manners, his punishment is at hand. You, perhaps, gentle reader, suppose that corporeal punishment is meant; but no—you are mistaken; 'tis in his self-love that the offender is punished. The day following the day of his offence, the dog dines, and even dines well; but not at milord's table, and as becomes a dog to dine; banished to the antechamber, and dressed in livery, he eats in sorrow the bread of shame, and picks the bone of mortification, while his place at table remains vacant till his repentance has merited a generous pardon.

THE BLESSINGS OF LIFE.

When the devil engaged with Job's patience in battle,
Tooth and nail strove to worry him out of his life,
He robb'd him of children, slaves, houses, and cattle,
But, mark me, he ne'er thought of taking his wife!

But heaven, at length, Job's forbearance rewards:
And in time double wealth, double honor arrives;
Heaven doubles his children, slaves, houses, and herds,
But we don't hear a word of a couple of wives!

A WHET BEFORE DINNER.

Too late for dinner by an hour,
The dandy enter'd—in a shower
Caught, and no coach when mostly wish'd,
The beau was, like the dinner, *dish'd.*

Mine host then, with fat capon lined,
Grinn'd and exclaim'd, "I 'spose you've dined.
Indeed, I see you took—'twas wrong—
A *whet*, sir, as you came along."

MANNERS *MAKES* THE MAN.

ANONYMOUS.

Know ye the wight one frequent meets,
With brazen lungs around the streets,
Soliciting a job?
His head in shovel-hat encased,
His legs in cotton hose embraced,
And nick-named "Dusty Bob?"

You hold in small account, no doubt,
One who "dust, ho!" doth bawl about,
Yet low as his estate,
Some philosophic thoughts belong
To him whose time is passed among
The ashes of the *grate.*

Still, these are matters all apart
From thy design, my muse, who art
Just now intent to tell
An episode of humble life,
That was with courtly manners rife,
And thus the chance befell.

"The rosy morn, with blushes spread,
Now rose from out Tithonus' bed,"
Which means, the world had set
(For these are unromantic days)
About its work, and gone its ways,
Forthwith to toil and sweat.

Among the many that arise,
To pay their morning sacrifice,
That is, to Juggernaut
Themselves beneath Aurora's car,
With Pagan zeal your dustmen are
Beyond all others fraught.

In sooth, to speak, we would not choose
To state these fellows *ever* snooze,
For bitter as the bore is,
Nor night, nor morn, in square or street,
Can one go forth, but he must meet,
These grim "*memento moris.*"

But to my tale: at break of day,
Up rose the hero of my lay,
With hope his spirits buoy'd;
And ever as he fill'd his cart,
He felt a space beneath his heart
Establishing a void.

Loud and more loud the murmurs rise,
Like an Æolian harp, whose sighs
At first breathe gently; but
Wild music from its bosom springs,
When the wind howls among the strings,
And agitates the gut.

Though Bob knew nought of Æolus,
He learnt, from this internal fuss,
'Twas time for breakfast now:
Or, as he said, "for bit and sup,
His innerds was a kicking up
Sich a unkimmon row."

'Twas thus intent on *dejeuner*,
Our hungry dustman took his way,
In search of fitting food:
Nor long his quest, until he came,
Where a spruce, gay, and buxom dame,
Behind a counter stood.

And, as with horny fist he smoothed his hair,
He thus bespoke that lady debonaire:
"Cut us a slap up slice of Cheshire cheese,
And tip's a twopenny burster, if you please."
Here, 'tis befitting to relate the guise,
In which Bob met the gentle lady's eyes.
A poll with matted carrots thatched,
A face with mud and smut bepatched,
A neck and chest scarce half begirt
With a lugubrious, yellow shirt,
A slip of waistcoat here and there,
Breeches, a demi-semi pair,
And not a vestige of a coat—
Such was our earthly *sans culotte.*

When such an apparition met her view,
What was most natural the dame should do?
Straightway address her dainty self,
To seek the treasures of her shelf?
Or clap some musty, antiquated crust,
Between the fingers of the man of dust?

The latter, doubtless, and it so fell out,
Turning, with ill-dissembled scorn, about,
The lady-baker hardly deigned to drop
Into his palm the patriarch of the shop;
A venerable roll, a fixture there—
A household nest-egg of the *boulangère.*

Here a domestic mouse had, long ago
(Soon after it was dough),
Wreathed him, as Thomas Moore would say,
"his bower"
Among the *flower;*
And happened, accidentally, to be
Chez lui,
When madame put the piece of antique bread
Into our dustman's hand, as hath been said.

Now, let me ask, had Chesterfield been placed,
What time his chyle with exercise was braced,
To make his meal from off a living mess,
D'ye think my Lord had kept his *politesse?*
Or acted, as did Bob, the man of dirt,
Who, on the instant that he did insert
His thumb and finger in that roll so stale,
Pull'd out the squeaking vermin by the tail;
And seeing that the bak'ress looked aghast
Upon the means she gave to break his fast—
Blandly observed, "There's some mistake in this,
I didn't ax you for a sandwich, Miss!"

BONAPARTE AT MISS FROUNCE'S SCHOOL.

BY GILBERT A. A'BECKETT.

THE mind of infancy is said to resemble wax, and certainly, from its excessive softness, there is reason in the simile. The impressions made upon children by public events are very curious, and warrant us in looking back upon boyhood as one of the very greenest spots of our existence. In the following chapter will be found a few JUVENILE REMINISCENCES OF THE WAR WITH FRANCE AND BONAPARTE.

During the very stirring events that were taking place on the Continent of Europe in the early part of the present century, my father, who was a respectable attorney, thought it prudent to place me at a preparatory school near Kensington. While Pitt was boldly contending against the revolutionary mania of France, I was engaged in a laborious contest with the difficulties of Lindley Murray. It was almost on the very day of Badajoz being taken, that I succeeded in mastering the last chapter of the Mother's Catechism; and the same post that brought news of Wellington having forced the enemy's lines, and secured his colors, gave intelligence of my having carried off the silver pen in triumph, as a prize for writing against my schoolfellows.

While Napoleon Bonaparte was taking lessons in the art of war, I was struggling in an establishment for "young gentlemen from three to eight," against being drenched from the Pierian spring, whose water is laid on to the youthful mind at the rate of about thirty guineas *per* annum. When the illustrious Wellington forced the enemy to lay down his arms, I had surrendered the customary spoon, fork, and six towels into the hands of my schoolmistress. I have no doubt the warlike character of the times in which she lived had impressed itself on her nature, for she was greatly addicted to the system of flogging, which is one of the necessary features of a military era. Often has the word been given to "march up" into the bedroom of the lady who presided over the school, and frequently have I obeyed the summons, when the birch, or a busk from the stays of my instructress, has expiated some piece of juvenile delinquency. In vain were the words "I will be good," reiterated amid screams and tears; for, until the avenging rod or the vindicatory whalebone—as the case might be—had done its office, it was hopeless to try to stay the hand of Miss Frounce, who took in young gentlemen from three to eight—and, ten to one, took in their parents also.

But while I am dwelling on the memory of the proceedings in the Hammersmith Road, I am forgetting the stirring events that were taking place on the Continent. Bonaparte had just escaped from Elba, and Miss Frounce, like an admirable politician, took advantage of this important event to overawe the "young gentlemen from three to eight" who were under her guidance. On all occasions, Bonaparte was held up as the great bugbear, and there was not a boy in the school who was not firmly convinced that Miss Frounce had Napoleon under her thumb—that, in fact, if any of "the young gentlemen" should prove refractory, Miss Frounce had it in her power to send for Bony with as much facility as she could order the sweeps or the dustman. If a boy, when spelling, knocked an *i* out of the word annihilate, he was threatened with being handed over to the tender mercies of Bonaparte; and every one of the pupils of Miss Frounce felt assured that, if Napoleon invaded England, he would knock at the door of the "establishment for young gentleman from three to eight" the very morning after his arrival.

MISS FROUNCE AND THE BOY.

Whatever might have been his feeling of hostility towards the Prince of Wales, or the members of the cabinet, my firm conviction was, that Master Snodgrass, who had been turned back in grammar, had much more to apprehend from Napoleon than the Regent and the ministers. Sometimes have I contemplated the possibility of hiding in case of the dreaded visit; but then it has flashed upon my juvenile mind that Bonaparte was not to be baffled, and that he would inevitably look under all the beds in the house, rather than be foiled in the vengeance which the "young gentlemen from three to eight" were convinced inspired him.

Never shall I forget the panic that seized on "all the boys" when the fact was announced that a leg of mutton had been stolen from the larder. Who could be the thief? Why, of course, nobody but Bonaparte. Miss Frounce, wishing to enhance the intimidating reputation of her great bugbear, favored the idea, and the whole of the "young gentlemen from three to eight" were under the firm impression that Bonaparte had landed in England during the night, secured the leg of mutton, and retreated before daylight into the bosom of his own army.

Such impressions as those I have related are strange and absurd; but there are many now living who, if they happened, during the time of the Bonaparte panic, to be inmates of a preparatory school for "young gentlemen from three to eight," will recognize the fidelity of the feelings I hav- described.

I never ate the lollipop which went by the name of his ribs, without being awed by a sort of unaccountable fear that Bonaparte might yet break from his captivity, and pay me off personally for the indignity offered him in purchasing a hap'orth of his anatomy, and sucking it, like Tom Trot or Everton Toffee.

SELECTIONS FROM "THE COMIC BLACKSTONE."

BY GILBERT A. A'BECKETT.

OF FELONIES INJURIOUS TO THE KING'S PREROGATIVE.

THE periodical lexicographers have puzzled themselves and each other as well as us, about the derivation of the word felony. As they all make different suggestions, we decline adopting any, and throw out on our own account the notion that felon is a corruption of fee-long, because a long fee is necessary to get up a defence for felony. This definition is, doubtless, far fetched, but not so far fetched as that of some of the legal antiquarians, who have travelled into Greece to get the word φηλος, an impostor, as the origin of the word alluded to. Our own suggestion we consider the best, because felony is on all hands allowed to be a crime involving a loss of property: and the fee-long or long fee certainly implies an enormous sacrifice of assets. The felonies against the king's prerogatives are six, which we shall briefly specify.

1st. Offences relating to the coin, which were formerly so severely dealt with that it was almost death to be found with a bad halfpenny in one's pocket, and to utter a suspicious sixpence was regarded as a piece of unutterable villany. All previous statutes have however been repealed by the act of William the 4th; and thanks to this measure, followed by that of the 1st of Victoria, the law now lies in a nutshell. We however always observe, that though the law does lie in a nutshell, it requires a good deal of jaw, and a long crack over it, before it is comeatable.

By the new Act it is an offence to manufacture coin, but there is no harm in making money; and it is also criminal to utter a white-washed halfpenny for a halfcrown, which would be a very desperate trick, for the uttering would probably turn out an utter failure. Having false money in your possession, with intent to utter, it is likewise a misdemeanor; but it is a minor offence for a singer to have a false note in his chest, and to utter it before an audience.

2d. Felonies against the king's council, which formerly included assaulting a privy councillor by a blow or even a kick; but these kicks are now on the footing of common assaults, and attempts to kill are felonies without any distinction as to the rank, except in the case of royalty, of the intended victim.

3d. Serving foreign states was formerly a felony, except, says Coke, "serving them out, which was always allowable." The statutes on this subject are now repealed, and any one may now enlist in the Kamtschatkan Grays, the Sandwich Island Buffs, or any other outlandish regiment, if he first provides himself with a royal license.

4th. Felony by embezzling the sovereign's stores, or rather his warlike stores; for if I go to his store closet, and steal a lump of his sugar, it is not felony under the statute. To set on fire any of the royal dock-yards or ships is a crime still punishable with death; and it is also arson to burn an arsenal.

5th. Desertion in time of war, by sea or land, is a felony, and in peace it is a grave offence; so that the sentinels in the park must not desert their posts to run after refractory boys who may irritate the military to any extent, by keeping just beyond the verge of the promenade to which the soldiery are limited. Endeavoring to seduce him from his allegiance is punishable with transportation or imprisonment, and holding a pot of beer up as a temptation to draw him off his beat, is probably within the statute.

6th. Administering oaths for a seditious purpose is felony punishable with transportation; but administering oaths indiscriminately when in a state of intoxication, to any one who happens to pass by, is only punishable with a fine of five shillings.

OF PRINCIPALS AND ACCESSORIES.

CRIMINALS are either principals or accessories; as, in a dramatic murder, the principal is he who enacts *Macbeth*, while the accessories are they who give him his cues, and otherwise aid or abet him. It is even doubtful whether the barber who dresses his wig is not an accessory before the fact, while the critic who praises his performance is clearly an accessory after it.

In some offences there are no accessories, but all are principals; and in the sort of murder we have just alluded to, all would no doubt wish to be. In high treason all are principals, because the offence is so great; and in trespass all are principals, because *de minimis non curat lex*, or in other words, because the offence is so little. Very small criminals are pounced upon all in a lump, and the law crushes them beneath its foot as an elephant would an ant-hill. *De minimis non curat legs* would be in each case appropriate. An accessory before the fact is one who causes the commission of a crime, and though he has suggested one crime, he may be accessory to another; as, if A orders B to shoot Titius, and B, instead of shooting Titius, gives him some British brandy, of which Titius dies, then A is accessory to the poisoning, and may be punished —like all accessories before the fact—in the same manner as the principal. Accessories after the fact are such as relieve or harbor a felon, knowing him to have committed a felony; or buy stolen goods, knowing them to be stolen. The purchaser of modern music is an accessory after the fact to a theft on the part of the composer, who has stolen the ideas of others. By the French law, receivers of stolen goods were punished with death, a law which, if put in force in this country, would have decimated Field Lane, and utterly depopulated the greater part of the Minories. Accessories before the fact are in most cases punished in the same way as principals, and it is very clear that in the case of *the crown on the prosecution of Banquo against Macbeth and wife*, the latter, though only an accessory before the fact, deserved as severe a punishment as her husband. In the case of *Friar Lawrence re Romeo on the demise of Paris*, the friar was only an accessory after the fact, and therefore in harboring and assisting Romeo he would, by the present law, have only rendered himself liable to two years' imprisonment.

A DEBT is a sum of money due; but, as we are not anxious to go very deeply into debt, we shall not attempt a minute description of what every one must be more or less acquainted with. An action of debt can only be brought for a specified sum; and if I claim 30*l*. I must not prove a debt of 20*l*., any more than I could recover an ox by an action of detinue if I claimed a horse; though it is certain that I might recover a pair of ducks if I claimed a pair of white trowsers.

A COVENANT is an obligation contained in a deed, to do or omit a certain act; as, if a man covenants, to go to Bath, he must either go to Bath, or be liable to a writ of covenant, which will plunge him into hot water. A promise is a sort of verbal covenant; as, if a builder undertakes to build Caius a pigsty by a certain day, and the pigs of Caius catch cold and die, because the sty is not completed, then the law not only takes the sty into its eye, but the pigs also, and will give damage to Caius for the injury he has sustained by the neglect of the builder.

OF OFFENCES AGAINST PUBLIC TRADE.

SMUGGLING is an offence against public trade; but it is so frequently practised by the fair sex, that it has been held to be a fair proceeding if it can be managed without detection.

Another offence of this class is fraudulent bankruptcy, like that of Antonio, the Venetian bankrupt, who having made an alarming failure and a terrific sacrifice of his friend, was compelled to take the benefit of the (fifth) act of the *Merchant of Venice*. Usury was formerly highly penal; but it may now be practised almost without restriction; for the law says, to protect yourself against usury, you must use—your—eye—and keep a good look-out after your own interest. Cheating is an offence against trade, which is very commonly practised; "for it is wonderful," says Roger Bacon, "how much lighter a pound of sugar becomes in your own scales;" and, indeed, the ingenuity of the tradesman is chiefly shown in attaching an undue weight to trifles.

Forestalling the market is an offence at common law; as if I were to waylay a cart full of turnips going towards Covent Garden and purchase them all, I should probably send turnips up to a frightful premium, by forestalling the market.

These are all the offences against trade which the law at present punishes; though perhaps the most serious offence against trade is the very ordinary one of getting into a tradesman's books without the smallest intention of paying him.

Rusticus wrote a letter to his love,
And filled it full of warm and keen desire;
He hoped to raise a flame, and so he did,
The lady put his nonsense in the fire.

MY CHRISTMAS DINNER.

ANONYMOUS.

It was on the twentieth of December last that I received an invitation from my friend, Mr. Phiggins, to dine with him in Mark Lane, on Christmay day. I had several reasons for declining this proposition. The first was that Mr. P. makes it a rule, at all these festivals, to empty the entire contents of his counting house into his little dining parlor; and you consequently sit down to dinner with six white-waistcoated clerks, let loose upon a turkey. The second was, that I am not sufficiently well read in cotton and sugar, to enter with any spirit into the subject of conversation. And the third was, and is, that I never drink Cape wine. But by far the most prevailing reason remains to be told. I had been anticipating for some days, and was hourly in the hope of receiving, an invitation to spend my

Christmas day in a most irresistible quarter. I was expecting, indeed, the felicity of eating plum-pudding with an angel; and, on the strength of my imaginary engagement, I returned a polite note to Mr. P., reducing him to the necessity of advertising for another candidate for Cape and turkey.

The twenty-first came. Another invitation—to dine with a regiment of roast-beef eaters at Clapham. I declined this also, for the above reason, and for one other, *viz.*, that, on dining there ten Christmas days ago, it was discovered, on sitting down, that one little accompaniment of the roast beef had been entirely overlooked. Would it be believed!—but I will not stay to mystify—I merely mention the fact. They had forgotten the horse-radish.

The next day arrived, and with it a neat epistle, sealed with violet-colored wax, from Upper Brook Street. "Dine with the ladies—at home on Christmas day." Very tempting, it is true; but not exactly the letter I was longing for. I began, however, to debate within myself upon the policy of securing this bird in hand, instead of waiting for the two that were still hopping about the bush, when the consultation was suddenly brought to a close, by a prophetic view of the portfolio of drawings fresh from boarding-school—moths and roses on embossed paper;—to say nothing of the album, in which I stood engaged to write an elegy on a Java sparrow, that had been a favorite in the family for three days. I rung for gilt-edged, pleaded a world of polite regret, and again declined.

The twenty-third dawned; time was getting on rather rapidly; but no card came. I began to despair of any more invitations, and to repent of my refusals. Breakfast was hardly over, however, when the servant brought up—not a letter—but an aunt and a brace of cousins from Bayswater. They would listen to no excuse; consanguinity required me, and Christmas was not my own. Now my cousins kept no albums; they are really as pretty as cousins can be; and when violent hands, with white kid gloves, are laid on one, it is sometimes difficult to effect an escape with becoming elegance. I could not, however, give up my darling hope of a pleasanter prospect. They fought with me in fifty engagements—that I pretended to have made. I showed them the Court Guide, with ten names obliterated—being those of persons who had *not* asked me to mince-meat and mistletoe; and I ultimately gained my cause by quartering the remains of an infectious fever on the sensitive fears of my aunt, and by dividing a rheumatism and a sprained ankle between my sympathetic cousins.

As soon as they were gone, I walked out, sauntering involuntarily in the direction of the only house in which I felt I could spend a "happy" Christmas. As I approached, a porter brought a large hamper to the door. "A present from the country," thought I; "yes, they *do* dine at home; they must ask me; they know that I am in town." Immediately afterwards, a servant issued with a letter: he took the nearest way to my lodgings, and I hurried back by another street to receive the so-much-wished-for invitation. I was in a state of delirious delight.

I arrived—but there was no letter. I sat down to wait, in a spirit of calmer enjoyment than I had experienced for some days; and in less than half an hour a note was brought to me. At length, the desired despatch had come: it seemed written on the leaf of a lily with a pen dipped in dew. I opened it—and had nearly fainted with disappointment. It was from a stock-broker, who begins an anecdote of Mr. Rothschild before dinner, and finishes it with the fourth bottle—and who makes his eight children stay up to supper and snap-dragon. In Macadamizing a stray stone in one of his periodical puddings, I once lost a tooth, and with it an heiress of some reputation. I wrote a most irritable apology, and despatched my warmest regards in a whirlwind.

December the twenty-fourth—I began to count the hours, and uttered many poetical things about the wings of Time. Alack! no letter came;—yes, I received a note from a distinguished dramatist, requesting the honor, etc. But I was too cunning for this, and practised wisdom for once. I happened to reflect that his pantomime was to make its appearance on the night after, and that his object was to perpetrate the whole programme upon me. Regret that I could not have the pleasure of meeting Mr. Paulo, and the rest of the *literati* to be then and there assembled, was of course immediately expressed.

My mind became restless and agitated. I felt, amidst all these invitations, cruelly neglected. They served, indeed, but to increase my uneasiness, as they opened prospects of happiness in which I could take no share. They discovered a most tempting dessert, composed of forbidden fruit. I took down "Childe Harold," and read myself into a sublime contempt of mankind. I began to perceive that merriment is only malice in disguise, and that the chief cardinal virtue is misanthropy.

I sat "nursing my wrath," till it scorched me; when the arrival of another epistle suddenly charmed me from this state of delicious melancholy and delightful endurance of wrong. I sickened as I surveyed, and trembled as I opened it. It was dated ——, but no matter; it was not *the* letter. In such a frenzy as mine, raging to behold the object of my admiration condescend, not to *eat* a custard, but to render it invisible—to be invited perhaps to a tart fabricated by her own ethereal fingers; with such possibilities before me, how could I think of joining a "friendly party,"—where I should inevitably sit next to a deaf lady, who had been, when a little girl, patted on the head by Wilkes, or my Lord North, she could not recollect which—had taken tea with the author of "Junius," but had forgotten his name—and who once asked me "whether Mr. Munden's monument was in Westminster Abbey or St. Paul's?"—I seized a pen, and presented my compliments. I hesitated—for the peril and precariousness of my situation flashed on my mind; but hope had still left me a straw to catch at, and I at length succeeded in resisting this late and terrible temptation.

After the first burst of excitement, I sunk into still deeper despondency. My spirit became a prey to anxiety and remorse. I could not eat; dinner was removed with unlifted covers. I went out. The world seemed to have acquired a new face; nothing was to be seen but raisins and rounds of beef. I wandered about like Lear—I had given up all! I felt myself grated against the world like a nutmeg. It grew dark— I sustained a still gloomier shock. Every chance seemed to have expired, and every-body seemed to have a delightful engagement for the next day. I alone was disengaged—I felt like the Last Man! To-morrow appeared to have already commenced its career; mankind had anticipated the future; "and coming mince pies cast their shadows before."

In this state of desolation and dismay, I called—I could not help it— at the house to which I had so fondly anticipated an invitation, and a welcome. My protest must here however be recorded, that though I called in the hope of being asked, it was my fixed determination not to avail myself of so protracted a piece of politeness. No: my triumph would have been to have annihilated them with an engagement made in September, payable three months after date. With these feelings, I gave an agitated knock—they were stoning the plums, and did not immediately attend. I rung—how unlike a dinner bell it sounded! A girl at length made her appearance, and, with a mouthful of citron, informed me that the family had gone to spend their Christmas-eve in Portland Place. I rushed down the steps, I hardly knew whither. My first impulse was to go to some wharf and inquire what vessels were starting for America. But it was a cold night—I went home and threw myself on my miserable couch. In other words, I went to bed.

I dozed and dreamed away the hours till daybreak. Sometimes I fancied myself seated in a roaring circle, roasting chestnuts at a blazing log: at others, that I had fallen into the Serpentine while skating, and that the Humane Society were piling upon me a Pelion, or rather a Vesuvius of blankets. I awoke a little refreshed. Alas! it was the twenty-fifth of the month—It was Christmas day! Let the reader, if he possess the imagination of Milton, conceive my sensations.

I swallowed an atom of dry toast—nothing could calm the fever of my soul. I stirred the fire and read Zimmermann alternately. Even reason—the last remedy one has recourse to in such cases—came at length to my relief: I argued myself into a philosophic fit. But, unluckily, just as the Lethean tide within me was at its height, my landlady broke in upon my lethargy, and chased away by a single word all the little sprites and pleasures that were acting as my physicians, and prescribing balm for my wounds. She paid me the usual compliment, and then—"Do you dine at home to-day, sir?" abruptly inquired she. Here was a question. No Spanish inquisitor ever inflicted such complete dismay in so short a sentence. Had she given me a Sphynx to expound, a Gordian tangle to untwist; had she set me a lesson in algebra, or asked me the way to Brobdignag; had she desired me to show her the North Pole, or the meaning of a melodrama:—any or all of these I might have accomplished. But to request me to define my dinner—to inquire into its latitude—to compel me to fathom that sea of appetite which I now felt rushing through my frame—to ask me to dive into futurity, and become the prophet of pies and preserves!—My heart died within me at the impossibility of a reply.

She had repeated the question before I could collect my senses around me. Then, for the first time it occurred to me that, in the event of my having no engagement abroad, my landlady meant to invite me! "There will at least be the two daughters," I whispered to myself; "and after all, Lucy Matthews is a charming girl, and touches the harp divinely. She has a very small, pretty hand, I recollect; only her fingers are so punctured by the needle—and I rather think she bites her nails. No, I will not even now give up my hope. It was yesterday but a straw—to-day it is but the thistledown; but I will cling to it to the last moment. There are still four hours left; they will not dine till six. One desperate struggle, and the peril is past; let me not be seduced by this last golden apple, and I may yet win my race." The struggle was made—"I should not dine at home." This was the only phrase left me; for I could not say that "I should dine out." Alas! that an event should be at the same time so doubtful and so desirable. I only begged that if any letter arrived, it might be brought to me immediately.

The last plank, the last splinter, had now given way beneath me. I was floating about with no hope but the chance of something almost impossible. They had "left me alone," not with my glory, but with an appetite that resembled an avalanche seeking whom it might devour. I had passed one dinnerless day, and half of another; yet the promised land was as far from sight as ever. I recounted the chances I had missed. The dinners I might have enjoyed, passed in a dioramic view before my eyes. Mr. Phiggins and his six clerks—the Clapham beef-eaters—the charms of Upper Brook street—my pretty cousins, and the pantomime writer—the stock-broker, whose stories one forgets, and the elderly lady who forgets her stories—they all marched by me, a procession of apparitions. Even my landlady's invitation, though unborn, was not forgotten in summing up my sacrifices. And for what?

Four o'clock. Hope was perfectly ridiculous. I had been walking upon the hair-bridge over a gulf, and could not get into Elysium after all. I had been catching moonbeams, and running after notes of music. Despair was my only convenient refuge; no chance remained, unless something should drop from the clouds. In this last particular I was not disappointed; for, on looking up, I perceived a heavy shower of snow. Yet I was obliged to venture forth; for being supposed to dine out, I could not of course remain at home. Where to go I knew not: I was like my first father—"the world was all before me." I flung my cloak round me, and hurried forth with the feelings of a bandit longing for a stiletto. At the foot of the stairs, I staggered against two or three smiling rascals, priding themselves upon their punctuality. They had just arrived—to make the tour of Turkey. How I hated them! —As I rushed by the parlor, a single glance disclosed to me a blazing fire, with Lucy and several lovely creatures in a semi-circle. Fancy, too, gave me a glimpse of a sprig of mistletoe—I vanished from the house, like a spectre at day-break.

How long I wandered about is doubtful. At last I happened to look through a kitchen window, with an area in front, and saw a villain with a fork in his hand, throwing himself back in his chair choked with ecstasy. Another was feasting with a graver air; he seemed to be swallowing a bit of Paradise, and criticising its flavor. This was too much for mortality—my appetite fastened upon me like an alligator. I darted from the spot; and only a few yards further discerned a house, with rather an elegant exterior, and with some ham in the window that looked perfectly sublime. There was no time for consideration—to hesitate was to perish. I entered; it was indeed "a banquet-hall deserted." The very waiters had gone home to their friends. There, however, I found a fire; and there—to sum up all my folly and felicity in a single word—I DINED.

an everlastin' hurry, drivin' away like one ravin' distracted mad?' 'A sick visit,' says he; 'poor Pat Lanigan, him that you mind to Bradore Lake; well, he's near about at the pint of death.' 'I guess not' said I, 'for I jist hear tell he was dead.' Well, that brought him up all standin', and he bouts ship in a jiffy, and walks a little way with me, and we

got a talkin' about this very subject. Says he, 'What are you, Mr. Slick?' Well, I looks up to him, and winks, 'a Clockmaker,' says I; well, he smiled, and says he, 'I see,' as much as to say I hadn't ought to have axed that are question at all, I guess, for every man's religion is his own, and nobody else's business. 'Then,' says he, 'you know all about this country—who does folks say has the best of the dispute?' Says I, 'Father John,' 'it's like the battles up to Canada lines last war, each side claims victory; I guess there ain't much to brag on nary way, damage done on both sides, and nothin' gained, as far as I can learn.' He stopt short and looked me in the face, and says he, 'Mr. Slick, you are a man that has see'd a good deal of the world, and a considerable of an understandin' man, and I guess I *can* talk to *you.* Now,' says he, 'for gracious sake, do jist look here, and see how you heretics (Protestants I mean,' says he,—for I guess that are word slipt out without leave), are by the ears, a drivin' away at each other, the whole blessed time, tooth and nail, hip and thigh, hammer and tongs, disputin', revilin', wranglin', and beloutin' each other, with all sorts of ugly names that they can lay their tongues to. Is that the way you love your neighbor as yourself? *We say this is a practical comment on schism*, and by the powers of Moll Kelly, said he, but they all ought to be well lambasted together, the whole batch on 'em entirely.' Says I, 'Father John, give me your hand; there are some things I guess you and I don't agree on, and most likely never will, seein that you are a Popish priest; but in that idee I do opinionate with you, and I wish, with all my heart, all the world thought with us.'

"I guess he didn't half like that are word, Popish priest, it seemed to grig him, like; his face looked kinder ryled, like well-water arter a heavy rain; and said he, 'Mr. Slick,' says he, 'your country is a free country, ain't it?' 'The freest,' says I, 'on the face of the airth—you can't ditto it nowhere. We are as free as the air, and when our dander's up, stronger than any hurricane you ever see'd—tear up all creation most; there ain't the beat of it to be found anywhere.' 'Do you call this a free country?' said he. 'Pretty considerable middlin',' says I, 'seein' that they are under a king.' 'Well,' says he, 'if you were seen in Connecticut shaking hands along with a Popish priest, as you are pleased to call me (and he made me a bow, as much as to say, mind your trumps the next deal), as you now are in the streets of Halifax along with me, with all your crackin' and boastin' of your freedom, I guess you wouldn't sell a clock agin in that State for one while,'—and he bid me good mornin', and turned away. 'Father John,' says I.—'I can't stop,' says he;' I must see that poor critter's family; they must be in great trouble, and sick visit is afore controversy in my creed.' 'Well,' says I, 'one word with you afore you go; if that are name Popish priest was an ongenteel one, I ax your pardon; I didn't mean no offence, I do assure you, and I'll say this for your satisfaction, tu; you're the first man in this Province that ever gave me a real right down complete checkmate since I first sot foot in it, I'll be skinned if you ain't.'"

ITALIAN PAINTINGS.

"In the latter eend of the year twenty-eight, I think it was, if my memory sarves me, I was in my little back studio to Slickville, with off coat, apron on, and sleeves up, as busy as a bee, abronzin' and gildin' of a clock case, when old Snow, the nigger-help, popped in his head in a most terrible of a conflustrigation, and says he, 'master,' says he, 'if there ain't massa Governor and the Gineral at the door, as I'm alive! what on airth shall I say?' 'Well,' says I, 'they have caught me at a nonplush, that's sartain; but there's no help for it, as I see—shew 'em in.' 'Mornin',' says I, 'gentlemen, how do you do? I am sorry,' says I, 'I didn't know of this pleasure in time to have received you respectfully. You have taken me at a short, that's a fact; and the worst of it is,—I can't shake hands along with you neither, for one hand, you see, is covered with ile, and t'other with copper bronze..' 'Don't mention it, Mr. Slick,' said his excellency, 'I beg of you;—the fine arts do sometimes require detergants, and there is no help for it. But that's a most a beautiful thing,' said he, 'you are adoin' of; may I presume to chatichise what it is!' 'Why,' said I, 'governor, that landscape on the right, with the great white two-story house in it, havin' a washin' tub of apple sarce on one side, and a cart chock full of punkin' pies on t'other, with the gold letters A. P. over it, is intended to represent this land of promise, our great country, Amerika; and the gold letters A. P. initialise it Airthly Paradise.' 'Well,' says he, 'who is that *he* one on the left?'—'I didn't intend them letters H and E to indicate he at all,' said I, 'tho' I see now they do; I guess I must alter that. That tall graceful figur',' says I, 'with wings, carryin' a long Bowie knife in his right hand, and them small winged figures in the rear, with little rifles, are angels emigratin' from heaven to this country. H and E means Heavenly Emigrants. Its alle-*go*-ry.' 'And a beautiful alle-*go*-ry it is,' said he, 'and well calculated to give foreigners a correct notion of our young growin' and great Republic. It is a fine conception that. It is worthy of West. How true to life—how much it conveys—how many chords it strikes. It addresses the heart—it's splendid.'

"'Hallo!' says I to myself, 'what's all this?' It made me look up at him. Thinks I to myself, you laid that soft sawder on pretty thick anyhow. I wonder whether you are in real right down airnest, or whether you are only arter a vote. Says he, 'Mr. Slick, it was on the subject of pictur's, we called. It's a thing I'm enthusiastic upon myself; but my official duties leave me no time to fraternize with the brush. I've been actilly six weeks adoin' of a bunch of grapes on a chair, and it's not yet done. The department of paintin' in our Atheneum,—in this risin' and flourishin' town of Slickville—is placed under the direction of the general and myself, and we propose detailing you to Italy to purchase some originals for our gallery, seein' that you are a na*tive* artist yourself, and have more practical experience than most of our citizens. There is a great aspiration among our free and enlightened youth for perfection, whether in the arts or sciences. Your expenses will be paid, and eight dollars a day while absent on this diplomacy. One thing, however, do pray remember,—don't bring any pictur's that will evoke a blush on female cheeks, or cause vartue to stand afore 'em with averted eyes or indignant looks. The statues imported last year we had to clothe, both male and female, from head to foot, for they actilly came start naked, and were right down ondecent. One of my factory ladies went into fits on seein' 'em, that lasted her a good hour: she took Jupiter for a rael human, and said she thought she had got into a bathin' room, among the men by mistake. Her narves received a heavy shock, poor critter; she said she never would forget what she see'd there the longest day she lived. So none o' your Potiphar's wives, or Susannahs, or sleepin' Venuses; such pictur's are repugnant to the high tone o' moral feelin' in this country.'

"Conceivin' an elective governor of a free and enlightened people to rank before an hereditary prince, I have given you letters of introduction to the *Eye*talian princes and the Pope, and have offered to reciprocate their attention should they visit Slickville. Farewell, my friend, farewell, and not fail to sustain the dignity of this great and enlightened nation abroad—farewell!'

"A very good man, the governor, and a genu*wine* patriot too," said Mr. Slick. "He knowed a good deal about paintin', for he was a sign painter by trade; but he often used to wade out too deep, and got over his head now and then afore he knowed it. He warn't the best o' swimmers neither, and sometimes I used to be scared to death for fear he'd go it afore he'd touch bottom ag'in. Well, off I sot in a vessel to Leghorn, and I laid out there three thousand dollars in pictur's. Rum-lookin' old cocks, them saints, some on 'em too, with their long beards, bald heads, and hard featur's, bean't they? but I got a lot of 'em of all sizes. I bought two madonnas I think they call them—beautiful little pictur's they were, too—but the child's legs were so naked and ondecent, that to please the governor and his factory galls, I had an artist to paint trowsers, and a pair of laced boots on him, and they look quite genteel now. It improved 'em amazin'ly; but the best o' the joke was those Macaroni rascals, seein' me a stranger, thought to do me nicely (most infarnal cheats them dealers, too,—walk right into you afore you know where you be). The older a pictur' was, and the more it was blacked, so you couldn't see the figur's, the more they axed for it; and they talk and jabber away about their Tittyan tints and Guido airs by the hour. 'How soft we are, ain't we?' said I. 'Catch a weasel asleep, will you? Second-hand furniture don't suit our market. We want pictur's, and not things that look a plaguy sight more like the shutters of an old smoke-house than paintin's, and I hope I may be shot if I didn't get bran new ones for half the price they asked for them rusty old veterans. Our folks were well pleased with the shipment, and I ought to be too, for I made a trifle in the discount of fifteen per cent. for coming down handsom' with the cash on the spot. Our Atheneum is worth seein' I tell you; you won't ditto it easy, I know; it's actilly a sight to behold."

SISTER SALL'S COURTSHIP.

"THERE goes one of them are everlastin' rottin' poles, in that bridge; they are no better than a trap for a critter's leg," said the Clockmaker. "They remind me of a trap Jim Munroe put his foot in one night, that near about made one leg half a yard longer than tother. I believe I told you of him, what a desperate idle feller he was—he came from Onion County in Connecticut. Well, he was courtin' Sister Sall—she was a real handsum looking gal; you scarce ever see'd a more out and out complete critter than she was—a fine figur' head, and a beautiful model of a craft as any in the state; a real clipper, and as full of fun and frolic as a kitten. Well, he fairly turned Sall's head; the more we wanted her to give him up, the more she wouldn't, and we got plaguy oneasy about it, for his character was none of the best. He was a universal favorite with the gals, and tho' he didn't behave very pretty neither, forgettin' to marry where he promised, and where he hadn't ought to have forgot, too, yet so it was, he had such an uncommon winnin' way with him, he could talk them over in no time—Sall was fairly bewitched.

"At last, father said to him one evening when he came a courtin', 'Jim,' says he, 'you'll never come to no good, if you act like old Scratch as you do; you ain't fit to come into no decent man's house, at all; and your absence would be ten times more agreeable than your company, I tell you. I won't consent to Sall's goin' to them are huskin' parties and quiltin' frolics along with you no more, on no account, for you know how Polly Brown and Nancy White ——?' 'Now don't,' says he, 'now don't, Uncle Sam; say no more about that; if you know'd all you wouldn't say it was my fault; and besides, I have turned right about, I am on t'other tack now, and the long leg, too; I am as steady as a pump bolt, now. I intend to settle myself, and take a farm.' 'Yes, yes, and you could stock it, too, by all accounts, pretty well, unless you are much misreported,' says father, 'but it won't do. I knew your father; he was our sargeant; a proper, clever and brave man he was, too; he was one of the heroes of our glorious revolution. I had a great respect for him, and I am sorry for his sake, you will act as you do; but I tell you once for all, you must give up all thoughts of Sall, now and for everlastin'. When Sall heard this, she began to nit away like mad, in a desperate hurry—she looked foolish enough, that's a fact. First she tried to bite in her breath, and look as if there was nothin' particular in the wind, then she blushed all over like scarlet fever, but she recovered that pretty soon, and then her color went and came, and came and went, till at last she grew as white as chalk, and down she fell slap off her seat on the floor, in a faintin' fit. 'I see,' says father, 'I see it now, you etarnal villain,' and he made a pull at the old fashioned sword, that always hung over the fire-place (we used to call it old Bunker, for his stories always begun, 'when I was at Bunker's Hill'), and drawin' it out, he made a clip at him as wicked as if he was stabbing a rat with a hay fork, but Jim, he outs of the door like a shot, and draws it too arter him, and father sends old Bunker right through the panel. 'I'll chop you up as fine as mince-meat, you villain,' said he, 'if ever I catch you inside my door agin. Mind what I tell you, *you'll swing for it yet.*' Well, he made himself considerable scarce arter that; he never sot foot inside the door agin, and I thought he had ginn up all hopes of Sall, and she of him; when, one night, a most particular uncommon dark night, as I was a comin' home from neighbor Dearborne's, I heerd some one a talkin' under Sall's window. Well, I stops and listens, and who should be near the ash saplin' but Jim Munroe, a tryin' to persuade Sall to run off with him to Rhode Island to be married. It was all settled, he should come with a horse and shay to the gate, and then help her out of the window, jist at nine o'clock, about the time she commonly went to bed. Then he axes her to reach down her hand for him to kiss (for he was proper clever at soft sawder), and she stretches it down, and he kisses it; and says he, 'I believe I must have the whole of you out, arter all,' and gives her a jirk that kinder startled her; it came so sudden like, it made her scream; so off he sot, hot foot, and over the gate in no time.

"Well, I cyphered over this all night, a calculatin' how I should reciprocate that trick with him, and at last I hit on a scheme. I recollected father's words at partin', '*mind what I tell you, you'll swing for it yet;*' and, thinks I, friend Jim, I'll make that prophecy come true, yet, I guess. So the next night, jist at dark, I gives January Snow, the old nigger, a nidge with my elbow, and as soon as he looks up, I winks and walks out, and he arter me—says I, 'January, can you keep your tongue within your teeth, you old nigger, you?' 'Why massa, why you ax that are question? my Gor Ormity, you tink old Snow he don't know that are yet; my tongue he got plenty room now, debil a tooth left, he can stretch out ever so far; like a little leg in a bed, he lay quiet enough, massa, never fear.' 'Well, then,' says I, 'bend down that are ash saplin' softly, you old Snowball, and make no noise.' The saplin' was no sooner bent than secured to the ground by a notched peg and a noose, and a slip knot was suspended from the tree, jist over the track that led from the pathway to the house. 'Why, my Gor, massa, that's a ——.' 'Hold your mug, you old nigger,' says I, 'or I'll send your tongue a sarchin' arter your teeth; keep quiet, and follow me in presently.'

"Well, jist as it struck nine o'clock, says I, 'Sally, hold this here hank of twine for a minute, till I wind a trifle on it off; that's a dear critter.' She sot down her candle, and I put the twine on her hands, and then I begins to wind and wind away ever so slow, and drops the ball every now and then, so as to keep her down stairs. 'Sam,' says she, 'I do believe you won't wind that are twine off all night; do give it to January, I won't stay no longer, I'm een a most dead asleep.' 'The old feller's arm is so plaguy onsteady,' says I, 'it won't do; but hark, what's that? I'm sure I heerd something in the ash saplin', didn't you, Sall?' 'I heerd the geese there, that's all,' says she; 'they always come under the windows at night,' but she looked scared enough, and says she, 'I vow I'm tired a holdin' out my arms this way, and I won't do it no longer;' and down she throw'd the hank on the floor. 'Well,' says I, 'stop one minute, dear, till I send old January out to see if any body is there; perhaps some o' neighbor Dearborne's cattle have broke into the sarce garden.' January went out, tho' Sall say'd it was no use, for she knew the noise of the geese: they always kept close to the house at night, for fear of the varmin. Presently in runs Snow, with his hair standin' up on eend, and the whites of his eyes lookin' as the rims of a soup plate; 'Oh! Gor Ormity,' said he, 'oh massa, oh Miss Sally, oh!' 'What on airth is the matter with you?' said Sally, 'how you do frighten me! I vow I believe you're mad—'oh my Gor,' said he, 'oh! massa, Jim Munroe he hang himself on the ash saplin' under Miss Sally's window—oh my Gor!!!' That shot was a settler, it struck poor Sall right atwixt wind and water; she gave a lurch ahead, and then heeled over and sunk right down in another faintin' fit; and Juno, old Snow's wife, carried her off, and laid her down on the bed—poor thing, she felt ugly enough, I do suppose.

"Well, father, I thought he'd a fainted too; he was so struck up all of a heap, he was completely bung-fungered; 'dear, dear,' said he, 'I didn't think it would come to pass so soon, but I knew it would come. 'I foretold it,' says he, 'the last time I see'd him; 'Jim,' says I, 'mind what I say, *you'll swing for it yet.*' Give me the sword I wore when I was at Bunker's Hill, 'may be there's life yet, I'll cut him down.' The lantern was soon made ready, and out we went to the ash saplin'. 'Cut me down, Sam, that's a good fellow,' said Jim, all the blood in my body has swashed into my head, and's a runnin' out o' my nose; I'm een a most smothered—be quick, for heaven's sake.' 'The Lord be praised,' said father, 'the poor sinner is not quite dead yet. Why, as I'm alive—well if that don't beat all natur', why he has hanged himself by one leg, and's a swingin' like a rabbit upside down, that's a fact. Why, if he ain't snared, Sam; he is properly wired, I declare—I vow this is some o' your doin's, Sam—well it was a clever scheme, too, but a little grain too dangerous, I guess.' 'Don't stand starin' and jawin' there all night,' said Jim, 'cut me down, I tell you—or cut my throat, and be d——d to you, for I'm chokin' with blood.' 'Roll over that are hogshead, old Snow,' said I, 'till I get a top on it and cut him down;' so I soon released him, but he couldn't walk a bit. His ankle was swelled and sprained like vengeance, and he swore one leg was near about six inches longer than tother. 'Jim Munroe,' says father, 'little did I think I should ever see you inside my door agin,

but I bid you enter now; we owe you that kindness, anyhow.'

"Well, to make a long story short, Jim was so chap-fallen and so down in the mouth, he begged for heaven's sake it might be kept a secret; he said he would *run* the state, if ever it got wind, he was sure he couldn't *stand* it. 'It will be one while, I guess,' said father, 'afore you are able to run or stand either; but if you will give me your hand, Jim, and promise to give over your evil ways, I will not only keep it secret, but you shall be a welcome guest, at old Sam Slick's once more, for the sake of your father—he was a brave man, one of the heroes of Bunker's Hill, he was our sarjeant and ——.' 'He promises,' says I, 'father (for the old man had stuck his right foot out, the way he always stood when he told about the old war; and as Jim couldn't stir a peg, it was a grand chance, and he was agoin' to give him the whole revolution, from General Gage up to Independence,) he promises,' says I, 'father.' Well it was all settled, and things soon grew as calm as a pan of milk two days old; and afore a year was over, Jim was as steady agoin' man as Minister Joshua Hopewell, and was married to our Sall. Nothin' was ever said about the snare till arter the weddin'. When the minister had finished axin' a blessin', father goes up to Jim, and says he, 'Jim Munroe, my boy,' givin' him a rousin' slap on the shoulder that sot him a coughin' for the matter of five minutes (for he was a mortal powerful man, was father), 'Jim Munroe, my boy,' says he, 'you've got the snare round your neck, I guess, now, instead of your leg; the saplin' has been a father to you, may you be father of many saplin's.'

"We had a most special time of it, you may depend, all except the minister; father got him into a corner, and gave him chapter and verse for the whole war. Every now and then as I came near them, I heard Bunker's Hill, Brandywine, Clinton, Gates, and so on. It was broad day when we parted, and the last that went was poor minister. Father followed him clean down to the gate, and says he, 'Minister, we hadn't time this hitch, or I'd a told you all about the *Evakyation* of New York, but I'll tell you that the next time we meet."

SLICKISMS; OR, YANKEE PHILOSOPHY.

FROM "THE CLOCKMAKER." BY JUDGE HALIBURTON.

Society is something like a barrel of pork. The meat that's at the top, is sometimes not as good as that that's a little grain lower down; the upper and lower ends are plaguy apt to have a little taint in 'em, but the middle is always good.

If a man don't hoe his corn, and he don't get a crop, he says 'tis all owing to the Bank: and if he runs into debt, and is sued, why he says the lawyers are a curse to the country.

We can do without any article of luxury we've never had, but when once obtained, it is not in human natur' to surrender it voluntarily.

When a feller is too lazy to work, he paints his name over his door, and calls it a tavern, and as like as not he makes the whole neighborhood as lazy as himself.

Our tree of liberty was a beautiful tree—a splendid tree—it was a sight to look at; it was fenced and well protected, and it grew so stately and so handsome, that strangers came from all parts of the world to see it. They all allowed it was the most splendid thing in the world. Well, the mobs have broken in and torn down their fences, and snapped off the branches, and scattered all the leaves about, and it looks no better than a gallows-tree.

I guess if you were at our factories at Lowell, we'd show you a wonder—*five hundred gals at work together, all in silence!* I don't think our great country has such a real natural curiosity as that—I expect the world don't contain the beat of it—for a woman's tongue goes so slick of itself, without water power or steam, and moves so easy on its hinges, that it is no easy matter to put a spring stop on it, I tell you. It comes as natural as drinking mint julep.

What *is* the use of reading the Proverbs of Solomon to our free and enlightened citizens, that are every mite and mortal as wise as he was? That are man undertook to say there was nothing new under the sun. I guess he'd think he spoke a little too fast, if he was to see our steamboats, railroads, and India-rubber shoes—three inventions worth more nor all he knew put in a heap together.

There are some folks who think a good deal and say but little, and they are wise folks; and there are others agin, who bleat right out whatever comes uppermost, and I guess they are pretty considerable superfine darned fools.

Never tell folks you can go ahead of 'em, but *do* it. It spares a great deal of talk, and helps them to save their breath to cool their broth.

It ain't them that stare the most that see the best, I guess.

An airly start makes easy stages.

Politics makes a man as crooked as a pack does a pedlar; not that they are so awful heavy, neither, but it *teaches a man to stoop* in the long run.

It's better never to wipe a child's nose at all, I guess, than to wring it off.

I'd rather keep a critter whose faults I do know, than change him for a beast whose faults I don't know.

There's nothing I hate so much as cant of all kinds; it's a sure kind of a tricky disposition. If you see a feller cant in religion, clap your hand into your pocket, and lay right hold of your *puss*, or he'll steal it, as sure as you're alive; and if a man cant in politics, he'll sell you if he gets a chance, you may depend. Law and physic are just the same, and every mite and morsel as bad. If a lawyer takes to cantin', it's like the fox preachin' to the geese; he'll eat up his whole congregation. And if a doctor takes to it, he's a quack, as sure as rates. The Lord have mercy on you, for he won't.

When a feller winks till his gal gets married, I guess it's a little too late to pop the question then.

Judge Beler put a notice over his factory gate, at Lowell, "no cigars or Irishmen admitted within these walls," for said he, "the one will set a flame agoin' among my cottons, and the t'other among my gals. I won't have no such inflammable and dangerous things about me on no account."

Natur' is natur' wherever you find it—in rags or in kings' robes—where butter is spread with the thumb as well as the silver knife.

All folks that grow up right off, like a mushroom, in one night, are apt to think no small beer of themselves. A cabbage has plaguy large leaves to the bottom, and spreads them out as wide as an old woman's petticoat, to hide the ground it sprung from, and conceal its extraction.

When a feller has run as fast as he can clip, he has to stop and take breath; you must do that or choke.

A long face is plaguy apt to cover a long conscience—that's a fact.

Nothin' sets up a woman's spunk like callin' her ugly—she gets her back right up, like a cat when a strange dog comes near her; she's all eyes, claws, and bristles.

Make a farmer of him, and you will have the satisfaction of seeing him an honest, independent, and respectable member of society—more honest than traders, more independent than professional men, and more respectable than either.

There are only two things worth looking at in a horse—action and soundness, for I never saw a critter that had good action that was a bad beast.

It's in politics as in racin', every thing depends upon a fair start. If you are off too quick, you have to pull up and turn back agin, and your beast gets out of wind and is baffled; and if you lose in the start, you ha'n't got a fair chance arterwards, and are plaguy apt to get jockeyed in the course.

There's a plaguy sight of truth in them are old proverbs. They are distilled facts steamed down to an essence. They are like portable soup, an amazin' deal o' matter in a small compass. They are as true as a plum' line, and as short and sweet as sugar candy.

When you've too many irons in the fire, some on 'em will get stone cold, and t'other ones will get burnt, and so they'll never be no good in natur'.

Now's the time to larn, when you are young. Store your mind well, and the fragrance will remain long arter the rose has shed its leaves. The otter of roses is stronger than the rose, and a plaguy sight more valuable.

The Yankees may stump the universe. We improve on every thing, and we have improved on our own species. You'll search one while, I tell you, afore you'll find a man that, take him big and large, is equal to one of our free and enlightened citizens. He's the chap that has got both speed, wind, and bottom; he's clear grit, ginger to the backbone, you may depend. It's generally allowed there ain't the beat of them to be found anywhere. Spry as a fox, supple as an eel, and 'cute as a weasel. Though I say it that shouldn't say it, they fairly take the shine off creation—they are actilly equal to cash.

BRIGHTON FAIR.

BY ALFRED FORRESTER. (A. CROWQUILL.)

I MUST confess a vagabond inclination for the vulgar pleasures of a fair. The mingled sounds of the mimic penny-trumpet, the rattle, and the toy-drum, the grinding of the barrel-organs, the clashing of cymbals, and the whole miscellaneous concert of discordant music is always very exhilarating, and never more so than when it breaks in upon the monotonous routine of a fashionable watering-place.

About eight o'clock on a fine warm September's evening, I quitted my temporary residence on the Marine Parade, and, crossing the Steyne, mingled in the parti-colored stream of boys and girls, and children of a larger growth, which was flowing on towards "Ireland's Gardens," where the fair was held.

The road, like a grocer's shop on a July day, was swarming with *flies*. All the beaux were unbent, and the belles bending to beaux, as they greeted each other on the way, ridiculing the idea of going to a fair, and yet all pushing forward to the scene of the annual Saturnalia. The countenances of the many fashionable females I recognized in the crowd encouraged me in the pursuit. "Sweet creatures!" thought I, "they at least will not censure my predilection in favor of such a pastime. Indeed, it would be sheer ingratitude in them to contemn my devotion to the fair!"

I entered the gardens. On two sides of the spacious green the cake and toy-booths and the shows were ranged, forming an angle. The children, who had parents or pence, were admiring the spice-nuts and gilt-gingerbread, and the fragile and many-colored allurements of the former; while a well-ordered mob were listening and laughing at the Stentorian invitations of the bawling proprietors of the latter places of scenic, dramatic, and intellectual entertainment. Every booth, with its neat white cloth, looked like the aproned lap of a capacious grandmamma, filled with nice things for distribution among her children's children. The laughing looks and the exclamations of the sunburnt little rogues filled my heart with pleasure, and emptied my pockets of the coppers wherewith I had stored them for the occasion.

As the twilight faded, the smaller part of the joyous multitude gradually disappeared from the festive scene; and the number of servant-maids, smart shopmen, sailors, and fishermen, almost imperceptibly increased. The colored lamps burned brighter, and gave the place the appearance of the jewel-bearing trees in the fruit-gardens of Aladdin. A party commenced a country-dance on the green, which was soon lengthened by new-comers; and even some of the genteeler people, inspired by the scene, contrived to get up a quadrille without the aid of a Master of the Ceremonies. Although admiring the freedom and good-humor with which they entered into the prevailing spirit of the hour, my dancing days were long since past, and I therefore moved on, and mingled with the motley mob before the principal show.

Here Mr. Merryman, having performed a *preludio* upon the salt-box with a rolling-pin, with all the *con spirito* and force which the compass of that favorite instrument allows, had just placed the box under his left arm, and was extending the rolling-pin *à la* truncheon in his right, when the proprietor of the adjoining booth, dressed in a white hat and red coat, extended his body over the show, in order to catch the attention of Mr. Merryman's customers, and bawled out,

"This is the show!"

"And this is the substance!" exclaimed Mr. Merryman. "Ladies and gentlemen! that man's a Radical—look at his hat!" A roar of laughter followed this allusion. "The only sign of good sense he has shown is his endeavor to thrust himself into our splendid and incomparable Thespian establishment! The only animal worth seeing is himself; for, as you observe, he is a kind of amphibious nondescript—being half beaver and half donkey, which is the cause of his exposing himself!"

Another peal of laughter followed this spirited expression of party feeling on the part of the indignant Mr. Merryman.

"Only tuppence, and children half-price!" emphatically exclaimed the rival.

"If you pay your money there," said Mr. Merryman, "you will most certainly be—let in. Here, here is the place, where all the money you lay out will produce a profit! We have travelled the country far and wide to gather materials for your amusement; and you will find, and must confess, that we have progressed with the march of intellect. We fearlessly challenge competition; and if any individual, ignorantly blind to our superior merit, shall declare he is dissatisfied, and that we have made a fool of him, we will refund his money! Walk up, ladies and gentlemen! and you will find a feast of wit here, where you may not only feed, but carry away scraps enough to entertain your friends for the next twelve months. Only threepence!—four a shilling! Why, it's as cheap as mackerel, and much more nourishing; for every one may 'laugh and grow fat,' if he *choose*, without the trouble of mastication. Walk up, ladies and gentlemen!—walk up!"

The wit and drollery of Mr. Merryman won upon his auditory, and they began to mount the wide-extended steps, from three to six abreast; and, having paid their money for admission, the platform was soon left clear of the performers, whose services were wanted on the stage, giving an opportunity to the "Radical," who had so unwarrantably ventured on the precincts of his neighbor, to "explain," and win over an audience from the crowd.

When I again approached the Thespian establishment, a "delighted and overflowing" audience were coming out.

"Now, my merry customers all!" exclaimed the unwearied clown, "walk up! walk up! and we will rejoice the very cockles of your hearts for the small cost of threepence! Is it not worth double the money, father?" exclaimed he, addressing a broad-shouldered Sussex farmer.

The rustic grinned at being addressed; and I heard the words "Deep as Garrick!"

"Not equalled since the days of Garrick, he says!" said the unblushing Mr. Merryman. The farmer grinned again, and descended with the crowd, leaving a "clear stage" for the antics of the outside performers.

The clown then proceeded to accompany a sort of six-handed reel, performed by his gorgeously-spangled brother-comedians, upon his favorite instrument. At the conclusion of the serpentine evolutions, Mr. Merryman began eating fire amid the loud applause of his ruder audience.

"Now doesn't that beat snap-dragon," cried he, "all to tinder? Don't be alarmed, young ladies! my heart's already in a flame with your charms, and this is the way I feed the combustion! Though no posture-master, I can put my *tow* in my mouth as cleverly as the best of 'em!"

After this *feat* with his *tow*, he turned to a be-rouged gentleman with a hat and feathers, a black velvet fly jacket, white pantaloons, and yellow boots, with a riding-whip in his hand.

"I say, Mister Master," said he.

"Well, Mr. Merryman, and what—do—you—say?" said the other.

"Why did the dun cow not know her tail when she saw it in the pond?"

"Don't—know—Mr.—Merryman."

"Why, 'cause she had never seen it—*before*—to be sure," replied the clown.

A laugh of course followed the solution of the query.

"Now here's a puzzler," continued he. "Why is a cabbage run to seed like a lover? Give it up? Because it has lost its heart!"

Another encouraging shout from the rustics succeeded.

"What were the last words of the trumpeter when he was gored by the parson's bull? Why, 'blow the horns!' to be sure; for that was in his vocation. I say, Gaffer," said he, addressing a 'joskin' in the crowd, whose mouth was extended from ear to ear with an awful grin of approbation, "if you've cut your teeth of wisdom, canst tell me what are the three domestic delights of a poor man on a cold day?"

"Noa," replied the party. "What be they, ey?"

"Why, a 'nagging' wife, the tooth-ache, and no chips to boil the pot withal!"

"Bravo, Mr. Merryman!" exclaimed 'the Master'; "you shall have a bowl of gooseberry fool."

"One fool at a time, if you please," cried Mr. Merryman. "Pray, can any other fool tell another fool what is the height of luxury? You—or you—or you? None! then I'll elucidate your ponderosity, and dazzle the eyes of your intellectuality with the brightness of my intelligence. Know, then, that the height of luxury is—a tight boot on a July day, with a sharp peg in the heel of it. Now, mend that boot if ye can, ye cobblers of conundrums!"

And he commenced capering among the dancers in the most agile and ludicrous manner, accompanied by the roars of his auditory. He certainly was a fellow of infinite humor, and I regret that my treacherous memory has let slip many bright specimens of his glittering nonsense.

At the conclusion of his Terpsichorean efforts, he again presented himself, assuming and caricaturing the character of a candidate at an election.

"Men of Sussex!" said he, oratorically sawing the air with his extended arms, "a dissolution of the house having just taken place, I again have the honor of appearing before you to solicit the favor of your suffrages! and I firmly trust that the manner in which I performed my arduous duties on the last occasion I had the honor of serving you, will have sufficiently testified my heartfelt zeal for your welfare and approbation. My principles are too well known to require me to pledge myself to the performance of my duties; and yet, should you require it, behold! I am ready to be 'put up the spout' for your benefit; although, in tenderness, I ought to resist such a request, because you would never be able to redeem me; for, without vanity, I may say there's no *duplicate* of your humble servant! Gallant men of Sussex! I call upon you to support the *fair*.

"Ladies of Sussex! 'tis your cause I advocate, and I deserve some support at your hands in gratitude, for all my life I have endeavored to uphold the interests of the *fair!* Then come to the poll! Remember a *fair* is like a lady's *ear-ring*, there being only *one* in a *year!* and now's your only chance! Walk up! walk up! threepence is a qualification! Here's reform and liberality! why, 'tis nothing less than universal suffrage! Come, then, and lay down your half-crowns, your shillings, and your sixpences, and you shall have all the *change* you desire. Yes, you shall find us Radicals in our promises, and true Tories in our performances!"

I felt that the "show" deserved patronage, and yet must confess I had no inclination to mount the stage; I was, however, determined that the concern should not be a loser by my *mauvaise honte*, and had no difficulty in finding a representation of four deputies among the urchins in the crowd. I am happy to say that my example was liberally followed by many of the "genteeler folk."

I now lounged along the range of cake and toy-booths, anxious for the repetition of the merry tricks, and quips, and quirks of our motley hero.

I had just yielded to the pressing instance of a smart *pâtissière* to purchase a bag of the "best spice-nuts," which she was "putting up" for me, when the sound of a gong suddenly startled me, and, turning hastily about, I observed that the performances were just over. I hurriedly threw down half-a-crown, and, seizing my "fairing," turned my steps eagerly to the chosen spot, fearful of losing a particle of Mr. Merryman's quaint and laughter-moving speech.

A young serving-lass was pushing, and anxiously endeavoring to penetrate the mob, evidently in pursuit of some object.

"Seeking for a lover, my dear?" asked Mr. Merryman.

"No; I've lost my shoe," pettishly replied the girl.

"A shoe!" said the clown; "it must be a slipper, and a very shabby one, too, to desert such a pretty foot. Yes, really 'tis barbarous—nay shocking!—to slip from such a fair—and well-darned stocking!"

Mr. Merryman now began to "hunt the slipper," which he soon found, and presented to the blushing damsel. The platform was speedily cleared again, and the same evolutions were recommenced by the untiring company to the boisterous clang of cymbals, drums, and trumpets.

"This is what I call life," exclaimed Mr. Merryman. "Cutting and shuffling is the order of the day! There they go! in and out, like so many wriggling eels in a fish-basket; and that's the way to make your way in the world, now-a-days! Your straight-forward fool only runs his head against a post, and comes to a stand-still! Commend me to a knave!—Knaves are sharp *blades*, and honest men their *handles!*"

"And pray, Mis-ter Merry-man—what—are—you!" demanded the master, laying an emphasis upon every syllable and word.

"A fool!" replied Mr. Merryman; "and every fool is an honest man, and every honest man a fool; that's my philosophy!"

"And pray, Mr. Merryman—what—am—I?" demanded the other.

"You're another!"

"Call me a fool?"

"To be sure," replied Mr. Merryman; "for, if you were a wise man, you'd 'know yourself,' and have no occasion to ask questions!" Hereupon, spinning round upon one leg, *à la pirouette*, he snatched up a hoop bound with red cloth, and began twisting himself through it, throwing it over his arms, legs, and head, with the most dexterous rapidity.

"That's what I call a 'round game,'" said he, breathless with his exertions, and offering it to his master; "would you like to take 'a hand?'"

"No; go on."

"Thank-ye," replied he; "but, if I go on, I shall go off for want of breath."

"Disobey me, and I'll discharge you directly, sirrah!" said the master, with mock authority.

"That's just what I want, Mister Master."

"What, to be *discharged?*"

"Yes; that is to say, *let off!* which is one and the same thing to a fool and a duck-gun!"

Here the indefatigable fellow again began capering among the *corps dramatique*, and at the conclusion immediately commenced the following invitation to the crowd:

"Now, my merry masters and mistresses all! walk up, and taste of the delightful banquet we have catered for your amusement! Here tragedy, comedy, and farce, are combined to move you to tears, and win your smiles! Here the thin may grow fat with laughter, and the fat sup full of horrors, and dwindle to the size of a Kentish hop-pole! Come, then, and down with your dust! only threepence. The only legitimate drama in the whole fair! All the rest are mere 'by-blows,' and fathered by fools! Here you will find not only the gold and glitter, but the gingerbread, good, spicy, and substantial. Allow me, sir, to lend you a hand!" continued he, stooping to a wooden-legged sailor, who was 'stumping' up the steps; "I would willingly lend you a leg to boot, had I one to spare. Walk up, ladies! the front row is still vacant; and there you may not only see, but be seen. Now, farmers of Sussex! ye first of corn-cutters! put your best legs foremost. It always delights my heart to welcome the agricultural interest; they are all sharp and good-tempered blades. Raisers of crops and crops of razors! walk up, walk up! the room and the 'company' are both extensive."

The booth was speedily filled, and I again sauntered from the spot, when one of those sudden showers, so frequent in Brighton, drove me from the scene of noise, bustle, and rude merriment; and hailing the first 'fly,' I drove home to my lodging, perfectly delighted with my evening's entertainment.

On the morning after the conclusion of the fair, I turned my steps towards the gardens. Most of the booths were dismantled, and many of the show-people had packed up and departed. The Thespian establishment, too, had nearly completed its travelling arrangements. A long cart covered with the scenery and paraphernalia of the drama alone remained, with its horseless shafts extended along the ground, like a couple of bony arms, waiting to embrace the lean ribs of the "hack" to transport it to the place of its next destination.

Several trunks were scattered over the path and green; and a man with sandy hair, deeply pitted with the small-pox, was issuing his orders to his assistants, diligently applying his hammer, to secure the "properties." He was in his shirt-sleeves, wore a pair of large corded, light-colored inexpressibles, dirty white cotton stockings, and high-low, heavy-nailed boots. He appeared the master of the concern, for he was ordering about him, and certainly in no very good humor.

"I hope," said I, "that you have made a good harvest?"

"Pretty well, sir, I thank you, considering the times," said he; "but fairs are not what they used to be: the people fancy themselves so clever that we find it difficult to please them now-a-days. The merest clown now sets up for a critic, and fancies, because he can read, he has brains, and feels much more pleasure in finding fault with what he don't understand, than with being pleased with what he does."

"Well, I am sure your 'clown' gave universal satisfaction," said I; "for my part, I must confess I was infinitely amused by his exertions."

"I'm sure I'm much obliged to you," said he; "for the praise of the judicious few compensates us for many disagreeables. You are not, perhaps, aware, sir, that you are now speaking to that 'gifted individual?'" continued he, smiling.

I was certainly what the old women call "thunder-struck" at this intelligence; and, no doubt, my stare of astonishment tickled the 'clown,' for he burst into a loud fit of laughter.

"Ah, sir," said he, "it's a wonder what a difference a little whitewashing makes in a man!"

When my amazement had abated, I continued the conversation, and found, upon inquiry, that he was the real and sole proprietor of the "Show." Though no beauty, I certainly discovered that he was no "ordinary" man, and, proffering him a gratuity for the pleasure he had afforded me, I took my leave, delighted with my strange encounter with the First Fool of Brighton Fair.

ON A ROMAN NOSE.

BY ALFRED A. FORRESTER. (A. CROWQUILL.)

Knows he, who never took a pinch,
Nosey! the pleasure thence which flows?
Knows he the titillating joys
Which my nose knows?

Oh, nose! I am as proud of thee,
As any mountain of its snows;
I gaze on thee, and feel that joy—
A Roman knows!

THE TALE OF THE ENGLISH SAILOR.

FROM "THE PACHA OF MANY TALES." BY CAPTAIN MARRYATT.

"I HAVE an infidel in the courtyard," replied Mustapha, "who telleth of strange things. He hath been caught like a wild beast; it is a Frank Galiongi, who hath travelled as far as that son of Shitan, Huckaback; he was found in the streets, overpowered by the forbidden juice, after having beaten many of your highness's subjects; and the cadi would have administered the bamboo, but he was as a lion, and he scattered the slaves as chaff, until he fell, and could not rise again. I have taken him from the cadi, and brought him here. He speaketh but the Frankish tongue, but the sun who shineth on me knoweth I have been in the Frank country, and Inshallah! please the Lord, I can interpret his meaning."

"What sort of a man may he be, Mustapha?"

"He is a baj baj—a big belly—a stout man; he is an anhunkher, a swallower of iron. He hath sailed in the war vessels of the Franks. He holdeth in one hand a bottle of the forbidden liquor, in the other he shakes at those who would examine him a thick stick. He hath a large handful of the precious weed which we use for our pipes in one of his cheeks, and his hair is hanging behind down to his waist, in a rolled up mass, as thick as the arm of your slave."

"It is well—we will admit him; but let there be armed men at hand. Let me have a full pipe. God is great," continued the pacha, holding out his glass to be filled; "and the bottle is nearly empty. Place the guards, and bring in the infidel."

The guards in a few minutes brought into the presence of the pacha, a stout-built English sailor, in the usual dress, and with a tail which hung down behind, below his waist. The sailor did not appear to like his treatment, and every now and then, as they pushed and dragged him in, turned to one side or the other, looking daggers at those who conducted him. He was sober, although his eyes bore testimony to recent intoxication; and his face, which was manly and handsome, was much disfigured by an enormous quid of tobacco in his right cheek, which gave him an appearance of natural deformity. As soon as he was near enough to the pacha, the attendants let him go. Jack shook his jacket, hitched up his trousers, and said, looking furiously at them, "Well, you beggars, have you done with me at last?"

Mustapha addressed the sailor in English, telling him that he was in the presence of his highness the pacha.

"What, that old chap muffled up in shawls and furs—is he the pacha? Well, I don't think much o' he;" and the sailor turned his eyes round the room, gaping with astonishment, and perfectly unmindful how very near he was to one who could cut off his head or his tail, by a single movement of his hand.

"What sayeth the Frank, Mustapha?' inquired the pacha.

"He is struck dumb with astonishment at the splendor of your majesty, and all that he beholds."

"It is well said, by Allah!"

"I suppose I may just as well come to an anchor," said the sailor, suiting the action to the word, and dropping down on the mats. "There," continued he, folding his legs in imitation of the Turks, "as it's the fashion to have a cross in your hawse, in this here country, I can be a bit of a lubber as well as yourselves; I wouldn't mind if I blew a cloud, as well as you, old fusty-musty."

"What does the Giaour say? What son of a dog is this, to sit in our presence?" exclaimed the pacha.

"He saith," replied Mustapha, "that in his country no one dare stand in the presence of the Frankish king; and, overcome by his humility, his legs refuse their office, and he sinks to the dust before you. It is even as he sayeth, for I have travelled in their country, and such is the custom of that uncivilized nation. Mashallah! but he lives in awe and trembling."

"By the beard of the prophet, he does not appear to show it outwardly," replied the pacha; "but that may be the custom also."

"Be chesm, on my eyes be it," replied Mustapha, "it is even so. Frank," said Mustapha, "the pacha has sent for you that he may hear an account of all the wonderful things which you have seen. You must tell lies, and you will have gold."

"Tell lies! that is, to spin a yarn; well, I can do that, but my mouth's baked with thirst, and without a drop of something, the devil a yarn from me, and so you may tell the old billy-goat perched up there."

"What sayeth the son of Shitan?" demanded the pacha, impatiently.

"The unbeliever declareth that his tongue is glued to his mouth from the terror of your highness's presence. He fainteth after water to restore him, and enable him to speak."

"Let him be fed," rejoined the pacha.

But Mustapha had heard enough to know that the sailor would not be content with the pure element. He therefore continued, "your slave must tell you, that in the country of the Franks, they drink nothing but the fire water, in which the true believers but occasionally venture to indulge."

"Allah acbar! nothing but fire water? What then do they do with common water?"

"They have none but from heaven—the rivers are all of the same strength."

"Mashallah, how wonderful is God! I would we had a river here. Let some be procured, then, for I wish to hear his story."

A bottle of brandy was sent for, and handed to the sailor, who put it to his mouth, and the quantity he took of it before he removed the bottle to recover his breath, fully convinced the pacha that Mustapha's assertions were true.

"Come, that's not so bad," said the sailor, putting the bottle down between his legs; "and now I'll be as good as my word, and I'll spin old Billy a yarn as long as the maintop-bowling."

"What sayeth the Giaour?" interrupted the pacha.

"That he is about to lay at your highness's feet the wonderful events of his life, and trust that his face will be whitened before he quits your sublime presence. Frank, you may proceed."

"To lie till I'm black in the face—well, since you wish it; but, old chap, my name ar'n't Frank. It happens to be Bill; howsomever, it warn't a bad guess for a Turk; and now I'm here, I'd just like to ax you a question. We had a bit of a hargument the other day, when I was in a frigate up the Dardanelles, as to what your religion might be. Jack Soames said that you warn't Christians, but that if you were, you could only be Catholics; but I don't know how he could know any thing about it, seeing that he had not been more than seven weeks on board of a man-of-war. What may you be—if I may make so bold as to ax the question?"

"What does he say?" inquired the pacha, impatiently.

"He says," interrupted Mustapha, "that he was not so fortunate as to be born in the country of the true believers, but in an island full of fog and mist, where the sun never shines, and the cold is so intense, that the water from heaven is hard and cold as a flint."

"That accounts for their not drinking it. Mashallah, God is great! Let him proceed."

"The pacha desires me to say, that our religion is, that there is but one God, and Mahomet is his prophet, and begs that you will go on with your story."

"Never heard of the chap—never mind—here's saw wood."

TALE OF THE ENGLISH SAILOR.

I was born at Shields, and bred to the sea, served my time out of that port, and got a berth on board a small vessel fitted out from Liverpool for the slave trade. We made the coast, unstowed our beads, spirits, and gunpowder, and very soon had a cargo on board; but the day after we sailed for the Havannah, the dysentery broke out among the niggers—no wonder, seeing how they were stowed, poor devils, head and tail, like pilchards in a cask. We opened the hatches, and brought part of them on deck, but it was no use, they died like rotten sheep, and we tossed overboard about thirty a day. Many others, who were alive, jumped overboard, and we were followed by a shoal of sharks, splashing, and darting, and diving, and tearing the bodies, yet warm, and revelling in the hot and bloody water. At last they were all gone, and we turned back to the coast to get a fresh supply. We were within a day's sail of the land, when we saw two boats on our weather bow; they made signals to us, and we found them to be full of men; we hove to, and took them on board, and then it was that we discovered that they had belonged to a French schooner, in the same trade, which had started a plank, and had gone down like a shot, with all the niggers in the hold.

"Now give the old gentleman the small change of that, while I just whet my whistle."

Mustapha having interpreted, and the sailor having taken a swig at the bottle, he proceeded.

We didn't much like having these French beggars on board, and it wasn't without reason, for they were as many as we were. The very first night, they were overheard by a negro who belonged to us, and had learnt French, making a plan for overpowering us, and taking possession of the vessel; so when we heard that, their doom was sealed. We mustered ourselves on deck, put the hatches over some o' the French, seized those on deck, and—in half an hour, they all walked a plank.

"I do not understand what you mean," said Mustapha.

That's 'cause you're a lubber of a landsman. The long and short of walking a plank is just this. We passed a wide plank over the gunnel, greasing it well at the outer end, led the Frenchmen up to it blindfolded, and wished them "bon voyage" in their own lingo, just out of politeness. They walked on till they toppled into the sea, and the sharks didn't refuse them, though they prefer a nigger to any thing else.

"What does he say, Mustapha?" interrupted the pacha. Mustapha interpreted.

"Good; I should like to have seen that," replied the pacha.

Well, as soon as we were rid of the Frenchmen, we made our port, and soon had another cargo on board, and after a good run, got safe to the Havannah, where we sold our slaves; but I didn't much like the sarvice, so I cut the schooner, and sailed home in summer, and got back safe to England. There I fell in with Betsy, and as she proved a regular out and outer, I spliced her, and a famous wedding we had of it, as long as the rhino lasted; but that wasn't long, the more's the pity; so I went to sea for more. When I came back after my trip, I found that Bet hadn't behaved quite so well as she might have done, so I cut my stick, and went away from her altogether.

"Why didn't you put her in a sack?" inquired the pacha, when Mustapha explained.

"Put her head in a bag—no, she wasn't so ugly as all that," replied the sailor. "Howsomever, to coil away."

I joined a privateer brig, and after three cruises I had plenty of money, and determined to have another spell on shore, that I might get rid of it. Then I picked up Sue, and spliced again; but, Lord bless your heart, she turned out a regular built tartar—nothing but fight fight, scratch scratch, all day long, till I wished her at old Scratch. I was tired of her, and Sue had taken a fancy to another chap; so says she one day, "As we both be of the same mind, why don't you sell me, and then we may part in a respectable manner." I agrees, and I puts a halter round her neck, and leads her to the market-place, the chap following to buy her. "Who bids for this woman?" says I.

"I do," says he.

"What will you give?"

"Half a crown," says he.

"Will you throw a glass of grog into the bargain?"

"Yes," says he.

"Then she's yours; and I wish you much joy of your bargain." So I hands the rope to him, and he leads her off.

"How much do you say he sold his wife for?' said the pacha to Mustapha, when this part of the story was repeated to him.

"A piastre, and a drink of the fire water," replied the vizier.

"Ask him if she was handsome?" said the pacha.

"Handsome," replied the sailor to Mustapha's inquiry; "yes, she was as pretty a craft to look at as you may set your eyes upon; fine round counter—clean run—swelling bows—good figure head, and hair enough for a mermaid."

"What does he say?" inquired the pacha.

"The Frank declareth that her eyes were bright as those of the gazelle—that her eyebrows were as one—her waist as that of the cypress—her face as the full moon, and that she was fat as the houris that wait the true believers."

"Mashallah! all for a piastre. Ask him, Mustapha, if there are more wives to be sold in that country?"

"More," replied the sailor, in answer to Mustapha: "you may have a ship full in an hour. There's many a fellow in England who would give a handful of coin to get rid of his wife."

"We will make further inquiry, Mustapha; it must be looked to. Say I not well?"

"It is well said," replied Mustapha. "My heart is burnt as roast meat at the recollection of the women of that country; who are, indeed, as he described, houris to the sight. Proceed, Yaha Bibi, my friend, and tell his—"

"Yaw Bibby! I told you my name was Bill, not Bibby; and I never yaws from my course, although I heaves to sometimes, as I do now, to take in provisions." The sailor took another swig, wiped his mouth with the back of his hand, and continued. "Now for a good lie."

I sailed in a brig for the Brazils, and a gale came on, that I never seed the like of. We were obliged to have three men stationed to hold the captain's hair on his head, and a little boy was blown over the moon, and slid down by two or three of her beams, till he caught the mainstay, and never hurt himself.

"Good," said Mustapha, who interpreted.

"By the beard of the prophet, wonderful!" exclaimed the pacha.

Well, the gale lasted for a week, and at last one night, when I was at the helm, we dashed on the rocks of a desolate island. I was pitched right over the mountains, and fell into the sea on the other side of the island. I swam on shore, and got into a cave, where I fell fast asleep. The next morning I found that there was nothing to eat except rats, and they were plentiful; but they were so quick that I could not catch them. I walked about, and at last discovered a great many rats together; they were at a spring of water, the only one, as I afterwards found, on the island. Rats can't do without water; and I thought I should have them there. I filled up the spring, all but a hole which I sat on the top of. When the rats came again I filled my mouth with water, and held it wide open; they ran up to drink and I caught their heads in my teeth, and thus I took as many as I wished.

"Aferin, excellent!" cried the pacha, as soon as this was explained.

Well, at last a vessel took me off, and I wasn't sorry for it, for raw rats are not very good eating. I went home again, and I hadn't been on shore more than two hours, when who should I see but my first wife Bet, with a robin-redbreast in tow. "That's he," says she. I gave fight, but was nabbed and put into limbo, to be tried for what they call *biggery*, or having a wife too much.

"How does he mean? desire him to explain," said the pacha, after Mustapha had conveyed the intelligence. Mustapha obeyed.

"In our country one wife is considered a man's allowance; and he is not to take more, that every Jack may have his Jill. I had spliced two, so they tried me, and sent me to Botany bay for life."

This explanation puzzled the pacha. "How! what sort of a country must it be, when a man can not have two wives? Inshallah! please the Lord, we may have hundreds in our harem! Does he not laugh at our beards with lies? Is this not all *bosh*, nothing?"

"It is even so, as the Frank speaketh," replied Mustapha. "The king of the country can take but one wife. Be chesm, on my eyes be it, if it is not the truth."

"Well," rejoined the pacha, "what are they but infidels? They deserve to have no more. Houris are for the faithful. May their fathers' graves be defiled. Let the Giaour proceed."

Well, I was started for the other side of the water, and got there safe enough, as I hope one day to get to heaven, wind and weather permitting; but I had no idea of working without pay, so one fine morning, I slipped away into the woods, where I remained with three or four more for six months. We lived upon kangaroos, and another odd little animal, and got on pretty well.

"What may the dish of kangaroos be composed of?" inquired Mustapha, in obedience to the pacha.

"Posed of! why a dish of kangaroos be made of kangaroos to be sure."

But I'll be dished if I talked about any thing but the animal, which we had some trouble to kill; for it stands on its big tail, and fights with all four feet. Moreover, it be otherwise a strange beast; for its young ones pop out of its stomach, and then pop in again, having a place there on purpose, just like the great hole in the bow of a timber ship: and as for the other little animal, it swims in the ponds, lays eggs, and has a duck's bill, yet still it be covered all over with hair like a beast.

The vizier interpreted. "By the prophet, but he laughs at our beards!" exclaimed the pacha, angrily. "These are foolish lies."

"You must not tell the pacha such foolish lies. He will be angry," said Mustapha. "Tell lies, but they must be good lies."

"Well I'll be—," replied the sailor, "if the old beggar don't doubt the only part which is true out of the whole yarn. Well, I will try another good un to please him."

After I had been there about six months I was tired, and as there was only twenty thousand miles between that country and my own, I determined to swim back.

"Mashallah! swim back!—how many thousand miles?" exclaimed Mustapha.

"Only twenty thousand—a mere nothing."

So, one fine morning, I throws a young kangaroo on my shoulder, and off I starts. I swam for three months, night and day, and then feeling a little tired, I laid to on my back, and then I set off again; but by this time I was so covered with barnacles, that I made but little way. So I stopped at Ascension, scraped and cleaned myself, and then after feeding for a week on turtle, just to keep the scurvy out of my bones, I set off again; and as I passed the Gut, I thought I might just as well put in here; and here I arrived, sure enough, yesterday, about three bells in the morning watch, after a voyage of five months and three days.

When Mustapha translated all this to the pacha, the latter was lost in astonishment. "Allah Wachbar! God is everywhere! Did you ever hear of such a swimmer? Twenty thousand miles—five months and three days. It is a wonderful story! Let his mouth be filled with gold."

Mustapha intimated to the sailor the unexpected compliment about to be conferred on him, just as he had finished the bottle, and rolled it away on one side. "Well, that be a rum way of paying a man. I have heard it said that a fellow *pursed* up his mouth; but I never afore heard of a mouth being a *purse*. Howsomever, all's one for that; only, d'ye see, if you are about to stow it away in bulk, it may be just as well to get rid of the dunnage." The sailor put his thumb and forefinger into the cheek, and pulled out his enormous quid of tobacco. "There now, I'm ready, and don't be afraid of choking me." One of the attendants then thrust several pieces of gold into the sailor's mouth, who, spitting them all out into his hat, jumped on his legs, and made a jerk of his head, with a kick of the leg behind, to the pacha; and declaring that he was the funniest old beggar he had ever fallen in with, nodded to Mustapha, and hastened out of the divan.

"Mashallah! but he swims well," said the pacha, breaking up the audience.

DOMESTIC DEMOCRACY.

FROM "MIDSHIPMAN EASY." BY CAPTAIN MARRYATT.

The packet anchored in Falmouth Roads. Jack, accompanied by Mesty, was soon on shore with his luggage, threw himself into the mail, arrived in London, and waiting there two or three days to obtain what he considered necessary from a fashionable tailor, ordered a chaise to Forest Hill. He had not written to his father to announce his arrival, and it was late in the morning when the chaise drew up at his father's door.

Jack stepped out and rang the bell. The servants who opened the door did not know him; they were not the same as those he left.

"Where is Mr. Easy?" demanded Jack.

"Who are you?" demanded one of the men, in a gruff tone.

"By de powers, you very soon find out who he is," observed Mesty.

"Stay here, and I'll see if he is at home."

"Stay here! stay in the hall like a footman? What do you mean, you rascal?" cried Jack, attempting to push by the man.

"O, that won't do here, master; this is Equality Hall—one man's as good as another."

"Not always," replied Jack, knocking him down. "Take that for your insolence, pack up your traps, and walk out of the house to-morrow morning."

Mesty, in the mean time, had seized the other by the throat.

"What I do with this fellow, Massa Easy?"

"Leave him now, Mesty; we'll settle their ac-

count to-morrow morning. I presume I shall find my father in the library."

"His father!" said one of the men to the other; "he's not exactly a chip of the old block."

"We shall have a change, I expect," replied the other, as they walked away.

"Mesty," cried Jack, in an authoritative tone, "bring those two rascals back to take the luggage out of the chaise; pay the postilion, and tell the housekeeper to show you my room and yours. Come to me for orders as soon as you have done this."

"Yes, sir," replied Mesty. "Now come here, you d—n blackguard, and take tings out of chaise, or by de holy poker, I choke your luff, both of you."

The filed teeth, the savage look, and determination of Mesty, had the due effect. The men sullenly returned and unloaded the chaise. In the mean time, Jack walked into his father's study; his father was there—the study was lighted up with argand lamps, and Jack looked with astonishment. Mr. Easy was busy with a plaster cast of a human head, which he pored over, so that he did not perceive the entrance of his son. The cast of the skull was divided into many compartments, with writing on each; but what most astonished our hero was the alteration in the apartment. The book-cases and books had all been removed, and in the centre, suspended from the ceiling, was an apparatus which would have puzzled any one, composed of rods in every direction, with screws at the end of them, and also tubes in equal number, one of which communicated with a large air-pump, which stood on a table. Jack took a short survey, and then walked up to his father and accosted him.

"What!" exclaimed Mr. Easy, "is it possible?—yes, it is my son John! I'm glad to see you, John, very glad indeed," continued the old gentleman, shaking him by both hands—"very glad that you have come home: I wanted you—wanted your assistance in my great and glorious project, which, I thank heaven, is now advancing rapidly. Very soon shall equality and the rights of man be proclaimed everywhere. The pressure from without is enormous, and the bulwarks of our ridiculous and tyrannical constitution must give way. King, lords, and aristocrats; landholders, tithe-collectors, church and state, thank God, will soon be overthrown, and the golden age revived—the millennium, the true millennium—not what your poor mother talked about. I am at the head of twenty-nine societies, and if my health lasts, you will see what I will accomplish now that I have your assistance, Jack;" and Mr. Easy's eyes sparkled and flashed, in all the brilliancy of incipient insanity.

Jack sighed, and to turn the conversation, he observed, "You have made a great change in this room, sir. What may all this be for? Is it a machine to improve equality and the rights of man?"

"My dear son," replied Mr. Easy, sitting down, and crossing his legs complacently, with his two hands under his right thigh, according to his usual custom when much pleased with himself—"why, my dear son, that is not exactly the case; and yet you have shown some degree of perception, even in your guess; for if my invention succeeds, and I have no doubt of it, I shall have discovered the great art of rectifying the mistakes of nature, and giving an equality of organization to the whole species, of introducing all the finer organs of humanity, and of destroying the baser. It is a splendid invention, Jack, very splendid. They may talk of Gall and Spurzheim, and all those; but what have they done? nothing but divided the brain into sections, classed the organs, and discovered where they reside; but what good result has been gained from that? the murderer by nature remained a murderer—the benevolent man, a benevolent man—he could not alter his organization. I have found out how to change all that."

"Surely, sir, you would not interfere with the organ of benevolence?"

"But indeed I must, Jack. I, myself, am suffering from my organ of benevolence being too large; I must reduce it, and then I shall be capable of greater things, shall not be so terrified by difficulties, shall overlook trifles, and only carry on great schemes for universal equality and the supreme rights of man. I have put myself into that machine every morning for two hours, for these last three months, and I now feel that I am daily losing a great portion."

"Will you do me the favor to explain an invention so extraordinary, sir?" said our hero.

"Most willingly, my boy. You observe that in the centre there is a frame to confine the human head, somewhat larger than the head itself, and that the head rests upon the iron collar beneath. When the head is thus firmly fixed, suppose I want to reduce the size of any particular organ, I take the boss corresponding to where that organ is situated in the cranium, and fix it on it. For you will observe that all the bosses inside of the top of the frame correspond to the organs as described in this plaster cast on the table. I then screw down pretty tight, and increase the pressure daily, until the organ disappears altogether, or is reduced to the size required."

"I comprehend that part perfectly, sir," replied Jack; "but now explain to me by what method you contrive to raise an organ which does not previously exist?"

"That," replied Mr. Easy, "is the greatest perfection of the whole invention, for without I could do that, I could have done little. I feel convinced that this invention of mine will immortalize me. Observe all these little bell-glasses which communicate with the air-pump. I shave my patient's head, grease it a little, and fix on the bell-glass, which is exactly shaped to fit the organ in length and breadth. I work the air-pump, and raise the organ by an exhausted receiver. It cannot fail. There is my butler, now; a man who escaped hanging last spring assizes on an undoubted charge of murder. I selected him on purpose; I have flattened down murder to nothing, and I have raised benevolence till it's like a wen."

"I am afraid my poor father's head is an exhausted receiver," thought Jack, who then replied, "Well, sir, if it succeeds, it will be a good invention."

"If it succeeds!—why, it has succeeded—it cannot fail. It has cost me near two thousand pounds. By-the-by, Jack, you have drawn very liberally lately, and I had some trouble, with my own expenses, to meet your bills; not that I complain—but what with societies, and my machine, and tenants refusing to pay their rents, on the principle that the farms are no more mine than theirs, which I admit to be true, I have had some difficulty in meeting all demands."

"The governor was right," thought Jack, who now inquired after Doctor Middleton.

"Ah, poor silly man! he's alive yet—I believe doing well. He is one who will interfere with the business of others, complains of my servants—very silly man, indeed—but I let him have his own way. So I did your poor mother. Silly woman, Mrs. Easy—but never mind that."

"If you please, sir, I have also a complaint to make of the servants for their insolence to me: but we will adjourn, if you please, as I wish to have some refreshment."

"Certainly, Jack, if you are hungry; I will go with you. Complain of my servants, say you?—there must be some mistake—they are all shaved, and wear wigs, and I put them in the machine every other morning; but I mean to make an alteration in one respect. You observe, Jack, it requires more dignity: we must raise the whole machinery some feet, ascend it with state as a throne, for it is the throne of reason, the victory of mind over nature."

"As you please, sir; but I am really hungry just now."

Jack and his father went into the drawing-room and rang the bell; not being answered, Jack rose and rang again.

"My dear sir," observed Mr. Easy, "you must not be in a hurry; every man naturally provides for his own wants first, and afterward for those of others. Now my servants—"

"Are a set of insolent scoundrels, sir, and insolence, I never permit. I knocked one down as I entered your house, and with your permission, I will discharge two, at least, to-morrow."

"My dear son," exclaimed Mr. Easy, "you knocked my servant down!—are you not aware by the laws of equality—"

"I am aware of this, my dear father," replied Jack, "that by all the laws of society we have a right to expect civility and obedience from those we pay and feed."

"Pay and feed! Why, my dear son—my dear Jack—you must recollect—"

"I recollect, sir, very well; but if your servants do not come to their recollection in a very short time, either I or they must quit the house."

"But, my dear boy, have you forgotten the principles I instilled into you? Did you not go to sea to obtain that equality foiled by tyranny and despotism here on shore? Do you not acknowledge and support my philosophy?"

"We'll argue that point to-morrow, sir—at present, I want to obtain my supper;" and Jack rang the bell furiously.

The butler made his appearance at this last summons, and he was followed by Mesty, who looked like a demon with anger.

"Mercy on me, who have we here?"

"My servant, father," exclaimed Jack, starting up; "one that I can trust to, and who will obey me. Mesty, I wish some supper and wine to be brought immediately—see that scoundrel gets it ready in a moment. If he does not, throw him out of the door and lock him out. You understand me."

"Yes, massa," grinned Mesty; "now you hab supper very quick, or Mesty know the reason why. Follow me, sar," cried Mesty, in an imperative tone, to the butler; "quick, sar, or by de holy poker, I show you what Mesty can do;" and Mesty grinned in his wrath.

"Bring supper and wine immediately," said Mr. Easy, giving an order such as the butler had never heard since he had been in the house.

The butler quitted the room, followed by the Ashantee.

"My dear boy—my Jack—I can make every allowance for hunger, it is often the cause of theft and crime in the present unnatural state of society—but really you are too violent. The principles—"

"Your principles are all confounded nonsense, father," cried Jack, in a rage.

"What! Jack—my son—what do I hear? This from you—nonsense! Why, Jack, what has Captain Wilson been doing with you?"

"Bringing me to my senses, sir."

"O dear, O dear! my dear Jack, you will make me lose mine."

"Gone already," thought Jack.

"That you, my child, so carefully brought up in the great and glorious school of philosophy, should behave this way—should be so violent—forget your sublime philosophy, and all—just like Esau selling his birthright for a mess of pottage. O Jack, you'll kill me! and yet I love you, Jack—whom else have I to love in this world? Never mind, never mind, we'll argue the point, my boy, I'll convince you—in a week all will be right again."

"It shall, sir, if I can manage it," replied Jack.

"That's right; I love to hear you say so—that's consoling, very consoling—but I think now I was wrong to let you go to sea, Jack."

"Indeed you were not, father."

"Well, I am glad to hear you say so; I thought they had ruined you, destroyed all your philosophy—but it will be all right again—you shall come to our societies, Jack—I am president—you shall hear me speak, Jack—you shall hear me thunder like Demosthenes—but here comes the tray."

The butler, followed by Mesty, who attended him as if he was his prisoner, now made his appearance with the tray—laid it down in a sulky manner, and retired. Jack desired Mesty to remain.

"Well, Mesty, how are they getting on in the servants' hall?"

"Regular mutiny, sar—ab swear dat dey no stand our nonsense, and dat we both leave the house to-morrow."

"Do you hear, sir, your servants declare that I shall leave your house to-morrow."

"You leave my house, Jack, after four years' absence!—no, no. I'll reason with them—I'll make them a speech. You don't know how I can speak, Jack."

"Look you, father, I cannot stand this: either give me a carte blanche to arrange this household as I please, or I shall quit it myself to-morrow morning."

"Quit my house, Jack! no, no—shake hands and make friends with them; be civil, and they will serve you—but you know upon the principles—"

"Principles of the devil!" cried Jack, in a rage.

"Of the devil, Jack; dear me! I wish you had never gone to sea."

"In one word, sir, do you consent, or am I to leave the house?"

"Leave the house! O no; not leave the house, Jack. I have no son but you. Then, do as you please—but you must not send away my murderer, for I must have him cured, and shown as a proof of my wonderful invention."

"Mesty, get my pistols ready for to-morrow morning, and your own too—do you hear?"

"All ready, massa," replied Mesty; "I tink dat right."

"Right—pistols, Jack! What do you mean?"

"It is possible, father, that you may not have yet quite cured your murderer, and therefore it is as well to be prepared. I will now wish you good night; but before I go, you will be pleased to summon one of the servants, that he may inform the others that the household is under my control for the future."

The bell was again rung, and was this time answered with more expedition. Jack told the servant, in presence of his father, that with the consent of the latter, he should hereafter take the whole control of the establishment, and that Mesty would be the major-domo from whom they would receive their orders. The men stared and cast an appealing look to Mr. Easy, who hesitated, and at last said,

"Yes, William; you'll apologize to all, and say that I have made the arrangement."

"You apologize to none, sir," cried Jack; "but tell them that I will arrange the whole business to-morrow morning. Tell the woman to come here and show me my bed-room. Mesty, get your supper, and then come up to me; if they dare to refuse you, recollect who does, and point them out to-morrow morning. That will do, sir; away with you, and bring flat candlesticks."

This scene may give some idea of the state of Mr. Easy's household upon our hero's arrival. The poor lunatic, for such we must call him, was at the mercy of his servants, who robbed, laughed at, and neglected him. The waste and expense was enormous. Our hero, who found how matters stood, went to bed, and lay the best part of the night resolving what to do. He determined to send for Doctor Middleton, and consult him.

The next morning, Jack rose early; Mesty was in the room with warm water, as soon as he rang.

"By de power, Massa Easy, your fader very silly old man."

"I'm afraid so," replied Jack.

"He not right here," observed Mesty, putting his fingers to his head.

Jack sighed, and desired Mesty to send one of the grooms up to the door. When the man knocked, he desired him to mount a horse and ride over to Doctor Middleton, and request his immediate attendance.

The man, who was really a good servant, replied, "Yes, sir," very respectfully, and hastened away.

Jack went down to breakfast, and found it all ready, but his father was not in the room: he went to his study, and found him occupied with a carpenter, who was making a sort of frame as a model of the platform or dais, to be raised under the wonderful invention. Mr. Easy was so busy that he could not come to breakfast, so Jack took his alone. An hour after this, Doctor Middleton's carriage drove up to the door. The doctor heartily greeted our hero.

"My dear sir—for so I suppose I must now call you—I am heartily glad that you have returned. I can assure you that it is not a moment too soon."

"I have found out that already, doctor," replied Jack; "sit down. Have you breakfasted?"

"No, I have not; for I was so anxious to see you, that I ordered my carriage at once."

"Then sit down, doctor, and we will talk over matters quietly."

"You, of course, perceive the state of your father. He has been some time quite unfit to manage his own affairs."

"So I am afraid."

"What do you intend to do then—put them in the hands of trustees?"

"I will be trustee for myself, Doctor Middleton. I could not do the other without submitting my poor father to a process, and confinement, which I cannot think of."

"I can assure you that there are not many in Bedlam worse than he is; but I perfectly agree with you; that is, if he will consent to your taking charge of the property."

"A power of attorney will be all that is requisite," replied Jack; "that is, as soon as I have rid the house of the set of miscreants who are in it; and who are now in open mutiny."

"I think," replied the doctor, "that you will have some trouble. You know the character of the butler."

"Yes, I have it from my father's own mouth. I really should take it as a great favor, Doctor Middleton, if you could stay here a day or two. I know that you have retired from practice."

"I would have made the same offer, my young friend. I will come here with two of my servants; for you must discharge these."

"I have one of my own who is worth his weight in gold—that will be sufficient. I will dismiss every man you think I ought, and as for the women, we can give them warning, and replace them at leisure."

"That is exactly what I should propose," replied the doctor. "I will go now, if you please, procure the assistance of a couple of constables, and also of your father's former legal adviser, who shall prepare a power of attorney."

"Yes," replied Jack, "and we must then find out the tenants who refuse to pay, upon the principles of equality, and he shall serve them with notice immediately."

"I am rejoiced, my dear young friend, to perceive that your father's absurd notions have not taken root."

"They lasted some time, nevertheless, doctor," replied Jack, laughing.

"Well then, I will only quit you for an hour or two, and then, as you wish it, will take up my quarters here, as long as you find me useful."

In the forenoon, Dr. Middleton again made his appearance, accompanied by Mr. Hanson, the solicitor, bringing with him his portmanteau and his servants. Mr. Easy had come into the parlor, and was at breakfast, when they entered. He received them very coolly; but a little judicious praise of the wonderful invention had its due effect; and after Jack had reminded him of his promise that in future he was to control the household, he was easily persuaded to sign the order for his so doing—that is, the power of attorney.

Mr. Easy also gave up to Jack the key of his secretary, and Mr. Hanson possessed himself of the books, papers, and receipts necessary to ascertain the state of his affairs, and the rents which had not yet been paid up. In the mean time, the constables arrived. The servants were all summoned; Mr. Hanson showed them the power of attorney, empowering Jack to act for his father, and, in less than half an hour afterward, all the men-servants, but two grooms, were dismissed: the presence of the constables and Mesty prevented any resistance, but not without various threats on the part of the butler, whose name was O'Rourke. Thus, in twenty-four hours, Jack had made a reformation in the household.

Mr. Easy took no notice of any thing; he returned to his study and his wonderful invention. Mesty had received the keys of the cellar, and had now complete control over those who remained. Dr. Middleton, Mr. Hanson, Mr. Easy, and Jack, sat down to dinner, and every thing wore the appearance of order and comfort. Mr. Easy ate very heartily, but said nothing till after dinner, when, as was his usual custom, he commenced arguing upon the truth and soundness of his philosophy.

"By-the-by, my dear son, if I recollect right, you told me last night that you were no longer of my opinion. Now, if you please, we will argue this point."

"I'll argue the point with all my heart, sir," replied Jack; "will you begin?"

"Let's fill our glasses," cried Mr. Easy, triumphantly; "let's fill our glasses, and then I will bring Jack back to the proper way of thinking. Now then, my son, I trust you will not deny that we are all born equal."

"I do deny it, sir," replied Jack; "I deny it *in toto*—I deny it from the evidence of our own senses, and from the authority of Scripture. To suppose all men were born equal, is to suppose that they are equally endowed with the same strength, and with the same capacity of mind, which we know is not the case. I deny it from Scripture, from which I could quote many passages; but I will restrict myself to one—the parable of the Talents: 'To one he gave five talents, to another but one,' holding them responsible for the trust reposed in them. We are all intended to fill various situations in society, and are provided by Heaven accordingly."

"That may be," replied Mr. Easy; "but that does not prove that the earth was not intended to be equally distributed among all alike."

"I beg your pardon; the proof that that was not the intention of Providence is, that that equality, allowing it to be put in practice, could never be maintained."

"Not maintained!—no, because the strong oppress the weak, tyrants rise up and conquer—men combine to do wrong."

"Not so, my dear father; I say it could not be maintained without the organization of each individual had been equalized, and several other points established. For instance, allowing that every man had, *ab origine*, a certain portion of ground. He who was the strongest or the cleverest, would soon cause his to yield more than others would, and thus the equality be destroyed. Again, if one couple had ten children, and another had none, then again would equality be broken in upon, as the land that supports two in the one instance, would have to feed twelve in the other. You perceive, therefore, that without rapine or injustice, your equality could not be preserved."

"But, Jack, allowing that there might be some diversity from such causes, that would be a very different thing from the present monstrous state of society, in which we have king, and lords, and people, rolling in wealth, while others are in a state of pauperism, and obliged to steal for their daily bread."

"My dear father, I consider that it is to this inequality that society owes its firmest cementation, that we are enabled to live in peace and happiness, protected by just laws, each doing his duty in that state of life to which he is called, rising above or sinking in the scale of society, according as he has been intrusted with the five talents or the one. Equality can and does exist nowhere. We are told that it does not exist in heaven itself—how can it exist upon earth?"

"But that is only asserted, Jack, and it is not proof that it ought not to exist."

"Let us argue the point, father, coolly. Let us examine a little what would be the effect if all was equality. Were all equal in beauty, there would be no beauty, for beauty is only by comparison—were all equal in strength, conflicts would be interminable—were all equal in rank, and power, and possessions, the greatest charms of existence would be destroyed—generosity, gratitude, and half the finer virtues would be unknown. The first principle of our religion, charity, could not be practised—pity would never be called forth—benevolence, your great organ, would be useless, and self-denial a blank letter. Were all equal in ability, there would be no instruction, no talent, no genius—nothing to admire, nothing to copy, to respect—nothing to rouse emulation, or stimulate to praiseworthy ambition. Why, my dear father, what an idle, unprofitable, weary world would this be, if it were based on equality."

"But, allowing all that, Jack," replied Mr. Easy, "and I will say you argue well in a bad cause; why should the inequality be carried so far? king and lords, for instance."

"The most lasting and imperishable form of building is that of the pyramid, which defies ages, and to that may the most perfect form of society be compared. It is based upon the many, and rising by degrees, it becomes less as wealth, talent, and rank increase in the individual, until it ends at the apex, or monarch, above all. Yet each several stone, from the apex to the base, is necessary for the preservation of the structure, and fulfils its duty in its allotted place. Could you prove that those at the summit possess the greatest share of happiness in this world, then, indeed, you have a position to argue on; but it is well known that such is not the case; and provided he is of a contented mind, the peasant is more happy than the king, surrounded as the latter is by cares and anxiety."

"Very well argued, indeed, my dear sir," observed Dr. Middleton.

"But, my dear boy, there are other states of society than monarchy; we have republics and despotisms."

"We have; but how long do they last, compared to the first? There is a cycle in the changes which never varies. A monarchy may be overthrown by a revolution, and republicanism succeed, but that is shortly followed by despotism, till, after a time, monarchy succeeds again by unanimous consent, as the most legitimate and equitable form of government; but in none of these do you find a single advance to equality. In a republic, those who govern are more powerful than the rulers in a restricted monarchy—a president is greater than a king, and next to a despot, whose will is law. Even in small societies, you find that some will naturally take the lead and assume domination. We commence the system at school, when we are first thrown into society, and there we are taught systems of petty tyranny. There are some few points in which we can obtain equality in this world, and that equality can only be obtained under a well-regulated form of society, and consists in an equal administration of justice and of laws to which we have agreed to submit for the benefit of the whole—the equal right to live, and not be permitted to starve, which has been obtained in this country. And when we are all called to account, we shall have equal justice. Now, my dear father, you have my opinion."

"Yes, my dear, this is all very well in the abstract; but how does it work?"

"It works well. The luxury, the pampered state, the idleness—if you please, the wickedness of the rich, all contribute to the support, the comfort, and employment of the poor. You may behold extravagance, it is a vice: but that very extravagance circulates money, and the vice of one contributes to the happiness of many. The only vice which is not redeemed by producing commensurate good, is avarice. If all were equal, there would be no arts, no manufactures, no industry, no employment. As it is, the inequality of the distribution of wealth may be compared to the heart, pouring forth the blood like a steam engine through the human frame; the same blood returning from the extremities by the veins, to be again propelled, and keep up a healthy and vigorous circulation."

"Bravo, Jack!" said Dr. Middleton. "Have you any thing to reply, sir?" continued he, addressing Mr. Easy.

"To reply, sir?" replied Mr. Easy, with scorn; "why he has not given me half an argument yet—why that black servant even laughs at him—look at him there, showing his teeth. Can he forget the horrors of slavery? can he forget the base, unfeeling lash?—no, sir, he has suffered, and he can estimate the divine right of equality. Ask him now, ask him if you dare, Jack, whether he will admit the truth of your argument."

"Well, I'll ask him," replied Jack, "and I tell you candidly that he was once one of your disciples. Mesty, what's your opinion of equality?"

"Equality, Massa Easy?" replied Mesty, pulling up his cravat; "I say d—n equality, now I major domo."

"The rascal deserves to be a slave all his life."

"True I ab been slave—but I a prince in my own country—Massa Easy tell how many skulls I have."

"Skulls—skulls—do you know any thing of the sublime science? are you a phrenologist?"

"I know man's skull very well in Ashantee country, any how."

"Then if you know that, you must be one. I had no idea that the science had extended so far—may be it was brought from thence. I will have some talk with you to-morrow. This is very curious, Dr. Middleton, is it not?"

"Very, indeed, Mr. Easy."

"I shall feel his head to-morrow, after breakfast, and if there is any thing wrong I shall correct it with my machine. By-the-by, I have quite forgot, gentlemen; you will excuse me, but I wish to see what the carpenter has done for me, and after that I shall attend the meeting of the society. Jack, my boy, won't you come and hear my speech?"

"Thank you, sir, but I cannot well leave your friends."

Mr. Easy quitted the room.

"Are you aware, my dear sir, that your father has opened his preserves to all the poachers?" said Mr. Hanson.

"The devil he has!"

"Yes, and has allowed several gangs of gipsies to locate themselves in his woods, much to the annoyance of the neighborhood, who suffer from their depredations," continued Dr. Middleton.

"I find by the receipts and books, that there is nearly two years' rental of the estate due; some tenants have paid up in full, others not for four years. I reckon fourteen thousand pounds still in arrear."

"You will oblige me by taking immediate steps, Mr. Hanson, for the recovery of the sums due."

"Most certainly, Mr. John. I trust your father will not commit himself to-night, as he has done lately."

When they rose to retire, Dr. Middleton took our hero by the hand. "You do not know, my dear fellow, what pleasure it gives me to find that, in spite of the doting of your mother, and the madness of your father, you have turned out so well. It is very fortunate that you have come home; I trust you will now give up the profession."

"I have given it up, sir, which, by-the-by, reminds me that I have not yet applied for either my discharge or that of my servant; but I cannot spare time yet, so I shall not report myself."

* * * * *

The next morning, when they met at breakfast, Mr. Easy did not make his appearance, and Jack inquired of Mesty where he was?

"They say down below that the old gentleman not come home last night."

"Did not come home!" said Dr. Middleton; "this must be looked to."

"He great rascal, dat butler man," said Mesty to Jack; "but de old gentleman not sleep in his bed, dat for sure."

"Make inquiries when he went out," said Jack.

"I hope no accident has happened," observed

Mr. Hanson; "but his company has lately been very strange."

"Nobody see him go out, sar, last night," reported Mesty."

"Very likely, he is in his study," observed Dr. Middleton; "he may have remained all night, fast asleep, by his wonderful invention."

"I'll go and see," replied Jack.

Dr. Middleton accompanied him, and Mesty followed. They opened the door, and beheld a spectacle which made them recoil with horror. There was Mr. Easy, with his head in the machine, the platform below fallen from under him, hanging, with his toes just touching the ground. Dr. Middleton hastened to him, and, assisted by Mesty and our hero, took him out of the steel collar which was round his neck; but life had been extinct for many hours, and, on examination, it was found that the poor old gentleman's neck was dislocated.

It was surmised that the accident must have taken place the evening before, and it was easy to account for it. Mr. Easy, who had had the machine raised four feet higher, for the platform and steps to be placed underneath, must have mounted on the frame modelled by the carpenter for his work, and have fixed his head in, for the knob was pressed on his bump of benevolence. The frame work, hastily put together with a few short nails, had given way with his weight, and the sudden fall had dislocated his neck.

A LITTLE TALK ABOUT BARTHOLOMEW FAIR—PAST AND PRESENT.

BY ALBERT SMITH.

By the time this sheet is in the hands of the reader, Bartholomew Fair will be spoken of as a festival that once was—an annual celebration, the account of which must henceforward be added, in the shape of an appendix, to the succeeding editions of Strutt's "Sports and Pastimes." For a long period its health has been visibly declining, from the effects of a shattered and depraved constitution. The same year that beheld the abolition of the climbing-boys—who whilome peopled the locality whereon it was held, for their yearly banquet, when the kind-hearted Charles Lamb felt it no degradation to sup with them,—has also witnessed the extinction of the *fête*, to celebrate whose return the "clergy imps" assembled amongst the cattle-pens, then and there to discuss the hissing sausages and small ale, which benevolence had provided for them.

Certainly better times and places for reflection might be found in London than Smithfield on a fair-day: and yet, we confess to have fallen into a day-dream on the fifth of the past month, when we paid what will probably be our last visit to this departed festival. We are indebted for our vision to no romance of poetic situation. We were sitting on the handle of a gaudily-painted hand-cart containing penny ginger-beer, by the side of a small perambulating theatre, which set forth "the vicissitudes of a servant-maid;" and, in spite of the unceasing noise on every side, we could not desist from indulging in a mental daguerreotype of events connected with the fair and its localities.

We first called to mind the period when Smithfield was "a plain, or smoothe fielde," from which circumstance, according to old Fitzstephen, it derived its name; and when, instead of the London butchers and country drovers, a gay train of gallant knights and tramping men-at-arms, whose harness gleamed in the sunlight of the glittering lists, together with a bevy of smiling, fair-haired "damosels" on their ambling palfreys, rode over its unpaved area to join the tournaments there held. We pictured them coming by "Gilt-spurre, or Knight-rider street,—so called because of the knights, who in quality of their honour wore gilt spurs, and who, with others, rode that way to the joustings and other feats of arms used in Smithfield." And then we thought what a fortune the events of these times would have been to the *boudoir* romancists of the present day, who write such pretty stories with dove's quills and otto of roses, for the annuals. Next, we lost ourselves in a reverie about the sly Rahere,—the founder of the monastery and fair, and minstrel to Henry the First,—who was in former days employed to tell stories to royalty (an office, it would seem, not altogether obsolete), and who once began one of so great a length that he himself fell asleep in the middle, and never finished it. Rahere, when he was sick, was frightened into this pious act by a supposed visitation of St. Bartholomew, and became the first head of the priory, within whose walls the drapers and clothiers invited to the fair were allowed to lock up their wares every night. Anon, we allowed ourselves to be carried in dreamy listlessness along the stream of time, until we were again halting, as we chuckled at the recollection of the humorous doings in the fair in the days of "Rare Ben Jonson,"—the puppet motions of Hero and Leander, altered from Sestos and Abydos to Puddledock and Bankside,—the Bartholomew pig, "roasted with fire o' juniper and rosemary branches,"—the court of *pié-poudre*, the "well-educated ape," and the "hare that beat the tabor,"—all hackneyed subjects to mouldy antiquaries, we allow; but, not being over-addicted to rummaging dusty records and worm-eaten volumes, still interesting to common-place every-day people like ourselves. And lastly, we pictured the fair as we had known it in our own days, of which poor Hone has left us so lively a specimen, and calling back some of the scenes we had therein witnessed, we began to think that the abolition was not altogether useless or disadvantageous.

Whether our reflections would now have taken a retrograde turn, and wandered back again to the days of the tournaments, we know not; but, having arrived close upon the present period, we were somewhat startled, upon wishing to use it, to find that our handkerchief had disappeared whilst we had been lost in our reveries; and, possibly, was already fluttering before one of the neighboring bandana-bazaars in Field-lane. Hereupon, we determined to give up ruminating in Smithfield, leaving that process to those animals in the cattle-market whose peculiar nature it is so to do; and having risen from our seat, and thanked the ginger-beer man for the accommodation his wagon afforded, we commenced making the tour of the fair, or rather, the ground once allotted to it.

There were no shows—no huge yellow caravans, or canvas pavilions, covered with wondrous representations of the marvels to be seen within: a few small portable theatres formed the leading exhibitions. One there was, to be sure, of higher pretensions, into which, upon payment of one penny, we were permitted to enter. The proprietor of the spectacle, who had pitched his theatre in the back-parlor of one of the houses near the Hospital-gate, stood at the street-door, and informed us that the entertainment set forth "The Bay of Naples in its native grander with the percession of the Ingian monarch and his elephint,—the sportsman and the stag as walked like life—the wild duck and the water-spanell, with the burning of Hamburg."

Here was enough to see, so we entered forthwith, and wedged ourselves in the corner of a room, small, and unpleasantly warm, where an audience of some five-and-twenty had already assembled before a small proscenium, about twelve feet high, having a painted drop-scene, which represented, as nearly as we could make out the localities, the Castle of Chillon moved to Virginia Water, with Athens and Mont Blanc in the background. After an Italian boy, who with his piano-organ formed the orchestra, had played "The days when we went gipsying," the drop rose, and discovered the Bay of Naples, with surrounding buildings, and something of a conical shape painted on the back scene—the *flat*, we think it is technically called—which we imagined to be a light-blue cotton night-cap, with a long tassel, until informed that it depicted "Vesuvius—the burnin' mounting, as it appears from the sea-shore." When the excitement caused by the rising of the curtain had somewhat subsided, a little figure dressed like a Turk, shuffled rapidly across the front of the stage, moving his legs backwards and forwards, both at once, and evidently by means of a crank connected with the wheels he ran on, which were invisible to the audience. Next, the "percession" commenced, which was extremely imposing, and would have been much more so if the manager had been less hasty in taking the figures off, and putting them on other stands to go across again, which gave them the appearance of being most unsteadily intoxicated upon their second *entrée*. Then, a little man came on in a boat, and shot a duck, which the "spanell" swam after; and, finally, the ignition of some red fire at the foot of Vesuvius formed the burning of Hamburg, which conflagration was exceedingly advantageous in rapidly clearing the room of the audience, by reason of its sulphurous vapor.

The principal traffic of the fair, beyond the business transacted in gingerbread-husbands, and wax-dolls from fourpence to three shillings each, was monopolized by several men in tilted carts, who were haranguing little mobs of people, and apparently disposing of their wares as fast as they could put them up for sale.

There were such frequent bursts of laughter from the buyers, that we were attracted towards one of these perambulating bazaars, in the hope of participating in their merriment. The proprietor of the cart was a tall burly fellow, in a round hat and knee-breeches, something like an aristocratic railway navigator, and the cart, in front of which he stood, was covered all over with a most curious display of goods, guns, braces, gimlets, waistcoats, saws, cruets,—in fact, specimens of almost every thing ever manufactured. The man was selling the goods by his own auction, and had a flow of ready low wit,—pure, unadulterated chaff—which was most remarkable. We recollect a few of his jokes, and these we chronicle to show the style of his address, even at the risk of being again accused of "exhibiting the coarsest peculiarities of the coarser classes, with such ultra accuracy." But it is in the lower orders, according to our own notion, that the natural character of a people is to be best discovered.

"Now, then, my customers," he exclaimed, advancing to the front of the cart, "I'll tell you more lies in five minutes than you can prove true in a week. Now, missus," he continued, addressing a female in the crowd, "no winking at me to get things cheap. My wife 's in the cart, and she's as sharp as the thick end of a pen'orth of cheese, as ugly as sin, and not half so pleasant."

A roar of laughter followed this sally as he took up a saw.

"Now, look here!—you never saw such a saw as this here saw is to saw in all the days you ever saw. This is a saw as *will* cut;—all you've got to do is to keep it back. If you was to lay this saw agin the root of a tree over night, and go home to bed—"

"Well, what then?" interrupted a fellow in the crowd, who wished to throw the dealer off his guard.

"Why," replied the man, "the chances are that when you came in the morning you wouldn't find it. Sold again!"

There was another laugh, and the would-be wag slunk away very crest-fallen.

"Now, I'm not going to take you in," he continued. "If you don't like these things, come again to-morrow, and I shan't be here. I'll charge you a pound for the saw, and if you don't like that, I'll say fifteen shillings. Come,—you've got faint hearts. Say twelve, ten, eight, five, three, *one!*—going for one! I'll ask no more, and I'll take no less. Sold again, and got the money!"

He now turned and picked out a cheap accordion, upon which he played some common air, and then proceeded.

"Now, look!—here's a young piece of music: the appollonicon in St. Martin's Lane lays a dozen every morning, and this is one of them. It's got the advantage that, when you're tired of it, it will blow the fire or mend your shoes. May I be rammed, jammed, and slammed into the mouth of a cannon, until I come out at the touchhole as thin as a dead rushlight, if it ain't cheap at five pound! But I'll only take five shillings, and if that won't do, I'll say one! Who's got the lucky shilling?"

Not fifteen feet from the cart of this man there was another similarly laden, and a constant fire of salutations and mock abuse passed between the two venders. The merchant, however, in this case was a mere boy—he could not have been above fourteen, but carrying an expression of the most precocious meaning we ever beheld. He was no whit inferior to his adversary in ready slang, as his following oration over a two-barrelled gun will testify:

"There's a little flaw in the lock, to be sure; but that don't hinder its going off. I sold the fellow for two pound to a farmer in Leicestershire, and

Albert Smith.

I'll tell you what it did. The first day he took it out, he fired one barrel, and killed six crows as he didn't see; he fired the second, and shot nine partridges out of five, and the kick of the gun knocked him back'ards into a ditch, and he fell upon a hare and killed that. These guns will shoot round a corner, and over a hay-rick; and they're used to fatten the paupers that are turned out of the Unions for not paying the Income Tax. They load the guns with fat bacon, and shoot it down their throats."

Of course, this was a safe *entamure* for a laugh. When he had done talking about the gun, which, however, he did not sell, he took up a whip, and, cracking it two or three times in front of his cart, recommenced:—

"Here's a whip, now, to make a lazy wife get up of a morning, and make the kettle boil before the fire's alight. It even makes my horse go, and he's got a weak constitution and a bad resolution; he jibs going up hill, kicks going down, and travels on his knees on level ground. When he means to go, he blows hisself out with the celebrated railroad corn as sticks sideways in his inside, and tickles him into a trot. Who says a crown for this whip!"

There did not appear much disposition to buy the article, so the seller commenced a fresh panegyric.

"You'd better buy it: you won't have another chance. There never was but two made, and the man died, and took the patent with him. He wouldn't have made them so cheap, only he lived in a garret, and never paid his landlord, but when he went home, always pulled the bottom of the house upstairs after him. If any man insults you, I'll warrant this whip to flog him from Newgate into the middle of next year. Who says a crown?"

There were two or three other carts of a similar description in different parts of Smithfield, but these fellows evidently enjoyed the supremacy. How many profits had to be made upon the articles, or what was their original cost, we know not, but we bought four pocket-knives, each containing three blades, with very fair springs, and horn handles, for sixpence! We had a little conversation afterwards with the first-mentioned vendor, who was, out of his rostrum, a quiet, intelligent person, and he assured us that at Wolverhampton the ordinary *curry-combs* of the shops were being made by families for ninepence a dozen, the rivets being clenched and the teeth cut by mere infants.

Beyond these features there was little to notice; —the vitality of the fair was evidently at its last gasp, and the civic authorities did not appear inclined to act as a humane society for its resuscitation. A little trade was maintained by the sale of portable cholera, in the shape of green-gages; but the majority of the stalls were sadly in want of customers. Even the Waterloo-crackers, unable to go off in a commercial point of view, failed to do so in a pyrotechnical one. Had we waited until midnight, when all became still, we might possibly have beheld the shades of Richardson, Saunders, Polito, and Miss Biffin, with their more ancient brethren, Fawkes the conjuror, and Lee, and Harper, waiting amongst the pens, or gathering together their audiences of old in shadowy bands to people the fair once more, as Napoleon collects his phantom troops in the Champs Elysées, where, since he has been buried in the Invalides, he must find it far more convenient to attend. But there was no inducement to stay until that period, and we left the fair about twenty minutes after we entered it, having seen every thing that it contained, and deeming ourselves fortunate in having been only once violently compelled to buy a pound of gingerbread-nuts, by the sheer force of a young lady who presided at the stall, and who appeared in a state of temporary insanity, caused by the lack of customers and limited incomes of the majority of the visitors.

SEPTEMBER 11, 1842.

THE LAUDANUM PATIENT.

BY ALBERT SMITH.

MR. CRIPPS was one of the best tempered men at the hospital, wherein he filled the post of house-surgeon, always ready for a piece of fun when there was any thing going on; and yet possessing sufficient tact and good sense to keep quiet when he thought it necessary for the support of the true dignity of his character. He was a universal favorite with all classes, both patients, surgeons and pupils; for he was kind to the first, attentive to the second, and never refused to join in the amusements of the third, when not interfering with his own duties. He was, in fact, what every medical student ought to be. Not on one side a careless idler, who sneered at every thing connected with study, and thought the chief happiness the world could give was to be found in a glass of brandy and water. Nor was he, on the other, one of those intense *potterers* who haunt the hospitals year after year, cringing to the officers, and thinking themselves above the pupils, with the sole hope of being at some very distant period elected assistant-surgeon —an aspiration which is never gratified. But he, Mr. Cripps, combined the best qualities of the two, and so kept very friendly with all. You could seldom go into his room without finding one or two of the choicest men in the medical school lolling about upon his chairs, and taking everlasting lunches; indeed his quarters appeared a perpetual scene of bread, cheese, and half-and-half, which were mingled upon the table in admirable confusion with scalpels, stethoscopes, bones, and manuals of surgery and anatomy.

Mr. Cripps' rooms—or rather his room, for the bedchamber was only a long narrow accidental appendix to his sitting apartment—were on the first floor of the hospital, and in the immediate vicinity of two of the wards. A strong smell of stale tobacco pervaded the interior; and indeed it would have been much stronger had there been any thing to retain it. But the carpet was so worn that it appeared to have been turned the wrong side upwards; and the pair of dingy window curtains had in all probability been hanging there ever since the hospital was first chartered; and now assumed a series of tints, varying in their color from dirty buff to dull red.

The furniture was admirably in keeping with the chamber, being dark with age, and of a fashion unknown in the memory of the oldest second-hand broker in London. The chairs mostly suffered from rickets, and the sofa was particularly unsteady, in consequence of an unreduced dislocation of one of its four hip joints, which was gradually wearing away a new socket for itself in a corner of the squab that formed its seat. There was an ancient bureau, in which Cripps kept his books; but the piece of furniture had lost its turned legs, which were supposed to have mortified at a period lost in antiquity; and now it stood by being propped up against the ledge of the wainscot behind, and was in consequence christened by Mr. Cripps his "upholsterous biped." One of its doors suffered from paralysis of the hinges; and the other had an artificial joint, ingeniously made from an old bent probe, which allowed it to close and open with tolerable facility. The windows commanded a fine view of the hospital garden, with its perambulating patients, consisting of convalescent amputations, ameliorated squints, recovered operations for club feet, and last stages but one of œdema, who were perpetually crawling up and down its formal walks, and over the parallelogram of hard black earth, which was by courtesy denominated the grass-plat. This area was bounded by the backs of the houses in the adjacent streets; all of whose occupants evinced indomitable perseverance in eternally washing their things at home, and then displaying them upon poles from their windows, where they fluttered all day long. By much observation, Mr. Cripps had become acquainted with a great deal of the domestic economy practised by his neighbors, through these signals. He knew perfectly when to look out for the appearance of the patchwork quilt, on the third floor of No. 12; and he discovered that the back attic of No. 7 possessed two pairs of sheets, which were washed in turns, being recognized by sundry patches and repairs.

He was sitting one morning in the surgery, waiting for some out-door patients to arrive, when the door opened, and Mr. Blake, a pupil of the hospital, having first thrust in a small portion of his head to see that the coast was clear, propelled the rest of his body after it, and saluted Cripps with a wink of the right eye, intended to express the compliments of the morning.

"What's the news, Cripps?" was the first question.

"Little enough from me," returned his friend. "My opinion of a house-surgeon is, that he's two degrees worse off than a prisoner in the Queen's Bench."

"Well, you have not much longer to stay," replied Blake, seating himself at the table, and playing with some tooth instruments. "What a room of torture this is!" he continued, after a momentary gaze around the surgery, and at the different objects hanging about.

There certainly was a great display of all kinds of articles, that any one skilled in the art of ingeniously tormenting would have delighted to contemplate. Gags for obstinate poison-takers; keys, elevators, forceps, and punches for the odontalgists: caustic for touching up refractory excrescences; long savage-looking bistouries; deeply-insinuating probes, and scalpels; with knives, lancets, and directors of every size and capacity.

"There only wants one thing to render all this apparatus perfect," said Blake, as he looked round him.

"And what's that?" asked Mr. Cripps.

"A twitch for the noses," replied Blake.

"I don't quite know what you mean."

"A twitch," returned Blake, "is a piece of broomstick with a string loop at the end, that you put over colts' noses, and screw up tight when they run rusty at being singed, or put into harness. You would find it a capital remedy for epistaxis."

"I don't doubt it," answered Cripps; "indeed, I think it would be a valuable addition to surgery. By the way, I've formed a beautiful diagnosis lately."

"What about?" asked Blake.

"Between various accidents," returned the house-surgeon. "For instance, broken legs always come on a shutter; fractured ribs in a patent cab; and dislocated shoulders usually walk."

"And what good does that do you?"

"Oh, nothing particular—only if you see a casualty coming, you know what it is, and what to get ready."

"Then you had better be looking after your apparatus now," said Blake, "for here's an accident coming in."

In confirmation of his statement, a crowd of dirty little boys, surrounding a group of three persons, the middle one of whom was being supported by the other two, crossed the court to the hospital, and came up to the surgery. As the nurse opened the door to admit them, the whole posse pressed forwards to obtain entrance with the patient; and the place would have been certainly carried by storm had not Blake gone to the assistance of the nurse, and vigorously repelled the assailants with a straw *junk*—an instrument used in the treatment of fractures, and which he liberally dealt about the heads of the intruders.

"Now, then, missus,—what is it?" asked Cripps, when Blake had succeeded in closing the door and bolting it, addressing himself to a woman who had come in with the patient.

"He's pisened himself with lodnum!" was the reply. Whereupon she began to moan after the most approved manner of poor people in a dilemma, thinking that she should have lived to have seen the day, and recollecting it was only last night he was saying, he meant to join the blessed Temperance.

"When did he take it?" asked Cripps, feeling in his waistcoat pocket for the key of his stomach-pump.

"Why, docthor," rejoined the woman, "last January twelvemonth——"

"When!" interrupted Blake, with some astonishment.

"Last January twelvemonth," continued the woman, "there was a benefit soeiety formed at the Corner Pin public house, and the members has some scursions on board the steam-boats——"

"My good woman," said Cripps; "I asked you when he took it;—can't you give me a simple answer?"

"I don't know, I don't know!" cried the woman, wringing the corner of her apron, as if she labored under a belief that it was wet. "All I can tell is, I'd been into Mrs. Watts' to help her wash, and when I come back the room was locked, and I looked through the keyhole, and there he was a sitting in an arm-chair with his hands hanging down just like a corpse. Oh dear! oh dear! what shall I do?"

"What makes you think he has taken laudanum?" asked Blake.

"I found this bottle on the floor," said the woman, producing an irregularly-shaped green phial with letters blown on it, and labelled "Laudanum Poison."

"I don't think that's opium," said Blake, smelling the bottle; "it's more like lacquer for brass work."

"He's evidently in a state of coma," replied Cripps; "and his breathing is any thing but what I should like mine to be. Well, there's only one plan—I suppose I had better perform a solo on the stomach-pump."

"And then we'll give him a promenade without the concert, in the garden, to keep him awake," added Blake. "Get a basin, Surgery, and some warm water."

"I think he's been sitting in the sun a little too much," observed the nurse addressed as 'Surgery,' with a knowing assent, as she tilted the kettle, implying by that delicate metaphor that the man was drunk.

The stomach-pump was soon in action, and the result convinced the students that there was a great deal more gin than laudanum in what the patient had taken. At the conclusion of the performance, the man appeared a little relieved. He opened his eyes, rolled them heavily about, gave a sulky grunt, and tried to raise himself from the chair.

"Do you think he'll recover, docthor?" asked the woman.

"I think so," said Cripps; "but he will require great care. Now, we must mind that he does not go to sleep again; and for that purpose he must be walked gently round the garden."

"You can stay here until we return," said Blake to the woman. And then, supporting the patient with Cripps' aid, they led him into the garden.

"How are you, old fireworks?" asked Blake, when they got out of earshot.

"I'm the marquis of Herne Bay, there and back; and Prince George of Peckham and Camberwell," growled the man, in the true accents of intoxication.

"Yes, yes! we know all that," said Blake. "Don't you think a little dash of Preissnitz would do him good, Cripps?"

"I should say so, decidedly," replied the house-surgeon; "and if I have a preference, it should be fresh from the pump."

Fortunately for their good intentions, there was a pump in the garden, principally used for the purpose of irrigating the esculent vegetables which grew there for the consumption of the matron, secretary, and house-apothecary; as well as for strengthening weak ligaments, and relaxed joints by its bracing stream. Towards this point, Blake and Cripps conducted their patient, and seating him opposite to it, upon the ground, propped up by the garden-roller, the first named gentleman worked at the handle, whilst the latter interrupted the stream with his hand, jerking it copiously into the face of their victim, until he was wet through and through.

"Now, I think we had better dry him," said Blake, when they had persevered in this innocent recreation about five minutes. Upon which—in spite of the struggles and remonstrances of the man, who having been in reality only dead-drunk, was coming to his senses again very quickly—Cripps and his companion took him by the arms, and ran him round and round the garden, until nearly every bit of breath was out of his body; and they themselves quite overcome with fatigue.

"Will you ever do it again?" asked Cripps, with as serious a face as he could command.

"Never, no more, s'help me eversomuch," was the answer. "I'll be a teetotaller,—if I don't I'm——"

"Hush!" cried Blake, gravely. "Recollect how

you have been snatched from the jaws of death by our united efforts. How came you to get drunk so early in the morning?"

"It's all along of the scursion as I was steward for," replied the man. "I had the grog to keep and couldn't help it."

"And how did you come by this bottle?" asked Cripps, taking the laudanum phial from his pocket.

"I keeps lacquer in it," was the answer; "I'm a gilder by trade."

"I said it was!" cried Blake, quite délighted at his prognosis; "I knew it all the while."

"How the deuce did you know what lacquer was?" asked Cripps.

"I was with a dentist once," replied Blake; "and we used it to set off the brass things that he kept in a little case on his street-door post, and made the people believe they were gold."

The man being pronounced recovered, was now led back to the surgery. He departed in a short time with the woman, accompanied by the cheers of such little boys as had waited outside the whole time, and looking very pale and repentant. It seems, however, that the ordeal he had undergone was not without its effect; for, three days afterwards, Blake saw him with a high clean shirt-collar, and a blue bow on his hat, entering the Temperance Coffee House, which was close to the hospital.

DELIGHTFUL PEOPLE.

BY ALBERT SMITH.

THERE are two sets of people in society—the amusers and the amused, who are both equally useful in their way, although widely different in their attributes. A *réunion*, to go off well, should contain a proper share of either class; because, notwithstanding the inability of the latter to contribute much to the festivity of the meeting, they make an excellent and patient audience, without which the powers of the amusers are cramped, and they feel they are not sufficiently appreciated.

Why all people, enjoying the same level of intellect, should not be equally sought after in society we do not pretend to decide; but we will endeavor to account for it by falling back upon our theatrical analogies. If you study the playbills, you see, year after year, the same names amongst the companies who keep at the same humble standard; whilst others, whom you recollect as their inferiors, ultimately arrive at big letters and benefits—in fact, that chance, tact, *forte*, and opportunity, come spontaneously to the latter, whilst the former are content to remain servants and peasants. They have been known to embody guests and mobs, and have sometimes arrived at first citizens; but this is by no means a common occurrence. The same union of circumstances that divides a theatrical commonwealth into stars and supernumaries, produces in our own circles delightful people and nobodies—for so are the listeners and admirers generally and uncourteously termed.

But there are various kinds of delightful people beyond the mere entertainers. If there is a family rather higher in life than yourselves, or moving in a sphere you think more of than your own, notwithstanding they may have formerly *snubbed* you, it is astonishing, when you get introduced to them, and at last asked to their house, what delightful people you find them. If you know two young persons who have tumbled into an engagement with one another, under tolerably favorable circumstances, and visit each other's friends for the first time, you will be enchanted with the accounts of what "delightful people" they are; how *very* friendly the mother was, and how well the sisters played, and made colored-paper dust-collectors. Persons who have large houses, give dinners, and keep carriages and private boxes—gentlemen who have been all along the coast of the Mediterranean, and tell most extraordinary anecdotes, until they themselves really believe that their adventures have happened—authors who have written a book which has proved a hit by chance, to the astonishment of every body, and no one more than the writers—acquaintances who have the happy knack of cordially agreeing with you upon every subject, and applauding every thing you do, thinking quite differently all the while—worn out "bits of quality tumbled into decay," as Miss Lucretia M'Tab says, who honor families of questionable *caste* with their acquaintance, and join all their parties by the tenor of relating stories of bygone greatness, and random recollections of defunct high circles; all these and many more, had we time to enumerate them, are "delightful people." But we proceed to consider the class that it is our wish to place more especially under the inspection of the reader.

We called one day upon a lady of our acquaintance, who was about to give a large evening party; and upon being ushered into the drawing-room, found the whole family in high glee at the contents of a note they had just received. Our intimacy prompted us to inquire the purport of the oblong billet that had so much delighted them.

"Oh!" said Ellen, the eldest daughter, "the Lawsons have accepted—all of them are coming!"

"And who are the Lawsons?" we ventured to ask.

"My goodness, Albert!" exclaimed every body at once, with an excitement which nearly caused us, being of a nervous temperament, to tilt backwards off the apology for a chair on which we were seated—one of those slim rickety specimens of upholstery, which inspire stout gentlemen with such nervous dread, when one is handed to them. "Is it possible you don't know the Lawsons?"

We confessed with shame our ignorance of the parties in question.

"They are such *delightful people*," continued the second female olive-branch, Margaret. "We were so afraid they would not come, because they are almost always engaged; so we sent their invitation nearly a month ago."

"And you have only just received their reply?" we subjoined. "It looks as if they had waited for something else that didn't come."

"Oh, no," said Ellen, almost offended. "Mrs. Lawson is always *so* charmed with every thing at our house, and says our parties are always *so* pleasant, and that we manage things *so* well."

"And she told me, the last time she was here,"

added Margaret, "that she could not have believed the whole of the supper was made at home, if she had not been told. And I am sure she liked it because she ate so much."

"And what does this family do to make them so delightful?" we inquired.

"Oh, almost every thing," said Ellen. "Mr. Lawson plays an admirable rubber, and Mrs. Lawson knows nearly all the great people of the day, and can tell a great deal of their private histories. Bessy is a perfect Mrs. Anderson on the piano, and Cynthia——"

"Who?" we interrupted, somewhat rudely.

"Cynthia—isn't it a pretty name? She is such a delightful girl—sings better than any one you ever heard in private."

"Then, Tom is such an oddity, and such a nice fellow," continued Margaret. "He imitates Macready and Buckstone, so that you would not know the difference, and sings the drollest songs! He can whistle just like a bird, play tunes upon a stick, and conjure with rout-cakes at supper."

"And you should hear him do the two cats, where he makes you believe that they talk real words!" chimed in Ellen.

"And what is this wonder?" we asked.

"He's a lawyer," said Ellen; "but I don't think he much likes his profession."

We thought so too. No man who did the two cats, or imitated Macready and Buckstone, ever did like his profession, unless he was an actor at once.

"You will see them here on Friday," said Margaret, "and then you can form your own opinions; but I am certain you will like them. Hark! there's a double knock at the door."

"Don't peep at the window, Margaret; they will see you," said Ellen to her sister, who was endeavoring to discover who the visitors were by taking a covert observation through the bars of a birdcage.

"It's those horrid Wiltons!" exclaimed Margaret. "Do ring again, Ellen. What a singular thing it is, servants are never in the way when a double knock comes at the door."

The new-comers entered the room, and at the same time we left: not, however, before our fair young friends had told "those horrid Wiltons" how angry they were with them for not calling more frequently, and how delighted they felt now they had come at last. We were sorry to find their pretty lips could let out such little falsehoods, and with such excellent grace.

Friday evening arrived, as in the common course of things every Friday evening must do if you wait for it; and about ten o'clock, after a shilling's-worth of shake, rattle, and altercation, we alighted from a cab at our friends' house, and tripped into the library, where tea and coffee were going on, with a lightness that only dress boots and white kids can inspire. Several visitors were there before us, as well as one of Margaret's brothers, who said, in a low voice, as we entered—

"My dear friend, let me introduce you to some delightful people. Mrs. Lawson, allow me to present to you Mr. ——"

"Will you take tea or coffee, Sir?" said the maid, at the same time.

We were so overcome with being thus suddenly confronted with the stars, that we think we bowed to the maid, and said we were happy to make her acquaintance; and merely exclaimed, "Coffee, if you please," as Mrs. Lawson inclined her head to ourselves.

We went up stairs, and entered the ball-room, where our friends had just received intelligence that "the Lawsons had arrived!"

The first portion of a party is always the same. And it was not until the evening was somewhat advanced, and they had made sure that every body was arrived, that the powers of the Lawsons came into full play,—at least, as regarded the young people; for the governor had been at whist ever since he first arrived, and Mrs. Lawson's feathers were ubiquitously perceptible, waving and bending apparently in every part of the room at once; talking to all the old ladies in turn, fishing for compliments for her own daughters by admiring theirs, and smiling, with angelic benignity, upon every young man concerning whose expectations she had been agreeably informed. The junior exhibition commenced by Bessy delighting the company with a rondo by Hertz, in the most approved skyrocket style of that great master; being a Parisian composition, introducing variations upon the popular airs, "*Rien, mes bons enfans, allez toujours,*" "*La Pierre de Newgate,*" and "*Joli Nez,*" from the opera of *Jacque Sheppard.* As it was not above twenty pages in length, every one was quite charmed,—indeed, they could almost have heard it again; and the manner in which Miss Lawson sprung at the keys, and darted up and down the flats and sharps, and twitched her shoulders, and tickled the piano into convulsions, and jerked about upon the music-stool, was really astonishing, and thunderstruck every body; except the young lady and gentleman who were flirting at the end of the room after a waltz, and actually appeared more engaged with their own conversation than they did with the fair Bessy's performance, which at last concluded amidst universal applause.

There was another quadrille, and then we were informed that Miss Cynthia Lawson was going to sing. The young lady was dressed in plain white robes, with her hair smoothed very flat round her head *à la Grisi*, whom she thought she resembled both in style of singing and features, and consequently studied all her attitudes from the clever Italian's impersonation of Norma. Of course, there was the usual delay attendant upon such displays. The musicians had to be cleared away from the piano, in which process their wine-bottle was knocked over; then the music was in a portfolio, in the room down stairs, which nobody could find; when found, it was all placed on the music-rest topsy-turvy; and many other annoyances. At last, the lady began a bravura, upon such a high note, and so powerful, that some impudent fellows in the square, who were passing at the time, sang out, "Vari-e-ty!" in reply. Presently, a young gentleman, who was standing at her side, chanced to turn over too soon, whereupon she gave him *such* a look, that, if he had entertained any thoughts of proposing, would effectually have stopped any such rash proceeding; but her equanimity was soon restored, and she went through the aria in most dashing style, until she came to the last note, whose appearance she heralded with a roulade of wonderful execution.

"Now, don't get up," said the lady of the house, in a most persuasive and winning manner, to Miss Cynthia, when she had really concluded. "*Do* favor us with one more, if you are not too fatigued. Or, perhaps you would like a glass of wine first—a very, very little glass."

The young lady declined any refreshment, and immediately commenced a duet with her brother, whose voice, however, she entirely drowned; nevertheless, the audience were equally delighted, and as soon as she had regularly concluded, and the murmur of approbation had ceased, six young men rushed up to Ellen, with the request that they might be introduced to Mis Lawson for the next waltz. But, unfortunately, Miss Lawson did not waltz, or rather she did not choose to do so. She was aware of her liability to be called upon to sing after every dance, and she had no notion of sitting down to the instrument with a red face and flustered *ensemble.*

"Delightful people, those Lawsons!" wheezed out a fat old gentleman in pumps and a white neckcloth, who was leaning against the wall, and looking as if he wanted a glass of ale.

"Do you know them, Sir?" we asked.

"Never had the pleasure of meeting them before, but they are a charming family. Mother a delightful person, Sir—woman of the world—appears to have been thrown early into good society, and profited by it. Clever fellow that young Lawson—ha! ha!—look at him!" And the old gentleman chuckled until he was almost choked.

We turned to gaze at the cause of his mirth, and saw Tom doing Pastorale in a most ballet-like style, jumping up and coming down upon one toe, turning round without touching the ground, and making every body afraid of coming within a yard of him.

There are many worse periods in our existence than the twenty minutes consumed at supper at an evening party. The reserve which prevailed at the commencement of the evening begins to wear off; you gain courage to make engagements for the first quadrille after supper, and think what a pity it is that the flight of time cannot be delayed by pleasure, with permission to make up his lost moments by hurrying doubly quick over periods of sorrow or *ennui.* Alas! the hoary old mower generally takes it into his head to act in precisely an opposite manner.

We went down to supper with a pretty specimen of feminine mortality, in white poplin, on our arm, and assisted her to a cubic inch of blancmange, and an homœopathic quantity of Moselle, which she affirmed was quite sufficient; as well as took the precaution to push the tongue to the other side of the table, opposite a man who had taken off his gloves to eat, and who was immediately "troubled for a slice" fifteen times in rapid succession. By the way, talking of taking off your gloves—what is the reason that, whenever you go out, and wish your hands to look more than ordinarily white, they generally resemble raw beefsteaks?

Our *devoirs* being for the time accomplished, we looked round the room, and the first object that caught our eye between the lines of wax-candles and trifle-dishes was Mrs. Lawson's turban, with herself attached to it, bobbing about at the head of the table, in most graceful affability to every body. Miss Lawson was flirting with a slim young man at the sideboard, where she preferred to sup, on the pretence of not being able to find a seat; and Miss Cynthia, no doubt much fatigued by her vocal exertions, was concluding the second patty, and thinking what she should send her *cavalier servente* for, next. Tom was in the centre of the table, in high glee, chirping at a sugar-plum bird in a barley-sugar cage, jerking bonbons into his mouth by slapping his hand, making little men out of raisins and preserved ginger, and sending them to different young ladies, with his compliments; playing the cornet-à-piston upon a wafer-cake, "and many other performances too numerous to mention," as they say at outside shows.

"My dear Mrs. Howard," said Mrs. Lawson to the hostess, "how delicious every thing is! You always do have such very fine lobsters—where *do* you contrive to get them?"

"I am very happy you admire them," returned the lady, "but I really don't know." Which affirmation was the more singular, as she had ordered them herself from a shop in Wigmore Street.

"Lady Mary Abbeville and yourself are the only two of my friends who contrive to get large lobsters," continued Mrs. Lawson. "Lady Mary is a charming creature—do you know her?"

"I have not that pleasure," replied our friend; "and yet I have heard the name somewhere."

"Between Boulogne and Paris," cried Tom, as he exploded a cracker bonbon. "The diligence dines there."

"Now, my dear Tom, do not be so foolish," said Mrs. Lawson, in a tone of admiring reproach. "How can a diligence dine?"

"Well, I've seen it *break-fast*, however, when it has been going down a hill, over-loaded," replied the "talented" son. "A glass of wine, Sir?" he continued, pitching upon some one opposite by chance, to make his wit appear off-hand.

The challenged individual was an overgrown young gentleman, with a very high shirt-collar. He stammered out, "With much pleasure!" and then filling up his half glass of sherry from the nearest decanter at hand, which contained port, he made a nervous bow, and swallowed the wine as if it had been physic.

"Here's you and I, Sir, and two more; but we won't tell their names," exclaimed Tom, winking to the young gentleman, whose blushes increased to a fearful pitch of intensity.

The ladies had been gradually leaving the room for the last ten minutes, and when they had all departed we sat down to our own supper. Tom never once flagged in his drolleries. He laughed, took wine with all the old gentlemen, did the two cats, imitated Macready and Buckstone—in fact, opened all his stores of facetiousness. He accompanied us upstairs, and after the ladies had finished the long quadrille they were having with themselves, he sang a song about "Wanted" a something, we do not exactly recollect what; being ourselves engaged in talking delightful absurdities to the belle in the white poplin, and endeavoring to reason down the antediluvian ideas she had formed, that it was improper to waltz with any one else but her brother; in which argument we finally succeeded. However, the song was eminently successful, and threw every body who witnessed the odd grimaces with which Tom accompanied it into delirious convulsions of laughter.

The "delightful people" left about half-past two; Mrs. Lawson declaring her girls went out so much that their health began to suffer from late hours. Tom saw them into their carriage, and then came back, pressing every other young man in the room to come to some tavern where there was a capital comic singer; but finding no one so inclined, he also took his leave. We waited until we saw the man who played the piano hammering away with his eyes shut, and gradually going to sleep over the keys, when we thought it time to depart ourselves; and in all the happiness of a latch-key in our pocket, and the same good hat we left in the hall upon our head, we bent our steps homeward.

Two or three weeks passed away, when one morning we received an application from a young medical friend, to use our interest in obtaining for him some votes for the situation of surgeon to a dispensary in the neighborhood, accompanied by a list of the governors. We obtained two or three promises, and at last determined to solicit Mr. Lawson, whose name we saw in the list: at the same time, we must confess that we were not a little anxious to see the "delightful people" at home—to track these lions to their own lair, and watch their natural instincts. We accordingly sallied forth, one fine day, in all the pride of unexceptionable boots and faultless gloves, and arriving at the family mansion, knocked at the door. A footman in his shirt sleeves ran out into the area, and having looked at us, ran back again; appearing the next minute at the door, with one arm still forcing its way down the sleeve of his coat. We found the Lawsons were at home, and were shown into the drawing-room, with the assurance from the servant that his mistress would be there directly. After looking over the card-basket, to see whom they knew, (which is one of our favorite employments when we are left to ourselves in a strange house,) we turned over the leaves of some albums that were lying about, in company with some theological works, which, being an enemy to religious display, we thought far better suited for the closet than the drawing-room table; and in which occupation we were interrupted by the sound of voices in angry dialogue below. This was suddenly cut short by the slamming of a door, and immediately afterwards Mrs. Lawson entered the room, looking a little red and excited, but all smiles and condescension; begging we would be seated, and telling us how very happy she was that we had called upon her.

After a few common-place observations and inquiries about the weather, the health of the family, the party we had lately met, and such-like exciting topics of conversation, Mrs. Lawson informed us her family were at luncheon, and begged we would join them. A strong smell of roast mutton greeted us as we descended to the dining-room, and tempted us to think that it was an early dinner. We expected to have been kept in a state of unceasing laughter throughout the whole meal, but were very much mistaken. We had not anticipated any immense fun from the papa Lawson, who was quietly enough discussing some bread and cheese; but, as the facetious Tom was there, and his gifted sisters, we calculated upon a repetition, in a certain degree, of their previous amusing powers. There was, however, nothing of the kind; the whole party were as flat as the jug of beer that has been left out for supper, covered with a cheese-plate, on returning from the play. Bessy had evidently been quarrelling with her sister; Cynthia contradicted her mother on every point or affirmation that Mrs. Lawson uttered; Tom sat back in his chair, with his hands in his pocket, and his legs stretched out straight under the table; and the good lady herself kept up such an alternation of smiles to us and black looks to the young people, that her command of countenance was perfectly marvellous. At first, we thought it probable that they were all recovering from influenza; but they looked so very healthy that we soon relinquished that opinion. They were, however, so very quiet, that when they retired, and we had mentioned the object of our visit to Mr. Lawson, who was a sensible man, (if the others had let him alone,) we summoned up courage to say that we feared we had intruded during some family discussion.

"My dear Sir," he replied, "we never have any thing else but family discussions here. I dare say you are surprised to see them so different from what they are in company; but the more they *show off* when they are out, the more cross they always are at home the next day."

In these few words was contained the whole history of "delightful people"—the melancholy truth, that those who in society carry all before them by their spirits and acquirements are, at home, the most uncomfortable beings upon the face of the earth, because they cannot there find the very excitement which is almost necessary to their existence.

We have met the Lawsons several times since, and we have begun to find that their attractions sadly want variety. Mrs. Lawson tells the same anecdotes, Bessy plays the same fantasias, Cynthia warbles the identical *arias* we last heard, and Tom has a certain routine of tricks and absurdities, which he plays off in regular order during the evening. We begin to weary of these lions; although, at every *réunion* where it is our lot to meet them, there are the same number of guests charmed at their talents, who never hesitate to pronounce them most "delightful people."

PHYSIOLOGY OF THE MEDICAL STUDENT.

BY ALBERT SMITH.

OF THE GRINDER AND HIS CLASS.

One fine morning, in the October of the third winter session, the student is suddenly struck by the recollection that at the end of the course the time will arrive for him to be thinking about undergoing the ordeals of the Hall and College. Making up his mind, therefore, to begin studying in earnest, he becomes a *pro tempore* member of a temperance society, pledging himself to abstain from immoderate beer for six months: he also purchases a coffee-pot, a reading-candlestick, and Steggall's Manual; and then, contriving to accumulate five guineas to pay a "grinder," he routs out his old note-books from the bottom of his box, and commences to "read for the Hall."

Aspirants to honors in law, physic, or divinity, each know the value of private cramming—a process by which their brains are fattened, by abstinence from liquids and an increase of dry food, (some of it *very* dry,) like the livers of Strasbourg geese. There are grinders in each of these three professional classes; but the medical teacher is the man of the most varied and eccentric knowledge. Not only is he intimately acquainted with the different branches required to be studied, but he is also master of all their minutiæ. In accordance with the taste of the examiners, he learns and imparts to his class at what degree of heat water boils in a balloon—how the article of commerce, *Prussian blue*, is more easily and correctly defined as the *Ferrosesquicyanuret of the Cyanide of Potassium*—why the nitrous oxide, or laughing gas, influences people to make such asses of themselves; and, especially, all sorts of individual inquiries, which, if continued at the present rate, will range from "Who discovered the use of the spleen?" to "Who killed Cock Robin?" for aught we know. They ask questions at the Hall quite as vague as these.

It is twelve o'clock at noon. In a large room, ornamented by shelves of bottles and preparations, with varnished prints of medical plants and cases of articulated bones and ligaments, a number of young men are seated round a long table covered with baize, in the centre of whom an intellectual-looking man, whose well-developed forehead shows the amount of knowledge it can contain, is interrogating by turns each of the students, and endeavoring to impress the points in question on their memories by various diverting associations. Each of his pupils, as he passes his examination, furnishes him with a copy of the subjects touched upon; and by studying these minutely, the private teacher forms a pretty correct idea of the general run of the "Hall questions."

"Now, Mr. Muff," says the gentleman to one of his class, handing him a bottle of something which appears like specimens of a chestnut colt's coat after he had been clipped; "what's that, sir?"

"That's cow-itch, sir," replies Mr. Muff.

"Cow what? You must call it at the Hall by its botanical name—*Dolichos pruriens*. What is it used for?"

"To strew in people's beds that you owe a grudge to," replies Muff; whereat all the class laugh, except the last comer, who takes it all for granted, and makes a note of the circumstance in his interleaved manual.

"That answer would floor you," continues the grinder. "The *dolichos* is used to destroy worms. How does it act, Mr. Jones?" going on to the next pupil—a man in a light cotton cravat and no shirt-collar, who looks very like a butler out of place.

"It tickles them to death, sir," answers Mr. Jones.

"You would say it acts mechanically," observes the grinder. "The fine points stick into the worms and kill them. They say 'Is this a dagger which I see before me?' and then die. Recollect the dagger, Mr. Jones, when you go up. Mr. Manhug, what do you consider the best sudorific, if you wanted to throw a person into a perspiration?"

Mr. Manhug, who is the wag of the class, finishes, in rather an abrupt manner, a song he was humming, *sotto voce*, having some allusion to a peer who was known as Thomas, Lord Noddy, having passed a night at a house of public entertainment

in the Old Bailey previous to an execution. He then takes a pinch of snuff, winks at the other pupils, as much as to say, "See me tackle him now;" and replies, "The gallery door of Covent Garden on Boxing-night."

"Now, come, be serious for once, Mr. Manhug," continues the teacher; "what else is likely to answer the purpose?"

"I think a run up Holborn-hill, with two Ely-Place knockers on your arm, and three policemen on your heels, might have a good effect," answers Mr. Manhug.

"Do you ever think you will pass the Hall, if you go on at this rate?" observes the teacher, in a tone of mild reproach.

"Not a doubt of it, sir," returns the imperturbable Manhug. "I've passed it twenty times within this last month, and did not find any very great difficulty about it; neither do I expect to, unless they block up Union Street and Water Lane."

The grinder gives Mr. Manhug up as a hopeless case, and goes on to the next. "Mr. Rapp, they will be very likely to ask you the composition of the *compound gamboge pill*: what is it made of?"

Mr. Rapp hasn't the least idea.

"Remember, then, it is composed of cambogia, aloes, ginger, and soap—C, A, G, S,—*cags*. Recollect Cags, Mr. Rapp. What would you do if you were sent for to a person poisoned by oxalic acid?"

"Give him some chalk," returns Mr. Rapp.

"But suppose you had not got any chalk, what would you substitute?"

"Oh, any thing; pipeclay and soapsuds."

"Yes, that's all very right; but we will presume you could not get any pipeclay and soapsuds; in fact, that there was nothing in the house. What would you do then?"

Mr. Manhug cries out from the bottom of the table—"Let him die and be ———!"

"Now, Mr. Manhug, I really must entreat of you to be more steady," interrupts the professor. "You would scrape the ceiling with the fire-shovel, would you not? Plaster contains lime, and lime is an antidote. Recollect that, if you please. They like you to say you would scrape the ceiling, at the Hall: they think it shows a ready invention in emergency. Mr. Newcome, you have heard the last question and answer?"

"Yes, sir," says the fresh arrival, as he finishes making a note of it.

"Well; you are sent for, to a man who has hung himself. What would be your first endeavor?"

"To scrape the ceiling with the fire-shovel," mildly observes Mr. Newcome; whereupon the class indulges in a hearty laugh, and Mr. Newcome blushes as deep as the red bull's-eye of a New Road doctor's lamp.

"What would *you* do, Mr. Manhug? perhaps you can inform Mr. Newcome."

"Cut him down, sir," answers the indomitable *farceur*.

"Well, well," continues the teacher; "but we will presume he has been cut down. What would you strive to do next?"

"Cut him up, sir, if the coroner would give an order for a *post mortem* examination."

"We have had no chemistry this morning," observes one of the pupils.

"Very well, Mr. Rogers; we will go on with it if you wish. How would you endeavor to detect the presence of gold in any body?"

"By begging the loan of a sovereign, sir," interrupts Mr. Manhug.

"If he knew you as well as I do, Manhug," observes Mr. Jones, "he'd be sure to lend it—oh, yes!—I should rather think so, certainly," whereupon Mr. Jones compresses his nostril with the thumb of his right hand, and moves his fingers as if he was performing a concerto on an imaginary one-handed flageolet.

"Mr. Rapp, what is the difference between an element and a compound body?"

Mr. Rapp is again obliged to confess his ignorance.

"A compound body is composed of two or more elements," says the grinder, "in various proportions. Give me an example, Mr. Jones."

"Half-and-half is a compound body, composed of the two elements, ale and porter, the proportion of the porter increasing in an inverse ratio to the respectability of the public house you get it from," replies Mr. Jones.

The professor smiles, and taking up a Pharmacopœia, says, "I see here directions for evaporating certain liquids 'in a water-bath.' Mr. Newcome, what is the most familiar instance of a water-bath you are acquainted with?"

"In High Holborn, sir; between Little Queen Street and Drury Lane," returns Mr. Newcome.

"A water-bath means a vessel placed in boiling water, Mr. Newcome, to keep it at a certain temperature. If you are asked at the Hall for the most familiar instance, they like you to say a carpenter's glue-pot."

And in like manner the grinding-class proceeds.

* * * *

Essential as sulphuric acid is to the ignition of the platinum in an hydropneumatic lamp, so is half-and-half to the proper illumination of a medical student's faculties. The Royal College of Surgeons may thunder and the lecturers may threaten, but all to no effect; for, like the slippers in the Eastern story, however often the pots may be ordered away from the dissecting-room, somehow or other they always find their way back again with unfliching pertinacity. All the world inclined towards beer knows that the current price of a pot of half-and-half is fivepence, and by this standard the medical student fixes his expenses. He says he has given three pots for a pair of Berlin gloves, and speaks of a half-crown as a six-pot piece.

Mr. Muff takes the goodly measure in his hand, and decapitating its "spuma" with his pipe, from which he flings it into Mr. Simpson's face, indulges in a prolonged drain, and commences his narrative —most probably in the following manner:—

"You know we should all have got on very well if Rapp hadn't been such a fool as to pull away the lanthorns from the place where they are putting down the wood pavement in the Strand, and swear he was a watchman. I thought the crusher saw us, and so I got ready for a bolt, when Manhug said the blocks had no right to obstruct the footpath, and, shoving down a whole wall of them into the street, voted for stopping to play at *duck* with them. Whilst he was trying how many he could pitch across the Strand against the shutters opposite, down came the *pewlice*, and off we cut."

"I had a tight squeak for it," interrupts Mr. Rapp; "but I beat them at last, in the dark of the Durham Street arch. That's a dodge worth being up to when you get into a row near the Adelphi. Fire away, Muff—where did you go?"

"Right up a court to Maiden Lane, in the hope of bolting into the Cider Cellars. But they were all shut up, and the fire out in the kitchen, so I ran on through a lot of alleys and back-slums, until I got somewhere in St. Giles's, and here I took a cab."

"Why, you hadn't got an atom of tin when you left us," said Mr. Manhug.

"Devil a bit did that signify. You know I only took the *cab*—I'd nothing at all to do with the driver; he was all right in the gin-shop near the stand, I suppose. I got on the box, and drove about for my own diversion—I don't exactly know where; but I couldn't leave the cab, as there was always a crusher in the way when I stopped. At last I found myself at the large gate of New Square, Lincoln's Inn, so I knocked until the porter opened it, and drove in as straight as I could. When I got to the corner of the square, by No. 7, I pulled up, and, tumbling off my perch, walked quietly along to the Portugal Street wicket. Here the other porter let me out, and I found myself in Lincoln's Inn's Fields."

"And what became of the cab?" asks Mr. Jones.

"How should I know?—it was no affair of mine. I dare say the horse made it right; it didn't matter to him whether he was standing in St. Giles's or Lincoln's Inn, only the last was the most respectable."

"I don't see that," says Mr. Manhug, refilling his pipe.

"Why, all the thieves in London live in St. Giles's."

"Well, and who live in Lincoln's Inn?"

"Pshaw! that's all worn out," continues Mr. Muff. "I got to the College of Surgeons, and had a good mind to scud some oyster shells through the windows, only there were several people about—fellows coming home to chambers, and the like; so I pattered on until I found myself in Drury Lane, close to a coffee-shop that was open. There I saw such a jolly row!"

Mr. Muff utters this last sentence in the same ecstatic accents of admiration with which we speak of a lovely woman or a magnificent view.

"What was it about?" eagerly demanded the rest of the circle.

"Why, just as I got in, a gentleman of a vivacious turn of mind, who was taking an early breakfast, had shied a soft-boiled egg at the gas-light, which didn't hit it, of course, but flew across the tops of the boxes, and broke upon a lady's head.

"What a mess it must have made?" interposes Mr. Manhug. "Coffee-shop eggs are always so very albuminous."

"Once I found some feathers in one, and a fœtal chick," observes Mr. Rapp.

"Knock that down for a good one!" says Mr. Jones, taking the poker and striking three distinct blows on the mantelpiece, the last of which breaks off the corner. "Well, what did the lady do?"

"Commenced kicking up an extensive shindy, something between crying, coughing, and abusing; until somebody in a fustian coat, addressing the assailant, said, 'he was no gentleman, whoever he was, to throw eggs at a woman; and that if he'd come out, he'd pretty soon butter his crumpets on both sides for him, and give him pepper for nothing.' The master of the coffee-shop now came forward and said, 'he wasn't a going to have no uproar in his house, which was very respectable, and always used by the first of company, and if they wanted to quarrel, they might fight it out in the streets.' Whereupon they all began to barge the master at once,—one saying 'his coffee was all snuff and chickweed,' or something of the kind; whilst the other told him 'he looked as measly as a mouldy muffin;" and then all of a sudden a lot of half-pint cups and pewter spoons flew up in the air, and the three men began an indiscriminate battle all to themselves, in one of the boxes, 'fighting quite permiscus,' as the lady properly observed. I think the landlord was worst off though; he got a very queer wipe across the face from the handle of his own toasting-fork."

"And what did you do, Muff?" asks Mr. Manhug.

"Ah, that was the finishing card of all. I put the gas out, and was walking off as quietly as could be, when some policemen, who heard the row outside, met me at the door, and wouldn't let me pass. I said I would, and they said I should not, until we came to scuffling, and then one of them calling to some more, told them to take me to Bow Street, which they did; but I made them carry me though. When I got into the office they had not any especial charge to make against me, and the old bird behind the partition said I might go about my business; but, as ill luck would have it, another of the unboiled ones recognized me as one of the party who had upset the wooden blocks—he knew me again by my d—d Taglioni."

"And what did they do to you?"

"Marched me across the yard and locked me up; when, to my great consolation in my affliction, I found Simpson, crying and twisting up his pocket-handkerchief, as if he was wringing it; and hoping his friends would not hear of his disgrace through the *Times*."

"What a love you are, Simpson!" observes Mr. Jones, patronizingly. "Why, how the deuce could they, if you gave a proper name? I hope you called yourself James Edwards."

Mr. Simpson blushes, blows his nose, mutters something about his card-case and telling an untruth, which excites much merriment; and Mr. Muff proceeds:—

"The beak wasn't such a bad fellow after all, when we went up in the morning. I said I was ashamed to confess we were both disgracefully intoxicated, and that I would take great care nothing of the same humiliating nature should occur again; whereupon we were fined twelve pots each, and I tossed sudden death with Simpson which should pay both. He lost; and paid down the dibs. We came away, and here we are."

The mirth proceeds, and, ere long, gives place to harmony; and when the cookery is finished, the bird is speedily converted into an anatomical preparation,—albeit her interarticular cartilages are somewhat tough, and her lateral ligaments apparently composed of a substance between leather and caoutchouc. As afternoon advances, the porter of the dissecting-room finds them performing an incantation dance round Mr. Muff, who, seated on a stool placed upon two of the tressels, is rattling some halfpence in a skull, accompanied by Mr. Rapp, who is performing a difficult concerto on an extempore instrument of his own invention, composed of the Scotchman's hat, who is still grinding in the museum, and the identical thigh-bone that assisted to hang Mr. Muff's patriarchal old hen!

THE DELUSION OF THREE DAYS.

BY R. BERNAL.

We are all, more or less, the slaves of prejudice, or the creatures of early habits and impressions; and, however wisely our resolutions may be framed in the hour of sober reflection, yet too often the impulse of a moment will entirely upset the influence of good sense and reason. How decidedly has the truth of this position been exemplified in the case of my friend Herbert, who, really amiable and pleasing, with every wish to escape from the pitiable condition of a bachelor, and with many advantages to assist him in his laudable and unremitting pursuit of a wife, still appears, at the age of thirty-five, as far distant from success as ever. For Herbert, from his first entrance into society, has been a devoted partisan of the fair sex, but an equally enthusiastic admirer of the arts of music and painting, and of all the other minor elegant accomplishments of the day; and he has always fettered himself by the singular notion that no female (whatever her mental or personal recommendations might be) could render him happy or contented, unless she were mistress of all or most of these desirable accomplishments.

Hence this caprice of my friend has been extended to so ridiculous a degree, that after every first introduction to any new and lovely votary of fashion, I have always found him ready to perplex himself and his associates with the same uniform set of interrogatories, of a *small part* of which the following may be an example.

"Does she sing, and play well on the piano or harp?—Were her masters Crivelli, Moscheles, or Bochsa?—can she paint in oil or water colors?—Did she study under Fielding or Prout?—Can she converse fluently in French, Italian, and German?" etc., etc.—In fact, so organized was this system in the mind of Herbert, and so notorious had he become by his unmitigated development of it, that in despite of his well-known and much-lauded eagerness to secure a wife, he became, at last, to be but coldly received by his female acquaintances.

The close of the spring, in the year 1827, found Herbert in a state of chagrin and disappointment: the slender encouragement held out to him by the offended spinsters of London, and one or two awkward repulses which he had experienced, had considerably abated his hopes and damped his ardor.

Under the pressure of ennui and low spirits, he took himself off to the baths of Ems in Germany. There, the bustle and liveliness of the well-frequented table d'hôte at the hotel de Russie, joined to its variety of faces, forms, and manners, contributed to restore his good humor with *le beau sexe*, and to revive his keenness for his old pursuit. But my friend's taste was vastly too fastidious for the atmosphere of a continental table d'hôte: one very fair and pretty Badoise horrified him by her *penchant* (however strictly patriotic) for eating stewed prunes with roast meat; while another black-eyed and interesting Alsacienne provoked him by her preference (however healthful) of the oysters of the dinner-table to all his small talk and attentions; in short, as far as the ladies were concerned, he had very little prospect of adding to his reputation at Ems.

By good fortune, Herbert met with an old acquaintance, the Baron de T——, whom he had formerly known, both in England and on the Continent, and who was upon terms of intimacy with many of the respectable families in the duchy of Nassau.

In the course of conversation, the baron mentioned the name of Madame de Steinbron, a lady residing in the neighborhood of Ems, and he described her as being a very young, lovely, and interesting widow. She had been contracted by her parents, at an early age, to a gentleman advanced in years, who died, leaving her in opulent circumstances, shortly after their marriage. The manner in which the baron spoke of the widow so wrought upon Herbert's feelings, that he would not quit the subject until he had obtained from the baron the promise of an introduction, on the next day, to the lady.

In consequence of this arrangement, the baron and Herbert, on the following morning, drove out to the Chateau de Steinbron; they found its fair mistress at home; when the baron, having been cordially welcomed, presented his friend, in flattering terms, to Madame de Steinbron.

Accustomed as Herbert had been to presentations to beautiful women, and critic *au fond* as he was upon every point, important or minute, connected with their personal appearance, he never before at least had been so immediately impressed with admiration, or so little disposed to criticise, as on the present occasion. The whole contour of Madame de Steinbron's countenance denoted youth and softness; dark brown hair, simply arranged, clustered round an oval face of the most transparent complexion, and a pair of eyes of the deepest hazel turned upon the beholder, with a penetrating expression of real feeling and intelligence; while the lines and proportions of her form appeared as round and correct as the poet or sculptor could desire. In addition, there was something striking and unusual in the style of her reception of the visitors, which, perhaps, from its very singularity, tended the more to produce a decided impression upon Herbert. Madame de Steinbron was reclined upon a handsome couch, beneath a canopy, the curtains of which were drawn back, and surrounded by all those elegant accessories of household decoration which the refinement and wealth of modern times have produced. She had only half raised herself upon the entrance of the two gentlemen, but resuming her recumbent position, she retained the same during the remainder of their stay. An animated conversation ensued, and was maintained for a considerable time, between Madame de Steinbron and her visitors. The history, literature, and topography of Germany were in turns talked over; and on all matters the lovely widow displayed so much unpretending knowledge and judgment, that Herbert was perfectly astonished at the fact of so youthful a female having been able to acquire an extent of information the more remarkable, as it was not alloyed by the slightest mixture of pedantry or affectation. Madame de Steinbron had been partly educated in France, and had travelled through the greater portion of Italy; the languages of these countries were quite familiar to her, and at her perfect command. Herbert was enchanted, and the current of his thoughts hardly found sufficient time to include in its flow all his notions and prejudices, as to the necessity of the acquisition of every species of accomplishment. An incidental remark on the beauty of the surrounding scenery of Nassau led to the subject of painting and drawing, when Madame de Steinbron confessed her utter want of knowledge of the art: but Herbert's excitement was too powerful to be much abated by this confession of a defect in his standard of excellence.

Unreasonably long as this first visit proved, Herbert did not suffer it to come to a conclusion without having obtained the lady's permission to repeat it; and at length he most unwillingly departed with the baron, being at least three parts, if not the whole, of a lover at first sight. During the rest of the day, Herbert persecuted the poor baron with the expression of his warm and passionate admiration of the charming Josephine de Steinbron, and with unceasing and innumerable questions concerning her, which the baron either could or would not satisfy.

Time dragged but heavily on with my enthusiastic friend until the next day arrived, when, at as early an hour as propriety could well sanction, Herbert, without soliciting the further escort of the baron, hurried off again to the Chateau, to pay his permitted visit to its interesting owner. To his great delight he was admitted, and he found Madame de Steinbron alone, occupying her couch in the same saloon, and nearly in the same manner as upon his first introduction. She received him, without any form or reserve, half sitting and lying on her sofa; the ease and elegance of her manner were so winning, and the charms of her conversation so seducing, that Herbert, in an hour, felt as if he had been acquainted with her for years. Every topic that could interest a cultivated and refined mind, was again brought forward and discussed; and if Herbert was fascinated on the former occasion, the seal of enchantment was certainly fixed on the present. One trifling incident, and one only, occurred, to disturb the serene and delicious harmony of his feelings: the conversation having branched off to the state of arts in Europe, Herbert's inveterate prejudices prompted him to introduce the subject of music, he not for a moment doubting but that his magician could exercise her influence over this delightful science. Herbert possessed a curious tact of applying generals to particulars, when any one of his old and favorite fancies came into action, and he thus addressed his fair companion:

HERB. What wonderful composers has Germany produced! Haydn, Mozart, and Winter.

M. DE STEIN. Yes, indeed, their reputation is deservedly great.

HERB. I feel delighted to think you rightly appreciate their merit. What heavenly compositions are the operas of La Clemenza di Tito and Il Ratto di Proserpina! You sing, I am certain, that charming duet of "Deh prendi un dolce amplesso?"

M. DE STEIN. I believe I have heard it, but really I do not remember it.

HERB. Not remember it! I could not have believed this. But you cannot forget the duet of "Ah Perdonna:" forgive me, but I am satisfied you must sing that piece of music to perfection!

M. DE STEIN. (*laughing.*) Pray moderate your expectations and enthusiasm, and, in mercy, grant me your *full pardon* when I assure you that I know not a single note of music, and that I am perfectly unable to sing or play on any instrument whatever.

Here it must be owned Herbert was silenced for a time, and his transports experienced no slight check; for it required all his fortitude, and a succession of the most enchanting smiles from the lovely widow, to restore him to his former composure and happy condition of mind. However, when the hour of taking leave arrived, Herbert was completely a lover, and a confirmed one, too; and though I cannot positively declare what was the exact state of the lady's heart, yet it is certain that Herbert, emboldened by the nature of his reception, ventured, after a very extended visit, to press her fair hand gently, and to request permission to return on the following day, and that such request was conceded, and the concession further established both by a blush and a sigh.

It would be a hopeless attempt to describe the feelings under which Herbert retired that night to rest, or rather to seek for rest; he was almost in an excess of delirium: he had at last found the woman he had been for nearly fifteen years seeking; the being, on whom all his hopes of happiness were to rest. The morning of the third day (every previous hour having been regularly counted) at last arrived; away flew Herbert, on the wings of love and sentiment, to the castle of his enchantress, as privately as he could, and keeping his intentions secret from the baron: for Herbert was determined, without further ceremony or delay, to make a proposition in form to Madame de Steinbron.

The weather was sultry and overpowering when he reached the chateau. Upon his admittance into the well-known saloon, he found the charming widow as usual upon her couch, her head resting on both her hands, with her arms extended on one of its pillows. Traces of thought and languor were apparent in her beautiful countenance, but her eyes were fraught with intense feeling. Herbert could hardly refrain from gazing on the lovely arms and hands exposed to his view, which were so white and perfect that Canova might have modelled from them. It was evident that Madame de Steinbron had been occupied in deep and serious meditation; her manner, though kind, partook of something between sorrow and embarrassment. A little time elapsed before the accustomed flow of conversation could be supported; for Herbert, on his part, bent on carrying his resolution into effect, expressed himself with a degree of confusion and hesitation. Madame de Steinbron having remarked how anxious she felt to travel in England, Herbert inwardly blessed his good fortune that so favorable an opportunity had been afforded for his project, and he was (after much conversation on the subject of society and amusements in Britain) in the act of replying to some inquiry of the lady, when the sound of a clarionet out of doors, playing the air of a favorite national dance, attracted his attention. The day of the week was Friday, and perhaps Herbert's evil genius, or some other demon of mischief, was then stalking abroad, or perhaps it was owing to the contemplation of a very pretty foot of Madame de Steinbron, which peeped out from under her robe, that Herbert all at once exclaimed, "What an enlivening air! and what an attractive sight it is, to behold an elegant woman waltz gracefully. I am sure you must be devoted to dancing?"

Madame de Steinbron cast down her lovely eyes, turned pale as marble, and dropping a tear, replied, with emotion, "I once was, but, alas! I am indeed unfortunate!"

Herbert became all romance and tenderness: he drew nearer to the couch, fully prepared to receive some interesting confession, or tale of past sorrows. How transporting, to be selected for such a mark of confidence! His beautiful widow appeared more fascinating than ever; and his senses were all concentrated in his eyes and ears. "Listen! my dear friend," continued Madame de Steinbron: "I have encountered most severe suffering: three years back my carriage was overturned; my right limb miserably fractured; it was amputated; and, alas! in its place I have only a *cork* leg!"

If a sudden thunderbolt from heaven had darted by Herbert without immediately destroying him, he could not have felt more overwhelmed and dismayed. Complete silence ensued for a few minutes, till, hardly conscious of his actions, he at last started from his seat, and absolutely screaming aloud, "A *cork* leg!" he darted out of the apartment, and in the shortest possible time, found himself at his hotel at Ems. In another half hour, his bill was discharged, his trunks were packed, and Herbert was in his travelling calèche, mentally ejaculating curses on the Baron de T. and his own wayward destiny, and audibly bestowing the same on the schwager and the post-horses, while he hurried over the road to Cologne to return to England, as fast as German travelling and English impetuosity could permit.

HOW TO FORM A STOCK COMPANY.

FROM "PICKWICK ABROAD." BY G. W. REYNOLDS.

Captain Walsingham, whom the reader has already known by the various names of Crashem, Sugden, and Boloski, was the happy tenant of a three-pair back sitting-room, and a four-pair back bed-room, *alias*, an agreeable and airy attic. The breakfast things had been swept away, there not being many to sweep—the room carefully dusted out—and the table duly covered with a green-baize cloth, which the landlady had borrowed from the pawnbroker's over the way. Captain Walsingham surveyed all these preparations with the most unfeigned delight; and when the little dirty servant, who ministered to his comforts and to those of the whole family (thirteen in all, besides the pigs in the back yard), had retired, Captain Walsingham placed about a dozen sheets of foolscap paper at equal distances round the table, and then laid a new pen, a small piece of blotting-paper, and a couple of wafers upon each of the sheets of foolscap thus disposed of. The inkstand was stood in the middle of the table, around which chairs were speedily arranged, a large Langham gracing the top, and a Windsor the bottom; and this being accomplished, Captain Walsingham expressed a wish to his landlady, whom he summoned to witness the preparations, "that the Directors would make their appearance."

No sooner were the words uttered, than a loud knock at the street door seemed to proclaim that the wish they expressed stood some chance of being immediately attended to. The landlady rushed down stairs—Captain Horatio Clarence Walsingham assumed a most business-like and sedate air, and a sober attitude—and in process of time, the vice-chairman was ushered into the room.

"Mr. Cherryburton, Sir, if you please," screamed the landlady, as she flung open the three-pair back door with as much importance as if it would admit the visitor into a palace.

"How are you, Mr. Cherryburton?" ejaculated the Captain, rushing forward to welcome the deputy-chairman of the infant Company, whereof he himself was the managing director. "You see that I do the thing economically; it is no use taking offices and all that, till some of the advances upon the shares are made. I expect the printer to send me up the book with the printed forms every minute."

"Very good," returned Mr. Cherryburton, who was a very short and very fat gentleman, with no neck, but plenty of head.

"Mr. Snuffery, Sir," cried the landlady, after a short interval of about five minutes; and the treasurer, whose place was quite a sinecure, walked into the room.

"Welcome, Snuffery, old boy," ejaculated Captain Walsingham, forgetting, in the excitement of the moment, the respect due to a treasurer, even by his great employer.

"*Mister* Snuffery, here," suggested the treasurer; "Snuffery at the ale-house, if you like;" it having been at the ale-house that the idea of establishing a Joint-stock Company first occurred to Captain Walsingham and Mr. Snuffery, as they discussed a pot of mild intermediate beer and a yard of clay, some weeks previous to this meeting.

"Very good, very good," exclaimed Mr. Cherryburton; "there's nothing like standing up for etiquette;" and with these words he stood himself exactly before the fire, so that neither Captain Walsingham nor Mr. Snuffery felt the slightest benefit from that fraction of a vast elementary whole.

"Mr. Stephen Muzzlewhite and Mr. Watkins Welladay," chanted the landlady, as two more full-grown directors of an infant project sallied into the room.

"Well, we shall be pretty numerous, I see," observed Mr. Cherryburton, pretending not to notice the desperate energy with which the new-comers rubbed their hands, and persisting in the retention of his enviable position in front of the fire.

"Yes, there'll be a tolerable sprinkle," coincided Mr. Snuffery; "and if every one will only subscribe for a certain number of shares and pay the earnest money, I may open my books at once."

"Oh! certainly—decidedly—we are all very ready to pay the earnest money," cried Captain Walsingham, instinctively glancing with great feeling to a pile of fourpence-halfpenny in coppers, with a sixpence upon the top, which he had prudently placed upon the mantel-piece, probably with an eye to a little display.

"Mr. Molesworthy," cried the landlady; and a very large nose, with an exceedingly small man behind it, entered the room; "and Mr. Muggins," continued the lessee of the house, in an unusually shrilly tone of voice.

"Come in, Mr. Muggins," ejaculated Captain Walsingham; "pray come in—don't stand in the passage."

"A-don't now be foolish," echoed the landlady's voice in a whisper, from the passage just alluded to; "I'll fetch you a slap over the face, I will. There now—you've quite tumbled my best cap, I declare."

Mr. Muggins, having been shrewdly suspected by his brother directors of perpetrating a kiss *vi et armis* upon the comely countenance of the landlady, now entered the room, and paid his respects to the company.

"I think we are all assembled now," observed Captain Horatio Clarence Walsingham; and, as if he had any moral doubt upon the subject, he pretended to count those present, referred to a list of names in his pocket-book, and then precipitated himself into the Langham chair. Mr. Snuffery fell into the Windsor ditto; and the remainder of the

directors slid into theirs without any farther invitation.

A general silence then prevailed throughout the room. This was at length broken by the chairman, who informed the meeting that they were sitting in Committee of Ways and Means, for the purpose of taking into consideration the financial department of the Universal Stone-Expelling and Asphaltum-Substituting Equitable Company.

"In opening the business of the day," observed Captain Horatio Clarence Walsingham, "I have to observe that the prospects of the Company are most smiling and favorable. When I calculate the immense advantages which the introduction and use of the asphalte will confer upon society in general, I am lost in a wide field of admiration and delight. To see the streets, not only of London, but of every town, village, and hamlet, throughout this vast empire, composed of asphalte instead of paving stones, is my most sanguine wish; and that such will be the result of our labors, Gentlemen, let us rest assured. (*Hear! hear.*) It may not be improper at this stage of the business," continued the worthy chairman, "to enumerate a few of the advantages attendant upon the use of the asphalte. In the first place, it will essentially benefit the pecuniary operations of many individuals resident in this vast metropolis; inasmuch as those discounters, whose methods of doing business have not unfrequently led them to offer half money and half paving-stones for suspicious bills, will suddenly find their rapacity deprived of the means of gratification; for what use will paving-stones be to any one when nothing but asphalte shall be in vogue? (*Loud cries of* 'Hear, hear;' *and* 'Bravo' *from Mr. Snuffery, who had done much in the discount way above described.*) Indeed," continued Captain Walsingham, affected almost to tears by the demonstrations of respect and admiration with which he was greeted,—"indeed, I may say, Gentlemen, that an universal good, as my friend the Great Cham used to observe to his prime minister Fiofunki-Khan, will be done to the nation by the use of our asphalte. Instead of shocking the ears of the delicate by noticing that such-and-such an unfortunate girl is compelled to walk the *pavé*, will it not be much more decent and becoming to hint that she promenades the asphaltum? Conceive, Gentlemen, the advantage attached to this circumstance alone, and rely upon our success as a thing certain—a self-evident proposition—an axiom—a—a result sincerely to be wished for by all." (*Loud cheers.*)

The Chairman resumed his lucid oration, after having been welcomed with the most deafening applause.

"Gentlemen," said he, "in categorizing the advantages which will accrue to society and, I may say to the cause of civilization, by the application of our measures, let me not forget to observe that had Paris been lined with asphalte instead of paving-stones, the Revolution of July would never have taken place, because the citizens could not have formed barricades of the precious substance which we so enthusiastically advocate. (*Hear, hear.*) There will be no danger of tripping on a loose stone, with our asphaltum, upon which all men will walk with that springiness and elasticity which to the ancient pavement never *did*—never *could* belong. Money is to be made out of the asphalte; but no blood ever came from the stone! Let us all remember this ancient proverb, and regard it as a species of prophecy relative to the present undertaking!"

Mr. Snuffery begged to ask the Chairman if he intended any thing personal by his allusion to the adage which states that one cannot get blood out a stone. Mr. Muggins supported Mr. Snuffery's demand, and "begged to inform the Cheerman and all present that he dared look any man in the face, that he didn't owe a blessed penny in the whole world, that no one could say black was the white of his eye, and that he would just like to know from the Cheerman's own lips who would say any thing to the contrary."

Captain Walsingham declared that his allusion was any thing but personal; Mr. Snuffery observed he was satisfied, but that if the explanation had not been given, he should most decidedly have resigned the post of treasurer to the Company—a statement, which, considering the nature of that Company's assets, filled the whole Committee with immediate alarm. This was only appeased by the production of a black bottle, and the imbibing of a little drop of brandy by each member; without which sudden remedy, the whole business might have been blighted in the bud. Mr. Muggins, indeed, was so affected by the temporary misunderstanding, that he was under the necessity of filling his glass and emptying it three times, before he could muster u psufficient strength to attend to business.

When something like order was restored, Captain Walsingham continued his truly wonderful oration as follows:—

"But, Gentlemen, I have only enumerated one half—indeed, I may safely say, only one quarter of the numerous advantages attending the substitution of asphalte for paving-stones. I have often remarked—and what gentleman present has not done the same?—I say, Gentlemen, that I have often remarked that the pavement, as it now exists, is frequently unsteady beneath the feet. Gentlemen, last evening only, I dined with a friend in the City—in fact, Gentlemen, to be candid with you, it was my old and much esteemed friend, Sir Barryl Punshun, the alderman and highly respected wine merchant of Portsoken Ward; and as I came home, I found that the pavement down Ludgate Hill was so unsteady, I could scarcely walk on it. Now, will you believe it, Gentlemen, when I assure you that by the time I arrived at the foot of Blackfriars Bridge, I was compelled to lie down in the very street; on account of the turn the inequality and bad state of the pavement upon Ludgate Hill had given me? (*Groans and hisses.*) Mr. Muggins," continued the worthy Chairman, "I hope you will help yourself. Yes, Gentlemen, I can myself vouch for the truth of the circumstance; the stone pavement *is* unsafe—very unsafe, Gentlemen; and the asphaltum must replace it. I repeat it, Gentlemen—" and Captain Walsingham smote the table with amazing violence—"I repeat it, that you cannot walk with safety upon stone-pavement—and all I know is, that there are times (particularly after dinner) when *I* myself cannot even stand upright upon it."

"Our worthy Cheerman's quite right," exclaimed Mr. Muggins; "this house o' his'n is built upon stones, and blowed if it ain't so unsteady, I can't sit upon my cheer."

Perhaps it struck Mr. Muggins at this precise moment, that he might be able to sit upon the floor, even if he could not retain his chair; at all events he placed himself comfortably under the table; and as the brandy he had drank was somewhat soporific in its effects, having been purposely hocussed by Captain Horatio Clarence Walsingham, he sank into a mild and tranquil slumber, to the extreme comfort of himself and to the unmitigated disgust of his companions.

"Printer's brought the prospecktesses, he says, please Sir," exclaimed the landlady, thrusting her hand in at the door, just as Mr. Muggins thrust himself under the table.

"Oh! very well," cried Captain Walsingham, being perfectly aware that it was very ill. "Tell him to leave them—I can't attend to him now."

"Please, Sir," ejaculated the printer's boy, who had followed the landlady up the stairs as far as the door of the Captain's three-pair back,—"please, sir, master said as how—"

"Very well, very well," interrupted the Chairman of the Universal Stone-Expelling and Asphaltum-Substituting Equitable Company; "I'll attend to it directly."

"That I vosn't to leave 'em without the money," added the boy, for the behoof of all the directors and the treasurer of the aforesaid eminent Company.

"Let him send in his bill to the Secretary," returned the Chairman; "the account shall be audited in due course."

"I am very much afeerd mas'er don't know nothink about the Secreterry," answered the boy, putting his right hand to his nose, and the left hand after the right, and extending the fingers of both in truly interesting puerile sport.

"What—do you mean to say that *we* ain't to be trusted, you young rascal?" demanded Captain Walsingham.

"No—I doesn't; but mas'er does," replied this unaccountable boy, perfectly unawed by the presence of that which intended to be the richest Company in the world.

"Oh! he does—does he?" said Captain Walsingham, rising in state from his Langham chair, and preparing to kick the little boy down stairs; "well, then—you may just tell your master—"

"Stay, stay," interrupted Mr. Muzzlewhite, "this affair will only do us harm. How much is your bill, youngster?"

"Three pound seven," returned the interesting youth, producing a dirty piece of paper.

"Well—here's ten bob towards it," exclaimed Mr. Muzzlewhite, throwing half-a-sovereign on the table.

The sum was soon made up amongst the directors, all of whom contributed something with the exception of Captain Walsingham and Messieurs Snuffery and Muggins—the first turning away to the window and whistling, with his hands in his pockets, as his friends subscribed for him; the second pretending to be asleep the moment any thing like payment was spoken of; and the third being really in a state of somnolency under the table.

"What is the amount of the capital upon which the Company works?" demanded Mr. Muzzlewhite, when the three pound seven had been with difficulty raised amongst the directors, and when the printer's boy had taken himself off.

"Capital—one million," answered Captain Walsingham. "We couldn't do it upon less."

"Oh! no—decidedly not," cried Mr. Muzzlewhite.

Rich men do things cautiously and by hundreds or thousands; but individuals without a *sou*, invariably found their speculations upon millions. Not that we would wish to disparage the eminent Company of which we are now treating; on the contrary, we believe it to have been as highly respectable as it was considered to be by any one of its directors.

"But how shall we dispose of the shares?" inquired Mr. Watkins Welladay.

"By advertisement, to be sure," returned Captain Walsingham. "We must placard all the walls —bill the Magazines—"

"But where is the money to come from, to do all this?" inquired Mr. Snuffery.

"Where?" echoed Captain Walsingham, assuming a tone and attitude of the deepest indignation; "where? Why from the Company's bankers, I should hope."

"Oh! very well," returned Mr. Snuffery, who was not however exactly aware that any account had been as yet opened at a banker's, or indeed that the Company was possessed of any account to open; but he did not choose, as he afterwards expressed himself, to irritate by useless interrogation the man to whom he owed his bread—and water, he might have added.

"Certainly," continued Captain Walsingham. "I have made arrangements with a capitalist, who will advance us five hundred pounds upon the strength of our firm, provided we take it out half in wine, and half in cigars. He *did* want to throw in a few pump-handles and patent axle-trees; but that did not suit my purpose. Now, the fact is—old Muggins must give us his acceptance—(there's no use my speechifying any longer, since he's asleep)—and I'll manage the rest."

"Yes," objected Mr. Welladay; "but will any bankers open an account with wine and cigars?"

"Well, you *are* green for the director of a Joint-Stock Company!" ejaculated Mr. Snuffery. "We must raise money upon them, don't you see?"

"I am sure you will all be delighted to hear that I have secured the patronage and support of Puffemorf, the sub-editor of the *Morning Tea-pot!*"

"No!" exclaimed several voices, in tones expressive of the deepest admiration.

"Do I, or do I not look like a man who is deceiving you?" calmly returned the Chairman, as he glanced complacently and philanthropically around upon his great co-operators.

"No—no," echoed from all present, save Mr. Muggins and the Chairman himself.

"Well, then," continued Captain Walsingham, "since I deserve all your confidence, as the Great Cham used to observe to those faithful slaves whom he intended to put to death,—I will show you that I mean to retain it. Here, Gentlemen—here is a paragraph which will appear in the *Tea-pot* of to-morrow morning. Mr. Snuffery, do me the favor, as treasurer, to read it."

Mr. Snuffery, who, notwithstanding the nature of his appointment, had nothing to treasure up but the speeches of the Chairman, immediately complied with that individual's request, and read the contents of a little piece of paper, which was handed to him, as follows:—

"THE DUKE OF WELLINGTON.—It is a well-known fact that this illustrious commander gave peace to Europe by the achievements he and his gallant followers performed at Waterloo. The reputation of his Grace is the most eminent that can be conceived; it seems to stand alone in the English annals of renown—its supernal lustre throws all others into a deep shade. Yet even this enviable and extensive reputation may eventually find a rival; and if such be the will of destiny, then will the honor of this great competition be decidedly awarded to Walsingham and Company's Asphaltum."

"Well, I never could have fancied what was coming," exclaimed Mr. Welladay, as the treasurer brought the perusal of this most erudite paragraph to a conclusion.

"It was Puffemorf's idea," exclaimed Captain Walsingham. "Why—it will create a more powerful sensation in the fashionable world than Twaddlehem's new novel."

"Very good, very good," observed Mr. Cherryburton, whose nose seemed to indicate that he was not indifferent to cherry-brandy.

"It ain't bad," kindly assented Mr. Molesworthy.

"What ain't?—the brandy?" murmured Mr. Muggins from beneath the table, where he had just awoke; "ask the Cheerman then to pour me out another thimble-full."

But the Chairman perceived that there was not another thimble-full, nor yet half a one, to pour out; so Mr. Muggins and his request were disregarded.

Matters having been brought to this very satisfactory point, and Mr. Muggins being too much overcome with liquor to give any acceptances at that moment, the meeting broke up; and Mr. Muggins himself was conveyed home on a shutter.

* * * * * *

In order that no time might be lost in establishing the celebrated Universal Stone-Expelling and Asphaltum-substituting Equitable Company upon a permanent foundation, its eminent originator, Captain Horatio Clarence Walsingham, sallied forth on the morning after and bent his way towards the abode of Mr. Muggins.

"Good morning, Mr. Muggins," was the Captain's amiable salutation; "how are you this morning?"

"Pretty tidy, thank'ee," returned Mr. Muggins. "Pray take a cheer."

"And how's Mrs. Muggins?" inquired the Captain with great feeling, as he sank into the proffered seat; "and all the family?"

"Hearty—quite hearty," replied Mr. Muggins. "But now to business. I was rayther sleepy yesterday, and did not hear all you had to say about your Asphalte institootion."

Captain Walsingham repeated many of the strong and very convincing arguments he had used the day before; and Mr. Muggins was so struck, not to say affected, by that one which related to the fact of the Captain's being unable to stand upright upon the pavement at times—particularly after dinner—that he immediately resolved upon giving the Company his fullest support. Indeed, he (Mr. Muggins) had not unfrequently noticed a similar coincidence in respect to himself; and he could not do otherwise than deeply deplore the existence of so great and crying an evil.

"And how much ready money shall we want to commence our operations?"

"The nominal capital is of course a million," ejaculated Captain Horatio Clarence Walsingham; "but all that we actually require at first is about five hundred to a thousand pounds."

"And where the deuce is it to come from?" demanded Mr. Muggins.

"The capitalist who will advance the cash," continued the Captain, without noticing the question, "is to receive a *bonus* of five *per cent.* more than any other person connected with the Company."

"Well—that is but fair," murmured Mr. Muggins.

"And he will have other perquisites and privileges too numerous to mention," added Captain Walsingham. "For instance, such capitalist shall have the right of advancing as much money to the Company, at the above-mentioned rate, as he chooses. What do you think of *that?*"

"Admirable!" exclaimed Mr. Muggins.

"And he shall have it in his power," proceeded the Chairman, "to prevent the Company from applying to any other individual for loans, so long as he chooses to furnish them himself."

"Very eligible—very eligible, indeed!" cried Mr. Muggins. "Them is tempting offers."

"And the company shall bind itself to receive, through its treasurer, all the sums he may be desirous of investing in the concern," said the chairman; "and you may depend upon it, that I will use my influence to induce the board of directors to accept of as large a loan as such capitalist may wish to advance. Nay, more, we will draw up a deed, by virtue of which the said capitalist shall have it in his power to *insist* upon the Company's receiving the loans."

"You know my capital is all locked up," began Mr. Muggins, whom these advantageous proffers greatly interested.

"And in order to accommodate such capitalist," hastily continued Captain Walsingham, "the money or moneys, to be furnished, shall be advanced upon bills; and, what is more—the Company shall pay for the stamps!"

The annals of Joint Stock Companies (even in the panic year) do not furnish such a remarkable instance of liberality and kindness on the part of any of those vast public enterprises which reflect so much honor upon the nation, as this which it is now our pleasure and our pride to put on record. Even Mr. Muggins himself was astonished at the generosity of the Chairman; and the production of the spirit-stand, with two small glasses, was the most emphatic proof of his gratitude which he could at the moment possibly think of.

"Taste this rum," said Mr. Muggins; and he filled two wine glasses with the juice of Jamaica's choicest production.

"Excellent!" cried the Captain, smacking his lips, and setting down the glass which he had emptied.

"Yes—it isn't bad," said Mr. Muggins. "But—I tell you what—an idea has entered my head."

"No!" ejaculated the Captain, with an affectation of the deepest astonishment.

"Honor bright!" exclaimed Mr. Muggins; and he bestowed a most sapient and cognoscent wink upon his companion.

"Well, what is it, now?" demanded the eminent Chairman; "something good, *I* dare say!"

"Why—I don't mind," began Mr. Muggins, speaking very deliberately, as he unfolded his plan, and refilled the glasses with equal caution,—"I don't mind if I let you have a little advance—a small loan, you know—myself!"

"Muggins," said Captain Walsingham, assuming

a most solemn expression of countenance,—"Muggins, I am your friend. I esteem you. I like you. I admire you. You are a man of the world, Muggins. Give me your hand."

By one of those strange coincidences which not unfrequently characterize mundane affairs, Captain Walsingham had a bill for five hundred pounds already drawn out upon the proper stamp, in his pocket. This little incident excited a great deal of laughter between the two gentlemen, on account of the strangeness of it; as it was not for a moment to be supposed that the result of the conference could have been anticipated by either.

"Odd—wasn't it?" observed the Captain.

"Very," returned Mr. Muggins.

"Just the amount, perhaps," said the Chairman.

"Exactly!" exclaimed the capitalist.

"You'll accept it, then?" inquired the Captain.

"On the conditions proposed," was the reply.

"Fire away, then," jocosely urged the gallant Captain Walsingham.

On the following morning, Captain Horatio Clarence Walsingham succeeded in discounting the acceptance of Mr. Peter Muggins in the City; and his first care was to treat himself with a basin of turtle-soup and a glass of iced punch at Birch's. He then purchased a watch at Mr. Cox Savory's, and a ring at Messieurs Griffin and Hyam's; and having thus ministered to his own necessities, he proceeded to attend to those of the Company. He began by hiring a splendid set of offices in Bartholomew-lane, and forthwith purchased desks, tables, and chairs to place in them. He procured a painter, who painted the words "Public Office" upon the door; "Waiting Room" upon another; and "Board Room" upon a third. He then hired three individuals, who, under the denomination of Clerks, were to sit at a desk in the Public Office, chatter and read the newspapers when they were alone, and apply themselves like madmen to three great books with clasps when a stranger came in. A servant in blue livery, with white buttons, was also engaged to lounge about in the passage outside the entrance door which led to the offices; and a man, with printed prospectuses to give away, was stationed in the street. A general meeting of the Directors was then called and advertised, to discuss the business of the Company; but as there was as yet no business to occupy their attention, they discussed a copious luncheon instead.

In a few days, a paragraph was drawn up by the excellent Chairman, and inserted (upon payment) in one or two of those daily papers which do not put the word "Advertisement" at the beginning; and this paragraph stated that they (the papers) were informed upon the best authority that the materials which composed the Asphaltum were derived from Asiatic sources: whereupon Mr. Snuffery, as treasurer and secretary, wrote a letter to all the journals to contradict this report; and as the said letters were inserted for nothing, the Company gained its aim in obtaining publicity at the least possible expense.

Another paragraph, tending to show that the Asphaltum would never be applied to universal use, was then paid for and inserted in the *Morning Teapot;* and at this the Company pretended to be in the most direful wrath; so much so, that Messieurs Rumrig and Sharp, the Company's solicitors, were instructed to bring an action against the aforesaid *Morning Teapot;* but, after a great deal of public display, letter-writing, pamphleteering, fending and proving, that eminent legal firm declared it was not necessary to proceed with the suit; and so the whole business was announced to have been arranged in the most amicable manner possible.

A few shares were next issued, and private friends were sent round to purchase up these shares at a *premium;* so that the transaction took wind, and the Company succeeded in getting itself blamed for allowing only the acquaintances of the Directors to profit by the speculation. The demand for shares was therefore immediate and great; and when a piece of the pavement fronting the house in which the offices of the Company were situate, was robbed of its stone and subjected to the process of the Asphalte, the enthusiasm and credulity of the public in favor of this great institution knew no bounds. A grand dinner was given by the Directors at the *City of London Tavern;* and Mr. Muggins was generously permitted by the worthy Chairman to advance the Company another five hundred pounds.

Of course, Captain Walsingham could no longer remain in the three-pair back, which he had formerly occupied in the New Cut. But Mr. Muggins had a ready-furnished house of his own in Broad street, to let; and into this the eminent Chairman of the Universal Stone-Expelling and Asphalte-Substituting Equitable Company speedily removed. With his usual prudence, he did not think it necessary to intimate to the public that he had just emerged from so vulgar a region as the New Cut; he accordingly had his arrival in town, from Walsingham Hall, Staffordshire, duly inserted in the fashionable columns of the *Morning Post*, and thence copied into the evening papers.

TOLD YOU SO

A farmer once, with many a comfort blest,
  Honest and plain—his plough too always going,
Still wanting something more to crown the rest,
  Took to himself a wife, active and knowing.
Their days they passed with harmony full fraught,
  And nothing knew of matrimonial strife,
Save from a cant phrase that his dear had caught,
  Which proved the torment of the poor man's life.
To cut the matter short, a curious power
  She boasted, of foretelling each event;
And did it rain, she knew there'd be a shower,
  If sinners turned, she knew that they'd repent.
Whene'er the good man, vexed, would say, "My dear,
  Old Hodge's hogs the corn-fields have been plundering,"
Or that the cows had eat the clover bare,
  "I told you so," she'd cry—"why are you wondering?"
When freshets rose, and swept a fence or gate,
  If barns blew down, or cattle went astray,
Or neighbor bowed beneath the stroke of fate—
  "I told you so," his loving spouse would say.
One day, to prove her wondrous foresight more,
  He hit upon a plan somewhat uncouth:
He ran into his house, and stoutly swore
  The hogs had eat the grindstone up smack smooth.
Up starts his rib, so ominous to prove it,
  And gazing in his agitated face,
Cries out, "*I told you so*, then, why not move it?
  I knew it stood in an improper place."

PICTORIAL HUMOR.

BY JOHN LEECH.

SOMETHING LIKE A HOLIDAY.

PASTRY COOK. What have you had, sir?

BOY. I've had two jellies, seven of *them*, and eleven of *them*, and six of *those*, and four Bath buns—a sausage roll, ten almond cakes, and a bottle of ginger beer.

NOTHING LIKE WARM BATHING.

Hollo! Hi! Here! Somebody! I've turned on the Hot Water, and I can't turn it off again!

HUNTING JOHN DORY.

BY GEORGE SOANE.

MATTHEW MUCHMORE was a fat little gentleman, on short legs, with a glistening eye, a round shiny face, and so unctuous withal that he involuntarily impressed you with the idea he must have oil in his veins instead of blood, like other people. He was a man of exquisite taste—not in music, nor yet of painting, and still less could it be said of him that he was particularly distinguished for his taste in dress, or dancing, or any such frivolities; no, it was in the matter of turtle and venison, champagne and Burgundy, that he was truly great; in these his taste was pre-eminent. Some foolish folks, whom I know, can see nothing to admire in this faculty of appreciating good things, and make it a great merit that their coarse throats can swallow any thing. But why should not taste be as much cultivated in the tongue as in any other organ? Surely there is quite as much merit in being able to point out and relish the various niceties of some exquisite dish—niceties imperceptible to the vulgar,—as in the faculty of enjoying pictures with the eye, or music with the ear. So thought and reasoned the great Matthew, and, by the beard of Plato, many worse systems of philosophy have been and still are current in the world. It unluckily, however, chanced with him as it has done with so many other people, Nature and Fortune could by no means agree in electing him for a common favorite, for, while the one had endowed him with this admirable delicacy of palate, the other had been exceedingly niggard in supplying him with the means of gratifying it. Hence it followed that he was obliged to be a regular diner-out, if he meant to dine at all; but, as he had a fund of good humor to back him, could tell a story well, and was besides no mean adept in the art of flattery, he was for the most part a welcome guest at the table of his acquaintance, whom, for his especial convenience, he took care should be as numerous as possible. They were chosen, moreover, with every attention to the qualities of their dinners, so that a certain malicious wag used to say that his dining frequently at any house was as good as a diploma to the cook of that particular establishment.

Still it would sometimes happen that his stomach got baffled and disappointed in its expectations; the meals even of his most valued friends were not at all times equally choice or well-supplied; and in more than one instance, when dropping in and invited to stop, the dinner which he fondly expected would consist at least of fish and fowl, in the absence of better things, proved to be that opprobrium on decent housekeeping, cold meat, eked out by the fragments of the day previous. Sorely was his patience tried, and his philosophy tasked by such occurrences; for, however good-humored a man may be, every human temper has limits to its powers of endurance, and this with him was the limit—the last straw on the back of the overloaded camel; it was the one evil of life that he could not bear without wincing, and his curses, like those of Macbeth's subjects, were not loud, but deep. At length, after long and serious reflection on the subject, he bethought him of a notable expedient by which he might be able to guess his bill of fare beforehand with some degree of certainty, instead of rashly accepting an invitation which might end, when too late to retreat, in cold orts and indigestible pickles. This was, to inquire at the various butchers and fishmongers who usually supplied his friends, what their several customers had ordered, and according to their replies, all duly entered and noted down, would he regulate his visits for the day.

It was in compliance with this laudable custom that our oleaginous little friend one day paid a visit to the King's fishmonger. On a marble slab at one side of the shop lay, as usual, several parcels of fish variously ticketed, according to their several destinations, and as he was by this time well known to the master, he was of course permitted to examine these important records, which he immediately fastened upon with all the *gusto* of an antiquary who has luckily discovered an illegible MS. There were soles—better never appeared at the table of a duke; cod-fish—the worst of them might have tempted a Jew to forswear his creed, and sit at a Christian's feast, even without the hope of cheating him; salmon—the Lord Mayor, and his whole court of aldermen, might have abandoned the greenest turtle, or the highest venison, only for the chance of a single mouthful. But, pre-eminent amongst them all was a John Dory—and oh! such a John! so magnificent in his proportions! so delicate in his complexion! so firm in his texture! of a verity he might have been eaten even as he lay there, in all his uncooked loveliness, unscathed by fire, untouched by water, unadulterated by sauce. The heart of Matthew leaped within him as he gazed upon this noble product of the salt seas; his eyes and mouth ran over from excess of rapture; his cheeks grew more oleaginous and shiny, the inward spirit lighting up his face as a farthing rushlight dimly burns through the yellow horn of a lantern. A moment's glance at the ticket in the fish's jowl sufficed to show him that John was intended for the table of Lord Spring. Here was a glorious chance! his lordship was one of those who constantly asked him to dinner, with the benevolent purpose of laughing at him. "But let him laugh who wins!" thought Matthew to himself, and off he posted, on the wings of love—his passion really deserved the name—and in less than half an hour he was to be seen knocking at his lordship's door,—not the loud, bullying dub-dub of an importunate dun, nor the consequential rat-a-tat-tat that so fitly announces an aristocratic visitor, nor yet the sneaking knock of a poor artist who seeks for patronage,—but a sort of conciliatory, yet firm tat-tat-tu, evincing that the knocker has great respect for the knockee, but still considers himself to be somebody in the world.

Now it happened to be just nine o'clock, consequently his lordship was at breakfast,—people kept shocking hours in those days to what they do now, —and Matthew was fortunate enough to gain a ready admission to him.

"I was just thinking of you, Mat!" he exclaimed, smiling benignantly on the epicure; "I have a score of jovial spirits to dine with me to-day. Suppose you join our party."

Most cheerfully did Matthew accept the invitation.

At this moment a servant entered, bearing on a silver tray a small pink-colored note, redolent with all the perfumes—not of Arabia, but of De la Croix, or some other of his odorous brethren. It was from Madame Pantalon, a fashionable Frenchwoman, in whom his lordship especially delighted. As he read her perfumed missive, a bland smile stole over his face, indicative of satisfaction with the writer, and he inquired of the servant what game there was in the house?"

"None," was the reply.

Whereat his lordship, giving a short, dissatisfied "humph!" demanded if there was any fish.

"Only a John Dory," said the gentleman's gentleman, "which has just come in for your lordship's table to-day."

"Is it a fine fish, Mortimer?"

"Remarkably, your lordship."

"That will do, then. Send it to Madame Pantalon, with my compliments, and say that I may perhaps see her to-morrow."

Mortimer accordingly departed. But Matthew, unfortunate Matthew! the color fled from his rubicund cheeks, and he sate the image of despair. Dido, abandoned by the false Æneas, did not look more disconsolately after the ship of the flying traitor.

"Why, what is the matter with you?" exclaimed his lordship. "Are you ill, Mat?"

"Only a little touch of my old complaint, a little vertigo, or so," said Matthew, the color bounding back again to his cheeks.

"God bless my soul!" exclaimed his lordship, starting up, and laying his hand on the bell-pull; "he's going to have a fit; I'll send for Dr. Stumps."

"Not at all necessary, my lord; I am much better now; a mouthful of fresh air is all that is requisite; so, with your leave, I'll just step into the park for an hour or so."

"Then I must not expect you to dinner to-day, I suppose?" said his lordship, in a tone of sympathy.

"I fear not; but, perhaps, as I shall be so close, I may look in upon Madame."

At this reply, carelessly and dexterously as it was given, the words seeming to slip from Matthew's lips almost without his consciousness, a sudden light flashed upon his lordship. He looked steadily at his visitor for a few moments, and then said, with a knowing laugh,

"Do so, Mat; John Dory is the best thing in the world for your complaint; and you can hint to Isabelle that the fish I have just sent will not keep till to-morrow."

Matthew now shuffled out of the room, with joy at his heart, and posted off to the little Frenchwoman's. Here, as his lordship's friend, he was of course made welcome, but not a word did the lady say about dinner, despite of all his hints about unoccupied time, and not knowing what to do with himself. Madame, baffled, as it seemed, by his long visit, at last begged he would stay and dine with her.

"But this is fast-day," she said, smiling, "with us Catholics, and I have nothing but my favorite dish of Maccaroni."

"Good heavens!" exclaimed the alarmed epicure, "then John has not come?"

"Jean!" said the lady, opening her eyes to the utmost, and giving a shrug, such as only a Frenchwoman can give. "What Jean?"

"The beautiful John Dory!" cried Matthew, more in the way of exclamation than reply.

"Monsieur Dory?" said Madame; "I shall not be acquaint with no Monsieur Dory."

"If any thing should have happened to him on the road!" exclaimed Matthew, without noticing the lady's disclaimer, fortified as it was by a double negative; "if that careless rascal should have dropped him in the mud!"

"Mais, mon Dieu!" exclaimed Madame, waxing impatient and irritable, "I shall not know him, no, nothing at all. Who is monsieur?"

"Bah!" said Matthew, angrily; "he's no monsieur, he's a fish, the loveliest that ever smoked upon a table!"

Madame burst out into a prolonged fit of laughing.

"Du poisson! ah! mon Dieu! à présent. Now I shall comprends,—you was intend an ugly monster, with a huge head, comme ça—ah! comme il étoit laid!"

"Ugly? he was beautiful!"

"Eh! mon Dieu! you shall have de taste bien extraordinaire; mais n'importe; I shall no like such poissons, and have send him to my old ami, Monsieur Dumas."

This was the unkindest cut of all. Of Monsieur Dumas he absolutely knew nothing, except that he was suspected of being a Catholic priest, a dangerous character to associate with in those days, when Popery was very generally believed to have an intimate connection with the cause of the Pretender, who, even then, according to the best intelligence from abroad, was preparing to make another struggle for the throne of his ancestors. Independently, then, of the peril, there would be no little difficulty in contriving for himself a place at the dinner-table of a perfect stranger.

It was a daring scheme which our epicure meditated; some may even feel disposed to call it a piece of matchless impudence: and in the very outset his confidence was destined to be put to a severe trial. Scarcely had he time to rejoice in his dexterity in obtaining his release from Madame and a maccaroni dinner, than he encountered the mischief-loving Sir Frederick Sands.

"My good fellow!" he exclaimed, in a tone that was meant to express much friendly anxiety, "what on earth could take you to the house of that Frenchwoman? Don't you know that to be seen going there is to be suspected of Jacobitism in these days, and that to be so suspected is the nearest way to a halter and gibbet of your own? But whither away so fast?"

"To Lord Spring!" answered Matthew, vainly endeavoring to free himself from the knight's grasp.

"Then I congratulate you," said the knight, "on the very fair chance you have of being hanged forthwith. Why, Lord Spring is one of the staunchest adherents of the Pretender! there was a talk only the other day of sending him to the Tower upon suspicion."

Matthew's jaw immediately dropped, and his whole face elongated prodigiously at this intimation. But yet, to give up his John Dory! it was impossible to entertain such an idea for a single moment.

"Come what may come," thought he to himself, "I must and will dine upon John this blessed day, —yea, though I should lose my head for it to-morrow."

Resolution worthy of a Roman! and by way of

tempering so much courage with a due mixture of caution and prudence, he communicated the whole history of his past and future wanderings to Sir Frederick, so that in case of any accident he might have a staunch loyalist and a true-blue Protestant to fall back upon for a character. To all these details did his mischievous auditor seriously incline, and having heard him out, commended with laudable gravity his pursuit of the fish—the *flying* fish, as he called it,—but all the time with the secret intention of leading him into a scrape before the day was over. Somehow or other, it generally happens that when a man is bent on any mischief, the devil is sure to be ready at his elbow with the means. And so it chanced now. Scarcely had Matthew bade farewell to his insidious adviser, than a certain secretary, well known as a Government spy, made his appearance on the scene. Touching his hat to Sir Frederick, he was about to pass on, as one who thought his absence was more likely to be agreeable than his company, when the latter, staying him, said,

"A word with you, Mr. Breedon!"

The spy started at the summons, not quite satisfied whether he was going to receive a bribe or a beating, for his conscience, without being asked, assured him he had quite as good a right to expect one as the other. He stopped, notwithstanding; blows being much too common an occurrence with him to let the fear of them stand in the way of any better chance.

"Well met, Mr. Breedon!" cried Sir Frederick, hastily; "you have come in the very nick to do a service to the state, and to yourself at the same time."

Mr. Breedon instantly called up a look of patriotism that would have done "honor to the noblest Roman of them all,"—it was absolutely Brutus in coat, waistcoat, and trowsers,—a great improvement on the costume of ancient Rome.

"You see that short, fat man, in the blue coat and grey trowsers? Yonder, I mean,—he is looking in at the pastrycook's window,—now he walks on again. Do you mark him?"

"I have him," said the spy, eagerly

"Then follow him; watch him; do not lose him for a moment."

"I won't."

"He's a Jesuit in disguise!" continued Sir Frederick, sinking his voice into a mysterious whisper.

"Is he, indeed!" said the spy, in a similar tone; "but truly I thought as much; he has all the air of St. Omer's about him, though he's much fatter than the breed in general."

"Fat as he is, he brings letters from the Pretender to the Jacobites on this side of the water. He has just come out of Madame Pantalon's—you must have heard of her—she corresponds with half the Catholics in England, and he is now going to Mr. Dumas, who is generally suspected for a Jesuit."

Off galloped the spy in pursuit of Matthew, who, in his no less eager pursuit of the John Dory, had by this time reached the house of Mr. Dumas. For a moment a qualm of bashfulness withheld his uplifted hand from the knocker, but he thought of John, and immediately was himself again. Down came the knocker, out came the servant, and in went the modest Matthew, with an intimation that he wished to see Mr. Dumas on a very urgent business. In a few minutes, a message was brought down from the master of the house, expressing his readiness to see the urgent gentleman, and up marched Matthew into the drawing-room, under the convoy of the servant, who, having placed a chair, again withdrew to the lower regions, leaving the two principals looking at each other in silence.

"I crave your pardon, sir," at length said the veracious Matthew; "when I asked for Mr. Dumas, I fully expected to see a very different person,—one, indeed, who is not half your years, and permit me to add, who is by no means so well calculated as yourself for the higher walks of life."

"There needs no apology, Mr. Muchmore," said the old gentleman, peering out the name from a furtive glance at the card, which he still held in hand.

"I am quite ashamed of my stupid blunder," replied the bashful visitant, "and fear I must give up all hope of ever seeing the object of my search. I have already been over half London."

The benevolent old gentleman took the hint, and politely requested him to be seated. Here was one point gained, at all events.

"You are too good," said Matthew; "I ought by this time to be with Lord Spring; but, no matter; I can put off that business to another day."

"Lord Spring!" exclaimed the old gentleman; "you are acquainted with that excellent nobleman,—my worthy friend, if I may presume to call him so?"

"Intimately," replied Matthew; "I was at his breakfast-table this very morning."

Our epicure had struck the right chord. The benevolent old gentleman came at once to look upon him as a friend's friend, and throwing off the last shades of reserve, earnestly pressed him to take some refreshments. "Would he like wine and biscuits? or did he prefer a sandwich?"

"Much obliged to you," said Matthew; "but, as I like to dine early, I seldom eat anything before that meal."

This was a wise forbearance, and showed the delicacy of his tact, but still did not produce the hoped-for invitation; so Matthew did all that could be done in such a dilemma. He made himself as agreeable as possible,—told a thousand pleasant anecdotes, at which, indeed, he was an adept,—discussed every subject that he thought most likely to prove interesting to his host,—and, in short, played his part so well, that the old gentleman at last requested the favor of his company to dinner.

"Oh! John Dory! John Dory!" mentally ejaculated the delighted Matthew, "at last I have thee! —*post tot casus, tot discrimina rerum*—after so many cruel disappointments, so many buffetings of unkind fortune!"

On his invitation being accepted, the old gentleman politely expressed a hope that his guest might be able to make a meal of the Lenten diet he had to set before him. "Not expecting," he said, "the pleasure of any company, he had nothing better for dinner than some *soup-maigre* and an *omelette*."

At this announcement, Matthew was thunderstruck—no John Dory, after all! Had Fate herself entered the lists against him, and vowed to make him a second Tantalus? He groaned inwardly at the idea. And what had become of the fish? —whither had it gone?—who was the lucky mortal destined by too partial fortune to feed upon its sweetness? It was no easy matter to get a solution of these knotty points, except, indeed, by putting the question directly to the old gentleman, and this was rather too much even for the modesty of our friend Matthew; so he fidgeted, and bit his fingers, and looked foolish, greatly to the surprise of his host, who could only attribute these symptoms to discontent with the Lenten fare he had announced. In his usual spirit of kindness, therefore, he said,

"'Tis a pity you did not happen to call a few minutes earlier, as in that case I might have amended our meal with a splendid John Dory. It had just come in from an old friend; but being much too great a treat for a bachelor dining alone, I sent it off to good Master Gillies."

"The hunchbacked tailor of Cheapside?" said Matthew, with sudden vivacity.

"The same," replied the old gentleman. "Odd enough that, high or low, you should seem to know all my acquaintance."

"Very odd," responded Matthew. "And now I think of it, I promised to see him to-day by one o'clock. It's on the matter of a bill of some standing;—and really I wonder how I came to forget it."

Great was the old gentleman's admiration of this spirit of punctuality,—so great, indeed, that he was not particularly urgent with Matthew to fulfil his first promise of dining with him on *omelette* and *soup-maigre;* so that our unctuous friend once more found himself in the street in pursuit of the fugitive John Dory. But in proportion as his speed brought him nearer and nearer to the tailor's well-known shop, so did his confidence in himself and his cause decline, the fact being that he was in Master Gillies' books, but not in his good books, and between the two there is a wide difference. Poor Matthew's appetite quailed for a moment when he remembered this circumstance, and how much worse than gout or rheumatism was the twinge from a bailiff's paw, however lightly laid upon the shoulder; but John Dory still gleamed to his fancy in the distance, marshalling him the way that he should go, as whilom the visionary dagger led Macbeth to the king's bed-room. On it beckoned him, and on he went, as if writs had been only innocent bits of parchment, with no more harm in them than so many strips for tailors' measures.

In this desperate mood, he entered the domicil of the redoubted fashioner, and though at the first glimpse of his visitant a dark cloud passed over the hunchback's face, yet this was transitory as an April shower, and like that was succeeded by a fair sunshine.

"I have not come to pay you," said Matthew, deeming it wisest to anticipate the attack that he knew else awaited him,—"I have not, indeed."

"I did not suppose you had," answered the hunchback, in a mild voice. "It's rather the old suit for a new suit, I should imagine." And the little man chuckled as gently at his own facetiousness, as if he were half ashamed of doing any thing so much out of character.

Matthew of course laughed, and in a much louder key, as in prudence bound; but the next moment, putting on a demure face, he gravely said, "No, no, Master Gillies; henceforth I intend incurring no fresh bills till I have paid off what I already owe."

"A very virtuous resolution," said the hunchback, with a smile. What that smile meant, it was no easy matter to divine; but it made Matthew feel any thing rather than comfortable.

"I have only called," he said, "that you might see I have not forgotten you, nor the little unsettled account between us."

Again the hunchback gave one of his inexplicable leers, and his voice lost none of its wonted gentleness, as he replied, "Well, that *does* show an honest mind; there's at least the intention to pay—when you can."

"Of course, of course," said Matthew, hastily.

"And now you are here," said the hunchback, "perhaps you will honor my poor house by taking your nooning with me?—some cake and a glass of sherry?"

"Nay, that were to spoil your dinner; for I know you keep early hours, and it's hard upon two already; but, if it does not put you too much out of your way, I'll take a snack with you when you sit down to dinner."

"I shall be proud of your company," said the tailor. "Excuse me, though, for a few minutes, I have some orders to give the men in the work-shop."

"Oh! don't let me interfere with business," exclaimed Matthew. "Do exactly as if I were not here."

To this the hunchback only replied by one of his uncomfortable smiles, and edged off, something after the fashion of a crab, into his back-parlor.

"Confound the little distortion!" muttered Matthew, as the door closed upon his host; "I hardly know what to make of him to-day. Now if he has gone out only to send for one of the city-officers, meaning to pack me off to the Compter, now that he has me in the rat-trap? Oh, John Dory! John Dory! what toils, what perils do I encounter for thy sake!"

This was a wise suspicion, all things considered, and it was not a little strengthened when, through the shop-window, he saw one of the hunchback's myrmidons hurrying along like one who is bound on a business that requires no ordinary despatch.

After such a hint, it would have been no very prudent measure to have trusted implicitly to his host's smiles: out, therefore, he darted, and followed, though not too closely, the steps of the flying tailor, till he saw him enter a house with grated windows, and a huge brass plate affixed. On the latter, even at that distance, he could plainly read, "Thomas Fangs, Officer to the Sheriffs of London and Middlesex,"—a proof that even in those days bailiffs had the grace to be ashamed of their vocation, and so endeavored to cloak a foul office by a fine name. Here was "confirmation strong as proof of holy writ;" and, as if that were not enough, the tailor's man had not been in the house more than a minute when he came out again with Mr. Fangs himself in his best top-boots, a dirty, bandy-legged follower bringing up the rear of this respectable party. Off flew Matthew the instant his eye caught them, up this alley and down another, till he was fairly brought to a stand, from want of breath, at a timber-yard on the river side. By a sort of blind impulse he dashed into the yard, and finding the door of communication open between that and the house adjoining, he entered without hesitation, and scampered up stairs to the drawing-room, much to the surprise of those who were sitting about the fire-place in expectation of their dinner.

"Mr. Muchmore!" cried the lady of the mansion.

"Matthew!" exclaimed the master; "where, in the name of wonder, do you come from?—and why in this strange fashion? One would fancy you had dropt down from the clouds amongst us."

The sound of these familiar voices acted upon Matthew like cold water dashed into the face of a patient just about to go off into a fit. His alarm at tailors and bailiffs passed away in a minute; and he at once saw that he had stumbled, without knowing it, into the house of an old friend,—no other, indeed, than John Gillies, the timber-merchant. It would be difficult to say which party looked the most astonished,—Matthew, or mine host and his family; but the former, with whom bashfulness was at no time a predominant failing, soon recovered himself enough to stammer out in excuse, that, wishing to cut a most unpleasant acquaintance, he had taken refuge in the merchant's dwelling. Now this certainly was the truth, only it happened to be truth in disguise, and it passed muster very well with the frank-hearted man of deals, who invited him, since he was there, to stay and take pot-luck with the family.

"By the by," he said, "we have had an odd accident to-day, that I was angry enough about at the time, but which I am not sorry for now that I find we are to have the pleasure of your company. A fine John Dory was brought to the house about half an hour ago, and, as it was directed to Mr. Gillies,—some namesake, of mine, I suppose,—the cook thought it had been sent in by me to eke out a short dinner, and without farther ceremony popped it into the fish-kettle. It was only from a few words dropped casually that I learned the mistake, and then it was too late to attempt rectifying it—the fish was nearly half-boiled; so, although somewhat against my conscience, I e'en left Master John where I found him—in hot water."

Here was a pleasant stroke of that whimsical jade, Fortune—after having hunted John Dory all the morning to no purpose, now to stumble upon him in a place and at a time when such a thing could be least expected. The heart of Mat, therefore, leaped and was glad within him at the messenger's stupidity in consigning the precious cargo to a wrong port, and internally he vowed to make himself amends by many a precious morsel for all his previous disappointments. But "*l'homme propose, et Dieu dispose*," says the proverb, and so it turned out on the present occasion.

It was past the usual dinner-hour, and the timber-merchant, having repeatedly consulted his watch at short intervals, and as often received from it a renewed assurance of the fact, began to be impatient; his wife smiled more and more languidly in answer to his increasing complaints of the cook's want of punctuality; the young ladies looked pale and dull from fasting; and when nearly half an hour had thus elapsed, and still no call came to dinner, even Matthew's previous hilarity and triumph gave way to certain unpleasant misgivings, though he, too, was silent, hiding in his bosom, as whilom did the Spartan boy, the foe that was devouring him.

At length, instead of dinner, two strangers were announced, the one a little, thin, dapper coxcomb, in a sky-blue coat, and the other a tall, broad-shouldered varlet, with legs and arms conformable, and a bull-neck, admirably calculated for the support of the huge head that rested on it.

"That's Mr. Muchmore," cried the sky-blue individual, pointing to our friend Matthew.

"Then you must come with me," said the more rugged personage, stepping forward.

"Not so, friend," replied the merchant. "I'll be his bail, and I hardly think you'll venture to refuse it."

"Bail!" said the man, with a sardonic grin; "it's much you know of these matters. Why, it ain't bailable,—not in no court."

"Not bailable!" cried the merchant. "I never heard of such a thing!"

"You hear it now, then," said the man, "and it's I that tells you—John Holdfast; so mind, old gentleman, you remember it another time."

Before the merchant could deliver himself of the angry reply that was at his tongue's end, Mr. Breedon—for it was no other than that worthy—gracefully stepped forward, and, with as much joy in his face as if he were communicating the pleasantest news imaginable, informed him that his friend was not arrested for debt, but apprehended on a charge of high treason.

"Me!" exclaimed the astonished Matthew,—"apprehend me upon a charge of high treason! There must be some mistake!"

"That 'ere's no consarn of mine," cried the Bow Street myrmidon. "Make the Old Bailey jury believe as much, and it may save you a ride to Tyburn."

"Are you sure that this gentleman is the person intended in your warrant?" asked the merchant, quite satisfied that his fat friend was the last person in the world to mix himself up in any thing of the kind.

"You're precious hard of belief," replied the man, with a sneer. "Read the warrant yourself."

The merchant took the sealed parchment, and seemed to scan it over and over again, his perplexity being any thing but lessened by the perusal. At length he said, "The warrant bears your name, sure enough. I should not wonder if some informing scoundrel has been trumping up this ridiculous charge, in the hope of somehow or other making money of you. There is no help for it, I fear," continued the merchant. "You must needs go, and I will go with you to see that you have fair play in this matter."

For the first time, in the whole course of that eventful day, was Matthew false to the memory of John Dory.

The magistrate, into whose awful presence Matthew was now led, or rather dragged, was devoted, as becomes a worshipful law-dispenser, soul and body to the powers that be. Short work was made with Matthew. He was fully committed to Newgate to take his trial, with a very fair chance of being hanged, unless some *Deus ex machinâ* descended, in this the fifth and last act, to save him from the gallows.

The hours passed sadly enough with the unlucky prisoner; confused visions of rope, and John Dory, and bailiffs, floated before his troubled brain, and even his appetite failed him, though the jailor very affectionately placed before him a nice loaf of sour black bread, and a large pitcher full to the brim of Thames water. Nor were matters much mended when night came. In spite of the accommodation afforded by a bundle of somewhat musty straw, poor Matthew could not for a long time compose himself to sleep; and even when, at a late hour, his eyes at length were closed, his dreams had just the same color as his waking fancies: they were made up of fish, bailiffs, and hangmen. In one of them he cut off his own head with his own hands, and held it up to the admiring multitude, the said head discoursing most feelingly all the time on the wisdom of eating apple-sauce with fish, and stuffing goose with parsley and red-herrings!

It was now the evening of the second day, and Mat, from want of his usual food and sleep, had grown more disconsolate than ever, when suddenly the dungeon-door opened, and Sir Frederick appeared, his finger on his lip to intimate the necessity of silence, and an expression of fear in his face, that effectually stifled the joyful exclamation that was rising to greet his presence.

"Bribery!—escape!—caution!" he whispered rapidly, and seizing Matthew's by no means unwilling hand, he led him forth from the dungeon.

At last he found himself whirled along the streets in Sir Frederick's own carriage. Then, and not till then, did he venture to ask how this wonderful escape had been contrived. Sir Frederick burst into a fit of laughter.

"My good fellow, your escape is all a hoax. I heard from Breedon what had happened—indeed, to own the truth, it was I who set him on—and immediately I went and explained all to my friend, Sir Robert Walpole, who gave me an order for your discharge. More than that, he is anxious to see you, and has invited you to dinner."

"To dinner!" sighed Matthew, for the thought of John Dory rushed full upon his memory, now that he felt himself safe, and the tears came to his eyes.

Matthew was duly introduced to the minister, and sat down to dinner with a select party of friends of both sexes. There was the welcome clatter of plates and glasses,—the delicious odor of soup from the yet uncovered tureen,—then the serving-men stepped noiselessly forward, and all the covers were simultaneously removed,—all, save one, and that one stood before Matthew. A moment's pause followed—every eye was fixed with an odd expression upon our unctuous friend, who actually gasped with expectation. His color went and came like a young lady when first listening to a lover, or like a dying dolphin, only the simile is somewhat the worse for wear—the servant, at a sign from his master, removed the cover—and what a glorious sight!—it was—yes, it was a John Dory!—a fresh John Dory!—a plump John Dory!—fresher, plumper than that for which he had gone through so many trials! Happy, happy, happy Matthew!

THESEUS AND ARIADNE.

BY J. R. PLANCHE.

So drained is every source of mirth, so low the muses' spring,
'Tis quite a puzzle now-a-days to find a theme to sing.
Of modern dames and heroes you have heard enough, and so
I'll sing of one or two who flourished many years ago.

In ancient times the Isle of Crete through all the world was famed,
And by a mighty monarch governed, who was Minos named.
On Athens he made war, and thrash'd her army and her fleet,
Until they wished with all their hearts that he was Minos Crete.

This monarch to a monster was allied in some degree;
A greater brute—the monster, mind—no eye did ever see:
If we may trust the poets, he was called the Minotaur,
And, half a man and half a bull, was reckon'd quite a bore!

A labyrinth he liv'd in, as said poets also say;
And never fasted save when he had nought whereon to prey.
This labyrinth was hard to thread, according to report,
And very like the one no doubt you've seen at Hampton Court.

King Minos, having thump'd his foes, politely did desire 'em
To day a yearly tribute to this *semi-bovemque virum:*
Seven fine young men, seven fair young maids—with cruel glee he drove 'em—
To furnish for an annual feast to this *semi-virumque bovem!*

But just as the Athenians had begun in fact to scorn hope,
Young Theseus nobly volunteered to lead this most forlorn hope;
The king's fair daughter saw him, and for love went almost mad; nei—
Ther had he seen a beauty like the Princess Ariadne.

She whisper'd softly in his ear, "My caution, do not mock it!
Be ruled by me, and put this ball of cotton in your pocket;
'Twill guide you through the labyrinth." The youth, for fame who thirsted,
Cried, "Lady, by this cotton shall the Minotaur be worsted!"

He vow'd eternal gratitude, as people always do;
And first he ran the labyrinth, and next the monster through,
Then starting with his *chère amie*, like beau of modern days,
Left no one in the labyrinth but all folks in amaze!

They stopp'd at Naxos by the way, and as he promised marriage,
The trusting fair was any thing but prudent in her carriage.
Imagine then her horror when she found at break of day
Her lover had levanted, and left her—the bill to pay!

She call'd, she bawl'd, she tore her hair—wigs then were not in fashion,
Or other heads had profited by this poor lady's passion;
When Bacchus, whom to post all night late revel often forces,
Stopped at that very Bunch of Grapes to breakfast and change horses.

To him with many a sigh she told her situation strange,
And down he threw a five-pound note, crying "Never mind the change.
Come, dry your eyes, I whining hate, though god of wine I am,
And I'll drown your real pain, my dear, in plenty of my Cham!"

She jump'd at such an offer, and his priestess soon was made,
And long with him she drove a roaring wine and spirit trade;
And thus by her example 'tis—at least, so I've been thinking—
That ladies, when they're cross'd in love, are apt to take to drinking.

OH, LOVE, YOU'VE BEEN A VILLAIN.

A Song.

BY J. R. PLANCHE.

Lovers who are young, indeed, and wish to know the sort of life
That in this world you're like to lead, ere you can say you've caught a wife;
Listen to the lay of one who's had with Cupid much to do,
And love-sick once, is love-sick still, but in another point of view.
Woman, though so kind she seems, will take your heart, and tantalize it—
Were it made of Portland stone, she'd manage to McAdamize it.
Dairy-maid or duchess
Keep it from her clutches,
If you'd ever wish to know a quiet moment more.
Wooing, cooing,
Seming, scheming,
Smiling, wiling,
Pleasing, teazing,
Taking, breaking,
Clutching, touching,
Bosoms to the core.
Oh, love, you've been a villain since the days of Troy and Helen,
When you caused the fall of Paris, and of very many more.

Sighing like a furnace, in the hope that you may win her still,
And losing health and appetite, and growing thin and thinner still;
Walking in the wet before her window or her door o' nights,
And catching nothing but a cold, with waiting there a score o' nights.
Spoiling paper by the ream, with rhymes devoid of reasoning,
As silly and insipid as a goose without the seasoning.
Running bills with tailors,
Locking up by jailers,
Bread and water diet then your senses to restore.
Sighing, dying,
Losing, musing,
Walking, stalking,
Hatching, catching,
Spoiling, toiling,
Rhyming, chiming,
Running up a score.
Oh, Love, you've been a villain, since the days of Troy and Helen,
When you caused the fall of Paris, and of very many more.

Finding all you've suffered has but been the sport of jilting jades,
And calling out your rival in the style of all true tilting blades.
Feeling, ere you've breakfasted, a bullet through your body pass,
And cursing, then, your cruel fate, and looking very like an ass.
Popped into a coffin, just as dead as suits your time of life;
Paragraphed in papers, too, as "cut off in the prime of life."
When the earth you're under
Just a nine days' wonder,
And the world jogs on again, exactly as before.
Jilting, tilting,
Calling, falling,
Swearing, tearing,
Lying, dying.
Cenotaphed and paragraphed,
And reckoned quite a bore.
Oh, Love, you've been a villain since the days of Troy and Helen,
When you caused the fall of Paris, and of very many more.

THE BOAT RACE.

FROM "THE LIFE AND TIMES OF PETER PRIGGINS." ANONYMOUS.

"ROBERT RURAL, ESQ., Rustic Grange, Rutlandshire.

"DEAR BOB,—I am very seedy, and rather stiff; nevertheless I cannot resist the inclination I feel to try to relieve the *ennui* under which you must be laboring in the country. The idea of being boxed up with your old governess at the Grange!—doing penance on barley-water and boiled chicken—no beer, no wine, no nothing—in submission to the orders of your medical, is rather a nuisance I calculate; but it's all your own fault, you will be so devilish fast there's no stopping you, until you run your head against some wall or other, and get pulled up all of a heap—just as if you could not have kept quiet for one week, and pulled in our boat, instead of larking off to Witney after Poll Stitch, the little ugly milliner's girl, and depriving us of the best No. 7 that ever turned oar in ro'llock, thereby losing your laurel crown (though one of *parsley* would be more congenial now with your chicken); for, to ease your doubts at once, Oxford won by a hundred yards at least; but I must give you an account of the whole thing, it was *res non parva* I can tell you.

"We found no little difficulty in getting a man to supply your place, but at last obtained a Jesus man, full of bone and beer; which last substance we succeeded in abstracting by a severe course of sudorifics and salts, under the advice and inspection of Stephen Dair, who got him into wind, by making him pull behind him, in a two-oar, down to Iffley and back, every other hour every day, as soon as he considered him medicinally *safe* for a start; giving him two sour plums, and a glass of acid Chablis between the heats, to keep his pluck up. He pulls stronger than you, old fellow, and that's saying a good deal for him; but, as Stephen says, 'rolls about in the boat like a barrel of beer in Squashy and Washy's dray;'—that will soon be rectified.

"The crew started two days before the race, and pulled gently down to Henley, merely trying a spirt now and then to prove their wind, when they came to a fine reach, and arrived at the Hart in splendid condition—their hands as hard as horn and without a blister, owing to Stephen's training and superior bees-wax. Not an ounce of spare flesh among them, even in the Welshman; but skin clear, and well strained over the starting muscles, with eyes as 'bright as bricks,' as Lord Nincompoop very ably remarked; he's always great at a simile. Stephen ordered the beefsteaks, and presided over the cooking of them, to insure their being properly *not* cooked; that is, merely just shown the fire to produce sufficient perfume and outside coloring to convince the consumers they were not performing an act of cannibalism. To wash down this *morçeau* each man was allowed half a pint of porter, and four glasses of port wine, and then Stephen undertook 'the character of chambermaid for that night only,' and saw every man safe in bed; an example he followed himself, after putting on his usual nightcap — fourteen glasses of cold without, and twenty-eight cigars—judiciously observing as he bit one end of the last, and missed the candle with the other, in endeavoring to light it, 'I'm not a going to pull nor steer, and it's very hard if I can't have a little rational recreation!'

"It was an understood thing throughout the university that any man, who chose, might go to Henley, provided he asked leave of the Dean of his college, was back before twelve o'clock, and did not go in a tandem, which was very rigidly and very properly forbidden. Our Dean, you know, is a regular trump, and though he keeps his teams to their work —never double thongs them unnecessarily, and is always ready to grant all reasonable indulgences. Upon the present occasion he showed his usual judgment and kindness, by bargaining with Costar and the other proprietors, for two coaches to carry all the men who wished to go, to Henley and back, at a certain moderate sum; thereby ensuring comfort and economy too. I got leave to go in Kickum's trap, with three other men—Dick Downe, who was to be wagoner, and wanted to use the long reins; but the Dean would not hear of it, though Dick brought up fifteen of his most intimate friends—presiding geniuses of the 'Tivy,' 'Tally-ho,' and other crack coaches, to certify to his proficiency in handling the ribbons; and could have produced their wives and families to strengthen his case, if requisite, for Dick is too fond of all connected with coaching to limit his attentions to the male branches of the profession. It was no go—so we had a pair, and a pair of good ones—Woodpecker, that kicked Sam Strapper's leg in two, and old Peter that bit a piece out of Will Wisp's breeches.

"Our two friends, who rode behind, were Solomon, the son of Sir Solomon Stingo, the great London porter brewer, who is generally known by the *sobriquet* of the Knight of Malta, and Tim Tripes, a fresh importation from Charterhouse; and, of course, a good judge of London entire.

"Now, I confess to a little malice in our motives for picking out these two men, we made sure of a good rise or two out of them during the day. Solomon is a great ass, very rich and very stingy; but he consented to pay pipes all the way, provided he was allowed to play a tune on a tin trumpet in every village we passed through, and to announce our approach to the various pikemen. He can't bear the slightest allusion to malt in any shape—small-beer, table-ale, XX, or stout, and would not be *seen* with a pewter in his hand, to get his governor a baronetcy. I knew from Tripe's talents in that line, he would insist on pulling up at every public on the road, to 'wash the dust out of his mouth,' and thereby drive the brewer's boy into hysterics or convulsions. Rise No. 1.

"You don't know Solomon, so I'll just give you an idea of him. Did you ever see a troop of yeomanry practising what is called *post* exercise; that is, learning to cut off human heads by chopping with their swords at a lump of wood like a barber's block stuck on a barber's pole? because that same pole with the block on it will give you no bad notion of Solomon's head and neck—shoulders he has none; but to compensate for the deficiency of his upper build, he displays what the sailors call a remarkable breadth of beam amidships, and his legs appear as if he had obtained a grace of the house, or a dispensation from the vice-chancellor to wear the calf downwards. His face seems as if it had been badly cut out of a frosty savoy, and thatched with red-wheat straw, ferret-eyes, and a mouth evidently designed to dispose of asparagus by the bundle. His dress in the worst possible *outré* taste of a Regent Street Sunday buck, with gold pins, rings, and chains, as ostentatiously displayed on all parts of his person as if he were training for bagman to a Brummagem jeweller. To crown all, on his nasty soapy red hair, he wears a white beaver tastily turned up with green eaves. He is no beauty, you'll allow.

"Tim Tripes, you know, as the best bow-oar in our boat—a little thick set fellow with splendid shoulders and deltoids well developed, full of pluck and science—not Aristotle's, but Mr. Jackson's running a little too much to middle from constitutional unwillingness to let go a quart of porter before he has seen the bottom of it; a trick acquired from tibbingout down the lane, *i. e.*, Charterhouse lane, to the Red Cow; the landlord of which noted public, generally a retired fighting man, looked with sovereign contempt on every man and boy who 'couldn't swallow a kevart hoff at vonce.'

"As I knew the little town of Henley would be full to overflowing, I took the precaution of writing to an old college friend to secure stables or stalls for the prads. In reply he told me he had succeeded in doing so, at the Bell or the Bull, but from the horrid nature of his scrawl, resembling Egyptian hieroglyphics, Sanscrit, and Arabic characters, I could not tell which, so I left it to chance, or Providence—which some of our senators consider the same thing.

"Just before we set off, I saw Solomon's tiger busily employed in wiping the moisture off his forehead (with the wash-leather intended for polishing his master's wine-glasses), caused, it appeared, from over exertion in trying to cram a large hamper under the trap, which Solomon kindly informed us, with as knowing a look as his ferrety eyes could convey, contained six bottles of gooseberry champagne, two of British brandy, and a large rook-pie, with bottled porter to match; 'for you know,' said he, 'they impose dreadful at inns, at public times, and we can slip out the back way, sit down in a field, and have a good dinner cheap, six bottles of sham champagne—it's very good, though—twelve shillings;—two of brandy—best British—nine;—that's a guinea.' (Making use of his fingers for ready reckoners.) The rooks I shot at Nuneham a week ago, and got Mother Priggins to put a cover over them, in exchange for an old waistcoat—so that don't count. My governor stands porter—we can beg a bit of salt, and buy a twopenny buster at a baker's shop. Now, if we had dined at the inn, we should have had to pay a guinea a-piece, instead of the same sum between four of us—for I don't mean to stand treat except for the crow-tart and porter.'

"We did not oppose the stingy dog's whim then, but got all our rattletraps into the pheaton, as Kickum's ostler (not to vary from his kind) called it, and started as soon as Woodpecker and Old Peter had done kicking and biting. They went off screwy at first, being groggy from overfast work: but as Kickum predicted, 'as soon as they got warm, and the *jint ile* began to act,' away they went, about twelve miles an hour, thus illustrating Virgil's '*vires acquirit eundo.*' We got along well till we came to the Harcourt Arms, at Nuneham. Solomon pulled out his tin trumpet, and had just commenced toot-toot-tooing, to the evident risk of blowing his front teeth out, when Tripes bawled out, 'Wo-ho!'—a sound Woodpecker and Old Peter willingly obeyed, in spite of Dick's persuasions lashingly applied. 'I say, old fellows, you don't think I'm going to pass the best glass of ale on the road? Hillo! Mother Bung! bring out four quarts of the best, in the pewters! What's one a-piece to begin with?' I turned round to get a glimpse of Solomon's savoy—he was looking daggers at Tripes, and holding the tin trumpet up in the air, like Mr. Harper preparing for a flourish, indicating a hostile descent on the head of his enemy—but Tim doubled his palm, which was ready extended for the malt, and merely observed, '*If you do*,' when the arm dropped listlessly by his side, and 'the music' into the road, where it performed a peculiar description of pirouette, for two minutes, in the dust, to Solomon's horror—as he had to give a quart of beer to the blacksmith's man for wiping it with his dirty apron.

"'Here's to you, Mr. Musician,' cried Tripes; 'come, sink your family failing for once, and taste the tap—won't you?—Then I'll do it for you.' The hand and head went gradually and beautifully back together, until the initials of Mary Thompson were visible at the bottom of the cup, and he found breath to say, 'All right, Dick! the gentleman with red hair will pay you as we come back, Mother Bung; by! by!'

"Solomon swore it was a shame, and said he'd be blowed if he would—and sulked and grumbled to Dorchester, where his conceit of his musical abilities got the better of his temper, and he blew his tin vociferously, till the White Hart appeared in view, when Tripes again cried 'Wo-ho! capital porter here. Landlord! four pints best stout.' It was only three miles from our last pull up, so we positively declined. But Tripes insisted on *his* allowance, taking especial care, in handing it into the tap, to drop a teacupfull over Solomon's new white kerseymeres, and drank it leisurely, to enjoy, with one eye, the spiteful look of vindictiveness depicted on his victim's face, as he carefully removed the 'stain upon his honor' with a refulgent red pocket-handkerchief, till Tripes cried out, 'All right, the gentleman in beery breeches will pay as we come back.'

"About a mile further is a little place called Shillingford, with two road-side houses just opposite each other, where Tripes wanted to stop again, to see whether a proper sense of competition had stimulated the respective landlords to brew something a little better than common, but his usual 'Wo-ho!' would not have succeeded, for Dick was awake to his plans by this time, and was cutting into Woodpecker and Old Peter unmercifully, had not the water-troughs on either side of the road proved as tempting to the nags, as the words 'real home brewed,' did to Tripes. There we were! Woodpecker, who was on the near side, making for the left-hand trough, and Old Peter doggedly determined to reach the other on the right—each horse being ably assisted in his struggles by the ostler and landlord of the house for which he was showing so decided a preference, when the landladies endeavored to seduce the gentlemen on their sides. Dick dropped his whip in despair, singing 'How happy could I be with either!' and the 'war of words' between the adherents of the *centre gauche* and the *centre droite*, was at length allayed by Tripes calling out 'A plague on both your houses—Mrs. left-hand house! bring two quarts of *your* best! Mrs. right-hand, ditto! ditto!—Left-hand ostler!—right hand ditto!—the gentleman in the harmonic line will give you sixpence a-piece, to bring each of those horses a pot of beer, and if they won't drink it, you can do it for them, and favor them with a bucket of water in exchange.' Solomon's demurrer was useless—we all swore we had no money, so he paid for all, taking his change to the uttermost farthing, and grumbling 'Here's a pretty go—I'm to stand Sam all day!'

"We got off again as quickly as we could, for fear we should be involved in a discussion with Tripes and the opposition landlords, as to which was the best brewer; a question he would not have ventured to decide without critically investigating the contents of every barrel in their cellars. However, he seemed willing to move on, as he knew that Benson was only a mile and a half further, and that we meant to stop and feed ourselves and the prads at the White Hart.

"As ill-luck would have it, just as we turned into the gateway of that inn in good style, Solomon melodiously saluting the house with evident self-satisfaction, and anticipating the praises of 'the boys,' the Alert was standing there, with the horses put to, and Black Will in the act of mounting the box with the reins and whip in his off-hand. Whether his team had no 'music in their souls,' or were anxious, and had a horror of horns, I can't say: but they all four began dancing out of tune and the yard, before Will had gained the box, whence he 'came down with a run,' as the Jack tars say, and was dragged some little distance by the reins before the horses could be stopped.

"Now those who know the 'Black *Prince*,' as Mr. Bowers was called when he worked on that coach (though one wag was wicked enough to suggest that the title was acquired from his having been seen at a battle of A-*gin*-court), must be well aware that his excessive politeness would be rather tried by so unpleasant an ejectment from 'his seat.' He rose gracefully—gave the reins and whip to the horsekeeper—made signs to boots to rub him down, and then walked deliberately up to poor Solomon, who had been viewing these proceedings with feelings verging on insanity; and touching his hat with his usual urbanity, and putting his heavy foot on the horn, and crushing it flat, said, 'Jim Spooney!—next time you want to prac*tise* on that there bugle, perch yourself somewhere or other, where there ain't no horses nor hasses to hear you.' Then turning round to Dick, who was looking deprecatingly, and shaking him by the hand much more affectionately than his own father would or could have done, whispered loudly enough for the whole assembly to hear, 'Dick! I thought as how you was too far advanced to put such an hass as that into a guard's place!—Why, his werry looks 'ud ruin the best consarn on the road.' Dick made an humble apology, and an offer of a libation, which Will accepted, in the shape of two glasses of cold brandy-and-water, concentrated into one, and then mounted his box and drove off for Henley, with his fourteen outside and six in—the supernumeraries being *shouldered*, in course!'

"Solomon was too deeply engaged in trying (fortunately without success—men being at a premium in Benson) to procure a new musical instrument, to join us in a quiet kidney and a glass of Curaçoa, though we made him pay, under the former successful plea of having no tin like himself, and a threat of Shrub's, suggested by ourselves, that he would detain him, and have him up before a beak, if he did not. Dick was so anxious to overtake the Alert, and beat his dark friend into Henley, that poor Woodpecker and Old Peter were forced to kick and bite in evident disgust at being put-to before they had properly digested their provender.

"Talking of provender, I must tell you a story: A juvenile commercial, out on his first journey, arrived at the inn to which he had been recommended by his predecessor, and to come it double strong, disdained to use the language of other men, telling the ostler to 'provender his quadruped while he discussed his chop.'

"Mr. Rub'emdown not knowing the precise interpretation of this oracular order, mentioned it to an old traveller in the Manchester line, who wickedly interpreted it to mean, 'crop his mane and ears close, and cut his tail down to a short dock,' which was accordingly done, much to the ostler's satisfaction, under the full anticipation of a double fee for despatch.

"When the gentleman ordered his gig, and having paid his score was about to mount, he swore in a most indecent manner, that 'that 'orse was not his'n, but another man's;' nor would he be convinced to the contrary until Rub'emdown fetched the stray attributes and replaced them as well as he could, making his identity undeniable. I need not say he never showed at the same house again.

"We got over the next five miles without a check, although it is all against collar; and Dick jockeyed Tripes at Nettlebed, by jerking his elbow violently against his mouth, just as we got to the Red Lion, thereby preventing the usual 'Wo-ho!' and by tipping Woodpecker and Peter a 'short Tommy,' *i. e.*, sticking an enormous large shirt-pin, in the shape of a coach-pole and splinter-bars, into their quarters, which engaged their attention too much to allow them to see the water-trough by the road-side, we got close up to the Alert just at the commencement of the fair-mile, where Dick began to make play to pass Will; but the old stager was too deep for him, and commenced the jostling system, which so amazed our charioteer, that seeing what he conceived a good opening to turn out on the turf, and give Will the go-by, he tried it on, and upset us very easily, but ludicrously, into a *ci-devant* gravel-pit, to the great amusement of every one but ourselves. However, the only harm done, was from a violent kick of Woodpecker's judiciously administered on Solomon's centre of gravity, and the ingratitude of Old Peter, who bit a piece out of Tripe's coat-tail, as he was kindly endeavoring to set him on his legs again. Amidst the shouts of the clods, 'we up and after them again,' getting into the town just as Will had touched his hat and his fees.

"We pulled up at the Bell, and found my friend had got us a capital two-stalled stable, in which we saw our nags comfortably locked up with full racks and mangers, and toddled off to the Hart to see how the crews looked, and hear the opinions as to the result. We ordered dinner at five, as the race was to take place at eight, without saying a word to Solomon, and on our return from viewing the natives and the boats, found a nice dish of stewed eels, fried perch, framed with gudgeons, cold lamb and salad, and roasted pigeons, with lots of Reading asparagus upon the table. Solomon was missing; and just as we had finished our fish, and the 'premier pop' of champagne was heard, he made his appearance, to tell us 'he had fixed on a nice quiet corner for the crow-tart and gooseberry,' but bolted again when he saw we were otherwise engaged, looking exasperated at our extravagance, and buttoning up both his trouser's pockets, as a hint we were to pay for ourselves this time.

"But to the race itself. About seven o'clock, the rival crews pulled gently down to the starting-place, about two miles below Henley Bridge, distinguished by their colors. Oxford, true blue; Cambridge, pink; and every thing was arranged by the umpires in a quiet gentlemanly way, without any wrangling. There was a toss for choice of sides, which was won by the Cambridge men; and of course, they chose the bank on their bows, as the river forms a rather sharp curve to the left, between the locks and the town. There was to be no fouling, and the victory was to belong to the party who passed first under the bridge.

"Just before the start, every inch of ground that could command a view of the river on either side, was occupied by gazers of all sorts and sizes—lords and ladies, Jans and Jinnies, saints and sinners, cockneys and country bumpkins—it was an universal holiday in that part of the world; and Miss Martineau might have applied her preventive check, without any fear of restraining the populace upon this occasion.

"The Oxford boat belonged to Baliol Coll., built by Davis and King; the Cambridge was a bran-new turn out of Serle's, and one of the neatest I ever saw; though it struck me, when I examined her on shore as she was being greased, that she was too crank for the crew that were to pull in her—all men of weight and inches; perhaps, two finer crews were never seen; but our men were rather the longer and lighter in their *corpuscula* of the two.

"At eight o'clock precisely, the order was given for 'Up with your oars;' and in two minutes at the word 'Off,' they dropped them in beautifully—as one man; but a cry of 'False start,' owing to some little dispute about the exact distance from blade to blade, caused them to backwater, and prepare again. In five minutes the referees made all right, and 'Off she goes,' was again cried. Away they went! and before they got three hundred yards, my experienced eye could see that my conjecture about the London boat, was quite correct. She dipped in the bows every stroke, as if they were going to pull her under water, and rocked fearfully until they got into good time. The short stroke too, with the back quite straight, and the arms doing all the work, would not do on *smooth* water, compared with the long pull *through* the water, and quick feather *out* of it, of the Oxford men, who gained rapidly upon, and soon passed their rivals, taking the inside place. I was close upon them both, and could hear the steady cry of the steersman, 'Go it, my blues—beautifully pulled!—three minutes more, and your work's done—they lose ground (water he meant) every moment—steady!—no hurry—keep the old stroke!—backs down on the thwarts,' from the Oxford boat; and the 'By George, we're beaten!—quicken your stroke—don't go back so, you No. 3—pull for heaven's sake!' of the Cambridge.

"I pulled up about a quarter of a mile from the bridge, being quite satisfied how it was going, and thoroughly blown from the speed and nature of my exertions; for no one, who has not tried it, knows what 'running up' with an eight-oar means—the snobs were wofully taken in that day, being shoved unreservedly, some into the river, others into ditches, by the more *au fait* Oxonians.

"A tremendous shout, and the striking up of the church bells, proclaimed the victory was won by the Oxford men, with one hundred yards to spare!!! I jumped into a punt with poor Stephen, and by dint of his superior generalship, got on the opposite bank in time to see our crew land; and the best proof of their excellent condition was, that not one man was so distressed as to be obliged to be helped out of the boat. Our opponents came in rather more distressed, but still not much the matter. Such a shouting was still going on, that it was impossible to hear any thing said, until Stephen thundered out 'Now, my true blues! as much porter as you like!' And I heard one of the victors say, as he set an emptied quart-cup on the table at Mrs. Dixon's, 'If nectar did not mean London porter, he did not know what did.'

"You, who have been so often at such scenes on the banks of Isis, will easily imagine the whole affair; nor will you require me to describe the supper given, by the vanquished to the conquerors—

the compliments mutually given and received—the toasts drank—and last, though by no means *least*, the quantity and quality of liquids absorbed. More unflinching candidates for the favor of father Bacchus never drained Cyathi. Nor were the muses neglected, 'Nine times nine' was the cry of the night! I shall finish my letter by recording the final adventures of our *partie carrée*.

"As for myself, I had an invitation to take coffee, at the house of my friend, whom I have mentioned before as the procurer of our nag's temporary domiciles, and being a little bit of a vocalist, passed two or three pleasant hours standing over a pianoforte, and a very fine girl, to whom I was well contented to sing second. However, when ten o'clock arrived, I tore myself away from my fair chantress or enchantress, whichever you please to call her, in order to get Dick, Tripes, and Solomon ready to start—for we had promised the Dean not to be later than twelve o'clock. This, however, I found to be no easy matter, and returned to my friend's house after half an hour's vain search, to consult him on the best means of getting out of my difficulties. One of the parties relieved me speedily if not pleasantly. Just fancy my horror on hearing a scuffling sort of noise at the door of the drawing-room, which was filled with company, and seeing my friend Tripes very bosky, holding on by the doorpost on either side, and in a husky, hiccupping tone, requesting to be informed 'if our drag was at the Bell or the Bull?—the Bull or the Bell?' adding, for the information of the ladies, that 'he'd tried every tap in the town, and never tasted such very bad beer in all his life.' I ran at him vicious, and carried him, *vi et armis*, with my friend's assistance, in spite of his spiteful kicks and bites, into the stable yard, where we laid him on a truss of straw, and sponged his head with cold pump-water, which soon had the desired effect. On his recovery, he laid it all to the beer being brewer's trash, and requested to taste my friend's private tap, assuring him half a pint would be the making of him. My expostulations were useless; and while my host was gone to give the necessary, or rather unnecessary orders, he entertained me with a discussion on the merits of a large two-handed pump, down Charterhouse, and its wonderful efficacy in remedying the effects of Red Cow—'pumps up ten gallons a minute, and as cold as ice,—hiccup!—never knew it fail!'

"I got him safe to the Bell at last, and locked him in with Woodpecker and Old Peter, giving the ostler strict charge not to supply him with any liquids but water. Then I proceeded on another voyage of discovery, and arrived at the White Hart just in time to see Will start with about half his cargo. With his usual judgment, he had stowed the soberest men outside; the very drunken ones, seven in number, were compressed inside with the doors screwed up to prevent their opening them, and tumbling out on the road, and the windows nailed down for fear they should cut themselves with the glasses. No objection was made to these arrangements, for none of the seven could articulate. When, however, he proceeded to strap three or four *half* bosky men to the roof of the coach, so firm and strong a resistance was made, that he found it necessary to borrow three of Bowling's kicking-straps, and a pair of darbies (*i. e.*, handcuffs) of the constable, before his endeavors were crowned with success. I inquired if he had seen Dick lately, and I heard with joy that he was then in the bar smoking a pipe with the coachman and guard of the Stroud mail *down*. He was sober at present, as he had been drinking tea with the coachman's wife, in his absence—coffee with the guard's sister, and was going to play at cribbage or dominoes with another Jehu's daughter, but left her in disgust when he discovered that her governor only *druv a pair*.

"I assisted him in finishing his glass of *twist*, which is coach-Latin for half gin and half brandy-and-water, and carried him off rather sulky, to assist in the search for Solomon. All our endeavors, for a time, were fruitless; he had not been seen since he left the yard, with the hamper under his arm, by any one. It struck me all of a sudden, that having intimated an intention of dining economically *al fresco*, he had made for the fields in the rear of the house, and as it was a brilliant moonlight night, we explored in that direction, with success; for being attracted by faint hip! hurrahs! uttered in 'childish trebles,' we directed our steps towards them, and discovered two little chimney-sweepers, and a charity-school boy, engaging themselves on the crow tart and gooseberry wine of poor Solomon, who was lying dead-drunk on his back, under the bushes, lovingly embracing a fly-driver, quite as drunk as himself.

"Dick, in spite of Mr. Martin's act, pulled him by the legs out of the bushes, with a stoical disregard of the lacerations caused by the thorns, and so strong was the sudden attachment formed between the two votaries of Bacchus, that in dragging Solomon out, he drew the fly-man with him.

"I afterwards learned that Solomon, finding the hamper rather heavy and inconvenient to carry, had engaged the assistance of the fly-man, who was idling about the yard, to carry it for him to his 'quiet corner,' under the promise of a bottle of porter as a reward. The flavor of the porter pleased his palate so well, that he returned after an hour's time, to offer his services in carrying the hamper back, in hopes of obtaining a second edition. To his great delight, he found Solomon so far gone from original sobriety, and in so generous a humor, that he unhesitatingly accepted his invitation to partake of the remainder of the crow-tart and a bottle of gooseberry. Though the rooks were not much the better for having been killed a week, and the steak on which they rested was very tough, they contrived between them to demolish nearly all of the pie and the porter; the wine, however, took a very sudden and powerful effect upon them, which they endeavored to remedy by imbibing nearly all the British brandy. The result was, both were so beastly drunk that they fell asleep in each other's arms. The little chummies and the charity-boy found them by accident, as they were cutting round the town the back way, to see the fireworks—being supposed by their fond parents to be safe in bed—and thought it a pity that two such intemperate beings should be exposed to further temptation if they chanced to recover; so they charitably resolved to remove the *irritamenta malorum* by finishing the little that was left. When we came up they were each engaged in guggling a bottle of gooseberry, to 'the health of the gen'l'-man as didn't know how to stop when he'd had enough.'

"We left them to take care of the hamper and the fly-man (who had to drive the Mayor of Maidenhead, his wife, and nine little aspirants for the mace to their home after the fireworks, which had just commenced, were over) and carried Solomon into the stable to Tripes, who was now nearly sober, and promised to behave well for the rest of the night, if we would let him out.

"What was to be done? it was folly to think of starting with Solomon in such a condition; so we agreed to let Tripes physic him, and stay one hour to see the effect of the dose, the fireworks, and the Stroud mail start. Tripes ran into the Bell in a state of ecstasy, and returned with a jug of hot water, into which he was industriously stirring the contents of two mustard-pots;—this he managed in a most scientific way, to administer as a drench to poor Solomon, after he had removed his stock, and unbuttoned his shirt collar: we then set him up in a corner, slanting-dicularly, and left him.

"The fireworks were very fine, but the night was finer, and spoiled their effect; it was too light for lights, so we humored Dick and ran to see the mail start. We were just in time—for there were about twenty Oxford men harnessed to it by ropes and all sorts of contrivances, dragging it off at about ten miles an hour—to the horror of Dick's friend the coachman, the insides and outs, and the guards who had to run with the bags in one hand and the pair of wheelers in the other, nearly a mile and a half before he could catch them.

"Tripes, who was gazing maliciously at the large image fixed over the inn-door, intended to represent a white hart (a sketch from nature, having golden hoofs, red eyes, nose, and ears, enormous green antlers, and no tail), suggested to about forty or fifty surrounding undergraduates that it was positively cruel to keep so noble an animal in a situation where he could get nothing to eat or drink, and proposed with their assistance to remove him to a more natural lay in Mr. Maitland's park. This act of disinterested benevolence was speedily effected by means of a cart-rope, amidst the cheers of a sympathizing mob of snobs and the useless expostulations of the landlord.

"An energetic *special* in his zeal for the maintenance of order, collared Tripes, who hates an authority at all times, and was not likely to submit quietly to a great overgrown baker, because he had a constable's staff in his hand, so he replied to his threat of 'pulling him up before the beaks,' by hitting him exceedingly hard in the wind, and calling out for 'a ring!' which was quickly formed, and the special carried home in less than five minutes after, with his face smashed to a pulp, and his molars rendered unfit for mastication.

"We took Stephen Davis's advice, and 'cut our lucky' at once. The dose had fortunately operated successfully on Solomon, who was just able to sit up in the trap when properly tied in with a halter; so we paid our bill and told Dick 'to slack his hand,' all the way to Benson, where we meant to sup. We arrived there about half-past twelve, and found them just shutting up. The cook was standing in the kitchen, flattering himself his work was over for the night, and about to wash down the fatigues of a hard day with a glass of warm brandy and water, when Dick rushed in, seized the goblet and swallowed its contents, before the puzzled *chef de cuisine* could stretch out his greasy fist to prevent him. He was so disgusted at the unceremonious usage he had met with, that he rudely declined broiling any ham for us, until Tripes knocked him down with the flat side of a 'best York,' weighing two or three and twenty pounds, seized his large knife, and proceeded to act as his deputy at the gridiron. This brought him to his senses and the fire. His ingenuity was displayed to our satisfaction, and his injured honor repaired by an unlimited order for brandy-and-water for himself and the waiter. When both these worthies were disposed of under the dresser, we yielded to the fascinating request of the barmaid and Mrs. Shrub, 'to let them have a *little* sleep,' and set off home about four in the morning.

"On the road, we, that is Dick and I, who were neither of us much amiss, were engaged in forming our plans for apologizing satisfactorily to the Dean. On one point we fully agreed: to lay all the blame on poor Solomon, who was fast asleep, lashed to the back of the trap and Tripe's arm. He, Tripes, being rather dozy, and afraid of falling out if he indulged in a nap without such due precautions.

"We got to college about five o'clock, and found the gates just opened, hurried Solomon to bed, undressing and locking him safe in his rooms; we then took his splash new coat, and the rest of his dress, and walked to the nearest meadow, where we immersed them in a green, muddy ditch, and then trailed them along the dusty road; giving them a friendly stamping with our dirty boots now and then, by way of variety, and finally strewed them about his room in drunken disorder. We then obtained a commons of new bread, and extracting a piece of crumb, about the size of a cricket-ball, entered Solomon's bedroom, and without his being at all conscious of the fact, tied it firmly on his right cheek, with a white pocket-handkerchief, to represent a swelled face; and by a judicious commixture of red and black ink, applied to his right optic, succeeded in making him a very effective black eye.

"All these arrangements being completed, I ran across quad to the Dean's rooms. He was up and dressing for chapel—I put on a very long face, and told him a very piteous tale of the trouble Solomon had given us all the day, and of his obstinate determination to have his share of driving, though unqualified for the art; the result of which was, that he had upset himself into a gravel-pit, after we had fortunately jumped out to avoid the danger which we saw was otherwise inevitable.

"'Is he hurt?"

"'A little, Sir, but we have put him to bed, and he is now asleep; will you look at him, and say if we can do any thing more for him?"

"'Certainly.' He returned with me, and found every thing as I had said—being satisfied from the horrid object he saw in bed, and the state of the 'clothing department,' that 'we must have experienced a great deal of annoyance from a man who gave way to such a disgusting vice as intoxication.'

"So ended our day at Henley, old fellow, and so ends the letter of

"Yours as ever,
"William Wydeawake.

"P. S.—Solomon's governess and two sisters, who had invited themselves to the commemoration, arrived very opportunely—they found him in the state we had left him, and are all three at this present moment in violent convulsions—dreading the irreparable loss of the 'dear sweet boy,' and relieving their consanguinal feelings, in the intervals between the fits, by threatening to take the law against the naughty young gentlemen who had seduced their beloved relative—the brutes—into so degrading and dangerous a state. Tripes 'wishes they may get it,' and Dick confidently affirms that 'that cock won't fight.'"

DRAFTS FROM "THE DOCTOR."

BY ROBERT SOUTHEY.

In that very entertaining work, "The Doctor," there is an abundance of pleasant gossip upon the odd and pitiful accidents, by which the "bubble reputation" has been raised. For example:—

"Whether the regular practitioner may sneer at Mr. Ching," says the historian of Cornwall, "I know not: but the Patent Worm Lozenges have gained our Launceston apothecary a large fortune, and secured to him perpetual fame!"

There would have been no other memorial of Richard Jaquett at this day, than the letters of his name in an old deed, and obsolete hand, if he had not, in the reign of Edward VI., been Lord of the manor of Tyburn, with its appurtenances, in which the gallows was included; wherefore, from the said Jaquett, it is presumed by antiquaries, that the hangman has ever since been corruptly called Jack Ketch.

A certain William Dowsing, who, during the great rebellion, was a Parliamentary visitor for demolishing images in churches, is supposed to have given rise to the expression of giving any one a *dousing.*

Johnson tells a story of a man, who was standing in an inn kitchen, with his back to the fire, and thus accosted a traveller, who stood next to him: "Do you know, sir, who I am?" "No, sir," replied the traveller, "I have not that advantage." "Sir," said the man, "I am the great Tramley, who invented the Floodgate Iron."

Who was Ludlam, whose dog was so lazy that he leant his head against a wall to bark?

And who was old Cole, whose dog was so proud that he took the wall of a dung cart, and got squeezed to death by the wheel? Was he the same person of whom the song says,

Old King Cole
Was a merry old soul,
And a merry old soul was he?

And was his dog proud because his master was called King?

Here are questions to be proposed in the Examination Papers of some Australian Cambridge, two hundred years hence.

Flogging at School.—If the dead have any cognizance of posthumous fame, one would think it must abate somewhat of the pleasures with which Virgil and Ovid regard their earthly immortality, when they see to what base purposes their productions are employed. That their verses should be administered to boys in regular doses, as lessons or compositions, and some dim conception whipped into the tail when it has failed to penetrate the head, cannot be just the sort of homage to their genius which they anticipated or desired.

Essays on Taste.—There are some readers who have never read an essay on taste, and if they take my advice they never will; for they can no more improve their taste by so doing, than they could improve their appetite or digestion by studying a cookery book.

School Learning.—I am sometimes inclined to think that pigs are brought up upon a wiser system than boys at a grammar-school. The pig is allowed to feed upon any kind of offal, however coarse, on which he can thrive, till the time approaches, when pig is to commence pork, or take a degree as bacon.

Lovers of Literature.—Your true lover of literature is never fastidious. I do not mean the *hellus librorum*, the swinish feeder, who thinks that every name which is to be found in a title-page, or on a tombstone, ought to be rescued from oblivion; nor those first cousins of the moth, who labor under a passion for black letter, and believe every thing to be excellent which was written in the reign of Elizabeth. I mean the man of robust and healthy intellect, who gathers the harvest of literature into his barns, thrashes the straw, winnows the grain, grinds it at his own mill, bakes it in his own oven, and then eats the true bread of Knowledge. If he take his loaf upon a cabbage-leaf, and eat onions with his bread and cheese, let who will find fault with him for his taste—not I!

Vanity of Human Fame.—An old woman in a village of the west of England, was told one day that the King of Prussia was dead, such a report having arrived when the great Frederick was in the noonday of his glory. Old Mary lifted up her great slow eyes at the news, and fixing them in the fulness of vacancy upon her informant, replied, "Is a! is a! the Lord ha' mercy! Well, well! the King of Prussia! and who's he?" The "who's he?" of this old woman might serve as a text for a notable sermon upon ambition. "Who's he?" may now be asked of men greater as soldiers in their day than Frederick and Wellington; greater as discoverers than Sir Isaac, or Sir Humphrey. Who built the pyramids? Who ate the first oyster? *Vanitas vanitatum! Omnia vanitas!*

Retirement.—It is neither so easy a thing, nor so agreeable a one, as men commonly expect, to dispose of leisure when they retire from the business of the world. Their old occupations cling to them even when they hope that they have emancipated themselves. Go to any seaport town, and you will see that the sea-captain, who has retired upon his well-earned earnings, sets up a weathercock in full view from his window, and watches the variations of the wind as duly as when he was at sea, though no longer with the same anxiety. A tallow-chandler, having amassed a fortune, disposed of his business, and took a house in the country, not far from London, that he might enjoy himself; and, after a few months' trial of a holiday life, requested permission of his successor to come into town and assist him on melting days. The keeper of a retail spirit-shop, having in like manner retired from trade, used to employ himself by having one puncheon filled with water, and measuring it off by pints into another. A butcher in a small town, for some time after he had left off business, informed his old customers, that he meant to kill a lamb once a week, just for amusement.

Preaching to the Poor.—A woman in humble life was asked one day on her way back from church, whether she had understood the sermon—a stranger having preached. "Wud I hae the presumption!" was her simple and contented answer.

"Well, Master Jackson," said his minister, walking homeward after service, with an industrious laborer, who was a constant attendant, "well, Master Jackson, Sunday must be a blessed day of rest for you, who work so hard all the week! And you make good use of the day, for you are always to be seen at church." "Aye, sir," replied Jackson, "it is, indeed, a blessed day; I works hard enough all the week; and then I comes to church o' Sundays, and sets me down, and lays my legs up, and *thinks o' nothing.*"

Voluminous Trifling.—Dr. Shaw, the naturalist, was one day showing to a friend two volumes written by a Dutchman, upon the wings of a butterfly, in the British Museum. "The dissertation is rather voluminous, perhaps you will think," said the Doctor, gravely, "but it is immensely important."

Parliamentary Jokes.—Of what use a story may be, even in the most serious debates, may be seen from the circulation of old *Joes* in Parliament, which are as current there as their current namesakes used to be in the city some threescore years ago. A jest, though it shall be as stale as last year's newspapers, and as flat as Lord Flounder's face, is sure to be received with laughter by the collective wisdom of the nation: nay, it is sometimes thrown out like a tub to the whale, or like a trail of carrion to draw off hounds from the scent.

Book Madness.—A collector of scarce books was one day showing me his small but curious hoard. "Have you ever seen a copy of this book?" he asked, with every volume that he put into my hands; and when my reply was that I had not, he always rejoined, with a look and tone of triumphant delight, "I should have been exceedingly sorry if you had!"

Utility of Pockets.—Of all the inventions of the tailor, (who is of all artists the most inventive,) I hold the pocket to be the most commodious, and saving the fig leaf, the most indispensable. Birds have their craw; ruminating beasts their first or ante-stomach; the monkey has his cheek, the opossum her pouch; and, so necessary is some convenience of this kind for the human animal, that the savage who cares not for clothing, makes for himself a pocket if he can. The Hindoo carries his snuff-box in his turban. Some of the inhabitants of Congo make a secret fob in their woolly toupee, of which, as P. Labat says, the worst use they make is—to carry poison in it. The Matolas, a long-haired race, who border upon the Caffres, form their locks into a sort of hollow cylinder, in which they bear about their little implements; certes a more sensible bag than such as is worn at court. The New Zealander is less ingenious; he makes a large opening in his ear and carries his knife in it. The Ogres, who are worse than savages, and whose ignorance and brutality are in proportion to their bulk, are said, upon the authority of tradition, when they have picked up a stray traveller or two more than they require for their supper, to lodge them in a hollow tooth as a place of security till breakfast; whence it may be inferred that they are not liable to toothache, and that they make no use of toothpicks. Ogres, savages, beasts, and birds, all require something to serve the purpose of a pocket. Thus much for the necessity of the thing. Touching its antiquity much might be said; for it would not be difficult to show, with that little assistance from the auxiliaries *must*, and *have*, and *been*, which enabled Whitaker of Manchester to write whole quartos of hypothetical history in the potential mood, that pockets are coeval with clothing: and, as erudite men have maintained that language and even letters are of divine origin, there might with like reason be a conclusion drawn from the twenty-first verse of the third chapter of the book of Genesis, which it would not be easy to impugn. Moreover, nature herself shows us the utility, the importance, nay, the indispensability, or, to take a hint from the pure language of our diplomatists, the *sinequanonniness* of pockets. There is but one organ which is common to all animals whatsoever: some are without eyes, many without noses; some have no heads, others no tails; some neither one nor the other; some there are who have no brains, others very pappy ones; some no hearts, others very bad ones; but all have a stomach—and what is the stomach but a live inside pocket? Hath not Van Helmont said of it, "*Saccus vel pera est, ut ciborum olla?*"

Dr. Towers used to have his coat pockets made of capacity to hold a quarto volume—a wise custom; but requiring stout cloth, good buckram, and strong thread well waxed. I do not so greatly commend the humor of Dr. Ingenhouz, whose coat was lined with pockets of all sizes, wherein, in his latter years, when science had become to him as a plaything, he carried about various materials for chemical experiments: among the rest, so many compositions for fulminating powders in glass tubes, separated only by a cork in the middle of the tube, that, if any person had unhappily given him a blow with a stick, he might have blown up himself and the doctor too. For myself, four coat pockets of the ordinary dimensions content me; in these a sufficiency of conveniences may be carried, and that sufficiency methodically arranged. For mark me, gentle or ungentle reader! there is nothing like method in pockets, as well as in composition: and what orderly and methodical man would have his pocket handkerchief, and his pocketbook, and the key of his door, (if he be a bachelor living in chambers,) and his knife, and his loose pence and halfpence, and the letters which peradventure he might just have received, or peradventure he may intend to drop in the post-office, twopenny or general, as he passes by, and his snuff, if he be accustomed so to regale his olfactory conduits, or his tobacco-box, if he prefer the masticable to the pulverized weed; or his box of lozenges, if he should be troubled with a tickling cough; and the sugar plums and the gingerbread nuts which he may be carrying home to his own children, or to any other small men and women upon whose hearts he may have a design; who, I say, would like to have all this in chaos and confusion, one lying upon the other, and the thing which is wanted first fated always to be undermost! —(Mr. Wilberforce knows the inconvenience:)—the snuff working its way out to the gingerbread, the sugar plums insinuating themselves into the folds of the pocket handkerchief, the pence grinding the lozenges to dust for the benefit of the pocket-book, and the door key busily employed in unlocking the letters?

Etymological Discoveries.—That the lost ten tribes of Israel may be found in London, is a discovery which any person may suppose he has made, when he walks for the first time from the city to Wapping. That the tribes of Judah and Benjamin flourish there is known to all mankind; and from them have sprung the Scripites, and the Omniumites, and the Threepercentites.

But it is not so well known that many other tribes noticed in the Old Testament are to be found in this island of Great Britain.

There are the Hittites, who excel in one branch of gymnastics. And there are the Amorites, who are to be found in town and country; and there are the Gadites, who frequent watering-places, and take picturesque tours.

Among the Gadites I shall have some of my best readers, who being in good humor with themselves and with every thing, else, except on a rainy day, will even then be in good humor with me. There will be the Amorites in their company; and among the Amorites, too, there will be some who, in the overflowing of their love, will have some liking to spare for the doctor and his faithful memorialist.

The poets, those especially who deal in erotics, lyrics, sentimentals, or sonnets, are the Ah-oh-ites.

The gentlemen who speculate in chapels are the Puhites.

The chief seat of the Simeonites is at Cambridge; but they are spread over the land. So are the Man-ass-ites, of whom the finest specimens are to be seen in St. James's-street, at the fashionable time of day for exhibiting the dress and the person upon the pavement.

The freemasons are of the family of the Jachin-ites.

The female Haggites are to be seen, in low life wheeling barrows, and in high life seated at card tables.

The Shuhamites are the cordwainers.

The Teamanites attend the sales of the East India Company.

Sir James Mackintosh, and Sir James Scarlett, and Sir James Graham, belong to the Jim-nites.

Who are the Gazathites, if the people of London are not, where any thing is to be seen? All of them are the Gettites when they can, all would be Havites if they could.

The journalists should be Geshurites, if they answered to their profession: instead of this they generally turn out to be Geshuwrongs.

There are, however, three tribes in England, not named in the Old Testament, who considerably outnumber all the rest. These are the High Vulgarites, who are the children of Rahank and Phashan: the Middle Vulgarites, who are the children of Mammon and Terade, and the low Vulgarites, who are the children of Tahag, Rahag, and Bohobtay-il.

With the Low Vulgarites I have no concern; but with the other two tribes, much. Well it is that some of those who are *fruges consumere nati*, think it proper that they should consume books also: if they did not, what a miserable creature wouldst thou be, Henry Colburn, who art their bookseller! I myself have that kind of respect for the consumers which we ought to feel for every thing useful. If not the salt of the earth, they are its manure, without which it could not produce so abundantly.

THE PIG.

A Colloquial Poem.

BY ROBERT SOUTHEY.

Jacob! I do not like to see thy nose
Turn'd up in scornful curve at yonder pig.
It would be well, my friend, if we, like him,
Were perfect in our kind! . . And why despise
The sow-born grunter? . . He is obstinate,
Thou answerest; ugly, and the filthiest beast
That banquets upon offal. . . Now I pray you
Hear the pig's counsel.
Is he obstinate?
We must not, Jacob, be deceived by words;
We must not take them as unheeding hands
Receive base money at the current worth,
But with a just suspicion try their sound,
And in the even balance weigh them well.
See now to what this obstinacy comes:
A poor, mistreated, democratic beast,
He knows that his unmerciful drivers seek
Their profit, and not his. He hath not learned
That pigs were made for man, . . born to be brawn'd
And baconized: that he must please to give
Just what his gracious masters please to take;
Perhaps his tusks, the weapons Nature gave
For self-defence, the general privilege;
Perhaps, . . hark, Jacob! dost thou hear that horn?
Woe to the young posterity of Pork!
Their enemy is at hand.
Again. Thou say'st
The pig is ugly. Jacob, look at him!
Those eyes have taught the lover flattery.
His face, . . nay, Jacob! Jacob! were it fair
To judge a lady in her dishabille?
Fancy it dressed, and with saltpetre rouged.
Behold his tail, my friend; with curls like that
The wanton hop marries her stately spouse:
So crisp in beauty Amoretta's hair
Rings round her lover's soul the chains of love.
And what is beauty, but the aptitude
Of parts harmonious? Give thy fancy scope,
And thou wilt find that no imagined change
Can beautify this beast. Place at his end
The starry glories of the peacock's pride,
Give him the swan's white breast; for his horn-hoofs
Shape such a foot and ankle as the waves
Crowded in eager rivalry to kiss
When Venus from the enamor'd sea arose; . .
Jacob, thou canst but make a monster of him!
All alteration man could think, would mar
His pig-perfection.
The last charge, . . he lives
A dirty life. Here I could shelter him
With noble and right-reverend precedents,
And show by sanction of authority
That 'tis a very honorable thing
To thrive by dirty ways. But let me rest
On better ground the unanswerable defence.
The pig is a philosopher, who knows
No prejudice. Dirt? . . Jacob, what is dirt?
If matter, . . why the delicate dish that tempts
An o'ergorged epicure to the last morsel
That stuffs him to the throat-gates, is no more.
If matter be not, but as sages say,
Spirit is all, and all things visible
Are one, the infinitely modified,
Think, Jacob, what that pig is, and the mire
Wherein he stands knee-deep!
And there! the breeze
Pleads with me, and has won thee to a smile
That speaks conviction. O'er yon blossom'd field
Of beans it came, and thoughts of bacon rise.

THE DEVIL'S WALK ON EARTH.

BY ROBERT SOUTHEY.

From his brimstone bed at break of day
A walking the Devil is gone,
To look at his snug little farm of the World,
And see how his stock went on.

Over the hill and over the dale,
And he went over the plain;
And backward and forward he swish'd his tail,
As a gentleman swishes a cane.

How then was the Devil drest?
Oh, he was in his Sunday's best.
His coat was red and his breeches were blue,
And there was a hole where his tail came through.

A lady drove by in her pride,
In whose face an expression he spied
For which he could have kiss'd her;
Such a flourishing, fine, clever woman was she,
With an eye as wicked as wicked can be,
I should take her for my Aunt, thought he,
If my dam had had a sister.

He met a lord of high degree,
No matter what was his name;
Whose face with his own when he came to compare
The expression, the look, and the air,
And the character, too, as it seem'd to a hair—
Such a twin-likeness there was in the pair,
That it made the Devil start and stare,
For he thought there was surely a looking-glass there,
But he could not see the frame.

He saw a Lawyer killing a viper,
On a dung-hill beside his stable;
Ha! quoth he, thou put'st me in mind
Of the story of Cain and Abel.

An Apothecary on a white horse
Rode by, on his vocation;
And the Devil thought of his old friend
Death in the Revelation.

He pass'd a cottage with a double coach-house,
A cottage of gentility,
And he own'd with a grin
That his favorite sin
Is pride that apes humility.

He saw a pig rapidly
Down a river float;
The pig swam well, but every stroke
Was cutting his own throat;

And Satan gave thereat his tail
A twirl of admiration;
For he thought of his daughter War,
And her suckling babe Taxation.

Well enough, in sooth, he liked that truth,
And nothing the worse for the jest;
But this was only a first thought;
And in this he did not rest:
Another came presently into his head,
And here it proved, as has often been said,
That second thoughts are best.

For as Piggy plied, with wind and tide,
His way with such celerity,
And at every stroke the water dyed
With his own red blood, the Devil cried,
Behold a swinish nation's pride
In cotton-spun prosperity.

He walk'd into London leisurely,
The streets were dirty and dim:
But there he saw Brothers the Prophet,
And Brothers the Prophet saw him.

He entered a thriving bookseller's shop;
Quoth he, we are both of one college,
For I myself sate like a Cormorant once
Upon the Tree of Knowledge.

As he passed through Cold-Bath Fields he look'd
At a solitary cell;
And he was well-pleased, for it gave him a hint
For improving the prisons of Hell.

He saw a turnkey tie a thief's hands
With a cordial tug and jerk;
Nimbly, quoth he, a man's fingers move
When his heart is in his work.

He saw the same turnkey unfettering a man
With little expedition;
And he chuckled to think of his dear slave-trade,
And the long debates and delays that were made,
Concerning its abolition.

He met one of his favorite daughters
By an Evangelical Meeting:
And forgetting himself for joy at her sight,
He would have accosted her outright,
And given her a fatherly greeting.

But she tipt him the wink, drew back, and cried,
Avaunt! my name's Religion!
And then she turn'd to the preacher,
And leer'd like a love-sick pigeon.

A fine man and a famous Professor was he,
As the great Alexander now may be,
Whose fame not yet o'erpast is:
Or that new Scotch performer
Who is fiercer and warmer,
The great Sir Arch-Bombastes.

With throbs and throes, and ah's and oh's,
Far famed his flock for frightening;
And thundering with his voice, the while
His eyes zigzag like lightning.

This Scotch phenomenon, I trow,
Beats Alexander hollow;
Even when most tame
He breathes more flame
Than ten Fire-Kings could swallow.

Another daughter he presently met;
With music of fife and drum,
And a consecrated flag,
And shout of tag and rag,
And march of rank and file,
Which had fill'd the crowded aisle
Of the venerable pile,
From church he saw her come.

He call'd her aside, and began to chide,
For what dost thou here? said he;
My city of Rome is thy proper home,
And there's work enough there for thee.

Thou hast confessions to listen,
And bells to christen,
And altars and dolls to dress;
And fools to coax,
And sinners to hoax,
And beads and bones to bless;
And great pardons to sell
For those who pay well,
And small ones for those who pay less.

Nay, Father, I boast, that this is my post,
She answered; and thou wilt allow,
That the great Harlot,
Who is clothed in scarlet,
Can very well spare me now.

Upon her business I am come here,
That we may extend our powers:
Whatever lets down this church that we hate,
Is something in favor of ours.

You will not think, great Cosmocrat!
That I spend my time in fooling;
Many irons, my sire, have we in the fire,
And I must leave none of them cooling;
For you must know state-councils here,
Are held which I bear rule in.
When my liberal notions,
Produce mischievous motions,
There's many a man of good intent,
In either house of Parliament,
Whom I shall find a tool in;
And I have hopeful pupils too
Who all this while are schooling.

Fine progress they make in our liberal opinions,
My Utilitarians,
My all sorts of —inians
And all sorts of —arians;
My all sorts of —ists,
And my Prigs and my Whigs
Who have all sorts of twists,
Train'd in the very way, I know,
Father, you would have them go;
High and low,
Wise and foolish, great and small,
March of-Intellect-Boys all.

Well pleased wilt thou be at no very far day,
When the caldron of mischief boils,
And I bring them forth in battle array,
And bid them suspend their broils,
That they may unite and fall on the prey,
For which we are spreading our toils.
How the nice boys all will give mouth at the call,
Hark away! hark away to the spoils!
My Macs and my Quacks and my lawless-Jacks,
My Shiels and O'Connells, my pious Mac-Donnells,
My joke-smith Sydney, and all of his kidney,
My Humes and my Broughams,
My merry old Jerry,
My Lord Kings, and my Doctor Doyles!

At this good news, so great
The Devil's pleasure grew,
That with a joyful swish he rent
The hole where his tail came through.

His countenance fell for a moment
When he felt the stitches go;
Ah! thought he, there's a job now
That I've made for my tailor below.

Great news! bloody news! cried a newsman;
The Devil said, Stop, let me see!
Great news! bloody news! thought the Devil,
The bloodier the better for me.

So he bought the newspaper, and no news
At all for his money he had.
Lying varlet, thought he, thus to take in old Nick!
But it's some satisfaction, my lad,
To know thou art paid beforehand for the trick,
For the sixpence I gave thee is bad.

And then it came into his head
By oracular inspiration,
That what he had seen and what he had said
In the course of this visitation,
Would be published in the Morning Post,
For all this reading nation.

Therewith in second sight he saw
The place and the manner and time,
In which this mortal story
Would be put in immortal rhyme.

That it would happen when two poets
Should on a time be met,
In the town of Nether Stowey,
In the shire of Somerset.

There while the one was shaving
Would he the song begin;
And the other when he heard it at breakfast,
In ready accord join in.

So each would help the other,
Two heads being better than one;
And the phrase and conceit
Would in unison meet,
And so with glee the verse flow free,
In ding-dong chime of sing-song rhyme,
Till the whole were merrily done.

And because it was set to the razor,
Not to the lute or harp,
Therefore it was that the fancy
Should be bright, and the wit be sharp.

But, then, said Satan to himself,
As for that said beginner,
Against my infernal Majesty,
There is no greater sinner.

He hath put me in ugly ballads
With libellous pictures for sale;
He hath scoff'd at my hoofs and my horns,
And has made very free with my tail.

But this Mr. Poet shall find
I am not a safe subject for whim;
For I'll set up a School of my own,
And my Poets shall set upon him.

He went to a coffee-house to dine,
And there he had soy in his dish;
Having ordered some soles for his dinner,
Because he was fond of flat fish.

They are much to my palate, thought he,
And now guess the reason who can,
Why no bait should be better than place,
When I fish for a Parliament-man.

But the soles in the bill were ten shillings;
Tell your master, quoth he, what I say;
If he charges at this rate for all things,
He must be in a pretty good way.

But mark ye, said he to the waiter,
I'm a dealer myself in this line,
And his business, between you and me,
Nothing like so extensive as mine.

Now soles are exceedingly cheap,
Which he will not attempt to deny,
When I see him at my fish-market
I'll warrant him, by-and-by.

As he went along the Strand,
Between three in the morning and four,
He observed a queer-looking person,
Who staggered from Perry's door.

And he thought that all the world over
In vain for a man you might seek,
Who could drink more like a Trojan,
Or talk more like a Greek.

The Devil then he prophesied—
It would one day be matter of talk,
That with wine when smitten,
And with wit moreover being happily bitten,
The erudite bibber was he who had written
The story of this walk.

A pretty mistake, quoth the Devil;
  A pretty mistake I opine!
I have put many ill thoughts in his mouth,
  He will never put good ones in mine.

And whoever shall say that to Porson
  These best of all verses belong,
He is an untruth-telling whore-son,
  And so shall be call'd in the song.

And if seeking an illicit connexion with fame,
  Any one else should put in a claim,
    In this comical competition;
  That excellent poem will prove
    A man-trap for such foolish ambition,
Where the silly rogue shall be caught by the leg,
    And exposed in a second edition.

Now the morning air was cold for him,
  Who was used to a warm abode;
And yet he did not immediately wish,
  To set out on his homeward road.

For he had some morning calls to make,
  Before he went back to Hell;
So, thought he, I'll step into a gaming-house,
  And that will do as well;
But just before he could get to the door
  A wonderful chance befell.

  For all on a sudden, in a dark place,
He came upon General ——'s burning face;
  And it struck him with such consternation,
That home in a hurry his way did he take,
Because he thought, by a slight mistake
  'Twas the general conflagration.

THE ANTI-PUNSTER.

ANONYMOUS.

The man who would scruple to make a pun, would not hesitate to commit a burglary. Why we think so, we don't know; but we have just as much right to our opinion that there is a distinct connection between a dislike of puns and a taste for burglaries, as Dr. Johnson had to his, when he chose, most arbitrarily and alliteratively, to confound a pun perpetrated with a pocket to be picked.

The anti-punster is the incarnation of the spirit of intolerance. His aversion knows no cold medium. He has no mercy for the man who differs from him —on the point of a pun. He is a man of one idea, and that, though an old one certainly, is no joke. His singleness of apprehension cannot stand the shock of a double meaning. One is as much as he can manage to comprehend; and he can no more stand up against the force and confusion of two, than he could brave the discharge of a double barelled gun at his head. Besides, he regards a pun as a most reckless and extravagant waste of meaning. He would rather you used a word that meant nothing. "The no meaning" does not puzzle *him* more than wit, and a passage that leads to nothing, affords him more profit and recreation than an insane attempt to walk in two paths at a time.

> Like to a man on double business bound,
> Who both neglects,

he would infinitely prefer a stroll in the dark through grounds beset with traps and spring-guns, to joining in conversation with a punster. He resents an unprovoked quibble as a personal insult. He never called anybody out on this score, because, in his opinion, a man once convicted of a premeditated pun, has forfeited all claims to be treated as a gentleman; but he never fails to kick the offender down stairs:—with his mind's foot, Horatio. Having discovered that his eldest son had called the cock an ornithological Cerberus—three birds at once, his throat being a swallow, and his voice a crow—he threatened to cut the culprit off with a shilling; and ascertaining that the young wag had remarked upon the difficulty of "cutting off" a son with a shilling—a shilling being undeniably "blunt"—he put his threat into execution. He sneers at Shakspere as an inspired idiot; and condemns as vicious, not only in taste but in morals, the final exit of Mercutio, who is sent into purgatory with a pun in his mouth. You increase his disgust if you tell him that the same thing has happened on the real stage of life—that Elliston's ending was even as that of Mercutio, whom he had so often represented—that when, an hour or two before the parting of soul and body, the patient's head was raised on his pillow, and, to seduce him into taking one more hopeless spoonful of medicine, he was told "he should wash it down with half a glass of his brown sherry"—that even then, the actor's glazed eye brightened under the influence of the ruling passion, as he articulated with almost moveless lips, "Bri-be-ry and Cor-rup-tion!"

Nothing incenses the anti-punster so much as detecting in a distaste to puns an incapacity for making them. Charge him with that, and he will immediately prove himself incapable by offering proof of capacity. He can neither make a genuine good pun, which is a good thing—nor a shocking bad one, which is a better. Whatever he hazards is bad, to be sure—but not bad enough; it is a wretched, dull piece of impotence, wholly innocent of drollery. He has no soul for a villanous quibble—he cannot for his life make it vile enough to succeed; he has not the grasp of mind required to gather up two remote meanings and compress them into a single word, which the eye, rather than the tongue, italicizes to the apprehension. In short, he is unconscious that the excellent and the execrable meet together upon a point which genius alone can reach; and that in the art of punning, to be good enough and bad enough are the same thing—the difficulty being as great, and the glory as unequivocal. In his attempt, therefore, he tries hard at working out a good one, and consequently fails to arrive at the proper pitch of badness. The anti-punster is an incapable; all he can do is, to take his hat because he can't take a joke. He breaks up a party because somebody breaks a jest. He thinks he shows his sense by not relishing nonsense; and seeks credit for profound thought, by authorizing a play upon words. He carries a sneer on his lip for want of a smile.

DIAMOND CUT DIAMOND.

FROM "THE YELLOWPLUSH CORRESPONDENCE." BY W. MAKEPEACE THACKERAY.

THE name of my nex master was, if posbil, still more ellygant and youfonious than that of my fust. I now found myself boddy servant to the Honrabble Halgernon Percy Deuceace, youngest and fifth son of the Earl of Crabs.

Halgernon was a barrystir—that is, he lived in Pump Court Temple; a wulgar nabrood, witch, praps my readers don't no. Suffiz to say, it's on the confines of the citty, and the choasen aboad of the lawyers of this metrappolish.

When I say that Mr. Deuceace was a barrystir, I don't mean that he went sesshums or surcoats, (as they call 'em,) but simply that he kep chambers, lived in Pump Court, and looked out for a commitionarship, or a revisinship, or any other place that the Wig guvvyment could give him. His father was a Wig pier, (as the landriss told me,) and had been a Toary pier. The fack is, his lordship was so poar, that he would be anythink, or nothink, to get previsions for his sons, and an inkum for himself.

I phansy that he aloud Halgernon two hundred a-year; and it would have been a very comforable maintenants, only he knever paid him.

Owever, the young gnlmn was a gnlmn, and no mistake; he got his allowents of nothink a-year, and spent it in the most honrable and fashnabble manner. He kep a kab—he went to Holmax and Crockfud's—he moved in the most xquizzit suckles —and trubbld the law-boox very little, I can tell you. Those fashnabble gents have ways of getten money, which comman pipple doant understand.

Though he had only a therd floar in Pump Cort, he lived as if he had the welth of Cresas. The tenpun notes floo abowt as common as haypince—clarrit and shampang was at his house as vulgar as gin; and verry glad I was, to be sure, to be a valley to a zion of the nobillaty.

Deuceace had, in his sittin-room, a large pictur on a sheet of paper. The names of his family was wrote on it: it was wrote in the shape of a tree, a groin out of a man-in-armer's stomick, and the names were on little plates among the bows. The pictur said that the Deuceaces kem into England in the year 1066, along with William Conqueruns. My master called it his podygree. I do beleev it was because he had this pictur, and because he was the *Honrabble* Deuceace, that he mannitched to live as he did. If he had been a common man, you'd have said he was no better than a swinler. It's only rank and buth that can warrant such singlarities as my master show'd. For it's no use disgysing it—the Honrabble Halgernon was a GAMBLER. For a man of wulgar family, it's the wust trade that can be—for a man of common feelinx of honesty, this profession is quite imposibill; but for a real thoroughbread genlmn, it's the easiest and most prophetable line he can take.

It may, praps appear curous that such a fashnable man should live in the Temple; but it must be recklected, that it's not only lawyers who live in what's called the Ins of Cort. Many batchylers, who have nothing to do with lor, have here their loginx; and many sham barrysters, who never put on a wig and a gownd twise in their lives, kip apartments in the Temple, instead of Bon Street, Pickledilly, or other fashnabble places.

Frinstance, on our stairkis (so these houses are called,) there was 8 sets of chamberses, and only 3 lawyers. These was, bottom floor, Screwson, Hewson, and Jewson, Attorneys; fust floor, Mr. Sergeant Flabber—opsit, Mr. Counslor Bruffy; and secknd pair, Mr. Haggerstony, an Irish counslor, pracktising at the Old Baly, and lickwise what they call reporter to the *Morning Post* nyouspapper.—Opsit him was wrote

MR. RICHARD BLEWITT;

and on the thud floar, with my master, lived one Mr. Dawkins.

This young fellow was a new comer into the Temple, and unlucky it was for him too—he'd better had never been born; for it's my firm apinion that the Temple ruined him—that is, with the help of my master and Mr. Dick Blewitt, as you shall hear.

Mr. Dawkins, as I was gave to understand by his young man, had jest left the Universary of Oxford, and had a pretty litttle fortn of his own—six thousand pound, or so—in the stox. He was jest of age, an orfin who had lost his father and mother; and having distinkwished hisself at collitch, where he gained seffral prices, was come to town to push his fortn, and study the barryster's bisniss.

Not bein of a verry high fammly hisself—indeed, I've heard say his father was a chismonger, or somethink of that lo sort—Dawkings was glad to find his old Oxford frend, Mr. Blewitt, yonger son to rich Squire Blewitt of Listershire, and to take rooms so near him.

Now, tho' there was a considdrable intimacy between me and Mr. Blewitt's gentleman, there was scarcely any betwixt our masters—mine being too much of the aristoxy to associate with one of Mr. Blewitt's sort. Blewitt was what they call a bettin man; he went reglar to Tattlesall's, kep a pony, wore a white hat, a blue berd's-eye hankercher, and a cut-away coat. In his manners he was the very contrary of my master, who was a slim, ellygant man, as ever I see—he had very white hands, rayther a sallow face, with dark sharp is, and small wiskus neatly trimmed, and as black as Warren's jet—he spoke very low and soft—he seemed to be watchin the person with whom he was in convysation, and always flattered every body. As for Blewitt, he was quite of another sort. He was always swearin, singin, and slappin people on the back, as hearty and familiar as posbill. He seemed a merry, careless, honest cretur, whom one would trust with life and soul. So thought Dawkins, at least; who, tho' a quiet young man, fond of his boox, novvles, Byron's poems, floot-playing, and such like scientafic amusemints, grew hand in glove with honest Dick Blewitt, and soon after with my master, the Honrabble Halgernon. Poor Daw! he thought he was makin good connexions, and real frends—he had fallen in with a couple of the most etrocious swinlers that ever lived.

Before Mr. Dawkins arrived in our house, Mr. Deuceace had barely condysended to speak to Mr. Blewitt: it was only about a month after that suckumstance that my master, all of a sudding, grew very friendly with him. The reason was pretty clear — Deuceace *wanted him.* Dawkins had not been an hour in master's compny, before he knew that he had a pidgin to pluck.

Blewitt knew this too; and bein very fond of pidgin, intended to keep this one entirely to himself. It was amusin to see the Honrabble Halgernon manuvring to get his pore bird out of Blewitt's clause, who thought he had it safe. In fact, he'd brought Dawkins to these chambers for that very porpus, thinking to have him under his eye, and strip him at leisure.

"My master very soon found out what was Mr. Blewitt's game. Gamblers know gamblers, if not by instink, at least by reputation; and though Mr. Blewitt moved in a much lower spear than Mr. Deuceace, they knew each other's dealins and caracters pufficklY well.

"Charles, you scoundrel," says Deuceace to me one day, (he always spoak in that kind way,) "who is this person that has taken the opsit chambers, and plays the flute so industrusly?"

"It's Mr. Dawkins, a rich young gentleman from Oxford, and a great friend of Mr. Blewittses, sir," says I; "they seem to live in each other's rooms."

Master said nothink, but he *grin'd*—my eye, how he did grin! Not the fowl find himself could snear more satannickly.

I knew what he meant.

Imprimish. A man who plays the floot is a simpleton.

Secknly. Mr. Blewitt is a raskle.

Thirdmo. When a raskle and a simpleton is always together, and when the simpleton is *rich*, one knows pretty well what will come of it.

I was but a lad in them days, but I knew what was what as well as my master; it's not gentlemen only that's up to snough. Law bless us! there was four of us on this stairkes, four as nice young men as you ever see; Mr. Bruffy's young man, Mr. Dawkinses, Mr. Blewitts, and me—and we knew what our masters was about as well as they did theirselfs.—Frinstance, I can say this for *myself*, there wasn't a paper in Deuceace's desk or drawer, not a bill, a note, or miserandum, which I hadn't read as well as he; with Blewitt's it was the same—me and his young man used to read 'em all. There wasn't a bottle of wind that we didn't get a glas, nor a pound of sugar that we didn't have some lumps of it. We had keys to all the cubbards—we pipped into all the letters that kem and went—we pored over all the bill-files—we'd the best pickins out of the dinners, the livvers of the fowls, the force-mit balls out of the soup, the egs from the sallit. As for the coals and candles, we left them to the landrisses.—You may call this robry—nonsince—it's only our rights—a suvvant's purquizzits is as sacred as the laws of Hengland.

Well, the long and short of it is this. Richard Blewitt, exquire, was sityouated as follows: He'd an inkum of three hundred a-year from his father. Out of this he had to pay one hundred and ninety for money borrowed by him at collidge, seventy for chambers, seventy more for his hoss, aty for his suvvant on bord wagis, and about three hundred and fifty for a sepprat establishmint in the Regency Park; besides this his pockit mony, say a hundred, his eatin, drinkin, and wine-merchant's bill, about two hundred moar. So that you see he laid by a pretty handsome sum at the end of the year.

My master was diffrent; and being a more fashnabble man than Mr. B., in course he owed a deal more money. There was fust:

	£	s.	d.
Account *contray*, at Crockford's	£ 3711	0	0
Bills of exchange and I. O. U.'s (but he didn't pay these in most cases,)	4963	0	0
21 tailor's bills in all,	1306	11	9
3 hossdealer's do,	402	0	0
2 coachbilder,	506	0	0
Bills contracted at Cambritch,	2193	6	8
Sundries,	987	10	0
	£14069	8	5

I give this as a curosity—pipple doant know how in many cases fashnabble life is carried on; and to know even what a real gnlmn *owes* is somethink instructif and agreeable.

But to my tail. The very day after my master had made the inquiries concerning Mr. Dawkins, witch I have mentioned already, he met Mr. Blewitt on the stairs, and byoutiffle it was to see how this gnlmn, who had before been almost cut by my master, was now received by him. One of the sweatest smiles I ever saw was now vizzible on Mr. Deuceace's countenence. He held out his hand, covered with a white kid glove, and said, in the most frenly tone of vice posbill, "What? Mr. Blewitt! It is an age since we met. What a shame that such near naybors should see each other so seldom!"

Mr. Blewitt, who was standing at his door, in a pe-green dressing gown, smoakin a segar, and singing a hunting coarus, looked surprised, flattered, and then suspicious.

"Why, yes," says he, "it is, Mr. Deuceace, a long time."

"Not, I think, since we dined at Sir George Hookey's. By the by, what an evening that was—hay, Mr. Blewitt? what wine! what capital songs! I recollect your 'May day in the morning'—cuss me, the best comick song I ever heard. I was speaking to the Duke of Doncaster about it only yesterday. You know the duke, I think?"

Mr. Blewitt said, quite surly, "No, I don't."

"Not know him!" cries master; "why, hang it, Blewitt! he knows *you*, as every sporting man in England does, I should think. Why, man, your good things are in every body's mouth at Newmarket."

And so master went on chaffin Mr. Blewitt. That genlmn at fust answered him quite short and angry; but, after a little more flumery, he grew as pleased as possbill, took in all Deuceace's flatry, and bleeved all his lies. At last the door shut, and they both went into Mr. Blewitt's chambers togither.

Of course I can't say what past there; but in an hour master kem up to his own room as yaller as mustard, and smellin sadly of backo smoke. I never see any genlmn more sick than he was; *he'd been smoaking segars* along with Blewitt. I said nothink, in course; tho' I'd often heard him xpress his horrow of backo, and knew very well he would as soon swallow pizon as smoke. But he wasn't a chap to do a thing without a reason: if he'd been smoakin, I warrant he had smoaked to some porpus.

I didn't hear the convysation between 'em; but Mr. Blewitt's man did: it was—"Well, Mr. Blewitt, what capital seagars! Have you one for a friend to smoak?" (The old fox, it wasn't only the *seagars* he was a smoakin!) "Walk in," says Mr. Blewitt; and then they began a chaffin together: master very ankshous about the young gentleman who had come to live in our chambers, Mr. Dawkins, and always coming back to that subject—sayin that people on the same stairkis ot to be frenly; how glad he'd be, for his part, to know Mr. Dick Blewitt, and *any friend of his*, and so on. Mr. Dick, howsever, seamed quite aware of the trap laid for him. "I really don't no this Dawkins," says he; "he's a chismonger's son, I hear; and tho' I've exchanged visits with him, I don't intend to continyou the acquaintance—not wishin to assoshate with that kind of pipple." So they went on, master fishin, and Mr. Blewitt not wishin to take the hook at no price.

"Confound the vulgar thief!" muttered my master, as he was laying on his sophy, after being so very ill; "I've poisoned myself with his infernal tobacco, and he has foiled me. The cursed swindling boor! he thinks he'll ruin this poor cheesemonger, does he? I'll step in, and *warn* him."

I thought I should bust a laffin, when he talked in this style. I knew very well what his "warning" meant—lockin the stable door, but stealin the hoss fust.

Nex day, his strattygam for becoming acquainted with Mr. Dawkins we exicuted, and very pritty it was.

Besides potry and the floot, Mr. Dawkins, I must tell you, had some other parshallities, wiz—he was wery fond of good eatin and drinkin. After doddling over his music and boox all day, this young genlmn used to sally out of evenings, dine sumptiously at a tavern, drinkin all sorts of wind along with his friend Mr. Blewitt. He was a quiet young fellow enough at fust; but it was Mr. B. who (for his own porpuses, no doubt,) had got him into this kind of life. Well, I needn't say that he who eats a fine dinner, and drinks too much over night, wants a bottle of soda-water, and a gril, praps, in the mornink. Such was Mr. Dawkinseses case; and reglar almost as twelve o'clock came, the waiter from Dix Coffy-House was to be seen on our stairkis, bringin up Mr. D.'s hot breakfast.

No man would have thought there was any think in such a trifling circkumstance; master did, tho', and pounced upon it like a cock on a barlycorn.

He sent me out to Mr. Morell's in Pickledilly, for what's called a Strasburg-pie—in French a "*patty defaw graw.*" He takes a card, and nails it on the outside case, (patty defaw graws come generally in a round wooden box, like a drumb;) and what do you think he writes on it? why, as follos:—"*For the Honorable Algernon Percy Deuceace, etc. etc. etc. With Prince Talleyrand's compliments.*"

Prince Tallyram's compliments, indeed! I laff when I think of it still, the old surpint! He *was* a surpint, that Deuceace and no mistake.

Well, by a most extrornary piece of ill luck, the nex day, punctially as Mr. Dawkinses brexfas was coming *up* the stairs, Mr. Halgernon Percy Deuceace was going *down.* He was as gay as a lark, humming an Oppra tune, and twizzting round his head his heavy gold-headed cane. Down he went very fast, and by a most unlucky axdent struck his cane against the waiter's tray, and away went Mr. Dawkinses gril, kayann, kitchup, soda-water, and all! I can't think how my master should have choas such an exact time; to be sure, his windo looked upon the cort, and he could see every one who came into our door.

As soon as the axdent had took place, master was in such a rage as, to be sure, no man ever was in befor; he swoar at the waiter in the most dreddfle way; he threatened him with his stick; and it was only when he see that the waiter was rayther a bigger man than hisself that he was in the least pazzyfied. He returned to his own chambers; and John, the waiter, went off for more grill to Dixes Coffy-House.

"This is a most unlucky axdent, to be sure, Charles," says master to me, after a few minnits paws, during which he had been and wrote a note, put it into an antelope, and sealed it with his bigg seal of arms. "But stay—a thought strikes me—take this note to Mr. Dawkins, and that pye you brought yesterday; and hearkye, you scoundrel, if you say where you got it I will break every bone in your skin!"

These kind of prommisses were among the few which I knew him to keep; and as I loved boath my skinn and my boans, I carried the noat, and of cors said nothink. Waiting in Mr. Dawkinses chambus for a few minnits, I returned to my master with an answer. I may as well give both of these documents, of which I happen to have taken coppies.

I.

"*The Hon.* A. P. DEUCEACE, *to* T. S. DAWKINS, *Esq.*

Temple, Tuesday.

"Mr. Deuceace presents his compliments to Mr. Dawkins, and begs at the same time to offer his most sincere apologies and regrets for the accident which has just taken place.

"May Mr. Deuceace be allowed to take a neighbor's privilege, and to remedy the evil he has occasioned to the best of his power? If Mr. Dawkins will do him the favor to partake of the contents of the accompanying case (from Strasburg direct, and the gift of a friend on whose taste as a gourmand Mr. Dawkins may rely,) perhaps he will find that it is not a bad substitute for the *plat* which Mr. Deuceace's awkwardness destroyed.

"It will, also, Mr. Deuceace is sure, be no small gratification to the original donor of the *pâté*, when he learns that it has fallen into the hands of so celebrated a *bon vivant* as Mr. Dawkins.

"*T. S. Dawkins, Esq., etc. etc. etc.*"

II.

"*From* T. S. DAWKINS, *Esq., to the Hon.* A. P. DEUCEACE.

"Mr. Thomas Smith Dawkins presents his grateful compliments to the Hon. Mr. Deuceace, and accepts with the greatest pleasure Mr. Deuceace's generous proffer.

"It would be one of the *happiest moments* of Mr. Smith Dawkins's life, if the Hon. M. Deuceace would *extend his generosity* still further, and condescend to partake of the repast which his *munificent politeness* has furnished.

"*Temple, Tuesday.*"

Many and many a time, I say, have I grind over these letters, which I had wrote from the original by Mr. Bruffy's copyin clark. Deuceace's flam about Prince Talyram was puffickly successful. I saw young Dawkins blush with delite as he red the note; he toar up four or five sheets before he composed the anser to it, which was as you read abuff, and roat in a hand quite trembling with pleasyer. If you could but have seen the look of triumth in Deuceace's wicked black eyes, when he read the noat! I never see a deamin yet, but I can phansy

I, a holding a writhing soal on his pitchfrock, and smilin like Deuceace. He dressed himself in his very best clothes, and in he went, after sending me over to say that he would xcept with pleasyour Mr. Dawkins's invite.

The pie was cut up, and a most frenly conversation begun betwixt the two genlmin. Deuceace was quite captivating. He spoke to Mr. Dawkins in the most respeckful and flatrin manner—agread in every think he said—prazed his taste, his furniter, his coat, his classick nolledge, and his playin' on the floot; you'd have thought, to hear him, that such a polygon of xlens as Dawkins did not breath—that such a modist, sinsear, honrabble genlmn as Deuceace was to be seen no where xcept in Pump Cort. Poor Daw was complitly taken in. My master said he'd introduce him to the Duke of Doncaster, and Heaven knows how many nobs more, till Dawkins was quite intawsicated with pleasyour. I know as a fack (and it pretty well shows the young genlmn's carryter,) that he went that very day, and ordered 2 new coats, on porpus to be introjuced to the lords in.

But the best joak of all was at last. Singin, swagerin, and swarink—up stares came Mr. Dick Blewitt. He flung open Mr. Dawkins's door, shouting out, "Daw, my old buck, how are you?" when, all of a sudden, he sees Mr. Deuceace; his jor dropt, he turned chocky white, and then burnin red, and looked as if a stror would knock him down. "My dear Mr. Blewitt," says my master, smilin, and offring his hand, "how glad I am to see you. Mr. Dawkins and I were just talking about your pony! Pray sit down."

Blewitt did; and now was the question, who should sit the other out; but law bless you, Mr. Blewitt was no match for my master; all the time he was fidgety, silent, and sulky; on the contry, master was charmin, I never herd such a flo of conversatin, or so many wittacisms as he uttered. At last, completely beat, Mr. Blewitt took his leaf; that instant master followed him; and passin his arm through that of Mr. Dick, led him into our chambers, and began talkin to him in the mos affabl and affecshnat manner.

But Dick was too angry to listen; at last, when master was telling him some long stoary about the Duke of Doncaster, Blewitt bust out—

"A plague on the Duke of Doncaster! Come, come, Mr. Deuceace, don't you be running your rigs upon me; I an't the man to be bamboozl'd by long-winded stories about dukes and duchesses. You think I don't know you; every man knows you, and your line of country. Yes, you're after young Dawkins there, and think to pluck him; but you shan't—no, by —— you shan't." (The reader must recklect that the oaths which interspussed Mr. B.'s convysatin I hav lift out.) Well, after he'd fired a wolley of 'em, Mr. Deuceace spoke as cool and slow as posbill.

"Heark, ye, Blewitt. I know you to be one of the most infernal thieves and scoundrels unhung. If you attempt to hector with me, I will cane you; if you want more, I'll shoot you; if you meddle between me and Dawkins, I will do both. I know your whole life, you miserable swindler and coward. I know you have already won two hundred pounds of this lad, and want all. I will have half, or you never shall have a penny." It's quite true that master knew these things; but how was the wonder.

I couldn't see Mr. B.'s face during this dialogue, bein on the wrong side of the door; but there was a considdrabble paws after these complymints had passed between the two genlmn—one walkin quickly up and down the room—tother, angry and stupid, sittin down, and stampin with his foot.

"Now listen to this, Mr. Blewitt," continues master, at last; "if you're quiet, you shall have half of this fellow's money; but venture to win a shilling from him in my absence, or without my consent, and you do it at your peril."

"Well, well, Mr. Deuceace," cries Dick, "it's very hard, and, I must say, not fair: the game was of my starting, and you've no right to interfere with my friend."

"Mr. Blewitt, you are a fool! You professed

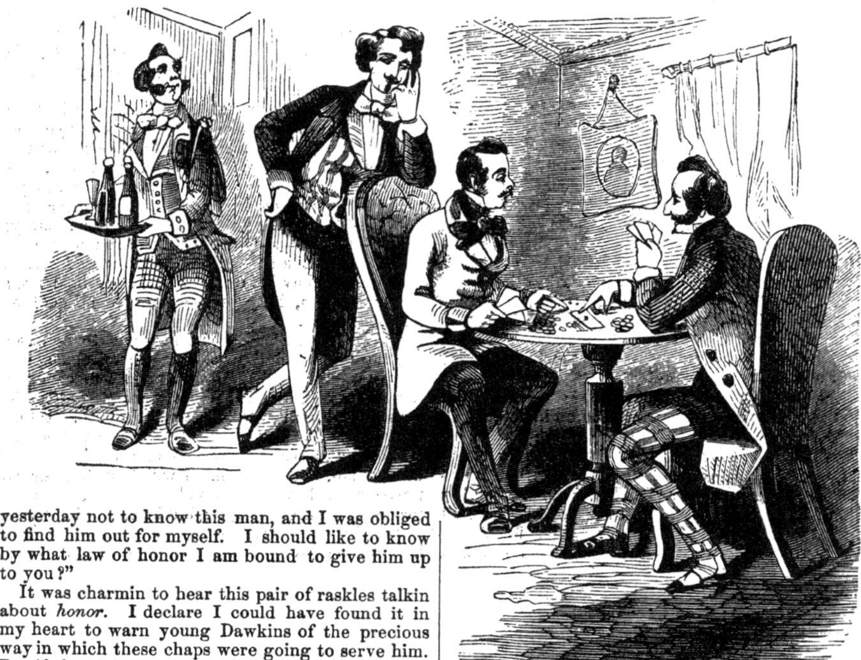

yesterday not to know this man, and I was obliged to find him out for myself. I should like to know by what law of honor I am bound to give him up to you?"

It was charmin to hear this pair of raskles talkin about *honor*. I declare I could have found it in my heart to warn young Dawkins of the precious way in which these chaps were going to serve him. But if *they* didn't know what honor was, *I* did; and never, never did I tell tails about my masters when in their sarvice—*out*, in cors, the hobligation is no longer binding.

Well, the nex day there was a gran dinner at our chambers. White soop, turbit, and lobster sos; saddil of Scotch muttin, grous, and M'Arony; winds, shampang, hock, madeira, a bottle of poart, and ever so many of clarrit. The company presint was three; wiz., the honrabble A. P. Deuceace, R. Blewitt, and Mr. Dawkins, Esquires. My i, how we genlmn in the kitchen did enjy it! Mr. Blewittes man eat so much grows (when it was brot out of the parlor,) that I reely thought he would be sik; Mr. Dawkinses gnlmn (who was only abowt thirteen years of age) grew so il with M'Arony and plumb-puddn, as to be obleeged to take sefral of Mr. D.'s pils, which half kild him. But this is all promiscuous: I an't talkin of the survants now, but the masters.

Would you bleev it? After dinner (and praps eight bottles of wind betwin the three) the genlmn sat down to *écarty*. It's a game where only two plays, and where, in coarse, when there's ony three, one looks on.

Fust, they playd crown pints, and a pound the bett! At this game they were wonderful equill; and about supper-time (when grilled am, more shampang, devld biskits, and other things, was brot in) the play stood thus: Mr. Dawkins had won two pounds; Mr. Blewit, thirty shillings; the Honrabble Mr. Deuceace having lost 3*l.* 10*s.* After the devvle and the shampang, the play was a little higher. Now it was pound pints, and five pound the bet. I thought, to be sure, after hearing the complyments between Blewitt and master in the morning, that now pore Dawkins's time was come.

Not so: Dawkins won always, Mr. B. betting on his play, and giving him the very best of advice. At the end of the evening (which was abowt five o'clock the next morning), they stopt. Master was counting up the score on a card.

"Blewitt," says he, "I've been unlucky. I ow you—let me see—yes, five-and-forty pounds!"

"Five-and-forty," says Blewitt, "and no mistake!"

"I will give you a cheque," says the honrabble genlmn.

"Oh! don't mention it, my dear sir!" But master got a grate sheet of paper, and drew him a check on Messeers Pump, Algit, and Co., his bankers.

"Now," says master, "I've got to settle with you, my dear Mr. Dawkins. If you had back'd your luck, I should have owed you a very handsome sum of money. *Voyons:* thirteen points, at a pound—it is easy to calculate;" and drawin out his puss, he clinked over the table 13 goolden suverings, which shon till they made my eyes wink.

So did pore Dawkinses, as he put out his hand, all trembling, and drew them in.

"Let me say," added master, "let me say (and I've had some little experience,) that you are the very best *écarté* player with whom I ever sat down.

Dawkinses eyes glissened as he put the money up, and said, "Law, Deuceace, you flatter me!"

Flatter him! I should think he did. It was the very thing which master ment.

"But mind you, Dawkins," continyoud he, "I must have my revenge; for I'm ruined—positively ruined—by your luck."

"Well, well," says Mr. Thomas Smith Dawkins, as pleased as if he had gained a millium, "shall it be to-morrow? Blewitt, what say you?"

Mr. Blewitt agread, in coarse. My master, after a little demurring, consented too. "We'll meet," says he, "at your chambers. But mind, my dear fello, not too much wind: I can't stand it at any time, especially when I have to play *écarté* with *you.*"

Pore Dawkins left our rooms, as happy as a prins. "Here, Charles," says he, and flung me a sovring. Pore fellow! pore fellow! I knew what was a comin!

* * * * * * * * * *

But the best of it was, that these 13 sovrings which Dawkins won, *master had borrowed them from Mr. Blewitt!* I brought 'em, with 7 more, from that young genlmn's chambers, that very morning: for, since his interview with master, Blewitt had nothing to refuse him.

* * * * * * * * *

Well, shall I continue the tail? If Mr. Dawkins had been the least bit wiser, it would have taken him six months befoar he lost his money; as it was, he was such a confounded ninny, that it took him a very short time to part with it.

Next day, (it was Thusday, and master's acquaintance with Mr. Dawkins had only commenced on Tuesday,) Mr. Dawkins, as I said, gev his party—dinner at 7. Mr. Blewitt, and the two Mr. D.'s as befoar. Play begins at 11. This time I knew the bisniss was pretty serious, for we suvvants was packed off to bed at 2 o'clock. On Friday, I went to chambers—no master—he kem in for 5 minutes at about 12, made a little toilit, ordered more devvles and soda-water, and back again he went to Mr. Dawkins's.

They had dinner there at seven again, but nobody seamed to eat, for all the vittals came out to us genlmn: they had in more wind though, and must have drunk at least 2 dozen in the 36 hours.

* * * * * * * * * *

At ten o'clock, however, on Friday night, back my master came to his chambers. I saw him as I never saw him before, namely, reglar drunk. He staggered about the room, he danced, he hickipd, he swore, he flung me a heap of silver, and finely, he sunk down exosted on his bed; I pullin off his boots and close, and makin him comfrabble.

When I had removed his garmints, I did what it's the duty of every servant to do—I emptied his pockits, and looked at his pockit-book and all his letters: a number of axdents have been prevented that way.

I found there among a heap of things, the following pretty dockyment:

> I. O. U.
>
> £4700.
>
> THOMAS SMITH DAWKINS.
>
> *Friday.* 16*th January.*

There was another bit of paper of the same kind—"I. O. U. four hundred pounds, Richard Blewitt:" but this, in cors, ment nothink.

* * * * * * * * * *

Nex mornin at nine, master was up, and as sober as a judg. He drest and was off to Mr. Dawkins. At 10, he ordered a cab, and the two genlmn went together.

"Where shall he drive, sir?" says I.

"Oh tell him to drive to the BANK."

Pore Dawkins! his eyes red with remors and sleepliss drunkenniss, gave a shudder and a sob, as he sunk back in the wehicle; and they drove on.

That day he soald out every hapny he was worth, xcept five hundred pounds.

* * * * * * * * * *

About 12, master had returned, and Mr. Dick Blewitt came stridin up the stairs with a sollum and important hair.

"Is your master at home?" says he.

"Yes, sir," says I; and in he walks, I in cors, with my ear to the keyhole, listning with all my mite.

"Well," says Blewitt, "we maid a pritty good night of it, Mr. Deuceace. You've settled, I see, with Dawkins."

"Settled!" says master. "Oh, yes—yes—I've settled with him."

"Four thousand seven hundred, I think?"

"About that—yes."

"That makes my share—let me see—two thousand three hundred and fifty; which I'll thank you to fork out."

"Upon my word—why—Mr. Blewitt," says my master, "I don't really understand what you mean."

"*You don't know what I mean!*" says Blewitt, in an axent such as I never befoar heard; "You don't know what I mean! Did you not promise me that we were to go shares? Didn't I lend you twenty sovereigns, the other night, to pay our losings to Dawkins? Didn't you swear, on your honor as a gentleman, to give me half of all that might be won in this affair?"

"Agreed, sir," says Deuceace; "agreed."

"Well, sir, and now what have you to say?"

"Why, *that I don't intend to keep my promise!* You infernal fool and ninny! do you suppose I was laboring for *you*? Do you fancy I was going to the expense of giving a dinner to that jackass yonder, that you should profit by it? Get away, sir! Leave the room, sir! Or, stop—here—I will give you four hundred pounds—your own note of hand, sir, for that sum, if you will consent to forget all that has passed between us, and that you have never known Mr. Algernon Deuceace."

I've sean pipple angery before now, but never any like Blewitt. He stormed, groned, belloed, swoar! At last, he fairly began blubbering; now cussing and nashing his teeth, now praying dear Mr. Deuceace to grant him mercy.

At last, master flung open the door (heavn bless us! it's well I didn't tumble, hed over eels, into the room!) and said, "Charles, show the gentleman down stairs!" My master looked at him quite steddy. Blewitt slunk down, as misrabble as any man I ever see. As for Dawkins, heaven knows where he was!

* * * * * * * * * *

"Charles," says my master to me, about an hour afterwards, "I am going to Paris; you may come, too, if you please."

THE SPECULATORS.

BY W. MAKEPEACE THACKERAY.

THE night was stormy and dark, The town was shut up in sleep: Only those were abroad who were out on a lark, Or those who'd no beds to keep.

I pass'd through the lonely street, The wind did sing and blow; I could hear the policeman's feet Clapping to and fro.

There stood a potato-man In the midst of all the wet; He stood with his 'tato-can In the lonely Haymarket.

Two gents of dismal mien, And dark and greasy rags, Came out of a shop for gin, Swaggering over the flags:

Swaggering over the stones, These shabby bucks did walk; And I went and followed those seedy ones, And listened to their talk.

Was I sober or awake? Could I believe my ears? Those dismal beggars spake Of nothing but railroad shares.

I wondered more and more: Says one—"Good friend of mine, How many shares have you wrote for In the Diddlesex Junction line?"

"I wrote for twenty," says Jim, "But they wouldn't give me one;" His comrade straight rebuked him For the folly he had done:

"O Jim, you are unawares Of the ways of this bad town; *I* always write for five hundred shares, And *then* they put me down."

"And yet you got no shares," Says Jim, "for all your boast;" "I *would* have wrote," says Jack, "but where Was the penny to pay the post?"

"I lost, for I couldn't pay That first instalment up; But here's taters smoking hot—I say Let's stop, my boy, and sup."

And at this simple feast The while they did regale, I drew each ragged capitalist Down on my left thumb-nail.

Their talk did me perplex, All night I tumbled and toss'd, And thought of railroad specs, And how money was won and lost.

"Bless railroads everywhere," I said, "and the world's advance; Bless every railroad share In Italy, Ireland, France; For never a beggar need now despair, And every rogue has a chance."

OTTILIA.

FROM "THE CONFESSIONS OF FITZ-BOODLE." BY W. M. THACKERAY.

OTHO SIGISMUND FREYHERR VON SCHLIPPENSCHLOPP, Knight Grand Cross of the Ducal Order of the Two-Necked Swan of Pumpernickel, of the Porc-et-Sifflet of Kalbsbraten, Commander of the George and Blue Boar of Dummerland, Excellency, and High Chancellor of the United Duchies, lived in the second floor of a house in the Schwapsgasse, where, with his private income and his revenues as chancellor, amounting together to some 300*l.* per annum, he maintained such a state as very few other officers of the Grand-Ducal Crown could exhibit. The Baron is married to Maria Antoinetta, a countess of the house of Kartoffelstadt, branches of which have taken root all over Germany. He has no sons, and but one daughter, the Fraülein OTTILIA.

The chancellor is a worthy old gentleman, too fat and wheezy to preside at the privy council, fond of his pipe, his ease, and his rubber. His lady is a very tall and pale Roman-nosed countess, who looks as gentle as Mrs. Robert Roy, where, in the novel, she is for putting Baillie Nicol Jarvie into the lake, and who keeps the honest chancellor in the greatest order.

Ottilia was pale and delicate. She wore her glistening black hair in bands, and dressed in vapory white muslin. She sang her own words to her harp, and they commonly insinuated that she was alone in the world,—that she suffered some inexpressible and mysterious heart pangs, the lot of all finer geniuses,—that though she lived and moved in the world, she was not of it,—that she was of a consumptive tendency, and might look for a premature interment. She even had fixed on the spot where she should lie: the violets grew there, she said, the river went moaning by; the grey willow whispered sadly over her head, and her heart pined to be at rest. "Mother," she would say, turning to her parent, "promise me, promise me to lay me in that spot when the parting hour has come!" At which Madame de Schlippenschlopp would shriek and grasp her in her arms, and at which, I confess,

I would myself blubber like a child. She had six darling friends at school, and every courier from Kalbsbraten carried off whole reams of her letter-paper.

In Kalbsbraten, as in every other German town, there are a vast number of literary characters, of whom our young friend quickly became the chief. They set up a literary journal, which appeared once a-week, upon light blue or primrose paper, and which, in compliment to the lovely Ottilia's maternal name, was called the *Kartoffelnkranz*. Here are a couple of her ballads, extracted from the *Kranz*, and by far the most cheerful specimen of her style. For in her songs she never would willingly let off the heroines without a suicide or a consumption. She never would hear of such a thing as a happy marriage, and had an appetite for grief quite amazing in so young a person.

* * * * *

Shall I tell how I became a poet for the dear girl's sake? Shall I tell what wild follies I committed in prose as well as in verse? how I used to watch under her window of icy evenings, and with chilblainy fingers sing serenades to her on the guitar? Shall I tell how, in a sledging party, I had the happiness to drive her, and of the delightful privilege which is, on these occasions, accorded to the driver?

Any reader, who has spent a winter in Germany, perhaps knows it. A large party of a score or more of sledges is formed. Away they go to some pleasure-house that has been previously fixed upon, where a ball and collation are prepared, and where each man, as his partner descends, has the delicious privilege of saluting her. O heavens and earth! I may grow to be a thousand years old, but I can never forget the rapture of that salute.

"The keen air has given me an appetite," said the dear angel, as we entered the supper-room; and to say the truth, fairy as she was, she made a remarkably good meal—consuming a couple of basins of white-soup, several kinds of German sausages, some Westphalia ham, some white puddings, an anchovy salad made with cornichons and onions, sweets innumerable, and a considerable quantity of old Stein Wein and rum-punch afterwards. Then she got up and danced as brisk as a fairy, in which operation I of course did not follow her, but had the honor at the close of the evening's amusement once more to have her by my side in the sledge, as we swept in the moonlight over the snow.

Kalbsbraten is a very hospitable place, as far as tea-parties are concerned, but I never was in one where dinners were so scarce. At the palace they occurred twice or thrice in a month, but on these occasions spinsters were not invited, and I seldom had the opportunity of seeing my Ottilia except at evening parties.

Nor are these, if the truth must be told, very much to my taste. Dancing I have forsworn, whist is too severe a study for me, and I do not like to play *écarté* with old ladies, who are sure to cheat you in the course of an evening's play.

But to have an occasional glance at Ottilia was enough; and many and many a napoleon did I lose to her mamma, Madame de Schlippenschlopp, for the blest privilege of looking at her daughter. Many is the tea-party I went to, shivering into cold clothes after dinner (which is my abomination) in order to have one little look at the lady of my soul.

At these parties, there were generally refreshments of a nature more substantial than mere tea—punch, both milk and rum, hot wine, *consommé*, and a peculiar and exceedingly disagreeable sandwich, made of a mixture of cold white puddings and garlic, of which I have forgotten the name, and always detested the savor.

Gradually a conviction came upon me that Ottilia *ate a great deal.*

I do not dislike to see a woman eat comfortably. I even think that an agreeable woman ought to be *friande*, and should love certain little dishes and nick-nacks. I know that though at dinner they commonly take nothing, they have had roast mutton with the children at two, and laugh at their pretensions to starvation.

No! a woman who eats a grain of rice like Amina in the *Arabian Nights*, is absurd and unnatural; but there is a *modus in rebus:* there is no reason why she should be a ghoul, a monster, an ogress, a horrid gormandizeress—faugh!

It was, then, with a rage amounting almost to agony, that I found Ottilia ate too much at every meal. She was always eating, and always eating too much. If I went there in the morning, there was the horrid familiar odor of those oniony sandwiches; if in the afternoon, dinner had been just removed, and I was choked by reeking reminiscences of roast meat. Tea we have spoken of. She gobbled up more cakes than any six people present; then came the supper and the sandwiches again, and the egg-flip and the horrible rum-punch.

She was thin as ever, paler if possible than ever; —but, by heavens! *her nose began to grow red!*

Mon dieu! how I used to watch and watch it! Some days it was purple, some days had more of the vermilion—I could take an affidavit that after a heavy night's supper it was more swollen, more red than before.

I recollect one night when we were playing a round game (I had been looking at her nose very eagerly and sadly for some time), she of herself brought up the conversation about eating, and confessed that she had five meals a-day.

"*That accounts for it!*" says I, flinging down the cards, and springing up and rushing like a madman out of the room. I rushed away into the night, and wrestled with my passion. "What! marry," said I, "a woman who eats meat twenty-one times in a week, besides breakfast and tea? Marry a sarcophagus, a cannibal, a butcher's shop?—Away!" I strove and strove, I drank, I groaned, I wrestled and fought with my love—but it overcame me; one look of those eyes brought me to her feet again. I yielded myself up like a slave; I fawned and whined for her; I thought her nose was not so *very* red.

Things came to this pitch that I sounded His Highness's minister to know whether he would give me service in the Duchy; I thought of purchasing an estate there. I was given to understand that I should get a chamberlain's key and some post of honor did I choose to remain, and I even wrote home to my brother Fitz in England, hinting a change in my condition.

At this juncture, the town of Hamburg sent His Highness the Grand Duke (*àpropos* of a commercial union which was pending between the two states) a singular present, no less than a certain number of barrels of oysters, which are considered extreme luxuries in Germany, especially in the inland parts of the country, where they are almost unknown.

In honor of the oysters and the new commercial treaty (which arrived in *fourgons* despatched for the purpose), His Highness announced a grand supper and ball, and invited all the quality of all the principalities round about. It was a splendid affair, the grand saloon brilliant with hundreds of uniforms and brilliant toilettes—not the least beautiful among them, I need not say, was Ottilia.

At midnight the supper-rooms were thrown open, and we formed into little parties of six, each having a table, nobly served with plate, a lackey in attendance, and a gratifying ice-pail or two of champagne to *égayer* the supper. It was no small cost to serve five hundred people on silver, and the repast was certainly a princely and magnificent one.

I had, of course, arranged with Mademoiselle de Schlippenschlopp. Captains Frumpel and Friedelberger of the Duke's Guard, Mesdames de Butterbrod and Bopp, formed our little party.

The first course, of course, consisted of *the oysters*. Ottilia's eyes gleamed with double brilliancy as the lackey opened them; there were nine a-piece for us—how well I recollect the number!

I never was much of an oyster-eater, nor can I relish them *in naturalibus* as some do, but require a quantity of sauces, lemons, cayenne peppers, bread and butter, and so forth, to render them palatable.

By the time I had made my preparations, Ottilia, the captains, and the two ladies, had well-nigh finished theirs. Indeed, Ottilia had gobbled up all hers, and there were only my nine left in the dish.

I took one—IT WAS BAD. The scent of it was enough—they were all bad. Ottilia had eaten nine bad oysters.

I put down the horrid shell. Her eyes glistened more and more, she could not take them off the tray.

"Dear Herr George," she said, "*Will you give me your oysters?*"

* * * * *

* * * * *

She had them all down—before—I could say—Jack—Robinson.

* * * * *

I left Kalbsbraten that night, and have never been there since.

THE YOUNG SCHOLAR.

ANONYMOUS.

A COUNTRY schoolmaster, hight Jonas Bell,
Once undertook of little souls,
To furnish up their jobber-knowls—
In other words, he taught them how to spell.
And well adapted to the task was Bell,
Whose iron-visage measur'd half an ell,
With huge proboscis, and eye-brows of soot,
Arm'd at the jowl just like a boar—
And when he gave an angry roar,
The little school-boys stood as fishes mute.
Poor Jonas, tho' a patient man as Job,
(Yet still, like Job, was sometimes heard to growl,)
Was by a scholar's adamantine nob,
Beyond all patience gravell'd to the soul.
I question whether Jonas in the fish
Did ever diet on a bitterer dish.
'Twas thus:—a lady who supported Bell,
Came unexpectedly to hear them spell;
The pupil fix'd on by the pedagogue,
Her son, a little round-faced, ruddy rogue,
Who thus his letters on the table laid—
M, I, L, K, and paused—"Well, sir, what's that?"
"I cannot tell," the boy all trembling said.
"Not tell! you little blind and stupid brat?
Not tell?" roared Jonas, in a violent rage,
And quick prepar'd an angry war to wage—
"Tell me this instant, or I'll flay thy hide—
Come, sir!
Dost thou this birchen weapon see?
What puts thy mother in her tea?"
With lifted eyes the quaking rogue replied—
"RUM, sir!"

THE MODERN SAINT.

ANONYMOUS.

HERE and there it is our fate,
To meet a sort of reprobate,
Who makes us feel the proverb lame,
That man and master are the same.
It chanced within a century,
There lived at B——
A saint, who well deserved
In rum to be preserved.
So pious and so fond of freedom,
No one to slavery would *he* doom.
But *whites* with him were not the crack ones,
His charity was all for *black* ones.
One day, a man—a common case—
Was looking out *to get a place*,
When he was told that there was room
In this said mansion for a groom.
He came—the master most observant,
Strict in the hiring of a servant,
Went thro' the forms inherent to the scene,
Of character, of wages, and of warning,
Good morals, sober, honest, steady, clean,
Shun plays, hate girls, rise early in the morning:
All which, though wisely he defined it,
He found just as he wished to find it;—
The man himself said so—
And *he* must know.
But now, though Thomas thought it all too much,
There yet remained this final master-touch.
He said—his visage graced with saint-like airs—
"When you have rack'd your horses up,
You'll comb your hair, and wash and sup,
And then, I shall expect, attend at prayers.
There like myself behave,
And sing a stave."
At this, the man—somewhat confused—
Scraped, scratched his head, and mused;
"Yes, sir—oh, yes—but if I must—
As it is right to do what one engages—
Your honor won't object, I trust,
To let it be considered in my wages."

A VISIT TO A CELEBRATED DIPLOMATIST.

FROM "VIVIAN GREY." BY BENJAMIN D'ISRAELI.

On the following morning, before sunrise, the Prince's valet roused Vivian from his slumbers. According to the appointment of the preceding evening, Vivian repaired in due time to a certain spot in the park. The Prince reached it at the same moment. A mounted groom, leading two English horses, of very showy appearance, and each having a travelling case strapped on the back of its saddle, awaited them. His Highness mounted one of the steeds with skilful celerity, although Arnelm and Von Neuwied were not there to do honor to his bridle and his stirrup.

"You must give me an impartial opinion of your courser, my dear friend," said the Prince to Vivian, "for if you deem it worthy of being bestridden by you, my son requests that you will do him the great honor of accepting it; if so, call it Max; and provided it be as thorough-bred as the donor, you need not change it for Bucephalus."

"Not worthy of the son of Ammon!" said Vivian, as he touched the spirited animal with the spur, and proved its fiery action on the springing turf.

A man never feels so proud or so sanguine as when he is bounding on the back of a fine horse. Cares fly with the first curvet; and the very sight of a spur is enough to prevent one committing suicide. What a magnificent creature is man, that a brute's prancing hoof can influence his temper or his destiny!—and truly, however little there may be to admire in the rider, few things in this admirable world can be conceived more beautiful than a horse, when the bloody spur has thrust some anger in his resentful side. How splendid to view him with his dilated nostril, his flaming eye, his arched neck, and his waving tail, rustling like a banner in a battle!—to see him champing his slavered bridle, and sprinkling the snowy foam upon the earth, which his hasty hoof seems almost as if it scorned to touch!

When Vivian and his companion had proceeded about five miles, the Prince pulled up, and giving a sealed letter to the groom, he desired him to leave them. The Prince and Vivian amused themselves for a considerable time, by endeavoring to form a correct conception of the person, manners, and habits of the wonderful man to whom they were on the point of paying so interesting a visit.

"I bitterly regret," said Vivian, "that I have forgotten my Montesquieu; and what would I give now to know by rote only one quotation from Machiavel! I expect to be received with folded arms, and a brow lowering with the overwhelming weight of a brain meditating for the control of millions. His letter has prepared us for the mysterious, but not very amusing style of his conversation. He will be perpetually on his guard not to commit himself; and although public business, and the receipt of papers, by calling him away, will occasionally give us an opportunity of being alone; still I regret most bitterly, that I did not put in my case some interesting volume which would have allowed me to feel less tedious those hours during which you will necessarily be employed with him in private consultation."

After a ride of five hours, the horsemen arrived at a small village.

"Thus far I think I have well piloted you," said the Prince; "but I confess my knowledge here ceases; and though I shall disobey the diplomatic instructions of the great man, I must even ask some old woman the way to Mr. Beckendorff's."

While they were hesitating as to whom they should address, an equestrian, who had already passed them on the road, though at some distance, came up, and inquired, in a voice which Vivian immediately recognized as that of the messenger who had brought Beckendorff's letter to Turriparva, whether he had the honor of addressing Mr. Von Philipson. Neither of the gentlemen answered, for Vivian of course expected the Prince to reply; and his Highness was, as yet, so unused to his incognito, that he had actually forgotten his own name. But it was evident that the demandant had questioned, rather from system, than by way of security; and he waited very patiently until the Prince had collected his senses, and assumed sufficient gravity of countenance to inform the horseman that he was the person in question. "What, Sir, is your pleasure?"

"I am instructed to ride on before you, sir, that you may not mistake your way;" and without waiting for an answer, the laconic messenger turned his steed's head, and trotted off.

The travellers soon left the high road, and turned up a wild turf path, not only inaccessible to carriages, but even requiring great attention from horsemen. After much winding, and some floundering, they arrived at a light and very fanciful iron gate, which apparently opened into a shrubbery.

"I will take your horses here, gentlemen," said the guide; and getting off his horse, he opened the gate. "Follow this path, and you can meet with no difficulty." The Prince and Vivian accordingly dismounted; and the guide immediately, with the end of his whip, gave a loud shrill whistle.

The path ran, for a very short way, through the shrubbery, which evidently was a belt encircling the grounds. From this, the Prince and Vivian emerged upon an ample lawn, which formed on the farthest side a terrace, by gradually sloping down to the margin of a river. It was enclosed on the other sides by an iron railing of the same pattern as the gate, and a great number of white pheasants were quietly feeding in its centre. Following the path which skirted the lawn, they arrived at a second gate, which opened into a garden, in which no signs of the taste at present existing in Germany for the English system of picturesque pleasure-grounds were at all visible. The walk was bounded on both sides by tall borders, or rather hedges, of box, cut into the shape of battlements; the sameness of these turrets being occasionally varied by the immovable form of some trusty warder, carved out of yew or laurel. Raised terraces and arched walks, aloes and orange trees, mounted on sculptured pedestals, columns of cypress, and pyramids of bay, whose dark foliage strikingly contrasted with the marble statues, and the white vases shining in the sun, rose in all directions in methodical confusion. The sound of a fountain was not wanting; and large beds of the most beautiful flowers abounded; but, in no instance did Vivian observe that two kinds of plants were ever mixed together. Proceeding through a very lofty berçeau, occasional openings, whose curving walks allowed effective glimpses of a bust or a statue, the companions at length came in sight of the house. It was a long, uneven, low building, evidently of ancient architecture. Numerous stacks of tall and fantastically shaped chimneys rose over three thick and heavy gables, which reached down further than the middle of the elevation, forming three compartments, one of them, including a large and modern bow-window, over which clustered in profusion the sweet and glowing blossoms of the clematis and the pomegranate. Indeed, the whole front of the house was so completely covered with a rich scarlet creeper, that it was almost impossible to ascertain of what materials it was built. As Vivian was admiring a large white peacock, which, attracted by their approach, had taken the opportunity of unfurling its wheeling train, a man came forward from the bow-window.

I shall be particular in my description of his appearance. In height he was about five feet eight inches, and of a spare, but well-proportioned figure. He had very little hair, which was highly powdered, and dressed in a manner to render more remarkable the extraordinary elevation of his conical and polished forehead. His long piercing black eyes were almost closed, from the fulness of their upper lids. His cheeks were sallow, his nose aquiline, his mouth compressed. His ears, which were quite uncovered by hair, were so wonderfully small, that it would be wrong to pass them over unnoticed; as indeed were his hands and feet, which in form were quite feminine. He was dressed in a coat and waistcoat of black velvet, the latter part of his costume reaching to his thighs; and in a button-hole of his coat was a large bunch of tuberose. A small part of his flannel waistcoat appeared through an opening in his exquisitely plaited shirt, the broad collar of which, though tied round with a wide black ribbon, did not conceal a neck which agreed well with his beardless chin, and would not have misbecome a woman. In England we should have called his breeches buck-skin. They were of a pale yellow leather, and suited his large and spur-armed cavalry boot, which fitted closely to the legs they covered, reaching over the knees of the wearer. A ribbon round his neck, tucked into his waistcoat pocket, was attached to a small French watch. He swung in his right hand the bow of a violin; and in the other, the little finger of which was nearly hid by a large antique ring, he held a white handkerchief, strongly perfumed with violets. Notwithstanding the many feminine characteristics which I have noticed, either from the expression of the eyes, or the formation of the mouth, the countenance of this individual generally conveyed an impression of the greatest firmness and energy. This description will not be considered ridiculously minute by those who have never had an opportunity of becoming acquainted with the person of so celebrated a gentleman as Mr. Beckendorff.

He advanced to the Prince with an air which seemed to proclaim, that as his person could not be mistaken, the ceremony of introduction was perfectly unnecessary. Bowing in the most ceremonious and courtly manner to his Highness, Mr. Beckendorff in a weak, but not unpleasing voice, said that he was honored "by the presence of Mr. Von Philipson." The Prince answered his salutation in a manner equally ceremonious, and equally courtly; for having no mean opinion of his own diplomatic abilities, his Highness determined that neither by an excess of coldness, nor cordiality on his part, should the Minister gather the slightest indication of the temper in which he had attended the interview. You see that even the bow of a diplomatist is a very serious business!

"Mr. Beckendorff," said his Highness, "my letters doubtless informed you that I should avail myself of your permission to be accompanied. Let me have the honor of presenting to you my friend Mr. Grey, an English gentleman."

As the Prince spoke, Beckendorff stood with his arms crossed behind him, and his chin resting upon his chest; but his eyes at the same time so raised as to look his Highness full in the face. Vivian was so struck by his posture, and the expression of his countenance, that he nearly omitted to bow when he was presented. As his name was mentioned, the Minister gave him a sharp, sidelong glance, and moving his head very gently, he invited his guests to enter the house. The gentlemen accordingly complied with his request. Passing through the bow-window, they found themselves in a well-sized room, the sides of which were covered with shelves of richly bound books. There was nothing in the room which gave the slightest indication that the master of the library was any other than a private gentleman. Not a book, not a chair was out of its place. A purple inkstand of Sevres china, and a very highly-tooled morocco portfolio of the same color, reposed on a rosewood table, and that was all. No papers, no despatches, no red tape, and no red boxes. Over an ancient chimney, lined with blue china tiles, on which were represented the most grotesque figures—cows playing the harp—monkeys acting monarchs—and tall figures all legs, flying with rapidity from pursuers who were all head—over this chimney were suspended some curious pieces of antique armor, among which an Italian dagger, with a chased and jewelled hilt, was the most remarkable, and the most precious.

"This," said Mr. Beckendorff, "is my library."

"What a splendid poniard!" said the Prince, who had no taste for books; and he immediately walked up to the chimney-piece. Beckendorff followed him, and taking down the admired weapon from its resting-place, proceeded to lecture on its virtues, its antiquity, and its beauty. Vivian seized this opportunity of taking a rapid glance at the contents of his library. He anticipated interleaved copies of Michael Vattel, and Montesquieu; and the lightest works that he expected to meet with were the lying memoirs of some intriguing Cardinal, or the deluding apology of an exiled Minister. To his surprise he found that, without an exception, the collection merely consisted of poetry and romance; and while his eyes rapidly passed over, not only the great names of Germany, but also of Italy and France, it was with pride that he remarked upon the shelves an English Shakspere; and perhaps with still greater delight, a complete edition of the enchanted volumes of our illustrious Scott. Surprised at this most unexpected circumstance, Vivian looked with a curious eye on the unlettered backs of a row of mighty folios on a corner shelf; "These," he thought, "at least must be royal ordinances, and collected state-papers." The sense of propriety struggled for a moment with the passion of curiosity; but nothing is more difficult for the man who loves books, than to refrain from examining a volume which he fancies may be unknown to him. From the jewelled dagger, Beckendorff had now got to an enamelled breastplate. Two to one he should not be observed; and so, with a desperate pull, Vivian extracted a volume—it was a herbal! He tried another—it was a collection of dried insects! He immediately replaced it, and staring at his host, wondered whether he really could be the Mr. Beckendorff of whom he had heard so much.

"And now," said Mr. Beckendorff, "I will show you my drawing-room."

He opened the door at the further end of the library, and introduced them to a room of a very different character. The sun, which was shining very brightly, lent additional brilliancy to the rainbow-tinted birds of paradise, the crimson mackaws, and the green parroquets that glistened on the splendid India paper, which covered not only the walls, but also the ceiling of the room. Over the fire-place, a black frame, projecting from the wall and mournfully contrasting with the general brilliant appearance of the apartment, inclosed a picture of a beautiful female; and bending over its frame, and indeed partly shadowing the countenance, was the withered branch of a tree. A harpsichord, and several cases of musical instruments were placed in different parts of the room; and suspended by very broad black ribbons from a wall on each side of the picture, were a guitar and a tambourine. On a sofa, of usual size, lay a Cremona; and as Mr. Beckendorff passed the instrument, he threw by its side the bow, which he had hitherto carried in his hand.

"We may as well now take something," said Mr. Beckendorff, when his guests had sufficiently admired the room; "my pictures are in my dining-room—let us go there."

So saying, and armed this time, not only with his bow, but also with his violin, he retraced his steps through the library, and crossing a small passage, which divided the house into two compartments, he opened the door into his dining-room. The moment that they entered the room, their ears were saluted, and indeed their senses ravished, by what appeared to be a concert of a thousand birds; yet none of the winged choristers were to be seen, and not even a single cage was visible. The room, which was very simply furnished, appeared at first rather gloomy; for though lighted by three windows, the silk blinds were all drawn.

"And now," said Mr. Beckendorff, raising the blind, "you shall see my pictures. At what do you estimate this Breughel?"

The window, which was of stained green glass, gave to the landscape an effect similar to that generally produced by the artist mentioned. The Prince, who was already very puzzled by finding one who, at the same time, was both his host and his enemy, so perfectly different a character to what he had conceived, and who, being by temper superstitious, considered that this preliminary false opinion of his was rather a bad omen,—did not express any very great admiration of the gallery of Mr. Beckendorff; but Vivian, who had no ambitious hopes or fears to affect his temper, and who was delighted with the character with whom he had become so unexpectedly acquainted—good-naturedly humored the fantasies of the Minister; and said that he preferred his picture to any Breughel he had ever seen.

"I see you have a fine taste," said Mr. Beckendorff, with a very serious air, but in a most courteous tone; "you shall see my Claude!"

The rich yellow tint of the second window, gave to the fanciful garden all that was requisite to make it look Italian.

"Have you ever been in Italy, sir?" asked Beckendorff.

"I have not."

"You have, Mr. Von Philipson?"

"Never south of Germany," answered the Prince, who was exceedingly hungry, and eyed with a rapacious glance the capital luncheon which he saw prepared for him.

"Well then, when either of you go, you will of course not miss the Laggo Maggiore. Gaze on Isola Bella at sunset, and you will not view as fair a scene as this! And now, Mr. Von Philipson," said Mr. Beckendorff, "do me the favor of giving me your opinion of this Honthorst?"

His Highness would rather have given his opinion of the fine dish of stewed game which still smoked upon the table, but which he was mournfully convinced would not smoke long; or of the large cucumbers, of which he was particularly fond, and which, among many other vegetables, his amorous eye had already detected. "But," thought he, "this is the last!" and so he very warmly admired the effect produced by the flaming panes, to which Beckendorff swore that no piece ever painted by Gerard Honthorst, for brilliancy of coloring and boldness of outline, could be compared; "besides," continued Beckendorff, "mine are all animated pictures. See that cypress, waving from the gentle breeze which is now stirring—and look! look at this crimson peacock!—look! Mr. Von Philipson."

"I am looking, Mr. Von—— I beg pardon, Mr. Beckendorff," said the Prince, with great dignity—making this slight mistake in the name, either from being unused to converse with such low people as had not the nominal mark of nobility, or to vent his spleen at being so unnecessarily kept from the refreshment which he so much required.

"Mr. Von Philipson," said Beckendorff, suddenly turning round; "all my fruits and all my vegetables, are from my own garden. Let us sit down and help ourselves."

The only substantial food at table was a great dish of stewed game, which I believe I have mentioned before. The Prince seized the breast and wings of a young pheasant, Vivian attacked a fine tender hare, and Beckendorff himself cut off the wing of a partridge. The vegetables and the fruits were numerous and superb; and there really appeared to be a fair prospect of the Prince of Little Lilliput making as good a luncheon as if the whole had been conducted under the auspices of Master Randolph himself,—had it not been for the confounded melody of the unseen vocalists, which, probably excited by the sounds of the knives and plates, too evidently increased every moment. But this inconvenience was soon removed by Mr. Beckendorff rising, and giving three loud knocks on the door opposite to the one by which they had entered. Immediate silence ensued.

"Clara will be here in an instant, to change your plate, Mr. Von Philipson," said Beckendorff—"and here she is."

Vivian eagerly looked up, not with the slightest idea that the entrance of Clara would prove that the mysterious picture in the drawing-room was a portrait; but it must be confessed with a little curiosity to view the first specimen of the sex who lived under the roof of Mr. Beckendorff. Clara was a hale old woman with rather an acid expression of countenance; very prim in her appearance, and evidently very precise in her manners. She placed a bottle, and two wine glasses with long thin stems, on the table; and having removed the game, and changed the plates, she disappeared.

"Pray what wine is this, Mr. Beckendorff?" eagerly asked the Prince, with a countenance glowing with delight—and his Highness was vulgar enough to smack his lips, which, for a Prince, is really shocking.

"I really don't know. I never drink wine."

"Not know! Grey, take a glass. What's your opinion?—I never tasted such wine in my life. Why I do declare it is real Tokay!"

"Probably it may be," said Mr. Beckendorff; "I think it was a present from the Emperor. I have never tasted it."

"My dear sir, take a glass!" said the Prince; his natural kind and jovial temper having made him completely forget whom he was addressing, the business he had come upon, and indeed every thing else except the astounding circumstance that there was an individual in the room who refused to take his share of a bottle of real Tokay:—"My dear sir, take a glass."

"I never drink wine; I'm glad you like it, I have no doubt Clara has more."

"No, no, no! we must be moderate, we must be moderate," said the Prince, who, though a great admirer of a good luncheon, had also a due respect for a good dinner,—and consequently had no idea at this awkward hour in the day of preventing himself from properly appreciating the future banquet. Moreover, his Highness, taking into consideration the very piquant sauce with which the game had been dressed, and the marks of refinement and good taste which seemed to pervade every part of the establishment of Mr. Beckendorff, did not imagine that he was much presuming, when he conjectured that there was a fair chance of his dinner being something very superior. The Prince, therefore, opposed a further supply of Tokay, and contented himself for the present with assisting his Gruyere with one of the very fine-looking cucumbers—his favorite cucumbers; which, though yet untasted, had not, in spite of the wine, been banished from his memory.

"You seem very fond of cucumbers, Mr. Von Philipson," said Beckendorff.

"So fond of them that I prefer them to any vegetable, and to most fruits. What is more cooling—more refreshing? What—"

"I never eat them myself; but I'll tell you, if you like, what I think the best way of treating a cucumber."

His Highness was the most ready, and the most graceful of pupils; and Vivian could scarcely suppress his laughter, when the Prime Minister, with a grave countenance, and in his peculiarly subdued voice and somewhat precise mode of speaking, commenced instructing his political opponent upon the important topic of dressing a vegetable.

"You must be careful," said Mr. Beckendorff, "to pick out the straightest thinnest-skinned, most seedless cucumber that you can find. Six hours before you want to eat it, put the stalk in cold water on a marble slab—not the whole cucumber—that's nonsense. Then pare it very carefully, so as to take off all the green outside and no more. Slice it as thin as possible, spread it over your dish, and sprinkle it with a good deal of white pepper, red pepper, salt, and mustard-seed. Mix some oil and common vinegar with a little Chili, and drown it in them. Open a large window very wide—and throw it all out!"

It was quite evident that Mr. Von Philipson was extremely disappointed, and perhaps a little offended at the unexpected termination of Mr. Beckendorff's lecture, to which he had listened with the most interested attention. As for Vivian Grey, he did not affect to contain himself any longer, but gave way to a long and loud laugh—a laugh not so much excited by the manner in which Beckendorff had detailed the desired information, although it was extremely humorous, as by the striking contrast which the speaker and the speech afforded to the conceptions which he and his companion had formed of their host during their ride. His rather boisterous risibility, apparently, did not offend Mr. Beckendorff, on whose upper lip, for an instant, Vivian thought he detected a smile or a sneer. It was, however, only for an instant; for the Minister immediately rose from table, and left the room by the same door on which his three loud knocks had previously produced so tranquillizing an effect.

The sudden arrival and appearance of some new and unexpected guests through the very mysterious portal by which Mr. Beckendorff had vanished, not only were the source of fresh entertainment to our hero, but also explained the character of the apartment, which, from its unceasing melody, had so much excited his curiosity. These new guests were a crowd of piping bullfinches, Virginia nightingales, trained canaries, Java sparrows, and Indian lories; which having been freed from their cages of golden wire by their fond master, had fled, as was their custom, from his superb aviary to pay their respects and compliments at his daily levée.

The table was immediately covered, and the Prince immediately annoyed. Nothing did he detest so much as the whole feathered race; and now, as far as he could observe, he might as well have visited a bird-catcher as Mr. Beckendorff. The white pheasants, and white peacock, could have been borne; but as for the present intrusion, a man had better live in Noah's ark than in the liberties of an aviary. The Prince was quite right; it was extremely annoying. A couple of bullfinches respectively perched on each of his shoulders, and commenced a most thrilling and jacobinical hymn of liberty, in celebration of their release; and an impudent little canary attacked his cucumber. As if this were not sufficient to produce instantaneous insanity, a long-tailed scarlet lory lighted on his head, and commenced its usual fondling tricks, by rubbing its beak in the Prince's hair, fluttering its wing on his cheek, and pecking his eye-brows. As it got more delighted, it shrieked its joy into his ear with such shrillness, that he started from his chair; and the little favorite consequently slipping down, to save itself from falling, hung upon his lip by his beak. As soon as his Highness had extricated himself from this unpleasing situation, the lory, making a perch on the back of his chair, regained its first position.

Just as the Prince was asking Vivian to hasten to his assistance, Mr. Beckendorff returned,—"Never mind, Mr. Von Philipson," said the Minister, "never mind; it only wants to make a nest, poor thing!"

"But I do mind, Mr. Beckendorff; I detest birds, and this annoying little animal, I beg to inform you, is exceedingly troublesome."

"Wheugh!" said the Prime Minister of Reisenberg, and the troublesome lory flew to his shoulder. "I am glad to see that you like birds, sir," said Beckendorff to Vivian; for our good hero, good-naturedly humoring the tastes of his host, was impartially dividing the luxuries of a peach among a crowd of gaudy and greedy little sparrows. "You shall see my favorites," continued Beckendorff, and tapping rather loudly on the table, he held out the forefinger of each hand. The two bullfinches, which were still singing on the shoulder of the Prince, recognized the signal, and immediately hastened to their perch.

"My dear!" thrilled out one little songster; and it raised its speaking eyes to its delighted master.

"My love!" warbled the other, making its affection by looks equally personal.

These monosyllables were repeated fifty times; at each one, Beckendorff, with sparkling eyes, and a countenance radiant with delight, triumphantly looked round at Vivian, as if the frequent reiteration were a proof of the sincerity of the affection of these singular friends.

At length, to the Prince's great relief, Mr. Beckendorff's feathered friends having finished their dessert, were sent back to their cages, with a strict injunction not to trouble their master at present with their voices—an injunction which, to Vivian's great surprise, was obeyed to the letter; and when the door was closed, few persons in the world could have been persuaded that the next room was an aviary.

"I am proud of my peaches, Mr. Von Philipson," said Beckendorff, recommending the fruit to his guest's attention; then, rising from the table, he threw himself on the sofa, and began humming a tune in a very low voice. Presently, he took up his Cremona, and using the violin as a guitar, accompanied himself in a very beautiful air, but not in a more audible tone. While Mr. Beckendorff was singing, he seemed quite unconscious that any person was in the room; and the Prince, who detested music, certainly gave him no hint, either by his approbation or his attention, that he was listened to. Vivian, however, like most unhappy men, did love music with all his spirit's strength; and actuated by this feeling, and the interest which he began to take in the character of Mr. Beckendorff, he could not, when that gentleman had finished his air, refrain from very sincerely saying "encore!"

Beckendorff started and looked around, as if he were for the first moment aware that any being had heard him.

"Encore!" said he, with a kind sneer; "who ever could sing or play the same thing twice! Are you fond of music, sir?"

"Very much so, indeed; I fancied I recognized that air. You are an admirer, I imagine, of Mozart?"

"I never heard of him; I know nothing of those gentry. But if you really like music, I'll play you something worth listening to."

Mr. Beckendorff began a beautiful air very adagio, gradually increasing the time in a kind of variation, till at last his execution became so wonderfully rapid, that Vivian, surprised at the mere mechanical action, rose from his chair in order better to examine the player's management and motion of his bow. Exquisite as were the tones, enchanting as were the originality of his variations, and the perfect harmony of his composition, it was nevertheless extremely difficult to resist laughing at the ludicrous contortions of his face and figure. Now, his body bending to the strain, he was at one moment with his violin raised in the air, and the next instant with the lower nut almost resting upon his foot. At length, by well-proportioned degrees, the air died away into the original soft cadence; and the player becoming completely entranced in his own performance, finished by sinking back on the sofa, with his bow and violin raised over his head. Vivian would not disturb him by his applause. An instant after, Mr. Beckendorff, throwing down the instrument, rushed through an open window into the garden.

As soon as Beckendorff was out of sight, Vivian looked at the Prince; and his Highness, elevating his eyebrows, screwing up his mouth, and shrugging his shoulders, altogether presented a very comical picture of a puzzled man.

"Well, my dear friend," said he, "this is rather different to what we expected."

"Very different, indeed; but much more amusing."

"Humph!" said the Prince, very slowly, "I do not think it exactly requires a ghost to tell us that Mr. Beckendorff is not in the habit of going to Court. I don't know how he is accustomed to conduct himself when he is honored by a visit from the Grand Duke; but I am quite sure, that as regards his treatment of myself, to say the least, the incognito is very well observed."

"Mr. Von Philipson," said the gentleman of whom they were speaking, putting his head in at the window; "you shall see my blue passion flower. —We'll take a walk round the garden."

The Prince gave Vivian a look, which seemed to suppose they must go; and accordingly they stepped into the garden.

"You do not see my garden in its glory," said Mr. Beckendorff, stopping before the bow-window of the library; "this spot is my strong point; had you been here earlier in the year, you might have admired with me my invaluable crescents of tulips —such colors! such brilliancy! so defined! And last year I had three king-tulips; their elegant formed creamy cups I have never seen equalled. And then my double variegated ranunculuses; my hyacinths of fifty bells, in every tint, single and double; and my favorite stands of auriculas, so large and powdered, that the color of the velvet leaves was scarcely discoverable! The blue passion-flower is, however, not very beautiful. You see that summer-house, sir," continued he, turning to Vivian, "the top is my observatory; you will sleep in that pavilion to-night, so you had better take notice how the walk winds."

The passion-flower was trained against the summer-house in question.

"There!" said Mr. Beckendorff, and he stood admiring with outstretched arms, "the latter days of its beauty, for the autumn frosts will soon stop its flower: Pray, Mr. Von Philipson, are either you or your friend a botanist?"

"Why," said the Prince, "I am a great admirer of flowers, but I cannot exactly say that—"

"Ah! I see you are no botanist. The flower of this beautiful plant continues only one day, but there is a constant succession from July to the end of the autumn; and if this fine weather continue— Pray, sir, how is the wind?"

"I really cannot say," said the Prince; "but I think the wind is either—"

"Ah! do you know how the wind is, sir?" continued Beckendorff to Vivian.

"I think, sir, that it is—"

"Ah! I see it's westerly.—Well, if this weather continue, the succession may still last another month. You will be interested to know, Mr. Von Philipson, that the flower comes out at the same joint with the leaf, on a peduncle near three inches long; round the centre of it are two radiating crowns; look, look, sir! the inner inclining towards the centre column—now examine this well, and I'll be with you in a moment." So saying, Mr. Beckendorff, running with great rapidity down the walk, jumped over the railing, and in a moment was coursing across the lawn, towards the river, in a desperate chase after a dragon-fly.

Mr. Beckendorff was soon out of sight; and after lingering half an hour in the vicinity of the blue passion-flower, the Prince proposed to Vivian that they should quit the spot. "As far as I can observe," continued his highness, "we might as well quit the house. No wonder that Beckendorff's power is on the wane, for he appears to me to be growing childish. Surely he could not always have been this frivolous creature!"

"I really am so overwhelmed with astonishment," said Vivian, "that it is quite out of my power to assist your highness in any supposition. But I should recommend you not to be too hasty in your movements. Take care that staying here does not affect the position which you have taken up, or retard the progress of any measures on which you have determined, and you are safe. What will it injure you, if, with the chance of achieving the great and patriotic purpose to which you have devoted your powers and energies, you are subjected for a few hours to the caprices, or even rudeness, of any man whatever? If Beckendorff be the character which the world gives him credit to be, I do not think he can imagine that you are to be deceived twice; and if he do imagine so, we are convinced that he will be disappointed. If, as you have supposed, not only his power is on the wane, but his intellect also, four-and-twenty hours will convince us of the fact; for in less than that time your highness will necessarily have conversation of a more important nature with him. I strenuously recommend, therefore, that we continue here to-day, although," added Vivian, smiling, "I have to sleep in his observatory."

After walking in the garden about an hour, the Prince and Vivian again went into the house, imagining that Beckendorff might have returned by another entrance; but he was not there. The Prince was very much annoyed; and Vivian, to amuse himself, had recourse to the library. After re-examining the armor, looking at the garden through the painted windows, conjecturing who might be the original of the mysterious picture, and what could be the meaning of the withered branch, the Prince was fairly worn out. The precise dinner hour he did not know; and notwithstanding repeated exertions, he had hitherto been unable to find the blooming Clara. He could not flatter himself, however, that there were less than two hours to kill before the great event took place; and so, quite miserable, and heartily wishing himself back again at Turriparva, he prevailed upon Vivian to throw aside his book, and take another walk.

This time they extended their distance, stretched out as far as the river, and explored the adjoining woods; but of Mr. Beckendorff they saw and heard nothing. At length they again returned; it was getting dusk. They found the bow-window of the library closed. They again entered the dining-room; and, to their surprise, found no preparations for dinner. This time the Prince was more fortunate in his exertions to procure an interview with Madam Clara, for that lady almost immediately entered the room.

"Pray, my good madam," inquired the Prince; "has your master returned?"

"Mr. Beckendorff is in the library, sir," said the old lady very pompously.

"Indeed! we don't dine in this room, then?"

"Dine, sir!" said the good dame, forgetting her pomposity in her astonishment.

"Yes—dine," said the Prince.

"La! sir; Mr. Beckendorff never takes any thing after noon meal."

"Am I to understand, then, that we are to have no dinner?" asked his highness, angry and agitated.

"Mr. Beckendorff never takes any thing after his noon meal, sir; but I'm sure if you and your friend are hungry, sir, I hope there's never a want in this house."

"My good lady, I am hungry, very hungry, indeed; and if your master, I mean Mr. Von—that is Mr. Beckendorff, has such a bad appetite that he can satisfy himself with picking, once a day, the breast of a pheasant; why, if he expects his friends to be willing, or even able to live on such fare,—the least that I can say is, that he is very much mistaken; and so, therefore, my good friend Grey, I think we had better order out our horses, and be off."

"No occasion for that, I hope," said Mrs. Clara, rather alarmed at the Prince's passion; "no want, I trust, ever here, sir; and I make no doubt you'll have dinner as soon as possible; and so, sir, I hope you'll not be hasty."

"Hasty! I have no wish to be hasty; but as for disarranging the whole economy of the house, and getting up an extemporaneous meal for me—I cannot think of it. Mr. Beckendorff may live as he likes, and if I stay here I am contented to live as he does. I do not wish him to change his habits for me, and I shall take care that after to-day, there will be no necessity for his doing so. However, absolute hunger can make no compliments; and therefore I will thank you, my good madam, to let me and my friend have the remains of that cold game, if they be still in existence, on which we lunched, or, as you term it, took our noon meal this morning; and which, if it were your own cooking, Mrs. Clara, I assure you, as I observed to my friend at the time, did you infinite credit."

The Prince, although his gentlemanly feelings had, in spite of his hunger, dictated a deprecation of Mrs. Clara's making a dinner merely for himself, still thought that a seasonable and deserved compliment to the lady might assist in bringing about a result, which, notwithstanding his politeness, he very much desired; and that was the production of another specimen of her culinary accomplishments. Having behaved, as he considered, with such moderation and dignified civility, he was, it must be confessed, rather astounded, when Mrs. Clara duly acknowledged his compliment by her courtesy, was sorry to inform him that she dared give no refreshment in this house, without Mr. Beckendorff's special order.

"Special order! why! surely your master will not grudge me the cold leg of a pheasant?"

"Mr. Beckendorff is not in the habit of grudging any thing," answered the housekeeper, with offended majesty.

"Then why should he object?" asked the Prince.

"Mr. Beckendorff is the best judge, sir, of the propriety of his own regulations."

"Well, well!" said Vivian, more interested for his friend than himself, "there is no difficulty in asking Mr. Beckendorff."

"None in the least, sir," answered the housekeeper, "when he is awake."

"Awake!" said the Prince, "why! is he asleep now?"

"Yes, sir, in the library."

"And how long will he be asleep?" asked the Prince, with great eagerness.

"It is uncertain; he may be asleep for hours—he may wake in five minutes; all I can do is to watch."

"But surely in a case like the present, you can wake your master?"

"I could not wake Mr. Beckendorff, sir, if the house were on fire. No one can enter the room when he is asleep."

"Then how can you possibly know when he is awake?"

"I shall hear his violin immediately, sir."

"Well, well! I suppose it must be so. Grey, I wish we were in Turriparva, that is all I know. Men of my station have no business to be paying visits to the sons of the Lord knows who! peasants, shopkeepers, and pedagogues!"

The Prince of Little Lilliput thought that mankind were solely created to hunt and to fight; and unless you could spear a boar or owned a commission, you were not included in his list of proper men. We smile at what we consider the narrow-minded ideas of a German Prince; yet, perhaps, if we inquire, we shall find that mankind, on an average, are influenced in all countries by the same feelings, and in the same degree; and the definition of *a gentleman* by a hero of St. James's Street, if not exactly similar, will not be less unwise and less ridiculous, than the Prince of Little Lilliput's description of a *proper man*. An officer in the guards once told me, that no person was a gentleman who was not the son of a man who had twenty thousand a year, landed property. Convinced that his declaration was sincere, I respected his prejudices, and did not dispute his definition. I should have behaved the same, had I been in Africa, and had a Hottentot dandy declared, that no person was to be visited who dared to devour the smoking entrails of a sheep in less than a couple of mouthfuls.

As a fire was blazing in the dining-room, which Mrs. Clara informed them Mr. Beckendorff never omitted having every night in the year, the Prince and his friend imagined that they were to remain there, and they consequently did not attempt to disturb the slumbers of Mr. Beckendorff. Resting his feet on the hobs, his Highness, for the fiftieth time, declared that he wished he had never left Turriparva; and just when Vivian was on the point of giving up, in despair, the hope of consoling him, Mrs. Clara entered, and proceeded to lay the cloth.

"Your master is awake, then?" asked the Prince, very quickly.

"Mr. Beckendorff has been long awake, sir! and dinner will be ready immediately."

His Highness's countenance brightened; and in a short time the supper appearing, the Prince again fascinated by Mrs. Clara's cookery and Mr. Beckendorff's wine, forgot his chagrin, and regained his temper.

In about a couple of hours, Mr. Beckendorff entered.

"I hope that Clara has given you wine you like, Mr. Von Philipson?"

"Excellent, my dear sir! the same bin, I'll answer for that."

Mr. Beckendorff had his violin in his hand; but his dress was much changed. His great boots being pulled off, exhibiting the white silk stockings which he invariably wore; and his coat had given place to the easier covering of a very long and handsome brocade dressing-gown. He drew a chair round the fire, between the Prince and Vivian. It was a late hour, and the room was only lighted by the glimmering coals, for the flames had long died away. Mr. Beckendorff sat for some time without speaking, gazing very earnestly on the decaying embers. Indeed, before many minutes had elapsed, complete silence prevailed, for both the endeavors of the Prince, and of Vivian, to promote conversation had been unsuccessful. At length, the master of the house turned round to the Prince, and pointing to a particular mass of coal, said, "I think, Mr. Von Philipson, that is the completest elephant I ever saw. We will ring the bell for some coals, and then have a game of whist."

The Prince was so surprised by Mr. Beckendorff's remark, that he was not sufficiently struck by the strangeness of his proposition; and it was only when he heard Vivian professing his ignorance of the game, that it occurred to him that to play at whist was hardly the object for which he had travelled from Turriparva.,

"An Englishman not know whist!" said Mr. Beckendorff; "ridiculous!—you do not know it. You're thinking of the stupid game they play here, of Boston whist. Let us play! Mr. Von Philipson, I know, has no objection."

"But, my good sir," said the Prince, "although previous to *conversation* I may have no objection to join in a little amusement, still it appears to me that it has escaped your memory that whist is a game which requires the co-operation of four persons."

"Not at all! I take dumbmy. I'm not sure it is not the finest way of playing the game."

The table was arranged, the lights brought, the cards produced, and the Prince of Little Lilliput, greatly to his surprise, found himself playing whist with Mr. Beckendorff. Nothing could be more dull. The Minister would neither bet nor stake; and the immense interest which he took in every card that was played, most ludicrously contrasted with the rather sullen looks of the Prince, and the very sleepy ones of Vivian. Whenever Mr. Beckendorff played for dumbmy, he always looked, with the most searching eye into the next adversary's face, as if he would read his cards in his features. The first rubber lasted an hour and a half—three long games, which Mr. Beckendorff, to his triumph, hardly won. In the first game of the second rubber Vivian blundered; in the second he revoked; and in the third, having neglected to play, and being loudly called upon, and rated both by his partner and Mr. Beckendorff, he was found to be asleep. Beckendorff threw down his hand with a loud dash, which roused Vivian from his slumber. He apologized for his drowsiness; but said that he was so extremely sleepy that he must retire. The Prince, who longed to be with Beckendorff alone, winked approbation of his intention.

"Well!" said Beckendorff, "you spoiled the rubber. I shall ring for Clara. Why you are all so fond of going to bed, I cannot understand. I have not been to bed these thirty years."

Vivian made his escape; and Beckendorff, pitying his degeneracy, proposed to the Prince, in a tone which seemed to anticipate that the offer would meet with instantaneous acceptation—double dumbmy;—this, however, was too much.

"No more cards, sir, I thank you," said the Prince; "if, however, you have a mind for an hour's conversation, I am quite at your service."

"I am obliged to you—I never talk—good night, Mr. Von Philipson."

Mr. Beckendorff left the room. His Highness could contain himself no longer. He rang the bell.

"Pray, Mrs. Clara," said he, "where are my horses?"

"Mr. Beckendorff will have no quadrupeds within a mile of the house, except Owlface."

"How do you mean?—let me see the man-servant."

"The household consists only of myself, sir."

"Why! where is my luggage, then?"

"That has been brought up, sir; it is in your room."

"I tell you I must have my horses."

"It is quite impossible to night, sir. I think, sir, you had better retire; Mr. Beckendorff may not be home again these six hours."

"What! is your master gone out?"

"Yes, sir, he is just gone out to take his ride."

"Why! where is his horse kept then?"

"It's Owlface, sir."

"Owlface, indeed! what, is your master in the habit of riding out at night?"

"Mr. Beckendorff rides out, sir, just when it happens to suit him."

"It is very odd I cannot ride out when it happens to suit me! However, I'll be off to-morrow; and so if you please, show me my bed-room at once."

"Your room is the library, sir."

"The library! why, there's no bed in the library."

"We have no beds, sir; but the sofa is made up."

"No beds! well! it's only for one night, You are all mad, and I am as mad as you for coming here."

The morning sun, peeping through the window of the little summer-house, roused its inmate at an early hour; and finding no signs of Mr. Beckendorff and his guest having yet arisen from their slumbers, Vivian took the opportunity of strolling about the gardens and the grounds. Directing his way along the margin of the river, he soon left the lawn, and entered some beautiful meadows, whose dewy verdure glistened in the brightening beams of the early sun. Crossing these, and passing through a gate, he found himself in a rural road, whose lofty hedge-rows, rich with all the varieties of wild fruit and flower, and animated with the cheering presence of the busy birds chirping from every bough and spray, altogether presented a scene which greatly reminded him of the soft beauties of his own country. With some men, to remember is to be sad; and unfortunately for Vivian Grey, there were few objects which with him did not give rise to associations of a most painful nature. Of what he was thinking, as he sat on a bank with his eyes fixed on the ground, it is needless to inquire. He was roused from his reverie by the sound of a trotting horse. He looked up, but the winding road prevented him at first from seeing the steed which evidently was approaching. The sound came nearer and nearer; and at length, turning a corner, Mr. Beckendorff came in sight. He was mounted on a very strong built, rough, and particularly ugly pony, with an obstinate mane, which, defying the exertions of the groom or ostler, fell in equal divisions on both sides of its bottle neck; and a large white face, which, combined with its blind, or blinking vision, had earned for it the euphonous and complimentary title of Owlface. Both master and steed must have travelled hard and far, for both were covered with dust and mud from top to toe—from mane to hoof. Mr. Beckendorff seemed surprised at meeting Vivian, and pulled up his pony as he reached him.

"An early riser, I see, sir. Where is Mr. Von Philipson?"

"I have not yet seen him, and imagined that both he and yourself had not yet risen."

"Hum! how many is it to noon?" asked Mr. Beckendorff, who always spoke astronomically.

"More than four, I imagine."

"Pray do you prefer the country about here to Turriparva?"

"Both, I think are very beautiful."

"You live at Turriparva?" asked Mr. Beckendorff.

"When I am there," answered Vivian, smiling, who was too practised a head to be *pumped* even by Mr. Beckendorff.

"Pray has it been a fine summer at Turriparva?"

"It has been a fine summer, I believe, everywhere."

"I am afraid Mr. Von Philipson finds it rather dull here?"

"I am not aware of it."

"He seems a ve—ry—?" said Mr. Beckendorff, looking keenly in his companion's face. But Vivian did not supply the desired phrase; and so the Minister was forced to finish the sentence himself—"a very—gentlemanly sort of man?" A low bow was the only response.

"I trust, sir, I may indulge the hope," continued Mr. Beckendorff, "that you will honor me with your company another day."

"You are most exceedingly obliging, sir!"

"Mr. Von Philipson is fond, I think, of a country life?" said Beckendorff.

"Most men are, I think, sir."

"I suppose he has no innate objection to live occasionally in a city?"

"Few men have, I think, sir."

"You probably have known him long?"

"Not long enough to wish our acquaintance at an end."

"Hum!"

They proceeded in silence for about five minutes, and then Beckendorff again turned round, and this time with a direct question.

"I wonder if Mr. Von Philipson can make it convenient to honor me with his company another day. Can you tell me?"

"I think the best person to inform you of that, sir, would be his Highness himself," said Vivian, using his friend's title purposely to show Mr. Beckendorff how very ridiculous he considered his present use of the incognito.

"You think so, sir, do you?" answered Beckendorff, very sarcastically.

They had now arrived at the gate by which Vivian had reached the door.

"Your course, sir," said Mr. Beckendorff, "lies that way. I see, like myself, you are no great talker. We shall meet at breakfast." So saying, the Minister set spurs to his pony, and was soon out of sight.

When Vivian reached the house, he found the bow window of the library thrown open; and as he approached, he saw Mr. Beckendorff enter the room and bow to the Prince. His Highness had passed a most excellent night, in spite of not sleeping in a bed; and he was at this moment commencing a most delicious breakfast. His ill-humor had consequently all vanished. He had made up his mind that Beckendorff was a madman; and although he had given up all the secret and flattering hopes which he had dared to entertain when the interview was first arranged, he nevertheless did not regret his visit, which on the whole had been very amusing, and had made him acquainted with the person and habits, and, as he believed, the intellectual powers of a man with whom, most probably, he should soon be engaged in open hostility. Vivian took his seat at the breakfast table, and Beckendorff stood conversing with them with his back to the fire-place, and occasionally, during the pauses of conversation, pulling the strings of his violin with his fingers. It did not escape Vivian's observation that the Minister was particularly courteous, and even attentive to his Highness; and that he endeavored by his quick, and more communicative answers, and occasionally by a stray observation, to encourage the good humor which was visible on the cheerful countenance of the Prince.

"Have you been long up, Mr. Beckendorff?" asked the Prince; for his host had resumed his dressing-gown and slippers.

"I generally see the sun rise."

"And yet you retire late!—out riding last night, I understand?"

"I never go to bed."

"Indeed!" said the Prince. "Well, for my part, without my regular rest, I am nothing. Have you breakfasted, Mr. Beckendorff?"

"Clara will bring my breakfast immediately."

The dame accordingly soon appeared, bearing a tray with a basin of boiling water, and one very large thick biscuit. This, Mr. Beckendorff having well soaked in the hot fluid, eagerly devoured; and then taking up his violin, amused himself until his guests had finished their breakfast.

When Vivian had ended his meal, he left the Prince and Mr. Beckendorff alone, determined that his presence should not be the occasion of the Minister any longer retarding the commencement of business. The Prince, who by a private glance had been prepared for his departure, immediately took the opportunity of asking Mr. Beckendorff, in a very decisive tone, whether he might flatter himself that he could command his present attention to a subject of great importance. Mr. Beckendorff said that he was always at Mr. Von Philipson's service; and drawing a chair opposite him, the Prince and Mr. Beckendorff now sat on each side of the fire-place.

"Hem!" said the Prince, clearing his throat; and he looked at Mr. Beckendorff, who sat with his heels close together, his toes out square, his hands resting on his knees, which, as well as his elbows were turned out, his shoulders bent, his head reclined, and his eyes glancing.

"Hem!" said the Prince of Little Lilliput. "In compliance, Mr. Beckendorff, with your wish, developed in the communication received by me on the — inst., I assented in my answer to the arrangement then proposed; the object of which was, to use your own words, to facilitate the occurrence of an oral interchange of the sentiments of various parties interested in certain proceedings, by which interchange it was anticipated that the mutual interests might be respectively considered and finally arranged. Prior, Mr. Beckendorff, to either of us going into any detail upon these points of probable discussion, which will, in all likelihood, form the fundamental features of this interview, I wish to recall your attention to the paper which I had the honor of presenting to his Royal Highness, and which is alluded to in your communication of the — inst. The principal heads of that document I have brought with me abridged in this paper."

Here the Prince handed to Mr. Beckendorff a MS. pamphlet, consisting of about sixty foolscap sheets, closely written. The Minister bowed very graciously, as he took it from his Highness's hand; and then, without even looking at it, he laid it on the table.

"You, sir, I perceive," continued the Prince, "are acquainted with its contents; and it will therefore be unnecessary for me at present to expatiate upon their individual expediency, or to argue for their particular adoption. And, sir, when we observe the progress of the human mind, when we take into consideration the quick march of intellect, and the wide expansion of enlightened views and liberal principles—when we take a bird's eye view of the history of man from the earliest ages to the present moment, I feel that it would be folly in me to conceive for an instant, that the measures developed and recommended in that paper, will not finally receive the approbation of his Royal Highness. As to the exact origin of slavery, Mr. Beckendorff, I confess that I am not, at this moment, prepared distinctly to speak. That the divine author of our religion was its decided enemy, I am informed, is clear. That the slavery of ancient times was the origin of the feudal service of a more modern period, is a point on which men of learning have not precisely made up their minds. With regard to the exact state of the ancient German people, Tacitus affords us a great deal of most interesting information. Whether or not, certain passages which I have brought with me marked in the Germania, are incontestable evidences that our ancestors enjoyed or understeod the practice of a wise and well regulated liberty, is a point on which I shall be happy to receive the opinion of so distinguished a statesman as Mr. Beckendorff. In stepping forward, as I have felt it my duty to do, as the advocate of popular rights and national privileges, I am desirous to prove that I have not become the votary of innovation and the professor of revolutionary doctrines. The passages of the Roman author in question, and an ancient charter of the Emperor Charlemagne, are, I consider, decisive and sufficient precedents for the measures which I have thought proper to sanction by my approval, and to support by my influence. A Minister, Mr. Beckendorff, must take care that in the great race of politics, the minds of his countrymen do not leave his own behind them. We must never forget the powers and capabilities of man. On this very spot, perhaps, some centuries ago, savages clothed in skins were committing cannibalism in a forest. We must not forget, I repeat, that it is the business of those to whom Providence has allotted the responsible possession of power and influence—that it is their duty, our duty, Mr. Beckendorff—to become guardians of our weaker fellow-creatures—that all power is a trust—that we are accountable for its exercise—that, from the people, and for the people, all springs, and all must exist; and that, unless we conduct ourselves with the requisite wisdom, prudence, and propriety, the whole system of society will be disorganized; and this country, in particular, fall a victim to that system of corruption and misgovernment, which has already occasioned the destruction of the great kingdoms mentioned in the Bible; and many other States beside—Greece, Rome, Carthage, etc.

Thus ended the peroration of an harangue consisting of an incoherent arrangement of imperfectly remembered facts, and misunderstood principles; all gleaned by his Highness from the enlightening articles of the Reisenberg journals. Like Brutus, the Prince of Little Lilliput paused for a reply.

"Mr. Von Philipson," said his companion, when his Highness had finished, "you speak like a man of sense." Having given this answer, Mr. Beckendorff rose from his seat, and walked straight out of the room.

The Prince, at first, took the answer for a compliment; but Mr. Beckendorff not returning, he began to have a very faint idea that he was neglected. In this uncertainty, he rang the bell for his old friend Clara.

"Mrs. Clara! where is your master?"

"Just gone out, sir."

"How do you mean?"

"He has gone out with his gun, sir."

"You are quite sure he has gone out?"

"Quite sure, sir. I took him his coat and boots myself."

"I am to understand, then, that your master has gone out?"

"Yes, sir, Mr. Beckendorff has gone out. He will be home for his noon meal."

"That is enough!—Grey!" hallooed the indignant Prince, darting into the garden; "Grey! Grey! where are you, Grey?"

"Well, my dear Prince," said Vivian; "what can possibly be the matter?"

"The matter! insanity can be the only excuse; insanity can alone account for his preposterous conduct. We have seen enough of him. The repetition of absurdity is only wearisome. Pray assist me in getting our horses immediately."

"Certainly, if you please; but, remember, you brought me here as your friend and counsellor. As I have accepted the trust, I cannot help being sensible of the responsibility. Before, therefore, you finally resolve upon departure, pray let me be fully acquainted with the circumstance which has impelled you to this sudden resolution."

"Willingly, my good friend, could I only command my temper; and yet to fall into a passion with a madman is almost a mark of madness; but his manner and his conduct are so provoking and so puzzling, that I cannot altogether repress my irritability. And that ridiculous incognito! why I sometimes begin to think that I really am Mr. Von Philipson! An incognito, forsooth! for what? to deceive whom? His household, apparently, only consists of two persons, one of whom has visited me in my own castle; and the other is a cross old hag, who would not be able to comprehend my rank if she were aware of it. But to the point! When you left the room, I was determined to be trifled with no longer, and I asked him in a firm voice, and very marked manner, whether I might command his immediate attention to very important business. He professed to be at my service. I opened the affair by taking a cursory, yet definite, review of the principles in which my political conduct had originated, and on which it was founded. I flattered myself that I had produced an impression. Sometimes, my dear Grey, we are in a better cue for these expositions than at others, and to-day I was really unusually felicitous. My memory never deserted me. I was, at the same time, luminous and profound; and while I was guided by the philosophical spirit of the present day, I showed, by my various reading, that I respected the experience of antiquity. In short, I was perfectly satisfied with myself; and with the exception of one single point about the origin of slavery, which unfortunately got entangled with the feudal system, I could not have got on better had Sievers himself been at my side. Nor did I spare Mr. Beckendorff; but on the contrary, my good fellow, I said a few things which, had he been in his senses, must, I imagine, have gone home to his feelings. Do you know I finished by drawing his own character, and showing the inevitable effects of his ruinous policy; and what do you think he did?"

"Left you in a passion?"

"Not at all. He seemed very much struck by what I had said, and apparently understood it. I have heard that in some species of insanity the patient is perfectly able to comprehend every thing addressed to him, though at that point his sanity ceases, and he is unable to answer or to act. This must be Beckendorff's case; for no sooner had I finished, than he rose up immediately, and saying that I spoke like a man of sense, he abruptly quitted the room. The housekeeper says he will not be at home again till that infernal ceremony takes place, called the noon-meal. Now do not you advise me to be off as soon as possible?"

"It will require some deliberation. Pray did you not speak to him last night?"

"Ah! I forgot that I had not been able to speak to you since then. Well! last night, what do you think he did? When you were gone, he had the insolence to congratulate me on the opportunity then afforded of playing double dumbmy; and when I declined his proposition, but said that if he wished to have an hour's conversation I was at his service, he very coolly told me that he never talked, and bade me good night! Did you ever know such a madman? He never goes to bed. I only had a sofa. How the deuce did you sleep?"

"Well, and safely, considering that I was in a summer-house without lock or bolt."

"Well! I need not ask you now as to your opinion of our immediately getting off. We shall have, however, some trouble about our horses, for he will not allow a quadruped near the house, except some monster of an animal that he rides himself; and by St. Hubert! I cannot find out where our steeds are. What shall we do?" But Vivian did not answer. "Grey," continued his Highness, "what are you thinking of? Why don't you answer?"

"Your Highness must not go," said Vivian, shaking his head.

"Not go! why so, my good fellow?"

"Depend upon it, you are wrong about Beckendorff. That he is a humorist, there is no doubt; but it appears to me to be equally clear, that his queer habits and singular mode of life are not of late adoption. What he is now, he must have been these ten, perhaps these twenty years, perhaps more. Of this there are a thousand proofs about us. As to the overpowering cause which has made him the character he appears at present, it is needless for us to inquire. Probably some incident in his private life, in all likelihood connected with the mysterious picture. Let us be satisfied with the effect. If the case be as I state it, in his private life and habits Beckendorff must have been equally incomprehensible and equally singular at the very time that, in his public capacity, he was producing such brilliant results, as at the present moment. Now then, can we believe him to be insane? I anticipate your objections. I know you will enlarge upon the evident absurdity of his inviting his political opponent to his house, for a grave consultation on the most important affairs, and then treating him as he has done you; when it must be clear to him that you cannot be again duped, and when he must feel that were he to amuse you for as many weeks as he has days, your plans and your position would not be injuriously affected. Be it so.—Probably a humorist like Beckendorff cannot, even in the most critical moment, altogether restrain the bent of his capricious inclinations. However, my dear Prince, I will lay no stress upon this point. My opinion, indeed my conviction, is that Beckendorff acts from design. I have considered his conduct well; and I have observed all that you have seen, and more than you have seen, and keenly. Depend upon it, that since you assented to the interview, Beckendorff has been obliged to shift his intended position for negotiation. Some of the machinery has gone wrong. Fearful, if he had postponed your visit, you should imagine that he was only again amusing you, and consequently listen to no future overtures, he has allowed you to attend a conference for which he is not prepared. That he is making desperate exertions to bring the business to a point, is my firm opinion; and you would perhaps agree with me, were you as convinced as I am, that since we parted last night our host has been to Reisenberg and back again.

"To Reisenberg, and back again!"

"Ay! I rose this morning at an early hour, and imagining that both you and Beckendorff had not yet made your appearance, I escaped from the grounds, intending to explore part of the surrounding country. In my stroll I came to a narrow winding road, which I am convinced lies in the direction towards Reisenberg; there, for some reason or other, I loitered more than an hour, and very probably should have been too late for breakfast, had I not been recalled to myself by the approach of a horseman. It was Beckendorff, covered with dust and mud. His horse had been evidently hard ridden. I did not think much of it at the time, because I supposed he might have been out for three or four hours, and hard-worked, but I nevertheless was struck by his appearance; and when you mentioned that he went out riding at a late hour last night, it immediately occurred to me, that had he come home at one or two o'clock, it was not very probable that he would have gone out again at four or five. I have no doubt that my conjecture is correct—Beckendorff has been at Reisenberg."

"You have placed this business in a new and important light," said the Prince, his expiring hopes reviving; "what, then, do you advise me to do?"

"To be quiet. If your own view of the case be right, you can act as well to-morrow or the next day as this moment; on the contrary, if mine be the correct one, a moment may enable Beckendorff himself to bring affairs to a crisis. In either case, I should recommend you to be silent, and in no manner to allude any more to the object of your visit. If you speak, you only give opportunities to Beckendorff of ascertaining your opinions and your inclinations; and your silence, after such frequent attempts on your side to promote discussion upon business, will soon be discovered by him to be systematic. This will not decrease his opinion of your sagacity and firmness. The first principle of negotiation is to make your advèrsary respect you."

After long consultation, the Prince determined to follow Vivian's advice; and so firmly did he adhere to his purpose, that when he met Mr. Beckendorff at the noon meal, he asked him, with a very embarrassed voice and manner, "what sport he had had in the morning?"

The noon meal again consisted of a single dish, as exquisitely dressed, however, as the preceding one. It was a splendid haunch of venison.

prised when Mr. Beckendorff asked him the magnitude of Mirac in Boötes; and the Prince confessing his utter ignorance of the subject, the Minister threw aside his unfinished Planisphere, and drew his chair to them at the table. It was with great pleasure that his Highness perceived a bottle of his favorite Tokay; and with no little astonishment he observed, that to-day, there were three wine-glasses placed before them. They were of peculiar beauty, and almost worthy, for their elegant shapes and great antiquity, of being included in the collection of the Duke of Schloss-Johannisberger.

"Your praise of my cellar, sir," said Mr. Beckendorff, very graciously, "has made me turn wine-drinker." So saying, the Minister took up one of the rare glasses and held it to the light. His keen, glancing eye, detected an almost invisible cloud on the side of the delicate glass, and jerking it across him, he flung it into the farthest corner of the room—it was shivered into a thousand pieces. He took up the second glass, examined it very narrowly, and then sent it, with equal force, after its companion. The third one shared the same fate. He rose and rang the bell.

"Clara!" said Mr. Beckendorff, in his usual tone of voice, "some clean glasses, and sweep away that litter in the corner."

"He is mad, then!" thought the Prince of Little Lilliput, and he shot a glance at his companion, which Vivian could not misunderstand.

"This is my dinner, gentlemen," said Beckendorff; "let it be your luncheon; I have ordered your dinner at sunset."

After having eaten a slice of the haunch, Mr. Beckendorff rose from table, and said, "We will have our wine in the drawing-room, Mr. Von Philipson, and then you will not be disturbed with my birds."

He left the room.

To the drawing-room, therefore, his two guests soon adjourned. They found him busily employed with his pencil. The Prince thought it must be a chart or a fortification at least, and was rather sur-

After exhausting their bottle, in which they were assisted to the extent of one glass by their host, who drank Mr. Von Philipson's health with cordiality, they assented to Mr. Beckendorff's proposition of visiting his fruitery.

To the Prince's great relief, dinner time soon arrived; and having employed a couple of hours on that meal very satisfactorily, he and Vivian adjourned to the drawing-room, having previously pledged their honor to each other, that nothing should again induce them again to play dumbmy whist. Their resolutions and their promises were needless. Mr. Beckendorff, who was sitting opposite the fire when they came into the room, neither by word nor motion acknowledged that he was aware of their entrance. Vivian found refuge in a book; and the Prince, after having examined and re-examined the brilliant birds that figured on the drawing-room paper, fell asleep upon the sofa. Mr. Beckendorff took down the guitar, and accompanied himself in a low voice for some time; then he suddenly ceased, and stretching out his legs, and supporting his thumbs in the arm-holes of his waistcoat, he leaned back in his chair, and remained perfectly motionless, with his eyes fixed upon the picture. Vivian, in turn gazed upon this singular being, and the fair pictured form which he seemed to idolize. Was he, too, unhappy? Had he, too, been bereft in the hour of his proud and perfect joy? Had he, too, lost a virgin bride?—His agony overcame him, the book fell from his hand, and he groaned aloud! Mr. Beckendorff started, and the Prince awoke. Vivian, confounded, and unable to overpower his emotions, uttered some hasty words, explanatory, apologetical, and contradictory, and retired. In his walk to the summer-house, a man passed him. In spite of a great cloak, Vivian recognized him as their messenger and guide; and his ample mantle did not conceal his riding-boots, and the spurs which glistened in the moonlight.

It was an hour past midnight when the door of the summer-house softly opened, and Mr. Beckendorff entered. He started when he found Vivian still undressed, and pacing up and down the little chamber. The young man made an effort, when he witnessed an intruder, to compose a countenance whose agitation could not be concealed.

"What, are you up again?" said Mr. Beckendorff. "Are you ill?"

"Would I were as well in mind as in body! I have not yet been to rest. We cannot command our feelings at all moments, sir; and at this, especially, I felt that I had a right to consider myself alone."

"I most exceedingly regret that I have disturbed you," said Mr. Beckendorff, in a very kind voice, and in a manner which responded to the sympathy of his tone. "I thought that you had been long asleep. There is a star which I cannot exactly make out. I fancy it must be a comet, and so I ran to the observatory; but let me not disturb you," and Mr. Beckendorff was retiring.

"You do not disturb me, sir. I cannot sleep;—pray ascend."

"Oh, no! never mind the star. But if you really have no inclination to sleep, let us sit down, and have a little conversation; or perhaps we had better take a stroll. It is a very warm night." As he spoke, Mr. Beckendorff gently put his arm within Vivian's and led him down the steps.

"Are you an astronomer, sir?" asked Beckendorff.

"I can tell the Great Bear from the Little Dog; but I confess that I look upon the stars rather in a poetical than a scientific spirit."

"Hum! I confess I do not."

"There are moments," continued Vivian, "when I cannot refrain from believing that these mysterious luminaries have more influence over our fortunes than modern times are disposed to believe. I feel that I am getting less sceptical, perhaps I should say more credulous, every day; but sorrow makes us superstitious."

"I discard all such fantasies," said Mr. Beckendorff; "they only tend to enervate our mental energies, and paralyze all human exertion. It is the belief in these, and a thousand other deceits I could mention, which teach man that he is not the master of his own mind, but the ordained victim, or the chance sport of circumstances; that makes millions pass through life unimpressive as shadows; and has gained for this existence the stigma of a vanity which it does not deserve."

"I wish that I could think as you do," said Vivian; "but the experience of my life forbids me. Within only these last two years, my career has, in so many instances, indicated that I am not the master of my own conduct, that, no longer able to resist the conviction which is hourly impressed on me, I recognize in every contingency the preordination of my fate."

"A delusion of the brain!" said Beckendorff, very quickly. "Fate, Destiny, Chance, particular and special Providence—idle words! Dismiss them all, sir! A man's Fate is his own temper; and according to that will be his opinion as to the particular manner in which the course of events is regulated. A consistent man believes in Destiny—a capricious man in Chance."

"But, sir, what is a man's temper? It may be changed every hour. I started in life with very different feelings to those which I profess at this moment. With great deference to you, I imagine that you mistake the effect for the cause; for surely temper is not the origin, but the result of those circumstances of which we are all the creatures."

"Sir, I deny it. Man is not the creature of circumstances. Circumstances are the creatures of men. We are free agents, and man is more powerful than matter. I recognize no intervening influence between that of the established course of Nature and my own mind. Truth may be distorted —may be stifled—be suppressed. The invention of cunning deceits may, and in some instances does, prevent man from exercising his own powers. They have made him responsible to a realm of shadows, and a suitor in a court of shades. He is ever dreading authority which does not exist, and fearing the occurrence of penalties which there are none to enforce. But the mind that dares to extricate itself from these vulgar prejudices, that proves its loyalty to its Creator by devoting all its adoration to His glory—such a spirit as this becomes a master-mind, and that master-mind will invariably find that circumstances are its slaves."

"Mr. Beckendorff, yours is a very bold philosophy, of which I, myself, was once a votary. How successful in my service, you may judge by finding me a wanderer."

"Sir! your present age is the age of error; your whole system is founded on a fallacy; you believe that man's temper can change. I deny it. If you have ever seriously entertained the views which I profess; if, as you lead me to suppose, you have dared to act upon them, and failed; sooner or later, whatever may be your present conviction and your present feelings, you will recur to your original wishes and your original pursuits. With a mind experienced and matured, you may in all probability be successful; and then I suppose, stretching your legs in your easy chair you will at the same moment be convinced of your own genius, and recognize your own Destiny!"

"With regard to myself, Mr. Beckendorff, I am convinced of the erroneousness of your views. It is my opinion, that no one who has dared to think, can look upon this world in any other than a mournful spirit. Young as I am, nearly two years have elapsed since, disgusted with the world of politics, I retired to a foreign solitude. At length, with passions subdued, and, as I flatter myself, with a mind matured, convinced of the vanity of all human affairs, I felt emboldened once more partially to mingle with my species. Bitter as my lot had been, as a philosopher, I had discovered the origin of my misery in my own unbridled passions; and, tranquil and subdued, I now trusted to pass through life as certain of no fresh sorrows, as I was of no fresh joys. And yet, sir, I am at this moment sinking under the infliction of unparalleled misery—misery which I feel I have a right to believe was undeserved. But why expatiate to a stranger on sorrow which must be secret? I deliver myself up to my remorseless Fate."

"What is Grief?" said Mr. Beckendorff;—"if it be exhibited by the fear of some contingency, instead of grieving, a man should exert his energies, and prevent its occurrence. If, on the contrary, it be caused by an event, that which has been occasioned by any thing human, by the co-operation of human circumstances, can be, and invariably is, removed by the same means. Grief is the agony of an instant; the indulgence of Grief, the blunder of a life. Mix in the world, and in a month's time you will speak to me very differently. A young man, you meet with disappointment,—in spite of all your exalted notions of your own powers, you immediately sink under it. If your belief of your powers were sincere, you should have proved it by the manner in which you struggled against adversity, not merely by the mode in which you labored for advancement. The latter is but a very inferior merit. If in fact you wish to succeed, success, I repeat, is at your command. You talk to me of your experience; and do you think that my sentiments are the crude opinions of an unpractised man? Sir! I am not fond of conversing with any person; and therefore, far from being inclined to maintain an argument in a spirit of insincerity, merely for the sake of a victory of words. Mark what I say; it is truth. No minister ever yet fell, but from his own inefficiency. If his downfall be occasioned, as it generally is, by the intrigues of one of his own creatures, his downfall is merited for having been the dupe of a tool, which, in all probability he should never have employed. If he fall through the open attacks of his political opponents, his downfall is equally deserved, for having occasioned by his impolicy, the formation of a party; for having allowed it to be formed; or for not having crushed it when formed. No conjecture can possibly occur, however fearful, however tremendous it may appear, from which a man, by his own energy, may not extricate himself—as a mariner by the rattling of his cannon can dissipate the impending water-spout!"

ABERNETHYANA.

FROM VARIOUS SOURCES.

ABERNETHY's mind disqualified him from adopting that affected interest which distinguishes many of the well-bred physicians, and he heartily despised their little arts to acquire popularity. He seemed to feel as if he mentally expressed himself thus:—"Here I am, ready to give my advice if you want it; but you must take it as you find it, and if you don't like it, egad (his favorite word), you may go about your business—I don't want any thing to do with you; hold your tongue and be off." In some such mood as this, he received a visit from a lady one day, who was well acquainted with his invincible repugnance to her sex's predominant disposition, and who therefore forbore speaking but simply in reply to his laconic queries. The consultation was conducted during three visits in the following manner:—First day.—Lady enters and holds out her finger. Abernethy: "Cut?" Lady: "Bite." A.: "Dog?" L.: "Parrot." A.: "Go home and poultice it." Second day.—Finger held out again. A.: "Better?" L.: "Worse." A.: "Go home and poultice it again." Third day.—Finger held out as before. A.: "Better?" L.: "Well." A.: "You're the most sensible woman I ever met with. Good-by. Get out."

Another lady, having scalded her arm, called at the usual hour to show it three successive days, when similar laconic conversations took place. First day.—Patient, exposing the arm, says—"Burnt." A.: "I see it," and having prescribed a lotion, she departs. Second day.—Patient shows the arm, and says—"Better." A.: "I know it." Third day.—Again showing the arm. Patient: "Well." A.: "Any fool can tell that. What do you come again for? Get away."

A very talkative lady, who had wearied the temper of Mr. Abernethy, which was at all times impatient of gabble, was told by him, the first time that he could get a chance of speaking, to be good enough to put out her tongue. "Now, pray, madam," said he, playfully, "*keep it out.*" He rarely met with his match except upon one occasion, when he was sent for by an inn-keeper, who had had a quarrel with his wife, and who had scored his face with her nails, so that the poor man was bleeding and much disfigured. Mr. Abernethy considered this an opportunity not to be lost for admonishing the offender, and said, "Madam, are you not ashamed of yourself to treat your husband thus, who is the head of you all—your *head*, madam?" "Well, Doctor," fiercely retorted the virago, "and may I not scratch my own head?"

A patient consulted Mr. Abernethy for a pain in the arm, and holding it up in the air, said, "It always gives me pain when I hold it up so." A.: "Then why the devil do you hold it up so?"

In all cases of obesity and repletion, Mr. Abernethy was especially impatient, and indisposed to prescribe. A portly gentleman from the country once called on him for advice, and received the following answer:—"You nasty beast, you go and fill your g—, and then you come to me to empty them."

A young lady was brought one morning by her

mamma, complaining of difficulty of breathing when taking exercise, and after her meals. Perceiving her to be very tightly laced round the waist, Mr. Abernethy seized a pair of scissors, and, without saying a word, ripped up the stays from top to bottom, and then desired her to walk about for ten minutes. The injunction being complied with accordingly, he demanded how she felt. "Better," was the reply. The mandate was repeated, and the walk being finished, he asked, "How now?" "Quite well," was the answer. Abernethy: "That will do. Take her away, and don't let her wear tight stays." In such a case a common physician would probably prescribe to oblige the apothecary, and to please the patient. The eccentric professor went directly to the cause at once, and removed it, without caring who was pleased or who not so, having no sinister object in view. Another young lady was one summer morning brought to him by her mother, in consequence of the former having swallowed a spider. Mr. Abernethy dexterously caught a blue-bottle fly as it flew by him, and told the patient to put it into her mouth, and if she spit it out in a few minutes, the spider would come out with it.

A lawyer having called to show the state of his leg, proceeded to remove the bandages, which Mr. Abernethy endeavored to prevent, every now and then repeating, "No, no, that will do; shut it up—shut it up." Accordingly, the lawyer yielded at length, but determined on revenge. Mr. Abernethy having simply prescribed for the stomach, without regard to the leg, the patient tendered a shilling, and prepared to depart, when the former, missing the expected sovereign, observed that there must be some mistake. "No, no," said the lawyer, advancing to the door, "that will do—that will do; shut it up—shut it up."

The Sublime and the Ridiculous.—"Now," (said Mr. Abernethy, in a lecture upon the muscles of the scalp,) "I will tell you a perfectly ridiculous story about this, with a view to impress this part of the subject on your minds. It happened in the early part of my time, to become quite the fashion to put half a pound of grease, and another half-pound of flour, on a man's head—what they called hair-dressing; it was the fashion, too, to bind this round with a piece of tape or riband, and make a tail of it, and it was the mode to wear those tails very thick and rather short. Now, a gentleman who possessed great power in the motion of his *frons occipitalis*, used to go to the boxes of the theatre when Mrs. Siddons first appeared, and I don't believe there ever will be such an actress again as she was, nor do I believe there ever was her equal before her. However, when people were affected beyond all description, and when they were all drowned in tears at her performance, this chap wagged his tail enormously, and all the people burst out into a roar of laughter. In vain did they cry, 'Turn him out!" in vain did they cry, 'Throw him over!' When he had produced this effect upon the audience, then he kept his tail quiet; but again, no sooner was their attention engaged, than wag went his tail, and again were the bursts of laughter re-echoed."

CHARLES MATHEWS, THE ELDER.

The Silver Spoon.—Amongst Mathews's pranks of younger days, that is to say, when he first came from York to the Haymarket theatre, he was invited, with F—— and some other performers, to dine with Mr. A——, now an eminent silversmith, but who, at that period, followed the business of a pawnbroker. It so happened that A—— was called out of the parlor, at the back of the shop, during dinner. Mathews, with wonderful celerity, altering his hair, countenance, hat, etc., took a large gravy-spoon off the dinner-table, ran instantly into the street, entered one of the little dark doors leading to the pawnbroker's counter, and actually pledged to the unconscious A—— his own gravy-spoon. Mathews contrived with equal rapidity to return and seat himself, (having left the street door open,) before A—— re-appeared at the dinner-table. As a matter of course, the spoon was made the subject of a wager. An *eclaircissement* took place before the party broke up, to the infinite astonishment of A——.

The First Dead-Head.—"Who was the first man recorded in history who didn't pay?" said Mathews, as he was handing a theatrical order to a friend. "Why, really, I never gave it a thought," replied the friend. "Why, Joseph, of course," said Mathews; "did not his brothers put him in the pit for nothing?"

Outpipped.—Melvin, the comedian, was a *bon-vivant*, and fond of a game at whist. One day, he brought a bottle of choice brandy into the green room, with his name and direction written on the back of the seven of clubs, attached to the neck of the bottle. Mathews, observing the bottle on the table, said, "Are you not afraid of losing that brandy?" "How so?" "Why, some one might come into the room with the *eight* of clubs, and take it."

Lots of Berries.—Our comedian was served by a green-grocer, named Berry, and generally settled his bill once a quarter. At one time the account was sent in before it was due, and Mathews, laboring under an idea that his credit was doubted, said, "Here's a pretty *mull, Berry*. You have sent in your *bill, Berry*, before it is *due, Berry*. Your father, the *elder Berry*, would not have been such a *goose, Berry;* but you need not look so *black, Berry*, for I don't care a *straw, Berry*, and shan't pay you till *Christmas, Berry*."

The Builder of his own Fortune.—Charles Mathews, Jr., was brought up as an architect. The father was once asked by a friend, what profession the young man was to be. "Why," said the comedian, "he is to *draw houses*, as his father does."

Queer Comfort.—Mathews used to tell, with great zest, a remark made to him by a Warwick goaler, while exhibiting the specialities of the prison. When he came to "the place of execution,"

Mathews remarked that, considering the extent of the country, and the number of executions which might take place, the drop struck him as being very small? "I don't know," said the man, "to be sure, six 'ould be crowded, but foive 'ould hang very comfortable!"

A Spanish Ambassador.—Mathews once personated a Spanish Ambassador; a frolic enacted by him at an inn at Dartford. An account of the freak was written by the late Mr. Hill, who took part in the joke, acting as Mathews's interpreter. He called it his "Recollections of his Excellency, the Spanish Ambassador's visit to Captain Selby, on board the *Prince Regent*, one of his Majesty's frigates stationed at the Nore, by the Interpreter."

The party hired a private coach, of large capacity, and extremely showy, to convey them to Gravesend, as the *suite* of Mathews, who personated an ambassador from Madrid to the English Government; and four smart lads, who were intrusted with the secret by the payment of a liberal fee. The drivers proved faithful to their promise. When they arrived at the posting-house at Dartford, one of the drivers dismounted, and communicated to the inn-keeper the character of the nobleman (Mr. Mathews) inside the coach, and that his mission to London had been attended with the happiest result. The report spread through Dartford like wildfire, and in about ten minutes the carriage (having by previous arrangement been detained) was surrounded by at least two hundred people, all with cheers and gratulations, anxious to gain a view of the important personage, who, decked out with nearly twenty different stage jewels, representing sham orders, bowed with obsequious dignity to the assembled multitude. It was settled that the party should dine and sleep at the Falcon Tavern, Gravesend, where a sumptuous dinner was provided for his excellency and *suite*. Previously, however, to dinner-time, and to heighten the joke, they promenaded the town and its environs, followed by a large assemblage of men, women, and children, at a respectful distance, all of whom preserved the greatest decorum. The interpreter (Mr. Hill) seemed to communicate and explain to the ambassador whatever was of interest in their perambulation. On their return to the inn, the crowd gradually dispersed. The dinner was served in a sumptuous style, and two or three additional waiters, dressed in their holiday clothes, were hired for the occasion.

The ambassador, by medium of his interpreter, asked for two soups, and a portion of four different dishes of fish, with oil, vinegar, mustard, pepper, salt, and sugar, in the same plate, which, *apparently* to the eyes of the waiters, and to their utter astonishment and surprise, he eagerly devoured. The waiters had been cautioned by one of the *suite* not to notice the manner in which his Excellency ate his dinner, lest it should offend him; and their occasional absence from the room gave Mathews or his companion an opportunity of depositing the incongruous medley in the ashes under the grate—a large fire having been provided. The ambassador continued to mingle the remaining viands, during dinner, in a similar heterogeneous way. The chamber in which his Excellency slept was brilliantly illuminated with wax candles, and in one corner of the room a table was fitted up, under the direction of one of the party, to represent an oratory, with such appropriate apparatus as could best be procured. A private sailing-barge was moored at the stairs by the Fountain early the next morning, to convey the ambassador and his attendants to the *Prince Regent*, at the Nore. The people again assembled in vast multitudes to witness the embarkation. Carpets were placed on the stairs at the water's edge, for the state and comfort of his Excellency, who, the instant he entered the barge, turned around and bade a grateful farewell to the multitude, at the same time placing his hand upon his bosom, and taking off his huge cocked hat. The captain of the barge, a supremely illiterate, good-humored cockney, was introduced most ceremoniously to the ambassador, and purposely placed on his right hand. It is impossible to describe the variety of absurd and extravagant stratagems practised on the credulity of the captain by Mathews, and with consummate success, until the barge arrived in sight of the King's frigate, which, by a previous understanding, recognized the ambassador by signals. The officers were all dressed in full uniform, and prepared to receive him. When on board, the whole party threw off their disguises, and were entertained by Captain Selby with a splendid dinner, to which the lieutenants of the ship were invited. After the banquet, Mathews, in his own character, kept the company in a high state of merriment by his incomparable mimic powers for more than ten hours, incorporating with admirable effect the entire narrative of the journey to Gravesend, and his "acts and deeds" at the Falcon. Towards the close of the feast, and about half an hour before the party took their departure, in order to give the commander and his officers a "touch of his quality," Mathews assumed his ambassadorial attire, and the captain of the barge, still in ignorance of the joke, was introduced into the cabin, between whom and his Excellency an indescribable scene of rich burlesque was enacted. The party left the ship for Gravesend at four o'clock in the morning—Mathews, in his "habit as he lived," with the addition of a pair of spectacles, which he had a peculiar way of wearing to conceal his identity, even from the most acute observer. Mathews again resumed his station by the side of the captain, as a person who had left the frigate for a temporary purpose. The simple captain recounted to Mathews all that the Spanish ambassador had enacted, both in his transit from Gravesend to the Nore, and whilst he (the captain) was permitted to join the festive board in the cabin, with singular fidelity, and to the great amusement of the original party, who, during the whole of this ambassadorial excursion, never lost their gravity, except when they were left to themselves. They landed at Gravesend, and from thence departed to London, luxuriating upon the hoax.

John P. Kemble and his Cat.—Mr. Mathews and Mr. Kemble had been dining together at Mr. Charles Kemble's house. Mr. John Kemble had taken much wine, and when the party broke up, Mr. Mathews determined to accompany the tragedian to his own door. Giving him his arm, therefore, they proceeded slowly to Mr. Kemble's house in Great Russell street, Bloomsbury. The tragedian was full of talk, and '*very happy*,' as it is *called;* and although the hour was late, his pressing invitation to his friend to enter the house with him induced the comedian to obey. It was evident that the man who opened the door was the only person who was up in the establishment. Mr. Kemble went into his library, accompanied by Mr. Mathews, and desired the attendant to bring a tray, at the same time with great formality introducing him to the notice of his guest as the 'gentleman who did him the honor to take care of his wine,' etc. It was in vain that Mr. Mathews protested against further hospitality. Mr. Kemble was too much excited to have his spirits easily laid: and, surrounded as he was with books, he began a disquisition upon their authors, above all, his '*beloved Shakspere*,' on whom he discoursed most eloquently, after taking a volume from the shelf, and devoutly kissing the binding. At length, the tray was brought in with wine, wine and water, etc., and with it entered an enormous cat, decorated with a red collar and a bell.

The appearance of his favorite cat called forth its master's most affectionate notice, and many relations of its extraordinary power of understanding, its devoted attachment to its master's person, etc., were detailed to Mr. Mathews. *Mustapha*, Mr. Kemble declared, had much of human feeling of the best kind in his composition; he described how he watched his return home, mourned his absence, etc., and grew maudlin in his praise. The animal seemed happy in its master's presence, and looked up in his face, as it composedly lay down before him. Mr. Mathews mewed; Mr. Kemble, turning round at this sound, which he believed to proceed from the cat, observed, 'There, my dear Mathews, do you hear that? Now that creature knows all I say of him, and is replying to it.' This amused the comedian, and he repeated the experiment in all the varieties of feline intonation, mewing, purring, etc. Mr. Kemble at last said to him, in his slow and measured tones, 'Now, you don't know what he means by *that*, but *I do.* Mus! Mus! (on every reiteration of this affectionate diminutive raising his voice to its most tragic expression of tenderness)—'umph! My dear sir, that creature *knows* that it is beyond my usual time of sitting up, and he's uneasy! Mus! Mus!'—but Mus was sleepy and inattentive, and his master resumed his criticisms upon the different readings of Shakspere; talked also of Lope de Vega, and was again interrupted by a *mew*, as he believed, from the dissatisfied Mus. 'What,' asked his fond master, looking down upon him, 'what is it you desire, my good friend!' (Mus, *alias* Mathews, mewed once more, in a more supplicating and more touching tone.) 'Well, well! I understand you; you want to go to bed. Well, I suppose I must indulge you.'

Here Mr. Kemble deliberately arose, put down his book upon the table, with its face open at the page to which he referred, took a measured pinch of snuff, and tottered to the door, which he with difficulty opened. He then awaited Mustapha's exit; but Mustapha, having no *voice* in the affair, preferred remaining where he was; and his master kindly reproached him with being a '*little capricious* in first asking to go, and then preferring to stay.' With a smile and look at Mr. Mathews of the gentlest indulgence towards his favorite's humor, he tottered back again to his chair, resumed his declamatory observations upon the relative powers of dramatic writers and their essential requisites, till the troublesome Mustapha again renewed his mewing solicitations. Mr. Kemble once more stopped, and looking again at the imaginary cause of his interruption, with philosophic patience, asked: 'Well, Mus, what would you have?' Then, after another pause, turning to his guest, said: 'Now, my dear Mathews, you are fond of animals, and ought to know this one; he's a perfect character for you to study. Now, sir, *that cat* knows that I shall be ill to-morrow, and he's uneasy at my sitting up.' Then, benevolently looking at the cat, he added: 'Umph! my dear Mus, I must beg your indulgence, my good friend; I really cannot go to bed yet.' Mus whined his reply, and his master declared that the cat asked to be allowed to go away.

On the door being a second time opened, after similar exertion on Mr. Kemble's part to effect this courtesy, and several grave chirpings in order to entice Mus from the fire-place, the animal at length left the room. Mr. Kemble then returned, as before, to his seat, drank another glass of wine and water, and just as he was comfortably established, the incorrigible Mus was heard in the passage again, in loud lament and importunate demand for re-admittance. 'Umph!' said Mr. Kemble, with another pinch of snuff, 'now that animal is not happy, after all, sir, away from me.' (Mus was louder than ever at this moment.) 'Why, what ails the creature? Surely there is more in this than we dream of, Mathews. You, who have studied such beings, ought to be able to explain.' Poor Mus made another pathetic appeal for re-admission, and his master's heart was not made of flint. Mr. Kemble apologized to his guest for these repeated interruptions, and managed once more to make his way to the door. After opening it, and waiting a minute for the re-entrance of his favorite, but not seeing it, he smiled at the comedian with the same indulgent expression as before, and remarked:—'Now, would you believe it, Mathews, that *extraordinary* animal was affronted at not being let in again on his first appeal! and now it is his humor not to come at all! *Mus! Mustapha! Mus!*' But as no Mus appeared, the door was closed with the same deliberation, and Mr. Kemble once more contrived to regain his chair, and recommenced, quite unobservant of the almost hysterical fit of laughter to which the comedian was by this time reduced, at the imposition he had so successfully, though in the first place so unintentionally, practised upon the credulity of his grave and unsuspecting friend. But it did not end here; for Mr. Mathews reiterated his imitations, and Mr. Kemble again remarked upon his favorite's peculiarities of temper, etc., again went to the door—again returned, till even 'Mr. Midnight' (as some intimate friends christened Mr. Mathews, from his love of late hours) felt it time to retire, and leave Mr. Kemble, which he did as he saw him fall asleep, in the act of representing his idea of the sick king in 'Henry IV.,' with his pocket handkerchief spread over his head as a substitute for the characteristic drapery of the dying monarch.

HIS LAST JOKE.—Mathews's attendant, in his last illness, intended to give the patient some medicine, but, a few moments after, it was discovered that the medicine was nothing but ink, which had been taken from the phial by mistake, and his friend exclaimed, "Good Heavens! Mathews, I have given you ink." "Never—never mind, my boy—never mind," said Mathews, faintly—"*I'll swallow a bit of blotting-paper.*" This was the last joke Mathews ever made.

THOUGHTS AND OPINIONS OF S. T. COLERIDGE.

Jews.—Coleridge relates: "I have had a good deal to do with Jews in the course of my life, although I never borrowed any money of them. The other day, I was what you may call *floored* by a Jew. He passed me several times, crying for old clothes in the most nasal and extraordinary tone I ever heard. At last, I was so provoked, that I said to him: 'Pray, why can't you say "old clothes" in a plain way, as I do now?' The Jew stopped, and, looking very gravely at me, said, in a clear and even fine accent, 'Sir, I can say "old clothes" as well as you can; but if you had to say so ten times a minute, for an hour together, you would say *ogh clo* as I do now;' and so he marched off. I was so confounded with the justice of his retort, that I followed and gave him a shilling, the only one I had.

"Once, I sat in a coach opposite a Jew; a symbol of old clothes-bags; an Isaiah of Holywell-street. He would close the window; I opened it. He closed it again; upon which, in a very solemn tone, I said to him: 'Son of Abraham! thou smellest; son of Isaac! thou art offensive; son of Jacob! thou stinkest foully. See the man in the moon! he is holding his nose at that distance: dost thou think that I, sitting here, can endure it any longer?' My Jew was astounded, opened the window forthwith himself, and said, 'he was sorry he did not know before I was so great a gentleman.'"

School Discipline.—In Coleridge's time, the discipline at Christ's Hospital was ultra-Spartan; all domestic ties were to be put aside. "Boy!" Coleridge remembered Bona saying to him once, when he was crying, the first day after his return from the holidays, "Boy! the school is your father! Boy! the school is your mother! Boy! the school is your brother! the school is your sister! the school is your first cousin, and your second cousin, and all the rest of your relations! Let's have no more crying."

Thelwall and Coleridge were sitting once in a beautiful recess in the Quantock hills, when the latter said, "Citizen John, this is a fine place to talk treason in!" "Nay, citizen Samuel," replied he; "it is rather a place to make a man forget that there is any necessity for treason!"

Stammering is sometimes the cause of a pun. Some one was mentioning in Lamb's presence the cold-heartedness of the Duke of Cumberland, in restraining the Duchess in rushing up to the embrace of her son, whom she had not seen for a considerable time, and insisting on her receiving him in state. "How horribly *cold* it was," said the narrator. "Yes," said Lamb, in his stuttering way, "but you know he is the Duke of *Cu-cum-ber-land*."

The Poets in a Puzzle.—Cottle, in his life of Coleridge, relates the following amusing incident:—"I led my horse to the stable, where a sad perplexity arose. I removed the harness without difficulty; but, after many strenuous attempts, I could not remove the collar. In despair I called for assistance, when Mr. Wordsworth brought his ingenuity into exercise; but, after several unsuccessful efforts, he relinquished the achievement as a thing altogether impracticable. Mr. Coleridge now tried his hand, but showed no more skill than his predecessor; for, after twisting the poor horse's neck almost to strangulation, and the great danger of his eyes, he gave up the useless task, pronouncing that the horse's head must have grown since the collar was put on; 'for,' he said, 'it was a downright impossibility for such a huge *os frontis* to pass through so narrow an aperture.' Just at this instant, a servant-girl came near, and understanding the cause of our consternation, 'Ha! masters,' said she, 'you don't go about the work in the right way. You should do like this,' when, turning the collar upside down, she slipped it off in a moment, to our great humiliation and wonderment, each satisfied afresh that there were heights of knowledge in the world to which we had not yet attained."

False Estimate.—Kean once played *Young Norval* to Mrs. Siddons's *Lady Randolph:* after the play, as Kean used to relate, Mrs. Siddons came to him, and patting him on the head, said, "You have played very well, sir, very well. It's a pity,—but there's too little of you to do any thing." Coleridge said of this "little" actor:—"Kean is original; but he copies from himself. His rapid descents from the hyper-tragic to the infra-colloquial, though sometimes productive of great effect, are often unreasonable. To see him act, is like reading Shakspere by flashes of lightning. I do not think him thorough-bred gentleman enough to play *Othello*."

Coleridge "Done Up."—"It is not easy to put me out of countenance, or interrupt the feeling of the time by mere external noise or circumstance; yet once I was thoroughly *done up*, as you would say. I was reciting, at a particular house, the 'Remorse;' and was in the midst of *Alhadra's* description of the death of her husband, when a scrubby boy, with a shining face set in dirt, burst open the door and cried out—'Please, ma'am, master says, Will you ha', or will you *not* ha', the pin-round?'"

Ear and Taste for Music.—"An ear for music is a very different thing from a taste for music. I have no ear whatever; I could not sing an air to save my life; but I have the intensest delight in music, and can detect good from bad. Naldi, a good fellow, remarked to me once at a concert, that I did not seem much interested with a piece of Rossini's which had just been performed. I said it sounded to me like nonsense verses. But I could scarcely contain myself when a thing of Beethoven's followed."

Shakspere.—It is Shakspere's peculiar excellence that, throughout the whole of his splendid picture-gallery, (the reader will excuse the confessed inadequacy of this metaphor,) we find individuality every where, mere portrait nowhere. In all his various characters we still feel ourselves communing with the same human nature, which is every where present, as the vegetable sap in the branches, sprays, leaves, buds, blossoms, and fruits,—their shapes, tastes, and odors.

Criticism.—As soon as a critic betrays that he knows more of his author than the author's publications could have told him;—as soon as from this more intimate knowledge, elsewhere obtained, he avails himself of the slightest *trait* against the author, his censure immediately becomes personal injury—his sarcasms personal insults. He ceases to be a CRITIC, and takes on him the most contemptible character to which a rational creature can be degraded—that of a gossip, backbiter, and pasquilant: but with this heavy aggravation, that he steals with the unquiet, the deforming passions of the world, into the museum; into the very place which, next to the chapel and oratory, should be our sanctuary, and secure place of refuge; offers abominations on the altar of the muses, and makes its sacred paling the very circle in which he conjures up the lying and profane spirit.

MODERN SATIRISTS.—In this age of personality—this age of literary and political gossiping, the meanest insects are worshipped with a sort of Egyptian superstition, if only the brainless head be atoned for by the sting of personal malignity in the tail. The most vapid satires have become the objects of a keen public interest, purely from the number of contemporary characters named in the patchwork notes, (which possess, however, the comparative merit of being more poetical than the text,) and because, to increase the stimulus, the author has sagaciously left his own name for whispers and conjectures.

MATERIALS OF POETRY.—Good sense is the *body* of poetic genius, fancy its *drapery*, motion its *life*, and imagination the *soul* that is every where, and in each; and forms all into one graceful and intelligent whole.

ILL-DESERVED COMMENDATION.—Praises of the unworthy are felt by ardent minds as robberies of the deserving.

SHAKSPERE AND MILTON.—Shakspere, no mere child of nature—no automaton of genius—no passive vehicle of inspiration, possessed by the spirit, *not* possessing it,—first studied patiently, meditated deeply, understood minutely, till knowledge became habitual and intuitive, wedded itself to his habitual feelings, and at length gave birth to that stupendous power, by which he stands alone, with no equal or second in his own class—to that power which seated him on one of the two glory-smitten summits of the poetic mountain, with Milton as his compeer, not rival. While the former darts himself forth, and passes into all the forms of human character and passion,—the one Proteus of the fire and the flood; the other attracts all forms and things to himself, into the unity of his own *ideal*.

THE REPROOF AND REPLY:

Or, the Flower-thief's Apology for a Robbery committed in Mr. and Mrs. ——'s Garden, on Sunday Morning, 25th of May, 1833, between the Hours of Eleven and Twelve.

BY S. T. COLERIDGE.

"FIE, Mr. Coleridge!—and can this be you?
Break two commandments? and in church-time too?
Have you not heard, or have you heard in vain,
The birth-and-parentage-recording strain?
Confessions shrill, that shrill-cried mack'rel drown—
Fresh from the drop—the youth not yet cut down—
Letter to sweet-heart—the last dying speech—
And didn't all this begin in Sabbath-breach?
You, that knew better! In broad open day
Steal in, steal out, and steal our flowers away?
What could possess you? Ah! sweet youth, I fear,
The chap with horns and tail was at your ear!"

Such sounds, of late, accusing fancy brought
From fair C—— to the poet's thought.
Now hear the meek Parnassian youth's reply:—
A bow—a pleading look—a downcast eye—
And then:
"Fair dame! a visionary wight,
Hard by your hill-side mansion sparkling white,
His thought all hovering round the muses' home,
Long hath it been your Poet's wont to roam.
And many a morn, on his bed-charmed sense,
So rich a stream of music issued thence,
He deem'd himself, as it flow'd warbling on,
Beside the vocal fount of Helicon!
But when, as if to settle the concern,
A nymph too he beheld, in many a turn,
Guiding the sweet rill from its fontal urn;
Say, can you blame?—No, none, that saw and heard,
Could blame a bard, that he, thus inly stirr'd,
A muse beholding in each fervent trait,
Took Mary H—— for Polly Hymnia?
Or, haply, as thou stood beside the maid,
One loftier form in sable stole arrayed,
If with regretful thought he hail'd in *thee*,
C——m, his long lost friend, Mol Pomonè?
But most of *you*, soft warblings, I complain!
'Twas ye, that from the bee-hive of my brain
Did lure the fancies forth, a freakish rout,
And witched the air with dreams turn'd inside out.

Thus all conspired—each power of eye and ear,
And this gay month, th' enchantress of the year,
To cheat poor me (no conjurer, God wot!)
And C——m's self accomplice in the plot.
Can you then wonder if I went astray?
Not bards alone, nor lovers mad as they—
All nature *day-dreams* in the month of May,
And if I pluck'd 'each flower that *sweetest* blows'—
Who walks in sleep, needs follow most his *nose*.
Thus long accustomed on the twy-fork'd hill,
To pluck both flower and floweret at my will;
The garden's maze, like No-man's land, I tread,
Nor common law, nor statute in my head;
For my own proper smell, sight, fancy, feeling,
With autocratic hand at once repealing
Five acts of Parliament 'gainst private stealing!
But yet from C——m, who despairs of grace?
There's no spring-gun nor man-trap in *that* face!
Let Moses then look black, and Aaron blue,
That look as if they had little else to do:
For C——m speaks. "Poor youth! he's but a waif!
The spoons all right? The hen and chickens safe?
Well, well, he shall not forfeit our regards—
The Eighth Commandment was not made for Bards!"

AN EXPECTORATION,

Or, Splenetic Extempore, on my joyful Departure from the City of Cologne.

BY S. T. COLERIDGE.

As I am Rhymer,
And now at least a merry one,
Mr. Mum's Rudesheimer
And the church of St. Geryon
Are the two things alone
That deserve to be known
In the body-and-soul-stinking town of Cologne.

EXPECTORATION THE SECOND.

In Coln, a town of monks and bones,
And pavements fang'd with murderous stones;
And rags, and hags, and hideous wenches;
I counted two-and-seventy stenches,
All well-defined, and several stinks!
Ye nymphs that reign o'er sewers and sinks,
The river Rhine, it is well known,
Don't wash your city of Cologne;
But tell me, nymphs! what power divine
Shall henceforth wash the river Rhine?

OUR FIGHTING EDITOR.

The "John Bull" newspaper, a high Tory weekly, edited by Theodore Hook, frequently indulged in offensive personalities in remarking on the conduct and character of public men. A military hero, who would persist in placing himself conspicuously before the world's gaze, received a copious share of what he considered malignant and libellous abuse, in the columns of the said "Bull." His soldier's spirit resolved on revenge. An officer and a gentleman could not demean himself by calling on a hireling scribbler for honorable satisfaction! no; he would horsewhip the miscreant in his own den! the Bull should be taken by the horns! Donning his uniform, and arming himself with a huge whip, he called at the office of the paper, and, scarcely concealing his agitation, inquired for the editor. He was invited by a clerk to take a seat in an inner room—he complied, and was kept waiting while the clerk, who recognized the visitor, ran up stairs and informed the editorial responsibilities of his name and evident purport. After an aggravating delay, which served considerably to increase the ill-temper of the officer, the door opened, and a coarse, rough looking man, over six feet in height, with a proportionate breadth of shoulder, and armed with a terrific bludgeon, entered the room; walking up to the surprised and angry visitor, he said, in a voice of thunder,—"Are you the chap as wants to see me?"

"You! no. I wish to see the editor of the paper."

"That's me! I'm the werry man."

"There must be some mistake."

"Not a morsel! I'm the *head-hitter* of the Bull," said the fellow, bringing the nobbed end of his bludgeon within fearful proclivity to the officer's *caput.*

"You, the editor? impossible!"

"Do you mean to say as I'm a telling a lie?" roared the ruffian, as he again raised his "knotty argument."

"Certainly not—by no means!" said the officer, rapidly cooling down; and dropping the horsewhip and his wrath at the same time.

"Werry well, then! what are you wanting wi' me?"

"A mistake, my dear sir! all a mistake. I expected to meet another person. I'll call some other time." And the valiant complainant backed towards the door, bowing politely to the brawn before him.

"And don't let me ketch you coming again without knowing *what* you want and *who* you want. We're always ready here for all sorts o' customers—army or navy—civil or military—horse, foot, and drag-goons."

The officer retired, resolving to undergo another goring by the "Bull," before he again ventured to encounter the Herculean proportions of the fighting editor.

When the clerk informed the occupiers of the editorial sanctum of the visit of the irate colonel, neither Hook nor his publisher cared to face the horsewhip. A well-known pugilist, the landlord of a tavern in the vicinity, was instantly sent for; a slight preparation fitted him for the part, in which he acquitted himself with complete success. The story rapidly circulated; and the reputation of the *fighting editor of the Bull* prevented further remonstrances from persons who fancied themselves aggrieved by the *liberty* of the press.

THE STAGE COACHMAN.

BY C. J. APPERLEY (NIMROD).

Let us revert to the old-fashioned Coachman of former days; and we know not how we can better develop his character and calling, than by letting him at once speak for himself. We will, then, introduce him in conversation with his box-passenger, on his first start from a country town, a hundred and fifty miles west of the metropolis. But, reader, observe this:—no coachman of the old school, nor many of the new, say a word to their passengers for the first two miles of the journey. They have sundry important matters to occupy, if not monopolize, their ideas for the time. There is the way-bill; the parcels to be dropped on the road; the state of the horses since their last journey; a calculation of their own lawful receipts, together with how much may be added to them by the help of the short pocket; and sundry other affairs which concern only themselves. Let us, however, suppose the ice to be broken, and after a slight survey of his person, imagine our Jehu of the old school, thus addressing his fellow-traveller:—

Coachman.—Booked through, sir?

Passenger.—Yes.

C. Nice day for your journey, and you'll find this a good coach.

P. Not very fast.

C. If she aint fast, she aint slow; and though she loads heavy, she keeps her time. You'll be in Lunnun to-morrow morning, sir, as the clock hits nine.

P. A good coach for coachman and guard, I'll be bound.

C. No great things, sir. We does contrive to make tongue and buckle meet, as the saying is, and that's all; although I have been a coachman thirty years come next May, I am worth next to nothing. Then, to be sure, I've had a heavy family, and if it wasn't for the help of the short pocket now and then, I know not what would have 'come on us.

P. Short pocket!

C. Some calls it shouldering, sir.

P. O, I understand you; you mean occasionally putting some money into your own pockets, instead of into your employer's?

C. Why, to be sure, sir; I can't say but it is a bit wrong, but a coachman's place is no 'heritance, and there aint half-a-dozen in England as doesn't do it, and very few proprietors as doesn't know it.

P. And will they stand it?

C. Not all on 'em, sir; nor some passengers wont if they knows it. For instance:—the last journey but one, I axed a passenger who sat behind me on the roof, if he would walk on a little way on the road, while I changed horses, and he said he would. At last, he asked me *why?* "Why, sir," said I, "I means *to swallow you this morning.*" "Swallow me," said he, "what do you mean?" On my telling him I meant to put his fare (it was but a trifle, as he warnt going very far, nor warnt on the bill) into my own pocket, he said, he should do no sich thing. Now, says I to myself, what sort of a chap can this be? And who do you think he was? Why, a Methodist parson! Blow me, says I to the guard, but I didn't think there was as much honesty in all the Methodist parsons in the world.

P. Then all proprietors will not stand shouldering?

C. No, sir. I lost a sarvice by only shouldering a soldier two stages, and made it a rule never to shoulder another of that sort of live lumber. A proprietor can see 'em a mile off by the color of their coat, and the feathers in their cap.

P. Well, it was no feather in your cap?

C. No, nor out of it, for the coach was no great things, and I've been on this ever since.

P. Driving must be a healthy occupation, and as you say you have been a coachman nearly thirty years, you prove it to be such, for you look hale and hearty.

C. No doubt but it's healthy, sir; that is to say, provided a man takes his natural rest, and keeps the right hand down. For my own part, I never lay rest a score journeys in my life, except when I broke this here leg, and had my hand frost-bitten.

P. What do you mean by keeping the right hand down?

C. Why, you know, sir (*smiling*), we takes the glass in the right hand; what I means is, not to take too much liquor.

P. What do you call too much liquor?

C. Why, sir, d'ye see, we stands in need, and especially o'er this high and cold ground, of something comfortable to keep out the weather. For my own part, I never called myself much of a drinker; but what curious notions some persons have about what a man like me should drink.

P. You rather might say, what a man like you does drink, or *ought* to drink.

C. Well, sir, have it that way, if you like; a few journeys back, I had a doctor on the box along with me, and he would have it that hot rum-and-water—and that's the liquor I always takes on the road—is poison.

P. Poison!

C. Yes, sir, downright poison; so much so, he said, he was quite sure that two glasses every day would kill a man in three years.

P. And what did you say to that remark?

C. Why, you know, sir, it warnt for me to contradict a doctor; but I made bold to ask him, what sort of stuff he thought I must be made of, for, said I, I have drunk no less than six every day, on the road, for the last nineteen years, besides what I takes with my dinner and supper, and something comfortable with my pipe at night; and I don't know now, whether the 'surance office people wouldn't have my life before the doctor's, for he looks as white in the face as my near leader does.

P. You must meet with all sorts of people in your daily vocation.

C. Yes, and of all sizes, too; I consider myself no small weight; but I had a gentleman alongside me on the box a few journeys back, that made me look like a shrimp. I axed him what he weighed, and he said, six-and-twenty stone *on the weigh-bridge*—for no scales would hold him.

P. Now what description of passengers pay you best?

C. Why, sir, next to a drunken sailor, just paid off, there is nothing like Eton schoolboys and Oxford gentlemen. You see, sir, when they leaves school, or the 'varsity, they are very happy at the thoughts af getting away from the big wigs, and their books; and when they returns, they are full of money, and don't think much of a few shillings.

P. But the drunken sailor?

C. Pardon me, sir; I don't mean to say all sailors are drunkards, but I mean to say this, there's nothing, in our line, comes near a sailor, a *little sprung*, with money in his pocket. When I drove the old "Liverpool Marcury," commonly called on the road (saving your presence), the "Lousy Liverpool," I have sacked two pounds on a journey for weeks together, in the time of war; and the landlord of the inn, at which the coach stopped to breakfast, has been heard to say, it was worth five hundred a-year to him.

P. How could that be?

C. How, sir? Why, Jack, you see, could never eat nothing at that time in the morning; but calling for something to drink for himself and messmates, would chuck down half-a-guinea, saying he never took no change.

P. And how came you to lose such a coach as that?

C. Aye, that's the job, sir. I told you before our place is no 'heritance; we had a bad mishap; we had four horses and three passengers all drowned at one go.

P. And was you the cause of it?

C. Worse luck, I was.

P. Drunk, I fear.

C. No, sir, I warnt drank, nor warnt sober.' I wos what we calls stale drunk; the liquor wos a dying in me, like; but that warnt the cause. It wos a terrible foggy night; we had a terrible awkward bridge to go over; and as bad luck would have it—we were shocking badly horsed in that coach—every one of the team that night was blind. Now what could be expected in such a case as this, with only one eye among us, and that one wos mine? I missed the bridge; into the river we went, drowning all the horses, and three drunken sailors asleep, in the inside. Of course, I got the sack.

P. And what are your worst payers?

C. Why, God bless them, sir—for I loves them to my very heart, for all that, and have had two heavy families by two wives—women are the worst, and parsons next. Many a woman thinks she behaves handsome if she gives a coachman sixpence for driving her fifty miles, and helping her to swear that her child aint seven years old, when she knows it is ten, and ought to pay full fare; and as to parsons, you might as well expect to squeeze blood out of turnips, as more than a shilling out of them, especially those who have their hats turned up behind, and a bit of a rose in front, like that at the side of our coach-horse's bridle-fronts. But I sarved one of them out, some years back. I happened to swear twice on the journey, when he made that an excuse for not giving me any thing. Well, sir, when I sets him down at his house, he wanted his carpet-bag; and also a heavy trunk that was on the roof: "You shall have your carpet-bag, sir," said I; "but as *you* have done your duty, I must do *mine*. I shall take your trunk to the office, and you will have seven-and-sixpence to pay for it." If he had given me something, you see, he would have had nothing to pay for his trunk.

P. I am at a loss to know how you distinguish your horses, when you have occasion to speak of them to the various horse-keepers on the road.

C. You see, sir, some on 'em are named by us, and others by the horse-keepers. For example:—this here near-wheeler wos christened Alderman in the stable, because he is such a devil to eat; and his partner, I calls Lawyer, because he wont do nothing without being well paid for it, and as little as he can help then. In short, he is a shifty rascal, and no more minds the whip than a lobster does a flea-bite.

P. And what do you call your present leaders?

C. Why, sir, I christened them both myself. The little bay horse on the near-side, I calls Barleycorn, because he was bought of a publican, who brews the best ale on this road; and his partner, the gray mare, Virago.

P. Why Virago?

C. Well; to tell you the plain truth, sir, she is much like my first wife; God rest her soul, she warnt a bad kind of woman neither; but terrible violent if put out. And that's the case with that there mare. If I was to hit her two or three times, smartly, under the bars—not that I am a-going to insinuvate that my poor missis and I ever came to blows—she wouldn't be herself again for all the rest of the stage. Then again you see, she wears something like a shade before her eyes, what we calls a mope, and this because she's apt to be what we calls megrimy.

P. What do you mean?

C. Why, if she runs with the sun in her face, she is apt to be taken with the megrims, and then she's down on her back in a crack, if not pulled up.

P. Has that any thing to do with temper?

C. I shouldn't wonder if it has, for the neighbors used to say, my wife was very full of megrims, and I see no reason why it shouldn't be the same case with horses.

P. From what does it proceed?

C. I can't say exactly; but our farrier says it has something to do with the head. Now if I was to give my opinion, it comes from the head in horses, and from the heart in women; but both are apt to be queer in their temper, and difficult to handle, so as always to keep them in the straight road. Both, you know, sir, are given to bolt at times, and now and then kick over a trace, or jump over the pole; not that I am a-going to insinuvate that my first missis ever went so far as this, at least, not to my knowledge.

P. But, Coachman, I fear your trade will soon be over; they tell me we are to have steam-carriages on the road as well as elsewhere.

C. Oh, sir, that wont be in my time nor in yours; the guard tells me, though, that our Lunnun man has been talking about them.

P. Who do you mean by your London man?

C. He who drives over the upper ground into Lunnun. These Lunnun men, you see, sir, knows a many things that we down in the country knows nothing about.

P. Was you never in London?

C. Never could reach it, sir; never could get beyond the middle ground. It aint on account of coachmanship, for I wouldn't turn my back to any man in England, in our line, and that our proprietors knows, or I shouldn't have been on this coach for the last nineteen years; the stock speaks for that; but the truth is, we country coachmen arnt thought quite 'cute enough to bring a coach—especially a night coach—in and out of Lunnun: so many thieves, you know. A brother of mine, who druv the Holyhead mail through Wales, where a man aint hanged above once in fifty years, was done brown the first week he druv a coach into Lunnun: a man comes up to him in Piccadilly, with fine lace on his hat, and says,—"Now, coachman, *be alive:* my master's luggage; there it is, that ere carpet bag; so, taking the first that was handed down to him, *off* he goes with it; and of course, before night, my brother was *off* the coach. Then they tells me, some of them Lunnun coachmen are quite like gentlemen, and able to talk with gentlemen on any matter, and in any language. Our Lunnun man, indeed, the passengers tells me, speaks Greek and Latin, and that which the Jews talks, as well. But for my part, I thinks some of those fine Lunnun coachmen are a little above their situvation; not but what I would have every man, in our line, keep himself respectable. Indeed, I could not help saying to our guard, t'other day, when he told me he met one of what they calls the "swell-dragsmen" out of Lunnun, at work in kid gloves, and with a bunch of curls sticking out on the off-side of his hat, that I should like to put a twitch on his nose, and trim him about the head as we do a horse. I'd put the dog-skins on him, too; what real coachman ever druv in any thing but dog-skin gloves? It's coming it too strong, sir. Then our guard told me another queer go. He said an old fellow-servant of mine had given notice to quit his place at the end of the month, and what do you think that place is? Why no less than thirty miles in and out of Lunnun, two coaches in twenty-four hours, and all night-work! Why, I reckon the blockhead wants a place in the House of Commons.

P. I think your friend is somewhat unreasonable; but I don't understand one expression of yours. You speak of "night-work," as a recommendation.

C. Nothing like "night-work," sir, for a coachman. Proprietors snug in bed arter a certain hour; always something to be picked up on such a road as his.

C. But you must suffer in cold weather?

C. Can't say we doesn't, sir. I've had my box-coat so froze that it could not be unbuttoned; actually obliged to have the buttons cut off before I could get out of it, and then it would stand up for all the world as stiff as if I had been in it. Then meeting a storm of hail—sore work for the eyes, because, you see, sir, we are obliged to raise the eyelid, or we can't—

P. I don't comprehend you.

C. Why, sir, if you'll try, you will find that, though you can see the wheel-horses, and half way along the leaders' backs, with your eyelids down, and your head in its natural place, you can't see their heads, still less the road before them, unless you raise your eyelids, and then you expose your eyes to the storm. I have had a pellet of hail strike my one good eye, ready to knock it out of the socket, and what a pretty go would that have been.

P. Well, driving and guarding a coach through a winter's night, or even a winter's day, must be punishing work, and doubtless attended with no small degree of danger. It is on this consideration that I always feel disposed to reward coachmen and guards well; here are three shillings for yourself, and I shall pay the guard where we leave him.

C. Much obliged to you, sir; I shall drink your health after my dinner, with my usual toast.

P. Pray what may be your usual toast?

C. "As we travel through life, may we live on the road."

P. (*to himself*). *Dum vivimus, vivamus;* and very well translated.

CELESTIAL CONFUSION.

Of Juno the shrew, Jove was husband and brother—
Minerva's papa, too, without any mother,
Thus playing the part of himself and another:
How strange!

Venus was Vulcan's half wife and half sister,
And proved to his breast a perpetual blister:
Had he sold her, he ne'er, by the bye, would have missed her—
How strange!

Such things are recorded in heathenish song;
Such things, we on earth say, to scandal belong,
But the gods—oh! they're always *above* doing wrong.
How strange!

EPIGRAMS.

"You're a thief," said a wag, "and I'll show it,"
To a butcher, with angry feeling;
"'Tis a scandalous fact, and you know it,
That knives you are constantly *steeling!*"

Cries Sue to Will, 'midst matrimonial strife,
"Cursed be the hour I first became your wife!"
"By all the powers," said Will, "but that's too bad!
You've cursed the only civil hour we've had."

A cockney sportsman, gunning, to a country squire declares,
That he, one morn, 'ere breakfast time, shot three and thirty hares.
"Indeed! shot three and thirty hares?" "Yes, truly!" looking big;
"Then," says the squire, "you surely must have *fired at a wig!*"

PROVERBS OF SOLOMON LEVI, ESQ., ATTORNEY-AT-LAW.

REMEMBERED AND EDITED BY HIS ARTICLED PUPIL. ANONYMOUS.

Our surprise that Mr. Levi had never married was participated in by Mr. Levi's friends. In early youth, he is reported to have loved—aye, loved madly, deeply (he gave her a watch and chain, which cost him thirty pounds). Miss Maud Doggery was not what might strictly be called handsome, owing to a large port wine stain on the left cheek, shaped exactly like a huge red gooseberry. (It appears that two days before Miss Maud was born, her mother felt an inordinate desire to drink champagne. It was not gratified, and hence the poor child was marked with a gooseberry.)

Mr. Levi has since confessed that whenever he made love to her, it was always on the right side, with the damaged cheek turned to the wall. He invariably spoke of her as one who, even if she had a stain upon her cheek, had none upon her character; and who, if not positively handsome (even on the other side of her face there were freckles as big as chocolate drops), at least was the perfection of maidenly modesty. But she deceived Mr. Levi in a most shameful manner. She had always led him to suppose that her fortune amounted to £15,000; and it was only a few days before the wedding was to have taken place that he fortunately discovered that the money was invested in Pennsylvanian bonds. One morning, twenty years after his love fit, somebody told Mr. Levi that Miss Maud Doggery was still living. I fancy I can see the governor—pale as a ground-glass lamp shade—throw up his hands as he exclaimed, "Living? Heavens! what an escape I have had! and the villains told me she was consumptive!" In the afternoon, he came into our office, and spoke the following wonderful proverbs:

ON WOMAN, ETC.

Remember this, my boys. In Eden there was only one woman, and it is the symbol of happiness. Would that it had been a *Pear*adise, for then the apple had not been there. The source of all evil was apple sauce.

With the rib of man was woman made. In her daughters you may easily trace the love of ribbones.

At the first wedding ceremony, the bridegroom slept. How many have since been led to the altar lulled by some soft soap-orific.

Woman shared the apple with man, but she took the first bite.

This was the curse of the world: "Woman shall love fine clothes, and man shall pay for them."

No sooner had Eve seen Sat(i)n than she wished to clothe herself.

Ask a woman what is meant by happiness, and she will reply, "A velvet dress, with fourteen breadths to the skirt."

How many marry that they may wear rich garments! Cambric handkerchiefs are not the only things that can be drawn through a wedding ring.

This is the vanity of women: "Court plumes and the largest bussel."

When cats wash their faces, bad weather is at hand; when women use washes to their complexions, it is a true sign that the beauty of the day is gone.

Many powder their faces, that their skins may seem white; it is as a poulterer flours an old hen, that it may pass for a tender chicken.

How many women have been ruined by diamonds, as bird-catchers entice the lark from heaven to earth with sparkling glass.

As the child crows at the shining candle, so do women at glittering gems; and both shall burn their fingers if they touch them.

The stepping-stone to fortune is not to be found in a jeweller's shop.

Some women have hearts brittle as glass; he that would engrave his name on them must use diamonds.

Brilliants of the first water are those given to stay the wife's first flood of tears.

Any woman will listen to your suit if you first give her an 'earing; but it must be an emerald one.

There are some men who beat their wives, and then seek the hand of forgiveness by placing jewels upon their fingers. They follow the inscriptions on their street-doors, "Knock and ring!"

All women have hearts, but often it is with them as with oaks—the heart is the hardest part.

No chain is so strong as the banns of marriage.

She who wears false ringlets is like a fire of green wood; it has curls of smoke, but he who would kindle the flame must puff vigorously.

As birds are snared with hairs, so are many men with a woman's head-dress.

She who dyes her locks, is like a desperate gambler, who makes his last venture, and risks all upon the hazard of the die:

You may tell the ages of horses and of women by their teeth—with a horse by looking at them, with a woman by asking how old she is; and if she shows her teeth, be sure that she is advanced in years.

Like the colored bottles in a chemist's window, is rouge on the cheeks of a maiden; it attracts the passers by, but all know the drug they advertise.

Shun vermilion cheeks. They are the red danger signals on the marriage lines.

Beware of the hare's foot—it leaves the footprints of Time behind it.

Showmen hang paintings before their booths, and women carry color on their faces. Let any examine the inward worth, and it shall be nothing to the outward show.

She who is in haste for the wedding says, "The more bussel the more speed."

The voice of the virgin is soft as the cooing of the wood-pigeon on St. Valentine's day. Her laughter is like the sound of distant bells ringing for a wedding.

She is timid as a Highland doe. He who would creep near to her must do it—as deer-stalkers do—on his knees.

At the voice of a man she flies, as a gazelle at the roaring of a lion.

But no sooner has she tasted wedding-cake, than she grows bold, as the tiger that has eaten raw food.

Henceforth she shall be bold, as a servant that has discovered your secret.

Her voice shall sound like a circus-gong at a fair, telling that the scenes in the ring are about to commence.

Choose not your wives as you do grapes, from the bloom on them.

He who marries a pretty face only, is like a buyer of cheap furniture—the varnish that caught the eye will not endure the fire-side blaze.

Better is love and gingham, than coldness and cashmeres.

Woman is the only female in creation that sings: have no piano in your house.

How many go to be married because there will be a carriage to bring them home from church.

None can tell how much they love their husbands as those that marry for money.

To be married, women will endure much. Though they be caged up as a parrot, still they complain not if they have the ring to play with.

The house-keeping book is the thunder-cloud of marriage. It is accompanied with the lightening of the husband's purse.

It is as the magic portfolio shown by conjurers. The trick consists in getting out of it—without being found out—bonnets, shawls, and dresses enough to fill a wardrobe.

The girl who chooses her husband for his gold, has a heart of quartz attached to a nugget.

Every woman leaves her husband "for ever" at least three times in her life, as folk striking a bargain pretend to leave the shop, hoping to be called back, and gain by the artifice.

The heart that breaks too easily is like an empty nut, that cracks readily from its very emptiness.

As harp-strings snap with the damp, so do a husband's strongest resolves with the tears of his wife.

Beware of girls with red hair: they are deceitful as foxes.

Shun them, as the mariner shuns the lighthouse with its head of flames. For there are the hidden rocks of deceit that would wreck your happiness.

Though they should grease their curls into darkness: still will their redness be shown by their actions.

The foolish virgins were red-haired girls who had no oil; so that the bridegroom discovered their locks of fire.

Avoid dark-haired girls: their love is as the blow of a cudgel.

They are fierce as strong drink, but lack sweetness; sugar will not dissolve in their high spirit.

They remember long an angry word; as ale turns sour with thunder.

Maidens with brown hair are pleasant as bread that has been well baked—all kissing crust.

She who has golden hair should be loved by a heart of leather, for that cannot break.

They are loving as spaniels, and as faithless; and he who whistles last shall be followed.

Remember this, ye wives. Be not too affectionate; without bitters there were no sweets.

As men take sour olives that they may relish their wine the more, so well-administered crossness will give fresh flavor to your love.

Women, beware of scandal, or it will crush you; as sometimes a word spoken in the snowy Alps will bring down an avalanche.

The girdle of beauty is not a stay-lace.

This is the only excuse for tight lacing. A good housewife should have no waste.

The wisest man is a batch o'lore.

All women dislike the words, "Love, honor, and obey." According to them it should be, "Love, honor, and a ba-*be*."

Forty is the turnpike-gate on the road to the church; none can pass it unless they have money.

When a maid takes to spaniels or parrots, it means that her beauty is gone to the dogs, and that henceforth her life is a *bird*en to her.

The mouth of a wise woman is like a money-box which is seldom opened, so that much treasure comes forth from it.

Store up this truth, O woman! Be charitable unto thy fallen sister. Imitate not the stags, that chase from their herd their wounded companion.

The wise wife opposes wrath with kindness. A sand-bag will stop a cannon-ball by its yielding.

The smell of the dinner is the incense of domestic love.

A good woman is like a Cremona fiddle; age only makes its tone the sweeter.

DID YOU EVER?

Did you ever know a sentinel who could tell what building he was keeping guard over?

Did you ever know a cab-man, or a ticket porter, with any change about him?

Did you ever know a tradesman asking for his account, who had not "a bill to take up on Friday?"

Did you ever know an omnibus cad who would not engage to set you down within a few yards of any place within the bills of mortality?

Did you ever know a turnpike man who could be roused in less than a quarter of an hour, when it wanted that much of midnight?

Did you ever see a pair of family snuffers which had not a broken spring, a leg deficient, or half an inch of the point knocked off?

Did you ever know a lodging-house landlady who would own to bugs?

Did you ever know the Boots at an inn call you too early for the morning coach?

Did you ever know a dancing-master's daughter who was not to excel Taglioni?

Did you ever know a man who did not think he could poke the fire better than you could?

Did you ever know a Frenchman admire Waterloo Bridge?

Did you ever know a housemaid who, on your discovering a fracture in a valuable China jar, did not tell you it was "done a long time ago," or that it was "cracked before?"

Did you ever know a man who didn't consider *his* walking-stick a better walking-stick than *your* walking-stick?

Did you ever know a penny-a-liner who was not on intimate terms with Lytton Bulwer, Capt. Marryatt, Sheridan Knowles, Tom Hood, Washington Irving, and Rigdum Funnidos?

Did you ever know a hatter who was not prepared to sell you as good a hat for ten and sixpence as the one you've got on at five and twenty shillings?

Did you ever know a red-haired man who had a very clear notion of where scarlet began and auburn terminated?

THE SAYINGS OF SYDNEY SMITH.

Habitual Bore.—Lord Chesterton we have often met with, and suffered a good deal from his lordship: a heavy, pompous, meddling peer, occupying a great share of the conversation—saying things in ten words which required only two, and evidently convinced that he is making a great impression; a large man with a large head, and a very candid manner. Knowing enough to torment his fellow creatures, not to instruct them; the intimate of young ladies, and the natural butt and target of wit. It is easy to talk of carnivorous animals and beasts of prey; but does such a man, who lays waste a whole civilized party of beings by prosing, reflect upon the joy he spoils, and the misery he creates, in the course of his life? and that any one who listens to him through politeness, would prefer toothache or earache to his conversation? Does he consider the extreme uneasiness which ensues when the company have discovered a man to be an extremely absurd person, at the same time that it is absolutely impossible to convey, by words or manner, the most distant suspicion of the discovery? And, then, who punishes this bore? What sessions or what assizes for him? What bill is found against him? Who indicts him? When the judges have gone their vernal and autumnal rounds, the sheep-stealer disappears—the swindler gets ready for the Bay—the solid parts of the murderer are preserved in anatomical collections. But after twenty years of crime, the bore is discovered in the same house, in the same attitude, eating the same soup—untried—unpunished—undissected.

Monk Lewis's Tragedy of Alfonso.—This tragedy delights in explosions. Alfonso's empire is destroyed by a blast of gunpowder, and restored by a clap of thunder. After the death of Cæsario, and a short exhortation to that purpose by Orsino, all the conspirators fall down in a thunderclap, ask pardon of the king, and are forgiven. This mixture of physical and moral power is beautiful! How interesting a water-spout would appear among Mr. Lewis's kings and queens. We anxiously look forward, in his next tragedy, to a fall of snow, three or four feet deep, or expect a plot shall gradually unfold itself by means of a general thaw.

American Ice.—Shortly after the repudiation of the Pennsylvanian bonds, Sydney Smith was shown a lump of American ice, upon which he remarked, "That he was glad to see any thing solvent come from America."

Cannibals.—Sydney Smith is said to have given some advice to the bishop of New Zealand, previous to his departure, recommending him to have regard to the minor as well as to the more grave duties of his station—to be given to hospitality—and, in order to meet the tastes of his native guests, never to be without a smoked little boy in the bacon sack, and a cold clergyman on the side-board. "And as for myself, my lord," he concluded, "all I can say is, that I hope you will not disagree with the man that eats you!"

A Dinner Party.—An excellent and well-arranged dinner is a most pleasing occurrence, and a great triumph of civilized life. It is not only the descending morsel and the enveloping sauce, but the rank, wealth, wit, and beauty which surround the meats; the learned management of light and heat; the silent and rapid services of the attendants; the smiling and sedulous host, proffering gusts and relishes; the exotic bottles; the embossed plate; the pleasant remarks; the handsome dresses; the cunning artifices in fruit and farina! The hour of dinner, in short, includes every thing of sensual and intellectual gratification, which a great nation glories in producing.

Duelling.—Though barbarous in civilized, is a highly civilized institution among barbarous people; and when compared to assassination, is a prodigious victory gained over human passions.

Burning Chimney-Sweeps.—A large party are invited to dinner, a great display is to be made; and about an hour before dinner, there is an alarm that the kitchen chimney is on fire! It is impossible to put off the distinguished persons who are expected. It gets very late for the soup and fish; the cook is frantic; all eyes are turned upon the sable consolation of the master chimney-sweeper; and up into the midst of the burning chimney is sent one of the miserable little infants of the brush! There is a positive prohibition of this practice, and an enactment of penalties in one of the acts of Parliament which respect chimney-sweepers. But what matters acts of Parliament, when the pleasures of genteel people are concerned? or what is a toasted child, compared to the agonies of the mistress of the house with a deranged dinner?

Enjoyment of Life.—Ennui, wretchedness, melancholy, groans, and sighs, are the offering which these unhappy Methodists make to a Deity, who has covered the earth with gay colors, and scented it with rich perfumes; and shown us, by the plan and order of his works, that he has given to man something better than a bare existence, and scattered over his creation a thousand superfluous joys, which are totally unnecessary to the mere support of life.

Bulls.—A bull is exactly the counterpart of a witticism: for as wit discovers real relations that are not apparent, bulls admit apparent relations that are not real. The pleasure arising from bulls, proceeds from our surprise at suddenly discovering two things to be dissimilar in which a resemblance might have been suspected. The same doctrine will apply to wit and bulls in action. Practical wit discovers connection or relation between actions, in which duller understandings discover none: and practical bulls originate from an apparent relation between two actions which more correct understandings immediately perceive to have none at all. In the late rebellion in Ireland, the rebels, who had conceived a high degree of indignation against some great banker, passed a resolution that they would burn his notes;—which they accordingly did, with great assiduity; forgetting, that in burning his notes, they were destroying his debts, and that for every note which went into the flames, a correspondent value went into the banker's pocket. A gentleman, in speaking of a nobleman's wife, of great rank and fortune, lamented very much that she had no children. A medical gentleman who was present observed, that to have no children was a great misfortune, but he thought he had remarked it was *hereditary* in some families. Take any in-

Sydney Smith

N.Y. D. Appleton & Co.

stance of this branch of the ridiculous, and you will always find an apparent relation of ideas leading to a complete inconsistency. There are some bulls so extremely fallacious, that any man may imagine himself to have been betrayed into them; but these are rare; and, in general, it is a poor, contemptible species of amusement; a delight in which evinces a very bad taste in wit.

Classical Glory.—Dr. Gonge, the celebrated Grecian, upon hearing the praises of the great king of Prussia, entertained considerable doubts whether the king, with all his victories, knew how to conjugate a Greek verb in μ.

Charades.—If they are made at all, they should be made, without benefit of clergy, the offender should be instantly hurried off to execution, and be cut off in the middle of his dulness, without being allowed to explain to the executioner, why his first is like his second, or what is the resemblance between his fourth and his ninth.

Materialism.—Sydney Smith was once dining with a French gentleman, who was indulging, not, perhaps, in the best possible taste, both before and during dinner, in a variety of freethinking speculations, and ended by avowing himself a materialist. "Very good soup this," said Mr. Smith. "*Oui, Monsieur, c'est excellente.*" "Pray, sir, do you believe in a cook?"

Official Dress.—The Americans, we believe, are the first persons who have discarded the tailor in the administration of justice, and his auxiliary the barber—two persons of endless importance in codes and pandects of Europe. A judge administers justice, without a calorific wig and party-colored gown, in a coat and pantaloons. He is obeyed, however; and life and property are not badly protected in the United States. We shall be denounced by the laureate as atheists and jacobins; but we must say, that we have doubts whether one atom of useful influence is added to men in important situations by any color, quantity, or configuration of cloth and hair. The true progress of refinement, we conceive, is to discard all the mountebank drapery of barbarous ages. One row of gold and fur falls off after another from the robe of power, and is picked up and worn by the parish beadle and the exhibitor of wild beasts. Meantime, the afflicted wiseacre mourns over equality of garment, and wotteth not of two men, whose doublets have cost alike, how one shall command and the other obey.

Pulpit Eloquence.—Pulpit discourses have insensibly dwindled from speaking to reading; a practice, of itself, sufficient to stifle every germ of eloquence. It is only by the fresh feelings of the heart, that mankind can be very powerfully affected. What can be more ludicrous than an orator delivering stale indignation, and fervor of a week old; turning over whole pages of violent passions, written out in German text; reading the tropes and apostrophes into which he is hurried by the ardor of his mind; and so affected at a preconcerted line and page, that he is unable to proceed any further!

Impertinence of an Opinion.—It is always considered as a piece of impertinence in England, if a man of less than two or three thousand a year has any opinions at all upon important subjects.

Prison Retirement.—Since the benevolent Howard attacked our prisons, incarceration has become not only healthy, but elegant; and a county jail is precisely the place to which any pauper might wish to retire, to gratify his taste for magnificence as well as comfort. Upon the same principle, there is some risk that transportation will be considered one of the surest roads to honor and wealth; and that no felon will hear a verdict of "*not guilty*," without considering himself as cut off in the fairest career of prosperity.

Parasites.—Nature descends down to infinite smallness. A great man has his parasites; and if you take a large, buzzing blue-bottle fly, and look at it in a microscope, you may see twenty or thirty little ugly insects crawling about it, which, doubtless, think their fly to be the bluest, grandest, merriest, most important animal in the universe; and are convinced the world would be at an end if it ceased to buzz.

The Theatre.—There is something in the word *Playhouse* which seems so closely connected, in the minds of some people, with sin and Satan, that it stands in their vocabulary for every species of abomination. And yet why? Where is every feeling more roused in favor of virtue than at a good play? Where is goodness so feelingly, so enthusiastically learned? What so solemn as to see the excellent passions of the human heart called forth by a great actor, animated by a great poet? to hear Siddons repeat what Shakspere wrote? To behold the child and his mother—the noble and the poor artisan—the monarch and his subjects—all ages and all ranks convulsed with one common passion—wrung with one common anguish, and, with loud sobs and cries, doing involuntary homage to the God that made their hearts! What wretched infatuation to interdict such amusements as these! What a blessing that mankind can be allured from sensual gratification, and find relaxation and pleasure in such pursuits!

Use and Abuse.—A certain authoress interdicts cards and assemblies. No cards, because cards are employed in gaming; no assemblies, because many dissipated persons pass their lives in assemblies. Carry this but a little further, and we must say, no wine, because of drunkenness; no meat, because of gluttony; no use, that there may be no abuse!

Men and Beasts.—I have sometimes, perhaps, felt a little uneasy at Exeter 'Change, from contrasting the monkeys with the 'prentice-boys who are teazing them; but a few pages of Locke, or a few lines of Milton, have always restored me to tranquillity, and convinced me that the superiority of men had nothing to fear.

Narrow-minded Persons.—A narrow-minded person has not a thought beyond the little sphere of his own vision. "The snail," say the Hindoos, "sees nothing but his own shell, and thinks it the grandest palace in the universe."

Frightful to Think of.—An injudicious adherent of Mr. Percival, the colleague of Canning, having mentioned drugs among the articles to be intercepted by the English ships, in order to make the French more disposed for peace, the opportunity which it offered to Sydney Smith for displaying his powers of ridicule, was too tempting to be lost, and he has thus 'shown up' the affair, in the 'Letters of Peter Plumley:' "What a sublime thought," exclaims Peter, "that no purge can now be taken between the Weser and the Garonne; that the bustling pestle is still, the canorous mortar mute, and the bowels of mankind locked up for fourteen degrees of latitude! When, I should be curious to know, were all the powers of crudity and flatulence fully explained to his majesty's ministers? At what period was this great plan of conquest and constipation fully developed? In whose mind was the idea of destroying the pride and the plasters of France first engendered? Without castor oil they might, for some months, to be sure, have carried on a lingering war; but can they do without bark? Will the people live under a government where antimonial powders cannot be procured? Will they bear the loss of mercury? 'There's the rub.' Depend upon it, the absence of materia medica will soon bring them to their senses, and the cry of *Bourbon and bolus* burst forth from the Baltic to the Mediterranean."

EDUCATION AT BOTANY BAY.—Sydney Smith, in enforcing the necessity of educating the children of the convicts at Botany Bay, humorously remarks, "Nothing but the earliest attention to the habits of children, can restrain the erratic finger from the contiguous scrip, or prevent the hereditary tendency to larcenous abstractions."

ECCLESIASTICAL JOKES.—Sydney Smith has been blamed for pushing his jests to an extremity that deserved Dr. Johnson's rebuke on the employment of "idle and indecent applications of sentences taken from the Scriptures; a mode of merriment which a good man dreads for its profaneness, and a witty man disdains for its ease and vulgarity." For instance, his description of Rogers' dining room—"a blaze of light above, and below nothing but darkness and gnashing of teeth." Also, the oft-quoted reply to Landseer, the great animal painter, who wished him to sit for his picture—"Is thy servant a dog that he should do this thing?" And again, his well-known answer to a friend, who, at the time of the non-payment of the Pennsylvania interest, congratulated him on his happy circumstances. "And you," said Smith, in the words of Paul, "Would that you were altogether such as I am—except these bonds!"

VIRGILIAN PUN.—Smith proposed, as a motto for Bishop Burgess, brother to the well-known fish sauce purveyor,

Gravi jampridem *saucia* curâ.

THE WRONG WORD.—Preaching a charity sermon, he frequently repeated the assertion that Englishmen were distinguished for the love of their species. The collection happened to be inferior to his expectations, and he said that he had evidently used the wrong word—his expression should have been, that they were distinguished for their love of their specie.

SAMARITANS.—Yes! you find people ready enough to do the Samaritan, without the oil and two pence.

STAGE-COACH TRAVELLING.—Most people sulk in stage-coaches; I always talk. I have had some amusing journeys from this habit. On one occasion, a gentleman in the coach with me, with whom I had been conversing for some time, suddenly looked out of the window as we approached York and said, 'There is a very clever man, they say, but a d— odd fellow, lives near here—Sydney Smith, I believe.' 'He may be a very odd fellow,' said I, taking off my hat to him, and laughing, 'and I dare say he is; but odd as he is, he is here, very much at your service.' Poor man! I thought he would have sunk into his boots, and vanished through the bed of the carriage, he was so distressed; but I thought I had better tell him at once, or he might proceed to say I had murdered my grandmother, which I must have resented, you know.

On another occasion, some years later, when going to Brougham Hall, two raw Scotch girls got into the coach in the dark, near Carlisle. 'It is very disagreeable getting into a coach in the dark,' exclaimed one, after arranging her bandboxes; 'one cannot see one's company.' 'Very true, ma'am, and you have a great loss in not seeing me, for I am a remarkably handsome man.' 'No, sir! are you really?' said both. 'Yes, and in the flower of my youth.' 'What a pity!' said they. We soon passed near a lamp-post: they both darted forward to get a look at me. 'La, sir, you seem very stout.' 'Oh no, not at all, ma'am, it's only my great coat.' 'Where are you going, sir?' 'To Brougham Hall.' 'Why, you must be a very remarkable man, to be going to Brougham Hall.' 'I am a very remarkable man, ma'am." At Penrith they got out, after having talked incessantly, and tried every possible means to discover who I was, exclaiming as they went off laughing, 'Well, it is very provoking we can't see you, but we'll find out who you are at the hall; Lord Brougham always comes to the hall at Penrith, and we shall certainly be there, and shall soon discover your name.'

YOUTH AND FAMILIARITY.—One evening, at a dinner party, he was excessively annoyed by the familiarity of a young fop, who constantly addressed him as "Smith."—"Smith, pass the wine," and so forth. Presently the young gentleman stated that he had received an invitation to dine with the Archbishop of Canterbury, and asked the reverend canon "what sort of a fellow" he was.

"A very good sort of a fellow, indeed," replied the satirist; "only, let me give you a piece of advice—don't call him Howley."

This rebuff vastly amused the company; but the object of it, being a fool at all points, did not see this point, and talked on in happy unconsciousness. Soon after, one of the company rose to depart, pleading an engagement to a soiree at Gore House.

"Take me with you," roars young hopeful. "I've the greatest possible desire to know Lady Blessington."

This request was very naturally demurred to, on the ground that a visitor was not authorized to introduce uninvited guests.

"Oh!" said Sydney Smith, "never mind; I'm sure that her ladyship will be delighted to see our young friend: the weather's uncommonly hot, and you can say that you have brought with you *the cool of the evening*.

DOGS.—"No, I don't like dogs; I always expect them to go mad. A lady asked me once for a motto for her dog Spot. I proposed, 'Out, damned Spot!' but she did not think it sentimental enough. You remember the story of the French marquise, who, when her pet lap-dog bit a piece out of her footman's leg, exclaimed, 'Ah, poor little beast! I hope it won't make him sick.' I called one day on Mrs. ——, and her lap-dog flew at my leg and bit it. After pitying her dog, like the French marquise, she did all she could to comfort me, by assuring me the dog was a Dissenter, and hated the Church, and was brought up in a Tory family. But whether the bite came from madness or dissent, I knew myself too well to neglect it; and went on the instant to a surgeon and had it cut out, making a mem. on the way to enter that house no more.

Dinner in the Country.—What misery human beings inflict on each other under the name of pleasure! We went to dine last Thursday with Mr. ——, a neighboring clergyman, a haunch of venison being the stimulus to the invitation. We set out at five o'clock, drove in a broiling sun, on dusty roads, three miles in our best gowns, found squire and parsons assembled in a small hot room, the whole house redolent of frying; talked, as is our wont, of roads, weather, and turnips; that done, began to grow hungry, then serious, then impatient. At last, a stripling, evidently caught up for the occasion, opened the door and beckoned our host out of the room. After some moments of awful suspense, he returned to us with a face of much distress, saying, 'The woman assisting in the kitchen had mistaken the soup for dirty water, and had thrown it away, so we must do without it;' we all agreed it was perhaps as well we should, under the circumstances. At last, to our joy, dinner was announced; but oh, ye gods! as we entered the dining-room what a gale met our noses! The venison was high, the venison was uneatable, and was obliged to follow the soup with all speed.

Dinner proceeded, but our spirits flagged under these accumulated misfortunes: there was an ominous pause between the first and second course; we looked each other in the face—what new disaster awaited us? The pause became fearful. At last, the door burst open, and the boy rushed in, calling aloud, 'Please, sir, has Betty any right to leather I?' What human gravity could stand this? We roared with laughter; all took part against Betty, obtained the second course with some difficulty, bored each other the usual time, ordered our carriages, expecting our post-boys to be drunk, and were grateful to Providence for not permitting them to deposit us in a wet ditch. So much for dinners in the country!

JEREMY SCRAP, THE OPTIMIST.

BY LAMAN BLANCHARD.

Morning Song:—It all happens for the best!
Evening Song:—It all happens for the best!

Such are the songs of Jeremy, the only ones (or one) he ever heard, sang, or knew in this or any world. Nay, it is the only bit of Queen's English that he has by heart; and at the very core of that heart, whenever it may stop, will the sanguine letters be found stamped.

He said the thing soon after he was weaned, and he will say it with his last breath. He says it in spring, summer, autumn, and winter. It is his cry at Lady-day, Midsummer, Michaelmas, and Christmas. He utters the same note at breakfast, dinner, tea, and supper. He would alike proclaim the identical fact, or sentiment, at bridal or funeral, whether in Europe, Asia, Africa, or America. The song is equally poured into the ear of man, woman, and child. He has but the one salutation, the one comfortable maxim, for friend, enemy, or stranger. He goes to bed with it sticking in his throat, and wakes up with it slipping from his lips. He trumpets his favorite maxim in clubs, highways, steamboats, churches, theatres, omnibuses, parlors, sleeping-rooms, ball-rooms, libraries, and holes and corners. He gives breath to the assertion in other people's houses, and in his own. He avows a like conviction on 'change, on race-courses, in cities, and in country quarters. He said it when he was robbed of a thousand pounds, and he would say it if he stood in the felon's dock at the Old Bailey, charged with robbery in turn. If his mutton chop were done up to a chip, or if the Bank of England were to break; if he had taken a bad half-crown, or if the universal sky had fallen, his cry then, and in all cases, would infallibly be the same:—"It all happens for the best."

It is a grand idea, to be sure; but then it is only *one*. No matter for its not being quite new,—if it were divisible—if it admitted of modification—if it were less rigid, arbitrary, positive.

To have but one idea, and that not your own, is better than to be quite notionless; yet this system of measuring every crooked line of life by one straight rule, does involve some difficulties and inaccuracies, no doubt. It may be very true—true as truth, in every imaginable application of it—always right when applied upon that particular principle which renders it impossible to be wrong; yet truth itself, we know, is sometimes attended with infinite (apparent) anomalies and contradictions, arising out of the time chosen for the utterance of it. The truth of one hour seems gross falsehood the next, though truth still. The rule of right here, is the wrong rule there, though in principle right as ever.

Thus, the expression, "It all happens for the best," may well become the lips of a father, when the exulting nurse places in his surprised and insufficient arms, two little new-born copies of him instead of one; but the remark does not so well apply years afterwards, when one of the twins pushes the other into a lime-kiln, or both conspire to effect a most successful forgery of the paternal hand-writing lodged at the banker's.

Again, it all happens for the best, has a noble and hospitable sound, when your wife's mother, and her three unmarried daughters, come to stay a month or two with you in your snug retreat, they having by various cross purposes been turned temporarily out of their own house; yet it has not so sweet a sound, but indeed a very cracked and hollow one at times, when you find that they do not intend ever to go away again.

It all happens for the best, is not by any means

an unreasonable remark, as times go, when we are told that our deadly enemy has been caught, while trespassing, in a man-trap; but it has a horrid click, it falls with a painful report upon the ear, when we discover that our dearest friend has been accidentally shot by a spring gun, while pursuing the rascal.

But the two circumstances would be treated as one by the philosophic, single-thoughted Jeremy Scrap. It all happens for the best, is his song and his sermon. He has some party predilections; but whether Whig or Tory come in, he is satisfied that it happens for the best. He is capable of ardent friendship; but whether the sharer of his heart win or lose the prize of honor and power aimed at, moves not the deep spring of feeling within him—either way, he is sure that the best has happened. He is a fond husband, but if his wife were to run off with the penny-postman next St. Valentine's day, his wound would gape to receive the same balm, and the same balm would be poured into it profusely:—It all happens for the best.

When Jeremy was horsewhipped by mistake, simply because he happened to put on a blue coat with bright buttons, he found immense comfort—it all happened for the best:—the right man had been spared a flogging, and the intemperate whipper had to pay damages all the same.

When he lost fifteen hundred at whist at a sitting, he rubbed his palms together within a few weeks, and chuckled at the agreeable recollection. With that same sum of money, he had been on the eve of buying a little place in Essex; and the gentleman who had taken it in his stead, had just been tossed by a bull.

Nobody has a right to find fault with Jeremy Scrap's practice in all its particulars: every one is privileged if he chooses, without injury to another, thus to turn his wrongs, losses, and miseries into gains and comforts: and he is wise in so doing, provided his philosophy prevent him not from seeing, that one thing is in itself—apart from its "happening" to the wrong person, or out of season—decidedly better than another, and more worthy the endeavor to secure it. Jeremy has a free-born Englishman's perfect and unadulterated right to rejoice, when his fields are flooded, and his crops are destroyed; when his uninsured house is burnt to the ground; when he takes a leap too much, and, breaking his hunter's neck, risks his own;—in these cases, let him cry as loud as he will, "It all happens for the best," and be as happy as the new year!

But his right is not so natural and clear, to raise the same cry, when his stack of hay or wheat is destroyed, not by accident, but the incendiary; when his favorite mare is poisoned on the eve of a race, in which he was sure to lose; when a villain knocks half his brains out on the highway, but only robs him of three-and-sixpence after all! It all happens for the best, is his sure note of comfort under wrongs and calamities such as these; but what right has he to rejoice in another's wrong-doing, or to assert that the wickedness of his fellow-creatures happens for the best.

Jeremy is decidedly in the wrong: every thing does *not* happen for the best. It may soothe his bruised and aching head to reflect, that although he was sorely beaten on the sconce by the highwayman, he had left his purse of gold at home; but the good little Christian philosopher should not forget, though the remembrance may trouble his tranquil doze, that one who feels heat and cold, as he does—who had father and mother, as he had—who has thought, passion, nerves, sinews, hopes, fears, as he has—who has frail flesh, and soul indestructible, as he has—had committed a robbery and outrage upon his fellow—broken, rashly, wilfully broken, the bond of brotherhood!

No, Jeremy Scrap; that never yet happened for the best on any highway of the world, and it is of no use to seek comfort in your favorite cry, or to attempt a universal cure with one precious medicine.

But the good easy world does not hear the maxim in that key. It puts no such restraint upon Jeremy.

It considers that Scrap's wrongs and injuries, however received, are his personal property, and that he may dance at his own funeral if he likes, without being at all bound to consider the shock to be sustained by the injured and disappointed mourners. The world would not esteem him to be one bit in the wrong, if he were to treat the very worst that could befall himself with the extreme of levity;—if, for example, he were to walk off consciously and deliberately to a ball and supper, having within him a large poisoned dumpling which had been administered by his housekeeper, to whom he had given notice that he had no idea of marrying at present. No, no; people would only admire his magnanimity and resignation; and however large the dumpling, and replete with sugar of lead, they would be apt not merely to approve, but to echo his cry of content—"It *all* happened for the best."

The cool world, however, as we all know, warms up fast enough upon occasions; and quarrel it will, and does, with Jeremy Scrap as often as he applies the balm of his maxims to any other wounds than *his own.* This is the point—this is where his doctrine leads him into dilemmas, some of them the most grave, some the most whimsical. If Scrap had his head in the lion's mouth when the lion's tail wagged, his inward expiring cry, "It all happens for the best," would be echoed from without, with "All right." But when Jeremy is but a bystander—mark this difference!—and when he sees a hungry wolf scampering off with a mouthful of calf and black silk stocking, taken from the leg of an unsuspecting clergyman, perambulating among his flock—then this pious ejaculation, "It all happens for the best," has an unfailing and natural tendency to render the mutilated prop of the church more wild, with passion and resentment, than his four-legged assailant. We don't care what fortitude and heroism clerical flesh may be capable of at other seasons, when it is not undergoing any suffering at all; but certain we are that no flesh and blood could bear that terrible and exasperating combination of tooth and tongue; the balm must be an enormous aggravation of the bite.

This, nevertheless, to the present hour, is the gentle Jeremy's mode of prescribing comfort, under every form of trouble, difficulty, and affliction by which man, or woman either, can be visited. To bear sorrow is the common lot—but to bear such consolation quietly is not common. In the case which we have already taken the great liberty of supposing—that Mrs. Scrap might run away with the postman on the 14th of February, Jeremy, if it so please him, must indulge his old reflection; but to go forth in the garb of Christian philosophy, and raise this consoling, this vindicatory outcry at another gentleman's door, is, to use a strong expression—another thing.

To the weary, way-worn man, wandering in search of a workhouse to his taste, or a parish that has within its boundaries even a pump of a Christian turn of mind—with scores of miles yet to walk, wet, cold, famine-smitten—to such a wretch when, footsore already, he runs a thorn through the crack in his bit of shoe—the healing maxim, "It all happens for the best," is worse than a mockery—it is a thorn run into his heart.

Tell not such a tale to the seaman, when the ship is on fire; it won't do even, in this case, to tell it to the marines. Tell it not to the struggling trader, when his chief debtor drops headlong into ruin, dragging him after; nor to the inventor who lives to see the completed work of his brain enriching half the world, and leaving him a beggar; nor to the author whose manuscript performs the grand tour of the great publishers and is still "at home"—until, publishing at his own cost, the critics, like savages, come out on the war-path, track him by the print he makes, and then scalp him. Whisper it not in the sandy desert (in fact, never go there, if you can help it) when the great winds arise; nor to the dwellers by Etna when the lava rushes down; nor to a luckless gentleman who loses his place under government, before he has had time to save his country; nor to the soldier with his frozen wounds; nor to an actor when he loses three pounds seven by his annual benefit; nor to a nice little boy with the toothache. Children are often very credulous, and have strong and flexile imaginations; but when you have told a kind, trusting little darling with the toothache, that "it all happens for the best," and he has believed you, bake him in a pie—he's not fit to live!

However, Scrap does this. Jeremy does it every day, as sure as you're born. He told Kitty so when Job broke off the match after a nine years' acquaintance—she would have slapped his face, only she fainted. He said the same thing when his brother, of six persons who went up in a balloon, was the only one who fell out. When the "devouring element," which long threatened to burn down his house, burnt the next door instead, he called upon his neighbor and coolly apprised him that it had happened for the best.

Jeremy dined with us on Christmas-day. Then, when the fatal tidings reached the assembled party—when the shell exploded upon the dinner-table—when the one pang pierced through all hearts, like a hot circling wire—when the festival had turned to funeral, and ocular demonstration had convinced all that "the pudding had broken," and that Smash, the first-born of Chaos, had spificated that celestial globe—then, in the deepest gulf of our mortification and agony, a deeper was opened, by the old familiar tone—"It all happens for the best!" "Last Christmas-day (cried Jeremy,) Tom Gulp took plum-pudding three times, and he died at Michaelmas, just as the goose was coming up!"

Puddings will break, so will banks, and some say hearts—but that these things should happen for the *best!* Bless the little Scrap, what must his *worst* be!

INGENIOUS DEFENCE.—An inveterate tippler, in a provincial town in England, was fined five shillings, and costs, for being found in a state of inebriation. He made an elaborate appeal to the magistrate, in mitigation of punishment—and, although confessing his fault, demanded his immediate discharge, as he had already been fined four several times for the same offence.

QUID PRO QUO.—Turner, the painter, was at a dinner, where several artists, amateurs, and literary men were convened. A poet, by way of being facetious, proposed as a toast, "*The Painters and Glaziers of England.*" The toast was drunk; and Turner, after returning thanks for it, proposed "*Success to the Paper Stainers,*" and called on the poet to respond.

WOMEN AND THEIR MASTERS.

BY LAMAN BLANCHARD.

Most women have no characters at all.—POPE.

No characters! What then, thought I the other evening, as Martha entered to light the reading-lamp, whilst I again took up the volume which had been laid down as the shadows of twilight came on, and prepared to pursue my pleasant way through the curious and original pages of "Woman and her Master,"—what then must become of that hapless majority of the female race (poor things!) who depend upon servitude in some shape or other for existence—who, in infinite forms, and endless diversities of occupation, are handmaidens unto us the masculine ringers of bells and issuers of mandates, and who, if destitute of "characters," can have no situation in society—no place in creation!

It was, perhaps, the entrance of Martha that turned the tide of my thoughts into this channel, suddenly diverting the course of speculation from the grand subjeet of woman and her master to a single branch of it—to the condition of one great class of womankind, maids of all-work, mop-spinners multitudinous, household varieties, all coming under one sweeping denomination, though all ranking in due degree, whether as plain cooks or pretty nursemaids—Betty Finnikins *ad infinitum.*

Lady Morgan's researches and reflections had previously suggested a train of ideas associated, not with Woman and her Master, but with Man and his Mistress, which it would here be irrelevant to pursue at any length. Enough, if we turn from any historical facts that may be adduced in proof of the injustice and barbarity of the mastership which man has claimed and established over woman, to contemplate the state and condition of the half-dozen powdered and gold-laced lackeys whose souls hang on the breath of any mortal dowager that shall be named! Turn we to that picture, and see what a fearfully avenging spirit it portrays! It may be perfectly true, for aught we know quite positively to the contrary, that the profligate Menelaus deserted his fond and faithful wife, and then accused her of eloping with the Trojan youth; and it may be equally true that Mr. Brownrigg, about a century ago, was in reality the perpetrator of that atrocity in the coal-hole upon two unfortunate apprentices, of which it was the fate of poor innocent Mrs. B. to bear the punishment and ignominy. Still that pair of flashy footmen yonder—specimens of lordly superiority of man—having a soul apiece, and hanging on behind my Lady Lacklustre's carriage, as it is whisked from shop to shop and house to house, on errands the most frivolous and enterprises the least dignified imaginable—those two samples of the "beauty of the world," the "paragon of animals," the "quintessence of dust," reduced to that extremity, are evidences of a horrible system of retaliation, and prove woman to be exceedingly well inclined to pull down, wherever she may, the boasted dignity of the master, man.

——Man to man so oft unjust
Is always so to woman,

insists another great authority; but man is not so unjust as to dress up two women in the most grotesque and ludicrous finery, and set them swinging behind the vehicle he lolls in. Great conqueror and despot as he is, he does not absolutely drag the other sex victims at his chariot-wheels in triumph. From what is, we infer what would be. Every woman would be a lady of quality if she could, and where is the lady of quality that would be content with two beings of the "superior race" behind her coach, if she could conveniently have four? Who are so fond of parading the costly trappings of a crowd of wretched coxcombs in livery as women? What fine people take such pride in their footmen as fine ladies? It would be pleasant to know what Mrs. Sparkle's rascals in peach-colored plush think upon the great question between woman and her master.

But, passing all such considerations, let us return to the race of female domestics, of whom there are about a dozen rushing at once to memory, as you may see them crowding round the door of a registry office, waiting, as they would phrase it, to be put into black and white. "No characters at all!" Why, every man, bachelor or Benedick, who has looked or listened to any purpose, must have detected in the genus "Maidservant," instances of the most extraordinary character—character as strongly marked, as widely various, and as richly comic, as in any heroine of farce that has been seen realized to the very life on the stage by our most popular actresses. What exquisite oddities and what outrageous opposites have we not all beheld, if we would only take the trouble to call them to mind. It is their mistresses generally who vow that they are all alike—the mistresses, who do bear a striking resemblance to each other, in the view they take of the characters of the maids! Poor drudges! If one be slovenly, the cry is, it's the way with them all. If another purloin the tea and sugar, for which she has received an allowance in her amount of wages, the particular judgment involves a general censure, and the impossibility of finding one that is honest is established. But so far from being like each other, the variety extends even to the bounds of a probability that you can't find two alike. The class-likeness goes scarcely further than certain habits and usages common to most people—the disposition to lie in bed of a morning as long as they are allowed—to go to the play or the fair as often or oftener than possible—to relieve the tedium of a domesticated lot by letting in frequent visitors, seeing that their entertainment is as cheap as it is cordial. All maidservants are alike perhaps in other points—each possesses a box, which is thought to contain a prayer book, a dream book, and six yards of songs—with probably a lock of hair, or a valentine, much worn at the folds, and certainly the holiday ribbons. They are all alike moreover—all under forty-five—in a taste for flirting with the genteeler section of the various purveyors who pull the area-bell every morning. But else how opposite is each to each—how broadly distinct—as different as their eyes are from their ears!

The maidservants in large towns, and in quiet

country residences, in great families, and in tradesmen's houses, are all separate classes, of course—as apart from each other as the servant of the inn may be from the servant of the court, or as the drudges of the inns of court are from the select society of ladies'-maids. But the difference does not end here; for the lady's-maid does not less resemble the fat scullion than one individual of a class resembles another. It was my fortune, in those days when independent bachelorship had succeeded to parental subjugation, to note in one queer lodging-house a succession of Sarahs and Betsies that was almost as rapid as the transformations on the stage when six characters are sustained by one performer, but the characters themselves formed a variety beyond the ordinary reach of such representations. Some are wholly forgotten, but of several the recollection remains to this hour, rendered vivid and complete by some saying or doing that serves as a key-note to the peculiarity of the character.

For an example to begin with—the first that comes to mind; and it happens that the catalogue, like the list of the ladies (not to be more particularly alluded to) whom the poet loved, opens with Kitty. What a curiosity she was! She ought to be a cabinet-minister, or a representative of the people in parliament at least; not because she was distinguished for punctuality in the discharge of her

duties, but because she was so wonderfully expert in the art of making excuses for neglecting it. She was certainly the most careless little chit that ever spilt hot water over you, or left your new boots burning in the fender; but it could not be otherwise; so unceasingly and so profoundly must her mind have been intent on devising excuses for negligence and vindications of her conduct. Her small, keen, fixed gray eye told you plainly before you began to find fault, that she had made up her mind not to admit she was in the wrong, and her lips, the instant she opened them to explain, confirmed the ocular assertion. It was not merely that her excuses were generally first-rate, but that she was never without one. A dozen times a day she would be put upon her defence; but you might be sure, in that case, of witnessing exactly twelve apparently unstudied exercises of startling ingenuity in clearing herself from the charge. She threw her flip-flaps—if the metaphor may be allowed—with the readiest grace in the world, and so quickly, that you could never catch her off her feet. Her figments were uttered with the most inartificial air ever witnessed. When you thought she had not a word to say for herself, out she would come with a volume. Her system of excuse involved a most philosophical supposition, that as human nature is a more precious thing than aught else in creation, animate or inanimate, so any thing was to be blamed rather than that. If this be not new in theory, it was at least novel in practice, to the extent to which she carried it. Mats if she tripped, coals if she scorched any thing, bore the blame. As the feminine is more worthy than the neuter, the neuter was of course shown to be in fault.

You complained of her bringing you an unpolished tumbler—"Kitty, whenever you bring me a glass, see that it is quite bright—of all things I hate a dull glass." Yes, I think I see her taking the glass, holding it up to the light, and pretending to examine it with a puzzled look, saying half to herself, "Curious tumblers these are, somehow; I never seed glasses catch the *fluf* off the napkin like these do." I was rash enough to set her to bring me down a rare old china jug, prized for the sake of a former possessor. Of course she broke it, and had there been two she would have broken both. Into the room she came with the beautiful handle swinging upon her fingers, saying with the most delicious air of simplicity and wonderment that can be conceived, "Dear me, well! If I wasn't coming so softly down stairs, and had hold of it so, when just as I set my foot on the very last stair, the jug *let go of my hand!*" She could never be brought to admit more upon such occasions than what in effect amounted to this—that the smash was an act of pure volition on the part of the broken jug—

that she, innocent as she was, had been sent to fetch a very wilful and obstinate utensil, a piece of china resolutely bent on self-destruction.

There were traces of a curious perception of certain zoological distinctions, in some of Kitty's self-defences and evasions. I remember that some small delicacy, or what remained of it at dinner, had been specially put by for me as a relish for my breakfast; but when Kitty, to whose care it had been consigned, produced it next morning, the edge of the dish bore evident marks of the excursion of some small four-footed invaders. "Oh, the mice!" exclaimed my landlady in horror. "Why, Kitty, how could you now —?" etc. But Kitty was quite certain that the muscipular footmarks could have no connection with the feet of a mouse; no, the dish had been where mice could never be—it was quite impossible.

"Well, Kitty, look—do look, and believe the evidence of your own eyes."

"I'm right, ma'am," said Kitty, after she had taken a careful and conscientious survey all round the edge. "I'm right—and if I wasn't positive certain, I wouldn't say so—no, *they're not our mice.*" Our mice! To detect a difference between other people's mice and our own! Why, all the zoological council assembled couldn't have done it!

Kitty was succeeded by a little damsel who was called Ellen, a sprightly, bright-eyed thing, far too slight for the coarse offices allotted to her, and with something of a childish elegance about her air that might have graced a lot far different from a life of servitude. Her character was as strikingly seen in all she did as Kitty's was. In her, the ruling principle was politeness. To be polite was an instinct which she could not but obey. The first glimpse I had of the girl, was on the morning after she came, when glancing from the window while dressing, I saw her running down the steps very prettily, and in sweet clear tones calling out, "Sir! sir, if you please!" to the dustman. His bell drowned the small voice, but she went springing after him a little way, and I could perceive that she brought him back with an air not less full of natural grace, but less ostentatious, than that of the nymphs who precede the great princes in romantic operas and ballets, and throw flowers in their path. The scene ended in her smilingly begging his pardon, and *would* he have the kindness to come in and take away the dust that morning! The next day, I heard her tell the fishmonger's boy when he called for orders, "Soles, sir, if it's quite convenient." So completely was this principle of excessive urbanity and deference a part of her nature, that it was in operation on all occasions, and extended to all comers. It was no respecter of persons, recognized no distinctions, real or false;

But like the sun, it shone on all alike.

There was nothing—no, not a dash of the high-life-below-stairs vulgarity in her courtesies to the gardener or the stable-boy. The chimney-sweep was just as sure of a gentle and gracious reception. In short, little Ellen could not, though she had tried, have laid aside the bland and most urbane qualities of her manner. As little was she capable of divesting them of their real grace, or of having them mistaken for affected airs and mock civilities. She was polite merely because she could not help it. True, her politeness was excessively ludicrous sometimes, and now and then rather embarrassing, when it implicated others by taking upon herself to speak for them. Thus I overheard her one morning prefacing a message I had given her for the boot-cleaner, with my "compliments" (she was polite enough to call me her master, which I was not), her master's compliments, and he thought the boots had not been quite so well polished of late! She never received even a command from any one without a "thankee," and she always took a letter from the postman with a nice little courtesy, and a smile of acknowledgment that implied a sense of obligation for his kindness in bringing it. "My master's much obliged," she would sometimes say as she handed the twopence. I'm not sure that she did not, one wet day, crown her politeness by offering to come and ask me to lend the postman my umbrella—she was certain he would get wet—and carrying other people's letters too!

One occasion I particularly recollect, and it affords a good illustration of Ellen's sensitiveness on the score of giving trouble. A man had brought me some books, for which, on delivery, she impressively thanked him; when, as he was turning away, it occurred to him that he had a letter to deliver with the packet, and he began to search industriously in his bag. Observing the anxiety with which he pried into the corners of it, she said to him, in her excess of good-nature, "Oh, sir, pray don't trouble yourself."

"Trouble myself!" returned the honest man, elevating his eyebrows rather contemptuously, "why, if I have a letter to deliver as well as the books, I must deliver it, mustn't I?" and he proceeded with his search for a minute or two, when Ellen's good-natured concern for him broke out again, with, "I'm sorry to keep you waiting."

"Waiting!" muttered the messenger; "why, it ain't you that keeps me waiting. But no, there's no letter here—certainly not—well, I thought I had one."

"Oh, sir!" cried Ellen, bent on tranquillizing his mind, and settling the matter with the truest politeness and delicacy of feeling,—"oh, sir, never mind —I dare say it doesn't signify—*another time, perhaps!*"

Ellen's stay in my landlady's service was not of long duration; for my landlady herself was taken suddenly ill, was dying. A friend of the invalid sent twice a day to inquire how she had slept and how she had sat up. Ellen regularly brought down the answer, "My missis's compliments, and she has had a very indifferent night;" or, "My missis's compliments, and she feels very weak to-day." This went on for six weeks, twice a day for six weeks, and Ellen seemed to grow more and more sensible of the kindness and attention every time the messenger came. The compliments were sent back as usual, but the intelligence became sadder and sadder. At length, one day, when the friendly inquiry after the health of her mistress came as before, poor Ellen crept to the door with swollen eyes streaming with tears, and sobbed out the melancholy answer, "My missis's compliments, and she died this morning at eight o'clock."* Here is the

* A friend, to whom I related this story, thinks he has heard something like it before. That may be, but it does not disturb my fact. In recording these little whimsicalities of character, I am recollecting, not inventing, and will vouch for every word of them.

"ruling passion" displaying its strength, not exactly in death, but in its close neighborhood.

This change brought other servants, though it did not render my removal necessary. Among them, came a girl of a most literal and matter-of-fact turn of mind, who persisted in calling herself Sophonisba, because she was so christened, but who, for that reason, I remorselessly cut down to Soph. She never could comprehend why the other three syllables should be lopped off—why people should be called "out of their names." The first specimen of her "characteristics" that I noticed, was when I sent her to Longman's (years ago) to get some old book, and she brought back the answer in these terms; "Please sir, Messrs. Longman, Hurst, Rees, Orme, Brown, and Green, say that the work is out of print." She would rather have perished than omitted a partner, and she would have added "and Co." had she found it on the doorpost.

The gentleman who denied that the Duke of Wellington could ever have reaped any of his laurels in India, seeing that the laurel does not grow there, was less literal than Soph. It was absolutely necessary to speak by the card when you spoke to her; but even then you were not safe. Her capacity for not comprehending, was as profound as Kitty's ingenuity in framing an excuse. You took especial pains—say—to warn her against the hard-egg-boiling principle; you picked the plainest words out of the dictionary to impress upon her mind the simple fact in natural philosophy, that three minutes will suffice for the boiling of an egg. At last, you make her clearly comprehend, and feel that you may safely calculate on a breakfast. No, the eggs come up as before, hard as undertakers' hearts. "Now, Soph," I cried out, on such an occasion, "how is this? Here they are, boiled fit for a salad, in spite of every direction. What did I tell you?"

"Oh! sir, I remember exakly what you told me, and acted according. The eggs was in the water, to a moment, precisely nine minutes."

"Nine! I told you three."

"Yes, sir, but there's three eggs. Of course, if one takes three minutes boiling, three *must* take nine. I may be a fool, sir, but I happen to know what three-times-three makes for all that!" Soph was incorrigible; she was a plague perpetually, and longer.

But though Soph had not an *iota* of imagination, the excess of the matter-of-fact of which she was made sometimes bordered on the imaginative, as the ridiculous approaches the confines of the sublime. She understood no more of Life and Death than a great philosopher. If she ever conceived an idea in connection with them, it was perhaps that the second is what we may call a mere "carrying out" of the principle of the first—the continuation of what *is*. She had no notion of their being distinct or dissimilar. It was impossible that she could imagine a different state of being to that which, living, she experienced; nor could she more readily understand how the present state should terminate. The somebody that was dead, she could never picture to herself as in the slightest degree changed from the somebody that had been alive. A winged angel was not more unapproachably raised beyond the scope of her ideas, than was a mass of senseless clay, mute and motionless matter, cut off for ever from the life it had held and enjoyed. She knew nothing of either. She only knew that Susan Hicks, deceased, had been her fellow-servant in this world, and she considered that Susan Hicks, when she was carried to the churchyard, had simply taken another situation—in short, that she had gone to another place. We all know with what blank and unspeculative eyes a primrose by a river's brim would be seen by Peter Bell,

And what it was to Wordsworth's oaf,
A yellow primrose was to Soph,
And it was nothing more.

But then, as was observed above, the acuteness of her sense of the actual, touched sometimes upon the verge of the ideal, and it might be said that she dived profoundly into the very surface of things.

A simple anecdote will help to explain all this. When the day fixed for the funeral of her old fellow-servant came, Soph evinced considerable sensi-

bility on the score of the weather, which looked dreadfully unpromising. I suspected that Soph's feelings were enlisted on behalf of the bombazin of the mourners, but it was not that, as I found out presently. From my place near a window, it happened that I could see her coming every five minutes to the garden door, to look at the clouds. "It'll rain presently, and preciously too," was the first cry. Then, with her hand stretched out into the pelting shower, to feel whether it was real water or not, "Ah! here it comes down, sure enough." Then, in ten minutes more, "It's set in for the day, that *I* can see, with my two eyes." (Some Sophs would have said, "with half an eye," but our Soph had no idea of such optical subdivisions.) However, the day began to promise better presently, and out she came again, ogling the scattered clouds, and decided that she shouldn't wonder if it were to clear up after all; till at last, when it began to brighten beyond mistake, she came once more, with her mind now made up, "Yes, yes, it's giving over now—*Susan will have a fine day to be buried!*" Not a thought about the followers in bombazin—the living clad in crape at so much per yard—but only about the late Miss Hicks, who was to set out on a long journey. She thought of Susan as having some business of importance to perform that day, as a traveller *nolens volens*, or as being doomed to take, without further delay, a very serious step in life. She would have said the same thing, had it been a wedding that was to take place. "Susan will have a fine day to be married!" Here, again, is the ruling passion strong in affinity with death.

What is the name of the good doctor, who, propped up on his pillow, desired his servant to stir the fire and shut the door gently, for he was going to die? How scrupulously, and as a matter of regular business, would Soph have obeyed his orders. Rare Soph! How she used to make me laugh! When she leaves her last place, and her name is headed with a large "WANTED," in death's list of advertisements, all I can say is, may she have a fine day to be buried!

The next name in my catalogue is Jane, who was old enough to have had a system of her own, and who invariably acquired one in whatever place she happened to be, but never acted upon it until she found herself in another service. What you expressly desired her to do in your own way, she did in point blank opposition to your orders, and according to the instructions she had received in her previous situation. This had evidently been her rule through life. She was a pattern of a servant, after she had left your house. All your regulations were sure to be observed, when she quitted your service. Her rule of pleasing you was simply a dutiful observance of the whims of other people.

Jane was quite as original in all her proceedings as any of them, an odd mixture of the tractable and the obstinate. She blundered unceasingly upon the strictest system, and was so anxious to give satisfaction that she would never do what she was told, for fear it should be wrong. Her best conscience was, that as she served you, so she had served her previous master; and though she had been inattentive to his desires, she was doing him ample justice in your family. She interfered with every thing and every body in the house, because all was not arranged in the order observed in Mr. Fitzcox's establishment. She worried the cook out of her life.

"Lor! do you put citron into that pudding? Mr. Fitzcox's cook never did. I'm sure I should never send up currant jelly with the haunch; Mr. Fitzcox couldn't abear it."

In defiance of the strictest injunction, she contrived to smuggle a climbing-boy up the chimneys, because Mr. Fitzcox's flues could not be swept nicely by a machine. Thus, the rules of her last place, which she had rigidly disregarded there, were in your house brought into conscientious operation, and what you wished her to do would be faithfully done for your successor.

The only prank that she played off at my expense was, first, when she was caught tampering with the newsman, and endeavoring to exclude the *Morning Chronicle* from the house—I fancied from a horror of Whig principles—but it turned out that Mr. Fitzcox had always taken in the *Morning Post;* and, secondly, during my absence for a day or two, when she must needs carry my letters and newspapers down to the Travellers' Club, to which I did not belong, because she had been in the habit of leaving Mr. Fitzcox's there, when he was not expected to return home. I told her she wanted a much more arbitrary mistress than the one she served; to which she answered, "I often wonder, sir, why *you* don't marry, and have an establishment of your own."

"Good heavens! why?"

"Why, sir, Mr. Fitzcox did!"

Rebecca succeeded Jane, but Rebecca was overmuch religious, and did not stay long. I believe I frightened her by a habit, not very moderately indulged in at that period, of spouting *Hamlet's* soliloquies and *Othello's* address, before the looking-glass of a morning, sometimes during the perilous operation of shaving. This profane practice, with the duty of setting out a card-table, two evenings a week, for a rubber at whist, was a shock she couldn't stand. All I can relate of her with certainty is comprised in her address to the cat, that was muttering "deep-mouthed thunder" at the door of the room, as she was quitting it one day.

"Ur—r—r—rh!" Rebecca growled forth as she went down stairs, "ur—r—rh you! Where do you expect to go to when you die? *swearing* in that manner!"

How little do any of us remember compared with the quantity we forget! These, such as they are, and a dozen more quite as strongly marked, as distinct from each other, and as consistent with themselves, were noted within the space of two or three years. How many maid-servants worthy to be noted might the reminiscence of a lifetime recall to view! The Cloes, Flavias, and Narcissas of Pope live in the rare and exquisite beauty of the painting; but else how common! How much of the extraordinary in character is unseen in women of all ranks, merely because it is not looked for or expected, or because it has not been fashionable to recognize it! Is it detected in the drawing-room only? Look into the kitchen, "up stairs and down stairs, and in my lady's chamber;" and wherever there is a woman there is a wonder.

"Of all the girls that were so smart," in one sense or other, I have a vivid recollection of fair Fanny. She was a curiosity of the Nervous School. How she used to faint away! Fainting is, in other girls, a weakness, an accident, or an expedient; in her it was a principle—it was her destiny. Her ruling passion pointed ever to a little purple cut-glass bottle, filled with pungent salts, the stopper of which was seldom allowed to remain in it more than an hour at a time. Exactly half her wages were spent in the purchase of staylaces, which were continually being cut. It came out, upon inquiry, that she was the victim of sensibility. Fanny had fallen head over heels in love—yet decorously withal—with some gentleman's gentleman, who, insensible to the value of his conquest, had accompanied his master abroad, and left her to pine and wither in single uncomfortableness. But this would not have been her lot either, had she not, one fatal Whit-Monday, resolved on spending the evening of her holiday in the two-shilling gallery at Drury-lane. There, for the first time in her life she saw a popular actor performing the character of *Rolla.* Now it might have happened to any other actor—at all events that particular actor is not responsible for the result—but it did so fall out that Fanny discovered, or fancied she discovered, something in the face, or voice, or manner, or the soul that shone through the eyes of *Rolla*, so strangely, so startlingly like the faithless gentleman's gentleman in Italy, that her heart leaped up as it never did when she beheld

A rainbow in the sky.

One long, shrill, piercing cry of "Richard," rang through the crowded theatre, setting the dear little child of *Cora* (a stunted babe of eleven) screaming with sudden terror, and then Fanny fainted. From that moment, fainting became a passion. It was a propensity that grew upon her with use, and she could no more have got through a day without it than she could have got through a week without sleep. It was her constant relief, her sweetest recreation. Merely to mention the name of *Rolla's* representative was at all times more than enough. Even the first syllable of that agitating name, as articulated by some pigeons that recreated in the next garden, sufficed to send her off six times a day. Nay, so strong is the sympathy, so subtle the affection, in these nervous cases, that, believe it or not, I only happened to make some allusion to "the Last of the Mohicans," while she was in the room, without mentioning the author's name, which she could never have heard of, when I saw her turn pale, and the little purple bottle was in additional requisition that morning. She used to tremble every time she saw the water butt for the supply of the garden—thinking from whose hands it came. My landlady was obliged to have her intermediate taken in in bottles—the barrel would have been heart-breaking.

Poor Fanny! she used to enjoy her holiday now and then so much, it afforded her such leisure for going off; she allowed herself a double supply of the pungent essence on those days. It was quite a matter of course to be told of a morning, "Fanny will finish dusting your books directly; she's only going to faint;" or to hear the sensitive creature, when desired by her mistress to light the candles, cry out, "I'll bring them in a minute or two, ma'am, as soon as I've fainted!" Little did she resemble

Her who in sweet vicissitudes appears,
Of mirth and opium, ratafie and tears.

Here there was no vicissitude. If there was a minute of the day when she was not "going," it was when she was gone. But it agreed with her, like a good cry.

There was a Sarah, too, who stayed a few days, and claims to figure in the queer collection. She was noticeable chiefly for her prodigious volubility, and a genius for the obscure. Unless she made a long speech, she was wholly unintelligible. The first words I heard from her, ran thus: "There's never an umbrella in the house but two in the world, and t'other two's in use." She would have been Irish, if any one country could have claimed such a compound. What Sarah said, you might not understand, but you must hear, for her voice was loud enough to proclaim her quarrel with some "first cousin," one evening, outside the gate.

"It's not," she remarked on that occasion, "as if I'd been an infidel to you, in fact it's rather more not than t'other."

The "t'other," in both cases, is characteristic of the exquisite confusion of meaning. But when she could let her tongue fairly loose, to wander at its own sweet will, then was Sarah in her glory. The windows open, we could hear her holding forth to her companion below:—

"This Easter Sunday! Bless my soul, and such bad weather! I assure you I remember the time having gooseberry-pudding for dinner on Easter Sunday; it was the time my poor mother was out nursing at Kingston—yes, it was Kingston, Kingston-on-Thames—and my sister made a gooseberry-pudding, and I know I didn't like it; yes, my poor dear mother, who's dead and gone now, was nursing of Mrs. Hadlington, and I know it was Easter Sunday, for I had a new frock on, a pink stripe it was, because I remember it had wire buttons down the back—it was too late on Saturday night to get cambric ones, so I put wire, and Mr. Macintosh came to see my sister Kate, and father wouldn't let him in, for he'd never seen him in his life before; but I went out for the dinner-beer—I know it was the dinner-beer, for it rained, and I had my green-silk bonnet on—so as I was a saying, as I came back, Mr. Macintosh gave me twopence to tell Kate to come out if she could, and my grandmother used to encourage it. Well, my sister made the pudding, for poor dear mother that's dead and gone, this time eleven year, was nursing, and so Mr. Macintosh used to come and stand opposite. I often think of that time when mother was alive, and we all had a mother then, though we havn't now—yes, we've got a mother-in-law, because father married agin—he married the cook at Waterloo House, you know Hodgson's,—and I'm sure I shall never forget Easter Sunday; for if you believe me, that day five weeks Kate was Mrs. Macintosh!"

Call her off you might, but she would return three-quarters of an hour after to the scene, and take up another thread of the story—"Ah! yes—and well do I remember father saying one day, 'Here, hem me these two white neck-handkerchiefs,' just as I'm telling you, for it was a square of muslin he gave me, so I had to cut it in half; because he told me he was going out on Sunday at eight o'clock on a day's pleasure. Well, that happened on the 8th of May, and so I got up the next morning with something on my mind that told me, 'Sally, all isn't right.' So I was standing by the pump, and a lady comes up and says to me, 'Good morning, I think your name's Sarah?'—'Yes, Sarah Dixon is my name, I was born, bred, and christened so, and I shall carry it to my grave with me.' 'Well, Sarah,' she says, 'if you look on the table in your father's bed-room, that with the looking-glass, you will see a parcel, it's for you.' Well, sure enough there was —something wrapped up in paper, foolscap paper, and a white wafer above all things. You might have knocked me down with a feather. Lo and behold a piece of cake—wedding cake, and they'd actually been and married. You may be sure my blood was up, for you must know I'm rather fiery; I take after my poor dear mother for that; but she was a good creature, though she's dead and gone." Quiet home was ours, when the head of the class of clacks were gone also.

—But I must come to a close, or my picture will be growing too large for its frame. Many a maid, besides this handful of Sophs and Sallys, whether of the cook, the housemaid, the servant of all-work, or the first-rate waiting-woman tribe, "wants a situation" in this little collection, and might say what the insulted sweep said to the dashing highwayman at the drop, "I've as much right to be here as you have." But all this time, while attracted by the "women," we have neglected their "masters." The subject at its commencement had suggested the inditing a few paragraphs, which shall now be a few sentences on that theory of gallantry and devotion to "the sex," the maintenance of which is, in many handsome words, held by youthful, middle-aged, and elderly masculines alike, to be both a pleasure and a duty, but the practice of which, in so many handsome acts, is held to be neither one nor the other.

The sex! What does any one of us understand by "the sex?" What proportion of the female race does the word include in our ideas of its practical meaning? How many women do we mean to admit the existence of, as having a right and title to the exercise of that generous gallantry which we call a duty and a delight, when we speak of the sex? Just those comparatively few members of it who can afford to employ the rest to wait upon their wills, and do their spiritings gently. The "sex," as the claimant of the exercise of gallantry, and the inspirer of devotional respect, means women who hire other women as servants, and who don't live by arranging the caps and curls, or dusting the chairs and curtains, of other people. Where were those gentlemen educated, and at what hour of the day may they be met with, and in what city of Europe do they chiefly abide, who are gallant and tender to a maiden with a mop, unless with a view to injure and degrade her? The gallantry of man to the other sex, is simply a narrow-class feeling, not a sentiment as universal as the eyes and breath, and language and motions of woman. It is the principle that stands by its order, and stops there. The lady drops her glove, and a dozen cavaliers would sacrifice theirs, how white and well-fitted soever, in the dust, to spare her the fatigue of even glancing at it where it lies; but the cavalier who drops his glove on the staircase, will allow any waiting-maid in the house to descend and pick it up for him. He will rush with an armful of shawls to save the lady "of his order" from a breath of air too much in her way from the door to her carriage; but you shall observe afterwards, that he is not at all shocked when the maid-servant runs out into the rain, uncovered, to bring him his umbrella. He must not serve his sister so, he dares not serve his wife so; still less would he dream of serving his friend's wife so; but what does he care for Sue? "Who on earth," would the man of gallantry internally exclaim, if required to put himself a hair's breadth out of the way,—"who on earth, I should like to know, is Sue!" That she was mere woman, would go exactly for nothing.

NOTELETS OF SAMUEL ROGERS.

FROM DYCE'S "TABLE TALK."

Lord Dudley and Ward was celebrated in Parliament for his fine studied speeches. Rogers burlesqued his method in an exceedingly neat, malicious epigram, which Byron, in conversation with Lady Blessington, pronounced "one of the best in the English language, with the true Greek talent of expressing, by implication, what is wished to be conveyed:"—

Ward has no heart, they say, but I deny it;
He has a heart, and gets his speeches by it.

Dudley (as Lockhart remarks), took capital revenge, in a review of Rogers' Columbus, in the Quarterly, a specimen of cool, exhausting criticism. Rogers comes out of it like a cat taken, at the last gasp, from the receiver of an air-pump.

Tuthill, by the way, has his couplet on "the joke about Lord Dudley speaking by heart." Moore preserves it in his Diary:—

In vain my affections the ladies are seeking:
If I give up my heart, there's an end to my speaking.

Lady Blessington also tried an adaptation of it:—

The charming Mary has no mind they say;
I prove she has—it changes every day.

It was Lord Dudley who made the remark, when he heard of Sir Walter Scott's pecuniary disasters: "Scott ruined! the author of Waverley ruined! Let every man to whom he has given months of delight, give him a sixpence, and he will rise to-morrow morning richer than Rothschild."

Rogers says, "I was to dine on a certain day with the Princess of Wales, at Kensington, and, thinking that Ward (Lord Dudley) was to be of the party, I wrote to him, proposing that we should go together. His answer was, "Dear Rogers, I am not invited. The fact is, when I dined there last, I made several rather free jokes, and the Princess, taking me perhaps for a clergyman, has not asked me back again."

Lady Holland, when she wanted to get rid of a fop, used to say, "I beg your pardon,—but I wish you would sit a little further off; there is something on your handkerchief which I don't like."

When any gentleman, to her great annoyance, was standing with his back close to the chimney-piece, she would call out, "Have the goodness, sir, to stir the fire!"

Charade.—What is it that causes a cold, cures a cold, and pays the doctor? A draft.

Gilt Un-Comfort.—Mr. ——'s house, the ——,

is very splendid; it contains a quantity of or-molu. Now, I like to have a kettle in my bed-room, to heat a little water if necessary; but I can't get a kettle at the ——, though there is a quantity of or-molu. Lady —— says, that when she is at the ——, she is obliged to have her clothes unpacked three times a day; for there are no chests-of-drawers, though there is a quantity of or-molu.

No Right Here.—A friend of mine in Portland Place has a wife who inflicts upon him every season two or three immense evening parties. At one of those parties, he was standing, in a very forlorn condition, leaning against the chimney-piece, when a gentleman, coming up to him, said, "Sir, as neither of us is acquainted with any of the people here, I think we had best go home."

High Gambling.—When I was living in the Temple, the chimneys of one of my neighbors were to be swept. Up went two boys; and at the end of an hour they had not come down again. Two other boys were then sent up; and up they remained also. The master of the boys was now summoned, who, on his arrival, exclaimed, "Oh, the idle little rascals! they are playing at all-fours on the top of the chimney." And to be sure, there they were, trumping it away at their ease. I suppose *spades* were their favorite cards.

Double Dumbmy.—Lord Seaforth, who was born deaf and dumb, was to dine one day with Lord Melville. Just before the time of the company's arrival, Lady Melville sent into the dining-room a lady of her acquaintance, who could talk with her fingers to dumb people, that she might receive Lord Seaforth. Presently Lord Guilford entered the room; and the lady, taking him for Lord Seaforth, began to ply her fingers very nimbly: Lord Guilford did the same; and they had been carrying on a conversation in this manner for about ten minutes, when Lady Melville joined them. Her female friend immediately said, "Well, I have been talking away to this dumb man." "Dumb!" cried Lord Guilford; "bless me, I thought *you* were dumb." I told this story (which is perfectly true) to Mathews; and he said that he could make excellent use of it at one of his evening entertainments; but I know not if he ever did.

A Duel in the Dark.—An Englishman and a Frenchman having quarrelled, they were to fight a duel. Being both great cowards, they agreed (for their mutual safety, of course) that the duel should take place in a room perfectly dark. The Englishman had to fire first. He groped his way to the hearth, fired up the chimney, and brought down—the Frenchman, who had taken refuge there.

A "Natural" Excuse.—A certain man of pleasure about London received a challenge from a young gentleman of his acquaintance; and they met at the appointed place. Just before the signal for firing was given, the man of pleasure rushed up to his antagonist, embraced him, and vehemently protested that "he could not lift his arm *against his own flesh and blood!*" The young gentleman, though he had never heard any imputation cast upon his mother's character, was so much staggered, that (as the sagacious man of pleasure had foreseen) no duel took place.

A Naked Fact.—Humphrey Honarth, the surgeon, was called out, and made his appearance in the field stark naked, to the astonishment of the challenger, who asked him what he meant. "I know," said H., "that if any part of the clothing is carried into the body by a gunshot wound, festering ensues; and therefore I have met you thus." His antagonist declared, that fighting with a man *in puris naturalibus* would be quite ridiculous; and accordingly they parted without further discussion.

The Back Track.—Lord Alvanley, on returning home, after his duel with young O'Connel, gave a guinea to the hackney-coachman who had driven him out and brought him back. The man, surprised at the largeness of the sum, said, "My lord, I only took you to ——." Alvanley interrupted him, "My friend, the guinea is *for bringing me back*, not for taking me out."

Three Irishmen (I am glad that they were not Englishmen) went up Vesuvius. They stopped at the hermitage to refresh themselves; and while they were drinking Lachrima Christi there, the Emperor and Empress of Austria arrived. The three Irishmen positively refused to admit them; but afterwards, on being told that a lady was outside, they offered to give up half the apartment. Upon this, the attendants of the Emperor (though against his wish) speedily cleared the hermitage of the three Irishmen, who, in a great passion, proceeded up to the crater. As they were coming down again, they met the royal personages, whom they abused most heartily, calling the Empress a variety of names under her bonnet. No notice of all this was ever taken by the Emperor: but, the story having got wind immediately, the three Irishmen thought it best to decamp next morning from Naples, their conduct having excited the highest indignation among the British who were resident there. I once told this anecdote at Lord Lonsdale's table, when Lord Eldon and Lord Castlereagh were present; and the remark of Lord Castlereagh was, "I am sorry to say that it is too true."

Witticisms are often attributed to the wrong people. It was Lord Chesterfield, not Sheridan, who said, on occasion of a certain marriage, that "Nobody's son had married Everybody's daughter."

Lord Chesterfield remarked of two persons dancing a minuet, that "they looked as if they were hired to do it, and were doubtful of being paid."

A Scotch Lady, hearing that it was desirable in any danger *to have presence of mind*, replied, "I had rather *have absence of body*."

Horne Tooke, when at school, was asked by the boys, "what his father was?" Tooke answered, "A Turkey merchant." (He was a poulterer.)

He once said to his brother, a pompous man, "You and I have reversed the natural course of things; you have risen by your gravity; I have sunk by my levity."

To Judge Ashhurst's remark, that the law was open to all, both to the rich and to the poor, Tooke replied, "So is the London Tavern."

He said that Hume wrote his History as witches say their prayers—backwards.

Vernon was a capital story-teller. He invented the story about the lady being pulverized in India by a *coup de soleil:*—When he was dining there with a Hindoo, one of his host's wives was reduced to ashes; upon which, the Hindoo *rang the bell*, and said to the attendant who answered it, "Bring fresh glasses, and sweep up your mistress."

Another of his stories was this. He happened to be shooting hyenas near Carthage, when he stumbled, and fell down an abyss of many fathoms' depth. He was surprised, however, to find himself unhurt; for he lighted as if on a feather-bed. Presently he perceived that he was gently moved upwards; and, having by degrees reached the mouth of the abyss, he again stood safe on *terra firma*. He had fallen upon an immense mass of bats, which, disturbed from their slumbers, had risen out of the abyss and brought him up with them.

Beauty of Youth.—One afternoon, at Court, I was standing beside two intimate acquaintances of mine, an old nobleman and a middle-aged lady of rank, when the former remarked to the latter that he thought a certain young lady near us was uncommonly beautiful. The middle-aged lady replied, "I cannot see any particular beauty in her." "Ah, madam," he rejoined, "to us old men, youth always appears beautiful!" (a speech with which Wordsworth, when I repeated it to him, was greatly struck). The fact is, till we are about to leave the world, we do not perceive how much it contains to excite our interest and admiration: the sunsets appear to me far lovelier now than they were in other years; and the bee upon the flower is now an object of curiosity to me, which it was not in my early days.

Curran.—I once dined with Curran in the public room of the chief inn at Greenwich, when he talked a great deal, and, as usual, with considerable exaggeration. Speaking of something which he would *not* do on any inducement, he exclaimed vehemently, "I had rather be hanged on twenty gibbets." "Don't you think, sir, that *one* would be enough for you?" said a girl, a stranger, who was sitting at the table next to us. I wish you could have seen Curran's face. He was absolutely confounded,—struck dumb.

Grattan's Uncle, Dean Marley, had a good deal of the humor of Swift. Once, when the footman was out of the way, he ordered the coachman to fetch some water from the well. To this the coachman objected that, *his* business was to *drive*, not to run on errands. "Well, then," said Marley, "bring out the coach and four, set the pitcher inside, and *drive* to the well;"—a service which was several times repeated, to the great amusement of the village.

Lord Ellenborough had infinite wit. When the income-tax was imposed, he said that Lord Kenyon (who was not very nice in his habits) intended, in consequence of it, to lay down—his pocket-handkerchief.

A lawyer one day pleading before him, and using several times the expression "my unfortunate client," Lord Ellenborough suddenly interrupted him, —"There, sir, the court is with you."

Lord Ellenborough was once about to go on the circuit, when Lady E. said that she should like to accompany him. He replied that he had no objections, provided she did not encumber the carriage with bandboxes, which were his utter abhorrence. They set off. During the first day's journey, Lord Ellenborough, happening to stretch his legs, struck his feet against something below the seat. He discovered that it was a bandbox. His indignation is not to be described. Up went the window, and out went the bandbox. The coachman stopped; and the footmen, thinking that the bandbox had tumbled out of the window by some extraordinary chance, were going to pick it up, when Lord Ellenborough furiously called out, "Drive on!" The bandbox accordingly was left by a ditch side. Having reached the county town where he was to officiate as judge, Lord Ellenborough proceeded to array himself for his appearance in the court-house. "Now," said he, "where's my wig,—where *is* my wig?" "My Lord," replied his attendant, "it was thrown out of the carriage window."

A COLLEGE LAY.

ANONYMOUS.

Here let me read; and reading, try
To picture these old authors in my eye:
But to begin with, here's an unknown word—
I ought to know it, but—oh! how absurd!
I'll look it out; and as with specs I con
The well-thumb'd dogs'-ears of my Lexicon,
I'll say—oh! dash it! some one's been and torn it;
And there's that wretch begun to play the cornet!
He's overhead, and will wear on his feet
Thick boots, with which he will try time to beat.
How can I ever read enough to pass,
While that infern—I mean eternal brass
Pumps out that ever-varying key,
Which makes attempts to say, "Remember me."
Lydia and Chloe, Horace' and Ovid's flames,
Are so mix'd up with waltz-suggestive names,
Let me but try the former's "lines upon her,"
I construe "*mater pulchra*" "*prima donna*."
I lose my place, and straight the mocker plays
"Thou'rt gone," in fitful quavers, "from my gaze."
O, that by some stern dean those notes were stopp'd!
It's full ten minutes that that weazel's popp'd.
And here's his bed-maker! I can't be left alone!
What is she wanting now? Well, Mrs. Bone,
"If y' please, sir, Mr. Swift, the gent up stairs,
As says he's just a trying some new airs,
Would be oblig'd if you'd not read so loud."
And here with solemn mental oath I vow'd
I'd buy a kettle-drum. Revenge is sweet!
I'll try if I can't his concertos beat.
Honors divided. I'll so loudly thump it,
He'll soon revoke, without the heart to trumpet.

AUTHORS AND THEIR DIETETICS.

FROM "TABLE TRAITS." BY DR. DORAN.

IT is all very well for Mr. Leigh Hunt to write a poem on the "Feast of the Poets," and to show us how Apollo stood "pitching his darts," by way of invitation to the ethereal banquet. This is all very well in graceful poetry, but the account is no more to be received, than the new gospel according to *ditto* is likely to be by the Lord Primate and orthodox Christians. It is far more difficult to tell the matter in plain prose; for, where there are few dinners, many authors cannot well dine. It is easier to tell how they fasted than how they fed; how they died, choked at last by the newly-baked roll that came too late to be swallowed, than how they lived daily,—for the daily life of some would be as impossible of discovery, as the door of the "Cathedral of Immensities," wherein Mr. Carlyle transacts worship. The soul of the poet, says an Eastern proverb, passes into the grasshopper, which sings till it dies of starvation. An apt illustration, but our English grasshoppers must not be used for the illustrative purpose, seeing that they are far too wise to do any thing of the sort. A British grasshopper no more sings till he dies, than a British swan dies singing: these foolish habits are left to foreigners and poetry. Let us turn to the more reliable register of our ever-juvenile friend, Mr. Sylvanus Urban.

More than a century ago, Mr. Urban, who is the only original "oldest inhabitant," gave a "Literary Bill of Mortality for 1752," showing the casualties among books as well as among authors. Touching the respective fates of the former, we find the productions of the year set down as, "Abortive, seven thousand; still-born, three thousand; old age, naught." Sudden deaths fell upon three hundred and twenty. Three or four thousand perished by trunk-makers, skyrockets, pastry-cooks, or worm; while more than half that number were privily disposed of. If such were the fortunes of the works, how desperate must have been the diet of the authors! So also was their destiny. As a class, they are fixed, in round numbers, at three thousand; and a third of these are registered as dying of lunacy. Some twelve hundred are entered as "starved." Seventeen were disposed of by "the hangman," and fifteen by hardly more respectable persons, namely *themselves!* Mad dogs, vipers, and mortification, swept off a goodly number. Five pastoral poets, who could not live by the oaten pipe, appropriately died of "fistula." And, as a contrast to the multitude "starved," we find a *zero* indicating the ascertained quantity of authors who had perished by the aldermanic malady of "surfeit."

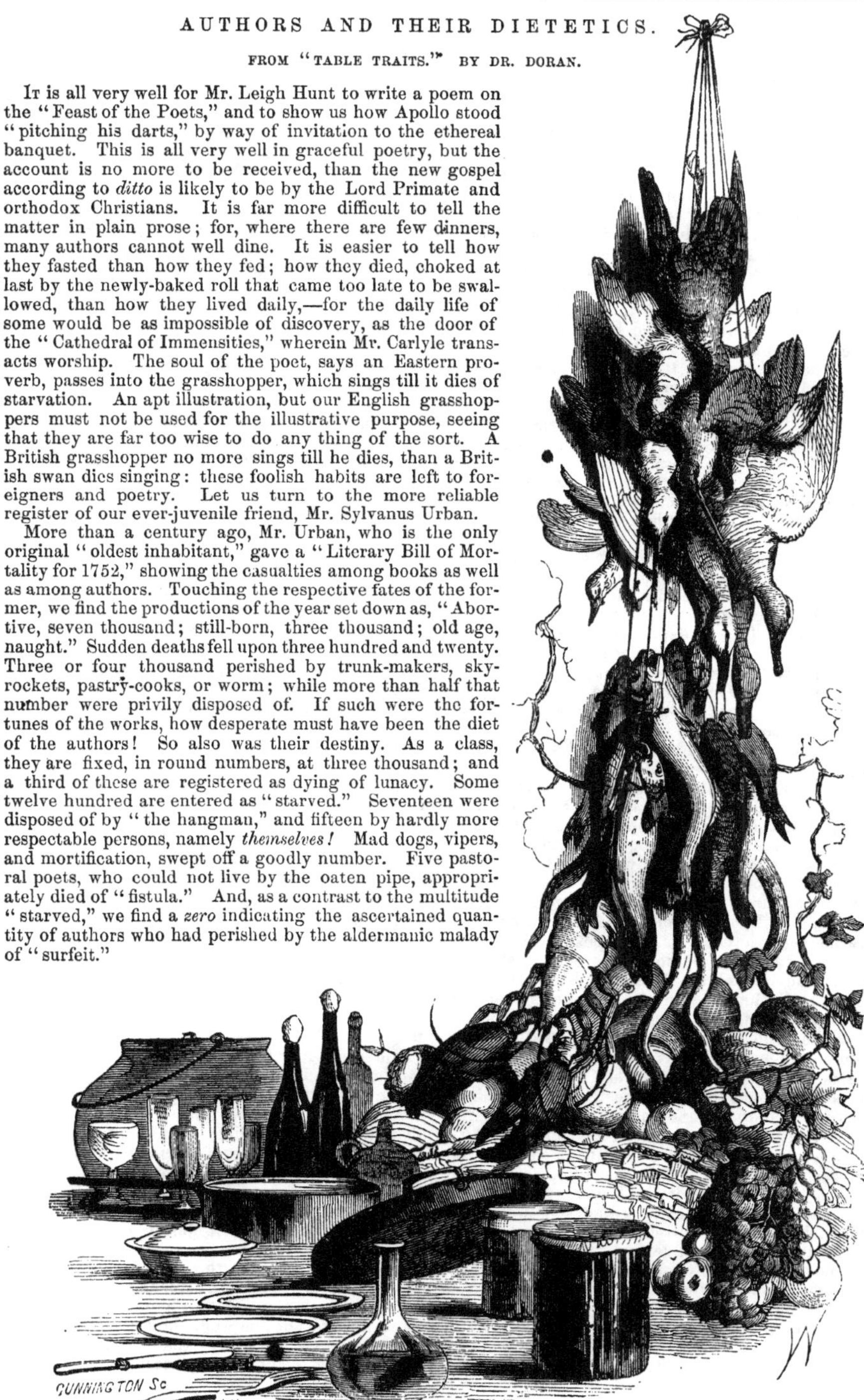

There is, perhaps, more approximation to truth than appears at first sight in this *jeu d'esprit.* It was only in Pagan days that authors could boast of obesity. They dined with the *tyranni*, as Persian poets get their mouths stuffed with sugar-candy by the Shah Inshah. And yet Pliny speaks of poets feeding sparingly, *ut solent poetæ.* Perhaps this was only an exception, like that of Moore, who smilingly sat down to a broil at home when not dining with "right honorables;" or contentedly thanked heaven for "salt fish and biscuits" with his mother and sister in Abbey Street, the day after he had supped with the ducal viceroy of Ireland, and half the peerage of the three kingdoms.

Still, in the old times, authors took more liberty with their hosts. In Rome they kept more to the proprieties; for a nod of the head of the imperial entertainer was sufficient to make their own fly from their shoulders. In presence of the Roman emperor of old, an author could only have declared that the famous invasion of Britain, which was productive of ship-loads of spoil, in the shape of sea-shells, was a god-like feat. So, at the table of the czar, all the lyres of Muscovy sing the ode of eternal sameness, to the effect that the dastardly butchery of Sinope was an act that made the angels of God jubilant! The Russian lyres dare not sing to any other tune. It was not so of yore. Witness what is told us of Philoxenus, the ode writer, whose odes, however, are less known than his acts. He was the author of the wish that he had a crane's neck, in order to have prolonged enjoyment in swallowing. This is a poor wish compared with that of Quin, elsewhere recorded, that he might have a swallow as long as from here to Botany Bay, and palate all the way! He was a greedy fellow, this same Philoxenus. He accustomed himself to hold his hands in the hottest water, and to gargle his throat with it scalding; and, by this sutble training, he achieved the noble end of being able to swallow the hottest things at table, before the other guests could venture on them. He would have conquered the most accomplished of our country bumpkins in consuming hasty-pudding at a fair. His mouth was as though it was paved, and his fellow-guests used to say of him, that he was an oven and not a man. He once travelled many miles to buy fish at Ephesus; but, when he reached the market-place, he found it all bespoke for a wedding banquet. He was by no means embarrassed; he went uninvited to the feast, kissed the bride, sang an epithalamium that made the guests roar with ecstasy, and afforded such delight by his humor, that the bridegroom invited him to breakfast with him on the morrow. His wit had made amends for his devouring all the best dishes. It is a long way from Philoxenus to Dr. Chalmers forgetting his repast in the outpouring of his wisdom, and entering in his journal the expression of his fear that he had been intolerant in argument. What a contrast, too, between Philoxenus and Byron, who, when dining with a half-score of wits at Rogers's, only opened his mouth to ask for biscuits and soda-water, and not finding any such articles in the bill of fare, silently dining on vegetables and vinegar! The noble poet's fare in Athens was often of the same modest character; but we know what excesses he could commit when his wayward appetite that way prompted, or when he wished to lash his Pegasus into fury, as, after reading the famous attack on his poetry in the Edinburgh Review, when he swallowed three bottles of claret, and then addressed himself to the tomahawking of his reviewers and rivals.

Philoxenus, however, had his counterpart in those abbés and poets who used, in the hearing of Louis XV., to praise Madame de Pompadour. He was writing a poem called "Galatea," in honor of the mistress of Dionysius of Sicily, when he was once dining with that tyrant. There were a couple of barbels on the royal board, a small one near the poet, and a larger one near the prince. As the latter saw Philoxenus put his diminutive barbel to his ear, he asked him wherefore, and the poet replied that he was asking news of Nereus, but that he thought the fish he held had been caught too young to give him any. "I think," said Philoxenus, "that the old fish near your sacredness would better suit my purpose." This joke has descended to Joe Miller, in whose collection it is to be found in a modified form. But the story is altogether less neat than the one told of Dominic, the famous Italian harlequin and farce writer. He was standing in presence of Louis XIV. at dinner, when the Grand Monarque observed that his eyes were fixed on a dish of partridges. "Give that dish to Dominic," said the king. "What!" exclaimed the *farceur*, "partridges and all!" "Well," said the monarch, smiling with gravity, "yes, partridges and all!" This reminds me of another anecdote, the hero of which is the Abbé Morallet, whom Miss Edgeworth in her "Ormond" praises so highly, and praises so justly. But Morallet, if he loved good deeds, loved not less good dinners, and he shone in both. His talents as a writer, and his virtues as a man, to say nothing of his appetite, made him especially welcome at the hospitable table of Monsieur Ansu. The abbé had learned to carve expressly that he might appropriate to himself his favorite portions, —a singular instance of selfishness in a man who was selfish in nothing else. It was on one of these occasions that a magnificent pheasant excited the admiration of the guests, and of the abbé in particular, who nevertheless sighed to think that it had not been placed close to him. Some dexterity was required so to carve it, that each of the guests might partake of the oriental bird; and the mistress of the house, remembering the abbé's skill as a carver, directed an attendant to pass the pheasant to M. l'Abbé Morallet. "What!" exclaimed the latter, "the whole of it? how very kind!" "The whole of it?" repeated the lady; "I have no objection, if these ladies and gentlemen are willing to surrender their rights to you." The entire company gave consent, by reiterating the words, "the whole of it!" and the man, who might have gained the Monthyon prize for virtue, really achieved a piece of gluttony which hardly confers honor on a hungry clown at a fair.

La Fontaine at table was seen in a better light than the Abbé Morallet. A fermier-general once invited him to a dinner of ceremony, in the persuasion that an author who excited such general admiration would create endless delight for the select company, to entertain whom he had been invited. La Fontaine knew it well, during the whole repast ate in silence, and immediately rose, to the consternation of the convives, to take his departure. He was going, he said, to the Academy. The master of the house represented to him that it was by far too early, and that he would find none of the members assembled. "I know that," said the fabulist, with his quiet smile and courteous bow; "I know that, but I will go a long way round." If this seemed a trifle uncourteous—and it was so more in seeming than reality—it was not so much so as in the case of Byron, who used to invite a company to dinner, and then leave them to themselves to enjoy their repast. Noble hosts of the past century used to do something like this when they gave masquerades. Fashion compelled them to adopt a species of amusement which they detested; but they vindicated personal liberty nevertheless, for when their rooms were at their fullest, the noble host, quietly leaving his guests to the care of his wife, would slip away to some neighboring coffee-house, and over a cool pint of claret enjoy the calm which was not to be had at home. The late Duke of Norfolk used habitually to dine at one of the houses in Covent Garden, out of pure liking to it. He was accustomed to order dinner for five, and to duly eat what he had deliberately ordered; but, as he one day detected a waiter watching him in his gastronomic process, he angrily ordered his bill, and never entered the house again.

It was a common practice with Haydn, like his Grace of Norfolk, to order a dinner for five or six, and then eat the whole himself. He once ordered such a dinner to be ready by a stated hour, at which time he alone appeared, and ordered the repast to be served. "But where is the company?" respectfully inquired the head waiter. "Oh!" exclaimed Haydn, "*I* am de gompany!" But if he ate all, he also paid for all. Moore and Bowles, in their visits together to Bath, used sometimes to dine at the White Hart, where, as Moore records, he paid his share of the dinner and pint of Madeira, and then Bowles magnificently "stood" a bottle of claret, at dessert. And a pleasant dinner the two opposite, yet able, poets, made of it—far more pleasant than Coleridge's dinner with a party at Reynolds's, when he bowled down the glasses like nine-pins, because they were too small to drink from copiously!

The name of Coleridge reminds me of Dufresny, an author of the time of Louis XVI., who was full of sentiment and majestic sounds, but who was content to live at the cost of other people, and who never achieved any thing like an independence for himself. After the death of his royal patron, he was one day dining with the Regent Duke of Orleans, who expressed a wish to provide for him. Caprice inspired the author to say, "Your royal highness had better leave me poor, as I am, as a monument of the condition of France before the regency." He was not displeased at having his petition refused. A guest at his side did indeed remark, by way of encouragement, that "poverty was no vice." "No," answered Dufresny, sharply, "but it is something very much worse." In act and spirit, he was not unlike a prince of wits and punsters among ourselves, who used to set up bottles of champagne on his little lawn and bowl them down for nine-pins; and who, of course, left his wife and children pensioners on the charity of the state and the people.

I have spoken of La Fontaine; he was as absent at table as poor Lord Dudley and Ward, whose first aberrations so alarmed Queen Adelaide. La Fontaine was also like Dean Ogle, who, at a friend's table, always thought himself at his own, and if the dinner were indifferent, he would make an apology to the guests, and promise them better treatment next time. So La Fontaine was one day at the table of Despreaux; the conversation turned upon St. Augustin, and after much serious discourse upon that Christian teacher, La Fontaine, who had till then been perfectly silent, turned to his neighbor, the Abbé Boileau, one of the most pious men of his day, and asked him "if he thought that St. Augustin had as much wit as Rabelais?" The priest blushed scarlet, and then contented himself with remarking, "M. de la Fontaine, you have got on one of your stockings the wrong side out"—which was the fact.

The poet's query to the priest was no doubt as startling as that put by the son of a renowned reverend joker to the then Lord Primate. The anxious parent had informed his somewhat "fast" offspring, that as the archbishop was to dine with him that day, it would be desirable that the young gentleman should eschew sporting subjects, and if he spoke at all, speak only on serious subjects. Accordingly, at dessert, during a moment of silence, the obedient child, looking gravely at his grace, asked him "if he could tell him what sort of condition Nebuchadnezzar was in, when he was taken up from grass?" The Lord Primate readily replied, that he should be able to answer the question by the time he who had made it, had found out the name of the man whom Samson ordered to tie the torches to the foxes' tails, before they were sent in to destroy the corn of the Philistines!

Moore loved to dine with the great; but there have been many authors who could not appreciate the supposed advantages of such a distinction. Lainez was one of these, and there were but few of his countrymen who resembled him. One day, the Duke of Orleans met him in the park at Fontainbleau, and did him the honor of inviting him to dinner. "It is really quite impossible," said Lainez; "I am engaged to dine at a tavern with half-a-dozen jolly companions; and what opinion would your royal highness have of me if I were to break my word?" Lainez was not like Madame de Sevigné, who, after having been asked to dance by Louis XIV., declared in her delight that he was the greatest monarch in the world. Bussi, who laughed at her absurd enthusiasm, affirms that the fair authoress of the famous "Letters" was so excited at the supper after the dance, that it was with difficulty she could refrain from shrieking out "Vive le Roi!"

Had the famous "petit père André" kept down his impulses as successfully as Madame de Sevigné did at the supper, where, after all, she did *not* exclaim, "Vive le Roi," it would have been more to his credit, and less to our amusement. The good father, like a better man, St. Vincent de Paul, was excessively fond of cards, but he did not cheat, like the saint, for the sake of winning for the poor. He had been playing at *piquet*, and in one game had won a considerable sum by the lucky intervention of a fourth king. He was in such ecstasy at his luck, that he declared at supper he would introduce his lucky fourth king into his next day's sermon. Bets were laid in consequence of this declaration, and the whole company were present when the discourse was preached. The promise made at the supper was kept in the sermon, though somewhat profanely: "My brethren," said the abbé, "there arrived one king, two kings, three kings; but what were they?—and where should I have been without the fourth king, who saved *me*, and has benefited you? That fourth king was He who lay in the manger, and whom the three royal magi came but to worship!" At the dinner which followed, the author of the sermon was more eulogized than if he had been as grand as Bourdaloue, as touching as Massillon, or as winning as Fenelon.

There was more wit in a curé of Bassa Bretagne, who was the author of his diocesan's pastorals, and who happened to hold invitations to dinners for the consecutive days of the week. He could not take advantage of them and perform his duty too, but he hit on a method of accomplishing his desire. He gave out at church, an intimation to this effect:—"In order to avoid confusion, my brethren, I have to announce that to-morrow, Monday, I will receive at confession the liars only; on Tuesday, the misers; on Wednesday, the slanderers; on Thursday, the thieves; Friday, the libertines; and Saturday, the women of evil life." It need not be said that the priest was left during *that* week to enjoy himself without let or hindrance. And it was at such joyous dinners as he was in the habit of attending that most of the sermons, with startling passages in them, like those of Father André, were devised. Thus, the Cordelier Maillard, the author of various pious works, at a dinner of counsellors, announced his intention of preaching against the counsellors' ladies,—that is, against their wives, or such of them that wore embroidery. And well he kept his word, as the following choice flowers from the bouquet of his pulpit oratory will show: "You say," he exclaimed to the ladies in question, "that you are clad according to your conditions; all the devils in hell fly away with your conditions, and you too, my ladies! You will say to me, perhaps, Our husbands do not give us this gorgeous apparel, we earn it by the labors of our bodies. Thirty thousand devils fly away with the labors of your bodies, and you too, my ladies!" And, after diatribes like these against the ladies in question, the Cordelier would dine with their lords, and dine sumptuously too. The dinners of the counsellors of those days were not like the Spanish dinner to which an author was invited, and which consisted of capon and wine, two excellent ingredients, but unfortunately, as at the banquet celebrated by Swift, where there was nothing warm but the ice, and nothing sweet but the vinegar, so here the capon was cold and the wine was hot. Whereupon, the literary guest dips the leg of the capon into the flask of wine, and being asked by his host wherefore de did so, replied, "I am warming the capon in the wine, and cooling the wine with the capon."

The host was not such a judge of wine, apparently, as the archbishops of Salzbourg, who used not indeed to write books, nor indeed read them, but who used to entertain those who did, and then preach against literary vanity from those double-balcony pulpits which some of my readers may recollect in the cathedral of the town where Paracelsus was wont to discourse like Solon, and to drink like Silenus; and before whose tomb I have seen votaries, imploring his aid against maladies, or thanking him for having averted them! It is said of one of these prince primates that when, on the occasion of his death, the municipal officers went to place the seals on his property, they found the library sealed up exactly as it had been done many years before, at the time of the decease of his predecessor. Such, however, was not the case with the wine-cellars. What the archiepiscopal wine is at Salzbourg, I do not know, but if it be half as good as that drank by the monks of Mölk, on the Danube, why the archbishops may stand excused. Besides, they only drank it during their leisure hours,—of which, as Hayne remarks, archbishops have generally four and twenty daily.

But to return nearer home, and to our own authors:—Dr. Arne may be reckoned among these, and it is of him, I think, that a pleasant story is told, showing how he wittily procured a dinner in an emergency, which certainly did not promise to allow such a consummation. The doctor was with a party of composers and musicians in a provincial town, where a musical festival was being celebrated, and at which they were prominent performers. They proceeded to an inn to dine; they were accommodated with a room, but were told that every eatable thing in the house was already engaged. All despaired in their hunger, save the "Mus. Doc." who, cutting off two or three ends of catgut, went out upon the stairs, and observing a waiter carrying a joint to a company in an adjacent room, contrived to drop the bits of catgut on the meat, while he addressed two or three questions to the waiter. He then returned to his companions, to whom he intimated that dinner would soon be ready. They smiled grimly at what they thought was a sorry joke, and soon after, some confusion being heard in the room to which the joint which he had ornamented had been conveyed, he reiterated the assurance that dinner was coming, and thereupon he left the room. On the stairs he encountered the waiter bearing away the joint, with a look of disgust in his face. "Whither so fast, friend, with that haunch of mutton?" was the query. "I am taking it back to the kitchen, sir; the gentlemen cannot touch it. Only look, sir," said William, with his nose in the direction of the bits of catgut; "it's enough to turn one's stomach!" "William," said Arne, gravely, "fiddlers have very strong stomachs; bring the mutton to our room." The thing was done, the haunch was eaten, the hungry guests were delighted, but William had ever afterwards a contempt for musical people; he classed them with those barbarians whom he had heard the company speak of where he waited, who not only ate grubs, but declared that they liked them.

Martial was often as hardly put to it to secure a dinner as any of the authors I have hitherto named. He was fond of a *good* dinner, *ut solent poetæ;* and he knew nothing better than a hare, followed by a dish of thrushes. The thrush appears to have been a favorite bird in the estimation of the poets. The latter may have loved to hear them sing, but they loved them better in a pie. Homer wrote a poem on the thrush; and Horace has said, in a line, as much in its favor as the Chian could have said in his long and lost poem,—"nil melius turdo." Martial was, at all events, a better fed and better weighted man than the poet Philetas of Cos, who was so thin that he walked abroad with leaden balls to his feet, in order that he might not be carried away by the wind. The poet Archestratus, when he was captured by the enemy, was put in a pair of scales, and was found of the weight of an obolus. Perhaps this was the value of his poetry! It was the value of nearly all that was written by a gastronomic authoress in France; I allude to Madame de Genlis, who boasts in her Memoirs, that having been courteously received by a certain German, she returned the courtesy by teaching him how to cook seven different dishes after the French fashion.

The authors of France have exhibited much caprice in their gastronomic practice; often professing in one direction, and acting in its opposite. Thus, Lamartine was a vegetarian until he entered his teens. He remains so in opinion, but he does violence to his taste, and eats good dinners for the sake of conforming to the rules of society! This course in an author, who is for the moment rigidly republican when all the world around him is monarchical, is singular enough. Lamartine's vegetarian taste was fostered by his mother, who took him when a child to the shambles, and disgusted him with the sight of butchers in activity on slaughtering days. He for a long time led about a pet lamb by a ribbon, and went into strong fits at a hint from his mother's cook, that it was time to turn the said pet into useful purposes, and make *tendrons d'agneau* of him. Lamartine would no more have thought of eating his lamb, than Emily Norton would have dreamed of breakfasting on collops cut from her dear white doe of Rylston. The poet still maintains, that it is cruel and sinful to kill one animal in order that another may dine; but, with a sigh for the victim, he can eat heartily of what *is* killed, and even put his fork into the breast of lamb without compunction,—but all for conformity! He knows that if he were to confine himself to turnips, he should enjoy better health and have a longer tenure of life; but then he thinks of the usages of society, sacrifices himself to custom, and gets an indigestion upon truffled turkey.

Moore, in his early days in London, used to dine somewhere in Marylebone with French refugee priests, for something less than a shilling. Dr. Johnson dined still cheaper, at the "Pine Apple," in New-street, Covent Garden—namely, for eightpence. They who drank wine paid fourpence more for the luxury, but the lexicographer seldom took wine at his own expense; and sixpennyworth of meat, one of bread, and a penny for the waiter, sufficed to purchase viands and comfort for the author of the "Vanity of Human Wishes." Boyce, the versifier, was of quite another kidney; when he lay in bed, not only starving, but stark naked, a compassionate friend gave him half-a-guinea, which he spent in truffles and mushrooms, eating the same in bed under the blankets. There was something atrociously sublime about Boyce. Famine had pretty well done for him, when some one sent him a slice of roast-beef, but Boyce refused to eat it, because there was no catsup to render it palatable.

It must have been a sight of gastronomic pleasure to have seen Wilkes and Johnson together over a fillet of veal, with abundance of butter, gravy, stuffing, and a squeeze of lemon. The philosopher and the patriot were then on a level with other hungry and appreciating men. Shallow, with his short-legged hen, and Sir Roger de Coverley over hasty-pudding, are myths; not so Pope with stewed regicide lampreys, Charles Lamb before roast pig, or Lord Eldon next to liver and bacon, or Theodore Hook bending to vulgar pea-soup. These were rich realities, and the principal performers in them had not the slightest idea of affecting refinement upon such subjects. Goldsmith, when he could get it, had a weakness for haunch of venison; and Dr. Young was so struck with a broiled bladebone, on which Pope regaled him, that he concluded it was a foreign dish, and anxiously inquired how it was prepared. Ben Jonson takes his place among the lovers of mutton; while Herrick, wandering dinnerless about Westminster, Nahum Tate enduring sanctuary and starvation in the Mint, Savage wantonly incurring hunger, and Otway strangled by it, introduce us to authors with whom "dining with Duke Humphrey," was so frequent a process, that each shadowy meal was but as a station towards death.

When Goldsmith "tramped" it in Italy, his flute ceased to be his bread-winner, as it had been in France; the fellow-countrymen of Palestrina were deaf to "Barbara Allen," pierced from memory through the vents of an Irish reed. Goldsmith, therefore, dropped his flute, and took up philosophy; not as a dignity; he played it as he had done his flute, for bread and a pillow. He knocked at the gate of a college instead of at the door of a cottage, made his bow, gave out a thesis, supported it in a Latin which must have set on edge the teeth of his hearers, and, having carried his exhibition to a successful end, was awarded the trifling and customary honorarium, with which he purchased bread and strength for the morrow. No saint in the howling wilderness lived a harder life than Goldsmith, during his struggling years in London; the table traits, even of his days of triumph, were sometimes colored unpleasingly. I am not sure if Goldsmith was present at the supper at Sir Joshua's, when Miss Reynolds, after the repast, was called upon as usual to give a toast, and not readily remembering one, was asked to give the ugliest man of her acquaintance, and thereon she gave "Dr. Goldsmith;" the name was no sooner uttered than Mrs. Cholmondeley rushed across the room, and shook hands with Reynolds by way of approval. What a sample of the manners of the day, and how characteristic the remark of Johnson, who *was* present, and whose wit, at his friend's expense, was rewarded by a roar, that "thus the ancients, on the commencement of their friendships, used to sacrifice a beast between them!" Cuzzoni, when found famishing, spent the guinea given her in charity, in a bottle of tokay and a penny roll. So Goldsmith, according to Mrs. Thrale, was "drinking himself drunk with Madeira," with the guinea sent to rescue him from hunger by Johnson. But let us be just to poor Oliver. If he squandered the eleemosynary guinea of a friend, he refused roast beef and daily pay, offered him by Parson Scott, Lord Sandwich's chaplain, if he would write against his conscience, and in support of government; and he could be generous in his turn to friends who needed the exercise of generosity. When Goldsmith went into the suburban gardens of London to enjoy his "shoemakers' holiday," he generally had Peter Barlow with him. Now Peter's utmost limit of profligacy was the sum of fifteen-pence for his dinner; his share would sometimes amount to five shillings, but Goldsmith always magnificently paid the difference. Perhaps there are few of the sons of song who dined so beggarly, and achieved such richness of fame, as Butler, Otway, Goldsmith, Chatterton, and, in a less degree of reputation, but not of suffering, poor Gerald Griffin, who wrestled with starvation till he began to despair. Chatterton *did* despair, as he sat without food, hope, and humility; and we know what came of it. Butler, the sturdy son of a Worcestershire farmer, after he had astonished his contemporaries by his "Hudibras," lived known but to a few, and upon the charity or at the tables of *them.* But he did not, like the heartless though sorely-tried Savage, slander the good-natured friends at whose tables he drew the support of his life. As for Otway, whether he perished of suffocation by the roll which he devoured too greedily after long fasting, or whether he died of the cold draught of water, drank when he was overheated, it is certain that he died in extreme penury at the "Bull," on Tower Hill,—the coarse frequenters of the low public-house were in noisy revelry round their tables, while the body of the dead poet lay, awaiting the grave, in the room adjacent.

The table life of Peter Pindar was a far more joyous one than that of much greater poets. At Truro he was noted for his frugal fare, and he never departed from the observance of frugality of living throughout his career. He would sometimes, we are told, when visiting country patients, and when he happened to be detained, go into the kitchen and cook his own beefsteak, in order to show a country cook how a steak was done in London,—the only place, he said, where it was properly cooked. He laughed at the faculty as he did at the king, and set the whole profession mad by sanctioning the plentiful use of water, declaring that physic was an uncertain thing, and maintaining that in most cases all that was required on the doctor's part was "to watch nature, and when she was going right, to give her a shove behind." He was accustomed to analyze the drugs which he had prescribed for his patients, before he would allow the latter to swallow them; and he gave a decided county bias against pork by remarking of a certain apothecary that he was too fond of bleeding the patients who resorted to him, and too proud of his large breed of pigs. The inference was certainly not in favor of pork. Peter's practical jokes in connexion with the table were no jokes to the chief object of them. Thus, when a pompous Cornish member of parliament issued invitations for as pompous a dinner to personages of corresponding pomposity, "Peter," recollecting that the senator had an aunt who was a laundress, sent her an invitation in her nephew's name, and the old lady, happy and proud, excited universal surprise, and very particular horror in the bosom of the parliament-man, by making her appearance in the august and hungry assembly, who welcomed her about as warmly as if she had been a "boule asphyxiante" of the new French artillery practice.

It is going a long way back to ascend from "Pindar" to Tasso, but both poets loved roasted chestnuts,—and *there* is the affinity. Peter never drank any thing but old rum; a wine glass, (never beyond a wine glass and a half,) served him for a day, after a dinner of the plainest kind. The doctor eschewed wine altogether, at least in his latter days, as generating acidity. Tasso, however, unlike our satirical friend, was a wine-bibber. During the imprisonment which had been the result of his own arrogance, he wrote to the physician of the Duke of Ferrara, complaining of intestinal pains, of sounds of bells in his ears, of painful mental images and varying apparitions of inanimate things appearing to him, and of his inability to study. The doctor advised him to apply a cautery to his leg, abstain from wine, and confine himself to a diet of broths and gruels. The poet defended the sacredness of his appetite, and declined to abstain from generous wine; but he urged the *medico* to find a remedy for his ills, promising to recompense him for his trouble, by making him immortal in song. At a later period of his life, when he was the guest of his friend Manco, in his gloomy castle of Bisaccio, the illustrious pair were seated together, after dinner, over a dessert of Tasso's favorite chestnuts and some generous wine; and there he affrighted his friend by maintaining that he was constantly attended by a guardian spirit, who was frequently conversing with him, and in proof of the same, he invited Manco to listen to their dialogue. The host replenished his glass and announced himself ready. Tasso fell into a loud rhapsody of mingled folly and beauty, occasionally pausing to give his spirit an opportunity of speaking; but the remarks of this agathodæmon were inaudible to all but the ears of the poet. The imaginary dialogue went on for an hour; and at the end of it, when Tasso asked Manco what he thought of it, Manco, who was the most matter-of-fact man that ever lived, replied that, for his part, he thought Tasso had drunk too much wine and eaten too many chestnuts. And truly I think so too.

The greatest of authors are given to the strangest of freaks. Thus, one of the most popular of the teachers of the people presided at a gay tavern supper the night before the execution of the Mannings. The feast concluded, the party (supplied with brandy and biscuits) proceeded to the disgusting spectacle, where they occupied "reserved seats;" and when all was done, the didactic leader of the revellers and sight seers thought he compensated for his want of taste, by pronouncing as "execrable" the taste of those who, like George Selwyn, could find pleasure in an execution. But there are few men so inconsistent as didactic authors. Pope taught, in poetry, the excellence of moderation; but he writes to Congreve, in 1715, that he sits up till two o'clock over burgundy and champagne; and he adds, "I am become so much of a rake that I shall be ashamed, in a short time, to be thought to do any sort of business." But Pope's table practice, like Swift's, was not always of the same character. The dean, writing to Pope, in the same year, that the latter tells Congreve (a dissolute man at table, by the way) of his sitting over burgundy and champagne till two in the morning, speaks of quite another character of life: "You are to understand that I live in a corner of a vast unfurnished house. My family consists of a steward, a groom, a helper in my stable, a footman, and an old maid, who are all at board wages; and when I do not dine abroad, or make an entertainment,—which last is very rare,—I eat a mutton pie, and drink half a pint of wine." Pope's habit of sleeping after dinner did not incline him to obesity, and it was a habit that the dean approved. Swift told Gay that his wine was bad, and that the clergy did not often call at his house; an admission in which Gay detected cause and effect. In the following year to that last named, Swift wrote a letter to Pope, in which I find a paragraph affording a table trait of some interest: "I remember," he says, "when it grieved your soul to see me pay a penny more than my club, at an inn, when you had maintained me three months at bed and board; for which, if I had dealt with you in the Smithfield way, it would have cost me a hundred pounds, for I live worse here (Dublin) upon more. Did you ever consider that I am, for life, almost twice as rich as you, and pay no rent, and drink French wine twice as cheap as you do port, and have neither coach, chair, nor mother?" Pope illustrates Bolingbroke's way of living as well as his own some years later. The reveller till two in the morning, of the year 1715, is sobered down to the most temperate of table men, in 1728. "My Lord Bolingbroke's great temperance and economy are so signal, that the first is fit for my constitution, and the latter would enable you to lay up so much money as to buy a bishopric in England. As to the return of his health and vigor, were you here, you might inquire of his haymakers. But, as to his temperance, I can answer, that, for one whole day, we have had nothing for dinner but mutton broth, beans and bacon, and a barn-door fowl;" after all, no bad fare either, for peer or poet! Swift too, at this period, boasts no longer of his "French wines." His appetite is affected by the appalling fact, that the national debt amounts to the unheard-of sum of seven millions sterling! and thereupon he says: "I dine alone on half a dish of meat, mix water with my wine, walk ten miles a-day, and read Baronius."

ANECDOTES OF JAMES SMITH.

The Rejected Addresses.—"The fame of the brothers, James and Horatio Smith, was confined to a limited circle, until the publication of "The Rejected Addresses." James used to dwell with much pleasure on the criticism of a Leicestershire clergyman: "I do not see why they ('The Addresses') should have been rejected; I think some of them very good." This, he would add, is almost as good as the avowal of the Irish Bishop, that there were some things in "Gulliver's Travels" which he could not believe.

A Close Escape.—One of James Smith's favorite anecdotes related to Colonel Greville. The Colonel requested young James to call at his lodgings, and, in the course of their first interview, related the particulars of the most curious circumstance in his life. He was taken prisoner during the American war, along with three other officers of the same rank; one evening they were summoned into the presence of Washington, who announced to them that the conduct of their government in condemning one of his officers to death, as a rebel, compelled him to make reprisal; and that, much to his regret, he was under the necessity of requiring them to cast lots, without delay, to decide which of them should be hanged. They were then bowed out, and returned to their quarters. Four slips of paper were put into a hat, and the shortest was drawn by Captain Asgill, who exclaimed, "I knew how it would be; I never won so much as a hit at backgammon in my life." As Greville told the story, he was selected to sit up with Captain Asgill, under pretext of companionship; but in reality to prevent him from escaping, and leaving the honor amongst the remaining three. "And what," inquired Smith, "did you say to comfort him?" "Why, I remember saying to him, when they left us, '*D—n it, old fellow, never mind*,'' but it may be doubted (added Smith) whether he drew much comfort from the exhortation. Lady Asgill persuaded the French Minister to interpose, and the Captain was permitted to escape.

Top and Bottom.—The following playful colloquy in verse took place at a dinner-table between Sir George Rose and James Smith, in allusion to Craven street, Strand, where he resided:—

J. S.—At the top of my street the attorneys abound,
And down at the bottom the barges are found:
Fly, honesty, fly, to some safer retreat,
For there's craft in the river, and craft in the street.

Sir J. R.—Why should honesty fly to some safer retreat,
From attorneys, and barges, od rot 'em?
For the lawyers are *just* at the top of the street,
And the barges are *just* at the bottom.

Unfair Advantage.—One of the best things lately said upon age—a very ticklish subject, by the way—was the observation of James Smith to Thomas Hill. "Hill," said the former gentleman, "you take an unfair advantage of an accident; the register of your birth was burnt in the great fire of London, and you avail yourself of the circumstance to give out that you are younger than you are."

Temperance Cruets.—James Smith was often seen at the Garrick Club, restricting himself at dinner to half a pint of sherry; whence he was designated an incorporated temperance society. To do him justice, however, this was not his choice; he diluted it with frequent tears; he was restricted, not by virtuous sobriety, but by vicious gout, of which he stood, or rather sat, in awe. But for this, there would have been no such small bottle of that liquid, to remind the observer of Pope's Avidien and his wife (Lady M. W. Montague, and her then antiquated spouse):—

One frugal cruet served them both to dine,
And pass'd at once for vinegar and wine.

The late Sir William Aylett, a grumbling member of the Union, and a two bottle-man, observing Mr. Smith to be thus frugally furnished, eyed his cruet with contempt, and exclaimed, "So I see you have got one of those d—d life-preservers."

The Gouty Shoe.—James Smith used to tell, with great glee, a story showing the general conviction of his dislike to realities. He was sitting in the library at a country house, when a gentleman proposed a quiet stroll in the pleasure grounds:—"Stroll! why don't you see my gouty shoe?" "Yes, I see that plain enough, and I wish I'd brought one, too; but they are all out now." "Well, and what then?" "What then? why, my dear fellow, you don't mean to say that you have really got the gout? I thought you had only put on that shoe to get off being shown over the improvements."

The Blood.—Two gentleman were discussing, in James Smith's company, the color of the blood. "You say," cried one, "that our blood is at first quite white. I will credit it, if you can also tell me in what stage (of circulation) it becomes red?" "Tell him," whispered Smith, "in the Reading stage, of course."

James Smith and Justice Holroyd.—Formerly, it was customary, on emergencies, for the judges to swear affidavits at their dwelling-houses. Smith was desired by his father to attend a judge's chambers for that purpose, but being engaged to dine in Russell-square, at the next house to Mr. Justice Holroyd's, he thought he might as well save himself the disagreeable necessity of leaving the party at eight, by dispatching his business at once; so, a few minutes before six, he boldly knocked at the judge's, and requested to speak to him on particular business. The judge was at dinner, but came down without delay, swore the affidavit, and then gravely asked what was the pressing necessity that induced our friend to disturb him at that hour. As Smith told the story, he raked his invention for a lie, but finding none fit for the purpose, he blurted out the truth:—"The fact is, my lord, I am engaged to dine at the next house—and—and"—"And, sir, you thought you might as well save your own dinner by spoiling mine?" "Exactly so, my lord, but—" "Sir, I wish you a good evening." Though Smith brazened the matter out, he said he never was more frightened.

The Two Smiths.—A gentleman with the same Christian and surname, took lodgings in the same house with James Smith. The consequence was, eternal confusion of calls and letters. Indeed, the postman had no alternative but to share the letters equally between the two. "This is intolerable, sir," said our friend, "and you must quit." "Why am I to quit more than you?" "Because you are James the Second, and must *abdicate*."

THE CLAPHAM CHALYBEATE.

BY JAMES SMITH.

Who has ne'er been at Clapham must needs know the pond
That belongs to Sir Barnaby Sturch;
'Tis well stock'd with fish; and the knight's rather fond
Of bobbing for tench or for perch.

When he draws up his line, to decide if all's right,
Moist drops o'er his pantaloons dribble;
Though seldom, if ever, beguiled by a bite,
He now and then boasts of a nibble.

Vulgar mud, very like vulgar men, will encroach
Unchecked by the spade and the rake;
In process of time it enveloped the roach
In Sir Barnaby's Lilliput lake.

Five workmen, well armed, and denuded of shoes,
Now fearlessly delved in the flood;
To steal unawares on the Empress of Ooze,
And cart off her insolent mud.

The innocent natives were borne from the bog,
Eel, minnow, and toad felt the shovel,
And lizard-like eft lay with fugitive frog
In a clay-built extempore hovel.

The men worked away with their hands and their feet,
And delved in a regular ring;
When lo! as their taskwork was all but complete,
They wakened a mineral spring.

"We've found a *Chalybeate*, sir," cried the men;
"We halt till we know what your wish is"—
"Keep it safe," quoth the knight, "till you've finish'd, and then
Throw it back with the rest of the fishes."

MY WIFE'S MOTHER.

BY JAMES SMITH.

My uncle George was never easy till he got all the males of the family married. He has said to me, at least a hundred times, "John, I'm surprised you don't settle." I did not at first understand his meaning. I was walking with him in the Temple Gardens, and while we were in the act of contemplating the beauties of the majestic Thames—I allude to a man in a red night-cap walking to and fro on a floating raft of tied timbers, and a coal-barge embedded in mud—he stopped short on the gravel walk, and said, "John, why don't you settle?" Concluding that he was tired, I answered, "Oh, by all means," and sat down in the green alcove at the eastern extremity of the footpath. "Pho!" said my uncle, "I don't mean that; I mean, why don't you marry? There's your brother Tom settled, and has had seven children, not reckoning two who died of the measles; and Charles is settled, and he has nine; his eldest boy, Jack, is tall enough to thump him; and Edward is settled, at least he will be, as soon as Charlotte Payne has made up her mind to live in Lime-street. I wonder why you don't settle." "Pray, uncle," said I, "of what Bucks Lodge are you a noble brother?" "Why do you ask?" said he. "Because," replied I, "you seem to think men are like masonry—never to be depended upon till they settle."

As we walked homeward, we saw that adventurous aëronaut Garnerin flying over our heads; and while we were wondering at his valor, he cut the rope that fastened his balloon to his parachute, and began to descend in the latter towards the earth. My uncle George began to run as fast as his legs could carry him, looking all the while so intently upwards, that he did not advert to a nurse-maid and two children, whom he accordingly upset in his course, and nearly precipitated into the subjacent ooze. "What's the matter, uncle?" said I. "Matter!" answered my outinian relative, "why, I'm going to look after Garnerin; I shall never be easy till I see him settled."

In process of time, my uncle began to be seriously displeased at my not settling. Population, he seemed to opine, was on the wane; and if anything should happen to my brothers Tom and Charles, and their respective families, not omitting Edward and his issue, when his intended wife should have conquered her repugnance to Lime-street, what would become of the House of Jackson? It might be dead, defunct, extinct, like the Plantagenets and Montmorencies of other days, unless I, John Jackson, of Finsbury Circus, underwriter, became accessary to its continuation.

The dilemma was awful, and my uncle George had money to leave. I accordingly resolved to fall in love. This, however, I found to be a matter more easily resolved upon than accomplished. A man may fall in a ditch whenever he pleases—he must fall in love when and where he can.

My mother recommended Susan Roper to me as a suitable match; and so she was, as far as circumstances extend. Her father was a reputable coal-merchant, living in Chatham-place; I tried very much to be in love with her, and one warm evening when she sang "Hush every breeze," in a boat under the second arch of Blackfriars bridge, and accompanied herself upon the guitar, I thought that I was in love—but it went off before morning. I was afterwards very glad it was so, for Susan Roper turned out very fat, and ate mustard with her roast beef. She married Tom Holloway, the Policy Broker, and I wished him joy. I wish it him still, but I doubt the efficacy of my prayers, inasmuch as his wife's visage bears a strong resemblance to the illuminated dial-plate of St. Giles's church clock.

My next affair was more decisive in its result. Old Mrs. Cumming, of St. Helen's-place, Bishopsgate-street, had a daughter named Jane, who taught me some duets. We sang "When thy bosom heaves a sigh,"—"Take back the virgin page,"—and "Fair Aurora," with impunity; but when it came to "Together let us range the fields," where the high contracting parties talk about "tinkling rills" and "rosy beds," the old lady, who had hitherto sat in seeming carelessness on the sofa, hemming doyleys, requested to speak with me in the back-drawing-room, and, after shutting the door, asked me my intentions. My heart was in my mouth, which plainly implied that it was still in my own keeping. Nevertheless, I had no answer ready; so Jane Cumming and I were married on that day month.

My uncle George was so delighted at my being settled, that, after making us a present of a silver coffee-pot, he exclaimed, "I shall now die happy;" an intention, however, which he has since shown himself in no hurry to carry into effect.

Now came my wife's mother into play. Sparrows leave their daughters to shift for themselves the moment they are able to take to the wing. (My uncle George calls this barbarous, and says they should wait till they are settled.) But in Christian countries, like England, one's wife's mother is not so unnatural. Mrs. Cumming lives, as I before mentioned, in St. Helen's-place; I reside in Finsbury Circus; so that the old Lady has only to cross Bishopsgate-street, pass the churchyard, and issue through the iron bars at the base of Broad-street-buildings, and here she is. This makes it so very convenient, that she is never out of my house. Indeed, all the congratulations of my wife's friends, verbal and epistolatory, ended with this apophthegm, "Then it must be so delightful to you to have your mamma so near!"

It is, in fact, not only delightful, but quite providential. I do not know what my wife would do without my wife's mother. She is the organ-blower to the organ—the kitchen jack to the kitchen fire—the verb that governs the accusative case. Mrs. Cumming has acquired, from the pressure of time, rather a stoop in her gait; but whenever my wife is in the family-way, my wife's mother is as tall and perpendicular as a Prussian life-guardsman. Such a bustling about the house, such a cry of "hush" to the pre-existent children, and such a bevy of directions to Jane! The general order given to my wife is to lie flat upon her back and look at nothing but the fly-trap, that hangs from the ceiling. For five months out of the twelve, my wife is parallel to the horizon, like a good quiet monumental wife in Westminster Abbey, and my wife's mother is sitting beside her with a bottle of eau de Cologne in one hand, and one of my book-club books in the other.

By the way, talking of book-clubs, it makes a great difference, as to the utility of those institutions, whether the members of them are married or single. My wife's mother is a woman of uncommon purity of mind, and so consequently is my wife. We have accordingly discarded our Malone and Steevens, to make way for Bowdler's Family Shakspere. My expensive quarto edition of Paradise Lost, printed in the year 1794, is dismissed to an empty garret, because it contains cuts of our first parents undecorated by the tailor and milliner. It is to be succeeded by a Family Milton, edited by the late Mr. Butterworth, in which our aforesaid progenitors are clad, like the poet's own evenings, "in sober gray." My wife's mother is herself editing a Family Æsop, in which old Menenius Agrippa's fable of the belly and the members is denominated the stomach and the members. Our family nomenclature is equally unexceptionable. Water, according to us, is the elemental fluid; a mad dog is a rabid animal; little Charles was yesterday rebuked for alleging that he had seen a mad bull, and informed by my wife's mother that the animal, which had excited his fears, was an over-driven ox. A pair of trousers is the rest of a man's dress; newspaper reporters are gentlemen connected with the press; and a sheep-stealer, making his exit under the gallows, is not hanged, but launched into eternity.

Neither do our obligations to my wife's mother end here. Our workmen she has changed too peratives; and by parity of reasoning she would have denominated the parish workhouse an opera-house, had she not been apprehensive in doing so she might then cause Miss Fanny Ayton, in error, to call upon us in quest of a re-engagement. Old Bethlem is already Liverpool-street, and we only wait to see Edinburgh fairly launched as the modern Athens, to call Broker's Row Cabinet Crescent.

But to return a while to our book-club. My wife and my wife's mother have an amazing knack of grasping all the quartos and octavos that come to my share. They all get into my wife's boudoir, as my wife's mother has christened it, where they seldom emerge till a week or ten days after they are transferable. This costs me an extra sixpence per book per diem—but that's a trifle. I sent up stairs yesterday for something to amuse me, hoping for De Vere, and down came little Billy with Baverstock on Brewing, with a portrait of the author prefixed. I myself drink nothing but water, but the secretary of the club brews his own beer. I sent back Baverstock on Brewing, with a request for something more funny; whereupon my wife's mother sent me down Sermons by the Rev. Something Andrews, of Walworth, with a portrait of the author likewise prefixed.

Mr. Burridge, the indigo broker, happened to be with me when this latter publication arrived; and when we happened also to be discoursing about what trade my nephew Osgood should be brought up to, Mr. Burridge cast his eye upon the portrait, and said, "Has your nephew got a black whisker?" "Yes," I answered. "And a white shirt collar?" "Yes." "Then bring him up to the church." It appears to me that a book-club would be a good thing if we could but get the books we want, and when we want them. But perhaps I am too particular.

We never have a dinner, without, of course, inviting my wife's mother. Indeed, she always settles the day, the dishes, and the party. Last Wednesday I begged hard to have Jack Smith invited; but no—my wife's mother was inexorable. The last time he dined with us he was asked for a song. Mrs. Cumming wanted him to sing "My mother had a maid called Barbara;" thinking that daughters should bear in mind not only their mothers, but their mother's maids; whereupon what does Jack do but break cover as follows:—

The Greeks they went fighting to Troy;
  The Trojans they came out to meet 'em:
'Tis known to each little schoolboy
  How the Greeks they horse-jockey'd and beat 'em.

No house in that day was secured;
  They made them too hot for their holders;
And Æneas, not being insured,
  Pack'd off with his dad on his shoulders,
    Singing Rumpti, etc.

This was intolerable. A man who would mention a husband's father thus irreverently, could only wait for an opportunity in order to lampoon a wife's mother. Jack is, consequently, suffering under the ban of the Finsbury empire.

This reminds me of an odd incident that happened under my cognizance before I had a wife's mother. I went one night into the green-room of Drury Lane theatre. When young girls are called upon to perform in London playhouses, it is customary for their mothers to come to look after them, to adjust their dress, rub their cheeks with a rouged hare's foot, and prevent viscounts from falling in love with them. It so happened that five young girls were wanted in the drama; the consequence was, that five black-bonneted mothers blockaded the green-room. "Did you ever see any thing like it?" ejaculated Munden, in an under tone; "I'll bring my own mother to-morrow night; I've as much right as they have!"—Munden's mother!!!

I own I am puzzled to know what my wife will do when my wife's mother dies, which, in the course of nature, she must do first. The laws of this country prevent her from mounting the pile, like a Hindoo widow, or descending into the grave, like Sinbad, the sailor. But I will not anticipate so lamentable an epoch.

Two incidents more, and I have done. We went, last Wednesday, with my uncle George and my wife's mother, to Covent Garden theatre, to see "Peter Wilkins, or the Flying Indians," whom, by the way, my wife's mother mistook for defeated Burmese. Miss M. Glover and Miss J. Scott, acted two flying Gowries, and were swinging across the stage when Mrs. Cumming expressed a wish to go home. "No, no, wait a little," said my uncle, looking upward to the theatrical firmament, "I'm quite uneasy about those two girls; I hope they'll soon settle."

Last Sunday Doctor Stubble gave us an excellent sermon; the subject was the fall of man; in which he descanted eloquently upon the happiness of Adam in Paradise. "Alas!" ejaculated I to myself as we walked homeward, "his happiness even there must have been incomplete! His wife had no mother!"

THE HAUNCH OF VENISON.

BY JAMES SMITH.

At Number One dwelt Captain Drew,
George Benson dwelt at Number Two,
  (The street we'll not now mention:)
The latter stunn'd the King's Bench bar,
The former, being lamed in war,
  Sang small upon a pension.

Tom Blewit knew them both; than he
None deeper in the mystery
  Of culinary knowledge;
From turtle soup to Stilton cheese,
Apt student, taking his degrees
  In Mrs. Rundell's college.

Benson to dine invited Tom;
Proud of an invitation from
  A host who "spread so nicely."
Tom answer'd, ere the ink was dry,
"Extremely happy—come on Fri-
  Day next, at six precisely."

Blewit, with expectation fraught,
Drove up at six, each savory thought
  Ideal turbot rich in;
But, ere he reach'd the winning-post,
He saw a haunch of ven'son roast
  Down in the next-door kitchen.

"Hey! zounds! what's this? a haunch at Drew's
I must drop in; I can't refuse;
  To pass were downright treason;
To cut Ned Benson's not quite staunch;
But the provocative—a haunch!
  Zounds! it's the first this season.

"Ven'son, thou'rt mine! I'll talk no more."
Then, rapping thrice at Benson's door,
  "John, I'm in such a hurry;
Do tell your master that my aunt
Is paralytic, quite aslant,
  I must be off for Surrey."

Now Tom at next door makes a din:
"Is Captain Drew at home?"—"Walk in."
  "Drew, how d'ye do?" "What! Blewit?"

"Yes, I—you've ask'd me, many a day,
To drop in, in a quiet way,
So now I'm come to do it."

"I'm very glad you have," said Drew,
"I've nothing but an Irish stew"—
Quoth Tom (aside), "No matter;
'Twon't do—my stomach's up to that,—
'Twill lie by, till the lucid fat
Comes quiv'ring on the platter."

"You see your dinner, Tom," Drew cried.
"No, but I don't though," Tom replied;
"I smok'd below."—"What?"—"Ven'son—
A haunch."—"Oh! true, it is not mine;
My neighbor has some friends to dine."
"Your neighbor! who?"—"George Benson.

"His chimney smoked; the scene to change,
I let him have my kitchen range,
While his was newly polish'd;
The ven'son you observ'd below,
Went home just half an hour ago;
I guess it's now demolish'd.

"Tom, why that look of doubtful dread?
Come, help yourself to salt and bread,
Don't sit with hands and knees up:
But dine, for once, off Irish stew,
And read the 'Dog and Shadow,' through,
When next you open Æsop."

BOUNCE MOLLOY AND CRAZY CRAB.

FROM "ADAM BROWN." BY HORACE SMITH.

"My good sir," began Captain Molloy, assuming a somewhat patronizing and consequential air, as he bowed himself, not ungracefully, into the parlor, "I should have done myself the honor of calling sooner, for I am well aware that the leading people of the locality should always be the first to welcome a new neighbor, as the rank and file will of course follow the example of their superior officers—you'll excuse my military language, being an old soldier—but the fact is, I have an apology to offer, which—"

"Which I will not trouble you to offer at all," interposed Brown, who hated all flummery and finery, and felt rather nettled at the airs assumed by his visitant. "You might have stayed away longer if you liked, and you needn't have called now, if you didn't like; for, though I shall be always happy to see the good folks of Woodcote and its vicinity, I rather think I can do without them. My name, sir, is Adam Brown, late of the firm of Brown, Gubbins, and Co.; and the books of the Bank of England will vouch, I believe, for my respectability and independence." This was not a very polite speech, but the worthy merchant did not pique himself upon his courtesy, and did pique himself upon the money which he had so hardly earned, and which he thought ought to secure him a position in society, wherever he might settle, and whosoever might be his neighbors. "But you have not introduced me to these young ladies," he continued, in a blander tone; "your daughters, I presume?"

"Yes, sir, yes," replied the father, looking at them with a smile of pride; "and the finest and the most fashionable, as well as the most accomplished girls in this part of the country, though I say it that shouldn't say it." Matilda endeavored to look modest at this speech, and, not feeling quite sure that she had succeeded, for that particular expression was not her *forte*, she determined to appear girlish and simple by giving her father a tap with her fingers, and affectedly ejaculating, "La, pa! how can you?" Ellen's eyes were fixed on the ground, her usually faint bloom undergoing a deeper suffusion as she listened to the coarse praises of her father.

"I suppose," resumed the latter, "that you have seen most of our immediate neighbors: *old* Penfold the parson, and *old* Dawson the apothecary, and *old* Roger Crab of Monkwell"—for the Captain was in the habit of applying this term to his contemporaries, and even to his juniors, imagining that it would assist him in passing himself off for a younger man than he really was.

"The former gentlemen have called, but I have not yet seen any thing of Mr. Crab."

"No loss, Mr. Brown—no loss, if he never comes near you; for a more sneering, snarling, sarcastic, ill-tempered old hunks it would be difficult to find. I don't know which is the sourest, his looks or his temper."

"I verily believe," cried Matilda, "that the two together turned our beer, the last time he paid us a visit."

"Ha, ha, ha! well done, 'Tilda. My eldest daughter, you see, is a wit—always had a jocular turn. By the powers! it must have been as she says: nothing could have done it but old Crab's verjuice face, for I brew my own beer, and capital stuff it is—all malt and hops, no water. I hope you'll do me the favor of tasting it one of these days."

"I wonder you suffer so disagreeable and dangerous a fellow to visit you," observed the merchant.

"Well, Sir, I am good-tempered to a fault—always was; and if the leading person of the place was to turn his back upon old Crab, he might as well turn hermit at once, and become the monk of Monkwell. Ha, ha, ha! Besides, he is as bilious as a nabob, his wife is a confirmed invalid, neither of them likely to live long—their money must go somewhere: and then he has purchased the right of shooting over an extensive manor; he often invites me to accompany him; and as he is too sickly to eat all the game he shoots, he is compelled to give it to his acquaintance."

"Why, then, it would appear that he does possess some good qualities."

"Not he; not any, at least, that he can help—an old cynical curmudgeon!"

"Nay, dear papa," urged Ellen, "you forget that he makes a most affectionate husband to a sick wife, and that he is very kind and generous to the poor, though he does scold them pretty sharply when he thinks they deserve it. Everybody says that his bark is worse than his bite; and besides, he is so absent, that I do think he hardly knows at times what ill-natured things he is saying."

"Ay, Nell, and that's the reason why I never notice his impertinence. If I thought he *meant* to be insolent—*By* the powers!" In delivering his favorite adjuration, the Captain was accustomed to accumulate the emphasis on the first word with a vehemence proportioned to the gravity of the occasion; his present stress upon the "*by*," evidently implying that, if there were sufficient ground for the process, he would make no bones of the offender, but swallow him up whole, or cut him up into mince-meat, according to the state of his digestive functions. "Egad, Nell!" he continued, "both his bark and his bite are bad enough."

"I have heard Ellen maintain," cried Matilda, "that there was sweetness at his heart, even when there was sourness in his mouth. If it is so, I can only say that his barley-sugar drops are very highly acidulated. Ha, ha, ha!"

"D'ye hear that? d'ye hear that!" exclaimed the father. "Didn't I tell you 'Tilda was a wit? As to old Crab, with his venomous jibes and jeers, and his malignant—" The conclusion of his speech was arrested by the opening of the door, and the appearance of John Trotman, ushering in the very party thus bitterly vituperated. "Ha, my good friend Crab?" cried the unabashed Captain, "I was just singing your praises to Mr. Brown. Allow me to introduce you to him." And he went through the form of presentation with as much pomposity as if he were in his own house, and were conferring a favor upon both parties. Brown, after gazing for a minute on the face of his new visitant, a little shrivelled man of an atrabilarious hue and sufficiently acid expression, turned towards Matilda, exclaiming, with a significant smile, "It *is* fortunate, Miss Molloy, that I have not yet brewed my beer."

"Oh—ay—true!" cried the Captain, whose self-possession was almost the only one that he retained. "We were talking, Mr. Crab, of my famous table ale—capital stuff, and yet never gets up into the head."

"That *is* a recommendation," replied the party addressed, "for I have a great horror of water on the brain."

"Curious old mansion this," pursued the Captain, pretending not to hear the last inuendo; "on a small scale it reminds me, in some respects, of my own patrimonial seat. Ah, Mr. Crab! you were never at my fine place—Clognakilty House, in the county Down."

"No, Captain; were *you?*" And then, as if talking to himself, the old gentleman ejaculated, as he counted his fingers, "There are estates in Ayrshire, and in the Isle of Skye, and in the Scilly Islands; and there are *Châteaux en Espagne;* and Ariosto tells us that all lost things are collected together in the moon; but where is there a depôt for the things that are very circumstantially described, but which never existed? It ought to be capacious. Yours is a large estate, I believe?"

"Immense, sir! immense! I forget the exact number of acres—Irish acres, you know, are larger than yours—but it is certainly one of the finest places in Ireland, though I say it that shouldn't say it."

"Nay, there we differ; for if you didn't say it, nobody would. If you assert the fact, I believe it; if I had seen the place with my own eyes, I might perhaps have doubted: but it's all the same; it's all the same. How say the logicians? *De non apparentibus et non existentibus eadem est ratio.*"

"And such hunting!" resumed the Captain, addressing himself to Brown: "I must give you an account some day of my celebrated hunter Paddy-whack, and my famous race-horse Skyscraper. Faith and troth! I played first fiddle at the meetings in Ireland."

"The Irish, I believe, have their lyres, as well as their fiddles," muttered Crab, again counting his fingers with a vacant look of absence. "Some say that the lyre of Mercury had three strings, some say four, some say seven. Amphion built up the walls of Thebes by means of a lyre—Quære: Was Amphion an Irishman? The lyre of Orpheus was thrown into the sea—Quære: Did you live near the coast in Ireland?"

"The great steeple-chase that I rode at Clognakilty," resumed Molloy, "is admitted to be the most wonderful thing of the sort ever performed. Skyscraper would climb up a stone-wall of twelve feet high like a cat: well, sir, he took ten of these walls; and after I had rode him at speed for seven hours without drawing bit, he cleared at a leap a river twenty-four feet wide. But the ground was low on the opposite side; the shock deranged my digestive functions; and for upward of five months—ay, just five months and four days—I could never eat more than an ounce at a time, so that I was known among my friends by the nickname of Ounce Molloy."

"Are you quite sure it was not *Bounce* Molloy?" asked Crab, in a tone and with a look of innocent curiosity. "'Bounce, Jupiter, bounce,' are the words of Midas, in O'Hara's burletta of The Golden

Pippin. High nonsense, says Addison, is like beer in a bottle, which has in reality no strength or spirit, but frets, and flies, and bounces, and imitates the passions of a much nobler liquor."

It might have been thought that the Captain would have taken offence at these splenetic and pointed sallies, but he was not a man to quarrel with a neighbor from whom he occasionally borrowed money, besides deriving various other advantages from his propinquity. Crab, moreover, had a sort of charter, as a humorist subject to strange fits of absence, for thinking aloud, and uttering whatever vagaries suggested themselves to his wandering thoughts; nor was it easy to believe that there was any raillery, badinage, or intentional offence in his effusions, however caustic; for his countenance never lost the grim seriousness of its expression, if we may except an occasional twinkle of his small, sharp eye, and his manner was invariably respectful. Rude and inopportune as his escapades appeared, they might, indeed, have been taken for the unconscious babblings of one who imagined that he was talking to himself and by himself, were it not manifest to a keen observer that he never gave them utterance unless when he was provoked by some display of arrogance, folly, or pretension.

Some farther gasconades of the incorrigible Captain having drawn down upon him a renewal of oblique sarcasms from Crab, Ellen, in order to protect her father, engaged the attention of his assailant by detailing a case of distress; a subject which never failed to elicit from her auditor an angry diatribe against the improvidence of the poor, and to secure some eventual relief to the sufferers, if, on a strict inquiry, they proved to be real objects of charity. Availing himself of this temporary diversion, the father whispered to Brown, as he pointed towards the delinquent, "I hope you don't mind his saucy sallies; I don't, for he really doesn't know what he is saying. Flighty, sir, flighty—we call him Crazy Crab. Even when he means to be splenetic, and caustic, and waspish, we only laugh at his impertinence. You're not offended with his wanderings, I trust?"

"Certainly not, if *you* are not," replied Brown, chuckling till he grew red in the face. "On the contrary, I think his wanderings, as you call them, are very like home-thrusts, or shots in the bull's eye. Depend upon it, he's a good bowler, for he seems to know that, if you would hit the Jack at last, you must seem at first not to be taking aim at it." At this moment, Matilda alluded to some private theatricals about to be performed at Gloucester, when the Captain, utterly unable to lose any opportunity of bragging, exclaimed, "Ah, sir! nothing like Kilkenny for private theatricals—never was and never will be. Egad, I starred it there famously—took all the first characters. 'Tilda, dear, what was that celebrated Spanish character that all the world declared I acted to the very life?"

"Ferdinand Mendez Pinto," ejaculated Crab, breaking off from his colloquy with Ellen, "was a celebrated Spaniard, and a surprising economist—of truth; being ever the first to visit non-existent cities, and to receive the most circumstantial intelligence of things that had never happened. His travels are extant, and written in choice Castilian."

"We were a jolly party of us," resumed the Captain, not heeding this interruption; "and, faith! we kept it up famously. There was the Marquis of Mayo, Lord Ormonde, Walter Butler, and I; we agreed to dine with one another in turn—that is to say, when I was not engaged to dine with the Duke of——Psha! I shall forget my own name next. 'Tilda, dear, what *is* the name of that duke I dined with so often at Kilkenny?"

"Duke Humphrey—Duke Humphrey! Eureka! it is found!" exclaimed Crab. "Douce, in his Illustrations of Shakspere, explains the first phrase; the second was uttered by Archimedes, when, on entering a full bath, he discovered that the quantity of water displaced depended upon the weight and volume of the body immersed in it."

"The last time I went to a match of pigeon-shooting," cried Molloy, making his rattan perform the sword exercise with such slashing animation that his companions kept at a prudent distance, "I remember I rode to the place of meeting on my famous hunter Paddy-whack; and *by* the powers! I never shot so well in all my life. Killed every bird but one, and he was knocked all to pieces. Beat all my competitors hollow, and yet the others had double-barrelled guns, while I had nothing in the world to shoot with but—"

"The long-bow," interposed Crab, "was once considered the best weapon to shoot with. The ancient ones were of a single piece; the modern long-bows have a thin piece of ash joined to them; but perhaps I interrupt you—pray go on."

"I was only about to add that mine was a single-barrel—and a famous cold I caught that same day, by shooting without my hat; but I'm always catching cold in my head."

"His own fault—he's always going out without anything in it," whispered Crab to Brown.

"And that same day," pursued Molloy, "I made a party with General Hooker to go fishing in the River Newry—by-the-by, Crab, what was the weight of that fine jack you caught last week in Langholme Water?"

"Twelve pounds."

"By the powers! is that all? The very last jack I caught in the River Newry weighed twenty-four pounds."

"Hang it!" muttered Crab, aside, "I wish I could catch my jack again; I would double the Captain's weight instantly, and make him a forty-eight pounder."

"As for the poor General, he would hardly have hooked a fish if I hadn't been at his elbow abetting and aiding."

"Rodomont-*ading* and gascon-*ading*," said Crab, patting the tops of his fingers, and looking up to the sky, as if lost in an etymological reverie, "are derived, I think, from the boastful hero of Ariosto, and the braggadocio character of the Gascon French."

"I brought the General home with me to Clognakilty House," pursued Molloy: "there was a party of six of us at dinner, and each of us drank five bottles of claret to his own cheek."

"That's more than I can swallow," observed Crab, very quietly.

"And yet I was as sober as a judge—must have been, for I won twenty pounds afterward at cards, though I'm no great hand at whist."

"If you had played at brag, you must have won forty at the very least; it's a *very* gambling game."

THE GOUTY MERCHANT AND THE STRANGER.

BY HORACE SMITH.

In Broad Street Buildings, on a winter night,
Snug by his parlor fire, a gouty wight,
Sat all alone, with one hand rubbing
His leg, wrapped up in fleecy hose,
While t'other held beneath his nose
The Public Ledger, in whose columns, grubbing,
He noted all the sales of hops,
Ships, shops, and slops,

Gums, galls, and groceries, ginger, gin,
Tar, tallow, turmeric, turpentine, and tin;

When lo! a decent personage in black
Entered, and most politely said—
"Your footman, sir, has gone his nightly track,
To the King's Head,
And left your door ajar, which,
Observed in passing by,
And thought it neighborly to give you notice."

"Ten thousand thanks! how very few get
In time of danger,
Such kind attentions from a stranger!
Assuredly that fellow's throat is
Doomed to a final drop at Newgate.
He knows, too, the unconscionable elf!
That there's no soul at home except myself."

"Indeed!" replied the stranger, looking grave;
"Then he's a double knave.
He knows that rogues and thieves by scores
Nightly beset unguarded doors:
And see how easily might one
Of those domestic foes,
Even beneath your very nose,
Perform his knavish tricks,
Enter your room as I have done,
Blow out your candles—*thus*, and *thus*
Pocket your silver candlesticks—
And walk off *thus*!"

So said, so done—he made no more remark;
Nor waited for replies,
But marched off with his prize,
Leaving the gouty merchant in the dark.

THE FARMER AND THE COUNSELLOR.

BY HORACE SMITH.

A counsel in the Common Pleas,
Who was esteemed a mighty wit,
Upon the strength of a chance hit
Amid a thousand flippancies,
And his occasional bad jokes
In bullying, bantering, browbeating,
Ridiculing, and maltreating
Women, or other timid folks,
In a late cause resolved to hoax
A clownish Yorkshire farmer—one
Who, by his uncouth look and gait,
Appeared expressly meant by Fate
For being quizzed and played upon:
So having tipped the wink to those
In the back rows,
Who kept the laughter bottled down,
Until our wag should draw the cork,
He smiled jocosely on the clown,
And went to work.
"Well, Farmer Numscull, how go calves at York?"
"Why—not, sir, as they do wi' you,
But on four legs, instead of two."
"Officer!" cried the legal elf,
Piqued at the laugh against himself,
"So pray keep silence down below there.
Now look at me, clown, and attend;
Have I not seen you somewhere, friend?"
"Yees—very like—I often go there."
"Our rustic's waggish—quite laconic,"
The counsel cried, with grin sardonic;
"I wish I'd known this prodigy,
This genius of the clods, when I
On circuit was at York residing.
Now, Farmer, do for once speak true—
Mind, you're on oath, so tell me, you,
Who doubtless think yourself so clever,
Are there as many fools as ever
In the West Riding?"
"Why—no, sir, no; we've got our share,
But not so many as when *you* were there!"

FINE BROWN STOUT.

BY HORACE SMITH.

A BREWER in a country town
Had got a monstrous reputation;
No other beer but his went down.
The hosts of the surrounding station
Carv'd its great name upon their mugs,
And painted it on every shutter;
And tho' some envious folks would utter
Hints that its flavor came from drugs,
Others maintained 'twas no such matter,
But owing to his monstrous vat,
At least as corpulent as that
At Heidelberg—and some said fatter.

His foreman was a lusty Black,
An honest fellow,
But one who had an ugly knack
Of tasting samples as he brewed,
Till he was stupefied and mellow.
One day, in his top-heavy mood,
Having to cross the vat aforesaid,
(Just then with boiling beer supplied,)
O'ercome with giddiness and qualms, he
Reeled, fell in, and nothing more was said,
But in his favorite liquor died,
Like Clarence in his butt of Malmsey.

In all directions round about
The negro absentee was sought,
But as no human noddle thought
That our fat Black was now Brown Stout,
They settled that the rogue had left
The place for debt, or crime, or theft.

Meanwhile the beer was, day and day,
Drawn into casks, and sent away,
Until the lees flow'd thick and thicker;
When lo! outstretch'd upon the ground,
Once more their missing friend they found,
As they had often done, in liquor.

"See," cried his moralizing master,
"I always knew the fellow drank hard,
And prophesied some sad disaster.
His fate should other tipplers strike:
Poor Mungo! there he wallows like
"A toast at bottom of a tankard!"

Next morn a publican, whose tap
Had help'd to drain the vat so dry,
Not having heard of the mishap,
Came to demand a fresh supply—
Protesting loudly that the last
All previous specimens surpass'd,
Possessing a much richer gusto
Than formerly it ever used to,
And begging as a special favor
Some more of the exact same flavor.

"Zounds!" said the brewer, "that's a task
More difficult to grant than ask.
Most gladly would I give the smack
Of the last beer to the ensuing,
But where am I to find a Black
And boil him down at every brewing?"

THE INTERRUPTED DUEL.

FROM "THE ADVENTURES OF HARRY AUSTIN." ANONYMOUS.

"IN case you happen to be killed, have you any particular directions to leave relative to the disposal of your remains?" inquired Daillie, on the following morning, while journeying in his curricle in the direction of Chalk Farm—"because, if you have, my dear fellow, now's your time, for it only wants ten minutes to eight."

Such a question, even, when addressed by a lawyer, on making out a rough sketch of your will, strikes rather harshly on the ear, but when spoken with the utmost nonchalance, some ten or twenty minutes prior to the probability of your being shot, grates most particularly unpleasant on the auricular nerve; and the cold, foggy atmosphere of a London December, at so early an hour in the morning, tends but in a very small degree to exhilarate the spirits.

So thick and substantial was the icy mist, that even objects within a short distance, were difficult to be discerned with accuracy, a circumstance which, my friend informed me, was highly favorable to the accomplishment of the object in hand, since there was not a sufficiency of fog to obscure the view of my opponent's outline—yet, at the same time, there would be no other visible object to distract my attention.

This was very satisfactory, truly; but, although I made no comment on the information thus afforded, it struck me that if any great benefit was to accrue to me individually, by reason of the state of the atmosphere, such advantage must unavoidably be shared in common with my adversary, in consequence whereof I could not so plainly discern any great cause for rejoicing on my part; but, as my friend appeared to think otherwise, it was not necessary to damp his pleasure, especially on an occasion where too much hilarity is not often the prevailing annoyance.

Individually, I experienced a sensation akin to any thing rather than merriment, and, as I traced all my misfortunes to the one source, my benedictions on the pale-faced cornet "fell thick as hail;" for, added to my other miseries and dilemmas, already recounted, I was now about to fight a duel with a man whom I never quarrelled with, and could not have engendered the slightest animosity against; and even should I escape from this ordeal, which, within a quarter of an hour, it seemed more than probable I should have to pass through, how was it possible for me to foretell, or in any way calculate upon, the many dangers and vexations which might still remain in store! How devoutly

I wished the cornet in my place—but wishing did not retard our progress, and, after a few seconds occupied in further reflections, Daillie informed me it was time to descend. So, divesting ourselves of our wet, clammy outer-garments, we walked onward towards the place appointed for the rencontre.

Having left the high road, and quitted the lanes branching from it, we traversed a slippery, muddy pathway, across two fields, at the end of which I was assured was the spot fixed on for the exhibition; but had I not had a guide, and one so conversant with the localities as my friend, I might have wandered about in the fog for a century, before I could have discovered the place of rendezvous. But Daillie was no novice, and the confidence with which he threaded his way, proclaimed his thorough knowledge of the premises.

"Here we are, Austin," said my companion, "not more than a hundred yards farther, and then we'll set to work—but don't forget to aim low—whatever you do, aim low—mark that. Even should your ball hit the ground, it may rebound and mark him, but if you fire over his head, no chance of such luck coming to pass. Cursed damp, isn't it? My dear fellow, don't forget, whatever you do, to keep your eye steadily on him, that is, if you *can* see him in this infernal fog—good thing the fog, though—always like a fog, on these occasions. Don't you feel hungry, Austin? This air and exercise would create an appetite in a skeleton—but look there—don't you see them? Sure enough that's them—now for it."

Straining my eyes in the direction pointed out by the captain, I at last discovered divers figures moving about, as indistinct and questionable as Shakspere's ghosts in Macbeth, but, as we soon discovered, somewhat more substantial.

"Austin!" exclaimed my friend earnestly, "by Jove, we are not the only ones this morning bent on a shooting excursion—very annoying that—however, can't be helped—must shift our ground, I suppose, if both sides of the other party have arrived before us. But let's see, how many are there?"

"Six, as well as I can make out," was my reply.

"Six," echoed the captain, "then all's right. I suppose Gregory, his friend, and the doctor are three—the others, not having as yet made up their number, we are of course entitled to the ground; and, if we get our affair over speedily, we may chance to see the next—that is, those who survive, of course—ah, here they come." And, issuing from the obscure coterie, two individuals advanced, but, as the decreasing distance between us diminished the doubt as to their identity, we discovered a couple of persons very different from Mr. Gregory and Sir Henry Stivers, whose society we had travelled thus far to enjoy.

One of the advancing gentlemen was habited in a pair of dark corduroy breeches, having a profusion of bunches of tape and ribbon affixed to the outside of each knee, which multiplicity of bindings aided and abetted in supporting a pair of large brick-dust colored top-boots, the feet of which were large and heavy enough to have macadamized more stones in an hour, than all the sinners at Brixton could accomplish in a year. He was large and portly in person, to make which the more evident, he had clothed himself outwardly in a huge, rough, white coat, somewhat resembling a blanket, and on the shaggy wool of which the damp hung in small brilliant particles, as you may sometimes see on the back of a Newfoundland dog when first emerging from an aquatic libation. Round his neck was bound an enormous belcher handkerchief of many colors, which, enveloping his chin in its ample fold, twined itself round and round the throat of its owner, as a boa constrictor is said to embrace its victim, till its course was arrested immediately under the bright variegated nose, forming the principal feature of this gentleman's face. On his head appeared a low-crowned hat of enormous and disproportionate expanse of brim: and altogether he looked as unlike my gentlemanly opponent, or the elegant baronet, as it was possible for two extremes to be.

The dress of the other person, who closely followed in the wake of the former, differed but in some trifling and immaterial points from the first; and, in whatever genus the leader might have been classed, it was palpably evident that the same description was applicable to each.

"Captain," commenced the voice from within the capacious folds of the neckcloth, "how d'ye do, captain—didn't expect to see me and my pall here, at this time o' day, I warrant? but, howsomedever, you see as how things will out sometimes, captain, as the terrier said to the badger when he draw'd him."

"What, Grabum!" loudly exclaimed Daillie, "What the devil brings you here?"

"Small matter of business, captain, as the hangman said to the culprit, when he fitted the halter."

"By heavens! I don't understand it—who gave information?" inquired the gallant officer.

"That's tellings, captain, as the informer said when he hanged his mother," replied the other.

"Come, Grabum, like a good fellow," coaxingly rejoined Daillie, "here's a five pound note for old acquaintance sake, only just tell me who the cursed rascal was; this is not the first time we've met, you know that, Grabum?"

"True, captain, I've seen you afore now, as the tread-mill said to the pickpocket, nevertheless duty's duty; and you knows, as well as I does, that it arn't my business to peach; I knows a trick worth two of that, and, after all, may be I can't tell who gived the information—may be I can; but, howsomedever, that's neither here nor there, as the man said of his wife's good temper—so, d'ye see, captain, there's no good in chaffing about it."

"Not much, truly," replied Daillie; "but where are the other gentlemen?"

"Quiet enough now, as the chap said when he cut the old woman's head off," was the answer.

"Well, Grabum," exclaimed my friend, "at least you'll allow me to speak to them?"

"With all my heart, captain, but don't be long about it, as the bride said to the parson, cause as how I'm tarnation cold and hungry, and it's full time as we was a jogging, for I see no fun in this here, as the pig said when he stood in the pillory."

My second accordingly advanced to the conference, and was immediately accosted by Sir Henry Stivers, when, after mutual expressions of astonishment, as to how the arrangements could have become so far public as to have enabled any person to give information of our intended proceedings, it was decided that no particle of suspicion of our *disappointment* having originated either in the principals or seconds could exist; and, to make doubly sure, the four persons most interested in the business willingly pledged their honors to that effect.

To attempt carrying the "little affair" through in presence of three Bow-street officers would have been ridiculous, even had it been in any degree feasible, which, however, it was not; for the three gentlemen alluded to, in order to set that question finally at rest, pointed out a few similarly apparelled individuals, who, they assured us, were always left by Mr. Grabum, as a sort of reserve, in case of his finding the influence of his warrant, backed as its presentation invariably was with elegant and appropriate similies, insufficient to carry his instructions into effect, without the aid of the corporeal arm of the law.

Under these circumstances, nothing remained but to deliver ourselves up at the police office, then and there to have our cases taken into the consideration of probably not the wisest and most courteous of God's creatures upon earth.

"That's right, gentlemen," vociferated Mr. Grabum, on seeing an inclination manifested on the part of all concerned to adjourn, "that's all right, the worst of the business is ended—and now it's all down-hill work, as Mr. Sadler said when he fell out of the balloon."

On pledging our words that no attempt at hostilities should be made by either party, we were permitted to return to town unaccompanied by Mr. Grabum and his friends, and as in honor bound, between ten and eleven o'clock, we made our appearance before the officiating mass of wisdom condensed into one solid ball, and deposited in the scull of Mr. Nonnant.

"Are these the offending parties against whom the information was laid?" pompously inquired the magistrate, on our appearing before him, and at the same time, running his eye quickly round the group.

"Yes, your worship;" answered a thin, greasy-looking thing, called by the presiding dignitary a clerk.

"Who apprehended these people?" asked the bench.

"Me! your worship, as the chap said when the man asked who he owed money to," sang out the melodious tones of Mr. Grabum's voice.

"Very well, Grabum, you're an intelligent and meritorious officer, always extremely diligent and active;" whereupon Mr. Grabum made divers attempts to emerge his chin from its imprisonment, as if desirous of developing the satisfaction which suffused his entire countenance.

"Did you find them in the act of committing a breach of the peace, Grabum?" inquired Mr. Nonnant.

"Summit near it, your worship; they was just a going to begin, and no mistake, as Boneyparte said at Salamanca, when he seed Lord Wellington a running after him."

"Well, gentlemen," said the magistrate, "I presume you are well acquainted with the reasons for appearing before me on this occasion?"

"We can tolerably surmise," replied the baronet. "But you will greatly oblige me by putting us in possession of the name of the party who lodged the information."

"Don't doubt it in the least, sir,—dare say you would," continued the man in power, "in order, I suppose, that he likewise should be called upon to satisfy what, in fashionable jargon, you call honor."

"I presume," sharply retorted the other, "that we were not forcibly arrested and brought up here for the exclusive purpose of furnishing an opportunity for an exhibition of elocution, since, if such *is* the case, I for one decline making part of the audience."

"Your remarks, sir," answered the justice, highly exasperated, "and the tone in which you have just uttered them, are, to say the least, uncalled for and extremely offensive; and," here his worship began to wax warm, "allow me to observe that a repetition of such insulting behavior will most assuredly call down upon the perpetrator an order for committal—sir, d'ye mark that? Perhaps you think, because you're a baronet, sir, that your words and inuendoes will pass without animadversion; but, I'll give you to understand, sir, that in this place, that is, as long as I fill the chair, mere rank shall never claim difference of treatment at my hands; no, sir, never; I consider all ranks, sects, and persuasions, as equal." And there was every prospect of the whole of our party being incarcerated in one of the secure private apartments belonging to the establishment, had not my friend Daillie, unperceived by the magistrate, intimated to his acquaintance, Mr. Grabum, that the period had arrived for his interference, and to do that individual justice, notwithstanding the anxiety which he showed in bringing about our interview with his superior, yet he seemed the very reverse of wishing our freedom to be further circumscribed; and, confident in his own oratorical powers, together with the privileged license of a necessary, and therefore highly useful, inferior, he boldly stepped forth and accosted Mr. Nonnant.

"I axes your worship's pardon for obtruding, but, as your worship very correctly says, there's no difference of sexes here, and therefore it isn't to be argued, for an instant, that, because a gentleman has had the misfortune to become a barrow-knight, that he's to take upon himself to come for to go for to flounder about, as if he was the lord mayor's footman in livery. No, no, certainly not, your worship, that won't do—people must stick in their places, as the officer said to the soldier when he was tired and wanted to go home. But the matter of that there is neither more nor less than this here. When I went to take these gentlemen, instead of making a tarnation blundering and row, as some on 'em sometimes does when they sees they're safe, off they comes along of me and my pal as quietly as possible, though to be sure they looked at me when I grabbed them, as much as to say, I'm blowed if I'm as fond of you as you seems of me, as the cake said to the school-boy; but then your worship knows I'm not considered generally the most pop'lor character what is. But I can't help that—know me better, like me more, as the fox said to the turkey poult as he could not reach at;—so, your worship, you sees that, as these ere gentlemen behaved civilly at the beginning, may be I can take upon myself to promise they'll behave genteelly to the last, so that their feelings may be spared the agonization of the lock-up; for, as you' worship knows, all living creatures have got fee' ing, as the lobster said to the cook when she was biling him."

"True, true," replied the magistrate, "I don't wish to incommode them more than can be helped; so, Grabum, if you guarantee their silence, possibly I may allow them to remain where they are, until the arrival of the bail."

Thus, through the intercession of Mr. Grabum, we were spared the infliction of the lock-up, and permitted to witness further instances of the worthy magistrate's impartiality and excellent judgment, in the disposal of divers cases brought before him.

Bail had been sent for, when on our road to the office; for my companions, far more experienced than myself, well knew the almost certain finale to the invitation, from the man in power, to attend him.

Eventually we were bound over to keep the peace for six months, in two hundred pounds each, and a couple of householders had the honor of appearing for every one at the forfeit of half that amount. There was a considerable degree of signing and feeing, and at length we were permitted to depart. But, the moment the edict for our discharge had irrevocably gone forth, Daillie approached the man of power, and, as if he had known him for ages, requested the pleasure of his society at dinner.

"Delighted to see you, at eight, old Nonnant, if that hour suits you, only a few friends—two Blenheims and a poodle—champagne in ice—no inconvenience to me, none whatever," he continued, seeing the persecuted about to speak, "happy to mount you, if you'll come earlier—send carriage to take you up—set you home—do any thing for you—love you greatly—do 'pon my honor—quite an original—best bear I ever met—"

"Turn these people out *instantly*," vociferated the enraged receiver of the public money, "turn them out of the office *instantly*," and forthwith divers brawny hands were applied to our shoulders, and we hurried through the passage with most miraculous rapidity.

"Not long about that, as the snail said when the garden roller crushed him," murmured Mr. Grabum, as we flew into the street; and, with merely a formal bow, exchanged between the adverse parties, the intended actors of a probable tragedy had no option but to return home, loudly and unasked for, lamenting their intentions having terminated in nothing.

DOUGLAS JERROLD.

The depth of his insight, the subtlety of his analysis, the vividness of his presentation, must strike every one who reads. His place among the wits of our own time is clear enough. He had less frolic than Theodore Hook, less elaborate humor than Sydney Smith, less quibble and quaintness than Thomas Hood. But he surpassed all these in intellectual flash and strength. His wit was all steel point—and his talk was like squadrons of lancers in evolution. Not one pun we have heard is to be found in his writings. His wit stood nearer to poetic fancy than to broad humor. The exquisite confusion of his tipsy gentleman, who, after scrapping the door for an hour with his latch-key, leans back and exclaims, "By Jove! some scoundrel has stolen—stolen—the keyhole!" comes as near farce as any of his illustrations. His celebrated definition of Dogmatism as "Puppyism come to maturity," looks like a happy pun—but is something far more deep and philosophic. Between this, however, and such fancies as his description of Australia—"A land so fat, that if tickled with a straw, it laughs with a harvest"—the distance is not great. In his earlier time, before age and success had mellowed him to his best, he was sometimes accused of ill-nature, a charge which he vehemently resented, and which seemed only ludicrous to those privileged with his friendship. To folly, pretence, and assumption he gave no quarter, though in fair fight; and some of those who tried lances with him, long remembered his home thrust. We may give two instances without offence, for the combatants are all gone from the scene. One of those playwrights who occupied Old Drury, under the French, against whom he waged ceaseless war of epigram, was describing himself as suffering from fever of the brain. "Courage, my good fellow," says Jerrold, "there is no foundation for the fact." When the flight of Guizot and Louis Philippe from Paris was the fresh talk of London, a writer of no great parts was abusing the Revolution and pitying Guizot. "You see," he observed, "Guizot and I are both historians—we row in the same boat."—"Aye, aye," says Jerrold, "but not with the same sculls." Yet such personal encounters were but the play of the panther. No man ever used such powers with greater gentleness. Indeed, to speak the plain truth, his fault as a man—if it be a fault—was a too great tenderness of heart. He never could say No. His purse—when he had a purse—was at every man's service, as were also his time, his pen, and his influence in the world. If he possessed a shilling, somebody would get sixpence of it from him. He had a lending look, of which many took advantage. The first time he ever saw Tom Dibdin, that worthy gentleman and song-writer said to him—"Youngster, have you sufficient confidence in me to lend me a guinea?"—"Oh, yes," said the author of 'Black Eyed Susan,' "I have all the confidence, but I haven't the guinea." A generosity which knew no limit—not even the limit at his bankers—led him into trials from which a colder man would have easily escaped. To give all that he possessed to relieve a brother from immediate trouble was nothing; he as willingly mortgaged his future for a friend as another man would bestow his advice or his blessing. And yet this man was accused of ill nature! If every one who received a kindness at his hands should lay a flower on his tomb, a mountain of roses would rise on the last resting-place of Douglas Jerrold.

"George," said Jerrold to the inimitable Cruikshank, "I hear that you are every where preaching temperance tee-total. Although I am glad to hear of your temperance, I am sorry you have taken the pledge, as it will be quite impossible for you to go to Heaven!" "Nonsense, Jerrold," replied George, "what do you mean by such stuff?" "Why," continued Jerrold, "you'd be a hypocrite, if you do; for there is nothing but *pure spirit* in Heaven!"

One sunny morning, a quidnunc and a bòre was sauntering down Regent Street, seeking whom he might devour with his interminable twaddle. At length he espies, approaching in hot haste, the witty and no less busy Douglas Jerrold. He stops and fastens on him. The bore puts his usual question—"Well, my dear Jerrold, what's going on?" Releasing himself, the wit strides hastily away, exclaiming, "I am."

Heraud, the writer, was another bore who inflicted "all his tediousness" on Jerrold. The satirist was asked if he had read Heraud's "Descent into Hell?" "No," was the answer, "but I should like to see it."

MRS. CAUDLE'S CURTAIN LECTURES.

BY DOUGLAS JERROLD.

INTRODUCTION.

Poor Job Caudle was one of the few men whom nature, in her casual bounty to women, sends into the world as patient listeners. He was, perhaps, in more respects than one, all ears. And these ears, Mrs. Caudle—his lawful, wedded wife, as she would ever and anon impress upon him, for she was not a woman to wear chains without shaking them—took whole and sole possession of. They were her entire property; as expressly made to convey to Caudle's brain the stream of wisdom that continually flowed from the lips of his wife, as was the tin funnel through which Mrs. Caudle in vintage time bottled her elder wine. There was, however, this difference between the wisdom and the wine. The wine was always sugared: the wisdom, never. It was expressed crude from the heart of Mrs. Caudle; who, doubtless, trusted to the sweetness of her husband's disposition to make it agree with him.

Philosophers have debated whether morning or night is most conducive to the strongest and clearest moral impressions. The Grecian sage confessed that his labors smelt of the lamp. In like manner, did Mrs. Caudle's wisdom smell of the rushlight. She knew that her husband was too much distracted by his business as toy-man and doll-merchant to digest her lessons in the broad day. Besides, she could never make sure of him; he was always liable to be summoned to the shop. Now from eleven at night until seven in the morning, there was no retreat for him. He was compelled to lie and listen. Perhaps there was little magnanimity in this on the part of Mrs. Caudle; but in marriage, as in war, it is permitted to take every advantage of the enemy. Besides, Mrs. Caudle copied very ancient and classic authority. Minerva's bird, the very wisest thing in feathers, is silent all the day. So was Mrs. Caudle. Like the owl, she hooted only at night.

Mr. Caudle was blessed with an indomitable constitution. One fact will prove the truth of this. He lived thirty years with Mrs. Caudle, surviving her. Yes, it took thirty years for Mrs. Caudle to lecture and dilate upon the joys, griefs, duties, and vicissitudes comprised within that seemingly small circle—the wedding-ring. We say, seemingly small; for the thing, as viewed by the vulgar, naked eye, is a tiny hoop made for the third feminine finger. Alack! like the ring of Saturn, for good or evil it circles a whole world. Or to take a less gigantic figure, it compasses a vast region: it may be Arabia Felix, and it may be Arabia Petrea.

A lemon-hearted cynic might liken the wedding-ring to an ancient Circus, in which wild animals clawed one another for the sport of lookers-on. Perish the hyperbole! We would rather compare it to an elfin ring, in which dancing fairies made the sweetest music for infirm humanity.

Manifold are the uses of rings. Even swine are tamed by them. You will see a vagrant, hilarious, devastating porker—a full-blooded fellow, that would bleed into many, many fathoms of black pudding—you will see him, escaped from his proper home, straying in a neighbor's garden. How he tramples upon the heart's-ease: how, with quivering snout, he roots up lilies—odoriferous bulbs! Here he gives a reckless snatch at thyme and marjoram—and here he munches violets and gillyflowers. At length the marauder is detected, seized by his owner, and driven, beaten home. To make the porker less dangerous, it is determined that he shall be *ringed.* The sentence is pronounced—execution is ordered. Listen to his screams!

> Would you not think the knife was in his throat?
> And yet they're only boring through his nose!

Hence, for all future time, the porker behaves himself with a sort of forced propriety—for in either nostril he carries a ring. It is, for the greatness of humanity, a saddening thought, that sometimes men must be treated no better than pigs.

But Mr. Job Caudle was not of these men. Marriage to him was not made a necessity. No; for him call it if you will a happy chance—a golden accident. It is, however, enough for us to know that he was married; and was therefore made the recipient of a wife's wisdom. Mrs. Caudle, like Mahomet's dove, continually pecked at the good man's ears; and it is a happiness to learn from what he left behind, that he had hived all her sayings in his brain; and further, that he employed the mellow evening of his life to put such sayings down, that, in due season, they might be enshrined in imperishable type.

When Mr. Job Caudle was left in this briary world without his daily guide and nocturnal monitress, he was in the ripe fulness of fifty-two. For three hours at least after he went to bed—such slaves are we to habit—he could not close an eye. His wife still talked at his side. True it was, she was dead and decently interred. His mind—it was a comfort to know it—could not wander on this point; this he knew. Nevertheless, his wife was with him. The Ghost of her Tongue still talked as in the life; and again and again did Job Caudle hear the monitions of by-gone years. At times, so loud, so lively, so real were the sounds, that Job, with a cold chill, doubted if he were really widowed. And then, with the movement of an arm, a foot, he would assure himself that he was alone in his holland. Nevertheless, the talk continued. It was terrible to be thus haunted by a voice: to have advice, commands, remonstrances, all sorts of saws and adages still poured upon him, and no visible wife. Now did the voice speak from the curtains; now from the tester; and now did it whisper to Job from the very pillow that he pressed. "It's a dreadful thing that her tongue should walk in this manner," said Job, and then he thought confusedly of exorcism, or at least of counsel from the parish priest.

Whether Job followed his own brain, or the wise direction of another, we know not. But he resolved every night to commit to paper one curtain lecture of his late wife. The employment would, possibly, lay the ghost that haunted him. It was her dear tongue that cried for justice, and when thus satisfied, it might possibly rest in quiet. And so it happened. Job faithfully chronicled all his late wife's lectures; the ghost of her tongue was thenceforth silent, and Job slept all his after nights in peace.

When Job died, a small packet of papers was found inscribed as follows:—

"*Curtain Lectures delivered in the course of Thirty Years by Mrs. Margaret Caudle, and suffered by Job, her Husband.*"

That Mr. Caudle had his eye upon the future printer, is made pretty probable by the fact that in most places he had affixed the text—such text for the most part arising out of his own daily conduct—to the lecture of the night. He had also, with an instinctive knowledge of the dignity of literature, left a bank-note of very fair amount with the manuscript. Following our duty as editor, we trust we have done justice to both documents.

MR. CAUDLE HAVING LENT FIVE POUNDS TO A FRIEND.

You ought to be very rich, Mr. Caudle. I wonder who'd lend you five pounds! But so it is; a wife may work and may slave. Oh, dear! the many things that might have been done with five pounds! As if people picked up money in the streets! But you always were a fool, Mr. Caudle! I've wanted a black satin gown these three years, and that five pounds would have pretty well bought it. But it's no matter how I go—not at all. Every body says I don't dress as becomes your wife—and I don't; but what's that to you, Mr. Caudle? Nothing. Oh no! you can have fine feelings for every body but those that belong to you. I wish people knew you, as I do—that's all. You like to be called liberal—and your poor family pays for it.

All the girls want bonnets, and when they're to get 'em I can't tell. Half five pounds would have bought 'em—but now they must go without. Of course, *they* belong to you; and any-body but your own flesh and blood, Mr. Caudle.

The man called for the water-rate to-day; but I should like to know how people are to pay taxes who throw away five pounds to every fellow that asks them.

Perhaps you don't know that Jack, this morning, knocked the shuttle cock through his bedroom window. I was going to send for the glazier to mend it; but after you lent that five pounds, I was sure we couldn't afford it. Oh, no, the window must go as it is; and pretty weather for a dear child to sleep with a broken window. He's got a cold already on his lungs, and I shouldn't at all wonder if that broken window settled him—if the dear boy dies, his death will be upon his father's head; for I'm sure we can't now pay to mend windows. We might though, and do a good many more things, if people didn't throw away their five pounds.

Next Tuesday, the fire insurance is due. I should like to know how it's to be paid! Why, it can't be paid at all. That five pounds would have just done it—and now, insurance is out of the question. And there never were so many fires as there are now. I shall never close my eyes all night—but what's that to you, so people can call you liberal, Mr. Caudle? Your wife and children may all be burnt alive in their beds—as all of us to a certainty shall be, for the insurance must drop. After we've insured for so many years! But how, I should like to know, are people to insure who make ducks and drakes of their five pounds?

I did think we might go to Margate this summer. There's poor Caroline, I'm sure she wants the sea. But no, dear creature, she must stop at home; she'll go into a consumption, there's no doubt of that; yes, sweet little angel. I've made up my mind to lose her now. The child might have been saved; but people can't save their children and throw away five pounds, too.

I wonder where little Cherub is! While you were lending that five pounds, the dog ran out of the shop. You know I never let it go into the street, for fear it should be bit by some mad dog, and come home and bite the children. It wouldn't at all astonish me if the animal was to come back with the hydrophobia, and give it to all the family. However, what's your family to you, so you can play the liberal creature with five pounds?

Do you hear that shutter, how it's banging to and fro? Yes—I know what it wants as well as you: it wants a new fastening. I was going to send for the blacksmith to-day. But now it's out of the question: now it must bang of nights, since you have thrown away five pounds.

Well, things have come to a pretty pass!—This is the first night I ever made my supper of roast beef without pickles. But who is to afford pickles when folks are always lending five pounds?

Do you hear the mice running about the room? I hear them. If they were only to drag you out of bed, it would be no matter. Set a trap for 'em. But how are people to afford the cheese, when every day they lose five pounds?

Hark! I'm sure there's a noise down stairs. It wouldn't surprise me if there were thieves in the house. Well, it may be the cat; but thieves are pretty sure to come some night. There's a wretched fastening to the back door: but these are not times to afford bolts and bars, when fools won't take care of their five pounds.

Mary Anne ought to have gone to the dentist's to-morrow. She wants three teeth pulled out. Now, it can't be done. Three teeth that quite disfigure the child's mouth. But there they must stop, and spoil the sweetest face that was ever made. Otherwise, she'd have been the wife for a lord. Now, when she grows up, who'll have her? Nobody. We shall die and leave her alone and unprotected in the world. But what do you care for that? Nothing; so you can squander away five pounds.

And now, Mr. Caudle, see what a misery you've brought on your wretched family! I can't have a satin gown—the girls can't have new bonnets—the water-rate must stand over—Jack must get his death through a broken window—our fire insurance can't be paid, so we shall all be victims to the devouring element—we can't go to Margate, and Caroline will go to an early grave—the dog will come home and bite us all mad—that shutter will go banging forever—the soot will always fall—the mice never let us have a wink of sleep—the thieves be always breaking in the house—and our dear Mary Anne be forever left an unprotected maid—and all, all, Mr. Caudle, because *you will go on lending five pounds!*

MR. CAUDLE HAS BEEN TO THE TAVERN WITH A FRIEND.

Poor me! Ha! I'm sure I don't know who'd be a poor woman! I don't know who'd tie themselves up to a man, if they knew only half they'd have to bear. A wife must stay at home, and be a drudge, whilst a man can go anywhere. It's enough for a wife to sit like Cinderella by the ashes, while her husband can go a drinking and singing at a tavern. You never sing! How do I know you never sing? It's very well for you to say so; but if I could hear you, I dare say you're amongst the worst of 'em.

And now, I suppose, it will be the tavern every night. If you think I'm going to sit up for you, Mr. Caudle, you are much mistaken. No: I'm not going to get up out of my warm bed to let you in, either. No; nor Susan shan't sit up for you; nor you shan't have a latch key. I'm not going to sleep with the door upon the latch, to be murdered before the morning.

Faugh! Pah! Whewgh! That filthy tobacco smoke. It's enough to kill any decent woman. You know I hate tobacco, and yet you will do it. You don't smoke yourself! What of that? If you go among people who *do* smoke, you're just as bad, or worse. You might as well smoke—indeed, better. Better smoke yourself, than come home with other people's smoke in your hair.

I never knew any good come to a man who went to a tavern. Nice companions he picks up there! Yes; people who make it a boast to treat their wives like slaves, and ruin their families. There's that wretch Prettyman.

See what he's come to. He doesn't now get home till two in the morning; and then in what a state! He begins quarrelling with the door mat, that his poor wife may be afraid to speak to him. A mean wretch! But don't you think I'll be like Mrs. Prettyman. No: I wouldn't put up with it from the best man that ever trod. You'll not make me afraid to speak to you, however you may swear at the door mat. No, Mr. Caudle, that you won't.

You don't intend to stay out till two in the morning! How do you know what you'll do when you get among such people? Men can't answer for themselves when they get boozing with one another. They never think of their poor wives, who are grieving and wearing themselves out at home. A nice headache you'll have to-morrow morning—or rather *this* morning; for it must be past twelve. You won't have a headache! It's very well for you to say so, but I know you will; and then you may nurse yourself for me. Ha! that filthy tobacco again. No: I shall not go to sleep, like a good soul! How's people to go to sleep when they're suffocated?

Yes, Mr. Caudle, you'll be nice and ill in the morning! But don't you think I'm going to let you have your breakfast in bed, like Mrs. Prettyman. I'll not be such a fool. No: nor I won't have discredit brought upon the house for sending for soda water early, for all the neighborhood to say, "Caudle was drunk last night!" No: I've some regard for the dear children, if you haven't. No: nor you shan't have broth for dinner. Not a neck of mutton crosses my threshold, I can tell you.

You won't want soda, and you won't want broth. All the better. You wouldn't get 'em if you did, I can assure you.——Dear, dear, dear! That filthy tobacco! I'm sure it's enough to make me as bad as you are. Talking about getting divorced—I'm sure tobacco ought to be good grounds. How little does a woman think, when she marries, that she gives herself to be poisoned! You men contrive to have it all your own side, you do. Now, if I was to go and leave you and the children, a pretty noise there'd be! You, however, can go and smoke no end of pipes. You didn't smoke! It's all the same, Mr. Caudle, if you go among smoking people. Folks are known by their company. You'd better smoke yourself, than bring me home the pipes of all the world.

Yes, I see how it will be. Now you've once gone to a tavern, you'll always be going. You'll be coming home tipsy every night; and putting out your shoulder; and bringing all sorts of disgrace and expense upon us. And then you'll be getting into a street fight—oh! I know your temper too well to doubt it, Mr. Caudle—and be knocking down some of the police. And then I know what will follow. Yes, you'll be sent, for a month or six weeks, to the treadmill. Pretty thing that, for a respectable tradesman, Mr. Caudle, to be put upon the treadmill with all sorts of thieves and vagabonds, and—there, again that horrible tobacco! and riff raff of every kind; I should like to know how your children are to hold up their heads, after their father has been upon the treadmill? No: I won't go to sleep. And I'm not talking of what's impossible. I know it will all happen, every bit of it. If it wasn't for the dear children, you might be ruined, and I not so much as think about it, but—oh! dear, dear! at least, you might go where they smoke *good* tobacco—but I can't forget that I'm their mother. At least, they shall have *one* parent.

Taverns! never did a man go to a tavern who did not die a beggar. And how your pot companions will laugh at you when they see your name in the Gazette! For it must happen,—your business is sure to fall off; for what respectable man will buy toys for his children of a drunkard? You're not a drunkard! No: but you will be—it's all the same.

You've began by staying out till midnight. By-and-by, 'twill be all night. But don't you think, Mr. Caudle, you shall ever have a key. I know you. Yes; you'd do exactly like that Prettyman, and what did he do, last Wednesday? Why, he let himself in about four in the morning, and brought home with him his pot companion, Leanly. His dear wife woke at six, and saw Prettyman's dirty boots at her bedside.—And where was the wretch, her husband? Why, he was drinking down stairs—swilling. Yes: worse than a midnight robber, he'd taken the keys out of his dear wife's pockets—ha! what that poor creature has to bear!—and had got the brandy. A pretty thing for a wife to wake at six in the morning, and instead of her husband, to see his dirty boots!

But I'll not be made your victim, Mr. Caudle. You shall never get at my keys, for they shall be under my pillow—under my own head, Mr. Caudle.

You'll be ruined; but if I can help it, you shall ruin nobody but yourself.

Oh! that hor—hor—i—ble tob—ac—co!

CAUDLE HAS BEEN MADE A MASON—MRS. CAUDLE IS INDIGNANT AND CURIOUS.

Now, Mr. Caudle; Mr. Caudle, I say: oh, you can't be asleep already, I know. Now, what I mean to say is this: there's no use, none at all, in our having any disturbance about the matter; but, at last, my mind's made, Mr. Caudle: I shall leave you. Either I know all you've been doing to-night, or to-morrow morning I quit the house. No, no: there's an end of the marriage state, I think—an end of all confidence between man and wife—if a husband's to have secrets and keep 'em all to himself. Pretty secrets they must be, when his own wife can't know 'em. Not fit for any decent person to know, I'm sure, if that's the case. Now, Caudle, don't let us quarrel; there's a good soul, tell me what it's all about? A pack of nonsense, I dare say; still, not that I care much about it—still, I *should* like to know. There's a dear. Eh! Oh, don't tell me there's nothing in it; I know better. I'm not a fool, Mr. Caudle; I know there's a good deal in it. Now, Caudle, just tell me a little bit of it. I'm sure I'd tell you anything. You know I would.—Well?

Caudle, you're enough to vex a saint! Now, don't you think you're going to sleep; because you're not. Do you suppose I'd ever suffered you to go and be made a mason, if I didn't suppose I was to know the secret, too? Not that it's any thing to know, I dare say, and that's why I'm determined to know it.

But I know what it is; oh, yes, there can be no doubt. The secret is, to ill-use poor women: to tyrannize over 'em; to make 'em your slaves; especially your wives. It must be something of the sort, or you wouldn't be ashamed to have it known. What's right and proper never need be done in secret. It's an insult to a woman for a man to be a freemason, and let his wife know nothing of it. But, poor soul! she's sure to know it somehow, for nice husbands they all make. Yes, yes; a part of the secret is to think better of all the world than their own wives and families. I'm sure men have quite enough to care for—that is, if they act properly—to care for them they have at home. They can't have much care to spare for the world besides.

And I suppose they call you *Brother* Caudle? A pretty brother, indeed! Going and dressing yourself up in an apron like a turnpike man—for that's what you look like. And I should like to know what the apron's for? There must be something in it not very respectable, I'm sure. Well, I only wish I was Queen for a day or two. I'd put an end to freemasonry and all such trumpery, I know.

Now, come, Caudle; don't let us quarrel. Eh! you're not in pain, dear? What's it all about? What are you lying laughing there at? But I'm a fool to trouble my head about you.

And you're not going to let me know the secret, eh? You mean to say, you're not. Now, Caudle, you know it's a hard matter to put me in a passion; not that I care about the secret itself, no, I wouldn't give a button to know it, for it's all nonsense, I'm sure. It isn't the secret I care about; it's the slight, Mr. Caudle; it's the studied insult that a man pays to his wife, when he thinks of going through the world keeping something to himself, which he won't let her know. Man and wife one, indeed! I should like to know how that can be when a man's a mason—when he keeps a secret that sets him and his wife apart? Ha, you men make the laws, and so you take good care to have all the best of 'em to yourselves; otherwise a woman ought to be allowed a divorce, when a man becomes a mason. When he's got a sort of corner-cupboard in his heart, a secret place in his mind, that his poor wife isn't allowed to rummage.

Caudle, you shan't close your eyes for a week—no, you shan't—unless you tell me some of it. Come, there's a good creature; there's a love. I'm sure, Caudle, I wouldn't refuse you anything; and you know it, or ought to know it by this time. I only wish I had a secret. To whom should I think of confiding it, but to my dear husband? I should be miserable to keep it to myself, and you know it. Now, Caudle?

Was there ever such a man? A man indeed! A brute! yes, Mr. Caudle, an unfeeling, brutal creature, when you might oblige me, and you won't. I'm sure I don't object to your being a mason; not at all, Caudle; I dare say it's a very good thing; I dare say it is; it's only your making a secret of it that vexes me. But you'll tell me; you'll tell your own Margaret? You won't! You're a wretch, Mr. Caudle.

But you know why: oh, yes, I can tell. The fact is, you're ashamed to let me know what a fool they've been making of you. That's it. You, at your time of life—the father of a family—I should be ashamed of myself, Caudle.

And I suppose you'll be going to what you call

your Lodge, every night, now. Lodge, indeed! Pretty place it must be, where they don't admit women. Nice goings on, I dare say. Then you call one another brethren. Brethren! I'm sure you had relations enough; you didn't want any more.

But I know what all this masonry's about. It's only an excuse to get away from your wives and families, that you may feast and drink together, that's all. That's the secret. And to abuse women, as if they were inferior animals, and not to be trusted. That's the secret, and nothing else.

Now, Caudle, don't let us quarrel. Yes, I know you're in pain. Still, Caudle, my love; Caudle! Dearest, I say, Caudle? Caud——

"I recollect nothing more," says Caudle, "for here, thank Providence, I fell asleep."

MY HUSBAND'S "WINNINGS."

A Household Incident.

BY DOUGLAS JERROLD.

Most men in something cheat their wives.—The Honeymoon.

"There, Mary, my love, take my winnings," said Mr. Joseph Langshawe; at the same time laying a sovereign and a sixpence upon the breakfast-table.

"Won again, Joseph!" cried Mrs. Langshawe, with one of her prettiest looks of astonishment. "Won again!"

"Take my winnings," repeated Mr. Langshawe; and, suppressing a sigh, he languidly stirred his coffee.

The reader may be assured that, for a winning man, Mr. Joseph Langshawe had one of the longest faces out of Chancery; yet, at the time at which our story commences, he appeared to his wife the chosen of good fortune; there never was such a lucky man! It seemed enough for him to touch the cards to turn them to trumps. Joseph Langshawe had won again!

Certainly the continued prosperity of Langshawe was to his wife marvellous; he never sat down to cards that he did not rise money in pocket. Had Joseph made a terrible compact with that crafty general dealer who continually roams about the earth, seeking cheap pennyworths? Had he trucked his immortal jewel for pasteboard diamonds as he chose to evoke them in this world? Had he surrendered himself to the great demon for a magical influence over tens, and fives, and sequences? In a word, was Joseph Langshawe become the fated Faust of five-card cribbage? Mysterious fears of future evil mingled in the marvellings of Mrs. Langshawe!

"When I think of Joseph's continued good fortune," observed Mrs. Langshawe to a female friend, "I own to you it sometimess makes me tremble."

"Why, my dear?" asked Mrs. Bridgeman. "Why? I thought you told me, like a good creature as he is, he always gave you his winnings."

"And so he does," replied Mrs. Langshawe; "invariably."

"What a good soul!" exclaimed Mrs. Bridgeman. "Dear fellow! it proves him so free from any selfish motives—shows that he merely plays for innocent excitement. And does Langshawe never lose?"

"Never," replied Mrs. Langshawe; "and it is that which makes me so very unhappy."

"Makes you unhappy! Well, you are the strangest creature," cried Mrs. Bridgeman.

"That is," rejoined Mrs. Langshawe, "when I fear that his continued good luck may some day tempt him to play for a ruinous sum; for it is impossible, my dear, that such fortune as Joseph's can last. I should be so happy if he'd never touch a card again."

"Why, you bought that beautiful chain, and your diamond drops, and all out of your husband's winnings," exclaimed Mrs. Bridgeman.

"Very true," allowed Mrs. Langshawe; and then she repeated, with a deep sigh, "but such fortune as Joseph's *can't* last."

Certain we are that the reader, after some further acquaintance with Langshawe, would not wish Joseph's fortune to continue. A brief extract from the conversation of the night previous to the presentation of the sovereign and sixpence, may explain the mystery of Langshawe's winnings.

"Well, Langshawe," cried a friend from an opposite table, as Joseph rose to go home, "how have you fared to-night?"

"As usual," said Joseph, and he tried to whistle; "as usual—there's no standing Bridgeman's luck."

"What!" exclaimed Fourpoints, "lost again? why, you always lose."

"I should say always," replied Joseph; "never mind—it's all right; yes, I've just enough;" and Langshawe held in his hand a sovereign, a half-crown, and a sixpence.

"Brought down to that, eh?" asked Flush, looking at the three pieces of coin.

"All that's left," answered Langshawe, "out of five-and-twenty pounds. Never mind, there's just enough; half-a-crown will pay for my coach home, and then—yes, that will make a very good show;" and Joseph surveyed at a distance the little piece of gold and lesser piece of silver in his palm; "a very good show for my winnings."

"Winnings!" exclaimed a new member of the club—"winnings! I thought, sir, you had nothing but losses?"

"That's very true, sir," replied Longshawe; "notwithstanding, I always make it a point in my domestic economy, whatever my losses may be, to take home my profits to my wife. You perceive," and Joseph exhibited the coin, "when the coach is paid, although I've lost to Bridgeman nearly four-and-twenty pounds, here's just a sovereign and sixpence for my winnings."

"A sixpence! why be so particular with the sixpence?" inquired the new member.

Mr. Joseph Langshawe looked one of his gravest

looks in the face of the new member, and, after a compassionate shake of the head, observed, "I should say, sir, you are a bachelor—I should say, pardon me if I'm wrong, that as yet you know nothing of conjugal confidence, otherwise you would perceive that the sixpence was a—a clincher."

"A clincher!" repeated the simple new member.

"The sovereign by itself," observed Joseph, might appear suspicious; but don't you perceive there's a reality in odd money? Mrs. Langshawe will see truth, sir, truth in the tester."

And the next morning, as we have already shown, Joseph handed over to the partner of his worldly goods a sovereign and a sixpence—his winnings!

"And who played last night?" asked Mrs. Langshawe—we must again ask the reader's attendance at the breakfast-table—"who played? Bridgeman?"

"Bridgeman," answered Joseph, shortly.

"My dear Joseph," said Mrs. Langshawe, very gravely, "I wish you'd exert the influence of a friend over Bridgeman; he confesses nothing to his wife, poor dear woman!—but I'm sure his losses must be very heavy. Every body hasn't your good fortune, Joseph."

Langshawe buried that expressive feature, his mouth, and half his nose, in his tea-cup.

"It would make me truly unhappy, Joseph, if I thought you won any of his money," said Mrs. Langshawe.

"Make yourself perfectly easy on that point, my dear," said Langshawe, internally wincing at the absurd suspicion; "my hands are clean of Bridgeman, though I played with him."

"I'm delighted to hear it," cried Mrs. Langshawe. "And now, Joseph, if you'll promise me to leave off play altogether ——"

"I have serious thoughts of it," said Joseph——

"You'll make me completely happy. For, depend upon it, as I have said again and again, your present fortune can't last."

"I've thought so, too," said Langshawe; who might have added, "and that's why I have gone on."

"And if you give up cards, perhaps the example may have a good effect upon Bridgeman; for the Bridgemans are not like us, Joseph; they want, I fear, that mutual confidence in one another, without which marriage must be——"

"To be sure, my dear," said Langshawe, acutely anticipating his wife's period—"to be sure. No—I shall give up play."

"I hope you will—I sincerely hope," said Mrs. Langshawe, as she took up the sovereign and the sixpence, "that this will be the last of your winnings."

Noon had scarcely passed, ere a passionate knocking at the door of the Langshawes announced a visitor. "Bless me! yes, it is—it is dear Mrs. Bridgeman," said Mrs. Langshawe, with unmingled surprise aud pleasure, as she heard the silvery voice of her friend on the staircase. "Dear Mrs. Bridgeman!"

As the visitor was introduced, Mrs. Langshawe jumped from her chair to run and kiss her best acquaintance, when Mrs. Bridgeman smiled somewhat severely, half-dropped a curtesy, put her hand to her brow, and sank into a seat.

"What's the matter, dear?" asked Mrs. Langshawe.

Mrs. Bridgeman entered into no details of her complaint, but simply observed, "I shall be better presently."

"Any thing happened at home?" inquired Mrs. Langshawe. "How's Bridgeman?"

Hath the reader beheld the countenance of an invalid when prescribed a certain drug, of all drugs his worst abhorrence? Hath the reader himself felt the cold shiver running through his vitals, twisting the very tips of his toes—the indescribable nausea that hath puckered up his countenance divine, and given his head a shake of most expressive loathing? Any one, so experienced, would have thought from Mrs. Bridgeman's manner that Mrs. Langshawe had spoke, it might be, of rhubarb, and not of Bridgeman—of assafœtida, perhaps, and not of a husband.

"I hope he's well?" said Mrs. Langshawe, anxiously.

"I believe Mr. Bridgeman is very well," said his wife; "but you know he never tells me any thing. Yes, last night I did gather from him that he had played at cards only with Mr. Langshawe."

"So Joseph told me," observed the innocent Mrs. Langshawe.

"Ha! you are blessed with a fortunate husband," said Mrs. Bridgeman, drily. "Some people, it is plain, are born with lucky fingers."

"I'm afraid it is so; however, Joseph has almost promised me never, never to play again."

"'Twill be a happy circumstance for some of his friends," remarked Mrs. Bridgeman, significantly.

"If, however, he will play and win, I am resolved—for it lies heavily upon my conscience to spend the money upon myself—I am determined to devote the money to some benevolent purpose; and, since the thought has taken me, I am so delighted that you are come to advise me. What do you think, my dear Mrs. Bridgeman," and Mrs. Langshawe drew herself nearer to her friend; "what do you think of the Society for the Conversion of the Jews?"

"Do you intend to subscribe Mr. Langshawe's winnings of last night to that estimable body?" asked Mrs. Bridgeman, biting her lips.

"How kind the suggestion!" exclaimed Mrs. Langshawe. "What a good creature you are! I did not think to do so, but now I certainly shall."

"For five-and-twenty pounds," said Mrs. Bridgeman, with a terrible smile, "no doubt you may be a life governess."

"Five-and-twenty pounds!" cried Mrs. Langshawe, laughingly.

"The losses of Mr. Bridgeman last night," remarked his wife; "he played with Mr. Langshawe, and, I presume, as usual, the fortunate man gave you his winnings." This was said in a cold, cutting tone, sharp enough to sever every silver tie of female friendship.

"My dear Mrs. Bridgeman, there must he some mistake. Joseph gave me his winnings, certainly, but they were only a sovereign——"

"A sovereign!" exclaimed Mrs. Bridgeman contemptuously.

"And a—sixpence," added Mrs. Langshawe, with her usual meekness.

"And a sixpence! A sovereign and a sixpence! My dear," said Mrs. Bridgeman, with awakened sympathy, "you are deceived, an injured woman."

"Do you really think so?" asked Mrs. Langshawe, unconscious of her calamity.

"Mr. Langshawe won five-and-twenty pounds—I have secret, but certain means of knowing—of poor innocent Bridgeman; five-and-twenty pounds, Madam; and the crafty man makes his winnings a sovereign and a—a——well, the effrontery of some people! And had you no suspicion of your husband's falsehood? Why, that very sixpence—the affected scrupulousness of the thing—would have made me doubt him. My love, I have seen more of the marriage state than you, and I know that men are never so very particular, except when they mean to deceive us."

"I'm sure I can't see why Joseph should misrepresent his winnings. I don't see the motive," said the artless Mrs. Langshawe.

"Perhaps not, my love; perhaps not. How should you know what he does with all his money? It's plain he has some object in deceiving you," was the charitable opinion, expressed with more than sufficient force, of Mrs. Bridgeman.

"It would really seem so," said Mrs. Langshawe, almost trembling at her doubts.

"Be sure of it," said Mrs. Bridgeman; "you hav'n't a twentieth part of his winnings, and where they go——"

"Many pardons," cried Langshawe, who had suddenly opened the door; "trust I break upon no secrets. How's Bridgeman?"

Mrs. Bridgeman looked at one hand, then at the other, and, with an effort, said, "I hope—that is, very well."

"Where are you going, love?" asked Langshawe, as his wife moved towards the door.

"Entertain Mrs. Bridgeman for a minute; I'll return directly," said Mrs. Langshawe; for she felt her eyes filling with tears as she looked upon Joseph, and thought of his duplicity, the sovereign, and the sixpence.

"Bridgeman, very well, eh?" said Langshawe, in his easy, pleasant style.

"All things considered, remarkably well," answered Mrs. Bridgeman.

"Nothing happened?" inquired Langshawe, struck by the serious manner of the lady. "Eh? bless me! all right at home I hope?—no domestic loss—no——"

"Some people, Mr. Langshawe, would call it one. Mr. Bridgeman's income, though sufficient for all reasonable enjoyments, is hardly adequate to the calls made by cards upon it, together with the constant good fortune of his bosom friends."

"Bridgeman plays now and then, to be sure," said Langshawe, in mollifying voice, "but then he always wins."

"Wins!" exclaimed Mrs. Bridgeman; "you know—better than anybody, you know—that last night he lost five-and-twenty pounds."

"Is it possible?" cried Langshawe.

"Possible!" echoed the lady. "Losing would seem a matter of certainty when he plays with some people. It is as certain for Mr. Bridgeman to lose as for Mr. Langshawe to win."

Langshawe, hurt by the words, yet more by the piercing looks of Mrs. Bridgeman, resolved to clear himself of the odium of constant success. With this determination, first glancing towards the door, he took the lady's hand. "My dear Mrs. Bridgeman, I'm sure you can keep a secret."

The compliment at once disarmed Mrs. Bridgeman; she, too, looked towards the door, and then said, "I can, Mr. Langshawe."

"Then, between ourselves, my dear madam," said Langshawe, in a low, soft voice, "I never win."

"Never win, Mr. Langshawe!"——

"Never. The truth is, Mary,—bless her!—is such a rigid economist in every thing that concerns herself—is so averse to laying out a shilling upon the smallest trinket, that I am compelled to use a little harmless deceit, to induce her to commit the least expense."

"Then your winnings last night, Mr. Langshawe?"——

"Quite apocryphal, I assure you—all, what I may call," said Langshawe, "a conjugal fiction."

"Mr. Langshawe,"—said Mrs. Bridgeman, with a subdued fierceness that made Joseph stare,—"a man may from habit consider himself justified in attempting the most unblushing fraud upon his own wife—habit goes far, in all matters—but, sir, that you should hold my common sense in so contemptuous a light"——

"My dear madam, I protest," exclaimed Langshawe, coloring to the eyelids; "I protest that I have the profoundest sense of"——

"Adds, sir—adds to the meanness of your first duplicity. You know that Mr. Bridgeman, your dear friend, as you are pleased to call him, last night lost five-and-twenty pounds."

"I vow I know nothing of the matter," cried Joseph.

"And more, and worse than all, that Mr. Langshawe was the winner."

"Now, my dear Mrs. Bridgeman," said Joseph, almost amused at the extravagance of the charge, he himself having been the sufferer,—"it is very true that I spoke of winnings to Mary—I"——

"I know, sir—I know; one piece of gold and a sixpence. Mr. Langshawe," cried Mrs. Bridgeman, for a lady, very sternly—"I am astounded at your double falsehood—I blush for your meanness—I"——

Langshawe could say nothing. For the first time he regretted that he had ever appeared to his wife a winning man.

"Mr. Langshawe," exclaimed Mrs. Bridgeman, with new energy, "may I solicit of you one—a last—favor?"

"Twenty, my dear Mrs. Bridgeman," answered the obliging Joseph.

"One—one will suffice, Mr. Langshawe. Promise me never to play with my unfortunate husband again. Heaven knows what his losses may have been! His poor wife knows nothing. But where there are great winnings, there must consequently be—you understand me, dear Mr. Langshawe?"—and Mrs. Bridgeman tried to forget her passion, and to smile Langshawe into acquiescence. "Poor Bridgeman," she added in a very equivocal tone, "is really no match for you. You are—you know you are—I hear it upon all hands—such an invincible player; whilst simple Bridgeman in the vanity of his heart thinks himself your equal. Now, do, pray take pity of his weakness—don't, don't play with him;" and Mrs. Bridgeman solicited the compassion of Langshawe, as she would have entreated the mercy of a highwayman; indeed, despite of the peculiarity of Joseph's winnings, he felt himself before Mrs. Bridgeman somewhat in the situation of a pickpocket. "There is a fate about you," said Mrs. Bridgeman—"as might be said of Macbeth, you bear 'charmed' cards—therefore, do spare my silly man—do spare "——

"Mr. Bridgeman," said the servant, opening the door.

"Bridgeman!" cried his wife and Langshawe.

"My mistress is with him, sir," said the domestic, and disappeared.

It was too true. Whilst Mrs. Bridgeman and Mr. Langshawe had been left to conversation, Mrs. Langshawe and Mr. Bridgeman—the gentleman entered the house as Mary quitted Joseph—had discoursed of the gain and loss of the preceding evening.

"Mr. Bridgeman, I am so glad you are come," said the gentle Mrs. Langshawe. "Your dear wife is up stairs."

"Indeed!" observed Bridgeman, very tranquilly; he then asked—"how's Langshawe?"

"Very well; he's with your lady. Oh! Mr. Bridgeman, I cannot express to you how much I am annoyed at the circumstances of last night."

Mr. Bridgeman put his hand to his chin, gently exalted his shoulders, and spoke not.

"I wish to my heart that Joseph would not play, for his fortune is so extraordinary," said Mrs. Langshawe.

Now, as Mr. Bridgeman was fully aware that, although Joseph always lost to him, he invariably, as in the case of the sovereign and the sixpence, took home winnings to some amount to Mrs. Langshawe, he did not feel quite at ease in his present situation with that lady. "Fortune," he endeavored to observe, "does act extraordinarily with Langshawe."

"And then there is something to me so uncomfortable, to say the least of it, in winning money of our friends;" and Mrs. Langshawe looked innocently in the perturbed face of Bridgeman.

"Cards are like love, Mrs. Langshawe, as I take it; friends are not to be considered in the matter," replied the impartial Bridgeman.

"I can't think so. I think there is something almost mean and sordid in these continual attempts on the purse of those for whom we profess an esteem, a friendship," said Mrs. Langshawe.

Mr. Bridgeman, with the weight of many pounds of his friend Langshawe about the neck of his conscience, began to think the interview less pleasant than it might have been. It was plain, however, from her looks, that Mrs. Langshawe expected some reply; therefore Mr. Bridgeman nodded his head affirmatively.

"But the worst of all is, Mr. Bridgeman," said Mrs. Langshawe, with animation, "that falsehood, positive falsehood, comes of the practice. Never—never before has Joseph deceived me!" (Poor little dear!) "And now I have found him capable of the least deceit—of misrepresentation in the simplest thing—it has made me truly wretched. Without mutual confidence, Mr. Bridgeman, there can be no happiness in the marriage state."

Mr. Bridgeman bowed very solemnly—perhaps it was so.

"To be sure, he may have been ashamed of the sum—really, too much to win of anybody, and more than all, of a friend."

"Has Langshawe really confessed to having lost? Did he bring home *no* winnings?" thought Bridgeman.

"Tell me, pray tell me, Mr. Bridgeman, was not the loss between you last night five-and-twenty pounds?"

Mrs. Langshawe's manner had so surprised Bridgeman—her sudden energy had so confused him, that the color rose to his face, and he began to stammer, as he thought—"It's plain, Joseph has confessed his losses—it's plain "——

"Five-and-twenty pounds?" again pressed Mrs. Langshawe.

"Not—not quite," answered Bridgeman.

"It is true, then," cried Mrs. Langshawe; "Mrs. Bridgeman is right!"

"Mrs. Bridgeman!" said her husband.

"It was she who told me the real amount of money lost, and not Mr. Langshawe. That Joseph should have won nearly five-and-twenty pounds of you—of you, his old, his early friend! I shall hardly know how to look in Mrs. Bridgeman's face again—I shall——"

To the inexpressible relief of Bridgeman—who, really being the winner of his friend's money, felt with double acuteness the reproaches inveighed against the innocent—Langshawe entered the apartment,—Mrs. Langshawe instantly quitting it.

"Bridgeman," said Langshawe, in a low voice, and with an accusing shake of the head, "this is really very wrong."

"There's something wrong, somewhere," replied Bridgeman.

"My dear fellow," cried Langshawe, "if you wanted to account for five-and-twenty pounds to your wife, you needn't have laid the loss upon my shoulders."

"I account to Mrs. Bridgeman! I lose five-and-twenty pounds! 'Twas just my winnings. The fact is, Langshawe—not that I am under the influence of my wife——"

"No more am I—not at all—no man less," said Langshawe. "If I have fabled a little as to my winnings, it was out of affection, not fear—no, no, it was to keep Mary happy, and the house quiet—nothing more."

"I was about to say, if you must win large sums of money, you might, out of respect to the feelings of Mrs. Bridgeman, win them of anybody but her husband."

"But I never win large sums; never, never but once, when I told Mary that I had won thirty guineas, because I wanted her to buy a pair of diamond drops, which otherwise she wouldn't consent to purchase. Never a large sum, but then," said Langshawe.

"Nonsense! Mrs. Langshawe feels assured at this minute that you won a large sum of me last night," cried Bridgeman.

"And if she does," replied Langshawe, "it is because Mrs. Bridgeman told her as much; and who told Mrs. Bridgeman I needn't declare to you."

"Langshawe," said Bridgeman, "we have known one another many years, and I should be sorry to quarrel with you."

"Should equally regret it, Bridgeman," answered Langshawe; "but when men can't keep matters like these to themselves—when their wives must be made parties to every thing—there's an end to every principle of manly friendship.'

"I think so, too," was the gloomy reply of Bridgeman.

"At all events, then, Mr. Bridgeman," said Langshawe, endeavoring to clothe his lengthened face with dignity—"at all events,"——

Unhappily, or we should rather say happily, the

appearance of the ladies not only cut short the wordy encounter of the gentlemen, but the smiles and beamy looks of the wives suddenly lighted up the faces of their husbands. The ladies requested that nothing more might be said of the matter, and, hoping that their husbands would leave filthy cards for ever, all shook hands, and, at the usual hour, sat down happily to dinner.

Mr. and Mrs. Bridgeman had departed from their home, and Mr. and Mrs. Langshawe still sat at their hearth.

"I forgive you, Joseph, this time, but never tell me a fib again," said the pretty Mrs. Langshawe. "Moreover, if you must play, promise me not to win of Bridgeman. His wife found out his loss in the oddest way; he had taken out fifty pounds to pay a bill, and returned home—how she discovered that I can't tell—with less than half the money; the bill, however, was not paid, for 'twas called for before he was up." (The truth is that Bridgeman had not taken the note with him, but replaced it in his desk.) "When she heard that he had played with you, knowing that you always won, she of course concluded that you had the money. And how naughty of you to tell me such a tale about a sovereign, and——but I have promised not to scold you;" and Mrs. Langshawe patted the blushing cheek of Joseph.

"She's a very violent woman, Mrs. Bridgeman," said Langshawe.

"Very; I was quite surprised at her passion—besides, it showed an avarice that—oh, Joseph, I wouldn't have had you keep those winnings for any consideration."

"Keep them! Why—eh?—Mrs. Bridgeman seemed suddenly in excellent spirits—you never returned the money—you——"

"Not exactly the money, Joseph," said Mrs. Langshawe, who smiled with some meaning.

Mr. Langshawe gaped, stared, and said, "Not exactly money—what then?"

"Oh! I hit upon an excellent plan. You know my diamond drops, that I bought out of your winnings?"

"Thirty guineas!" cried Joseph Langshawe, turning a little pale.

"Mrs. Bridgeman was always admiring them. So, to-day, whilst you and her husband were alone, after a little persuasion, I induced Mrs. Bridgeman—to accept them."

"You did, Mary?"

"I did, Joseph!" said Mrs. Langshawe, delighted at her dexterity.

"Your diamond drops!" cried Langshawe.

"And as they cost thirty guineas, and as last night you took less than five-and-twenty of Bridgeman, why, his wife having the diamonds, you may now be said to have won less than nothing," said Mrs. Langshawe.

"Much less," groaned Joseph.

We believe, though we cannot vouch for him, that from that time Langshawe forswore cards. Of this, however, we are certain; if he did play, Mrs. Langshawe was never again perplexed with her—"husband's winnings."

Young hearts and old hearts
  Cannot live together;
Warm hearts and cold hearts
  Make but foul weather.
Young hearts and old hearts
  Are deadly foes—
Young hearts are Poetry!
  Old hearts are Prose!

Young hearts have freshness,
  Beauty, and joy—
Young hearts are *pure gold!*
  Old hearts *alloy!*
Old hearts are sadness,
  Young hearts are mirth—
Young hearts are Heaven!
  Old hearts are Earth.

THE ADVENTURES OF A TALE.

BY THE HON. MRS. ERSKINE NORTON.

I could [and will] a tale unfold.—HAMLET.

It is with indignation such only as a literary composition, conscious of its own high value, and smarting under injustice and neglect, can be supposed to feel, that I lift up my voice from behind the serried ranks of my companions, long tales and short, the light effusion of three pages, or the decided weight of three volumes; serious tales or gay; moral or profane; fine French or low Irish; tales without an end, and tales that ought never to have had a beginning; tales in ponderous verse or in gossamer prose; the delicate and brittle ware called travellers' tales; or those more substantial and important-looking matters, political economy tales. I say, that from behind this prodigious phalanx, I rise up like Erskine from the big-wigs of the first law-court he addressed, elevating myself as the young counsellor on his bench, and making myself heard,—not, it is true, in the general cause of justice, liberty, humanity, etc., but in that cause in which all, if not eloquent, are at least earnest and sincere—in the cause of self.

It is said that Minerva (a goddess) sprang from the brain of Jupiter without a mamma; I, Seraphina (a tale,) issued forth from the lovely head (I am not quite so sure of the brain) of a fair romantic young lady, without a papa;—at least, so I presume, for my composition is purely feminine; my slight and delicate texture could only have been woven by an unassisted female imagination.

While yet in embryo, I was christened Seraphina, and was to be composed in three or four reasonably long letters (ladies' letters, crossed and recrossed with different colored inks,) to Clementina. My respected parent decided that there was nothing equal to the epistolary form for describing the sentiments and adventures of a heroine; for, who like herself *can* lay open all those finer and minuter feelings of the inmost heart, pouring into the ear of sympathizing friendship every wish, every hope, every thought! Soul meets soul, even through the vulgar medium of pens, ink, and paper; "thoughts that glow and words that burn" are traced by the delicate fingers that "resume the pen," with a celerity altogether surprising; no agitation can delay, no fatigue can excuse; the half-dozen sheets of foolscap that are to be run over before she can lay her throbbing temples on her pillow, her white drapery (i. e. her night-gown) floating round her, her long hair unbound (very much out of curl,) her snowy feet on the cold marble (she has lost her slippers,) her door carefully locked, but the trellised casement left open that the pale moonbeams may peep through it; her lamp is decaying, her hands are trembling, her eyes swimming in tears:—*n'importe*, the six sheets of foolscap are finished! O, there is nothing like the epistolary form! Seraphina shall be in letters to Clementina:

> Sure, letters were invented for some wretch's aid,
> Some absent lover, or some captive maid.—POPE.

I can just recollect, as I began to assume form and consistency, how much and how dearly I was fondled by my young and doting mother; indeed, at times, I ran some danger of being killed by kindness. While transcribing some of the deeply affecting scenes and sentiments with which I abound, I was nearly obliterated by her tears, my material parts being composed with a very fine pen and very pale ink; at other times, when the stronger passions took possession of the scene, and revenge, hatred, and fury predominated, she would crush me in her hand, "her eyes in a fine frenzy rolling," and throw me to the other end of the room. Of course she had some difficulty in smoothing me out again. Nevertheless I grew in stature, and in favor with mamma, myself, and four young ladies, her neighbors, (all under fifteen,) who were at home for the holidays. On the assembling of this little coterie, I was mysteriously brought forth from my perfumed drawer, where I lay covered with dry rose-leaves; and read by the author of my being, in a way in which an author only can read. My young auditory listened in profound attention and admiration, secretly resolving that they too would try their unfledged wings in authorship, when they had left off school and finished their education. Except to these four interesting girls, my existence was a profound secret.

My composition is certainly enough to excite emulation, however hopeless. I am (though I say it myself) an exquisite tale. My heroine is a model of beauty, virtue, tenderness, and thrilling sensibility; "a perfect wonder that the world ne'er saw;" therefore the world ought the more to appreciate so rare a conception. Her mother was a suffering angel on earth; but, happily for herself, she removed to a more congenial abode, while her cherub child was yet in infancy. The surviving parent is, of course, a horrid tyrant, who cannot comprehend the highly-wrought sensibilities of his daughter, and therefore will not give way to them. There is the suitor favored by the father, and the lover favored by the daughter. There are a locking up, an elopement, delicate and dubious situations full of excitement, misapprehensions of all kinds, a false female friend, libertine lords, fine unfeeling ladies, dark stormy nights, and a catastrophe of the most extraordinary, pathetic, and soul-subduing interest. Add then, my descriptions of nature! my silver moon and diamond stars! my rustling trees! my woodbine, jessamine, and violets!

A little conceit I acknowledge to, when copied on pale pink, gilt-edged paper, curiously ornamented with embossed loves and doves, written in a neat, small running-hand, the tails of my letters prettily curled, plenty of dashes, and a very few stops, I was thus headed:

SERAPHINA; OR, SUFFERING SENSIBILITY.

A TALE. BY A FAIR UNKNOWN.

> Love rules the camp, the court, the grove,
> And man below, and saints above,
> For love is heaven, and heaven is love.
> LAY OF THE LAST MINSTREL.

I was highly scented, and sealed in green wax, with a device of Cupid tormenting a heart.

The dignified half-yearly was selected for my debut. It rarely admitted literature of my class, and such only of acknowledged merit; consequently it was considered my proper and natural medium. From it, I was to be commented on and extracted in the monthlies, as well in Edinburgh and Dublin as in London; I was to be pirated by the Americans, and translated by the French; and at the end of the year I was, by express permission, to appear in one of the most fashionable annuals, my tenderest scene forming the subject of a gorgeous frontispiece, on which the most celebrated artists were to lavish their talents. The identification of the "Fair Unknown," was to become the puzzle of the season; and already many scenes of admiring wonder on the part of others, and of dignified modesty on her own, had been played off in the active imagination of my dear parent: the acknowledgment of Evelina by its young authoress to her father, and the final recognition of the *Great* Unknown, were her models.

At length, with this dazzling perspective before me, I was dismissed from the maternal embrace. Betty, the house-maid, slipped with me out of the street-door, holding me with a piece of white paper between her finger and thumb, to prevent her soiling my envelope; while my mother watched us from the window with tears in her eyes. On reaching the two-penny post-office, Betty, without any ceremony, pushed me through a slit beneath a window, and, to my great discomposure, I fell head over heels into a dirty box full of all sorts of queer-looking epistles. As might be expected, I painfully felt this my first tumble (for I cannot call it *step*) into real from imaginary life. I had scarcely time to recover from the shock, before the box was withdrawn, and we were all turned out by a fat woman on a horrid thing called a counter, where we were *sorted*, as she termed it, and distributed, with a rapidity that was quite confounding, to three or four shabby-looking men having bags under their arms. I, being the first turned out, was the last the post-mistress clawed up. She retained me a full minute, twirled me round, examined my seal, thrust her great finger between my delicate side folds, and brought me up to her eye to peer if possible into my inside, when the monster who held his bag open to receive me, called out,

"Come, mistress—can't wait no longer!"

"Well," she replied, "bless me, if this don't look for all the world like a walentine!" and into the bag she reluctantly dropped me, writhing as I was with pain and indignation.

When I had somewhat smoothed my ruffled plumes, I ventured to look round on my fellow-travellers, in search of some congenial spirit with whom I might beguile the tediousness of time, as we jolted along on the shoulders of the postman; but I looked round in vain. My nearest neighbor, to my great annoyance, was a butcher's bill, with whom every jolt brought me in contact; the dirty thing had a wet wafer pressed down by a greasy thumb. I shrank from it with horror, and fell back on an epistle from a young gentleman at school, which was at least clean, and in fair, round characters; so I attended to what it had to say. The date took up a large portion of the paper, and then: "My dear mamma—I have the pleasure to inform you that our Christmas vacation begins on the 20th. I am very well. I hope you are very well. I hope my papa is very well; and my brothers and sisters, my uncles, aunts, and cousins. I beg my duty to my papa, my love to my brothers and sisters, my respects to my uncles and aunts, and my remembrances to my cousins; and believe me your dutiful son." I sighed, and turned to a business-like looking letter, directed in a precise hand to Messrs. ——, in some dark lane in the city. The names of the persons addressed, and a very exact date, took up, as in the school-boy's letter, a vast deal of room, and then it began: "Gentlemen—We beg to acknowledge your *favor* of the 1st instant—" I could not get any farther, for I was suddenly attracted by a smart-looking and very highly scented affair, sealed, and directed to a lord; but was disappointed on finding it was only a Bond-street perfumer's little yearly account of one hundred and fifty pounds for perfumes, fine soaps, cold-cream, and tooth-brushes. There was no other very close to me, so I ventured gently to push my way to a curiously folded epistle directed to Miss Matilda Dandeville, Oxford-street: "Dear Tilly—Pray send me, as soon as you can, my close bonnet, for my nose is nearly off from wearing my pink silk and blonde this freezing weather. Full of life and fun here! Shall tell you all when we meet. It will be your turn next; meantime, business, business! money, money! Love to all inquiring friends." I felt disgusted. Do not gentlemen and ladies write by the twopenny-post? Nothing but duns, bills, business, and money! Is there no sense, sentiment, or sensibility, to be found in a twopenny-post-bag? I certainly did observe some fashionable-looking letters, and one decidedly with a coronet, but they were too far down, quite unattainable; so I drew myself up as much apart as possible from the things by which I was so unhappily surrounded, and remained the rest of the way in dignified stillness. My wounded feelings were somewhat soothed by observing the awe, mingled with curiosity, with which I was regarded; and somewhat amused by the perfumer's genteel account turning its back on the butcher's bill, and the lady of the pink and blonde squeezing herself into a corner to avoid contact with a house-maid. The school-boy alone was at perfect liberty—and a great annoyance he was—evidently delighting to jumble us all together by a single jump, and constantly peering at my seal, trying to read my address, and touching my embossed and gilded edges.

At length, we reached our district, and that nervous sound, the postman's rap, was heard in rapid succession down the street; heads were popped out at windows, and doors were opened, and pence ready, before we reached. Out hopped the house-maid, out jumped the school-boy; and, as my fellow-travellers departed, I sank gradually lower, until I arrived among the genteel-looking letters I had spied at a distance; a slight shuffle was perceptible among them: their black and red seals were erected with great gravity, and my pink dye became almost crimson when I found that, from the gaiety of my attire, they evidently thought me "no better than I should be;" however, I had scarcely time to feel uneasy, so swift were our evolutions, and so completely were we all turned topsy-turvy every time the postman's hand was introduced among us, and that was every minute; the big-wigs lost their dignity, and as to me, I felt my seal crack like a lady's stay-lace; I thought my envelope was torn away, and that I myself would have been displayed. Shocked at the very idea of such a catastrophe, I sank senseless to the bottom of the bag, and only recovered on being violently shaken from it, and hearing my brutal conductor exclaim: "Why, here it is, to be sure; and if it isn't the walentine itself, I declare!" He seized his pence, and, folding up his empty bag, strode off.

I found myself in the hands of a respectable man-servant out of livery, who, after having examined me with a look of surprise, introduced me up stairs into rather a dark and heavy drawing-room, with, however, a cheerful fire, book-cases, and portraits of distinguished authors. I lay for some time on a circular table, which was covered with newspapers and periodicals; there was a dead silence; if I had had a heart, it would have beaten audibly. At length, a side-door opened, and a young gentleman stept in from an adjoining room; he glanced his eyes over the table, evidently in search of letters from the post; and, when he saw me, he smiled, and, picking me up, carried me into the room he had just left. I am sure he must have felt me tremble in his grasp. In this apartment, the only furniture was chairs and three writing-tables, the two smaller of which were occupied by my bearer and another young gentleman; but at that in the centre was seated a grave, elderly personage, rather large in person, with bushy eye-brows, and keen, penetrating eyes. I, who was extremely ignorant at that time, and had heard much of the knowledge, power, and dignity, of the Half-yearly, without exactly knowing what it was, took this gentleman for it himself. My introducer held me up to his young companion, and a stifled laugh passed between them; but, recovering his gravity, he laid me on the Half-yearly's desk, as near under his spectacles as he could bring me without interrupting his pen. The old gentleman started, frowned, and, lowering his head, looked at me from above his spectacles, (an awful way of looking, as is well known,) inquired gruffly, "What's this?" "A letter by the two-penny, sir; a lady's verses, I should think, by its appearance." "D—— ladies' verses! Take it away." "Shall *we* open it, sir?" "Don't pester me!" and in an instant afterwards he was lost in his important meditations.

The two young gentlemen cut round my seal, and perused the note of the Fair Unknown, with tears—but not of sympathy. *I* was then taken up, and passages here and there recited in an undertone with mock gravity, eliciting, in spite of their superior, bursts of irrepressible laughter; these, at last, attracted his attention, and looking over his shoulder he angrily inquired what they were about. "Pray, sir, do look at this! it is quite a curiosity;" and my note was handed to him.

"A fair unknown, with that modesty which ever accompanies genius; with faltering accent, timid step, and eyes that seek the ground, presumes to lay at the feet of the great Half-yearly the first-born of her imagination! She prays him not to spurn the babe: but to take it, cherish it, and usher it into the world! It is his own!"

"Mine!" exclaimed the Half-yearly, settling his wig; "I hope she does not mean to swear it to me; such scrapes are marvellously difficult to get out of. Wafer up the babe, if you please, gentlemen, in a sheet of foolscap, (its proper swaddling band,) and add a sentence to our Notices to Correspondents."

In a few weeks after this memorable scene, my young and tender parent was at breakfast with her family, when her father entered, carrying a new Half-yearly, with leaves uncut, and hot from the press under his arm. My mother's heart leaped in her bosom, her face became scarlet, and her mouthful of bread and butter nearly choked her. Her father dawdled a little over the advertisements and answers to correspondents; at the latter he smiled. "What amuses you, sir?" inquired his anxious daughter in a tone of forced calmness: he read, "A Fair Unknown is earnestly requested to send for her babe immediately; the Half-yearly having no intention of cherishing, fostering, furthering, or fathering it in any way whatever." It was well for his thunder-stricken auditor that the reader became immediately too much absorbed in a political paper to notice the effect of this appalling blow. She made her escape unobserved; I was instantly sent for, torn from my coarse envelope, and pressed to her agonized bosom.

Her four friends had returned to school; she could not therefore have the benefit of their advice and condolence; and, to tell the truth, she did not appear much to regret this circumstance—the mortification of their presence would have been too great.

Betty was not even let into the secret; I was placed in a plain white envelope, accompanied by a note much less romantic than the first, addressed to a Monthly: and, being sealed with a more respectable and well-behaved seal, she hid me in her muff, and dropped me herself into the same dirty box as before.

The Monthly was not nearly so terrible a person as the Half-yearly. He was not at home on my arrival in the evening, and I was laid with several other very literary-looking letters on a table in his dressing-room, near a good fire, with a lamp ready to light, a pair of slippers on the hearth-rug, and a large easy chair with a dressing-gown thrown over it. All this looked sociable and comfortable; and, feeling quite in spirits, I curtsied respectfully to a moral paper, shook hands with a political argument, chatted with a *jeu d'esprit*, and flirted with a sonnet.

The Monthly returned home about midnight in exceeding good humor, humming an opera tune; he lit his lamp, donned his dressing-gown, thrust his feet into his slippers, and, having mused a little while over the fire, ventured a glance at the table. "The deuce take it, what a lot there are of them!' he exclaimed; "politics, morality, and poetry, I am not fit for to-night, that's very clear; something entertaining—what's this?" (taking up me)—"a woman's hand—prose—a tale—just the very thing!" and forthwith I was begun.

Reader, can you imagine—no, you cannot, so there is no use in appealing to your sympathy—the state of agitation I was in? He read amazingly fast, and hummed and ha'ed as he proceeded; and, to my utter astonishment, at one of my most pathetic appeals he burst into a fit of laughter; in short—I grieve to say it—but I fear the Monthly, as indeed he himself had hinted, had indulged a little too freely,—had taken a little drop too much; for, soon after this unaccountable explosion of merriment, he yawned, settled himself more decidedly in his chair, read very much slower, and at last, on observing that he turned over two of my pages at once without finding it out, I ventured to look up, and, behold! his eyes were closing—sleep was creeping over him! I lay aghast, every moment inclining more and more backwards, till I reposed upon his knee. The pangs of wounded pride, acute as they were, began to give way to apprehensions of the most serious nature; his hold momentarily relaxed, and at length I fell—fell over the fender, reader! and there I lay roasting like a Spanish priest cooked by a French soldier, (the French, they say, are excellent cooks,) until he should discover the hidden treasures of his monastery.

Alas! I thought *my* treasures were lost for ever to the literary world! There they lay, scorching and melting, until at last fortunately a cinder, inspired no doubt by the Muses, leaped out to my protection, and, by destroying a small portion, saved the remainder; for the smell of fire became so strong, that a servant, who had just let himself into the house from a high-life below stairs party, came rushing in with a nose extended to its utmost width, rousing and alarming his sleeping master. "Deuce take it!" exclaimed the Monthly on perceiving me, "in ten minutes more we should have been all set on fire by this d—d *soporific* (I think that is what he called me.) Who would have thought it had spirit enough to burn!" The next morning I was despatched home, without a single line, not even an apology, for my miserable condition.

The curse of Cain was upon me; my own mother (who had become engaged in the creation of another offspring) received me with mortifying coolness, and beheld my burnt and disfigured tale with horror and contempt. She gave up all thoughts of the London annuals, (her new pet was intended for one of them,) and, having coarsely repaired me, I was put into the general post, addressed to a country annual, the "Rosebud" of Diddle-town.

The glowing aspirations of youth were chilled, misfortune had set her seal upon me; but, although hope was diminished, pride remained unquelled, for, as I glided over high-ways, and jolted over by-ways, in the Diddle-town coach, I recalled to my recollection all that I had heard (especially while I lay smothered up for six weeks on the learned Half-yearly's table,) of the many great luminaries of literature who had struggled into light and life through the dark and chilling mists of neglect, ignorance, and envy. I had no doubt but that I should yet burst forth from my cloud, astonishing and dazzling the weak eyes which had hitherto refused to encounter, or were incapable of dwelling upon, my beauty and brilliancy.

On being presented to the Diddle-town editor, he immediately seized upon me with great glee, and carried me off, without reading me, to the printer's devil; and, to my utter astonishment, I found myself in the process of printing, an hour after my arrival. Although this consummation had long been devoutly wished, I cannot say I was much flattered at its mode.

I appeared in the "Rosebud" of Diddle-town. The editor gave out that I was the production of a celebrated lady-author, anonymous on the occasion to all but him. I was demurely listened to by a coterie of old maids, who, on my conclusion, curtsied to the reader and curtsied to each other, sighed, and inquired if there were a picture; I was hummed over by two or three lazy half-pay officers; I was spelt over by a cottage-full of young lace-makers; and I was wept over by the Diddle-town milliner's apprentice girls.

But my desire for a larger and nobler sphere of action can no longer be suppressed; I am determined to make known that I exist, and to inform the reading world, and all who, like many great philophers of old, are eager to seek what they are never likely to find, that the Tale of Seraphina reposes in all its neglected sweetness, and unappreciated, because unappreciable, beauty, on the leaves of the "Rosebud" of Diddle-town.

THE DOG FANCIER.

FROM "REVELATIONS OF LONDON." BY WM. HARRISON AINSWORTH.

The Rookery! Who that has passed Saint Giles's, on the way to the city, or coming from it, but has caught a glimpse, through some narrow opening, of its squalid habitations, and wretched and ruffianly occupants! Who but must have been struck with amazement, that such a huge receptacle of vice and crime should be allowed to exist in the very heart of the metropolis, like an ulcerated spot, capable of tainting the whole system! Of late, the progress of improvement has caused its removal; but whether any less cogent motive would have abated the nuisance, may be questioned. For years the evil was felt, and complained of, but no effort was made to remedy it, or to cleanse these worse than Augean stables. As the place is now partially, if not altogether, swept away, and a wide and airy street passes through the midst of its foul recesses, a slight sketch may be given of its former appearance.

Entering a narrow street, guarded by posts and cross-bars, a few steps from the crowded thoroughfare brought you into a frightful region, the refuge, it was easy to perceive, of half the lawless characters infesting the metropolis. The coarsest ribaldry assailed your ears, and noisome odors afflicted your sense of smell. As you advanced, picking your way through kennels flowing with filth, or over putrescent heaps of rubbish and oyster-shells, all the repulsive and hideous features of the place were displayed before you. There was something savagely picturesque in the aspect of the place, but its features were too loathsome to be regarded with any other feeling than disgust. The houses looked as sordid, and as thickly crusted with the leprosy of vice as their tenants. Horrible habitations they were, in truth. Many of them were without windows, and where the frames were left, brown paper or tin supplied the place of glass; some even wanted doors, and no effort was made to conceal the squalor within. On the contrary, it seemed to be intruded on observation. Miserable rooms almost destitute of furniture; floors and walls caked with dirt, or decked with coarse, flaring prints; shameless and abandoned-looking women; children without shoes and stockings, and with scarcely a rag to their backs: these were the chief objects that met the view. Of men few were visible—the majority being out on business, it is to be presumed; but where a solitary straggler was seen, his sinister looks and mean attire were in perfect keeping with the spot. So thickly inhabited were these wretched dwellings, that every chamber, from garret to cellar, swarmed with inmates. As to the cellars, they looked like dismal caverns, which a wild beast would shun. Clothes-lines were hung from house to house, festooned with every kind of garment. Out of the main street branched several alleys and passages, all displaying the same degree of misery, or, if possible, worse, and teeming with occupants. Personal security, however, forbade any attempt to track these labyrinths; but imagination, after the specimen afforded, could easily picture them. It was impossible to move a step without insult or annoyance. Every human being seemed brutalized and degraded; and the women appeared utterly lost to decency, and made the street ring with their cries, their quarrels, and their imprecations. It was a positive relief to escape from this hot-bed of crime to the world without, and breathe a purer atmosphere.

Such being the aspect of the Rookery in the day time, what must it have been when crowded with its worst denizens at night! Yet at such an hour it will now be necessary to enter its penetralia.

After escaping from the ruined house in the Vauxhall Road, the two ruffians shaped their course towards Saint Giles's, running the greater part of the way, and arriving at the Broadway just as the church clock struck two. Darting into a narrow alley, and heedless of any obstructions they encountered in their path, they entered a somewhat wider cross street, which they pursued for a short distance, and then struck into an entry, at the bottom of which was a swing door that admitted them into a small court, where they found a dwarfish person wrapped in a tattered watchman's great-coat, seated on a stool with a horn lantern in his hand, and a cutty in his mouth, the glow of which lighted up his hard, withered features. This was the deputy porter of the lodging-house they were about to enter. Addressing him by the name of Old Parr, the ruffians passed on, and lifting the latch of another door, entered a sort of kitchen, at the further end of which blazed a cheerful fire with a large copper kettle boiling upon it. On one side of the room was a deal table, round which several men of sinister aspect and sordid attire were collected, playing at cards. A smaller table of the same material stood near the fire, and opposite it was a staircase leading to the upper rooms. The place was dingy and dirty in the extreme, the floors could not have been scoured for years, and the walls were begrimed with filth. In one corner, with his head resting on a heap of coals and coke, lay a boy almost as black as a chimney-sweeper, fast asleep. He was the waiter. The principal light was afforded by a candle stuck against the wall, with a tin reflector behind it. Before the fire, with his back turned towards it, stood a noticeable individual, clad in a velveteen jacket, with ivory buttons, a striped waistcoat, drabknees, a faded black silk neckcloth tied in a great bow, and a pair of ancient Wellingtons ascending half-way up his legs, which looked disproportionately thin when compared with the upper part of his square, robustious, and somewhat pursy frame. His face was broad, jolly, and good-humored, with a bottle-shaped nose, fleshy lips, and light gray eyes, glistening with cunning and roguery. His hair, which dangled in long flakes over his ears and neck, was of a dunnish red, as were also his whiskers and beard. A superannuated white castor, with a black hatband round it, was cocked knowingly on one side of his head, and gave him a flashy and sporting look. His particular vocation was made manifest by the number of dogs he had about him. A beautiful black and tan spaniel, of Charles the Second's breed, popped its short snubby nose and long silken ears out of each coat pocket. A pug was thrust into his breast, and he carried an exquisite Blenheim under either arm. At his feet reposed an Isle of Sky terrier, and a partly-cropped French poodle, of snowy whiteness, with a red worsted riband round its throat. This person, it need scarcely be said, was a dog fancier, or, in other words, a dealer in, and a stealer of, dogs, as well as a practiser of all the tricks connected with that nefarious trade. His self-satisfied air made it evident he thought himself a smart clever fellow,—and adroit and knavish he was, no doubt, —while his droll, plausible, and rather winning manners helped him materially to impose upon his customers. His real name was Taylor, but he was known among his companions by the appellation of Ginger. On the entrance of the Sandman and the Tinker, he nodded familiarly to them, and with a sly look inquired—"Vell, my 'arties—vot luck?"

"Oh, pretty middlin'," replied the Sandman, gruffly. And seating himself at the table, near the fire, he kicked up the lad who was lying fast asleep on the coals, and bade him fetch a pot of half-and-half. The Tinker took a place beside him, and they waited in silence the arrival of the liquor, which, when it came, was disposed of at a couple of pulls.

* * * * * *

"Arter all," said the Tinker, "there's no branch o' the purfession so safe as yours, Ginger. The law is favorable to you, and the beaks is afeerd to touch you. I think I shall turn dog fancier myself."

"It's a good business," replied Ginger, "but it requires a edication. As I wos sayin', we gets a high price sometimes for restorin' a favorite, especially ven ve've a soft-hearted lady to deal vith. There's some vimen as fond o' dogs as o' their own childer, and ven ve gets one o' their precious pets, ve makes 'em ransom it as the brigands you see at the Adelphi or the Surrey sarves their prisoners, threatenin' to send first an ear, and then a paw, or a tail, and so on. I'll tell you wot happened t'other day. There wos a lady—a Miss Vite, as wos desperate fond of her dog. It wos a ugly warmint, but no matter for that,—the creater had gained her heart. Vell, she lost it; and, somehow or other, I found it. She wos in great trouble, and a friend o' mine calls to say she can have the dog agin, but she must pay eight pound for it. She thinks this dear, and a friend o' her own adwises her to wait, sayin' better terms will be offered; so I sends vord by my friend that if she don't come down at once, the poor animal's throat will be cut that werry night."

"Ha!—ha!—ha!" laughed the others.

"Vell, she sent four pound, and I put up with it," pursued Ginger; "but about a month arterwards she loses her favorite agin, and strange to say, I finds it. The same game is played over agin, and she comes down with another four pound. But she takes care this time that I shan't repeat the trick; for no sooner does she obtain possession of her favorite, than she embarks in the steamer for France, in the hope of keepin' her dog safe there."

"Oh! Miss Bailey, unfortinate Miss Bailey!—Fol-de-riddle-tol-ol-lol—unfortinate Miss Bailey!" sang the Tinker.

"But there's dog-fanciers in France, ain't there?" asked the Sandman.

"Lor' bless 'ee, to be sure there is," replied Ginger; "there's as many o' the Fancy i' France as here. Vy, ve drives a smartish trade wi' them through them foreign steamers. There's scarcely a steamer as leaves the port o' London but takes out a cargo o' dogs. Ve sells 'em to the stewards, stokers, and sailors, cheap—and no questions asked. They goes to Ostend, Antverp, Rotterdam, Hamburg, and sometimes to Havre. There's a Mounseer Coqquilu as comes over to buy dogs, and ve takes 'em to him at a house near Billinsgit market."

"Then you're always sure o' a ready market somehow," observed the Sandman.

"Sartin," replied Ginger, "cos the law's so kind to us. Vy, bless you, a perliceman can't detain us, even if he knows ve've a stolen dog in our persession, and ve svears it's our own; and yet he'd stop you in a minute if he seed you vith a suspicious-looking bundle under your arm. Now, jist to show you the difference atwixt the two perfessions:—I steals a dog—walue, may be, fifty pound, or p'raps more. Even if I'm catched i' the fact, I may get fined twenty pound, or have six months' imprisonment; vile if you steals an old fogle, walue three fardens, you'll get seven years abroad, to a dead certainty."

"That seems hard on us," observed the Sandman, reflectively.

"It's the *law!*" exclaimed Ginger, triumphantly. "Now ve generally escapes by payin' the fine, cos our pals goes and steals more dogs to raise the money. Ve alvays stands by each other. There's a reg'lar horganization among us; so ve can alvays bring vitnesses to svear vot ve likes, and ve so puzzles the beaks, that the case gets dismissed, and the constable says, 'Vich party shall I give the dog to, your vorship?' Upon vich, the beak replies, a shakin' of his vise noddle, 'Give it to the person in whose persession it was found. I have nuffin' more to do vith it.' In course, the dog is delivered up to us."

"The law seems made for dog-fanciers," remarked the Tinker.

"Wot d'ye think o' this?" pursued Ginger. "I wos a-standin' at the corner o' Gray's Inn-lane vith some o' my pals near a coach-stand, ven a lady passes by vith this here dog—an' a beauty it is, a real long-eared Charley—a follerin' of her. Vell, the moment I spies it, I unties my apron, whips up the dog, and covers it up in a trice. Vell, the lady sees me, and gives me in charge to a perliceman. But that si'nifies nuffin'. I brings six vitnesses to svear the dog vos mine, and that I'd actilly had it since it vos a blind little puppy, and wot's more, I brings it's *mother*, and that settles the pint. So, in course, I'm discharged; the dog is given up to me; and the lady goes avay lamentin'. I then plays the amiable, an' offers to sell it her for twenty guineas, seein' as how she had taken a fancy to it, but she von't bite. So, if I don't sell it next week, I shall send it to Mounseer Coqquilu. The only vay you can go wrong is to steal a dog wi' a collar on, for if you do, you may get seven years' transportation for a bit o' leather and a brass plate vorth a shillin', vile the animal, though vorth a hundred pound, can't hurt you. There's *law* again—ha, ha!"

"Dog-fancier's law!" laughed the Sandman.

"Some of the Fancy is given to cruelty," pursued Ginger, "and crops a dog's ears, or pulls out his teeth to disguise him; but I'm too fond o' the animal for that. I may frighten old ladies sometimes, as I told you afore, but I never seriously hurts their pets. Nor did I ever kill a dog for his skin, as some on 'em does."

"And you're always sure o' gettin' a dog, if you vants it, I s'pose?" inquired the Tinker.

"Always," replied Ginger. "No man's dog is safe. I don't care how he's kept, ve're sure to have him at last. Ve feels our vay with the sarvents, and finds out from them the walley the master or missis sets on the dog, and soon after that the animal's gone. Vith a bit o' liver, prepared in my partic'lar vay, I can tame the fiercest dog as ever barked, take him off his chain, an' bring him arter me at a gallop."

"And do respectable parties ever buy dogs, knowin' they're stolen?" inquired the Tinker.

"Ay, to be sure," replied Ginger, "sometimes first-rate nobs. They put us up to it themselves; they'll say, 'I've just left my Lord So-and-So's, and there I seed a couple o' the finest pointers I ever clapped eyes on. I vants you to get me *jist sich another couple.*' Vell, ve understands in a minnit, an' in doo time the identicle dogs finds their vay to our customer."

"Oh! that's how it's done?" remarked the Sandman.

"Yes, that's the vay," replied Ginger. "Sometimes a party 'll vant a couple o' dogs for the shootin' season; and then ve asks, 'Vich vay are you a-goin'—into Surrey or Kent?' And accordin' as the answer is given ve arranges our plans."

"Vell, yourn appears a profitable and safe employment, I must say," remarked the Sandman.

"Perfectly so," replied Ginger. "Nothin' can touch us till dogs is declared by statute to be property, and stealin' 'em a misdemeanor. And that won't occur in my time."

"Let's hope not," rejoined the other two.

JOLLY NOSE.

BY WILLIAM H. AINSWORTH.

Jolly nose! the bright rubies that garnish thy tip
 Are dug from the mines of canary;
And to keep up their lustre I moisten my lip
 With hogsheads of claret and sherry.

Jolly nose! he who sees thee across a broad glass
 Beholds thee in all thy perfection;
And to the pale snout of a temperate ass
 Entertains the profoundest objection.

For a big-bellied glass is the palette I use,
 And the choicest of wine is my color;
And I find that my nose takes the mellowest hues,
 The fuller I fill it—the fuller!

Jolly nose! there are fools who say drink hurts the sight;
 Such dullards know nothing about it;
'Tis better, with wine, to extinguish the light,
 Than live always in darkness, without it.

MY OLD COMPLAINT.

Its Cause and Cure.

BY WILLIAM H. AINSWORTH.

I'm sadly afraid of my Old Complaint—
Dying of thirst. Not a drop I've drunk
For more than an hour:' Tis too long to wait,
Wonderful how my spirits have sunk!
Provocation enough it is for a saint,
To suffer so much from my Old Complaint!

What is it like, my Old Complaint?
I'll tell you anon since you wish to know.
It troubles me now, but it troubled me first,
When I was a youngster years ago;
Bubble-and-squeak is the image quaint
Of what it is like, my Old Complaint!

The Herring, in a very few minutes we're told,
Loses his life, ta'en out o' the sea;
Rob me of wine, and you will behold
Just the same thing happen to me.
Thirst makes the poor little herring so faint;—
Thirst is the cause of my OldComplaint!

The bibulous Salmon is ill content,
Unless he batheth his jowl in brine:
And so, my spirits are quickly spent,
Unless I dip my muzzle in Wine!
Myself in the jolly old Salmon I paint:
Wine is the Cure of my Old Complaint.
Give me full bottles and no restraint,
And little you'll hear of my Old Complaint!

I never indulge in fanciful stuff,
Or idly prate, if my flagon be full;
Give me good Claret, and give me enough,
And then my spirits are never dull.
Give me good Claret and no constraint
And I soon get rid of my Old Complaint!
Herring and Salmon my friends will acquaint
With the Cause and Cure of my Old Complaint.

ALE AND SACK.

BY W. H. AINSWORTH.

Your Gaul may tipple his thin, thin wine,
And prate of its hue, and its fragrance fine,
Shall never a drop pass throat of mine,
Again—again!

His claret is meagre (but let that pass),
I can't say much for his hippocrass,
And never more will I fill my glass
With cold champagne.

But froth me a flagon of English ale,
Stout, and old, and as amber pale,
Which heart and head will alike assail—
Ale—ale be mine!

Or brew me a pottle of sturdy sack
Sherris and spice, with a toast to its back,
And need shall be none to bid me attack
That drink divine!

THE AUTOCRAT OF THE PARLOR FIRE.

FROM "THE PRIORS OF PRAGUE." BY W. JOHNSON NEALE.

On arriving at the village, and alighting at the only inn, I ordered the landlord to spread for us, in the coffee-room, the best dinner he could provide.

With a true landlord's bow, my host ushered us forthwith into the little parlor; there, with plenteous promises of speed and glorious fare of beef-steak and onions, he shut the door upon us. Hastening after him to countermand the appearance of the fragrant vegetable he had mentioned, I returned in time to see Jeremy walk towards the fire-place and take up the poker.

"Touch that fire if you dare, sir," said a shrill, sharp, ill-natured voice, proceeding from a portly figure comfortably ensconced in the ingle-nook.

"There are few things, my good friend, not to be dared by Jeremy the honest," returned the latter, very coolly thrusting the poker into the fire without even deigning to turn round.

In an instant, the querulous old fellow's cane was lifted on high, and had I not caught it in my hand, it would certainly have descended on the head of my good valet with no slight rap.

Naturally incensed at such an unprovoked outrage, I said, "Excuse me, sir, but learn to use your cane with more discretion, or else I must take the liberty of thrusting it into the fire, and bundling your good rotundity of person on the top of it."

"Curse ye both! ye impudent rascals—do you know who I am?" cried the old fellow with an oath, as, starting on his legs, he kicked his chair over behind him.

"Not a whit, and care just as little," replied Jeremy, who having turned round, fully comprehended all that had passed.

"Then curse ye, you vagabond, I'm steward of the parlor fire!"

"Likely enough," quoth Jeremy, in his impenetrable manner, "and a warm, comfortable berth too for this life!—though, for aught I know, your worship may have earned a hotter one in that to come."

At this repartee several people present burst into a loud laugh, which so irritated our opponent that he once more lifted his cane, but thinking there were two to one, he contented himself with an impotent grin of rage, and applying heartily to the bell-pull, brought in the landlord.

"Turn these vagabonds out of the house, landlord, this instant!"

My host looked at us with mingled dismay and deprecation.

"Turn them out of the house, I say, this instant, or I'll leave ye to-morrow morning!"

"Why, sir, I hope they haven't been defending the French?"—"No!"—"or abusing the government?"—"No!"—"or protecting the flies?—or—"—"No, sir; no, sir; curse ye—no, sir, they've done worse!—a thousand times worse!—they've been poking the parlor fire!"

Mine host shook his head with evident signs of sorrow, and turning to us, said in a most lachrymose tone, "Oh, gentlemen! if you've been so imprudent as to do that, you must indeed withdraw!"

"Mr. Landlord," said Jeremy, in great amazement, "I beg you distinctly to understand, that I'll see you at the devil first!"

"Turn 'em out! turn 'em out!" still more noisily vociferated the original cause of the fray, now more angry than ever, as he observed his influence—though why I could not divine—preponderating with the landlord. "Fight it out, gemmen! fight it out!" interposed the spectators, so greatly amused as to wish to be more so.

"Only please to retire, sir, and you shall have—another pot of beer there, boy, for number six—a private room," whispered the landlord.—"Let me beg of you, sir, and I will explain all this."

This was enough—I saw mine host was more to be pitied than blamed in the matter—so, making a sign to Jeremy to follow, I withdrew from the scene of strife, and followed my landlord into a more peaceful, and as it happened, into better quarters.

"Landlord! landlord!" was now heard in the voice of the enemy below.

"Coming, sir, coming!—no fool like an old fool, gentlemen!—be with you in a moment,"—and the unhappy arbiter of the house vanished with wonderful celerity down stairs.

"Now, may it please your worship, we can have a fire of our own to poke," said Jeremy, ringing the bell and taking a seat without further notice of what had happened.—The fire was accordingly lit, and by the time that its flames were roaring merrily up the chimney, our host once more appeared, bearing in his hands our intended meal.

"Landlord, may you live for ever!" said Jeremy, slapping that worthy functionary upon the back, and then smacking his lips and slightly rubbing his hands at the hot tempting dish before him.

"Sit down, Jeremy, and eat," said I, seeing he was about to wait behind my chair. Jeremy obeyed—the landlord opened his eyes—for being unable from my companion's language to take him for any thing less than a gentleman, though an odd-looking one, he doubtless wondered of what rank might be the master, setting me down, perhaps, for aught I knew or cared, as one of the blood-royal.

"Gentlemen," said he, after the last adjusting touch of the potato dish, and bowing low as he whipped his white napkin of office under the left arm,—"Gentlemen, I humbly beg your pardon for the unfortunate scene below—Did you say the bread, sir?—but the fact is—we've excellent bottled ale, sir—the fact is, sir, that gentleman below is the most extraordinary—Glass of porter?—certainly, sir—character that ever came to—drink up quickly, sir—the house. Ever since he first came he's always been saying—Change your plate directly, sir,—'Landlord!'—'Sir,' says I—'Send in my bill to-night, I'm off to-morrow morning'—and would you believe it, sir—the pudding will be up presently, sir—he's lived in my house seventeen years come Michaelmas.—He's the most curious—Cheese, sir?—ay, sir, not better cheese in the country—most curious character that ever I met."

"Then prithee, my good friend, in mercy halt," said I, perceiving what a curious mode of parlance mine host's calling had imparted to him, and presuming to interrupt this singular detail.—"Of all things, Mr. Landlord, I admire character—but not the parenthetical character with which you seem so much inclined to season your discourse—I can easily imagine it to make the worst of stories very droll, but believe me, it would also murder the very best. Have a moment's patience, then, till these dinner things are cleared away, and put me a bottle of port on the table; bring your chair, take your glass, and tell your tale fairly to an end."

"Excuse me, gentlemen, couldn't think of being guilty of such an indecency as sitting down to your table—bottle of port you said, sir,—such a thing was never done yet in the Jolly Traveller, for I always say to gentlemen—get the cork-screw directly, sir,—doesn't become a landlord, such familiarity—and, so as I was going to say, the gentleman below stairs is one of the whimsicallest people that you could never meet; for, seventeen years ago, as I said before, come Michaelmas, he drops into my house one morning, dines and spends the day, 'and' says he—'your health, gentlemen!'—'landlord,' says he, 'give me a bed and be cursed to you.' 'The curse to yourself,' says I, 'you may get a bed where you can, but it shan't be in my house, for I have none to give you.' 'It's a lie,' says he, 'you have—' 'Well, whether I have or no,' said I, 'you shan't have it.' 'There you lie again,' said he, and before I could hold out an arm to stop him, whip me, gentlemen, if he wasn't past me up the stairs, into the first bed-room, and locked was the door—the best bottle of port in my cellar, gemmen—in the turning of a bed-post. Well, gemmen, I stormed and he raved—I'd have the blacksmith to break open the lock. He wheels round the bed, and barricadoes it against the door.—'Twas another gentleman's room who wanted his things—he opens the window and flings them out into the yard—well, thinks I, if the Jolly Traveller isn't to become a lunatic asylum, my name is not Muggins, and so said I—thank ye, gentlemen, no more than this glass,—'He may stay there to-night, but hang me if I don't have the fox out of his hole to-morrow.' So I went to show the gentleman who'd been turned out of his own room into the one that was next it, and as 'twas only a lath and plaster partition, the first thing that I heard was Mr. Domitian saying to himself as he got into bed,—'Hang me if I don't stay here all my life, to plague this grumbling fellow.' Old Nick himself, gemmen, could scarcely have frightened me more, and for aught I know, this might be his first cousin; so I solemnly determined, in the first place, to make him pay double for his bill. In the second place, to put him out of the Jolly Traveller, and in the third to—drink your very good health once more, gemmen,—send for a constable.

"Well, sir, up I got, at five o'clock next morning, though 'twas a dark winter's morning; and while I was fumbling about there in the little parlor, for a tinder box, and just thinking over these matters, I felt a heavy grip on my shoulder, and heard Mr. Domitian's voice.

"Well, Mr. Landlord," said he, "who's to be master in this house, think ye, you or I?"

"You, sir! you, sir!" says I, not thinking of what I was saying, and shaking from head to foot. —"Right, you rascal, right," says he, "I'm glad you've come to your senses at last, curse ye—what's my bill?"

"Five pounds, sir," said I, at a round guess.

"Here, keep ten," says he, "for the bother you've given me, and see that my breakfast is on the table at eight o'clock to a second. I'm off to take a walk."

"Gemmen, you may be sure I trembled very sufficiently, but having looked very hard—for I had now lighted the candle—and being able to see neither hoofs nor tail, I pocketed—Another bottle?—yes, sir!—the money, and lit the fire. However, gentlemen, to make short of a long story, here he's been in my house ever since. Every day determined to—Step down the cellar in a moment, gentlemen—set off next morning, and every morning, just as firm by the ingle nook, as he was the day before. Seeing he's been very kind in giving me heavy sums of cash, gemmen,—for he says he won't lend—why I've been very particular to humor his whims—one of which is to let no one touch the parlor fire except himself; so he's elected steward, and provided he can kill all the flies—praise the British constitution—cut his jokes upon the customers, and abuse the French—he's perfectly happy,—Ay, a true old liberal English gentleman he is, every inch of him, I warrant ye, and worth a power of money too—fifty thousand pounds they say—made up there in London in the hosiery line."

"A good customer then, landlord, doubtless."

"Not a better have I to my back, sir!—though ten to one that ever I had any of his money. He came down into these parts to buy some snug cottage, and if so be we hadn't chanced to have a row at first, two or three nights would have been the outside of his stay—and as to regularity, sir, never was such a regular man—not a drop does he drink, not a morsel does he eat to-day, that he doesn't eat and drink to-morrow."

"Then, Mr. Landlord, let me tell you there's one great fault about your friend."

"What, sir?" demanded mine host, in great alarm.

"Why, that he evidently has been born a few centuries too late; for clearly, nature's only reason for producing such a being was to give mankind a rude notion of clockwork."

"Rude enough, and may it please your worship!" said Jeremy, with a hem. The landlord grinned applause, and with a low bow departed for the—But why should I here narrate the history of the second bottle? Was it not, after the inviolable custom of British landlords, vastly inferior to the first? Most indubitably it was; so we wasted no farther time upon its contents, but ordering our horses to be put to, forthwith—paid our bill, and once more set off upon our travels.

A Persian's Paradise.—When the Persian ambassador and his suite left England, a few years since, many of them shed tears. One of the suite, who had been struck with the quiet of an Englishman's life, compared it with that of a Persian, exclaiming, that he could not wish for a better Paradise than Chelsea Hospital, where, for the remainder of his days, he could sit under the trees, do nothing, and drink as much porter as he liked.

An Old Soldier.—An elderly gentleman in a coffee-room one day, when it was raining very hard and the water running down the streets, said that it reminded him of the general deluge. "Zounds, sir," said an old veteran officer near him, "who's he? I have heard of all the Generals in Europe but him." This reminds one of the print-collector inquiring for a portrait of Admiral Noah, to illustrate Lord Byron's "Don Juan."

A GREENWICH PENSIONER;

BY THOMAS HOOD. WITH A CUT, FROM G. CRUIKSHANK.

A Greenwich Pensioner is a sort of stranded marine animal, that the receding tide of life has left high and dry on the shore. He pines for his element like a sea bear, and misses his briny washings and wettings. What the ocean could not do, the land does; for it makes him sick. He cannot digest properly, unless his body is rolled and tumbled about like a barrel-churn. Terra-firma, he thinks, is good enough to touch at for wood and water, but nothing more. There is no wind, he swears, ashore—every day of his life is a dead calm, a thing above all others he detests. He would like it better for an occasional earthquake. Walk he cannot, the ground being so still and steady that he is puzzled to keep his legs; and ride he will not, for he disdains a craft whose rudder is forward and not astern.

Inland scenery is his especial aversion. He despises a tree "before the mast," and would give all the singing-birds in creation for a boatswain's whistle. He hates prospects, but enjoys retrospects. An old boat, a stray anchor, or a decayed mooring ring, will set him dreaming for hours. He splices sea and land ideas together. He reads of "shooting off a tie at Battersea," and it reminds him of a ball carrying away his own pig-tail. "Canvassing for a situation," recalls running with all sails set for a station at Aboukir. He has the advantage of our economists as to the "standard of value," knowing it to be the British ensign. The announcement of "an arrival of foreign vessels, with our ports open," claps him into a paradise of prize money, with Poll of the *Pint*. He wonders sometimes at "petitions to be discharged from the fleet," but sympathizes with those in the Marshalsea Court, as subject to a Sea Court Martial. Finally, try him even in the learned languages, by asking him for the meaning of "Georgius Rex," and he will answer, without hesitation, "The wrecks of the Royal George."

LUTTRELL.

Rogers said that Luttrell's epigram on Miss Tree, the singer, was "quite a little fairy tale."

> On this Tree when a nightingale settles and sings,
> The Tree will return her as good as she brings.

Washington Irving was walking with Moore and Luttrell, near Paris, when the conversation turned on a female aeronaut, who had not been heard of since her recent ascent. Moore described her upward progress—the last seen of her, she was still ascending, ascending. "Handed out, at last, I suppose," said Luttrell, "by Enoch and Elijah."

Walking with Luttrell, one day, Moore referred to a saying on Sharp's very dark complexion, that he looked as if the dye of his old trade (hat-making,) had got engrained into his face. "Yes," said Luttrell, "darkness that may be *felt*."

Luttrell gave this illustration of the English climate: "On a fine day, like looking up a chimney —on a wet day, like looking down it."

Luttrell wrote the following epitaph on a man who was run over by an omnibus:

> Killed by an omnibus! Why not?
> So quick a death a boon is:
> Let not his friends lament his lot—
> *Mors omnibus communis!*

Some one said to Sir F. Gould, "I am told you eat three eggs every day at breakfast." "No," answered Gould, "on the contrary." Some of us asked, "What was the contrary of eating three eggs?" "Laying three eggs, I suppose," said Luttrell.

When Mr. Croker had charged the public with his war salary, on account of the doings at Algiers, and thereby excited much indignation, it happened that some one at dinner talked of the name of Croker mountains given to land supposed to be seen in one of the voyages to the North Pole. "Does any thing grow on them?" said some one. "Only a little wild celery (salary)," said Luttrell.

In talking of the Eumelian Club, of which Ashe was the founder, somebody said that a son of that Ashe was at present chairman of it. "Still in its *ashes* live their wonted fires," said Luttrell.

A DAY OF DISASTERS.

A Conversation between Peter and Zedekiah.

BY MARY HOWITT.

PETER. Zedekiah, come here!
ZEDEKIAH. Well now, what's the matter?
PETER. Look at my hat; the more I set it right, it only gets the flatter.
ZEDEKIAH. Why, Peter, what's come to your hat? I never saw such a thing.
PETER. I've had nothing but ill-luck to-day; I did this with the swing;
I've been tossed into the apple-tree just as if I was a ball,
And though I caught hold of a bough, I've had a terrible fall;
I'm sure I should have cracked my skull, had it not been for my hat.
You may see what a fall it was, for the crown's quite flat;
And it never will take its shape again, do all that ever I may!
ZEDEKIAH. Never mind it, Peter! Put it on your head, and come along, I say!
PETER. Nay, I shall not. I shall sit down under this tree;
I've had nothing but ill-luck to-day. Come, sit down by me,
And I'll tell you all, Zedekiah, for I feel quite forlorn;
Oh dear! oh dear! I'm lamed now!—I've sat down upon a thorn!
ZEDEKIAH. Goodness sake! Peter, be still—what a terrible bellow—
One would think you'd sate on a hornet's nest; sit down, my good fellow.
PETER. I'll be sure there are no more thorns here, before I sit down;
Pretty well of one thorn at a time, Master Zedekiah Brown!
There, now, I think this seat is safe and easy—so now you must know
I was fast asleep at breakfast-time; and you'll always find it so,
That if you begin a day ill, it will be ill all the day.
Well, when I woke, the breakfast things were clattering all away;
And I knew they had eggs and fowl, and all sorts of good things;
But then none may partake who are in bed when the morning bell rings;
So, sadly vexed as I was, I rolled myself round in bed,
And, "as breakfast is over, I'll not hurry myself," I said,
So I just got into a nice little doze, when in came my mother;
And "for shame, Peter," she said, "to be a-bed now, well, you can't go with your brother."
Then out of the door she went without another word;
And just then a sound of wheels, and of passing horses' hoofs I heard;
So I jumped up to the window to see what it was, and I declare
There was a grand party of fine folks setting off somewhere:
There was my brother, mounted on the pony so slick and brown,
And Bell in her white frock, and my mother in her satin gown;
And my father in his best, and ten gentlemen beside;
And I had never heard a word about it, either of drive or ride!
I really think it was very queer of them to set off in that way—
If I'd only known over-night, I'd have been up by break of day!
As you may think, I was sadly vexed, but I did not choose to show it,
So I whistled as I came down stairs, that the servants might not know it;
Then I went into the yard, and called the dog by his name,
For I thought if they were gone, he and I might have a good game.
But I called and called, and there was no dog either in this place or th' other;
And Thomas said, "Master Peter, Neptune's gone with your brother."
Well, as there was no dog, I went to look for the fox,
And sure enough the chain was broke, and there was no creature in the box;
But where the fellow was gone nobody could say,
He had broken loose himself, I suppose, and so had slipped away;
I would give any thing I have, but to find the fox again—
And was it not provoking, Zedekiah, to lose him just then?
ZEDEKIAH. Provoking enough! Well, Peter, and what happened next?
PETER. Why, when I think of it now, it makes me quite vexed;
I went into the garden just to look about
To see if the green peas were ready, or the scarlet lychnis come out;
And there what should I clap my eyes on but the old sow,
And seven little pigs making a pretty row!
And of all places in the world, as if for very spite,
They had gone into my garden, and spoiled and ruined it quite!
The old sow, she had grubbed up my rosemary and old-man by the root,
And my phlox and my sunflowers, and my hollyhocks, that were as black as soot;
And every flower that I set store on was ruined for ever;
I never was so mortified in all my life—never!
ZEDEKIAH. You sent them off, I should think, with a famous swither!

PETER. Grunting and tumbling one over the other, I cared not whither.
Well, as I was just then standing, grieving over the ruin,
I heard Thomas call, "Master Peter, come and see what the rats have been doing—
They've eaten all the guinea-pigs' heads off!"
ZEDEKIAH. Oh, Peter, was it true?
PETER. Away I ran, not knowing what in the world to do!
And there—I declare it makes me quite shudder to the bone—
Lay all my pretty little guinea-pigs as dead as a stone!
"It's no manner of use," says Thomas, "setting traps, for you see
They no more care for a trap, than I do for a pea;
I'll lay my life on't, there are twenty rats now down in that hole,
And we can no more reach 'em, than an underground mole!"
I declare, Zedekiah, I never passed such a day before—not I;
It makes me quite low-spirited, till I'm ready to cry.
All those pretty guinea-pigs! and I've nothing left at all,
Only the hawk, and I've just set his cage on the wall.
ZEDEKIAH. Hush! hush now! for Thomas is saying something there,
PETER. What d'ye say, Thomas?
THOMAS. The hawk's soaring in the air!
The cage door was open, and he's flown clean away!
PETER. There now, Zedekiah, is it not an unfortunate day?
I've lost all my favorites—I've nothing left at all,
And my garden is spoiled, and I've had such a dreadful fall!
I wish that I had been up in the morning as early as the sun,
And then I should have gone to Cammonley, nor have had all this mischief done!
I'm sure it's quite enough to make me cry for a year—
Let's go into the house, Zedekiah; what's the use of sitting here?

HIGH LIFE IN THE TAP-ROOM.

FROM PUNCH.

ADJOINING the House of Lords is a public-house which enjoys the exclusive patronage of the coachmen and footmen in waiting upon the hereditary wisdom of the empire.

Some years ago, it was discovered that one-third of these motley gentlemen rejoiced in the name of Smith, one-sixth in the name of Brown, and one-sixth in the name of Jones, whilst the remaining third had their patronymics from the varied columns of Pigot's Directory.

In order to remedy the confusion consequent upon this unfortunate similarity of names, it was enacted:

"That on and from the 12th day of June, 1839, every Member of this Honorable Public House shall be spoken of and spoken to by the title and designation of the fortunate individual who has the honor of paying him his wages, and supplying him his livery. And be it further enacted, that should any Member of this Honorable Public House infringe the above regulations, he shall be liable to pay for as many glasses of 'hot with' or 'cold without,' as there are gentlemen's gentlemen present."

Signed,

GEORGE SMITH,	OWEN JONES,
JONES JONES,	HECTOR SMITH,
JOHN SMITH,	PAUL BROWN,
PETER BROWN,	SMITH SMITH,
ISAAC SMITH,	ABRAHAM HALL.

Members of the Privy Council.

In consequence of this politic arrangement, it very seldom occurs that any person pays twice, as was the case formerly—sometimes. During the hours that are occupied in debate by their noble and honorable masters, a colloquy something like the following may be heard:—

1ST FOOTMAN.—Waiter—a go of gin.

WAITER.—Very well, my lord—*(calls)*—A go of gin for the Bishop of London!

2D FOOTMAN.—A pint of mild ale and a shee-root.

WAITER.—Yes, Sir James—*(calls)*—A pint of mild ale and a shee-root for Sir James Graham.

1ST FOOTMAN.—I say, Sir James.

2D FOOTMAN.—What *is* it, my Lord?

1ST FOOTMAN.—Lord Melbourne and Sir Robert Peel have made it up again; they smoked a pipe together last night.

3D FOOTMAN.—I shall be happy to toss the Duke of Wellington for six pen'orth of rum and water.

4TH FOOTMAN.—I never take rum, but the Lord Chancellor does.

5TH FOOTMAN.—I'm your man, Mr. Roebuck; Newmarket, of course.

6TH FOOTMAN.—I say, Mr. Speaker, you owe me a shilling.

7TH FOOTMAN.—So I do, Mr. Hume; and I must continue to owe it. Who's eating onions?

6TH FOOTMAN.—Lord Londonderry.

8TH FOOTMAN.—It's not me, it's Lord Palmerston; I'm having part of a cowheel with the Duke of Devonshire.

4TH FOOTMAN.—Any body seen Lord John Russell to-night?

6TH FOOTMAN.—I have—he's gone to lay down. He's taken something that has disagreed with him. I believe it's six glasses of gin and water.

WAITER.—The Chancellor of the Exchequer's wanted.

9TH FOOTMAN.—Am I?—somebody lend us a penny.

THE GOSSIP.

BY CATHERINE FRANCES GORE.

Why are the English—the grave English—the rational English—the moral English—the greatest gossips in the world? No one conversant with the social life of other nations will deny the fact;—but who will adduce the cause? Doctor Johnson defines to gossip is "to chat, to spend time idly." A more correct definition of the word, as used in modern parlance, would be, "to spend time idly in chatting of other people's affairs." Yet the English are not a people addicted to spending time idly. It must be some overmastering influence which inspires them with the vague curiosity, leading to so vile a waste of the impalpable treasure, more precious than silver or gold.

Is it that the desire of knowledge, so extensively cultivated among us by the high-pressure power of universal education, begets in weak minds, incapable of retaining solid information, a restless craving after intelligence? Does learning, like the wind which extinguishes a candle while it stimulates a great fire, strengthen the strong mind, but enfeeble the weak? No matter! By some defect of organization, the English, taken as a mass, are gossips—decided gossips. Is it not written in the book of the chronicles of their public journals—those bulletins of the national mind? Is it not attested by the avidity with which the most trivial anecdotes of domestic life are circulated and eagerly swallowed, by that yawning gulf, the reading public? Is it not pointed out with a sneer by the foreign world—rejoicing to detect in our details of private parties and descriptions of court-trains and feathers, a counterbalance to the sageness of our councils, and the vastness of our scientific achievements? The scandal of personality would be put down in continental countries by the strong arm of the law; but the froth of every-day "fashionable intelligence" would be simply blown aside by the contemptuous lips of common sense!

But it is the appetite for gossip, and not the food which the yearnings of that appetite bring into the market, with which we have to deal. The press gossips for society, because society gossips for itself and makes no secret of its love of gossiping, pretending that a mere tattler is a merely harmless person. But the taste thus established, is any thing but harmless. Like the bind-weed, which, when once suffered to take root, extinguishes the growth of more profitable plants, it intertwines itself irretrievably with all the product of the soil.

Critics boast of a new work as "a pleasant gossiping book;" people boast of a new acquaintance, as "a pleasant gossiping fellow;" and the most valuable of our periodicals was a few years ago redeemed from decadence by a series of "pleasant gossiping articles."

When a new work of fiction issues from the press, in a style called by the French *un roman de mœurs*, by ourselves, a fashionable novel, be sure that it is either personal, or will pretend to be personal, or will be said to be personal. Without some such *nota bene* to "The Gossip," the piquancy of its general hits at the foibles of general society, would be thrown away. At this very moment, half our readers are running on impatiently through our prosiness, hoping that some especial Gossip, male or female, will be pointed out to shame, and some entertaining anecdote cited, in order to fasten the label round the right neck! "Have at ye all, my gossips!" Not *one* of you, ladies, but is the original of the horrible Lady Pagginton we are about to describe; not *one* of you, gentlemen, but has your sympathetic part in "that amusing, gossiping fellow," Flutter, of whom more anon.

You are all gossips! You gossip every where, of every thing; not alone of the dinner-party and ball-room—the pink satin dress and flirtation in the balcony; but after visiting a condemned cell, you gossip concerning the morose anguish of the being, contemplating the terrors of eternity! You obtain an order for Bethlem Hospital; and, unawed by the spectacle of one of the overmastering scourges of the human race, garnish your discourse at the gay dinner-table with pleasant anecdotes of the comicalities of madmen! You hie to the factory, and after shuddering at the blue faces and pinched noses of the suffering population, hie home and gossip pleasantly at the conversation concerning the curious dialect of the overseer, or the quaint comments of some droll little victim promoted to the honors of interrogation.

An infirm nobleman is murdered at dead of night in his chamber. With what hosts of entertaining anecdotes and clever puns do the gossips recount the narrative of his assassination! A woman elopes from her husband, leaving her infants motherless: what joy for the gossips in all the concomitant details of the wig and broken spectacles of the paramour! On such occasions, regardless of the influence of such histories on their own minds and the minds of their hearers, the gossips overrun both town and country, scattering the seed of their tares in all directions.

The most awful catastrophes—suicide, battle, murder, sudden death—become reduced to the same trifling consistency—the same chaff—after being ground in the mill and winnowed through the sieve of a gossip.

Be patient, gentle reader; we promised you "a light gossiping article;" you shall come to Lady Pagginton and Felix Flutter in time. Allow us, however, to begin with the gossip of an humbler sphere.

There is Miss Bargeham, the favorite milliner of the well-known market-place of B. ("B?—B. certainly stands for Birmingham!" murmurs some gossiping reader.) For the last thirty years, the counters of Kitty Bargeham have obtained a remarkable preference over a succession of new comers in the immediate neighborhood. Vainly have the windows of her rivals displayed the most unquestionable superiority of cap and turban, hat, and bonnet, plaid ribbons, and chantilly veils. These parti-colored attractions have invariably given place within the year to a placard of "To Let, Unfurnished;" or, "To be Sold under Prime Cost, by order of the Assignees." One rash firm even went as far as to advertise the attraction of a Parisian assistant, "A young lady from the eminent French house of Mesdames Follette et Cie., Rue Vivienne." In vain! In six months, the shop was shut up, and the Parisian assistant shut out.

There was no standing against the "light gossiping articles" of Kitty Bargeham.

Oh! that back-parlor! Oh! the inedited anecdotes of Brush Park and Lark Hall, conveyed from their respective ladies'-maids, to the ears of the milliner, and from the milliner to the ears of all the tradesmen's wives and farmers' daughters of the neighborhood of B.! The shoe-ribbon purchased of Mesdames Brown, or the green veil of Mrs. Smith, might be of worthier texture, or even by sixpence a better bargain; but what was that compared with the joy of having been seated face to face with Kitty Bargeham, in her little stuffy, dingy sanctum, listening to charming innuendos about Sir Thomas Lark's London losses at play, or hints that "something would be sure to come of Miss Melusinda Brush's early walks in the green lane." Kitty "knew it from the best authority,"—but Kitty "would say no more!" More reputations were "done to death by slanderous tongues" in Kitty Bargeham's back-parlor, than in the whole county besides; a perpetual twitter of chit-chat being emitted therefrom on every opening of its sacred door, to tantalize the less-privileged customers not yet initiated into the gossip-shop. But Brush Park is now to be let, and Lark Hall to be sold; too hot to hold the respective proprietors, martyrized *à coup d'épingles* by the milliner of the market-place—by THE GOSSIP!

Lady Pagginton—(draw your chair closer to the fender, courteous gossip—we have got to Lady Pagginton at last!—) is a widow, and a London lady—that is, a Marylebonian, the most diluted and colorless species of the London lady. Mediocrity personified, whether as regards mind, body, or estate, Lady P. has managed to make herself heard of as the gnats do—by humming and stinging. The creature means no harm—'tis in its nature; but the sting is not the less irritating, nor the noise less tiresome. So is it with Lady P. Her perseverance in making her way into your house—her perseverance in communicating in emphatic whispers idle sayings concerning still idler doings in which you have not the slightest interest—her perseverance in attributing to her last auditor the comments with which she has herself embroidered the intelligence derived from her first informant, are worthy a better cause; you might cut a canal with almost half the labor.

Nothing too great—nothing too little—to be caught up and carried off in her ladyship's budget. To the little matters, like the bits of worthless glass which acquire beauty in a kaleidoscope, she imparts importance by a species of scientific illusion; while the great ones she brings within her paltry compass, as the body of De Rance's mistress was forced into the leaden coffin, by cutting off the head. She contrives to gossip about the affairs of the East, by garnishing them with secret anecdotes of our lady of Cairo, the renowned widow of Mehemet Ali's eldest son; or sets her mark upon the politicians of the West, by rumors pilfered from the Charivari, about the domestic life of a minister whose whole life is public—or the secret cabinet of Metternich, through whose key-hole not even the winds of heaven are permitted to whistle. But without this mischievous occupation—this perpetual cobbling of colloquial shreds and patches—what would become of the vapid, unmeaning, unconnected Lady P.? Devote her leisure to some useful purpose—condescend to knit—sew—read? Why, she would sink into a second-rate person of respectability! losing all pretext for intruding upon your more serious occupations, in her capacity of "a most lively, agreeable woman—knowing every body,—full of anecdote,—in short, the very perfection of A GOSSIP!"

Felix Flutter is a more dangerous individual. *His* story and note savor of the rattlesnake rather than the gnat; *his* smatterings consist of steel filings, rather than of chaff; *his* pourings forth are *aqua Tofana*, rather than milk-and-water; but all dispensed under the same delusive head, of "light, pleasant gossip!" Men might be brought to the scaffold, or condemned to the cart, for the crimes "pleasant but wrong," imputed in the light anecdotes which Flutter impels like shuttlecocks from his smart-racket, from house to house. Like the snake-charmers of the East, who amuse your leisure with the display of reptiles, that seem to curl and play in their adroit hands, he ties love-knots with adders! Worse still, when like the cunning seers of Egypt, who, by pretended incantations, seem to withdraw from beneath the very cushions of your divan, the serpent they have cunningly introduced into the chamber to accredit their power, Felix Flutter contrives to inspire your mind with terror and mistrust, by ascribing to the treachery of a bosom friend the mischief concocted by his own malice!

But Flutter is such an amusing fellow! Nothing like him for a morning visit—a dull dinner-party! Like Mr. Merryman at Gyngell's, his pockets are always full of squibs and crackers, to be discharged at intervals when the wit of the company runs low. And then he is so plausible! His most improper little stories make their appearance in the most decent attire; like one of Congreve's gallants arrayed in the gown and cassock of Dr. Spintext, or Cartouche dressed up as one of the Maréchaussée, to rob a house! Nothing more decorous—nothing more deadly! He runs you through the body with a regulation small-sword; or, if you insist on committing suicide, sells you your arsenic with "poison" labelled on the packet, as per order of the magistrates established.

My public! know ye not this Felix Flutter? Has he not related *sub rosa* of each of you to the other, that your grandfathers were one shocking thing, and your grandmothers the other shocking thing! —that you have overdrawn your bankers—that you have injured your early friends—that you have blasphemed the Church, or conspired against the State? Know ye not Felix Flutter?—know ye not *ten* Felix Flutters—*twenty* Felix Flutters? Know ye not, in short, in some shape or other, the concentrated essence of A MODERN GOSSIP?

A RE-BUS.

"What is a rebus?" I asked of dear Mary,
As close by my side the fair maiden was seated:
I saw her eyes sink, and her countenance vary,
As she said in reply, "'Tis a kiss, sir, repeated."

DEATH'S INJUNCTION.

Pinto *lies here*. 'Tis natural he should,
Who *lied* through life as often as he could:
He thought of mending, but, to spite his will,
Death came unlooked for, and bade him *lie still!*

CAPTURING A FORT.

A True Story.

BY H. R. ADDISON.

Many years ago it was found necessary to besiege the fort called Budge-Budge, some few miles from Calcutta down the river, which the natives held in spite of our remonstrances, probably supported in their hostile obstinacy by the Dutch and French governments, who, as all the world knows, have several settlements in the East Indies. These settlements we could wrest from them in an instant, but, for some unaccountable reason or other, we have allowed them to remain in their hands, to the no small hindrance of justice and equity; since it frequently happens that characters deserving punishment for their offences have merely to cross the river, and in ten minutes are beyond the pale of British law, having found refuge in Chinsurah, or some other foreign town. The existence of these little colonies has a still worse effect in case of disaffection amongst the Indians, inasmuch as they are ever ready to pour forth foreign emissaries, who urgently foment the feud, and mislead the poor natives, by holding out hopes of assistance from their respective countries.

Such had been the case with Budge-Budge, the aforesaid fort, before which a couple of frigates and some armed boats were lying at the time of my sketch. The native garrison, which amounted to about six hundred men, had vainly been summoned to surrender. They vowed they would rather die than do so. For three days, long shots had been fired at them; but, as the fortress was built of mud, no sooner was the smallest breach made than it was instantly closed up, and rebuilt stronger than ever. One of the commanders advised the adoption of a storming party; his brother officer, however, differed from him, urging that the place was too well garrisoned to be easily carried by assault. The opinions of the two leaders were forwarded to Calcutta, and the reply expected to be returned on the morrow.

James Bunting (so we will call the old tar) heard all these *palavers*, as he styled them, and looked very knowing. He understood there was a chance of fighting, so he felt perfectly delighted. To his berth he descended, and as usual, when he was particularly happy, managed to get particularly drunk, and turned in evidently the worse for liquor. Now, it so happened that in about an hour after he had thus settled himself in his hammock, he suddenly awoke. A burning fever, an agonizing thirst parched his mouth, so he arose, and went to his locker; but, alas! he had drunk every drop of liquid he possessed, and where to find more he knew not. On board the vessel he had no hopes; shore was his only chance; so, unseen by any one, he made his way into the water by lowering himself from the chains, or from a port-hole, or some such place, and struck out for the beach, where he landed safely, in spite of alligators, sentinels, and all other similar oppositions.

When he had shaken the water from his hair, and hitched up his trowsers, he began to look around for a toddy-shop, where he could purchase some of that liquor, or some arrack, to take the chill off the water he had swallowed; but, alas! no building of the kind met his view,—not a single habitation could he see. The fort frowned gloomily over him in sullen grandeur; no other place where spirits were likely to be found could he discover, though he peered anxiously round on every side. To lose his time, to be laughed at by his comrades on his return from the wild-goose chase he had undertaken, was by no means palatable to Bunting. To be balked is a maxim unknown to a British sailor; so, rather than lose his grog, he determined to lose his life, or at all events, risk it. Without further ado, he began scaling the walls of the fort. This he easily managed, and in a few moments found himself at the top of the glacis. Elated at his success, he began shouting as loud as ever he could bawl, to the horror of the garrison, who instantly fancying themselves assailed, started up, and were about to run to the spot where they supposed the attacking party had made good a lodgment, when Jim, who had scampered round the defences, again began to shout from the opposite side, and suddenly lowering himself into the town itself, commenced cheering as loud as he could, intermingling his vociferations with cries for liquor.

Assailed, as they supposed, on both sides, the enemy actually *in* the fortress, surprised in the middle of the night, expecting nothing less than to be cut to pieces in the dark, what could they do? The bravest well might hesitate; unable to get their forces together, confused, and astounded, they naturally believed they had been betrayed. They had but one course left to pursue. They opened the gates, and fled as fast and as far as their feet would carry them, leaving the town in the quiet and peaceable possession of James Bunting, who, after shouting vainly for some time, fell down, and slept for a couple of hours, when he awoke, perfectly sober, though about as much puzzled at finding himself alone, and in the enemy's fort, as the poor man was in the Arabian Nights, when he suddenly found himself transformed into an eagle.

Jim rubbed his eyes. He pinched his legs, and walking up to a tank, actually drank three mouthfuls of water before he could believe that he was awake. He then strutted up to the ramparts: and convinced himself he was in his proper senses, for there lay the two frigates, and there floated the union-jack, for which he had so often risked his life. "Shiver my timbers! but this is a queer go!" said he, and with that he twitched up his trowsers as usual, and shook the pigtail—which then hung from every sailor's head.

The vessels, perceiving a man thus expose himself, began to fire on him.

"Avast there!" shouted Jim; but as they did not hear him, or attend to him, he ran to the principal battery, and, climbing up the flagstaff, pulled down the Dutch colors, and hoisted up a ragged old turban he found lying in one of the streets. The commanders of the vessels thought this extremely odd. Something strange had evidently happened: so they sent a boat on shore, bearing a flag of truce, carried by the first lieutenant of one of the frigates. Unmolested the party marched *up* to the fort; and, as the gates were open, unmolested they marched *into* it. Not a soul did they meet till Jim strutted up to them.

"Holloa, you sir, what's the meaning of this?" said the first lieutenant to Bunting, in a voice of anger; for it was sadly *infra dig.* for an officer of his rank to have been thus sent off to parley with a common sailor. "What's the meaning of this?"

"Please your honor, I hope you won't be angry, Leeftenant, but, somehow or other, I've taken this place. The enemy have cut the painter, and sheered off."

"What!" cried the superior. "*You* took the fort?"

Jim nodded.

"And, pray, who the devil gave you leave to do so, I should like to know? Get on board, sir, directly."

"Ay, ay, sir," replied Jim respectfully, instantly doing as he was desired.

In the mean time, the lieutenant went and formally took possession of the place by running up the British colors; then writing a most pompous dispatch, in which he recommended the real captor to be tried for leaving his ship without permission, he sent it back by a young midshipman, remaining behind himself with a half-a-dozen sailors, in order, as he expressed it, to garrison the fort.

Strange to say, his recommendation was attended to, and Jim Bunting brought to a court-martial, who most reluctantly were compelled to find him guilty, adjudging him, however, to undergo the least possible punishment that could be inflicted for so glaring a breach of discipline. Jim felt highly indignant at the turn things had taken. He could not help fancying himself an ill-used man; but he bore it stoically. When, however, he heard the verdict delivered; when he heard himself pronounced guilty, he once more hitched up his nether garments, and exclaimed in an audible voice as he left the cabin, "D—n my eyes, if ever I take another fort as long as I live."

Need I add that, though, to satisfy the strictness of the law, to which all in the navy must bow, the verdict of guilty was brought in, he was afterwards amply praised, and rewarded by his superiors?

PICTORIAL HUMOR.

BY JOHN LEECH.

Angelina. Will my darling Edwin grant his Angelina a boon?

Edwin. Is there any thing on earth her Edwin would not do for his pet?—Name the boon, oh, dearest—name it!

Angelina. Then, love, as we dine by ourselves to-morrow, let us, oh! let us have roast pork, with plenty of sage and onions!

ALL FOR WANT OF A HALFPENNY.

A Financial Sketch.

BY J. PALGRAVE SIMPSON.

I AM not fond of old proverbs. For the most part, they have grown wondrously inapplicable to practical life in the present day. It might be a matter of curious research to trace the reasons why so many of them have become trivial truisms, worn-out saws, or utterly false scraps of futile philosophy—taking it for granted, of course, that, once upon a time, they really *were* true, and fitted manners in their application. But this research is not my purpose now. There are, however, some old axioms, the profundity of which I am never tired of admiring, much as they may, at first sight, appear to touch nearly, like their cousins, the proverbs, upon triviality of truism. One, with which I have always been most peculiarly impressed, is that which has flowed into metre in the words, "From little causes great effects arise." It is, perhaps, my childish cuiiosity as regards the hidden mainsprings of men's actions, the exercise of which has always been, from my boyhood, one of my favorite pastimes, that has led me to consider this axiom as one of the most profound in its practical application. From its constant study, I have arrived at the conviction that there are none of the greatest events of history which could not be traced to a primary starting point, in its nature so trivial and frivolous, that, by comparison, it would be as the grain of sand to the mountain—that the great memorable facts on record have all grown from some slight cause, as the oak from the acorn. I was, early in life, practically convinced of this truth, by an adventure which happened to myself. Pardon me! Let it not, for a moment, be supposed that I have the vanity to think I have ever appeared, as a prominent figure, in any great historical event, or that I have even been the grain of sand which eventually led to the formation of the mountain, or the acorn which formed the seed for the wide-spreading oak. Far from it; the events I am about to relate, if "events" such trivialities as the incidents of an adventure may be called, are the smallest of the small in the world's great sum. But all things are comparative; and to me these paltry events were great at the time, as regarded their temporary effect upon the equilibrium of one man's state of mind and body during several hours; and, as circumstances turned out, they might have easily exercised a mighty influence on my own little destiny. The simple words, "*might have*," even if they did not, is sufficient to prove the truth of my axiom.

To proceed. I was, at that time, an undergraduate of the University of Cambridge. Parental authority asserted, in those days, a sway seemingly unknown in later years, or but seldom asserted in its pristine rigor, and comparatively but feebly exercised. The despotic announcement from the parental throne, that I was expected to remain in college, and lose no time in reading for honors, during the short Easter vacation, was a ukase from which there was no escape. An infringement was sure to be met by a punishment of a long exile to a moral Siberia. But even Russian subjects sometimes revolt; and several little demons were insidiously whispering to my heart, that infringement is only punishable if the infringement is known. Now, these demons were the demons of pleasure, curiosity, love of change, desire for excitement, and, if last, not least, the demon of contrariety—the demon that urges weak mortals to do certain deeds, simply and solely because those deeds are forbidden. These demons, like the witches in Macbeth, with one finger on their skinny lips, intimating that secrecy was sure, with the other outstretched, in a southerly direction, towards the crown of my ambiton, were always whispering "London! London!" The "parental" were safe in the country. No one would be likely to meet or know me in town. The metropolitan theatres—the dreams of my childhood, my boyhood, and my youth—were looming in the distance, gorgeous and tempting visions! Other pleasures rose before my eyes—day-dreams of my constant aspirations—fair *mirages* of a collegiate desert! The demons were powerful—the will was weak—discovery improbable—gratification certain. It were useless to detail all the rounds of the great stand-up fight between Duty and Inclination. Of course, Inclination pummelled Duty, until Duty's eyes were completely "bunged up," and Duty's ears were deafened by the terrible back-hitters it received. The result of the combat was inevitable. "A few days in town!"—ye gods of youthful anticipations, what a glorious symphony of delight was in the words!—so a few days in town were resolved upon. Finances were, however, prudently counted, and found available. A last letter—another would not be expected for a week—was despatched to the parental penates; and, with a heart beating with anticipated joys, and also with some of that fluster of nervous apprehension, which the little "tic-tac" of conscience will, after all, be always hammering, under such circumstances, about that same region, I started for town. "Only for a few days," I repeated.

Those were not the days of that rapid locomotion, which, with a little contrivance, now enables an undergraduate to have his "spree in town," and yet be "up" again to be marked for hall-dinner. Railways had not lent to gownsmen their demoniac aid to drive "high pressure express" through the barriers of parental authority; and, by the way, it might be another matter of curious research to trace how far the facilities of railway travelling may have proved facilities in the relaxation of morals and social ties—a research which, also, cannot be entered upon now. The old coach—the "slow and seedy," the most available for my purpose, was even then called as a thing too much behind the requirements of the age, not to merit contempt—was the public conveyance, which was to prove the gilded chariot of desire and hope. Perhaps, the difficulties and delays of locomotion in those days, only added to the charms of a forbidden *escapade:* it is in human nature that difficulties should do so; and, may be, easiness of execution now diminishes the zest with which an under-graduate of either university formerly regarded a "bolt off to the village." But this is, again, beside my purpose.

I am not going to enter now upon a description

of all I did, all I saw, all I enjoyed—for I enjoyed *every thing* in those days, and have not yet entirely lost that happy faculty—during those "few days" (of course, prolonged beyond my first intention) of charming but somewhat agitated truancy; although a fast man's doings in those days made, in so many respects, a notable contrast with a fast man's doings in the present, that a description of them might form a *tableau de mœurs*, almost sufficiently lost to moderners to give it the piquancy of a page of Pepys's. My last day had arrived—my very last. I was just able, by "slow and seedy," to reach Cambridge in time to send off an epistle, duly dated with the old hieroglyphics, "C. C. C. C.," and duly stamped with the official post-mark, to prove that I was at my post, and a willing martyr to the inflictions of duty—just able, and no more! My "traps"—I forgot, however, whether a man's travelling necessaries were called "traps" in those days—had been duly packed at the obscure hotel, where I had taken up my abode, as less likely to be discovered. A few hours were still free, before the departure of "slow and seedy." I remember that I had been indulging *pour passer le temps*, in a flirtation with a pretty shopwoman, and an indigestible bun, at a pastrycook's in the Strand; and I stood by the shop door and carefully looked over the contents of my purse, to assure myself, once more, that I had still more than sufficient to pay my hotel bill, and the demands of "slow and seedy." Yes! they were ample. They still consisted of a few sovereigns, a five-shilling piece, a half-crown, a shilling, a sixpence, and a halfpenny! That common, vulgar, dirty, brown halfpenny, lying along with its aristocratic gold and silver brethren, excited my most supercilious contempt. As I gazed upon the paltry coin, why was there no good genius near me, to whisper, "Nothing so small but may aid in time of need"—another axiom, which I have since cherished and observed to the personal incumbrance of shelves, drawers, and pockets, in the preservation of trifles. Why did no warning spirit suggest to my mind, not yet outgrown from childhood's love, the fable of the lion and the mouse? Alas, I had but recently cut all acquaintance with my good genius, and repudiated all right to the influence of warning voices? But I must not anticipate. That common, vulgar, dirty, brown halfpenny, at that moment, was in my eyes, I say, an object of disgust. A little ragged girl was passing the shop-door; and before her feet I "chucked" away the obnoxious halfpenny. Of course it was pounced upon by eager hands. The child's eyes glistened wistfully—perhaps, also, with a glance of gratitude. But I must solemnly confess, that I was not actuated by the slightest feelings of charity. I cannot take that "flattering unction" to my soul. Had that halfpenny of destiny rolled into a drain, I should not have less considered its mission on earth accomplished—I should not have felt one feeling of remorse that it had not done its work of benevolence. But I had no time for reflections, even had I been inclined to make them—which I in no way was—for, at that moment, such a jaunty, sprightly female figure passed me, that I was immediately all eyes for that pattern of slim elegance. If I mistook—and I was not mistaken—she had turned her head suddenly towards me, and started with visible emotion. I could not see her face. It was but for a second she had turned her head; and a veil was drawn down and held tightly before her. Now, I always had a cruelly susceptible heart, a treacherously vivid imagination, and an all absorbing love of adventure. I darted after the lovely female immediately; for lovely I was most positively convinced she was, by my heart's instincts, although I never saw her face. Besides, there was no mistaking the grace of that exquisite *tournure*—the elegance of that lady-like apparel—the neatly turned delicacy of that foot and ankle, as with one hand she held up her dress to avoid that slight layer of mud, which seems indispensable to the well-being of the Strand, even in bright weather. What a light, springy step she had, too! She must be a Hebe! She was as young as beautiful. She walked briskly; I followed with quick steps, but unwilling to alarm her by too evident a pursuit—I followed like one fascinated by a witch-spell. She turned the corner of Wellington Street, and made for Waterloo Bridge. Between that corner and the bridge I was never once able to pass her, so as directly to turn round and gaze upon her lovely face. She reached the bridge rapidly, paid her halfpenny, passed the turnstile—and there I stood on the other side! I felt for a halfpenny—my last and only coin of that value had been recklessly flung away! But was I to be detained in my pursuit of that beauteous creature for the want of such a paltry piece of money? Gallantry forbid! I pulled out my purse, hunted out my sixpence, flung it down, and, furious at the dilatory precision of the toll-keeper, as he fumbled for my fivepence-halfpenny worth of balance, dashed through the turnstile, with the hasty objurgation of—"Confound you!—keep your change!"

During this delay, the "lovely one" had considerably gained upon me in her rapid course. She had just reached the further extremity of the bridge, and was proceeding, with that peculiar fascinating jauntiness of step, along the Waterloo Road, when I found myself sufficiently near to make a plunge in advance of her, and turn. This rapid act of footmanship was executed to my entire satisfaction; and I faced round! Fatality! At the very same moment my fair unknown mounted the steps of a large house, and knocked at the door. During the interval that ensued, before the appearance of a slipshod maid in answer to that knock, the object of my pursuit was not even influenced by that powerful motive of curiosity, which is supposed to be so essentially feminine, to turn her head and look at her pursuer; and yet she *must* have been aware that a gentleman, and one of decent personal appearance, he flattered himself, was behind her. The door was opened—an inquiry was made—she disappeared behind that closing door. I felt myself profoundly humiliated. My *amour propre* was now, however, strongly called into play, as ally and auxiliary to my previous love of excitement. I was not going to renounce my piquant adventure upon the first slight defeat. Oh, no! I commenced, then, the duty of performing, what the Germans so significantly call "*fenster-parade*"—window parade—before that house. But not a glimpse could I catch of any lovely form at any window of any story of the house. I did considerable damage to the soles of my boots with the continuous friction of my impatience. Time—precious time—elapsed. She did not come. Did she, perhaps, reside in that house? Had I hunted my fox to earth? Might I not spend the rest of the day without unearthing her? But no. The elegance of that lady-like attire never *could* belong to a house in the Waterloo

Road! I resumed my *fenster-parade.* Suddenly my eye fell upon a grinning pot-boy, who stood with the empty attributes of his peripatetic calling, evidently laughing at me and my occupation. My first feeling was that of wrath at this vulgar ridicule—my first impulse that of pommelling. But these first feelings were crushed by the bright idea that this probable denizen of the neighborhood might be able to give me some information with regard to the inmates of that house.

So I accosted my satirical observer, and propounded to him boldly the necessary questions. Confound the fellow! he only scratched his head and grinned the more. Indignation, however, again gave way to another bright idea. There is a certain race of beings, whose powers of speech are so feeble, that their tongues cannot be loosened, until a charm, much recommended by gipsies, is exercised upon it—that, namely, of crossing the palm with silver. My purse was again put in requisition. Now it is perfectly evident that, for this purpose, a "little sixpence" would have amply sufficed. But that "little sixpence" had already been sent to look after that halfpenny, the contemptuous treatment of which was already bringing down upon my destined head its just retaliation—that halfpenny, the true value of which was now beginning to be felt. So a shilling was compelled to take the place of the "little sixpence." The proof of the infallibility of gipsies was shown, however, on the spot. The charm operated like a miracle. The pot-boy's power of speech was suddenly restored; although that obnoxious grinning was not for a moment modified by the sudden revulsion. The information I received was of a most miscellaneous character; the different stories of the house were inhabited by personages of the most varied description—in the first floor lived a "curious old chap," —pot-boy could not tell me what he was; some said he was a conjurer—others a doctor—only he didn't doctor like other doctors—he was supposed to doctor by magic signs with his fingers. He had no family. In the second floor dwelt a celebrated actress, with her husband. In the third was a tailor's establishment. In the garrets—but no! I would not have the *prestige* of my beauteous creature destroyed by a supposition that she could have any connection with garrets! I waived all further information of so lofty a description. I could not believe that she had come to have her fortune told by the conjurer—I would not so cruelly malign her good sense; and I was ignorant at that time of the new profession of mesmeric pathology, just then struggling into notice. She could not be—she was not the celebrated actress. I knew all the celebrated actresses at all the theatres in London by heart, and the celebrated actress named in particular. My fair unknown wanted very many inches of her volume of waist. She could not have come to the tailoring establishment to order a coat or a pair of —no! no!—I was bewildered. I renewed my *fenster-parade* once more. Exit pot-boy, still grinning over the charm which crossed the palm of his hand, with the evident conviction impressed upon every feature of his face, that the "young chap was awful green."

The beat of my *fenster-parade* was getting more and more elongated—for its exercise had evidently attracted the notice of various passengers, and among others, of a guardian of the public peace; and I was troubled by the little flattering attention I was receiving. I had almost reached the bridge, when, on turning, I saw at last, to my delight, my fair unknown descending the steps of the mysterious house. Now I should meet her! But no! She turned in the other direction. I again pursued her. But, oh! and again fatality! she hailed a coach, got into it, and proceeded along the Waterloo Road. Now the old "hackney" of those days was as devoid of the fleetness of movement possessed by the public vehicles of the present time, as were all other means of locomotion. With a slight exertion I might have followed and kept in sight the heavy old "jarvey," on foot. But at the time a cab passed—a cab—then a modern conveyance. An evil genius prompted me to hail the driver—my good genius, you know, had long since left me, very deservedly, perhaps, in the lurch. I imagined that I could continue my pursuit in a far more satisfactory manner, as regarded both body and mind, by this seemingly more commodious proceeding. Giving the cabman directions to follow the vehicle immediately before us, keep it in sight, and stop a little short of the place where it might stop, I flung myself upon the seat. Our *avant courier* turned down a street to the right—Lambeth Marsh, I have since been led to believe, was its muddy appellation—we followed. Suddenly we were arrested in our career by a brewer's dray, a costermonger's donkey cart, and sundry other obnoxious vehicles. But, by Jove! the jarvey had got past before the thick of the obstruction came;—the jarvey *had* got past! and we were blocked up as with an avalanche—a fallen Rossberg, which no human efforts could have removed. What availed my frantic curses on the head of the cabman, who was not in fault?—or on my own, although far nearer to justice in this last fulmination? We were pitilessly locked in! Nothing was to be done but to pursue the coach on foot. I sprang from the cab, and telling the cabman to go—never mind where—tendered him hastily his fare. In those days, his fare would have been eightpence. The smallest coin now left in my possession, since the reckless bestowal of that shilling upon the grinning pot-boy—that shilling which might have been replaced by a sixpence, if the sixpence had not been tendered to the toll-keeper, and all for want of that unlucky halfpenny!—the smallest coin now left was half a crown. Of course the cabman had no change—a cabman never has, more especially when he sees a fare in a fluster of hurry—to say nothing of a fare who has just sent him—never mind where! If I could wait, he might, perhaps, get change at the nearest "public." Wait! wait! impossible! so the cabman grinned and pocketed the half-crown—he, too, grinned! And again behold me on my feet, in pursuit of that creaky, crazy, crawling vehicle, which contained the object of my admiration. Yes! there it was still before me! Pursuing my way through opposing throngs—never surely was London thoroughfare so encumbered before—I reached the corner of Bridge Street, just as jarvey turned the same corner. I rushed round at a sharp angle. Then came a crash—an outcry—a grasp of my collar—a struggle, and a fall!

In my sharp turn of that unlucky corner, my feet had come into conflict with a mass of crockery exposed to view, and, perhaps, not unwittingly, to accident, before a paltry shop door. The master of the establishment, seeing that I paid no heed to the mischief I had done, by smashing sundry plates and other utensils of the coarsest fabric, had seized me by the collar and rudely dragged me back with an impetus, to which the hurried movement of my desperate impatience lent a resistless force. In vain was my frantic cries—in vain was my struggle! A powerful arm held me captive, until I should make ample compensation for the damage. I promised all that was desired, if my antagonist would but make a rapid estimate of the injury inflicted upon his dirty crockery. A sulky, but keen glance was thrown over the fragments; and I was informed that half-a-crown would about pay for the unlucky smash. I am convinced—I was convinced at the moment—that tenpence would have been an ample remuneration. But I attempted no resistance to the extortion. My purse was again opened for the half-crown demanded. But my only half-crown was already gone to replace the shilling, that had replaced the sixpence, that had replaced the unlucky and self-avenging half-penny! It was a very "House that Jack built," (could I have laughed, I could have chuckled, a very "house that Jack demolished")—of financial disaster! I tendered the five-shilling piece. My rude brittleware enemy was fumbling in his pockets for change, when a vile twenty-stone blowsy female helpmate of the small dealer came forward, and, without even deigning to cast one of her squinting eyes upon the destroyed ware, impudently asserted that the five shillings tendered would scarcely cover the price of the damage. Now, this began to be too much for my exasperated spirit! I angrily resisted the further claim, which, could I have paid the half-crown at once, would visibly never have been made. I was more angrily treated as a malefactor. The reeking crowd of all ages and of both sexes, which had gathered around us, uplifted their "greasy voices," and howled "Shame! shame!" at *me!* me, the victim! Hideous hootings arose upon the air; and the guardian of the public peace—an apparition, whom only an evil destiny could have raised at a juncture when interference was really necessary—again suddenly stood by my side, and, by a grasp of my collar, appeared inclined to side with the clamorous populace, and drag me to "durance vile," as a positive or a probable criminal. But, by this time I had become frantic. I made a "grand rush of one," tore myself from the hands of the tyrannical myrmidon, dashed through the crowd with the violence of a young elephant, and rushed desperately along Bridge-street, pursued by cries of "Stop thief! stop thief!"—cries admirably illustrative of the diabolical injustice of the divine "*vox populi*,"—for had I not have left my five shilling piece in the hands of my extortioner?

I ran as a man will run before the howlings of a mass of other men, however unjust the popular execration, when he is unaided and has lost his head. I ran. The pursuit was still behind me; the howlings still rang in my ears. I felt myself a hare fleeing from a pack of mangy hounds. Suddenly the thought crossed that I might double. I turned, and darted into an open house door, tore up the first flight of stairs, dimly discovered a brass plate upon a door, setting forth the words, "Screw, Dentist,"—rang frantically, and was admitted without further molestation. Ushered into the presence of Mr. Screw, dentist, I stammered and blushed, and could find no excuse for my intrusion. I was too young and foolish to do what I should have now done—could I, with any possibility, find myself in a similar dilemma—simply tell the truth, laugh over it, and beg ten minutes' hospitality. But, no. I could find no available reason for my entry, but the natural one, which the occupation of my host suggested. Besides, I feared that he too might misinterpret my story. I declared that I had called, in an extremity of agony, to have a tooth extracted. Now, I solemnly assert that all my teeth were in the finest possible condition; and, I believe, I had a kind of conviction on my mind that my honest operator would immediately declare that there was, in reality, no tooth to extract. In answer to his inquiries as to where I felt the pain, I gasped, in an embarrassed manner, "Every where." Upon this the rascal audaciously asserted that he descried the cause of the pain in one of my molars; and, before I could expostulate, an instrument was inserted into my mouth, to prevent further explanation, and a molar was wrenched from my jaws. *Par paranthese*, I am fully convinced that all the evils that have since happened to as splendid a set of teeth as originally ever adorned a human mouth, are wholly attributable to the untimely dislocation of that one molar—another illustration of causes and effects, upon which I cannot now dwell. However, the operation had been performed; and, still maddened with pain and mortification, I hunted in my purse for payment. A circular lay upon the table of the vile Screw; and I had occasion to see that the sum of five shillings was professionally demanded for the extraction of a tooth. My five-shilling-piece, however, had disappeared, upon the "house that Jack demolished" principle. I laid one of my sovereigns on the table. What did that audacious fellow mean by smiling with that false smile, and transferring the sovereign to his pocket? He evidently meant to insinuate that it was no more than his accustomed fee. I have said that I was young and foolish. So, instead of politely speaking my mind to the traitor, I merely blushed again awkwardly, and allowed myself to be bowed out of the room; and I found my way down again into the street, *minus* a fine molar, and with the horrible conviction dawning upon me that the funds necessary for the payment of my bill and the fare of "slow and seedy"—necessary to allow me to escape from London, and return to those college rooms, whence I was bound to indite my weekly epistle, without which detection and disgrace were inevitable—were already frightfully entrenched upon. I was a lost man! My mind was far from relieved by the further conviction that, but for the reckless disregard of that poor despised halfpenny, sixpence would have saved a shilling, a shilling half-a-crown, half-a-crown five shillings, five shillings a pound, and that my sovereign would have been still safe in my purse. All my financial misfortunes had arisen simply "*for the want of a halfpenny!*"

When I reached the street my pursuers had dispersed. Of course, my beauteous unknown had long since disappeared for ever in that treacherous coach. Still I seemed the object of unpleasant attention. The truth slowly dawned upon me that my coat had been torn up my back by the late struggle in the matter of the crockery. There was nothing to be done but to purchase, at the nearest salesman's, a hideous ready-made outer garment. With these further entrenches upon my finances, the smallest hope of meeting my liabilities would have vanished, even had not all hope vanished before. I now looked upon myself completely as an outcast, a beggar, a discovered and degraded being. I could not reach Cambridge without an appeal to friends or family for funds. I was utterly lost! "*All for the want of a halfpenny!*"

Repentance and regret were now, however, vain. In this state of mind I crossed Westminster Bridge, and found myself in the regions of Charing Cross, wandering despondingly towards my hotel. So absorbed in my dilemma was I that I no longer looked upon any of the passers-by. What instinct, then, was it that made me start suddenly and look around? Yes! it was again my fair unknown, who had passed me with another lady. It was the same elegant attire—the same charming figure—the same lady-like *tournure*. Again my reckless fit seized me! —and why should it not? Was I not utterly lost already? I followed once more. The ladies entered the National Gallery. I was quickly behind the object of my pursuit in the first room. Suddenly she turned, and uttered an exclamation of surprise at seeing me. But that exclamation was nothing in intensity to my own. It was my own mother!—my own mother, whose youthful elegance of figure had often been the theme of general admiration, but, probably, had never before attracted the attention of her son—my own mother, whom I had fancied safely domiciled in the country! My consternation, confusion, anguish, I cannot attempt to expatiate upon now.

After some minutes of awkward embarrassment, and a few preliminary stammered sentences, my mother took my hand, and spoke kindly. "My dear John," she said, "should your father ever discover that you have committed so great an act of disobedience, he would certainly remove you from the University for ever, and make you expiate your fault in some position of wretched drudgery." See! what great effects in my destiny might have arisen from one trivial cause. "But, for once, I will conceal your delinquency," she continued, like a good, dear, indulgent, liberal little mother, as she was. "I saw you at a glance in the Strand, as, being for a few days in town, I passed on my way to visit our poor old housekeeper, Mrs. Hewett, who lies sick and in poverty in the garrets of a house in Waterloo-road, but thought it best to ignore your presence, and refuse to see what it pained me to see. Why did you persist in following me?"—(Could I say?)—"I then took a coach, visited your cousins in Parliament-street, with one of whom I have come on here. I little thought to see you again; but you seem to force yourself upon me. I ought to speak harshly to you. There is one trait of your conduct, however, my boy, which has given me pleasure in the midst of my distress about you, and bids me be indulgent. I have seen you charitably disposed to the unfortunate." Oh! how I blushed at this unmerited praise! But, oh! lucky halfpenny! "You may want money, my child, after such a journey. Here, take this!" She thrust a five-pound note into my hand, bless her! "and remember, we have not seen each other." We parted.

So I paid my hotel bill, and got back by "slow and seedy:" and my father remained in ignorance of my *escapade*. And I have learned never again, by recklessness in trifles, to plunge myself into embarrassment, "*all for the want of a halfpenny!*"

THE SERIOUS JOE MILLER.

BY DUDLEY COSTELLO.

The wide spread of intellect, which distinguishes the present generation from all that have preceded it, and the intense desire for knowledge which pervades all classes of society, have impressed upon the writer of the following lines the necessity of ministering to the wants of an educated public in a manner hitherto unattempted. Frivolity has, until now, characterized by far too large a proportion of our literature, and familiarity of style has bred contempt in the minds of the majority of readers. Antiquity has ceased to be venerated, and old age has been held in disesteem. Our best comic authors have suffered from this cause—and more particularly one who is identified, not only with the English language, but with the daily intercourse and intimate conversation of Englishmen, in all our relations of life, and particularly—after dinner! Is it necessary that the name of *Joseph Miller* should be mentioned? He to whom we owe the most, has met with the least gratitude in return. A witticism is uttered,—not the very newest, perhaps,—and straightway the listener curls his lip, and scornfully exclaims, "A Joe!" as if it were a crime to repeat that which, when first it was told, imparted the keenest delight! This false feeling arises, not from any defect in the jokes themselves, but from the manner of putting them; and this we purpose, according to our present system, to remedy.

Instead of descending to the common-place level of prose, it is our intention to raise the respected Miller to the dignity of blank-verse; to impart a tone of lofty sentiment to the exordium which heralds his poignant anecdotes, and by the force of startling antithesis, to enhance the value of the witticism.

With this view, the following specimens are respectfully submitted to the discerning public.

THE MASQUERADE.

'Tis merry in Lord William's hall to-night;
The dance, the song, the garlands, and the lamps,
Make night a summer day. Fair forms are there,
Graceful as houris fresh from Paradise.
The guests are clothed in garbs of many lands:
The Pole, the Russ, the Turk, the Highlander,
With step majestic tread the marble floor;
And di'monds flash from many a haughty brow;
And all is pride, and pomp, and revelry.
The board is glittering with a gorgeous pile
Of viands, form'd to lure the appetite,
And make the anchorite forget his vow.
One sat beside that table.

He was pale—
As though the blight of sorrow had too soon
Pass'd o'er the blossom of his youthful hopes:
His glance was wand'ring and irresolute,
As if he sought—and found not. By his garb,
You might have said Armenia called him son—
Ample his sleeve, and large his mantle's folds.
Sudden a flash, as of a gem illumined,
Broke from his eye; his hand with rapid motion
Clutches some object, and again supine

Sinks into quietude:—but where it pass'd
There is a void—a space—where something was,
And is no more!—
Who gazes fixedly,
As though the scowl of hate were in that look?
Suspicion—of a nameless character—
Curls the sardonic look, and sharp and fierce
Flow forth the words from that envenom'd tongue,
As, seizing from the board a vase brimful
T' o'erflowing,—he accosted the Armenian,
And, dashing the contents into his breast,
Exclaim'd, "Perhaps,—as you have *stolen the fowls*,
You'd like *some melted butter* with them, sir!"

THE CARAC.

Keen blew the blast across the dreary waste,
The driving sleet, and cold, sharp piercing rain,
Beat in the trav'ller's face, and numb'd his limbs,
As onward still he sped, to gain the roof
Where he might safely house;—the prowling wolf,
Alone abroad, howl'd wildly for his prey,
And mock'd the wat'ry moon that gleam'd above.

Anselmo stood within his ancient hall:
He paced the marble floor,—then wistfully
Turn'd his dark eyes to where no cheerful blaze
Gleam'd forth as it was wont;—his household gods
Were shiver'd all; gloom darken'd o'er his hearth,
And desolation reign'd, where once was joy!

Sudden the trampling of a steed was heard;
The loud-toned bell gave warning of approach;
The portal open'd.—Dripping, from the storm,
A stranger enter'd; from his vest he drew
A scroll, inscribed with mystic characters:
"Behold," he cried, "this token of my zeal!
I come but now, from yonder distant mart,
To tell thee that a carac, long consign'd,
Has safely made the port—and there she lies,
Her precious cargo waiting thy award.
But 'tis a costly price thou'lt have to pay
For what thou lack'st;—*coals now are coals indeed.*"

Anselmo's brow grew dark, his breath came short;
He seized the paper with a trembling hand,
And gazed upon those characters of fire—
Then, with a scowl of fearful augury,
He slowly mutter'd to the messenger,
"I'm glad 'tis so—the last you sent were *slates!*"

THE ILLUMINATION.

London was in a blaze—great Wellington
Had made his name immortal, and the swords
Of our brave warriors had done mighty things;
The enemy was crush'd, and Victory
Raised her enamelled crest, and crow'd for joy!

London was in a blaze—Saint James's Street
Was all one meteor, gems of ev'ry hue
Sent forth their flashing coruscations round,
In myriad lamps of letters, stars, and suns.
A shouting multitude is gazing upward:
'Twould seem as if the world had but one mouth,
And that was open in amazed delight.
One window—*window* did I say—a score
Of crystal casements glitter'd like a lake
On which the planets shine. 'Twas in a house
Where even in daylight rainbow hues were seen
On vases ranged in rows symmetrical:
Mysterious forms of instruments were there,
Such as the Druids in their sacred rites
Might well have used. Within—but let me not
Lift the dim curtain from that secret place—
'Tis with the windows of that temple now
I have to do: and so had he, yon chief,
Whose brawny arm is raised with fell intent;
Whose hands grasp missiles dangerous and dire,
While with a force worthy a Titan's strength,
He dash'd them at th' illuminated windows.
Loud
And terrible the crash; pane after pane
Fell rattling down, lamp follow'd blazing lamp,
In wild confusion—fired with fiendlike rage,
The giant, madden'd with his first success,
Pursued his proud advantage. All had felt
His vengeance, when a blow, quick, heavy, telling,
Came down upon him with the speed of light.
"Why do you break my windows, ruffian, say?"
Exclaim'd a voice—"Because I am a glazier,"
Return'd the Titan, with a fiendish laugh.
"And I a surgeon," cried the enraged assailant;
"And for this cause 'tis mine to break thy head."

THE LANE.

'Twas a green lane, the primrose was in bloom,
And the sweet violet, with purple blush,
Starr'd ev'ry bank: the hawthorn hedges gave
Their perfumed garlands to the flattering wind
That fondled them: the golden buttercup
And white-ray'd daisy looked up from the grass,
Emerald and glistening with the morning's tears.
The steer, with spotted hide, peep'd o'er the fence,
And low'd a welcome to the rising day;
The tit sprang from a tiny twig, and woke
A fairy lay of love; the fleecy flock
Their ceaseless labor, 'midst the thymy mead,
Pursued, with heads bent down, as though they sought
Some treasure strew'd along the flow'ry way.
Thrice happy searchers! finding what they seek,
Food—ever food—fragrant and fresh and springing,
Like youthful hopes and wishes.
Who approaches,
With buoyant step and countenance, where blend
The rich vermilion and the purple tint
Of health and exercise? Young boy, thy face
Is round and ruddy, and thy garments scarce
Conceal those limbs robust and strongly knit.
There is a sparkle in that eye of thine
Might make the warbler on his topmost bough
Tremble for those within the downy nest.

Another form comes pacing from afar,
Severe and lordly, portly and austere:
In sable clad, and hat of mystic form,
Bespeaking reverence.

But no sign of awe
That blooming boy displays—he passes on—
Yes, on—nor turns aside, nor bows his head,
But whistling, runs as though no clergyman
Existed under Nature's canopy!
"Ill-nurtured urchin!" cries the reverend man,
"Methinks that thou art *better fed than taught.*"

The boy of rosy countenance turn'd round,
And with a glance in which respect was not,
And an unfolding of his fingers four
And thumb depress'd, placed on his curling nose,
Replied—"You're right for once, old gentleman;
For mother feeds me, and *I'm taught by you!*"

WHIMSICALITIES OF ROBERT WILLIAM ELLISTON.

FROM VARIOUS SOURCES.

ROBERT WILLIAM ELLISTON was the most gentlemanly comedian upon the stage. In the warm-hearted, eccentric heroes of the sterling comedies he has never been excelled; and his success in Sir Edward Mortimer, in Colman's play of The Iron Chest, after John Kemble had failed in it, stamped him as a tragedian of considerable pretension. He afterwards went through the whole range of first-rate parts, but I must confess that his tragedy always seemed vapid and heavy, even in his proud and palmy days. He had a pompous delivery in all serious characters, with a labored and frequent emphasis; and the beautiful language of Shakspere came from his mouth like the fustian of modern melo-drama. He played for some time at London and Bath upon alternate nights, travelling each day a distance of more than one hundred miles; this procured him the name of "the telegraph actor." He was at all times an industrious and persevering man, honest in his payments when he could, but too often lavish of promises which he never intended to perform. As an actor of first-rate talent, he was deservedly a general favorite; but as a manager, no man could be more despised. His domineering temper involved him in continual strife. His management at Drury Lane Theatre was marked with an eternal string of police cases, horse-whippings, squabbles and fights; yet he was without animosity in his disposition, and in social life was bland, conversational, and agreeable.

Elliston had a rage—a passion—a perfect mania for addressing the audience, which he did most impudently, and generally most effectually. He was once manager of the Olympic, a band-box theatre, with a small pit then enclosed, and not bigger than a decent-sized drawing-room. The house had been moderately attended in the early part of the evening in question, but the second or half-price customers crammed it to suffocation. The pit was so full that many persons became alarmed, and endeavored to climb into the boxes; but as they were already sufficiently crowded, the intruders were pushed back again, and the confusion became uproarious. Elliston was acting the hero in Moncrieff's drama of "Rochester." He was on the stage, singing or endeavoring to sing to his lady-love, the ballad of "I love thee, and that is enough." The over-crowded pitites were too noisy to be passed over. Dropping the lady's hand, and advancing to the very front of the stage, he looked all around with an authoritative and school-master sort of stare, and in a pompous manner said, "What is the meaning of this disgraceful disturbance?" "Too full—over-crowded,—shame!—shame!—robbery! give us back our money!" were some of the numerous responses. "Do I understand aright, that you complain of the house being too full? Who dare assert it?"—and he drew himself up as if he felt that it was impossible any one could contradict him. "I do," said a gentleman in the pit; "there are more of us here now than the place was ever intended to hold, and your door-keepers still keep admitting others." Elliston pointed his finger at the speaker, and thus addressed him: "How dare you, sir, contradict me *in my own house?* I say the pit is not too full; and to your confusion I say it, that I have had one hundred pounds more in that pit than there is at the present moment." The barefaced effrontery of this lie absolutely dumbfounded the audience. The pit never held twenty pounds at any one time. Before the collecting wrath could explode, Elliston turned round to his companion, and taking her hand with his blandest and most insinuating smile, resumed the *réfrain* of his song.—"E-e-e-enough—e-e-e-enough—and that—and that is—enough." The transition was so abrupt, and the words so ridiculously appropriate, that the thunder-cloud burst in a roar of laughter, and the over-crowded audience settled legs as well as they could.

While he was lessee of Drury Lane theatre, some comedy failed upon the first representation, and was most unequivocally damned. It was close upon the time of the famine in Ireland, consequent upon the failure of the potato-crop. Elliston was annoyed at the non-success of the piece. He expected it would have had a long run, and have brought money to the treasury. He therefore insisted on one of the performers announcing it for further representation. The audience felt insulted, and raised a cry of "Manager!" He threw open the stage-door, and stalked on. "What is the reason you have condemned this comedy? I am a better judge of plays than you can be, and I aver it to be an excellent play, a capital play, and it must and shall be again performed." He retired toward the stage door; a roar of indignation followed him. He felt he had gone too far. The yells were redoubled; he trembled for the safety of his chandeliers; so drawing out his white cambric handkerchief, an excellent adjunct when you wish to be pathetic, he advanced again to the front, assuming a penitential and deprecatory air. The groans were loud and long, but he kept his ground, looking beseechingly to the right and left. He triumphed; a pause ensued, when he began: "My countrymen!—thousands of our fellow-creatures are now starving in Ireland. A Benefit will take place at this theatre in the course of next week, when I shall present the whole of the proceeds to the committee appointed to receive subscriptions for their relief. When I appeal to you as Englishmen for coöperation in this glorious cause, my heart tells me that I shall not appeal in vain." A burst of approbation followed; John Bull was tickled; the insult forgiven; and Elliston retired amidst loud and vehement shouts of applause.

In the stage representation of George the Fourth's coronation, which ran some two or three hundred nights, Elliston personated the King. This spectacle was produced with extraordinary splendor; the principal actors walked in procession as members of the Royal Family; a platform extended across the immense pit; and the mimic monarch, gorgeously dressed in exact imitation of his royal patron, marched over the heads of that portion of the audience, and received the shouts of applause and the homage of his acted subjects, with a graceful and dignified acknowledgment. The frequent repetition of all this "pride, pomp, and circumstance" of kingly assumption, mingling with the fumes of much brandy and water, and the natural hauteur of his managerial dignity, so conglomerated our actor's ideas, that he frequently fancied himself the monarch he was representing. It has been said that he offered to confer the dignity of knighthood upon his stage manager, steady John Cooper; but if the proposal was ever made, it must have been when Elliston was most royally drunk. More than once did he leave the crowd of kneeling courtiers, and advancing to the front of the stage, extend his arms toward the audience as if in the act of benediction, and say, "God bless you, my people!"

So firmly was this impression of royalty fixed in the mind of this eccentric man, or so agreeable was the assumption to his usual pomposity, that it would frequently appear, even in matters of business,—and in the early part of the day, too, when charity would lead us to suppose that the spiritual movement could scarcely have commenced. A boy was sent to him with a note from a friend, requesting a free admission for the evening. He waved his hand and said, in a dignified voice, "Child, quit the council chamber; we cannot now receive petitions."

This regal display procured him the title of King Robert William, and even his friends nick-named him His Majesty. A curious remark by old Spring, the box-book keeper, added to the jeer. At this time the rivalry between the two large houses was carried to extremes. An habitual frequenter met Spring in the lobby of Drury one evening, and accosted him with, "Well, Spring, what sort of a house have you to-night?—pretty full, eh?" "Middling, my dear, sir, middling; that is, not *very* good; but we don't grumble; indeed we have no right to grumble. God is very good to us, for they have a miserable house at Covent Garden." The wags said, with more wit than reverence, that Drury was managed by a monarch, and patronized by Providence.

Richard the Third was reproduced under Elliston's management, with a revision of text, and a total alteration in the usual style of dress. Soane produced his authorities, and Kean jumped about in an iron skull-cap and a "close-bodied gown, the sleeves curiously cut," looking more like a Tartar amazon than the Richard of our idea. Elliston appeared as Richmond in a new suit of shining armor, and strutted about the stage, grasping a terrific pole-axe and a bright shield,—very much to his own delight, Kean's annoyance, and the amusement of the audience. In the last scene, when Harry Tudor inquires of his friend, Lord Stanley, after his son, the safety of whose head had been threatened by the tyrant, Elliston should have said:

Pray tell me, is young George Stanley living?

To which the grateful parent replies:

He is, my liege, and safe in Leicester town.

Mr. Powel, a respectable veteran, played Lord Stanley. He was the usual representative of gray-headed pappies, quiet old guardians, and fifth act uncles. He was always scrupulously perfect, but could no more go out of his way, even to the alteration of a syllable, than he could have walked up a rope stretched from the stage to the gallery, in the style of that god of grace and agility, Herr Cline. Elliston, instead of asking Powell if young Stanley was living, said

Is young George Stanley *slain?*

To which Powell replied, with his usual accuracy:

He is, my liege, and safe in Leicester town.

The audience roared, and Kean, lying on the stage as the dead tyrant, muttered an emphatic oath, which drew the attention of the front rows of the pit.

Elliston was told of his error. Upon the repetition of the piece, Wilmot, the prompter, cautioned him before he went on, and repeated the words of the line to him that he might impress them upon his memory: "Not *slain*, sir, but *living*,—young Stanley was not killed." "No, no,—I know, sir,—I know," said Elliston; "d'ye think I am drunk, or a fool?" On he went, and inquired of the elder Stanley if his son was—*missing!* and Powell answered, with painful correctness:

He is, my liege, and *safe* in Leicester town.

When the queen of ballad singers, Mrs. Bland, was unable to pursue her professional exertions, Elliston gave her a benefit at Drury Lane, and all the talent in the metropolis volunteered assistance to help an old favorite. Mathews sang a couple of songs. Through some fault in the arrangements, all the rest of the intermediate amusements were over before Mathews' first song came on. He sang it, and was encored. "Now what next?" said Mathews.

"Why, my dear boy," replied Elliston, "my stupid blundering prompter has made a little mistake,—a small error. We have nothing now but your other song and the farce."

"D—— it, sir," said Mathews, who was always irritable in business, "I can't and won't sing two comic songs close together. There must be something between them to relieve the thing. Nobody serves up two courses at dinner, exactly alike, one after the other; besides, I want to change my dress."

"Never mind dressing, my dear boy; the same dress will do for both."

"What do you mean, Mr. Elliston, by 'Never mind dressing?' Sir, I always mind dressing. When you give a dinner, and send down the venison and the salmon to the cook, do you say 'Never mind the *dressing*,' or do you tell her that the same dressing will do for both. This stupid business is done on purpose to tease me. Hop on and sing a long song, and then hop off. Encored, and hop on, and sing it again. Hop off, out of wind, fagged to death, and then you want me to hop on again, and sing another d——d long song."

"But on a night like this—charity——"

"Curse charity! Charity begins at home. I said I'd sing, and I will; but you don't want me to be all night singing, and hopping, and screeching, like a lame parrot. It's done on purpose. I did say I'd never enter your plaguy patent theatres again."

"Well, what time do you want?"

"Ten minutes to change my dress."

"You shall have it."

"But how?—the curtain has been down five minutes now; can't keep them waiting a quarter of an hour, and nothing doing. They'll pull up the benches,—pelt me,—knock my eye out,—serve me right,—I had no business to come."

"Well, well, Mr. Mathews, go and dress; I'll keep them in a good humor for you; *I'll make a speech!*"

Mathews went to his dressing room, and Elliston took out his watch. He suffered three minutes more to elapse, then, with his watch concealed in the palm of one hand, and his white handkerchief in the other, he gravely threw open the stage door, and walked slowly to the centre of the stage. A round of applause, three dignified bows, and a short pause. In his usual grandiloquent style, he thanked them for their presence on that evening, in the name of their old favorite, Mrs. Bland, who was desirous of evincing her gratitude for their heart-cheering generosity. He glanced at his watch, and to the wing; but as Mathews was not there, he felt bound to proceed. He spoke of the uncertain tenure of an actor's prosperity,—many chances of dreadful vicissitudes,—no resource when faculties fail. Another glance at watch and wing. He adverted to the extra talent he had the honor of offering to their notice that evening,—instanced Mathews, who was the first on such occasions to evince a promptitude truly praiseworthy. ("Curse him, he's not ready yet!") He then congratulated the audience upon seeing this popular comedian once more on the boards of a theatre royal; hoped the arrangements of the evening were entirely to their satisfaction; were his generous patrons but pleased, he cared not what time he spent in the task. (Ten minutes exactly.) Then winding up with a splendid peroration, he bowed himself off amidst thunders of applause. "There," said he to Mathews, who had just arrived at the wing, and was greeted with a hearty slap on the back,—"there, listen to that—now, my grumbler, go on and sing. They are in a better humor than ever; my speech against your song for next week's receipts."

In the old Drury Lane theatre, many of the dressing-rooms were level with the landing beneath the stage. During the representation of some piece, wherein Dowton had to be lowered by means of a trap through the stage, his face being turned towards the audience, Elliston and De Camp, who were concealed below, had provided themselves with small rattan canes, and as their brother actor, who was playing a serious part, was slowly descending to solemn music, they applied their sticks sharply and rapidly to the thinly-clad calves of his legs.

Poor Dowton, whose duty it was to look as dignified and intrenchant as a ghost, smarting under the pain, could scarcely refrain the expression of it by a positive screech, whilst he curveted with his heels, like a horse in Duncan's arena. Choking with rage, he was at length wholly let down, and being now completely out of sight of the audience, he looked earnestly round to discover the base perpetrators of the violence. Elliston and his companion had of course absconded—it was to *decamp* with each of them; but at this moment Charles Holland, dressed to the very finish of fashion, worthy of Cibber himself, was crossing from one of the rooms. The enraged actor, mistaking his man, and believing, by Holland's imperturbability of manner, he was in fact the real offender, seized a mop at that moment immersed in most unseemly water, and thrusting it in his face, utterly destroyed wig, ruffles, point lace, and every particular of his elaborate attire. In vain Holland protested his innocence, and implored for mercy — his cries only whetted the appetite of the other's revenge, and again and again the saturated mop was at work on his finery. Somewhat appeased at last, Dowton quitted his victim; but in the mean time, the prompter's bell had announced the commencement of the piece in which Holland was to have appeared. What was to be done? The drama was proceeding —Holland already called to the stage! All was confusion thrice confounded. An apology for "*the sudden indisposition of Mr. Holland*" was made, and the public informed that De Camp had "*kindly undertaken to go on for the part!*"

In the vicinity of the Abbey Church, Bath, resided a Mr. Sims, an opulent woollen-draper—a man of strict probity in all transactions of life—whose active benevolence and unassailable good humor, had acquired to him the esteem of a wide circle of acquaintances.

This personage was a bachelor, and at this time about sixty-five years of age. His figure was tall, his step airy, his deportment the flower of politeness, and in disputes he was the very Atticus of parties. His dress was usually a suit of gray; and his hair, of which there was a profusion, being perfectly white, whereunto a queue appended, gave him somewhat of a *Sir Joshua* contour; though perhaps he bore a nearer resemblance to the more modern portrait of that precise merchant, as personated by the late Mr. Terry, in Poole's admirable little comedy of "Simpson and Co."

While he paid a marked deference to all men's opinions, he had a mistrust of his own, which was singularly curious. On a sudden torrent, for instance, which some people would denominate "cats and dogs," he would merely *apprehend that it rained;* and if the house were as suddenly enveloped in flame, he would *suggest the expediency of quitting the tenement.* His respect for the other sex was so profound, as to keep in awful subjection every gentler impulse of the bosom—for he was far from a woman-hater; on the contrary, he could not honor them too highly; but it was all honor.

His "menage" consisted of a duplicate female attendant, that is, two separate beings, but with brains under the same meridian, whose autumnal time of life, and counterpart in attire, rendered them perfectly homogeneous.

The great characteristic of Mr. Sims was a painful precision in all things. His hat always occupied the left peg in respect of his coat. His parlor furniture was cased in cotton covers, which covers were again involuted by divers sheets of brown paper, resembling the pendant patterns in a tailor's shop. Every thing, according to him, was "to wear even;" if he pulled *this* bell-rope on the first occasion, he would bear in mind to handle *that* on the second; every chair, tea-cup, and silver spoon, had its day of labor and relaxation; and had he discovered that, by misadventure, he had worn a pair of shoes or gray stockings out of turn, he would positively have lost his stomach.

In his dressing-room, he was constantly attended by his two waiting-women; not that he actually required the services of both, but by such means the reputation of each was kept in a state of preservation; and, to conclude, whenever he retired to bed, he invariably crept up the foot of it, that his linen might be without a wrinkle.

It may not at once appear, how any sympathies could have existed between a *Milesian* like Elliston and such a character as this; but Mr. Sims was by no means an ascetic: he was never as wise as Ximenes, and not always as moderate as Fleury; and in respect of his little indulgences, like the country wench, he looked very much as though he had rather sin again than repent. And why not? an extra glass of punch, or a visit prolonged to midnight, constituted his excess; though once, indeed, he had been known to have so far mystified himself, as to toast a certain female of no extraordinary virtue, in a tumbler of toddy. He, however, confessed he went for three days unshaved, from the above event, as he had not the assurance to look on himself in the glass, after so peccant an action.

Mr. Sims was fond of a play, and had some taste for the drama. He had seen the best actors of Garrick's day, and could talk critically on the genius of "rare Ben Jonson." Mr. Sims, therefore, became, with other Bath people, known to the Elliston family.

Mrs. Elliston being absent for a few days on a visit to Mrs. Collins, Elliston was consequently left at Bath, *en garçon.* On one of his widowed afternoons, his knocker announced some visitor, and Mr. Sims himself deferentially entered.

"My dear Mr. Elliston," cried he, as he advanced, with a step lighter than a roebuck, "have I indeed caught you?—this is charming!—and how well you look! Listen: I promised your excellent wife to have an eye on you during her absence, and so I will, for you positively must—must, I say, dine with me to-day."

"Dine with you, Mr. Sims?" exclaimed Elliston, in a tone which must have been truly comic. "My good Mr. Sims——"

"—— Nay, nay—I shall be downright riotous if I hear any excuses. I absolutely must—must have you. In fact," continued he, making a leg, as he advanced, and tapping the tip of his left fore-finger with the corresponding extremity of the right, "my dinner is already ordered—within one hour will be served—see, with what little ceremony I treat you."

There was something irresistibly grotesque even in the proposition; for though Mr. Sims was by no means a stranger in the house, yet the very suggestion of a *tête-à-tête* repast with the precise woollen-draper, appeared one of those things which, although clearly possible, had still never yet been known to have transpired. As for instance, A man shall not marry his grandmother.

"To-day! said you, worthy neighbor?" demanded Elliston, as he passed his hand thoughtfully across his forehead—"to-day—that is—*this* day is——"

"Thursday, I would suggest," interposed Sims, most apologetically.

"Just so; and here comes my friend Quick, who reminds me of his promised visit. Dinner on table punctually at five—" continued Elliston, addressing himself to Quick, just as he entered—"not a minute later;" which was of course the first notice the other had had at all of the matter, while Elliston himself was quite aware he had not a solitary cutlet in the house.

"But—but—" interrupted Sims, with his fingers as before—"my humble fare is preparing—is nearly ready——"

"—— And will be excellent when eaten cold to-morrow," rejoined Elliston; "but to-day—to-day, Sims, you are *my* guest!"

The draper having recovered from the shock which these words occasioned, was evidently as pleased as Punch at the proposition, though he looked on the affair as one of the maddest pranks ever yet attempted—quite a Camelford exploit of that day, or Waterford of the present; the challenge, however, he accepted, but to no one's surprise more than his own.

"I will at least apprise my domestics," said Sims, catching up his hat and cane, with the intention of tripping off to his own abode; but Elliston, grasping his arm with considerable melodramatic effect, said, "Not so, friend Sims; this is a point easier settled; and our time is short. Take your own card, neighbor, and just inscribe in pencil, '*remains to-day with Mr. Elliston*,' and I will despatch it instantly."

The expedient was no sooner suggested than adopted, and Elliston, taking Mr. Sims's card, vanished instantly from the room, for the purpose already named, but secretly interpolated certain other words to the protocol in question, so that it ran thus—"*Mr. Sims remains to-day with Mr. Elliston, and begs that the dinner he had ordered, may be carefully delivered, just as prepared, to the bearer.*"

This being achieved, Elliston returned to the apartment; and Quick being, by this time, well assured some *belle plaisanterie* was in blossom, took part in the amicable contest of civil things, till dinner was announced; and thus, within a quarter of an hour of five, the happy trio sat down together.

But no sooner was the first cover removed, than Sims, with some little look of surprise, and great show of satisfaction, exclaimed—"A trout! Mr. Elliston. Well, and I protest a very fine one! but the fishmonger's a rogue, for he told me *mine* was the only one in the market!"

"Fishmongers do lie most infernally," observed Elliston; "why, he told me the very same thing. Come, a glass of wine! Had you been a married man now, this little annoyance had never reached you. Ah! you bachelors! But peradventure you are one who, in searching for female perfection, can only find it in the wives of his friends."

Here Sims hid his face.

"And then as to a nursery," interposed Quick, "your bachelor, by adoption, may pick and choose his heir; but if he marries, he must put up with any booby that providence assigns him."

"Excellent!" cried Elliston. "Come, a glass of wine!"

A second cover was now removed, and a shoulder of mutton, admirably dressed, was presented; at the sight of which, Sims, clasping his hands in token of renewed astonishment, exclaimed,

"A shoulder of mutton!—why, it *is* a shoulder—the very dish I had ordered myself."

"Similar, similar," interposed Quick, laughingly; "a coincidence."

Sims acknowledged the correction by one of the blandest smiles in nature.

"Coincidences are indeed extraordinary," observed Elliston. "I remember in May, —99, the very day Seringapatam was taken, our sexton's wife was brought to bed of twins."

"With great humility, my dear Mr. Elliston," observed Sims, "that may be a coincidence; but is it, think you, so very—very remarkable?"

"Why, Hindostan does not yield us cities every spring," replied Elliston, "nor are sexton's wives brought to bed of twins, as a matter of course."

"And that both of these events should have happened on the same day, is at least extraordinary," added Quick.

"Say no more—say no more; I am completely answered," rejoined Sims.

Here Elliston suggested another glass of wine all round.

By this time a third cover was removed, and a tart, very temptingly served, succeeded, which Elliston having commenced dividing, Sims rose from his chair, and extending his hands over the dismantled *tourte de pommes*, screamed out,

"An apple-pie, as I live! Forgive me for swearing, but I gave special orders for an apple-pie myself. Apple—apple, said I to Mrs. Green and Mrs. Blowflower, and here it is!"

"Yes, I'll give up Seringapatam after this!" said Elliston, mysteriously; "but when fruit is in season you know——why, I'll be bound they have an apple-tart next door."

"Apples are unusually plentiful this year," observed Quick.

"Come, another glass of wine! It shall at least be no apple of discord."

The repast was now drawing to a close, and Elliston, who had promised his guests a bottle of superior port wine, gave orders for its immediate introduction; but in the mean time, a half Stilton cheese, in prime condition, was placed on the table.

We are told that a certain maréchal of France was always taken in convulsions at the sight of a sucking pig, that Tycho Brahe swooned at the very glimpse of a hare, and that the philosophic Bayle was seized with sickness at the sound of water running from a cock; but the concentrated force of all these phenomena could scarcely have produced a more electric shock, than the sudden appearance of the said Stilton cheese on the nerves of Mr. Sims. Springing from his seat, as though stung by an adder, he gazed upon the dish before him in breathless stupefaction, and was no sooner restored to strength of utterance, than he shrieked aloud,

"A cheese! a cheese!—and, is it possible, a Stilton cheese, too?"

"My good Sims——" interrupted Elliston.

"——'Tis magic! magic! Excuse me for swearing; but I—I, myself, my dear Mr. Elliston, have a Stilton too!"

"And what more probable?"

"But the mould!—that fine blue mould!—and all this marble tracing—'tis most positively the same!"

"Similar, similar," interposed Quick, a second time.

"Tell me," said Elliston, with an ineffable look of wisdom, "where did you purchase your half Stilton?"

"At Coxe's," was the reply.

"Then, upon my honor, the cheese before you was bought at the same place. Why, 'tis the other half! and your fine blue mould and marble veining must inevitably correspond to the minutest speck. The fact is, we have been lucky to-day in hitting each other's taste. Come, the port!"

This lucid judgment was acquiesced in by Sims, with a smile of the most lavish admiration, and the cloth being removed, the host began to push the bottle.

In vain have we collected all the fine things that transpired from this moment. The three friends were in considerable force, and the decanter circulated as briskly as a hat in a mountebank's ring. As the wine sank, their spirits rose; Mr. Sims so far forgot himself as to remember a song, and by ten o'clock there was not a happier gentleman of threescore in the four parishes.

Mr. Sims being now sufficiently far gone—ripe as his own Stilton, for the purpose—Elliston gave directions for a sedan chair to be in waiting, and collecting the crockery of the woollen-draper, which had lately graced the dinner-table, he placed the pyramidal pile on a wooden tray, flanking the edifice by the four black bottles they had just emptied.

All things being now in readiness, Mr. Sims, much against his inclination, was assisted into the chair, and being secured therein, the tray and porcelain, borne on the head of a porter, like a board of black plumes in advance of a solemn hearse, led the procession to the Abbey Churchyard. The body of Mr. Sims, dancing between the poles, came next in order, while Elliston and his friend, as chief mourners, brought up the rear. In this way they reached the mausoleum of the illustrious departed, and having "made wet their eyes with penitential tears," left the rites of sepulture to the care of Mrs. Green and Mrs. Blowflower.

THE PRINCE OF DARKNESS.

"—— is a gentleman."

BY GEORGE RAYMOND.

I am better to-day. How much so do I feel by a visit from my friend Charles Bamfylde! His companionable qualities minister to my spirit a transient reinvigoration, in which I ever find the bodily frame participates. Charles is really a feature in the drama of life, contributing little, perhaps, to the great business of the scene, which, mechanically, would go on as well without him; but his character bears with it an agreeable variety, by which, though the world itself may not be materially benefited, yet I undoubtedly am. Though frequently a butt, he is always a hero; and in various instances his good-natured blundering begets him as much applause as though he were a positive wit. The anecdote which he has just related, though not of the first order, even after his own way, occupies still a page in the social adventures of my friend; and here it is:

In the early part of the present week, he had accidentally encountered a certain acquaintance, a gentleman with whom his father and himself had originally fallen in, during their short stay at some one of our large mercantile cities, and in whose power it had been to confer on the Bamfylde family much useful attention and considerable gratification. This gentleman, though neither marvellously intelligent himself, nor deeply skilled in the mysteries of science or commercial strife, was still known to others who were so; and by his means, therefore, Mr. Bamfylde, and my favorite friend Charles, passed a fortnight in the city of ——, very much to their satisfaction. Unexpectedly delighted was each at their occurrence in this place, Hastings, and after a hearty shake of recognition, Charles invited his companion to a dinner for the following day, at his father's house.

When I say recognition, I mean thereby of face, lineaments, and person; but as to the *name* of the individual, my young friend confessed, much to his annoyance, that he had altogether forgotten it. He felt, however, assured, on relating the circumstance at his family conclave, one and all of them would immediately remind him of it. On reaching home, he described the pleasing apparition of his morning ramble, and, true enough, every circumstance so well recollected by the son had been equally treasured up by the worthy family circle; but on a declaration of his precise dilemma, his mother, with a ludicrous look of embarrassment, observed, "This is, indeed, very untoward, for Sophia and myself are in the same predicament—*we also have forgotten the gentleman's name!*"

The family began now to find their situation becoming not a little perplexed; and on the morrow, as the hour of six p. m. was approaching, with that rapidity which time usually chooses when he promises to bring evil along with him, the general uneasiness was by no means abated. Every project was thought of which might be likely to unravel the distressing mystery. The alphabet was first put into requisition; "Atkins, Batskins, Catskins—Armstrong, Bachelor, Coxheath,"—all, all in vain. "Brown, Jones, and Robinson," were equally of no avail, and each experiment was "a deed without a name."

Charles, however, stated a suggestion which might lead to their rescue, which was to lay a special mandate on the foot-boy, to give due emphasis on announcing the name of each guest, at his introduction to the drawing-room; and this he further enforced by actually telling the lad the necessity for it. This arrangement tended in some degree to compose their minds, and they now only awaited the arrival of their dinner-company. In due time, the umber-clouded street-door shook again by the operation of the first knocking. Breathless was the silence in the drawing-room, and "*Mr. Cincinnatus Wharton*" was announced in so altisonant a key, as to challenge some slight suffusion into the countenance of the young gentleman, as he made his way to the upper end of the apartment. But Cincinnatus Wharton was not the material which composed the interest of the moment. Again were the panels startled; a second knocking —a third, quick upon its heels. "*Colonel and Mrs. Lomax!*"—in they came. "*Mr Pipkin!*"—and in glided Mr. Pipkin. Mr. Pipkin passed through a reduplication, and in a tone which might have entitled the boy Davidson to no less an office than that of toastmaster at Guildhall; but neither Pipkin nor the Colonel was the man. By this time, the whole party, with the exception of the tardy *Unknown*, were arrived. The interest grew warmer. Like Fabius, the loiterer gained mightily by delay; indeed, the family began to entertain great hopes that their friend might have been afflicted nowise dissimilarly with themselves, and had either forgotten his invitation altogether, or had been providentially detained elsewhere. But another and final rattling at the panels proclaimed him here. Bamfylde, his wife, Charles, and the fair Sophia, moved in a family knot in the direction of the door, making assurance doubly sure by catching the full force of Davidson's announcement; when, whether suddenly unmanned by this family array, or paralyzed by overwrought anxiety, which oftentimes o'erleaps itself, it would be as difficult as immaterial to say, but in walked the substance of a man, to the phantom of a name! Tongue-tied was the bewildered foot-boy, and ——— "stuck in his throat!" What was to be done? What could now be done?

Fortunately, the fashion for general introductions had fallen into disuse, and this *was* something. Yet what was to be *done?* Some one present—Pipkin, for instance, so fond of going from place to place, and being considered a great diner out—might possibly be acquainted with him, and so accost him by name; or it might turn out, if the *Undiscovered* were but a bit of an egotist, he would indulge in some narration of "himself and times," whereby his obnubilated patronymic might transpire to the fullest content.

A thought, worth a jewel, suddenly invested Charles. "Gentlemen not unfrequently have their names written in their hats; an initial will speak the rest; I'll go into the hall and find it. Or, peradventure, he may have come in a great-coat, which, not very unlikely, may contain his card-case—I'll pick his pocket!" And away he ran out of the room, leaving his benighted parents to grope their way as well as they could, until the announcement for dinner.

Nothing, however, could be found to give any clue to this sphinx of a name. The hat disclosed only "water-proof," at the bottom, and a cloak, containing a pair of those most useful articles, goloshes, had been brought instead of a great-coat. "My usual and own peculiar luck!" mentally exclaimed Charles, when observing Davidson supporting the family tureen into the dining-parlor. "I can't tell how it was, sir," mournfully said the lad; "but, oh! sir! the gentleman's name!"

In the mean while, the master of the house was endeavoring to make light of the matter with the Prince of Darkness. He talked of London, of acquaintance, and past occurrences, hoping thereby the deeply-imbedded word, by some coincidence or other, would be rooted up and fully discovered. But no such thing—"Oh! no, we never mentioned him!" and dinner was served. The *Prince*, under the delusion that the entertainment had been fixed for the special honor of his company, offered his arm to his amiable hostess, and the rest of the gentlemen, with appropriation of partners, after a little amicable contest as to precedence, followed in a rush towards the parlor; an act altogether as clumsy as ridiculous.

The stranger was placed on Mrs. Bamfylde's right hand; those who followed dropped into their respective chairs. The unfolding of napkins, tinkling of glasses, and collision of soup-plates, which constitute the preliminary buzz of a dinner-party, took the field; and matters appeared at least to commence tolerably well.

The *Unconfessed* had very gallantly taken on himself the severance of a Dover turbot, passing on it the favor of his own especial admiration, when Bamfylde, being desirous of making the polite apprehension that "Mr. ——— had gotten into a troublesome corner," found himself painfully curtailed of the bland address; for not being in possession of his name, the intended civility could not be forthcoming. Yet it soon became necessary to say something, and directing, therefore, his voice to the upper end of the table, and fixing his eye steadfastly on his friend, said, "Shall I have the honor of helping you, *sir*, from my *ragoût?*" but unfortunately, not having caught even a glance in return, no answer was the result. Conversation was, nevertheless, carried on, and the stranger, with an *empressement* peculiar to some people, was whispering a common stock of small-talk into the ear of the lady; declaring the Madeira was of the rarest quality in a confidential manner, worthy a cause of a far softer interest.

Bamfylde now made a second effort like the former.

"A little wine, sir, after your trouble at the top of the table?" But Colonel Lomax, who, at that moment happened to look up, and who had hitherto been completely lost in thought, or rather lost for the want of it, replied, "With great pleasure!" He thereupon chose his wine, stooped his head, and raised his glass.

The great *Ignote* now decidedly took the lead at table, and well satisfied with his single listener, Mr. Pipkin, by whose obsequious attention he was sufficiently compensated for the total absence of it in the rest of the company, he at length established his exclusive privilege to every word that was uttered.

Pipkin had a vague conjecture he had somewhere encountered his fellow-guest on a former occasion—at some Toxophilite meeting or Fancy-fair; but not having the courage to put the question, the interesting fact was "smothered in surmise."

As to the other division of the party, they had but little interest in any names which did not affect their appetites, and had been perfectly content had "sherry" and "champagne" been the only words uttered during the repast.

And now the *Prince*, bursting from the silken trammels of his hostess, into which he had once more fallen, and having rendered Pipkin happy for the rest of the evening, addressed himself somewhat abruptly to the master of the mansion, saying,

"I believe, Mr. Bamfylde, you have a son who has just sailed for India?"

"Last month," was the reply; "my youngest—Percival."

"Yes, I remember," continued the former; "I was at Liverpool about the time. By the bye, did he not go out in a ship *named after my family?*"

Poor Bamfylde staggered even in his chair, and putting the wing of a pheasant, intended for the Colonel's lady, into his own plate, which already contained a sufficient portion of *omelette sucrée*, stammered forth, "Ye—yes—he did so—he did so."

Here a most involuntary burst of laughter from my young friend Charles, caused the company to turn round, somewhat to the mortification of Pipkin, who was never desirous of missing a joke. But Charles, having by no means the confusion of his father before his eyes, announced to him in a measured whisper, "Then his name, after all, is *Agamemnon!*"

The illustrious *Obscure*, for an instant, was taken rather aback, and with a certain fixed direction of the eyes, and indescribable extension of the nether lip, appeared to say, "Surely, I have uttered something mightily ridiculous!"

But our host, resolving to acquire a lesson by this untoward *contretemps*, and say as little as possible for the future, did not even venture to raise his head; and, that he might have ample pretence for not doing so, betook himself to the pheasant and sweet sauce, unconscious of flavor and involuntary in mastication.

With great precaution, things went on tolerably well until the ladies were about to retire. Pipkin was hastening to the door, when his wine-glass, already too near the *gros de Naples* of Mrs. Lomax, acquired a totter by the general movement, which placed the contents at once in the lady's lap; and having, on his sudden recoil of horror, fixed himself with no equivocal positiveness on the toe of his other neighbor, Cincinnatus Wharton, the confusion which attended the attempt of a double apology, rendered perhaps the unfortunate aggressor quite as much an object of merriment as the sufferers of pity.

And now our host, having but little desire for the renewal of an attack in any wise similar to the last, and entertaining about as much affection for his guest of the visor, as a scalded cat for a family tea-kettle, instead of taking the post of honor just vacated by his lady, remained where he was, at the lower end of the table, addressing himself wholly to Mr. Wharton and the Colonel. But the former, who had for some months past cast an eye of desire upon a certain schedule B borough, was far more inclined to indulge his thoughts on his mistress aforesaid, though far away in Dorsetshire, and for the present in the embraces of a profligate anti-church-rater, than to listen to his host; and for the latter, the Colonel, he appeared not only like his entertainer, disposed to forget others, but likewise himself, and had dropped off into a comfortable snooze for the remainder of the sitting.

Poor Bamfylde, with that senseless courage which frequently distinguishes the coward, opened now with a volubility on the whole rank and file of the party present, by pouring in anecdote after anecdote, and amongst them one of some interest; the facts having recently transpired on this immediate coast. It was the loss of a poor fisherman at sea—native of the place—much respected—leaving a wife to deplore his loss, with six children, and another expected some time about quarter-day. Our host, in his narrative, was both animated and impressive; painting the desolate condition of the marine family of seven, in striking colors, and describing the turbulence of the night in question with the force of true eloquence. The *Prince* was duly invested with becoming pity—Cincinnatus was recalled from Dorsetshire—and the Colonel begged pardon for being so rude.

"A mother and six children!" exclaimed the *Nameless*, "all desolate—fatherless—dear me! and the widow expecting within a few weeks to—— dear me!"

"Just so," responded Bamfylde, "and it is moreover one of those melancholy facts by no means uncommon here."

"But has there been no assistance given—no subscription raised for the helpless ones?" demanded the other.

"Oh! yes," was the reply; "a subscription was immediately set on foot, and many have contributed."

"Then, my worthy friend Bamfylde," continued his august visitor, thrusting his hand into his pocket, and pulling out two sovereigns, "may I request you will add *my name* to-morrow to the list already—you know I am off early in the morning—and Heaven send them further comfort!"

What was the "Agamemnon" dilemma to this! Unhappy Bamfylde! he wished heartily he had been a companion in that identical boat, and perished too. With his friend's money already in his hand, he was the very picture of despair.

"Hadn't you rather—wouldn't it be better—" he was beginning; "but no, no," thought he, "worse and worse will follow—I'll hazard no more—disaster comes upon disaster—and yet, 'the worst remains behind!'"

The great *Obscure* looking on all this as the sudden effect of his munificence, took up, therefore, the general line of remark as his friend Bamfylde had left it, pouring in such a torrent of eloquence on the great Christian duty of benevolence, that Pipkin modestly requested to be permitted a partaker in the delight of doing good; and a third sovereign was thereupon added.

The cry of "Land! land!" at sea, after a long voyage, is a most heartfelt sound; and so I apprehend is that of "Reprieve!" within the narrow walls of a condemned cell; but I much question whether either of these could be a more welcome hearing than "Coffee is waiting in the drawing-room!" to our despairing master.

"Coffee is waiting!" His countenance verily did brighten, and, springing on his feet with greater eagerness to be gone than quite befitted the giver of a feast, exclaimed, "Come, a glass of Madeira round!" and thus firing his challenge into the covey of his friends, he felt himself once again on shore. The very transit from one place to another was a relief, and the whole party were presently restored to the drawing-room.

With a little precaution, Bamfylde now calculated on getting through the residue of the night undisturbed. Certainly he took extreme pains to avoid his friend altogether, and, under the firm conviction of *tutus cavendo*, occupied a corner in the room with the immovability of a plaster divinity.

The clock indicated ten—coffee had passed away

—"chasse" had followed, and the *Prince*, with his wonted *impressement*, had just concluded a sly anecdote to Sophia, begging she would not divulge his name as authority for the scandal, when sundry vehicles were heard rolling up to the door. "Colonel Lomax's carriage" was presently announced; at the sound of which the Colonel suddenly shook his head, as though the fibres of his nodding plume impeded his vision, and starting up, stood erect, as if about to undergo the ceremony of admeasurement. His placid lady languidly whispered she was ready; and while making her farewell, heard many regrets thereupon expressed, which, if they possessed half the sincerity of Pipkin's delight, must indeed have been highly flattering to the lady.

Soon after this "division," Cincinnatus Wharton, of course, "quitted the house," leaving the honorable member, "whose name we could not learn," in possession of the chair. The sublime *Obscure* still lingered—a moration which failed not to raise some misgivings with certain parties—with all, in fact, now remaining, except the supple and re-encouraged Pipkin.

But the dread *Undiscovered*, now suddenly jumping up, and interrupting himself in the midst of an inquiry respecting the publication of the list of donations to the survivors, in the county "Mercury," gently laid his hand on the bell-rope, and pulling it at the time he spoke, demanded if he might be permitted to ask for the footman. The lad presently appeared; Bamfylde peeped from behind the damask hangings of the window, and my friend Charles exhibited a coolness which would have become a tactician of far graver years than his own.

"Pray, does it rain?" demanded the *Man of Mystery*.

"Yes, sir, it pours."

"Then you will be so good as to inquire if my carriage is at the door?"

"*Your* carriage, sir?"

"If you please—'tis a wet night; but we have indeed been happy;" the latter part of which, being addressed to the fair Sophia, was also intended to imply, "I know you will think of me when I am gone."

"*Your* carriage!" repeated the attendant, looking towards the great *Occult*. "*His* carriage!" still continued he, turning in the direction of his master.

"Idiot!" vociferated the enraged head of the Bamfyldes, when, springing on his feet, he sprang also to the door, and pushing the consterned serving-lad aside, plunged down the staircase, and passing the hall, spite of wind and weather, rushed uncovered into the street. Sure enough, a hired carriage and driver were in attendance; on perceiving which, Bamfylde, in rapid accents, exclaimed—"Flyman, my man, my good man, harkye!—You were ordered to be in waiting at this house by a certain hour?"

"Yes, sir—half-past ten; and I'm somewheres about my time," replied the man, deliberately drawing out his watch.

"Good, good," proceeded the other, "punctual and right; but listen: what was the name of the gentleman for whom you were to inquire?"

"The name of the gentleman!—what, the gentleman's name who bid me come?"

"Yes, yes, I tell you!"

"A tall gentleman, you mean, sir: rather pockmarked?"

"Cannot you answer me?—what name did he give you?"

"Why, sir, to say the truth, I didn't pay much account to that, seeing he would be sure to know this here fly again, for he picked me out o' the whole lot. But here's *my* name, sir, and address too," continued the driver, pulling from his greatcoat a pocket-book of small printed cards, "White Lion Yard, sir, down by the bathing-rooms."

Ill-starred Bamfylde! He did not rave—no, he was past that; but putting his hand to his forehead trickling with rain, and stamping in bitter earnest at every step, forced his way again into the house. The family-lad, who was still waiting in the hall, as his disordered master entered, and seeing him turn distractedly into the dining-parlor, presented himself once more at the drawing-room entrance.

"Did you say my carriage was waiting?" he was again asked.

"Yes, sir," replied the man, with a slight exhibition of doggedness. "*Your* carriage *is* waiting; but as to master, sir, he appears to have been taken——"

"My father is subject to them," opportunely interrupted Charles—"attacks of dizziness, which at times are absolutely alarming."

"Not brought on by our meeting to-day?" was the hope of him whose name none could remember, and equally responded to by "Pipkin," which no one could forget.

After indulging in certain indications of departure, the *Prince* made his obeisance to the lady of the mansion, and smiling an "adieu" to Sophia, which again appeared to imply, "I'm sure you'll think of me," he took his leave.

"'Tis all over at last!" exclaimed one of the family quartette, and each dropped with thankfulness into a seat.

Three minutes had not elapsed, when "*le grotesque malheureux*," poor Bamfylde himself, entered the apartment.

"Heaven be praised! this day of *pleasure* is at an end," cried he; "and what a day has it been! If there be gratitude in man, I am prepared to show it now."

But Charles and his sister laughed with the most joyous freedom.

"Come, come! you make too much of this affair," observed the mamma.

"Oh, no! I was upon thorns—writhing on stinging-nettles; I'm blistered from top to toe. And his money too—a couple of sovereigns!"

Here again the party laughed aloud, and so hearty was the peal, that no one had heard the door abruptly opened, until the elder gentleman, turning about, to his horror discovered the *Prince of Darkness* standing in the middle of the apartment!

A faint scream burst from the ladies. Bamfylde was once more a plaster divinity; while I verily believe his son entertained the unfilial persuasion of the present being the richest portion of the feast.

"Go on, go on!" murmured Bamfylde; "let him proceed." And he buried his face between his hands.

"I am here only for an instant," said the *Undeparted*, "with a request that my young friend, in executing a slight commission for me to-morrow, will at the same time confer a considerable favor."

But no comment being offered, he proceeded.

"In my stroll, yesterday, I accidentally went into a sale-room, just by, and could not resist bidding for a very charming ormolu time-piece—the subject, Bacchus and Ariadne—worthy Cellini himself. 'Twas knocked down to me, and is to be packed for travelling, by the auctioneer. Every thing is paid; but as I cannot conveniently carry it to-morrow with me, I have taken the liberty of saying that you, my friend Charles, would receive it. May I therefore beg you will do this, and see it properly addressed, that I may find it safely delivered on my return home from London? No, no! I'll not sit down again—'tis late—egad! I'd nearly forgotten my errand. Now, don't stir! good night, and farewell till we meet again! Happy dream, Miss Sophia!—adieu! adieu!" and again he left the room.

This second exit was by no means distinguished like the first, by the eruption of merriment. Matters had at length become serious, and Sophia began to apprehend that the joke might be carried too far with poor papa. Once more raising his head, he appeared to question with the appalled Macbeth, "Which of you have done this?" and throwing his eyes in the direction of the door, he shuddered even by the fireside.

"Have courage, sir," exclaimed Charles; "he is gone whence he came; has scented the morning air, and the ghost's furlough is at an end."

"At an end?" interrupted his father. "Misery has no end. Children, my resolution is fixed. To-morrow, early, I am resolved to discover this legate of Erebus, confess the whole, appeal to his humanity—if the devil have one—create a proper trust for the money in my hand, take a new assignment of Bacchus and Ariadne; nor will I refuse, on assurance of his forgiveness, to receive in bond every molten deity in the Pagan mythology."

And the morrow did arrive. The clock had already struck eight, when Bamfylde prepared for passing his threshold, with that artificial composure which a man who is about to fight a duel flatters himself is most exemplary courage. At this moment, a loud single rap was heard at the yellow entrance, and Davidson announced a waiter from the —— Hotel. Holding between the thumb and finger of his right-hand a small oblong piece of pasteboard, "The gentleman," said the messenger, "who slept at our house last night, and dined here yesterday, has left for London early this morning, by the 'Taglioni,' and desired me to bring you this card, sir, hoping that you may have found yourself better after a night's rest."

Bamfylde, seizing the card and gazing an instant upon it with straining eye-balls, exclaimed, "MR. JOHN PUZZLETHWAIT!"

PICTORIAL HUMOR.

BY JOHN LEECH.

TOM. Ah, Bill! I'm quite tired of the dissipation of the gay and fashionable world. I think I shall marry and settle.

BILL. Well, I'm devilish sick of a Bachelor's Life myself, but I don't like the idea of throwing myself away in a hurry.

THE JESTER'S SERMON.

BY GEORGE W. THORNBURY.

THE jester shook his hood and bells, and leaped upon a chair,
The pages laughed, the women screamed, and tossed their scented hair;
The falcon whistled, stag-hounds bayed, the lap-dog barked without,
The scullion dropped the pitcher brown, the cook railed at the lout;
The steward, counting out his gold, let pouch and money fall,
And why? because the jester rose to say grace in the hall!

The page played with the heron's plume, the steward with his chain,
The butler drummed upon the board, and laughed with might and main;
The grooms beat on their metal cans, and roared till they turned red,
But still the jester shut his eyes, and rolled his witty head;
And when they grew a little still, read half a yard of text,
And waving hand, struck on the desk, then frowned like one perplexed.

"Dear sinners all," the fool began, "man's life is but a jest,
"A dream, a shadow, bubble, air, a vapor at the best.
"In a thousand pounds of law I find not a single ounce of love:
"A blind man killed the parson's cow in shooting at the dove;
"The fool that eats till he is sick must fast till he is well;
"The wooer who can flatter most will bear away the belle.

"Let no man halloo he is safe till he is through the wood;
"He who will not when he may, must tarry when he should.
"He who laughs at crooked men should need walk very straight;
"O he who once has won a name may lie a-bed till eight,
"Make haste to purchase house and land, be very slow to wed;
"True coral needs no painter's brush, nor need be daubed with red.

"The friar, preaching, cursed the thief (the pudding in his sleeve).
"To fish for sprats with golden hooks is foolish, by your leave—
"To travel well—an ass's ears, ape's face, hog's mouth, and ostrich legs.
"He does not care a pin for thieves who limps about and begs.
"Be always first man at a feast and last man at a fray;
"The short way round, in spite of all, is still the longest way.

"When the hungry curate licks the knife, there's not much for the clerk;
"When the pilot, turning pale and sick, looks up—the storm grows dark."
Then loud they laughed, the fat cook's tears ran down into the pan;
The steward shook, that he was forced to drop the brimming can;
And then again the women screamed, and every stag-hound bayed—
And why? because the motley fool so wise a sermon made!

AN EX-ALE-ATION, HOT AND COLD.

A POOR poet, desirous of a cask of ale, sent the following epistle to the brewer:—

Dyott, brewer of good ale,
May thy custom never fail:
How I love that draught of thine!
Clear as amber, rich as wine.
While I sip, it flows along
Sweetly o'er my pleased tongue,
Making every trouble cease,
Lulling soft my soul to peace.
Thy delicious beverage
Makes a youth of crippled age;
Banishes all misery,
And sets the loaded bosom free.
Let me whisper in thine ear—
Send me, friend, a cask of beer!

The Brewer paid no attention to the poet's request, who then sent him the following:—

Hail! thou cause of aches and pains;
Hail! destroyer of men's brains;
Hail! thou origin of riot,
Hail! thou fat and vulgar Dyott!
A beast thyself, thou makest others
Look just like thy beastly brothers.
Bodies are by thee enlarged,
Heads are palsied, stomachs charged.
Pleurisies, asthmatic breath,
Gout, and want, and sudden death,
Madness, fevers, misery
Of every kind, arise from thee!
Drink, wicked wretch, thy poisonous ale,
Drink till you burst, and go to h—.

GIDEON OWEN; OR, TIMING A SHIPWRECK.

BY W. H. HARRISON.

Taking care of the main chance, I have elsewhere attempted to define, the keeping one hand on your own pocket, and the other in your neighbor's, a definition which, whatever it may want of truth in its general application, was in exact accordance with the practice and opinions of Gideon Owen. He was one of those who, very early in life, discovered the inconveniences attendant upon having a good character, a quality, he would observe, in such universal request, that the possessor is liable to be robbed of it at every turn. Nay, it was even an incumbrance to a man of his peculiar genius, which, when relieved from the restraint, developed itself in a manner which promised to secure him a distinguished place in that calendar which is more remarkable for heroes than saints. He was one of the honorable fraternity of British merchants, though like a true genius, he altogether rejected those common-place notions by which that respectable body have the universal reputation of being governed. The halter and the gibbet were the line and rule by which Gideon was regulated in his dealings, and it is admitted that he was exact, to a nicety, in his measures. The accounts of a man who trusted no one, and whom none ever thought of trusting, must, necessarily, have lain in a nutshell; and it was Owen's boast that his pocket was his counting-house, and his journal and ledger a two-penny memorandum-book.

For a description of his person, as I cannot hope, with my feeble pen, to rival the pencil of Mr. Rowlandson, I must e'en refer the reader to the illustration of this article. Behold hlm plodding his way through the street, regardless of every external object, but in chuckling self-gratulation on having completed some advantageous and overreaching bargain; observe the pleased, but unpleasing expression, so purely animal, of his countenance; remark, too, his left hand clenched upon his bosom—a sinister attempt to keep down the upbraidings of conscience; or, perhaps, to guard his heart from the possibility of its being assailed by any of those sympathies by which ordinary and grovelling minds are sometimes turned from their purposes. His vigilance was at once useless and misplaced; useless, because his heart was as hard as a brickbat, and misplaced, because, with him, the seat of feeling was the neck.

One of his latest commercial transactions was of so remarkable a character, that I shall venture to conclude this sketch by putting it upon record. Gideon was, on a sudden, seized with a passion for speculation to the East Indies, and, accordingly, purchased a vessel, loaded her to the very hatches, and, like a prudent man, insured ship and cargo to a considerable amount. It is true, there were some trifling discrepancies between the invoices and the shipments, but such things will occur in the hurry of business, and underwriters are not particular so long as the ship stands A 1, and they get their premiums.

Two months afterwards, news arrived that the vessel had foundered, to the great dismay of Gideon, who alleged that he had insured too little, and of the underwriters, who found that they had assured too much. Some of them had taken heavy lines upon the risk, and one man in particular, had ventured to an amount the exaction of which would have left him and his family without a shilling in the world, and Gideon, unluckily, was not slow in advancing his claim. A meeting was appointed between Owen and the underwriters, at a coffee-house, for the purpose of discussing certain matters connected with the loss, when his documents were produced, and found to be altogether unchangeable. One of the parties, however, ventured to express a doubt as to the total loss of the vessel.

"Nay," exclaimed a voice from an adjoining box, "if it be the loss of the Hopewell, I can vouch for that."

"And pray," inquired one of the parties interested, regarding the volunteer witness with no complacent look, "what makes you so knowing about the loss of the ship?"

"The simple fact of my having had the pleasure of being in her company at the time," rejoined the first speaker, a fashionably dressed young man, with a very handsome but sunburt countenance, rising, and leaning carelessly against the partition of the boxes, so as to confront the party, one of whom, the individual who had at first addressed him, took upon himself the office of spokesman, and continued his interrogatories by saying, "Why you were surely not one of the crew?"

"No," answered the young gentleman, bowing in acknowledgment of the compliment intended, "I was only a passenger, and so, when the Hopewell struck, the captain and crew took to the long boat, and, paradoxically enough, alleging that I did not belong to the ship, left me in undisputed command of her."

"And you were picked off from the wreck afterwards, I presume?" said the querist.

"Within an ace of it, by a shot from a Dutch man-of-war, fired for no earthly reason that I could guess, except that I did not answer their first signal.'

"You should have waved your handkerchief."

"I should have been waved myself, then," was the reply, "seeing that it was the only tie which bound me to life and the main-top-mast, from which it was not exactly convenient for me, just at that time, to part company."

"And pray, sir," continued the inquisitor, "how many hours did you continue in that perilous situation?"

"Upon my honor, sir, I am unable to answer your question with any degree of precision, as I committed my watch to the trusteeship of the deep, for the precious metals, however they may contribute to keep a man's head above water on the Royal Exchange, have a marvellously anti-buoyant tendency in the Atlantic. Besides, to let you into a secret, I had, at that particular juncture, a strong impression that Time and I had very nearly done with each other."

"And may I inquire, then, by what miracle you escaped?"

"By no miracle at all, sir, but by simply waiting until the tide turned, when the vessel was left, high and dry, upon the sand, and I took the opportunity of stepping on shore."

"Upon my word," exclaimed another of the party, "you were in high luck to have been able to hold out so long."

"Luck, you call it?" replied the person addressed; "well, we will not cavil about terms; I have been accustomed to call it by another name though."

"But, sir," interrupted the first interrogator, "did the crew make no effort to save the cargo?"

"Oh, yes! their exertions were wonderful, and their success complete—in saving themselves, which they seemed to consider the most valuable part of it, and, as far as my observation went, they were about right, for, always excepting myself, there appeared to be little else in the ship worth caring for."

"The goods then must have been wretchedly packed."

"Quite the contrary, I assure you; had they been the crown jewels they could not have been more beautifully cased: I had the curiosity to examine a few of them while the tide was subsiding."

"And what, may I ask, were the contents?"

"Why the boxes, for the most part, contained mineralogical specimens—chiefly of silex or flint, which appeared an appropriate article of exportation to a country whither we had already sent so much steel."

"And the bales—what did they contain?"

"Oh! rags—principally rags, which I thought also a very proper article of export from a country in which there appears a superfluity of the commodity."

"And do you imagine that the rest of the cargo was of the like materials?"

"Can't say as to the materials, but, I apprehend, of pretty much the same value, for I remarked that some of the inhabitants of the coast, who ran down to the wreck, at low water, to see if they could be useful, returned empty-handed."

"And pray, sir," continued the querist, "is it your opinion that the loss of the vessel was occasioned by the captain's bad management and ignorance of the coast?"

"Oh no! I never saw any thing better managed in my life, and nothing but a most intimate acquaintance with the seas could have enabled him to run her upon the only rock which was to be found within ten leagues of the spot."

"And do you think the captain and his crew got safely to land?"

"I have no reason to doubt it, for they chose a fine day and a fair wind for the excursion. Besides, I saw the captain, six months after, at New York, in high feather, and living away, *en prince*, at one of the principal hotels in the city."

"Indeed! that is somewhat extraordinary for a shipwrecked mariner: whence think you he derived the means?"

"I cannot, for the life of me, imagine; unless, by the way, it was from a huge pocket-book which I observed him to stow away carefully in his bosom, about ten minutes before he made the notable experiment on the ship's bottom."

"He must have been somewhat abashed at seeing you."

"Not a whit! he shook me cordially by the hand, alluded frankly to the auspicious circumstances in which he had left me, apologized for the oversight, and concluded by asking me to dinner."

"And you immediately denounced him to the police."

"Not I! for our brother Jonathan is much too jealous a dry nurse of his adopted children to admit of any interference in their education; so I sat down to a *partie quarrée*, consisting of the captain, his chief mate, an under secretary, and myself, and we laughed immeasurably over the claret and the story of my escape."

"Upon my word, young gentleman," exclaimed the other, gravely, "that is what we should call, in England, compromising a felony."

"Very like it, I confess; but it was better than compromising my safety, and I knew my nautical friend too well not to feel assured that, if he had had the least suspicion of my attention to the cargo he left in my charge, he would scarcely have allowed me to quit America without some testimonial of his gratitude."

During this dialogue, Gideon, who found the young gentleman so well informed on the subject under discussion, as to render any explanation from himself superfluous, took an opportunity of withdrawing, leaving the matter entirely in the hands of the underwriters. The latter worthies held a consultation, continued by three several adjournments, which ended, on the fourth day, in their obtaining a warrant for Gideon's apprehension. He, however, having only his own safety to consult, had availed himself of certain paper wings which he kept in his pocket-book, and had sailed from Gravesend, with a fair wind, on his passage to join the captain, just three days before the arrival of the officer in pursuit.

He was overtaken, however, not by Mr. Lavender, but by a storm, by which he was shipwrecked in good earnest, and found his way to New York, in so wretched and dilapidated a condition, that his old friend could not be prevailed on to believe he was the same person, and positively refused him assistance, alleging that it was a principle with him never to encourage impostors.

JONES AT THE BARBER'S SHOP.

ANONYMOUS. FROM "PUNCH."

SCENE—*A Barber's Shop. Barber's men engaged in cutting hair, making wigs, and other barberesque operations.*

Enter JONES, *meeting* OILY *the barber.*

JONES. I wish my hair cut.
OILY. Pray, sir, take a seat.
[OILY *puts a chair for* JONES, *who sits. During the following dialogue* OILY *continues cutting* JONES'S *hair.*
OILY. We've had much wet, sir.
JONES. Very much, indeed.
OILY. And yet November's early days were fine.
JONES. They were.
OILY. I hoped fair weather might have lasted us
Until the end.
JONES. At one time—so did I.
OILY. But we have had it very wet.
JONES. We have.
[*A pause of some ten minutes.*
OILY. I know not, sir, who cut your hair last time;
But this I say, sir, it was badly cut:
No doubt 'twas in the country.
JONES. No! in town!
OILY. Indeed! I should have fancied otherwise.
JONES. 'Twas cut in town—and in this very room.
OILY. Amazement!—but I now remember well.
We had an awkward, new provincial hand,
A fellow from the country. Sir, he did
More damage to my business in a week
Than all my skill can in a year repair.
He must have cut your hair.
JONES (*looking at him*). No—'twas yourself.
OILY. Myself! Impossible! You must mistake.
JONES. I don't mistake—'twas you that cut my hair.
[*A long pause, interrupted only by the clipping of the scissors.*
OILY. Your hair is very dry, sir.
JONES. Oh! indeed.
OILY. Our Vegetable Extract moistens it.
JONES. I like it dry.
OILY. But, sir, the hair when dry
Turns quickly gray.
JONES. That color I prefer.
OILY. But hair, when gray, will rapidly fall off,
And baldness will ensue.
JONES. I would be bald.
OILY. Perhaps you mean to say you'd like a wig.—
We've wigs so natural they can't be told
From real hair.
JONES. Deception I detest.
[*Another pause ensues, during which* OILY *blows down* JONES'S *neck, and relieves him from the linen wrapper in which he has been enveloped during the process of hair-cutting.*
OILY. We've brushes, soaps, and scent, of every kind.
JONES. I see you have. (*Pays 6d.*) I think you'll find that right.
OILY. If there is nothing I can show you, sir.
JONES. No; nothing. Yet—there may be something, too,
That you may show me.
OILY. Name it, sir.
JONES. The door. [*Exit* JONES.
OILY (*to his man*). That's a rum customer at any rate.
Had I cut him as short as he cut me,
How little hair upon his head would be!
But if kind friends will all our pains requite,
We'll hope for better luck another night.
[*Shop-bell rings and curtain falls.*

AN INVITATION TO THE ZOOLOGICAL GARDENS.

BY A STUTTERING LOVER. ANON. FROM "PUNCH."

I HAVE found out a gig-gig-gift for my fuf-fuf-fair,
I have found where the rattle-snakes bub-bub-breed;
Will you co-co-come, and I'll show you the bub-bub-bear,
And the lions and tit-tit-tigers at fuf-fuf-feed.

I know where the co-co-cockatoo's song
Makes mum-mum-melody through the sweet-vale;
Where the mum-monkeys gig-gig-grin all the day long
Or gracefully swing by the tit-tit-tail.

You shall pip-play, dear, some did-did-delicate joke
With the bub-bub-bear on the tit-tit-top of his pip-pip-pip-pole;
But observe, 'tis forbidden to pip-poke
At the bub-bub-bear with your pip-pip-pink pip-pip-pip-pip-parasol!

You shall see the huge elephant pip-pip-play,
You shall gig-gig-gaze on the stit-stit-stately racoon;
And then did-dear, together we'll stray
To the cage of the bub-bub-blue-faced bab-bab-boon.

You wished (I r-r-remember it well,
And I lul-lul-loved you the m-m-more for the wish)
To witness the bub-bub-beautiful pip-pip-pelican swallow the l-l-ive little fuf-fuf-fish!

ANONYMOUS.

FROM "PUNCH'S" ALMANAC.

Of ANON, but little is known, though his works are excessively numerous. He has dabbled in every thing. Prose and Poetry are alike familiar to his pen. One moment he will be up the highest flights of philosophy, and the next he will be down in some kitchen-garden of literature, culling an Enormous Gooseberry, to present it to the columns of some provincial newspaper. His contributions are scattered wherever the English language is read. Open any volume of Miscellanies at any place you will, and you are sure to fall upon some choice little bit signed by 'Anon.' What a mind his must have been! It took in every thing like a pawnbroker's shop. Nothing was too trifling for his grasp. Now he was hanging on to the trunk of an elephant, and explaining to you how it was more elastic than a pair of India-rubber braces; and next he would be constructing a suspension bridge with a series of monkey's tails, tying them together as they do pocket-handkerchiefs in the gallery of a theatre when they want to fish up a bonnet that has fallen into the pit.

Anon is one of our greatest authors. If all the things which are signed with Anon's name were collected on rows of shelves, he would require a British Musuem all to himself. And yet of this great man so little is known that we are not even acquainted with his Christian name. There is no certificate of baptism, no mouldy tombstone, no musty washing-bill in the world on which we can hook the smallest line of speculation whether it was John, or James, or Joshua, or Tom, or Dick, or Billy Anon. Shame that a man should write so much, and yet be known so little. Oblivion uses its snuffers, sometimes, very unjustly. On second thoughts, perhaps, it is as well that the works of Anon were not collected together. His reputation for consistency would not probably be increased by the collection. It would be found that frequently he had contradicted himself—that in many instances when he had been warmly upholding the Christian white of a question he had afterward turned round, and maintained with equal warmth the Pagan black of it. He might often be discovered on both sides of a truth, jumping boldly from the right side over to the wrong, and flinging big stones at any one who dared to assail him in either position. Such double-sidedness would not be pretty, and yet we should be lenient to such inconsistencies. With one who had written so many thousand volumes, who had twirled his thoughts as with a mop on every possible subject, how was it possible to expect any thing like consistency? How was it likely that he could recollect every little atom out of the innumerable atoms his pen had heaped up?

Anon ought to have been rich, but he lived in an age when piracy was the fashion, and when booksellers walked about, as it were, like Indian chiefs, with the skulls of the authors they had slain hung round their necks. No wonder, therefore, that we know nothing of the wealth of Anon. Doubtless he died in a garret, like many other kindred spirits, Death being the only score out of the many knocking at his door that he could pay. But to his immortal credit let it be said he has filled more libraries than the most generous patrons of literature. The volumes that formed the fuel of the barbarians' bonfire at Alexandria would be but a small bookstall by the side of the octavos, quartos, and duodecimos he has pyramidized on our book-shelves. Look through any catalogue you will, and you will find that a large proportion of the works in it have been contributed by Anon. The only author who can in the least compete with him in fecundity is Ibid.

FINIS.

INDEX.

AMERICAN.

72

INDEX.

IRISH.

INDEX.

SCOTCH.

INDEX.

ENGLISH.